THE UNIVERSITY OF CHICAGO
ORIENTAL INSTITUTE PUBLICATIONS
VOLUME 101

Series Editors

Thomas A. Holland

and

Thomas G. Urban

Protoliterate Orchestra Seal Impression from Chogha Mish

ORIENTAL INSTITUTE PUBLICATIONS • VOLUME 101

CHOGHA MISH
Volume I

The First Five Seasons
of Excavations
1961–1971

Part 1: Text

by

PINHAS DELOUGAZ[†] *and* HELENE J. KANTOR[†]

edited by

ABBAS ALIZADEH

THE ORIENTAL INSTITUTE OF THE UNIVERSITY OF CHICAGO
CHICAGO • ILLINOIS

Library of Congress Catalog Card Number: 95-72170

ISBN: 1-885923-01-5

ISSN: 0069-3367

The Oriental Institute, Chicago

Series Editors' Acknowledgments

We acknowledge the assistance of the following individuals in the production of this volume: Professor Robert D. Biggs, The Oriental Institute; Valery Braun, Photographer, University of Chicago Printing Services, who expertly prepared all of the artwork contained herein for printing; Cheryl Corey and Davis Scott, McNaughton & Gunn, Inc.; Charles E. Jones, Research Archivist and Bibliographer, Oriental Institute; Sue Ormuz, University of Chicago Printing Services; Emily Teeter, Assistant Curator, Oriental Institute Museum; and especially Abbas Alizadeh. Kamyar Abdi and Christopher G. B. Kahrl provided invaluable assistance on various aspects of the manuscript.

Printed by McNaughton & Gunn, Inc., Saline, Michigan

TABLE OF CONTENTS

LIST OF ABBREVIATIONS

AS	Archaic Susiana
B.F.	Boneh Fazili
B.S.	below surface (measured in meters unless otherwise noted)
ca.	*circa* (approximately)
cm	centimeter(s)
E	east
e.g.	*exempli gratia* (for example)
el.	elevation
ES	Early Susiana
ex(x).	example(s)
fig(s).	figure(s)
i.e.	*id est* (that is)
km	kilometer(s)
KS	Khuzestan Survey
LS	Late Susiana
m	meter(s)
mm	millimeter(s)
MS	Middle Susiana
N	north
n(n).	note(s)
N/A	not available
n.d.	no date
no(s).	number(s)
n.p.	no publisher
p(p).	page(s)
pers. comm.	personal communication
PL	Protoliterate
pl(s).	plate(s)
S	south
sq.	square
Tr(s).	Trench(es)
vol(s).	volume(s)
W	west

LIST OF FIGURES

LIST OF TABLES

FOREWORD

Pinhas Delougaz

Originally the series of Oriental Institute Communications (OIC) was intended for publishing the results of excavations in a popular vein to acquaint the public with the activities of the Oriental Institute. However, the energy of some of the field archaeologists and the need for publishing promptly not only the most spectacular but also the most significant scholarly results soon turned this series into an effective organ of archaeological literature. In retrospect, this series admirably fulfilled its function, because some of the most important discoveries in Near Eastern archaeology during the 1930s were made known though it, and in some cases it is still the only source of such information. On the other hand, the relatively temporary character of these publications is demonstrated by various instances in which the results as understood and interpreted during one phase of the excavations have been radically changed by the subsequent progress of the work.

It is purely a matter of accident that the last volume in this series before its interruption in 1939 (OIC 21) and the present volume both deal with excavations in Iran. But there is no accident in the choice of sites and consequently the archaeological materials with which each deals. Persepolis, the subject of OIC 21, one of the major ancient sites in the Near East, had been selected for the work of the Oriental Institute in Iran in the 1930s in accordance with the Institute's ambitious program and considerable means at that time. In contrast, the changed conditions after the Second World War and the greatly reduced means available for archaeological research have entailed working on a much smaller scale and at a fewer number of sites. Therefore, it becomes essential to devote the resources available to attempts at solving the most significant archaeological problems.

In particular, the development of prehistoric cultures and the rise of urban civilization in southwestern Iran led us to central Khuzestan and there to one of the most promising sites of the region, which luckily had remained untouched. After five campaigns at irregular intervals, the results both in quantity and quality of material have far surpassed our most sanguine expectations.

Our interest in excavations in Khuzestan goes back to the middle 1940s when, as soon as it became practical to resume excavations in the Near East after the war, I planned for work there. Indeed, in 1947 I was generously granted by the government of Iran a permit to work in Khuzestan. Various circumstances prevented me from taking advantage of this permit and Dr. D. McCown, who was to have been a member of my staff, went out for two seasons of survey and excavation in the Ram Hormuz area of Khuzestan (Tall-e Ghazir). Not until 1961 did I have the opportunity to initiate excavations in Iran with Professor Helene J. Kantor as co-director.

The first three campaigns at Chogha Mish were conducted under the auspices of the Oriental Institute. After my transfer to the University of California, Los Angeles (UCLA) in 1967, the administration of UCLA agreed to become a cosponsor of the expedition and to share its financing. In addition the late Professor Gustav von Grunebaum, director of the Middle Eastern Center of UCLA, and Professor Ann Kilmer, Dean of the Division of Humanities at the University of California, Berkeley, made much appreciated and helpful contributions to the expedition out of their own budgets. Since the establishment of the Joint Iranian Expedition in 1968, several personal friends of the expedition, including Mr. and Mrs. Albert T. Haas, Maurice D. Schwartz, and Mr. Charles D. Kantor, have generously contributed sums that have constituted welcome additions to rather limited operating budgets which the two sponsoring universities were able to provide. To every person concerned with its financial support, the expedition owes a debt of gratitude, for without this support its work would have been much less fruitful.

Since 1968, when the Ford Foundation made available to both the University of California and the University of Chicago funds for training graduate students in archaeological field work abroad, the Joint Iranian Expedition has availed itself to this opportunity. Thus, in the fourth and fifth seasons eight students participated in the excavations as Ford Foundation trainees.

During the decade since we began work in Khuzestan, we have been fortunate in acquiring many friends and receiving much encouragement and assistance from them. We have incurred many more debts of gratitude than we can possibly enumerate here. We wish to acknowledge the cordial help extended to us by His Excellency, Mr. Mehrdad Pahlbod, the Minister of Culture and Arts, and members of his Ministry, particularly Mr. A. A. Pourmand, Director of the Archaeological and Folklore Service, Mr. S. M. Khorramabadi, Assistant Director, and all other members of the Archaeological Service with whom we have come in contact. Professor Ezat Negahban, Director of the Archaeological Institute of the University of Tehran and Advisor to His Excellency, the Minister of Culture, gave us generously of his time and advice on archaeological matters. We owe a special debt of gratitude to the Iranian collaborators assigned to us each season for their interest in our work and for the manner in which they carried out their duties when sharing with us the sometimes onerous conditions of work in the field, especially during the final and rushed days of the season. To the American ambassadors in Iran beginning with Ambassador J. C. Holmes and his successors, and to the members of the Embassy staff in Tehran and the consular staff in Khorramshahr we owe much for their constant interest and friendly assistance. Although as we write, the old Presbyterian Mission complex in Tehran is no longer active on the same scale as when we began our work in Khuzestan, we cannot but record our warm feelings for this institution and our gratitude for the hospitality that was offered us on many occasions and for the many close and lasting ties of friendship which we established under its roof.

We have also received much kindness from the local authorities in Khuzestan, from the Governor-general of the province, the chiefs of the gendarmerie, the police, and representatives of the Ministeries of Culture and Arts and of Education in Ahvaz and Dezful.

A few days after our first arrival in Khuzestan, while looking for a possible place to stay in the vicinity of Chogha Mish, we were fortunate to meet Mr. Bahman Samsam, who happened to be in residence in his home in the village of Shalgahi. Only a few minutes after we made his acquaintance, he, with the most striking and typical Iranian generosity, invited us to be his guests. We availed ourselves to his hospitality and, in fact, he put his house at our disposal not only for the few weeks of the first season, but also for the six months of the lengthy second season. Since in good weather Mr. Samsam's comfortable house is only about a twenty-minute drive from Chogha Mish, his hospitality made it possible not only to begin the two first seasons without delay, but also to reach the site quickly, a feat that would not have been possible had we had to stay in the nearby town of Dezful.

During the first three seasons while the Khuzestan Development Service was active, we received very generous practical aid from the organization as such and personally from a number of its staff members. We are grateful to the successive directors, Mr. Leo L. Anderson and Mr. Alan McCulloch, as well as to Dr. F. G. L. Gremliza, medical officer, Mr. Robert Kreiss and Mr. Alan Craig, irrigation engineers, and many others for their continuous interest in our work and unfailing practical assistance. Mr. Stoop of the Konigklike Heidemy Company, which worked in association with the Khuzestan Development Service, had the responsibility for preparing the contour map of Chogha Mish; in addition he assisted the expedition with his skill in photographic processing and provided a line of communication with Dezful.

Mr. A. K. Rashidian, whom we met within a few days of our first arrival in Khuzestan, was then manager of the Khuzestan Development Service guest house in Andimeshk and is now director of the Khuzestan Water and Electricity Authority facilities in Andimeshk and Dezful. During the years, he rendered the expedition innumerable services and became a close and trusted friend. Dr. Gremliza and his wife, Frau Maria Gremliza, had been in Khuzestan for thirteen years when we first met them and knew the area and its inhabitants intimately. Until their departure from Iran in 1966, they were invaluable friends of the expedition, giving unstinting aid in many ways.

We wish to thank also the colleagues, students, and volunteers who worked with us during the various seasons for their hard work and many contributions to the results.

During the years of our work we have had the pleasure of getting acquainted with many persons in the towns and villages around Chogha Mish and of establishing friendly relations with them. Except for our faithful driver, Muhammad Basirifar, who was a taxi driver from Dezful, our small domestic staff and all our workmen have been from these villages. Our workmen were trained by us, some of them from boyhood, and many of them have developed an interest in the work and its results. At first our operations seemed pointless, if not outright ridiculous to them, but in the course of time many acquired not only excellent technique, but also a considerable understanding of the aims of our work and its significance for the understanding their own past. We are grateful to them for their work and loyalty to the expedition, and to all those who have helped the expedition in its work and who cannot be named individually, we wish to extend our cordial thanks.

PREFACE

Helene J. Kantor

The present publication has been enormously delayed. When Pinhas Delougaz wrote his preface, around 1974, the publication was to be an interim report. In his preface he described how it was first planned to be an Oriental Institute Communication (OIC) preliminary report. In the summer of 1974, we worked on the interim report and considered that it was ready to go to the editorial office. Since then many vicissitudes have prevented the appearance of the publication. Among the personal ones, the most overwhelming was the death of Pinhas Delougaz on Chogha Mish in the final days of our ninth season (March 29, 1975).

Shortly after that great loss, it was decided that the projected volume should be a final report on the first five seasons. This decision entailed the publication of a great quantity of data not present in the "interim report" version. In his architectural chapters,[1] Delougaz discussed only those loci that formed a meaningful pattern. However, such loci formed only a small proportion of the total number, which appeared in the interim version only as proveniences in the plate catalogs. Accordingly, it was necessary to create a large new section in the publication, an index of loci and finds. There, every locus number assigned in the first five seasons is defined and the objects found in it are listed according to their absolute depth. The loss of Delougaz, the person primarily responsible for the stratification and architecture, made the preparation of this index a tremendously time-consuming and difficult task. In the earliest seasons, the daily excavation notes were not as standardized and complete as in later seasons. The loss of information that only Delougaz possessed is incalculable.

The collecting of objects by provenience was also in those pre-computer days another daunting task, in which I was greatly aided by the collaboration of Guillermo Algaze and Abbas Alizadeh. During those years, it was necessary to trace and photograph or draw as many objects as possible from the various loci. A large number of new plates were assembled, most of them consisting of new drawings. A number of difficult ones were prepared by Yousef Majidzadeh in the year immediately after the loss of Delougaz. Thereafter, I was fortunate in having the aid of Abbas Alizadeh, who made a large number of drawings. The result of our efforts was a major rewriting and expansion of all chapters except for the architecture. The latter remain much as Delougaz left them; the one major change is the dating of the Circular Structure, done on the basis of evidence not yet known before the death of Delougaz (see *Chapters 2* and *3*).

Some time ago, during a too-optimistic projection for the volume's completion, a cut-off date of 1981 was set for the citation of comparative materials and discussion. Since now again years have elapsed, it is necessary to bring in some of the more important recent materials, such as, for example, work at Susa, Jebel Hamrin, Tell el-'Oueili, and in the Protoliterate sites on the middle Euphrates in western Syria. Even so, the citation of publications after 1982 is less comprehensive.

---

1. Originally *Chapters 2* and *7*, now *Chapters 2, 3,* and *8*. AA

EDITOR'S PREFACE

Abbas Alizadeh

The appearance of this publication creates mixed feelings for those who personally knew Helene J. Kantor. It is sad that Helene Kantor died before she could complete this publication, on which she spent close to one-third of her life. On the other hand, she would be pleased to know that her work has finally been published.

The task of editing and completing an unfinished manuscript is problematic and is always surrounded by a number of academic, technical, and ethical issues. When I resumed work on the Chogha Mish publication, I found some chapters were complete and in final draft form (*Chapters 2–4, 8–9*), some complete but tentative (*Chapters 1, 5–6, 10*), and some both tentative and incomplete. The complete chapters are only edited and are published much as Helene Kantor left them. The tentative and incomplete chapters I have reconstructed and completed based on the available data and on my understanding of her thoughts. In the beginning, I thought of specifying all of my additions, deletions, and reconstructions in the text, but it soon proved to be both impractical and in many cases confusing to the reader. As a result I decided to add my initials to only the specific items that appear either in the footnotes or in the descriptions of objects and pottery. However, a major revision of the chronological position of the close-line ware of the Archaic Susiana 3 *vis-à-vis* the Samarra and Chogha Mami Transitional wares and the omission of Middle Susiana 2 from the Susiana sequence must be explained here.

For a number of years, Helene Kantor held the opinion that Archaic Susiana 3 close-line ware was earlier than Samarra and Chogha Mami Transitional wares. Excavations at Tell el-'Oueili in southern Mesopotamia forced a strong variable into this chronological equation, which Professor Kantor could not ignore. Although she never published her opinion on this question, in our informal talks she appeared to be leaning toward the idea of abandoning her previous position. On this basis, I have revised *Chapter 12* accordingly.

I also have omitted the problematic Middle Susiana 2 phase and have renamed the subdivisions in this period as Early Middle Susiana and Late Middle Susiana phases. When Helene Kantor introduced Middle Susiana 2 in her chronological sequence of Susiana, she was not intimately familiar with the Susiana pottery sequence and had based the presence of an intermediate phase between an early Middle Susiana and late Middle Susiana period on a few painted motifs that occurred only at Chogha Mish. As she became more familiar with the material, she began to doubt the existence of such a phase, though she never totally gave up the idea. No architectural features or even pits can be safely assigned to this presumably transitional phase. Its existence was solely based on certain painted decorations that do not comfortably fit in either Early Middle Susiana or Late Middle Susiana pottery assemblages, and which, it should be noted, are exclusive to Chogha Mish. Such painted decorations include lattices[1] and filled ovals painted on the interior base of some Middle Susiana bowls (pl. 179:A–J). The four reserved ovals of the central cross design of the Early Middle Susiana may be filled with small representational motifs such as fish, birds, or quadrupeds (pl. 179:A–J). The attenuation of the tips of the outer ring of the cusps of these central motifs would be another characteristic of "Middle Susiana 2" pottery (pl. 168:A–D).

"Middle Susiana 2" has been eliminated here and the materials originally assigned to it have been reassigned to either Early Middle Susiana or Late Middle Susiana (Middle Susiana 1 and Middle Susiana 3, respectively, in the previous chronology). This should solve the problem of the Middle Susiana 2 phase that has entered the literature and which is floating in chronological charts with no stratigraphic or architectural position.

It should be noted here that a "Middle Susiana 3c phase," which has been erroneously introduced into the literature (Dollfus 1983a:166; Dittmann 1984), has no archaeological basis. The introduction of this phase stems from a misunderstanding of a notation in the unpublished plate catalog of Chogha Mish that was made available by Helene Kantor to some of her colleagues.[2]

---

1. The open lattice decoration (pl. 179:A) has one parallel at Haji Muhammad (Ziegler 1953, pl. 32:b).
2. The "c" in Middle Susiana 3c stands for "context" and was intended to denote that the piece was recovered from a primary context.

I have argued elsewhere (Alizadeh 1992) for the subdivision of the Late Susiana period into two phases: Late Susiana 1 and Late Susiana 2, corresponding respectively to Susa 1 and to a transitional phase from Middle Susiana to the Late Susiana period. When I presented the evidence to Professor Kantor, she agreed with my argument and felt that this phase may also be represented at Chogha Mish, although she did not have much material to support it.

Except for a couple of sherds typical of the Late Susiana 1 phase, I have not been able to find enough material from the first five seasons to justify the presence of this phase at Chogha Mish. Nonetheless, a small section is devoted to the description of this phase, which may be represented in the materials excavated in seasons 6–11.

Helene Kantor followed Delougaz' terminology for the Uruk period. This terminology is retained here, but when references are made to sites or materials that are earlier in date than the Protoliterate (Protoliterate *a*), the term Early Uruk, rather than "early Protoliterate" is used to avoid confusion.

The tremendous variety of Protoliterate pottery types, which result from the combination of different body forms and wares with numerous different accessories, is worked out and presented in this publication based on the "system of pottery classification" that was used in the publication of the pottery from the Diyala region (Delougaz 1952:1–26), including its specific definition and terminology. For example, a rim is not simply the opening of a vessel but "an opening accentuated either by a variation in thickness or by changing of curvature" (ibid., p. 17, n. 22). Wash and slip are distinguished as coats of pigment and clay respectively.

The designation of forms by a letter and six digits also follows the same system of classification. The letter prefixes indicate the size category, A = miniature (less than 6 cm in height), B = small (less than 12 cm in height), C = medium (less than 30 cm in height), D = large (over 30 cm in height), and E = very large. The six digits following the letters represent the essential characteristics of the pottery form. Body shapes are divided into ten major categories (first digit), each category having ten subdivisions (second digit). Every body shape so defined can occur with different proportions (third digit). The bases and the mouths of the vessels and the accessories are indicated by the remaining digits. Not all of the illustrated pieces have shape designation numbers either because these pieces were added after Helene Kantor died or their original shapes could not be reconstructed with certainty.

Insofar as possible, numbers have been assigned to pottery families according to the order of the shape designations of the vessels included in them and the same principle has governed the arrangement of the plates. However, the clustering of individual types into families has precluded the presentation of the pottery in a single continuous corpus order as in the publication of the Diyala pottery. Even within families, space or other exigencies have sometimes interfered with a systematic arrangement of individual specimens on the plates by order of shape designation. Occasionally a vessel not shown in the plates serves as the representative of a family on the synoptic figures 8–13, 15, 23, 26, 30–31, 33–35, and 37, interspaced in relevant chapters.

Parallels for the Archaic Susiana-Protoliterate ceramics from Chogha Mish are usually cited at the end of the discussion of individual families. Not all of the pertinent material has been included; stratified finds and those from outlying geographical areas have been emphasized.

When ceramic families are discussed under specific rubrics, only their family numbers are given. When they are discussed under different categories or in connection with other families, their chronological periods are specified by the initials representing that period, i.e., Archaic Susiana Family VI, Early Susiana Family XX, Middle Susiana Family VII, etc. Plates illustrating pottery of various periods are arranged in ascending sequence numbers within individual phase. This arrangement will make it easy for the reader to find a specific piece without even knowing the plate number.

Sometimes objects are discussed but not illustrated. Such objects are indicated by their field registration numbers. These numbers are preceded by either roman or arabic numerals. They both indicate season number. The arabic numerals are almost always used to indicate potsherds, and roman numbers to indicate objects and whole vessels. A few plates (pls. 81 and 93 for examples) include items for which I have not been able to locate any stratigraphic information. These items have been retained for comparative and reference purposes.

In the object numbers, the first digit, whether written as a roman or arabic numeral, gives the season in which the item was found. For example, III-1 is the first object registered in the third season and 3.001 the first sherd or fragment cataloged that season. Normally the first digit of the object number is the same as the first digit of the loci where they were found. Occasional exceptions are items found in areas of a previous season where excavation was not continued. In the absence of current locus numbers the old ones are used; for example, 4.001 has the provenience of K22:201 and is a fragment found in the fourth season after it had been washed into the small trench dug in the second season. The items with discrepant first digits in their provenience and field numbers are those either washed into or partially exposed in discontinued areas between seasons.

The first number in a grave designation indicates the season during which the grave was excavated and the subsequent numbers identify the grave, e.g., 4.08 indicates the eighth grave to be excavated during the fourth season. The season number should be separated from the grave number by a period; however, this period was occasionally omitted in the plans.

Sometimes some objects are included in the *Index of Loci* but not illustrated. In such cases, the date (if known) is indicated. Occasionally objects excavated after the fifth season are illustrated in this volume, either because of their individual importance or because they provide better examples of a specific type than was found in seasons 1–5. The greater part of such later-season objects consist of Archaic Susiana pottery. It seemed advisable to present a relatively comprehensive corpus of Archaic Susiana pottery. The proveniences of such pieces are listed in the plate catalogs but the loci are not included in the *Index of Loci*. In addition, the presentation of certain categories of material includes the examples from later seasons, namely: stone objects, Seasons I–X (*Chapter 11*); spindle whorls, Seasons I–IX; and potters' marks, Seasons I–XI.

The present volume contains chapters by three specialists, Daniel M. Shimabuku (*Chapter 11*) on ground stone implements, Anne I. Woosley (*Chapter 13*) on the plant remains, and Dr. Donald Ortner (*Appendix A*) on the deformed skull from Trench XXII. Daniel Shimabuku's analysis was done in the field where a great mass of implements were available and he dealt with all of them, through Season 8. The registered ground stone implements which were not available to him working in the field are dealt with in the chapters on Protoliterate and Susiana small finds. Likewise, Woosley dealt with all the plant remains up through Season 8. The faunal remains were given to Jane Wheeler for detailed analysis, and she also covered all available specimens, working both in Chicago and in the field. Her original record cards were coded and put into the mainframe computer here in Chicago. On behalf of Helene Kantor I would like to thank Mr. James Lichtenstein, senior programmer at the University of Chicago computer center, for his aid and interest in processing the Wheeler records and creating a comprehensive list of all the bones recovered from Chogha Mish. This list is based on Wheeler's analysis and identification of some 40,000 bones representing various species with stratigraphic information.

Several years ago, Jane Wheeler had sent a short chapter on the faunal remains to be included in the manuscript. When I contacted her to go over that chapter for final revision, she unfortunately withdrew it as she felt it was not up-to-date and that after so many years she would be unable to go back to the available data. The comprehensive computer-generated list will be published in the next volume dealing with the materials from the sixth to eleventh seasons.

Professor James S. Phillips analyzed the flints. The results of his analysis were to be published as a chapter on flint blades in this volume. Unfortunately that chapter does not seem to be forthcoming and I had to submit the manuscript without it.

In the course of the preparation of the Chogha Mish manuscript many individuals have contributed to the completion of this publication. Apart from working for a number of years on the preparation of Chogha Mish materials, Guillermo Algaze kindly read *Chapters 4* and *12* and made a number of valuable suggestions. The illustrations are primarily the work of Helene Kantor, Abbas Alizadeh, and W. Raymond Johnson. I would like to thank Yousef Majidzadeh, Carlene Friedman, and Donald Whitcomb, who also prepared a number of illustrations. I am also thankful to Melanie Jansen, who patiently checked and corrected the bibliographic references, footnote citations, and prepared a number of tables. The late Carolyn Livingood worked as a volunteer with Helene Kantor for a number of years. She was primarily responsible for the painstaking task of typing the *Index of Loci*. Her efforts are greatly appreciated.

There is no doubt in my mind that the manuscript would have been published in greater detail and perhaps error-free had Professor Kantor lived long enough. I am also certain that Helene Kantor would have been the first to point to the flaws in this publication. The greatest weakness I felt in the course of the preparation of the manuscript was my lack of first-hand knowledge of a number of issues for which, unfortunately, no information was recorded and with which Professor Kantor was intimately familiar. Despite this I felt that the publication of the Chogha Mish material has long been overdue and that it should be published without further delay. Nevertheless, I take full responsibility for any errors and misinterpretations presented in the chapters that were completed after Helene Kantor's death.

BIBLIOGRAPHY

Adams, Robert McCormick

    1962   "Agriculture and Urban Life in Early Southwestern Iran." *Science* 136:109–22.

    1965   *Land Behind Baghdad*. Chicago: University of Chicago Press.

    1981   *Heartland of Cities: Surveys of Ancient Settlement and Land Use in the Central Floodplain of the Euphrates*. Chicago: University of Chicago Press.

Adams, Robert McCormick and Nissen, Hans J.

    1972   *The Uruk Countryside: The Natural Setting of Urban Societies*. Chicago: University of Chicago Press.

Alden, John R.

    1979   "Regional Economic Organization in Banesh Period Iran." Ph.D. dissertation, Department of Anthropology, University of Michigan.

Algaze, Guillermo

    1989   "The Uruk Expansion: Cross-Cultural Exchange in Early Mesopotamian Civilization." *Current Anthropology* 30:571–608.

    1993   *The Uruk World System: The Dynamics of Expansion of Early Mesopotamian Civilization*. Chicago: University of Chicago Press.

Algaze, Guillermo, editor

    1990   *Town and Country in Southeastern Anatolia, Volume II: The Stratigraphic Sequence at Kurban Höyük*. Oriental Institute Publications, Vol. 110. Chicago: The Oriental Institute.

Alizadeh, Abbas

    1985a   "A Tomb of the Neo-Elamite Period at Arjan, near Behbahan." *Archäologische Mitteilungen aus Iran* 18:49–73.

    1985b   "A Protoliterate Kiln from Chogha Mish." *Iran* 23:39–50.

    1988a   "Mobile Pastoralism and the Development of Complex Societies in Highland Iran: The Evidence from Tall-i Bakun A." Ph.D. dissertation, Department of Near Eastern Languages and Civilizations, University of Chicago.

    1988b   "Socio-economic Complexity in Southwestern Iran during the Fifth and Fourth Millennia B.C.: The Evidence from Tall-i Bakun A." *Iran* 26:17–34.

    1992   *Prehistoric Settlement Patterns and Cultures in Susiana, Southwestern Iran: The Analysis of the F. G. L. Gremliza Survey Collection*. Technical Report, No. 24. Ann Arbor: The Museum of Anthropology, University of Michigan.

Amiet, Pierre

    1957a   "Glyptique susienne archaïque." *Revue d'assyriologie et d'archéologie orientale* 51:121–29.

    1957b   "Les Intailles orientales de la collection Henri de Genouillac." *Cahiers de Byrsa* 7:35–73.

    1961   *La Glyptique mésopotamienne archaïque*. Paris: Centre National de la Recherche Scientifique.

    1963a   "Argenterie d'époque Achéménide." In *Collection Helene Stathatos, Tome 3: Objets antiques et byzantines*, by H. A. Stathatou. Strasbourg: n.p.

Amiet, Pierre (*cont.*)

1963b   "La Glyptique syrienne archaïque: Notes sur la diffusion de la civilisation mésopotamienne en Syrie du nord." *Syria* 40:57–83.

1966a   *Elam.* Auvers-sur-Oise: Archée Éditeur.

1966b   "Il y a 5000 ans les Elamites inventaient l'écriture." *Archéologia* 12:10–22.

1970/71   "Sceaux syriens découvertes à Suse." *Mélanges de l'Université Saint-Joseph* 46:131–35.

1972   *Glyptique susienne des origines à l'époque des perses achéménides: Cachets, sceaux-cylindres et empreintes antiques découverts à Suse de 1913 à 1967.* Mémoires de la délégation archéologique en Iran, Mission de Susiane, Tome 43. Paris: Paul Geuthner.

1973   "La Civilisation du désert de Lut." *Archéologia* 60:20–27.

1974   "Antiquités du désert de Lut: À propos d'objets de la collection Foroughi." *Revue d'assyriologie et d'archéologie orientale* 68:97–110.

1977   "Bactriane proto-historique." *Syria* 54:89–121.

Andrae, Walter

1930   *Das Gotteshaus und die Urformen des Bauens im alten Orient.* Studien zur Bauforschung, Heft 2. Berlin: Hans Schoetz.

Andrae, Walter and Lenzen, Heinrich

1933   *Die Partherstadt Assur.* Wissenschaftliche Veröffentlichung der Deutschen Orient-Gesellschaft, Band 57. Leipzig: J. C. Hinrichs.

Arnold, Dorothea

1976   "Wandbild und Scherbenbefund: Zur Töpfertechnik der alten Ägypter vom Beginn der pharaonischen Zeit bis zu den Hyksos." *Mitteilungen des Deutschen Archäologischen Instituts, Abteilung Kairo* 32:1–34.

Avi-Yonah, Michael and Stern, Ephraim, editors

1978   *Encyclopedia of Archaeological Excavations in the Holy Land, Volume 4.* Jerusalem: Israel Exploration Society and Massada Press.

Balcz, Heinrich

1932   "Die Geffässdarstellungen des Alten Reiches." *Mitteilungen des Deutschen Instituts für ägyptische Altertumskunde in Kairo* 3:50–87, 98–114.

1933   "Die Gefässdarstellungen des Alten Reiches." *Mitteilungen des Deutschen Instituts für ägyptische Altertumskunde in Kairo* 4:18–36, 207–27.

1934   "Die Gefässdarstellungen des Alten Reiches." *Mitteilungen des Deutschen Instituts für ägyptische Altertumskunde in Kairo* 5:45–94.

Balfet, Hélène

1980   "À propos du métier de l'argile: Example de dialogue entre ethnologie et archéologie." In *L'Archéologie de l'Iraq du début de l'époque néolithique à 333 avant notre ère*, edited by M.-T. Barrelet, pp. 71–83. Colloques Internationaux du Centre National de la Recherche Scientifique, No. 580. Paris: Éditions du Centre National de la Recherche Scientifique.

Bar-Adon, Pessah

1980   *The Cave of the Treasure: The Finds from the Caves in Nahal Mishmar.* Judean Desert Studies. Jerusalem: Israel Exploration Society.

Barnett, Richard D.

    1976   *The Sculptures from the North Palace of Ashurbanipal at Nineveh (668–627 B.C.).* London: British Museum.

Beale, Thomas W.

    1978   "Bevelled Rim Bowls and Their Implications for Change and Economic Organization in the Later Fourth Millennium B.C." *Journal of Near Eastern Studies* 37:289–313.

Behm-Blancke, Manfred R., et al.

    1981   "Hassek Höyük: Vorläufiger Bericht über die Grabungen in der Jahre 1978–1980." *Istanbuler Mitteilungen* 31:5–93.

    1984   "Hassek Höyük: Vorläufiger Bericht über die Grabungen in den Jahren 1981–1983." *Istanbuler Mitteilungen* 34:31–149.

Belaiew, N. T.

    1943   "Poids archaïques." In *Archéologie susienne*, by R. de Mecquenem, G. Contenau, R. Pfister, and N. T. Belaiew, pp. 195–207. Mémoires de la mission archéologique en Iran, Mission de Susiane, Tome 29. Paris: Presses Universitaires de France.

Berry, A. Caroline; Berry, R. J.; and Ucko, Peter J.

    1967   "Genetical Change in Ancient Egypt." *Man* 2:551–68.

Biggs, Robert D.

    1968   "The Sumerian Harp." *American Harp Journal* 1:6–12.

Blackwood, B. and Danby, P. M.

    1956   "A Study of Artificial Cranial Deformation in New Britain." *The Journal of the Royal Anthropological Institute of Great Britain and Ireland* 86:173–91.

Blegen, Carl W.; Caskey, John L.; Rawson, Marion; and Sperling, Jerome

    1950   *Troy, Volume 1: General Introduction. The First and Second Settlements.* Princeton: Princeton University Press.

Bliss, Frederick Jones

    1898   *A Mound of Many Cities, or Tell el Hesy Excavated.* London: Palestine Exploration Fund.

Boehmer, Rainer Michael

    1972a   "Die Keramikfunde im Bereich des Steingebäudes." In *XXVI. und XXVII. vorläufiger Bericht über die von dem Deutschen Archäologischen Institut und der Deutschen Orient-Gesellschaft aus Mitteln der Deutschen Forschungsgemeinschaft unternommenen Ausgrabungen in Uruk-Warka*, by J. Schmidt et al., pp. 31–42. Berlin: Gebr. Mann Verlag.

    1972b   "Kleinfunde." In *XXVI. und XXVII. vorläufiger Bericht über die von dem Deutschen Archäologischen Institut und der Deutschen Orient-Gesellschaft aus Mitteln der Deutschen Forschungsgemeinschaft unternommenen Ausgrabungen in Uruk-Warka*, by J. Schmidt et al., pp. 70–76. Berlin: Gebr. Mann Verlag.

    1974   "Das Rollsiegel in prädynastischen Ägypten." *Archäologischer Anzeiger* 89:495–514.

Boese, Johannes

    1971   *Altmesopotamische Weihplatten: Ein sumerische Denkmalsgattung des 3. Jahrtausends v. Chr.* Untersuchungen zur Assyriologie und vorderasiatischen Archäologie, Ergänzungsbande zur Zeitschrift für Assyriologie und vorderasiatische Archäologie, Neue Folge, Band 6. Berlin and New York: Walter de Gruyter.

Boese, Johannes (*cont.*)

1986/87   "Excavations at Tell Sheikh Hassan: Preliminary Report on the 1987 Campaign in the Euphrates Valley." *Les Annales archéologiques arabes syriennes* 36/37:67–101.

Boucharlat, Rémy and Labrousse, Audran

1979   "Le Palais d'Artaxerxès II sur la rive droite du chaour à Suse." *Cahiers de la délégation archéologique française en Iran* 10:19–136.

Braidwood, Robert J.

1960   "Seeking the World's First Farmers in Persian Kurdistan." *The Illustrated London News*, October 22, pp. 695–97.

Braidwood, Robert J. and Braidwood, Linda S.

1960   *Excavations in the Plain of Antioch, Volume I: The Earlier Assemblages: Phases A–J*. Oriental Institute Publications, Vol. 61. Chicago: University of Chicago Press.

Braidwood, Robert J.; Braidwood, Linda S.; Howe, Bruce; Reed, Charles; and Watson, Patty Jo

1983   *Prehistoric Archeology Along the Zagros Flanks*. Oriental Institute Publications, Vol. 105. Chicago: The Oriental Institute.

Braidwood, Robert J.; Çambel, Halet; Schirmer, Wulf; et al.

1981   "Beginnings of Village-Farming Communities in Southeastern Turkey: Çayönü Tepesi, 1978 and 1979." *Journal of Field Archaeology* 8:249–58.

Braidwood, Robert J. and Howe, Bruce

1960   *Prehistoric Investigations in Iraqi Kurdistan*. Studies in Ancient Oriental Civilizations, No. 31. Chicago: University of Chicago Press.

Brandes, Mark A.

1968   *Untersuchungen zur Komposition der Stiftmosaiken an der Pfeilerhalle der Schicht IVa in Uruk-Warka*. Baghdader Mitteilungen, Beiheft 1. Berlin: Gebr. Mann Verlag.

1979   *Siegelabrollungen aus den archäischen Bauschichten in Uruk-Warka, I–II*. Freiburger altorientalische Studien, Band 3. Wiesbaden: Franz Steiner Verlag.

Brothwell, Don R.

1963   *Digging Up Bones*. London: British Museum.

Buchanan, Briggs

1966   *Catalogue of Ancient Near Eastern Seals in the Ashmolean Museum, Volume 1: Cylinder Seals*. Oxford: Oxford University Press.

Burkholder, Grace

1972   "Ubaid Sites and Pottery in Saudi Arabia." *Archaeology* 25:264–75.

Burkholder, Grace and Golding, Marny

1971   *Surface Survey of al-'Ubaid sites in the Eastern Province: Contribution to the Anthropology of Saudi Arabia*. Coconut Grove: Field Research Projects.

Burney, Charles

1980   "Aspects of the Excavations in the Altınova, Elazığ." *Anatolian Studies 30*:157–67.

Cajori, Florian

1928   *A History of Mathematical Notations, Volume 1: Notations in Elementary Mathematics*. Chicago: Open Court Publishing.

Caldwell, Joseph R., editor

1967   *Investigations at Tal-i-Iblis.* Illinois State Museum Preliminary Reports, No. 9. Springfield: Illinois State Museum Society.

1968   "Tell-i Ghazir." *Reallexikon der Assyriologie und verderasiatischen Archäologie* 3:348–55.

Calvet, Yves

1983   "Le Sondage profond en Y. 27 (1981)." In *Larsa et 'Oueili. Travaux de 1978–1981*, edited by J.-L. Huot, pp. 15–70. Recherche sur les Civilisations, Mémoire, No. 26. Paris: Éditions Recherche sur les Civilisations.

1985/86   "The New Deep Sounding X 36 at Tell el-'Oueili." *Sumer* 44:67–87.

1986   "Le Niveau Obeid 1 de Tell el-'Oueili." In *Préhistoire de la Mésopotamie: La Mésopotamie préhistorique et l'exploration récente du Djebel Hamrin,* edited by J.-L. Huot, pp. 129–39. Colloque international du Centre National de la Recherche Scientifique. Paris: Éditions du Centre National de la Recherche Scientifique.

1987   "Le Sondage X 36 de Tell el-'Oueili." *Rapport préliminaire,* edited by J.-L. Huot, pp. 33–94. Mémoire de la Centre National de la Recherche Scientifique, No. 73. Paris: Éditions du Centre National de la Recherche Scientifique.

Canal, D.

1978   "La Haute terrasse de l'acropole de Suse." *Paléorient* 4:169–76.

Carter, Elizabeth

1971   "Elam in the Second Millennium B.C.: The Archaeological Evidence." Ph.D. dissertation, Department of Near Eastern Languages and Civilizations, University of Chicago.

1979   "Elamite Pottery, ca. 2000–1000 B.C." *Journal of Near Eastern Studies* 38:111–28.

1980   "Excavations in Ville Royale I at Susa: The Third Millennium B.C. Occupation." *Cahiers de la délégation archéologique française en Iran* 11:11–134.

Carter, Elizabeth and Stolper, Matthew

1984   *Elam: Survey of Political History and Archaeology.* University of California Publications in Near Eastern Studies, Vol. 25. Los Angeles: University of California Press.

Cleuziou, Serge

1977   "Les Pointes de flèches 'scythiques' au Proche et Moyen-Orient." In *Le Plateau iranien et l'asie centrale des origines à la conquête islamique,* edited by J. Deshayes, pp. 186–99. Colloques internationaux du Centre National de la Recherche Scientifique, No. 567. Paris: Éditions du Centre National de la Recherche Scientifique.

Cohen, J. M., trans.

1959   *Don Quixote.* By Miguel de Cervantes. Bungay: Richard Clay.

Cowper, William, trans.

1913   *The Odyssey.* By Homer. New York: E. P. Dutton.

Delougaz, Pinhas

1938   "A Short Investigation of the Temple at al-'Ubaid." *Iraq* 5:1–11.

1940   *The Temple Oval at Khafājah.* Oriental Institute Publications, Vol. 53. Chicago: University of Chicago Press.

1952   *Pottery from the Diyala Region.* Oriental Institute Publications, Vol. 63. Chicago: University of Chicago Press.

1968   "Animals Emerging from a Hut." *Journal of Near Eastern Studies* 27:184–97.

Delougaz, Pinhas and Lloyd, Seton

1942 *Pre-Sargonid Temples in the Diyala Region.* Oriental Institute Publications, Vol. 58. Chicago: University of Chicago Press.

Delougaz, Pinhas; Hill, Harold D.; and Lloyd, Seton

1967 *Private Houses and Graves in the Diyala Region.* Oriental Institute Publications, Vol. 88. Chicago: University of Chicago Press.

de Mecquenem, Roland

1912 "Catalogue de la céramique peinte susienne conservée au Musée du Louvre." In *Céramique peinte de Suse et petits monuments de l'époque archaïque*, edited by J. de Morgan, pp. 105–58. Mémoires de la mission archéologique en Perse, Cinquième série, Tome 13. Paris: Ernest Leroux.

1928 "Notes sur la céramique peinte archaïque en Perse." In *Numismatique, épigraphie grecque, et céramique élamite*, edited by M. F. Allotte de la Fuÿe, F. Cumont, and R. de Mecquenem, pp. 99–132. Mémoires de la mission archéologique de Perse, Mission en Susiane, Tome 20. Paris: Ernest Leroux.

1934 "Fouilles de Suse 1929–1933." In *Archéologie, métrologie et numismatique susienne*, edited by M. F. Allotte de la Fuÿe, N. T. Belaiew, R. de Mecquenem, and J.-M. Unvala, pp. 177–237. Mémoires de la mission archéologique de Perse, Mission en Susiane, Tome 25. Paris: Ernest Leroux.

de Mecquenem, Roland, et al.

1943 "Fouilles de Suse, 1933–1939. " In *Archéologie susienne*, edited by R. de Mecquenem, G. Contenau, R. Pfister, and N. T. Belaiew, pp. 3–161. Mémoires de la mission archéologique en Iran, Mission de Susiane, Tome 29. Paris: Presses Universitaires de France.

de Morgan, Jacques

1900 "Appendice No. 1: Céramique archaïque" In *Fouilles à Suse en 1897–98 et 1898–99*, by J. de Morgan, G. Lampre, and G. Jéquier, pp. 183–90. Mémoires de la mission archéologique de Perse, Recherches archéologiques, Première série, Tome 1. Paris: Ernest Leroux.

1905 "Découverte d'une sépulture achéménide à Suse." In *Recherches archéologiques*, edited by J. de Morgan, pp. 29–58. Mémoires de la mission archéologique de Perse, Troisième série, Tome 8. Paris: Ernest Leroux.

1912 "Observations sur les couches profondes de l'acropole à Suse." In *Céramique peinte de Suse and petits monuments de l'époque archaïque*, edited by J. de Morgan, pp. 1–25. Mémoires de la mission archéologique de Perse, Cinquième série, Tome 13. Paris: Ernest Leroux.

Deshayes, Jean

1960 *Les Outils de bronze, de l'Indus au Danube (IVe au IIe millénaire)*, I–II. Institut français d'archéologie de Beyrouth, Bibliothèque Archéologique et Historique, Tome 71. Paris: Paul Geuthner.

1977 "À propos des terrasses hautes de la fin du IIIe millénaire en Iran et en Asie centrale." In *Le Plateau iranien et l'Asie centrale des origines à la conquête islamique*, edited by J. Deshayes, pp. 95–111. Colloques internationaux du Centre National de la Recherche Scientifique, No. 567. Paris: Éditions du Centre National de la Recherche Scientifique.

DeVries, Carl E.

1969   "A Ritual Ball Game?" In *Studies in Honor of John A. Wilson, September 12, 1969*, edited by E. B. Hauser, pp. 25–35. Studies in Ancient Oriental Civilization, No. 35. Chicago: University of Chicago Press.

Dingwall, Eric John

1931   *Artificial Cranial Deformation: A Contribution to the Study of Ethnic Mutilations.* London: J. Bale and Danielesson.

Dittmann, Reinhard

1984   *Eine Randebene des Zagros in der Frühzeit: Ergebnisse des Behbehan-Zuhreh Surveys.* Berliner Beiträge zum Vorderen Orient, Band 3. Berlin: Dietrich Reimer Verlag.

1986   "Seals, Sealings, and Tablets: Thoughts on the Changing Pattern of Administrative Control from the Late-Uruk to the Proto-Elamite Period at Susa." In *Ǧamdat Naṣr: Period or Regional Style?*, edited by U. Finkbeiner and W. Röllig, pp. 332–66. Beihefte zum Tübinger Atlas des Vorderen Orients, Reihe B, No. 62. Wiesbaden: Dr. Ludwig Reichert.

Dollfus, Geneviève

1971   "Les Fouilles: Djaffarabad de 1969 à 1971." *Cahiers de la délégation archéologique française en Iran* 1:17–161.

1975   "Les Fouilles: Djaffarabad de 1972 à 1974, Djaffarabad, périodes I et II." *Cahiers de la délégation archéologique française en Iran* 5:11–222.

1978   "Djaffarabad, Djowi, Bandebal: Contribution à l'étude de la Susiane au début V^e millénaire et au début du IVe millénaire." *Paléorient* 4:141–67.

1983   "Djowi et Bandebal: Deux villages de la plaine centrale du Khuzistan, Iran, V^e millénaire avant J.-C., Travaux de 1975, 1977, 1978." *Cahiers de la délégation archéologique française en Iran* 13:17–284.

1987   "Peut-on parler de 'Choga Mami Transitional' dans le sud-ouest de l'Iran?" In *Préhistoire de la Mésopotamie: La Mésopotamie préhistorique et l'exploration récente du Djebel Hamrin*, edited by J.-L. Huot, pp. 181–88. Colloque international du Centre National de la Recherche Scientifique. Paris: Éditions du Centre National de la Recherche Scientifique.

Dollfus, Geneviève and Encreve, P.

1982   "Marques sur poteries dans la Susiane du Ve millénaire: Réflexions et comparaisons." *Paléorient* 8:107–15.

Dollfus, Geneviève and Hesse, Albert

1977   "Les Structures de combustion du Tépé Djaffarabad, périodes I à III." *Cahiers de la délégation archéologique française en Iran* 7:11–47.

Dyson, Robert H., Jr.

1965   "Problems in the Relative Chronology of Iran, 6000–2000 B.C." In *Chronologies in Old World Archaeology*, edited by R. W. Ehrich, pp. 215–56. Chicago: University of Chicago Press.

1968   "Annotations and Corrections on the Relative Chronology of Iran, 1968." *American Journal of Archaeology* 72:308–13.

Ehrich, Robert W., editor

1965   *Chronologies in Old World Archaeology.* Chicago: University of Chicago Press.

Egami, Namio and Masuda, Seiichi

    1962   *Marv-Dasht I: The Excavation at Tall-i-Bakun 1956*. The Tokyo University Iraq-Iran Archaeological Expedition, Report, No. 2. Tokyo: Yamakawa Publishing.

Egami, Namio and Sono, Toshihiko

    1962   *Marv-Dasht II: The Excavation at Tall-i-Gap 1959*. The Tokyo University Iraq-Iran Archaeological Expedition, Report, No. 3. Tokyo: Yamakawa Publishing.

Ellis, Richard S.

    1968   *Foundation Deposits in Ancient Mesopotamia*. Yale Near Eastern Researches, No. 2. New Haven and London: Yale University Press.

el-Wailly, Faisal and Abu es-Soof, Behnam

    1965   "Excavations at Tell es-Sawwan, First Preliminary Report (1964)." *Sumer* 21:17–32.

Esin, Ufuk

    1974   "Tepecik Excavations, 1971." In *Keban Project 1971 Activities*, edited by Middle East Technical University. Keban Project Publications Series, Vol. 1, No. 4. Ankara: Turkish Historical Society Press.

Falkenstein, Adam

    1936   *Archäische Texte aus Uruk*. Ausgrabungen der Deutschen Forschungsgemeinschaft in Uruk-Warka, Band 2. Leipzig: Otto Harrassowitz.

Ferioli, Piera and Fiandra, Enrica

    1979a   "Stamp Seals and the Functional Analysis of their Sealings at Shahr-i Sokhta II–III (2700–2200 B.C.), Part 2." In *South Asian Archaeology 1975*, edited by J. E. Van Lohuizen-De Leeuw, pp. 12–26. Leiden: E. J. Brill.

    1979b   "The Administrative Functions of Clay Sealings in Proto-historical Iran." In *Iranica*, Series minor, No. 10, edited by G. Gnoli and A. V. Rossi, pp. 307–12. Naples: Istituto Universitario Orientale, Seminario di Studi Asiatici.

Fiandra, Enrica

    1975   "Ancora a proposito delle cretule di Festòs: connessione tra i sistemi amministrativi centralizzati e l'uso delle cretule nell'età del bronzo." *Bollettino d'Arte*, Serie 5, Anno 60:1–25.

    1981a   "Attività a Kish di un Mercante di Lagash in Epoca Presargonica." *Oriens Antiquus* 20:165–74.

    1981b   "The Connection between Clay Sealings and Tablets in Administration." In *South Asian Archaeology 1979*, edited by H. Härtel, pp. 29–43. Berlin: Dietrich Reimer Verlag.

Finet, André

    1975   "Les Temples sumériens du Tell Kannâs." *Syria* 52:157–74.

    1979   "Bilan provisoire des fouilles belges du Tell Kannâs." In *Excavation Reports from the Tabqa Dam Project—Euphrates Valley, Syria*, edited by D. N. Freedman, pp. 79–95. Annual of the American Schools of Oriental Research, No. 44. Cambridge, Massachusetts: American Schools of Oriental Research.

Finet, André, editor

    1982   *Lorsque la royauté descendit du ciel: Les Fouilles belges du Tell Kannâs sur l'Euphrate en Syrie*. Brussels: Musée royale de Mariemont.

Forbes, Robert J.

    1964   *Studies in Ancient Technology, Volume 4*. Leiden. E. J. Brill.

Frankfort, Henri

   1935   *Oriental Institute Discoveries in Iraq, 1933/34: Fourth Preliminary Report of the Iraq Expedition.* Oriental Institute Communications, No. 19. Chicago: University of Chicago Press.

   1936   *Progress of the Work of the Oriental Institute in Iraq, 1934/35: Fifth Preliminary Report of the Iraq Expedition.* Oriental Institute Communications, No. 20. Chicago: University of Chicago Press.

   1939a   *Cylinder Seals: A Documentary Essay on the Art and Religion of the Ancient Near East.* London: MacMillan.

   1939b   *Sculpture of the Third Millennium B.C. from Tell Asmar and Khafājah.* Oriental Institute Publications, Vol. 44. Chicago: University of Chicago Press.

   1943   *More Sculpture from the Diyala Region.* Oriental Institute Publications, Vol. 60. Chicago: University of Chicago Press.

   1951   *The Birth of Civilization in the Near East.* Bloomington: Indiana University Press.

   1954   *The Art and Architecture of the Ancient Orient.* Harmondsworth: Penguin Books.

   1955   *Stratified Cylinder Seals from the Diyala Region.* Oriental Institute Publications, Vol. 72. Chicago: University of Chicago Press.

Friberg, Jöran

   1978/79 *The Third Millennium Roots of Babylonian Mathematics, Volume 1: A Method for the Decipherment, through Mathematical and Metrological Analysis, of Proto-Sumerian and Proto-Elamite Semi-Pictographic Inscriptions.* Göteborg: Department of Mathematics, Chalmers University of Technology and University of Göteborg.

   1984   "Numbers and Measures in the Earliest Written Records." *Scientific American,* February 1984:110–18.

   1994   "Preliterate Counting and Accounting in the Middle East. A Constructively Critical Review of Schmandt-Besserat's *Before Writing.*" *Orientalische Literaturzeitung* 89:477–502.

Frifelt, Karen

   1975   "On Prehistoric Settlement and Chronology of the Oman Peninsula." *East and West* 25:359–423.

Fujii, Hideo

   1981   "Preliminary Report of Excavations at Gubba and Songor." *Al-Rāfidān,* pp. 131–242.

Garstang, John

   1904   *Tombs of the Third Egyptian Dynasty at Reqaqnah and Bet Khallaf.* Westminster: A. Constable.

   1953   *Prehistoric Mersin: Yümük Tepe in Southern Turkey* (The Neilson Expedition in Cilicia). Oxford: Oxford University Press.

Gasche, Hermann

   1973   *La Poterie élamite du deuxième millénaire a.C.* Mémoires de la délégation archéologique en Iran, Mission de Susiane, Tome 47. Leiden: E. J. Brill; Paris: Paul Geuthner.

Gautier, J. E. and Lampre, G.

   1905   "Fouilles de Moussian." In *Recherches archéologiques,* edited by J. de Morgan, pp. 59–148. Mémoires de la mission archéologique de Perse, Troisième série, Tome 8. Paris: Ernest Leroux.

Genouillac, Henri de, et al.

   1934   *Fouilles de Telloh, Tome 1: Époques présargoniques.* Paris: Paul Geuthner.

Ghirshman, Roman

  1935   *Fouilles du Tépé-Giyan près de Néhavend: 1931 et 1932*. Musée du Louvre, Département des an-
            tiquités orientales, Série archéologique, Tome 3. Paris: Paul Geuthner.

  1938   *Fouilles de Sialk près de Kashan, Volume 1: 1933, 1934, 1937*. Musée du Louvre, Département
            des antiquités orientales, Série archéologique, Tome 4. Paris: Paul Geuthner.

  1954   *Village perse-achéménide*. Mémoires de la mission archéologique en Iran, Mission de Susiane,
            Tome 36. Paris: Presses Universitaires de France.

  1966   *Tchoga Zanbil (Dur-Untash), Volume 1: La Ziggurat*. Mémoires de la délégation archéologique
            en Iran, Mission de Susiane, Tome 39. Paris: Paul Geuthner.

  1970   "The Elamite Levels at Susa and Their Chronological Significance." *American Journal of Ar-
            chaeology* 74:223–25.

Goff, Clare L.

  1963   "Excavations at Tall-i-Nokhodi." *Iran* 1:43–70.

  1968   "Luristan in the First Half of the First Millennium B.C.: A Preliminary Report on the First Sea-
            son's Excavations at Baba Jan and Associated Surveys in the Eastern Pish-i-Kuh." *Iran* 6:105–
            34.

  1970   "Excavations at Baba Jan, 1968: Third Preliminary Report." *Iran* 8:141–56.

  1971   "Luristan Before the Iron Age." *Iran* 9:131–52.

  1976   "The Excavations at Baba Jan: The Bronze Age Occupation." *Iran* 14:19–40.

Gordon, Cyrus H.

  1939   "Western Asiatic Seals in the Walters Art Gallery." *Iraq* 6:3–34.

Gotch, Paul

  1968   "A Survey of the Persepolis Plain and Shiraz Area." *Iran* 6:168–70.

  1969   "Persepolis Plain and Shiraz: Field Survey 2." *Iran* 7:190–92.

Groenewegen-Frankfort, H. A.

  1951   *Arrest and Movement: An Essay on Space and Time in the Representational Art of the Ancient
            Near East*. Chicago: University of Chicago Press.

Haerinck, Ernie

  1979   "Contribution à l'étude de la céramique d'époque parthe en Iran." In *Proceedings of the Seventh
            International Congress for Iranian Art and Archaeology, München 7–10 September 1976*, pp.
            286–93. Archäologische Mitteilungen aus Iran, Ergänzungsband 6. Berlin: Dietrich Reimer Ver-
            lag.

  1983   *La Céramique en Iran pendant le période parthe*. Gent, Iranica Antiqua Supplément 2. Leuven:
            Imprimerie Orientaliste.

Hall, Harry Reginald Holland; Woolley, Leonard; Gadd, C. J.; and Keith, Arthur

  1927   *Ur Excavations 1: Al-'Ubaid*. Publications of the Joint Expedition of the British Museum and of
            the Museum of the University of Pennsylvania to Mesopotamia. Oxford: Oxford University
            Press.

Haller, Arndt von

  1932   "Die Keramik der archäischen Schichten von Uruk." In *Vierter vorläufiger Bericht über die von
            der Notgemeinschaft der Deutschen Wissenschaft in Uruk unternommenen Ausgrabungen*, by A.
            Nöldeke et al., pp. 31–47. Berlin: Verlag der Akademie der Wissenschaften.

1954 *Die Gräber und Grüfte von Assur.* Wissenschaftliche Veröffentlichung der Deutschen Orient-Gesellschaft, Band 65. Berlin: Verlag Gebr. Mann.

Hamilton, R. W.

1966 "A Silver Bowl in the Ashmolean Museum." *Iraq* 28:1–17.

Hampe, Roland and Winter, Adam

1962 *Bei Töpfern und Töpferinnen in Kreta, Messenien und Zypern.* Mainz: Verlag des Römisch-germanischen Zentralmuseums.

Hansen, Donald P.

1963 "New Votive Plaques from Nippur." *Journal of Near Eastern Studies* 22:145–66.

1965 "The Relative Chronology of Mesopotamia, Part 2: The Pottery Sequence at Nippur from the Middle Uruk to the End of the Old Babylonia Period." In *Chronologies in Old World Archaeology*, edited by R. W. Ehrich, pp. 201–13. Chicago: University of Chicago Press.

Hansen, Donald P. and Dales, George F.

1962 "The Temple of Inanna Queen of Heaven at Nippur." *Archaeology* 15:75–84.

Hansman, John

1978 "Seleucia and the Three Dauraks." *Iran* 16:154–61.

Hansman, John and Stronach, David

1970 "Excavations at Shahr-i Qūmis, 1967." *Journal of the Royal Asiatic Society*, pp. 29–62.

1974 "Excavations at Shahr-i Qūmis, 1971." *Journal of the Royal Asiatic Society*, pp. 8–22.

Hartmann, Henrike

1960 *Die Musik der sumerischen Kultur.* Dissertation, Universität Frankfurt. Frankfurt am Main: J. W. Goethe-Universität.

Heath, Martha C.

1958 "Early Helladic Clay Sealings from the House of the Tiles at Lerna." *Hesperia* 27:81–121.

Heinrich, Ernst

1932 "Die Schichten und ihre Bauten." In *Vierter vorläufiger Bericht über die von der Notgemeinschaft der Deutschen Wissenschaft in Uruk unternommenen Ausgrabungen*, by A. Nöldeke et al., pp. 6–24. Berlin: Verlag der Akademie der Wissenschaften.

1934 "Arbeiten in Eanna, im Stadtgebiet und im Südbau." In *Fünfter vorläufiger Bericht über die von der Notgemeinschaft der Deutschen Wissenschaft in Uruk unternommenen Ausgrabungen*, by A. Nöldeke et al., pp. 5–38. Berlin: Verlag der Akademie der Wissenschaften.

1935 *Sechster vorläufiger Bericht über die von der Deutschen Forschungsgemeinschaft in Uruk-Warka unternommenen Ausgrabungen.* Berlin: Verlag der Akademie der Wissenschaften.

1936 *Kleinfunde aus den archäischen Tempelschichten in Uruk.* Ausgrabungen der Deutschen Forschungsgemeinschaft in Uruk-Warka, Band 1. Leipzig: Otto Harrassowitz.

1937 "Die Grabung im Planquadrat K XVII." In *Achter vorläufiger Bericht über die von der Deutschen Forschungsgemeinschaft in Uruk-Warka unternommenen Ausgrabungen*, by A. Nöldeke et al., pp. 27–55. Berlin: Verlag der Akademie der Wissenschaften.

1938 "Grabungen im Gebiet des Anu-Antum-Temple." In *Neunter vorläufiger Bericht über die von der Deutschen Forschungsgemeinschaft in Uruk-Warka unternommenen Ausgrabungen*, pp. 19–30. Berlin: Verlag der Akademie der Wissenschaften.

Heinrich, Ernst (*cont.*)

1939   "Grabungen im Gebiet des Anu-Antum-Tempels." In *Zehnter vorläufiger Bericht über die von der Deutschen Forschungsgemeinschaft in Uruk-Warka unternommenen Ausgrabungen*, by A. Nöldeke et al., pp. 21–34. Berlin: Verlag der Akademie der Wissenschaften.

1957   *Bauwerke in der altsumerischen Bildkunst*. Schriften der Max Freiherr von Oppenheim-Stiftung, Heft 2. Wiesbaden: Otto Harrassowitz.

Heinrich, Ernst and Falkenstein, Adam

1938   "Forschungen in der Umgebung von Warka." In *Neunter vorläufiger Bericht über die von der Deutschen Forschungsgemeinschaft in Uruk-Warka unternommenen Ausgrabungen*, by A. Nöldeke et al., pp. 31–38. Berlin: Verlag der Akademie der Wissenschaften.

Helbaek, Hans

1969   "Plant Collecting, Dry-farming, and Irrigation Agriculture in Prehistoric Deh Luran." In *Prehistory and Human Ecology of the Deh Luran Plain: An Early Village Sequence from Khuzistan, Iran*, by F. Hole, K. V. Flannery, and J. A. Neely, Appendix 1, pp. 383–426. Memoirs of the Museum of Anthropology, No. 1. Ann Arbor: University of Michigan.

1972   "Samarran Irrigation Agriculture at Choga Mami in Iraq." *Iraq* 34:35–48.

Helms, Svend Walter

1976   "Jawa Excavations 1974: A Preliminary Report." *Levant* 8:1–35.

1981   *Jawa: Lost City of the Black Desert*. Ithaca: Cornell University Press.

Herzfeld, Ernst

1930   *Die Ausgrabungen von Samarra: Die vorgeschichtlichen Töpfereien von Samarra*. Berlin: Verlag Dietrich Reimer.

Hoffman, Marta

1964   *The Warp-weighted Loom: Studies in the History and Technology of an Ancient Implement*. Studia Norvegica, No. 14. Oslo: Universitetsforlaget.

Hoh, Manfred R.

1981   "Die Keramik von Hassek Höyük." In "Hassek Höyük: Vorläufiger Bericht über die Grabungen in der Jahre 1978–1980," by M. Behm-Blancke et al. *Istanbuler Mitteilungen* 31:31–82.

1984   "Die Keramik von Hassek Höyük." In "Hassek Höyük: Vorläufiger Bericht über die Grabungen in den Jahren 1981–1983," by M. Behm-Blancke et al. *Istanbuler Mitteilungen* 34:66–91.

Hole, Frank

1974   "Tepe Tula'i: An Early Campsite in Khuzistan, Iran." *Paléorient* 2/2:219–42.

1975   "The Sondage at Tappeh Tula'i." *Proceedings of the Third Annual Symposium on Archaeological Research in Iran*, pp. 63–76. Tehran: Iranian Centre for Archaeological Research.

1977   *Studies in the Archaeological History of the Deh Luran Plain: The Excavation of Chagha Sefid*. Memoirs of the Museum of Anthropology, No. 9. Ann Arbor: University of Michigan.

1987   *The Archaeology of Western Iran: Settlement and Society from Prehistory to the Islamic Conquest*. Edited by F. Hole. Smithsonian Series in Archaeological Inquiry. Washington, D.C.: Smithsonian Institution Press.

Hole, Frank; Flannery, Kent V.; and Neely, James A.

1969   *Prehistory and Human Ecology of the Deh Luran Plain: An Early Village Sequence from Khuzistan, Iran*. Memoirs of the Museum of Anthropology, No. 1. Ann Arbor: University of Michigan.

Homès-Fredericq, D.

1970 *Les Cachets mésopotamiens protohistoriques*. Documenta et Monument Orientis Antiqui, Vol. 14. Leiden: E. J. Brill.

Huot, Jean-Louis

1987 *Préhistoire de la Mésopotamie*: *La Mésopotamie préhistorique et l'exploration récente du Djebel Hamrin*. Colloque international du Centre National de la Recherche Scientifique. Paris: Éditions du Centre National de la Recherche Scientifique.

Huot, Jean-Louis; Bachelot, L.; Braun, J. P.; Calvet, Yves; Cleuziou, Serge; Forest, J. D.; and Seigne, J.

1980 "Larsa: Preliminary Report of the Seventh Campaign at Larsa and the First Campaign at Tell el-'Oueili (1976)." *Sumer* 36:99–127.

Ippolitoni, Fiorella

1970/71 "The Pottery of Tell es-Sawwan, First Season." *Mesopotamia* 5–6:105–79.

Johnson, Gregory Allan

1973 *Local Exchange and Early State Development in Southwestern Iran*. Anthropological Papers, Museum of Anthropology, No. 51. Ann Arbor: University of Michigan.

1975 "Locational Analysis and the Investigation of Uruk Local Exchange Systems." In *Ancient Civilization and Trade*, edited by J. A. Sabloff and C. C. Lamberg-Karlovsky, pp. 285–339. Albuquerque: University of New Mexico Press.

Jordan, Julius

1928 *Uruk-Warka*. Wissenschaftliche Veröffentlichung der Deutschen Orient-Gesellschaft, Band 51. Leipzig: J. C. Hinrichs.

1932 *Dritter vorläufiger Bericht über die von der Notgemeinschaft der Deutschen Wissenschaft in Uruk unternommenen Ausgrabungen*. Berlin: Verlag der Akademie der Wissenschaften.

Kalsbeek, J.

1980 "La Céramique de série du Djebel 'Aruda (à l'époque d'Uruk)." *Akkadica* 20:1–11.

Kantor, Helene J.

1952 "Further Evidence for Early Mesopotamian Relations with Egypt." *Journal of Near Eastern Studies* 11:239–50.

1965 "The Relative Chronology of Egypt and its Foreign Correlations Before the Late Bronze Age." In *Chronologies in Old World Archaeology*, edited by R. W. Ehrich, pp. 1–46. Chicago: University of Chicago Press.

1972/73 "Excavations at Chogha Mish." *Oriental Institute Annual Report*, edited by J. A. Brinkman, pp. 10–17. Chicago: The Oriental Institute.

1974 "Ägypten." In *Frühe Stüfen der Kunst,* edited by M. J. Mellink and J. Filip, pp. 227–56, pls. 188–225. Propyläen Kunstgeschichte, Band 13. Berlin: Propyläen Verlag.

1975/76 "Excavations at Chogha Mish." *Oriental Institute Annual Report,* edited by J. A. Brinkman, pp. 12–21. Chicago: The Oriental Institute.

1976 "The Prehistoric Cultures of Chogha Mish and Boneh Fazili." In *The Memorial Volume of the Sixth International Congress of Iranian Art and Archaeology, Oxford, September 11–16th, 1972*, edited by M. Y. Kiani, pp. 177–93. Tehran: Iranian Centre for Archaeological Research.

1976/77 "Excavations at Chogha Mish and Chogha Banut." *Oriental Institute Annual Report*, edited by J. A. Brinkman, pp. 15–24. Chicago: The Oriental Institute.

1984 "The Ancestry of the Divine Boat (Sirsir?) of Early Dynastic and Akkadian Glyptic." *Journal of Near Eastern Studies* 43:277–80.

Kirkbride, Diana

    1972   "Umm Dabaghiyah 1971: A Preliminary Report." *Iraq* 34:3–19.

    1974   "Umm Dabaghiyah: A Trading Outpost?" *Iraq* 36:85–92.

Klebs, Luise

    1915   *Die Reliefs des alten Reiches.* Heidelberg: Carl Winters Universitätsbuchhandlung.

Korfmann, Manfred

    1972   *Schleuder und Bogen in Südwestasien.* Antiquitas, Band 3. Bonn: Rudolf Habelt Verlag.

Kraus, Fritz Rudolf

    1948   "Ein altakkadisches Festungsbild." *Iraq* 10:81–92.

Labrousse, Audran and Boucharlat, Rémy

    1974   "La Fouille du palais du Chaour à Suse en 1970 et 1971." *Cahiers de la délégation archéologique française en Iran* 2:61–167.

Lamberg-Karlovsky, C. C.

    1971   "The Proto-Elamite Settlement at Tepe Yahya." *Iran* 9:87–95.

Lamberg-Karlovsky, C. C. and Tosi, Mario

    1974   "Shahr-i Sokhta and Tepe Yahya: Tracks on the Earliest History of the Iranian Plateau." *East and West*, New Series, 24:21–57.

Lambert, Wilfred George

    1979   "Near Eastern Seals in the Gulbenkian Museum of Oriental Art, University of Durham." *Iraq* 41:1–45.

Landsberger, Benno

  1947–52   "Assyriologische Notizen 2: Das Symbol der verflochten Schlangen." *Die Welt des Orients* 1:366–68.

Langsdorff, Alexander and McCown, Donald E.

    1942   *Tall-i-Bakun A, Season of 1932.* Oriental Institute Publications, Vol. 59. Chicago: University of Chicago Press.

Layard, Austin Henry

    1846   "Description of the Plain of Khuzistan." *Journal of the Royal Asiatic Society* 16:78–86.

    1894   *Early Adventures in Persia, Susiana, and Babylonia.* London: John Murray.

Lebeau, Marc

  1985/86   "A First Report on Pre-Eridu Pottery from Tell el-Oueilli." *Sumer* 44:88–108.

Le Breton, Louis

    1947   "Note sur la céramique peinte aux environs de Suse et à Suse." In *Archéologique susienne*, by R. de Mecquenem, L. Le Breton, and M. Ruten, pp. 120–219. Mémoires de la mission archéologique en Iran, Mission de Susiane, Tome 30. Paris: Presses Universitaires de France.

    1948   *Essai de classification de la céramique peinte de Suse II.* Thèse de l'École du Louvre 1947–48.

    1957   "The Early Periods at Susa, Mesopotamian Relations." *Iraq* 19:79–124.

Le Brun, Alain

    1971   "Recherches stratigraphiques: L'Acropole de Suse 1969–1971." *Cahiers de la délégation archéologique française en Iran* 1:163–216.

1978a   "Le Niveau 17B de l'acropole de Suse." *Cahiers de la délégation archéologique française en Iran* 9:57–156.

1978b   "Suse, Chantier 'Acropole I.'" *Paléorient* 4:177–92.

1978c   "La Glyptique du niveau 17B de l'acropole (Campagne de 1972)." *Cahiers de la délégation archéologique française en Iran* 8:61–79.

1980   "Les 'Ecuelles grossières': État de la question." In *L'Archéologie de l'Iraq du début de l'époque néolithique à 333 avant notre ère,* edited by M.-T. Barrelet, pp. 59–70. Colloques internationaux du Centre National de la Recherche Scientifique, No. 580. Paris: Éditions du Centre National de la Recherche Scientifique.

Le Brun, Alain and Vallat, François

1978   "L'Origine de l'écriture à Suse." *Cahiers de la délégation archéologique française en Iran* 8:11–59.

Legrain, Léon

1921   *Empreintes de cachets élamites.* Mémoires de la mission archéologique de Perse, Mission en Susiane, Tome 16. Paris: Ernest Leroux.

1936   *Ur Excavations, Volume 3: Archaic Seal-Impressions.* Publications of the Joint Expedition of the British Museum and of the University Museum, University of Pennsylvania, Philadelphia to Mesopotamia. Oxford: Oxford University Press.

1951   *Ur Excavations, Volume 10: Seal Cylinders.* Oxford: Oxford University Press.

Lenzen, Heinrich

1932   "Die Kleinfunde." In *Vierter vorläufiger Bericht über die von der Notgemeinschaft der Deutschen Wissenschaft in Uruk unternommenen Ausgrabungen,* by A. Nöldeke et al., pp. 25–30. Berlin: Verlag der Akademie der Wissenschaften.

1959a   "Die Ausgrabungen an der Westecke von E-anna." In *XV. vorläufiger Bericht über die von dem Deutschen Archäologischen Institut und der Deutschen Orient-Gesellschaft aus Mitteln der Deutschen Forschungsgemeinschaft unternommenen Ausgrabungen in Uruk-Warka,* by H. Lenzen et al., pp. 8–19. Berlin: Verlag Gebr. Mann.

1959b   "Kleinfunde aus dem Bezirk des Steinstifttempels." In *XV. vorläufiger Bericht über die von dem Deutschen Archäologischen Institut und der Deutschen Orient-Gesellschaft aus Mitteln der Deutschen Forschungsgemeinschaft unternommenen Ausgrabungen in Uruk-Warka,* by H. Lenzen et al., pp. 20–23. Berlin: Verlag Gebr. Mann.

1960   "Die Kleinfunde." In *XVI. vorläufiger Bericht über die von dem Deutschen Archäologischen Institut und der Deutschen Orient-Gesellschaft aus Mitteln der Deutschen Forschungsgemeinschaft unternommenen Ausgrabungen in Uruk-Warka,* by H. Lenzen et al., pp. 47–56. Berlin: Verlag Gebr. Mann.

1961   "Die Kleinfunde." In *XVII. vorläufiger Bericht über die von dem Deutschen Archäologischen Institut und der Deutschen Orient-Gesellschaft aus Mitteln der Deutschen Forschungsgemeinschaft unternommenen Ausgrabungen in Uruk-Warka,* by H. Lenzen et al., pp. 24–37. Berlin: Verlag Gebr. Mann.

1963a   "Die archäischen Schichten von E-anna." In *XIX. vorläufiger Bericht über die von dem Deutschen Archäologischen Institut und der Deutschen Orient-Gesellschaft aus Mitteln der Deutschen Forschungsgemeinschaft unternommenen Ausgrabungen in Uruk-Warka,* pp. 8–14. Berlin: Verlag Gebr. Mann.

Lenzen, Heinrich (*cont.*)

1963b   "Die Siegelarollungen aus E-anna." In *XIX. vorläufiger Bericht über die von dem Deutschen Archäologischen Institut und der Deutschen Orient-Gesellschaft aus Mitteln der Deutschen Forschungsgemeinschaft unternommenen Ausgrabungen in Uruk-Warka*, pp. 17–24. Berlin: Verlag Gebr. Mann.

1964   "Die Siegelabrollungen." In *XX. vorläufiger Bericht über die von dem Deutschen Archäologischen Institut und der Deutschen Orient-Gesellschaft aus Mitteln der Deutschen Forschungsgemeinschaft unternommenen Ausgrabungen in Uruk-Warka*, by H. Lenzen et al., pp. 22–23. Berlin: Verlag Gebr. Mann.

1965   "Zwischenschicht zwischen Archäisch III und Archäisch IV." In *XXI. vorläufiger Bericht über die von dem Deutschen Archäologischen Institut und der Deutschen Orient-Gesellschaft aus Mitteln der Deutschen Forschungsgemeinschaft unternommenen Ausgrabungen in Uruk-Warka*, by H. Lenzen et al., pp. 13–15. Berlin: Verlag Gebr. Mann.

1974   "Terrakotten." In *XXV. vorläufiger Bericht über die von dem Deutschen Archäologischen Institut und der Deutschen Orient-Gesellschaft aus Mitteln der Deutschen Forschungsgemeinschaft unternommenen Ausgrabungen in Uruk-Warka*, by H. Lenzen et al., pp. 27–30. Berlin: Verlag Gebr. Mann.

Lenzen, Heinrich, et al., editors

1958   *XIV. vorläufiger Bericht über die von dem Deutschen Archäologischen Institut und der Deutschen Orient-Gesellschaft aus Mitteln der Deutschen Forschungsgemeinschaft unternommenen Ausgrabungen in Uruk-Warka.* Berlin: Verlag Gebr. Mann.

1960   *XVI. vorläufiger Bericht über die von dem Deutschen Archäologischen Institut und der Deutschen Orient-Gesellschaft aus Mitteln der Deutschen Forschungsgemeinschaft unternommenen Ausgrabungen in Uruk-Warka.* Berlin: Verlag Gebr. Mann.

1966   *XXII. vorläufiger Bericht Über die von dem Deutschen Archäologischen Institut und der Deutschen Orient-Gesellschaft aus Mitteln der Deutschen Forschungsgemeinschaft unternommenen Ausgrabungen in Uruk-Warka.* Berlin: Verlag Gebr. Mann.

1967   *XXIII. vorläufiger Bericht über die von dem Deutschen Archäologischen Institut und der Deutschen Orient-Gesellschaft aus Mitteln der Deutschen Forschungsgemeinschaft unternommenen Ausgrabungen in Uruk-Warka.* Berlin: Verlag Gebr. Mann.

Levine, Louis and Young, T. Cuyler

1987   "A Summary of the Ceramic Assemblages of the Central Western Zagros from the Middle Neolithic to the Late Third Millennium B.C." In *Préhistoire de la Mésopotamie: La Mésopotamie préhistorique et l'exploration récente du Djebel Hamrin*, edited by J.-L. Huot, pp. 15–53. Colloque international du Centre National de la Recherche Scientifique. Paris: Éditions du Centre National de Recherche Scientifique.

Lieberman, Stephen J.

1980   "Of Clay Pebbles, Hollow Clay Balls and Writing: A Sumerian View." *American Journal of Archaeology* 84:339–58.

Lloyd, Seton

1948   "Uruk Pottery: A Comparative Study in Relation to Recent Finds at Eridu." *Sumer* 4:39–50.

1978   *The Archaeology of Mesopotamia from the Old Stone Age to the Persian Conquest.* London: Thames and Hudson.

Lloyd, Seton and Safar, Fuad

    1940   "Iraq Government Soundings at Sinjar." *Iraq* 7:13–21.

    1943   "Tell Uqair: Excavations by the Iraq Government Directorate of Antiquities in 1940 and 1941." *Journal of Near Eastern Studies* 2:131–58.

    1945   "Tell Hassuna: Excavations of the Iraq Government Directorate General of Antiquities in 1943 and 1944." *Journal of Near Eastern Studies* 4:255–84.

    1948   "Eridu: A Preliminary Communication on the Second Season's Excavations, 1947–1948." *Sumer* 4:115–27.

Loftus, William Kennett

    1857   *Travels and Researches in Chaldaea and Susiana*. London: James Nisbet.

Loud, Gordon

    1948   *Megiddo, Volume II: Seasons of 1935–39*. Oriental Institute Publications, Vol. 62. Chicago: University of Chicago Press.

Lucas, Alfred and Harris, J. R.

    1962   *Ancient Egyptian Materials and Industries*. 4th ed. London: Edward Arnold.

Ludwig, W.

    1980   "Mass, Sitte und Technik des Bauens in Habuba Kabira-Süd." In *Le Moyen Euphrate: Zone de contacts et d'échanges. Actes du Colloque de Strasbourg 10–12 mars 1977*, edited by J.-C. Margueron, pp. 63–74. Travaux du Centre de Recherche sur le Proche-Orient et la Grèce Antiques, No. 5. Leiden: E. J. Brill.

Luschey, Heinz

    1939   *Die Phiale*. Bleicherode am Harz: C. Nieft.

Lythgoe, Albert M. and Dunham, Dows

    1965   *The Predynastic Cemetery N 7000: Naga-ed-Der, Part 4*. Berkeley and Los Angeles: University of California Press.

Mackay, Ernest

    1925   *Report on the Excavation of the "A" Cemetery at Kish, Mesopotamia, Part 1*. Field Museum of Natural History, Anthropology Memoirs, Vol. 1, No. 1. Chicago: Field Museum Press.

    1929   *A Sumerian Palace and the "A" Cemetery at Kish, Mesopotamia, Part 2*. Field Museum of Natural History, Anthropology Memoirs, Vol. 1, No. 2. Chicago: Field Museum Press.

    1931   *Report on Excavations at Jemdet Nasr, Iraq*. Field Museum of Natural History, Anthropology Memoirs, Vol. 1, No. 3. Chicago: Field Museum Press.

Majidzadeh, Yousef

    1976   "The Early Prehistoric Cultures of the Central Plateau of Iran: An Archaeological History of Its Development During the Fifth and Fourth Millennia B.C." Ph.D. dissertation, Department of Near Eastern Languages and Civilizations, University of Chicago.

    1979   "An Early Prehistoric Coppersmith Workshop at Tepe Ghabristan." In *Akten des VII. Internationalen Kongresses für iranische Kunst und Archäologie, München 7.–10. September 1976*, edited by Wolfram Kleiss, pp. 82–92. Archäologische Mitteilungen aus Iran, Ergänzungsband 6. Berlin: Dietrich Reimer Verlag.

Malek-Shahmirzadi, Sadegh

    1977   "The Excavation of Sagzabad Mound, Qazvin Plain, Iran, 1970–71." *Marlik* 2:67–79.

Malek-Shahmirzadi, Sadegh (*cont.*)

    1979   "A Specialized Housebuilder in an Iranian Village of the VIth Millennium B.C." *Paléorient* 5:183–92.

    1980   "Tepe Zagheh and the Problem of the Fugitive Painted Pottery." *Survey and Excavations* 3:13–21.

Mallowan, M. E. L.

    1936   "The Excavations at Tell Chagar Bazar and an Archaeological Survey of the Habur Region, 1934–35." *Iraq* 3:1–86.

    1937   "The Excavations at Tell Chagar Bazar and an Archaeological Survey of the Habur Region, Second Campaign, 1936." *Iraq* 4:91–177.

    1947   "Excavations at Brak and Chagar Bazar." *Iraq* 9:1–269.

    1963   "The Amuq Plain." *Antiquity* 37:185–92. A review of *Excavations in the Plain of Antioch, Volume 1. The Earlier Assemblages: Phases A–J.* R. J. Braidwood and L. S. Braidwood. Oriental Institute Publications, Vol. 61.

    1966   *Nimrud and Its Remains.* London: Collins.

    1969   "Alabaster Eye-Idols from Tell Brak, North Syria." *Mélanges de l'Université Saint-Joseph* 95, fascicule 23:392–96.

Mallowan, M. E. L. and Rose, J. Cruikshank

    1935   "Excavations at Tell Arpachiyah, 1933." *Iraq* 2:1–178.

Margueron, Jean-Claude

    1977   *Le Moyen Euphrate: Zone de contacts et d'échanges. Actes du Colloque de Strasbourg 10–12 mars 1977.* Travaux du Centre de Recherche sur le Proche-Orient et la Grèce Antiques 5. Leiden: E. J. Brill.

Marshack, Alexander

    1972a   *The Roots of Civilization: The Cognitive Beginnings of Man's First Art, Symbol and Notation.* New York: McGraw-Hill Book Company.

    1972b   "Upper Paleolithic Notation and Symbol." *Science* 178:817–28.

Marschner, Robert F. and Wright, Henry T.

    1978   "Asphalts from Middle Eastern Sites." In *Archaeological Chemistry, Volume 2*, edited by G. F. Carter, pp. 150–71. Advances in Chemistry Series, Vol. 171. Washington, D.C.: American Chemistry Association.

Martin, Richard A.

    1935   "Description of Painted Pottery from Jemdet Nasr." *American Journal of Archaeology* 39:312–20.

Martin, Alexander C. and Barkley, William D.

    1961   *Seed Identification Manual.* Berkeley and Los Angeles: University of California Press.

Martin, John H. and Leonard, Warren H.

    1967   *Principles of Field Crop Production.* New York: Macmillan.

Masson, V. M. and Sarianidi, V. I.

    1972   *Central Asia: Turkmenia before the Achaemenids.* Ancient Peoples and Places, Vol. 79. London: Thames and Hudson.

Masuda, Seiichi

1972   "Excavations at Tappeh Sang-e Čaxmāq." In *Proceedings of the First Annual Symposium on Archaeological Research in Iran*, edited by F. Bagherzadeh, pp. 1–5. Tehran: Iran Bustan Museum.

1974   "Excavations at Tappeh Sang-e Čaxmāq." In *Proceedings of the Second Annual Symposium on Archaeological Research in Iran*, edited by F. Bagherzadeh. pp. 23–33. Tehran: Iranian Centre for Archaeological Research.

Matthews, R. J.

1992   "Defining the Style of the Period: Jemdet Nasr 1926–28." *Iraq* 54:1–34.

McCown, Donald E.

1942   *The Comparative Stratigraphy of Early Iran*. Studies in Ancient Oriental Civilization, No. 23. Chicago: University of Chicago Press.

McCown, Donald E. and Haines, Richard C.

1967   *Nippur, Volume 1: The Temple of Enlil, Scribal Quarter, and Soundings. Excavations of the Joint Expedition to Nippur of the University Museum of the University of Pennsylvania and the Oriental Institute of the University of Chicago*. Oriental Institute Publications, Vol. 78. Chicago: University of Chicago Press.

Mehringer, Peter J., Jr.

1965   "Late Pleistocene Vegetation in the Mojave Desert of Southern Nevada." *Journal of Arizona Academy of Sciences* 3:172–88.

Mehringer, Peter J., Jr.; Martin, Paul S.; and Haynes, C. Vance, Jr.

1965   "Murray Springs: A Mid-Postglacial Pollen Record from Southern Arizona." *American Journal of Science* 265:786–97.

Meldgaard, Jorgen; Thrane, Henrik; and Mortensen, Peder

1963   "Excavations at Tepe Guran, Luristan." *Acta Archaeologia* 34:97–133.

Mellink, Machteld J. and Filip, Jan

1974   *Frühe Stüfen der Kunst*. Propyläen Kunstgeschichte, Band 13. Berlin: Propyläen Verlag.

Mesnil du Buisson, Robert

1935   *Le Site archéologique de Mishrifé-Qatna*. Paris: E. de Boccard, Éditeur.

Michel, Rudolph H.; McGovern, Patrick E.; and Badler, Virginia R.

1992   "Chemical Evidence for Ancient Beer." *Nature* 360:24.

1993   "The First Wine and Beer: Chemical Detection of Ancient Fermented Beverages." *Analytical Chemistry* 65:408 A–413 A.

Miroschedji, Pierre de

1976   "Un Four de potier du IVe millénaire sur le tell de l'Apadana à Suse." *Cahiers de la délégation archéologique française en Iran* 6:13–46.

1978   "Stratigraphie de la période néo-élamite Suse (c. 1110–c. 540)." *Paléorient* 4:213–28.

Moorey, P. R. S.

1967   "Some Aspects of Incised Drawing and Mosaic in the Early Dynastic Period." *Iraq* 29:97–116.

1974   *Ancient Persian Bronzes in the Adam Collection*. London: Faber and Faber.

1975   "Iranian Troops at Deve Hüyük in Syria in the Earlier Fifth Century B.C." *Levant* 7:108–17.

Moorey, P. R. S. (*cont.*)

1980   *Cemeteries of the First Millennium B.C. at Deve Hüyük, near Carchemish, Salvaged by T. E. Lawrence and C. L. Woolley in 1913*. British Archaeological Reports, International Series 87. Oxford: British Archaeological Reports.

Moortgat, Anton

1940   *Vorderasiatische Rollsiegel*. Berlin: Verlag Gebr. Mann.

1960   "Tell Chuēra im Nordest-Syrien." In *Wissenschaftliche Abhandlungen der Arbeitsgemeinschaft für Forschung des Landes Nordheim, Westfalen, Volume 24*. Cologne: Westdeutscher Verlag.

1969   *The Art of Ancient Mesopotamia*. London: Phaidon.

Morales, Vivian Broman

1990   *Figurines and Other Clay Objects from Sarab and Çayönü*. Oriental Institute Communications, No. 25. Chicago: The Oriental Institute.

Mortensen, Peder

1974   "A Survey of Early Prehistoric Sites in the Hulailan Valley in Lorestan." *Proceedings of the Second Annual Symposium on Archaeological Research in Iran*, edited by F. Bagherzadeh, pp. 34–52. Tehran: Iranian Centre for Archaeological Research.

1976   "Chalcolithic Settlements in the Holailan Valley." *Proceedings of the Fourth Annual Symposium on Archaeological Research in Iran*, edited by F. Bagherzadeh, pp. 42–62. Tehran: Iranian Centre for Archaeological Research.

Moss, Melvin L.

1958   "The Pathogenesis of Artificial Cranial Deformation." *American Journal of Physical Anthropology* 16:269–86.

Munchaev, R. M. and Merpert, N. J.

1981   *Earliest Agricultural Settlements of Northern Mesopotamia: The Investigations of the Soviet Expedition in Iran*. Moscow: Nauka. (In Russian with English summary)

Negahban, Ezat O.

1973   "Preliminary Report of the Excavation of Sagzabad." *Marlik* 1:1–9.

1977   "Preliminary Report of Qazvin Expedition: Excavations of Zaghe, Qabrestan, and Sagzabad 1971–72." *Marlik* 2:26–44.

Newberry, Percy E.

n.d.   *Bersheh 1: The Tomb of Tehuti-Hetep*. Archaeological Survey of Egypt, Vol. 3. London: Egypt Exploration Fund.

Nicholas, Ilene Mildred

1980   *A Spatial/Functional Analysis of Late Fourth Millennium Occupation at the TUV Mound, Tal-e Malyan, Iran*. Ph.D. dissertation, University of Pennsylvania.

1990   *The Proto-Elamite Settlement at TUV*. University Museum Monograph, No. 69. Philadelphia: University of Pennsylvania Press.

Nissen, Hans J.

1970   "Grabung in den Quadraten K/L XII in Uruk-Warka." *Baghdader Mitteilungen* 5:101–91.

1980   "Commentaires." In *L'Archéologie de l'Iraq du début de l'époque Néolithique à 333 avant notre ère*, edited by M.-Th. Barrelet, p. 95. Colloques internationaux du Centre National de la

Recherche Scientifique, No. 580. Paris: Éditions du Centre National de la Recherche Scientifique.

Nissen, Hans J.; Damerow, Peter; and Englund, Robert K.

1991   *Frühe Schrift und Techniken der Wirtschaftsverwaltung im alten Vorderen Orient: Informationsspeicherung und verarbeitung vor 5000 Jahren.* Bad Salzdetfurth: Franzbecker.

Oates, Joan

1959   "Late Assyrian Pottery from Fort Shalmaneser." *Iraq* 21:130–46.

1960   "Ur and Eridu: The Prehistory." *Iraq* 22:32–50.

1968   "Prehistoric Investigations near Mandali, Iraq." *Iraq* 30:1–20.

1969   "Chogha Mami 1967–68: A Preliminary Report." *Iraq* 31:115–52.

1973   "'Ubaid Mesopotamia and Its Relation to Gulf Countries." In *Qatar Archaeological Report: Excavations 1973*, edited by B. de Cardi, pp. 39–52. Oxford: Oxford University Press.

1983   "Ubaid Mesopotamia Reconsidered." In *The Hilly Flanks and Beyond: Essays on the Prehistory of Southwestern Asia Presented to Robert J. Braidwood, November 15, 1982*, edited by T. C. Young, Jr., P. E. L. Smith, and P. Mortensen, pp. 251–82. Studies in Ancient Oriental Civilization, No. 36. Chicago: The Oriental Institute.

1987a   "The Choga Mami Transitional." In *Préhistoire de la Mésopotamie*: *La Mésopotamie préhistorique et l'exploration récente du Djebel Hamrin*, edited by J.-L. Huot, pp. 163–80. Colloque international du Centre National de la Recherche Scientifique. Paris: Éditions du Centre National de la Recherche Scientifique.

1987b   "Le Choga Mami transitional et l'Obeid 1: Synthèse de la séance." In *Préhistoire de la Mésopotamie*: *La Mésopotamie préhistorique et l'exploration récente du Djebel Hamrin*, edited by J.-L. Huot, pp. 199–206. Colloque international du Centre National de la Recherche Scientifique. Paris: Éditions du Centre National de la Recherche Scientifique.

Ochsenschlager, Edward

1973   "Mud Objects from al-Hiba: A Study in Ancient and Modern Technology." *Archaeology* 27:162–74.

Oppenheim, A. Leo

1959   "On an Operational Device in Mesopotamian Bureaucracy." *Journal of Near Eastern Studies* 18:121–28.

Oren, E. D.

1978   "Esh-Shari'a, Tell." In *Encyclopedia of Archaeological Excavations in the Holy Land, Volume 4*, edited by M. Avi-Yonah and E. Stern, pp. 1057, 1059–69. Jerusalem: Israel Exploration Society and Massada Press.

Orthmann, Winfried, et al.

1975   *Der Alte Orient.* Propyläen Kunstgeschichte, Band 14. Berlin: Propyläen Verlag.

Ortner, Donald J. and Putschar, William G. J.

1981   *Identification of Pathological Conditions in Human Skeletal Remains.* Smithsonian Contributions to Anthropology, No. 28. Washington, D.C.: Smithsonian Institution Press.

Osten, Hans Henning von der

1934   *Ancient Oriental Seals in the Collection of Mr. Edward T. Newell.* Oriental Institute Publications, Vol. 22. Chicago: University of Chicago Press.

Özbek, Metin

    1974   "Étude de la déformation crânienne artificielle chez les chalcolithiques de Byblos (Liban)." *Bulletins et Mémoires de la Société d'Anthropologie de Paris,* Tome premier, 13ᵉ série, pp. 455–81.

Özgüç, Tahsin

    1950   *Kültepe Kazisi Raporu 1948: Ausgrabungen in Kültepe.* Türk Tarih Kurumu Yayınlarindan, Seri 5, No. 10. Ankara: Türk Tarih Kurumu Basımevi.

Özgüç, Tahsin and Özgüç, Nimet

    1953   *Kültepe Kazisi Raporu 1949: Ausgrabungen in Kültepe.* Turk Tarih Kurumu Yayınlarindan, Seri 5, No. 12. Ankara: Türk Tarih Kurumu Basımevi.

Pabot, H.

    1960   *The Native Vegetation and its Ecology in the Khuzestan River Basins.* Ahwaz, Iran: Khuzestan Development Service. (Mimeographed)

Palmieri, Alba

    1973   "Scavi nell'area sud-occidentale di Arslantepe: ritrovamento di una struttura templare dell'antica età del bronzo." *Origini* 7:55–179.

    1977   "The 1973 and 1975 Campaigns at Arslantepe (Malatya)." *Türk Arkeoloji Dergisi* 24:123–32.

    1981   "Excavations at Arslantepe (Malatya)." *Anatolian Studies* 31:101–19.

Parrot, André

    1948   *Tello: Vingt Campagnes de Fouilles (1877–1933).* Paris: Albin Michel.

    1968   *Mission archéologique de Mari, Tome 4: Le 'Trésor' d'Ur.* Institut français d'archéologie de Beyrouth, Bibliothèque archéologique et historique, Tome 87. Paris: Paul Geuthner.

Parrot, André and Lambert, Maurice

    1954   *Glyptique mésopotamienne: Fouilles de Lagash (Tello) et de Larsa (Senkereh) (1931–1933).* Paris: Paul Geuthner.

Peet, T. Eric

    1915   "A Remarkable Burial Custom of the Old Kingdom." *Journal of Egyptian Archaeology* 2:8–9.

Peet, T. Eric and Loat, W. L. S.

    1913   *Cemeteries of Abydos, Part 3: 1912–1913.* Thirty-fifth Memoir of the Egypt Exploration Fund. London: The Egypt Exploration Fund.

Pelon, O.; Courtois, J.-C.; Lagarce, E.; Lagarce, J.; and Schaeffer, C. F. A.

    1971   "Rapport sommaire sur la XXIᵉ campagne de fouilles à Enkomi-Alasia (Chypre), Mars-Avril 1971." *Syria* 48:323–35.

Petrie, Flinders

    1928   *Gerar.* British School of Archaeology in Egypt, Publication, No. 43. London: British School of Archaeology in Egypt.

    1930   *Beth Pelet 1 (Tell Fara).* British School of Archaeology in Egypt, Publication, No. 48. London: British School of Archaeology in Egypt.

Porada, Edith

    1948   *Corpus of Ancient Near Eastern Seals in North American Collections, Volume 1: The Collection of the Pierpont Morgan Library.* New York: Pantheon Books.

    1965   *The Art of Ancient Iran: Pre-Islamic Cultures.* New York: Crown Publishers.

1967　"Battlements in the Military Architecture and in the Symbolism of the Ancient Near East." In *Essays in the History of Architecture Presented to Rudolf Wittkower,* edited by D. Fraser, H. Hibbard, and M. J. Lewine, pp. 1–12. London: Phaidon Press.

Pottier, Edmond

1912　"Étude historique et chronologique sur les vases de l'acropole de Suse." In *Céramique peinte de Suse et petits monuments de l'époque archaïque,* edited by J. de Morgan, pp. 27–103. Mémoires de la mission archéologique de Perse, Cinquième série, Tome 13. Paris: Ernest Leroux.

1923　*Corpus Vasorum Antiquorum: France, Musée du Louvre, Fascicule 1.* Paris: Librairie Ancienne Edouard Champion.

Powell, Marvin Adell, Jr.

1971　"Sumerian Numeration and Metrology." Ph.D. dissertation, University of Minnesota.

Quibell, J. E.

1913　*Excavations at Saqqara (1911–12): The Tomb of Hesy.* Cairo: Imprimerie de l'Institut Français d'Archéologie Orientale.

Ralph, E. D.; Michael, H. H.; and Han, M. C.

1973　"Radiocarbon Dates and Reality." *MASCA Newsletter* 9 (1):1–20.

Rathbun, Ted A.

1975　*A Study of the Physical Characteristics of the Ancient Inhabitants of Kish, Iraq.* Coconut Grove: Field Research Projects.

Renfrew, Jane M.

n.d.　*Identification of Carbonized Seed Material from Chagha Sefid, Iran.* (Unpublished)

1973　*Palaeoethnobotany: The Prehistoric Food Plants of the Near East and Europe.* New York: Columbia University Press.

Reynolds, Peter J.

1974　"Experimental Iron Age Storage Pits: An Interim Report." *Proceedings of the Prehistoric Society* 40:118–31.

Risdon, D. L.

1939　"A Study of the Cranial and Other Human Remains from Palestine Excavated at Tell Duweir (Lachish) by the Wellcome-Marston Archaeological Research Expedition." *Biometrica* 31:99–166.

Sabloff, J. A. and Lamberg-Karlovsky, C. C.

1975　*Ancient Civilization and Trade.* Albuquerque: University of New Mexico Press.

Safar, Fuad; Mustafa, Mohammed Ali; and Lloyd, Seton

1981　*Eridu.* Baghdad: Republic of Iraq, Ministry of Culture and Information, and the State Organization of Antiquities and Heritage.

Schäfer, Heinrich and Andrae, Walter

1925　*Die Kunst des alten Orients.* Propyläen Kunstgeschichte, Band 2. Berlin: Propyläen Verlag.

Schmandt-Besserat, Denise

1974　"The Use of Clay Before Pottery in the Zagros." *Expedition* 16:11–17.

1977a　"An Archaic Recording System and the Origin of Writing." *Syro-Mesopotamian Studies* 1:1–32.

1977b　"The Beginnings of the Use of Clay in Turkey." *Anatolian Studies* 27:133–50.

Schmandt-Besserat, Denise (*cont.*)

1992   *Before Writing, Volume 1: From Counting to Cuneiform.* Austin: University of Texas Press.

Schmidt, Erich F.

1932   *Researches in Anatolia, Volume IV: The Alishar Hüyük Seasons of 1928 and 1929, Part 1.* Oriental Institute Publications, Vol. 19. Chicago: University of Chicago Press.

1937   *Excavations at Tepe Hissar, Damghan.* Publications of the Iranian Section of the University Museum. Philadelphia: University of Pennsylvania Press.

1957   *Persepolis, Volume II: Contents of the Treasury and Other Discoveries.* Oriental Institute Publications, Vol. 69. Chicago: University of Chicago Press.

Schott, E.

1934   "Die Siegelbilder der Uruk-Schicht IV." In *Fünfter vorläufiger Bericht über die von der Notgemeinschaft der Deutschen Wissenschaft in Uruk unternommenen Ausgrabungen,* by A. Nöldeke et al., pp. 42–54. Berlin: Verlag der Akademie der Wissenschaften.

Shahideh, Elahe

1979   "The Susiana Period on the Izeh Plain." In *Archaeological Investigations in Northeastern Xuzestan,* edited by H. T. Wright, pp. 50–58. Museum of Anthropology, Technical Reports, No. 10. Ann Arbor: University of Michigan.

Sheffer, Avigail

1981   "The Use of Perforated Clay Balls on the Warp-Weighted Loom." *Tel Aviv: Journal of the Tel Aviv University Institute of Archaeology* 8:81–83.

Smeltzer, Donald

1953   *Man and Number.* London and New York: Emerson Books.

Smith, Philip E. L.

1976   "Reflections on Four Seasons of Excavations at Tappeh Ganj Dareh." *Proceedings of the Fourth Annual Symposium on Archaeological Research in Iran,* edited by F. Bagherzadeh, pp. 11–22. Tehran: Iranian Centre for Archaeological Research.

Speiser, Ephraim A.

1935   *Excavations at Tepe Gawra, Volume 1.* Joint Expedition of the Baghdad School, the University Museum, and Dropsie College to Mesopotamia. Philadelphia: University of Pennsylvania Press.

Stager, Lawrence E.

1971   "Climatic Conditions and Grain Storage in the Persian Period." *Biblical Archaeologist* 34:86–88.

Starr, Richard F. S.

1937   *Nuzi: Report on the Excavation at Yorgan Tepe Near Kirkuk, Iraq, Volume 2: Plates and Plans.* Cambridge: Harvard University Press.

Stauder, Wilhelm

1957   *Die Harfen und Leiern der Sumerer.* Frankfurt am Main: J. W. Goethe-Universität.

1970   "Die Musik der Sumerer, Babylonier und Assyrer." In *Orientalische Musik,* edited by H. Hickmann and W. Stauder, pp. 174–78. Handbuch der Orientalistik, Erganzungsband 4. Leiden and Cologne: E. J. Brill.

Stein, Gil

1995   "Excavations at Hacinebi Tepe 1993." *Kazi Sonoçlari Toplantasi* 16:121–40.

Stein, Sir Mark Aurel

  1940   *Old Routes of Western Iran.* New York: Greenwood Press.

Stern, Ephraim

  1980   "Achaemenian Tombs from Shechem." *Levant* 12:90–111.

Steve, M. J. and Gasche, Hermann

  1971   *L'Acropole de Suse: Nouvelles fouilles (Rapport préliminaire).* Mémoires de la délégation archéologique en Iran, Mission de Susiane, Tome 46. Leiden: E. J. Brill; Paris: Paul Geuthner.

Stewart, T. D.

  1941   "The Circular Type of Cranial Deformity in the United States." *American Journal of Physical Anthropology* 28:343–51.

  1950   "Deformity, Trephining, and Mutilation in South American Indian Skeletal Remains." In *Handbook of South American Indians, Volume 6: Physical Anthropology, Linguistics, and Cultural Geography of South American Indians,* edited by J. H. Steward, pp. 43–48. Bureau of American Ethnology Bulletin, No. 143, 6. Washington, D.C.: Smithsonian Institution Press.

Strommenger, Eva

  1961   "Rollsiegelfälschungen." *Berliner Jahrbuch für Vor-und Frühgeschichte.* 1:196–200.

  1962a   "Die Kleinfunde aus dem Gebiet von E-anna, dem Bīt Rēš sowie von der Oberfläche." In *XVIII. vorläufiger Bericht über die von dem Deutschen Archäologischen Institut und der Deutschen Orient-Gesellschaft aus Mittlen der Deutschen Forschungsgemeinschaft unternommenen Ausgrabungen in Uruk-Warka,* by H. J. Lenzen, pp. 18–20. Berlin: Verlag Gebr. Mann.

  1962b   *Fünf Jahrtausende Mesopotamien: Die Kunst von den Anfängen um 5000 v. Chr. bis zu Alexander dem Großen.* Munich: Hirmer Verlag.

  1963   "Archäische Siedlung." In *XIX. vorläufiger Bericht über die von dem Deutschen Archäologischen Institut und der Deutschen Orient-Gesellschaft aus Mittlen der Deutschen Forschungsgemeinschaft unternommenen Ausgrabungen in Uruk-Warka,* by H. J. Lenzen, pp. 45–55. Berlin: Verlag Gebr. Mann.

  1975   "Habuba Kabira-Süd 1974." *Les Annales arhéologiques Arabes Syriennes* 25:155–64.

  1980a   *Habuba Kabira: Eine Stadt vor 5000 Jahren. Ausgrabungen der Deutschen Orient-Gesellschaft am Euphrat in Habuba Kabira, Syrien.* Mainz am Rhein: Philipp von Zabern.

  1980b   "The Chronological Division of the Archaic Levels of Uruk-Eanna VI to III/II: Past and Present." *American Journal of Archaeology* 84:479–99.

Strommenger, Eva and Sürenhagen, Dietrich

  1970   "Die Grabung in Habuba Kabira-Süd." *Mitteilungen der Deutschen Orient-Gesellschaft zu Berlin* 102:59–71.

Stronach, David

  1959   "The Development of the Fibula in the Near East." *Iraq* 21:181–206.

  1961   "The Excavations at Ras al ʿAmiya." *Iraq* 23:95–137.

  1974   "Achaemenid Village I at Susa and the Persian Migration to Fars." *Iraq* 36:239–48.

  1978   *Pasargadae: A Report on the Excavations Conducted by the British Institute of Persian Studies from 1961 to 1963.* Oxford: Oxford University Press.

Stronach, Ruth

    1978   "Excavations at Tepe Nush-i Jan, Part 2: Median Pottery from a Fallen Floor in the Fort." *Iran* 16:11–24.

Sumner, William

    1974   "Excavations at Tall-i Malyan, 1971–72." *Iran* 12:155–80.

Sürenhagen, Dietrich

    1974/75   "Untersuchungen zur Keramikproduktion innerhalb der Spät-Urukzeitlichen Siedlung Habuba Kabira-Süd in Nordsyrien." *Acta Praehistorica et Archaeologica* 5/6:43–164.

    1986   "Archäische Keramik aus Uruk-Warka, Erster Teil: Die Keramik der Schichten XVI–VI aus den Sondagen 'Tiefschnitt' und 'Sägengraben' in Eanna." *Baghdader Mitteilungen* 17:7–95.

    1987   "Archäische Keramik aus Uruk-Warka, Zweiter Teil: Keramik der Schicht V aus dem 'Sägengraben'; 'Keramik der schichten VII bis II' in Eanna; die registrierte Keramik aus den Sondagen O XI–XII und K–L XII–XIII; Keramik von der Anu-Zikkurat in K XVII." *Baghdader Mitteilungen* 18:1–92.

Talalay, Lauren

    1987   "Rethinking the Function of Clay Figurine Legs from Neolithic Greece: An Argument by Analogy." *American Journal of Archaeology* 91:161–69.

Thompson, R. Campbell and Mallowan, M. E. L.

    1933   "The British Museum Excavations at Nineveh, 1931–32." *University of Liverpool Annals of Archaeology and Anthropology* 20:71–186.

Tobler, Arthur J.

    1950   *Excavations at Tepe Gawra, Volume 2: Levels IX–XX*. Philadelphia: University of Pennsylvania Press.

Thrane, Henrik

    1964   "Excavations at Tepe Guran, Luristan." *Acta Archaeologica* 34:97–133.

Tufnell, Olga

    1953   *Lachish 3 (Tell ed-Duweir): The Iron Age*. The Wellcome-Marston Research Expedition to the Near East. London: Oxford University Press.

Ussishkin, David

    1982   *The Conquest of Lachish by Sennacherib*. Tel Aviv: The Institute of Archaeology.

Vaiman, A. A.

    1974   "Über die Protosumerische Schrift." *Acta Antiqua Academiae Scientiarum Hungaricae* 22:15–27.

Vallois, H. V.

    1937   "Note sur les ossements humains de la nécropole enéolithique de Byblos." *Bulletin du Musée de Beyrouth* 1:23–33.

Van Beek, G. W.

    1972   "Tel Gamma." *Israel Exploration Journal* 22:245–46.

Van Buren, E. Douglas

    1940   *The Cylinder Seals of the Pontifical Biblical Institute*. Analecta Orientalia, Vol. 21. Rome: Pontificium Institutum Biblicum.

Vanden Berghe, Louis

    1959   *Archéologie de l'Iran ancien*. Leiden: E. J. Brill.

    1970   "La Nécropole de Kalleh Nisar." *Archéologia* 32:64–73.

    1973   "Le Luristan avant l'âge du bronze: La Nécropole de Hakalan." *Archéologia* 57:49–58.

    1987   "Luristan, Pusht-i-Kuh au chalcolithique moyen (les nécropoles de Parchinah et Hakalan)." In *Préhistoire de la Mésopotamie: La Mésopotamie préhistorique et l'exploration récente du Djebel Hamrin*, by J.-L. Huot, pp. 91–106. Colloque international du Centre National de la Recherche Scientifique. Paris: Éditions du Centre National de la Recherche Scientifique.

van Driel, Govert

    1982   "Tablets from Jebel Aruda." In *Zikir Šumim: Assyriological Studies Presented to F. R. Kraus on the Occasion of his Seventieth Birthday*, edited by G. van Driel, Th. J. H. Krispijn, M. Stol, and K. R. Veenhof, pp. 12–25. Leiden: E. J. Brill.

    1983   "Seals and Sealings from Jebel Aruda 1974–1978." *Akkadica* 33:34–63.

van Driel, Govert and Van Driel-Murray, Carol

    1979   "Jebel Aruda 1977–1978." *Akkadica* 12:2–28.

    1983   "Jebel Aruda: The 1982 Season of Excavation, Interim Reports." *Akkadica* 33:1–26.

van Driel, Govert; Krispin, Th. J. H.; Stol, M.; and Veenhof, K. R.; editors

    1982   *Zikir Šumim: Assyriological Studies Presented to F. R. Kraus on the Occasion of his Seventieth Birthday*. Leiden: E. J. Brill.

Vernier, Émile

    1927   *Nos. 52001–53855: Bijoux et orfèvreries, Tome 2*. Catalogue général des antiquités égyptiennes du Musée du Caire, Vol. 79. Cairo: Imprimerie de l'Institut Français d'Archéologie Orientale.

Voigt, Mary

    1983   *Hajji Firuz Tepe, Iran: The Neolithic Settlement*. University Museum Monograph, No. 50. Philadelphia: The University Museum, University of Pennsylvania.

Volk, Joyce Geary

    1979   *Habib Anavian Collection: Ancient Near Eastern Cylinder and Stamp Seals from the Early Sixth Millennium B.C. to 651 A.D.* New York: Habib Anavian Galleries.

Von Luschan, F. and Andrae, Walter

    1943   *Die Kleinfunde von Sendschirli*. Mitteilungen aus den orientalischen Sammlungen, Heft 15, Ausgrabungen in Sendschirli, Band 5. Berlin: Walter de Gruyter.

Von Oppenheim, Max Freiherr

    1943   *Tell Halaf (erster Band): Die prähistorischen Funde*. Berlin: Walter de Gruyter.

Ward, William Hayes

    1910   *The Seal Cylinders of Western Asia*. Washington, D.C.: Carnegie Institute of Washington.

Warren, Peter

    1972   *Myrtos: An Early Bronze Age Settlement in Crete*. Oxford: The Alden Press.

Weber, O.

    1920   *Altorientalische Siegelbilder*. Der Alte Orient, Band 17–18. Leipzig: J. C. Hinrichs.

Weiss, Harvey

    1976   "Ceramics for Chronology: Discriminant and Cluster Analyses of Fifth Millennium Ceramic Assemblages from Qabr Sheykheyn, Khuzistan." Ph.D. dissertation, University of Pennsylvania. Ann Arbor: University Microfilms.

Weiss, Harvey and Young, T. Cuyler, Jr.

    1975   "The Merchants of Susa: Godin V and Plateau-Lowland Relations in the Late Fourth Millennium B.C." *Iran* 13:1–17.

Wenke, R. J.

    1975/76   "Imperial Investments and Agricultural Developments in Parthian and Sasanian Khuzestan, 150 B.C. to A.D. 640." *Mesopotamia* 10–11:31–221.

Woolley, C. Leonard

    1934   *Ur Excavations, Volume 2: The Royal Cemetery*. London: British Museum; Philadelphia: The University Museum.

    1955   *Ur Excavations, Volume 4: The Early Periods*. Philadelphia: Allen, Lane and Scott.

    1962   *Ur Excavations, Volume 9: The Neo-Babylonian and Persian Periods*. London: Charles Skilton.

Woosley, Anne I.

    1976   "Pollen Studies in Archaeology: Correlation of the Prehistoric Pollen and Cultural Sequences of the Deh Luran Plain, Southwestern Iran." Ph.D. dissertation, University of California, Los Angeles.

    1978   "Pollen Extraction for Arid-land Sediments." *Journal of Field Archaeology* 5:349–55.

Wright, Henry T.

    1981   "The Southern Margins of Sumer: Archaeological Survey of the Area of Eridu and Ur." In *Heartland of Cities*, by R. McC. Adams, pp. 295–345. Chicago: University of Chicago Press.

    1984   "Prestate Political Formation." In *On the Evolution of Complex Societies: Essays in Honor of Harry Hoijer 1982*, edited by T. Earle, pp. 41–77. Other Realities, Vol. 6. Malibu: Undena Publications.

    1987   "The Susiana Hinterlands during the Era of Primary State Formation." In *The Archaeology of Western Iran: Settlement and Society from Prehistory to the Islamic Conquest*, edited by F. Hole, pp. 141–49. Smithsonian Series in Archaeological Inquiry. Washington, D.C.: Smithsonian Institution Press.

Wright, Henry T. and Johnson, Gregory A.

    1975   "Population, Exchange, and Early State Formation in Southwestern Iran." *American Anthropologist* 77:267–89.

Wright, Henry T., et al.

    1979   *Archaeological Investigations in Northeastern Xuzestan, 1976*. Museum of Anthropology, Technical Reports, No. 10. Ann Arbor: University of Michigan.

    1981   *An Early Town on the Deh Luran Plain: Excavations at Tepe Farukhabad*. Memoirs of the Museum of Anthropology, No. 13. Ann Arbor: University of Michigan.

Wulff, Hans E.

    1966   *The Traditional Crafts of Persia: Their Development, Technology, and Influence on Eastern and Western Civilizations*. Cambridge and London: Massachusetts Institute of Technology Press.

Yadin, Yigael

 1972 "The Earliest Representation of a Siege Scene and a 'Scythian Bow' from Mari." *Israel Exploration Journal* 22:89–94.

Yeivin, Shemuel

 1960 "Tell Gath." *Revue Biblique* 67:391–94.

 1961 *First Preliminary Report on the Excavations at Tel 'Gat' (Tell Sheykh 'Ahmed el-'Areyny): Seasons 1956–1958.* Jerusalem: The Gat Expedition.

Young, T. Cuyler, Jr.

 1965 "A Comparative Ceramic Chronology for Western Iran, 1500–500 B.C." *Iran* 3:53–83.

 1969 *Excavations at Godin Tepe: First Progress Report.* Royal Ontario Museum, Art and Archaeology, Occasional Paper, No. 17. Toronto: The Royal Ontario Museum.

 1974 "Excavations at Godin Tappeh 1973." In *Proceedings of the Second Annual Symposium on Archaeological Research in Iran*, edited by F. Bagherzadeh, pp. 80–90. Tehran: Iranian Centre for Archaeological Research.

Young, T. Cuyler, Jr. and Levine, Louis D.

 1974 *Excavations of the Godin Project: Second Progress Report.* Royal Ontario Museum, Art and Archaeology, Occasional Paper, No. 26. Toronto: The Royal Ontario Museum.

Ziegler, Charlotte

 1953 *Die Keramik von der Qal'a des Haǧǧi Moḥammed.* Ausgrabungen der Deutschen Forschungsgemeinschaft in Uruk-Warka, Band 5. Berlin: Verlag Gebr. Mann.

Zeist, Willem van

 1967 "Late Quarternary Vegetation History of Western Iran." *Review of Paleobotany and Palynology* 2:301–11.

Zohary, Michael

 1963 "On the Geobotanical Structure of Iran." *Bulletin of the Research Council of Israel, Section D: Botany*, Vol. 11D, Supplement: 1–113.II.

 1973 *Geobotanical Foundations of the Middle East, Volume 2.* Geobotanica Selecta, Band 3.2. Stuttgart: Gustav Fischer Verlag; Amsterdam: Swets and Zeitlinger.

CHAPTER 1

INTRODUCTION

The accelerated archaeological activities in the Near East after the First World War extended our understanding of the beginnings of civilization in the lands at the head of the Persian Gulf back from biblical times into the third and then into the fourth millennium B.C. While many excavations were conducted at Mesopotamian sites by teams of various nationalities, the adjacent regions in Khuzestan were largely reserved for French archaeologists. Our own interest in this region goes back to the 1930s, when it became clear that certain major cultural-historical problems could perhaps be solved in Khuzestan. With the end of the Second World War it appeared that the opportunity for an American expedition to work in Khuzestan had arisen as a result of our efforts. The excavations of D. E. McCown at Tal-i Ghazir, interesting as were they, were discontinued after the second season and did not produce the results hoped for in our original plan (Caldwell 1968:348–55). In 1960, R. McC. Adams, after a surface survey related to ancient irrigation patterns in central Khuzestan under the auspices of the Khuzestan Development Service, reported that he observed numerous beveled-rim bowl fragments on the surface of Chogha Mish (Adams 1962:109–22). The site had already been mentioned by Layard (1846:87) and was indicated on maps of the Délégation Française as second in size only to Susa (de Mecquenem et al. 1943, fig. 106). Fortunately, Chogha Mish had remained intact. A brief first season at the site at the end of the Oriental Institute Archeological Reconnaissance Expedition in the Near East[1] proved convincingly that, in contrast to Susa and to many sites in Mesopotamia, where Protoliterate remains were covered by thick later deposits, at Chogha Mish Protoliterate materials were to be found at or close below the surface. Moreover, the abundance of painted sherds of many types indicated that this site would offer an excellent opportunity to test the relationship of the Protoliterate civilization to the cultures of preceding periods and to verify the validity of the prehistoric Susiana sequence as built up by a number of archaeologists on the basis of largely unstratified materials.

Chogha Mish, 32°13′ north, 48°33′ east, is the largest pre-Sasanian site in its area and is strategically located between the outlets of the large perennial streams of the Dez and Karun Rivers in the plain (pl. 283). Although well within the Susiana area, it is not far from the lowest foothills of the Bakhtiari mountains. Closer to the site are two important tributaries of the Dez River, the beds of which are now dry in the summer; the Siah Mansur, some 10 km to the west, just beyond the western boundary of Jundi Shapur; and the Shur, slightly less than 1 km to the east.

Chogha Mish consists of two parts, the High Mound on the north and the long terrace extending to the south (pl. 1:A–B). In the winter of 1963 a contour map was prepared for the expedition by the K. Heidemy Surveying Company of The Netherlands under the supervision of Mr. Stoop. The original, on a scale of 1:2000, shows 0.50 m contours. The smaller-scale map (pl. 260) shows 1.00 m contours. On the original map a grid of 20.00 m squares was superimposed, oriented to the magnetic north of the spring of 1963. Each square is marked by a letter reading from west to east and a number reading from north to south. The base of the bench mark at the summit of the site[2] was chosen to correspond to the northwest corner of Square O6 (i.e., the intersection of Squares N5–6 and O5–6). The map extends only over those parts of the ancient site clearly discernible on the surface, but not over those presumably covered by wash from higher parts and now lying under cultivated fields. According to the information provided by the surveyors, the summit of the High Mound is at el. 100.54 m above the mean sea level at the head of the Persian Gulf. It is about 27 m above the surrounding plain and over 30 m above the riverbed of the Shur to the east (el. 70.30 m). Eleven massive concrete blocks were buried in the ground at convenient points for triangulation and leveling purposes. A number of secondary points were also set out.

The High Mound, measuring ca. 200 × 150 m, is steepest toward the north and northwest, where it slopes ca. 23 m in 60 m, i.e., an incline of nearly 1 in 3. Its

---

1. Archaeological Reconnaissance Expedition of 1961 under the direction of Pinhas Delougaz with the participation of Professors Helene J. Kantor and Hans G. Güterbock and Mr. James E. Knudstad briefly published in the *Oriental Institute Report for 1961/62*, pp. 10–14. AA

2. As the highest landmark in the area, Chogha Mish was constantly used as a datum point during the surveying undertaken in connection with the work of the Khuzestan Development Service.

western edge is fairly regular, but on its northeast, east, and southeast sides it has four irregularly shaped lobes separated by deeply eroded gullies. The terrace, about 400 × 300 m, has four less prominent peaks in Squares H14 (el. 82–83 m), R16 (el. 84–85 m), O25 (el. 84–85 m), and H27 (el. 82–83 m).

From the beginning of the excavation we identified small soundings by capital letters and more extensive trenches by roman numerals. We continued this practice after the contour map had been made and the grid superimposed on it. By the end of the fifth season there were nine soundings (A–I) and thirty-two trenches (I–XXXII). Some were carried down to virgin soil, while others were extended to cover considerable areas, especially when architectural remains were encountered. Sometimes the trenches were absorbed, as it were, by the larger areas (e.g., Trenches IX, XIX, XX, and XXI). Before the map of the site and the grid on it were available, the trenches were divided into plots for more accurate documentation of the finds. Subsequently, such preliminary designations were replaced by normal locus numbers and elevations in relation to the established datum point of 100.54 m.[3]

With the introduction of the grid system, the location of each find or feature is given in terms of loci. A locus is a relatively small area on the map with definite limits of elevation and usually defined by specific features (e.g., a room, well, kiln, drain) or by finds. According to this system,[4] loci are numbered consecutively within one 20 m square; e.g., the locus N9:302 indicates the second locus (N9:**302**) in Square N9 (**N9**:302) assigned during the third season (N9:**3**02). Parts of architectural features might be assigned different locus numbers, especially if they extend over more than one square (e.g., parts of a large room in different squares, various parts of a street, a court, or a drain). Sometimes a room contains a feature such as a kiln or hearth with a different locus number (e.g., K22:405 in K22:407 and K22:408 in K23:403). Objects are recorded as either found in or in definite relation to a locus (i.e., north, south, etc.).

In order to cope adequately with the ever-increasing quantities of pottery from both the prehistoric phases and the remarkably prolific Protoliterate period, a method of using tabular recording sheets was devised after the second season, which enabled both a detailed

qualitative and quantitative record of the ceramic finds to be kept. In brief, the system was based on an analysis of the most frequent combinations of salient features, for instance, specific necks or rims with surface finishes or with spouts. By listing a number of such features in the horizontal lines and vertical columns of recording sheets, it was possible to note the number of occurrences of characteristic combinations in the appropriate box where the two defining features meet. These records were kept by loci and by elevations within them. This method was based largely on the actual field experience and finds during the first two seasons, which permitted some extrapolation as to the range of variants that could be expected. The system was used successfully in subsequent seasons. It permitted the inclusion of new materials with only minor supplements in the six Protoliterate sheets. The refinement of knowledge of the prehistoric periods and in particular the discovery of the Archaic Susiana period naturally required the preparation of sheets additional to the three originally devised for the prehistoric Susiana periods. The pottery was processed on the site, where extensive sherd yards were laid out in groups according to provenience and depth. Washing and preliminary sorting made possible the retrieval of complete or semi-complete forms, often reconstructed from large numbers of fragments scattered in antiquity in different locations or at varying depths.[5] Only after completion of this work did the final sorting and recording proceed.

In addition to the records of sherds, a corpus of complete and recognizable incomplete forms was kept, the analysis and designation of the shape being based on the system introduced in the publication of the Diyala pottery (Delougaz 1952:1–26), with each occurrence of a type entered by locus and elevation. The corpus replaced the need for repetitive drawings of identical or nearly identical forms and made it possible to divide both the Protoliterate and the prehistoric Susiana pottery into families composed of vessels that share a cluster of specific attributes.

It was obvious that a numerical record based on a sherd count was not sufficient to give the actual number of any specific type of vessel (since the same vessel could be broken into quite a different number of fragments), except that each such single feature as a complete base or spout represented one vessel. However, when the types of vessels could be identified from their sherds, the varying proportions of specific types in either different levels or localities might reflect a meaningful

---

3. In the field, it was often simpler to record finds by depth from fixed points on the surface (B.S.). The actual elevation of these points are given in relation to our datum point, and the conversion of B.S. depths to actual elevations is then a matter of simple arithmetic. "El." is used throughout to indicate the actual elevations in relation to the datum point.

4. Already introduced in the Diyala records and publications (see, e.g., Delougaz 1940).

5. Throughout the course of the years, a number of workers were gradually trained for these tasks. The skill of many of them in discriminating between different wares and vessel shapes and in retrieving and joining the fragments of individual specimens has a high level and was a major aid in dealing with the pottery.

change caused by specific factors such as variation in fashion in the course of time or differences in type resulting from different practical requirements in contemporary locations (e.g., the difference between kitchenware, storage vessels, and tableware).

In addition to the general aims of the expedition, a major specific problem was the establishment of the settlement patterns on the site from the earliest occupations to the latest preserved. When the work began, it could not be assumed *a priori* that the whole site (ca. 15 hectares) was regularly settled over its entire area during all the various periods of occupation. Indeed, it was more likely that the area of settlement varied at different times, both in location and size. To obtain adequate answers to this problem, excavations had to be spread over various areas. Consequently, trial excavations were made in a variety of strategic points on the site at some distance from each other, but not at regular intervals or mechanically in straight lines. In twelve areas virgin soil was reached, while in some other deep stratigraphic trenches, the earliest settlements were located.

The following summary of the first five seasons of excavation indicates the location and character of the various operations on the site and lists the collaborators.

FIRST SEASON (CHOGHA MISH I): NOVEMBER 6, 1961–DECEMBER 18, 1961

During this season the Expedition enjoyed the hospitality of Mr. B. Samsam. Work began with our group consisting of Delougaz, Kantor, James E. Knudstad (architect), and M. Shahnazi, the Iranian representative assigned to the Expedition by the Archaeological Service.

The field activities during this short campaign were confined to the High Mound while the rest of the site was still under cultivation. In the beginning the workmen had to be trained to collect the surface potsherds and to handle the excavation tools, which were entirely new to them. The actual excavation began with the opening of a preliminary trench in the lower end of the gully between two spurs in the northeastern part of the mound (Squares R–S6). This was abandoned almost immediately since it cut into a thick deposit of debris washed down from higher slopes, and it was not assigned a trench number. Of the two parallel Trenches I and II laid out on the eastern slope of the southeastern lobe of the High Mound, mostly in Square R11, only Trench II was developed into a large step trench, giving us our first detailed stratigraphic test of the mound, while Trench I was left as an exit for the upper step of Trench II. Trench II established that Protoliterate remains overlay many meters of prehistoric Susiana deposits.

Trench III on the eastern slope of the eastern lobe of the High Mound in Squares R–S8 had at its summit large Elamite bricks with some pottery overlying prehis-

toric debris, into which we did not dig deeply. There was no distinct intervening Protoliterate layer.

Trench IV, in a hollow in Squares Q9–10 had some Protoliterate remains at its top and an accumulation of prehistoric levels below. On the southeastern slope just below the present surface were remains of an Old Elamite (Sukkalmaḫ) burial, dated by its pottery, and also a smoothed surface with traces of fire, presumably of the same date.

SECOND SEASON (CHOGHA MISH II): JANUARY 30, 1963–JULY 18, 1963

The Expedition was again invited to settle in the house of Mr. Samsam. Other than ourselves and the representatives sent to the Expedition by the Archaeological Service there was no regular staff. We were joined by some colleagues for various lengths of time. Clare Goff, then of the British Institute of Persian Studies, was able to spare us a few weeks to give valuable assistance in drawing pottery. Robert Biggs spent a fortnight working with us. Robert McC. Adams, Donald Hansen, and Edward Keall, then of the British Institute of Persian Studies, stayed with us in the house of Mr. Samsam while surveying and making test excavations at the great site of Jundi Shapur. Our Iranian colleague for the first part of the season was Mr. Shahnazi, who was joined by Mr. M. Moshirpur when the work at Jundi Shapur was terminated.

In this season Trench II on the High Mound was carried down to virgin soil. However, the exploration of the terrace, which was no longer under cultivation, occupied most of the season. A 65 m long trench (Trench V) running southwest to northeast and divided into 5 m long plots,[6] revealed near the surface a few fragmentary walls, some of them consisting of no more than two or three layers of mudbrick of a relatively small size. In most of the length of Trench V we encountered fallen brickwork, ashes, and mixed debris, together with masses of Protoliterate sherds. In Q18:202 there appeared a short segment of a rounded wall belonging to an important building that was completely traced in the following season (Chogha Mish III). The northeastern end of Trench V was enlarged on both sides to an area of about 200 sq. m, and several building levels were discerned, all of them Protoliterate. A large pit, R17:207 and 208, next to fragmentary walls and a small kiln, R17:210, contained an enormous amount of Protoliterate potsherds as well as numerous complete or semi-complete beveled-rim bowls. From this pit a sounding,

6. The locus numbers for the plots of Trench V are as follows:

Plot A = P18:202	Plot F = Q17:202	Plot J = R17:203
Plot B = P18:203	Plot G = Q17:203	Plot K = R17:204
Plot C = Q18:201	Plot H = R17:201	Plot L = R17:205
Plot D = Q18:202	Plot I = R17:202	Plot Z = P18:201
Plot E = Q17:201		

R17:209, was dug into the underlying prehistoric levels. Another prehistoric test pit, P18:204, was dug in the southwestern end of Trench V.

In the northwestern part of the terrace, Trenches VI and IX and Sounding C were opened in Squares K–J14 and J15 and showed that, as in the East Area, Protoliterate building remains with masses of pottery began immediately below the surface. Dug into the Protoliterate remains were Parthian burials containing distinctive large "torpedo" jars and smaller glazed vessels accompanying burials. The small nearby Soundings A, B, and D provided some pottery but no special features and were shortly discontinued. Sounding E, somewhat to the south, in J18, had Parthian pottery and a presumably contemporary fireplace with flimsy walls immediately below the surface and was not continued to a lower depth.

Farther to the south along the western edge of the terrace, Trenches VIII and X corroborated the existence of Protoliterate remains above prehistoric deposits. Trench XIV contained rich deposits of Protoliterate pottery and was not carried down to deeper levels. At the foot of the southwestern corner of the terrace the modest Trench XV began with prehistoric pottery; no overlying Protoliterate levels existed. The relatively flat central parts of the terrace were tested by Sounding F and Trenches VII, XI, and XIII. Of these, only Trench XIII was carried down to any considerable depth and yielded important stratigraphic information. Trench XI had a number of small fragmentary walls and hearths close to the surface.

Trenches XII and XVI were driven into the eastern slope and southeastern corner of the terrace. In neither of these narrow trenches were any substantial building remains traced, although XVI penetrated fairly deep.

Trench XII, though relatively small, is of special importance since it was the first area to reveal sherds of types quite new for Susiana, unknown at the time from any other site and not represented even at Chogha Mish among the abundant prehistoric surface sherds. These were our first samples of the Archaic Susiana plain and decorated wares.

THIRD SEASON (CHOGHA MISH III): NOVEMBER 5, 1965–APRIL 5, 1966

During the five months of our third season, an innovation was the housing of the Expedition in a new house in Dezful. The advantages of electricity, running hot and cold water, and other city comforts were, however, offset by the need of commuting to and from the site every day, which required nearly an hour each way. For the first time we were able to bring out student assistants, Elizabeth Carter and Father Stanislao Loffreda, who worked ably and tirelessly. Our government collaborators were, first, Mr. Manuchehr Imani, who unfortu-

nately had to leave us in mid-season because of ill health, and, thereafter, Mr. Rahbar Modami, who stayed with us through the most difficult part of the season and whose enthusiastic, cheerful help was invaluable. In February before Miss Carter and Father Loffreda left to resume their studies in Chicago, we were fortunate to secure the participation of two experienced and highly devoted archaeologists as volunteers, Mrs. H. A. Frankfort from England and Miss Ruth Vaadia from Israel.

During this season Trenches XVII–XXX were added. Some of these (XVIII, XXI, XXII, XXIII, and XXV) were deep trenches in the usual sense of the word. Other areas were designated as trenches when started, but did not develop in depth (XXIV, XXVI, and XXVII). Still other trenches were absorbed, as it were, into contiguous areas of excavation. Thus, Trenches V, Va, XVIII, XIX, and XX are within the eastern area of the terrace excavations, the various parts of which were designated by normal loci. Trenches VI, IX, XVII, and XVII and Sounding C were within the large western area of the terrace excavations.

In the third season work was resumed on the High Mound, chiefly by clearing large areas of brickwork that revealed monumental Old Elamite walls (Trenches XXIV and XXVI) and beneath them substantial Protoliterate remains. Two small, deep test pits in the central hollow of the High Mound (O7:301, 302) demonstrated the sequence of Parthian, Old Elamite, Protoliterate, and prehistoric Susiana periods. The sherds of the two later periods were often mixed together in the uppermost debris. For considerations of safety, these narrow pits were discontinued well above the level where we could expect virgin soil.

On the terrace the enlarged Protoliterate areas on the east and the west produced house remains badly destroyed by erosion and extensive pits of the same general period. Several architectural levels could be distinguished within an accumulation of about 2 to 3 m, the lower ones on the whole better preserved than the higher ones. In the East Area the excavation of the Circular Structure was finished. On the western side of the terrace we succeeded in tracing most of the outline of a polygonal platform of which only the lowermost foundations remain. In all cases the Protoliterate walls rest directly upon remains of the Middle Susiana period.

Of the isolated trenches, Trench XXIII, in the lower part of the southern slopes of the High Mound, had some evidence of Protoliterate occupation immediately below the surface and a thick accumulation of Susiana deposits. Trench XXII, not far away on the terrace, also gave a good sequence of Susiana remains with hardly any Protoliterate overburden. In contrast, Trench XVIII had a shallow but massive Protoliterate deposit at the surface above the Middle Susiana levels. Close to the deepest gully of the terrace, on the eastern side, Trenches XXI and XXV were laid out, flanking Trench XII of the previous season, where the Archaic Susiana pottery had been discovered. Both produced the hoped-for results. In fact, Trench XXV produced not only Archaic Susiana pottery but also a new type of architecture using exceptionally long bricks.

FOURTH SEASON (CHOGHA MISH IV): OCTOBER 1, 1969–MARCH 30, 1970

The circumstances of the excavation changed considerably with the formation of the Joint Iranian Expedition in 1968. The joint sponsorship of the Oriental Institute and the University of California at Los Angeles made it possible to build an expedition house in the vicinity of Chogha Mish, thus fulfilling a long-felt need. We spent June 1969 in Khuzestan finding a suitable location for the house at the edge of Ghaleh Khalil, a small village 3 km west of Chogha Mish, making the final plan and specifications for the house and supervising the construction of the wall up to the level of the windows. Thanks to the kindness of our friend, Mr. A. K. Rashidian, who inspected the building periodically, the house was ready when the Expedition returned for the fourth season of work at the end of September, 1969.

The excavations began in November. The staff consisted of six Ford Foundation student trainees, Charles Adelman, Edward Brovarski, Yousef Majidzadeh, Shapur Malek-Shahmirzadi, Harriet Osborn, and Cynthia Sheikholeslami, as well as two volunteers, Donald D. Bickford (artist) and H. A. Groenewegen-Frankfort (archaeologist). Two other volunteers were with us for shorter periods of time, Maggie van Nierop and Mary C. McCutchan. Yousef Majidzadeh, who, like Shapur Malek-Shahmirzadi, had just completed his M.A. degree at the University of Chicago, served as the representative of the Archaeological Service.

During the fourth season we returned to the High Mound to clean the brickwork on the southwestern slope of the southern slope in Square P10 in order to check whether the brickwork there corresponded in its alignment to that of the Old Elamite brickwork cleared across the gully in Square N10 in the third season. On the terrace the eastern and western areas of private houses were considerably enlarged, reaching about 1,300 sq. m and 450 sq. m respectively. Protoliterate remains were found in the upper layers of Trench XXV, which was doubled in area to about 200 sq. m. The ubiquitous large pits, which are the scourge of the house areas, were more frequent in the enlarged area of Trench XXV than in the previously dug portion and had destroyed not only much of the earlier Protoliterate building remains but also the earlier levels beneath them.

In the center of the terrace, Trench XIII, which had not been touched since the second season, was enlarged to about ten times its original size. The first important results concerned late periods, represented by a cem-

etery presumably Sasanian in date and the traces of a small settlement of the Achaemenid period. The Protoliterate deposits into which the late graves had been dug were relatively sparse in comparison with the East and West Areas. Below were remains of the Middle Susiana period including a series of architectural levels; the upper levels were much disturbed by the Late Cemetery, but the lower levels had relatively well-preserved walls. Middle Susiana and Early Susiana remains were found in Trench XXI, but time did not allow expansion of the work there.

One of the main problems that occupied us since the second season was the Archaic Susiana period. In enlarging Trench XXV, after removal of the overlying Protoliterate remains, we had expected to follow the Archaic Susiana walls discovered at its western edge during the third season. In this we were only partly successful because much of the early brickwork had been destroyed by Protoliterate pits. To test a still lower part of the site and to save some labor in removing top levels we began a new trench at the eastern foot of the mound (S22–23), an area which has retained its original toponym of "Gully Cut" and has never received a trench number. The Gully Cut provided a stratified sequence of Archaic Susiana ceramics and small objects, continuing down to virgin soil and lying under washed-down debris of the other Susiana and Protoliterate periods. In the very gentle, lowest slopes of the terrace not far from the Gully Cut, in Square T20, two small soundings, G and H, also provided excellent ceramic sequences and, in G, building remains as well.

FIFTH SEASON (CHOGHA MISH V): JANUARY 19, 1971–APRIL 1, 1971

On returning we found the expedition house in perfect order, which enabled us to begin work promptly. The staff consisted of two Ford Foundation student trainees, Susan J. Allen and Hal Roberts, and James Phillips of the Anthropology Department of the Chicago Circle Campus,[7] University of Illinois, who was responsible for the lithic remains and for collecting organic materials. Mr. Zabihollah Rahmatian of the Archaeological Service was an able and devoted collaborator in all phases of the expedition's work and he trained some of our workmen in pottery restoration. In this relatively short season work was concentrated on areas important for the prehistoric sequence. Trench XIII was enlarged to follow the walls of the Middle Susiana complex beyond the confines of the fourth season's area. We also penetrated into deeper levels, which also have complex building remains. Trench XXI became one of the major areas this season, yielding good structures on two levels, Middle Susiana and Early Susiana, which were traced

---

7. Now, University of Illinois at Chicago. AA

considerably beyond the limits of the expansion planned for the area. In addition, an exceptional find of complete and semi-complete Early Susiana vessels was discovered adjacent to a house wall. In Trench XXV a considerable area was added on the north, and progress was made in unraveling architectural units of the Archaic Susiana period from the portions of walls spared by the Protoliterate pits. In the northern half of the enlarged Gully Cut, below relatively sparse Protoliterate deposits and mixed debris, a mass of jumbled brickwork apparently represents the final phase of the Archaic Susiana period. From there down we found excellent stratified ceramics, which add considerably to the formulation of our subdivisions of the Archaic Susiana period.

The three areas new in the fifth season are the deep Sounding I (S26) and Trenches XXXI and XXXII. Sounding I revealed washed debris about 8 m deep at the eastern edge of the terrace. The small Trench XXXI on the southeastern slope of the terrace, after a shallow but ashy Protoliterate deposit, yielded superimposed Middle Susiana and Early Susiana remains. Portions of relatively well-preserved walls occurred. Trench XXXII, shortly down the slope from Trench XXI in Square R23, showed the usual Protoliterate sherds on the surface, but the standard Susiana deposits had been considerably eroded so that the walls of long Archaic Susiana bricks were the first substantial building remains to appear below the surface.

CHAPTER 2

THE HISTORICAL PERIODS

The sherds of the prehistoric and Protoliterate periods are so prominent on the surface of Chogha Mish, particularly on the terrace, that at first the existence of later materials was hardly noticed. As work progressed a fairly clear idea as to the distribution of these later remains has been gained.

THE LATEST REMAINS

What seems to be the latest phase represented by structural remains, albeit very scanty ones, occurs just at the surface of the southeastern spur of the High Mound in Squares M–N9. Here there were traces of walls and of a lime- or gypsum-plastered floor, but no plan remained. No artifacts were definitely associated with this floor, which is not surprising since it was at the surface. These traces of occupation could be of very recent date. Even during the present century it was customary for the grandfather and father of Mr. Bahman Samsam, our generous host for the first two seasons, to erect tents on the top of Chogha Mish during the celebration of the Naw Ruz (Persian New Year, March 21) and to review from there the maneuver of the Bakhtiari horsemen on the plain below. Apparently in preparation for such occasions the uppermost parts of the High Mound were flattened and probably also the plaster floor laid down. It does not represent a period of real occupation.

A few burials near the summit of the High Mound were not part of a cemetery but single scattered graves. They were covered in rough gabled fashion with irregular stone slabs and broken baked bricks of various periods that could have been picked up on the surface of the mound at anytime during the last two and a half millennia. The much decayed skeletons showed no definite orientation and thus might be pre-Islamic. The graves contained no objects with the exception of a silver and gold ornament with an incised design, perhaps a face (pl. 5:A) and a shell pendant in the shape of a bird (pl. 5:F), both from P6:304. It appears that during the Islamic and Sasanian periods no part of Chogha Mish itself had been occupied. However, about 300 m to the west of Chogha Mish there is a long slightly raised area with late sherds, the eastern outcrop of a huge, flat settlement extending far to the west.[1] Islamic sites are also to be found in the vicinity. Only some 6 km to the northwest of the site lies Jundi Shapur, the famous metropolis and cultural center of Sasanian and Islamic times.

THE LATE CEMETERY

Almost immediately below the surface in Squares K–L22 and K–L23 (Trench XIII) burials were discovered, some of them dug into loose soil and others into earlier mudbrick constructions of poor quality. During the fourth season twenty-eight such graves were found, clearly a part of a cemetery.[2] Nine additional ones were found during the fifth season. The skeletons, very poorly preserved because of proximity to the surface, were mostly of adults; all were single burials. The great majority had been placed on the right side with the head to the northwest. Nearly all the graves had along the north-northeast side of the burial pit, at the back of the skeleton, a thin screen wall made of four large mudbricks standing on edge (average size: $50 \times 50 \times 10$ cm; cf. pl. 262). No traces of such construction were found at the head, feet, or front of the skeletons. However, a mudbrick found in a horizontal position near the head of the skeleton of Grave 4.16 might be an indication that many, if not all, of the burials were covered by bricks resting on earth ledges above the narrower pit with the body. If this was indeed the case, the closeness of many of the burials to the modern surface presumably accounts for the disappearance of the covering bricks. The bottoms of the higher of these burials (Graves 4.01, 4.03, 4.11, 4.13, 4.15) were only 0.34–0.55 m below the modern surface (el. 83.30–83.09). Thus, the tops of the screen walls were exposed at the surface and often denuded by rain and recent plowing. The lower graves (4.23, 4.26) were not more than 1.29 m below the modern surface (el. 82.35). All the others were distributed in

---

1. Higher standing parts of this area have been assigned site numbers, KS (= Khuzestan Survey) 367, 384, 385, in the comprehensive surveys initiated by Robert McC. Adams and continued some years later by Henry T. Wright and his collaborators (Wenke 1975/76, maps 43–46). Other low mounds to the north and northwest, KS 363–366 and 396–397, might also have been part of the same general urban area.

2. In the fourth season the depth of the graves in Trench XIII was measured from a surface point of 83.54 (southeastern corner).

the 1 m of debris between the two levels. There was no stratification that distinguished individual graves as earlier or later, with one exception (Grave 4.28). It was clear that the original surface level from which these graves were dug had been denuded. It was also clear from their relative density, number, and regularity of orientation that they represent part of a cemetery and were not dug in from houses. Whether the variation in depth reflected the topography of the mound when the cemetery was in use or whether there was no standard as to the depth of the burials is uncertain.

The date of this cemetery remains in doubt. Its burials contained no objects; the absence of pottery distinguishes them from Parthian graves and they are presumably later. Their proximity to the surface suggests that they belonged to a relatively late period in the history of the site. Since the use of horizontal bricks on earth ledges to form a kind of coffin is customary in Islamic graves, this arrangement, assuming that it existed, and the general orientation of the faces of the burials to the south or southwest suggest that the Chogha Mish terrace might have served as a cemetery for nearby early Islamic communities. This is perhaps a likely conclusion even though it must remain tentative in view of the considerable variety of attitude of the bodies, for instance, the crossed legs and the hands against the face, which distinguishes them from traditional Muslim burials.

THE PARTHIAN PERIOD

On the High Mound sherds of gritty buff ware attributable to the Parthian period, particularly the roll rims and corrugated bodies of large torpedo-shaped jars, occurred in mixed debris near the modern surface. In Sounding P7:301 the debris covering a floor at el. 93.66, about 1.20 m below the modern surface at that point, consisted almost entirely of Parthian sherds mixed with ashes. Unlike the similar sherds from surface debris and from the upper levels of soundings in O7:301 and 302, they constitute an uncontaminated group of typically Parthian pottery.

The presence of some glazed potsherds on the surface of the mound on the northwestern tip of the terrace in Squares G–K 13–15 first suggested that there might be traces of Islamic structures in the vicinity. However, as soon as excavations there began, it became clear that no Islamic remains occurred beneath the surface and that the few Islamic glazed sherds were probably carried over in the course of time from the late mound to the west.

Among the Parthian remains that can be dated with certainty in the West Area are a fair number of large torpedo-shaped jars. It gradually became clear that they belonged to graves dug through Protoliterate brickwork from a surface that had been completely denuded. The one horizontal and five vertical torpedo jars of H14:305

(pl. 2:A) were above the northwest edge of H15:407 (Grave 4.31), which had been dug into deposits of the Protoliterate period; consequently, Parthian vessels (pls. 70:B, D–G, L; 71:I) occurred at the same level or even lower than typical Protoliterate pottery. One skeleton was in a peculiar attitude, interred in an almost seated position with its legs and feet lowered into a pit (pl. 2:C). The other skeleton had only half a skull, the front having been sharply cut away.

A second group of vertical torpedo jars, some upright, some mouth down, in J15:306 were close to a burial of which only faint traces of a skeleton remained, but to which three small glazed vessels (III-632, 883–84; pl. 70:A, C) and an iron blade (III-633; pl. 4:D) can be attributed. A short distance away, in J14:302, a rather large two-handled glazed jar (III-950; pls. 4:C; 71:G) was found, apparently marking the position of another grave although no traces of a body were preserved. Near the surface in J14:404 South the skeletons of an adult (woman?) and a child lay alongside a torpedo jar (pl. 2:F; Grave 4.30). Two torpedo jars in K14:302 had no traces of a burial (pl. 2:B). In J14:301 North a torpedo jar appeared at a considerably lower depth than any of the others. Since the adjacent area was not dug, it is unknown whether or not the jar was associated with a burial, although this seems likely since a fragmentary eggshell bowl (III-58) was also found. Although most of the torpedo jars or fragments found *in situ* at Chogha Mish were associated with burials, the bodies were not placed inside the jars as at Susa (Labrousse and Boucharlat 1974, pl. 27:1).

During the Parthian period the terrace was used not only for burials but in some places was actually occupied. In Sounding E (J18) there were traces of domestic installations such as hearths. In the fourth season a roughly-laid pavement of pebbles and Parthian potsherds appeared under a deposit of very hard clay in the enlarged Sounding A, to the east of Trench VI. The most impressive of the Parthian architectural remains, however, is the pottery kiln, J15:301. It consisted of a round combustion chamber, the oven of which was not preserved, 1.90 m in diameter, with a floor about 1.20 m below the present surface of the mound (el. 81.35). The kiln's walls were plastered and its grate had twenty-one holes. The stoke hole was traced but was not excavated so as to avoid leaving it exposed at the end of the season. However, by investigating through some of the holes, it was determined that the combustion chamber must have been at least 50 cm deep. The kiln was filled with a considerable amount of pottery, both glazed and unglazed, and provided excellent samples for the period (pls. 70:H, J–K; 71:J–M; 72:E, H–I, L).

The bulk of the Parthian pottery is of a buff fabric, which ranges in tint from greenish to somewhat orange; the clay was mixed with varying amounts of grits or sand. This basic ware appears either plain, with in some cases a slip, or glazed. The repertory of forms is rather limited. Medium- or large-sized bowls were common in the unglazed ware. They might have either lips or rims of various profiles: blunt (pl. 70:G, N) or channeled (pl. 70:H) lips or rims of various profiles (pls. 70:I–J; 71:J, L), including a slightly beveled, ribbed, variety (pl. 71:J). One specialized open form, a funnel, occurs (pl. 70:O).[3] An open vessel of barrel shape (pl. 71:A) is not exactly dated by its context. It was found just below the surface in the eastern part of Trench XIII, where Parthian torpedo jar sherds were common but normally mixed with some earlier fragments. It represents a simple form that began earlier than the Parthian period— examples occurred at Susa in Achaemenid levels,[4] but the shape is also known in the Parthian period.[5] The plain ware closed vessels of medium size have the same basic shape, a barrel-shaped body (cf. pl. 71:A) elongated above into a wide (pl. 71:C–D) or, in one case, a narrow (pl. 71:E) neck. The addition of a large loop handle produced the most distinctive type, the pitchers (pl. 71:F, H–I). Among the large plain ware vessels the torpedo jars, with exterior corrugations, are the most frequent. They appear to have been made in sections (pl. 72:I, L). Large bag-shaped vessels also occur (pl. 72:G–H). Disc or ring bases are common accessories on both open and closed vessels. Moldings (pl. 71:E) or scoring (pl. 71:C, I) sometimes adorn or demarcate parts of closed vessels. Another decorative feature of the plain ware is the thick plastic band with finger imprints placed at the lip of a large bowl (pl. 71:N).

Although the glazed variant of the buff ware shares bowl (pl. 70:K) and pitcher (pl. 70:D) forms with the plain ware, the outstanding glazed forms are specialized narrow-necked flasks with two handles. Those with bag-shaped bodies were more common (pls. 70:B–C; 71:G), but the square-shouldered pilgrim flask also occurred (pl. 70:E).[6] Another glazed vessel is the wide-mouthed carinated jar with two loop handles (pl. 70:A). At Chogha Mish the glazed vessels of closed form are found primarily in the graves, where they form the bulk of the pottery gifts.

In addition to the standard buff ware in its plain and glazed variants, two specialized and rare wares occur. One is a dense fine ware, buff or greenish buff in color, appearing in the form of simple bowls of eggshell thinness (pl. 70:F, L–M). In addition to bowls, other shapes were probably also made in fine ware. The pitcher (pl. 71:I) has walls approaching in thinness to that of the fine ware. The second specialized ware is characterized by the presence of variously sized grits and of white inclusions; despite its grit the fabric is dense. It is grayish black or brown but can grade to orange at the surface. The exterior is irregularly smoothed and stroke burnished. Only globular, hole-mouthed vessels with small loop handles at the mouth were made in this ware (pl. 71:B). An example with two handles and much of the body preserved, 3.836 (Trench XXIV), indicates that the base was round. The vessels can be identified with confidence as cooking pots. They have a long genealogy both in ware and shape. At Chogha Mish itself a small loop handle of brownish-gray paste full of large grits found in an Achaemenid context could have belonged to a cooking pot of this type (3.914; Q18:305). In Mesopotamia both the cooking-pot ware and the hole-mouthed shape with loop handles at the lip already occur in Late Assyrian levels at Nimrud.[7] Since globular vessels with a wide mouth and round base are so well-adapted for cooking, it is no surprise that they are widely distributed without being necessarily related.[8]

Aside from pottery, the bronze and iron tools and pin from H15:407 (IV-76–79), and the iron lance head from J15:306 (pl. 4:D), there are hardly any objects that can be attributed to the Parthian occupation. One, from the surface of the West Area, appears to be the figurative appliqué of a large glazed vessel; it shows the head and bust of a woman dressed in a draped robe. Less certain in date but possibly Parthian are the upper part of a terra-cotta plaque and the head from another (pl. 5:D, J). Unfortunately, neither their contexts or stylistic characteristics are sufficiently distinctive to date them without doubt.

The materials just described represent the latest regular occupation at Chogha Mish. Their position within the long range of the Parthian dynasty must be determined by the ceramic evidence. Considerable attention is now being devoted to the analysis of Parthian pottery in Iran and as this work progresses it will probably become possible to date various phases within the period with relative precision.[9] Although at present the Parthian occupation at Chogha Mish can hardly be assigned exact absolute dates, it does seem to belong in the latter part of the period, perhaps even at the end if weight is placed on the similarities between some of the Chogha Mish material and that from Level 2 of the Pal-

3. Utensils of the same general type and size, but different in details of shape, already appear in Late Assyrian contexts at Nimrud (Oates 1959, pl. 39:109).

4. Village perse-achéménide, Level 2 (Ghirshman 1954, pl. 38:G. S. 1230); Ville royale II, Levels 5–3 (Miroschedji 1978:224, fig. 55:13).

5. Shahr-e Qumis (Hansman and Stronach 1970:58, fig. 14:10).

6. On the square-shouldered pilgrim flask, see D. Stronach 1978:242, figs. 106:B; 243, no. 13 (Pasargadae).

7. Fort Shalmaneser (Oates 1959:17, pl. 39:108).

8. For example, see the vessels of Middle Susiana Family XXXIX at Chogha Mish, one specimen of which had lugs close to the lip (pl. 193:T), and an Early Dynastic III hole-mouthed vessel with lugs near the lip from Temple Oval II at Khafajah (Delougaz 1952, pl. 187:C.654.503).

9. Compare the proposals of Haerinck 1979.

ace of Artaxerxes II on the Shaur at Susa,[10] which is assigned a long range from the Late Parthian to the Sasanid period.[11]

The evidence available indicates that the Parthian settlement was rather sparse and confined primarily to the High Mound and the western parts of the terrace, as far as Trench XIII. In fact, the occupation on the mound of Chogha Mish was probably only the outlying eastern edge of a large Parthian settlement, the central quarters of which lay in the more level areas to the west.[12]

THE ACHAEMENID PERIOD

In the eastern half of the terrace, Achaemenid sherds are scattered over the surface or found close to it in excavated areas, chiefly Trench XIII and the East Area, except for some special cases such as pits. No house walls were recovered, although a few structural elements marked some floor levels near the surface. The settlement from which these Iron Age remains came had, as the uppermost layer of the terrace, been particularly vulnerable to weathering. Moreover, since it was established directly on top of Protoliterate levels that had themselves been suffering from erosion for over two millennia, it is not surprising that Iron Age remains were normally mixed with Protoliterate material. The absence of primary context makes more difficult the establishment of the precise date within the later part of the Iron Age of the Chogha Mish settlement. However, there is considerable evidence to date it to the Achaemenid period, although the possibility that it began earlier should not be excluded.

THE EAST AREA

In the East Area Achaemenid sherds occur throughout the higher terrain toward the north, usually in levels close to the surface. However, the scattered distribution of Achaemenid materials in eastern[13] and middle[14] sectors contrasts markedly with their abundance in the northwestern part of the East Area. In the exploratory Trench V of the second season, Plot D (Q18:202) crossed the southeastern part of a round structure, the excavation of which was later continued as Q18:305. The finds from both Q18:202 and 305 belong to the Circular Structure or to the below-surface debris above it; Achaemenid sherds are prominent among them. Just to the north, in Trench V A in Square P17, typical late sherds appeared near the surface and in a pit (pl. 75:D, I, Q, S, V). When the Trench V A area was enlarged traces of simple domestic features were found. To the west in P17:401 two round baked bricks, ca. 30 cm in diameter and 5 cm thick, perhaps the bases for posts, appeared 35 cm below the surface at el. 82.27. Next to and flush with one of them were a small baked brick and a rather flat oval stone; although no floor was distinguished, it is possible that these elements indicate the approximate level of an Achaemenid installation at this point. In addition to Achaemenid sherds, a frit scaraboid (pl. 76:M) and a large fragment of a bituminous stone bowl were found in P17:401.

Adjacent to the original Trench V A on the east within a space of ca. 1 × 2 m was a cluster of shallow depressions, two oval (20 × 50 cm) and one circular (50 cm in diameter and about 30 cm deep; P17:402 Northeast, Pits 1–3). They were all filled with ashy gray-black earth and were probably fire holes. Less than 2 m distant was a larger pit about 1.25 m in diameter and about 75 cm deep, also filled with ashy debris (P17:402 Northeast, Pit 4); in it were an iron projectile point (pl. 76:H) and a bronze trilobate arrowhead (pl. 76:F).

The two larger pits had been dug from a hard surface at el. 82.65 and the two smaller pits from a slightly higher elevation; these apparently represent an Achaemenid occupation level sunk into Protoliterate debris. Immediately adjacent in the southeastern corner of P17:402 at a higher level (82.96–82.76) was a deposit with a number of complete beveled-rim bowls. A fragmentary fibula (pl. 76:B) and sherds were found to the

---

10. Note the similarities in the following forms: Bowl with finger-imprinted band: at Chogha Mish (pl. 71:N) and at Shaur, Level 2 (Boucharlat and Labrousse 1979:103, fig. 26:11). Bag-shaped jar: at Chogha Mish (pl. 72:G) and at Shaur, Level 2 (Labrousse and Boucharlat 1974:123, fig. 34:17). Torpedo jars: at Chogha Mish (pl. 72:I–L) and at Shaur, Level 2 (ibid., figs. 35:8; 37:10). Glazed footed bowls: at Chogha Mish (pl. 70:K) and at Shaur, Level 2 (ibid., fig. 35:5; Boucharlat and Labrousse 1979, fig. 28:6). For unglazed prototypes, see Shaur, Level 3 (ibid., figs. 29:11 [beveled base similar to pl. 70:K]; 3:1–2). Glazed two-handled jars: at Chogha Mish (pls. 70:C; 71:G) and at Shaur, Level 2 (Labrousse and Boucharlat 1974, fig. 37:2, 5, 9). Fine ware bowl: at Chogha Mish (pl. 70:F) and at Shaur, Level 2 (ibid., fig. 36:9 [Cachette 417]).

11. In a personal communication, R. Boucharlat noted that in a forthcoming study the Susa materials providing Middle Parthian are dated around the first century B.C.

12. In a later season torrential rains provided some supporting evidence for this assumption by revealing several torpedo jars and a pitcher in the low area adjacent to Chogha Mish on the west.

13. Compare the eastern plots of Trench V, their southern extension (R17:215), and in the northern extension the large Protoliterate pit (R17:208).

14. Compare R17:303 and 306; R17:301, 304–05, 307; and Q18:302. In the primarily Protoliterate pit (R18:305) Achaemenid sherds penetrated from 0.50 to 1.70 m B.S. Close by, in R18:304, a few Achaemenid sherds and a tablet were found. Perhaps originally Achaemenid materials had been sufficiently abundant in this vicinity for some sherds to have reached the lower parts of the pit during the activity of rodents or by some other agency.

south and east of the Circular Structure,[15] but aside from the grave material in Trench XIII, the most notable concentration of Achaemenid remains found during the first five seasons was in the northwestern part of the East Area.

The Circular Structure: A regular, circular building, Q18:305, extending into Squares P17, P18, Q17, and Q18, stands out among the agglomeration of rooms around it. Its curved walls were first discovered in Trench V at the end of the second season, being then extremely hard to trace with the help of the still relatively untrained workmen. The task was of particular difficulty because of the exceedingly bad quality of the brickwork. Individual bricks were rarely distinguished, as they were soft and crumbly and contained ashes, pebbles, and small sherds. The walls would have been almost impossible to trace if it were not for patches of a reasonably distinguishable coating of mud plaster. Accordingly, in the course of the third season we were able to clear the structure both inside and outside (pls. 8:A; 9:A). It is almost perfectly circular, with a diameter of ca. 11.0 m outside and 7.5 m inside. The walls average about 1 m in thickness and the top of the foundation is at about el. 80.00 m. Parts of the foundations could be traced outside on the northern end as well as on the inside. To the southeast of the Circular Structure and disappearing beneath it was a pavement made of broken baked bricks in somewhat of a "crazy pavement" pattern, Q18:315 (pl. 9:B). The bricks are of typical Protoliterate format and dimensions, but they are all incomplete, which shows that here they were used secondarily. Some 20 cm below the baked-brick pavement is an earlier pavement made of pebbles. It appears that both pavements were laid in a street or on courts (pl. 9:B).

Despite very careful examination of the wall surfaces both inside and outside, no entrance to this structure could be found. It must therefore be assumed that it was entered from above the preserved level that was well over 1 m in height.[16] On the inside several floors could be discerned, but the number of finds was surprisingly small, with relatively little pottery. Beginning with the third floor from the foundation and continuing almost to the whole height now preserved, the structure contained masses of animal bones.

15. Compare also, somewhat to the east, Q17:202 (Trench V, Plot F) and 304, and Q18:301.

16. A third-season field note of Delougaz records the discovery "at the north end of the Circular Structure at ca. 0.60 m B.S." of many reed impressions representing a fallen ceiling. Since he did not specify that the fragments were found *inside* the structure, they might have been found just to the north in the Trench V A area. Thus, it is not possible to establish that the reed fragments came from the roof of the Circular Structure.

Delougaz concluded that the Circular Structure was, indeed, Protoliterate and that the enormous accumulation of bones was secondarily deposited in the upper part of it. His reasons were as follows. First, the walls of the nearby houses were clearly built directly against it or occasionally bonded into it without any interval, such as would have occurred if the structure had been sunk into a circular hole cut from a higher level. Secondly, great masses of Protoliterate pottery of various forms were piled directly against the building on its southwestern side (pl. 8:A–B). The proportion of complete and fragmentary beveled-rim bowls was very large, but other types of Protoliterate pottery were represented. The debris also contained large numbers of clay jar and bottle stoppers and fragments of some of the more interesting clay sealings from the site. Third, small sections of drains built of baked bricks of the usual Protoliterate format (about 42 × 18 × 7 cm) seem to have run over part of this structure. Although these could have been remains of later structures using early building material, it seems more likely that they were built after the Circular Structure had been abandoned and that they give it a date *ante quem*.

The original conclusion that the Circular Structure was an integral part of the Protoliterate city was shaken after the third season. It was then that the existence of an Achaemenid settlement at the modern surface was recognized. In addition, a large representative collection of samples from the bone deposit was examined preliminarily by Dr. Sandor Bökönyi of the National Museum, Budapest. Many of the identifications could have been expected, but the appearance of the skull bones of a domesticated horse and the leg bones of a camel was startling. Furthermore, the pelvis of a horse appeared in an immediately adjacent Achaemenid deposit that was preserved to a somewhat higher elevation than the Circular Structure. The presence of those species in a late fourth-millennium context would contradict the known history of their first appearance in the Near East. Neither do they appear in the enormous repertory of animals in Protoliterate art. Thus, the faunal remains made a reassessment of what had seemed the unquestionable Protoliterate date of the structure.

The pottery from the interior of the Circular Structure, though it included many beveled-rim bowl fragments, was not as abundant as in various Protoliterate loci in the immediate vicinity (Q18:301; P18:301) and in particular did not contain complete or semi-complete vessels (see *Index of Loci and Finds*). Achaemenid sherds occurred with the bone deposit, which yielded the horse and camel bones whose presence has provided a serious obstacle to an early date for the building. It seems that in the Achaemenid period the upper part of a much older structure was cleared and eventually used as a dump for bones. In the course of these activities, it would be natural for some contemporary sherds to be mixed with the fill. However, a recheck of the Q18:305 pottery shows that Achaemenid sherds also appear in the deepest part of the structure, some 2 m below the modern surface. This strongly suggests that the entire fill of Q18:305 is late, which would explain why it contains less and more fragmentary pottery than much normal Protoliterate debris.

The great contrast between the form of the Circular Structure and the walls and rectangular rooms normal for the Protoliterate houses surrounding it does not necessarily speak against a Protoliterate date, since its function, presumably as a granary, was different. On the other hand, the presence of the late faunal remains and of Achaemenid sherds throughout the fill, makes the evidence of comparable structures in Achaemenid contexts at southern Palestinian sites pertinent. These are brick-lined underground granaries found at sites in the general area of Gaza and Beersheba. Two large examples at Tell Jemmeh (Gerar), 11.50 and 10.75 m in diameter (Petrie 1928, pl. 13) provide the best parallels for the 11.00 m diameter of the Circular Structure. One, discovered in 1971–72, had an interior diameter of over 6.00 m (Van Beek 1972:245). At Jemmeh the walls of the large granaries and of eight smaller granaries ranging from 7.75 to 7.00 m in diameter are all about 1.50 m thick (Petrie 1928:8–9, pl. 13). At Tell esh-Shari the Persian Stratum, V, had a granary of about 5.00 m in diameter with a brick floor covered by vegetal remains (Oren 1978:1060, color plate on p. 1057). The smaller mud-lined or simple pits, ca. 1.50–2.50 m in diameter, were found in Persian contexts at several other sites, although also apparently used for storing grain, are not directly comparable to the Circular Structure.[17] Despite the absence at Chogha Mish of certain structural features found in Tell Jemmeh (interior steps, recessed ledges, and lower courses of conical roofs) and Tell esh-Shari (brick floor) granaries, their general similarity to the thick-walled Circular Structure is striking and strongly corroborates the Achaemenid date already suggested by the late sherds and faunal remains found in it.

At Chogha Mish no evidence for the roofing of the Circular Structure was discovered, nor were traces of grain preserved, but its interpretation as a granary, as suggested by Delougaz, is reinforced by the Palestinian parallels. The storage of grain in the Persian period was discussed by Stager (1971), who also drew attention to an experimental study by Reynolds (1974) on the underground storage of grain which demonstrated that even unlined pits are suitable and that a conical shape is preferable to a cylindrical one.

There seems now to be no way to reconcile such a late dating of the building with the factor on which Delougaz finally placed overriding weight, namely the corner of Protoliterate Room Q17:305 bonded into the structure's southeastern side. Only he would have been in a position to assess how binding these observations are or whether it would have been possible to reinterpret them in the light of the additional evidence just cited. Although these contradictory considerations must be placed aside as an insoluble problem, the coincidence between the presence of late pottery and bones inside the structure and the existence of late parallels for it seems too striking to be accidental. Accordingly, the Circular Structure can be assigned to the Achaemenid period with great probability. The structure fits very well into its setting immediately adjacent to the Trench V A habitation remains. They indicate that the Achaemenid occupation level was close to the modern surface and that the surviving walls of the Circular Structure had been underground originally. This explains the absence of an entrance and suggests that the structure was entered from above. When the Circular Structure was constructed, its walls were probably built directly against the sides of the pit, which would explain the undisturbed Protoliterate remains directly adjacent in Q18:301.

TRENCH XIII AREA

Settlement Remains: In the east end of Trench XIII, in a small area not so badly disturbed by burials of the Late Cemetery as elsewhere, two hard floors appeared at 37 cm (el. 83.27) and 48 cm (el. 83.16) below the surface respectively (L22:401). On the lower floor was a door socket made of part of a baked brick resting on a cluster of small pebbles and a complete baked brick (37 × 37 × 10 cm). Another complete baked brick (34 × 34 × 7 cm) was set flush with the floor a little distance south of the socket. The occupational debris above and just below the lower floor yielded characteristic potsherds (pls. 73:E; 75:O, U, Y), a trilobate and bronze arrowhead (pl. 76:E), and the front part of an animal figurine (pl. 76:A). The head is so badly damaged as to make identification difficult; the two short projections could be taken as the horns of a bull or the ears of a lion. The rudimentary modeling is supplemented by decorative incisions. The legs are reduced to mere stubs or else, a less likely alternative, are intended to represent a couchant pose.

In the fifth season a small area immediately adjacent to L22:401 was dug. About 50 cm below the surface (el. 83.06) in L22:501 were some trapezoidal bricks with one curved side, designed for constructing round features such as columns or wells and made of a distinctive heavy reddish clay mixed with sand. At the western edge of L22:501, 1 m below the surface (el. 82.06), was

---

17. Tell el-Hesy: Bliss 1898:109–11; Lachish, City III: Tufnell 1953:1151–58; pls. 17:4, 115, 116: Tell Gath = Tell Sheikh el-Areini; Yeivin 1960:392; 1961:4, fig. 2.

the mouth of a kiln, varying from 90 to 75 cm in diameter (pl. 3:A left). The 1.25 m deep structure was slightly conical in section, but very irregular in the interior. The rim and sides had been plastered with mud in which finger marks show. The kiln still contained fragments of a thick grate. Small irregular projections from the walls about 80 cm below the mouth indicate the position of the grate.

The Graves: In another part of Trench XIII, K23:400, a late grave (Grave 4.25) had been cut down into a lower burial, Grave 4.28 (el. 82.15), truncating one of the latter's large pottery vessels (pl. 3:B). Grave 4.28 is recognizable as Achaemenid from its pottery and small objects (pl. 263). It contained the skeleton of an individual over six feet tall (pl. 3:C). A small band of gold foil was over the mouth (pl. 4:E) and a large undecorated agate bead nearby at the chin (pl. 263:10).[18] Fragments of a few corroded silver rings were found among the bones (pl. 4:K). The grave also contained two corroded copper or bronze vessels—a small jar with a wide neck (pl. 4:J) and a bowl found in the crossed arms (pls. 3:E; 4:M), a bundle of eleven projectile points—most of them corroded together in groups of two or three (pls. 4:L; 263:12 b–e), two trilobate bronze arrowheads (pl. 263:12 a), an iron spear head (pl. 4:F; 263:7), and pottery (pls. 73:I; 74:A; 75:X; 263:4). Across the legs of the skeleton lay that of an animal, apparently a sheep or goat (pl. 3:C–D).

Fragmentary remains from a robbed Achaemenid burial, Grave 5.08 (1 m below surface = el. 82.23), the skeleton of which had disappeared, were found in the fifth season some 30 cm below a grave of the Late Cemetery, Grave 5.01. The finds of Grave 5.08 consisted of a copper or bronze cup (pl. 74:P), the fragments of a corroded bowl with petal ornaments (pl. 4:N), a pair of silver bracelets in the form of a broad band with three ridges and open ends (pl. 76:J), four rings of silver wire, an oval and a round pendant of silver foil, a small shapeless fragment of an iron blade, and some beads.

OTHER AREAS

Other areas that yielded Achaemenid sherds were Trench VII in the western side of Squares O20–21, Sounding F nearby in the northeastern corner of Square N22, and Trench XI in O23–24, where some traces of fragmentary walls close to the surface might accordingly be attributed to that period (pl. 260). All three were small test areas dug only briefly during the second season. However, they are of significance in suggesting that the Achaemenid settlement was probably continuous over at least the eastern part of the terrace and that the high terrace in the southeast, around Trench XI, might shelter somewhat better traces of late structures

18. For the fragment of a similar bead, see Schmidt 1957, pl. 43:22 (Persepolis, Treasury).

than have been so far found elsewhere. In contrast to the situation in the eastern half of the terrace, there is only some rather tenuous evidence for an Achaemenid presence in the west, in the form of various sherds from mixed debris (Protoliterate with late intrusions: J15:402 and 403; K14:403; K15:402). The case for considering them as Achaemenid rather than Parthian versions of long-lived types are indicated below at the end of the discussion of the pottery.

THE POTTERY

The wares of the Iron Age pottery range widely in quality. Some sherds of coarse ware contain so many multicolored grits that they can, at first glance, be easily confused with the gritty buff ware of the Early Susiana period. The ordinary fabrics include both fairly sandy pastes and more purified, denser pastes. This color ranges considerably from brownish or grayish-buff to light buff shades with characteristic undertones of greenish-yellow or orange. Dense, highly refined pastes without visible grits occur in light red, buff, grayish-buff, and gray colors. Cream slips or orange or red washes were applied to vessels of both common and fine wares. Some of the fine ware vessels were highly burnished; partial smoothing or stroke burnish also occurs on the common ware.

The quality of the ware is correlated with the size and shape of the vessels, as is indicated by the frequency with which small or sharply-articulated open shapes occur in varieties of fine ware. High burnish also seems to be characteristic for sharply profiled forms such as a small, incurved lip bowl with an exterior ledge (pl. 73:A) and a ridged gray ware bowl (pl. 73:H).

Vessels of small (B) size are rare. Two almost identical red-washed globular jars, both with broken necks, are representative of small-sized closed forms (pl. 73:D); they might have come from a plundered grave. Bowls of medium (C) size form the largest component of the Achaemenid pottery corpus at Chogha Mish. Among those whose walls can be taken as forming basically a continuous curve, no individual shape predominates. Convex-sided bowls range from the thin-walled, rimless vessel in Grave 4.28 (pl. 73:I) to thicker-walled varieties with varying treatment of the mouth (pl. 73:E–F, K–L) and examples with a specialized ribbing on the exterior (pl. 73:H, J). A different kind of ribbing decorated the upper part of a bowl with an overhanging and ribbed rim (pl. 73:N). Rather globular rims occur on bowls with vertical upper walls or sinuous sides (pl. 73:P–R).

It is among the bowls with angled shape that we find the types dominating the Achaemenid pottery of Chogha Mish. The bowls vary greatly, however, in the character of the angles, ranging from examples with very slight (pl. 74:A–B) or rounded (pl. 74:C–E, L, N) angles to more sharply carinated forms (pl. 74:F–K, M, O). The angled bowls can also be divided into rimless and rimmed categories, but there is no sharp division between them. Blunt lips (pl. 73:E) merge into thickened rims (pl. 74:I, L–N) and these in turn into overhanging rims (pl. 74:G–H, J). Occasionally there are sophisticated details such as ribbing on the exterior of the thickened rim (pl. 74:K). As far as body shapes go, forms with fairly straight upper bodies (pl. 74:A–C, J–K) appear to be rarer than those with a concavity, either slight or pronounced, above the angle. The lower body seems normally to have been taller than the portion above the angle, in so far as can be determined when so many examples are mere fragments. One sherd (pl. 74:O) seems to have a relatively high upper body but is too broken to provide a mouth diameter and to be claimed as a certain example of the typical Achaemenid milk bowls.[19]

The presence of horizontal loop handles delimits a prominent class of open vessels. One fairly small example was recovered (pl. 75:N), as well as some fragments of medium size (pl. 75:M, Q, T). The large, D size, basins have massive handles that could hardly have been functional unless they were in pairs (pl. 75:O, R–S). The upper part of the body where the handles were attached tends to be fairly vertical. The shapes vary from simple convex (pl. 75:Q) to sharply carinated (pl. 75:R) profiles. Rims might be thickened (pl. 75:O, Q), but are more commonly everted and blunt (pl. 75:M, S–T). The everted rim of one of the basins was so flattened on top as to form a slanting ledge (pl. 75:R).

A fragmentary ring-based object found on the Achaemenid floor in Trench XIII has on the interior ridges, some of which taper out on one side, the stumps of two loop-handles; an evenly-spaced third handle must have once existed (pl. 75:U). On the basis of the three "handles," the object might be tentatively considered as a tripod stand suitable for use beneath, for example, a large, porous water jar.[20]

The medium-sized closed vessels normally have wide necks. Fine ware vessels with a wide, high neck sharply differentiated from the body form a specialized class (pl. 75:A–C). The quality of the ordinary domestic vessels is represented by one-handled jars (pl. 75:D, G) and by trefoil spouts (pl. 75:H–L, P). Although these are unfortunately all broken away from their bodies, they belong to a well-known family of jars. Three of the Chogha Mish examples retain enough of their necks to show that the latter had been fairly high and wide (pl.

75:J–K, P). The spouts were placed either vertically, so that lip and spout approached or touched each other (pl. 75:J–K, P), or diagonally (pl. 75:H–I). One of the diagonal spouts has a pronounced gullet (pl. 75:L).

The standard type of large jar is ovoid with a relatively narrow neck. It is represented by a complete and an almost complete example from Grave 4.28 in Trench XIII (pls. 75:X; 263:3–4) and by fragments (pl. 75:V–W, Y). The rims vary from a simple thickening (pl. 75:V) to more differentiated, overhanging roll rims (pl. 75:W–Y). A club rim type, concave on top, is more rare (pl. 75:BB). Rimless necks also occur; one of the examples has sloping walls suggesting a globular or bag-like body (pl. 75:Z).

The dating of the Iron Age settlement at Chogha Mish depends to a great extent upon the evidence of the pottery which, however, includes many long-lived types. Achaemenid levels at both provincial centers[21] and the capitals provide good parallels for many of the bowl types from Chogha Mish.[22] The Chogha Mish representative of the long-lived class of bowl with horizontal handles, which persisted as late as the Parthian period

---

19. Typical examples are found at Pasargadae (D. Stronach 1978:184, figs. 106:13; 243, note 13); Susa, Ville royale II, Levels 5–4 (Miroschedji 1978:242, fig. 55:1); and Persepolis (Schmidt 1957, pl. 89:8).

20. A Period II sherd from Godin, consisting of a fragment of a ring-based tray or stand with molding can be taken as a distant analogy (Young and Levine 1974:133, fig. 48:3).

21. Period II of Godin had a range from ca. 800 B.C. to the early Achaemenid period and a considerable amount of Period II pottery probably belongs to the later part of the range; Period I (or Iron III, late) of Baba Jan corresponds to the Achaemenid period (D. Stronach 1978:11).

22. For parallels to pl. 72:K, see Miroschedji 1978:224, fig. 55:6 (Susa, Ville royale II, Levels 5–4); and D. Stronach 1978:252, fig. 111:9 (Pasargadae, late Achaemenid or immediately post-Achaemenid); similar forms are found at Susa, Village achéménide, Level II (Ghirshman 1954, pl. 37:G. S. 1222). For beveled rims on bowls of simple convex shapes (cf. pl. 73:E), see ibid., pl. 37:G. S. 1219a (Susa, Village achéménide, Level II); and D. Stronach 1978:254, fig. 112:2 (Pasargadae, late Achaemenid). For the overhanging channeled rim (cf. pl. 73:N), see ibid., p. 252, fig. 111:7 (Pasargadae, Achaemenid). For parallels to pl. 73:O, see Miroschedji 1978:224, fig. 55:2–3 (Susa, Ville royale, Levels 5–4); for a distant analogy, see Young 1969:119, fig. 42:12/03 with three ribs (Godin, Period II). For similar shape and ribbing, without overhanging rim (cf. pl. 73:Q), see Ghirshman 1954, pl. 36:G. S. 1218e (Susa, Village achéménide, Level II). For parallels to pl. 75:S–U, see ibid., pl. 37:G. S. 1221a, 1219c, 1225 (Susa, Village achéménide, Level II); for a distant analogy, see Young 1969:123, fig. 44:16 (Godin, Period II). For a form similar to pl. 74:B, see D. Stronach 1978, fig. 111:19 (Pasargadae, late Achaemenid). For parallels to pl. 74:E, L, see ibid., p. 244, fig. 107:7 (Pasargadae, presumably Achaemenid) and ibid., fig. 107:8 (Achaemenid); and Schmidt 1957, pl. 74:1 (Persepolis). For parallels to pl. 74:I, see Goff 1970:154. fig. 8:7 (Baba Jan, Period 1); and Miroschedji 1978:224, fig. 55:9 (Susa, Ville royale II, Levels 5–4); cf. also D. Stronach 1978:246, fig. 108:3 (Pasargadae, post-Achaemenid). For a body similar to pl. 74:K, see ibid., p. 246, fig. 108:2 (Pasargadae). For a form similar to pl. 74:M, see ibid., p. 244, fig. 107:10 (Pasargadae, post-Achaemenid).

(Hansman and Stronach 1974:20, fig. 4:3), are allied by their everted rim types more closely to examples from Period I at Baba Jan than to the earlier, Late Median examples from Nush-i Jan with their predominantly incurved lips of rims.[23] Among the closed forms the small globular jars, the trefoil-spouted jars, and the large, relatively narrow-necked jars in fine ware, the wide, high-necked jar, and the band-rim neck all have good Achaemenid parallels, as does also the general type of squat, one-handled jar.[24]

The comparisons for the pottery (see footnotes 22, 24, above and below) indicate an Achaemenid date for much of the Iron-age corpus of pottery from Chogha Mish. The possibility that it contains some earlier elements should be mentioned, however. Although a discussion of the extent to which pottery types found in the Achaemenid period might have begun earlier is beyond the scope of this study, Chogha Mish does provide some types with pre-Achaemenid affinities. One rather small bowl of fine ware with an exterior ledge close to the lip (pl. 73:A) has parallels at Ziwiye and also at Godin during Period II.[25] The second type is the bridge-spout. One example consists only of the stump of the spout attached to the wide, concave lip of an open bowl (pl. 75:E).[26]

Another example was originally attached to the wide neck of a jar (pl. 75:F) and has parallels at Susa in Level I of the Village perse-achéménide and Level 7 of the Ville royale II.[27] A ring-based carinated bowl (pl. 74:A) is, aside from minor variations, the same as a bowl type that was common and distinctive for Late Assyrian pottery of the seventh century.[28] The bituminous stone bowl fragment (pl. 74:Q), described below, is a variation of the general type in which the height of the body above the carination has been enlarged at the expense of that below. The questions raised by the presence of these types can probably best be dealt with when the Iron Age pottery found after the fifth season of excavation can be published. Although it might thus be premature to exclude completely the possibility that the Iron Age settlement at Chogha Mish began earlier than the Achaemenid period proper, the apparent shallowness of the occupational debris certainly suggests strongly that the occupation was short-lived.

The Achaemenid settlement seems to have been concentrated in the eastern half of the terrace, where angled-bowl sherds occur on the surface and characteristic sherds are found either in secondary deposits or associated with floors or other traces of occupation in the East Area, in Trenches VII, XI, and XIII, and in Sounding F. On the High Mound no reliable evidence for Achaemenid occupation has been recovered; two horizontal handled sherds (pl. 75:N, T), not from well-dated contexts, could be strays or possibly later, Parthian, examples of this persistent class. Similarly, in the West Area the problem of distinguishing Achaemenid and Parthian pottery arises. There, in addition to the prominent Parthian materials, some Achaemenid fragments might have also intruded into debris of much earlier, Protoliterate date. The pieces in question are as follows. A fragment of a red-washed, sharply carinated bowl (pl. 74:F) from J15:403, a Protoliterate context with some intrusive Parthian pottery, is best matched by examples from Period II at Godin.[29] The mixed debris of K14:402 provided several fragmentary or semi-complete bowls with parallels ranging in date from somewhat before to

23. Cf. Baba Jan, Period I (Goff 1970:154, fig. 8:11–12); Nush-i Jan, Late Median (R. Stronach 1978:17–18, figs. 6:28, 29; 7:2, 4). The small horizontal-handled bowls from Nush-i Jan have incurving mouths (ibid., fig 6:3–8) different from the everted mouth of Chogha Mish (cf. pl. 75:N).

24. For parallels to pl. 75:V–W, see Ghirshman 1954, pl. 38:G. S. 1177 (Susa, Village achéménide, Level II) and ibid., pl. 49:G. S. 830, G. S. 1278a (Level III–IV); and D. Stronach 1978:262, fig. 116:3 (Pasargadae, Achaemenid). For a form similar to pl. 74:B (common ware), see Ghirshman 1954, pl. 39:G. S. 1242b (Susa, Village achéménide, Level III). For parallels to pl. 75:AA, see D. Stronach 1978:264, fig. 117:10 (closest parallel; Pasargadae, late Achaemenid) and perhaps ibid., fig. 117:30 (post-Achaemenid). For parallels to pl. 75:BB, see Ghirshman 1954, pl. 40:G. S. 1246e (Susa, Village achéménide, Level III); and Young and Levine 1974:127, fig. 45:10 (Godin II). For parallels to pl. 75:V, see Ghirshman 1954, pl. 40:G. S. 1246f (Susa, Village achéménide III); and Young and Levine 1974, fig. 44:13 (Godin II). For parallels to pl. 75:X, see Ghirshman 1954, pl. 39:G. S. 2155 (Susa, Village achéménide III); and D. Stronach 1978:272, fig. 121:9 (Pasargadae, Achaemenid). For a form similar to pl. 75:Z, see ibid., fig. 117:2 (Pasargadae, Achaemenid). For a general type (cf. pl. 75:D), see Miroschedji 1978:224, fig. 55:16 (Susa, Ville royale II, Levels 5–4).

25. Cf. Ziwiye, Iron III (Young 1965:58, fig. 3:4); Godin Tepe II (Young 1969:119, fig. 43:11 [fine ware, but slightly carinated]; 123, fig. 44:12 [common ware bowl with ledge]); Godin II (Young and Levine 1974:127, fig. 45:19).

26. The sherd was found in a Protoliterate context but presumably was close to the surface. The pierced lug projecting below the spout is strikingly similar to those characteristic for the Protoliterate bowls with open trough spout of Family XXXIV (pl. 85:E–H, J); however, this must be an unrelated

similarity; the late date of 2.574 (pl. 75:E) is assured by its bridged spout and its wide concave rim notched along the exterior edge. These are features alien to Protoliterate ceramic.

27. Cf. Susa, Achaemenid Level I (Ghirshman 1954, pl. 29:G. S. 2242); Ville royale II, Level 7 (Miroschedji 1978:223, fig. 54:7). For discussion of the date of Level 1, see D. Stronach 1974. Two other Chogha Mish bridge spouts similar to 3.334 (pl. 75:F) were found on the surface near Trench V (2.660, 2.661).

28. Cf. Nimrud, Fort Shalmaneser (Oates 1959:132, 141, pl. 36:31).

29. For parallels to pl. 74:F, see Young 1969:123, fig. 44:18; Young and Levine 1974:131, fig. 47:11 (Godin, Period II).

somewhat after the Achaemenid period (pl. 73:L, P).[30] Also from K14:402, from the same depth as the carinated bowl with overhanging rim (pl. 74:H) is a wide, high-mouthed jar of a type paralleled at Persepolis (Schmidt 1957, pls. 71:3, 72:9). Another variation of the same general type from the West Area has a molding separating neck and body (pl. 75:C), as does the third Chogha Mish example of this class (pl. 75:B), for which a parallel at Susa has already been cited. Less satisfactory are the distant parallels for a fragment of a large jar, also from K14:402 (pl. 75:CC).[31] The comparisons available for these specimens from the West Area justify their inclusion, although with a certain amount of reservation, in the Achaemenid corpus and suggest that there was some Achaemenid occupation on the western side of the terrace.

STONE AND METAL VESSELS

Vessels of materials other than pottery are also represented. The western part of the East Area provided a fragment of a bowl of bituminous stone (pl. 74:Q), and four metal vessels were found in Trench XIII in Graves 4.28 and 5.02. The bituminous bowl's ring base and straight-walled carinated shape relate it to one of the pottery bowls from Grave 4.28 (pl. 74:A), although the enlargement of the upper body at the expense of the lower part gives it a different appearance. Similar to the pottery bowl, the bituminous bowl has Late Assyrian parallels in pottery and glazed frit bowls from graves at Assur.[32]

The corroded metal bowl that rested under the crossed forearms of the skeleton of Grave 4.28 (pls. 3:E; 4:M; 263:6) and the bowl reconstituted from corroded fragments found in the destroyed Grave 5.08 (pl. 4:N) both have shallow, convex shapes. Such simple undifferentiated forms can be expected to occur widely without being necessarily connected. Nevertheless, it is of interest that graves of the Persian period at Deve Hüyük

contained undecorated bowls of similar shallow shape.[33] The petal decoration on one of the bowls (pl. 4:N) links it with vessels of more differentiated character, the phialai which were typical for western Asia in the Iron Age and which sometimes have elaborate decoration.[34] Good parallels in body shape and decoration are a bronze phiale from Deve Hüyük[35] and silver phialai from Susa and Tell el-Fara (South).[36] All of these have mouths slightly offset from the decorated portion of the body; this also seems to have been true of the example from Chogha Mish (pl. 4:N), although its severe corrosion has left only slight and not completely certain traces at some spots of such an offset. The bowl's frieze of obovate petals with a second whorl of petals filling the corners of the outer one is best paralleled by the two-whorled frieze of the Deve Hüyük bowl.[37]

A third metal vessel from the same destroyed grave as the bowl with the petal frieze is a simple cylindrical cup with two metal pellets and the stumps of a loop handle (pl. 74:P). A parallel for the shape is provided by a mug of different proportions and smaller size from Deve Hüyük.[38] The fourth of the metal vessels, the beaker from Grave 4.28, has a wide, flaring neck, ovoid body, and very slight ring base (pls. 4:J; 263:5). It belongs to a prominent family of pottery and metal vessels with a lineage extending back to Middle Assyrian and Kassite ceramics of the second millennium B.C.[39] In the Late Assyrian period examples occur in both Palace and standard wares; beakers from Assur are particularly close in shape and proportion to the beaker found at Chogha Mish (pl. 4:J).[40] The shape also appeared in metal; a silver example with button base and vegetal ornament in gold foil was found at Nimrud in Fort

30. For parallels to pl. 73:L, see Young 1965:58, fig. 3:3 (Ziwiye, Iron III); Miroschedji 1978:224, fig. 55:4 (more definitely carinated; Susa, Ville royale II, Levels 5–4, Achaemenid); and D. Stronach 1978:244, fig. 107:12 (Pasargadae, unstratified, probably Achaemenid). For later Parthian-Sasanian beveled rims, see Jan-i Shin, Khuzestan (Hansman 1978:157, fig. 19:4). For parallels to pl. 74:H, see D. Stronach 1978:246, fig. 108:3–4 (Pasargadae, post-Achaemenid not later than 280 B.C.); and Young 1969:123, fig. 144:10; Young and Levine 1974:129, fig. 46:13 (Godin II).

31. Cf. Godin II (Young 1969:121, fig. 43:2,5,7,12 [necks with moldings or ridges and, in one case, a loop handle]).

32. Cf. Haller 1954, pls. 6:r (pottery; profile almost identical to pl. 74:Q except squatter; also higher ring base; Grave 442); 13:a (frit; Grave r a). A similar shape in bronze was found in the Neo-Babylonian temple of Enunmah at Ur (Woolley 1962, pl. 32:1 [U 124A; on top of wall of Room 9]).

33. Deve Hüyük II (Moorey 1980:33, fig. 6:79 [group 13], 82 [group 11]; cf. pp. 7–8 for discussion of the dating of the inhumation burials of Deve Hüyük to ca. 480–350 B.C.).

34. For discussion of this class of vessel, see Luschey 1939; Hamilton 1966; Moorey 1974:147–51; idem 1980:32–36. The presence of a basal omphalos or umbo is so common as to be practically a defining feature of the phialai.

35. Moorey 1980:33, fig. 6:85, p. 32, for parallels.

36. Susa (de Morgan 1905:43, pl. 3); Tell el-Fara (South), Tomb 650 (Petrie 1930, pl. 44:3–5 = Avi-Yonah and Stern 1978, vol. 4:1080); both have basal rosettes in place of the omphaloi.

37. Examples with simple petal friezes are numerous: cf. Senjirli (von Luschan and Andrae 1943:118, pl. 56:b, e, i [around the omphalos]); Deve Hüyük II, group 9 (Moorey 1980:33, fig. 6:92); Nippur (McCown and Haines 1967, pl. 108:8–9); and Ur (Woolley 1962, pl. 32:9 [U.113, U.6666, U.14438]).

38. Deve Hüyük II, group 9 (Moorey 1980:39, 41, fig. 7:123 [with separately made round base]).

39. Assur, Crypt 9 (Haller 1954, pl. 2).

40. Assur, Crypt 30 (ibid., pl. 5:b); cf. also Nimrud (Oates 1959:133–34, pl. 37:60–61, 79).

Shalmaneser.[41] Although the Achaemenid period has bequeathed to us a surprisingly large number of vessels of precious metals and also specialized stone vessels, the corpus of more modest metal and stone forms is rather limited.[42] This is a handicap when considering whether the existence of Late Assyrian parallels should be taken as indication of a pre-Achaemenid date for the Chogha Mish examples (pl. 4:J, M). The more likely conclusion seems to be that they are comparable to other cases in which Achaemenid potters and metal workers continued to produce traditional types.[43]

SMALL OBJECTS

Various small objects such as the weapons and jewelry from Graves 4.28 and 5.08, the animal figurine and arrowhead from L22:401, and the scaraboid and arrowheads from P17:401 and 402, have already been mentioned in connection with their findspots. A small corpus of weapons is provided by Grave 4.28 and by scattered individual finds. The largest piece is a 36.5 cm long iron dagger blade with a mid-rib and tang (pls. 4:F; 263:7). It is paralleled by a somewhat longer and less pointed blade from Persepolis.[44] Tanged iron arrowheads[45] are represented by a cluster of ten corroded examples of an oval shape paralleled by an example from Persepolis (pl. 263:12 c–e),[46] and two examples of more triangular shapes (pls. 4:L and 263:12 b; 76:H).

The bronze arrowheads with a socket and three flanges (pls. 76:D–G; 263:12 a) belong to a well-known class with a long history, the trilobate arrowhead often called Scythian; the Chogha Mish examples, which are rather badly corroded, appear to represent a typical Achaemenid variety in which the socket is somewhat longer than the lobes.[47] In addition to the examples from Grave 4.28 (pl. 263:12 a), the surface of P23:501 (pl.

76:D), L22:401 (pl. 76:E), and P17:402 (pl. 76:F), there were three others scattered in the East Area. An arrowhead from the surface of the High Mound represents a type without a projecting socket (pl. 76:C).

Of considerable interest was a fragment of a fibula, which is much corroded and whose pin is missing (pl. 76:B). The arm seems to be plain; the catch is preserved. The bow is semicircular and resembles Stronach's Type I (D. Stronach 1959:185–86). Unlike the specimens of this type, the apex of the Chogha Mish fibula is flattened and might have been decorated. Such fibulae are dated to the eighth–sixth century B.C.

There remain for discussion several objects of more complex character than those just reviewed. The first is a cuneiform tablet found in R18:304 close to the modern surface in an area with a scatter of late pottery (pl. 5:K).[48] Richard T. Hallock examined the photographs of the tablet and on that basis wrote the following comments:

> The tablet of unbaked clay is inscribed with Elamite cuneiform writing of the Achaemenid period. There are eleven lines of text, eight with one or more legible signs, three with only traces. Unfortunately, not a single word can be clearly identified, and there seems to be no good clue to the nature of the text.

Although it is disappointing that the damaged tablet cannot be read, the object is still of importance both as an indication of date and of the existence of literacy in the late settlement of Chogha Mish. Though we cannot specifically prove that the tablet was written at the site, its appearance there indicates the presence of some literate individual or individuals.

A small sealing was found somewhat to the northeast of the tablet's findspot, but not far away. The clay is dense gray with no visible vegetal inclusions; one mica speck. The upper and side surfaces were smoothed; the lower surface is very uneven with string or knot impression entering from one side. An extremely shallow and incomplete impression covers part of the upper surface.

The third object remaining to be discussed is unfortunately from a secondary context. It is a cylinder seal (pl. 5:B) found either in the vicinity of the High Mound or on the dump of P8:302. The seal is so worn that not all the details of the engraving of a kneeling hunter aiming his arrow at a rampant goat are clear. Although the theme of a kneeling archer and his prey was used from the Middle Assyrian to the Achaemenid period, the possible range of the seal is from Late Elamite to Achaemenid. The following diagnostic features are important. The empty field against which one or two figures are silhouetted, although sometimes found on Neo-

---

41. Ibid., pl. 34:b = Mallowan 1966, vol. II, p. 428, fig. 356.

42. For a summary of what is known of Achaemenid metal vessels and a reference to the rarity of ordinary examples from Iran itself, see Moorey 1980:28–30.

43. For example, the unbroken line of metal phialai or the Achaemenid metal and pottery vessels with wide flaring necks derived from comparable Late Assyrian Palace Ware shapes. Cf. Hamilton 1966:3–6, figs. 3–6; D. Stronach 1978:242, figs. 106:1–4, 6–8; 243, notes 1–3.

44. Schmidt 1957, pl. 75:6 (42.4 cm long).

45. For a discussion of the discrimination of arrow and javelin heads, see Moorey 1980:60, where specimens over 10 gr in weight are considered as javelin heads.

46. Schmidt 1957, pl. 76:4 (length = 7.6 cm).

47. Cleuziou 1977, Type F 17 with socket extending beyond the lobes; cf. ibid., p. 189, fig. 1:194–96 for a thorough discussion of "Scythian" arrowheads, including the characteristics and distribution of the Achaemenid types. At Persepolis F 17 was the commonest type (Schmidt 1957:99, table IX, #8, pl. 76:8); cf. also, among many others, examples from Pasargadae (D. Stronach 1978:180–81, 218, fig. 94:2–13) and Deve Hüyük (Moorey 1980:63–66, fig. 10:202, 206).

48. Photographs courtesy of the Iranian Center for Archaeological Research, Tehran.

Babylonian seals, is common in Achaemenid glyptic (Frankfort 1939a, pl. 37:a, e, g, i–j, m). The rendering of the archer for the most part by unretouched gouges and without details of clothing is in contrast with his modeled and tuniced compeer on seal impressions from the Treasury at Persepolis (Schmidt 1957, pl. 10, Seal No. 33); however, a kneeling archer executed in a simple style does occur on a Walters Art Gallery seal that is identified as Achaemenid by a cross of heads with typical tiaras (Gordon 1939, pl. 13:108 [no provenience]). Of three other seals with similar scenes of kneeling archers, two from Susa are dated by Amiet to Late Elamite and one in the Walters Art Gallery with a particularly animated hunter might well be Achaemenid.[49] The alignment of the hind legs, body, and forelegs of the goat depicted on a cylinder seal (pl. 5:C) along the same markedly diagonal lines give it a vivacity that is paralleled on a seal in the Morgan Collection, where the animal hunted by an equestrian is rendered in the same way.[50] On the seal only one hind leg remains visible; the other was probably originally indicated by a staggered outline as on the Morgan seal and one of those from Susa (Amiet 1972, pl. 188:218b). The characteristics and comparisons just indicated suggest that another seal (pl. 5:B) belongs in the later, Achaemenid, end of its possible range.

CONCLUSION

A final statement on the date of the Iron Age settlement at Chogha Mish cannot be made until evidence found after the fifth season is analyzed. At this juncture, however, the combined evidence of the pottery, the cuneiform tablet, the objects such as the trilobed arrowheads, the frit scaraboid, and the cylinder seal supports the Achaemenid date assigned to the settlement. On the other hand, some typical Iron III ceramic features which either do not continue later, such as the open trough spouts and ridged bowl sherds of gray ware, or are hardly known in the Achaemenid period, such as the horizontal-handled bowl fragments, are prominent among our finds. Although these fragments cannot, unfortunately, be stratigraphically distinguished from the bulk of the Iron Age pottery,[51] their presence suggests that the settlement might have begun earlier than the Achaemenid dynasty. Thus our materials are pertinent to the problem of the transition from the Late Elamite

ceramic tradition[52] linked with the Iron III tradition of the highlands and presumably introduced by Iranians.[53] The settlement at Chogha Mish might not in reality have been the small, transitory village, as visualized at first from its scanty remains, but was a more long-lived settlement occupied from the later part of Iron III into the Achaemenid period.[54] By that time its inhabitants, or some of them at least, had achieved the rather prosperous scale of living illustrated by the finds from Grave 4.28 and 5.08 and were sophisticated enough to utilize written records.

THE OLD ELAMITE PERIOD

Chogha Mish had lain deserted for many centuries prior to the Achaemenid settlement. The preceding phase of occupation, the Old Elamite (Sukkalmaḫ), was confined to the High Mound. There, in the first season a portion of an Old Elamite wall built of well-made, large square bricks was found at the surface of the eastern spur at the top of Trench III in Square R8 (pl. 260). In the third season much more massive Old Elamite remains were revealed. Starting at the base of the southwestern slope of the High Mound in Square M9 masses of brickwork were located immediately below the surface. The work of articulating individual bricks was carried on to the northeast up the slope as Locus N9:301 (pl. 10:A–C). Another team of workmen was placed to the north, west of the central gully of the High Mound, in Squares N–O 7–8, and soon discovered a very substantial mudbrick wall of the Old Elamite period (pls. 6:A; 7:A left background). In the fourth season exploration of the Old Elamite remains was continued by clearing brickwork in Squares P–Q:9–11.

The Old Elamite remains known so far are as follows. The very massive brickwork of a long wall ranging between 8 and 11 m in width and fairly straight except for a jog in Squares N7 and O8 was cleared on top of the western ridge of the High Mound in Squares N6–8 and O8. The outline of this wall could be traced for about 60 m from north to south. Its preserved height diminished with the slope of the mound until, finally, its lower courses of brickwork merged with the upper

---

49. Seal No. 12 (no provenience). The same theme is rendered in a rather different fashion on two seals in the Morgan Collection (Porada 1948, pl. 122:813–14 [dated as Proto-Achaemenid]).

50. Porada 1948, pl. 122:812 (dated as Proto-Achaemenid but in stylistic feeling belonging with the equestrians on Achaemenid glyptic [Frankfort 1939, pl. 37:i] rather than with normal Neo-Babylonian figures).

51. The trough spouts, for example, are mostly surface finds.

52. See, for example, Susa, Ville royale II, Levels 9 and 8 (Miroschedji 1978:222, fig. 53:226–27).

53. In this connection discussions with D. Stronach, who shortly after the first finds of late pottery at Chogha Mish noted their possible relevance to this problem, and with T. Cuyler Young, Jr., have been very helpful. For the date of Level 1 of the Village perse-achéménide at Susa, see D. Stronach 1974; Young 1965.

54. The parallels for the Circular Structure cited above are additional evidence to support an Achaemenid date for the village at Chogha Mish. In addition, the presence of such a structure, the identification of which as a granary is almost certain, implies a community of some size and importance.

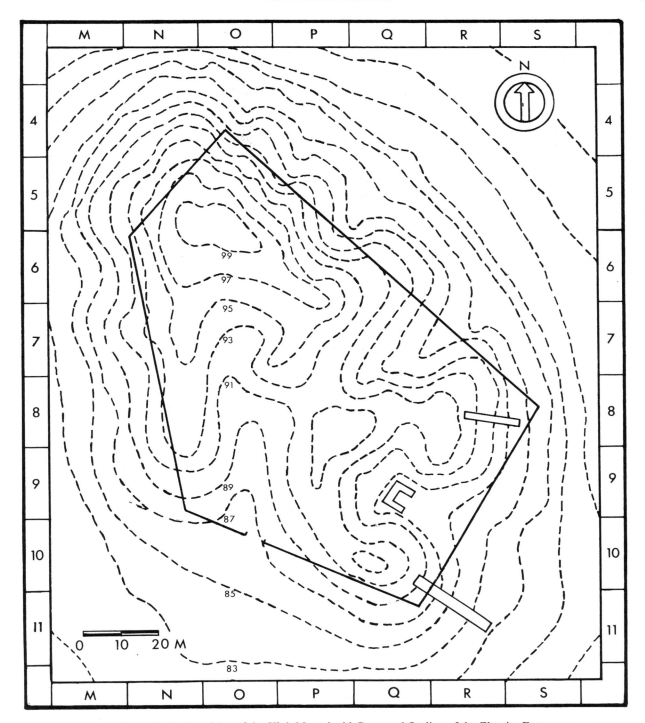

Figure 1. Contour Map of the High Mound with Proposed Outline of the Elamite Fort

courses of the brickwork of the Protoliterate period preserved in N9 (pl. 7:A top right corner). Thin cross walls, roughly at right angles to the massive Old Elamite wall, appeared on its eastern inner side at a somewhat lower level. Since it is not clear whether they were inner walls of the same building or belonged to an earlier one, they are not shown on the plan. It appears that there were no intermediate layers of debris or construction between the Old Elamite walls and the Protoliterate brickwork. Rather, Protoliterate remains seem to have stood exposed to the elements for so long that they had been denuded down to their foundations when Old Elamite

walls were founded directly above them. Only by carefully clearing individual bricks and observing the change in the size of bricks and the lines of orientation of the walls was it possible to distinguish the line of separation between the brickwork of the two periods many centuries apart in date.

The great partially preserved wall, which must have been the western wall of an Old Elamite fort, shows evidence of not having been constructed in a single phase. Along its western face there are several remains of towers and buttresses, some bonded to the brickwork of the original wall, and some built against its mud plaster on the outside. In a few places traces of fire have blackened and hardened this plaster and made it relatively easy to follow; in others the rain has completely washed the surface away. Floors remain only for short distances in the immediate vicinity of the outer face of the wall before they are destroyed by the slope of the mound. Since all of the walls are considerably higher than the present level of the plain, presumably this was also true in antiquity, and there must have been some access in the form of stairs or ramps from the walls to the exterior floors. Possibly these floors belong to a space between the preserved wall and a now completely vanished outer wall farther out nearer the perimeter of the mound. The level of the floors inside, that is to the east of the preserved wall, is somewhat higher than on the west, but again, most of these floors and the walls above them have disappeared since the slope to the inner gully is rather abrupt.

The brickwork in Square R8 at the top of Trench III must also have been part of the circuit walls of the fort. In addition, on the southeastern slope of the High Mound in Squares Q10–11, a solid mass of still-bonded bricks that had fallen as one piece, about 1.5 m wide and over 3 m in length, can be taken as part of the fort and testifies to the massive character of the walls on that side also. Individual bricks standing on their edges at various angles could be distinguished only by the very thin lines of mortar between them and their slight differences in color. This large mass might have tumbled down when the fort was still standing in ruins with parts of it probably being undermined by rain gullies.

East of the gully in Squares O–P8 (Trench XXVI) a wall some 5.5 m thick and in places still more than 3 m high runs in a southwest-northeast direction (P8:301; pl. 7:A–C). We were unable to trace this wall to its foundations because the rainwater that accumulated in the foundation trench did not dry out before the end of the season. This wall is completely denuded at its southwestern end, and on the northeastern side it is cut by a breach now filled with rubbish and ashes. This breach might indicate a violent end for the Old Elamite fortress of which the P8:301 wall was presumably a part.

Although only in the west did we uncover a long stretch of wall, it looked as if the High Mound had been encircled by a massive circuit enclosing various interior rooms and forming a fort. Indeed, the present configuration of the High Mound (see contour lines on pl. 260) might reflect the general outlines of such a fort. Because of the tremendous erosion that has occurred in the center and on the slopes of the High Mound (Squares O–P7, 9) it will never be possible to recover the complete plan, but the configuration of the High Mound might reflect the general character of the edifice that was the last to exist there. Consequently, in addition to the general map of the High Mound (pl. 260), the area in question is illustrated on a large scale with the contour lines; it includes the summit of the site at the corner of Squares N–O:506 (fig. 1). The thick west wall, parts of which are preserved in Squares N6–9 at elevations 95.00–94.00 m, is roughly paralleled by the lower contour lines 92.00–87.00 m. These lower contours were followed around the whole area beginning from the point in Square M5 at the northern end of the thick wall. For reasons that are explained below, in drawing the abstracted lines, not only the minor irregularities in these contours but also their major incurvatures in gullies on the northeast and east sides, in Squares Q–R7 and Q–R9–10, were ignored. From Square M5 these contours continue in a fairly straight line for about 4 m before turning to the southeast (in O4) and reaching Square R8 after about 120 m to include the massive brickwork at the top of the promontory in which Trench III was cut. Here a second turn, to the southwest, is noticeable. On this side the southeastern corner of the polygon lies in Q11; from there a turn of more than 90 and 85 m leads to the partially preserved western wall at its southern end in N9; the entire southern part of the High Mound is surrounded, both the southeastern lobe with its own high point in Square Q10 and the southwestern lobe. Finally, along the southern line in O9 these contour lines turn to the north, marking the gully that runs from the south of the mound to its center. The central part of the High Mound in Squares O–P7 is marked by higher contour lines in an approximately 20 m square area. This might have been the central court and it is from its southern end that the gully runs southward, descending from an elevation of about 91.00 m to about 86.00 m.

If the assumption that the present configuration of the mound corresponds to the mostly vanished Old Elamite fort that once stood there is correct, the above discussion leads to the conclusion that the structure was not a regular square or rectangle but rather a polygon, apparently an irregular one with walls of unequal length. The maximum length of the fort from northwest to southeast would have been approximately 140 m with its width from southwest to northeast varying up to a maximum of about 95 m.

The situation of the gully in Squares O8–10 is probably a key to the location of the gateway to the fort. Ghirshman's (1966:57–58) postulate—that the channels eroded in the ruins of the Chogha Zanbil ziggurat reflect the position of the stairways and gates—can be applied here also. In brief, Ghirshman proposed that when walls or brick massifs are pierced by openings that allow rainwater to drain from an enclosed area, such openings tend to be gradually enlarged until gullies of considerable dimensions are eroded.[55] Eventually such gullies

---

55. The undulation of some of the contour lines, especially on the northern side of the mound, is due to minor channels dug out by the runoff of the rainwater at fairly regular intervals. The two larger gullies between the eastern and southeastern

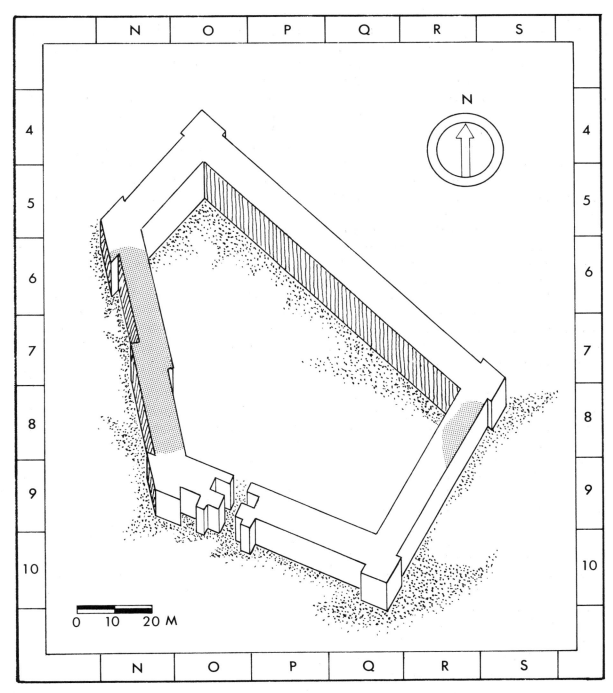

N O P Q R S

N

4 4

5 5

6 6

7 7

8 8

9 9

10 10

0 10 20 M

N O P Q R S

Figure 2. Proposed Isometric Plan of Elamite Fort

might destroy large parts of a building. At Chogha Mish in even one field season small regular channels cut to divert rainwater from areas under excavation widen and deepen and tend to become noticeable features of the topography of the site. Accordingly, we assume that the gully of Squares O8–10 arose in such a fashion and can thus be taken as an indication that a gate or breach in

the southern wall of the Old Elamite fort existed at this point.

In accordance with the above considerations a tentative isometric reconstruction of the fortress walls is shown in figure 2. The preserved parts of the western wall as well as the segment of the wall in Trench III are indicated by dark shading. Corner towers are assumed to have existed but no buttresses are shown. The hypothetical gate in the southern wall follows the type known from Chogha Zanbil.

On the southwestern and southeastern slopes of the High Mound brickwork masses at a lower level than the partly preserved western wall extended for considerable

lobes of the mound in Squares R–S7 are smaller than the major gully just discussed and were probably created after the fort was abandoned. The hollow in Square Q9 with a gully to its southeast is rather square and might reflect a feature of the original building.

areas and depths. However, no wall faces could be distinguished in them. It is not yet certain whether such brickwork represents an Old Elamite structure of a somewhat earlier phase than the western wall or is merely the remains of an artificial terrace that filled in the irregularities of the tepe in preparation for erecting the fortress. However, the first alternative that the various remains are of somewhat different dates, seems to be more likely. On the southwest in Squares N–O9 the alignment of this lower brickwork is not the same as that of the preserved upper part of the western wall. The fact that floors, burnt areas, and burials were found inside or below the lower brickwork masses suggests the existence of several construction phases. On the southeastern slope floors paved with sherds were found just below the brickwork masses in P10:401 (pls. 6:B; 7:D) and to the north of P19:402. Two burials, Graves 4.32 and 4.33, appeared in P10:402 and P10:403 South. In the same area the stumps of walls demarcating P10:402 and P10:403 South and East establish the existence of rooms below the brickwork massif in this area (pl. 260). Thus, it seems apparent that the lower Old Elamite brickwork must have already involved at least two building phases. In turn, the addition to the higher western wall of towers and buttresses, sometimes against a burnt outer surface, indicates that the building to which it belonged must have been of considerable duration. The function and relative dating of the fragmentary thick wall inside the fortress Squares O–P8 are still not clear. Nonetheless, the cumulative evidence available shows that the Old Elamite occupation of the High Mound must have lasted for a considerable time.

Although the general identification of the structural remains on the High Mound as Old Elamite is obvious, in the absence of inscriptions the pottery must serve as the primary evidence for more precise dating. A considerable sample of pottery, chiefly in the form of sherds, was found associated with both the higher walls and with the lower brickwork massifs. The coherence of the pottery indicated that however many building phases might be represented on the High Mound, the same ceramic tradition appears in all of them.

THE POTTERY

The standard ware is basically buff, with the shades varying from orange or yellow on one side to brown or gray on the other. The tempering frequently consists of grit and straw used together, with the larger vessels as the vats containing proportionally more straw. Smaller pieces might have only grit tempering. Occasionally a slip of a shade differing somewhat from that of the paste occurs; it is difficult to determine whether such examples are true slips added to the surface or wet-smoothing with the variation in color resulting from firing. On the whole, however, finely smoothed surfaces are not characteristic. A relatively coarse surface combined with marked wheel striations on the base and lower body is standard on smaller forms (pls. 77:A–B, K–P). Ridges in one or more groups serve to emphasize the carinations (pl. 78:D–E) or the upper bodies of various types of jars (pl. 78:L, N–O) and, in at least one case, to mark different segments of a vat (pl. 79:J). Scrabbled lines and imprints also occur on vats (pl. 79:M, O–R, U) and thick body sherds (pl. 4:G–I).

The repertory of forms is limited. Much of the material falls into three main categories that, despite the difficulties of comparing sherds and complete forms, have excellent parallels in the pottery of the Ville royale at Susa (Gasche 1973). Open vessels of medium size are represented by two practically identical complete bowls found together (pl. 77:A; III–567). Such semi-carinated bowls with almost vertical upper walls and disc base were standard forms, as indicated by a variant found in a later season (pl. 77:B) and by examples from Susa, where they are assigned by Gasche to Group 3 of his pottery forms.[56] Among the sherds belonging to larger size bowls, one (pl. 77:E) has a close parallel at Susa,[57] while the other (pl. 77:C) might be related to bowls of Gasche's Group 4.[58]

The dominant closed form is the shouldered jar, characterized by a high neck either vertical or flaring, a sharp shoulder carination, a ring base or foot, and wheel striations on the lower body (pls. 77:K–P; 78:A–J). At Susa such vessels constitute Gasche's Group 21. The only complete example found at Chogha Mish in the first five seasons is a small jar (I-38; pl. 77:J) washed out on the surface of the High Mound; some small shouldered jars from Susa are in general similar to it, but differ in details of body shape and proportion of the neck.[59] Susa provides parallels for a number of the individual fragments from Chogha Mish, including the shoulders with ribbing just below the carination (pl. 78:D–E).[60]

---

56. For pl. 77:A, see Gasche 1973, pl. 3:15 (group 3, variant a; Ville royale, Level B V); for pl. 77:B, see ibid., pl. 3:10 (group 3, variant a; Ville royal, Level A XV).

57. See ibid., pl. 10:3 (Ville royale, Level A XV).

58. See ibid., pl. 4:17 (group 4; Ville royale, Level A XV).

59. For shouldered jars from Susa, see ibid., p. 40–41, plan 8, group 21; Carter 1979:119. For examples from the Ville royale I Sounding, Level 3, see Carter 1980, figs. 45:7–9; 46:1–8; 47:1–3. For a parallel to pl. 75:J, see Gasche 1973, pl. 24:23 (group 21 variant b; squatter, wider neck, and stepped shoulder; Ville royale, Level A XV). For parallels to pl. 77:L, see ibid., pls. 17, 19, 24 (group 21, variant b; Level A XV).

60. For a parallel to pl. 77:M, see Gasche 1973, pl. 24:11 (group 21, variant a; Ville royale, Level A XV). For a parallel to pl. 77:N, see ibid., pl. 25:20 (group 21, variant a; Level B VI). For parallels to pl. 77:O, see ibid., pls. 25:11 (group 21, variant a; Level B V); 25:39 (group 21, variant b; Level B V); 25:18–19 (group 21, variant a; Level B VI).

Jars without shoulders, subsumed by Gasche under his Group 25, are represented among the Chogha Mish sherds, but much less commonly than the shouldered jars. The club rim of a plain jar (pl. 78:M) has a general parallel at Susa, and the shoulders with ridges (pl. 78:L, N–O) have more specific parallels.[61]

The two more prominent groups of Old Elamite pottery at Chogha Mish are the shouldered jars already discussed and the large vats and storage jars characterized by heavy rims and, in many cases, prominent ledges near the rims. The shape of the rim varies according to the stance of the upper body; relatively vertical walls have ledge or club rims with usually a pronounced overhang (pl. 79:A–F, H–I, M, O, R), while incurving walls have normally recumbent rims (pl. 79:G, J, P, T). The former represent the types of rims typical for Gasche's Groups 33–35 at Susa, but in the absence of bodies it is difficult to attribute the Chogha Mish rim and ledge fragments to his individual groups.[62] The recumbent rims are at Susa characteristic for Groups 36 and 37. The most complete of the large Old Elamite vessels from Chogha Mish, which was reconstructed from the sherd paving of P10:401 (pl. 79:J), is paralleled at Susa by a jar with a fairly similar body shape and ridges below the rim; Susa also provides parallels for the next largest fragment (pl. 79:G), and for a sherd with ridges and notches immediately below the recumbent rim (pl. 79:T).[63] The complete examples from Susa indicate that this type of vessel had a ring base.

At Susa the analogies for the Chogha Mish Old Elamite pottery appear in two parts of the Ville royale

in strata that can be assigned to the early centuries of the second millennium B.C. with the aid of inscriptions.[64] The earliest of these levels, B VI, dated by a seal with the name of the wife of the Shimashkian king Tan-Ruhuratir (1970 B.C.), provides parallels for three shapes (pl. 79 M–N, P). The next level, B V, which yielded tablets with the name of Addahushu, who is connected through Ebarat and Shilhaha to the period of Sumu-abum of Babylon (1894–1881 B.C.; Carter and Stolper 1984:16–30), provides parallels for three other forms (pl. 79:A–B, J). However, the majority of the Chogha Mish pieces (pls. 78:B, J–L; 79:A–H, P) are paralleled by vessels from A XV, a level without inscriptions, but fitting in between B V and A XIV, the latter with letters of Kutur-Nahhunte I, a contemporary of Samsu-iluna of Babylon. Level A XIV provides only a few parallels (pls. 77:E; 79:C, P). Thus, the Old Elamite remains at Chogha Mish can be assigned to the first two or three centuries of the second millennium B.C., that is to the earlier part of the Sukkalmaḫ period in general contemporary with the First Dynasty of Babylon in Mesopotamia. An attempt to subdivide the material into successive subphases would be premature in view of both the limited number and fragmentary condition of the Old Elamite pottery recovered during the first five seasons and the very coherent character of the Old Elamite ceramic tradition at Susa during the Shimashki and early Sukkalmaḫ periods.

SMALL OBJECTS

Several fragments of the typical mold-made terracotta female figurines were found on the High Mound, unfortunately either on the surface or in mixed contexts (pl. 5:I, M). Nonetheless, they can be considered to be Old Elamite with considerable confidence. Plaques of the Sukkalmaḫ period from Susa provide analogies for the upper part of a figure with clasped hands, necklace, and face surrounded by hair (pl. 5:I), for the torso with hands clasping the breasts (pl. 5:L), and for the fragment of a lower body (pl. 5:M; Amiet 1966:300–01, figs. 224–25). The most elaborate of the Chogha Mish figures (pl. 5:I) has features such as large eyes with wide borders and a necklace and a headdress rendered in detail that have parallels on a more elegantly modeled plaque from Susa (ibid., p. 302, fig. 226).

For a parallel to pl. 77:P, see ibid., pl. 25:1 (group 21, variant a; Level B V). For a parallel to pl. 77:P, see ibid., pl. 25:23 (group 21, variant a; Level B VI). For a parallel to pl. 78:B–C, I, see ibid., pl. 24:9–10 (group 21, variant a; Level A XV). For a parallel to pl. 78:G, see ibid., pl. 24:25 (group 21, variant b; Level A XV). For a parallel to pl. 78:J, see ibid., pl. 24:11 (group, variant a; Level A XV). For a parallel to pl. 78:D–E, see ibid., pl. 24:14 (group 21, variant a; Level A XV).

61. For parallels to pl. 78:M, see ibid., pl. 28:20–21, group 25; 17, group 25 (Ville royale, Level B VI). For parallels to pl. 78:L, N, see ibid., pls. 28:10, 11, group 25, one cluster of ridges only; 24:18, two clusters (Level A XV).

62. See ibid., pls. 42–48, plan 9. For a parallel to pl. 79:A–F, H., see ibid., pl. 45:7 (group 36, variant a; Ville royale, Level A XV). For parallels to pl. 79:C, see ibid., pls. 43:2 (group 34; Level A XIV); 43:6–7 (group 34; Level A XV).

63. For a parallel to pl. 79:J, see ibid., pl. 47:3 (group 36, variant c; Ville royale, Level B V). A second block of ridges lower on the body, as on plate 79:J, occurs at Susa on several jars that otherwise are not as similar as the first parallel cited and are from A XIV, higher than A XV; cf. Level A XIV (ibid., pls. 47:1 [group 36, variant c]; 48:2–3 [group 36]). For a parallel to pl. 79:G, see ibid., pl. 45:5 (group 36, variant a; Level A XV). For parallels to pl. 79:T, see ibid., pls. 46:4 (group 36, variant b; Level A XV); 47:1 (group 36, variant c; Level A XIV).

64. For stratification and chronology, see Ghirshman 1970:224–25; Gasche 1973:9–15; Carter 1979, *passim*, and p. 115, table I. The divergences between the chronologies of Carter and Gasche involve only the later part of the Sukkalmaḫ period (Ville royale A XIII and higher levels). For the earlier periods pertinent for Chogha Mish the corresponding Carter and Gasche terminologies are as follows:

Shimashki phase =	*Elamite ancien IIb* =	Ville royale B VII–VI + I, Levels 6–3
(ca. 2100–1900 B.C.)	(ca. 2040–1900 B.C.)	
Sukkalmaḫ phase =	*Elamite ancien III* =	Ville royale B V + A XV–XIII (Carter)
(ca. 1900–1600 B.C.)	(ca. 1920–1500 B.C.)	Ville royale B V + A XV–XII (Gasche)

Other than terra-cotta plaques and the cylinder seal discussed below, practically no small objects were recovered in primary Old Elamite contexts. Stone objects are represented by a small biconical mace-head (pl. 29:M), which might be contemporary with the massive Old Elamite fortification wall in P8:301 in the vicinity of which it was found, or might represent an earlier type out of context.

There remains to be discussed a worn stone cylinder seal found on the surface of the High Mound (pl. 5:C). On it a seated figure faces an adorant who approaches from the left; both wear long robes. The group is completed on the right by an unnaturalistic squat figure in a robe represented as three hatched tiers of, presumably, flounces. A bent arm extended to the left probably holds a small cup; the irregular line parallel with the forearm appears to be only an accidental blemish, not part of the original design. Beside the squat figure a plant rises from a broadened base to the top of the seal where it grows horizontally to the left. Five irregularly ovoid leaves turn downward on one side of the stem; there might have been a few more at its tip. Excrescences on the right side of the stem and between the heads of the seated and squat figures represent evidently secondary damage.

A close parallel for the Chogha Mish seal is provided by a Susa cylinder seal of bituminous stone belonging to the "Popular" Elamite class typical for the period of the Sukkalmaḫ (Amiet 1972, pl. 169:1899, cf. pp. 239–40, 248). The excellent preservation of the Susa seal clarifies various unclear details on the Chogha Mish seal, for example, that the left arm of both long-robed figures is not seen but only suggested by horizontal ridges and that both the seated and the squat figure hold a cup in their right hands. The only appreciable differences between the two examples are in a few details such as the Susa seal's table and duck between the worshipper and seated figure where the Chogha Mish seal has only an irregular vertical stroke. Both seals have a crescent at the upper edge between the two left-hand figures and plants rendered in the same way, although the Chogha Mish seal retains only traces of the ribbing of the leaves, which is very clear on the Susa example.

The essential outline of the third, squat, figure, unbroken on the right and indented on the left, is the same on both seals. Its inorganic character is particularly evident at Susa, where it has no feet and is set on a low platform or cushion. These details indicate that the irregular line at the lower left corner of the squat Chogha Mish figure should not be interpreted as a leg, but as a secondary gash. The rest of the surface below the figure is intact and plain. Since the squat figure, similar to the seated one, holds a cup, it might also be ranked as a deity approached by the adorant. Despite the fairly debased form of the squat figures on these two seals, they

are reminiscent of both legless, squatting goddesses on earlier cylinder seals from Shahdad[65] and Yahya,[66] and of the three figures on a chalcedony seal with a damaged inscription attributed to the Ebarat, the founder of the Sukkalmaḫ dynasty.[67] In the round the same type of rotund flounce-clad figure exemplified by composite statuettes attributed to Fars and Bactria and, in the absence of archaeological contexts, is only datable to an approximate range of late third to early second millennium B.C.[68] Related figures occur on a silver vase said to have been found in Bactria (Deshayes 1977:104–05, figs. 7–8). It is clear that such unrealistically rotund figures are characteristic for local traditions of art in eastern Iran and Afghanistan, which had been considerably influenced by the example of Mesopotamian art of the Early Dynastic period (Amiet 1974, 1977; Deshayes 1977:106). Elam must have been a major intermediary in the diffusion of Mesopotamian influence; thus, it is not surprising to find the rotund figures recurring on glyptic of the Sukkalmaḫ period. The leafy stem sheltering the squat figure depicted on the seal (pl. 5:C) and its Susa analog indicate that here she appears as a vegetation goddess, even though the plant attribute does not spring directly from her body as on earlier seals from Shahdad and Yahya. The goddess appears with her leafy shelter and a worshipper on a stamp seal from Malyan (Sumner 1974:172, fig. 12:1 [Kaftari phase]). The composition shown on the seal from Chogha Mish (pl. 5:C) was standard for the Sukkalmaḫ period. In addition to the Chogha Mish and Susa examples, it occurs on a seal in a private collection (Volk 1979, number 125 [Habib Anavian Collection]). The meaning of the motif seems clear—the adoration of a god and his consort, a vegetation goddess.

CONCLUSION

The cylinder seal corroborates the Sukkalmaḫ date already established for the Old Elamite structures at Chogha Mish by the pottery. The architectural remains themselves require much additional evidence and they might eventually contribute useful historical information. Already, even the facts that the Old Elamite occu-

65. Orthmann 1975, pl. 283:b; Amiet 1973:25, top two figures = Amiet 1974:105, figs. 9–10. For other decorated objects from Kerman province which indicate that the legless squatting woman was a standard motif, see Amiet 1974:102, fig. 6 (lapis lazuli disc); 104, fig. 8 (copper pin).

66. Orthmann 1975, pl. 283 b = Lamberg-Karlovsky 1971, pl. VI (Period IVB).

67. Lambert 1979:15–17, 38–44, pl. V 42 (Gulbenkian Museum of Oriental Art, University of Durham); Carter and Stolper 1984:24–32.

68. Ghirshman 1968; Orthmann 1975, pl. 281:b (Louvre A 22918, former Foroughi Collection); Amiet 1977:103–05, 107, fig. 13; pls. 3–4.

pation was limited to the High Mound and that the remains discovered so far are characteristic of a fortress rather than a normal town have historical implications.

The extent to which the plan suggested in figure 2 actually corresponds to the original structure is less important than the circumstance that a fort approximating this character existed in this part of the country. The fort's presence is thus of considerable historical interest as an indication that conditions in the region during the early part of the second millennium B.C. required such structures. Forts are often established to guard trade routes between distant points when the countryside is not safe for traders and travelers. Chogha Mish lies at a strategic point on the route between southern Elam and the nearest mountain passes to the north. The choice of the place for the fort is not surprising since in the Old Elamite period the High Mound must have been the highest tepe in the region, covering not only the accumulations of the prehistoric periods but also the possibly substantial structures of the Protoliterate city. Thus, it was suitable not only for fortification but also for the transmission of signals. Even now on clear days the top of the Chogha Zanbil ziggurat is clearly visible from the summit of the High Mound, which is considerably lower than the roof of the fortress would have been. Although the ziggurat of Chogha Zanbil postdates the fortress, its visibility from Chogha Mish today indicates that light signals could easily have been transmitted to some points on the hills near Chogha Zanbil and relayed from there to points farther south and east.

CHAPTER 3

THE PROTOLITERATE TOWN

THE HIGH MOUND

(Pls. 260–61)

The first architectural feature of the Protoliterate period found by the expedition at Chogha Mish was a portion of a wall near the summit of the southeastern spur of the High Mound in Square Q10 at ca. 90.00 m elevation (pl. 46:A). It was located at the beginning of the first season when beveled-rim bowls were exposed *in situ* in the eroding slope. At this spot a number of such bowls, some complete, and other examples of the coarser Protoliterate fabrics were imbedded in a soft ashy deposit upon which the wall was founded. Some of the beveled-rim bowls were found immediately adjacent to the wall in a fashion that would have been impossible if it had been built at a later time; thus its dating to the Protoliterate period is certain. Since only a short length of this wall was preserved, it is not known to what kind of installation it belonged. The large Trench II was placed at the bar of this wall and carried down the slope of the southeastern spur as far as Square S11, and reached virgin soil in a small area.

In the third season remains of Protoliterate architecture of rather imposing proportions were found on the southwestern slope of the High Mound in Squares M–N9 by articulating individual bricks in an area of about 30 m down the slope from the preserved Old Elamite brickwork (N9:301, pl. 10:A). A chamber, about 2.4 × 4.6 m with walls apparently over 3 m thick, was cleared (N9:302; pl. 10:B). No trace of a doorway was found in any of the walls, which are denuded with the slope being preserved to a height of only a few centimeters on the western side and just over 1.0 m on the east (pl. 10:A–B). We assume that these walls are the lower courses of foundations below the floor of a building whose actual walls above floor level have completely disappeared. A very slight difference in color between the inside of this chamber and its walls was observed on the surface even before digging had revealed its presence. However, if it was part of the foundation complex, then the quantity and variety of pottery types that it contained are astonishing. In fact, several new types of vessels not found elsewhere on the site occurred, some of them in "duplicate." The continuation of the Protoliterate brickwork to the south (N9:304) and the north (N9:303) of N9:302 is not clear, because there seem to

have been some changes and additions that complicated the original plan.

On the southern side of the High Mound, two round cesspits (O9:301 and 302) built of small baked bricks, are located close to each other (pl. 10:C–D). It is of interest to note that the size of the bricks of which these cesspits were built is closer to that of unbaked bricks than to that of the ordinary baked bricks. A stone cut to imitate one of the smaller bricks was found nearby. Baked bricks of normal large size were used in paving one of the cesspits. Part of a terra-cotta drain now almost at the modern surface comes from the northern slope but is destroyed before reaching the cesspits.

The cesspits were filled primarily with beveled-rim bowls. A few other pottery types were also represented, as well as one almost complete stone bowl (pl. 29:AA). All the pottery from these pits was heavily coated with a characteristic green encrustation quite different from the lime coating of sherds long exposed to moisture near the surface. The same type of encrustation occurs on pottery from cesspits of various other periods.

Two small test pits sunk into the deeply eroded surface of the High Mound (O7:301 and 302) area provide evidence of the existence of Protoliterate materials there. Below mixed levels with later sherds, many of them lime coated, Protoliterate sherds and pottery mosaic cones are predominant in the debris between 2.80 m and 5.00 m below surface at ca. 93.00 (i.e., 90.20–88.00). An interesting feature that distinguishes the finds from these test pits is the relatively high proportion of mosaic cones to potsherds. The implication is obvious, but considering the fact that there was a very long gap between the occupation of the site in the Protoliterate period and the Old Elamite building activities, it is not at all certain that the edifice to which these cones were applied is still preserved to any extent.

Somewhat higher than the two test pits in Square O7 is an area at the head of a narrow trench in Squares O–P7 (P7:301), which provided an example of very neat stratification. The excellent deposit of Parthian pottery in P7:301 was underlaid by a barren layer about 1 m thick. Below that on a floor at el. 91.74 was a dense deposit of Protoliterate pottery with a wide variety of typical forms. This deposit and the hard floor on which it rested petered out in the central eroded hollow of the High Mound. It is clear that the Protoliterate occupation was on several different levels, that of P7:30 being some 6 m higher than N9:302 outside the mass of brick-work at the southwestern lobe of the High Mound.

THE TERRACE

Wherever there were excavations on the terrace, with the exception of certain greatly eroded areas on the eastern slope, traces of Protoliterate remains appeared. Much of the information comes from the large areas of stratified houses on the northeastern and northwestern sides of the terrace. Features common to the Proto-literate remains on the various parts of the terrace are discussed first.

For the most part Protoliterate sherds and other re-mains lie just below the surface. Since the entire terrace was being cultivated, even after the beginning of exca-vations, complete vessels or even large sherds had been fragmented by the plows. Intact vessels began to appear about 0.30–0.40 m below the surface. Where traces of later occupation occurred, they were clearly dug down into Protoliterate levels.

Scattered densely over the main excavated Proto-literate areas, especially the East Area, are the abun-dant "refuse" pits (pls. 11:B, D; 264) that contribute greatly to the difficulty of disengaging complete or even coherent architectural plans at Chogha Mish. These "refuse" pits are similar to pits in modern villages, which were dug originally to supply the clay for the mudbricks of the houses and are usually left open in courtyards to receive household refuse until they are filled. However, the ancient pits at Chogha Mish are on the whole smaller than what we consider to be their modern counterparts. They are not confined to court-yards; in fact, the very existence of courtyards in the an-cient houses is still problematical. Usually the occu-pation level from which these pits were dug is not pre-served, having been above the present surface of the site. In depth they often extend more than 2 m below the modern surface, which means that they were originally considerably deeper. They are of irregular shape and vary from about 2 to more than 4 m in width. The an-cient pits also cut through walls, and sometimes new secondary pits of smaller size were dug into the existing ones before they had been filled (e.g., R18:310). The secondary pits might be as little as 0.70 cm in diameter. Occasionally the pits were sealed by ancient pavements or walls (see West Area).

The fill of the pits was usually darker in color and less compact than the soil around them. They often con-tained a large proportion of ashes and some charcoal and were the richest source for pottery. Frequently it ap-peared that their fill consisted mostly of pottery (e.g., R17:208; pl. 11:B, D). Normally the vessels were bro-ken, but often sufficient fragments of a vessel were found in a pit to enable the vessel's nearly complete re-

construction. Pits also contained fragments of unbaked and baked bricks, jar stoppers, sealings, unbaked frag-ments of animal figurines, and kneaded lumps of puri-fied clay. The last mentioned could have served both in pot making and in the sealing of vessels.

On the whole the building remains of the Proto-literate period were in an exceptionally poor state of preservation. A combination of factors contributed to this situation. One is the destruction caused by the many pits sunk from the now-eroded upper levels. Others are the character and construction of the buildings them-selves. They were undoubtedly rather modest private dwellings, the walls of which were on the average only between 30 to 50 cm thick and of rather indifferent workmanship. The walls consisted for the most part of small-format mudbricks, the materials for which were not chosen with great care since the clay used for their making often contained ashes and potsherds. Still an-other factor is that the uppermost walls have been not only so denuded as to leave very little of their original height but that which does remain has been affected by rain, frost, plant roots, and recent plowing. Thus such walls are normally preserved only one or two bricks high and usually soon peter out with the slope of the ground.

Under the highest walls and the floors belonging to them there were walls and floors of at least two earlier building phases within the Protoliterate period. Not all the floors of a single occupation were at exactly the same levels. Although no stairs were found, the differ-ence in levels between floors in different rooms sug-gests the existence of some steps within the same phase of occupation. The walls of the earlier buildings were reduced, probably by intentional leveling, to about 0.60–0.70 m in height before the subsequent rebuilding took place. In most cases the builders seem to have been aware of the earlier ruins underground, because, as of-ten happened in Mesopotamia, stumps of earlier walls were frequently used as foundations. However, entirely new rebuildings with a disregard for earlier plans were also observed. Such walls were built directly on accu-mulated rubbish without special foundations.

The rooms in both areas were rather small and not very regular in shape. Apparently, as in somewhat later periods in Mesopotamia, the individual houses, as well as the rooms within each house, had to accommodate themselves both in size and shape to the available space. In contrast to Mesopotamia, at least in the Diyala region, no burials were found beneath the house floors. Mudbrick was the common building material in the Protoliterate period. The bricks vary somewhat in size, but tend to be rather small (10–12 cm wide × 20–22 cm long × 7–8 cm thick). No bricks of unusual shapes or sizes, such as the prismatic *Riemchen* found in the sec-ond half of the Protoliterate period in Mesopotamia, were observed. Baked bricks, though less numerous, were by no means scarce. They were freely used in connection with water, especially in drains. On the average, they were somewhat larger than the sun-dried bricks, often measuring 7.00–8.00 × 18.20 × 39.44 cm.

THE DRAINS

Both open-channel drains and drains covered with bricks laid crosswise are very numerous. Frequently when a drain was being rebuilt the older structure was left nearly intact, although it could have provided usable building material if taken apart. Some of the drains were quite long, as at the northeastern side of Trench IX (pl. 265) and in the East Area (pl. 12:A–B) and were presumably laid in the middle of narrow streets or alleys. Some had subsidiaries draining into them from side alleys or individual houses (pl. 12:A).

In addition to drains made of baked bricks, effective use was made of terra-cotta drains constructed of lengths of pipes varying between 40–75 cm in length and 12–35 cm in diameter, the end of each having been made so as to fit into the mouth of the following one (fig. 9:Family LV; R18:309 [pl. 12:E]). Although bitumen was known, being occasionally applied to waterproof a floor or to mend broken objects, no evidence was found of its use for waterproofing drain joints. Pipe drains might sometimes have been used in conjunction with baked bricks, as in Q19:301 (pl. 12:C) and H14:305 South (pl. 12:D).

At some points on the terrace the incline of the ancient drains was in the opposite direction to the incline of the modern surface. The accumulation and analysis of such evidence might eventually provide valuable information concerning the topography of the site in the Protoliterate period.

THE KILNS AND FIREPLACES

A considerable variety of fireplaces and kilns was found among the architectural remains of the Protoliterate period. Usually the term *kiln* is applied to the larger or more complex structures with distinct architectural components such as grate, walls, and combustion chamber. There is ample evidence for identifying pottery kilns through the discovery in their immediate vicinity of overfired wasters and fragments of shaped but unfired pottery. Fireplaces were simpler structures, presumably used chiefly for cooking.

The normal fireplace was circular, varying in size from a few centimeters to about 1 m in diameter, usually consisting of a floor hardened by fire. Occasionally the floor had turned a typical reddish color. No fire chamber and no walls were found with these fireplaces. One must assume that the material to be heated or fired was arranged on a prepared surface; the fuel, probably straw or dung, was piled between and above the vessels and ignited. If such fireplaces were used for pottery firing,

perhaps temporary low walls with apertures in them to maintain a flow of air were built around the pile of pottery. One load of fuel would hardly suffice for a firing and one can imagine that fuel continued to be added until the vessels were completely baked. Examples of such fireplaces occur in both the East and West Areas (e.g., Room Q17:305, northeastern end; H15:409).

A simple type of kiln, also relatively small, is ovoid in shape but in such examples walls are usually preserved. Actually, the walls do not consist of brickwork but of several layers of mud plaster,[1] each baked to fairly high temperature until the inside surface began to fuse and melt, acquiring a glazed effect. Two kilns had an opening or an air duct at the narrow end (Q18:316 and 317). One of these kilns was built on a low platform consisting of a small retaining wall of mudbricks and mudbrick fragments and a fill of earth mixed with potsherds and fragments of mudbricks (Q18:316 [pl. 13:B]). The narrow end of these small structures provided a flue for the intake of air. The first kiln found in the excavations (R17:210; pl. 11:C) was of this type and it had been partly cut away by the large pit, R17:208 (pl. 11:D). It was at el. 83.70 immediately below the surface and was built above the wall of Room R17:414. It contained many wasters, including some misshapen beveled-rim bowls. This was the first proof both that such kilns were used for firing pottery and that the innumerable beveled-rim bowls had been produced at the site. Similar wasters and pieces of shaped but unfired pottery were found later in the vicinity of other kilns.

A considerably larger and more complex oval kiln was found in Trench XXV, R21:404 (pls. 272–73).[2] The lower part consisted of walls roughly built of mudbricks. It had a well-preserved arched opening low in its southeastern side (pl. 13:C), indicating the presence of a separate combustion chamber. The oven was either domed or vaulted. Its sides above the rough brick wall consisted of several layers of mud plaster originally exposed to temperatures high enough to produce a rough glaze on each layer. An exceptional elaboration found so far only in this structure is the "ribbing" of the upper chamber, apparently carried out in each successive building of the kiln (pl. 13:C). The kiln in R21:404 was full of masses of slag and cinders, as well as spongy hard lumps or clots, both usually partially vitrified. A large pile of the same material was found just south of the kiln (pls. 13:C, left edge; 273). It might have accumulated by periodic cleaning of the kiln after firings, but it has consolidated into a single mass with quite a hard surface. Analysis of these lumps of slag might indicate what this kiln was used for. However, the first impression that it

---

1. The first layer presumably covered a pile of fuel.
2. See Alizadeh 1985b:39–50 for a detailed discussion of this kiln.

could have been a lime-burning kiln is not supported by the evidence in the excavations, since no lime plaster, waterproofing material, or mortar was found in any of the areas excavated so far.

Yet another type of kiln was found in the West Area, H14:201. This, too, was built on a low platform and, while rather poorly preserved, was clearly rectangular with a central combustion chamber below and a series of holes, presumably in the floor of a now-destroyed oven, above. On the other hand, a combustion chamber with such holes could have been simply a "cooking range" on which vessels containing food to be cooked were placed, without any upper chamber.

THE EAST AREA

As mentioned in the *Introduction*, the excavation of East Area (pl. 264) began with the digging of the long exploratory Trench V (pl. 11:A). The highest part of the northeastern lobe of the terrace is at the level of ca. 84.50 m, that is about 16.00 m lower than the highest point of the site (High Mound, northwestern corner of Square O6). There is a gradual slope of about 1.20 m to the southeast and west and a more pronounced slope to the east and northeast, going down to the lowest surface level of about 81.50 m. At least three phases of building within the Protoliterate period can be distinguished in the East Area. Only in a small space near the summit of this sector were building remains of the uppermost level preserved. Lower down the slope, especially on the southeast side of Trench V, this building level had been eroded and the remains of earlier Protoliterate phases came to light immediately below the modern surface. To the south and southeast of the Circular Structure (Q18:305) the Protoliterate architectural remains thin out markedly. Here large areas near the surface were covered by masses of fallen mudbrick that might conceal yet unreached articulated walls. Farther to the south fragmentary walls close to the surface appear to belong to the Middle Susiana occupation (Q18:308).

Since not all of the remains of the uppermost levels have been removed, the plans of the underlying buildings are not complete. Consequently, the plan as shown on plate 264 combines some structures that are not contemporaneous. However, the observation that it was common practice in this period to follow a single general plan during several consecutive rebuildings and the evidence provided by the pottery that all the building phases in question fall within a relatively narrow time range add to the probability that the plans at somewhat different levels in this area did not vary greatly. Accordingly, the combined plan can be taken as a fair representation of any single phase within this time range. Nonetheless, when different building phases can be separated, they are marked by different shadings in the plan.

The rooms vary greatly not only in size but also in shape from nearly square (R17:715, perhaps R18:424, S17:701) to rather oblong rectangles (S17:404). While right-angle corners were undoubtedly the aim of the builders, it was frequently not attained, so that some rooms are trapezoidal (cf. Q17:304, 307 ["closet"], 308, 313). The irregularities of such rooms were the result of either the shape of the available space or the position and orientation of walls of earlier buildings, of which the builders often seem to have been aware. However, despite minor irregularities the rooms are, on the whole, oriented with their corners toward the cardinal points of the compass. This general orientation of the corners and thus of the walls, together with the alignment of the preserved fragments and their relatively uniform thickness, helped to clarify the handicaps created by the poor preservation of the walls, their interruption by the pits, and the fact that no doorways were found between rooms. Thus three main units are distinguishable: one to the northwest of long straight drain R17:314 and the street through which it runs (Squares R17 and S17); a second to the southwest of the first unit, between it and the Circular Structure (Q18:305); and a third to the southeast of the long street drain (R17:310 + 314). In the rest of the excavated area the close spacing of the pits and the large areas of fallen brickwork near the surface have left nothing but scattered fragmentary walls and occasional fragments of baked-brick or terra-cotta pipe drains. In this southwestern section, too, because of the slope, the Protoliterate remains were somewhat thinner than at the higher point to the north and the surface of the Middle Susiana occupation was reached in some spots.

THE HOUSES

While no complete plans of individual houses are preserved, separate architectural units can be distinguished. In the first one, near the highest point of Square R17, a series of small rooms, R17:305, 413, 410, and 414, are traceable for a length of about 12 m. One of these rooms, R17:305, has a small bitumen-plastered area at its northwestern edge. Below the room there had once existed a small subdivided closet, R17:404 + 403. Several pits dug from an eroded upper level have penetrated into both R17:305 and 404. To the northeast of R17:305 and the adjoining room R17:402 are small and somewhat irregular rooms, R17:401, 403, and 410. This group of rooms is delimited on the southeast by a perfectly straight wall preserved to a length of more than 14 m, but partially destroyed by pits R17:214 and 412. This wall is almost exactly parallel to the narrow street and the drain some 4.5 m to the southeast mentioned above. The highest preserved floor is in R17:401 at el. 83.60 m. To the northeast of these rooms a new series of rooms, including R17:704 West and 714, were partially cleared during the seventh season of excavation and, though yet incompletely excavated, it appears that they might have belonged to the same unit.[3] The rectangular area between the straight wall to the southwest of R17:401, 402, and 404 and the street with the drain is still largely unexcavated except for the uppermost level. A few rooms, R17:715, S17:701 and 702, at the northeastern edge of this rectangular area were cleared during the seventh season, but these are from a building phase preceding that which was preserved at the highest point some 10 m to the west (R17:401) and are outside the scope of this report.

The second likely architectural unit consists of a number of rooms to the southwest of the first unit, between it and the Circular Structure at the junction of Squares P17, P18, Q17 and Q18. The rooms that can be attributed to this unit are Q17:304, 308 and another at the junction of four squares, Q17:303 + R17:306. They were considerably larger than those of the first unit, being ca. 3 × 4 m. Their walls are also somewhat thicker than the average walls of the houses to the northeast, attaining sometimes 0.80 m in breadth. As preserved the walls are at a somewhat lower level than those of the rooms to the northeast and apparently belong to an earlier building phase. An oblong room, Q17:305, approximately 6.00 m long by 2.20 m wide, has considerably thinner walls measuring only ca. 0.40 m, but its northwestern wall lines up almost exactly with the north walls of rooms Q17:308 and 304, and it might have thus belonged to the same architectural unit as those rooms. The western corner of this oblong room abuts the eastern side of the Circular Structure above the baked-brick pavement, Q18:315.

A series of rooms and fragmentary walls to the southeast of the narrow street with the long drain (R17:314) probably formed a third architectural unit. Two fragments of a straight wall preserved at R18:421 and R17:415 have been cut by pits R18:408 and S17:202. This wall apparently defined the southeast edge of the narrow street at this point. To the southeast of the broken wall are walls, that on the northeast being almost 1 m thick, which together form an almost perfect square, about 6.50 × 6.50 m. This square is divided somewhat unequally by a thin partition wall, ca. 0.30 m wide, into two regular oblong chambers of rather unusual size, R18:411 and S17:404, with respectively interior widths of about 2.70 and 2.00 m. An oblong projection that forms a large niche on the southwestern end of this square in Room R18:411 is probably from a somewhat later phase of the building. Against the opposite, northeastern, wall of the room was a well, S18:404 (pl. 14:B).

---

3. On pl. 264 rooms R17:704 West and 714 are assigned to the highest preserved and the middle phase respectively of the Protoliterate occupation. Nonetheless, it is quite likely that they belonged to a similar structure that went through two building phases. AA

Aligned with the southeastern wall of Squares R18:411 and S17:404, but south of it, are two exactly parallel walls forming an oblong room over 6.00 m long by 2.20 m wide, R18:410. At its southwestern end this long room is divided by a thin and somewhat oblique partition wall to form a small trapezoidal chamber, R18:313. To the southeast of this oblong room and at right angles to it are walls whose southeastern ends peter out in the eroded slope; the areas delimited by them, R18:409 and S18:401, might have been rooms belonging to the same architectural unit.

Abutting the southwestern corner of R18:410 is a wall about 0.60 m thick, which is not greatly different from the thickness of the walls in most of the rooms discussed above. However, since this wall is placed at a sharp angle of about 60° to the general orientation of those walls it might belong to a different architectural unit. This wall could be traced for a length of about 8 m, though it is cut into by three refuse pits, R18:405, 407, and 414. Parallel to it at a distance of about 1.20 m is a thinner wall that is joined by a second thin wall at an angle of about 60°. Thus, the latter is parallel with the southwestern walls of R18:312 and 313, which might have belonged to the same unit as rooms R18:412 and S17:404. Almost in line with this second thin wall, about 4.00 m to the northwest of it and at a considerably higher level, is a thick wall near the surface, of which only the northeastern face could be articulated (R18:304). Although its orientation is the same as the rooms just described, the nature of the thick wall segment remains unclear.

Several of the individual rooms contained special features. Fairly common were the simple fireplaces marked by burnt patches on the floor already discussed. Specially constructed fireplaces with an elevated ridge and traces of fire also occurred, e.g., against the northern wall of R17:305 and the western wall of R17:715. Bitumen-coated areas, mostly rounded, appeared in several of the rooms, as in the northern corner of Q18:308. The northeastern end of Q17:305 was filled by a semicircular floor of hard earth, two levels of which were traced (pl. 14:A). Small bench-like or table-like structures occurred as in the southeastern corner of Q17:303, the western corner of R17:305, and against the northeastern wall of Q17:402. An especially interesting feature was the shelf against the southeastern wall in R17:313, on which had been placed a row of twelve beveled-rim bowls with a subsidiary row of one pouring-lip bowl and four beveled-rim bowls (pl. 15:A). On a small lower bench against the northeastern wall were three additional beveled-rim bowls; a few others were scattered on the floor. Another example of regularly laid out beveled-rim bowls occurred in R19:401 East, but these were not associated with any architectural elements (pl. 15:B).

THE DRAINS

A prominent feature in the East Area is the considerable number of drains, constructed of either baked bricks or of segments of pottery pipes. Many of these drains were so close to the modern surface that the original buildings which they served have completely disappeared. However, the long drain constructed of baked bricks of the average normal Protoliterate format (42 × 17 × 7) and cut by two pits (R17:408; S17:202) could be traced for over 10 m in a straight line and apparently continued on the same line until it joined, some 22 m distant from its southwestern end, the brickwork preserved on the northeastern slope at S17:407, where there was possibly a sump. There were remains at R17:310 of the juncture of the long drain and a branch from the houses on the southeast (pl. 12:A). As already mentioned on several occasions, it is clear that this drain ran through a narrow street or lane with houses on both sides. If it were possible to establish with certainty whether such drains served for the disposal of sewage or only of rainwater, this would be of considerable importance for understanding the organization of a Protoliterate town in its apparently less affluent living quarters. The numerous other fragmentary drains, whether of baked bricks or pottery pipes or a combination of the two, attest to the organized distribution of large quantities of water. Some partly preserved installations such as R17:405 apparently served as ablution places. Others, such as the drains near kilns, might have been used in connection with pottery manufacture. The excavations at the slope of the East Area where earlier strata were reached indicate that they also contained drains which might be better preserved and eventually provide additional information as to their function.

The relative abundance of water that is suggested by the numerous drains provided a problem. It seemed unlikely that so many substantial drains would be constructed for use only during the rainy season, yet it has been hard to visualize how large quantities of water could have been obtained, if then, as now, the nearest running water supply was the Shur water course, almost 1 km to the east.[4] Even though the geological work of the Khuzestan Development Service has revealed a gradual shift of the water courses of the area to the west, so that anciently the Shur drainage system was closer to Chogha Mish, there remains the question of whether it was the sole source of water in the Protoliterate period.

In this context the well S18:404, found in R18:411, is of exceptional importance (pl. 14:B). It is a squared-off shaft, about 0.80 m wide by 1.40 m long. Except for

its squarish shape, it is not greatly different from wells in modern villages; it even has in its sides characteristic footholds similar to those still used today by well diggers in the villages around Chogha Mish. Unfortunately, it could not be cleaned to its full depth and the ancient water table at this point could not be established. The well was excavated during a particularly active rainy season; the rain not only filled the lowest part excavated but it also softened the exposed sides, endangering anyone who might try to climb down. This well might be a key to the abundance of drains of various types at Chogha Mish during the Protoliterate period. If individual households had their own wells, then considerably more water would have been readily available than if all of it had to be transported from outside the settlement.

To the southeast of the Circular Structure and disappearing beneath it was a pavement made of broken baked bricks in somewhat of a "crazy pavement" pattern (Q18:315, pl. 9:B). The bricks are of typical Protoliterate format and dimensions, but they are all incomplete, which shows that here they were used secondarily. Some 20 cm below the baked-brick pavement is an earlier pavement made of river pebbles. It appears that both pavements were laid in a street or on courts.

THE WEST AREA[5]

The excavations of the West Area, as mentioned in the *Introduction*, developed from the preliminary trial Trenches VI and IX and Sounding C between them (pl. 265). The structural remains can be divided into two main categories, the polygonal platform and the small-scale buildings and features.

THE POLYGONAL PLATFORM

In extending the excavations over the area between Trenches VI and IX (Squares J–K14) what seemed to be a platform constructed of very hard mudbricks was encountered in Square J14. There were no lines marking walls, nor any space free of the hard brickwork in an area extending over at least 350 sq. m. While the articulation of individual bricks was very difficult it seems that they were of the normal small format found in the Protoliterate period (12 × 23 × 5–7 cm). The edges of this structure on its eastern, northern, and northwestern sides were located in the third season. Its outline was not rectangular; apparently it was a polygon of a somewhat irregular shape. At the edges the structure was pre-

---

4. For much of the year the Shur does not have running streams of water above the ground. However, water wells up into shallow depressions dug in the gravel at suitable points along the banks and serves as the regular supply for large villages nearby such as Dowlati.

5. Certain features not recorded on the Chogha Mish III and IV plane table sheets have been added to the plan from field notes and measured sketches: the location of IV-39 and of the torpedo jars of H14:305 and J15:306, the loci H14:403 and 404, and the southwestern drains. However, the possible range of error involved in the process was small. AA

served in places only to a height of one or two bricks. Two large projections to the east might be all that remain of buttresses on towers. Several thinner walls abut the structure at its northeastern and northern edges. A thin wall runs parallel to the northwestern edge of the platform in Trench XVII A, separated from it by a space of only about 0.70 m, for a distance of about 10 m (pl. 265, between H13:301 and J13:301).

Because of the considerable quantity of Parthian pottery found in the vicinity and even embedded in the brickwork of the platform itself, we were inclined to date it to this period until nearly the close of the third season. But then, in tracing the platform's western edge toward the south a breach in the solid brickwork was found that led into a circular pit about 3 m in diameter (H14:308). It was filled with debris; ashes and potsherds were piled against the brickwork of the platform. Both the passage and the pit into which it led were clearly later than the brickwork into which they were cut, and both contained in their fill nothing later than Protoliterate pottery. In this way the date of the platform can be established without doubt. Unfortunately, any structure that might have once been built on it would have been higher than the surface of the mound in this area.

THE SMALL-SCALE BUILDINGS AND FEATURES

At the denuded southwestern corner of the platform, near H14:308, there appeared immediately below the surface the westernmost preserved part of a drain constructed of baked bricks of typical Protoliterate format (H14:404). This drain extended for at least 20 m from the northwest (H14:404 + J14:304) to the southeast (J15:303), apparently roughly parallel with the preserved southern edge of the platform. Various lengths of terra-cotta pipe drains and baked-brick drains opened into it on the northeast from under the platform (J14:303) and on the southeast from structures that have been completely denuded (J14:401). The long drain's channel sloped down from 81.11 in the northwest to 80.52 just to the east of the juncture with the wide drain J14:401, and on down to 80.19 at the southeastern end, about 1.70 m below the modern surface. Although greatly destroyed and broken at various points (particularly in J14:303), on the northwest (H14:404 + J14:304 North) one side of it was still well preserved to a length of about 11 m. It appeared as a continuous line of bricks laid lengthwise on edge; in at least one spot there were also traces of some lower bricks. Better preserved drain segments, particularly those of H14:403 and J14:401 and the long drain of the East Area, indicate that such drains consisted of bricks laid flat, lengthwise; with others standing on edge on both sides, and, apparently, in turn covered with the same type of brick, also laid lengthwise. On the southeast J15:303, the structure was different, with the sides of the channel being formed by

three courses of bricks laid flat, the lowest course consisting of relatively complete bricks predominantly laid as stretchers and those of the two upper courses of mostly broken bricks laid as both headers and stretchers. The sides of the tributary drain J14:401 were formed by baked bricks laid on edge lengthwise. The top was unique, consisting of irregular stone slabs. A segment of a well-constructed baked-brick wall with a corner at the east (H14:304 South) was parallel to the drain at a higher level and might have been the foundation of a wall marking the outline of a lane below which the drain originally was constructed; the corner perhaps was part of the foundation of a doorway in that wall.[6]

In addition to the main drainage system just described, numerous segments of drains built of baked bricks appeared over the area, some of them superimposed (H14:403; H14:305 South; H15:402). None could be traced for any length to their origin and it would seem that in most cases in building the later phase of drains the material of earlier drains lying immediately below was reused freely, thus making the recording of both phases extremely difficult.

Generally speaking the building remains at or immediately below the surface of the site at this point were in an even poorer state of preservation than those of the East Area and for the most part only very short segments of unconnected mudbrick walls could be distinguished. It is possible that some of these could have belonged to the Parthian period. In this area, in contrast to the East Area, later walls built over accumulations of loose debris rather than continued on the foundation of earlier structures were observed, for example, in Hl4:201 and J15:305. At levels somewhat lower under the surface fairly regular walls began to appear. Most were between 40 and 60 cm wide and preserved to a height also of 40 to 60 cm, but even the earlier walls were not preserved to their full length and they cannot be grouped into clear architectural units. However, in J15 the angles between pairs of walls forming the corners of the two rooms at the lower level were nearly perpendicular, although the two pairs of walls were irregularly aligned to each other. They apparently represent two different architectural units separated by an open space or street (J15:304), which probably continued to the south (J15:403).

Close to the southern edge of the excavated area were found two round structures with traces of burning, apparently a large hearth and a kiln (H15:409, 405 respectively) and one step-like construction with, to the south, patches of a clay pavement on a foundation of sherds (J15:402), also burnt. The stepped structure cannot easily be explained as a domestic installation. One

---

6. Since some drains had sides three-courses high (H14:305 South; J14:303), it is possible that J14:304 South was a fragment left over from a drain later than the long drain.

would have been inclined to consider it as an altar of sorts if its situation within a building could have been ascertained. Objects such as the "hut symbol" found in a lower level in about the same location (pl. 31:Q) and the jar with two spouts found about 7 m to the north at a higher level (pls. 26; 108:F) are clearly of non-domestic character. Their presence together with the fairly well-preserved walls at the lower level and the appearance of such an installation as the kiln in H14:201 perhaps lend some credence to the interpretation that part of the West Area was of ritual significance in the Protoliterate period.

At the western part of the excavations, where nothing but loose debris occurred to a considerable depth, a round structure about 2.50 m in diameter, in the form of a low ridge made of clay (H14:202), was found at about 1.65 m below the surface. It might mark the end of the occupation of the Middle Susiana period or the beginning of the settlement of the Protoliterate period.

The northeasternmost part of the West Area is Trench VI, which in the second season was started at the gully in K14 to ascertain whether some glazed sherds found on the surface of the northwestern promontory of the terrace corresponded to the remains of a later period existing in situ. No glazed pottery was discovered there, but immediately below the surface great masses of Protoliterate pottery began to appear. Only about 0.60 m below the surface at el. 79.57 m a floor of packed earth was reached and on it a round structure plastered with bitumen (K14:201). As the excavation continued toward the south into the higher part of the northwestern terrace the accumulation of sherds became thicker. The characteristic feature of the pottery at this spot is that, although it contained a large number of beveled-rim bowls, as did every other part of the site excavated, the proportion of the flower pots (pl. 83:Z–DD) was greater. Also, there was a considerable proportion of fragments of tall spouted bottles with collared rims ranging in height from about 25.0 cm to nearly 1.00 m (pl. 111). No architectural features of the Protoliterate period were found in this trench, but a few meters to the southwest of it in K14:402 were traces of walls too fragmentary to support any speculation as to their character (K14:403).

PROTOLITERATE FINDS IN THE SMALLER AREAS ON THE TERRACE

TRENCH XVIII (PL. 260)

In the middle of the terrace at the juncture of Squares M–N13–14 an ashy area was discernible on the surface. This proved to be a sign of a typical Protoliterate deposit consisting of masses of complete and fragmentary beveled-rim bowls and many other partially reconstructible vessels (pl. 16:A). These were scattered in a shallow layer only about 9.40 m deep below the present surface. No Protoliterate pits or traces of walls occurred in Trench XVIII.

TRENCH XIII (PLS. 268–69)

It will be recalled that there was evidence of an Achaemenid domestic installation in the northeastern part of this trench (L22:401). It yielded more substantial traces of Protoliterate occupation even though no coherent architectural remains seem to have survived the disturbance caused by the intrusive graves of the Late Cemetery. However, Protoliterate pottery occurred in significant quantities, including intact beveled-rim bowls, between the late graves (e.g., K23:401, 501, 502; L23:402, 503, 505). The southwestern part of the trench had in K23:503 a circular plastered floor at el. 82.12 and, just to the south, a large pit, not yet completely excavated, of the type which is so common in other parts of the site. This pit had penetrated from an eroded Protoliterate level to a considerable depth (ca. 1.75 m) through the remains of a Middle Susiana house, destroying parts of its walls (K23:506, southern wall; K23:507, southwestern corner).

OTHER TRENCHES (PLS. 260, 267, 272)

In the small Trench X, located in Squares G26–27 in the southwestern part of the terrace, pottery deposits consisting of intact beveled-rim bowls testify to the Protoliterate occupation. There were no structural remains in the limited area of this test trench.

Trench XIV in Square E23, another small area dug in the second season, contained beveled-rim bowls lined up with a few other vessels as if on a shelf (pl. 15:C). Though this arrangement is reminiscent of the beveled-rim bowl shelf in R17:313, here no adjacent walls were distinguished. Near the line of vessels was one of the usual good deposits of Protoliterate pottery, but no structural elements were found until a heavy rain in the third season revealed an almost complete spouted vessel lying on top of a rather considerable pottery deposit. The removal of this deposit revealed that it had been lying immediately to the southwest of two courses of badly decayed bricks. However, further excavation in this area was not undertaken.

Various small trenches in the western and eastern slopes of the terrace, VIII (H–J21), XV (F27), XVI (O27), XII (P–Q22), and XXI (P–Q23), were mostly on parts of the site too eroded to have preserved Protoliterate occupation floors in situ, although Protoliterate sherds were abundant immediately below the surface. On the other hand, in Trench XXV (R20–21), also located in a considerably eroded spot, the strata underlying the scantily preserved Protoliterate occupation level had been penetrated by deep pits filled with pottery and ashy debris (R20:402, 513; R21:408, 405, 503, 505, 509). This is in marked contrast to the absence of such pits in the small trenches just mentioned and suggests that the Protoliterate town contained quarters of somewhat varying character. In addition to the pits, the other Protoliterate features in Trench XXV were the kiln R21:404 and its ash heap (pls. 272–73) and the stumps of two roughly parallel walls in the upper part of R21:300 Southwest and Center West (pl. 272). They might have outlined a passage way.

SUMMARY OF THE ARCHITECTURAL EVIDENCE FOR THE PROTO-LITERATE TOWN

The general topography of the Protoliterate town is clear. It was divided into an upper and a lower town, with varying intermediate levels in each. It has already been pointed out that the Protoliterate floor of P7:302 was considerably higher than room N9:302, which can be explained because structures were built into the slopes of the acropolis as well as crowning it. Also on the terrace the difference in level between Protoliterate structures on the higher segments and on the slopes is too considerable to be interpreted as marking merely later and earlier phases. The remains in the East Area show how the successive building phases were so closely intermeshed; therefore, the larger differences in level can be interpreted as reflecting the clustering of buildings on the flat surfaces and lower slopes of the terrace.

The presence of public buildings at Chogha Mish is indicated by the clay cones scattered abundantly over the surface of the site and in the Protoliterate strata. Some still retain red or black paint on their heads (pl. 31:S–T). Others are light buff or dark gray; many of the latter are large in size and have a central hollow for inlay (pl. 31:KK–LL). They were once used to form cone mosaic-wall decoration similar to that typical of Protoliterate temples at Warka; so far none have been found *in situ* at Chogha Mish. It seems likely, however, that at least one temple would have crowned the High Mound. The apparently solid mudbrick area underlying the Elamite brickwork at N9:301 on the southwestern lobe of the High Mound could have been part of a temple platform; further investigation is needed to test this possibility. The two baked-brick cesspits, 09:301, 302, placed side-by-side at a low point in the same area are unparalleled on the terrace and might have served a public building. On the terrace, the Polygonal Platform of the West Area stands out from the house remains. The platform was built above an area that yielded some ritual objects and contained large round hearths and a small altar-like feature. It was perhaps intended as the foundation for a temple replacing simpler, earlier shrines.

The general character of the other architectural remains is quite clear although thus far it has been impossible to establish coherent complete plans for individual units. In addition to the rather indifferent workmanship, the sizes of the rooms so far excavated, which vary between about 1.5 × 1.5 m (e.g., R17:401, 404) to about 2.5 × 5.5 m (e.g., Q17:401; R18:410, 411; S17:404), show that these were private houses. The contiguous arrangement of rooms of various shapes and sizes over a relatively large area with only small areas functioning as narrow streets or lanes or open spaces between built-up areas, definitely indicates a dense urban population in a confined space, perhaps within a walled city,[7] rather than a smaller, less dense population with more extensive open areas available for individual dwellings, as is the case in modern villages in this region. Thus Chogha Mish in the Protoliterate period qualifies as a town because of both its size and the character of its "town planning."

7. A small part of a heavy fortification wall found subsequent to the fifth season might, when its character and date are further investigated, clarify whether the town was fortified in the Protoliterate period.

CHAPTER 4

THE POTTERY OF THE PROTOLITERATE PERIOD

The amounts of pottery recovered in the Proto-literate levels are overwhelming. On the surface of the site, particularly in the terrace area, masses of sherds from both the prehistoric Susiana and the Protoliterate periods had been uncovered by erosion. Accordingly in the first season, even before trenches were made in the terrace, a good Protoliterate series of special spout, handle, and rim sherds were collected. In addition to the ubiquitous fragments of beveled-rim bowls, nearly complete examples were not far to seek. In subsequent seasons the excavations on the terrace have provided huge quantities of sherds as well as numerous complete or semi-complete vessels representing many pottery families (see figs. 3–7).

THE WARES

All the Protoliterate pottery from Chogha Mish seems to have been made at the site from local deposits of clay. Several wares can be distinguished, primarily on the basis of the quality of the clay and the ingredients mixed with it as tempering materials.[1] The main varieties are: coarse ware filled with vegetal tempering and sometimes grit; standard ware containing considerable sand and grit; fine ware consisting of well-levigated clay tempered with very fine sand; and shatter ware of almost pure clay with little or no mineral tempering. There is no sharp line of demarcation between these various categories of pastes. In particular, the standard ware shows many gradations from the normal gritty examples to denser, better-levigated examples that approach in their quality the fine ware.

To a considerable degree, shapes and wares tend to dovetail so that some forms normally occur only in coarse ware and many others only in standard ware. However, as one might expect in non-mechanized products, there is a certain amount of overlapping. It is obvious, nevertheless, that the potters at Chogha Mish had very clear craft traditions and standards.

COARSE WARE

The presence of considerable amounts of vegetal tempering is the defining characteristic for the bulk of the coarse ware. Sand and grit sometimes appear in minor amounts alongside the straw or occasionally form the primary tempering. The paste consisted of relatively unpurified clay, which was fired to shades of brown, as well as of buff and orange or reddish buff. This ware was used for everyday containers, particularly simple open forms such as beveled-rim bowls, flower pots, straight or convex sided bowls, and trays (see pl. 84:A–C, N). Although examples of the common coarse ware forms are so abundant as frequently to form the bulk of individual pottery groups, the total number of coarse ware types made in coarse ware is quite small, even though a few specialized shapes do appear in it.

The vessels are either hand- or wheel-made, depending upon their shape and function. Usually the surfaces received no special treatment, although a kind of slip seems sometimes to have been produced by wet-smoothing during the shaping of the vessels. The firing was relatively low; frequently the core is darker than the outer surfaces.

STANDARD WARE

The clay of the standard ware is not greatly different from that of the coarse ware, but it tends to be of a better quality. Unlike that of the coarse ware, it contains no vegetal tempering but only grit, which appears in widely varying amounts and with a considerable range in the size of the particles. The colors range from very light or yellowish cream, through buff or greenish buff, to light pink, orange, or red. On a single vessel several of these shades might blend into each other, apparently reflecting variations in temperature and gases during firing. Frequently standard ware vessels were not fired at high enough temperatures to do away with a black core.

---

1. In the use of "ware" as applied to define various categories of pottery, this report follows the practice adopted in the publication of the pottery of the Diyala region (Delougaz 1952), in which "ware" is associated with a distinctive epithet denoting some specific characteristics. These can pertain to fabric, mode of manufacture, a geographic entity (Jemdet Nasr pottery), a type of decoration (scarlet ware), or a combination of such characteristics as defined in each case. For a discussion of Protoliterate wares on the basis of the pottery from Habuba Kabira South, see Sürenhagen 1974/75:60–61, in which twenty-three varieties are distinguished and the manufacturing technique discussed in considerable detail (pp. 81–95).

Standard ware vessels were normally wheel-made. Nonetheless, clear wheel marks frequently appear only on the rim and upper part of the interior of a vessel while the rest, inside and out, is smoothed, finger imprinted, scraped, pared, or scratched in such a way as to obliterate wheel marks. The interiors of closed forms usually have no special additions to the marks left by the shaping procedures just mentioned. The exception is the addition of wedges or lumps of clay in one family of storage jars (pl. 28:V). On exterior surfaces, slips appear, but it is often difficult to distinguish true slips from slips produced by wet-smoothing. The best examples of slips are those belonging to a well-known specialized category in which part of the surface coating has been removed to expose narrow strips of the underlying fabric. Such reserve slips are quite unobtrusive when paste and slip are similar in color, but much more prominent when those shades differ.[2] The strokes are usually diagonal, with their lower ends often becoming vertical if they reach the middle of the body (pls. 28:A–B; 86:C, E; 87:H; 89:I, S–T, V; 92:B, D, G; 93:D; 94:C; 107:K–N; 108:A, I; 110:J–K), but sometimes the strokes are vertical (pls. 19:E; 28:C; 86:G; 89:B). Normally the reserve slip does not extend onto the lower part of a vessel. As it is described in the discussion of forms, there is considerable correlation between surface treatment and shape. In particular, the reserve slip is characteristic for one family of open forms and for certain families of closed vessels without major accessories or with spouts, but it never appears on handled or four-lugged vessels. Painted decoration is almost nonexistent in the Protoliterate pottery of Chogha Mish, with isolated examples occurring on only two families (pls. 24:E; 123:C, F), but various forms of incision, punctuation, rocker, and imprints are frequent. Plastic decoration is typical of the period but rarer than the various categories of incised decoration.

The variety of types is enormous, ranging from open bowls and plates through pots with various types of handles, lugs, and spouts to large pithoi. These were the practical kitchenware and other domestic vessels.

FINE WARE

There is no sharp demarcation between the standard and the fine ware, but in the latter both the amount of the mineral tempering and also the size of individual grains of sand or grit are reduced. An occasional large grit might appear, but never in the quantity normal for the standard ware. Frequently the tempering is not discernible to the eye alone. Fine ware vessels tend to be smaller and more sharply profiled in shape than many of

the standard ware vessels, the normal colors range from light cream through greenish or yellow buff to pink. The surface color carries through the core, possibly because the thin walls allowed more uniform firing. Characteristic for the fine ware are the marks of throwing on a fast wheel covering the whole interior (pl. 24:J). The exterior walls are normally more evenly finished than those of the standard ware. However, even on the fine ware vessels the lower part of the exterior tends to be not quite so regularly shaped or so carefully smoothed as the upper part. In addition to wet-smoothing, fine light-cream slips appear, as well as an occasional reserve slip.

The fine ware shapes are less numerous than those of the standard ware. Obviously this ware was not appropriate for cooking vessels or large storage jars. The great standard ware classes of vessels with vertical or horizontal handles are unrepresented except for rare specimens of strap-handled ovoid jars made in a ware intermediate between the standard and fine grades and finely scored on their upper bodies. Some types such as pouring-lip bowls, narrow-based ovoid jars of miniature or small size, and four-lugged vessels of several families can appear in either standard or fine ware. Only one type, certain very rare conical cups (Protoliterate Family V), occurs only in an especially refined variant of the fine ware. Among spouted vessels a large number of the smaller and medium-sized examples of fine ware have very sharply profiled necks or rims and carefully inserted spouts in a great variety of shapes.

SHATTER WARE

A ware characterized by negligible or complete absence of tempering is indistinguishable from fine ware in complete vessels. Only when such vessels have been broken can the typical, sharply angular fractures be observed. Even the sherds are extremely brittle and tend to shatter under slight pressure into small angular fragments, hence the ware's name. It is a distinct, though as far as observed, relatively rare ware. The highly purified paste resembles the layers of fine clay silt deposited in a depression after rain, which shatter in exactly the same way when dried out by the sun. Shatter ware tends to be reddish or tan in color, particularly in the fractures. The vessels are of medium or small size and are frequently very carefully made. Obviously this was considered to be one of the better wares of the period.

GRAY WARE

The rarest of the Protoliterate wares has a fine dense paste without noticeable grits and uniformly light gray surfaces and cores. The color is presumably due to deliberate control of the firing conditions, perhaps with the intention of producing pottery imitations of stone vessels, as in the case of a band-rim bowl fragment

---

2. Delougaz (1952:33) pointed out that some reserved slip was produced merely by scraping a wet-smoothed surface. For discussion of the chronological range of reserved slip and related matters, see ibid., pp. 53, 125, 133–34, 141, 143.

(4.989). The shapes, in so far as they are known, correspond to those of the standard ware, but only a very few sherds and semi-complete vessel fragments were found (e.g., pl. 90:A). Despite its rarity, the gray ware is definitely characteristic of Chogha Mish and of considerable significance in view of the famous Uruk gray wares.

RED WARE

A prominent but rather rare surface treatment is a red wash, sometimes bright in color: it is usually matt but can be burnished. In itself the red wash does not necessarily define a ware of distinctive fabric since it was applied to both standard and fine wares, as well as to a brown fabric that often slivers into many thin layers. Only the combination of this fabric with a red wash is here termed red ware. It is, as in the case of the shatter ware, usually impossible to recognize from intact specimens. The red ware seems to have been limited to medium-sized four-lugged jars (pl. 114:H, L–M).

SHAPES

The classification of the shapes of individual vessels was the basic first step in analyzing the Protoliterate pottery from Chogha Mish.[3] However, the great amount and variety of the material provided an unwieldy number of single types even though several vessels were often so similar as to fall under one shape number. A systematic overview of the Protoliterate ceramics could only be achieved by assembling related types into families, each consisting of a group of individual vessels or types that share common characteristics in defined combinations. Shape is used as the fundamental characteristic with which are associated those other features, whether of size, ware, accessorial elements, or decoration, that give the group in question a specific individuality. Since shape and function are inextricably connected, the families defined on this relatively formal basis do in great part represent functional units, such as storage jars, kitchen and table utensils, and ritual vessels whose general use, at least, is clear. The specialized features of some families apparently correspond to specific functions that can hardly be reconstructed with the evidence at hand.[4] Other variations among families and individual types, particularly in the

spouted and four-lugged classes, might reflect the creativity of the potters rather than functional requirements.

These families are presented in two major groups, the wide-mouthed open forms such as plates, bowls, or cups and the small-mouthed closed forms such as jars or bottles. On the whole there is no problem in distinguishing between the two categories except for borderline forms. Since the ancient potters had no rigid demarcation between open and closed vessels, a somewhat arbitrary definition of open form is used: a form in which the diameter of the mouth is 80% or more of the widest diameter of the vessel. To allow for some flexibility, however, a general rule is followed that in classifying borderline cases the majority prevails. Thus, exceptional specimens that differ from the majority of the examples of a family of open vessels only in having mouths of somewhat less than 80% are, nonetheless, classified with the majority as open forms.

THE FAMILIES OF OPEN FORMS[5]
(Figs. 8–9)

Size is an important element in defining the families into which the open vessels can be grouped. Vessels of markedly varying dimensions are placed in the same family only when a few exemplars of a specific shape occur in an atypical size. An example of such an exceptional case is the large-sized pouring-lip bowl included in Protoliterate Family VII (pl. 80:FF). Although size and the finer or coarser quality of the ware and fabric combine to indicate the general function of various families of vessels as either tableware, domestic or craft utensils, or relatively immovable storage vats, it is impossible to specify precise and differing functions for each major type or family. The diversity of form probably often reflects various predilections of taste as much as the needs of practical functions.

Protoliterate Family I

A.00, .03; proportion 2, coarse and standard ware

Figure 8; plate 80:A–B

Miniature open vessels were of little importance in Protoliterate ceramics. They are extremely rare and for

---

3. See Delougaz 1952:11, 18 (tables I–II) for the definitions of the six classification digits used here. More detailed explanations and illustrations for the application of this system, including a device by means of which the third proportion digit can be determined quickly without calculation, can be found in the original publication (ibid., pp. 14–15, figs. 4–6).

4. Cf. Balcz 1932, 1933, 1934, where the functions of Egyptian pottery types are established with the aid of tomb representations and written evidence.

5. Much of the comparative material has been collected by Guillermo Algaze and Abbas Alizadeh. In addition, Algaze kindly agreed to the utilization here of comparisons between the ceramics of Chogha Mish and unpublished pottery from Nippur that emerged during his preparation of an unpublished study, "Inanna Temple Ceramic Sequence," 1978. McGuire Gibson, Director of the Nippur Expedition, and Richard Zettler, who is responsible for the publication of Inanna Temple materials, have generously permitted the citation of unpublished vessels from Nippur by field numbers and the use of the Nippur data in the tables below.

OPEN VESSELS

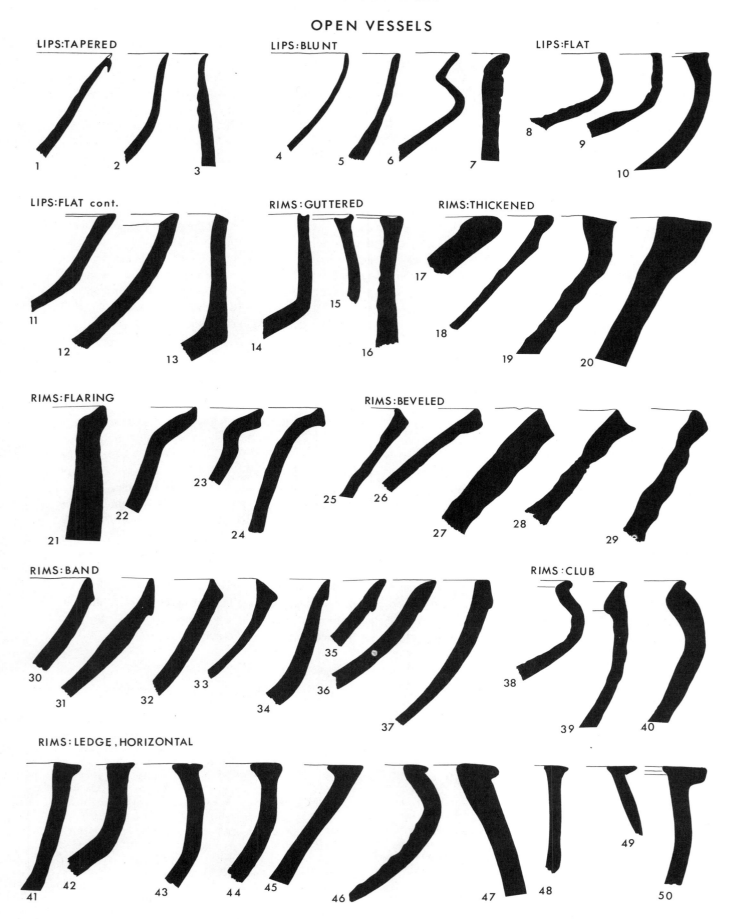

Figure 3. Profiles of Protoliterate Open Forms: Lip and Rim Types

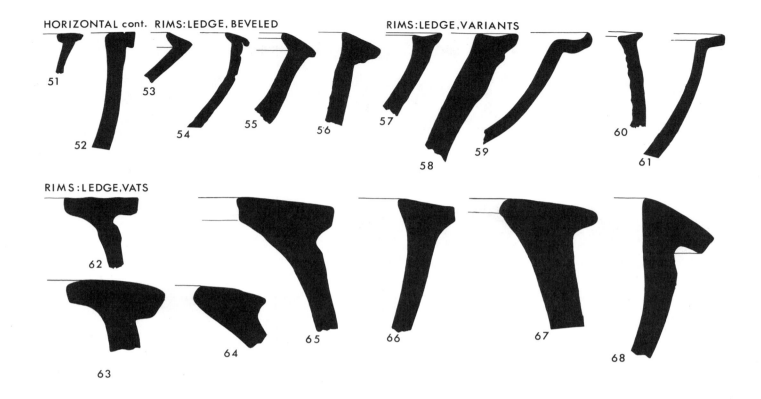

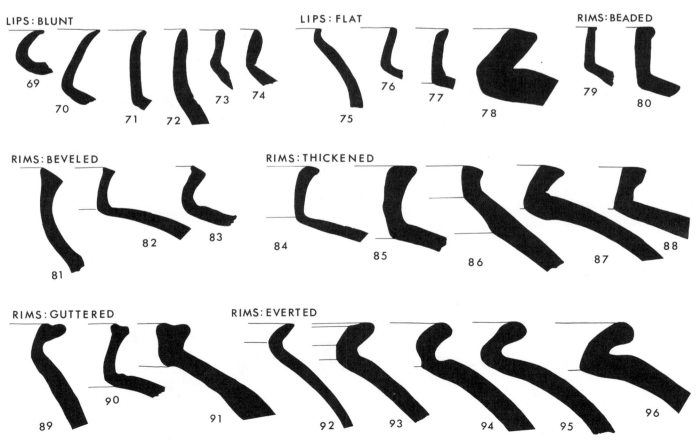

Figure 4. Profiles of Protoliterate Open and Closed Forms: Rim Types

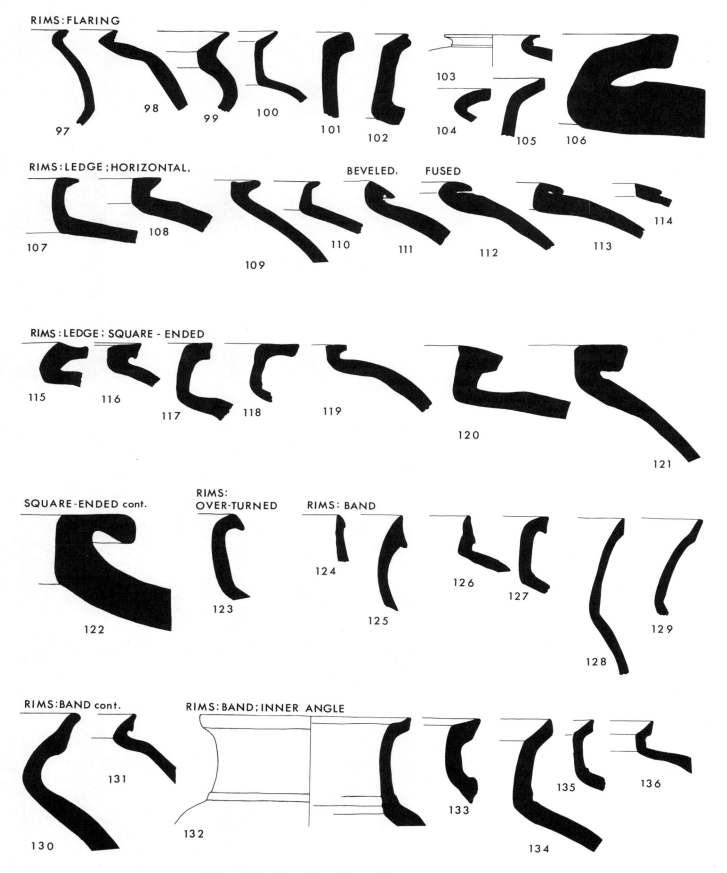

Figure 5. Profiles of Protoliterate Closed Forms: Rim Types

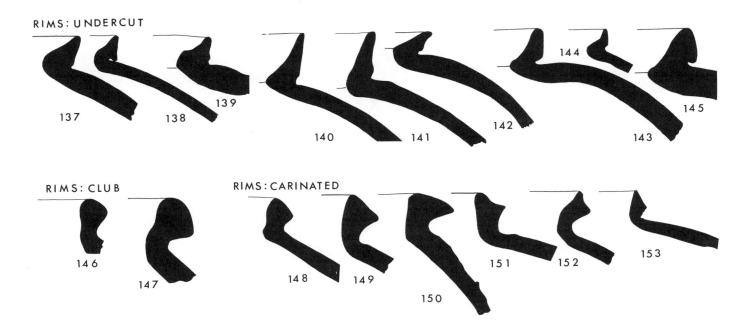

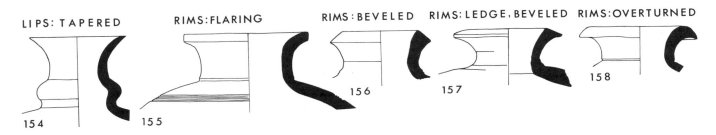

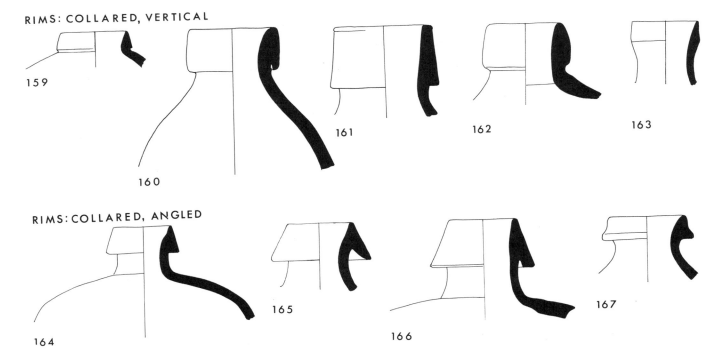

Figure 6. Profiles of Protoliterate Closed Forms: Rim Types and Narrow Necks

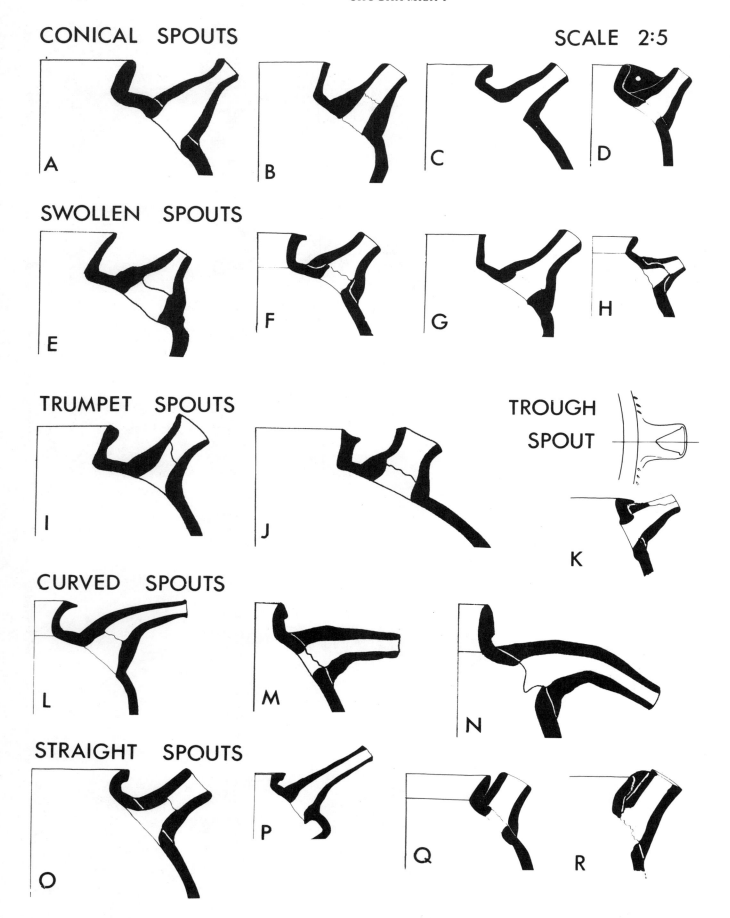

Figure 7. Profiles of Protoliterate Spout Types

the most part appear only as isolated single examples of various shapes rather than as clusters of forms. Tiny bowls of squat proportions are placed in Family I.

Protoliterate Family II

A.24; proportions 4, 6, standard and fine ware

Figure 8; plate 80:C–D

Two miniature cylindrical vessels provide the basis for distinguishing Family II. They are isolated examples, but the squatter one (pl. 80:C) is, however, a small-scale version of the vessels of Family XX (pl. 83:A–E), which are in turn allied to Family LXVI (pl. 89:D–G). The little vessel (pl. 80:D) represents essentially the same shape as the vessels just cited except that the main part of its body is sinuous.

Protoliterate Family III

B.11; proportion 3, standard ware

Figure 8; plate 80:E

Family III was set up to accommodate miscellaneous bowls of a slightly more practical size than those of Families I and II, but so far has only a single representative.

Protoliterate Family IV

A–B.30; proportion 1, standard to fine ware

Figure 8; plate 80:F–I

The first of the well-defined, coherent open families is that containing shallow forms with nearly vertical walls, slightly convex "bases," and diameters of about 4 to 12 cm. The size and shallowness of these objects make them impractical as ordinary containers. They apparently served as lids and are well known at several Protoliterate sites.[6]

Protoliterate Family V

B.00, .04, .06; normally proportion 3, fine ware

Figure 8; plate 80:J–N

Small bowls characterized by their standardized size, fine ware, and markedly thin walls form a distinctive, although rare, class. The ware is a particularly refined variant of fine ware, without visible tempering, and greenish or light brownish buff in color. The vessels

were made on a fast wheel; striations appear prominently on the interior of the base and sometimes on the interior of the walls, although these are more frequently elegantly smooth. The regular and evenly flat bases have sharp edges; they were probably carefully pared with a knife. Striations on the exterior of the walls and bases suggest that the bowls were replaced on the wheel, mouth down, for a final shaping that left prominent (fragment 3.650) or faint striations (pl. 80:K–L) on the base.

Relatively straight-sided or slightly sinuous profiles combined with broad flat bases are typical for Family V. Also included in the family because of size, distinctive ware, and eggshell thinness is a convex bowl with a relatively narrow and uneven base (pl. 80:N). Although it is not a standard type at Chogha Mish, parallels occur elsewhere.[7]

Protoliterate Family VI

B.00, .03; proportion 2 or lower range of 3, blunt lips, string-cut base, usually standard ware

Figure 8; plate 80:O–X

One of the major groups of Protoliterate open forms consists of conical bowls of a size and shape suitable for tableware. Although the exterior profiles are often rather irregular, they can be taken as either straight-sided (pl. 80:O–S, U, X) or slightly convex (pl. 80:T–V, W) forms. Occasionally the base was shaped into a slight foot (pl. 80:Q). The Family VI bowls fall normally into the upper range of proportion 2 and the lower range of proportion 3. Their standardized size, proportions, and shapes are apparent (see pl. 80). A squat example (pl. 80:O) is quite atypical. Small-sized variants occur extremely rarely and their exceptional character is enhanced by their fine ware and thin walls (pl. 80:R and 3.027 [height 6.4, diameter 8.50 cm]). A thin-walled example of standard size was also found (pl. 80:T). Typical for Family VI are fast-wheel striations and corrugation, the latter usually on the interior (pl. 17:B). The bases are normally string-cut. Very rare anomalous examples have plain bases on which the striations have probably been obliterated by subsequent smoothing. Remnants of the original lump of clay remaining around the base were trimmed away by either rough (pl. 80:V–W) or quite regular paring, in the latter cases apparently done while the bowls were rotated mouth down on the wheel.

Some Family VI bowls might have been secondarily utilized as funnels. The incidence of anciently-made holes in the base seems too great to have been accidental. Nine out of thirty-two complete or fragmentary

6. For parallels to plate 80:G–I, see Haller 1932, pl. 19 C:h (Warka, Eanna, Level VI); Nissen 1970, pl. 101:30 (Warka, K/L XII Sounding, Layer 40); Strommenger 1963, pl. 38:m–o (Warka, Archaic Settlement Trench); 7N P223 and 7N 745 (both plum red wash; Nippur, Inanna Temple XIV); Mackay 1931, pl. 66:20–21 (Jemdet Nasr). For parallels to plate 80:H, see 7N P312 (diameter 14 cm; Nippur, Inanna Temple XIX); de Genouillac et al. 1934, pl. 5:4729 (Tello); Thompson and Mallowan 1933, pl. 49:6 (Nineveh).

7. For parallels, see Le Brun 1978a, fig. 19:19 (Susa, Acropole I, Level 17B); Sürenhagen 1974/75, pl. 22:67–68 (Habuba Kabira South).

specimens in the Oriental Institute are perforated. Holes also occur in examples of the closely allied Family VIII (pl. 81:B). Parallels for the bowls of Family VI are to be found at a number of sites.[8]

Protoliterate Family VII

> B.00, .03; normally proportion 2, pouring lip, standard to fine ware

> Figure 8; plate 80:Y–FF

The bowls of Family VII, similar to those of Family VI, which they resemble in general size, shape, and proportion, must have been ubiquitous household utensils. Their outstanding characteristic is the opening formed by folding over part of the lip (pl. 17:C). Even when this feature is not preserved, however, various characteristics usually associated with it in complete examples identify fragments as belonging to Family VII rather than Family VI. Thus, the pouring-lip bowls are distinguished from Family VI bowls by a tendency to be squatter and to have more rounded profiles and thinner walls without interior corrugation. In contrast to Family VI, the pouring-lip bowls were often made in fine ware and their surfaces wet-smoothed or covered with a light buff slip. Fairly tapered lips are common for Family VII although blunt lips also occur, in which case they are, as a corollary of their thinner walls, more delicate than the blunt lips of Family VI. The bases are strikingly diagnostic; unlike the string-cut Family VI bowls, the majority of Family VII bases bear the straight, parallel marks of an instrument, apparently serrated, with which they were cut from the potter's wheel.

Exceptions are two string-cut examples, which also have the interior corrugation typical for Family VI (III-160–61), and several vessels whose smoothed bases no longer bear traces of how they were separated from the wheel. The clusters of specific characteristics that enable small bowls of simple, undifferentiated shapes to be separated into two well-defined families testify to the standardized categories and professionalism of the potter's craft in the early Protoliterate period.

Two pouring-lip bowls (pl. 80:FF and 4.333) are considerably larger than the normal examples, which have a maximum diameter of about 12 cm. The pouring lips of the standard-sized bowls vary in width from

about 2 to 3 cm. Some are well shaped with projecting flaps, but others are more vestigial. When complete bowls are filled to the brim with water, it tends to spill over on the sides as one pours, but falls in a narrow stream from less full bowls, particularly if their pouring lips are well formed. Perhaps the Family VII bowls were used with viscous fluids. One might also speculate that they served as drinking vessels, a possibility perhaps supported by the existence of at least one example of stone (pls. 29:O; 124:M).[9]

Protoliterate Family VIII

> B.03, .04, .06; upper range of proportion 3 and lower range of 4, blunt lip, standard ware

> Figure 8; plate 81:A–F

Bowls that share many characteristics such as corrugated interiors, blunt lips, string-cut bases, and secondary perforations in the bases (pl. 81:B) with the vessels of Family VI are given a separate identity by their higher proportions. They are much rarer than the squatter, Family VI bowls and appear to be early examples of the relatively high conical bowls or cups which are characteristic for the later part of the Protoliterate period.[10]

Protoliterate Family IX

> B.00, 03; perforation for stick handle, standard ware

> Figure 8; plates 17:H; 81:G–K

Small bowls, normally convex in profile, although occasionally straight-walled (pl. 81:G) are given a special character by a perforation in the base. Such bowls were once interpreted as funnels or colanders. However, the holes are normally off center and their sides might slant. They were evidently intended for the insertion of wooden handles that made the bowls into ladles. The straight imprints sometimes remaining on the interiors (pls. 17:H; 81:G–I, K–L) suggest that the holes were made by inserting a stick while the bowls were still wet. This process often made the bowls slightly asymmetrical. After firing, sticks must have been reinserted and fastened at the center. Additional security was some-

8. For parallels to plate 80:O–X, see Le Brun 1978b, fig. 32:8 (Susa, Acropole I, Level 18); Le Brun 1978a, fig. 19:1–2 (Susa, Level 17B); Haller 1932, pl. 20 A:w (Warka, Eanna IV); 7N 795 (Nippur, Inanna Temple XVIII–XVII); 7N 787 (Nippur, Inanna Temple XVII–XVI); 7N 769 (Nippur, Inanna Temple XVb); 7N P245 (Nippur, Inanna Temple XV); Sürenhagen 1974/75, pl. 1:4–5 (both are of the less typical proportion 3 and are not included in Sürenhagen's section on mass-produced pottery; Habuba Kabira South). The standard Family VI bowls, ubiquitous at Chogha Mish, do not yet occur in the published Habuba Kabira pottery.

9. For parallels to plate 80:Y, FF, see Le Brun 1978b, fig. 32:7 (Susa, Acropole I, Level 18); Le Brun 1978a, fig. 19:6 (Susa, Acropole I, Level 17B); Miroschedji 1976, fig. 4:15–17 (Susa, Apadana, Trench 1038); Lenzen 1961:28, pl. 16:b (Warka, Eanna VI–V); Nissen 1970, pls. 93:16; 100:5; 104:10 (Warka, K/L Sounding Layers 34, 39–40).

10. For parallels to plate 81:A–F, see Le Brun 1978a, fig. 19:12–15 (Susa, Acropole I, Level 17B); Le Brun 1971, fig. 47:1–3 (Susa, Acropole I, Level 17); Haller 1932, pl. 20 A:x–y (Warka, Eanna IV); 7N 774 (Nippur, Inanna XV); 8N 217 (Nippur, Inanna XII).

times provided by a pair of supplementary holes for lashing the stick handle to the wall (pl. 81:K).[11]

Protoliterate Family X

> B.04; fine ware
>
> Figure 8; plate 81:M

The sole representative of Family X is a bowl with a combination of features that prevent it from being placed in any other family. Although its fine ware and thin walls are shared with the vessels of Family V, its proportions and hemispherical shape set it sharply apart from them.

Protoliterate Family XI

> B.04; with perforations, standard ware
>
> Figure 8; plate 81:N

A colander or strainer in the form of a small bowl of standard ware with many perforations represents a utensil of such an obvious and useful function that it is surprising that only one example appeared. It resembles examples found in Mesopotamia in later contexts.[12]

Protoliterate Family XII

> B–C.04, .20, .22; large loop handle, standard ware
>
> Figure 8; plates 17:D; 81:O–P

Vessels with rounded base, band rim, and large vertical strap handle, though rare, represent a distinctive group in which the body shape varies from slightly conical to cylindrical. Such vessels would have served as ladles or dippers, or possibly, drinking cups. The rather careful execution, including the setting off of the mouth by a rim, suggests that they were tableware rather than simply utilitarian utensils, such as the rougher-made ladles of Subfamily XVIIIa. Specimens of Family XII appear to be uncommon not only at Chogha Mish, but also in the corpus of Protoliterate pottery as a whole.[13]

Protoliterate Family XIII

> B.05; with rims, standard ware
>
> Figure 8; plate 81:Q

Bowls with incurving near the mouth are rare in Protoliterate pottery, but there is one small-sized example with a slightly slanting ledge rim (pl. 81:Q).

Protoliterate Family XIV

> B.07; proportion 5, standard ware
>
> Figure 8; plate 81:R

So far unique is a small tumbler-like vessel with a pouring lip (pl. 81:R). Despite its small size and presumably special function, its paste is grittier than the usual standard ware. At Warka a tumbler of rough fabric, only 4 cm high, has a shape somewhat reminiscent of the Chogha Mish example, although not as splayed at the top and without the latter's concave base or pouring lip.[14] The similarity is not close enough to establish the two examples as representatives of the same type. The pouring-lip tumbler remains as a distinctive but isolated piece.

Protoliterate Family XV

> B.20; flat lip with one knob, flat base, standard ware
>
> Figure 8; plate 81:S–T

Small bowls with low, nearly vertical walls have a small globular knob placed at the lip, thus making them a distinct type.

Protoliterate Family XVI

> B–C.31; proportions normally 0–1, standard or fine ware
>
> Figure 8; 3.998 and plate 81:U–W

Small-sized open rings are rather rare. Examples with diameters of 8–10 cm predominate and are usually of fine ware. The larger specimens of Family XVI are of standard ware (pl. 81:W; fig. 8); their upper lips are somewhat thicker than those of the smaller fragments (pl. 81:U–V). The latter usually have a thickened lower wall with the lower edge varying considerably from a simple flat lip to inbeveled ones, some of which were shaped into interior moldings.[15]

---

11. For parallels to plate 81:G–L, see Le Brun 1978a, fig. 34:8–9 (Susa, Acropole I, Level 17B); Le Brun 1978b, fig. 34:4 (Susa, Acropole I, Level 17); Haller 1932, pl. 20 A:k′, B:d″ (Warka, Eanna IV, III–II); Lenzen 1965, pls. 22:k, 25:e–f, cf. pp. 36–37, 39 for identification as colander or lid (Warka, Eanna III, I); Strommenger 1963, pl. 41:m–n (Warka, Archaic Settlement Trench); Mackay 1931, pl. 66:16–19; cf. p. 248, Type J where, despite a reference to the possible attachment of a stick to form a ladle, the objects are still termed strainers (Jemdet Nasr); Sürenhagen 1974/75, pl. 19:158–59 (Habuba Kabira South).

12. Delougaz 1952, pl. 147:B.032.500 (Early Dynastic II/III, Larsa), B.041.200 (Akkadian), B.042.500a (Akkadian). For contemporary parallels, see Le Brun 1978a, fig. 34:10 (Susa, Acropole I, Level 17B); Le Brun 1971, fig. 45:3 (Susa, Acropole I, Level 17).

13. For parallels to plate 81:O–P, see 7N 793 (Nippur, Inanna XVII–XVI); Mackay 1931, pl. 64:26 (Jemdet Nasr).

14. Lenzen 1961:27–28, pl. 17:f ("Late Jemdet Nasr period to early Early Dynastic").

15. For parallels to figure 8:3.998 and plate 81:U–W, see Alden 1979:276, fig. 54:1–24 (Malyan, Banesh period); Carter 1980, fig. 33:9 (Susa, Ville royale I); Sürenhagen 1974/75, pls. 19:157; 32:1 (Habuba Kabira South); Hoh 1981, fig. 24:1–6 (Hassek Hüyük, Early Bronze Age I); Braidwood and Braidwood 1960:270, fig. 212:5 (Amuq, Phase G, "Earliest Phase").

The Family XVI rings are well paralleled by pottery rings of the Banesh period in Fars, whose originally sharp lips were subsequently much worn. The Banesh rings have been interpreted by John Alden (1979:89–90) as potter's tools. At Chogha Mish likewise some of the fragments have chipped upper edges.

Protoliterate Family XVII

> B.30, .31; inner beveled ledge rim, standard and fine ware

> Figure 8; plate 81:X–Z

Bowls with the greater part of the body conical and tapering toward the mouth are borderline forms between the open and closed vessels (pl. 81:X–Z). The inbeveled ledge rim is diagnostic for this family of rare bowls, although on one example (pl. 81:Y) it is not as well defined as on the two others. Despite its fine ware, careless workmanship made one example (pl. 81:W) relatively shapeless. A closed form (pl. 88:AA) reminiscent of the Family XVII bowls (particularly pl. 81:Z) is quite distinct in its narrower mouth and different type of rim.

Protoliterate Family XVIII

> A.31, B.24; large horizontal loop handle, standard ware

> Figure 8; plates 17:G, M–N; 82:A–G

Large-handled ladles constitute one of the more striking Protoliterate ceramic types. Their upper walls curve somewhat inward, which sharply distinguishes them from the handled cups of Family XII. The bases are flattened or slightly convex. Loop handles, attached to the lip and lower body or base, were huge in proportion to the bodies and, because of their vulnerability, have hardly ever survived intact. The Family XVIII bodies are fairly similar, the only atypical example being the narrow-mouthed example (pl. 82:E),[16] but two distinct types of handles were used. The ladles are, accordingly, divided into two subfamilies, XVIIIa with flat strap handles and XVIIIb with round rod handles. No complete examples of the XVIIIa handles were found. At least three stumps (pl. 82:A–B, D) suggest that the handles projected diagonally in a large and wide loop. One example (pl. 82:C) might have had a more vertical

handle, similar to those of Family XII. Complete examples of Subfamily XVIIIb—one miniature (pl. 17:G), one full size (pl. 82:G), and a semi-complete example (pl. 82:F)—show that the rod handles swept out horizontally from the body in an extravagantly long curve. Despite the apparent impracticability of these fragile handles, fragments indicate that the rod-handled ladles were fairly common. Both types of ladles presumably served specific functions that determined the shape of their handles.[17]

Protoliterate Family XIX

> B.82; convex spoon bowl and strap handle, standard ware

> Figure 8; plates 17:O; 82:H–L

Among the variety of handled utensils of the Protoliterate period the type immediately recognizable as a spoon is reminiscent of modern Chinese soup spoons. The bowls are usually ovoid, but a circular example exists (pl. 82:L). The variations in details occur in the stance and curvature of the handle (pl. 82:H, K). One handle might have been longer than indicated in the drawing (pl. 82:H).[18]

Protoliterate Family XX

> B.20, .22, .23, .24; proportion usually 5–6, flaring lip, standard ware

> Figure 8; plate 83:A–E

Cylindrical vessels with walls tending to taper slightly toward the mouth from a low point of greatest diameter form a recognizable group. However, such beakers constitute the "open" part of a continuous line of shapes, the "closed" part of which is represented by Family LXVI (pl. 89:D–G). There is no sharp break between any two contiguous forms in the series, so that individual specimens are somewhat arbitrarily placed on one side or the other, depending on the extent to which the upper walls taper and the lower body widens (cf. pls. 83:D; 89:E).

In size the beakers range from small to medium. They vary also in the care with which they were shaped and the quality of their surface treatment, often being rough, particularly below the point of greatest diameter.

---

16. The Family XVIII ladles can be taken as round-based .3 shapes, i.e., cones tapering toward the opening, as is clear in two cases (pl. 82:D, F). In some instances (pl. 82:A, E, G) the round base must be considered to comprise about half of the total height of the ladle's container. Because of the latter's wide mouth, it is classified as a cylindrical .2 form rather than a conical .3 form. The miniature ladle (pl. 82:E) could, particularly in view of the presence of a neck, be assigned the shape number A.655.521, except that this would separate it from the group to which it belongs, including a very similar example (pl. 82:A).

17. For parallels to plate 82:A, see Miroschedji 1976:37, fig. 8:8 (Susa, Apadana, Trench 1038); Haller 1932, pl. 19 B:u (Warka, Eanna VI).

18. For parallels to plate 82:H, see Haller 1932, pl. 18 D:i′ (Warka, Eanna VII). For parallels to plate 82:I, see Steve and Gasche 1971, pl. 30:17, for end of handles, see 15, 16 (Susa, 1965 Acropole Sounding, "Jamdat Nasr ancien-Uruk récent"). For parallels to plate 82:K, see Haller 1932, pl. 19 C:a, d (Warka, Eanna VI); Lloyd 1948, fig. 4:43 (Grai Resh, Level II). For parallels to plate 82:L, see Miroschedji 1976:37, fig. 8:7 (Susa, Apadana, Trench 1038).

Protoliterate Family XXI

B–C.00, .02; beveled rim, coarse ware, handmade

Figure 8; plates 17:J–K; 83:F–S

The most frequent shape of the coarse ware is the beveled-rim bowl, which might be considered the hallmark of the Protoliterate period. It was discussed at some length many years ago by Delougaz (1952:39, 127–28); these bowls are always handmade,[19] rough on the outside, wet smoothed on the inside, and bear characteristic finger imprints on the bottom (pl. 17:F, H). The fabric contains a very large proportion of chaff or straw temper, sometimes with grain imprints; and it would appear that the paste from which it was fashioned was softer than the normal clay used on the wheel. In color, there is quite a range from the brown or buff to quite light cream, orange, or pink; some specimens are variegated. In part, at least, the different colors resulted from variations in firing. Some beveled-rim bowls are very well fired and have a metallic ring, while others are very soft, being either under or overfired. Some of a light-colored fabrics are markedly lighter in weight than the normal orange buff, brown, or pinkish bowls.[20]

The beveled rims are always pronounced and usually have a projecting or sharp outer edge. These attributes are important since they distinguish the beveled rims of Family XXI from the more rounded beveled rims of the Family XXIV flower pots, which sometimes have bodies similar to those of the beveled-rim bowls (cf. pl. 83:M, CC).[21]

19. Nissen (1970:137–38) suggested that the beveled-rim bowls were made in molds. The absence of any molds or mold fragments would be explained by the view of Johnson (1973:130–31) that the bowls were shaped in depressions in the ground, a process which Sürenhagen (1974/75:73–74) also considers feasible. Two ceramic specialists, Kalsbeek (1980:3–4, 10 illustrations, fig. 2) and Balfet (1980:76–78), consider the beveled-rim bowls to be handmade. The latter discusses specific reasons against the manufacture in a mold. See also Beale 1978.

20. Compare the weights of similar size, one of 542.25 gr (unnumbered; R21:300 Southeast; diameter 16.5 cm, height 7.0 cm, reddish buff) and one of only 351.70 gr (II-507; E23:Trench XIV; diameter 15.5 cm, height 6.5 cm).

21. Beveled-rim bowls (pl. 83:F–S) are so well known both at Protoliterate sites and as an intrusive Protoliterate element in other cultures that it is almost superfluous to quote parallels. For examples additional to those cited below, see Delougaz 1952, pl. 168:C.002.210 comparanda. For discussions of the type see Nissen 1970:136–38 and Sürenhagen 1974/75:72–75, 91–92, 95, 100–02. For parallels, see Le Brun 1978b, fig. 32:6 (Susa, Acropole I, Level 18); Le Brun 1978a, fig. 20:8 (Susa, Acropole I, Level 17B); Le Brun 1971, fig. 47:8–12 (Susa, Acropole I, Level 17); Steve and Gasche 1971, pls. 29:5; 30:5, 14; 32:1–5 (Susa, Acropole 1965 Sounding, "Jamdat Nasr ancien-Uruk récent"); Miroschedji 1976, fig. 3:1–6 (Susa, Apadana, Trench 1038); Haller 1932:41, pls. 18 A:c, 19 A:t, 19 C:o; Lenzen 1965, pls. 23:m–n; 25:p (Warka, Eanna XII–IV); Nissen 1970, pl.

One feature that was noticed in the 1930s was the markedly standardized size of these bowls (diameter ca. 19–20 cm) throughout the wide geographical area in which they occur. However, at Chogha Mish, their diameter has a much wider range. To be sure, Chogha Mish has two relatively standard sizes, the more common being about 20 cm in diameter and about 8 cm in height, and the other averaging about 14 cm in diameter. Rarer are the extremely large and small variations. The largest beveled-rim bowls from Chogha Mish might reach a diameter of about 30 cm; some of these are shallow in comparison to those of the standard proportions. The smallest beveled-rim bowls measure about 8–10 cm in diameter and are very rare. Rarest of all are the small beveled-rim bowls with conical projections in the interior; only three examples occur among many tens of thousands of beveled-rim bowls and fragments so far recorded (pl. 81:I). The knobbed beveled-rim bowls must have served as lids.[22] Even examples of standard size could be so used, similar to that set into the neck of a large jar (pl. 16:B), or those occasionally placed upside down on top of another beveled-rim bowl.

Unbaked fragments and many wasters (pl. 17:E, L) of beveled-rim bowls were recovered, for example, in the vicinity of small pottery kilns such as R17:210 and Q18:316. Although such finds leave no doubt that beveled-rim bowls were being produced at Chogha Mish, in any case the tremendous quantities of fragments found was in itself sufficient to prove that they were not imported. A count for the third and fourth seasons brings to nearly a quarter of a million the number of beveled-rim bowl sherds recorded. The great majority of complete examples were found in pits and deposits of pottery,

104:7 (Warka, K/L XII Sounding, Layers 42–34); Hansen 1965:202 (Nippur, Inanna Temple XIV–XII); Mackay 1931, pl. 67:22–23 (Jemdet Nasr); Thompson and Mallowan 1933:168 (Nineveh III–IV); Lloyd and Safar 1940, pl. 3, fig. 7:13 (Grai Resh, Level II); Sürenhagen 1974/75, pl. 1:19 (Habuba Kabira South); Kalsbeek 1980:10, fig. 1 (Gebel Aruda); Hoh 1981, fig. 8:9 (Hassek Hüyük, Late Chalcolithic); Palmieri 1981:105, fig. 2:5 (Arslan Tepe VIa); Esin 1974, pl. 107:3 (Keban Dam area, Tepecik, Late Chalcolithic); Weiss and Young 1975:7, fig. 3:3–4 (Godin V); Ghirshman 1938, pl. 90:S.34 (Sialk IV); Majidzadeh 1976:288, fig. 37:1, 3 (Qabrestan Period IV); Sumner 1974:162, fig. 4:d (Malyan, Banesh period); Lamberg-Karlovsky and Tosi 1974, figs. 101, 104:D (Yahya, Period IVc).

22. Parallels do not seem to have been found elsewhere but analogous types, small- or medium-sized bowls with interior projections, do exist in the later part of the Protoliterate period. For examples, see Haller 1932, pl. 20 B:d′ (Warka, Eanna III–II), Lenzen 1961:27, pl. 16:d ("Late Jemdet Nasr-early Early Dynastic"; Warka, Eanna II–I); Mackay 1931, pl. 67:24–27 (Jemdet Nasr).

mostly jumbled in upright, upside down,[23] and sideways positions. In three instances they were found lined up, twice without apparent architectural setting, and once on a ledge along the wall of a room (pl. 15:A–C).

In the light of their prodigious numbers at Chogha Mish, the question of the function of the beveled-rim bowls is no less topical today than in the 1930s when Delougaz denied their ritual character and indicated their fitness for simple dairy-manufacturing purposes (Delougaz 1952:39, 127–28). A colleague from north-western Iran has indicated that even now bowls of similar shape and porosity are used in the province of Gilan, northern Iran, for making a kind of cottage cheese. Women walk along rows of such bowls, pouring a small amount of milk into each in turn until gradually all are filled to the proper height. The bowls are then left to stand until the liquid has filtered through the porous walls while leaving the curds to develop into *mast* (yogurt) or into soft cheese. The great number and ubiquity of beveled-rim bowls can be explained by the fact that, in addition to a specialized use for dairy foods, they were also adaptable for a large variety of household and industrial purposes.[24]

Protoliterate Family XXII

C.00, .02; beveled rim, wheel-made, standard ware

Figure 8; plate 83:T–V

This is a standard type that usually appears—in a simple line drawing—to be similar to a refined beveled-rim bowl. The actual bowls are, however, quite different in ware, make, and small individual details. They are wheel-made of standard ware, with sometimes wheel corrugations on the exterior. One example (pl. 83:U) is

somewhat more irregular than is normal for these pseudo beveled-rim bowls. A notable characteristic is the wheel-made gutter encircling the base on the interior.[25]

Protoliterate Family XXIII

C.00, .02; flat bases, normally blunt lips, coarse to standard ware

Figure 8; plate 83:W–Y

Relatively straight-sided conical bowls, their walls sometimes slightly undulated, appear in both coarse and standard wares and could have served a variety of everyday uses. They are characterized by their simplicity of shape and blunt lips. There is, however, one specialized variant in which a clay partition with some small perforations divides the vessel (pl. 83:X).[26]

Protoliterate Family XXIV

C.00, .02, .08; blunt or beveled lip, string-cut base, wheel-made, body often corrugated, coarse ware

Figure 8; plate 83:Z–DD

The flower pots[27] form a standard type of coarse ware but are by no means so evenly distributed on the site as the beveled-rim bowls. They were ubiquitous in some deposits (K14:Trench VI; R17:203, 208, 210), but in most others they were not found at all. This distribution might eventually be explained by functional differences. There is no chronological distinction between the two types; neither is the ancestor of the other. Al-

---

23. The apparent preponderance of upside-down examples has been explained by Delougaz (1952:127, note 6).

24. It should be noted that one or two examples from Chogha Mish still contain bitumen. There has been much discussion of the possible functions of the beveled-rim bowls, which is summarized by Le Brun (1980:60), who argues for a multiplicity of uses. Nissen (1970:137) suggested that beveled-rim bowls were used to distribute rations to a large part of the population. The application of this theory to data from Khuzestan by Johnson (1973:129–39; 1975:304–05) has been challenged by Beale (1978:9). Sürenhagen (1974/75:73, 101–02) states that the beveled-rim bowls of Habuba Kabira South do not fall into standard size groups and gives some other considerations speaking against the identification of the vessels as ration bowls. Shimabuku, in an extensive study of beveled-rim bowls from Chogha Mish originally scheduled for publication in the *Proceedings of the Fifth Annual Symposium on Archaeological Research in Iran 1980,* demonstrated in detail their great variability in size and the absence of markedly standardized groups. Sürenhagen considers that the use of beveled-rim bowls for making curdled milk (*mast*) or cheese would fit their distri-

bution at Habuba Kabira South and that clogging of the pores might have made their usefulness short-lived and hence explain their frequency. This possibility is rejected by Nissen (1980:95) on the basis of some analyses of sherds made by the chemistry department of the Free University of Berlin.

25. For parallels to plate 83:T–V, see Le Brun 1978a, fig. 19:24–25 (Susa, Acropole I, Level 17B); Lenzen 1965:38, pls. 22:i; 25:i (the occurrence of such a specifically Protoliterate form at the edge of an Early Dynastic foundation is so unexpected as to suggest that the bowl is out of context; Warka, Eanna I); 3N P279 (Nippur, Inanna Temple XVII); Sürenhagen 1974/75, pl. 1:19 (Habuba Kabira South).

26. See Haller 1932, pl. 19 B:g (Warka, Eanna VI) for a generally similar example to plate 83:W–X.

27. The colloquial term, "flower pot," was not originally intended for this type of vessel because of the likelihood of confusion with the use of the term "*Blumentopf*" in the Warka publications. However, Nissen (1970:132–36, 139–42) discussed in detail the applications of the term in the Warka reports and introduced the term "*Grosse Blumentopf*" to correspond to "flower pot." See also Sürenhagen 1974/75:72–73 and Kalsbeek 1980:5, "*pot de fleurs.*" Accordingly, there now seems to be no danger of confusion.

though fully comparable in ware to the beveled-rim bowls, the cut bases of the flower pots prove them to be wheel-made. They might have spiral wheel marks on the base of the interior. Their flaring sides are usually rather corrugated and their lips rounded or beveled. The difference between the latter and the standard beveled rims of Family XXI has been noted above. The flower pots do not range nearly as much in size as the beveled-rim bowls, their average diameter being about 20 cm. Their shapes are frequently quite irregular. Often finger imprints appear near the base on the exterior, and they are usually wet-smoothed.[28]

Two vessels from the West Area resemble the flower pots of Family XXIV in shape except that their proportions are more elongated and their lips more flaring (pl. 83:EE). Their ware is unusually dense even though it seems to have only vegetal tempering. Corrugations on the exterior and interior show that the vessels were wheel-made. They remain as isolated specimens not assigned to a family.

Protoliterate Family XXV

C.00, .03, .05; proportion 3, predominantly blunt
lips, coarse ware, rough surface

Figure 8; plate 84:A–C

Bowls of simple straight- or convex-sided shape are made into a clearly recognizable class by their coarse ware and crude finish. Also characteristic for the family are the irregularity of the walls and the blunt lips. One example has a slight disc base (pl. 84:C).

Protoliterate Family XXVI

C.01, .03, .06; shallow, proportion 1, standard ware

Figure 8; plate 84:D–E

Unlike the three preceding families, Family XXVI does not consist of a substantial group of distinctive vessels. It includes assorted examples of shallow bowls, some of them superficially reminiscent in profile to the small trays (pl. 18:B–C).

Protoliterate Family XXVII

C.03; upper body developed into slight rim, standard ware

Figure 8; plate 84:F–G

Some flat-based bowls with flaring convex walls have rather slight, but distinctive rims and an exterior fluting that sets off the mouth from the body proper. Such bowls seem to be rare.[29]

Protoliterate Family XXVIII

C.03, .04; rimless, with blunt lip only, standard ware

Figure 8; plate 84:H–N

Flat-based, flaring bowls, for the most part with fairly deep proportions (2), although in general shape similar to those of Family XXVII, are distinguished by their blunt lips. The Family XXVIII vessels constitute a standard class of Protoliterate bowls.[30]

Protoliterate Family XXIX

C.03, .04; band rims, standard ware

Figure 8; plate 84:O–P

In body shape those bowls are similar to those of the preceding family, but they are distinguished as a separate group by their band rims. Exactly the same type of rim appears on similarly shaped bowls, which were probably the prototypes for the less expensive imitation in pottery.[31]

Protoliterate Family XXX

C.03, .04; triangular sloping rim, standard ware

Figure 8; plates 18:A; 84:Q–S

Triangular outward-sloping, slightly overhanging rims set some bowls apart from the band-rim bowls

28. For parallels to plates 17:P; 83:Z–DD, see Le Brun 1978a, fig. 21:1–11 (Susa, Acropole I, Level 17B); Le Brun 1971, fig. 47:4–5 (Susa, Acropole I, Level 17); Steve and Gasche 1971, pl. 31:5–7 (Susa, 1965 Acropole Sounding "Jamdat Nasr ancien-Uruk récent"); Haller 1932, pls. 19 A:w′, B:h, D:y (Warka, Eanna V); 7N 773 (Nippur, Inanna Temple XVa); 7N 775 (Nippur, Inanna Temple XVb); de Genouillac et al. 1934, pl. 8:4386, 4244 (Tello); Sürenhagen 1974/75, pls. 1:20–21; 2:24 (Habuba Kabira South); Kalsbeek 1980:11, fig. 3 (Gebel Aruda); Hoh 1981, fig. 8:7 (Hassek Hüyük, Late Chalcolithic/Early Bronze Age I); Palmieri 1973:160, fig. 65:3, 5–6, 10, 12 (Arslan Tepe VIa); Young 1969, fig. 9:14 (Godin V).

29. For parallels to plate 84:F–G, see Haller 1932, pl. 18 D:e (Warka, Eanna VII); Sürenhagen 1974–75, pls. 1:15–16; 20:28–31 (some examples have more slender and slanting rims; Habuba Kabira South).

30. For parallels to plate 84:I–M, see Le Brun 1978b, fig. 32:5 (Susa, Acropole I Sounding, Level 18); Le Brun 1978a, fig. 22:12 (Susa, Acropole I Sounding, Level 17B); Le Brun 1971, fig. 45:4, 13–14; idem 1978b, fig. 34:6 (Susa, Acropole I Sounding, Level 17); Steve and Gasche 1971, pl. 30:38 (Susa, Acropole 1965 Sounding, "Jamdat Nasr ancien-Uruk récent"); Miroschedji 1976, fig. 4:4 (Susa, Apadana, Trench 1038); Haller 1932, pl. 18 A:b (Warka, Eanna XII); Nissen 1970, pl. 100:10 (Warka, K/L XII Sounding, Layer 40). For a parallel to plate 84:N, see Steve and Gasche 1971, pl. 32:9 (Susa, Acropole 1965 Sounding, "Jamdat Nasr ancien-Uruk récent").

31. For parallels to plate 84:P, see Miroschedji 1976, fig. 4:2–3 (Susa, Apadana, Trench 1038); Nissen 1970, pl. 88:9 (Warka, K/L XII Sounding, Layer 38); Hoh 1981, fig. 12:2–3 (Hassek Hüyük, Early Bronze Age I).

(e.g., pl. 84:P) to which the group is closely allied. The vessels of Family XXX do not seem to have been very frequent.[32]

Protoliterate Family XXXI

C.05; standard ware

Figure 8; plate 84:T–X

Bowls with walls incurving near the mouth are rare. Nonetheless, we can distinguish three subfamilies. The first, Subfamily XXXIa, consists of the basic family type, a bowl without any accessories save for a rim (pl. 84:T). In Subfamily XXXIb a strap handle has been added (pl. 84:U–W), a feature also found on the more developed, necked bowls of Family XXXVII; the line of demarcation between Subfamilies XXXIa and b is quite slight. The third, Subfamily XXXIc, is characterized by the addition of a straight spout to the bowl and is represented so far by only one example (pl. 84:X).[33]

Protoliterate Family XXXII

C–D.07; flaring rim, standard ware

Figure 8; plate 84:Y–Z

Bowls with a .07 profile, which distinguishes them from usually larger basins of Family XLV, are accommodated in Family XXXII. It is not a populous group. One example was found in the same locus and depth as a funnel (pl. 85:GG). Another, larger example has a notched rim (pl. 84:Z).

Protoliterate Family XXXIII

C.11; ledge rim with incised decoration, standard ware

Figure 8; plate 85:A–C

Bowls closely defined by their angled profile and thickened ledge rim with simple incised decoration, such as crosshatching, constitute Family XXXIII. In one case the rim has a row of very shallow oval depressions, similar to finger imprints, each crossed by three or four short incised lines (pl. 85:B). These bowls are relatively thick walled and their surfaces, particularly the lower

exterior, might be rather roughly finished. On one example the root of a spout has been preserved (pl. 85:A).[34]

Protoliterate Family XXXIV

C–D.11; channeled or slightly beveled lip, trough spout, standard to fine ware

Figure 9; plates 18:E; 85:D–M

Cylindrical spouts appear in Subfamily XXXIc and Family XXXIII as isolated examples, but in Family XXXIV trough spouts, usually with a basal pierced lug, are one of the main defining characteristics of a specific type of vessel. They were added to the vertical walls of carinated bowls, flush with the lips. The latter are normally slightly channeled or cut and either horizontal or slightly out-beveled. So diagnostic is the combination of carinated body, sharply profiled lip, and trough spout that wall or lip sherds can be identified as belonging to this family even though the spouts themselves are not preserved; spouts could safely be restored on four examples (pl. 85:I, K–M). Separate spouts are also attributable to this group, since trough spouts are almost completely unknown otherwise. Ring bases appear to have been characteristic. The average diameter is about 24 cm, but occasionally larger (pl. 85:M) or smaller (pl. 85:D) examples occur. Their highly differentiated shape, and usually, smooth finish make the trough spouted bowls into one of the more outstanding families of relatively frequent Protoliterate open vessels.[35]

Protoliterate Family XXXV

C.12; standard ware

Figure 9; plate 85:N–P

Only a few individual bowls of slightly carinated shapes are contained in this family. Their upper walls flare out instead of being almost vertical as in Family XXXIV.[36]

---

32. For parallels to plate 84:Q, see Le Brun 1978a, fig. 22:4 (Susa, Acropole I Sounding, Level 17B); Miroschedji 1976, fig. 4:1 (Susa, Apadana, Trench 1038); Steve and Gasche 1971, pl. 32:7 (Susa, Acropole 1965 Sounding, "Jamdat Nasr ancien-Uruk récent" phase); Nissen 1970, pls. 93:27; 99:114 (Warka, K/L XII Sounding, Layer 39); Hoh 1981, fig. 11:7–8 (chaff-tempered; Hassek Hüyük, Late Chalcolithic); Habuba Kabira South (Sürenhagen 1974/75, pl. 20:39). For a closely related form to plate 82:R, see 7N P289 (shallower; Nippur, Inanna Temple XVII).

33. For parallels to plate 84:X, see Miroschedji 1976, fig. 7:2 (Susa, Apadana, Trench 1038); Haller 1932, pl. 19 A:h′ (pl. 19 A:g′ is a closely related form; Warka Eanna VI).

34. For a parallel to plate 85:A, see Le Brun 1978a, fig. 23:12 (Susa, Acropole I, Level 17B); 7N P232 and 7N P236 (Nippur, Inanna Temple XIV). For forms related to plate 85:A–B, see Le Brun 1978a, fig. 22:5, 7 (Susa, Acropole I, Level 17B); Le Brun 1971, fig. 46:13 (Susa, Acropole I, Level 17); idem 1978b, fig. 34:5 (Susa, Acropole I, Level 17); Sürenhagen 1974/75, pl. 20:18 (Habuba Kabira South).

35. For parallels to plate 85:E–H, J, see Haller 1932, pl. 19 D:f (atypical—very shallow, no lug, red ware; Warka Eanna VI); 7N P315, 7N 808, Hansen 1965:202, fig. 3 (Nippur, Inanna Temple XX, XIX). For parallels to plate 85:J, M, see Haller 1932, pl. 19 A:u′ (Warka, Eanna VI). For parallels to plate 85:M, see 7N P292, 7N P283 (Nippur, Inanna Temple XVII–XVII, XVIII).

36. For parallels to plate 85:O, see Miroschedji 1976, fig. 4:10 (different proportions; Susa, Apadana, Trench 1038).

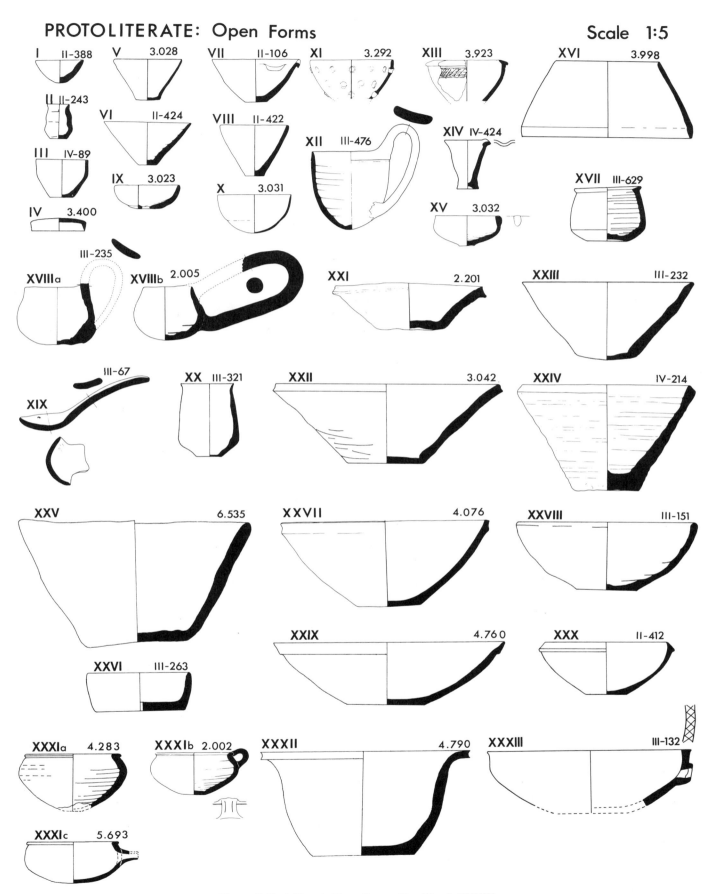

Figure 8. Protoliterate Open Forms, Families I–XXXIII

Table 1. Open Vessels, Similar to Chogha Mish Protoliterate Families IV–XXXIc, Present at Other Sites

	IV	V	VI	VII	VIII	IX	XI	XII	XVI	XVIIIa	XIX	XXI	XXII	XXIII	XXIV	XXVII	XXVIII	XXIX	XXX	XXXIc
SUSA																				
Acropole 1965																				
"Jamdat Nasr récent"	—	—	—	—	—	—	—	—	—	—	—	×	—	—	—	—	—	—	—	—
"Jamdat Nasr ancien-Uruk récent"	—	—	—	—	—	—	—	—	—	—	×	×	—	—	×	—	×	—	×	—
Apadana Trench 1038	—	—	—	×	—	—	—	—	—	×	×	×	—	—	—	—	—	×	×	—
Acropole I																				
17	—	—	—	—	×	×	×	—	—	—	—	×	—	×	×	—	×	—	—	—
17B	—	×	×	×	×	×	—	—	—	—	×	×	×	×	—	×	×	—	—	×
18	—	—	×	×	—	—	—	—	—	—	—	×	—	—	—	—	×	—	—	—
WARKA																				
Md XV4: Archaic Settlement "Jemdet Nasr"	×	—	—	—	×	—	—	—	—	—	—	—	—	—	—	—	—	—	—	—
K/L XII Sounding "Spät-Uruk"	×	—	×	×	—	—	—	—	—	—	—	×	—	—	×	—	×	×	×	—
Eanna Precinct and Test Pit																				
III–II	—	—	—	—	×	—	—	—	—	—	—	—	—	—	—	—	—	—	—	—
IV	—	—	×	—	×	×	—	—	—	—	—	×	—	—	×	—	—	—	—	—
V	—	—	—	×	—	—	—	—	—	—	—	×	—	—	×	—	—	—	—	—
VI	×	—	—	×	—	—	—	—	×	×	×	×	—	—	—	—	—	—	—	×
VII	—	—	—	×	—	—	—	—	—	—	×	×	—	—	—	×	—	—	—	—
IX–VIII	—	—	—	—	—	—	—	—	—	—	—	×	—	—	—	—	—	—	—	—
XII	—	—	—	—	—	—	—	—	—	—	—	×	—	—	—	—	×	—	—	—
NIPPUR																				
Inanna Temple																				
XII	—	—	—	—	—	×	—	—	—	—	—	×	—	—	—	—	—	—	—	—
XIII	—	—	—	—	—	—	—	—	—	—	—	×	—	—	—	—	—	—	—	—
XIV	×	—	—	—	—	—	—	—	—	—	—	×	—	×	—	—	—	—	—	—
XV	—	—	×	—	—	×	—	—	—	—	—	×	—	—	×	—	—	—	—	—
XVI	—	—	×	—	—	—	—	×	—	—	—	×	—	—	—	—	—	—	—	—
XVII	—	—	×	—	—	—	—	—	—	—	—	×	×	—	—	—	—	×	—	—
XVIII	—	—	—	—	—	—	—	—	—	—	—	×	—	—	—	—	—	—	—	—
XIX	×	—	—	—	—	—	—	—	—	—	—	×	—	—	—	—	—	—	—	—
XX	—	—	×	—	—	—	—	—	—	—	—	×	—	—	—	—	—	—	—	—
TELLO	—	—	×	—	—	—	—	—	—	—	—	×	—	—	×	—	—	—	—	—
JEMDET NASR	×	—	—	—	×	—	—	—	—	—	—	—	—	—	—	—	—	—	—	—
KHAFAJAH Protoliterate c–d	—	—	—	—	—	—	—	—	—	—	—	×	—	—	—	—	—	—	—	—
NINEVEH																				
IV	×	—	—	—	—	—	—	—	—	—	—	×	—	—	—	—	—	—	—	—
III	—	—	—	—	—	—	—	—	—	—	—	×	—	—	—	—	—	—	—	—
GRAI RESH II	—	—	—	—	—	—	—	—	—	—	×	×	—	—	—	—	—	—	—	—
HABUBA KABIRA SOUTH	—	×	×	—	×	—	—	—	×	—	—	×	×	×	×	×	—	—	×	—
GEBEL ARUDA	—	—	—	—	—	—	—	—	—	—	—	×	—	—	—	—	—	—	—	—
HASSEK HÜYÜK																				
Early Bronze Age I	—	—	—	—	—	—	—	×	—	—	—	—	—	—	—	—	—	×	—	—
Late Chalcolithic	—	—	—	—	—	—	—	—	—	—	—	×	—	—	×	—	—	—	×	—
ARSLAN TEPE VIa	—	—	—	—	—	—	—	—	—	—	—	×	—	—	×	—	—	—	—	—
TEPECIK (KEBAN)																				
Late Chalcolithic	—	—	—	—	—	—	—	—	—	—	—	×	—	—	—	—	—	—	—	—
GODIN V	—	—	—	—	—	—	—	—	—	—	—	×	—	—	×	—	—	—	—	—
GIYAN Surface Collection	—	—	—	—	—	—	—	—	—	—	—	×	—	—	—	—	—	—	—	—
SIALK IV	—	—	—	—	—	—	—	—	—	—	—	×	—	—	—	—	—	—	—	—
QABRESTAN IV	—	—	—	—	—	—	—	—	—	—	—	×	—	—	—	—	—	—	—	—
MALYAN Banesh Period	—	—	—	—	—	—	—	—	×	—	—	×	—	—	—	—	—	—	—	—
YAHYA IVc	—	—	—	—	—	—	—	—	—	—	—	×	—	—	—	—	—	—	—	—

Protoliterate Family XXXVI

C.14, .17; standard ware

Figure 9; plate 85:Q–R

Bowls with body walls varying in thickness so as to produce a carination on the exterior while still curving smoothly on the interior are assigned to Family XXXVI. They are very rare. One example has a lump of clay at the lip reminiscent of similar appliqués on other bowls (cf. pl. 81:R–T).[37]

Protoliterate Family XXXVII

C.17; standard ware

Figure 9; plate 85:S–T

The bowls of Family XXXVII, though apparently of squatter proportions, have exterior profiles similar to those of the Family XXXVI bowls. However, a basic difference between the two families is in the formation of the carinations; it is created in the preceding family merely by a thickening of the body wall, but in Family XXXVI by the curvature of the entire wall. Although the rare examples of Family XXXVI belong without doubt among the open forms, such as the strap-handles, one bowl (pl. 85:T) is intermediate between open forms such as the strap-handled bowls of Subfamily XXXIb (pl. 84:U–W) and closed ones such as the strap-handled jars of Subfamily LXXXVIIa (pl. 95:E). Instead of classifying the bowl with intermediate form (pl. 85:T) as a carinated bowl, its two parts could be considered as a flaring neck and a markedly squat ovoid body.[38]

Protoliterate Family XXXVIII

C.20; coarse to standard ware

Figure 9; plate 85:U–V

Relatively straight-sided cylindrical vessels appear predominantly as trays, either oval or varying from round to oval. In addition, however, there occur a few examples of straight-sided cylindrical vessels that cannot be classified as trays and are subsumed under Family XXXVIII.

Protoliterate Family XXXIX

B–C.20; usually proportions 4 and 5; ledge rim projecting to the exterior, at least slightly, flat base; standard ware

Figure 9; plates 18:F; 85:W–AA

Characteristics for the various shapes included here are the practically vertical stance of the upper walls, the carination, which is frequently rather round, and the rim (pl. 85:Y), which is somewhat reminiscent of Protoliterate beakers (pl. 83:B), but other examples with vertical walls, rims, and squatter proportions sharply distinguish this family. Two atypically squat examples are included (pl. 85:W–X); the smaller of these has a thickened out-beveled rim rather than an overhanging ledge rim.

Protoliterate Family XL

C.20, .22, .24, atypical .03; proportion 4, standard ware

Figure 9; plate 85:BB–FF

Rather deep vessels with thick and predominantly vertical walls can be separated as a group by the treatment of their mouths. These might be formed by ledge rims or flat lips, sometimes channeled, or beveled. The characteristic features of the family are the small holes or socket-like clay bosses spaced at intervals around the mouth. These do not seem to be decorative, but their function remains unexplained. They are absent on one vessel (pl. 85:FF) that is also atypically small.[39]

Protoliterate Family XLI

C.22; ledge rim, open base, standard ware

Figure 9; plate 85:GG–HH

Two fairly deep vessels with bases specialized for use with liquids so far remain unique. The more complete example (pl. 85:HH) has a funnel base. What little exists of the base of one example (pl. 85:GG) preserves part of what was apparently a perforation of small diameter. As indicated in the reconstruction, the base probably had several perforations making the utensil into a sieve or colander. The vessels were found fairly close together in the West Area where a Parthian burial (H15:407) had been dug into debris containing Protoliterate pottery. The disturbed character of the findspot raises the question of a late date for these unusual vessels. This seems unlikely, however, since their fragments were not found among the Parthian grave goods and since their fabric falls within the normal range of the Protoliterate standard ware.

37. For a form similar to plate 85:R, see Sürenhagen 1974/75, pls. 1:10; 21:63 (a form that in exterior shape and proportion is an excellent parallel but nonetheless belongs with Family XXXVII because of its structure; Habuba Kabira South).

38. For a parallel to plate 83:S, see ibid., pl. 21:62 (Habuba Kabira South).

39. For a parallel to plate 85:BB–EE, see Haller 1932, pl. 19 A:v′ (Warka, Eanna VI). For a parallel to plate 85:DD, see de Genouillac et al. 1934, pl. 19:1 (Tello).

Protoliterate Family XLII

C.20, .22, .24; blunt lip; exterior with band of scrabbled or incised decoration near lip, below, reserve slip or scraped, standard ware

Figure 9; plates 28:A–C; 86:A–G

This group is so distinctive that even small sherds from lips or upper bodies can be identified. Proportions (4) are fairly high. The upper walls are nearly vertical; lower down the sides taper inward to a flat base. At the top the walls end in plain blunt lips. The exterior treatment is elaborate. Below a horizontal lip band, usually filled with a scrabbled wavy line, the upright portion of the body is covered by reserve slip or by pare or scrape marks that simulate reserve slip.[40]

Protoliterate Family XLIII

C.23; open ends, standard ware

Figure 9; plate 86:H

Uncommon is the open stand, flaring at both ends but with the presumed lower lip blunt and the other one somewhat beveled.[41]

Protoliterate Family XLIV

C.80, .83; shallow, oval, almost vertical or slightly flaring walls, thick blunt or cut lip, standard ware

Figure 9; plates 18:B–C, G–H; 86:I–J

A distinctive class of tray is distinguished from the ordinary oval trays (Family XLVI) by its standard ware and medium size (averaging about 20 cm in length) as well as by the absence of rims and the presence on a number of examples of specialized features. The latter are the heavily sanded floor (pl. 18:G), the incised lip patterns (pls. 18:G–H; 86:J), and the miniature bowl mounted on the lip (pls. 18:B, G; 86:J).[42] A narrow tray with two pairs of beak lugs is unique (pl. 86:I). In general, the trays of this family are much rarer than the large oval ones of Family XLVI.

Protoliterate Family XLV

C–D.01, .80; low wall, simple thickened rim with notched lip, standard to coarse ware

Figure 9; plate 86:K–M

Similar to the preceding group, this family consists of rare and specialized low-walled trays. They are set off from the common trays of Family XLVI by rather better ware and by the addition of notched lips, presumably in pairs, as in the case of the closed vessels of Family LXXVI. No example is complete. The largest fragment (pl. 86:M) appears to have belonged to a circular tray, but in view of the many irregularities observable in the complete or partly complete trays of other families this is not altogether certain. On the whole, the low-walled trays appear to have been oval. The smallest example (pl. 86:K) is definitely oval; in view of its size and sanded floor, it would have been included among the small oval trays of Family IV if it had not possessed a notched lip.

Protoliterate Family XLVI

D.80; proportion 0, coarse ware

Figure 9; plate 86:N–BB

Large handmade trays of coarse ware are one of the more typical and widespread components of Protoliterate ceramics. Though often represented only by small fragments, one diagnostic feature almost always discernible is the height of the walls, which are either low, about 6–7 cm or somewhat higher, up to about 12 cm. The wall height is correlated with other characteristics, as is shown by larger fragments or complete examples and is thus an extremely useful diagnostic feature for distinguishing between the two major families of trays, low walled and high walled respectively. The low walls always end in some types of thickening so that such trays can be divided into several subgroups according to their rim type: XLVIa ledge (pl. 86:N–P), XLVIb club (pl. 86:Q–R), XLVIc incurved (pl. 86:T–W), XLVId thickened (pl. 86:X–Z), XLVIe guttered (pl. 86:AA), and XLVIf exterior rounded (pl. 86:S, BB). The trays are so shallow on some examples (pl. 86:S, AA–BB) that no proper walls exist; the sides are formed by the rims. In addition to the presence of rims, another outstanding characteristic of the low-walled trays is their oval shapes.[43]

---

40. For parallels to plate 86:A–E, see Le Brun 1978a, fig. 23:2, 11, 14 (Susa, Acropole I Sounding, Level 17B); Le Brun 1971, fig. 46:11 (Susa, Acropole I Sounding, Level 17); 7N P267b (Nippur, Inanna Temple XVI). For a parallel to plate 86:G, see Sürenhagen 1974/75, pl. 39:88 (Habuba Kabira South).

41. For a parallel to plate 86:H, see ibid., pl. 9:153 (Habuba Kabira South).

42. For parallels to plate 18:H, see Le Brun 1971, fig. 46:5 (Susa, Acropole I, Level 17); Nissen 1970, pl. 103:1 (Warka, K/L XII Sounding, Layer 42); 7N 784 (Nippur, Inanna Temple XVII–XVI). For parallels to pls. 18:B, G and 86:J, see Le Brun 1971, fig. 46:6 (Susa, Acropole I, Level 17); de Genouillac et al. 1934, pl. 22:3 (Tello); Sürenhagen 1974/75, pl. 3:45, 47 (Habuba Kabira South).

43. For parallels to plate 86:N–P, see Haller 1932, pl. 19 A:h′ (Warka, Eanna VI); Steve and Gasche 1971, pl. 32:55 (Susa, Acropole 1965 Sounding, "Jamdat Nasr ancien-Uruk récent"). For parallels to plate 86:Q–R, see ibid. pl. 32:54 (Susa, Acropole 1965 Sounding, "Jamdat Nasr ancien-Uruk récent"); Nissen 1970, pl. 92:11 (Warka, K/L XII Sounding Layer 39); Sürenhagen 1974/75, pl. 23:11 (Habuba Kabira South); Young 1969, fig. 9:1–2 (Godin V). For parallels to plate 86:T–W, see Steve and Gasche 1971, pl. 32:52 (Susa,

Protoliterate Family XLVII

> D.01, .03, .08, .23, .80; proportion 1, coarse ware

> Figure 9; plate 86:CC–HH

The high-walled trays have simple blunt or cut lips in contrast to the variety of rims characteristic for the low-walled trays. Another major distinction between these two big groups is that the high-walled trays were for the most part round in shape, as indicated by several complete and semi-complete examples. However, it would be rash to claim that all of them were round. There is at least one fragment from an oval example (2.255; P18:203). Often it is impossible to determine with certainty whether small sections of irregular lips originally belonged to round or to oval forms. This is not surprising in view of the fact that the large trays were handmade and rough in execution. Some of the round trays were as large as 77 cm in diameter (pl. 86:GG).

The high-walled trays can be subdivided into three subfamilies: XLVIIa with blunt lips (pl. 86:CC–DD, GG);[44] XLVIIb with flattened lips (pl. 86:EE–FF); and XLVIIc with an internal divider (pl. 86:HH). In contrast to the other groups, the latter are very rare.

The trays could have served a variety of purposes even though they are simple primitive forms. Round

---

Acropole 1965 Sounding, "Jamdat Nasr ancien-Uruk récent"); Miroschedji 1976, figs. 3:11–13, 8:1 (Susa, Apadana, Trench 1038); Haller 1932, pl. 19 A:g′ (Warka, Eanna VI); Nissen 1970, pls. 85:1; 92: 12 (Warka, K/L XII Sounding, Levels 36, 39); Hansen 1965:202, fig. 8 (Nippur, Inanna Temple XX–XVII); 7N P174 (Nippur, Inanna Temple XII). For parallels to plate 86:X–Z, see Le Brun 1978a, fig. 23:10 (Susa, Acropole I, Level 17B); Le Brun 1971, fig. 46:8 (Susa, Acropole I, Level 17); Steve and Gasche 1971, pl. 32:43–44, 48–51 (Susa, Acropole 1965 Sounding, "Jamdat Nasr ancien-Uruk récent"); Miroschedji 1976, figs. 3:14, 8:2 (Susa, Apadana, Trench 1038); Haller 1932, pl. 18 D:c (Warka, Eanna VII); Nissen 1970, pl. 92:11–15 (11 is intermediate between pl. 86:Q–R and X–Z; Warka, K/L XII Trench, Layer 39); Alden 1979:255, fig. 33:1, 5–7, 11, 13–14, 17, 22, 24, 28, 30; Sumner 1974:163, fig. 5:f (Malyan, Banesh period). For a parallel to plate 86:Z, see 7N P286 (Nippur, Inanna Temple XVII). For similar, but flat-lipped examples, to plate 86:AA, see Steve and Gasche 1971, pl. 32:45–47 (Susa, Acropole 1965 Sounding, "Jamdat-Nasr ancien-Uruk récent"); Haller 1932, pl. 18 D:b (Warka, Eanna VII). For parallels to plate 86:S, BB, see Le Brun 1978a, fig. 23:9 (Susa, Acropole I, Level 17B); Miroschedji 1976, fig. 3:10 (Susa, Apadana, Trench 1038); Haller 1932, pl. 19 A:e′–f′ (Warka, Eanna VI).

44. For parallels to plate 86:CC–DD, see Nissen 1970, pls. 83:6 and 99:112 (Warka, K/L XII Sounding Layers 34, 39); Alden 1979:257, fig. 35:10–11 (Malyan, Banesh period); Miroschedji 1976, fig. 3:8 (Susa, Apadana, Trench 1038). For parallels to plate 86:EE–FF, see ibid. fig. 3:9 (Susa, Apadana, Trench 1038); Haller 1932, pl. 19 A:c′ (Warka, Eanna VI); Sürenhagen 1974/75, pl. 23:13 (Habuba Kabira South); Alden 1979:257, fig. 35:3–8, 12–13 (Malyan, Banesh period).

---

trays of similar shape are still made today in the vicinity of al-Hiba in southern Mesopotamia and used as unfired, sun-dried utensils.[45]

Protoliterate Family XLVIII

> D.31; proportions 0–1, open top and bottom, standard ware

> Figure 9; plate 86:II–KK

Fragments with horizontal or beveled ledge rims at both top and bottom can be restored as thick pottery rings. Those of about 40 cm in diameter and 10 cm in height might well have been pot stands, but others seem too large and low to have served such a purpose. For instance, the widest and shallowest example is about 65 cm in diameter and only 7.5 cm in height (pl. 86:JJ). Thus, the use of at least the larger Family XLVIII rings remains uncertain even though these specialized and standardized objects must have been made for a specific purpose.[46]

Protoliterate Family XLIX

> C–D.01, .03, .04; proportions 2–3, ledge rim, fairly wide base, standard ware

> Figure 9; plate 87:A–E

The basins are a standard and practical Protoliterate utensil, sometimes attaining a diameter of 40 cm or more. They are fairly deep with either straight or convex walls. The surfaces vary from smooth to somewhat rough. With their large flat bases and overhanging ledge rims, these basins could have been mixing vessels for the preparation of food or have been used in a variety of domestic or craft procedures.[47]

Protoliterate Family L

> D.03; standard ware

> Figure 9; plate 87:F

A large bowl with widely flaring convex walls does not fall within any of the standard families of large open

---

45. See Ochsenschlager 1973, for illustrations of *sahans*; these mud trays have bases spreading out similar to those from Chogha Mish (pl. 86:CC–EE).

46. For parallels to plate 86:II–KK, see Algaze 1990, pls. 22:I (grit-tempered), 34:C (straw-tempered) (Kurban Höyük, Area A, Period VI); cf. also a related but not identical chaff-tempered example from Habuba Kabira South (Sürenhagen 1974/75, pl. 32 H:2).

47. For a similar form to plate 87:A–B, combined with incised rim decoration analogous to that of Family XXXIII, see Alden 1979:259, fig. 37:9 (Malyan, Banesh period). For parallels to plate 87:D–E, see Nissen 1970, pl. 100:7 (Warka, K/L XII Sounding, Layer 40); 7N P304 (Nippur, Inanna Temple XIX); Thompson and Mallowan 1933, pl. 49:42 and probably 3 (Nineveh III8).

vessels. It remains so far the only example of Family L, which is defined to accommodate any large splaying bowls with simple or thickened lips.

Protoliterate Family LI

D.04; standard ware

Figure 9; plate 87:G

As in the case of the preceding group, Family LI was created to provide a niche for a single unusual specimen, a large deep bowl with an interior beveled rim.

Protoliterate Family LII

D.22, .24; ledge rim, normally band of imprinted decorations, coarse to standard ware

Figure 9; plates 18:J; 87:H–I

The deep vats, which form one of the major groups of the size D open forms, were probably standard storage utensils. Those made of coarse ware often contain a larger proportion of sand and grit than of vegetal temper. Some have fairly cylindrical upper bodies (pl. 18:J); others are barrel-shaped (pl. 87:H–I). The rims are wide flat ledges, usually sloping slightly downward and one is set off from the body by plastic imprinted bands. Though many specimens are represented only by small fragments, the complete vessel (III-515; pl. 18:J) indicates the proportions of such vats and the character of the base. Such thick irregularly flat bases, once one of them has been seen as part of a complete vat, can be identified when they appear in isolated fragments. Occasionally a vat occurs in a smaller size and with reserve slip in addition to the plastic band (pl. 87:H).[48]

Protoliterate Family LIII

D.31; open both ends, standard ware

Figure 9; plate 87:J

A pottery object whose unique character sets it apart in a family of its own has an asymmetrical body and is open at the top and the base. Its use is uncertain; although it is somewhat reminiscent of the far more elaborate elements used to top vertical drains in later periods,[49] Chogha Mish has provided no evidence for the existence of vertical drains in the Protoliterate period.

Protoliterate Family LIV

E.22; open both ends, standard ware

Figure 9; plate 87:K

Medium-sized pipes of standard ware and elongated barrel shape are rare in contrast to the standard drain pipes of the following family.

Protoliterate Family LV

E.24; open both ends, coarse ware

Figure 9; plate 12:C, E

Drain pipes of coarse ware with one wider than the other so that they could be laid in overlapping fashion were common in this family. The drains constructed of pipes are discussed in *Chapter 3*.[50]

Protoliterate Family LVI

E.80; trough-shaped, usually holes for attachment at one end, coarse ware

Figure 9; plate 87:L–N

Spouts are common but often appear only as relatively small sherds that resemble those of trays until the straightness of the lips is noticed. When complete, the larger spouts were probably some 75 cm long and about 18 cm wide. Their sides slope down at the ends. One end might have holes through which wooden or perhaps terra-cotta spikes were presumably rammed to hold the spouts in place on the roof. It is possible that such objects were sometimes sunk into the ground to form channels useful for household or other purposes.[51]

The families of Protoliterate open vessels reviewed above vary greatly in their coherency and populousness. Many of the families have been defined on the basis of specific features, but some consist of only one individual type, while others consist of a cluster of related types. Only a few of the families are so ubiquitous as to be represented in practically every group, large or small, of Protoliterate pottery. About one-third of the families consist of specific and fairly common pottery types, and another one-third of specific but less common varieties. The remainder of the families are defined on the basis of a single specimen or contain assortments of pottery types that are in general similar but not sufficiently differentiated in shape to constitute coherent groups. Family numbers LVII–LIX have been reserved for additional types of open vessel; the families of closed vessels begin with number LX.

---

48. For parallels to plates 18:J and 87:H–I, see Miroschedji 1976, fig. 5:11–13 (Susa, Apadana, Trench 1038); probably 7N P309 (Nippur, Inanna Temple XIX); Sürenhagen 1974/75, pl. 24:3 (Habuba Kabira South). All parallels are without finger impressed molding.

49. For example, see Delougaz 1952:119; pl. 198:E.313.040 (Isin-Larsa period).

50. For a parallel to plates 12:C, E, and 87:K, see Ludwig 1980, fig. 6 (Habuba Kabira South).

51. For parallels to plate 87:L–N, see Le Brun 1978a, fig. 34:13 (Susa, Acropole I, Level 17B); Steve and Gasche 1971, pl. 29:23 (Susa, Acropole 1965 Sounding, "Jamdat-Nasr ancien-Uruk récent"); Ludwig 1980, fig. 6 (Habuba Kabira South); Alden 1979:257, fig. 35:14 (Malyan, Banesh period).

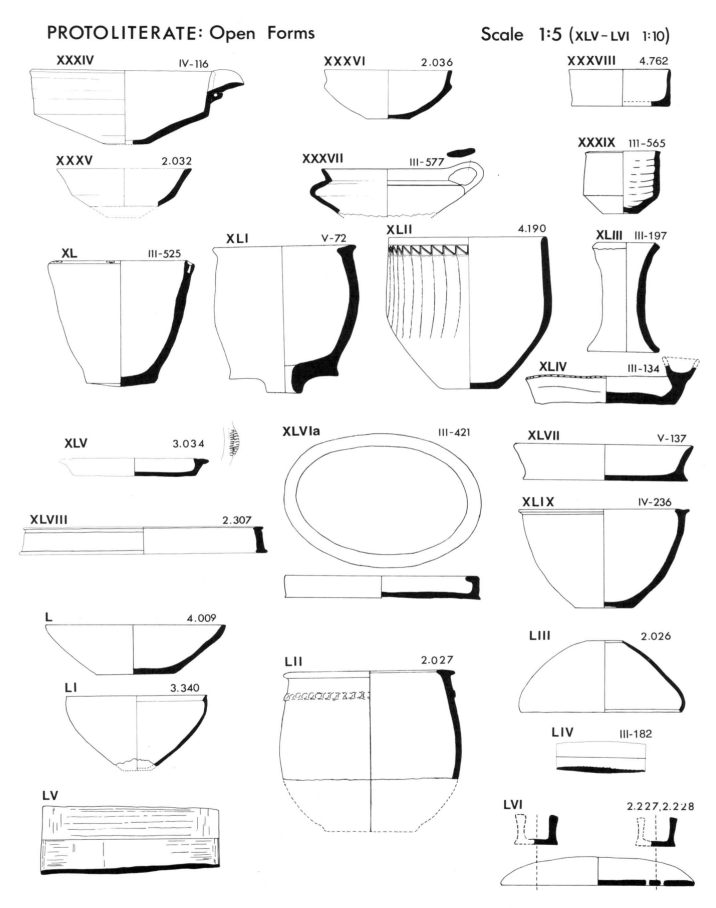

Figure 9. Protoliterate Open Forms, Families XXXIV–LVI

Table 2. Open Vessels, Similar to Chogha Mish Protoliterate Families XXXIV–LVI, Present at Other Sites

PROTOLITERATE FAMILIES

	XXXIV	XXXV	XXXVII	XL	XLII	XLIII	XLIV	XLVI a	b	c	d	e	f	XLVII a	b	XLVIII	XLIX	LII	LIV	LV	LVI
SUSA																					
Acropole 1965																					
"Jamdat Nasr récent"	—	—	—	—	—	—	—	—	—	—	—	—	—	—	—	—	—	—	—	—	—
"Jamdat Nasr ancien-Uruk récent"	—	—	—	—	—	—	—	×	×	×	×	×	—	—	—	—	—	—	—	—	×
Apadana Trench 1038	—	×	—	—	—	—	—	—	—	×	×	—	×	×	×	—	—	×	—	—	—
Acropole I																					
17	—	—	—	—	×	—	×	—	—	×	×	—	—	—	—	—	—	—	—	—	—
17B	—	—	—	—	×	—	—	—	—	×	×	—	×	—	—	—	—	—	—	—	×
18	—	—	—	—	—	—	—	—	—	—	—	—	—	—	—	—	—	—	—	—	—
WARKA																					
K/L XII Sounding																					
"Spät-Uruk"	—	—	—	—	—	—	×	—	×	×	×	—	—	—	—	—	—	—	—	—	×
Eanna Precinct and Test Pit																					
III–II	—	—	—	—	—	—	—	—	—	—	—	—	—	—	—	—	—	—	—	—	—
IV	—	—	—	—	—	—	—	—	—	—	—	—	—	—	—	—	—	—	—	—	—
V	—	—	—	—	—	—	—	—	—	—	—	—	—	—	—	—	—	—	—	—	—
VI	×	—	—	—	×	—	×	—	×	×	—	×	—	—	—	—	—	—	—	—	—
VII	—	—	—	—	×	×	—	—	—	—	—	—	—	—	—	—	—	—	—	—	—
XII	—	—	—	—	—	—	—	—	—	—	—	—	—	—	—	—	—	—	—	—	—
NIPPUR																					
Inanna Temple																					
XII	—	—	—	—	—	—	—	—	—	×	—	—	—	—	—	—	—	—	—	—	—
XIII	—	—	—	—	—	—	—	—	—	—	—	—	—	—	—	—	—	—	—	—	—
XIV	—	—	—	—	—	—	—	—	—	—	—	—	—	—	—	—	—	—	—	—	—
XV	—	—	—	—	—	—	—	—	—	—	—	—	—	—	—	—	—	—	—	—	—
XVI	—	—	—	—	—	×	—	—	—	—	—	—	—	—	—	—	—	—	—	—	—
XVII	×	—	—	—	—	—	—	—	—	—	×	—	—	—	—	—	—	—	—	—	—
XVIII	×	—	—	—	—	—	—	—	—	—	×	—	—	—	—	—	—	—	—	—	—
XIX	×	—	—	—	—	—	—	—	—	—	×	—	—	—	—	—	?	×	—	—	—
XX	×	—	—	—	—	—	—	—	—	—	×	—	—	—	—	—	—	—	—	—	—
TELLO	—	—	—	×	—	—	×	—	—	—	—	—	—	—	—	—	—	—	—	—	—
NINEVEH																					
IV	—	—	—	—	—	—	—	—	—	—	—	—	—	—	—	—	—	—	—	—	—
III	—	—	—	—	—	—	—	—	—	—	—	—	—	—	—	—	×	—	—	—	—
HABUBA KABIRA SOUTH	?	—	×	—	×	×	×	—	×	—	—	—	—	—	×	×	×	×	×	×	×
GODIN V	—	—	—	—	—	—	—	—	×	—	—	—	—	—	—	—	—	—	—	—	—
MALYAN Banesh Period	—	—	—	—	—	—	—	—	—	×	—	—	—	×	×	—	?	—	—	—	×

Table 3. Coherency and Relative Frequency of the Families of Protoliterate Open Vessels
(Specific and Related Types in One Family Assorted)

Ubiquitous	Common		Less Common		One Only	Assortment
VI	IX	XXXIX	IV	XXXIII	X	I
VII	XVIII	XL	V	XXXV	XI	II
XXI	XIX	XLII	VIII	XXXVI	XIII	III
XLVI	XX	XLVII	XII	XXXVIII	XIV	XXVI
	XXII	LII	XV	XLI	XLIII	XXXVIII
	XXIII	LIII	XVI	XLIV	L	
	XXIV	LV	XVII	XLV	LI	
	XXV	LVI	XXIX	XLVIII	LIII	
	XXVIII		XXX	XLIX		
			XXXII	LIV		
7%	32%		37%		14%	9%

THE FAMILIES OF CLOSED FORMS
(Figs. 10–15)

The great variety of types and families of closed vessels in the Protoliterate period should not obscure the fact that the potters of that period at Chogha Mish had a predilection for a limited number of basic shapes. Dominant is the ovoid form in which the greatest diameter is above the middle of the vessel (.5 form). The innumerable variations in ware, proportion, size, and accessories do not affect the prevalence of this basic shape. Less common, but also numerous, are symmetrical vessels, those with their greatest diameter in the middle (.6 form). Bag-shaped jars (.7 form) are relatively rare.

The closed forms fall into the following major classes: vessels without major accessories such as handles and spouts (fig. 10), handled vessels (fig. 11), spouted vessels (figs. 12–13), and four-lugged vessels (figs. 14–15). They are discussed in that sequence with, on the whole, the families following one another in the general order of the pottery classification system, that is, subdivided according to size, and within each size range usually in the order of the shape numbers. Occasionally, however, some inconsistencies might be introduced in order to avoid separating related groups.

In the definitions and discussion that follow it is understood that all vessels fall within the limits of the standard ware unless there is an explicit statement to the contrary. Rims are always mentioned in the definitions if they exist as a significant feature; when only necks are cited that indicates no rims exist.

VESSELS WITHOUT MAJOR ACCESSORIES

Protoliterate Family LX

A.54; rare

Figure 10; plate 88:A

Ovoid or globular vessels up to a greatest dimension of about 7 cm occur as isolated, individual examples but are too rare to constitute a cluster of similar specimens. They must have been fortuitous pieces, not serving any regular purpose, although capable of containing a substance used in small quantities. However, this seems to have been performed by A or B sized vessels of more differentiated shapes belonging to Families LXI–LXV.

Protoliterate Family LXI

A–C.53; B most common size, normal proportion 6, narrow, flaring necks, narrow flat bases

Plate 88:B–J

The vessels of one of the outstanding closed families derive their distinctive character from their high ovoid bodies tapering to narrow bases and necks. They are usually of good standard or fine ware with smoothly

finished surfaces. In some examples the neck flares markedly, adding to the elegance of the form. Three vessels (pl. 88:E–F, J), with their smoothly curving bodies, can be taken as classical examples of this family shape. B or small C sizes are typical. A miniature example occasionally appears (pl. 88:D). At the other extreme, its relatively large size and wide neck mark one example (pl. 88:I) as an exceptional specimen. Another large example (pl. 88:F) is also atypical, not only in size but also for the almost horizontal stance of the uppermost part of the body.[52]

The smaller jars are evidently closely related to the small stone vessels of similar or identical shapes that are known to have served as cosmetic containers (pl. 125:H). The pottery examples were probably used in the same way.

Protoliterate Family LXII

B.41,[53] .50, .51; proportions 5–6, high neck, shoulder

Figure 10; plate 88:K–L

The shapes of some small jars, although in general similar to those of Family LXI, have rather wider and higher necks and either a marked curve or carination that sets off the upper part of the body as a shoulder. These features are sufficiently distinctive to place the vessels possessing them in a separate family, LXII, despite the existence of intermediate examples (pl. 88:E). The difference between Families LXI and LXII is particularly clear in the sharply carinated example (pl. 19:F). The jars of Family LXII are closely related to the larger-sized vessels of Family LXVIII, even though the latter tend to have wider necks, straighter bodies, and higher proportions.[54]

Protoliterate Family LXIII

B.53, .54, .64, .65; rather wide neck, convex or flat base

Figure 10; plate 88:M–Q

Several types of small uncarinated vessels with their greatest diameter in either the upper or middle part of the body make up Family LXIII. They tend to be squat, but one tall example exists (pl. 88:Q). The ves-

---

52. For parallels to plate 88:C–D, G, see Haller 1932, pl. 19 C:w, y (Warka, Eanna VI); de Genouillac et al. 1934, pl. 18:1b (Tello). For a parallel to plate 88:F, H, see ibid., pl. 20:1b (Tello).

53. The only significant difference between .41 and .50 forms is the profile of the body, straight and somewhat convex respectively. Although .41 examples are not in hand, they might well have existed.

54. For parallels to plate 88:K–L, see Haller 1932, pl. 19 C:t (neck shorter; Warka, Eanna VI); Sürenhagen 1974/75, pl. 18:138–39, 143 (Habuba Kabira South).

sels of this family might be well made and provided with special elements such as a pair of knobs (pl. 88:M) or a band of notches (pl. 88:P).

Protoliterate Family LXIV

> B.76; proportion 6, pointed base
>
> Figure 10; plate 88:R

A small vessel with its greater diameter in the lower part of the body and mostly covered by reserve slip is the only example of this family. The vessel is too distinctive to fit in elsewhere, but it might be only a unique specimen rather than the representative of a group.

Protoliterate Family LXV

> B–C.60, .63, .70, .74, .75; neck or rim or combination of the two, normally at least one marked carination, standard or fine ware
>
> Figure 10; plates 88:S–AA; 89:A–C

In contrast to the vessels with continuously curving bodies (pl. 88:M–R), others (pls. 88:S–AA; 89:A–C) are for the most part markedly carinated 6 and 7 shapes, with varieties of the latter more frequent. There is no sharp line of demarcation between vessels with the greatest diameter in the middle of the body and those with it lower. The vertical-walled vessel (pl. 88:S) is closely related to the other double-angled vessels which, however, have flaring lower walls (pls. 88:V–W; 89:B). These vessels in turn grade into others with rounded instead of carinated upper bodies (pls. 88:X–Z; 89:C). Proportions vary from squat to relatively tall and necks from round to wide. The double-angled vessels and their cousins are for the most part small and carefully made of dense paste, with niceties such as lines of notches (pls. 88:M, V, X; 89:C), reserved slip (pls. 88:W; 89:B), or a blob of clay at the mouth (pls. 88:Z; 89:C). They could have been containers for cosmetics or ointments. Such a function might also have been served by a small vessel of the same general character, but of simpler shape than the carinated vessels (pl. 88:AA). A vessel with only one carination in the middle of the body (pl. 89:A) remains so far as an isolated specimen standing apart from the other members of the family.[55]

Protoliterate Family LXVI

> B–C.71; proportion 6, wide mouths without rim, flat bases
>
> Figure 10; plate 89:D–G

The vessels of Family LXVI are equivocal in the sense that they form one part of a typological series in which there is no natural break between any two similar shapes. However, while the walls of the vessels considered as open beakers are relatively vertical (Family XX), those of Family LXVI taper above the carination, producing containers of narrower, higher proportions. In some cases the mouth flares. There are thus intimations of a body and neck, even though the forms are still quite unsegmented. The interiors usually bear prominent wheel striations; no special surface treatment was given to the exteriors.

Protoliterate Family LXVII

> C.75, .78; proportion 6, rounded lower body
>
> Plate 89:H–J

Vessels related to Family LXVI (pl. 89:D–G), but with a rounded lower body instead of a carinated body, are grouped in this family. One example (pl. 89:I) is intermediate between the two families. Another with a markedly narrowed upper body (pl. 89:H) belongs at the "closed" end of the typological series formed by the vessels of Families XX, LXVI, and LXVII.

Protoliterate Family LXVIII

> C.45, .51;[56] proportions 6–7, wide, high neck
>
> Figure 10; plate 89:K–M

Tall shouldered vessels with large necks form a distinctive but rare group. They are closely related to the small vessels of Family LXII, the only significant difference in shape being the taller proportions. The elegantly concave profile of the neck of one example (pl. 89:L), which is reminiscent of that of the Family LXI jars, is less typical than the straighter neck of another (pl. 89:K).[57]

---

récent"); Le Brun 1978a, fig. 31:3 (less carinated, rimless; Susa, Acropole I, Level 17B).

55. For a parallel to plate 88:S, see Haller 1932, pl. 19 C:g′ (Warka, Eanna VI). For a parallel to plate 88:T, see 7N 783, 7N P254 (Nippur, Inanna Temple XVI, XV). For parallels to plate 88:X, see Haller 1932, pl. 19 C:g′ (Warka, Eanna VI); Sürenhagen 1974/75, pl. 19:147 (Habuba Kabira South). For parallels to plate 89:Y, see Haller 1932, pl. 19 D:x (Warka, Eanna VI); Sürenhagen 1974/75, pl. 18:115 (more elongated, narrow mouth; Habuba Kabira South). For a parallel to plate 88:Z, see ibid., pl. 19:149–50 (more elongated; Habuba Kabira South). For parallels to plate 89:A, see Steve and Gasche 1971, fig. 29:2 (Susa, Acropole 1965 Sounding, "Jamdat-Nasr ancien-Uruk

56. Shapes .45 and .51 are very similar; the primary distinction is the outline of the body below the carination, relatively straight and relatively convex, respectively.

57. For parallels to plate 89:K, see Le Brun 1978a, fig. 29:4 (Susa, Acropole I, Level 17B); 7N 770 (related type; Nippur, Inanna Temple XVb); de Genouillac et al. 1934, pl. 6:4938 (Tello); Sürenhagen 1974/75, pls. 15:91 and 16:92 (both C.51 shapes; Habuba Kabira South). For a parallel to plate 89:L, see ibid., pl. 16:93 with (shorter neck and red wash). For parallels to plate 89:M, see ibid., pl. 13:85 (with pointed base); Le Brun 1978a, fig. 24:5 (Susa, Acropole I, Level 17B). For coarser D-sized variations of plate 89:L–

Protoliterate Family LXIX

C.54; proportion 3, undercut rim, reserve slip

Figure 10; plate 89:N

A jar characterized by its squat ovoid form, undercut rim, and reserve slip remains so far the only representative of a type so well defined that it must be accommodated in a family of its own. Usually reserved-slip vessels of squat ovoid shapes have a spout (pl. 110:O) and might be an aberrant example without the normal accessory.

Protoliterate Family LXX

C.53; proportion 6, narrow neck, flat base

Figure 10; plate 89:O

A medium-sized vessel of tall rounded shape appears to be an isolated example rather than the representative of a group.

Protoliterate Family LXXI

C.53, .54, .55; medium to wide neck, proportions 5 to 6

Plate 89:P

The medium-sized (C) ovoid jars are distinguished from the narrow-necked jar of the preceding family by their wide necks. One example is very simple in form and has a rough surface (pl. 89:P). Others are closely related by the shape of the body and the gracefully flaring neck to the jars of Family LXI.

Protoliterate Family LXXII

C.64; medium to wide neck

Figure 10; plate 89:Q–R

Like the preceding family, Family LXXII has been established for medium-sized jars with quite large mouths, but in this group the greatest diameter is in the middle of the body.

Protoliterate Family LXXIII

C.64, .70; proportions 5–6, high necks, reserve slip typical, flat bases

Figure 10; plate 89:S–V

The larger-sized relatives of the Family LXV vessels form a distinctive group of shouldered jars with sharply profiled necks and rims. The necks are of either medium or narrow width, and they end in overhanging rims of somewhat varying types. A single lump of clay is sometimes added to the rim (pl. 89:U). Adding further to the individuality of this family is the reserve slip that

often covers the body. One fragment (pl. 89:T) has a pseudo-reserve slip consisting of slight ridges left as the body surface was pressed down with the same type of strokes as in true reserve slip.[58]

Protoliterate Family LXXIV

C.66, rarely B.55; proportion 4, narrow neck, slight rim possible, base slightly flat or convex

Figure 10; plate 90:A–D

Globular or squat flasks with short narrow necks form a rare, but unmistakable, class. The necks end in a blunt lip or a small beveled rim. One example stands out because of its gray ware (pl. 90:A) and another because of its red wash and two painted bands decorating its neck (pl. 90:D). The same shape also appears with four lugs.[59]

Protoliterate Family LXXV

C–D.54, .55; proportion 4, everted rims, convex base, rough surface

Figure 10; plates 19:S; 90:E–J

Among the more ubiquitous varieties of Protoliterate pottery are the squat, round-bottomed, wide-mouthed jars with everted rims that flare either directly from the body or form a minimal neck. The ware of these jars represents the coarser, grittier range of standard ware; the paste of some examples also contains straw and in this resembles coarse ware. A distinctive feature of this family, in addition to the form, is the rough surface created by the dragging along of the grits of the paste as the jars were scraped; there was no subsequent wet-smoothing. A number of the jars bear fire smudges or mottling. This circumstance, the suitability of the form, the considerable number of complete or semi-complete examples,[60] and the appearance of frag-

---

M, see Lenzen 1958, pls. 49:a–e; 50:d–e, g–i (Warka, Eanna IVa, *Riemchengebäude*).

58. For a parallel to plate 89:S, see Le Brun 1978a, fig. 29:7 (different rim and no reserve slip; Susa, Acropole I, Level 17B). For a parallel to plate 89:U, see Sürenhagen 1974/75, pl. 16:97, proportion 5 (Habuba Kabira South). For a parallel to plate 89:V, see ibid., pl. 16:98 (taller, proportion 7). For related example, see a false-spouted jar (Family CIXe) from Nippur, Inanna Temple XVII–XVI (7N 786 = Hansen 1965:204, fig. 19).

59. For parallels to plate 90:B, see Le Brun 1971, fig. 48:10 (Susa, Acropole I, Level 17); Nissen 1970, pl. 101:22 (Warka, K/L XII Sounding, Layer 40). For a parallel to plate 90:C, see Sürenhagen 1974/75, pl. 18:13b (and pl. 12:80 for related but larger examples; Habuba Kabira South).

60. In the fourth season, for instance, in addition to 4.1077 (R18:303/304; pl. 90:G) and IV-418 (R17:408; pl. 90:H), the following examples were found: IV-230 (R18:307); IV-231 (R18:301); IV-232 (R18:307); IV-419 (R17:408 Northwest); IV-420 (R17:408 Northwest).

ments of such jars everywhere indicate that they were cooking pots.[61]

Occasionally a specimen has a plastic band with finger imprints (pl. 90:J), the walls of which were also wet-smoothed after being scraped. However, only exceptional pieces lack the rough surface normal for the family.

Protoliterate Family LXXVI

C–D.64; proportion 4, everted rims with pair of notched lips, convex base, rough surface, or plastic shoulder band

Figure 10; plates 19:I–R; 90:K–M

Vessels that are fundamentally the same as the Family LXXV cooking pots (pl. 90:E–J), sharing with them globular round-based bodies and wide mouths with everted rims, are distinguished as a separate group by the addition of two notched lips to the rim. The presence of one such lip on a handled vessel from the Diyala region was interpreted as facilitating the pouring of liquid.[62] The paired lips of the jar probably helped in lifting the vessels. The lips take their name from the notches that were often imprinted on them in one or two rows (pls. 19:A–B, J–K; 90:K, M). This feature was interpreted on the basis of one example found in the Diyala region as a notation of volume.[63] In addition to the long imprints, neat rows of triangular notches (pl. 19:L–M) or more haphazardly placed crossing strokes (pls. 19:N–R; 90:L) occur on the lips. An example with finger-imprinted pellets is unusual (pl. 19:I). The interpretation of the diverse markings of the notched lips call for a detailed study that should include the occurrence of the same kinds of notching on the lips of the vertical-handled jars and on the strap handles.

Like their Family LXXV cousins, the jars with notched lips often have grit-roughened surfaces (pls. 19:A, I, M; 90:L).[64] Finger imprinted plastic bands are

quite standard, both on normal examples (pl. 90:J–K) and on one atypical for its coarse ware and wide mouth (pl. 90:M). Scored lines similar to those on the vertical handled vessels occur occasionally (pl. 19:R). Although many of the Family LXXVI jars are made of gritty varieties of standard ware, there is an example of a gritty gray ware with irregularly horizontal stroke burnish (III-785).

Protoliterate Family LXXVII

C–D.54, .55; proportions 5–6, everted rim, convex base, rough surface

Figure 10; plates 19:G; 91:A–C

Only one essential feature, their higher proportions, distinguishes the jars of Family LXXVII from the cooking pots of Family LXXV. Otherwise, both groups share the same everted rim types, rounded bases, and rough surfaces. The similarity is such that if only rims or fragments are preserved, it might not be possible to distinguish between Families LXXV and LXXVII specimens. Like the cooking pots, these jars are common. They are frequently of large (D) sizes.[65]

Protoliterate Family LXXVIII

C–D.52, .54, .55; proportions probably 4, exceptionally wide mouth

Plate 91:D

A fragment of a large vessel has a mouth so unusually wide that it has been set apart in a family of its own, although in its general shape and everted rim it is related to the jars of Families LXXV and LXXVI. A large band of rocker imprints decorates the upper body.

---

61. For possible parallels to plate 90:E–I, see Le Brun 1978a, fig. 25:8–10 (Susa, Acropole I, Level 17B); Miroschedji 1976, fig. 6:8 (Susa, Apadana, Trench 1038); Sürenhagen 1974/75, pl. 24:19, 24–25 (Habuba Kabira South). It is difficult to distinguish Families LXXV and LXXVII on the basis of rim fragments only. For types related to plate 90:J, see Le Brun 1971, fig. 50:7 (Susa, Acropole I, Level 17).

62. Delougaz (1952:38, pl. 20:a–b) termed these elements pouring lips. At Chogha Mish the term is preempted for the specialized lips of the Family VII bowls and the term notched lips is adopted for use with Family LXXVI.

63. Ibid., p. 38, pl. 20:b (twisted-handle jar fragment from Tell Khubair near Tell Agrab).

64. For parallels to plate 90:K–L, see Steve and Gasche 1971, pl. 30:7 (Susa, Acropole 1965 Sounding, "Jamdat Nasr ancien-Uruk récent"); Nissen 1970, pls. 83:9 (the diagonal stance of the attachments is more similar to that of twisted handles [pl. 101:D, F] than of the normally horizontal stance of the notched lips); 102:14 (Warka, K/L Sounding, Layers

34, 41). Notched lips on incomplete rims might have belonged to either Family LXXVI or XCIIIb jars. The apparent rarity of Family LXXVI jars at other sites is probably accidental. At Habuba Kabira South a notched lip appears on a vessel of quite different form (Sürenhagen 1974/75:92–93, fig. 53; pl. 16:97). The notched lips were ancestral to later forms, some of which have plain surfaces; cf. Frankfort 1936, pl. 3:4, 6, 23 (Tell Asmar, Abu Temple, Archaic Shrine 3, Early Dynastic I); Delougaz 1952, pl. 64:24 (H 18:14 Sounding, Protoliterate d level); Kh. III 505, unpublished, cf. Delougaz, Hill, and Lloyd 1967:51 and note 44 (Khafajah, P 42:2, unstratified area of robbers' pits).

65. For a parallel to plate 91:A, see Le Brun 1978a, fig. 26:10 (Susa, Acropole I, Level 17B). For parallels to plate 91:B–C, see ibid., fig. 25:13 (Susa, Acropole I, Level 17B); Le Brun 1971, fig. 50:6 (Susa, Acropole I, Level 17); Sürenhagen 1974/75, pl. 5:57 (Habuba Kabira South).

Table 4. Closed Vessels without Major Accessories, Similar to Chogha Mish Protoliterate
Families LXI–LXXVI, Present at Other Sites

	PROTOLITERATE FAMILIES													
	LXI	LXII	LXV	LXVIII	LXXIII	LXXIV	LXXV	LXXVII	LXXIX	LXXX	LXXXII	LXXXIII	LXXXV	LXXXVI
SUSA														
Acropole 1965														
"Jamdat Nasr récent"	—	—	—	—	—	—	—	—	—	—	—	—	—	—
"Jamdat Nasr ancien-Uruk récent"	—	—	×	—	—	—	—	—	—	—	—	×	—	×
Apadana Trench 1038	—	—	—	—	—	—	×	—	×	×	—	×	—	—
Acropole I														
17	—	—	—	—	—	×	—	—	×	—	—	—	×	—
17B	—	—	×	×	×	—	×	×	×	×	—	—	×	—
18	—	—	—	—	—	—	—	—	—	—	—	×	—	—
WARKA														
K/L XII Sounding														
"Spät-Uruk"	—	—	—	—	—	×	—	—	—	—	—	—	—	×
Eanna Precinct and Test Pit														
III–II	—	—	—	—	—	—	—	—	—	—	—	—	—	—
IV	—	—	—	×	—	—	—	—	—	—	—	—	—	—
V	—	—	—	—	—	—	—	—	—	—	—	—	—	—
VI	×	×	×	—	—	—	—	—	—	—	—	—	—	—
VII	—	—	—	—	—	—	—	—	—	—	—	—	—	—
IX–VIII	—	—	—	—	—	—	—	—	—	—	—	—	—	—
XII	—	—	—	—	—	—	—	—	—	—	—	—	—	—
NIPPUR														
Inanna Temple														
XII	—	—	—	—	—	—	—	—	—	—	—	—	—	—
XIII	—	—	—	—	—	—	—	—	—	—	—	—	—	—
XIV	—	—	—	—	—	—	—	—	—	—	—	—	—	—
XV	—	—	—	×	×	—	—	—	—	—	—	—	—	—
XVI	—	—	—	×	—	—	—	—	—	—	—	—	—	—
XVII	—	—	—	—	—	—	—	—	—	—	—	—	—	—
XVIII	—	—	—	—	—	—	—	—	—	—	—	×	—	—
XIX	—	—	—	—	—	—	—	—	—	—	—	—	—	—
XX	—	—	—	—	—	—	—	—	—	—	—	—	—	—
TELLO	×	×	×	×	×	×	×	×	—	—	×	—	—	—
HABUBA KABIRA SOUTH	—	×	×	×	×	×	×	×	—	—	×	—	—	—

Protoliterate Family LXXIX

C–D.54, .55; proportions 4–5, rim, predominantly ledge, usually low neck, flat base, better grades of standard ware

Figure 10; plate 91:E–L

Vessels reminiscent of the cooking pots of Family LXXV in the broad ovoid shape of the body are sharply distinguished from them by the rim types (guttered, carinated, flaring, and ledge) and by the presence in most cases of a low neck. The bases of the Family LXXIX jars might be either convex (pl. 91:K) or flat (pl. 91:E, H–I); since the bottom is so often incomplete, it is impossible to determine which type of base was more common, or whether jars with carinated rims always had convex bases and ledge-rimmed jars had flat bases. The smooth surfaces of the Family LXXIX jars provide another distinction from those of Family LXXV. Upper walls are sometimes adorned by scored lines (pl. 91:J), finger indentations (pl. 91:G), or horizontal reserve slip (pl. 91:L). The Family LXXIX jars are relatively common.[66]

Protoliterate Family LXXX

C–D.54, .65; proportion 5, high neck, flat base, usually better grades of standard ware

Figure 10; plate 92:A–D

High necks distinguish a group of ovoid or spherical vessels as different from the low-necked jars of the preceding family. In addition, the Family LXXX jars tend to be of slightly taller proportions than those of Family LXXIX. The necks usually end in rims, although not always (pl. 92:A). One specimen is rather thin-walled in proportion to its size (pl. 92:C), or a finger-imprinted band (pl. 92:A), the latter being a large-sized relative of a medium-sized jar with a large mouth (pl. 89:R). Although these high-necked jars are relatively rare among the forms without major accessories, somewhat smaller-sized versions of this type with the addition of spouts constitute a prominent group of spouted vessels.[67]

Protoliterate Family LXXXI

D.53; proportion 4, high neck with rim, plastic decoration, interior with buttresses

Figure 10; plates 28:V; 92:E–F

Large jars which in their high necks and rims resemble Family LXXX have, however, wider upper bodies and are in general larger. The curve of the walls of the most completely preserved example (pl. 92:F), as they approach close to the base, indicates that, similar to the pithoi of Family LXXXIII, the Family LXXXI jars had convex bases. In addition to the form, the treatment of the exterior and interior surfaces gives this group a very specific individuality. The exteriors were roughened by pronounced scrape marks, in one case forming a quadrant pattern when viewed from the top (III-592). A pair of bosses, supplemented on one jar by a snake, were added. On the interior irregular lumps or bars of clay were applied in haphazard arrangement (pl. 28:V); the purpose might have been to strengthen the walls, which are relatively thin and light for vessels of such large size. The necks were made separately and welded to the body (pl. 28:V).

The buttressed pithoi are quite rare, though they are represented by individual sherds in addition to the three semi-complete examples.

Protoliterate Family LXXXII

D.53; proportion 6, medium mouths, undercut rim, flat base, plain body or reserve slip

Figure 10; plate 92:G–H

Some ovoid jars with undercut rims are given special character by their rather high proportions. They seem to have been rare in contrast to the squat jars with undercut rims. In addition, a complete example of this family (pl. 92:H) suggests that these tall jars had flat bases.

Protoliterate Family LXXXIII

D.53, .54, .55, .56; usually proportion 4, no neck, predominantly undercut, convex bases, standard or occasionally coarse ware

Figure 10; plates 19:S; 93:A–H; 94:A–C

One of the more prominent groups of Protoliterate pottery consists of jars reminiscent in their bulbous shapes and convex bases of the cooking pots. However, there are significant distinctions that give the vessels of this family a quite different character. First, they are large-sized pithoi; only one (pl. 93:G) is on the borderline between medium and large. Second, undercut rims prevail, with only a minority of other types appearing (everted rim: pl. 93:D; square-ended ledge rim: pl. 94:C). Third, rough-surfaced bodies are rare (pls. 19:S; 94:B); one example also has an everted rim and thus conforms to the specifications for Family LXXV except for its great size (pl. 94:B). Many examples of this common group have somewhat smoothed bodies, particularly above the point of greatest diameter. Two rim sherds assignable to this family have reserve slip (pls. 93:D; 94:C), but this kind of body treatment does not seem to be frequent on the pithoi. Sometimes decorative elements appear close to the rim, rocker impressions (pl. 19:S), plastic thumb-imprinted bands on rim sherds (pl. 93:C–E), and notches (pl. 93:F). The latter is also an example of an unusually tall shape. The bases are always convex, but might be either round or pointed.[68]

---

66. For a parallel to plate 91:I, see Le Brun 1978a, fig. 27:1 (rim fragment; Susa, Acropole I, Level 17B). For parallels to plate 91:G–H, K–L, see ibid., fig. 27:2, 4, 8; Miroschedji 1976. fig. 6:4 (Susa, Apadana, Trench 1038).

67. For parallels to plate 92:B, see Le Brun 1978a, fig. 26:1 (neck rimless, reserve slip), 2 (rimless, no reserve slip), 6 (band-rim neck; Susa, Acropole I Sounding, Level 17B). For a parallel to plate 92:C, see Miroschedji 1976, fig. 6:16 (neck fragment, no decoration; Susa, Apadana, Trench 1038). For a parallel to plate 92:D, see Le Brun 1978a, fig. 27:3 (no reserve slip; Susa, Acropole I, Level 17B).

68. For a parallel to plate 93:B, see Miroschedji 1976, fig. 6:1 (undercut rim fragment from Susa, Apadana, Trench 1038). For parallels to plate 93:C, see Le Brun 1978b, fig. 32:2 (rim diameter = 35 cm; Susa, Acropole I Sounding, Level 18); Steve and Gasche 1971, fig. 29:3 (Susa, Acropole 1965 Sounding, "Jamdat Nasr ancien-Uruk récent"). For a parallel to plate 93:D, see 7N P299 (no reserve slip; Nippur, Inanna Temple XVIII). For a parallel to plate 93:H, see Le Brun 1978b, fig. 32:2 (with imprinted molding; Susa, Acropole I, Level 18). For a parallel to plate 94:C, see Miroschedji 1976, fig. 6:2 (smaller, no reserve slip or notches; Susa, Apadana, Trench 1038).

Protoliterate Family LXXXIV

D.54; proportion 7, low neck with rim, convex base

Figure 10; plate 94:D

A so far unique tall jar with a sharply profiled short neck and a rim is such a specific type that it cannot be subsumed under any family but one of its own.

Protoliterate Family LXXXV

D.55; proportion 8, wide neck

Figure 10; plate 94:E–F

Vessels of a simple but characteristic shape, proportions, and an elongated ovoid body with a high, wide neck are rare. They resemble a somewhat larger vessel, which differs in some details of its neck and in the presence of a rim, that has been tentatively placed with the Parthian pottery (pl. 73:E). It was found in a mixed Protoliterate/Parthian context. In view of the general similarity in the vessels (pls. 73:E; 94:E–F), a Protoliterate date for all three is possible.[69]

HANDLED VESSELS (Fig. 11; Pls. 20–21, 95–101)

In addition to the handles which define the second major category of closed vessels, other features characteristic of it are standard ware, wide predominantly rimless necks, and scored decoration. The scoring was done as the pot turned on the wheel and when the handles were added afterward it was often completely or partially covered at the point of attachment (pl. 20:S). Basic and most common is continuous spiral scoring, producing the effect of three or more horizontal lines executed either regularly (pls. 20:B–C, G; 95–101; passim) or somewhat carelessly (pls. 95:H; 100:B). A rare variant of the horizontal scoring is the "fine-line" type done with the tip of a sharp instrument and, unlike the normal scoring, carried down to the middle part of the body (pl. 96:B). More frequent is the type of decoration in which the horizontal scoring is crossed by diagonal or zigzag lines (pls. 20:S; 97:E; 98:I–K).[70] Much

rarer is punctuated decoration (pl. 97:B) and rarest of all is combing over the upper body of the vessel (pl. 96:E). Various examples of incised, notched, and punctuated decoration also occur sporadically on regular-sized vessels (pls. 97:B; 98:B, D; 100:F) and perhaps somewhat more regularly on small vessels (pls. 95:A, D–E; 97:A).

The handle types provide the basic subdivisions for this category of closed vessels.[71] The two major shapes are the strap handles with a flattened, approximately rectangular section and the twisted handles with a round section. The latter usually consist of a single strand of clay twisted on its axis (pl. 20:M, O), but they occasionally were formed by two or more intertwined strands. Many examples were secondarily grooved to accentuate the twisted effect (pl. 20:B, F–R). Occasionally single twisted handles approach the flattened shape of the strap handles (pl. 20:B, H). Sometimes two or three twisted handles (pl. 20:I–K, R; 101:N) or, much more rarely, plain clay rods (pls. 20:Q; 97:A) were combined to form multiple handles. The rod handles, which seem never to have been used as single strands, show what the rolls of clay used to make the twisted handles were like.

Both strap and twisted handles could be set either vertically or horizontally, with the vertical position by far preponderant. The vertical strap and twisted handled vessels form two parallel series with the families and actual examples of the former far outnumbering those of the latter, being, in fact, among the more ubiquitous groups of Protoliterate vessels at Chogha Mish. The standard-sized vessels with multiple twisted or rod handles are placed in the same families as the single vertical twisted handles. Miniature or small vessels with all types of vertical handles are placed together in the same families, since the small-sized vessels with twisted and rod handles are both rare and often represented only by handle fragments (pl. 20:L–Q). The vertical handles quite often have embellishments at the top where they join the neck. The twisted handles can have one or three round imprints (pls. 20:E, M; 100:A), a perforation (pls. 97:A; 100:G), or notches (pl. 20:I). The strap handles might be notched (pls. 96:E; 97:B; 98:I) or, if unusually wide, perforated (pl. 20:D).

As a whole, horizontal handles are much rarer than vertical handles; and rod or multiple handles were never used in this position. However, pairs of horizontal twisted handles are the defining feature of one of the more outstanding of the handled families (fig 11:Family XCVIII). Horizontally-placed strap handles are extremely rare, being limited to the scoops (fig. 11:Family C) and to one unusual family of small spouted vessels.

69. For a parallel to plate 94:E, see Le Brun 1971, fig. 50:5 (Susa, Acropole I, Level 17). For a parallel to plate 92:F, see Le Brun 1978a, fig. 29:6 (Susa, Acropole I, Level 17B).

70. Crossed scoring decorated the strap-handled vessel in which the famous Protoliterate statuette of a city ruler was found at Warka (Lenzen 1960:38, pl. 24:a). At the time of the excavation the jar, which had a small Protoliterate bowl (Family VI) covering its broken upper body, was considered to be of late date (first millennium B.C., Seleucid). Despite the fact that such types were identified as Protoliterate in the publication of the Diyala pottery (Delougaz 1952, pl. 20:a–b), the vessel continued for many years thereafter to be ascribed to a late period (Moortgat 1969:8). For an example of fine-point scoring from Khafajah, see Delougaz 1952, pl. 17:R.

71. On Protoliterate handles, see Sürenhagen 1974/75:92–93, figs. 51–52; pl. 33 F:1–12.

PROTOLITERATE: No Major Accessories   Scale 1:5 (LXXVII–LXXXIII 1:10)

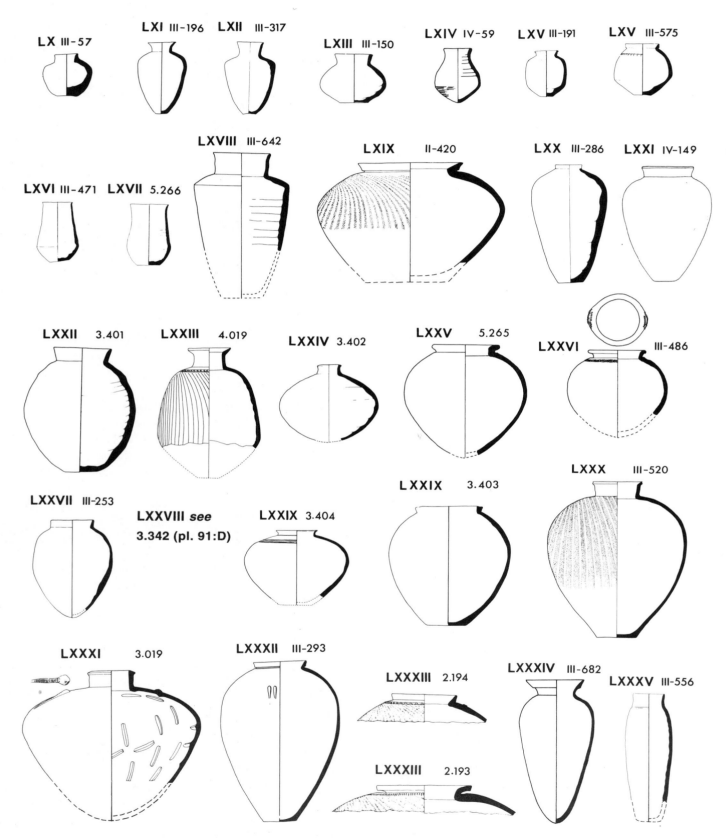

Figure 10. Protoliterate Closed Forms with No Major Accessories

Table 5. Handled Vessels, Similar to Chogha Mish Protoliterate Families LXXXVI–C, Present at Other Sites

	LXXXVI	LXXXVII a	LXXXVII b	LXXXVIII	LXXXIX	XC	XCII a	XCIII b	XCV	XCVI	XCVII	XCVIII	XCIX	C
SUSA														
Acropole 1965														
"Jamdat Nasr récent"	—	—	—	—	—	—	—	—	—	—	—	—	—	—
"Jamdat Nasr ancien-Uruk récent"	—	—	—	—	—	—	—	—	—	—	—	—	—	—
Apadana Trench 1038	—	—	×	—	×	×	—	—	—	—	—	—	—	—
Acropole, Old Excavations, "Susa C"	—	—	—	—	—	—	—	—	—	—	—	—	×	—
Acropole I														
17	—	—	—	×	×	—	—	×	—	—	—	×	—	—
17B	—	×	—	—	—	—	—	×	—	—	×	×	—	—
18	—	—	—	—	—	—	×	—	—	—	—	—	—	—
WARKA														
Md XV4: Archaic Settlement "Jemdet Nasr"	—	—	—	—	—	—	—	×	—	—	—	—	—	—
K/L XII Sounding "Spät-Uruk"	×	—	×	—	—	—	—	—	—	—	—	—	—	—
Eanna Precinct and Test Pit														
III–II	—	—	—	—	—	—	—	—	—	—	—	—	—	—
IV	—	—	—	—	—	—	—	—	—	—	—	—	—	—
V	—	—	—	—	—	—	—	—	—	—	—	—	—	—
VI	—	—	×	—	—	×	—	—	—	—	—	—	—	—
VII	—	—	—	—	—	—	×	—	—	—	—	—	—	—
IX–VIII	—	—	×	—	—	—	—	—	—	×	—	—	—	—
XII	—	—	—	—	—	—	—	—	—	—	—	—	—	—
NIPPUR														
Inanna Temple														
XII	—	—	—	—	—	—	—	—	—	—	—	—	—	—
XIII	—	—	—	×	—	—	—	—	—	—	—	—	—	—
XIV	—	—	—	—	—	—	—	—	—	—	—	—	—	—
XV	—	—	—	×	—	—	—	—	—	×	—	—	—	—
XVI	—	—	—	—	×	—	—	—	—	—	—	×	—	—
XVII	—	—	—	—	—	—	—	—	—	×	—	×	—	—
XVIII	—	—	—	—	—	—	—	—	—	—	—	—	—	—
XIX	—	—	—	×	×	—	—	—	—	—	—	—	—	—
XX	×	—	×	—	—	—	×	—	—	—	—	—	—	—
TELLO	—	—	—	×	×	—	—	—	—	—	—	—	—	—
JEMDET NASR	×	—	×	×	×	—	—	—	—	—	—	—	—	×
KHAFAJAH Protoliterate c–d	—	—	—	—	—	—	—	×	—	—	—	—	—	×
AGRAB Early Dynastic I	—	—	—	—	—	—	—	×	×	—	—	—	—	—
NINEVEH IV	—	—	—	×	—	—	—	—	—	—	—	—	—	—
HABUBA KABIRA SOUTH	—	—	—	—	×	—	—	—	—	×	—	—	—	—

The handled vessels range in size from miniatures to about 30 cm in width (4.088). Some examples occur in every Protoliterate pottery group. They were clearly household vessels that would have served a variety of uses.

Protoliterate Family LXXXVI

A.53, .54, .60, .64, .70; wide to medium necks, varying proportions, vertical strap or twisted handle

Figure 11; plate 95:A–E

Miniature vessels range from impractical tiny ones (pl. 95:A) to examples about 7 cm high. Many are squat, but an example of proportion 6 exists (pl. 95:D). Stumps indicate that broken examples had strap handles (pl. 95:A–D); a twisted (pl. 95:E) handle also occurs. These miniatures were too small to decorate by wheel scoring; instead they might have punctuations (pl. 95:A) or a single or double band of rocker imprints (pl. 95:D–E).[72]

Protoliterate Family LXXXVII

B–C, .53, .55; proportion 3, size to small C only, low neck, flat base, strap handle, plain or scored shoulder

Figure 11; plate 95:F–I

The examples of this family are squat and rather small, being for the most part of size B or only a few centimeters larger. Two groups can be distinguished according to the proportions of the mouth. Subfamily LXXXVIIa is defined on the basis of one example, a vessel with a mouth so wide as to make it intermediate between the open bowls of Subfamily XXXIb (pl. 84:U–W) and Family XXXVIII (pl. 85:T) and the normal strap-handled vessels. One example (pl. 95:F) is rather more carefully shaped than many of the other members of the family, is also somewhat oversize, and most importantly, has a markedly tapering lower body (shape .53), which is atypical for the rest of the family. Subfamily LXXXVIIb contains the vessels with normal-sized mouths, which form the bulk of the family (pl. 95:G–I). They tend to be thick walled and often quite crude. The fire smudges preserved on some of them suggest that they were used in cooking; it is easy to imagine them placed in the coals of a hearth to warm small quantities of food. One of the smaller vessels had notches on its handles (pl. 95:H), which presumably denoted its capacity. However, it has a rather unusually large number of notches, fifteen parallel to the mouth and fifteen or sixteen in three rows on the handle.[73]

Protoliterate Family LXXXVIII

B–C.54; proportion 4–5, low neck, body tapering markedly to flat base only ca. 33% of maximum diameter, strap handle, shoulders mostly scored

Figure 11; plate 95:J–N

Only a few members of Family LXXXVIII are small (pl. 95:J), the great majority being of medium size (C). Their normally larger dimensions distinguish them from the vessels of plate 95:E–H, but a more significant difference is their shape. The lower part of their bodies tapers toward the base (shape .54) and provides much of their height, thus setting them clearly apart from the globular vessels of Families LXXXVI–LXXXVII (pl. 95:F–I). Many are of proportion 4, but an occasional example is of proportion 5. The upper body is almost always emphasized by scored lines. Examples of this family are very common.[74]

Protoliterate Family LXXXIX

B–C.55; proportion 4, low neck, body rounded, flat base, strap handle, both plain and scored shoulders common

Figure 11; plate 96:A–G

Another big group of strap-handled vessels consists of those which have the same rounded ovoid body shape as Subfamily LXXXVIIb specimens but are less squat and for the most part of larger size. Appropriately enough, in view of their rounded shape and thus less pronounced distinction between the upper and lower body, scoring is much rarer in this family than in Family LXXXVIII. Frequently the vessels are plain or, more rarely, have fine-line scoring covering the upper half of the body (fig. 11:Family LXXXVIII 4.014 and 4.132). One example with random combing is also known (pl. 96:E); it has notches on its handle and an atypically narrow, high neck.[75]

---

72. For a parallel to plate 95:C, see 7N 818, Hansen 1965, fig. 2 (two rows of rocker decoration; Nippur, Inanna Temple, Level XX). For other miniatures, see Nissen 1970, pl. 98:109 = shape A.654.221 with scoring (Warka, K/L XII Sounding, Layer 39); Mackay 1931, pl. 64:25 (Jemdet Nasr).

73. For a parallel to plate 95:E, see Le Brun 1978a, fig. 28:3 (Susa, Acropole I, Level 17B). For a parallel to plate 95:F, see Miroschedji 1976, figs. 8–9 (Susa, Apadana, Trench 1038). For parallels to plate 95:G, see Nissen 1970:35 (Warka, K/L XII Sounding, Layer 38); Mackay 1931, pl. 64:22 (smaller; Jemdet Nasr). For parallels to plate 95:H, see Haller 1932, pls. 18 C:u; 19 B:k (Warka, Eanna IX–VIII, VI); Nissen 1970, pl. 90:36 (Warka, K/L XII Sounding, Layer 38); 7N P316 (notches on shoulder and handle), 7N 817 (plain), 7N 778 (scored) (Nippur, Inanna Temple, Levels XX and XVI–XV); Mackay 1931, pl. 64:23 (Jemdet Nasr).

74. For an example with a narrower base (cf. pl. 95:I), see Mackay 1931, pl. 64:21 (Jemdet Nasr). For parallels to plate 95:J, see Le Brun 1971, fig. 49:2 (Susa, Acropole I, Level 17); de Genouillac et al. 1934, pl. 6:4304 (Tello); Thompson and Mallowan 1933, pls. 51:6; 52:14 (cross scored; Nineveh IV). For a probable parallel to plate 95:K, see 7N P215 (Nippur, Inanna Temple XIII).

75. For a parallel to plate 96:B, see Sürenhagen 1974/75, pl. 5:48 (Habuba Kabira South). For a parallel to plate 96:D, see de Genouillac et al. 1934, pl. 7:4603 (Tello); for possible parallels, see Miroschedji 1976, fig. 8:13 (Susa, Apadana, Trench 1038); 7N 779 (Nippur, Inanna Temple, Level XVI). For a parallel to plate 96:E, see 7N P320 (more open and thinner combing, shorter neck; Nippur, Inanna Temple XIX). For parallels to plate 94:F–G, see Le Brun 1971, fig. 49:10 (fig. 49:3–7, 9 are fragments that could have belonged to either Family LXXXVIII or LXXXIX; Susa, Acropole I, Level 17); Mackay 1931, pl. 64:27 (Jemdet Nasr); de Genouillac et al. 1934, pls. 23:1; 7:4603 (Tello).

Protoliterate Family XC

> B–C.60, .64; proportions 3–5, low neck of large or medium width, strap, multiple rod handle

> Figure 11; plates 20:Q, S; 97:A–C; 101:N

A small, but distinctive group consists of vessels with their center of gravity in the middle of the body. They seem to be predominantly of small size. In their biconical shape they are similar to some vessels without major accessories (pl. 89:A–B). Almost all examples have decorated upper bodies—either notched (fig. 11:Family XC, IV-46), pocked (pl. 97:B), notched and incised (pls. 20:Q; 97:A), or scored (pl. 20:S). It is quite likely that multiple rod handles are typical for the group (pls. 20:Q; 97:A). In fact, the examples of Family XC stand out as having combinations of less common body forms and varieties of decoration and handle types. The smallest of the vessels with a notched handle (pl. 97:C) is undecorated, similar to a vessel of somewhat taller proportions (IV-58).[76]

Protoliterate Family XCI

> B–C.70; proportions 4–5, low neck, flat base, strap handle

> Figure 11; plate 97:D–F

Handled vessels with their greatest diameter below the middle of the body are very rare. Good parallels for their shapes are to be found in Families LXV and LXXII of the vessels without major accessories. The bodies might be either plain (pl. 97:F) or scored (pl. 97:D–E).

Protoliterate Family XCII

> a = C.53, .54, .55; b = C.63; c = C.65; varying proportions, high neck, medium mouth, flat base, strap handle, frequently high swung, many plain shoulders

> Figure 11; plates 97:G–J; 98:A–D

The strap-handled families discussed so far have all been characterized, aside from a few exceptions (pl. 97:D), by wide low necks. In contrast, the necks of the Family XCII vessels are higher and frequently narrower. Despite the variation in the proportions of the necks within this family, their difference from the standard necks of the other strap-handled vessels is evident. Concomitant with the heightening of the neck is that of the strap handle which almost always rises above the mouth and occasionally becomes markedly extended (pl. 98:A). Also adding to the individuality of the family is the circumstance that its members are frequently of very good standard ware or of fine ware with plain

---

76. For a parallel to plate 97:A, see Miroschedji 1976, fig. 8:12 (undecorated; Susa, Apadana, Trench 1038). For a parallel to plate 97:C, see Haller 1932, pl. 19 B:n″ (Warka, Eanna VI).

---

smoothed surfaces and no scoring. This family is divided into three parts according to the shape of the body, but so far only the first category is represented by more than one example.

> *a.* (C.53, .54, .55): The ovoid vessels of Subfamily XCIIa occur rather commonly in proportion 4; only one squatter example is at hand; it also stands out for its definite shoulder with crossed scoring (pl. 98:A).

> *b.* (C.63): The single example of Subfamily XCIIb, a double-angled vessel with an unusual decoration of carefully incised *xs* on its flat shoulder (pl. 98:C), is allied by both its shape and decoration with a four-lugged vessel (pl. 121:F).

> *c.* (C.65): Only one example of a high-necked ellipsoidal strap-handled vessel is so far at hand (pl. 98:D). The unusual shape is accompanied as in the preceding specimens by crossed scoring, a decoration unusual for Family XCII.

Protoliterate Family XCIII

> C.53, .54, .55; proportions 4–5, convex base, strap handle, plain or scored upper body

> Figure 11; plates 21:B–C; 98:E–K

Sometimes strap-handled vessels disobey the "rules" by appearing with convex bases. Two families of such jars can be distinguished and the first of these, Family XCIII, is subdivided by the absence or presence of a notched lip.

> *a.* (C.53, .54; proportion 4; low necks with rims; without notched lip) plate 98:E–F: The presence of a well-differentiated rim is characteristic for the Subfamily XCIIIa jars. Both of the two complete examples are very sharply contoured. The crossed scoring of the larger vessel is similar to that of other vessels (pls. 97:E; 98:I, K). The apparent rarity of Subfamily XCIIIa vessels might be partly an accident of preservation since the recognition of one of the defining features, the convex base, depends on the state of preservation of the body.

> *b.* (C.54, .55; proportions 4–5; necks usually rimless; semicircular lip) plates 21:B–C; 98:G–K: The only group of convex-based handled vessels that is fairly common consists of those with a semicircular lip attached to the neck opposite the handle. These lips can be plain (pl. 98:G) but are usually notched (cf. pl. 90:K–M). It is assumed that these, similar to the notches on the lips and handles of other families, pertain to the volumes of the vessels. However, as the number of examples increases, so does the

diversity of the markings. The five round imprints on III-879, the five irregularly-placed short notches on a fragment (pl. 21:B), and the rows of wedges on a complete vessel (pl. 98:J) differ considerably from the quite regular long notches on the lips of other examples (pl. 98:K [12 notches], H [13 or 14 notches], I [14 notches]). One of the latter also has notches on the handle (pl. 98:I), but these would presumably not be part of the volume notation. Their existence and the diversity of the markings on this subfamily and on the handles of other families suggest that sometimes the purpose was primarily decorative. The treatment of the bodies of the Subfamily XCIIIb jars varies. One is undecorated (pl. 98:G); one has fine-point scoring (pl. 98:H). The preferred treatment appears to have been crossed scoring (pl. 98:I–K).[77]

The assumption that the notched lips facilitated the handling of liquids is strengthened by a Protoliterate c jar from Khafajah similar in shape and crossed scoring to a vessel of this family (pl. 98:I) but with a small beak spout in place of the notched lip.[78]

Protoliterate Family XCIV

> D.55; proportion 6, low neck, convex base, strap handle
>
> Figure 11; plate 98:L–M

The vessels of Family XCIV are in general shape comparable to those of the preceding family, but their larger size, considerably higher proportions, rimless necks, and coarser ware give them a distinctive character. In fact they can be considered as variants of an example of Family LXXVII (pl. 91:A) with handles added. Both examples have lost their bases, but enough is preserved of one (pl. 98:M) to justify the restoration of a pointed base.

Protoliterate Family XCV

> D.55; flat base, strap handle
>
> Plates 16:B; 20:D; 21:K; 99:B–C

Rare among the strap-handled vessels are those of large size. In size and shape one example (pl. 21:K) is comparable to the high-necked jars of Subfamily XCIIa. Even when empty, it could not have been lifted by the handle alone. The vessel is overfired, with a sunken, warped wall on one side (pl. 99:B). An imprinted plastic band rings the neck and the root of the handle. Although the broad handle itself is missing, its attachment remains to show that it was perforated where it joined the rim. A fragment with two perforations shows that the strap handles of such outsize vessels were sometimes decorated (pl. 20:D).

A fragmentary large jar is unique at Chogha Mish for its combination of features definitive for two major Protoliterate categories, handles and a spout. The latter is now represented only by its hole surrounded by bits of welding clay. Not only is the presence of two handles unusual, but also is the attachment of their upper ends to the body of the jar rather than to its mouth. The rim is of undercut type, as so often on spouted vessels (pl. 99:C). The rough surface and imprinted plastic band encircling the rim are reminiscent of vessels described above (pl. 90:J, K). Two lines of incisions connect the ends of the handles. Isolated though it is at Chogha Mish, the jar (pl. 99:C) is by no means outside the mainstream of the Protoliterate ceramic tradition judging by some striking parallels—the fragments of two large vessels from the Shara Temple at Tell Agrab dated to the end of the Early Dynastic I phase.[79] One has a pair of large strap handles and the other a pair of two-strand twisted handles. Both pairs of handles are placed on their jars in the same position as the handles of the Chogha Mish vessel and have their ends connected by narrow bands of ornament.[80] These striking similarities between vessels separated from each other both geographically and chronologically suggest strongly that this jar (pl. 99:C), rather than being unique, represents a Protoliterate type that was common enough to have descendants in the Early Dynastic period.

Protoliterate Family XCVI

> B–C.54, .55; proportions 3–4, low neck, flat base, twisted vertical handle, shoulder scored
>
> Figure 11; plates 20:B–C, E–R; 100:A–E, G.

The jars with twisted handles are not only considerably rarer than the strap-handled jars, but also much less varied in size and shape. They are of medium size except for one miniature example assigned to Family LXXXVI (pl. 95:D). Low necks, flat bases and scored decoration are standard. There is some variation in the twisted handles from those with a circular section to

---

77. For parallels to plate 98:I–K, see Le Brun 1971, fig. 49:8, pl. 18:1 (rocker incision on lower body; Susa, Acropole I Sounding, Level 17), and Le Brun 1978a, pl. 28:9–11 (Susa, Acropole I Sounding, Level 17B); Strommenger 1963, pl. 38:a (Warka, Archaic Trench). For a variant with a vertical twisted handle instead of a strap handle, see Delougaz 1952, pl. 20:b (fragment from Tell Khubair near Khafajah).

78. See Delougaz 1952, pls. 20:a–a'; 194:D.545.626 (Khafajah, Sin Temple II, Kh. VII 116).

79. For a parallel to plate 99:C, see Delougaz 1952:60; pls. 51:a–b, 65:37–38 (Tell Agrab, lower level of Earlier Building of Shara Temple).

80. Similar vessels from Godin are considered by Virginia Badler to be beer containers. Badler has also demonstrated that the interior scorings in such vessels were intended to collect beer residue (Michel, McGovern, and Badler 1992; 1993; and personal communication). AA

those with an oblong section similar to that of the strap handles (pl. 20:B, H). However, the single twisted handles afforded little space for the notches characteristic of the strap handles; instead they were quite commonly marked by a round imprint at the point where the handle joins the lip (pl. 100:A) or were completely perforated (pl. 100:G). However, fragments of small twisted handles suggest that more small-sized vessels might have existed than are represented among the restorable vessels now available (pl. 20:E, L–P). One fragment has a round imprint plus notching (pl. 20:E) and another three imprints (pl. 20:M). In addition to the single twisted handles double and triple ones appear (pl. 20:I–K, R).

Protoliterate Family XCVII

B–C.63, .70; proportion 4, low neck, twisted vertical handle

Figure 11; plate 100:F

Double-angled vessels with twisted handles are extremely rare and related in body form to other rare families (LXV, XCI). It is interesting to note that the upper half of the single example (pl. 100:F) bears punctuations similar to its biconical strap-handled cousins of Family XC; unusual shapes tend to have rarer types of decoration. Another example of Family XCVII has ordinary crossed scoring (III-228).[81]

Protoliterate Family XCVIII

C–D.54, .55; proportion 4; low neck; carinated or ledge rim with two horizontal twisted handles, convex base, often rough surface

Figure 11; plates 21:D–I; 101:A–G, I

The vessels of Family XCVIII combine features of two major groups of pottery, the convex-based shape and rough surface of the Family LXXV cooking pots with the handles and incised decoration of the handled category. In fact, the horizontal-handled jars can, similar to those with notched lips, be considered as a specialized class of cooking pot. The handles are firmly attached at the middle to the rim and at the ends to the uppermost part of the body; thus they were clearly functional, providing a good grip for lifting the vessels. In contrast to the norm for handled vessels, the Family XCVIII jars always have rims, with a wide variety of ledges being common. A few examples have preserved their convex base (pl. 21:I).[82]

Protoliterate Family XCIX

C.54; low neck, convex base, one twisted horizontal and one strap handle

Figure 11; plate 101:J

The combination of one horizontal twisted and one strap handle on vessels otherwise analogous to those of Subfamily XCIIIb and Family XCVIII is exceptional at Chogha Mish (pl. 101:J). It apparently has not been found elsewhere except for one example from the 1929–1933 excavations of de Mecquenem at Susa.[83]

Protoliterate Family C

C.64, .75; basket handle, convex base

Figure 11; plate 101:H, K–M

Strap handles placed horizontally to form basket or bail handles occur only on the scoops of Family C and the rare small-sized spouted jars of Family CII. One example preserves only the stumps of the handle, welded to a slight neck (pl. 101:L). On another most of the handle and body fragments down almost to the round base remain (pl. 101:H). Detached handles preserved down to the juncture with the mouth indicate the existence of other examples (pl. 101:K, M). It is striking that three of the examples (pl. 101:H, L–M) were found in the same locus, R18:305. A highly specialized function presumably explains the great rarity of the scoops. They can be taken, however, as a standard type, since they recur, with slightly different details, at Khafajah and Jemdet Nasr in the late Protoliterate period.[84]

SPOUTED VESSELS (Figs. 12–13)

Spouted vessels are among the more numerous and characteristic forms of the Protoliterate period. While the possible combinations of size, ware, body shape, and accessories such as necks, rims, and spouts are almost unlimited, in actuality the vessels tend to cluster into a relatively small number of major families. Neck and rim types prove to be quite consistently correlated with certain fabrics, body shapes, and even sizes of vessels, so that they have, unexpectedly, provided somewhat more specific criteria for delimiting families than the spout types themselves (fig. 12). Accordingly, after the first family of miniature vessels (CI); necks and rims are used to delimit certain major orders of spouted vessels within each of which the usual arrangement according to size and body shape is followed. The determining fea-

81. For a parallel to plate 100:F, see Le Brun 1978a, fig. 28:2 (Susa, Acropole I, Level 17B).

82. For parallels to plate 101:A–G, I, see Le Brun 1971, fig. 49:12 (Susa, Acropole I, Level 17), and Le Brun 1978a, fig. 28:7 (Susa, Acropole I, Level 17B); 7N P278 and 7N P265 (everted rim) (Nippur, Inanna Temple XVII, XVI).

83. For a parallel to plate 101:J, see de Mecquenem 1934:197, fig. 33:3 (Susa, Acropole 1929–1933).

84. For parallels to plate 101:H, see Delougaz 1952:42, pls. 24:b, 166:B.757.605 (Khafajah, Houses 12, Protoliterate d); Mackay 1931:242f., pl. 64:32 (Jemdet Nasr).

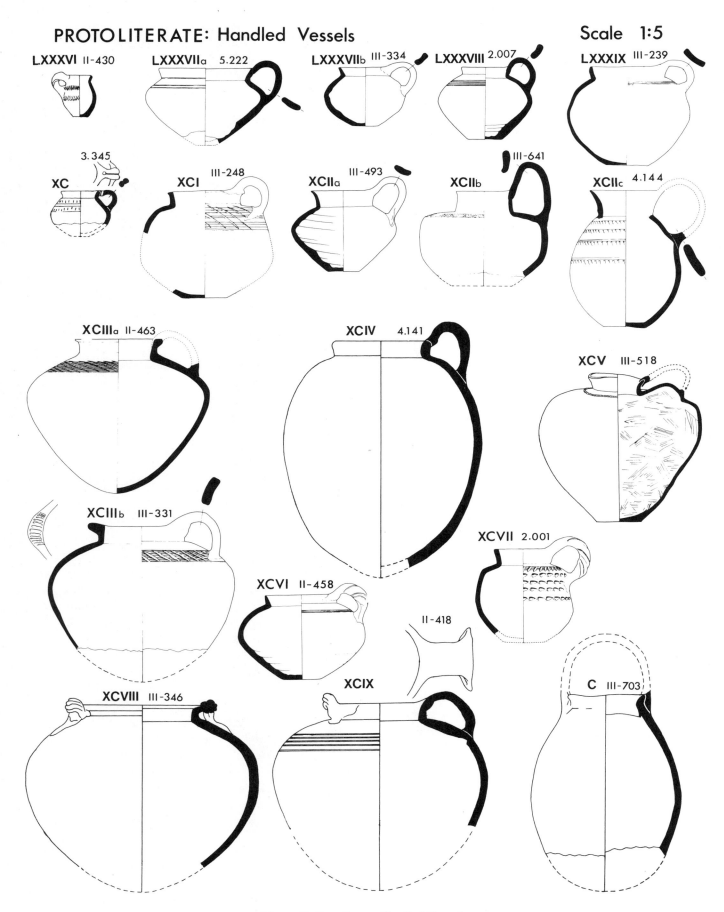

Figure 11. Protoliterate Handled Vessels

tures are as follows: vertical or almost vertical straight-sided necks without rims; flaring, concave-sided necks without rims; necks with rims; and minimal necks with rims or rims only.

Within each cluster of families, insofar as possible, the progression is from wide low necks to narrow high ones. As in the case of the distinction between open and closed forms, it is necessary to choose somewhat arbitrary definitions in order to divide the families between individual merging examples. The necks with inner diameters of more than 33% of the greatest inner diameter of the vessel are defined as wide, those with an inner diameter of 33–25% as medium, and those with an inner diameter of 25% or less as narrow.[85] In borderline cases the rule that "the majority prevails" can be followed. Only the miniature vessels remain outside these categories.

Protoliterate Family CI

A.54, .63, .75; varying proportions and accessories

Figure 12; plates 22:A–B, D–E; 102:A–D

Among the miniature spouted vessels ovoid shapes are more common (pl. 102:A–B). The double-angled example (pl. 102:C) is related in body shape to a Family LXV vessel (pl. 88:X). The baggy body of another example (pl. 102:D) is exactly the same shape as the vessel (pl. 88:AA). The miniature spouted vessels seem to be, for the most part, carefully made and several bear incised decoration.[86]

Protoliterate Family CII

B.54, .65; proportions 4–5, straight neck, vertical or diagonal; flat base, basket handle

Figure 12; plate 102:E–F

Small jars with essentially straight necks are given marked individuality by their basket handles. None is completely preserved; an example gleaned from the sherd yard of Trench V A has its entire body and flat base but only one root of the basket handle (fig. 12:IV-56). In only one case is most of the handle preserved

(pl. 102:E). Although spouted jars with basket handles were very rare, they nonetheless have descendants in the late Protoliterate period.[87]

Protoliterate Family CIII

C.5, .6; necks low to medium high and straight, usually vertical, flat bases

Figure 12; plates 22:F; 102:G–J; 103:A–F

This family is one of the large families of spouted vessels. The great majority of examples are of medium (C) size. They are normally of relatively gritty and roughly finished standard ware with quite thick walls, though more carefully finished examples do occur. For the most part the bodies are undecorated, except for occasional scoring on the shoulder (pl. 22:F). The spout types vary; curved and conical shapes are more common and a few swollen ones also occur. This family is divided into three subfamilies. The first two contain ovoid vessels of squat and taller proportions respectively. The third contains the ellipsoidal vessels.

a. (C.51, .53, .54; proportion mostly 4; with a few atypical examples; occasional B sizes) plate 102:G–J: This group is the most common of the Family CIII subfamilies. In proportions and the combination of ovoid bodies with fairly wide, rimless vertical necks, these vessels closely resemble the strap-handled vessels. A basic unit of the Protoliterate potters was the ovoid, straight-necked vessel of standard ware to which varying accessories could be added. The straight necks of Subfamily CIIIa jars sometimes deviate slightly from a strictly vertical stance.[88]

b. (C.55; proportion 5 or more) plates 22:F; 103:A–D: The straight-necked ovoid jars of relatively high proportions are rarer than the squat ones. Included here are jars with definitely ovoid bodies (pl. 103:A, D) and others that are almost ellipsoidal (pl. 103:B–C).[89]

---

85. These dimensions, derived from the Chogha Mish spouted vessels and defined in terms of interior diameter, vary somewhat from the definition of wide, medium, and narrow necks set up by Delougaz to distinguish shapes .64, .65, and .66 (Delougaz 1952:9, n. 15). These are based on exterior dimensions and are, of course, used in assigning shape numbers while the interior neck proportions, whenever pertinent, determine assignment to spouted families or subfamilies.

86. For a parallel to plate 22:D, see Mackay 1931, pl. 63:7 (Jemdet Nasr). For miniature spouted vessels not comparable to any specific Chogha Mish example, see Nissen 1970, pls. 38:f, 101:32 A.603.212 (Warka, K/L XII Sounding, Layer 40).

87. For parallels to plate 102:E–F, see Mackay 1931:240, pl. 63:30 (Jemdet Nasr); Delougaz 1952:42, pl. 178:C.515.265 (Protoliterate burial; Khafajah).

88. For parallels to plate 102:G, see Le Brun 1971, fig. 52:7 (Susa, Acropole I, Level 17); 7N 777 and 7N P233 (Nippur, Inanna Temple XVI–XV, XV); all with more rounded shoulders. For parallels to plate 102:I–J, see Le Brun 1971, fig. 52:8 (Susa, Acropole I, Level 17); de Genouillac et al. 1934, pl. VII 4806 (Tello).

89. For a parallel to plate 103:A, see Mackay 1931, pl. 63:1 (wall of neck slants inward; Jemdet Nasr). For a parallel to plate 103:C, see Haller 1932, pl. 18 D:g (Warka, Eanna VII). For a distantly related parallel, see Mackay 1931, pl. 63:4 (Jemdet Nasr). For a parallel to plate 103:D, see Mackay 1931, pl. 63:3 (Jemdet Nasr). For related form, see Le Brun 1971, fig. 52:6 (Susa, Acropole I, Level 17).

c. (C.64; proportions 5–6; conical or swollen spouts) plate 103:E–F: The vessels of Subfamily CIIIc have tall barrel-shaped bodies and characteristic blunt-lipped necks (pl. 103:E–F; fig. 4:74). Although the combination is distinctive, there is no break between these jars and others that are identical except that their bodies are slightly ovoid so that they have been placed in Subfamily CIIIb (pl. 103:C–D).[90]

Protoliterate Family CIV

D.53, .56; proportions 5–6, straight neck, flat base

Figure 12; plate 103:G–H

Large-sized spouted vessels with simple necks with either a vertical or diagonal stance are very rare. The body of one example is unusual because of its straight walls below the shoulder (pl. 103:G).[91]

Protoliterate Family CV

B–C.5, .5, .7; varying proportions, flaring neck, flat base

Figure 12; plates 22:K; 103:I; 104:A–L; 105:A–H

The necks of Family CV vessels flare, not only because of their stance, but also in many cases, because they have a concave profile. Spouted vases with such rimless necks are very common and can be divided into a number of distinct groups. When taken as a whole, however, they form such a minutely graduated series of shapes that it seems better to subsume them under one family heading.

In contrast to Families CII and CIII, in which vessels with their greatest diameter in the middle of the body are either absent or form only a small minority, in Family CV they are frequent. Furthermore, many of the ovoid (.5) vessels approach ellipsoidal (.6) shapes.

The defining feature of this family, the flaring neck, in itself a sharply profiled accessory often ending in a tapered lip, was frequently set on a sharply profiled or elegantly curving body. Associated with the clear definition of the shapes is the frequency of fine fabric. Very fast wheel marks are common (pl. 22:K) and the outer surface, particularly of the upper parts of the body, is well smoothed but normally without decoration.

The subfamilies are distinguished by size, width of neck, and proportion. Although the majority of forms are of middle size, constituting Subfamilies b–f, there is a substantial number of small vessels that are set apart as Subfamily a. Subfamily b contains the numerous vessels which are of proportions 4–5 and have either wide or medium-sized necks. The defining characteristics of Subfamily c are the high proportions, 6, and the wide mouths. The vessels of Subfamily d are also of high proportions, 6–7, and provide the transition from medium-sized to narrow necks. The last two subfamilies, e and f, contain the vessels with narrow necks and are differentiated from each other by lower, 4–5, or higher, 6, proportions.

a. (B.54, .55, .60, .65; proportions mostly 4 but rarely 3; low necks, wide to medium in diameter) plates 104:A–G, J; 105:D: The small-sized vessels are also squat, the result being that even the ovoid forms approximate biconical or globular forms. Some of the jars are of relatively rough quality, comparable to that normal for the squat one-handled vessels of the same size range, but others have sharper and smoother profiles (e.g., pl. 104:B–C, E). One vessel (pl. 104:F) is disgracefully asymmetrical for this family. The bow neck of one example (pl. 104:E) and the straight neck of another (pl. 104:J) are atypical. The spouts are for the most part either conical or curved.[92]

b. (C.50, .51, .52, .53, .54, .55, .60, .61, .65, .66; proportions 4–6, wide or medium neck) figure 12:IV-412; plates 104:H–L; 105:A–B, G: In their paste the vessels of Subfamily CVb vary from examples made of ordinary gritty standard ware to those of refined dense buff or greenish-buff fine ware (pl. 104:I); the latter tend to have sharper profiles and to be well smoothed. In general, many examples of this group are better in quality than most of the vessels of Subfamily CVa. Ellipsoidal shapes are very common (fig. 12:IV–412; pl. 105:A, G) and some of the ovoid vessels are themselves almost ellipsoidal (pls. 104:L; 105:B). An example unusual for its slightly concave lower walls (pl. 104:K) is allied by its sharp

---

90. For parallels to plate 103:E–F, see Miroschedji 1976, fig. 7:6 (Susa, Apadana, Trench 1038); Haller 1932, pl. 19 B:g′ (Warka, Eanna VI). For related forms with rounded bottom, see Haller 1932, pl. 18 D:k (rounded base; Warka, Eanna VII); and 7N P311 (.7 body; Nippur, Inanna Temple XIX).

91. For more cylindrical, but related parallels to plate 103:G, see Le Brun 1978b, fig. 31:5–7 (Susa, Acropole I, Level 17B); Le Brun 1971, fig. 52:6 (Susa, Acropole I, Level 17); Lenzen 1961, pl. 17:b (small, degenerate neck; Warka, Md XV4, "Jemdet Nasr").

92. For a parallel to plate 104:A–C, see 7N P266 (Nippur, Inanna Temple XVI). For a parallel to plate 104:B, E, see Miroschedji 1976, fig. 7:9 (Susa, Apadana, Trench 1038). For a parallel to plate 104:D, see Haller 1932, pl. 198:v (Warka, Eanna VI). For a parallel to plate 104:G, see Le Brun 1978a, fig. 31:10 (Susa, Acropole I, Level 17B). For a parallel to plate 104:H, see Haller 1932, pl. 19 B:x (Warka, Eanna VI). For a parallel to plate 104:I, see 7N 766 (Nippur, Inanna Temple XV). For a parallel to plate 105:D, see Haller 1932, pl. 19 D:c′ (Warka, Eanna V).

carination to the vessels on plate 109:B–C, E; it has not been classified with them since in place of their conical spouts it has a curved one and since it might have possessed only a flaring neck. Curved spouts predominate in Subfamily CVb, although occasional conical (fig. 12:IV-412) and swollen (pl. 104:I) examples occur.[93]

c. (C.47, .55; proportions 6, wide neck) plate 103:I: Tall spouted vessels with wide flaring necks form Subfamily CVc. They are, in contrast to the squatter jars of Subfamily CVb, very rare.[94]

d. (C.55, .65; proportions 6–7; medium to narrow necks) figure 12:IV-371; plates 22:K; 105:C, F: The range in shape in Subfamily CVd is strikingly limited, particularly if contrasted to that in Subfamily CVb. Here the vessels are barrel-shaped. The occasional very slightly ovoid example (fig. 12:IV-371) is hardly distinguishable from the completely ellipsoidal shapes (pl. 105:C, F). The normal proportions fall within the range of 6, but some taller examples exist (pl. 105:F). The necks tend to be higher and to flare in a more pronounced curve than do those of the preceding subfamilies. Many specimens are of fine ware and well made. The long conical spout both interrupts and accentuates the bold and elegant curves of the body and neck.[95]

e. (C.54, .55, .65; proportions 4–5, narrow neck) figure 12:III-31; plate 105:H: Vessels of relatively squat proportions and with narrow necks, usually less exuberant in shape than those of the preceding group, form Subfamily CVe. One example is, except for its spout, is a globular flask (pl. 105:H). Another, of a refined grade of standard ware with only a few scattered grits, is

somewhat taller (fig. 12:III-692). A type that can be described as a squat variant of the Subfamily CVd jars also exists (III-242).[96]

f. (C.54, .55, .66; proportions 6, narrow neck) figure 12:III-692; plates 105:I; 106:A: The vessels of Subfamily CVf are distinguished from those of CVe by their higher proportions. In one case (pl. 106:A) the body is similar to those of some Subfamily CVe jars, but the neck is very tall; it has in addition a large bulge at the juncture of the body and neck, which gives the jar a striking individuality. The shape of a tall ovoid jar (pl. 105:I) is, except for its large size, similar to that of the vessels of Family LXI. Although narrow necks occur only rarely without rims, they appear with rims in some of the more populous of the spouted families.[97]

Protoliterate Family CVI

C.70, .74; proportions 4–5, medium or narrow neck

Figure 12; plate 105:E

Vessels with their greatest diameter in the lower part of the body, the rarest category of shapes in Protoliterate pottery, sometimes appear with a spout (pl. 105:E), which is a somewhat larger version of a narrow-necked vessel (cf. pl. 88:X). The shape of the fragmentary 2.430 (fig. 12) can be restored by analogy with some Closed Form pottery (pl. 88) and it shares its reserve slip with several double-angled vessels without accessories (pls. 88:W; 89:B, S–V).[98]

Protoliterate Family CVII

C–D.54, .55, .66; narrow necks, varying rims, flat bases, frequently good standard or fine ware

Figure 12; plate 106:B–E

The presence of a narrow neck with a slight rim is the diagnostic feature of Family CVII. Examples are rare but can be subdivided according to their squat or high proportions and size.

a. (C.54, .55; proportion 4; curved or swollen spouts) plate 106:B–C: Two squat, narrow-

93. For body shape parallel to plate 104:N, see Haller 1932, pl. 19 B:h″ (with strap handle), and C:k′ (curved spout) (Warka, Eanna VI). For parallels to plate 105:A, see Haller 1932, pl. 19:B:z (Warka, Eanna VI); Strommenger and Sürenhagen 1970:65, fig. 22:C (Habuba Kabira South). For parallels to plate 105:B, see Le Brun 1978a, fig. 31:9 (Susa, Acropole I, Level 17B); 7N 791 (Nippur, Inanna Temple XVII). For parallels to plate 105:G, see Miroschedji 1976, fig. 7:8 (Susa, Apadana, Trench 1038); Lenzen 1961, pl. 17:a (Warka, Eanna VI–V).

94. For parallels to plate 103:I, see Haller 1932, pl. 19 A:k″ (smaller, taller neck with beveled rim; Warka, Eanna VI); 7N 788 (vertical, flat-lipped neck; Nippur, Inanna Temple XVII–XVI); de Genouillac et al. 1934, pl. 7:4937 (vertical, tapering neck; Tello).

95. For parallels to plate 105:C, F, see Miroschedji 1976, fig. 7:7 (Susa, Apadana, Trench 1038); possibly Haller 1932, pl. 19 C:z (neck missing, no spout indicated; Warka, Eanna VI); de Genouillac et al. 1934, pl. 17:3 (Tello).

96. For forms related to figure 22:III-31, see Nissen 1970, pl. 98:98 (Warka, K/L XII Sounding layer); Strommenger 1975:163, fig. 6 (Habuba Kabira South). For a parallel to plate 105:H, see Nissen 1970, pl. 98:99 (Warka, K/L XII Sounding layer).

97. For a parallel to plate 105:I, see Mackay 1931, pl. 63:6 (Jemdet Nasr). For a parallel varying in some details to plate 106:A, see Mackay 1931, pl. 63:29 (C.746.272, neck bulge carinated; Jemdet Nasr).

98. For a form related to figure 12:2.430, see Sürenhagen 1974/75, pl. 16:99 (narrow neck, long curved spout, reserve slip; Habuba Kabira South). For a parallel to plate 105:E, see Haller 1932, pl. 19 B:w (Warka, Eanna VI).

necked vessels vary in the details of their body, necks, and spout. They seem to be individual specimens rather than representatives of recurring types.[99]

b. (C.55; proportion 6, curved spouts) plate 106:D and 5.223: A rare but very specific group of narrow-necked vessels is characterized by its good ware and high ovoid shape. The bodies have marked wheel corrugations on the interior and approach in character the bodies of both the bottles with rimless necks (pl. 105:G) and those with collared rims (pl. 111). The necks are also similar to those of the bottles but have beveled ledge rims. The long curved spouts provide still another similarity to the bottles of Families CVe and CXVI.[100]

c. (D.66; proportion 6) plate 106:E: A unique vessel (pl. 106:E) stands out from the other members of Family CVII because of its size and ellipsoidal body shape and is therefore assigned to a subfamily of its own. Its narrow neck is quite high and more vertical than the other necks in this family. The beveled-ledge rim resembles those of Subfamily CVIIb.[101]

Protoliterate Family CVIII

C.55, .63, .65; proportions 4, 6, medium neck and rim with one, exceptional, or two, normal, pierced lugs, presumably flat base, normally conical spout

Figure 12; plate 106:F–H.

The diagnostic feature of Family CVIII, the neck lug, is outstanding and rare. One example (pl. 106:F), which is included here even though its neck is rimless, has a flat base, which is presumably standard for the group. The other incomplete examples (pl. 106:G–H) were probably globular (.6), but could have been rounded ovoids (.55). The neck and its accessories give the vessels of Family CVIII an unmistakable individuality. The usual arrangement appears to be a pair of pierced lugs attached to the neck, with a conical or curved spout projecting asymmetrically from underneath one of them, which thus forms a buttress between spout and neck (pl. 106:G–H). In one case the spout is separate, placed at a right angle to the lugs (fig. 12:IV-182). The example with the rimless neck (pl. 106:F) is atypical in having only one lug. Rare rim fragments with only one lug preserved presumably belong to this family (4.207). Another, 5.307, has reserve slip. The other decoration so far associated with the group is scoring, either horizontal (pl. 106:G) or vertical (pl. 106:F).[102]

Protoliterate Family CIX

C–D.5, .6; proportions 4–5, a few 6, low to high necks with rims, usually flat bases, varying spout types

Figures 12; 13; plates 107:A–N; 108:A–E

Many types that have in common relatively straight-sided and usually vertical necks ending in a variety of small rims, frequently ledges, constitute Family CIX. Included here is a vessel that conforms to the specifications of Family CIX except that its neck has no defined rim (pl. 107:L); such examples are rare. The necks range from wide to medium in diameter with the latter being more common. Ovoid bodies predominate, and the large sizes (D) are rarer than the medium sizes (C).

In keeping with their well-formed rims, these vessels are usually of good quality and frequently have distinctive surface treatment. The first four subfamilies are distinguished on the basis of their low or high necks combined with the absence or presence of reserve slip (Subfamilies CIXa–d); the last two are defined by the presence of specific special features.

a. (C.50, .53, .54, .55, .64, .65; low neck of wide to medium diameter, no reserve slip) plates 23:A–B; 107:A–B, I: Vessels with low neck but no reserve slip constitute the first of the CIX subfamilies. Since these low-necked examples grade into the higher-necked examples of Subfamily CIXb, the dividing line between the two subfamilies must be fairly arbitrary. The only small example of Subfamily CIXa (pl. 107:A) is just over B size; it has an unobtrusive thickened rim (cf. fig. 4) and a line of notches at the lip of the spout. A finger-imprinted plastic band (pl. 23:B) and rocker incision (pls. 23:A; 107:I) are found on other vessels. Trumpet spouts appear to be particularly characteristic for Subfamily CIXa.[103]

99. For a related form to plate 106:C, see Le Brun 1978b, fig. 32:12 (Susa, Acropole I, Level 18).

100. For parallels to plate 106:D, see Le Brun 1978b, fig. 32:15 (Susa, Acropole I, Level 18); de Genouillac et al. 1934, pl. 4:5497 (Proportion 7; Tello); Palmieri 1977, fig. 8 (Arslan Tepe VIa).

101. For parallels to plate 106:E, see Strommenger 1963, pl. 37:e (D.547.242; Warka, Archaic Settlement); 7N P322 (D.536.242; Nippur, Inanna Temple XV); Sürenhagen 1974/75, pl. 17:100 (more elongated, D.667.272; Habuba Kabira South).

102. For a parallel to plate 106:G–H, see Sürenhagen 1974/75, pl. 33:10–12 (lug only preserved; Habuba Kabira South).

103. For parallels to plate 107:A, see Haller 1932, pl. 19 D:a′ (Warka, Eanna VI); Strommenger 1975, fig. 8 (Habuba Kabira South). For forms related to plate 107:B, see Steve and Gasche 1971, pl. 30:24 (Susa, Apadana, 1965 Sounding, "Jamdat Nasr ancien-Uruk récent"); Mackay 1931, pl. 63:9 (Jemdet Nasr).

b. (C.50, .54, .55, .65, .66; high neck of medium diameter, no reserve slip) plate 107:C–H: The high necks of Subfamily CIXb are prominent except for those of some transitional examples (pl. 107:D, F). The CIXb vessels are, with one exception (pl. 107:C), of proportions 5 and 6, and thus higher than the Subfamily CIXa jars, which are commonly of proportion 4. The bodies vary, some being plain and some having horizontal scoring at about the lip of the spout (pl. 107:C) or notches (pl. 107:G) or rocker incision (pl. 107:H) covering the upper body. Curved, swollen, and straight spouts appear on Subfamily CIXb vessels.[104]

c. (C–D.53, .54; low neck of medium diameter, rim, reserve slip) figure 13; plates 19:E; 107:J–K: The addition of reserve slip distinguishes Subfamily CIXc from CIXa, to which it otherwise corresponds. On one example (pl. 107:J) the reserve slip begins at the neck, but on two others the uppermost part of the body is set off by a scored line (pl. 107:K) or by a finger-imprinted plastic band (pl. 19:E) below which the reserved slip begins. The latter also has two circles of notches just below the plastic band. Trumpet spouts are favored.[105]

d. (C–D.53, .54, .65; high neck of medium diameter, usually with rim, reserve slip) figure 13; plate 107:L–N: The vessels of Subfamily CIXd have essentially the same combination of body, neck, and rim as the CIXb jars, with the addition of reserve slip. Curved (pl. 107:L, N) and swollen (pl. 107:M) spouts appear. A large-sized relative without major accessories (pl. 92:D) belongs to Family LXXX.[106]

e. (C.64, .65, D.60, .65; high neck, usually with rim, buttressed spout, proportions normally 6–7) figure 13:V-40; plate 108:A–D: Subfamily CIXe consists of rare vessels distinctive for their combination of ellipsoidal bodies and high necks with specialized, buttressed spouts.

These are straight or swollen spouts set directly against the neck, with any empty space filled by a wedge of clay. Some examples, though hollow, are false spouts not opening into the interior of their vessels. The proportions of the jars are usually tall, with one exception (pl. 108:A), whose body should probably be restored as squatter, proportion 5. Both examples have a line of notches with reserve slip below. The latter has a true spout, but that of the former is false. The attenuation of the taller examples has left their spouts clinging to the neck and in two cases (pl. 108:C–D) opening into it; the vessel (pl. 108:C) found in the ninth season serves to identify a tiny and puzzling spout fragment found earlier. Another completely preserved tall specimen has a false spout (pl. 108:D). The buttressed spout jars of proportion 7 are closely related in form to one of the rare families of vessels without major accessories (pl. 94:E–F).[107]

f. (C–D.5; high neck, incised decoration or other atypical features) figure 13; plate 108:E: The niche for high-necked vessels with atypical features provided by Subfamily CIXf has at present only one occupant, a fragment of a large vessel with a sharply curved spout and two registers of incised geometric decoration of a type normally reserved for four-lugged vessels (cf. pl. 122:B). Although at Chogha Mish this piece remains unique, at Susa a four-lugged fragment with the same design had a spout, now broken, and thus provides an analogy for the appearance on one vessel of features usually only found separately on different major categories of Protoliterate pottery.[108]

Protoliterate Family CX

C.54, .55, .56; multiple spouts

Figure 13; plates 26; 108:F–H

Vessels with more than one spout are extremely rare and must have had specialized functions. Only

---

104. For a guttered rim similar to plate 107:E, see Nissen 1970, pl. 91:37 (Family CXV pithos fragment; Warka K/L XII Trench, Layer 38). For undecorated fragments of simple vessels parallel to plate 107:F, see Le Brun 1978a, fig. 31:8 (Susa, Acropole I, Level 17B); Le Brun 1971, fig. 52:1 (Susa, Acropole I, Level 17). For related forms, see Mackay 1931, pl. 63:11 (wide neck, undecorated; Jemdet Nasr), and 13 (taller proportions, scored). For an example related to plate 107:G, but squatter with scoring, see Sumner 1974:106, fig. 4:a (Malyan, Banesh period).

105. For a parallel to plate 107:J, see 7N P274 (Nippur, Inanna Temple XVII, XVI).

106. For a parallel to plate 107:M, see Sürenhagen 1974/75, pl. 12:76 (Habuba Kabira South).

107. For parallels to figure 12:IV-182, see Nissen 1970, pl. 98:102 (Warka, Square K/L XII Sounding, Layer 39); Hansen 1965:204, fig. 15 (7N P296 [neck and false spout fragment]; Nippur, Inanna Temple XVIII). For a parallel to plate 108:C, see Steve and Gasche 1971, pl. 32:62 (Susa, Acropole 1965 Sounding, "Jamdat Nasr ancien-Uruk récent"). For a parallel to plate 108:D, see 7N 786 (C.7 body and reserve slip; Nippur, Inanna Temple XVII–XVI). For a related form to figure 13:V-40 (R21:509), also with reserve slip, see Le Breton 1957:96, fig. 10:16 (Susa, Acropole, older excavations, Susa B).

108. For a parallel to plate 108:E, see Le Brun 1971, fig. 51:7 (Susa, Acropole I, Level 17).

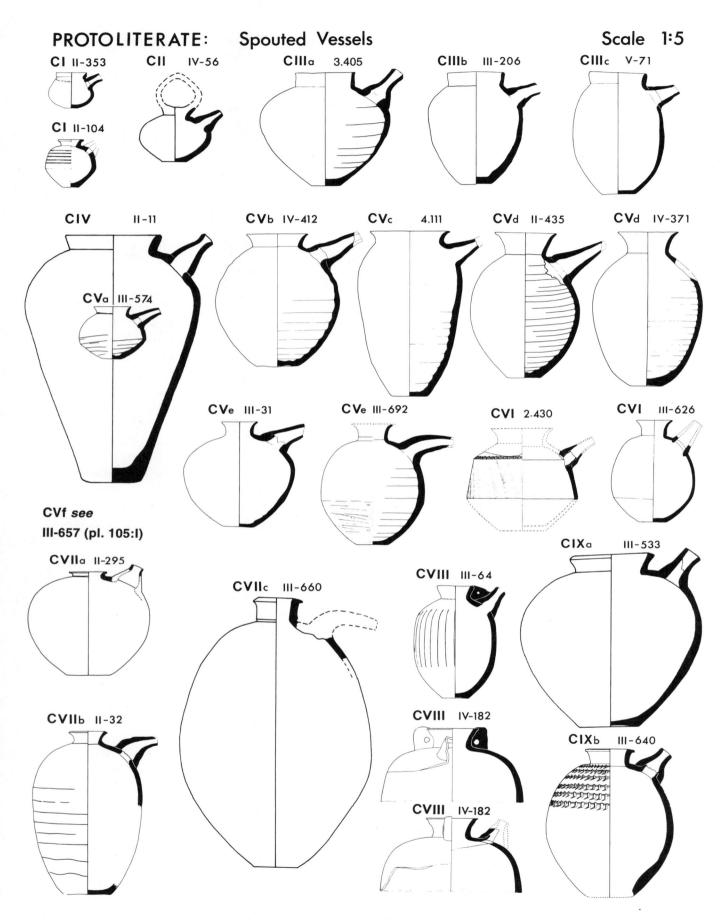

Figure 12. Protoliterate Spouted Vessels, Families CI–CIXb

Table 6. Spouted Vessels, Similar to Chogha Mish Protoliterate Families CI–CIXa–b, Present at Other Sites

	CI	CII	CIII a	CIII b	CIII c	CIV	CV a	CV b	CV c	CV d	CV e	CV f	CVI	CVII a	CVII b	CVII c	CVIII	CIX a	CIX b
SUSA																			
Acropole 1965																			
"Jamdat Nasr récent"	—	—	—	—	—	—	—	—	—	—	—	—	—	—	—	—	—	—	—
"Jamdat Nasr ancient-Uruk récent"	—	—	—	—	—	—	—	—	—	—	—	—	—	—	—	—	—	×	—
Apadana Trench 1038	—	—	—	—	×	—	×	×	—	×	—	—	—	—	—	—	—	—	—
Acropole I																			
17	—	—	×	×	—	×	—	—	—	—	—	—	—	—	—	—	—	—	—
17B	—	—	—	—	—	×	×	×	—	—	—	—	—	—	—	—	—	—	—
18	—	—	—	—	—	—	—	—	—	—	—	—	—	—	—	—	—	—	—
WARKA																			
Md XV4: Archaic Settlement																			
"Jemdet Nasr"	—	—	—	—	—	×	—	—	—	—	—	—	—	—	—	×	—	—	—
K/L XII Sounding																			
"Spät-Uruk"	×	—	—	—	—	—	—	—	×	×	—	—	—	—	—	—	—	—	—
Eanna Precinct and Test Pit																			
III–II	—	—	—	—	—	—	—	—	—	—	—	—	—	—	—	—	—	—	—
IV	—	—	—	—	—	—	—	—	—	—	—	—	—	—	—	—	—	—	—
V	—	—	—	—	—	—	×	×	—	—	—	—	—	—	—	—	—	—	—
VI	—	—	—	—	×	—	×	×	×	×	—	×	—	—	—	—	—	×	—
VII	—	—	—	×	×	—	—	—	—	—	—	—	—	—	—	—	—	—	—
IX–VIII	—	—	—	—	—	—	—	—	—	—	—	—	—	—	—	—	—	—	—
XII	—	—	—	—	—	—	—	—	—	—	—	—	—	—	—	—	—	—	—
NIPPUR																			
Inanna Temple																			
XII	—	—	—	—	—	—	—	—	—	—	—	—	—	—	—	—	—	—	—
XIII	—	—	—	—	—	—	—	—	—	—	—	—	—	—	—	—	—	—	—
XIV	—	—	—	—	—	—	—	—	—	—	—	—	—	—	—	—	—	—	—
XV	—	—	×	—	—	—	×	—	—	—	—	—	—	×	—	×	—	×	—
XVI	—	—	—	—	—	—	×	—	×	—	—	—	—	×	—	—	—	×	—
XVII	—	—	—	—	—	—	×	—	—	—	—	—	—	—	—	—	—	—	—
XVIII	—	—	—	—	—	—	—	—	—	—	—	—	—	—	—	—	—	—	—
XIX	—	—	—	—	×	—	—	—	—	—	—	—	—	—	—	—	—	—	—
XX	—	—	—	—	—	—	—	—	—	—	—	—	—	—	—	—	—	—	—
TELLO	—	—	×	—	—	—	—	—	×	—	×	—	—	—	×	—	—	—	—
JEMDET NASR	×	×	×	×	—	—	—	—	—	—	—	—	×	—	—	—	—	×	—
KHAFAJAH Protoliterate c–d	—	×	—	—	—	—	—	—	—	—	—	—	—	—	—	—	—	—	—
HABUBA KABIRA SOUTh	—	—	—	—	—	—	—	×	—	×	—	—	×	—	—	×	×	×	—
ARSLAN TEPE VIa	—	—	—	—	—	—	—	—	—	—	—	—	—	—	×	—	—	—	—

three have been recovered from Chogha Mish. The most elaborate of them has appliquéd decoration of snakes and goats around the emplacements for two now lost spouts (pls. 26; 108:F). This jar and the Mesopotamian evidence for double spouted vessels is discussed in detail below. A small vessel had originally two spouts projecting at opposite sides of the body, but only their stumps remain; the neck is also missing (pl. 108:G). The third example is the most enigmatic one, consisting of a convex wall from which spring three spouts. Even the correct orientation of this fragment is not certain (pl. 108:H).

Protoliterate Family CXI

C–D.64; wide mouth with ledge or undercut rim, no neck, cut spout

Figure 13; plate 108:I–L

The defining features of the rare Family CXI jars are shape and a specialized type of spout. The globular vessels have mouths so wide that they approach open forms. Although none is intact, almost complete examples of C (pl. 108:I) and D (III-552a) sizes might be used to reconstruct the small fragments (pl. 108:J–L). The cut spouts are limited to this family alone. The rims are set directly on the bodies without any necks. The larger examples differ from the smaller types in having undercut rim types instead of small horizontal ledges and spouts set just below the rim rather than flush with it (pl. 108:K). Notched and reserve-slip decoration are characteristic (pl. 108:I, L). The latter also has centered on its spout asymmetrical pairs of curving notched lines similar to a Family CIX example (pl. 108:A).[109]

Protoliterate Family CXII

B–C.5; varying proportions, minimal neck with rim, swollen spouts and flat bases predominate

Figure 13; plate 108:M–P

Ovoid jars with rims resting on minimal necks constitute Family CXII. Medium (C) sizes predominate. The fabric varies from the ordinary to the finer grades of standard ware. Swollen spouts are usual. Two subfamilies are distinguished on the basis of the proportions, the first containing the squatter vessels and the second the taller vessels.

a. (B–C.55; proportions 2–3, flat base) figure 13; plate 108:M–N: A quite small vessel (pl. 108:M) is also particularly squat (2). It is decorated by a scored line with notches. A larger example (pl. 108:N) has scoring only.[110]

b. (C.53, .54, .55; proportions 4–5, flat base) figure 13; plate 108:O–P: Among the taller vessels of Family CXII, one has a flaring rim (pl. 108:P) and another a beveled edge rim (pl. 108:O). The more complete one is remarkable as it combines features that do not usually occur together. Its globular rough-surfaced body and everted rim link it with the cooking pots (cf. pl. 90:F), but it has the pair of notched lips (cf. pl. 90:K). The missing base of one vessel (pl. 108:P) can accordingly be restored as convex, which instead of the single plastic bands that sometimes occur on Families LXXV and LXXVI vessels has an unparalleled group of six bands covering the upper half of the body. The addition of the spout comes as an unexpected climax. Unfortunately no sherds from the base were found; it has been restored as flat, similar to those of the majority of the spouted vessels. However, if the vessel was made primarily as a Family LXXVI jar with the spout as a secondary addition, then its base must have been convex.

Protoliterate Family CXIII

C.6; biconical or ellipsoidal, minimal necks with ledge or band rims, flat bases, proportions 3–4, better grades of standard or fine ware

Figure 13; plates 22:G; 109:A–H

Vessels with rims attached to minimal necks make up both Families CXII and CXIII, but in the first the center of gravity is in the upper part of the body (.5) and in the second in the middle of the body (.6). Throughout the description of the spouted vessels, the contrast between these two main body shapes is evident even though other features have at times taken precedence in defining groups.[111] That the distinction between these two categories of shape is no mere modern nicety but a major difference recognized anciently is proven by two archaic signs representing spouted vessels, the one ovoid and the other spherical (Falkenstein 1936, signs 149 and 153).

A biconical or ellipsoidal shape alone does not place a vessel in Family CXIII since identical or similar shapes occur commonly among the flaring-necked vessels of Subfamily CVc (pl. 103:I). A specimen must also have either a square-ended ledge rim (cf. fig. 5:116 [pl. 109:A–C]) or a band rim (fig. 5:125 [pl. 109:F]; 5:127 variants [pl. 109:D, G–H]; 5:131 [pl. 109:E]) to qualify as a member of Family CXIII. Within the family two groups are distinguished by the shape of the body, first that containing definitely biconical forms and second that with rounded globular forms. While the contrast between the pure types is clear (pl. 109:E versus H), other examples are intermediate and harder to classify (pl. 109:D, G). Examples of both are rare.

a. (C.60; biconical, proportion 3–4) plate 109:A–E: Subfamily CXIIIa vessels are notable for their pronounced shapes, from the biconical bodies, which are markedly carinated in the squatter forms, to the sharp angles of the rims and the long spouts sweeping in a bold diagonal line well above the mouth. It is likely that the spouts were always conical, but this cannot be proved without additional examples. One example (pl. 109:B) is unusually small but otherwise a splendidly characteristic example of the subfamily.[112]

109. For parallels to plate 108:I–J, see Miroschedji 1976, fig. 5:8 (rim fragment; Susa, Apadana, Trench 1038); Haller 1932, pl. 18 D:n (Warka, Eanna VII). For later versions with neck added, see Steve and Gasche 1971, pls. 27:13–14, 84:4, 9 (Susa, Acropole 1965 Sounding, "Jamdat Nasr finale").

110. For a type similar to plate 108:N, see Le Brun 1971, fig. 62:3 (narrower mouth, undercut rim, proportion 3, row of notches; Susa, Acropole, Level 14B).

111. For groups in which body form is a primary element of classification, see Subfamilies CIIIa and b versus CIIIc, CVIIa and b versus CVIIc, or CIXe. For groups in which other features take precedence over body form, see Subfamilies CVa–e (size, width of neck, proportions) or CIXa–d (height of neck and presence or absence of reserve slip).

112. For a parallel to plate 109:A, see Haller 1932, pl. 19 C:a′ (body more rounded; Warka, Eanna VI). For a parallel to plate 109:B, see ibid., 19 C:h′ (concave below carination similar to plate 104:M, of taller proportions, herein). For a

b. (C.65; bodies rounded, proportion 4) plate 109:F–H: Although the profiles of Subfamily CXIIIb vessels are smoothly curving, a comparison of shapes (pl. 109:D and G) shows that there is no sharp demarcation between these two subfamilies. In the CXIIIb group the spouts, either straight (pl. 109:F–G) or conical (pl. 109:H), are shorter than those of Subfamily CXIIIa. One vessel has a scored line marking the middle of its body and a row of notches encircling the neck and spout as is clear in the top view (pl. 109:F).[113]

Protoliterate Family CXIV

C.65; spouts set at mouth and frequently buttresses

Figure 13; plate 110:A–C, G–H

The defining characteristics of Family CXIV are a spout set directly at the neck or rim of a vessel of medium size. The family is so far represented only by one complete specimen and a handful of detached spouts. Although the unusual position of the spout links them, these examples are not sufficient to provide an adequate family description. In shape, one example (pl. 110:G) is intermediate between examples from Family CIIIb–c (pl. 103:B, F), but the position of its spout allies it with various detached buttressed spouts similar to those attached to the high necks of elongated jars of Subfamily CIXe. In Family CXIV, however, the buttressed spouts are set against either simple necks or rims or against minimal necks with rims of various types (pl. 110:A–C, H). Some of the detached spouts might have belonged to vessels shaped similar to III-790 (pl. 110:G).[114]

Protoliterate Family CXV

D.5, .6; wide to medium mouth with rim or rim and neck

Figure 13; plates 23:D; 110:D–F, I–O

An important group of large vessels and pithoi, many of which when filled would have been too heavy to move, make up Family CXV. In both general character and various specific features some of the examples resemble the pithoi without accessories of Families LXXX–LXXXII. They would have made good stationary storage vessels, the big mouths facilitating access to the interior and the projecting rims providing a good hold for tying on lids or cloth covers. The spouts are usually placed in a fairly vertical position on the highest and flattest part of the body.

Since often only the upper parts of examples are preserved, it is difficult to subdivide the family according to body shape or proportions. As in other spouted families, a useful diagnostic feature is the treatment of the mouth. Examples with an undercut rim are set apart as Subfamily CXVc, while the remaining examples, which display a variety of rims and necks, are subdivided by proportion, the higher proportions forming Subfamily CXVa and the squatter proportions Subfamily CXVb.

a. (D.54, .55; proportion 6) plate 110:D–E: In addition to the high proportions, variations in the shape of the neck and base are typical for Subfamily CXVa. The neck can be either minimal (pl. 110:D) or substantial (pl. 110:E). The former preserves part of its flat base; the latter's missing base can be confidently restored as convex by analogy with a more complete example, 4.793 and a specimen from Warka. Such jars are rare at Chogha Mish, but representatives of the subfamily are well known in the pottery of the later Protoliterate period.[115]

b. (D.54, .55, .65; proportions not higher than 5, rim sometimes with minimal neck) plate 110:I–K: Although mostly incomplete, the examples of Subfamily CXVb are clearly of squatter proportions than those of the preceding group. A semi-complete example, V-83, is of great importance for its pointed base, which indicates that some, at least, of the incomplete forms might have had convex bases. The example (pl. 110:F) with a buttressed spout is combined with the paired knobs of Family LXXXI and the imprinted band found in various of the families without major accessories. The decoration of another jar (pl. 110:J) is unusual in having horizontal reserve slip below the neck and a

---

form related to plate 109:E, see Lenzen 1961, pl. 17:e (rounded instead of carinated, curved spout, pointed base, C.603.642; Warka, Eanna VI–V).

113. For a parallel to plate 109:G, see Haller 1932, pl. 19 C:a′ (combines features of both pl. 109:A and G; Warka, Eanna VI).

114. For a parallel to plate 110:B, see Hansen 1965:205, fig. 20 (neck and spout only; 7N P264, P268; Nippur, Inanna Temple XVI). For a parallel to plate 110:G, see Nissen 1970, pl. 87:14 (neck and spout only; Warka, K/L XII, Layer 37).

115. For rim and spout fragments probably belonging to vessels similar to plate 110:D, see Steve and Gasche 1971, pl. 30:24 (Susa, Acropole 1971 Sounding, "Jamdat Nasr ancien-Uruk récent"); Nissen 1970, pls. 101:28, 91:45 (Warka, K/L XII Sounding, Layers 40, 38). For parallels to plate 110:E and 4.793, see Haller 1932, pl. 19 A:1″ (proportions similar to pl. 110:E; absence of neck similar to 4.793; Warka, Eanna VI), B:a (proportion 6, minimal neck; Warka, Eanna VI); see also a similar but squatter 7N P218 (Nippur, Inanna Temple XIV–XIII). For related type, see Sürenhagen 1974/75, pl. 14:84 (Habuba Kabira South).

scrabbled line instead of the few notches standardly typical (V-83; 4.196). The largest spouted vessel so far found at Chogha Mish is represented by a fragment with a mouth about 32 cm wide and a spout 12 cm in diameter (pl. 110:I). Seven slightly raised and slashed moldings cover the portion of the body preserved.[116]

c. (D.53, .54, .55; proportions 4–6, undercut rim) plate 110:L–O: The pithoi with undercut rims vary considerably in their proportions, with one example as high as 6 (III-670). Although its base (see also pl. 110:M, O) is flat, some convex bases might have existed, as in Subfamilies CXVa–b. The bodies can be altogether plain (pl. 110:M) or decorated at the neck by an imprinted plastic band (pl. 110:L). However, reserve slip appears to have been particularly common (pl. 110:K, O). Swollen spouts seem to have been favored over straight and conical spouts.[117]

Protoliterate Family CXVI

D.55, .66; proportions 7–8, minimal necks with collared rims, curved spouts, flat base

Figure 13; plates 23:E–F; 111:A–L

Large, narrow storage vessels are some of the more common and more easily distinguished of the spouted forms. Even small body sherds or bases of such bottles can be recognized by their almost cylindrical shape and specific interior appearance, pronounced wheel ridges if the fragment is from the lower part of the vessel or a smoothed surface if it is from the upper part. The greatly elongated proportions might occasionally obscure the fundamental ovoid form of most of the bottles (pl. 111:G–H). True ellipsoidal examples are rare (pl. 111:L). In addition to the body shapes, other defining features are the narrow necks and the collared rims, appearing in both vertical (fig. 6:160–162) and angled versions (fig. 6:164–167). The varying shapes of the collared rims seem to have no chronological significance. The collared necks, aside from the atypical (fig. 6:159, 163), are specific for the bottles and do not occur on the nearest relatives of the bottles, the smaller and squatter

jars (pl. 106:D; cf. fig. 6:156–158). Bottles always have down-curving spouts, forming one of the rare cases of a family with a diagnostic spout type. The walls of the bottles are sturdy and their bases quite thick. The external walls were left plain except for occasional scored lines that seem to be haphazard occurrences without decorative intent (pl. 111:E, H). The complete bottles found range from 32 cm to 80 cm in height. An even larger fragmentary example (pl. 111:J) would have been about 1 m high when complete.[118]

The bottles were obviously designed to store liquids and to be easily closed. The imprints of narrow mouths often remain on the clay stoppers that are ubiquitous in the Protoliterate town area (pl. 130:N–V). Since other narrow-mouthed vessels are relatively rare, many of the stoppers must have sealed bottles. The shape and sturdiness of the bottles made them suitable for transport in slings, carried either by pack animals or, attached to a pole, by two men, as shown by a cylinder seal impression from Warka.[119] The bases of the bottles are too narrow for them to stand unsupported; they were probably stacked against walls, perhaps sometimes massed in storerooms. It should be noted that, common as the bottles are, their distribution is irregular. In some loci they are abundantly represented but are entirely missing in others.

FOUR-LUGGED VESSELS (Fig. 15)

The variety in size and execution displayed by these vessels is extraordinary. They range from large jars over 0.50 m in diameter to miniatures smaller than the lugs of the large jars. They occur in many types of ware: coarse, standard, fine, and the specialized red. The surfaces vary from plain or rough in the larger-sized vessels to smoothed, wet-smoothed, elegantly cream-slipped, or red-washed in the smaller ones. The most common shapes are squat ovoids, but flat-shouldered

116. For general parallels to plate 110:C, but varying in details and smaller, see Le Brun 1971, fig. 52:9 (Susa, Acropole I, Level 17); Haller 1932, pl. 19 A:m″ (Warka Eanna VI). For a parallel to plate 110:J, see Sürenhagen 1974/75, pl. 5:60 (wide mouth, flat base, reserve slip; Habuba Kabira South).

117. For spouted pithos fragment with rim close to undercut types similar to plate 110:O, see Nissen 1970, pl. 86:27 (plain body; Warka, K/L XII Trench, Layer 36); 7N P274 (notches and reserved slip; Nippur, Inanna Temple XVII); see ibid. pl. 91:37 for a fragment of a similar pithos with guttered rim (Warka, K/L XII Trench, Layer 38).

118. For parallels to plate 111:A–L, see Le Brun 1978b, fig. 34:8 (Susa, Acropole I, Level 18); Le Brun 1978a, fig. 30:7–14 (Susa, Acropole I, Level 17B); Le Brun 1971, fig. 52:5 (Susa, Acropole I, Level 17); Steve and Gasche 1971, pls. 30:25; 32:32–34 (Susa, Acropole 1965 Sounding, "Jamdat Nasr ancien-Uruk récent"); Haller 1932, pls. 18 D:a′; 19b″, p″; 19 D:v; 20 A:o, r (Warka, Eanna VII, VI, V, IV); Lenzen 1959a, pl. 21:f (Warka, *Steinstiftempel*); Nissen 1970, pls. 96:84; 87:9–11, 17, 18 (Warka, K/L Sounding, Layers 39, 37); 7N 785 and 7N P257 (Nippur, Inanna Temple XVII–XVI, XVI); Lloyd 1948:51f., figs. 3:9; 4:23–24 (Uqair VII–VI); de Genouillac et al. 1934, pl. IV 5434 (Tello); Thompson and Mallowan 1933, pl. 50:3 (collared rim; Nineveh IV); Sürenhagen 1974/75, pl. 17:101–04 (Habuba Kabira South); Hoh 1981, fig. 23:7 (Hassek Hüyük, Late Chalcolithic).

119. Lenzen 1960, pl. 29:h–i; the vessel carried here is of wider and squatter proportions than the bottles.

PROTOLITERATE: Spouted Vessels

Scale: 1:5 (cxvₐ,ᵦ 1:10)

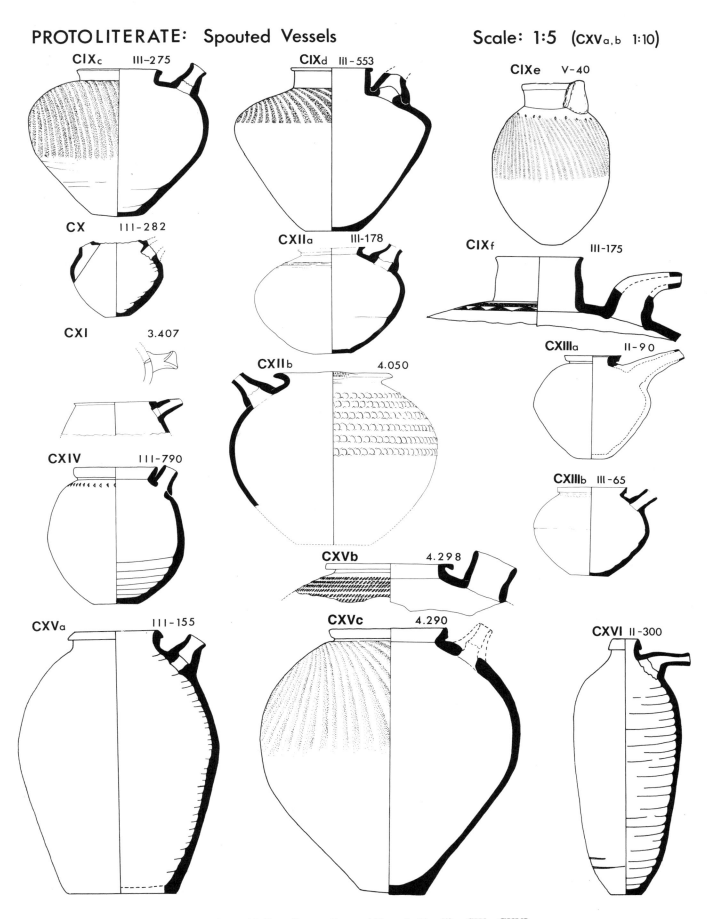

Figure 13. Protoliterate Spouted Vessels, Families CIXc–CXVI

Table 7. Spouted Vessels, Similar to Chogha Mish Protoliterate Families CIXc–f–CXVI, Present at Other Sites

| | PROTOLITERATE FAMILIES | | | | | | | | | | | | | | |
| | CIX | | | | CX | CXI | CXII | | CXIII | | CXIV | CXV | | | CXVI |
	c	d	e	f			a	b	a	b		a	b	c	
SUSA															
Acropole 1965															
"Jamdat Nasr récent"	—	—	—	—	—	×	—	—	—	—	—	—	—	—	—
"Jamdat Nasr ancien-Uruk récent"	—	—	×	—	—	—	—	—	—	—	—	×	—	—	×
Apadana Trench 1038	—	—	—	—	—	×	—	—	—	—	—	—	—	—	—
Acropole I															
17	—	—	—	×	—	—	—	—	—	—	—	—	×	—	×
17B	—	—	—	—	—	—	—	—	—	—	—	—	—	—	—
18	—	—	—	—	—	—	—	—	—	—	—	—	—	—	×
WARKA															
K/L XII Sounding															
"Spät-Uruk"	—	—	×	—	—	—	—	—	—	—	×	×	—	×	×
Eanna Precinct and Test Pit															
III–II	—	—	—	—	—	—	—	—	—	—	—	—	—	—	—
IV	—	—	—	—	—	—	—	—	—	—	—	—	—	—	×
V	—	—	—	—	—	—	—	—	×	—	—	—	—	—	×
VI	—	—	—	—	—	—	—	—	×	×	—	×	—	—	×
VII	—	—	—	—	—	×	—	—	—	—	—	—	—	—	×
IX–VIII	—	—	—	—	—	—	—	—	—	—	—	—	—	—	—
XII	—	—	—	—	—	—	—	—	—	—	—	—	—	—	—
NIPPUR															
Inanna Temple															
XII	—	—	—	—	—	—	—	—	—	—	—	—	—	—	—
XIII	—	—	—	—	—	—	—	—	—	—	—	—	—	—	—
XIV	—	—	—	—	—	—	—	—	—	—	—	×	—	—	—
XV	—	—	—	—	—	—	—	—	—	—	—	—	—	—	—
XVI	×	—	×	—	—	—	—	—	—	—	×	—	—	—	×
XVII	×	—	×	—	—	—	—	—	—	—	—	—	—	×	×
XVIII	—	—	×	—	—	—	—	—	—	—	—	—	—	—	—
XIX	—	—	—	—	—	—	—	—	—	—	—	—	—	—	—
XX	—	—	—	—	—	—	—	—	—	—	—	—	—	—	—
UQAIR VII–VI	—	—	—	—	—	—	—	—	—	—	—	—	—	—	×
UR Late Protoliterate Graves	—	—	—	—	×	—	—	—	—	—	—	—	—	—	—
ERIDU "Late Uruk"	—	—	—	—	—	—	—	—	—	—	—	—	—	—	×
TELLO	—	—	—	—	—	—	—	—	—	—	—	—	—	—	×
NINEVEH IV	—	—	—	—	—	—	—	—	—	—	—	—	—	—	×
HABUBA KABIRA SOUTH	—	×	—	—	—	—	—	—	—	—	—	×	×	—	×
HASSEK HÜYÜK															
Late Chalcolithic	—	—	—	—	—	—	—	—	—	—	—	—	—	—	×

and carinated bodies also occur. The four lugs are placed on the shoulder at approximately equal distance from one another, but asymmetrically spaced lugs also occur (pls. 114:E–F, J). Often an incised or punctuated decoration in one or more horizontal bands connects the lugs, the specific character of the ornament varying according to the size and type of the individual vessels. The shape of the lugs themselves varies considerably from rather broadly triangular to attenuated, the latter reminiscent of long-beaked bird heads (pl. 25:F, L, N).

Furthermore, on red-washed vessels, paired lugs sometimes replace the normal single ones.

Such pierced lugs have been considered as devices for suspension, but it is pointed out that in many cases such a use would have been impractical and that pierced lugs were probably used to fasten lids (Delougaz 1952:41, 53). The pottery from Chogha Mish supports this view. The size of the large four-lugged jars is such that one person could hardly have lifted one of them when filled; much less could they have been suspended by their lugs. Moreover, the lugs were not riveted or otherwise firmly fastened to the body. On one large vessel a lug was found in place but detached since it had been joined to the body by nothing more than a little wet clay (III-695).

Protoliterate Family CXVII

A.53, .54, .55; proportions 3–4, wide to narrow necks, sometimes with rim, bases flat or convex

Figure 15; plates 24:A–B; 112:A–J

The miniature four-lugged vessels usually have a proportion of 3 but are occasionally slightly squatter or taller. A few examples with a diameter somewhat over 6 cm have been included in the miniature class. The necks or mouths vary from wide to medium. Bases are round or flat. The shoulder decoration is normally a simple row of notches (pls. 24:A; 112:E–G, J) or variations such as notches strung on a scored line (pl. 112:C) or narrow hatched bands (pl. 112:B, H). The wide bands of incised decoration (pls. 24:B; 112:A, D, I) and the row of knobs (IV-219) are unusual for miniatures. In general, the four-lugged miniatures are more carefully made than most of the miniature vessels of less specialized types; one example (pl. 112:A) is atypically crude.

Protoliterate Family CXVIII

B.53; proportion 3, wide to medium necks, flat base, usually notches or narrow hatched band on shoulder

Figure 15; plate 113:A–E

Squat ovoid vessels with relatively wide low necks and flat bases form Family CXVIII. Though undecorated shoulders can appear (pl. 113:E), normally rows of notches either alone (pl. 113:A, D), strung on scoring (pl. 113:B), or placed within a narrow band (pl. 113:C) adorn them. It should be noted that the lines were scored as the vessels turned on the wheel and hence were circular, while the simple notches were sometimes added after the attachment of the lugs and form a "square" when seen from above (pl. 113:A).[120]

Protoliterate Family CXIX

B.54; proportion 2, wide rimless mouth with cut lip, flat base, four holes corresponding to four lugs

Figure 15; plate 113:F

The Family CXIX niche accommodates an aberrant vessel shaped similar to a small, squat four-lugged jar,

but without rim or lugs. Instead, four irregularly spaced holes pierce the upper part of the vessel.

Protoliterate Family CXX

B.54; proportions 3–4, narrow neck usually with rim, convex base usual

Figure 15; plates 113:G–I; 114:A–F

The vessels of Family CXX are similar to those of Family CXVIII except for two distinguishing features, the narrow neck, frequently ending in a cut lip or an outbeveled ledge rim, and the prevalence of the convex base. The flat bases of two vessels (pl. 113:G–H) are exceptional. In addition to the various notched decorations normal for the small four-lugged vessels, scored lines (pl. 113:G–H) and a hatched band appear (pl. 113:I). There is an excellent example of the rarer pattern of a wide hatched band (pl. 24:D), which was clearly incised after the attachment of the lugs.[121]

Protoliterate Family CXXI

B.60, .63, .74, .75; proportion 4, wide to narrow necks, sometimes with slight rim, flat or slightly concave bases, lines of notches on shoulder

Figure 15; plate 114:G–J

Several examples of the rarer body shapes appear among the smaller four-lugged vessels and are well paralleled among the other major classes of Protoliterate pottery. A miniature strap-handled vessel (pl. 97:C) provides a model for the reconstruction of the lower part of another vessel (pl. 114:F). One example has an extremely rare shape (pl. 114:G) that is paralleled by a small jar (pl. 88:S) without accessories. The red-washed jar (pl. 114:H) is a squatter version of a Family LXV example (pl. 88:S). The shape and row of notches on II-434 (pl. 114:J) are well paralleled by a vessel without accessories (pl. 88:W) and by a small spouted jar (pl.

---

120. For parallels to plate 113:A, see Haller 1932, pl. 19 D:b (with broad crosshatched band similar to pls. 109:A and 114:A herein; Warka, Eanna VI); Nissen 1970, pl. 98:110 (Warka, K/L XII Sounding, Layer 39). For parallels to plate 113:E, see Le Brun 1978b, fig. 32:11 (red wash; Susa,

Acropole I Sounding, Level 18); 7N P321 (body diameter 13.5 cm, row of notches; Nippur, Inanna Temple XIX).

121. For a form related (perhaps a local imitation) to plate 113:G, see Palmieri 1977:131, fig. 12 (Arslan Tepe VIa). For parallels to plate 114:A, see Thompson and Mallowan 1933, pl. 52:9 (red ware; Nineveh IV); Sürenhagen 1974/75, pl. 18:124 (Habuba Kabira South); Helms 1981:227, fig. B4:7 (Jawa, "Late Chalcolithic"). For parallels to plate 114:B–D, see Hoh 1981, fig. 23:1–2 (Hassek Hüyük, Late Chalcolithic); Esin 1974, fig. 107:4 (probably a local imitation; Keban Dam area, Tepecik, Late Chalcolithic); Kantor 1965:28, fig. 4:A (Egypt, Mostagedda, Gr. 1837, Gerzean). For parallels to plate 114:E, see Hansen 1965:203, fig. 11:a (7N 801; Nippur, Inanna Temple XIX); Mackay 1931, pl. 64:4, 6 (Jemdet Nasr). For parallels to plate 114:F, see Miroschedji 1976, fig. 8:6 (Susa, Apadana, Trench 1038); Hansen and Dales 1962, fig. 14 (7N 806; Nippur, Inanna Temple XIX burial).

102:D). The simple line of notches is the normal decoration for Family CXXI.[122]

Protoliterate Family CXXII

> C.51, .56; proportion 3, necks wide to medium, bases flat, disc, or ring, shoulders mostly undecorated, red wash typical

Figure 15; plates 24:I; 114:K–M

The main diagnostic feature for Family CXXII is the flattened shoulder, which is sometimes sharply carinated (pl. 114:K–L). The medium-sized vessels are made of dense standard or of fine ware and tend to be red-washed. In keeping with this trait is the absence of decoration. Another feature often linked with red wash is the ring base (pl. 114:L–M). The lips of the necks usually widen into small ledge rims. This is one of the rarer families of the four-lugged jars.[123]

Protoliterate Family CXXIII

> C.51, .54, .56; proportions 2–3, 6, medium necks tending to be high, strap handle in addition to four lugs, bases flat

Figures 14; 15; plate 115:A–E

A very rare but important special class of four-lugged vessels is characterized by the addition of a vertical strap handle, usually attached to the shoulder but in the smallest example to shoulder and lip as on the ordinary strap-handled vessels (pl. 115:A). Four of the five examples are flat-shouldered vessels (fig. 14; pl. 115:A, C–E). The range in proportions is very wide, from 2 to 6. All examples have vertical necks; apparently the flatter the shoulder, the taller the neck became. The tapering or blunt lips might flare out slightly.

In ware the Family CXXIII vessels vary from standard to fine. The surface can remain completely plain (pl. 115:A), have scoring with notches at the shoulder

(pl. 115:B), or be covered with red wash (pl. 115:E), which does not exclude the use of a band of incised decoration (fig. 14). The latter also exemplifies the narrow, elongated lugs, here arranged in pairs, which are linked with the use of a red wash (pl. 25:F). The most outstanding example of this family (pl. 27:A–B) has several unusual features, above all the incised decoration covering its tall body; see the discussion below.[124]

Protoliterate Family CXXIV

> C. 53, .54, .65; proportions normally 3, medium low neck, small ledge rim, hatched bands, often with knobs below, on shoulder, standard, fine, and red wares

Figure 15; plates 24:K; 120:A–D

Fairly wide ovoid vessels usually made of finer wares and sometimes covered with a cream slip or a red wash are typical of Family CXXIV. Gritty ware and a plain surface are atypical. Some bases are flat or slightly concave; small ring bases also appear. Much attention was paid to the sharp profiling of the necks and ledge rims. Normally the careful execution of the body is paralleled by the elegance of narrow hatched bands bordered below by a line of small pellets. Vessels so decorated are among the finer of the four-lugged vessels.[125]

---

122. For parallels to plate 114:I, see Strommenger 1963, pl. 39:h (squatter; Warka, Archaic Settlement); Hansen and Dales 1962, fig. 12/7N 803 (gray ware; Nippur, Inanna Temple XIX burial); de Genouillac et al. 1934, pl. VI 4936 (no notches; Tello); Sürenhagen 1974/75, pl. 18:132 (squatter, narrower neck, for related shapes, see also ibid., pl. 18:127–31; Habuba Kabira South). For related, but larger, squatter form, see Delougaz 1952, pl. 189:C.702.253 (Khafajah, Protoliterate d). For a parallel to plate 114:J, see Le Brun 1978a, fig. 24:12 (Susa, Acropole I, Level 17B).

123. For parallels to plate 114:K, see Le Brun 1978a, fig. 32:3 (only thickened rim; Susa, Acropole I, Level 17B); Le Brun 1971, fig. 51:1, 4–5 (variations of same body types; Susa, Acropole I, Level 17). For parallels to plate 114:L–M, see Le Brun 1978a, fig. 32:5 (Susa, Acropole I Sounding, Level 17B); 7N 782 (small, with no rim; Nippur, Inanna Temple XVI); Sürenhagen 1974/75, pl. 11:74 (Habuba Kabira South); idem 1975, fig. 7 (Habuba Kabira South).

124. See Sürenhagen 1974/75, pls. 9:69.1 (two false spouts opposite handle), 69.2 (false-spouted; unpierced lugs similar to those opposite handle in fig. 12.7), 10:70 (paired handles, false spouts), 12:75 (false spout, unpierced lug) (Habuba Kabira South). For high shape, see Alden 1979:272, fig. 50:4 (Malyan, Banesh period). For vertical bands dividing body of a vessel into panels, see Sürenhagen 1974/75, pl. 11:73 (red-washed jar similar to pl. 115:C, but broad punctuated bands substituting for lugs; Habuba Kabira South). For parallels to plate 115:A, see Le Breton 1957:98, fig. 11:35–36 (also spouted; Susa, Acropole, old excavations, Susa Cb–c); for stone examples, see ibid., p. 110, fig. 28:26, 32, 33 (with spout); Le Brun 1978a, fig. 28:1 (Susa, Acropole I, Level 17B). For an example with characteristics of plate 115:A–B, but lacking lugs, see de Genouillac et al. 1934, pl. 6:4976 (Tello). For a parallel to plate 115:C, see Le Brun 1978a, fig. 32:1 (Susa, Acropole I Sounding, Level 17B).

125. For parallels to plate 120:C, see Hansen and Dales 1962:84, fig. 14:7N 802, 804 (Nippur, Inanna Temple XIX burial), 7N P230 (Nippur, Inanna Temple XV burial); de Genouillac et al. 1934, pl. 24:3 (narrower mouth, flat lip; Tello). For parallels to plate 120:E, see Le Breton 1957:98, fig. 11:26 (Susa, Acropole, old excavations, Susa C); Le Brun 1978b, fig. 32:10 (Susa, Acropole I, Level 18); 7N P305 and 7N P273 (Nippur, Inanna Temple XIX, XVII–XVI); de Genouillac et al. 1934, pls. A, bottom; 25::2 (Tello); Kantor 1965:28, fig. 4:F (Egypt, Badari, Area 3800). For a parallel to plate 120:D, see Le Breton 1957:99, fig. 12:8 (Susa, Acropole, old excavations, Susa Cb).

Protoliterate Family CXXV

> C.55, .66; proportion 4, narrow neck, convex base, standard or fine ware

> Figure 15; plate 120:E–G

Narrow necks, medium-sized globular bodies, and round bases make the vessels of Family CXXV unmistakable. They are larger versions of some small-sized four-lugged vessels (pl. 114:B–D) and are also related to the flasks without accessories (pl. 90:A–B, D), although there both flat and convex bases occur. In both groups ellipsoidal bodies appear; one flask (pl. 120:E) is a .5 shape on one side and a .6 on the other, while both III-666 and 5.314 are ellipsoidal. The narrow necks sometimes end in slight rims; the beveled rim of one vessel (pl. 120:G) is the same as that on a flask (pl. 90:B). Similar to the flasks among the types without accessories, these vessels are among the rarer four-lugged forms. They are made of either a good quality standard ware or of fine ware, sometimes with a buff or cream slip. The standard shoulder decoration is a row of notches with or without a scored line.

Protoliterate Family CXXVI

> C.54; proportion 6, narrow neck, presumably flat bases, fine ware and special features

> Figure 15; plates 24:F, K; 121:A

The diagnostic character for Family CXXVI is the high ovoid form, which is extremely rare among the four-lugged vessels, one of which (pl. 121:A) has been combined with a narrow flaring neck and a small base, that is, exactly the shape typical for one of the common families of the closed vessels without accessories (pl. 88). The body of one small example of that family is covered by rocker imprints (III-676) and this specific type is well paralleled at other sites. However, there seems to be only one known example (pl. 121:A) of this shape to which four lugs have been added, although they do appear on a squat, rocker-decorated jar from Susa. A further refinement in the decoration—the red wash covering the base, shoul-

der, and undoubtedly the now missing neck—is standard for this type.[126]

The other example of this family (pl. 24:K) can even in its incomplete state be seen to have been of higher proportions than the normal four-lugged vessels. It is carefully made in a dense gray to buff ware. Between the lugs it has three knobs in place of the usual narrow lines of incised or notched decoration.

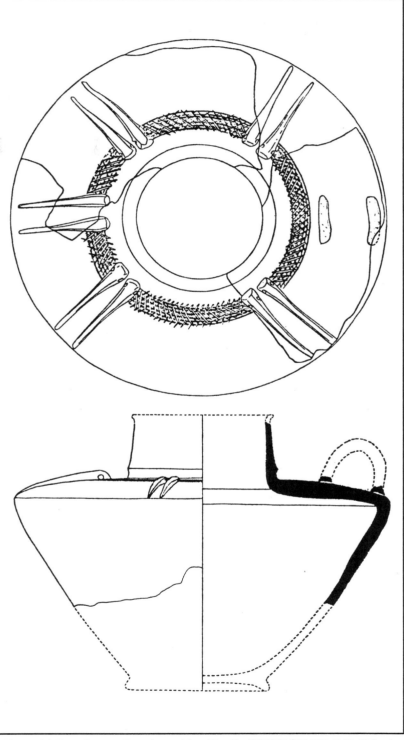

Figure 14. Protoliterate Four-lugged Jar: Family CXXIII (III-550; R18:301; el. ca. 82.60; Fine Ware; Orange-Buff Clay, Red Wash on Exterior)

126. For parallels to plate 121:A, see Le Breton 1957:99, fig. 13:1 (without lugs), 5 (atypical form, .734, with lugs) (Susa, Acropole, old excavations, Susa Ca); Haller 1932, pl. 19 D:a (Warka, Eanna VI); Hansen 1965:201, fig. 1 (7N 807; Nippur, Inanna Temple XIX burial).

Protoliterate Family CXXVII

> C.49, .63, .65, .70; proportions 3–4, flat base, standard, fine and red ware

> Figure 15; plates 24:J; 121:B–I

The rare vessels that are not ovoid but have wider necks than those of Family CXXV make up the present family. Three main types of bodies appear and provide the basis for subdivision.

> *a.* (C.65; proportions 3–4, vertical or flaring neck of medium diameter) plate 121:B–C: The vessels of Subfamily CXXVIIa have their center of gravity in the middle of the body, which is always rounded. The necks tend to be short and without defined rims. The usual decoration is a line of notches, but one large, squat example of red ware has between each pair of lugs a notched band with two knobs below.[127]

> *b.* (C.70; proportion 4, rimless necks) plate 121:D–E: So far there are only two specimens whose widest diameters are below the middle of the body at the point where the line of the profile changes direction—one has a definite angle (pl. 121:D) and the other only a gentle curve (pl. 121:E). Both are variants of the .70 shape that occasionally occurs among the small four-lugged vessels (pl. 114:H) as well as in the other major categories of Protoliterate pottery. Although the necks vary in shape and height, they are both rimless. One example has scoring, which in four-lugged vessels is a more unusual shoulder decoration than the row of notches.[128]

> *c.* (C.49, .63; proportions 3–4, low, rimmed necks of median diameter) plates 24:J; 121:F–I: Subfamily CXXVII includes vessels that are double-angled and for the most part sharply profiled. Though the body of one example is rather rounded, its shape is, nonetheless, fundamentally the same as that of the others (pl. 121:H). The squattish jar (pl. 121:G) is unusual for the marked inward slant of its walls below the shoulder but is otherwise quite similar to a

vessel of more standard shape (pl. 121:F). In contrast with the two preceding groups, here the necks are always low and tipped with slightly overhanging ledge rims. There is considerable variation in the shoulder ornament. However, the most remarkable of the individual elements are the tubular lugs that appear in place of the triangular ones on the well-made, fine ware vessel (pl. 121:I). The tubular lugs are unparalleled among the many lugged vessels and fragments from Chogha Mish, yet they cannot be considered as a unique aberrant variation since a vessel from Susa of almost identical shape and decoration has exactly the same type of lug.[129]

Protoliterate Family CXXVIII

> C.54, .54; proportions 3–4; wide to medium mouth, minimal neck with rim or rim only; flat base; broad band as bands with incised geometric decoration

> Figure 15; plates 24:H; 25:D–E, H–P; 122:A–J; 123:A–C

One of the more prominent classes of four-lugged vessels is that defined by both size and the presence of wide bands of incised geometric decoration. Such ornament is usually found on big vessels, either the D or large C sizes. Only rarely does it occur on medium-sized vessels (pl. 24:H) or, atypically, on miniatures (pl. 112:A, D). The motifs are, in order of frequency, crosshatching, hatched triangles, semicircles, herringbone (pls. 25:I; 122:C), zigzags (pl. 122:J), and crosshatched lozenges (3.266). Most common is the crosshatched band, occurring either singly (pls. 25:H; 122:A, D–E) or doubly (pl. 122:F, I). A band with crosshatching and one with hatches or crosshatched triangles are frequently combined (pls. 24:H; 25:D–E; 122:B, G–H). Less common are three-band (pls. 25:K, N; 122:J) or occasionally four-band (3.266) combinations. The most elaborate of the incised geometric motifs are the semicircular or peltate elements usually placed in one of several incised bands (pls. 25:L–N; 123:A–C).

The sturdy jars of Family CXXVIII were clearly storage vessels. Many of them would have been ex-

---

127. For a parallel to plate 121:B, see Le Breton 1957:98, fig. 11:23 (squatter; Susa, Acropole, old excavations, Susa Ca).

128. For parallels to plate 121:D, see Le Breton 1957:98, fig. 11:27, 28 (Susa, Acropole, old excavations, Susa Cb); Hansen 1965, p. 203, fig. 11b (7N 799; Nippur, Inanna Temple XIX); for a related form, see Delougaz 1952, pl. 186:C.634.253 (Khafajah, Protoliterate c). For parallels to plate 121:E, see Le Breton 1957:98, fig. 11:31 (Susa, Acropole, old excavations, Susa C); Strommenger 1963, pl. 39:h (squatter; Warka, Archaic Settlement). For larger vessel of related shape, see Weiss and Young 1975:7, fig. 3:1 (Godin V).

129. For a parallel to plate 121:G, see Le Breton 1957, fig. 11:3d (Susa, Acropole, old excavations, Susa Cb). For possibly related later forms in which the body turns inward slightly below the level of lugs, see Mackay 1931, pl. 64:7, 13 (Jemdet Nasr); Delougaz 1952, pl. 175:C.413.253b, C.413.253c (Khafajah, Protoliterate c). For a parallel to plate 121:F, see Le Breton 1957, fig. 11:29 (Susa, Acropole, old excavations, Susa Cb). For parallels to plate 121:I, see Steve and Gasche 1971, pls. 32:14, 86:13 (Susa, Acropole 1965 Sounding, "Jamdat Nasr ancien-Uruk récent"); 7N P263 and 7N P230 (Nippur, Inanna Temple XVI, XIV).

tremely heavy when full. Their rims and lugs would have facilitated the attachment of covers. Their prominent bands of incised decoration suggest that the vessels were kept in rooms where their attractive appearance could be appreciated rather than in purely utilitarian storage areas.[130]

Protoliterate Family CXXIX

> C.53, .54; proportion 4, neck with rim, flat base, painted shoulder decoration

> Figure 15; plates 24:E; 123:D–F

Four-lugged vessels with painted instead of incised decoration on their shoulders are extremely rare, amounting so far to only two complete specimens and a few sherds. However, several different types of decoration are represented. None can be equated with the painted Jemdet Nasr ware of the later part of the Protoliterate period.

Two sherds (pl. 123:F), one of them preserving the stump of a lug, represent a vessel that had first been painted in black just below the neck with a design of horizontal bands enclosing a crosshatched zigzag and afterward covered with a transparent red wash that extended upward over the four lowermost painted bands. The result is a bichrome decoration. Another sherd does not preserve a lug but unmistakably belongs to a four-lugged vessel. A slashed molding and a row of knobs were first applied; then a wide crosshatched band was painted between them and the decoration completed by upper and lower borders. Despite differences in size and proportions the close relationship of a complete vessel (pl. 123:E) to typical jars of Family CXXVIII is obvious.

The two crosshatched bands of two vessels (pls. 122:I; 123:E) are identical except that the first are incised and the second painted. The wavy bands on the other complete example (pl. 123:D) are not paralleled among the incised patterns and are more natural as brush strokes. The painted decoration was carried over the lugs.[131]

Protoliterate Family CXXX

> D.74; proportion 4, wide to medium neck thickened into ledge rim, coarse ware, rough surface with plastic, finger-indented bands

> Figure 15; plate 123:G–H

The last group of four-lugged vessels consists of large storage jars with rough surfaces and, usually, plastic bands with finger imprints connecting the lugs. Although fragments of the heavy ledge rims and sherds with both plastic bands and huge lugs prove that such pithoi were fairly common, few restorable specimens were found. The most complete (pl. 123:H) is an example of the rarest type of Protoliterate shape, that with its greatest diameter below the equator. The base of this vessel was not recovered but despite the enormous discrepancy in size, we might assume that it was flat by analogy with the bases of the similarly shaped vessels (pls. 88:Y; 89:T; 114:H, J).

Unlike the storage jars of Family CXXVIII, those of Family CXXX were huge, coarse, and apparently purely utilitarian. Even the plastic molding might have had a useful function as an anchor for ropes or slings when the vessels were to be moved.[132]

After this long review of the families of closed vessels it might be useful, as recorded above for the open forms, to review the character of the many groups.

THE DECORATION OF PROTOLITERATE POTTERY

In the review of the pottery vessels above a variety of decorations are noted in connection with certain families. The techniques and motifs used can be summarized as follows (cf. table 9).[133]

130. For a parallel to plate 24:H, see Sürenhagen 1974/75, pl. 7:67 (Habuba Kabira South; for incised designs, see also ibid., pls. 37:18, 20, 26, 28; 38:10–17, 22–23). For parallels to plate 122:B, see Le Brun 1978a, fig. 33:2, 7 (slightly different incision pattern; Susa, Acropole I, Level 17B); Le Brun 1971, fig. 51:9–10 (Susa, Acropole I, Level 17); Steve and Gasche 1971, pl. 30:18–19 (sherds; Susa, Acropole 1965 Sounding, "Jamdat Nasr ancien Uruk récent"); Miroschedji 1976, fig. 8:4 (sherd; Susa, Apadana, Trench 1038); Nissen 1970, pls. 102:9, 103:12 (Warka, K/L XII Sounding, Layers 41, 42); 7N P263 and 7N P230 (Nippur, Inanna Temple XVI, XIV); de Genouillac et al. 1934, pl. 23:2 (Tello). For a parallel to plate 122:C, see Sürenhagen 1974/75, pls. 6:65; 7:64, 66 (various combinations of bands with crosshatch and triangles; Habuba Kabira South). For parallels to plate 122:D, see Le Breton 1957c:99, fig. 12:9 (Susa, old excavations, Susa Cb); Weiss and Young 1975, fig. 3:1a (three bands of triangles; Godin V). For a parallel to plate 122:E, see Thompson and Mallowan 1933, pl. 50:9 (rim and crosshatch; Nineveh IV). For a parallel to plate 122:F, I, see Miroschedji 1976, pl. 3:2 (sherd; Susa, Apadana, Trench 1038). For parallels to plate 128 sherds, see Haller 1932, pls. 8 A:g'; C:i'; 19C:r; 20A:l', n' (Warka, Eanna XII, IX/VIII, VI, IV).

131. For parallels to plate 123:E–G, see Le Breton 1957, figs. 13:7 (Susa, Acropole, old excavations, Susa Cb), 14:3–4 (sherds; Susa, Acropole, old excavations, Susa C); Haller 1932, pl. 19 D:1 (sherd; Warka, Eanna VI). For forms and sherd related to plate 123:G, see Le Brun 1971, fig. 53:17 (Susa, Acropole I, Level 17); Nissen 1970, pl. 103:15 (Warka, K/L XII Sounding, Layer 42); Weiss and Young 1975:7, fig. 3:2 (Godin V).

132. For Family CXXX examples of ovoid shapes and squatter proportions parallel to plate 123:G–H, see Le Brun 1971, fig. 53:1 (Susa, Acropole I, Level 17); Weiss and Young 1975:7, fig. 3:2a (Godin V).

133. For the decoration of Protoliterate pottery, see Sürenhagen 1974/75, pls. 35–39 (Habuba Kabira South).

PROTOLITERATE: Four-lugged Vessels   Scale 1:5 (CXXX 1:10)

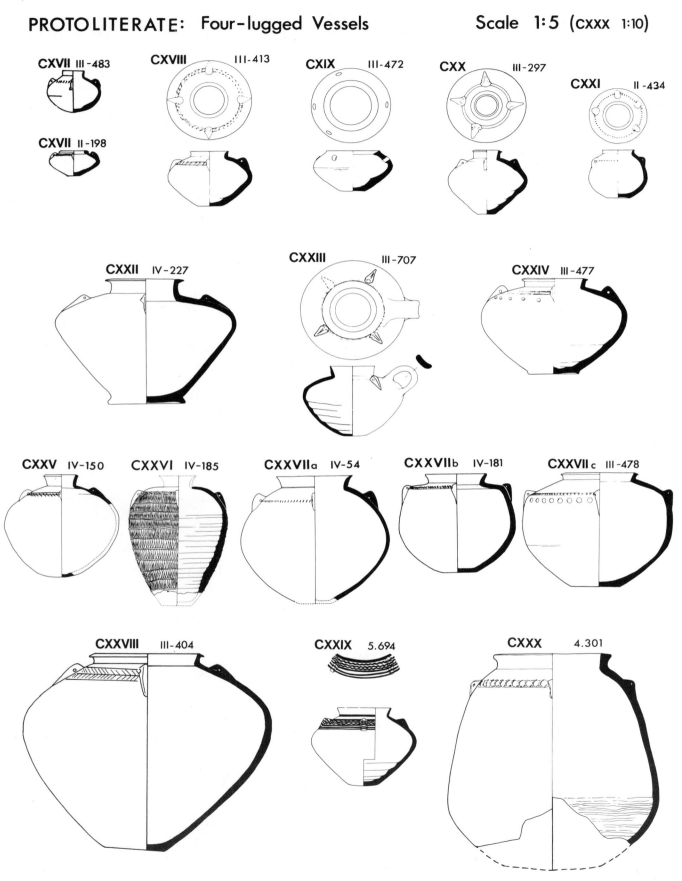

Figure 15. Protoliterate Four-lugged Vessels, Families CXVII–CXXX

Table 8. Four-lugged Vessels, Similar to Chogha Mish Protoliterate Families CXVIII–CXXX, Present at Other Sites

	CXVIII	CXX	CXXI	CXXII	CXXIII	CXXIV	CXXVI	CXXVII a	CXXVII b	CXXVII c	CXXVIII	CXXIX	CXXX
SUSA													
Acropole 1965													
"Jamdat Nasr récent"	—	—	—	—	—	—	—	—	—	—	—	—	—
"Jamdat Nasr ancien-Uruk récent"	—	—	—	—	—	—	—	—	—	×	×	—	—
Apadana Trench 1038	—	×	—	—	—	—	—	—	—	—	×	—	—
Acropole, Old Excavations,													
"Susa C"	—	—	—	—	×	×	×	×	×	×	×	×	—
"Susa B"	—	—	—	—	—	—	—	—	—	—	—	—	—
Acropole I													
17	—	—	—	×	—	—	—	—	—	—	×	×	×
17B	—	—	×	×	×	—	—	—	—	—	×	—	—
18	×	—	—	—	—	×	—	—	—	—	—	—	—
WARKA													
Md XV4: Archaic Settlement													
"Jemdet Nasr"	—	×	—	—	—	—	—	—	×	—	—	—	—
K/L XII Sounding													
"Spät-Uruk"	×	—	—	—	—	—	—	—	—	—	×	×	—
Eanna Precinct and Test Pit													
III–II	—	—	—	—	—	—	—	—	—	—	—	—	—
IV	—	—	—	—	—	—	—	—	—	—	×	—	—
V	—	—	—	—	—	—	—	—	—	—	—	—	—
VI	×	—	—	—	—	—	×	—	—	—	×	×	—
VII	—	—	—	—	—	—	—	—	—	—	—	—	—
IX–VIII	—	—	—	—	—	—	—	—	—	—	×	—	—
XII	—	—	—	—	—	—	—	—	—	—	×	—	—
NIPPUR													
Inanna Temple													
XII	—	—	—	—	—	—	—	—	—	—	—	—	—
XIII	—	—	—	—	—	—	—	—	—	—	—	—	—
XIV	—	—	—	—	—	—	—	—	—	—	×	—	—
XV	—	—	—	—	—	×	—	—	—	—	—	—	—
XVI	—	—	—	×	—	×	—	—	—	—	×	—	—
XVII	—	—	—	—	—	—	—	—	—	—	—	—	—
XVIII	—	—	—	—	—	—	—	—	—	—	—	—	—
XIX	—	×	×	—	—	×	×	—	×	—	—	—	—
XX	—	—	—	—	—	—	—	—	—	—	—	—	—
JEMDET NASR	—	×	—	—	—	—	—	—	—	×	—	—	—
TELLO	—	—	—	—	—	×	—	—	—	—	×	—	—
KHAFAJAH Protoliterate c–d	—	—	×	—	—	—	—	—	×	×	—	—	—
NINEVEH IV	—	×	—	—	—	—	—	—	—	—	×	—	—
HABUBA KABIRA SOUTH	—	×	×	×	×	—	—	—	×	—	×	—	—
HASSEK HÜYÜK Late Chalcolithic	—	×	—	—	—	—	—	—	—	—	—	—	—
ARSLAN TEPE VIa	—	×	—	—	—	—	—	—	—	—	—	—	—
TEPECIK (KEBAN) Late Chalcolithic	—	×	—	—	—	—	—	—	—	—	—	—	—
GODIN V	—	—	—	—	—	—	—	—	×	—	—	×	—
MALYAN Banesh Period	—	—	—	—	×	—	—	—	—	—	—	—	—
JAWA Late Chalcolithic	—	×	—	—	—	—	—	—	—	—	—	—	—

Painted decoration is extremely rare, occurring as an isolated instance on a Family LXXIV flask and regularly only in the four-lugged Family CXXIX, as a substitute for the broad bands of incision of the Family CXXVIII jars. Various types of plastic decoration are more common and are particularly characteristic for rough-surfaced jars and different types sometimes appear together on one vessel. Moldings with finger imprints are usually found on large vats and storage vessels, but sometimes also on spouted jars. Such bands can form simple patterns, mostly attached to or flanking major accessories. Occasionally a raised molding with slashes or crosshatching is used as a divider between body and shoulder (figs. 14; 15; pls. 24:F; 108:E); incised crosshatched bands serve the same function (pls. 24:J; 98:C; 121:F–I). One or more isolated knobs appear on vessels of various sizes but are particularly at home on large rough surfaced jars, often together with imprinted moldings. Small knobs in a row are, in contrast, typical for finely-finished four-lugged jars. Exceptional, but striking specimens of barbotine decoration occur; on IV-423 roughly conical lumps of clay project from the entire lower part of the spherical body. Sherds of large vessels with flattened wads of clay are very rare (pl. 28:I, K–M). Also unusual are curving plastic bands ending in flattened heads and forming appliqués resembling a snake. Clearly representational appliqués are exceedingly rare. A sherd from a large vessel bears a bird (III-955) and a spouted vessel discussed below has snakes and goats (pls. 26; 108:F). Animal forms in the round also appear. Small quadrupeds adorn a strap handle (III-953). Short necks originally connected animal heads to the shoulders of vessels (III-53). The tip of a spout is shaped similar to an animal head (III-183).[134]

Incised decorations are more common, ranging from simple scored lines to, in exceptional examples, representational designs. Scored lines, either a single one or a spiral producing the effect of several parallel horizontal lines, are typical for the handled vessels but occur sporadically in some other groups. Sometimes the horizontal scoring is crossed by hatching or zigzags to produce a more elaborate shoulder decoration on vertical and horizontal-handled vessels. On the whole, the incised decoration typical for handled families is quite distinct from the incised and notched decoration normal for the four-lugged vessels; thus even small sherds can usually be assigned to their respective classes, and sometimes families, on the basis of their decoration. Among the rarer types of ornament punctuations are limited to the handled class, but rocker decoration is to be found on all four classes of closed vessels.

An isolated and sometimes doodle-like incision sometimes occurs on sherds from the bodies of large vessels without accessories; unfortunately these are for the most part incomplete. Some appear to be geometric (pl. 28:F–G) and one represents a fish (pl. 28:O). Such sporadic occurrences of isolated incised motifs does not, however, provide any hint of the existence of elaborate incised representations such as those on a unique four-lugged vessel described below (fig. 16; pls. 27; 115:C).

RITUAL VESSELS

THE SNAKE VASE (Pls. 26; 108:F)

Sherds forming the greater part of an ovoid jar with the stumps of two spouts were found only about 30 cm below the surface in the West Area (pl. 265). The jar has a wide short neck; the missing base can be restored as flat by analogy with other vessels of Subfamily CIXe. On the upper body of a row of notches are the stumps of

the closely-spaced spouts, one sufficiently preserved to indicate that they were curved. Appliqués representing a snake biting the neck of a goat are placed symmetrically at the base of each spout. Between the spouts projects a broken pottery stump that presumably ended in an animal head; some detached pottery heads with similar stalks, which are different from the broader necks of the animal figurines, provide prototypes for the reconstruction of this element of the snake vase (III-53; IV-32). The pair of spouts and the representational appliqués give a special character to what would otherwise be a standard spouted vessel.

The only approximately contemporary parallels for the paired spouts appear to be the false spouts added to elaborate four-lugged jars of Family CXXIII at Habuba Kabira South,[135] but many analogies for the special features of this vessel exist in later periods. The ritual nature of double-spouted vessels and the association of snake appliqués with spouts are discussed in detail in the publication of the Diyala pottery, where it is pointed out that paired spouts occur at Ur in the Late Protoliterate period and appear with snake appliqués from Early Dynastic I to, probably, the Akkadian period.[136] The Early Dynastic I example was found at Tell Asmar in the Archaic Shrine IV of the Abu Temple and one of the Early Dynastic III double spouts was found below the Single Shrine I of the same temple. The occurrence of some examples in a temple area and the association with snakes can be taken as indications of the ritual character of the double-spouted jars.

The snake vase from Chogha Mish carries the association of double spouts and snake appliqués back to the earlier part of the Protoliterate period. On the Chogha Mish jar they are not isolated, but attack goats in a vulnerable spot. Since the importance of cattle in Protoliterate economy and the concern for their well-being are manifested in many works of art of the period, the snakes might be interpreted, very tentatively, as representative of chthonic forces that could be hostile to the flocks and should be propitiated. Whatever the significance of the appliqué groups, their presence further strengthens the case for considering double-spouted jars as ritual utensils.

134. For a similar example, see Steve and Gasche 1971, pl. 28:9 (Susa, Acropole, 1965 Sounding, "Jamdat Nasr finale").

135. Sürenhagen 1974/75, pls. 9:69.2; 10:70; 11:71. For a single spouted but otherwise very similar red-burnished jar, see Woolley 1955, pl. 26:f (U.14909; Ur, Jemdet Nasr Graves Stratum).

136. For parallels from Diyala sites, see Delougaz 1952:92, pls. 91:a (Tell Asmar, Abu Temple, below Single Shrine I, Early Dynastic III), b (Khafajah, Houses 6, Early Dynastic III), c (with snakes; Early Dynastic III), d (with snakes; Akkadian[?]); 92:d (Tell Asmar, Abu Temple Archaic Shrine IV, Early Dynastic I). For single spouts with snakes, see ibid., pl. 92:a–c, e–k; Woolley 1955, pl. 25: U.18722 (Pit W; [painted] 61; Jemdet Nasr Type 120 [unpainted]; Ur, Jemdet Nasr Graves Stratum); Mackay 1931:223.

FOUR-LUGGED VASE (III-225) INCISED WITH REPRESENTATIONAL DESIGNS (Fig. 16; Pls. 27; 115:C; 116–19)

The sherds of the most elaborate example of the rare family of four-lugged jars with a strap handle (Family CXXIII) were found in an ash pit in the East Area. The vessel is reconstructible although some sherds are missing. Its proportions are atypically high for a four-lugged vessel. A raised molding with incised crosshatch encircles the shoulder at the top of the lugs and is comparable to the molding on an unusual spouted fragment (pl. 108:E). This vessel also shares its high neck, flat shoulder, and crosshatched band with another jar of the same family but is unique in the treatment of the lugs and body. The four lugs, instead of being limited as normally to the upper part of the vessel, extend over the shoulder carination to form elongated bars dividing the body into four panels. These are completely filled with deftly incised decoration of exceptional interest. It is formed by large numbers of lines that must have been incised with a steady and swift hand in order to complete the designs before the vessel became too dry.[137]

The strap handle is balanced on the opposite side of the shoulder by a broken stump, which like the similar stump (pl. 26) must have ended in an animal head. Such heads in the round might be distant antecedents for the animals in the round on the upper parts of vessels of the Early Dynastic III phase (Delougaz 1952, pls. 93, 95 [Early Dynastic III]). In any case, the strap handle and the head of the four-lugged vase give this vessel an axial movement proceeding in the direction of the head. The panels below these features (I, III) are narrower than the two other panels (II, IV).

The front panel has the simplest design, a checkerboard of plain and crosshatched squares above crosshatched and plain vertical strips (pl. 116). Since some sherds of this panel are missing, it is not certain whether the two patterns were separated by a horizontal band of crosshatched and plain triangles similar to that on Panel III (pl. 118). In the center of Panel II is a large fish surrounded by checkerboard and lozenge designs that might

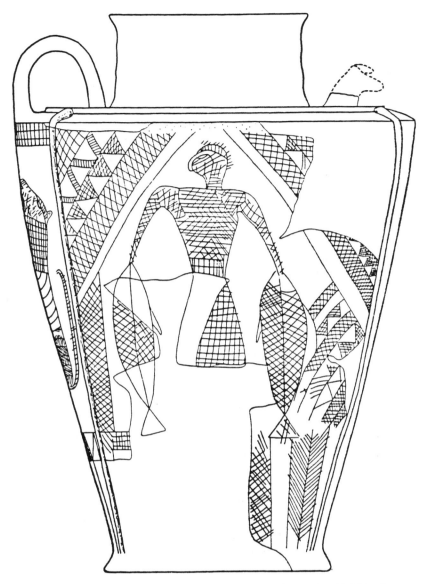

Figure 16. Protoliterate Incised Vase: Family CXXIII (III-225; R18:301; el. ca. 82.60; Fine Ware; Dense with Small White Grits; Brown Core Shading to Brownish-Buff toward Surface; White Slip; Fast Wheel Marks on Interior)

137. Figure 16 and plates 116–119 have been drawn with extraordinary patience and skill by Abbas Alizadeh using casts of the incised body sherds (cf. pl. 27) and color slides taken after the vessel had been restored (Iran Bastan Museum, Tehran).

be the representative of a net rather than purely geometric (pl. 117). On the opposite panel, IV (pl. 119), triangular areas filled with bands of geometric designs comparable to those of the four-lugged vessels frame the central theme of a man with two fish. He might be a fisherman returning with his catch or a porter bringing provisions for a feast. The two wide panels are linked by their common concern with fish. The fish of panels II and IV differ in the details of their rendering. On Panel II a curved crosshatched band demarcates the head and suggests the line of the gill opening; one set of the hatched lines covering the body follows the curve of the gills. On Panel IV a median line divides the fish into two sections that are crosshatched separately; in addition to the caudal fin, a ventral fin is shown. The human figure of Panel IV, whose legs are unfortunately missing, is rendered in a simplified geometric fashion. The hands are omitted and the bird-like appearance of the head can be attributed to the simple style rather than considered as an intentional rendering of a nonhuman head. Nonetheless, there is, as in the fish, some feeling for organic form, exemplified by the curving lines that demarcate the shoulders and the nose and face. A small oval apparently represents the eye. The different hatching on various parts of the body might represent a kilt, belt, and bare chest.

The back panel, III (pl. 118), seems unrelated in theme to the others. The geometric ornament, mostly destroyed, is limited to the upper edge and lower one-third of the panel. There is no obvious thematic relationship between the intertwined snakes and the felines flanking them. The latter, though represented in a couchant posture, are placed vertically on the vase.

The head, fore-, and hindquarters of the stockier animal on the right are separated from each other by curved lines and enclosing markedly different hatching. Well-represented claws tip the crosshatched legs; the wider crosshatching on the neck and forequarter presumably indicates the mane. On the other beast there is no such differentiation—the body as far as preserved is covered by curved hatched bands. Apparently the craftsman here represented a maned lion and a sleek-bodied lioness. On both animals the open mouths, oval eyes, and projecting ears are prominent. In these feline figures that feeling for organic structure characteristic for the modeling of Protoliterate glyptic and sculpture is expressed by the simpler technique of incised lines.

Although the use of incision to cover the entire body of a vessel with geometric and representational decoration remains so far unique, numerous parallels for individual motifs link the Chogha Mish vase closely with other manifestations of Protoliterate and later Mesopotamian art and help to interpret its significance. Parallels for the making of geometric designs by incised outlines and hatching are, of course, provided by the four-lugged vessels of Family CXXVIII. The similarity between their bands of geometric ornament and those in the upper corners of Panel IV and on the bodies of the felines of Panel III shows how the facility developed in the production of the common Family CXXVIII jars and provided the basis for the decoration of the incised vase. In the later part of the Protoliterate period parallels in other media can be found in the large scale checkerboards and the lozenge diapers painted on the altar of the temple at Tell Uqair (Lloyd 1943, pls. 10, 12) and in the small scale checkerboards[138] and narrow vertical bands (Delougaz 1952, pls. 6:8 Kh IX 153; 33) on Jemdet Nasr painted pottery.

The entwined snakes have good analogies in the glyptic of the early Protoliterate period (pl. 36:H).[139] The many lions on the seals, though usually active, were occasionally shown in the couchant pose of the Chogha Mish felines.[140] A large-scale painted and somewhat later parallel is the crouching leopard whose forepart and tail were preserved above the steps of the altar of the Tell Uqair temple.[141]

The second, sitting, leopard at Tell Uqair has his tail in the curl typical for the Protoliterate period as does the Chogha Mish lion, though for reasons of space his tail is pushed close to his back. Both at Tell Uqair and here the mouths are gaping, but, as is to be expected, the patterning of the body on the incised animals is quite different from that of the painted leopards.

Several versions of the theme of a man with fish occur in early Protoliterate glyptic. In a naturalistic boating scene on an impression from Warka a man seated in a boat holds up two fish by their heads.[142] A man on one impression from Susa holds a large fish with both hands and on another the figure has a fish in each hand.[143] In both of the Susa representations the man strides to the left and carries the fish in front of him, differing in these naturalistic features from the more abstract, heraldic arrangement on the Chogha Mish vase. In the late Protoliterate period two fish filling one of the panels on the upper body of a carinated polychrome jar from Jemdet Nasr might, though they are not carried by a man but only suspended from the ends of a rope, be taken as thematically related to Panel IV.[144] The same is true of a double-fish amulet from the *Kleinfunde* at Warka and its Early Dynastic I successors,[145] which are directly comparable to the pairs of fish carried by men on seal impressions from Ur attributable to Early Dynastic I[146] and on the inlaid Ur standard of Early Dynastic III.[147] Fish appear occasionally on Early Dynastic stone votive plaques as provisions being brought for banquets.[148]

138. See Martin 1935, pl. 31 (Jemdet Nasr); Delougaz 1952, pl. 28:a (panel filled by a lozenge diaper on a late Protoliterate monochrome painted jar; Khafajah, Sin Temple I).

139. See Heinrich 1938, pl. 30:i = Amiet 1961, pl. 13:228 (Warka); Amiet 1972, pls. 6:485, 488; 63:485, 486; 64:488 (Susa).

140. Amiet 1972, pls. 10:553, 69:553 (Susa).

141. Lloyd and Safar 1943, pl. 10 (Uqair).

142. Lenzen 1960, pls. 26:b, 31:g–h = Amiet 1961, pl. 13:bis G (Warka).

143. Amiet 1972, pls. 14:622, 623; 78:623 (Susa).

144. Martin 1935, pl. 31 (Jemdet Nasr).

145. Heinrich 1936, pl. 13:i (Warka); Frankfort 1936:38, fig. 30 (Khafajah, Sin Temple VI).

146. Legrain 1936, pl. 16:302 (two fish held by one hand, three by the other), 303 (two fish held by each hand).

147. Woolley 1934, pl. 91 (Ur).

148. Frankfort 1939b, pl. 109:193 (man carrying fish on pole; Khafajah, Temple Oval I, Early Dynastic II); Boese 1971, pl. 31:4 (presumably plaque fragment; man with two fish in one hand, three in the other; Tello, Early Dynastic III).

The parallels just cited for the representational motifs of the Chogha Mish vase have been relatively specific. The Early Dynastic analogies for the most elaborate theme, the man with fish, have explicit religious connotations. They occur on temple plaques and on the Ur standard, all showing banquets that were no ordinary secular feasts. If the roles played by felines in Protoliterate civilization are considered, not just the more specific motif of couchant lions, the implications of the lion of the incised vase can better be understood. Felines, especially lions, are among the more common animals in Protoliterate art, where they are embodiments of great power, often threatening the flocks but also in turn, subdued by hunters or heroes. Such representations are the background for the occurrence of felines in specifically religious contexts. The representation on a cylinder seal of a city ruler carrying to a temple the legless body of a feline, apparently as a sacrifice,[149] is strikingly paralleled by the discovery of actual feline leg bones that formed a foundation deposit beneath one corner of the White Temple at Warka (Ellis 1968:42–43). Among the representations of temple furnishings are a libation vessel in the form of a lion[150] and a lion figure supporting an altar topped by Inanna symbols and a human figure.[151] Snakes through the ages have been both dreaded and revered manifestations of nature. The motif of entwined snakes as known in Protoliterate glyptic and in later Mesopotamian art has been taken as a representation of mating and hence as emblematic of fertility. The representations of snake deities prominent in later Mesopotamian art, particularly in the Akkadian period, might be personifications of chthonic forces.[152] Thus, although it is impossible to offer exact and specific interpretations for the representational motifs of the Chogha Mish vase, when they are looked at from the vantage point of later times and a wide range of evidence, they have a nexus of religious connotations which makes them fitting ornaments for a vessel intended for use in ceremonies or in a shrine.

The Chogha Mish vase is important not only as a representative of a new type of Protoliterate decorative art, but also as a precursor of decorated pottery of the Early Dynastic period. Several examples of fairly intricate incised representation, such as a boar-hunting scene on sherds from Khafajah and a date palm scene on a fruit stand from Tello, exist.[153] The incised cross-hatching and fish on another fragmentary vessel from Khafajah appear as later simplifications of ornament such as that on the Chogha Mish vase and the vessels of Family CXXVIII.[154] The various examples with incised decoration, however, are not as standardized in form as the scarlet ware vessels of Early Dynastic I, which can be seen as more directly linked with the incised vase, despite the difference in technique and the chronological gap. Scarlet ware vessels with elongated bodies, high necks, and ring bases are similar in shape to this vase.[155] Even more striking similarities are the covering of the entire body below the shoulder with painted decoration and the frequent division of this surface into metopes with geometric and representational motifs.[156]

In addition to the correspondence between the placement and composition of the decoration on the Chogha Mish vase and scarlet ware vessels, there are specific resemblances in iconography and details of rendering. The bird-like heads of the women on a scarlet ware vase from Tell Agrab are similar to that of the Chogha Mish man with the fish.[157] Such simplification could, of course, occur independently. However, much the same type of head appears on the figure of a man painted on a Tell Agrab sherd;[158] his hourglass body, outstretched arms, and position in a metope compare too closely with features of the man of Panel IV on the Chogha Mish vase to be accidental. The entwined snakes of Panel III appear in a debased form in one of the shoulder metopes of a vase from Tell Agrab.[159] Still another specific parallel is the recurrence of the geometric pattern of Panel I of the Chogha Mish vase, the checkerboard with crosshatched squares above narrow vertical bands, on an early scarlet ware vessel from Khafajah[160] while the Jemdet Nasr painted ware was the direct root of the scarlet ware,[161] some of the latter's

representations, see Moorey 1967:97–116, and particularly pp. 109–10.

154. Delougaz 1952, pl. 71:a (Khafajah; Early Dynastic II).

155. Ibid., pls. 9:Kh. VI 69, Kh. IX 100, 11, and 56:b, Ag. 35:1032; 55:a–b; 137 (Khafajah and Tell Agrab).

156. Ibid., pls. 9:Kh. IX 164; 10, and 56 a:Kh IX 61; 12 and 57:Ag. 36:580 (with two wide panels and two narrow panels, one of the latter being subdivided; Khafajah and Tell Agrab); 14 and 59:Kh. IX 60; 15, 60, and 61:Kh. IX 150; 55:d and 137 a; 55 e; 58 b and 137 c.

157. Ibid., pl. 12:Ag. 36:580 (Early Dynastic I).

158. Ibid., p. 63, pls. 4:Ag. 36:520 and 53:c (Agrab Houses, Early Dynastic I).

159. Ibid., p. 62, pls. 53:b and 135:c (Early Dynastic I).

160. Ibid., pl. 14:Kh. IX 60 (Khafajah; Early Dynastic I). On the Chogha Mish vase the vertical bands are alternately crosshatched and plain; on the Khafajah vase they are hatched so as to produce a herring bone effect similar to that on an incised fragment of a Family CXXVIII vessel from Chogha Mish (pl. 115:B).

161. Ibid., pp. 50, 60–61.

149. Von der Osten 1934, pl. 29:669 = Frankfort 1939a:19, fig. 2 (Newell Collection).

150. Heinrich 1936, pl. 38 (stone vases; Warka).

151. Schott 1934, pl. 29:b = Amiet 1961, pl. 46:654 (Warka).

152. Frankfort 1939a, pl. 21:b; Landsberger (1947–52:366–68) did not consider *entwined* snakes to be a fertility motif.

153. Delougaz 1952, pl. 80:c (Khafajah), see also the temple facade and animals on plates 85:b and 139:a; de Genouillac et al. 1934:76ff., pls. 63–65 (Tello). For discussion of incised

Table 9. Types of Decoration on Protoliterate Pottery

Decoration	Family	Identification	Illustration(s)
PLASTIC			
FINGER-IMPRINTED BANDS			
Horizontal			
	Protoliterate LII	Vats	Pls. 18:J; 87:H–I
	Protoliterate LXXII	Jar, C.6	Pl. 89:R
	Protoliterate LXXV	Cooking pot	Pl. 90:J
	Protoliterate LXXVI	Notched-lip jar	Pl. 90:M
	Protoliterate LXXX	High-necked jar	Pls. 28:T; 92:A
	—	Jar fragment	Pl. 28:U
	Protoliterate LXXXIII	Pithoi	Pl. 93:C–E
	Protoliterate CIX	Spouted jar	Pl. 23:B
	Protoliterate CXIIb	Spouted notched-lip jar	Pl. 108:P
	Protoliterate CXIV	Spouted jar	Pl. 110:F
	Protoliterate CXVa	Spouted pithos	Pl. 110:E
	Protoliterate CXXX	Four-lugged pithoi	Pl. 123:G–H
Simple Patterns			
	Protoliterate LII	Vat	Pl. 28:J
	Protoliterate XCIV	Handled pithos	Pl. 21:K
	Protoliterate CXI	Spouted jar	Pl. 28:H
Slashed, Hatched, or Notched Bands			
	—	Jar fragments	Pl. 28:Q–S
	Protoliterate XCIV	Handled pithos	Pl. 98:M
	Protoliterate CIXf	Spouted fragment	Pl. 108:E
	Protoliterate CXVb	Spouted pithos fragment	Pls. 23:C; 110:I
	Protoliterate CXXIII	Four-lugged jar	Pl. 115:B
	Protoliterate CXXIV	Four-lugged jar fragment	Pl. 25:B
	Protoliterate CXXVI	Four-lugged jar	Pl. 24:F
	Protoliterate CXXIX	Four-lugged jar fragment	Pl. 24:E
1 TO 3 ISOLATED KNOBS			
	—	Pithos fragment(?)	Pl. 28:N
	—	Jar sherd	Pl. 28:P
	Protoliterate LXIII	B.5 jar	Pl. 88:M
	Protoliterate LXXXI	Buttressed pithoi	Pl. 92:E–F
	Protoliterate LXXXII	Undercut-rim jar	Pl. 92:H
	Protoliterate LXXXIII	Undercut-rim pithos	Pl. 93:H
	Protoliterate CXVb	Spouted pithos fragment	Pl. 110:F
ROW OF KNOBS			
	Protoliterate CXVII	Four-lugged jar	Pl. 112:I
	Protoliterate CXXIV	Four-lugged jars	Pls. 25:B–C, F–G; 115:B–C
	Protoliterate CXXVI	Four-lugged fragment	Pl. 24:K
	Protoliterate CXXVIIc	Four-lugged jar	Pl. 121:H
	Protoliterate CXXIX	Four-lugged fragment	Pl. 123:D–F
BARBOTINE			
	—	Jar fragments	Pl. 28:I, K–M
	Protoliterate XXVI	Notched-lip jar IV-423 (R17:408 Southeast)	—
REPRESENTATIONAL APPLIQUÉS			
	—	Jar fragments	Pl. 28:D–E
	Protoliterate CX	Spouted jar	Pl. 26
	—	Pithos fragment III-955 (North of R19:305)	—
ANIMAL ELEMENTS IN ROUND			
	Protoliterate CX	Spouted jar	Pl. 108:F
	Protoliterate CXXIII	Four-lugged jar	Pl. 24:C
	—	Strap-handled fragment III-953 (P18:301)	—
	—	Heads III-53 (Q18:201), IV-32 (H14:Trench IX)	—
	—	Spout III-183 (Q18:307)	—

Table 9. Types of Decoration on Protoliterate Pottery (*cont.*)

Decoration	Family	Identification	Illustration(s)
IMPRINTED OR INCISED			
COMBED ALL OVER			
	Protoliterate LXXXIX	Strap-handled jar	Pl. 96:E
ROCKER INCISION			
	Protoliterate LXXVIII	Storage jar fragment	Pl. 91:D
	Protoliterate LXXX	High-necked jar	Pl. 92:C
	Protoliterate LXXXIII	Pithos	Pl. 19:S
	Protoliterate LXXXVI	Miniature handled jar	Pl. 95:D–E
	Protoliterate CIXb	High-necked spouted jars	Pls. 23:A; 107:H–I
	Protoliterate CXXVI	Four-lugged jars	Pls. 24:F; 121:A
PUNCTUATIONS			
	Protoliterate XC	Strap-handled jar	Pl. 97:B
	Protoliterate XCVI, XCVII	Twisted-handled jars	Pls. 100:G; 100:F
FINGER IMPRINTS AND/OR INCISED			
	Protoliterate XXXII	Bowl, C.07	Pl. 84:Z
INCISED HATCHING AT LIP			
	Protoliterate XXXIII	Bowls, C.11	Pl. 85:A–B
MOUTH OR NECK			
	Protoliterate XLIV	Small trays	Pls. 18:G–H; 86:J
	Protoliterate LXXIX	Storage jar	Pl. 91:G
	Protoliterate LXXXII	Tall jar (above reserve slip)	Pl. 92:G
SCRABBLED HORIZONTAL LINE (USUALLY WITH RESERVE SLIP)			
	Protoliterate XLII	Deep bowls	Pls. 28:A–C; 86:A–F
	Protoliterate CXVa	Spouted pithos	Pl. 110:D
SCORED HORIZONTAL LINE			
Simple			
	Protoliterate LXXIX	Ovoid jars	Pl. 91:F, J
	Protoliterate LXXXVII–XCIIa, XCVI	Vertical strap and twisted handled vessels	Pls. 20:A–C, F–G; 21:I–J; 95–101 passim
	Protoliterate XCVIII	Horizontal handled jar	Pls. 21:I; 101:A–D, F
	Protoliterate XCIX	Horizontal + strap handled jar	Pls. 21:J; 101:J
	Protoliterate CI	Miniature spouted jar	Pl. 102:C
	Protoliterate CVa	Spouted jar	Pl. 104:J
	Protoliterate CVIII	Buttressed spouted jar	Pl. 106:G
	Protoliterate CIXb	Spouted jar	Pl. 107:D, F
	Protoliterate CXVIII	Small four-lugged jar	Pl. 113:C
	Protoliterate CXX	Small four-lugged jar	Pl. 113:G
	Protoliterate CXXII	Four-lugged jar	Pl. 114:K
	Protoliterate CXXVIIb	Four-lugged jar	Pl. 121:D
Crossed			
	Protoliterate XIII	Bowl	Pl. 81:N
	Protoliterate LXXXVIII	Strap-handled jar	Pl. 95:K
	Protoliterate XCI	Strap-handled jar	Pls. 20:S; 97:E
	Protoliterate XCIIa	Strap-handled jar	Pl. 98:A
	Protoliterate XCIIIa–b	Strap-handled jar	Pls. 21:B–C; 98:F, J
	Protoliterate XCVIII	Horizontal-handled jar	Pl. 101:E
Fine Point			
	Protoliterate XCIIIb	Jar with strap handled and notched lip	Pl. 98:J
Scored Vertical Lines			
	Protoliterate CVIII	Buttressed spouted jar	Pl. 106:F
NOTCHES			
Horizontal row(s) alone			
	Protoliterate LXV	B–C.7 jars	Pls. 88:V, Y, AA; 89:C
	Protoliterate LXXXVI	Miniature strap-handled jar	Pl. 95:A
	Protoliterate XC	Rod-handled jars	Pls. 20:Q; 97:A
	Protoliterate XCVIII	Horizontal-handled jar	Pl. 21:E
	Protoliterate CI	Miniature spouted jar	Pl. 102:A, D

Table 9. Types of Decoration on Protoliterate Pottery (*cont.*)

Decoration	Family	Identification	Illustration(s)
IMPRINTED OR INCISED (*cont.*)			
NOTCHES (*cont.*)			
Horizontal row(s) alone (*cont.*)			
Protoliterate CIXa	Spouted jar	Pl. 107:A	
Protoliterate CXIV	Spouted jar	Pl. 110:B	
Protoliterate CXVII	Four-lugged miniature jars	Pl. 112:E, G–H, J	
Protoliterate CXVIII	Small four-lugged jars	Pl. 113:A, D	
Protoliterate CXX	Small four-lugged jars	Pl. 114:D, F	
Protoliterate CXXI	Small four-lugged jars	Pl. 114:G–J	
Protoliterate CXXV	Four-lugged flask	Pl. 120:E	
Protoliterate CXXVIIa–b	Four-lugged jars	Pl. 121:B–C, E	
Above reserved slip			
Protoliterate LXXX	High-necked jar	Pl. 92:B	
Protoliterate LXV, LXXIII	B–C.7 jars	Pls. 88:W; 89:V	
Protoliterate LXXXIII	Pithos	Pl. 94:C	
Simple patterns, usually flanking an accessory			
Protoliterate LXXXIII	Pithos	Pl. 93:F	
Protoliterate XCVI	Twisted handle jar	Pl. 100:G	
Protoliterate CI	Spouted miniature jar	Pls. 22:E; 102:D	
Protoliterate CIXe	Spouted jar	Pl. 108:A	
Protoliterate CXIIIb	Spouted jar	Pl. 109:F, H	
Protoliterate CXIV	Spouted jar	Pls. 23:D; 110:B	
NOTCHES ON SCORED LINE(S)			
Protoliterate XCIIc	Strap-handled jar	Pl. 98:D	
Protoliterate CIXb	Spouted jar	Pls. 22:H; 107:G	
Protoliterate CX	Spouted jar	Pls. 26; 108:F	
Protoliterate CXIIa	Spouted jar	Pl. 108:M	
Protoliterate CXVII	Four-lugged miniature jars	Pls. 24:A; 112:B–C	
Protoliterate CXVIII, CXX	Small four-lugged jars	Pls. 113:B; 114:B–C	
Protoliterate CXXIII	Four-lugged jar + strap handle	Pl. 115:B	
Protoliterate CXXV	Four-lugged flask	Pl. 120:E	
NARROW BAND(S) WITH NOTCHES OR INCISED DESIGNS			
Alone			
Protoliterate LXIII	B.6 jar	Pls. 19:H; 88:P	
Protoliterate XCIIb	Strap-handled jar	Pl. 98:C	
Protoliterate CI	Spouted miniature jar	Pl. 102:A	
Protoliterate CXIIa	Spouted jar	Pl. 108:M	
Protoliterate CXVIII, CXX	Small four-lugged jar	Pls. 113:C, I; 114:E	
Protoliterate CXXIV, CXXVIIc	Four-lugged jars (also knobbed)	Pls. 25:B, C, G; 121:H	
Protoliterate CXXVIIc	Four-lugged jars	Pls. 24:J; 121:F, I	
Above reserve slip			
Protoliterate LXXIII	C.7 jars	Pls. 19:E; 89:T–U	
Protoliterate CIXd	Spouted jar	Pl. 107:L	
Protoliterate CXI	Cut-spouted jar	Pl. 108:I	
BROAD BAND(S) WITH INCISION			
Protoliterate CIXf	Spouted fragment	Pl. 108:E	
Protoliterate CXVII	Four-lugged miniature jars	Pls. 24:B; 112:A, D, I	
Protoliterate CXX	Small four-lugged jar	Pl. 25:D	
Protoliterate CXXVIII	Four-lugged C–D jars	Pls. 24:H; 25:D–E, H–P; 122:A–J; 123:A–C	
ISOLATED INCISED MOTIFS			
—	—	Pl. 28:F–G, O	
INCISED PANELS WITH GEOMETRIC AND REPRESENTATIONAL MOTIFS			
Protoliterate CXXIII	Four-lugged jars + strap handle	Pl. 115:B	
PAINTED			
HORIZONTAL LINES			
Protoliterate LXXIV	Flask	Pl. 90:D	
BROAD BANDS			
Protoliterate CXXIX	Four-lugged jars	Pls. 24:E; 123:D, F	

decorative syntax and motifs were derived from early Protoliterate prototypes which by the accident of discovery are so far represented only by the incised vessel from Chogha Mish.

CONCLUSION

When excavations were begun at Chogha Mish in 1961 the pottery of the earlier part of the Protoliterate period [a–b] was known in stratified context chiefly from Warka.[162] That of the later part of the period [c–d] was represented, in addition to some finds from Warka, by the pottery from the Diyala sites and from Jemdet Nasr, Kish, Tell Uqair, and to a lesser extent by material from other sites in both southern and northern Mesopotamia. Often, however, the stratification and sometimes even the exact provenience within a site were not clearly documented. Susa had also produced a considerable number of Protoliterate pottery types, which Le Breton attributed, for the most part on the basis of Mesopotamian comparisons, to phases termed Susa B and C (Le Breton 1957, figs. 10–13).

The excavations at Chogha Mish have yielded enormous quantities of Protoliterate pottery, including many complete or restorable shapes and innumerable sherds. Much of the pottery is stratified in terms of floors and building levels, but even more comes from the pits that pockmark the Protoliterate house areas of the site.

The pottery types specific for the late Protoliterate period [c–d] are well established from the Diyala area and other central Mesopotamian sites. After years of excavations at Chogha Mish, during which large areas of Protoliterate occupation were opened, no pottery definitely datable to the later part of the Protoliterate period as known in Mesopotamia has been found. Especially noticeable is the absence of the typical polychrome Jemdet Nasr wares [Protoliterate c]. Neither are there any representatives of the monochrome four-lugged jars, the slender red-washed spouted vessels, the solid pottery stands, or other typical Protoliterate [c–d] types such as have been found at Jemdet Nasr. In addition to the absence of diagnostic pottery types, the typical *Riemchen* bricks are not known at Chogha Mish. Accordingly, it is clear that during Protoliterate c–d, or what in the Susiana area can best be termed the Proto-Elamite period, Chogha Mish was no longer inhabited, as it certainly was not during any part of the following phases contemporary with the Early Dynastic period. No specimens that could be directly related to Early Dynastic pottery types have been discovered. No examples of scarlet ware or jars with upright handles, which later became the so-called goddess-handled vases, have ever been found, although some occurred at Susa (Le Breton 1957, pl. 26:9; figs. 10–11, 36). Chogha Mish apparently lay deserted until the Sukkalmaḫ period. There remains the question of where in the earlier part of the Protoliterate period the occupation of Chogha Mish belongs.

Although the volume of Protoliterate pottery known has now been immensely increased by materials of wide geographical distribution, the stratified excavations on which the relative dating of the early ranges of Protoliterate pottery to a great extent still depends on the materials from Nippur and the test pit dug at Warka more than fifty years ago.[163] In using the data from the pit, the inevitable incompleteness of materials from a limited area is still a handicap.[164] Above the final Ubaid level (Level XIV) come levels with unpainted sherds, including long, slender, straight spouts with either normal or cutaway tips (Haller 1932, pl. 17 D:p–q [Level XIII]) and narrow vessels with bodies sharply tapering toward the base (ibid., pl. 17 D:r [Level XIII]). These types thus appear as diagnostic for the Early Uruk period, intermediate between the final phases of the Ubaid period and the Protoliterate period proper (Adams and Nissen 1972:101, fig. 30:a–e; 109, fig. 33:4–7 [Early Uruk Site WS 022]).

At Chogha Mish the types diagnostic for the Early Uruk period do not occur, neither the tapered vessels nor the long narrow spouts close to or adjoining the rim, although examples of their near descendants do (Families CXI and CXIV). Since by now, tests or large-scale areas have been dug in many parts of the terrace and the High Mound, there is hardly any likelihood that these negative results are accidental. On the terrace there is no deposit intermediate between the prehistoric and Protoliterate settlements, which was begun directly on land that had been abandoned since the Middle Susiana period. On the High Mound, where the Protoliterate remains are covered by massive Sukkalmaḫ structures and

---

162. And later from Nippur as discussed by Hansen (1965).

163. Jordan 1932, pls. 7, 10–13; Heinrich 1932:18–19, pl. 2. Absolute precision cannot be expected from the pit's data, not only because its division into "levels" does not correspond to other parts of the site, but also because its small area— even Levels VI to VIII are only ca. 10.0 × 14.5 m—can provide only rather limited assemblages for each level. There might be, besides, some errors in the documentation, as for instance when the solid-footed goblet, which has since been established as a typical Early Dynastic I vessel, is attributed to Level IV (pl. 20:s). There is, therefore, little wonder that, on the one hand, the sampling does not include all the Protoliterate pottery types known from other sites and, on the other hand, that it does include some unique or rare types which have no exact parallels elsewhere.

164. The original Eanna pit in Square Pc-XVI4 has since been supplemented by another stratigraphic test pit in K/L XII (Nissen 1970); see also Sürenhagen 1987 and 1988 for additional new Protoliterate material and reanalysis of the published pottery from the "deep sounding." AA

consequently far less explored, the possibility of some occupation intermediate between Late Susiana and Protoliterate cannot be excluded. However, at present, it is far more probable that the new settlement was begun simultaneously on all parts of the Chogha Mish mound at some time after the Early Uruk period. With an early Protoliterate date for the occupation at Chogha Mish established negatively by the absence of pottery types characteristic for either the Early Uruk or the late Protoliterate period and positively by the many Warka parallels for the Chogha Mish assemblage from Levels VIII–VI in the test pit and V–IV in the East precinct, the next question to consider is whether the Chogha Mish pottery can be divided into chronological groups corresponding to Protoliterate a and b, which have never been definitively distinguished on the basis of stratified pottery. Because of the great wealth of the pottery material and because of the existence of several Protoliterate building levels in the East Area, some corresponding changes in ceramic forms and styles might be established. However, so far, the pottery seems to constitute a single assemblage without any items confined to an earlier or later building phase. For instance, specimens of distinctive types with rocker decoration, the miniature handled jars of Protoliterate Family LXXXVI and the slender ovoid jars of Families LVI and CXXVI occur both in pits and in earlier deposits. The rather numerous representatives of another distinctive type, the trough-spouted bowl, appear in the East and West Areas in deposits of both high and low levels.

The concentration of certain types of Protoliterate pottery in some areas and their scarcity in others could be taken as a chronological indication. A prize example is Family XXIV, the flower pots, which abound in Trench VI and in the most northeastern part of the East Area but are very rare elsewhere. However, in both areas these are associated with types standard everywhere and thus cannot serve as chronological indicators for the dates of the two areas where they are so common. The uneven patterns of distribution seem rather to be correlated with variations in the activities carried out in different areas.

For the present we regard the Protoliterate pottery from Chogha Mish as one coherent assemblage, but this conclusion remains to be tested by statistical analysis of all the Protoliterate pottery found at the site, both in the first five seasons and thereafter. Such analysis might reveal, for example, chronologically significant variations in the frequencies of types that have not yet been recognized.

There follows, in conclusion, a conspectus of our Protoliterate pottery typology in the form of figures with representatives of each family. Tables 1–7 summarize the parallels which are cited under the rubrics of the individual families. In the tables "×" indicates the presence of examples either almost indistinguishable from or extremely close to Chogha Mish vessels.

The close relationship of the Protoliterate pottery from Chogha Mish and that from Susa—particularly from Levels 17/17B at the Acropole I Sounding and from Trench 1038 of the Apadana, from Warka—particularly from Eanna VII–IV, and from Habuba Kabira South stands out in the tables.[165] The circumstance that many more parallels for Chogha Mish pottery are provided by Eanna VI at Warka than by Eanna V or IV might well be merely an accident of preservation and publication rather than an indication of chronological distinction. The more that is known of the ceramics of the Early Protoliterate period, the more apparent becomes the coherence of the pottery from different sites. This could, of course, be expected for sites as close as Chogha Mish and Susa, but is striking in the case of Habuba Kabira, some one thousand kilometers to the west. A great proportion of the vessels from that Syrian site, including specialized forms are well-nigh identical with those from Chogha Mish. Moreover, at these sites the coherence in tradition is not only limited to pottery, but includes also the other major manifestations of Protoliterate civilization. The integrity of material culture in such Protoliterate cities contrasts strongly with the situation in outlying sites in, for example, the coastal Amuq plain in southern Anatolia and in Iranian plateau and Kerman province sites. In such areas a few Protoliterate features, notably the beveled-rim bowls, occur out of their own context as individual borrowed items. Among the outlying sites Godin occupies a special position since there a number of Protoliterate elements occur together as a foreign enclave in the native culture; other such sites probably remain to be discovered. Already, however, the evidence now being recovered, a large part of it in the form of pottery, testifies to historical developments of profound importance. It is already evident that the impact of Protoliterate power and civilization was far more far-flung than anyone could have imagined a few years ago.

---

165. The majority of Chogha Mish Protoliterate parallels seem to be with Susa, Level 18, suggesting the maximum size of Chogha Mish was attained during Susa, Level 18 and probably Level 19. Both Algaze (1993:129) and Dittmann (1986) believe that Chogha Mish had contracted by the time of Susa, Level 17. AA

CHAPTER 5

STONE VESSELS AND SMALL OBJECTS OF THE PROTOLITERATE PERIOD

The pottery constitutes by far the bulk of the Protoliterate finds. However, other categories of objects are also important in the assemblage and they are surveyed in this chapter.

STONE VESSELS
(Pls. 29:O, AA–CC; 124:A–FF; 125:A–E)

Vessels were made of several types of stone: (1) a soft, black, bituminous stone, often found badly cracked; (2) a gray-green sandstone prone to disintegration; (3) ordinary white limestone, sometimes badly eroded; and (4) relatively hard and light-colored dense stones that could be given a high polish. Stone vessels were in common use, but are for the most part represented by fragments scattered individually in Protoliterate loci, the outstanding exception being nine bowls and cups, ranging in diameter from about 8–20 cm, found stacked inside a large, disintegrated sandstone bowl in debris between pit R18:310 and Q18:307 (III-900–08).[1] The group can be taken as an indication of the amount and type of stone vessels used in individual households.

The majority of the stone vessels are open forms, among which simple flat-based bowls with almost straight (pl. 124:B, L, CC) or somewhat convex sides (pl. 124:A, C, K) prevail. They vary in proportion from shallow, rather wide-based bowls to deeper, narrow-based cups. The character of the plain rimless bowls depends on their size and the type of stone of which they are made. Larger examples tend to be of sandstone and to have relatively thick walls and blunt lips (pl. 124:D, O, CC). A thick greenish-gray fragment is unusual for the gouges on both the exterior and interior (pl. 125:A); it might be from an unfinished vessel of the same shape (cf. pl. 124:CC). Bowls made of harder stones usually have thin walls and relatively tapered lips (pl. 124:G–J).

In addition to the simple bowls, four types of more differentiated open forms can be distinguished, the most common being the bowl with a band rim. Sometimes the band rims, particularly on larger or thicker-walled bowls, project beyond the body wall to form a vertical or almost-vertical band at the mouth (pl. 124:U–X). In other examples there is no noticeable shift in angle between the body wall and the rim. Rather both form part of the same general curve with a groove separating rim and body (pl. 124:P–T, Z–BB). To judge by frequency of occurrence, the band rim was a feature typical for stone bowls.[2] The pottery bowls with band rims occasionally found (pls. 17:I; 84:O–P) can be considered as imitations of stone prototypes. The opposite is true of a fragment of a stone pouring lip bowl (pls. 29:O; 124:M), which imitates an ubiquitous pottery shape (pls. 17:C; 29:P; 80:Y–Z, AA–FF). The third specialized open form, the rectangular trough, is represented only by fragments (pls. 29:BB; 124:EE–FF). Complete vessels from Susa and Warka demonstrate a range in proportions from rather square to elongated rectangular shapes. A monumental variant of the type is the trough from Warka now in the British Museum; its elongated proportions can be attributed to its special character and the need to accommodate the carved representation.[3] Trays, known only from fragments, constitute the fourth type of specialized forms. The most complete example is about half of a round tray with a horizontal tab handle, undoubtedly one of an original pair (pl. 125:C). A small section of an even larger tray has a more elongated tab handle (pl. 125:B). The closest pottery parallel is a tray with a notched lip (pl. 86:M). Two small segments of trays with flattened lips might well have belonged to specimens with tab handles (pl. 125:B–C). All four fragments are made of the same kind of greenish-gray limestone.

The closed stone vessels are almost all miniature containers for cosmetics such as kohl or red ocher. The four examples found inside a four-lugged pottery jar

---

1. For a parallel to plate 124:B, see Le Brun 1971, fig. 55:4 (Susa, Acropole I, Level 17A). For a parallel to plate 124:F, see ibid., fig. 55:4–5 (Susa, Acropole I, Level 17, 17B).

2. For a parallel to plate 124:P, W, see Mackay 1931, pl. 67:38 (Jemdet Nasr).

3. For parallels to plate 124:EE–FF, see Le Brun 1978a, fig. 36:9 (Susa, Acropole I, Level 17B); Le Breton 1957:110, fig. 28:14 (Susa, old excavations); Heinrich 1937, pl. 51:d (Warka, White Temple area); de Genouillac et al. 1934, pl. 5:3 (Tello); Delougaz and Lloyd 1942:141, Kh. VI-318–319 (Khafajah, Sin Temple IV, Protoliterate d). For the Warka trough, see Frankfort 1954, pl. 3:c.

from Trench XXV together with beads and a lump of red ocher show the normal range of shapes. Square or rectangular bodies with flaring necks are shapes specific to stone (pl. 125:D–E). Two squat ovoid pots with rather narrow necks, their lips unfortunately destroyed (pl. 125:A), are in general shape similar to some of the small squat vessels without accessories (pl. 88:M–O). A little jar of tall proportions (pl. 125:H) has a profile similar to that of vessels of Protoliterate Family LXI (pl. 88:D, G). It was a more durable and undoubtedly a more expensive version of such small pottery vessels.[4]

The one fragment of a large stone vessel of closed form was found on the surface at the southern foot of the High Mound (pl. 124:DD). Although from a secondary context, its shape and the traces of a lug indicate that it belonged to a four-lugged Protoliterate vessel, one which would have been impractically heavy for ordinary household use because of its size and thick walls.

STONE IMPLEMENTS
(Pls. 29:I–N, Q–Z; 125:K–KK)

The Protoliterate ground stone implements are presented separately by Daniel M. Shimabuku (*Chapter 11*), so that here only some examples or categories not discussed by him are given, as well as a few remarks on the flints.[5] Flints were in common use; the debris of P17:404 with its concentration of flint blades might have been part of the working area of a flint knapper. Some samples of flint blades still retaining their bitumen setting illustrate the flint sickles of Susiana type that continued in use alongside of the new terra-cotta sickles (III-942; IV-323).[6] Large round scrapers chipped from tabular flint are very rare, but characteristic (pl. 29:J).

Among the implements of ground stone, small perforated discs are characteristic. They are usually made from tabular gray river pebbles (pls. 29:Q–Z; 125:K–X; 247:F–H), but more rarely of stone bowl fragments (pls. 29:Q; 125:O, S–T, X). The examples made from pebbles are usually bored from both sides (pls. 125:V;

247:G), and the resulting perforation is somewhat biconical. The examples made from bowl sherds are usually of buff or tan colored stone and have a carefully bored cylindrical perforation. Except for their material these perforated stone discs are identical to somewhat more rare perforated terra-cotta discs (pl. 126:A–B, D).[7] The perforated stone discs and their possible functions are discussed more fully below in *Chapter 11* by D. Shimabuku.

Quite different from the perforated discs is a large solid disc completely flat on one side and on the other flat in the center and slightly convex at the periphery (pl. 125:AA). It was carefully made and probably originally polished all over. Now, however, the flat side has been roughened, except for some patches that are mostly in the center, by irregularly radial wear marks; most of the convex periphery of the other side has discontinuously concentric wear marks. In the absence of associated objects or of parallels, it is difficult even to speculate as to the function of this large solid disc (pl. 125:AA). The same is true of a tool that presumably had a specialized function in keeping with its well-defined shape (pl. 125:GG). The straight edge of the slender crescent is quite sharp. The convex and thick edge, now bruised, seems to have been rather flat. Two rectangular objects, both broken at the end opposite the perforation, were perhaps whetstones (pl. 125:Y–Z).[8] A finger-shaped pebble has its two narrow edges flattened and its smaller end finely honed for a sharp-edged tool that could have been useful in a number of crafts (pl. 125:EE). The narrow end of a fragment of reddish tabular stone has also been ground into a sharp working edge and it might have been a wider version of another (pl. 125:FF). The function of several perforated and well-smoothed hemispherical objects is uncertain (pl. 125:K–N). Although the largest one (pl. 125:N) resembles the terra-cotta spindle whorls in shape, they seem to be too small for such a purpose; they might have been ornaments rather than tools.

A somewhat convex rectangular slab cut from the fragment of a large band-rimmed stone bowl might have been a palette or a grinding stone (pl. 29:K). The polished narrow flat edge of a lunate-shaped object of tabular stone indicates that it was a rubbing or polishing tool (pl. 29:L). A crescentic object made of the conglomerate stone standard for grinding stones (pl. 125:KK) has a broad convex base on which it could be

---

4. For larger specimens of forms related to plate 125:A, see Le Brun 1971, fig. 55:3 (flat base; Susa, Acropole I, Level 17); Mackay 1931, pl. 117:C (Jemdet Nasr). For much larger vessels with related shapes, see Le Brun 1978b, fig. 37:3–4 (Susa, Acropole I, Level 17B). For other related vessels, see Le Breton 1957:110, fig. 28 (Susa); de Genouillac et al. 1934, pl. 6:36 (Tello). For parallels to plate 125:D–E, see Le Breton 1957:110, fig. 28:37 (Susa); Le Brun 1971, fig. 54:1 (higher proportion; Susa, Acropole I, Level 17).

5. It was hoped that Professor James S. Phillips would present the flint industry at Chogha Mish in detail.

6. See Steve and Gasche 1971, pl. 30:20–23 (Susa, Acropole, 1965 Sounding, "Jamdat Nasr ancien-Uruk récent"); Le Brun 1978a, fig. 40:12 (Susa, Acropole I, Level 17B).

7. See Le Brun 1978a, fig. 36:6 (Susa, Acropole I, Level 17B); Mackay 1931, pl. 70:2 (Jemdet Nasr).

8. For possible parallels, see Late Protoliterate pendants that were perhaps used as whet stones rather than merely for ornament: Strommenger 1963, pl. 34:f (length = 3.4 cm; Warka, Archaic Village); Mackay 1931, pl. 75:6 (Jemdet Nasr).

smoothly rocked; it could have been used in this way for crushing or mashing food or minerals. Another possibility is that it was a boring tool for making stone vessels, used with an abrasive and turned concentrically either by hand or by a cleft handle fitted over the concave edge.[9]

Several carefully polished celts widening toward a beveled, and originally sharp, cutting edge are dated to the Protoliterate period by their contexts. Two examples were elongated (pl. 125:JJ) and a third is smaller and squatter (pl. 125:II). A still smaller example comes from the surface of the terrace, but is so similar to the smaller and squatter example (pl. 125:II) that it can be assigned with confidence to the Protoliterate period (pl. 125:GG). More problematic is a miniature celt of unpolished gray stone from a mixed Protoliterate and Archaic Susiana context in Trench XXV (pl. 125:GG). Its size is similar to a purple celt (pl. 125:HH), but it differs from the other celts in that it tapers toward the cutting edge. Its date remains uncertain. Other sites have provided celts dated to the Protoliterate period.[10] They resemble the contemporary metal adzes (pl. 29:A) as well as much older prehistoric celts (pls. 65:RR; 234) in general shape and might have had similar functions.

One example of the typical Protoliterate solid mace-head with grooves, presumably for leather thongs, was found (pl. 29:I).[11] The only other mace-head from a good Protoliterate deposit is a highly polished fragment of a large specimen (pl. 125:DD).[12] Part of a small carinated mace-head of uncertain date was found on the High Mound in the vicinity of an Old Elamite wall, with which it would be presumed to be contemporary except that a Protoliterate cone at the surface of the locus in question indicates the presence of earlier objects out of

context (pls. 29:M; 125:CC). Also of uncertain date is the fragment of an unfinished mace-head found on the surface to the west of P18:301 (pl. 125:BB). On one side the boring had reached almost the middle of the object before it was stopped. On the bruised other end a tiny depression might mark the beginning of the second bore hole, at which point the stone might have split. On the exterior, slight ridges remain from the blocking out of the mace-head. A perforated gray stone object (III-360) with a polished surface has too squat a discoidal shape for it to be considered as a mace-head with any certainty.[13] The function of a peg-shaped object of variegated black-and-white stone with highly polished surfaces is unknown (pl. 29:N).

METAL OBJECTS
(Pls. 29:A–H; 128:A–S)

The Protoliterate period has provided a fair number of metal objects. None of the specimens has yet been analyzed, but it is assumed that they are made of copper. Five types of objects can be distinguished, the first represented by only a single fragment, a chisel-like tool (pl. 128:A); tools with a rectangular section (pl. 128:B); rods (pl. 128:C–D); pins (pl. 128:E–S); and adzes (pl. 29:A). Three examples of thin tools with a rectangular section occurred; they taper to a rounded point and might have served for piercing and reaming of leather or other materials (pl. 128:B).[14] Slightly more common are rods varying in length from 17.8 cm (III-30) to 9.2 cm (pl. 128:F). Three examples have blunt ends (pl. 128:C).[15] Another is similarly blunt ended, but twisted in the middle, a feature known at other sites.[16] Another type of rod, also represented by only one example, has thickened blunt ends (pl. 128:F).[17]

More common metal objects of the Protoliterate period are pins with one end tapered and, aside from one or two possible exceptions, a head at the other end, usually domed and separated from the shaft by a groove

9. For the cleft stick and bare stone used by the makers of stone vessels in Egypt, see Klebs 1915:82–83; Lucas and Harris 1962:423–26; also a bore stone of different shape from Protoliterate levels at Ur (Woolley 1955:14, fig. 5; pl. 13:U16405).

10. See Heinrich 1936, pl. 38:c (perforated; Warka. Eanna III); Mackay 1931, pl. 74 1:3401 (Jemdet Nasr); Woolley 1955:61, U.13737 (Ur, Pit F, Building Stratum E); Tobler 1950, pl. 177:23, 27–28 (Gawra XIII, X).

11. See Le Brun 1978a, fig. 39:1–7 (Susa, Acropole I, Level 17B); Steve and Gasche 1971, pl. 30:6 (Susa, Acropole, 1965 Sounding, "Djemdet Nasr ancien-Uruk récent"); Ghirshman 1938, pl. 28:1 (Sialk IV); Alden 1979:279, fig. 57:21 (Kur River Basin Survey, Banesh period); Strommenger 1963, pl. 34:i (Warka, "Archaic" settlement about 4 km to the northwest of the Eanna Ziggurat); Adams and Nissen 1972:211 (Warka Survey area, examples from fourteen sites ranging over the whole Protoliterate period); Mackay 1931, pl. 75:5 (Jemdet Nasr); de Genouillac et al. 1934, pl. 8:1a (Tello); Strommenger and Sürenhagen 1970:71, fig. 27 (Habuba Kabira South).

12. See Mackay 1931, pl. 70:7 (Jemdet Nasr).

13. J15:305, 79.66, diameter 7.8–8.0 cm, height 3.5 cm; perforation drilled from one side, diameter 3.0 cm, narrowing to 1.8 cm at the other.

14. See Le Brun 1971, fig. 42:7 (Susa, Acropole I, Level 25, Late Susiana); Ghirshman 1938, pl. 84:S.132 (Sialk III 4).

15. See de Genouillac et al. 1934, pl. 9:2 (Tello); Ghirshman 1938, pl. 84:S.132 (Sialk III 4).

16. See Le Brun 1971, figs. 57:2, 67:5 (Susa, Acropole I, Levels 17A, 15A); Nicholas 1980, fig. 86:e (Malyan TUV, Banesh period); Ghirshman 1938, pl. 84:S.1643 (Sialk III 7); Amuq, Phase G (Braidwood and Braidwood 1960, fig. 239:12).

17. See Ghirshman 1938, pl. 84:S.402, S.225, S.1804, S.1745 (Sialk III 1, 4, 7).

(pl. 128:G–P).[18] Examples in which the head end has been flattened and coiled are rare (pl. 128:Q–S).[19] A heavily corroded fragment of a large pin appears to have a double coiled head (pl. 128:R).[20]

One substantial metal object, an adze or ax, weighing about 600 gr and presumably cast in an open mold,[21] indicated that metal tools of considerable size were in use (pl. 29:A). A similar tool with a slightly more splayed cutting edge and a length of only 10.4 cm as opposed to the 20.0 cm of a metal chisel (pl. 29:A) was also found.[22]

BAKED AND UNBAKED CLAY IMPLEMENTS
(Pls. 30; 126:Y–II)

Terra-cotta sickles are prominent tools in the Protoliterate deposits at Chogha Mish (pl. 30:T–U, W).[23] Their ware is identical to that of the coarser grades of the standard pottery vessels. Frequently the broad sur-

faces of the sickles were sprinkled with sandy grit in the same manner as the interiors of the small oval trays. The sickles always have a definite handle end, narrower than the rest of the tool and with rounded sides to make it more easily held. The reverse side is flat while on the obverse the concave edge is strongly beveled. Some of these cutting edges are still quite sharp, indicating that the terra-cotta sickles were practical agricultural tools. Presumably they were fairly cheap to produce so that they could be easily replaced when their cutting edge chipped. Although the clay sickles resemble one another in shape, they fall into two types; the more common left-handed sickles in which the cutting edge curves to the right when the obverse side is up and the mirror-image right-handed sickles. This is an unexpectedly sophisticated feature.

At Chogha Mish sickles of the type described occur only in the levels of the Protoliterate period and this appears to hold true for the Susiana plain as a whole.[24] In contrast, when the sickles were first found in Mesopotamia, they were thought to date exclusively to the Ubaid period (Lloyd and Safar 1943:155; Adams 1965:127). It has since become clear that they were in use there in the Protoliterate period and that they might even have been most common at that time.[25]

Several types of objects typical for the Protoliterate areas can with varying degrees of certainty be connected with the crafts of spinning and weaving. The function of the spindle whorls is, of course, obvious; one is shown in use on a cylinder seal design reconstructible from several impressions (pls. 44:D, G; 146:E). The paste of the Protoliterate spindle whorls is dense, but varies from a grade with numerous small grits to fine with scarcely any tempering at all. Sometimes the bases were intentionally sanded, probably by placing the still moist objects on sand. The perforations are usually

18. See Le Brun 1971, fig. 57:1 (Susa, Acropole I, Level 17A); Le Brun 1978a, fig. 40:6 (Susa, Acropole I, Level 17B); Strommenger 1980a, fig. 42 (Habuba Kabira South); de Genouillac et al. 1934, pl. 9:2, E–F, I–L (Tello). Protoliterate pins with grooved heads were probably prototypes for the mushroom-shaped pins common in Early Dynastic III contexts, e.g., Woolley 1934, pl. 231:U = 7880, U = 8086 (Ur, Royal Cemetery area, pin Type 3); Mackay 1929, pl. 58:14, 17–18 (Kish A Cemetery); Parrot 1968, pls. 12–13 (Mari, Pre-Sargonid Palace area, "Tresor d'Ur").

19. See Le Brun 1978a, fig. 40:7 (Susa, Acropole I, Level 17B); Braidwood and Braidwood 1960, fig. 239:11 (Amuq, Phase G); Mackay 1925, pl. 19:7–8 (Kish, A Cemetery); Woolley 1934, pl. 231:U = 6144 (Ur, Royal Cemetery area, pin Type 4).

20. Such double coil-headed pins are known from Sialk IV (Ghirshman 1938, pl. 45:S.1602 a, e).

21. Open molds, including one for an adze, have been found in Iran as early as the middle of the fifth millennium B.C. (Majidzadeh 1979:82–92, figs. 2–3 [Tepe Qabrestan, Level 9, Middle Plateau C]). For open molds of the Banesh period, see Nicholas 1980:389–408, figs. 103, 108; idem 1990, pl. 14:c–d (Malyan TUV). In the third millennium B.C. they are common in Syria and northern Mesopotamia, see Strommenger 1980a, fig. 81 (Habuba Kabira Tell, Level 14); Mallowan 1947, pl. 29:A (Tell Brak, Sargonid, Site C. H.); Mallowan 1937, pl. 18:B (Chagar Bazar, Level 2); Speiser 1935, pl. 47 (Gawra VI).

22. Such adzes have a wide spatial and temporal distribution (Deshayes 1960:51–84). They occur in Late Susiana contexts at Susa (de Morgan 1912:11, figs. 27–29). For examples of the Protoliterate or contemporary periods, see Le Breton 1957:109 (Susa, old excavation); Ghirshman 1938, pl. 45:S.535 (Sialk IV); Strommenger 1980a:47, fig. 29 (Habuba Kabira South); van Driel and van Driel-Murray 1979:20 (Gebel Aruda); Tobler 1950, pl. 48:a, 1–2 (Gawra XII–XI).

23. For other examples, not illustrated, see III-188 (handle end missing, left-handed; III-189 (fragment, left-handed); III-

361 (left-handed); III-362; III-637 (handle missing, right-handed); III-688 (fragment, left-handed); III-691 (tip missing, left-handed); IV-438 (left-handed; IV- 439 (fragment, left-handed).

24. Miroschedji 1976, fig. 9:3–4; pl. 3:6, 8 (Susa, Apadana, Trench 1038); Steve and Gasche 1971, pls. 28:33–36; 85:17 (Susa, Acropole, 1965 Sounding, "Djemdet Nasr finale"). A fragmentary Late Susiana sickle from Jafarabad differs from Protoliterate sickels in details of shape, particularly in the presence of a groove into which flint blades were fastened with bitumen to form the cutting edge (Dollfus 1971, fig. 20:22).

25. Adams and Nissen (1972:208–09) in their survey of the Warka region used the sickles as an "undifferentiated indicator of the Ubaid, Uruk, and JN periods," but a later survey in the Nippur area led Adams (1981:121) to consider the sickles to have been most common in the Early and Middle Uruk periods. Wright (1981:304), on the basis of a survey of the Ur region, considers the sickles to have been most frequent in the Late and Terminal Ubaid periods.

sharp, smooth bore holes. Occasionally a spindle whorl was made of bituminous stone (pl. 30:N) or of cream-colored marble.[26] The spindle whorls, though varying somewhat in proportions and size, appear in only two standardized shapes, being either conical (pl. 126:J–M) or domed, with convex sides (pl. 126:N–V).[27] The squat example (pl. 126:C) is intermediate between the domed whorls and the rarer perforated terra-cotta discs (pl. 126:A–B, D). Except for their material, the latter are identical with the perforated discs of stone (pls. 29:Q–Z; 125:O–X) and cannot be automatically assumed to be spindle whorls. Incisions, punctations, and imprints sometimes appear on the tops of the spindle whorls (pl. 126:D–I) and on at least one of the terra-cotta discs (pl. 126:A), but are so simple that they are probably better interpreted as the identification marks of individual specimens rather than as decoration. The Chogha Mish terra-cotta spindle whorls and discs are readily paralleled in Protoliterate levels at other sites.[28]

Three distinctive and well-known categories of objects that are usually associated with weaving occur at Chogha Mish, although far less frequently than the spindle whorls. Spools, usually of terra-cotta but in at least one case of unbaked clay, range in length from 4.7 to 6.2 cm (pls. 30:A–G; 126:Y–CC).[29] They tend to occur in groups; half the loci where they were found yielded two or three examples.[30] In Mesopotamia spools occur in Late Ubaid and Protoliterate contexts, and in Anatolia and the Levant in later periods.[31] They might perhaps have actually served as spools on which thread was wound. The second type is the terra-cotta disc with

a perforation near one edge, normally interpreted as a loom weight (pl. 126:DD–FF).[32]

In Mesopotamia such discs occur already in the Late Ubaid period,[33] at Susa in the Proto-Elamite phase,[34] and in Crete, far to the west, in Early and Late Minoan contexts.[35] The third type is the tetrahedron of unbaked clay perforated at the narrower end (pls. 30:H–I; 126:GG). Though very rare at Chogha Mish and in Mesopotamia occurring apparently only at Jemdet Nasr, it is a widely distributed and long-lived type of loom weight in the west; particularly famous are the thirty-three examples found *in situ* at Troy.[36]

Similar objects (pl. 126:DD–FF) have been taken by Forbes as proof for the existence at Ur in the Early

---

26. For a parallel to plate 30:N, see Le Brun 1978a, fig. 38:7 (Susa, Acropole I, Level 17B). Alabaster and serpentine whorls are more common at Susa than at Chogha Mish (ibid., 38:1–6, 8–11).

27. Biconical spindle whorls, with or without notched edges, of Middle Susiana type sometimes occur in Protoliterate levels and apparently represent intrusions from earlier levels (III-25 [pl. 65:II] similar to 4.807 [pl. 65:HH]).

28. See Le Brun 1978a, fig. 35:1–9 (all incised or imprinted; Susa, Acropole I, Level 17B).

29. For other examples from Chogha Mish, all terra-cotta unless otherwise specified, see III-313; III-315, 316 (one end narrower); III-387; III-496; III-680; IV-126, 127, 128 (unbaked clay); IV-427 (one end smaller).

30. P17:Trench V A (two examples); R17:303 and environs (three examples); R18:310 (two examples); S17:301 (two examples); S18:402 (three examples).

31. See Lloyd 1943, pl. 16b (Tell Uqair); Lenzen 1974, pl. 21:K (Warka, no provenience); Mackay 1931, pl. 70:28–30 (Jemdet Nasr); de Genouillac et al. 1934, pl. 44:1 (Tello); Woolley 1955:66, U.14466; 67, U.14941; pl. 16, U.102, U.14466 (Ur, Pit F, Stratum H, Late Protoliterate contexts); Alishar, Assyrian Colony period (Schmidt 1932:122, fig. 150:b 2686–b 2687); Gawra VIII (Speiser 1935).

32. For the distribution and chronology of loom weights and for photographs of warp weights in recent use in Norway, see Hoffman 1964:17–22; 33–36, figs. 4–6:42–43; 9–10:46–50; 13–14; 16; 18; Professor Jack Davis kindly provided the reference to this publication.

33. See Boehmer 1972a, pl. 45:38, 38w (Warka, Square K XVII, Anu Ziggurat area, sounding in the southeastern side of the Steingebäude, Level 6); Lloyd 1943, pl. 16b = Lloyd 1978:46, fig. 14 (Tell Uqair, House A); Huot et al. 1980:123, fig. 30:g, i (Tell el-'Oueili). In the seventh season at Chogha Mish the discovery of such a disc in a primary Late Middle Susiana context (VII-22, G28:705, 78.87) showed that there, too, the type was known before the Protoliterate period. Discs that are similar to those just cited except in having a pair of perforations centrally placed might also have been loom weights; see Jordon 1932, pl. 20d (Warka, Eanna XVII); Boehmer 1972a, pl. 50:140 (Steingebäude Sounding, Layer 5); Woolley 1955:9, fig. 14 (al-Ubaid); Huot et al. 1980:123, fig. 30:H (Tell el-'Oueili). A disc of this type in the collection of the Field Museum (228389) comes from Kish, but its provenience is uncertain; it should be either Late Protoliterate or Early Dynastic. Ben Bronson kindly granted permission to refer to this object.

34. See Steve and Gasche 1971, pls. 28:23; 85:113 (Susa, Acropole, 1965 Sounding, "Djemdet Nasr finale").

35. See Warren 1972:212, 243, fig. 96:7, 75, 77–79; pl. 73:77, 7, 78 (one to three lateral perforations; Myrtos, Periods I and II, Early Minoan IIa and b). For an Early Minoan II example from Palaikastro and Late Minoan examples from Tylissos, see ibid., p. 212.

36. See Mackay 1931, pl. 70:19 (perhaps identical with an example in the Field Museum 228979 = JN 34581; Jemdet Nasr); Blegen et al. 1950:50, 338, 350; pls. 324, 333–34, 369, 461 (Troy I and II). For an earlier weaver's workshop with conical loom weights and some weaver's tools, see Garstang 1953:172–73, figs. 110–12; pl. 26:a–b (Mersin XIIB, Room 112, Late Chalcolithic approximately equivalent to Ubaid 4); Schmidt 1932:47, fig. 55 (Alishar, Early Bronze); Özgüç 1948, pl. 65:410, 415; 1949, pl. 58:644 (Kültepe, Assyrian Colony period); Palmieri 1973:81, 104; figs. 26:10, 105; 27:12, 13 (11 complete and fragmentary examples of weights intermediate in shape between tetra-hedrons and discs; Arslan Tepe Room A58, Late Colony period); Loud 1948, pls. 164:1; 169:2–16; 170:17–25 (Megiddo Strata XIIIA–IX, Middle Bronze IIA–Late Bronze I).

Dynastic period of the vertical warp-weighted loom.[37] In general, both the disc and the tetrahedral weights are usually assumed to have been used with such looms.[38] However, an indication that warp weights might not always necessarily indicate the presence of vertical looms is given by those used with horizontal looms in modern Iran (Wulff 1966:203). As it happens, cylinder seal impressions from Susa document the existence of horizontal looms in the early Protoliterate period (Amiet 1972, pls. 17:673; 82:673). Perhaps the most likely assumption is that both vertical and horizontal looms were in use during the Protoliterate period, a situation that has been suggested for prehistoric Europe and demonstrated for recent times in Norway and in Palestine and Syria (Hoffmann 1964:11, 23). There remains the question of whether two differently shaped types, the discs and the tetrahedrons, were used at Chogha Mish at the same time for the same purpose. Though there is not enough evidence to settle the question with certainty, it is noteworthy that at least one other Protoliterate site appears to have two similar types in the same context.[39]

Terra-cotta discs of biconical shape constitute a distinct category of objects, the use of which is uncertain. They could perhaps have been net sinkers; their perforations seem too small for mounting them on rigid sticks as maces. In so far as can be judged on the basis of a limited number of specimens, they cluster in three ranges of size, the smaller discs from about 6.0–7.0 cm in diameter (pl. 126:N–Q), the larger discs ca. 8.5–11.0 cm (pls. 30:C; 126:R–S), and one outsize example of 14.5 cm (pl. 126:T). Objects of a flattened spherical shape with a perforation seem to be rarer than the biconical discs. One (pl. 126:V) is of terra-cotta, but the other two are of unbaked clay (pl. 126:W, GG). It is clear that the latter, at least, could not have been net sinkers.[40]

A perforated rectangular object of unbaked clay, with a little lump of extra material on one side, is unique and of problematic function (pl. 126:W). Also one-of-a-kind is a cone with a relatively large flat base; it was probably a lid (pl. 30:V). Both examples of a crescent-shaped tool had been fired to a high degree of hardness (pl. 126:HH–II). The complete one has a roughly flattened concave side and a relatively sharp convex side. Slight indentations mark off the corners, one of which has two score marks on the flat side. Such crescentic tools are also known at Ur[41] and Habuba Kabira South, where they are considered to have been the tools of potters (Sürenhagen 1974/75:80, fig. 32 [two examples]). No signs of wear occur in the Chogha Mish examples except for two score marks at one corner on the flat side of one example (pl. 126:II), although without the hole characteristic of the bone needle-shuttles known in Palestine in the Chalcolithic period (cf. Bar-Adon 1980:177, fig. 50); the terra-cotta crescents might have been weaver's tools.

Unbaked clay slingshots indistinguishable in shape and size from earlier Susiana examples (pl. 65:L) were still in common use in the Protoliterate period. They occurred individually or in small groups in occupation debris and pits, for instance, in K23:501, 502; P17:Trench V A; and Q18:312. Numerous parallels for the Chogha Mish examples are to be found in both Early and Late Protoliterate contexts at other sites.[42]

37. See Woolley 1955:56, "circular clay loom weight"; 59, "two loom weights" (Ur, Pit F, Strata A, C, Early Dynastic). Forbes (1964:204), in the same connection, also cites spools found at Ur in Late Protoliterate contexts.

38. For discussion of the various types of looms and their chronological and geographical distribution, see Forbes 1964:198–206; Hoffman 1964:5–16, 297–336. For fragments of a horizontal loom and weaving tools found in the Nahal Mishmar and a discussion of the horizontal loom, see Bar-Adon 1980:177–82.

39. G. Algaze noted that in house ruins of Protoliterate date at Mereijib, some ten miles to the south of Ur, Woolley found what might have been the remains of a warp-weighted loom in situ, although he himself considered them to be net sinkers. His description is as follows: "... quantities of clay roundels, pierced each by one hole and in some cases decorated with incised circles, sometimes pierced with two holes, sometimes marked with an incised cross; they lay in piles and had evidently been strung together on a cord, though of that all traces had vanished" (Woolley 1955:84). The perforated discs were found in association with pierced weights (ibid., p. 84, fig. 21:d) similar to the Chogha Mish tetrahedrons (pl. 126:I) except for pointed bases.

40. Unbaked or slightly baked objects of the same general shape and size range as 2.743 (pl. 126:HH) are common in Iron Age Palestine and their suitability as loom weights has been experimentally verified (Sheffer 1981). Clearly such evidence is too far distant in time and space to have any direct pertinence for Chogha Mish, but even as a general analogy there is a difference; in the west the globular loom weights occur in large numbers, frequently in clusters, while at Chogha Mish such objects are rare.

41. See Woolley 1955:67, pl. 45:H (U.14938, Pit F, Square C6, Level 7.80-, Late Protoliterate). Of considerably later date and very likely different in function are three objects of similar shape, but much larger from Early Dynastic III private graves in the Royal Cemetery (Woolley 1934, pl. 221, U.8323 [two terra-cotta crescents 16.5 and 18.8 cm long from Grave PG/171/]; U.8213 [pinkish stone, 17.3 cm long, Gr. PG/159/]).

42. For a comprehensive study of slingshots, see Korfmann 1972. For Protoliterate examples, see Le Brun 1978a:84 (Susa, Acropole I, Level 17B); Steve and Gasche 1971, pl. 28:25 (Susa, Acropole, 1965 Sounding, "Djemdet Nasr" phase); Mackay 1931, pl. 70:20, 26–27; LXXI:24–27 (Jemdet Nasr); Lloyd and Safar 1940:15, pl. 2:21 (Grai Resh, Early Protoliterate context); Tobler 1950:173, pl. 87 (Gawra XI and XIA); Strommenger 1980a:47–48 (Habuba Kabira South).

Sherds were made into simple implements. The most striking are the round, sharp-edged scrapers, which were very neatly chipped into shape (pl. 30:P–R).[43] Two of the examples illustrated were made from fragments of large four-lugged jars with incised bands. The sherd scrapers might have been cheaper and commoner versions of the rare tabular flint scrapers (pl. 29:J). There are also sherds which, though apparently intentionally shaped into irregularly circular roundels, have thick edges quite distinct from the tapered ones of the scrapers. It is unlikely that such roundels were merely blanks for scrapers, since they have a greater size range, from ca. 10.0 to 4.5 cm. One example has about one-fourth of its periphery evenly abraded and must have been used as a rubber.[44] The perforated sherd roundels known in the Susiana periods seem to be represented in the Protoliterate levels only by a few rather large, curved examples with small holes (pl. 30:X).[45]

One of the more outstanding types of clay implements from the Protoliterate levels is the large pottery disc with a central projection on one side. Such discs were made of coarse ware and range in size from 34.0 cm (pl. 127:I) to about 41.0 cm (pl. 127:H). One example has a solid tang or boss and the disc itself is extended into a low wall on the tanged side (III-514, pl. 127:I). Three other examples have a socket, rather long in 3.033 (pl. 127:J) and the similar socket fragment 4.344, but considerably shorter in the fragmentary disc (pl. 127:H). The plain side was left rough and dimpled and seems usually to have been somewhat concave. The projections on the opposite side, whether of the boss or socket type, must have served as a means of attachment and suggest that the discs were potter's wheels, which pivoted with some kind of suitable lubricant on a wooden shaft.[46] Aid in visualizing the complete wheel is provided, despite great geographical and chronological gaps, by Egyptian tomb representations of the First Intermediate Period and the Twelfth Dynasty that show potters either squatting or sitting at their wheels. Of particular interest is a scene in the tomb of Djehutihotep at Bersheh, where the wheel consists of a disc with a ventral boss, analogous to that of III-514 (pl. 127:I), inserted into a vertical stand.[47] Although in the representations at Bersheh and Beni Hasan, the shaft of the wheel has a separate base, this seems to be merely an immovable support; it is not a treadle disc turned by the foot of the potter, as such relatively modern wheel types did not appear in Egypt, at least, until the Late period (Wulff 1966:154–56; Arnold 1976:25).

In addition to potter's wheels, a simple terra-cotta disc 42.0 cm in diameter and 2.5 cm thick was found (pl. 127:G). Although such an object could have been useful in a variety of ways, it is most likely to have been a potter's tool.[48] It could have rested on an immovable base and supported the clay to be shaped by hand, as shown in an Egyptian relief of the Old Kingdom (Arnold 1976:14, figs. 7 [Saqqara, Tomb of Ti, Dyn. V], 15). Alternatively, it could have been placed on top of the wheel proper, similar to the discs used by modern Cretan potters (Hampe and Winter 1962:16–17, figs. 12–14).

43. Compare also 3.1210 (Q18:313, ca. 81.51 [standard ware: small grits; yellowish buff, reserve slip; diameter 10.1–11.2 cm]); 3.1211 (R18:Trench XX Southeast, 0.30–0.50 B.S. [standard ware: dense, scattered small grits; yellowish buff, reserve slip; diameter ca. 10.2 cm]); 3.1212 (R17:305, 82.90 [standard ware: dense, scattered small grits; yellowish buff; diameter 7.9–8.1 cm]).

44. 3.1213 (West of R18:305, 83.00–82.75 [standard ware: dense scattered small grit; greenish buff; diameter 6.2 × 8.3 cm; bottle Protoliterate Family CXVI]). Compare also plain roundels listed according to descending size: 3.1215 (Northeast of Q18:301, ca. 81.65 [standard ware: dense, small grits; green waster; 7.2 × 9.9 cm]); 3.1214 (between R18:310 and Q18:312, ca. 82.10 [standard ware: small grits; greenish buff; 7.9 × 9.5; bottle, Protoliterate Family CXVI]); 3.1216 (Q18:301, ca. 81.20 [coarse ware: small to large grits; buff; 6.4 × 7.6 cm]); 3.1217 (Q18:313, 81.81 [Middle Susiana red ware: dense; light orange to brown at surfaces; 6.9 × 7.3; presumably reused]); 3.1218 (East of Q19:301, 81.10–80.60 [standard ware: small to medium grits; greenish buff; 4.4 × 4.5]); 3.1219 (Southeast of R19:303, 80.50] standard ware fragment: small grits; buff]).

45. Compare also III-353 (East of R18:308, ca. 82.10 [standard ware: grit tempered; buff; diameter 12.7 cm]); IV-132 (R18:405, ca. 82.20–82.00 [standard ware: large grits; yellowish buff; diameter 12.1 cm]).

46. Perhaps related although clearly not identical is a "potter's wheel" described but not illustrated by Woolley (1955:28) from Protoliterate contexts at Ur: "it was a disk of baked clay 0.075 m thick and 0.75 m in diameter, heavy enough therefore to spin freely of its own momentum; the central pivot hole was smoothed with bitumen (or perhaps the bitumen was for attaching a peg which itself revolved in a socket in the lower board) and at one point near the edge of the upper surface there were small holes into which would be put the stick handles that served to turn the wheel."

47. Arnold 1976:20–25, figs. 10–14; p. 24, fig. 13 = Newberry, no date, pl. 25 (Djehutyhotep, reign of Sesostris III).

48. A convex underside worn at the center distinguishes discs from Early Minoan II contexts at Myrtos from spindle whorl 3.1063 (pl. 126:N; see Warren 1972:213–14, 245, numbers 105, 116, 10, 12–15, pls. 75:A–D, 76:A–C). The Myrtos objects have been identified as a potter's turntable rotated by hand and "standing at the beginning of the potter's wheel tradition" (ibid., 213–15, 224). Eight were found together in a room of a complex taken accordingly to be a potter's workshop (ibid., pl. 6:A [room 49]). One Myrtos example had a slight depression in the underside and points forward to Middle Minoan and Middle Helladic I examples with a concavity for the shaft; for these and later Minoan potter's wheels, see ibid., 214, 223, #105; 245, fig. 98:105.

BONE OBJECTS
(Pl. 128:T–AA)

Bone tools of the Protoliterate period were scarce at Chogha Mish. A tanged arrowhead found below the surface at the southern edge of the East Area cannot be dated definitively to the period (pl. 128:Z).[49] Wide, flat spatula-like implements, probably made from ribs, are represented by one complete example and two fragments (pl. 128:Y, AA). They seem to have had pointed tips and more or less rounded butts—that of one fragment (pl. 128:Y) is worn by use. The two perforated needles seem too large for sewing normal textiles and one of them was perhaps big enough to have served as a needle shuttle (pl. 128:V–W; cf. Bar-Adon 1980:177). A pin, oval in section, has a head delimited by a groove and is similar to the metal pins with heads (pl. 128:T).[50] A very small fragment of an incised bone object (pl. 128:U) has decoration similar to that on a pin from Tello and long tubular beads from Late Protoliterate contexts at Warka and Jemdet Nasr.[51]

ORNAMENTS AND INLAYS
(Pl. 129:A–OO)

In view of the circumstances that no Protoliterate graves were discovered and that the settlement seems to have been abandoned rather than suddenly destroyed, it is hardly surprising that personal ornaments are rare. The majority of those that do occur are beads, occasionally made of terra-cotta or frit, but usually of varieties of stone obtainable locally from the riverbeds or from the nearby Zagros foothills. Of the rarer, imported stones, only carnelian appears for certain.[52]

The beads appeared as scattered specimens except for those from Trench XXV found inside a four-lugged jar together with four small alabaster jars and a lump of red ocher (pls. 31:R; 129:A, EE, KK). The group consisted of 144 small disc beads of frit, carnelian, and black stone (pl. 31:R), 1 larger and thinner stone disc bead, 13 cylindrical or barrel-shaped beads of frit and white or black stone, 1 spool-shaped bead of black stone, and, largest of all, a squat cylinder of white stone engraved with fish-like ovals (pl. 129:A). A tiny white stone pendant in the form of a fish also belongs to the group (pl. 129:EE). In addition, the jar contained 10 small and 6 large shells pierced for stringing (pl. 31:R)[53] and a 1 × 2 cm plaque of buff-colored stone inlay cut into 5 ribs on 1 side (pl. 129:KK).

Two general categories of beads can be distinguished, those with circular sections and those with noncircular sections. Among the former, tubular beads occur in stone (pl. 129:E, I), frit (pl. 129:G), and terra-cotta (pl. 129:F, H). A stone spacer bead with two perforations is paralleled at Susa (pl. 129:J).[54] A tubular bead of translucent brown stone decorated with irregular incisions provides a problem; although found in a primary Protoliterate context, its affinities seem to lie with prehistoric beads and it might be out of context or a holdover from earlier times (pl. 129:D).[55] Squat tubular beads with incised decoration constitute another special variety, in this case intermediate between beads and cylinder seals (pls. 41:E–F, K; 129:A–B). Barrel-shaped beads occur in stone (pl. 129:K–L) and in terra-cotta (pl. 129:M). A specialized variant in stone has an octagonal section (pl. 129:N). Large, coarse cylindrical beads appear only in terra-cotta (pl. 129:O–Q). Disc beads are best known from the small examples of the group of beads described above, but a larger example also occurs (pl. 129:S).[56]

Among the beads with noncircular sections, one subgroup consists of those with irregularly oval sections such as barrel shapes in frit and stone (pl. 129:U, X–Z) and a squat ovoid in translucent stone (pl. 129:T). The other subgroup is that in which one side is flat, thus creating a triangular or hemispherical section. This group provides some of the more characteristic of the Protoliterate beads. One flat example (pl. 129:W) is a simple lentoid in shape, but another (pl. 129:V) has protruding narrow ends similar to those of the larger and

49. A tanged bone arrowhead from Susa, Acropole I, Level 17, is different in shape (Le Brun 1971, fig. 58:8).

50. A more sophisticated pin with a rounded head separated from the shaft by a pronounced groove was found at Susa, Acropole I, Level 17 (Le Brun 1971, fig. 57:12).

51. See de Genouillac et al. 1934, pl. 34:3 (Tello); Heinrich 1936:41, pl. 31:W14636e (Warka, Kleinfunde); Mackay 1931, pl. 74:8 (Jemdet Nasr).

52. Disc bead (pl. 129:A) found inside a four-lugged jar. A disc bead (III-446) from below the surface of P17:Trench V A cannot be dated with certainty to the Protoliterate period because of the amount of Achaemenid material found in that area. An object preserved to a length of 1.2 cm might have been an animal-shaped bead or pendant and is made of a blue stone that looks similar to lapis lazuli (III-109). A roughly trapezoidal pendant, 1.2 cm long is probably of obsidian (III-461).

53. See Heinrich 1936, pl. 37 (Warka, Eanna III), for shells found with beads in the Kleinfunde and strung modernly as pendants.

54. See Le Brun 1971, fig. 57:22; idem 1978a, fig. 41:30 (Susa, Acropole, Levels 17A and 17B).

55. For a Late Protoliterate (Proto-Elamite) parallel, see Wright et al., 1981:151, fig. 75:F (shell; Farukhabad, Layer 23B). For prehistoric beads of related character, see Dollfus 1971, fig. 21:15–16 (Jafarabad, Levels 3 and 2); Le Breton 1948, fig. 32:17 (Bandebal, old excavation); Hole, Flannery, and Neely 1969, fig. 103:N (Tappeh Sabz, Bayat phase); Tobler 1950, pl. 171:15 (Gawra XIII).

56. The majority of the beads just enumerated represent simple and universally used forms, cf. Heinrich 1936:42, fig. 7 (Warka, Eanna III, Kleinfunde).

rounder stone bead (pl. 129:AA).[57] Two other stone beads resemble stamp seals (cf. pl. 41:H, J, M–N, R) in form, but their bases are plain except for some slight incision on the smaller of the two (pl. 129:BB–CC).

Pendants are even rarer than beads. Three rectangular or trapezoidal plaques are made of stone (pl. 129:GG–HH, JJ) and one from a potsherd (pl. 129:II).[58] Far more sophisticated and specific to the Protoliterate period is a circle of shell with six depressions filled with black paste (pl. 129:DD).[59] Theriomorphic pendants are represented by a small stone fish from the Trench XXV group (pl. 129:EE) and a bird carved from the spiral core of a shell, as attested by a groove remaining on the base and the side (pl. 129:FF).[60]

Among the few elements of inlay is a ribbed plaque of buff stone the shape and size of which are well paralleled elsewhere (pl. 129:KK);[61] although found with the group of beads from Trench XXV, it might originally have belonged to some architectural ornament such as the well-known golden frieze from the altar of the Eye Temple at Tell Brak (cf. Mallowan 1947, pl. 3). The remaining inlays are all made of mother-of-pearl. An eight-rayed rosette has in the center and at the tip of each petal round depressions, presumably for paste of a contrasting color (pl. 129:OO). It and two similar but smaller examples from Susa and Tell Agrab[62] appear to

be round-petaled variants of the rosettes with pointed petals that appear on Protoliterate cylinder seals as vegetation and, on a larger scale, as composite architectural inlays made of different-colored stones.[63] The eight-rayed rosette (pl. 129:OO), four to five times smaller than the stone rosette, is too small and of too delicate a material to have been an architectural inlay. Naturalistic shapes are represented by a fish (pl. 129:LL) and a pair of geometricized frogs or birds (pl. 129:MM–NN). The nature of the matrices into which these pieces might have been set is unknown. They differ in shape from the inlays that decorate stone vessels of the late Protoliterate period. The fashion of inlaying stone vases with colorful elements of other materials, which is represented so often by stone vases from the Diyala sites and from Warka, was probably not developed until a phase of the Protoliterate period later than the occupation at Chogha Mish.

FIGURINES
(Pl. 31:A–P)

Only animal figurines were found in the Protoliterate levels. The majority of them are of unbaked clay and not well preserved. In addition, they are usually very simply shaped, with a minimum of modeling and detail. Both their general quality and their state of preservation make the identification of the species intended difficult. Apparently all represent domestic cattle, but the shapes are so simple, particularly since in almost every case the horns are missing, that they cannot be distinguished as sheep or bovines. The exception is a figurine that is both considerably better shaped than the others and also purposely baked (pl. 31:A). Its horns identify it as a bovoid even though the shape of the head is more sheep-like.

Except for the horns, which appear to have been made separately, each figure seems to have been made from one lump of clay. The legs are not rendered individually but indicated by a solid mass of clay pulled down from the ends of the lump. Thus in profile the ventral contour of the figures is arched. Backs are usually at least slightly concave, except for one (pl. 31:C) whose back is not only as high as the head, but also pinched to a narrow notched edge. Despite these eccentricities, an identification as a boar seems to be ruled out by the broken stumps of horns. Tails were sometimes indicated, either as a projection (pl. 31:M) or as an asymmetrical and slight posterior bulge (pl. 31:K). Another feature

57. See de Genouillac et al. 1934, pl. 36:6b–c (Tello); Mallowan 1947, pls. 16:4; 20:13, 16 (Tell Brak, Late Protoliterate).

58. For Protoliterate parallels, see Strommenger 1963, pl. 34:F (Warka, Archaic Settlement, Late Protoliterate); de Genouillac et al., 1934, pl. 43:10 (Tello). At Gawra similar examples came from prehistoric and proto-historic contexts (Tobler 1950, pl. 91:1, 6). For still earlier examples of this simple types of ornament from early Neolithic contexts, see Hole, Flannery, and Neely 1969, fig. 100:C–D (Tappeh Ali Kosh, Bus Mordeh, and Ali Kosh phases).

59. See Le Brun 1978a, fig. 41:19, cf. p. 154 (Susa, Acropole I, Level 17B); de Mecquenem 1934:192, fig. 27:13 (Susa, old excavation); de Genouillac et al. 1934, pl. 37:1 e (plain), f (depressions for inlay) (Tello); Mackay 1931, pl. 72:17–18 (Jemdet Nasr); Gawra XII and XI (Tobler 1950, pl. 173:41–42); Delougaz and Lloyd 1942:139, Kh. VII:81, unpublished (in shell but no depressions for inlay; Khafajah, Sin Temple IV, Protoliterate d).

60. For an example larger than plate 129:EE, 2.5 cm long, see Woolley 1955, pl. 28:U.18499 (Diqdiqqeh, environs of Ur, period uncertain). For parallels to plate 129:FF, see de Mecquenem 1934:192, fig. 27:24 (Susa, old excavation); Mackay 1931, pl. 74:6, number 3314 (Jemdet Nasr).

61. See Lenzen 1959b = Lenzen 1959a, pl. 16:G (Warka, Eanna IV, *Riemchengebäude*); Heinrich 1936, pl. 34:F, H (Warka, Eanna III, *Kleinfunde*).

62. See de Mecquenem 1934:192, fig. 27:12 (shell, diameter 1.5 cm; Susa, old excavation); Delougaz and Lloyd 1942:272, N 13:5, Ag. 36:97, 30.20 (shell, diameter 1.1 cm; Tell Agrab, Shara Temple, Early Dynastic II).

63. For cylinder seals, see Frankfort 1939, pl. 3:a; Heinrich 1936, pl. 17:C. For inlays, see Heinrich 1936, pl. 32:a (Warka, Eanna III, *Kleinfunde*); Mallowan 1947, pl. 5 (stone; Brak, Late Protoliterate); cf. also Tobler 1950, pl. 175:76 (Gawra XIA, Grave 181 for a gold rosette).

that sometimes appeared although very rarely, is the eye; when it is rendered by a small perforation (cf. pl. 31:A, B), the figures take on an unexpected liveliness.

STRUCTURAL/ARCHITECTURAL ELEMENTS

Several widely different types of objects from the Protoliterate levels can be related either directly or indirectly with architecture. The more numerous and familiar are the terra-cotta cones used for the mosaic decorations of important buildings. Both rarer and more difficult to interpret are other types such as model bricks. One group found in Trench VI consisted of individually formed and subsequently baked pieces: 42 complete examples ranging in size from 2.8 × 1.5 × 1.1 to 3.3 × 1.8 × 1.2 cm, 6 chipped, and 37 fragmentary (pl. 30:S). The pieces of the second group, found in different seasons in the same room, approximately 40 in number, differ from those of the first group in being squared-off rim sherds of beveled-rim bowls. The sizes of some of the fragmentary model bricks (3.1247a–q) range from a minimum of 1.8 × 1.4 × 1.4 cm to a maximum of 4.0 × 1.5 × 2 8 cm, but the majority are about the same size as other bricks (pl. 30:S). An isolated example of the squared-off beveled-rim sherd type (3.1248) was found in pit Q18:312. The function of these objects is conjectural. They might have been toys for children or have served masons in laying out model plans.

A perforated terra-cotta fragment might be one quadrant of a roughly square plaque about 20 × 23 cm in size (pl. 127:K). Its sparsely scattered and irregularly shaped holes have a greatest dimension of 0.6–1.0 cm. Although perforated partitions occur in bowls of Protoliterate Family XXIII (pl. 83:X), the plaque is too thick, 2 to 4 cm, to have been part of a vessel. Its finished, though very uneven edge suggests that it was a grill set into some kind of architectural setting. If it were, indeed, a plaque of limited size, much later analogies from Akkadian contexts could be cited, for example, the plaque with slightly bigger holes found in the upper part of a wall at Susa[64] and the window grill with much larger perforations from the Archaic House at Tell Asmar (Delougaz, Hill, and Lloyd 1967, pl. 67:A). It is also possible, however, that the fragment belonged to a grillwork separating the fire pit and firing chamber of the kiln. A second fragment might have had rather longer rectangular openings (pl. 127:L). The original shape of a plaque fragment with two round perforations near one end is uncertain (pl. 127:M). The function of these three objects (pl. 127:K–M) is unknown.

Terra-cotta pegs with either hollow (pl. 127:A–C) or solid (pl. 127:D–F) shafts and flaring heads varying somewhat in shape are characteristic for the Protoliterate levels, though not very numerous. Many examples have been found in Susa, one of them inserted into a hole in the center of a square plaque.[65] Such objects were set into walls to serve either as fasteners or perhaps as decorations in their own right. At Susa, as Steve and Gasche (1971:51; pls. 38:1–12; 39:22–24; 94:37; 97:6–7) have pointed out, the Protoliterate pegs continue a custom already established in the Late Susiana period. At Warka hollow terra-cotta cornets, in a general way comparable to the Chogha Mish pegs but larger, with mouth diameters of 15–17 cm and lengths of 30–35 cm, were placed in rows at the top edges of the high platforms belonging to the successive phases of the White Temple complex; they served both as decoration and to strengthen the edges of the platforms.[66]

Chogha Mish has provided numerous examples of the two types of terra-cotta cones used in the Protoliterate period to form the mosaic wall decoration of important buildings. The first group consists of examples made of the ordinary standard and fine wares employed in Protoliterate ceramics; such cones range from yellowish buff to pink in color. They vary in size from a minimum length of about 7 cm and a greatest diameter of somewhat less than 1 cm to well over 15 cm in length and about 3 cm in diameter (pl. 31:U–Y, HH–JJ). Their flat ends were often dipped in black or red paint (pl. 31:S–T).[67] The second group consists of considerably larger cones made of dark gray clay. In color and consistency these cones often closely resemble gray stone. The greatest diameter of the gray cones is never less than 2 cm and often reaches 5 cm. Although the majority of the examples found were broken, it appears that some might have been at least 20 cm long. The conical depressions of the gray cones must have been

---

64. See Steve and Gasche 1971:71–81; pls. 12:15; 45:3; 71:3 (Susa, Acropole, 1965 Sounding). The wall in question was part of a group of square structures considered by Steve and Gasche to have been granaries; ventilated by a grill whose holes were too small for mice to enter.

65. See Steve and Gasche 1971:150–51, pls. 33:1–16, 38 (plaque and peg); 55:3 (pegs from Locus 331), 4 (plaque and peg); 89:1, 3, 5, 7, 8–12, 14 (all pegs), 15, 17 (plaques) (Susa, Acropole, 1965 Sounding "Djemdet Nasr ancien-Uruk récent"), cf. also Haller 1932, pl. 20 A:v (Warka, Eanna IV).

66. Jordan 1932:22–23, pls. 9 ("Flaschenwand"), 17:d; Heinrich 1937, pl. 44:b (most were conical, but there were also many of the jar-like shapes, with definite bodies); Lenzen et al. 1967:11–12, pls. 1:a, 2:b, 3:a, 4:b, 7a, 26 (plan).

67. Two cone fragments found in R21:401 North, an area of Protoliterate debris, are so atypical in being made of bitumen that it is not altogether certain that they should be identified as cones at all (IV-318, diameter of flat end, 2.3 cm preserved length 3.8 cm; IV-319, diameter of slightly domed end 2.4 cm; preserved length 4.2 cm).

intended for single- or multiple-ringed inlays. The materials used could have been of pottery, stone, shell, or mother-of-pearl, to judge by the inlays of stone vases known from the Diyala region and Warka in the Late Protoliterate period.

Cone mosaic is best known from Warka, where it was first discovered by Loftus over a century ago[68] and where systematic excavation has uncovered several structures with such decoration in the Eanna temenos. There solid-ended cones form geometric patterns on walls, niches, and engaged columns.[69] Large cones with hollowed ends were used on the pillared platform of Eanna IV to form a crowning frieze above the mosaic patterns (Heinrich 1932:14, pls. 8, 9:b). That such architectural ornament was known not only in southern Mesopotamia and the Susiana region but also far to the west is now attested by cones from Habuba Kabira South (Strommenger 1980:43–44, fig. 24) and by a fragment of mosaic and by terra-cotta plaques with imitation cone-mosaic from the Late Protoliterate Eye Temple at Brak (Mallowan 1947, pls. 3, 4 [b]).

Comparable public buildings must have existed at Chogha Mish although it has not yet yielded any cone mosaic *in situ*. This probably indicates that most of the buildings to which the cones belonged existed above the present surface of the site and have been completely eroded. The ubiquity of detached cones all over the site, either on the surface or in the Protoliterate levels, suggests that their use was not confined to a single area. On the terrace there is no evidence from the distribution of the cones to indicate any particular spot as the most likely location for a structure with cone mosaic. On the High Mound, however, in the two stratigraphic test pits in the central hollow, the cones either equaled or outnumbered the beveled-rim bowl sherds, which are usually by far the more numerous constituents of any Protoliterate group. Although undue reliance should not be placed on data from such limited areas, nonetheless, such a markedly high proportion of cones suggests that a temple with cone mosaic once crowned the High Mound.

HUT SYMBOLS

A number of objects with a bell-shaped body, usually somewhat oval in section, and a head in the form of twinned rings were found at Chogha Mish. Our name for the category is taken from Andrae's interpretation of similar objects as highly stylized renderings of reed huts similar to those still constructed today in the marshes of southern Mesopotamia (Andrae 1930, chapters 1, 3). The Chogha Mish examples can be divided into two groups according to their size and the material of which they are made. Small hut symbols ranging in height from 2.0 to 5.0 cm and made of stone are more numerous (pl. 31:AA–GG). Larger examples are made of terra-cotta and represented by two looped heads with tangs for attaching them to separately-made bodies. One is a flat heart-shaped plaque with small perforations (pl. 31:Z). The other is much more substantial, being 13.6 cm wide, 10.3 cm high, and 1.8 cm thick (tang 2.2 cm thick); its tang is broad and traces of the clay weld remain that once masked the juncture of head and body (pl. 31:Q). By analogy with the proportions of the small stone hut symbols, the total height of the terra-cotta examples can be estimated as approximately 9.0 and 21.5 cm respectively.

Close parallels for the small stone hut symbols have been found at Susa, Ur, Khafajah, Tell Agrab, and Brak.[70] Variant forms occur in northern Mesopotamia in levels contemporary with the late Protoliterate period. Three larger hut symbols made of stone from Gawra have a definite neck between the loops and the body.[71] The terra-cotta examples from Gawra, some of which are even larger than the stone examples, are abbreviated renderings consisting only of the neck and loops.[72] They were, unlike two examples from Chogha Mish (pl. 31:Q, Z), independent objects that could stand on their somewhat splayed bases. A similar large terra-cotta example was found at Grai Resh, as well as terra-cotta examples of related form at Brak.[73]

68. Loftus 1857:187ff.; cf. Heinrich 1932, pl. 7 (lower right).

69. For cones *in situ*, see Jordan 1932, pls. 1:16 a; Heinrich 1932, pls. 7–9 (the colonnade of the northwest terrace and the adjoining court, Eanna V); Lenzen 1966 et al., pls. 6:b, 7:a–b, 8:a–b, 9 a, 27; Brandes 1968, passim (Pillared Hall southeast of Temple C, Eanna IVa). For table with occurrences of cone mosaic at Warka, see Heinrich 1935, pl. 2. For stone cone mosaic, see Heinrich 1938:28; pl. 34; Lenzen 1959b:13–14, 16 (terra-cotta cones of court), pls. 6:a, 7:b, 20:a–b, 41) (Eanna IV, Steinstiftmosaik-Tempel).

70. See Belaiew 1943, tables I, III (Susa, old excavation); Woolley 1955, pl. 15:U.17836; out of context (Ur, Early Dynastic III level); Delougaz and Lloyd 1942:28–29, fig. 24, Kh VI.242 and 243 (Khafajah, Sin Temple IV, Protoliterate d); ibid., 268, 269, 274, Ag. 36.134 and 367; Ag. 35.805 (out of context) (Tell Agrab, Shara Temple, Early Dynastic II); Mallowan 1947, pls. 26:8, 51:2; pp. 26–28, 30–34, 150–56, 198–205, for Mallowan's typology of "spectacle idols" (hut symbols) and "eye-idols," evidence that the latter were special local variations of the earlier "spectacle" type, and extensive comparative and interpretative discussion (Brak, Eye Temple, Late Protoliterate).

71. See Speiser 1935:99–100; pl. 44:c (14.5 cm high; two other examples 9.6 and 9.8 cm high; Gawra IX).

72. See Tobler 1950, pl. 86:1–4, 8–9 (Gawra XI or XIA).

73. See Lloyd and Safar 1940, pl. 3, fig. 7:1 (Grai Resh, Level II); Mallowan 1947, pls. 25:10 (10.2 cm high), 11 (6.0 cm high) (Brak, Eye Temple).

The suggestion that these much-discussed objects are highly stylized renderings of reed structures remains the best clue for understanding their function and significance.[74] Reed huts and the associated elements, the bundle of reeds and the post with rings, appear in some detail in Protoliterate glyptic and relief and in simplified form among the archaic signs.[75] The most likely specific prototype for the hut symbols is the hut with two reed bundles projecting symmetrically from the top.[76] Though these bundles do not curl into a volute, they are clearly closely akin to the Inanna symbol proper, the voluted reed bundle.[77] The animals shown emerging from the huts underline the significance of the hut motif and of the hut symbols derived from it.[78] The small stone hut symbols must have been portable amulets emblematic of the principles of fertility and growth personalized as the goddess Inanna. The larger examples, whether of stone or terra-cotta, were probably stationary cult ob-

jects. Occasionally the hut symbols themselves appear on glyptic designs (pl. 45:Q),[79] but not together with the elaborate altars and other objects of temple repositories.[80] Thus the large hut symbols might well have been used primarily for private veneration in households rather than in the ceremonial worship of public sanctuaries.

The Protoliterate small objects surveyed in this chapter run the gamut from ordinary implements used in agriculture or various crafts through the finer household utensils such as the stone vessels and the personal adornments to objects with architectural or religious connotations. There still remains for discussion some of the more numerous and significant of the Protoliterate finds, those which provide evidence of fundamental importance both for economic and social developments, including writing, and also for the appearance of elaborate representational art.

74. See Heinrich 1957:33–34 and note 34 for a summary of the evidence and additional bibliography.

75. Heinrich 1957:11–30; Falkenstein 1936:51, 59–60, and signs 213, 236, 239, 244, 248–51.

76. Heinrich 1957:13, figs. 5:a (= Amiet 1961, pl. 42:623 = Frankfort 1954, pl. 3:c), 7 (= Amiet 1961, pl. 10:186 = Schott 1934, pl. 29), Lenzen 1961, pl. 15:e; Falkenstein 1936:51, sign 213.

77. Falkenstein 1936:58–59; signs 208–210. For hut with single volute bundle, see Heinrich 1957:11, fig. 2 (= Amiet 1961, pl. 43:632).

78. Delougaz (1968) suggested that these representations should not be interpreted literally but rather as symbolic renderings of the birth of animals from Inanna. Such an interpretation would make the transmutation of the hut symbols into the Late Protoliterate "Eye idols" of Brak easily understandable.

79. Amiet 1961:100, pl. 78:628 (rows of hut symbols alternating with rows of fish); Parrot (1948:51f.) suggested that a motif consisting of a conical or round element surmounted by two drill holes, found quite often on Jemdet Nasr-style seals of the late Protoliterate period, represents "Eye idols"; Amiet (1961:102–03) interprets the motif as a vessel since it often occurs together with unmistakable vessels (ibid., numbers 315, 320, 324, 329–30, 334–35, 338, 343, 345, 347, 443).

80. Heinrich 1936, pl. 38 (= Amiet 1961, pl. 45:644); Schott 1934, pl. 29:b (= Amiet 1961, pl. 46:654; Baghdad).

CHAPTER 6

CLAY STOPPERS, SEALINGS, AND RECORDS
OF THE PROTOLITERATE PERIOD

The various elements of unbaked clay, pertaining to Protoliterate administrative practices, constitute an important part of Protoliterate archaeological assemblage. The clay elements in question are particularly common in the soft ashy filling of refuse pits, along with sherds, small implements, and lumps of kneaded clay. Debris of this kind presumably accumulated in or near places where administrative activities occurred. Some of them are adjuncts, such as the vessel stoppers, usually without seal impressions, and the sealings attached to various types of objects. Others are independent objects, such as clay records in the form of tablets and balls containing tokens, almost all of which bear seal impressions.[1] Such clay elements need to be surveyed before the seals and glyptic designs are considered. Recognition of the types of sealings involved can help in reconstituting seal designs from fragmentary impressions. Moreover, the objects, part of whose basic function was to bear seal impressions, are of great interest and importance in themselves; they represent some of the more significant developments in the late prehistoric period that crystallized and became widespread during the Protoliterate period.

ACCESSORIAL ELEMENTS

JAR STOPPERS (Pls. 32:A–B; 130)

Rather substantial masses of clay were used to seal vessels with relatively large mouths, the imprints of which often remain on the lower side of the stoppers. They seem to fall into two main categories of size, those with diameters ranging from about 6.00 to 6.80 cm and those from about 8.00 to 10.75 cm. Some are made of the heavy, refined clay without visible tempering typical for cylinder seal impressions. Others are of coarse clay with vegetal tempering, sometimes in large amounts. Even the more carefully shaped examples are irregular; many are markedly rough or lumpy. Only a minority, usually those of refined clay, have smoothed surfaces.

The jar stoppers were for the most part essentially lids set on top of the mouths of the vessels with convex

or irregularly flat bases. They were at most pressed down only slightly into the jar neck (pls. 32:B; 130:B–D). A stopper whose lower part formed a thick plug in the neck of a jar is exceptional (pl. 130:A). The only imprint normally found on the lower side of a jar stopper is that of the jar neck and, sometimes, rim. By the time the stoppers were used their clay seems to have been solid enough to demand firm pressure to set them in place.

The tops of the jar stoppers vary in shape. They are sometimes irregularly flat (pl. 130:B–C) and occasionally impressed with a cylinder seal (pl. 36:A). The stoppers with convex tops can be divided into low domed shapes (pl. 130:A, D–E) and high conical shapes (pl. 130:F–G), but some of the examples are of intermediate forms blurring the distinction. The higher stoppers sometimes appear with two finger holds (pl. 130:H [very small], I–K) and in one case with four (pl. 130:M). Small perforations were occasionally made in jar stoppers. The most elaborate example (pl. 130:C) has a vertical perforation through the thin edge of the stopper that overlays the jar rim. The two perforations in the thick part of the stopper were produced by boring into the clay at different angles from top and bottom thus forming an angular channel. Two other stoppers have only a single small perforation each (pl. 130:A). The purpose of these perforations remains uncertain. They could have allowed either air to enter or steam to escape from the jar. The pair of perforations on one example (pl. 130:C) could perhaps have accommodated loops of string to allow the stopper to be repeatedly removed without injuring it. However, the smallness and crookedness of the perforations and the absence of signs of wear or of string imprints make this interpretation rather dubious.

BOTTLE STOPPERS

The small size of some clay stoppers and the imprints often remaining on their undersides indicate that they could have fitted only narrow necks such as are best known from the spouted bottles (Protoliterate Family CXVI). The small stoppers are frequently found intact; they seem to have been easily removed as they were not usually pushed deeply into the neck. Some examples had, however, plugged the neck; they have a vertical channel on one side, in one instance it is rather

---

1. The exceptions are tablets marked only with numerals, such as were found at Chogha Mish in the seventh season. AA

broad as if made by a thumb; others have narrower imprints, perhaps of sticks or reeds inserted to facilitate the withdrawal of the stopper or the contents of the bottles.

The tops of the bottle stoppers vary in shape more than do the jar stoppers. Some are irregularly flattened and occasionally have an irregular transverse groove; one example has two parallel grooves. The greater number of bottle stoppers are convex; the innumerable individual variations are all best subsumed under the rubric of "domed" as there is no natural dividing line between examples of rounded shape (pl. 130:I) and those of more pointed conical form (pl. 130:T). The imprints frequently found on the domed stoppers must have been practical finger holds. From one to seven imprints can occur on a single stopper (pl. 130:R–X).

Among the standard shapes of the bottle stoppers, only the flat-topped examples could have been impressed by a seal, and even they provided no scope for a single complete rolling of a cylinder seal. However, one bottle stopper with a seal impression was found (pl. 131:A). In addition, one other small-sized stopper is impressed, with atypically deep and, unfortunately, unrecognizable elements (pl. 131:B). Although its concave underside is atypical for a bottle stopper, it can be provisionally assigned to that class. Out of almost two thousand bottle stoppers recorded, only two exceptional examples (pl. 131:A–B) bear impressions. Clearly, the contents of bottles were not normally secured by seals. The bottle stoppers are very unevenly distributed in the Protoliterate areas. In many spots they are either absent or only sporadically represented, but in a few pits and pottery deposits, in particular P18:301, they are present in great quantities, as indicated in table 10.

DOOR SEALINGS (Fig. 17; Pls. 32:C, F–G; 33:A)

The most distinctive type of sealing is represented mostly by fragments. Its specific character is given by the irregularly conical outer shape and the imprints of string and a stick on the inner surface (pl. 32:C). Some fragments preserve part of the apex of the sealing with the lip surrounding the stick (pl. 32:C, F–G). The majority of the door sealings are small fragments preserving only bits of the original seal design, which often cannot be completely reconstructed in the absence of a number of examples impressed by the same seal. When large enough to be reconstructed, the door sealings varied considerably in size. Three joining fragments form about half of a sealing with a diameter of ca. 15 cm (pl. 33:A). On each door sealing a single cylinder seal was rolled radially several times, apparently without any concern for the quality of the impressions. Individual rollings sometimes overlap and obscure each other or are separated by a pronounced and characteristic wedge of plain clay (pl. 33:A).

The door sealings are a standard type with a wide geographical and temporal distribution. The earlier examples come from the prehistoric site of Tall-i Bakun A in Fars, where they are found together with actual stamp seals (Langsdorff and McCown 1942:66, pl. 7:13, 18–19; Alizadeh 1988b). The use of this type of sealing to secure doors has been demonstrated in detail by Enrica Fiandra (1975), who started with clues provided by Middle Minoan sealings from the palace of Phaistos and a knobbed door frame of Ramses II in Turin. A stick or knob set in a wall beside a door was lashed with string attached to the door and covered with clay so that it was

Table 10. Distribution of Clay Stoppers in Various Contexts (+ = seal impressions; cf. Table 13)

Provenience	Flat Plain	Flat Vertical Channeled	Domed Plain	Domed Grooved	1	2	3	4	5	6	7	Indeterminate	Indeterminate* Complete	Indeterminate* Fragment	Flat	Domed Plain	Domed Finger Impressed	Conical	Indeterminate	Number of Items in Locus
ROOMS AND FLOORS																				
Q17:304	—	—	1	—	—	1	—	1	—	—	—	--	2	—	—	—	—	—	—	5
R17:305	—	—	1	—	—	—	—	1	—	—	—	—	—	—	—	1	—	—	—	3
R18:307	—	—	1	—	—	—	—	—	—	—	—	—	—	—	—	1	—	—	—	2
R18:421	—	—	—	—	—	—	—	—	—	—	—	—	—	—	—	1+	—	—	—	1
H14:304	—	—	—	—	—	—	—	—	—	—	—	—	—	—	—	—	—	—	2	2
N9:302	—	—	—	—	—	1	—	—	—	—	—	—	—	35	1	1+	1	1	7	47
Totals	0	0	3	0	0	2	0	2	0	0	0	0	2	35	1	4	1	1	9	60
PITS																				
Q18:312	—	—	—	1	1	1	—	1	1	—	—	—	1	—	—	—	—	—	—	6
Q18:314	60	2	42	13	32	24	23	23	12	—	—	—	160	—	—	—	—	—	1	396
R17:208	1	—	—	—	2	—	2	1	—	—	—	—	—	—	—	1	—	—	—	7
R17:212	—	—	—	—	—	—	—	—	1	—	—	—	—	—	—	—	—	—	—	1
R17:302	—	—	—	—	—	—	—	—	—	—	—	—	—	—	—	1	—	—	—	1
R17:303	1	—	—	—	—	—	1	1	1	—	—	—	1	—	—	—	—	—	—	5
R18:305	4	1	6	3	1	3	—	2	1	—	—	—	3	33	2	2	—	—	—	61
R18:310	—	—	2	1	2	3	—	—	—	—	—	—	33	13	—	1	1	1	3	59
S17:201	—	—	—	—	—	—	—	—	—	—	—	—	—	—	—	2	1	2	—	5
Totals	66	3	50	18	38	31	26	28	16	0	0	0	198	46	2	6	2	3	4	537
POTTERY DEPOSITS																				
P18:301	32	—	178	9	33	24	19	28	14	1	—	141	750	24	—	—	—	—	6	1,259
P–Q18:301	—	—	—	—	1	—	—	—	—	—	—	—	—	—	—	—	—	—	—	1
Q18:301	2	—	1	—	—	1	—	—	—	—	—	—	1	—	—	—	—	—	1	6
Totals	34	0	179	9	34	25	19	28	14	1	0	141	751	24	0	0	0	0	7	1,266

Table 10. Distribution of Clay Stoppers in Various Contexts (+ = seal impressions; cf. Table 13) (*cont.*)

Provenience	BOTTLE STOPPERS															JAR STOPPERS					Number of Items in Locus
	Flat		Domed		Number of Finger Impressions								Indeterminate*		Flat	Domed		Conical	Indeterminate	
	Plain	Vertical Channeled	Plain	Grooved	1	2	3	4	5	6	7	Indeterminate	Complete	Fragment		Plain	Finger Impressed			
NEAR FEATURES																				
Q18:305	—	—	1+	1	—	1	—	—	—	—	—	—	—	—	—	—	—	—	—	3
R17:210	—	—	—	—	1	—	—	—	—	—	—	—	—	—	—	—	—	—	—	1
R18:302	—	—	—	—	—	—	—	1	—	—	—	—	—	—	—	—	—	—	—	1
Totals	0	0	1	1	1	1	0	1	0	0	0	0	0	0	0	0	0	0	0	5
OCCUPATIONAL DEBRIS																				
P17:Trench V A South	—	—	—	1	—	—	—	—	—	—	—	—	—	1	—	—	—	—	—	2
P18:203	—	—	1	—	—	2	—	1	—	—	—	—	—	—	—	—	—	—	—	4
P18:205	—	—	—	—	—	—	1	—	—	—	—	—	—	—	—	—	—	—	—	1
Q17:202	—	—	—	—	—	—	—	—	—	—	—	—	—	—	—	1	—	—	—	1
South of Q18:301	3	—	2	—	3	—	—	—	—	2	—	—	—	—	—	—	—	—	—	10
Q18:301; Q18:312	1	—	—	—	1	—	—	—	—	—	—	—	—	—	—	—	—	—	—	2
Q18:307	—	—	1	—	—	—	—	—	—	—	—	—	—	—	—	1+	—	—	—	2
Q18:307–08	—	—	—	—	—	1	—	—	—	—	—	—	—	—	—	—	—	—	—	1
Q18:308	—	—	—	—	—	—	—	—	1	—	—	—	1	—	—	—	—	—	—	2
North of Q18:308	—	—	1+	—	—	—	—	—	1	—	—	—	—	—	—	—	—	—	—	2
Q18:313	—	—	2	—	—	—	—	—	—	—	—	—	—	—	—	—	—	—	—	2
North of Q18:303	—	—	1	—	—	—	—	—	—	—	—	—	—	—	—	—	—	—	—	1
North of R17:203	—	—	1	—	1	2	1	2	2	—	—	—	—	—	—	—	—	—	—	9
R17:203–04	1	—	—	—	—	—	—	—	—	—	—	—	—	—	—	—	—	—	—	1
R17:204	—	—	—	—	1	—	—	—	—	—	—	—	—	—	—	1	—	—	—	2
North of R17:204	—	—	—	—	—	—	—	1	—	—	—	—	—	—	—	—	—	—	—	1
R17:204–05	—	—	—	—	—	—	—	1	—	—	—	—	—	—	—	—	—	—	—	1
North of R17:204–05	—	1	—	—	—	1	—	—	—	—	—	—	—	—	—	—	—	—	—	2
R17:205	1	—	—	—	—	—	—	—	—	—	—	—	—	—	—	—	—	—	—	1
R17:207	—	3	2	—	1	5	—	—	—	—	—	—	—	—	—	—	—	—	—	11
R17:215	1	—	2	1	—	1	—	—	—	—	—	—	—	—	1	—	1	—	—	7
North of R17:301	—	—	—	—	—	—	—	—	—	—	—	—	—	—	—	1	—	—	—	1
North of R17:302	—	—	—	—	—	—	—	—	—	—	—	—	—	—	—	1+	—	—	—	1
North of R17:303	—	—	—	—	—	—	—	1	—	—	—	—	—	—	—	—	—	—	—	1
R18:Trench XX	—	—	1	—	1	2	—	1	—	—	—	—	—	—	—	—	—	—	—	5
R18:Trench XX South	—	—	—	—	—	—	—	—	—	—	—	—	—	—	—	—	1	—	—	1
R18:301	—	—	—	—	1	—	—	—	—	—	—	—	—	—	—	—	—	—	—	1
West of R18:302	1	—	1	1	—	—	—	—	—	—	—	—	25	—	—	—	—	—	—	28
R18:304	—	—	—	—	1	—	—	—	—	—	—	—	1	—	—	—	—	—	—	2
R18:308	1	—	1	—	—	—	—	—	—	—	—	—	—	—	—	—	—	—	—	2
R19:301; Q18:307	—	—	—	—	—	—	—	—	—	—	—	—	—	—	—	—	1	—	—	1
R19:302	—	—	—	—	—	—	—	—	—	—	—	—	—	—	—	—	—	1	—	1
R19:304	—	—	8	—	—	—	—	—	—	—	—	—	—	—	—	—	—	—	—	8
North of R19:305	—	—	—	—	—	—	1	—	—	—	—	—	—	—	—	—	—	—	—	1
S17:301	1	—	—	—	2	—	—	—	—	—	—	—	1	—	—	—	—	—	—	4
H14:305	—	—	—	—	—	—	—	—	—	—	—	—	1	—	—	—	—	—	—	1
H14:306	5	—	1	1	—	—	—	—	1	—	—	—	—	9	—	—	—	—	—	17
J13:Northern Slope	1	—	—	—	—	—	—	—	—	—	—	—	—	—	—	—	—	—	—	1
J14:301 West	—	—	—	—	1	—	—	—	—	—	—	—	—	—	—	—	—	—	—	1
J15:Sounding C	—	—	—	—	—	—	—	—	—	—	—	—	—	—	—	—	—	1	—	1
J15:Sounding C East	—	—	—	—	—	—	—	—	—	—	—	—	—	—	1	—	1	—	—	2
J15:Sounding C South	—	—	1	—	—	—	—	—	—	—	—	—	—	—	—	—	—	2	—	3
G26–27:Trench X	—	—	4	—	2	2	2	—	1	—	1	—	—	—	—	—	—	—	—	12
R20–21:Trench XXV	—	—	—	—	—	—	—	—	—	—	—	—	1	—	—	—	—	—	—	1
R20:509	1	—	—	—	—	—	—	—	—	—	—	—	—	—	—	—	—	—	—	1
R20:511	—	—	—	—	—	—	—	1	—	—	—	—	—	—	—	—	—	—	—	1
R21:300 West	—	—	2	—	—	—	—	—	—	—	—	—	—	—	—	—	—	—	—	2
West of R21:405	—	—	—	—	—	—	—	—	—	—	—	—	—	—	—	1+	—	—	—	1
M–N/5–10:Trench XXIV	—	—	—	—	—	—	—	—	—	—	—	—	1	—	—	—	—	—	—	1
N10:Trench XXIII	—	—	1	—	—	—	—	1	—	—	—	—	—	—	—	—	—	—	—	2
P-Q9:Trench XXVII	—	—	—	—	—	—	—	—	—	—	—	—	1	—	—	—	—	—	—	1
Q6:Trench XXVII	1	—	—	—	—	—	—	—	—	—	—	—	1	—	—	—	—	—	—	2
Totals	18	4	33	4	15	16	5	9	6	2	1	0	33	10	2	6	4	4	0	172
Category Totals	118	7	266	33	93	76	51	69	35	3	1	141	989	116	5	14	7	8	22	2,040

*It was often difficult to assign fragments of bottle stoppers to individual categories. In addition, many complete bottle stoppers were unfortunately counted without recording their shape. It is assumed that this large number of "indeterminate" specimens would have consisted of an average mixture of types.

impossible to open the door without breaking the sealing. Casts made from the inner surfaces of door sealings
have enabled Fiandra to reconstruct varying types of
door fittings. At Shahr-e Sokhte, southeastern Iran, actual wooden pins have been preserved, as well as a wall
with space for a door and the adjacent holes for the
wooden pins.[2] Such evidence provides excellent analogies for the usage that prevailed earlier at Bakun
(Alizadeh 1988a, 1988b), Chogha Mish, and Susa
(Legrain 1921:286–93, pl. 19; Amiet 1972). Of particular interest in this connection are four fragments, found
in pit R17:208, which join to form an almost complete
door sealing with greatest dimensions of 9.3 × 11.2 cm.
The inside surfaces of the fragments preserve not only
the usual impressions of the stick and coil of string
around it, but also that of the single strand of string running off toward the door (fig. 17). This particular door
sealing has no seal impression. In this it is highly unusual, but at least one other, very small, fragment of a
door sealing also seems to have been unimpressed.

The door sealings, as Fiandra and her colleagues
have demonstrated in detail,[3] were widely used from
Crete in the west to eastern Iran over a long period of
time and provide extremely important information on
administrative and business procedures.[4]

JAR NECK AND OTHER SEALINGS

Narrow and relatively flat sealings with finished top
and bottom edges are identified by their profiles and the
impressions on their inner sides as sealings placed
around the necks of jars. On the inner surface the upper
and lower edges are smooth where the clay strip was
pressed against the rim and the upper body of a jar; the
rim imprint tends to be narrower than the body imprint.
The space between the two flattened areas is filled by
impressions of the string tied around the jar neck to hold
in place the cloth covering the mouth of the jar.[5] The
profile of one sealing (pl. 131:C) shows that it had been
attached to a jar with an undercut rim (pl. 131:D). The
jar neck sealings are usually small fragments, but the
type is sufficiently distinctive to permit the recognition
of even very small bits of clay that are preserved on the
inner surface.

A number of sealings are of less distinctive type
than those applied to doors or the necks of jars. Some,
such as a thick sealing (pl. 45:P), have flat inner surfaces considerably smoother than those normal for the
door sealings. Sometimes the flat inner surface has basketry imprints (pls. 32:E; 153:A). Some lumps of clay
have the impression of a single seal on a relatively flat
outer surface and imprints of string on the inner surface
(pl. 32:D). These, as well as at least some of the
sealings with flat inner surfaces, were probably attached
to various kinds of boxes or bales (pl. 35:G), such as can
be seen on the heads of porters on cylinder seals and on
a stela from Warka.[6]

A sealing with a relatively flat impressed side is
complete on all sides except for some old breaks on the
upper right (pl. 44:D). It has a roughly triangular section
formed by a horizontal bulge, 4.2 cm thick, which tapers
to thin edges. These are marked by widely-spaced ovoid
imprints. Despite such distinctive features, the nature of
the element to which the sealing had been attached remains uncertain.

The distribution of the various categories of
sealings as well as the objects with impressions still to
be discussed, is given in table 13. The door sealings are
by far the commonest of the types whose use is known,
forming 32% of all the attached sealings. The flattish
sealings that might have belonged to bales or packages
come next, forming 25%. The sealings from jar necks
constitute 7%. The unassigned category, which include a
number of very small and irregularly-shaped fragments,
forms 32% of the total number of attached sealings.

CLAY OBJECTS OF INDEPENDENT SHAPE USED IN KEEPING RECORDS

The discussion above deals with elements that were
merely accessories, the predominantly unimpressed clay
stoppers of pottery vessels and the impressed sealings
that secured the contents of rooms and various kinds of
containers and parcels. In addition, clay was formed into
objects of independent shapes and these, except for one
rare type, represent some of the more significant innovations of the Protoliterate period.[7]

---

2. Ferioli and Fiandra 1979a:18, fig. 6 (reconstruction of
sealed door), pls. 7 (door between rooms 12 and 18, Levels
II–III), 8 (wooden pins).

3. Ferioli and Fiandra 1979a:12–26; idem 1979b; Fiandra
1981a:165–74; idem 1981b:29–43.

4. At Chogha Mish itself a door sealing of the Sukkalmaḫ period was found on the High Mound in one of the later seasons of excavation. AA

5. The use of cloth and string to cover the mouths of vessels is
standard practice in the ancient Near East. Note the Egyptian Third Dynasty painting in the tomb of Hesy at Saqqara
(Quibell 1913, pl. 10).

6. A plain lump of clay with a string imprint on the inner surface might have been a package sealing that for some reason was never imprinted.

7. Aside from additional documentation of the Chogha Mish
finds and some references to specific parallels elsewhere,
the content of the following section remains as it was finished around 1970. The objects in question have by now
been the subject of intensive discussion by numerous scholars. For the variety and complexity of the interpretations
that have been proposed, see Amiet 1966b:21–22; idem
1972:69–70; Le Brun and Vallat 1978; Friberg 1978–79;
idem 1994a, idem 1994b; Lieberman 1980:339–58; Powell
1971; Schmandt-Besserat 1977a, idem 1992.

TALLYING SLABS

Objects of a type not found in any other locus occurred in the large pit, R17:208, in the northeastern corner of the East Area. One is an irregularly rectangular flat slab of clay (pl. 132:A). On one of its long sides are six imprinted wedges, on the other five wedges and a wide triangular indentation. The slab has two perforations running diagonally through it. In addition, each side has two punctations, resulting in two matching pairs of marks.

The other objects are much less complete. One is the end of a presumably ovoid slab of irregular thickness (pl. 132:B). Another is the curving end of a slab of ovoid section (pl. 132:C). They are marked by longitudinal incised lines separating rows of punctations. Both types of objects can be interpreted as tallying devices. In the case of one example (pl. 132:A) the marks are large and easily distinguished. On the thicker slabs, the multiplicity of the individual punctations raises the question of whether each indeed stood for an individual item. However, they can hardly be considered as mere decoration, as in the case of the far less regular punctations without dividing lines scattered on a fragment of an animal figurine from the same pit (II-328). On the contrary, the clay slabs in question seem to have been made as a vehicle for the incisions and punctations. Detailed reconstruction of the use of the tallying slabs is difficult since they are rare and far simpler in character than the well-defined and specialized groups of objects considered below.

BULLAE (Pl. 33:H–I)

Rather small lumps of clay are given a specific character by their ovoid and often faceted shape. The lumps were not, however, completely independent objects but appear to have been shaped around a thread or string by which they were attached to some other object (pl. 33:I; III-812; III-911a) and might thus be termed bullae.[8] Each facet of a bulla bears a seal

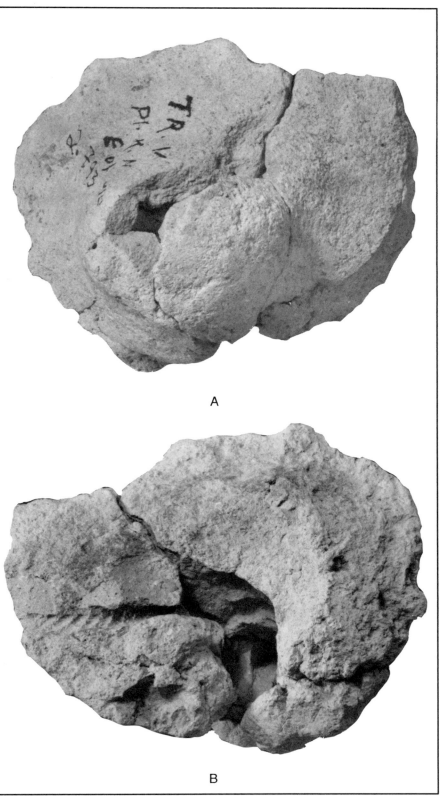

A

B

Figure 17. Top and Bottom Views of the Plain Door Sealing (2.793) from Trench V, Plot K. Photograph by Jean Grant

8. The term bulla is used here only for the ovoid faceted sealing; the same usage is also followed at Habuba Kabira South (Strommenger 1980:64). At Susa this type of object is termed "bulle oblongue" (Amiet 1972:70) and "scellément fusiforme" and "bulla" is used for the clay balls (Amiet 1972:69–70; Le Brun 1978c; Le Brun and Vallat 1978).

impression, necessarily incomplete because of the limited space. Individual bullae were impressed by a single seal only.

The bullae are rare at Chogha Mish but can be considered as typical Protoliterate elements. They are known also from Susa and Habuba Kabira South.[9] A considerably earlier analogy for the Protoliterate usage is provided by ovoid but unfaceted bullae with stamp seal imprints from early Halaf levels at Arpachiyah.[10] They exemplify the prehistoric background that underlay the widespread and often complex uses of clay sealings in the Protoliterate period.

TABLETS (Pl. 33:B–G)

Two relatively complete examples and a considerable number of fragments occurred as individual pieces in the East Area of private houses, usually in the ashy debris of the pits, which was also the richest source for sealings. The tablets are rectangular, blank on one side, and on the other impressed only with seals and numerals. In these characteristics they correspond to various tablets from Warka assigned to Eanna IV levels.[11] Such tablets also occur at Susa and Habuba Kabira South.[12] To judge by the more complete examples (pl. 33:D–E), it was normal for tablets to bear impressions of only one seal that was made before the numerals were imprinted.

HOLLOW BALLS AND TOKENS (Pls. 34–40; 134)

One of the more prominent Protoliterate vehicles for seal impressions is the exterior of clay balls, ranging in diameter from an unusually small 3.2 cm (pl. 34:A–D) through the standard sizes of some 5–6 cm (pls. 34:E–M; 35–37:E–G) to 7.3 cm (pl. 37:A–D) and 8 cm (pls. 38:A, E; 40:A). When the first Chogha Mish examples were found in 1963, it was not yet established that such objects were hollow. Four of the eight second-season balls were x-rayed in the Department of Radiol-

ogy at the University of Chicago's Medical Center. The x-rays (pl. 39:A–B) and broken balls found subsequently in the third season (pls. 35:K–L; 38:F–G) showed that the balls had well-formed central cavities, in one case covered with a bitumen stain (pl. 39:C). The hazy shapes of pellets appear in the x-rays and the ball fragments of the third season still retain spherical, discoidal, and pill-shaped pellets in place (pls. 39:C–D; 40:A, D) and in another the imprint of a pellet remained (pl. 38:E).

The x-rays and other evidence made it possible to associate with the hollow balls numerous small objects found loose at Chogha Mish and elsewhere and previously often identified as gaming pieces or amulets (Le Breton 1957:112, fig. 33; Lenzen 1965:32). These objects must have functioned as tokens, and Delougaz identified them as such when showing slides of the x-rayed balls in a lecture at the 1964 Rencontre assyriologique internationale in Paris. They were grouped together in clay balls and certified as untouched records by the seal impressions. In 1965, broken clay balls containing pellets found in the 1962/63 season at Warka were published; they had been, similar to the R18:312 balls at Chogha Mish, deposited at the base of a wall.[13] In the earlier years of the excavations at Susa both seal-impressed clay balls and loose pellets were found,[14] but the connection between the two categories of objects was not made until Amiet's definitive publication on glyptic from Susa.[15] Balls with tokens have also been found in recent excavations at Susa.[16] Since then, such objects have been much discussed. In a number of studies, Schmandt-Besserat (1974, 1977b, 1992) has proposed antecedents for the tokens in the clay pellets ubiquitous at prehistoric sites and a progression from hollow ball to tablet.

At Chogha Mish complete or semi-complete balls tend to appear in groups, in one case four on a floor near a wall at the western edge of R17:212. A much larger cluster was found close to the modern surface in a hole that had been scooped out anciently immediately below the bottom course of the almost completely eroded east wall of room R18:312. Of the group twenty-one complete or relatively complete examples and fragments

9. See Le Brun 1980a, fig. 10:1; pl. 8:1 (Susa, Acropole I, Level 17B); Le Brun and Vallat 1978, pl. 5:1–6 (Susa, Acropole I, Level 18); Amiet 1972, seals 510, 540–41, 544, 547, 585, 599, 644, 649, 665 (Susa, old excavations); Strommenger 1980a:64, figs. 56–57 (Habuba Kabira South).

10. See Mallowan and Rose 1935:98; pl. 9:b (Arpachiyah).

11. See Lenzen 1932, pl. 14:c–h (Warka, Eanna IV); idem 1961, pl. 26:f–k (Warka, Eanna IV); idem 1964, pls. 26:g = 28 c (Warka, Eanna IV); Heinrich 1934, pl. 14:b (numerals only), d (Warka, Suchgrabung north of Eanna in XI–XII); Jordan 1932, pl. 19:b (Warka, White Temple); Lenzen 1932, pl. 23:c (plaster tablet; Warka, White Temple). Falkenstein (1936:32–33) indicated that, although such tablets could be taken to represent a type of record used before the development of writing, there is no evidence that those actually found were earlier than the tablets with signs; he denied, in any case, that the tablets with only seal impressions and numerals were antecedents of writing. On the stratification of the tablets in question, see now Strommenger 1980b:480–81.

12. See Strommenger 1980b:64, fig. 56 (Habuba Kabira South); Le Brun and Vallat 1978 (Susa, Acropole I, Level 18), fig. 4:1–5; pl. 4); Le Brun 1980a, fig. 8:1, 5–6 (Susa, Acropole I, Level 17B).

13. See Lenzen 1965, pl. 19:a–b, cf. pls. 17:a–b, 18:a–d for intact balls and p. 32 where pellets are termed amulets; see also Brandes 1979:31.

14. See de Mecquenem 1934:19, fig. 16; Belaiew 1943:195–207 (pellets interpreted as weights); Amiet 1961, pl. A:7.

15. Amiet 1972:69–70, seals 460, 464–65, 467–70, 486, 488, 539, 549–50, 553, 555–56, 565, 568, 572, 574, 577, 580–83, 586, 596, 653–55, 660, 662, 678, 680, 682–83, 689, 691, 697, 700, 704.

16. See Le Brun and Vallat 1978, fig. 3:1–4, pl. 1:1–4 (Susa, Acropole I, Level 18); cf. also ibid., pls. 2:1–5; 3:1–4 for other balls.

representing at least four more balls were recovered: the large number of tokens from R18:312 suggests that the cluster might have originally consisted of even more balls. Such deposits of intact balls presumably represent records on file; the majority of the seal-impressed balls were broken open on purpose when it became necessary to check their contents. Thus, in addition to their general fragility their very purpose contributed to their destruction. It is no wonder, then, that we find them so often represented by small fragments, identifiable only by the curvature of their inner and outer surfaces, and that tokens are so widely scattered in the debris of the areas of private house quarters (tables 11–12).

The clay balls were made to hold together particular groups of tokens of varying sizes and shapes and to authenticate and protect them by seal impressions. The balls provide the context without which the variously-shaped tokens had remained relatively insignificant objects of obscure purpose. By the third season at Chogha Mish, it was realized that the discovery of such objects, particularly in numbers (cf. R18:309, Q18:315), implied the presence originally of balls in the same locus, or at least nearby. The balls, once they had been opened or accidentally broken, would crumble more easily than the compact pellets inside them and disappear while the latter was preserved.

Table 11. Distribution of Tokens in Loci with More than One Example (* = punctated; + = scored)

Provenience	Sphere	Cone	Pyramid	Pill-Shaped	Barrel	Disc	Triangle	Crescent	Pod	Rare Types	Number of Examples in Locus	Seal Impression from Table 13
ROOMS AND FLOORS												
Q18:315	15+ 7*	—	26+ 1* 2 nicked	5	—	—	—	—	1+	Quadruped: 1	58	—
R17:305	1	2	—	—	—	1	—	—	—	—	4	—
R18:307	1	—	—	—	—	—	—	—	—	Truncated cone: 1 Cashew: 1	3	—
R18:309	24	19	35	11	—	3	1*	—	—	Petal: 2	95	3
R18:312	43	12	4	7	—	2	—	—	1	Cashew: 1	70	25
S18:401	2	1	1 nicked	—	—	—	—	—	—	—	4	—
J15:305	—	1	—	1	—	1	—	—	—	—	3	—
From Table 12	1	2	—	—	—	1	—	—	—	—	4	—
Totals	94	37	69	24	0	8	1	0	2	6	241	28
PITS												
Q18:312	2+ 1*	6	1	1	—	—	—	—	—	—	11	11
Q18:314	1+ 4*	—	—	—	—	—	—	—	—	Quadruped: 2	7	13
R17:208	21	3	1	1	—	—	—	—	—	—	26	66
R17:212†	—	2	—	—	—	—	—	—	—	—	2	6
R17:303†	2	2	1	1	—	1	—	—	—	—	7	7
R18:305	6	2	—	—	—	—	—	—	—	—	8	21
R18:310	2	—	—	—	—	—	—	—	1+	—	3	2
R18:408	2	1	—	—	—	—	—	—	—	—	3	—
R15:401	3	2	—	1	—	—	—	—	—	Hemispherical: 1	7	6
From Table 12	1	5	—	—	—	—	—	—	1	—	7	—
Totals	43	25	3	4	0	1	0	0	2	3	81	132
POTTERY DEPOSITS												
P18:301	3	—	—	—	—	—	—	—	—	Hemispherical: 2	5	49
Totals	3	0	0	0	0	0	0	0	0	2	5	49
NEAR FEATURES												
Q18:402 (kiln area)	4	—	—	1	1	—	—	—	—	—	6	1
R14:404 (drain)	1	—	—	1	—	—	—	—	—	—	2	—
R15:405 (kiln area)	1	1	—	—	—	—	—	—	—	—	2	3
J15:304 (lane)	1	—	—	1	—	—	—	—	—	—	2	
R21:402 North (near wall)	4	—	—	1	7	14+ 6*	10	—	—	Rod: 4	46	—
D7:301 (cesspit)	—	1	—	1	—	—	—	—	—	—	2	—
From Table 12	1	1	—	1	—	—	—	—	—	—	3	—
Totals	12	3	0	6	8	20	10	0	0	4	63	4
OCCUPATIONAL DEBRIS												
P17:402	1	—	1+	1	—	—	—	—	1+	—	4	—
Q18:303	1	1	—	—	—	—	—	—	—	—	2	—
Q18:307	1	2	—	—	—	—	—	—	—	—	3	1

Table 11. Distribution of Tokens in Loci with More than One Example (* = punctated; + = scored) (*cont.*)

Provenience	Sphere	Cone	Pyramid	Pill-Shaped	Barrel	Disc	Triangle	Crescent	Pod	Rare Types	Number of Examples in Locus	Seal Impression from Table 13
OCCUPATIONAL DEBRIS (*cont.*)												
Q18:307/R19:301	1	1	—	—	—	—	—	—	—	—	2	2
Q18:313	1	—	—	—	—	—	—	—	1	Hemispherical: 1	3	—
Q19:402	2	—	—	—	—	—	—	—	—	—	2	—
North of R17:203	—	2	—	—	3	—	—	—	—	—	5	1
R17:215, 215 West	2	—	—	—	—	—	—	—	—	—	2	5
R18:Trench XX	1	4	—	—	—	—	—	—	—	—	5	—
R18:308	1*	2	—	—	—	—	—	—	—	—	3	—
R18:401	—	2	—	1	—	—	—	—	—	—	3	—
R18:406	—	1	—	1	—	1	—	—	—	—	3	—
R18:418	1	1	—	—	—	1	—	—	—	—	3	—
R19:301	1	3	1	—	—	—	—	—	—	—	5	—
S17:301	4+ 1*	4	—	2	—	—	1*	—	—	—	12	2
H14:Trench IX	7	2	1	3	—	—	—	—	—	—	13	—
H-J14:Trench IX East	—	2	1	2	—	—	—	—	—	—	5	—
H-J14:Trench IX South	1	1	—	—	—	—	—	—	—	—	2	—
H14:305	—	3	—	—	—	—	—	—	—	—	3	7
South of H14:306	2	—	—	—	—	—	—	—	—	—	2	—
H14:401	1	3	1*	1	1	—	—	—	—	—	7	1
Southwest of H14:401	2	—	—	—	—	—	—	—	—	—	2	—
H14:403	3	—	—	—	—	—	—	—	—	—	3	1
J13: Northern Slope	7	1	—	1	—	—	—	—	—	—	9	1
J15:Sounding C	1	—	—	1	—	—	—	—	—	—	2	—
J15:Sounding C South	26	—	—	25	—	—	—	—	—	—	51	1
J15:Sounding C Southern Extension	—	—	—	2	—	—	—	—	—	—	2	—
K14:Trench VI North	—	—	—	4	—	—	—	—	—	—	4	1
K14:Tr. VI South	6	1	—	—	—	—	—	—	—	—	7	—
K14:402	1	—	—	1	—	—	—	—	—	—	2	—
K23:400	1	1	—	—	—	—	—	—	—	—	2	—
L22:400	1	1	—	—	—	—	—	—	—	—	2	—
L23:400	1	1	—	1	—	—	—	—	—	—	3	—
P27:501 Southwest	1*	—	—	1	—	—	—	—	—	Plano-convex+: 1	3	—
R20:505	—	—	105	—	—	—	—	—	—	Cashew: 1	106	—
R21:300 Southeast	—	2	—	—	2+	—	—	—	—	—	4	—
R21:300 Northwest	—	—	—	1	—	—	—	—	1+	—	2	—
R21:300 Center West	—	1	—	1	—	1	—	—	—	—	3	—
R21:401 South	1	2	—	—	—	—	—	—	—	—	3	—
R21:402 South	1	—	—	—	—	1*	—	—	—	—	2	—
West of R21:402	1	—	—	—	—	1*	—	—	—	—	2	—
R21:403	2	—	—	—	—	—	—	—	—	—	2	—
R21:406	—	1	—	1	—	—	—	—	—	—	2	—
S22:403	2	—	—	—	—	—	—	—	—	—	2	—
N9:Trench XXIV	2	—	—	—	—	—	—	—	—	—	2	—
From Table 12	25	17	1	6	2	4	—	2	2+ 2*	3	64	—
Totals	113	62	111	56	8	9	1	2	7	6	375	23
NO CONTEXTS												
Provenience lost	14+ 2*	6	—	4	—	—	—	2	1	—	29	—
Surface	7+ 1*	1	—	7				1	1	1	19	—
Totals	24	7	0	11	0	0	0	3	2	1	48	0
Category Totals	289	134	183	100	17	39	11	6	12	22	813	236
Percentages	100%	100%	100%	100%	100%	100%	100%	100%	100%	100%	100%	100%
Relative frequency	289	134	183	100	17	39	11	6	12	22	813	—
of the token categories	35.5%	16%	22.5%	12%	2%	5%	1.5%	1%	1.5%	3%	100%	

†The R17:212 tokens were found just below the surface in a pit that forms the eastern part of R17:208. The four balls from R17:212 are listed in table 13 under "Rooms and Floors" since they were found at a remnant of the floor of a room cut by the pit. R17:303 is a pit, but one object assigned to the locus was found near a drain and accordingly listed under "Near Features" in table 13. There is no record of a drain in R17:303 itself and perhaps the drain in question is R17:310.

Table 12. Distribution of Tokens in Loci with Only One Example
(Loci = Occupational Debris Unless Otherwise Noted)

Sphere	Cone	Pyramid	Pill	Barrel	Disc	Crescent	Pod	Rare Types
P17:401	Q17:303 (room)	South of R17:305	R18:302 (drain)	P18:202	R17:215 East scored	R17:205 scored	P18:201 scored	Cashew: Q17:401
P17:402	West of Q18:312	—	R18:308 East	North of R17:204	R18:410 (room)	L22:501 scored	Q18:406 scored	Rectangle: North of Q18:313
South of Q17:305	R17:201	—	H13:Trench XVII A	—	S17:405	—	R18:310 S (pit)	Bilobed: Northeast of R18:302
South of Q18:301	South of R17:203	—	J15:Sounding C Southwest	—	S18:404 (room)	—	R19:303	—
Q18:308 East (punctations)	R17:203–04	—	K14:Trench VI	—	West of L23:403	—	R21:401 North scored	—
Q19:301	North of R17:203–04	—	R21:402	—	—	—	—	—
R18: Trench XX South	R17:206 probably	—	R21:405	—	—	—	—	—
R18:303/R17:305	R17:302 (pit)	—	—	—	—	—	—	—
North of H14:306	R17:408 (pit)	—	—	—	—	—	—	—
H14:310	R18:Trench XX Northeast	—	—	—	—	—	—	—
East of H14:401	R18:303 (pit)	—	—	—	—	—	—	—
West of H15:401	R18:407 (pit)	—	—	—	—	—	—	—
H15:402 (near drain)	R18:415 (pit)	—	—	—	—	—	—	—
J13:301	H14:306	—	—	—	—	—	—	—
J14:403 South	South of H14:404 East	—	—	—	—	—	—	—
J15:401	H–J14:Trench IX Northwest	—	—	—	—	—	—	—
J15:403	J14:403 East	—	—	—	—	—	—	—
J15:403 Northeast	J15:402 (room)	—	—	—	—	—	—	—
K14:Trench VI	K14:Trench VI	—	—	—	—	—	—	—
R20-21:Trench XXV	G27–28:Trench X	—	—	—	—	—	—	—
R20:402 (pit)	K22:402	—	—	—	—	—	—	—
R21:404	K22:402 above	—	—	—	—	—	—	—
S22:402	East of K23:402	—	—	—	—	—	—	—
S22:404	R20-21:Trench XXV West	—	—	—	—	—	—	—
N9:Slope Wash	M-N5-10:Trench XXIV East Slope	—	—	—	—	—	—	—
N9:302 (room)	—	—	—	—	—	—	—	—
South of N9:304	—	—	—	—	—	—	—	—
P-Q9:Trench XXVII	—	—	—	—	—	—	—	—
28	25	1	7	2	5	2	5	3 (= 78 Total)

The varieties of tokens so far found at Chogha Mish are shown on plates 40 and 134. The geometric shapes such as spheres (pl. 134:A 1–10), cones (pl. 134:B 1–10), pyramids (pl. 134:C 1–10), pills (pl. 134:D 1–7), and discs (pl. 134:E 1–6) are far commoner than those of more specialized forms such as the barrels (pl. 134:D 8–11), hemispheres (pl. 134:E 7–9), "cashews" (pl. 134:F 1–2), crescents (pl. 134:F 3–6), triangles (pl. 134:F 7–8), "petals" (pl. 134:G 1–2), and animals (pl. 134:G 11–12). The dimensions of the tokens appear to have been almost as standardized as their shapes. Thus, the spherical tokens, probably the most frequent type, fall into three recognizably distinct clusters of sizes: the small spheres with diameters of ca. 0.05 cm, the medium-sized spheres of ca. 1.00 cm, and the large spheres of ca. 1.50–2.00 cm. The analogous variations in the sizes of other types of tokens are indicated by the examples on plate 134. The cones differ among themselves not only in total dimensions but also in their squat or high proportions. The small-sized discs would fit well inside of clay balls, but those with diameters of ca. 3.0–3.5 cm are so large that clay balls of the sizes known from Chogha Mish could hardly have held them. The large discs occur sporadically as single examples except for those in a group of tokens found in the large Protoliterate pit, R20:402 North in Trench XXV. The tokens recovered were twelve large, plain discs (pl. 134:E 4) and five even larger scored discs (pl. 134:E 5), two small discs, four small spheres, and, finally, seven barrels (pl. 134:D 9) and ten triangles (pl. 134:F 8) of a size and proportion found nowhere else. A very large clay ball would have been needed to accommodate combinations of the large tokens from R20:402 North. It must be assumed either that such balls once existed or that the particularly large tokens were used in another context.

It is assumed that specific and standardized meanings and values were attached to the individual types of tokens. Were these conventions purely arbitrary, which would greatly increase the difficulties of attempts to reconstruct the meanings of the tokens, or can the existence of some logical links between the shapes and the values of the tokens be assumed? For example, it is noteworthy that the smooth cones and pills are comparable in shape to the representations of numerals on Protoliterate tablets, the horizontal wedge standing for a digit and the circle for a unit of a higher order. Accordingly, such tokens could well have possessed numerical values and have indicated the total number of whatever item was involved, the nature of which might have been conveyed by another type of token with a substantive rather than a numerical value. A recording system can be visualized in which certain sets of tokens had numerical values, others substantive values, and the record of "how many items of what" would have been achieved by sealing the appropriate combination of tokens in a ball.

An alternative, but not necessarily exclusive, system for recording such data might have existed. Markings of various sorts occur on a minority of tokens. For example, several of the rare crescent (pl. 134:F 3–6) and cashew-shaped tokens (pl. 134:F 1) bear scoring similar to that on the notched lips of some pottery vessels (pls. 19:A–B, J–K, R; 98:H–K). In addition to the crescents, tokens of other shapes are scored, the large discs from R20:402 North being particularly striking (pl. 134:C 3; E 5; G 3, 6, 9). The varying number of scored strokes must be meaningful. In the case of the vessels the strokes perhaps indicate the number of units of volume. The scored tokens might represent a system in which the shape of the tokens had a substantive meaning, while the scoring on them indicated the number of the particular elements in question. With conventions such as these it would have been possible to record within one ball transactions involving several different types of items.

Punctations occur on several types of tokens, for example, singly on one face of pyramids (pl. 134:C 4) or paired on three faces (pl. 134:C 8)[17] and as a line of six on a large disc (pls. 40:C; 134:E 6) and a triangle (pl. 134:F 7). Medium-sized or large-sized spheres have, rarely, a single (pl. 134:A 7) and somewhat more frequently two sets of three punctations (pl. 134:A 5, 9; cf. 3.858b, 3.1043–44, 3.295, V-116b), which in two cases are combined with equatorial scoring (pl. 134:A 6). Though marked tokens occur in various parts of the site, the pavements running under the Circular Structure, Q18:315, had a concentration of them: four spheres with triple punctations, the pyramid with three pairs of punctations, and, in addition, two pyramids with a wedge imprinted at one edge, a combination known only here (pl. 134:C 2, 7). The spherical tokens, for example, might have stood for some very frequent item, for example, sheep or goats, with the small examples referring to lambs or kids and the large ones to adults. Perhaps, then, the number of adults involved in a transaction was indicated by the marks on the larger spheres, while each young animal was recorded by a small token. Such speculation is intended only to exemplify a possible avenue of interpretation, not as a specific proposal establishable by the evidence at hand. In fact, there are two tokens, both the only examples of their kind at Chogha Mish, a disc (pl. 40:B) and a barrel (pl. 134:D 10) marked with a cross that can be tentatively equated with the archaic sign for sheep, a circle enclosing a cross (Falkenstein 1936, Sign 761).

---

17. For a pyramid with a deep punctation in two sides, see Le Brun and Vallat 1978, fig. 3:4, pl. 1:3 (Susa, Acropole, Level 18).

In addition to the standard token types, there are a few aberrant examples. The identity as tokens of smoothly shaped hemispherical examples (pl. 134:E 7–8) and of a truncated cone with a finger imprint on top (pl. 134:E 9) seems indubitable. This is not the case for several other objects all from secondary contexts. A rather tall hemispherical specimen has vertical panels of irregular slashes differing greatly from the standard token markings and might be earlier than the Protoliterate period (pl. 40:I; de Mecquenem et al. 1943, fig. 23:74). A surface find, a small smoothly-finished spool-shaped object, has a narrow perforation through the waist which seems impracticably narrow for stringing so that the object might have been a token (pl. 134:D 11).

Although for the most part the tokens do not have readily recognizable naturalistic shapes, so animal figures small enough to have fitted into clay balls occurred. The use, as tokens, at least occasionally, of such simplified animal representations is indicated by two examples found in a ball at Susa (Amiet 1972, pl. 61:460 bis) and by the occurrence at Chogha Mish of such small figures among the tokens from Q18:315 (pl. 134:G 11), Q18:314 (pl. 134:G 12), and R18:305 (III-732). Despite their rarity, these examples are sufficient to establish the existence of a category of figurative tokens analogous in general to the pictographic signs found on the archaic tablets at Warka.

THE ORGANIZATION OF MULTIPLE SEAL IMPRESSIONS ON CLAY BALLS

The process of making and sealing the balls must have required skill. Unfortunately, the breaks of the fragments did not yield evidence for the two main possibilities, that the balls were made in two halves and joined after the tokens were inserted, or that an opening to the exterior was reserved and then plugged. In a few intact balls tokens are loose enough to rattle (III-758–59), but for the most part they stick to the walls. The lower part of the cavity in half of a small ball from P17:Trench V A is shaped as if to fit a fairly large spherical token; the exterior surface is unimpressed so the ball was presumably never used (3.1049; diameter 4.6 cm). Since the balls would have had to be at least leather dry before they could hold tokens, their surfaces would have had to be moistened before rolling the seals. The low and indistinct impressions on some balls might well be a result of rolling seals on clay surfaces that had become too dry. Normally the entire ball was completely covered with impressions made according to a specific scheme (pls. 35:G–H, J; 133). One seal was rolled completely around the ball, as recognized by Brandes on the balls from Warka, thus producing an equatorial impression defining two polar areas. These can in most cases be termed upper and lower in accordance with the orientation of the designs on the equatorial seal. Each pole had space sufficient for rolling at

least two seals (pl. 133:B). When, as quite frequently, the impressions on the upper pole are at right angles to those on the equator and on the lower pole (pl. 133:A–F), the upper pole is given a slightly gabled shape (pl. 133:B). In making the polar seal, the integrity of the equatorial seal, normally the first seal to be rolled, was respected, with only slight, accidental encroachment on it (pls. 37:A; 133:B). There could perhaps be a purely technical reason for the equatorial rolling. If the balls were made in two halves, then an equatorial rolling would have consolidated and covered the joins. On the other hand, a more meaningful explanation for the equatorial seal is discussed below.

Although the equatorial and polar scheme is standard, the number of seals rolled on individual balls varies. On a few balls only one seal was used for both the equator and the poles (pl. 34:A–B). Some small fragments probably represent a pair of large balls impressed by only one seal showing lions (pl. 38:C–D). A large seal, approximately 3.7 cm high, was rolled discontinuously, leaving faint impressions of parts of addorsed rampant animals (pl. 34:E) and of a man facing to the left. The seal was then turned some 90° and another partial imprint of the addorsed animals was made. Whether the ball was so sparsely and faintly impressed because it had already dried out too much before rolling the seal or whether slight traces of the design were sufficient for the transaction in hand can only be speculated.

Balls with imprints of three seals, the equatorial one and two others appearing on both the upper and lower poles (pl. 133:A–F), are the most common, but many variations appear (pls. 135:A–C; 158). For example, on some three-seal balls, each of the two polar seals occupies its own pole, as on III-778 (pls. 149:G; 153:E) where the abraded upper pole has traces of two rollings of a cylinder seal with small animals and the lower pole two rollings of a seal with cloth bearers (III-778a–c; R18:312). It was hard to fit the impressions of three polar seals on each pole; on one example (pl. 36:E–I) the upper pole has antithetical lions and a master of snakes, a small section of which appears on the lower pole, which is mainly occupied by cloth carriers. In such cases it is particularly difficult to reconstruct the complete designs of the polar seals on the basis of a single incomplete rolling.

Occasionally stamp seals were used in addition to cylinder seals, in one case only a single stamp seal, and in another, three. That ball has the impressions of five different seals (pl. 133:A–C) and its lower pole was asymmetrically flattened by the pressure of the stamp seals.

The standard scheme and the variations in the number of seals used calls for some explanation. The deposit of twenty-four balls from R18:312 offers a closed group with which to work. The equatorial seals vary from ball to ball. Altogether at least fifteen different seals were rolled over the equator and these seals do not occur on the poles of any of the balls. The following hypothesis can therefore be suggested, that the equatorial seals belonged to the individuals/offices primarily concerned with the transaction recorded by the balls and that the polar seals belonged to witnesses or secondary offices. Perhaps, then, the R18:312 "archive" was stored by an individual in charge of receiving certain shipments or perhaps taxes or tithes.

The number of polar seals varies from ball to ball. Sometimes only one cylinder seal was used, impressed twice on each pole (pl. 35:B, F). If there were two polar seals each was normally impressed once on each pole, as on III-762 (pl. 133:A), where the polar rollings show respectively two rows of triangles and a man with what seem to be a saluki and a bear (for other examples, see pl. 35:G–H). An anomalous arrangement in which each of two polar seals appears on only one pole is apparently provided by a ball with a badly-preserved surface, where the upper pole has only traces of two rollings of a cylinder seal with small animals and the lower pole two rollings of a seal with men carrying cloth (III-778a–c; pls. 149:G; 153:E). If there are more than two polar seals, the upper and lower poles do not share designs (pl. 36:E–I). In such cases it is particularly difficult to reconstruct the complete designs of the polar seals rolled only once and usually incompletely. The standard scheme also prevailed when stamp and cylinder seals were used together as on a badly impressed and eroded ball from the West Area (pl. 37:A–D). There the equatorial impression shows a two-register design of a large lion and bull below three somewhat smaller figures: a squatting human being and a bushy-tailed predator, perhaps a fox, following a quadruped. The upper and lower poles bear portions of a cylinder-seal design with small animals, including antithetical rampant lions; the front thigh of the right-hand lion is visible as a palimpsest on the body of the "fox" of the equatorial impression (pl. 37:A). The remainder of the upper pole and the greater part of the lower pole have stamp-seal imprints, but the bad state of the ball makes it impossible to determine with certainty whether one or more stamp seals were used. The pressure exerted by the stamp seal(s) asymmetrically flattened the lower part of the ball.

Sometimes balls, particularly smaller ones, were impressed by only one cylinder seal. One (pl. 34:A), for example, only 3.8 cm in diameter, hardly had room for more than one equatorial rolling. Two certain and one possible example of balls impressed all over with only one seal came from the R18:312 deposit.[18]

___

18. III-760: diameter 4.9 cm, for design, see plate 151:C; III-771: diameter 5.5 cm, plate 35:C; III-772: diameter 5.9 cm, over half of surface either destroyed or badly weathered, but traces of three rollings of a cylinder seal with a file of men carrying bows and quivers remain.

It can hardly be doubted that the sealed balls containing tokens, similar to the early tablets, are economic documents, even though it is still impossible to determine with certainty the exact character of the accounts or transactions involved. The balls vary among themselves in some significant details—the number of seals used to impress them and the very rare appearance of numerals on the exterior (pl. 36:A)—and might have had a variety of functions. They might have been itemizations of taxes or records of contracts for the exchange of goods or services. They could have served as bills of lading indicating the character and number of the goods or animals being sent and thus ensuring full delivery. If, indeed, some of the balls corresponded to bills of lading, then the places where they are found were the receiving areas where they were kept on file and eventually discarded after the animals or goods had been checked. Presumably the cylinder seals used for sealing such balls were kept in the dispatching center or centers. Considerations of the function of the clay balls raises many questions concerning the economy of the site and of the settlement network in which it must have been, on the basis of its size, a major center. Before the questions can be answered, detailed analyses on various levels are needed, for example, (1) the relative distribution of the different categories of impressed elements in various types of loci or in various areas of excavation; (2) the character of seal designs occurring in different loci; (3) the distribution of individual seal designs on different categories of impressed elements found in one locus; (4) the arrangement of the rollings on individual clay balls; and (5) the distribution of individual seal designs within closed groups of balls. The discussion that follows can only begin the exploration of these topics.

THE DISTRIBUTION OF SEAL IMPRESSIONS AND INDIVIDUAL SEAL DESIGNS

A consideration of the percentages of the various categories of impressed elements found in different types of contexts provides, despite the rarity of examples in some categories, several striking contrasts. The distribution of seal impressions is documented in detail in table 13 and summarized in table 14. Because of their similar nature some categories of loci fall together: "Occupational Debris" with "Near Features" and "Pits" with "Pottery Deposits," the latter being similar to the pits except that they are wider areas without a definite periphery. The pits and pottery deposits account for 76% of the door sealings, 56% of the jar-neck sealings, 52% of the flattish sealings and 100% of the bullae. The two latter categories presumably represent sealings from bales or boxes. Rooms provide only 3% of the door sealings, and 13% and 7% respectively of the jar-neck and flattish sealings. This contrast can be taken as functional; broken door and package sealings were swept out of rooms and thrown outside or into pits, or else the clay was reused. The circumstance that pits and pottery deposits provided 70% of the unassigned seal impressions, the majority of which are so small as to be without clear diagnostic features, corroborates the assumption that such fragments were for the most part package or jar-neck sealings.

The distribution of tablets and clay balls constitutes a second striking contrast. The pits contained 79% of the tablets, but no complete balls, while the rooms produced no tablets and 71% of the complete balls. The presence of tablets in the pits and their absence from rooms might be a chronological contrast since many of the pits, such as R17:208, were dug down from a now-eroded occupation level and cut into the walls of rooms.[19] However, this interpretation remains provisional. The tablets are so rare that the "statistics" of their distribution might be misleading. In any case, they are not limited to the pits; examples were found in occupational debris. There is some evidence to link clay balls with pits, namely the 15% of the ball fragments and 100% of the loose tokens found in them. For example, twenty-six tokens were recovered from pit R17:208. The absence of complete balls from pits is definitely a functional, rather than a chronological matter. The function of the balls culminated when they were opened; until that time came they were important records which had to be kept intact. The 17% of the ball fragments and 20% of the loose tokens found in rooms might well represent, in part at least, accidental later damage to intact balls. The largest proportion of both ball fragments, 65%, and loose tokens, 54%, was found in occupational debris, including the debris near architectural features.[20] Once balls were opened, it was more likely for small fragments and little tokens to remain scattered where they had fallen or been swept, rather than to be slung with larger debris into pits.

One pit, R18:305, contained five tablet and two ball fragments. Undue weight should not be placed upon this circumstance; the fill of the pit cannot be taken as a tightly closed group since three Achaemenid sherds had intruded into the lower part of it at about the same elevation as one of the tablet fragments (cf. *Index of Loci*). Nonetheless, the appearance together of tablet and ball fragments, as well as loose tokens, can be tentatively taken as an additional indication that the absence of complete balls and the rarity of their fragments in pits is not necessarily a chronological indicator. The door sealings have already provided an example of a wide disparity of distribution in rooms and pits that must be interpreted as functional rather than chronological in view of the long range of that type of sealing.

The variations between the different areas is another important aspect of the distribution of the seal impressions (table 15). In general, the more outlying areas in the southern part of the terrace yielded almost no impressions (11 items) although almost all had a few tokens. The northern part of the terrace yielded the bulk of the impressions, in particular the East Area with 405 items. The High Mound provided 9 examples from a Protoliterate exposure that is, aside from solid brickwork, very small. In contrast, a larger exposure in Trench XIII provided only a handful of tokens. This difference between the central and outlying areas seems too great to be merely a factor of erosion or an accident of discovery. Rather it is one of character and function. The thickness of the Protoliterate deposits and the consequent greater height of areas in the northern terrace apparently derive from the presence there of more substantial structures than elsewhere; presumably the same was the case for the High Mound. The East Area was evidently a quarter occupied by individuals, whether officials or entrepreneurs, who kept accounts, sealed some of their doors, and opened sealed containers. The contrast is clear in the finds from pits; the pits in Trench XXV and the big one at the southern edge of Trench XIII contained no seal impressions comparable to those from the East Area pits R17:208 and R18:305. Even in the East Area the distribution of seal impressions is not even. Among the house units, the southeastern unit stands out, with a deposit of at least 25 clay balls in room R18:312, the fragments of 3 balls from the adjacent locus R18:413—probably the area of a destroyed room, assorted sealings and 96 tokens in a corner of room R18:309 (= 410) and the fragments of 2 balls from immediately adjacent debris (R18:302 and West of R18:302).

The West Area provided only 42 seal impressions in contrast to the 292 items from the East Area. Moreover, there is a striking difference in the relative proportions of the sealing categories from the two areas. Door sealings form only 7%[21] of the impressions from the West Area as opposed to 22% in the East Area, while the clay balls constitute 60% in the West as opposed to only about 18% in the East Area. These figures suggest the existence of some significant differences, which

19. For discussion of the relative chronology of the balls and tablets on the basis of recent finds at Susa, see Le Brun and Vallat 1978.

20. Eleven complete balls, amounting to 29% of those found, occurred in occupational debris. Occasionally intact balls might have been discarded. It is also possible that floors corresponding to rooms might have been missed in some loci, but perhaps the most likely source of possible error in the West Area is locus H14:310, which was the source of four complete balls. However, in this exceptional case, the exact context of the objects was not observed; they were brought in by the pickman subsequent to their discovery. AA

21. This situation fits well with the assumption that only few (and more important) individuals were in charge of warehouses (see Alizadeh 1988b). AA

Table 13. Distribution in Various Contexts of Sealings and Tokens and the Relative Frequencies of Sealings Categories

CONTENT	Stoppers	Jar Neck	Door Sealing	Sealings Flattish	Flat Bottom	Unassigned	Bullae	Tablets	Balls Complete	Balls Fragments	Impressed Total	Tokens	Number of Items in Locus
ROOMS AND FLOORS													
Q17:304	—	—	—	—	—	—	—	—	—	1	1	—	1
R17:212	—	—	1	1	—	—	—	—	4	—	6	2	8
R18:309	—	1	—	1	—	1	—	—	—	—	3	95	98
R18:312	—	—	—	—	—	—	—	—	21	4	25	70	95
R18:413	—	—	—	—	—	—	—	—	—	3	3	—	3
R18:421	1 = jar	—	—	—	—	—	—	—	—	—	1	—	1
R14:304	—	—	—	—	—	—	—	—	1	1	2	—	2
N9:302	1 = jar	1	1	2	—	2	—	—	1	—	8	1	9
Totals	2	2	2	4	0	3	0	0	27	9	49	168	217
PITS													
Q18:312, 312 North	—	3	—	2	1	2	1	—	—	2	11	11	22
Q18:314	—	—	7	2	—	2	1	1	—	—	13	7	20
R17:208	—	4	25	14	2	20	—	—	—	1	66	26	92
R17:408	—	—	—	—	1	—	—	—	—	1	2	1	3
R18:305	—	1	4	2	—	5	2	5	—	2	21	8	29
R18:310, 310 South	—	—	—	1	—	—	—	1	—	—	2	4	6
S17:201 West	—	—	—	—	—	—	—	1	—	—	1	—	1
S17:202	—	—	—	—	1	1	—	1	—	—	4	—	4
H14:308	—	—	—	—	—	—	—	—	—	—	1	—	1
H15:401, 401 South	1 = jar	1	—	1	1	1	—	—	—	1	6	7	13
R21:509	—	—	—	—	—	—	—	—	—	1	1	—	1
Totals	1	9	36	22	6	31	4	9	0	8	128	64	192
POTTERY DEPOSITS													
P18:301	—	—	18	7	1	19	3	—	—	1	49	5	54
Q18:301	—	—	2	—	—	—	—	—	—	—	2	—	2
Totals	0	0	20	7	1	19	3	0	0	1	51	5	56
NEAR FEATURES													
Q18:305 (Circular Structure)	1 = bottle	—	—	—	—	—	—	—	—	—	1	—	1
Q18:402 (Kiln Area)	—	—	—	1	—	—	—	—	—	—	1	6	7
R17:303 (Drain)	—	—	—	1	—	—	—	—	—	—	1	7	8
R17:310 (Lane)	—	—	—	—	—	—	—	—	—	1	1	1	2
H15:405 (Kiln Area)	—	—	—	1	—	—	—	—	—	2	3	2	5
J15:402 (Near Bin)	—	—	—	—	—	1	—	—	—	3	4	1	5
O9:302 (Cesspit)	—	—	—	—	—	1	—	—	—	—	1	—	1
Totals	1	0	0	4	0	2	0	0	0	6	12	17	29
OCCUPATIONAL DEBRIS													
East Area:Surface	—	—	—	1	—	—	—	—	—	2	3	—	3
East Area:Trench V	—	—	1	1	—	1	—	—	—	—	3	—	3
P17:Trench V A	—	—	—	1	—	—	—	—	—	—	1	—	1
P17:402	—	—	—	—	—	1	—	—	—	1	2	3	5
P18:203	—	—	—	—	1	—	—	—	—	1	2	—	2
Q17:202	—	—	1	—	—	—	—	—	—	—	1	—	1
West of Q17:304	—	—	—	—	—	—	—	—	—	1	1	—	1
South of Q18:303	—	—	—	1	—	—	—	—	—	—	1	—	1
R18:307													
Q18:307	1 = jar	—	—	—	—	—	—	—	—	—	1	3	4
Q18:307/R19:301	—	—	—	1	—	—	—	—	—	1	2	2	4
North of Q18:308	1 = bottle	—	1	1	—	—	—	—	—	2	5	—	5
Q18:318	—	—	2	—	—	1	—	—	—	2	5	—	5
R17:203	—	—	1	—	1	—	—	—	—	—	2	—	2
North of R17:203	—	—	—	—	—	—	—	1	—	—	1	5	6
R17:203–04	—	—	—	—	—	2	—	—	—	—	2	1	3

Table 13. Distribution in Various Contexts of Sealings and Tokens
and the Relative Frequencies of Sealings Categories (*cont.*)

CONTENT	Stoppers	Jar Neck	Door Sealing	Sealings Flattish	Flat Bottom	Unassigned	Bullae	Tablets	Balls Complete	Balls Fragments	Impressed Total	Tokens	Number of Items in Locus
R17:204	—	—	1	—	—	1	—	—	—	—	2	—	2
R17:207	—	1	4	3	2	3	—	—	—	—	13	—	13
R17:215, 215 West	—	2	—	—	—	—	—	—	—	3	5	—	5
North of R17:302	1 = jar	—	—	—	—	—	—	—	—	—	1	—	1
R17:303 East, Northeast	—	—	—	2	—	—	—	—	—	1	3	—	3
North of R17:303	—	—	—	2	—	—	—	—	—	1	3	—	3
R17:308	—	—	—	2	—	—	—	—	—	—	2	—	2
R18:Trench XX	—	—	2	—	—	—	—	—	—	—	2	5	7
West of R18:302	—	—	—	—	—	—	—	—	—	1	1	—	1
North of R18:304 West of R18:302	—	—	—	—	—	1	—	—	—	—	1·	—	1
West of R18:305	—	1	—	—	—	—	—	—	—	—	1	—	1
South of R18:309	—	—	1	—	—	—	—	—	—	—	1	—	1
R18:310/Q18:312	—	—	—	—	—	—	—	—	—	1	1	—	1
North of R19:301	—	—	—	—	—	1	—	—	—	—	1	—	1
R19:302	—	—	—	—	—	1	—	—	—	—	1	—	1
S17:301	—	—	1	1	—	—	—	—	—	—	2	12	14
S17:405	—	—	—	1	—	—	—	—	—	—	1	1	2
H13:301	—	—	—	—	—	—	—	1	—	—	1	1	2
H14:Trench IX	—	—	—	—	—	—	—	—	1	—	1	13	14
H14:Trench IX West	—	—	—	1	—	—	—	—	—	—	1	—	1
H14:302	—	—	—	—	—	—	—	1	—	—	1	—	1
H14:305	—	—	—	—	—	—	—	—	1	—	1	3	4
H14:310	—	—	—	—	—	—	—	—	5	2	7	1	8
H14:401	—	—	—	—	—	—	—	—	—	1	1	7	8
H14:403	—	—	—	1	—	—	—	—	—	—	1	3	4
H15:407–08	—	—	—	—	—	—	—	—	—	1	1	—	1
J13:Northern slope	—	1	—	—	—	—	—	—	—	—	1	9	10
J13:301	—	—	—	—	—	2	—	—	—	—	2	1	3
J14:403 South	—	—	—	—	—	—	—	—	—	1	1	1	2
J15:Sounding C	—	—	—	—	—	—	—	—	1	—	1	2	3
J15:Sounding C South	—	—	—	—	—	—	—	—	1	—	1	51	52
J15:403, 403 Southeast	—	—	—	—	—	—	—	—	1	1	2	1	3
K14:Trench VI	—	—	—	—	—	—	—	—	1	—	1	1	2
K14: Trench VI North	—	—	—	—	—	1	—	—	—	—	1	4	5
E23:Trench XIV	—	—	—	—	—	—	—	—	—	1	1	—	1
R21:300	—	—	—	—	—	1	—	—	—	—	1	—	1
West of R21:405	1 = jar	—	—	—	—	—	—	—	—	—	1	1	2
R21:407	—	—	—	—	—	—	—	—	—	4	4	—	4
East of R21:503	—	—	—	—	—	—	—	—	—	1	1	—	1
S22:507	—	—	—	—	—	1	—	—	—	—	1	—	1
Totals	4	5	15	19	4	17	0	3	11	29	107	131	238
Category Total	8	16	73	56	11	72	7	12	38	53	347	385	732

Table 14. Summary of the Distribution of Sealings, Tokens, and Stoppers by Context

CONTEXT	Jar Neck	Door Sealing	Sealings Flattish	Flat Bottom	Unassigned	Bullae	Tablets	Balls Complete	Fragments	Loose Tokens	Stoppers Jar	Bottle
Rooms and Floors	2	2	4	0	3	0	0	27	9	241	15	44
	13%	3%	7%	0%	4%	0%	0%	71%	17%	29%	27%	2%
Pits	9	36	22	6	31	4	11	0	8	81	17	524
	56%	49%	39%	55%	43%	57%	79%	0%	15%	10%	30%	26%
Pottery Deposits	0	20	7	1	19	3	0	0	1	5	7	1,259
	0%	27%	13%	9%	26%	43%	0%	0%	2%	1%	13%	63%
Near Features	0	0	4	0	2	0	0	0	6	63	0	5
	0%	0%	7%	0%	3%	0%	0%	0%	11%	8%	0%	0%
Occupational Debris	5	15	19	4	17	0	3	11	29	375	17	166
	31%	21%	34%	36%	24%	0%	21%	29%	55%	46%	30%	8%
Totals	16	73	56	11	72	7	14	38	53	765	56	1,998
	100%	100%	100%	100%	100%	100%	100%	100%	100%	100%	100%	100%

cannot as yet be specified, in the range of activities carried out in the two areas.

Apart from the distribution of the categories of sealings, the distribution of impressions made by seals of varying styles or by individual seals is also of importance. In general, there are no meaningful contrasts in style between the seal impressions from the various areas or from the different types of contexts within areas, or, for that matter, on the different categories of seal impressions. For example, the door sealings and the balls both bear impressions of seals cut in the finest modeled style of the early Protoliterate period and in a less sophisticated rustic style. Pits and rooms yielded impressions of the two styles, as well as those made by "Jemdet Nasr" type seals with staggered rows of motifs. The absence of stylistic distinctions between the impressions from pits and rooms indicates that no appreciable lapse of time separated the pits from the houses into which they were dug.

In studying the occurrences of individual seal designs in different loci and on various categories of impressions the basic assumption is, of course, that each seal belonged to a specific person/office whose activities are reflected in the distribution of its impressions. The comments and suggestions that follow must to some extent remain provisional until much additional analysis can be done. On the whole, so far as the distribution of the designs in different loci is concerned, each seal-impression locus seems to have its own group of designs and thus to reflect the activities of separate sets of individuals/offices. It should be noted, however, that this situation might also be due to the fact that our sample is extremely limited in proportion to what once existed and extends over at least two building phases.

Three loci near the Circular Structure that share impressions made by the same seals provide an exception

to the usual situation. Q18:314 is a well-defined pit about 9 m to the east of the big pottery deposit, P18:301. Between the two is Q18:318, which includes both occupational debris and a fringe of the pottery deposit in the section contiguous to the eastern end of P18:301 and above the pavements of Q18:315. P18:301 contains broken door sealings impressed by at least six different seals. Those with a lion and bull in rustic style (III-827a–b; pls. 43:C; 139:D) and with a finely-delineated version of the motif of cloth-offering bearer (III-869a–c; pls. 45:P; 153:F) occur only in the big pottery deposit. The impressions of the seals showing two lions attacking a goat,[22] men in activities of daily life,[23] and a niched building[24] occur in both the big pottery deposit and pit Q18:314, while the door sealing fragments of the orchestra seal (pl. 155:A) are scattered in P18:301, Q18:318, and Q18:314.[25] These six seals were used only on door sealings with the minor exception of a flattish sealing with part of the "daily activities" design and the major exception of three bullae, two from Near Q18:315 (III-911a, c) and one from Q18:318 (III-911b). The latter are imprinted by the seal showing two lions attacking a goat, which indicates that the bullae were made at the site and not brought in on shipments from outside.

The impressions from pit R17:208 document the securing of doors by, again, at least six persons/offices.[26] One of them, the owner of the seal engraved with a tree

22. III-823–24, 916 (all P18:301); III-835a–b (Q18:314).

23. III-828a–b, 833c, 915 (all P18:301); III-833b (Q18;314).

24. III-866a–b (P18:301); III-866c (Q18:314).

25. III-830a, 913b–c (P18:301); III-830c (Q18:314); III-830b, 913a (Q18:318).

26. Compare pls. 43:L, O (II-206a–b, e, i, k, q–s); 143:E (II-212a–b); 120:A (II-209a–b); 153:D (II-288a–b), 144:C; 145:C (II-316b; 360a–i, k–q); and II-99, a fragment showing a bull(?) and plants.

Table 15. The Distribution of the Stoppers, Sealings, and Tokens by Area

AREA	Stoppers	Jar Neck	Door Sealing	Sealings Flattish	Flat Bottom	Unassigned	Bullae	Tablets	Balls Complete	Fragment	Number of Seal Impressions in Locus	Tokens
East Area ca. 1,725 sq. m	4 1.3%	12 3.9%	65 22.2%	53 18.1%	10 3.4%	76 26%	7 2.3%	11 3.7%	30 10.2%	24 8.2%	292 100%	405 —
West Area ca. 1,207 sq. m	0 0%	0 0%	3 7.1%	5 11.9%	1 2.3%	5 11.9%	0 0%	3 7.1%	12 28.6%	13 30.9%	42 100%	150 —
Trench XXV ca. 309 sq. m	1 12.5%	0 0%	0 0%	0 0%	0 0%	1 12.5%	0 0%	0 0%	0 0%	6 75%	8 100%	180 —
Other Areas												
High Mound Terrace	1	1	1	2	0	3	0	0	1	0	9	9
E23:Trench XIV	0	0	0	0	0	0	0	0	0	1	1	0
K–L22–23:Trench XIII	0	0	0	0	0	0	0	0	0	0	0	13
G26–27:Trench X	0	0	0	0	0	0	0	0	0	0	0	1
P27:Trench XXXI	0	0	0	0	0	0	0	0	0	0	0	3
S22:Gully Cut	0	0	0	0	0	1	0	0	0	0	1	4
Other Areas Totals	1 9.1%	1 9.1%	1 9.1%	2 18.2%	0 0%	4 36.4%	0 0%	0 0%	1 9.1%	1 9.1%	11 100%	30 —

flanked on each side by two animals (pl. 43:L–O), also used it to secure a jar (II-206t; pl. 143:I) and other containers (pl. 43:M–N; II-206c–d, g, j, l–m). Another ball fragment from R17:208 has part of a design (pls. 45:K–L; 153:B) that does not recur on any of the other sealings from the pit. This is also the case in the four other loci that contained both ball and door sealing fragments (N9:302; P18:301; Q18:318; R18:305). Although the appearance of door sealings and balls with exactly the same designs would have been immediate proof for the sealing of balls at the site, the absence of such designs in common does not necessarily prove the converse.

Among all the categories of seal impressions, only the clay balls were normally impressed by more than one seal. In this respect the majority of the balls are strikingly different from the tablets, which have impressions of only one cylinder seal and, in addition, imprinted numerals. The latter hardly ever occur on the balls (pl. 36:A–B). These characteristics, as well as the other marked distinctions between balls and tablets, might well indicate that the two categories were more functionally than chronologically distinct. Except for a minority of examples covered by impressions of only one seal, the balls involved from two to five individuals and thus appear to be documents of a different character and function than the tablets. Furthermore, the regularity of the arrangement of the different seal impressions on the balls (pl. 133) implies that there was some meaning to the scheme. The primacy of the equatorial impression suggests that the owner of that seal was the person/office principally concerned with the circumstances of transactions being recorded. The usually less-complete polar imprints might have been made by witnesses.

Data for the analysis of the position and distribution of individual seal designs in a closed group of clay balls are provided by R18:312, with its twenty-one complete or semi-complete examples and the fragments of four, or possibly more, additional examples.[27] At least twenty different persons/offices are documented on the R18:312 balls, but no individual seal design recurs on more than four balls, with the possible exception of a motif, men carrying cloth, which is known in many versions at Chogha Mish. This theme appears on five balls, but the impressions do not remain in sufficient detail to prove with certainty that each was impressed by the same cloth-bearer seal (pls. 35:C; 36:I).

Over half of the R18:312 seal designs occur on only one ball. Among the equatorial designs are a rosette-filled interlace (pl. 36:G), a file of lions (pl. 35:A), and the victorious personage in a ship, whose status is indicated by his much larger size and whose authority by holding the captives (pl. 151:B). Seals with the siege scene (pl. 151:C) and a file of bowmen (pl. 151:A) were used to fill the polar areas as well as the equators of their respective balls. Among the polar impressions three designs occur only once: rampant lions (pl. 36:E, G), a master of snakes (pl. 36:F), and a row of angular men (pl. 35:F).

Each of four persons/offices used their seals twice to make equatorial impressions on balls of the R18:312 cache. The designs in question are a row of individual tall granaries (pl. 149:G), a file of men with right arms extended (pl. 35:D), domed multiple granaries (pl. 35:K), and porters carrying boxes on their heads (pls.

27. The discussion remains preliminary since many of the examples have not yet been analyzed in detail. AA

35:G; 133:B). The two balls with the equatorial multiple granaries form an identical pair, as do those with the porters. A polar seal common to both pairs of balls shows a man, a saluki, and a boar, all moving toward the left (pl. 35:H, J). It is partnered on one pair of balls with a free-field composition of small squatting and standing men (pl. 35:I) and on the other pair with a simple design of two rows of staggered triangles, presumably representing heaps of grain (pl. 35:G–H). The seal with triangles was also impressed on another ball (pl. 35:B) and on the fragments of III-773.

If we look to the equatorial impressions as indicators of the main protagonists involved in the R18:312 records, we find only four designs, out of at least ten equatorial impressions, which recur twice. Thus, there are no designs that could foster an interpretation of the balls as records executed by either one major protagonist or by a limited group of persons associated by their family or functions. Nonetheless, there are patterns to be seen in the distribution of the individual designs.

On all the balls with more than one design, no equatorial seal was impressed on the polar areas and *vice versa*. If we assume that the former represent the seals of protagonists and the latter those of witnesses or minor participants, then it follows that no protagonist on any record in this cache ever appeared on another as a witness for someone else. On the other hand, several persons serving as witnesses for various principals can be observed. The owners of the seals with a man, a saluki, and a boar and with triangles witnessed together on one pair of balls for the possessor of the file-of-porters seal and witnessed separately the balls of several other principals. Such evidence indicated that the R18:312 balls are not a family archive in the sense of being direct records of transactions conducted by one or a few individuals. Rather the unity of the balls as an archive stems from a connection between the persons represented by the equatorial impressions and the person who had custody of the balls, presumably the owner/administrator of the house/office in which they were found. Whether the transactions in question involved trading ventures, simple debts, or other types of dues can probably only be a matter of speculation for the moment. Likewise, the questions whether the persons who controlled groups of balls were entrepreneurs or officials, whether the balls recorded private concerns or involved relations with secular or religious institutions, and whether there is a meaningful correlation between the apparent concentration of the balls in the East and West Areas and the presumptive existence of shrines in those quarters of the town can only be raised, but not answered.

CONCLUSION

The great creative manifestations of the Protoliterate period do not necessarily possess a regularly graduated series of antecedents bridging the prehistoric and dawning historical periods. On the other hand, such inventions are not made in a vacuum. One could expect *a priori* that the exigencies of daily life would lead to the widespread parallel development, all over the world and at widely varying periods, of simple methods of recording numerical data by tallying with notches on a stick or with a collection of pebbles (cf. Cajori 1928; Danzig 1942, 1948; Smeltzer 1953:3, 7, 11–14). It has been suggested that incised notational systems had already been developed as early as the Aurignacian and Magdalenian[28] periods and that clay tokens widely distributed in prehistoric sites in pre-pottery and later stages are examples of tallying systems (Schmandt-Besserat 1974:11–17; 1977b:133–50). It is on the basis of such a general background of varied and widespread incipient record-keeping that the sophisticated numerical and writing systems of the Protoliterate period must have developed. The occasional persistence of simple tallying methods is exemplified by clay objects from Pit R17:208 discussed above (pl. 132).

Of the two specific types of record-bearing objects appearing in the Protoliterate period, the tablet was to remain for millennia the normal vehicle for writing in Western Asia. In contrast, the chronological and geographical distribution of the seal-impressed balls enclosing tokens appears to be limited primarily to early Protoliterate (Late Uruk) levels at sites belonging to the central Protoliterate tradition.[29] There are, however, two groups of surprisingly analogous objects from Upper Egyptian tombs datable to the Fourth Dynasty. At Abydos the sand core of Mastaba 124 (Cemetery D) yielded about forty small clay balls varying in diameter from 2 to 4 cm,[30] the majority of which had been impressed by a cylinder seal bearing, according to Peet, a simple design of six crosshatched rectangles. The balls had then been incised with a group of signs, always the same, reading *ḫtm*, the Egyptian word for seal.[31] Peet does not specifically refer to a hollow in the center, stating only that the balls had been blackened by organic matter and that three were opened; two contained fragments of reed and the third a fragment of cloth (Peet 1915:8–9, pl. 4). At nearby Reqaqna clay balls bearing the same cylinder seal pattern and incised inscription as

---

28. See the speculative proposals of Marshack (1972b:817–28), who suggests a far more advanced stage of development in the Upper Paleolithic than has been assumed hitherto; see also Marshack 1972a.

29. For a much later and much discussed hollow ball with pebbles, which is important for the interpretation of the Protoliterate balls, see Oppenheim 1959:121–28.

30. Peet and Loat 1913:20. The small mastaba of unbaked brick has one large niche on the southern part of the eastern facade and three small niches on the northern end.

31. Klaus Baer kindly identified the signs.

at Abydos were found in a hole bored into the top of the northwestern corner of Mastaba 50 (Peet 1915:9; Garstang 1904:32, 59, pl. 30). The two examples opened by Garstang and Peet contained bits of cloth "made up into pellets."[32]

The two groups of balls from provincial Upper Egyptian tombs do not seem to have any parallels in the far more numerous and developed mastabas of the Memphite cemeteries. Neither is the specific use of the objects clear, although an apotropaic function is possible.[33] Although as sealed receptacles for small elements the Upper Egyptian balls provide a striking general analogy for the Protoliterate clay balls, the two sets of objects must be considered merely as convergent phenomena. The Egyptian balls are over half a millennium later than the Protoliterate ones. Aside from the great chronological discrepancy, even in the Gerzean period when many Protoliterate features did reach Egypt, there would have been no occasion for clay balls to appear. They were records made only in the course of the normal transactions of a Protoliterate community,

unlike the easily portable and attractive engraved cylinder seals, which were introduced into Egypt in the Predynastic Gerzean period and thoroughly adopted and Egyptianized in the Protodynastic period.

In this chapter the widespread use of clay for protective and recording devices is surveyed. Variously shaped stoppers protected the contents of jars and bottles, while clay impressed by seals both protected and validated the intactness of packages, jars, and rooms. Among the variety of contexts in which seal impressions occur at Chogha Mish, the tablets and clay balls, with their associated tokens, stand out as two categories that exemplify outstanding developments of the dawning historical period, the appearance of elaborate economic and social systems and the beginning of writing. Equally characteristic of the new era is the crystallization of a highly sophisticated representational art. The greater part of the evidence for it is provided by the impressions on the tablets, balls, and various categories of sealings. These designs and the few actual seals recovered are discussed in the following chapter.

32. Peet (1915:9, n. 1) wrote "like our Abydos examples," but his statement in the text as to the contents of the Abydos balls is not so definite.

33. Klaus Baer drew our attention to the ritual use in later periods (New Kingdom, Ptolemaic, Roman) of balls, including clay ones, in a ritual game in which the smashing of the balls was linked to the destruction of the enemies of Egypt. See also DeVries 1969:25–35, especially p. 33.

CHAPTER 7
THE DESIGNS OF PROTOLITERATE GLYPTIC

The earliest school of elaborate representational art known in Western Asia is documented primarily by seals and seal impressions. Chogha Mish has a varied repertory of designs executed with considerable stylistic latitude, known only from impressions, not from extant seals. The same discrepancy between a wealth of elaborate impressions and a scarcity of extant cylinder seals of comparable character is to be observed at other sites of the Protoliterate period and presents a difficult problem. It hardly seems likely that at all sites only "receiving areas" have been dug, and no "dispatching areas" where the seals were being used. Since the situation at Chogha Mish is not unique, the seals of the impressions were surely both made and used at the site itself. The door sealings must, of course, have been impressed after they were placed around the door fastenings. Other impressions on the sealings of moveable objects (jar sealings, bale sealings, etc.) might have been made in "dispatching areas," either at the site or elsewhere, different from the "receiving areas" where they have been found. The few extant seals from Chogha Mish do illustrate the types in use there during the Protoliterate period and serve as an introduction to the richer documentation of the seal impressions.

STAMP SEALS

Three of the main types of Protoliterate stamp seals are represented at Chogha Mish. More elaborate are two theriomorphic seals, a goat with its head turned back carved in bone (pl. 41:S) and a more schematically-rendered animal cut in translucent green stone (pl. 41:T). The designs on their bases are consistent in style with the varying rendering of the animals' bodies. The disjointed drill-hole animals on the stone seal contrast with the full-bodied horned animals on the bone seal. Square stamp seals with simple gouged (pl. 41:Q) or drill-hole (pl. 41:O–P) designs on the base also occur.

Plano-convex and lentoid stamp seals appear with irregular gouges (pl. 41:L) or, more commonly, drill holes, sometimes suggesting animals (pl. 41:M–N, R). Such pieces might have functioned more as beads than as true stamp seals. Several examples with plain uncarved bases were found (pl. 129:AA–CC). The stamp seals from Chogha Mish represent types standard for the Protoliterate period. The majority of the compa-

rable examples come from contexts that either date to the Late Protoliterate period or are contemporary with it.[1]

Stamp seals are also exemplified at Chogha Mish by a few impressions showing animals or human beings. Arthropods are represented by a spider with a pair of chelicerae and four pairs of legs (II-235, pl. 135:H–I) and what seems to be an ant with three pairs of legs (pl. 42:A). An impression shows a man with a raised arm (III-864). In addition, impressions of stamp seals occur side-by-side with those of cylinder seals on clay balls: a turtle is depicted on one sealing (pl. 34:G) and apparently two seals, one with a turtle and one with perhaps a quadruped, are depicted on another (pl. 37:C).

Impressions of stamp seals are much rarer than those of cylinder seals. They were sometimes used side-by-side, as on clay ball II-97 (pl. 37:A–D). There the lower pole has three stamp seal impressions and only a slight portion of the seal that covered the upper pole (pl. 135:C). It is remarkable that two of these stamp seals

1. See Homès-Fredericq 1970 for a monograph devoted to stamp seals. For a parallel to plate 41:F, see Mackay 1931, pl. 73:27 (Jemdet Nasr). For a parallel to plate 41:H, see Amiet 1972, no. 275 (Susa, old excavation). For a parallel to plate 41:J, see Amiet 1972, no. 376 (Susa, old excavation); de Genouillac et al. 1934, pl. 38:1 d = Homès-Fredericq 1970, pl. 46:468 (Tello). For a parallel to plate 41:L, see (Amiet 1972, no. 287 (shape and incising somewhat different; Susa, old excavation). For a parallel to plate 41:N, see von der Osten 1934, pl. 1:3 (Newell Collection). For parallels to plate 41:N, see Amiet 1972, nos. 382 (no projections), 409–10 (feet on square stamp seal) (Susa, old excavation); Starr 1937, pl. 40:U = Homès-Fredericq 1970, pl. 38:415 (Nuzi); von der Osten 1934, pl. 1:10 (Newell Collection). For parallels to plate 41:P, see Amiet 1972, nos. 404–06 (Susa, old excavation); Strommenger 1962a, pl. 15:e = Homès-Fredericq 1970, pl. 44:455–56 (Warka, Archaic Settlement, surface); de Genouillac et al. 1934, pl. 38:2 b (Tello); von der Osten 1934, pl. 50:1 (Newell Collection). For a parallel to plate 41:R, see Starr 1937, pl. 40:H, N, Q = Homès-Fredericq 1970, pl. 39:427–29 (Nuzi). For parallels to plate 41:S, see Heinrich 1936, pl. 12:i = Homès-Fredericq 1970, pl. 43:452 (Warka area); Mallowan 1947, pls. 12:1 a–b; 46:6 = Homès-Fredericq 1970, pl. 29:341 (Brak). For parallels to plate 41:T, see Amiet 1972, no. 418 (Susa, old excavation); Legrain 1951, pl. 1:12 = Homès-Fredericq 1970, pl. 49:504 (Ur); de Genouillac et al. 1934, pl. 36:6h = Homès-Fredericq 1970, pl. 47:481 (Tello); von der Osten 1934, pl. 2:15–17 (Newell Collection).

share the same motif, a frog. There can be no question that there are two different seals since the frogs are considerably different in scale (pl. 135:D–E). In the smaller version, the webbed feet of the frog are clearly shown. The third stamp seal impression on this ball is badly eroded. However, the animal pictured is clearly an invertebrate. It represents, most probably, a scorpion, although it does not resemble closely other renderings of that arthropod. The symmetrical incurving elements probably represent the chelicerae and there are three pairs of legs. The main problem with identifying it as a scorpion is the absence of the curving tail with the sting. A sealing with a basketry imprint on the inside has two impressions of a stamped seal showing a spider or an ant (pl. 135:G). The body also with a head and abdomen is emphasized, in contrast to the broad triangular head plus body of the presumed scorpion (pl. 135:K). A square stamp seal also on a ball shows a turtle (pl. 135:J).

CYLINDER SEALS

The few cylinder seals found give no hint as to the complexity of the glyptic art documented by the impressions. The decoration is simple, in two cases there are irregular drill holes or gouges not forming any recognizable shapes (pl. 41:A–B) and in others rows of fish (pl. 41:C) or ovals (pl. 41:D, G),[2] one of which (pl. 41:G) is only 1.5 cm high but can still be accepted as a seal since we have impressions made by a slightly smaller seal of the same general type (pl. 42:M). Only the somewhat larger size distinguishes such cylinder seals from the 1.0–1.2 cm high cylindrical beads with similar ovals (pl. 41:E, I). The beads also appear with crosshatching (pl. 41:K) or random gouges (pl. 41:F).

The impressions illustrate a larger range in size than do the extant seals. Although smaller seals are represented (pl. 155:B), examples about 2.0 cm high are much more frequent. In cases where borders of the seals are not evident, the sizes of the animals reflect the vary-

---

2. Comparable seals are well known elsewhere, occurring in Protoliterate c–d contexts but sometimes surviving into later periods. For parallels to plate 41:C, see Amiet 1972, no. 794 (three rows; Susa, old excavation); Heinrich 1936, pl. 19:f (three rows; Warka, *Kleinfunde*). For parallels to plate 41:D, see Amiet 1972, no. 789 (Susa, old excavation); Frankfort 1955, pl. 32:329 (Khafajah, Houses 2, Early Dynastic III). For parallels to plate 41:E, see Amiet 1972, nos. 786, 788, 792 (Susa, old excavation); Frankfort 1955, pl. 18:180 (Khafajah, Sin Temple IV, Protoliterate d). For parallels to plate 41:G, see Amiet 1972, No 814 (Susa, old excavation); Frankfort 1955, pl. 36:376 (Khafajah, surface). For pattern related to that in plate 41:I, see Frankfort 1955, no. 51 (Khafajah, Sin Temple III, Protoliterate c). For parallels to plate 41:K, see Amiet 1972, nos. 852–54 (Susa, old excavation); Frankfort 1955, pl. 8:57 (Khafajah, Sin Temple III); and Frankfort 1955, pl. 72:788 (Tell Agrab, Shara Temple, Early Dynastic II).

ing sizes of the seals. Animals about 2.0 cm in height, which is average, imply a seal not much taller, as can be checked on a very clearly rolled impression where the lions are about 1.9 cm high and the seal itself about 2.2 cm high (pl. 35:A). The upper ranges of size are indicated by a sealing where a lion whose head is lost must have been originally at least 3.0 cm high (pl. 42:O) and by impressions with military themes between 3.8 and 4.0 cm high (pl. 150:A–F). However, such sizes seem to have been exceptional; the majority of the seals were probably between 2.0 and 3.0 cm high.

THE SEAL IMPRESSIONS

In the field, P. Delougaz cleaned each impression by hand, removing dirt and salt encrustations grain by grain. The reconstruction of seal designs from fragmentary impressions of the palimpsests of rollings on clay balls has been a lengthy process. The aim has been not only to reconstruct complete seal designs but also to do justice to their artistic style as far as is possible when impressions of often sensitively modeled designs are reduced to line drawings. To capture the refinements of contours and small details, all drawings of the impressions have been done at a scale of 5:2, and are illustrated at 3:2.

The problems of reconstituting the seal designs are heightened not only by the very fragmentary character of many of the sealings, but also by the differences in shape and proportions caused by varying degrees of pressure exerted during multiple rollings of a seal. The extremes of variation thus possible are shown by two impressions of an Akkadian seal made many years ago by P. Delougaz (fig. 18).

The horizontal and diagonal elements of the design are naturally most affected by the motion of the seal, while the vertical relationships of elements remain fairly constant. Thus, vertical dimensions provide fixed basic points of reference when working from impressions back to the reconstruction of the original seal design. Even though on ancient impressions the variations are not usually as extreme as shown in figure 18, they are still quite sufficient to make the reconstitution of a seal design represented by many fragments a complex and time-consuming process. The proportions and the spacing of individual elements vary, sometimes drastically, from impression to impression. Compositions as they were originally cut on the seals must be reconstructed on the basis of innumerable comparative measurements (see pl. 143:I for an outstanding example).[3]

When only one incomplete impression of a particular seal design exists, the outline of the sealing is given and the impression drawn as it is. The absence of any

---

3. See the description of plate 143:I for the manner in which it is reconstructed. AA

sealing outline usually indicates that the design has been reconstituted on the basis of several rollings of the seal, whether multiple rollings on one sealing or several individual sealings. Occasionally, a design represented by only one incomplete and contorted rolling can be reconstituted by using as guides the vertical relationships at a number of points; in such cases, also, the outline of the sealing is omitted.

The problems caused by variations in proportions are not so obvious as those arising from badly preserved surfaces. For example, the archive of balls from R18:312 was in an area where the denudation had been so great that the hoard was only about 40 cm below the modern surface. Accordingly, the impressions on many of the balls had been badly damaged by surface moisture and by the roots of plants and were in a few cases irretrievably lost.

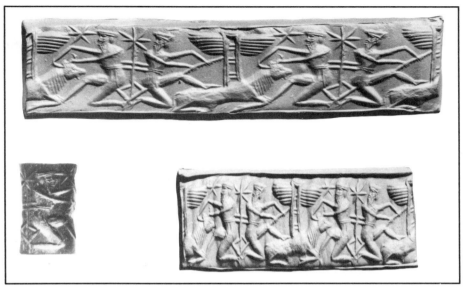

Figure 18. Elongated and Foreshortened Rollings of Akkadian Cylinder Seal (Oriental Institute A 29182), Made by P. Delougaz to Demonstrate the Effects of Varying Pressure

THE ICONOGRAPHY AND COMPOSITION OF THE SEAL DESIGNS

The Chogha Mish seal designs provide a good cross-section of themes already known to be typical for Protoliterate art. In addition, they add some outstanding new subjects. Abstract geometric motifs are extremely rare (pls. 41:D; 42:R; table 16).[4] Furthermore, representational interpretations are possible for several of the few that do exist (pls. 34:G; 35:B; 36:E, G, I; 45:F). The bulk of the designs can be divided into three general iconographic groups; those with only animals, including monsters; those with both animals and human beings; and those devoted exclusively to human beings and their concerns. The themes and the composition of the seal surfaces are intimately related. The compositional schemes used vary from the simple seriation of paratactic figures or groups to continuous friezes or formal heraldic groups. In all cases the desire was evidently to cast a fairly even net of representation across a blank background without either large vacant spaces or markedly dense agglomerations of motifs. Compositions in which the main standing figures, whether human or animal, extend to the full height of the seal predominate. Thus the edges of the seal, though not marked by engraved borders, establish a register in which the main figures stand or sit on an implicit ground line (pl. 150:E–F). Suitable accessorial elements(?) are added to fill excess empty space (pl. 150:F). However, in the representations of themes such as the more elaborate human

activities, some of the figures are freed from implicit ground lines and placed freely in the field of the representation. Examples are the attendants of the city ruler (pl. 151:B) and the prisoner (pl. 150:F). In one design (pl. 155:A), five of the figures are based on an implicit ground line, but no one—not even the focal group of the banqueter and his attendant—extends to the top of the seal. The harpist squats free in the field flanked by adjuncts of the feast that are almost as large as is he. Another incomplete example of a free-field composition is illustrated by the drawing on plate 155:C.

In addition to the single-register seals, others have several registers, though these are not separated by actual ground lines. Seals with the same motif repeated in two or three staggered rows are commoner. A considerable variety of motifs appear: geometric crescents (III-733), "kidneys" (pl. 138:I),[5] and ovals (pl. 41:D); scorpions (IV-390; pl. 135:K), fish (pls. 41:C; 42:L; 138:A, C), turtles (pls. 38:F; 138:B), and quadrupeds (pls. 42:M; 143); squatting men (pls. 138:J; 148);[6] granaries (pls. 35:K; 149), and the triangles that probably represent heaps of grain (pls. 35:B; 133:A). A fragment preserving a very small part of a design of coiled snakes is atypical in that the two rows are not staggered (pl. 42:S). Since these designs are found in the same contexts as the more elaborate designs, they establish that the staggered-rows typical of the Jemdet Nasr style

---

4. Squares with filling = III-811; for similar design, see Amiet 1972, no. 626 bis (Susa, old excavation).

5. For rows of kidney-shaped motifs, see Amiet 1972, pl. 19:714 (Susa, old excavation). The similarity between this motif and the similarly-shaped stamp seals known at Brak in a context contemporary with the later Protoliterate period is probably accidental.

6. For a similar staggered row in which the men hold alternately a large loop or fringed triangle to their mouths, see Le Brun and Vallat 1978, fig. 6:13 (Susa, Acropole I, Level 18).

originated in the earlier part of the Protoliterate period. While the rudimentary fish (pl. 41:C) and simple ovals (pl. 41:D, G) of the extant seals are indistinguishable from Jemdet Nasr examples, the motifs of the staggered rows known from impressions are rendered in a more detailed fashion (pls. 42:L, P; 138:A, C).[7]

Quite different from the abstract, single-motif rows of the Jemdet Nasr category are the multiple-register designs containing several motifs arranged fairly freely. Such designs are stylistically comparable to those of the single-register seals and can be considered standard. Normally, there are two registers. These might be of equal importance, as in the case of incomplete designs consisting of a lower file of animals walking left and an upper file walking right (pl. 42:I).[8] Probably somewhat more frequent are designs in which the figures of the upper registers are smaller than those of the main register (pl. 37:B, D).

In many of the Chogha Mish designs there is considerable uniformity in the direction in which figures face or move. The majority of paratactic files, whether animal or human, move toward the left. Paired figures of predator and prey also usually walk to the left, as do men guiding animals. On seals showing human figures engaged in various activities, individual groups might consist of asymmetrical pairs in which neither direction is emphasized. Designs with major and subordinate figures have more complicated compositions in which the main figure is on the right and forms the focal point toward which the action of the other figures moves. Examples are the compositions showing victory on the battlefield in which the city ruler faces to the left, while the active figures, his soldiers, turn to the right in the direction of their commander. Such compositions are represented at Chogha Mish by incomplete impressions (pl. 151:C) but are known in their complete form from Warka (Heinrich 1934, pl. 23:a–b). In a remarkable scene in which the city ruler himself participates in the movement of the design, he is enthroned in his boat, facing to the right, the direction in which the boat is moving (pl. 151:B).[9]

The iconography and composition of the glyptic at Chogha Mish are summarized in table 16. Various aspects of the classification used in it are considered above, but a few further points still need clarification.

Symmetrical pairs of animals or human beings are considered to be groups even if the individual elements do not actually touch, but in asymmetrical arrangements only figures that are actually joined are considered groups. Thus the figures of a bull followed by a lion are classified as a mixed file, although conceptually the two animals could be considered as a group consisting of the domesticated animal and its wild opponent. In most versions of the common motif of men carrying cloth the figures are identical and accordingly the compositions are classified as uniform files. However, in one elaborate rendering the two individuals carry different combinations of textiles and are separated by standards, so this version is classified under "groups" (pl. 153:B). The design of another seal (pl. 145:B) is in general a file but since it is made up of two clusters of elements, a man holding a container and the tail of a bull, it is also classified under "groups."

Two categories are distinguished, the "normal" category in which any symmetrical arrangement that might be present arises naturally from the subject matter and the "heraldic" category in which abstract considerations such as symmetry or continuous patterning dominate the arrangement. Impressions placed under the rubric of "Design Incomplete" are too small or unclear for the type of composition to be identified with certainty. Many of the examples classified under the other categories are also incomplete, but in these cases there are sufficient remains for the composition to be identified. In order to avoid a still lengthier table, many subsidiary elements, including the very common jars, have not been included. Certain groups of themes and outstanding individual seal designs are considered below.

Animal Files or Rows

Aside from the Jemdet Nasr category of staggered rows discussed above, the simplest seal designs are files of one species of animal. Ruminants (III-812, 839), boars (pl. 36:A), lions (pls. 35:A; 38:C–D), and horizontal-winged griffins (pls. 32:A; 42:H, N) all form uniform rows; the latter have at Chogha Mish feline forelegs rather than the bird talons typical for the Susa griffins.[10] Probably only two animals were cut on many seals; this is usually clear in mixed files, such as the lion and bull (cf. pl. 43:C),[11] but is difficult to check on the impressions of uniform files. However, sometimes almost undetectable differences provide clues. On the equatorial seal of III-735 (pl. 236:B) one lion has an attenuated

7. For a parallel to plate 42:L, see Amiet 1972, no. 773 (Susa, old excavation). For a parallel to plate 42:P, see ibid., no. 769, for a strikingly detailed rendering.

8. See also III-743 (dogs and other animals), and IV-2 (ruminants, the one most completely preserved with horns).

9. Note here an aspect of great interest and importance, namely, the circumstance that throughout the duration of Mesopotamian art, normally the primary direction of the action of the representations is toward the right, as in, for example, the Eannatum or Naram Sin stelae.

10. For lions in rows, see Amiet 1972, nos. 495, 498 (both lions; Susa, old excavation). For griffins, see ibid., nos. 585 and 692A (free-field composition), 587 (fragment); Le Brun and Vallat 1978:49, fig. 5:2 (attacking ruminant; XVIII).

11. For examples, see Amiet 1972, nos. 491, 493 (Susa, old excavation); Lenzen 1960, pl. 19:a (Warka, Eanna IV).

neck, pointed muzzle, an ear close to the upper border of the seal, and forelegs rather close together. The other lion's forelegs are more widely spread, its neck stocky, its muzzle square, and its ear lower than that of the first lion. The two lions share one unusual feature; their right forelegs are lifted above the implicit ground line, almost as high as the joint of the hind legs.

Designs showing horned animals tend to be a little more complex than those with carnivores. Different herbivorous species are sometimes combined on one seal, together with accessories. Plant sprays above the backs of animals (pls. 42:F; 143:C, E, H) or in front of them (pls. 42:C; 143:A) are not merely suitable naturalistic adjuncts but suggest the dependence of the herbivores on plants, one of the principal themes of Mesopotamian art from the Protoliterate period onward.[12] In contrast, the appearance of a pinnately branched trunk alongside a large lion seems incongruous (pl. 144:E). Nonetheless, a similar combination occurs on a Susa impression where a plant of the same habit growing on a hillock is flanked by lions[13] and suggests the possibility that the fragmentary design from Chogha Mish could have been part of an antithetical composition.

Occasionally ladder-like elements, both straight and curved, link the animals of a file (pls. 42:D, F; 143:B–G, I).[14] The most likely interpretation seems to be that they represent nets within which the animals are being either trapped or corralled. Many centuries later the theme occurs on a relief of Assurbanipal, where the fear of the trapped deer is vividly expressed.[15] On the Protoliterate cylinder seals the beasts proceed impassively on their way.

REALISTIC ANIMAL GROUPS

Designs showing lions attacking their prey can be characterized as realistic groups although the cases with two lions in symmetrical poses on either side of the victim are almost heraldic. Portions of designs showing a lion jumping at his prey from either the back or front occur (pls. 37:E; 140:A; III-917; IV-342). Groups in which an unfortunate animal is attacked from both sides by lions seem to have been slightly more frequent (probably pls. 43:A; 139:C; bull III-821; III-837; goat III-823–25). Such groups as the plants with animals, express one of the main preoccupations of the Protoliterate craftsmen, namely, the danger that threatened the flocks. The dep-

redations of lions were not an abstract threat in either the Susiana plain or Mesopotamia. Lions did not become extinct in Khuzestan until the nineteenth century.[16] The theme is known on impressions from Susa and Warka[17] and in the later part of the Protoliterate period on stone vessels decorated in relief.[18]

HERALDIC ANIMAL GROUPS AND COMPOSITIONS

In the heraldic compositions lions predominate; they appear in antithetical rampant pairs (pls. 36:E, H; 37:A–B; 43:H–I; 141) and are sometimes linked into continuous friezes by intertwined tails and crossed forelegs (pls. 43:D–E; 141:C–D).[19] Small fragments preserve parts of abstract compositions in which seated lions alternate with jars in two staggered rows, thus forming a pattern consisting of intersecting zigzag bands of lions and jars (pl. 43:J–K). Similarly abstract arrangements of lions and jars combined with other objects occur elsewhere.[20]

Ruminants occasionally appear in formal groups. In one case goats are arranged in symmetrical pairs (III-764). One of two designs with a plant as the central axis has finely-executed antithetical gazelles beside a trunk with a slightly knobbed head; leafy foliage appears over the back of the more completely preserved animal (pl. 43:G). The design is a forerunner of many later Proto-Elamite versions of the theme. In sharp contrast is the linear and clumsy style of an axial design represented by a number of fragmentary impressions (pl. 43:L–O). Pairs of small animals flank a stem with a sparse crown of drill holes. Above, a horizontal ladder-like element suggests the presence of a corral (pl. 143:I). The seal of this impression is already far developed in the direction of the Jemdet Nasr style and possesses a rather close relative in a seal from the Temple Oval at Khafajah.[21] Both are asymmetrical, the central plant element being flanked by two animals on one side and only one on the other. Another similarity is the appearance of two types of horns. The pattern, in which thick vertical bars form a panel enclosing what might be a quadruped with head

---

12. For examples, see Amiet 1972, nos. 523, 526–27 (Susa, old excavation); idem 1961, nos. 171, 174–75 (Warka, Eanna IVa).

13. See Amiet 1972, no. 472 (Susa, old excavation).

14. See ibid., nos. 511, 524–25.

15. Schäfer and Andrae 1925:535 (Nineveh, North Palace of Ashurbanipal) = Barnett 1976, pl. 44 (British Museum, no. 124871).

16. See the vivid description of lions and lion hunts in Layard 1894:185–90.

17. For examples, see Amiet 1972, nos. 507, 509, 521 (Susa, old excavations); Heinrich 1934, pl. 24:e (Warka, Eanna IV).

18. See Frankfort 1954, pls. 5:A (Warka, *Kleinfunde*); 6:A–B (Tell Agrab).

19. For examples, see Amiet 1972, pl. 5:474, 477 (Susa, old excavations); ibid. 1961, no. 196 A (Warka, Eanna IV or III); idem, no. 199 (Eanna IV).

20. See Amiet 1972, nos. 535–36, 561 (Susa, old excavations).

21. See Frankfort 1955, pl. 25:251 (Khafajah, Temple Oval, Jemdet Nasr style seal found in an Early Dynastic II context). For Jemdet Nasr files of animals with horizontal nets, see ibid. 1939a, pl. 8:h (Paris, Bibliothèque Nationale 504).

Figure 19. Examples of Cable (Entwined Snakes) Seal Designs

there and at Susa paratactic versions with heads and tails seem to be the norm.[23] A parallel for the rosette-filled coils (pl. 36:G, I) occurs at Susa.[24] Like the cable designs, the interlace (pl. 43:F) is probably a serpent motif rather than an abstract element; parallels from Warka and Susa have heads and tails (fig. 19).[25]

HUMAN BEINGS AND ANIMALS

Three main categories of themes might be distinguished. In the first, human and animal figures are combined asymmetrically in mixed, paratactic files. In a very elegantly cut design the figures are from right to left a man, a hound, and a boar; the space above the two latter elements is filled by smaller animals (pls. 35:H, J; 146:A). The species of the two main animals suggest that the man behind them should be a hunter; however, he has no weapon. The differences between the lively hunting scenes from Susa and Warka[26] and the Chogha Mish design, in which the regularly arranged figures move with a slow, dignified gait, are striking. Perhaps the clue to the subject-matter lies in the unidentified elongated motif beneath the right elbow of the man.

Much more abstract than the man with the hound and boar are the human beings squatting in the paratactic mixed rows of two-register seals. In one case the man is in the subsidiary register behind a bushy-tailed animal that follows a ruminant (pl. 37:A–B, D).[27] The main register of another design consists of three squatting human figures raising their forearms and a fourth leaning toward the lion in front of him (pl. 138:H). This animal has assumed as best it can the squatting pose of the human figures. It might, perhaps, be a precursor of the animals in human posture that are prominent in the Proto-Elamite glyptic of the following period. The squatting men here are so divorced from any understandable human context that the row seems similar to an arbitrary juxtaposition of figures even though the lion turns his head back toward the man who reaches in his direction. Two similar mixed rows, one with a lion in the same pose (cf. pl. 138:H),

turned back, falls outside the normal range in both design and execution (pl. 34:D).

Some unending cable designs should probably be interpreted as entwined snakes (pl. 142:A–B) comparable to those on the Chogha Mish incised vase but transmuted on the seals into unending motifs by the omission of heads and tails (pls. 34:G; 36:E, G, I). Similar, but not identical, designs occur elsewhere. At Warka continuous cables were sometimes used to form panels filled by eagles or, in one case, bucrania;[22] both

22. Brandes 1979, pls. 26–29 (found in Eanna III level, attributed to IVa [bucrania]), see pl. 25 where heads and tails appear (Warka, Eanna IVa).

23. See Amiet 1972, pl. 6:485–86, 488 (Susa, old excavations); Brandes 1979, pl. 14 (Warka, Eanna IVa).

24. See Amiet 1972, pl. 6:488 (Susa, old excavations).

25. See Brandes 1979, pl. 23 (Warka, Eanna IV); Amiet 1972, pl. 6:483–84 (Susa, old excavations).

26. See Amiet 1972, pls. 13:599–606 (Susa, old excavations).

27. For an impression from Susa with a similar two-register design, see ibid., no. 549 (a mixed file of lion and bull below and a man kneeling with animal above).

from Susa indicate that such compositions were standard at both sites.[28] Perhaps some meaning—long forgotten—underlaid the mixed rows of squatting men and animals. A subsidiary register (pl. 138:H) is formed by three animals whose size and poses are skillfully varied so as to fill the space left over by the irregular heights of the figures below. The horizontal position of the legs of the animals is probably an adaptation to the space available rather than a couchant pose.

A second category of themes is·that in which paired animals and human beings walk in a file. An excellent example is the impression of a finely modeled seal showing two bulls, each guided by a man who holds its tail in his left hand and a bag or a jar in his right (pls. 44:A–B; 145:B). The filling motifs, two bag-like containers and another two-handled jar, fit into the context of the main figures, the domesticated animals and the herdsmen. Susa provides an impression with a very similar design.[29]

Two carefully cut and modeled seals show human beings with animals, but unlike the groups of men holding animals, here the subject matter is uncertain. On III-762 (pls. 35:G–H, J; 133:A–C; 146:A; 149:C; 156:C) the man bends forward slightly over a cylindrical object, the character of which is completely uncertain. It is unwarranted to identify it as an altar, since there is nothing at all to identify it as such. The equatorial seal on ball II-147 (pls. 34:I–K; 146:B; 153:D) is a splendid example of the high quality of Protoliterate modeling. It also bears an unusual design without any close parallels. An object of some sort is being pulled forward by a bull (pl. 146:B). The human figure holds a rein that passes through a ring, the first documentation of an object shown in the inlaid standard of Early Dynastic III from Ur. The object being drawn remains problematical. It could not be a plow since that motif is already well known as a sign on the Protoliterate tablets from Warka and our motif does not have those characteristics. It is possible that the object is a body of a sledge or a chariot, but none of this can be proved. Above the bull are the legs and ventral outline of another animal of uncertain species.

The third category of compositions consists of those in which human and animal figures are woven into formal patterns, which usually express human dominion over animals. Outstanding here is the self-contained, symmetrical group where the master of the animals, forming the central axis, holds antithetical beasts of the

same species. Normally, the only asymmetrical element is the head of the central figure. One of the balls from the R18:312 hoard provides an excellent example of this motif, a master of snakes (pls. 36:F; 156:C).[30] A master of stags also occurs (III-746).

Figures are sometimes combined so as to produce a continuous pattern with no natural breaks. At first glance one design (pl. 145:C) seems to consist of groups of animals and men analogous to the men and cattle of another (pl. 145:B). Two men are shown, one grasping the wild goat behind him by the neck and the other holding his goat by a horn. But this is no ordinary realistic file. Each man holds with his right arm a head that emerges as a secondary element from the bodies of the wild goats and has gazelle horns since, presumably, there is no room for another long goat horn. Thus the men become axial figures faced on either side by horned animal heads and each animal figure belongs simultaneously to two masters. It is striking testimony to the range of Protoliterate art that superbly rendered naturalistic animals with well-observed details could suddenly be equipped with an extra head in order to conflate two discrete themes, the realistic group of an animal guided by a man and the heraldic master of animals into a continuous frieze. There is a masterful balance between the motifs and the background; the figures form an unending even web of pattern across the neutral field that contains them.

A different solution to the problem of transforming a file of men and animals into a continuous pattern is provided by a design reconstructed on the basis of an incomplete impression (pl. 145:D). Here, the two animals have become the primary elements and their escorts have been reduced to mere excrescences from the hindquarters of the animals; the arms of the human torsos grasp the horns of the animals thus creating a continuous pattern.[31] The designs of the four seals (pl. 145:A–D) all render essentially the same motif, but in one case it remains as a naturalistic scene, while in the others it has been transmuted into formal patterns.

HUMAN BEINGS

Themes involving only human figures are more frequently represented at Chogha Mish than those combining animal and human figures. The subjects range from very simple to complex, but almost always the representational aspect outweighs purely decorative considerations. Formal patterns are exceedingly rare, being repre-

28. Ibid., nos. 564–65. There are similar compositions from Susa (ibid., nos. 562–63) that have no squatting animals in the main register.

29. See Le Brun and Vallat 1978, fig. 6:4 (Susa, Acropole I, Level 18). The triangular stylization of the end of the bull's tail anticipates a typical feature of Proto-Elamite glyptic. See also Amiet 1972, pls. 24:996, 102:949 (Susa).

30. A strikingly similar master of snakes occurs on one of the balls of the Warka hoard and has been extensively discussed by Brandes (1979, pls. 17–18).

31. For an analogous composition in which the upper part of a man serves as a master of serpent-necked panthers, see Amiet 1972, pl. 5:475 (Susa, old excavations).

sented by only some of the simplest themes. For the most part the designs are "scenes."

Horizontal Figures: The simplest of all the human themes is that in which the figure of a man covers the entire surface of a seal. Though unusual, it appears in several versions at Chogha Mish, as a completely plain naked man (pl. 152:B), as a cloth bearer (pl. 153), and as a master of snakes (pls. 36:F; 156:C). Examples are found at Susa and Warka[32] and recur in the Early Dynastic and Old Babylonian periods.[33]

The Work of Women: Two large impressions and many small fragments allow the reconstitution of a seal design consisting of two seated women, each with her utensils (pls. 44:D, G; 146:E). The space between them is filled by a scorpion and a dog, whose specific significance, if any, cannot be recovered. Both of the women engage in activities hitherto not known in Protoliterate glyptic. The one on a footed stool spins, holding in her hands a whorl attached to a thread.[34] The other woman, perhaps of lesser status, since she squats only on a mat, extends her arms toward two vessels with large horizontal handles; the most likely interpretation is that she is churning. The type of container characterized by an elongated body and one or more narrow necks is well known among the earliest pictographs as the sign for milk or cream (cf. Falkenstein 1936:46–47, sign 176). Here, for the first time, is a representational scene that can be interpreted as connecting this sign with milk or cream. Of the actual vessels extant, one of pottery from Habuba Kabira South, is of practical size (Sürenhagen 1974–75, pl. 14:86); others are small stone containers, almost certainly for cosmetics.[35] The additional feature

on the representation, the long horizontal handle, might well belong not to the container itself but to a sling by means of which it could be both suspended and shaken back and forth. In the villages around Chogha Mish milk was recently still being churned in skins suspended from tripods of wooden poles (fig. 20).

The jar with large loop handles closing the scene on the left is similar to the two vessels depicted on the seal with herdsmen (pl. 145:B) and might be, as has already been suggested, of a type associated with dairy products. The impressions indicate that the original seal was not as fully modeled as the standard examples. The drill holes by which the base and stopper of the tall jar were formed are still obvious. The arms of the women are angular and stick-like (pl. 44:D, G).[36] This seal in its execution and in the motif of a figure squatting on a low stool provides early Protoliterate antecedents for the drill-hole technique and simplified seated figures characteristic for the Jemdet Nasr style of the later Protoliterate period. It has a relative in a more elaborate design from Susa where the squatting women have attendants.[37]

The Occupations of Men: Many of the seals that showed men engaged in various activities are represented only by a single sealing fragment, with but a small part of the original design, so that it is particularly

36. The same seal apparently impressed a fragment that retains only part of one woman (II-213). The contours of her arms are somewhat more curved, which suggests that the original seal might have had somewhat more detail than is to be seen in these rollings (pl. 44:D, G).

37. See Amiet 1972, no. 674 (Susa, old excavations).

32. See Amiet 1972, no. 595; Brandes 1979, pls. 17–18 (master of snakes; Warka, Eanna IVa). Other motifs were sometimes arranged in the same horizontal manner; see Le Brun and Vallat 1978, fig. 2 (Susa, Acropole I, Level 18).

33. See Early Dynastic example from Tell Asmar, older town wall (Frankfort 1955, no. 535 [master of snakes]) and Old Babylonian examples collected by Amiet 1961, pl. 111:1475 (Pontifical Biblical Institute; van Buren 1940, pl. 1:7), 1476 (Tello; Parrot and Lambert 1954, pl. 14:263), 1477, 1478 (no provenience; Ward 1910:77, fig. 206), 1479 (de Genouillac Collection; Amiet 1957b, pl. 18:106), 1480 (Ur; Legrain 1951, pl. 17:246).

34. The similarity of this scene and the suggested high status of the seated figure to the much later scene of a Neo-Elamite relief from Susa (Porada 1962, fig. 43) is striking. AA

35. See Le Breton 1957:110, fig. 28:40, 46 (Susa, old excavations).

Figure 20. Goat Skin Churn in the Village of Boneh Fazili Near Chogha Mish. Photograph by Diana Rasche-Olson

difficult to reconstitute complete compositions or to identify the activities that are shown. Many designs probably show craft and dairy scenes.

In general, the figures in designs showing activities tend to be relatively small in proportion to the surface of the seal and are accompanied by various objects that are presumably pertinent to the subject matter of the scene. These objects and sometimes the human figures also are arranged quite freely on the field. On the implicit ground line of three examples (pls. 35:I, K; 148:D), squatting men face each other while to the right a standing man bends forward; he might have had a symmetrical partner. Scattered above the figures are a box(?), two triangular elements, and a ring-shaped object. The free-field character of the composition shown on one example (pl. 45:O) and several other small fragments is even more marked. The design included horizontal bars flanked by squatting men with raised forearms and probably a symmetrical pair of standing men bending forward. Both the human figures and the accessorial objects are arranged freely on the field at different levels. Similar compositions are represented by the even smaller fragments (pls. 42:J; 44:C; 148:A–B). Susa provides generally analogous scenes of activities[38] and also parallels for specific elements.[39]

Two fragments show both figures and structures. On the one the lower part of a niched brick building has a ladder alongside it (pls. 44:F; 149:A) and on the other a simple hatched platform supporting domes forms a continuous frieze in the upper part of the seal (pls. 44:E; 149:B).[40] These structures can be identified as granaries on the basis of fairly complete compositions from Susa where men climb steps or a ladder to fill the domes of recessed buildings (cf. Amiet 1972, pl. 16:659–63). On the Chogha Mish fragment the men are presumably occupied with work related to the granaries, perhaps the threshing and measuring of grain (pl. 44:E).

The motifs of several designs consisting only of double or single rows of structures can also be identified as granaries. On the equatorial seal of one of the balls from R18:312, two or three small domes emerge from a plain building (pl. 149:D). On another of the R18:312 balls the equatorial seal consists of a continuous row of tall cylindrical granaries, each crowned with a dome

(III-767). Still another motif on balls of the same hoard, the triangles arranged in two staggered rows (pl. 35:B; 149:C), can be considered as belonging to the same context and interpreted as heaps of grain such as are to be seen today at harvest time dotting the threshing floors adjacent to the villages near Chogha Mish. The triangular element between two men depicted on a sealing (pl. 44:E) is probably also a heap of grain. This interpretation is strengthened by impressions from the old excavations at Susa in which convex heaps or triangles appear in scenes that are either certainly or probably connected with granaries.[41] The seal designs support the reconstruction of the only surviving traces of the lowest register of a Protoliterate stela from Warka as the flattened tops of heaps. Their interpretation as grain fits well with the representation of three mature stalks of grain and an irrigated field full of plants in the uppermost register of the stela.

Men and Jars: Compositions combining the figures of squatting men and jars appear to be the most abstract of the human themes from Chogha Mish. Somewhat more realistic is the design in which a row of squatting men leans forward as if to hold or shake the large jar in front of each of them (pl. 147:H). The tapering bases of the jars appear to be inserted into some kind of stand.[42] Although the vessel is of the same type as two of the jars on the herdsmen seal (pl. 145:B) and another beside the churns (pl. 146:E), it is unlikely that such vessels were linked exclusively with scenes of animal husbandry and the dairy.

The motif of a squatting man with a jar is well known at Susa, where the addition of a second figure sometimes makes the group antithetical.[43] However, the Chogha Mish version of the theme has some unique details. One is a long, narrow projection of uncertain nature emerging from the mouth of the jar. Still more unusual is the placing of large jars, similar to the main one except for their slings, on the heads of the squatting men. So unrealistic is this arrangement that the composition was probably to be affected by the more abstract designs of intersecting zigzags of jars and men. Both at Chogha Mish and Susa the impressions with this theme seem to have been made by seals modeled in a some-

38. See Amiet 1972, nos. 637, 642, 646; Le Brun and Vallat 1978, fig. 6:7, 9 (Acropole I Sounding, Level 18); Lenzen 1960, pl. 15:d (Warka, Eanna IVb); Boehmer 1972b, pl. 19:k (Eanna III).

39. Pair of squatting men flanking horizontal bars = IV-292a (pl. 148:B): for parallels, see Amiet 1972, no. 646 (Susa, old excavations); Le Brun and Vallat 1978, fig. 6:9 (Susa, Acropole I Sounding, Level 18). For a similar object in the form of a large loop (= pl. 42:J), see Le Brun and Vallat 1978, fig. 6:11, 13 (Susa, Acropole I Sounding, Level 18).

40. For a parallel, see Amiet 1972, no. 656 (Susa, old excavations).

41. Ibid., pl. 16:652 (three superimposed rows of three triangles each with a bull and niched building at the left), 656 (a triangular element, presumably a grain heap, flanked by squatting men with a granary at the left), 657 (a row of three convex heaps in a probable granary scene), 662 (two convex heaps beside a granary).

42. The fragments of low pottery rings that might have been used as stands occur among the Protoliterate sherds (pl. 86:U-W) but have much too large a diameter to have been used with jars of this shape.

43. See Amiet 1972, nos. 646 (one group in workshop scene), 650 (two registers; Susa, old excavations).

what simplified style. The motif traveled far beyond its homeland, as shown by peripheral renderings found in coastal Syria.[44]

Files, Porters, and Processions: Paratactic files of figures, usually so identical that it is difficult to determine when the seal design begins to repeat itself, always move to the left. Sometimes no accessories at all appear, as in a file of well-modeled men with bent left arms and extended right arms (pls. 35:D–E; 152:B). For the most part, however, the figures carry objects, the character of which is sometimes difficult to distinguish on poorly impressed or badly weathered impressions (pls. 33:D; 152:D, F). Occasionally, the objects carried might be of such a size and importance as to form a kind of group with their porter (pl. 153:D). In addition to the different subsidiary elements, there is also a considerable range in the style of the files.

One of the balls from the R18:312 deposit has a row of men carrying square box-like objects (pls. 35:G; 152:F). Good parallels for porters carrying their loads on their heads occur on seals[45] and on a larger-scale stone carving. The middle register of the fragmentary stela found during the first season at Warka shows men with loads on their heads. On the badly weathered surface details are uncertain; Brandes sees all the loads as baskets and Strommenger one of them as a jar. The porters of the middle register of the stone vase from the *Kleinfunde* deposit at Warka do not provide quite such a close parallel since they carry their jars and baskets in their hands, not on their heads (cf. Heinrich 1936, pls. 3, 38). However, they are important for their context. They appear in a carefully integrated cycle of representations centered on the functions and worship of the goddess Inanna, who, either herself or in the person of her priestess, received the city ruler in the top, and major, register of the vase. He is accompanied there by two principal offering bearers while the men of the register below are the continuation of his retinue. They thus provide a valuable indication of the ambiance in which the file of porters on the Chogha Mish sealing should be regarded. Though there is nothing in the design to indicate the context, whether secular or otherwise, of the representation, the analogy with the Warka vase suggests that the files of men in some sealings (pl. 33:D; 35:G; 152:D) are probably carrying offerings or tithes to a temple. On the Warka vase the man who follows the

city ruler carries a finely worked robe as the most important gift for the goddess (cf. Strommenger 1962, pl. 21). It has a border, a long fringe, and is crosshatched similar to the garment worn by the city ruler in small-scale scenes on cylinder seals showing him as the focal figure in the cult of Inanna[46] or, with one or two attendants, bringing gifts, among which a crosshatched textile appears.[47] The textile bearer of the Warka vase and the gift bearers of the seals identify one of the more common motifs in the glyptic repertory at Chogha Mish, a man carrying long asymmetrical objects in each hand. Each seal bearing the motif seems to have accommodated two such figures. The quality of the execution varies widely from seal to seal. The design of the most detailed and well-cut version can be completely restored (pls. 45:K–L; 153:B). One man carries asymmetrically-shaped objects ending in a long fringe, a motif frequent on Susa impressions in various contexts and also partly preserved on a Chogha Mish fragment (pl. 153:A–B).[48] The second porter holds aloft long and supple flounced elements[49] and has fringed triangles, corresponding to

---

44. See Amiet 1963b:66, fig. 8 (a more degenerated version: the men hold the tails of the scorpions rather than the handles of the jars; Biredjik; Ashmolean); p. 67, fig. 13 (Chatal Hüyük, Amuq).

45. For file of half-human, half-animal porters, see Amiet 1972, no. 679 (Susa, old excavations). For a single porter carrying a flat object, perhaps a basket, see ibid., no. 622. For a man with a box in a file of three porters, see Boehmer 1972b, pls. 18:c–d; 19:a; 42:a (procession to temple; Warka, Eanna IV-III).

46. See Frankfort 1939, pl. 3:a (Berlin, Vorderasiatische Abteilung 10537; vicinity of Warka), e (Warka, Eanna III, *Kleinfunde* = Heinrich 1936, pl. 17:a); Strommenger 1962a, pl. 16 bottom (Louvre AO 6620; ruler and attendant in a crosshatched kilt).

47. See Frankfort 1939a:19, fig. 2 (Newell Collection, no. 669); pl. 3:d (= Orthmann et al. 1975, pl. 126:d; Tell Billa, the ruler's atypical physiognomy and short robe betray a peripheral hand; his two attendants bring a string of beads and a crosshatched textile as gifts).

48. Held by the mouth and hands of a squatting man in workshop or heraldic compositions, compare Amiet 1972, pl. 15:642, 644–45 (Susa, old excavations); Le Brun and Vallat 1978, fig. 6:13 (Susa, Acropole I, Level 18). Doubled example with a central loop held aloft by a squatting man (ibid., fig. 7:3). Pair emerging symmetrically from vases in heraldic compositions, see Amiet 1972, pl. 15:629, 632–33, 640–41 (old excavations). For rectangularly-shaped variant, see ibid., pl. 15:630 (with other objects in fragmentary design), 646 (workshop scene); Le Brun and Vallat 1978, fig. 7:8 (presentation to temple; Susa, Acropole I, Level 18). In discussing the problem of identifying these fringed elements, Amiet (1972:78) concluded that the men holding them might be basket makers or weavers preparing lashing for jars; he also drew attention to the occurrence of the motif with animals. A sign of the same shape and presumably representing the same type of woven object occurs on an Eanna IV tablet (Falkenstein 1936:79, sign 273). When appearing diagonally over the backs of animals (pl. 42:F), the motif must represent a plant stem, analogous to the stalks of grain crossing the bulls on a seal in the Louvre (Strommenger 1962a, pl. 16, third row, right) and on a stone vessel from Ur (ibid., pl. 28). On crude late Protoliterate seals, one in the British Museum and one from the *Kleinfunde* at Warka, stalks of grain are depicted as approximately triangular, fringed heads (Heinrich 1936, pls. 17:d, 18:b).

49. For an element of the same shape, but emerging from the mouth of a jar, see Amiet 1972, pl. 8:534 (Susa, old excava-

the lower part of the objects carried by the other figure, suspended from his elbow. The same combination of elements is carried by a porter on a sealing from Susa (Amiet 1972, pl. 15:635). The best evidence for interpreting the objects as cloth or robes to be presented to the deity here represented by the standards, is provided by the detailed rendering on the Warka vase of the fringed presentation robe, which bends at the point where it is held.[50] In turn, the design (pl. 153:B) serves to identify the sketchy versions of the motif known from both Chogha Mish (pls. 35:C; 36:E; table 16) and from Susa,[51] in which the character of the objects carried could hardly be recognized without the aid of more precise renderings. These enable us to recognize in the porters of textiles a cult motif belonging to the cycle of themes represented in greatest detail on the Warka vase.

A class of file quite distinct from any of the designs described above is characterized by the sketchily modeled pig-tailed figures wearing robes; they have, in marked contrast to the naked figures of the seals so far discussed, drill-hole heads and stick-like arms. In one design each person bends forward to touch the hair and body of the one in front, forming the only hypotactic frieze of human beings from Chogha Mish (pls. 45:H; 152:C). The rather graceful vivacity of the poses suggests that this design might be a procession of women.[52] There are several other versions of the file of pig-tailed figures, empty-handed (III-921) or more often carrying staves with bulbous tops (pl. 152:G).

The more elaborate of the pig-tailed figures have at their waists what might be quivers (cf. pl. 45:D) and carry staves varying in detail; one is of standard shape but the stem of the other is thicker and ends in a compound head (pls. 45:F–G, I; 152:G). To the right of the two figures preserved are traces of unidentified elements. Neither is the nature of the staves carried by the pig-tailed men certain, but they probably are emblems rather than realistic sticks. Clues to their nature can be found in other representations. A similarly-shaped element serves as the presumably vegetal axis between two gazelles (pl. 43:G). Some figures in renderings of pig-tailed files from Susa carry emblems with the same bulbous tops as at Chogha Mish (Amiet 1972, pl.

19:705–06, and probably 707), but others bear three-branched stems that are clearly vegetal (ibid., pl. 19:718). Late Protoliterate seals from Warka, the majority of them very crudely cut, show the city ruler carrying a large ear of grain, in one case simplified into a bulbous-tipped stick, in the presence of the Inanna symbol.[53] Even more explicit is an impression from Susa where a pig-tailed figure with a stave approaches a niched-brick building.[54] Thus, the evidence available indicates that the pig-tailed files represent processions to a temple in which the participants carry emblems of vegetation, the context being that realm of fertility embodied by the goddess Inanna.

Ritual or Religious Themes: It would undoubtedly be a mistake to try to draw a sharp distinction between secular and religious themes in Protoliterate iconography. A number of the representations discussed above are not really secular, for example, the porters and offering bearers whose links with temple processions and festivals are also indicated above. More overtly ritual and a representative of a theme typical for Protoliterate glyptic is a design showing several figures, not very well preserved, advancing to the left toward a niched building (pls. 34:A–B; 154:A). The pair of gate post emblems[55] as well as analogous designs from other sites[56] identify the building as a temple. Presumably some, at least, of the fragmentary impressions with niched brick buildings belonged to similar designs (cf. table 16). The nature of the continuous niched facades that were the sole motif of some seals is less clear (pls. 38:F; 45:R–S). A fragmentary impression preserves part of what seems to have been a ritual scene with a number of small elements placed freely on the field (pl. 154:A). The nature of the tall conical motif on the left is unclear; although the lower part is somewhat similar to the emblems borne in procession by pig-tailed figures, the traces remaining of its top do not support the reconstruction of a bulbous head. Below the conical element is the upper corner of a niched building. The human figures on the

---

tions). It also appears as a looped double strand in the same craftsmen scenes as the fringed objects (ibid., pl. 15:642, 646).

50. For another version of the same general subject, see the composition showing a temple flanked by two men carrying respectively a double flounced strand and a rectangular fringed object (Le Brun and Vallat 1978, fig. 7:8; Susa, Acropole I, Level 18).

51. Amiet 1972, pl. 13:598 (Susa, old excavations).

52. Figures attendant on a tree assume the same pose at Susa, ibid., pl. 19:710–11.

53. Heinrich 1936, pls. 17:b, d (British Museum); 18:b–c (no Inanna symbol), d.

54. Le Brun 1978c, fig. 9:3 (Susa, Acropole I, Level 17B).

55. Amiet 1972, nos. 456 (stamp seal), 694 (alternating with snakes; Susa, old excavations); Le Brun and Vallat 1978, fig. 7:8 (temple flanked symmetrically by gate posts and figures bearing gifts; Susa, Acropole I, Level 18).

56. Le Brun 1978c, fig. 9:3 (temple on left approached by one figure bearing stave; Susa, Acropole I, Level 17B); Brandes 1979, pl. 30 (two figures advancing to temple at right; Warka, Eanna IVa); Boehmer 1972b:71, pls. 18:c, e; 19:a–c; 42:a (three offering bearers advancing to temple at right; cf. pl. 18:d for an almost exact duplicate; Warka, Eanna IV-III); Lenzen 1961:30–31 pl. 25:a–n, and idem 1960:22; pl. 16:a (procession to temple, with gate post, at left; Warka, Eanna IVa–III); Brandes 1979, pl. 31 (three figures advancing to temple at left; Warka, Eanna III).

fragment have contours of considerable refinement. Above are two persons wearing robes similar to those of the pig-tailed figures in some of the processional designs, but with different coiffures. They appear to be women who raise their arms, perhaps in a gesture of salutation. Below a standing man leans forward with arms outstretched. In front of him is part of what seems to be a kneeling man bending forward. The complete composition must have been a fairly elaborate scene of a ritual or perhaps a meeting of two groups in the area of a temple. Although tantalizing in its incompleteness, sufficient remains to exemplify an extremely rare type of composition in which small-sized figures were not strictly confined to implicit registers. Such a free-field method of composition was particularly suitable for rendering complex scenes involving many figures.[57]

Themes of Conflict: The number and variety of the seal impressions with martial themes suggests the existence of coercive forces and armed conflicts in the Protoliterate period. The simplest composition is the paratactic file of archers, marching to the right in one case and to the left in another (pls. 33:H; 37:F). This subject is also known at Susa.[58] The bows on a small fragment of a ball seem to have been made by two rollings of a seal engraved with either one or two rows of weapons (pls. 45:C; 150:B).[59] Although seal designs already discussed provide precedents for formal rows of a single motif, here it is perhaps possible to interpret the design somewhat more realistically as the contents of an armory. The same ball fragment bears traces of what seems to have been a free-field composition with small figures. Preserved are only a bowman, bending forward in a rather lively manner, and the feet of another figure on the upper right (pl. 150:C).

In the most elaborate rendering of a bowman from Chogha Mish the archer holds in front of him a bow as tall as he (pls. 45:D; 151:A). The marked double curvature of the weapon suggests that it is a compound bow; if so, it is the earliest known representation of that weapon (Yadin 1972:89–91). Projecting diagonally backward from the archer's waist are two narrow, pouch-like elements, which appear in a simpler form at the waists of archers (pl. 33:H) and men (pl. 150:A). These objects are probably quivers. The small-scale figure of a squatting prisoner indicates a scene (pl. 45:D) to be part of a composition showing a battlefield. Both the bowman and the prisoner face toward the left and were presumably once balanced by other figures.

Part of another version of the battlefield theme, occurring on two fragments belonging to different clay balls, shows a soldier facing right and brandishing a weapon, presumably a mace, with which he is about to kill the captive kneeling in front of him (pl. 150:F). In complete battlefield scenes from Warka the focus for analogous victor-and-prisoner groups is the city ruler, who stands on the right side of the representation and looks left toward his victorious soldiers.[60] The design of the battlefield scene (pl. 150:F) could be restored in this way, but in another design (pl. 45:D) the bowman himself faces left. In this case the composition might have lacked a focal figure and consisted instead of several soldiers and conquered enemies, as on two other battlefield designs from Warka.[61]

More complex than the designs described above are two unique representations on clay balls from the deposit in locus R18:312. On the first (pl. 151:B) the composition centers on the figure of the city ruler, a personage always clearly recognizable in Protoliterate monuments both by the major role he plays and by the way he is rendered, with hair in chignon, full beard, markedly muscular torso and arms, and kilt. Here he appears in a hitherto unknown situation, enthroned in a ship as he returns presumably in triumph from a military expedition. In his right hand he holds his mace and in the left the rope binding two supplicating prisoners kneeling in front of him. He is seated not on an ordinary stool but on a bull-shaped throne. The great difference in scale between the city ruler and the retinue surrounding him is extremely rare in Protoliterate art.[62] Several attendants are arranged irregularly in the field and the free-field aspect of the composition might be even more marked if the missing upper section of it were preserved. One of the men squatting at the stern of the ship holds the crescent-shaped standard (cf. pl. 154:B), on a Susa impression (Amiet 1972, pl. 18:691), and as a writing sign on a tablet from Eanna IV at Warka.[63] The crescent emblem adds a religious overtone to the scene of victory.

The second elaborate military scene can be completely reconstructed aside from some subsidiary details (pl. 151:C). The figures who stand on the two lower parts of a niched brick construction identify it as the representation of a fortified city with three tiers of battlements. Its inhabitants lean forward with arms raised in a universal gesture of despair and surrender. Beside the besieged city two conquerors appear to be dispatching a

---

57. The best example is probably an impression from the old excavations at Susa (Amiet 1972, no. 691).

58. Ibid. nos. 688–89; see also Gil Stein 1995, fig. 4, for an example from Anatolia.

59. For bow, see Falkenstein 1936:199, no. 871.

60. Heinrich 1934, pl. 23:a–b = Brandes 1979, pls. 2–3 (Eanna IVb).

61. Brandes 1979, pls. 6, 10 (Eanna IVb and end of Eanna IVa).

62. The nearest approach to it appears to be an impression from Susa, old excavations (Amiet 1972, pl. 18:695).

63. Falkenstein 1936, pls. 1–2, sign 305; interpreted as representing the sun (ibid., p. 60, n. 4).

smaller-scale defender of the city; the lower parts of the figures are missing, so it is not known whether he is kneeling, as it would be expected. The two parts of the composition are not simply juxtaposed, but graphically linked by the gesticulating soldier, who turns his head right toward the city. Two of the elements in the field might be greatly enlarged representations of the ovoid clay slingshots frequent at Chogha Mish in the Susiana and Protoliterate periods. Despite their simplicity, slingshots of the same shape, only made of stone or flint, were still being used by Assyrian armies of the first millennium B.C. They are shown in reliefs of Sennacherib[64] and numerous examples were excavated at Lachish.[65]

The Chogha Mish siege scene was a startling discovery from several points of view. At the time that it was found, it provided the only tangible evidence for the existence of city walls in the Protoliterate period, since those at Habuba Kabira had not yet been excavated (Strommenger 1980a:32, fig. 12 and end paper). Moreover, it showed that already in the initial period of Mesopotamian art the main features of a victorious siege scene had been formulated. The seal on which the siege was engraved was larger than usual, but even so it was a tour de force to visualize and fit so complicated a subject into such a small compass. In essentials the representation is comparable to the much later sieges of fortified cities shown on Assyrian reliefs of the ninth to seventh centuries B.C. Very little exists to fill the great gap of over twenty-five hundred years. An incomplete seal design from Ur, probably of the Early Dynastic I period, resembles the Chogha Mish siege scene in general composition: a pair of contestants and three figures on top of an architectural facade on which two men gesture their surrender and a woman tears her hair (Legrain 1936, pl. 388). One soldier engraved on a shell plaque of the Early Dynastic III period from Mari shelters behind a large shield and another aims his arrow upward, presumably toward a besieged fortress shown on another plaque.[66] On an incomplete Middle Assyrian seal impression from Assur a fortified city is actively defended by the small figures on its battlements.[67] Isolated though these examples are, they suggest that the theme of the beleaguered fortress did exist in the repertory of

Mesopotamian art. The elaborate character of the Middle Assyrian version implies that it was not an isolated work. Battle and siege scenes could have been executed in painting in the Middle Assyrian period, as military themes had been in the Old Babylonian palace at Mari. Painted siege scenes might have existed in the Akkadian period since representations of fortified cities in their settings were executed in relief (cf. Kraus 1948:81–92). Thus, it is quite likely that there was a more continuous tradition linking such Protoliterate scenes (e.g., pl. 151:C) and Assyrian art than is exemplified by extant examples.

There is an important contemporary parallel for the Chogha Mish siege scene. On an impression from Susa the city ruler plays an exceptionally active role. With his arrows he has slain three men, one rendered on a large-scale; their bodies lie between him and a niched structure, which Amiet interpreted as a platform supporting a temple decked with horns, perhaps the ruler's residence (Amiet 1972:82, 107, no. 695). However, if the Chogha Mish and Susa compositions are parallel in conception and composition, the latter can be considered as representing the moment at which the main defender of a fortified community has been vanquished and his city set afire.

The Orchestra Seal: Five small sealing fragments found near the bottom of the great beveled-rim bowl deposit on the southeastern side of the Circular Structure, P18:301 and the adjacent Q18:308, enable a remarkable composition to be reconstituted (pls. 45:N; 155:A). The main figure, perhaps a woman, is distinguished not by size but by her function as the focus of the entire composition. She squats on a cushion; in front of her is a low table with vessels. Like the city rulers of battlefield scenes, she is on the right side of the composition and looks toward the left. All but one of the five other figures face her. An attendant holding a spouted jar and a three-necked milk vessel bends toward her. This tightly knit group has as its pendant on the left four squatting musicians and various adjuncts of the feast[68] arranged in a free-field manner. One man plays a four-stringed harp, which here in its first appearance is already part of

---

64. Ussishkin 1982:78–79, fig. 66 (Segment I, slingers = left side); pp. 80–81, fig. 67 (Segment II, pair of small slingers with pile of sling stones in front of them; above near city wall large sling stones are silhouetted against "scaly" hills); p. 95, fig. 75 (detail of Segment I: slingers); p. 96, fig. 76 left (line drawing of slinger).

65. Ibid., p. 56, fig. 47 (pile of flint sling stones ca. 6 cm in diameter).

66. Yadin (1972:89–94) indicates the importance of the plaque as the representation of a siege.

67. Weber 1920, no. 531 (Berlin VAT 7847); cf. also Porada 1967, fig. 5.

68. Some are pottery vessels: a standard two-handled jar and, probably, two bowls. The identity of the round object with what appears to be two horizontal handles is unknown. Finally, an object resembling a fish except for the asymmetry of its tail rests on a mat. The identification is supported by evidence from the Early Dynastic period such as the fish represented in the field of a banqueting scene on a votive plaque from Nippur (Boese 1971, pl. 16:1) or the two pairs brought as part of the supplies on the inlaid standard from the royal tombs at Ur (Woolley 1934, pl. 91 = Strommenger 1962b, pl. 10). Imprints of this motif on both the fragments with the musicians and with the banqueter enabled the complete design of the seal to be reconstituted.

the ensemble.[69] Below, a man extends his arms over the flat top of an object which, though not completely preserved on the sealing, is restored as a drum. The third man holds two horn-shaped objects, the narrow part of one of them touching his mouth. He is blowing one horn or an instrument in that shape, while holding in reserve another, possibly one of a different pitch. The fourth person places his hand against his cheek in an attitude well known for both ancient and modern Near Eastern singers. We have here what appears to be the earliest known representation of an ensemble with the essential elements of an orchestra, musicians playing string, percussion, and wind instruments accompanying a singer. Furthermore, this ensemble appears as part of a feast, so that the whole seal design is the first known representation of the union of music and feasting so universal in later periods.[70] Here, though not explicitly indicated, we might assume that the music and banquet are in celebration of a religious festival, particularly since later Mesopotamian renderings of the theme have ritual connotations.

This representation is of exceptional interest for the history of music and as additional evidence for the scope of the cultural achievements of the Protoliterate period. In addition, it proves that yet another of the major themes of Mesopotamian art began in this formative stage. In the Early Dynastic period feasters entertained by music are frequently represented. They appear in relief on stone votive plaques[71] and cylinder seals,[72] as well as on the "peace" side of the standard from the royal tombs at Ur (Woolley 1934, pls. 90–93). The theme survived into much later times, as for example in the well-known Late Assyrian version, Assurbanipal's

banquet in celebration of his victory over Elam (Barnett 1976, pls. 63–65).

CONCLUSIONS

After this survey of the seal designs from Chogha Mish, a few words of summary concerning iconography and style are in order. Also the pertinence of the evidence from Chogha Mish for the question of regional and chronological groups in Protoliterate glyptic is briefly considered. It has already become clear that the motif and the compositional scheme of a seal are usually so intimately linked that, given the one, the other can often be visualized (cf. table 16). The range of motif is great. The rarer themes are the geometric elements that occasionally occur as the main element on a seal. The commoner themes are animals and human beings arranged in relatively realistic scenes. On the other hand, representational motifs were also frequently used as elements of formal heraldic designs. The homogeneity of the glyptic iconography from sites as close together as Chogha Mish and Susa is hardly surprising. In addition, it has been possible to cite numerous parallels between the Chogha Mish seal impressions and the glyptic; and other works of art from Warka or elsewhere in southern Mesopotamia have been cited above. Although the iconography of the Chogha Mish sealings and of Protoliterate art as known from Sumer is essentially the same, it is likely that there are some regional divergences between the Susiana and Mesopotamian repertories. Amiet pointed out some time ago that the horizontal-winged griffin popular at Susa, as it is also at Chogha Mish, hardly occurs in Mesopotamia.[73] Neither do we have from there as many scenes of men engaged in various activities. Also absent from Mesopotamia is the man squatting in a row with animals.

The absence of elaborate war scenes might be an accident; the "city ruler" in a chariot does occur on a tablet from Warka, although it might not be a war scene.[74] On the other hand, the serpent-necked panthers so popular at Warka are not known at all at Chogha Mish and occur only once at Susa.[75] Neither have the Susiana sites provided examples of the city ruler with flocks and vegetation or of animals emerging from huts, both being typical major themes at Warka nor does the scene with animals associated with the Inanna symbol occur in Susiana.

The majority of the seals documented by the Chogha Mish impressions were cut in a refined manner

69. For early representations of the harp, see Falkenstein 1936:96, sign 349; pl. 10:197; 28:331 Vs; 43:419; 47:501 Vs (Warka, Eanna IV tablets); Hartman 1960:298–300, figs. 2–5 (Ur, Archaic strata sealings, probably Early Dynastic I); ibid., p. 309, fig. 13 (Early Dynastic III). For later examples and discussions of harps and other instruments, see Biggs 1968:6–12; Hartman 1960; Stauder 1957; idem 1970.

70. For example, see the remarks of Odysseus to Eumaeus: "And I mark that in the house itself many men are feasting; for the savor of meat arises from it, and therewith resounds the voice of the lyre, which the gods have made the companion of the feast" (Homer, *The Odyssey,* Book XVII, lines 267–71 [Cowper 1913]); and of Sancho Panza to Don Quixote: "... but music is always a sign of feasting and merriment" (Miguel de Cervantes, *Don Quixote* [Cohen 1959]).

71. Boese 1971, pls. 1:AG2 (Tell Agrab, Shara Temple, Early Dynastic II), 5:CT2 (= Frankfort 1939a, pl. 107, 187; Khafajah, Temple Oval, House D, Room IX, Early Dynastic II), 9:CS7 (= ibid., pl. 108:188, Khafajah, Sin Temple IX, Early Dynastic II), 17:N6 (= Hansen 1963, pl. 6; Nippur, Inanna Temple VIIB, Early Dynastic IIIa), 38:K2 (Basel, Sammlung Erlenneyer).

72. Woolley 1934, pls. 193:18, 21; 194:222; 200:102 = Amiet 1961, nos. 1180, 1192–94 (Ur, Royal Cemetery, Early Dynastic III).

73. Amiet 1957a:126; idem 1972:76; see also Le Brun and Vallat 1978:224. For a horizontal-winged griffin, see Lenzen 1964, pls. 26:g, 28:c (Warka, Eanna IV).

74. Heinrich 1934, pl. 28:c; Amiet 1961, no. 663 (Warka, Eanna IVb).

75. Amiet 1972, nos. 475–76 (Susa, old excavations).

characterized by an elegance of linear outline and a sophistication of modeling described above in the discussion of various individual designs. Such seals represent what might be termed the standard style of early Protoliterate glyptic; it is essentially the same whether it appears in southern Mesopotamia, the Susiana area, or far away to the west at Habuba Kabira South. Nevertheless, within the standard style there seems to be some local variations. For example, in Susiana even the more elaborately cut seals rarely render such details as the eyes of animal and human figures or the ears of lions silhouetted against their necks, which do occur at Warka.[76] Until new evidence proves otherwise, it seems reasonable to assume some local variations in iconography between the Susiana and Mesopotamian areas.

A few impressions document seals cut in what appears to represent an inchoate manner and bear, for the most part, compositions that do not fit well into normal categories, except for the individual motif of the man carrying cloth. The exaggerated and awkward shapes, with which the theme is rendered on one sealing (pl. 45:M), are far removed from the carefully-observed body contours and assured symmetrical curves of cloth on another (pl. 153:D). One fragment (pl. 45:M) represents a coarse or rustic group of seals in which the figures do not have the sensitive outlines or modeling characteristic of the standard style. Bodies tend to be puffy and large in proportion to the size of the seal. There is little of that careful balance between motifs and the plain background against which they are silhouetted, a balance so characteristic for the seals of the standard style. Other certain and a probable renderings of a man carrying cloth were found; instead of the standard arrangement in a uniform file, he appears with a crude lion (pl. 34:G) or with a squatting man (pl. 38:A–B). Other designs show square-shouldered men in stolid rows lacking the movement in one direction that is characteristic of the normal Protoliterate files (pls. 34:F; 35:F). An impression made by a large seal provides a striking example of the rustic style (pl. 144:F). The two human figures crowded tightly together with various elements of uncertain nature conform to neither the iconographic or stylistic norms of standard Protoliterate glyptic. These iconographic and technical details do not necessarily represent a developmental stage. Rather, one can presume that the rustic-style impressions represent the attempts at seal cutting of undisciplined craftsmen. Such seals are rare in comparison with those of normal style and are unified only by the inchoate character of both their style and iconography.

It is possible to distinguish a third stylistic category which is not, however, sharply divided from the standard one but rather represents a subgroup characterized by a predilection for certain subjects executed in a relatively simple manner. What might be called the simplified style can be defined by the decreased emphasis on natural detail and modeling. Arms, for example, become stick-like, losing the natural contours of swelling muscles. Fewer details, whether they be elements of the main motifs or filling motifs, are included. The seals of the simplified style do not seem, similar to the rustic group, to be merely the products of less competent workmen, but to represent a real stylistic variation correlated with specific motifs. Such seals are important in connection with the emergence of the Jemdet Nasr style of glyptic characteristic for the later part of the Protoliterate period.

In place of the rich iconography of early Protoliterate glyptic, the themes of the representational Jemdet Nasr seals tend to be stereotyped and simple. Prototypes for three of the commoner categories occur at Chogha Mish. The Jemdet Nasr human figures seated on low stools and, hardly distinguishable as male or female, are descended from such seal designs (pl. 146:E), where the scene of two women possesses many more accessorial details than its successors.[77] Files of pigtailed figures[78] and the staggered rows of fish and quadrupeds of the Jemdet Nasr style are heralded at Chogha Mish by processions (pl. 152:C, G) and animal rows (pls. 41:C; 42:L–M; 138:C–E). In the later period the motifs arranged in staggered rows are for the most part limited to ovals and fish; they appear in innumerable versions, while quadrupeds are scarce and turtles[79] and scorpions[80] exceptional. In contrast, Chogha Mish shows that earlier a single site can provide a greater variety of staggered-row motifs, with triangles, granaries, and squatting men in addition to these just mentioned.[81] Moreover, though the Chogha Mish pig-tailed figures have stick-like arms and sometimes drill-hole heads,

76. For impressions from Susa showing eyes, see Le Brun 1978c, fig. 9:3, pl. 8:3 (Susa, Acropole I, Level 17B). Many ancient impressions are, of course, too carelessly made and too weathered to show the true quality of the execution of the seals in question.

77. See Amiet 1972, nos. 721–36 (Susa, old excavations); Frankfort 1955, nos. 480 (Tell Asmar, Single Shrine, Abu Temple), 871 (Tell Agrab, Shara Temple, Early Dynastic II context; both from Diyala sites); Amiet 1961, nos. 330–38 (various sites and collections).

78. See Amiet 1972, no. 718 (Susa, old excavations); Mackay 1931, pl. 73:24 (Jemdet Nasr); Frankfort 1955, No 872 (Tell Agrab, Shara Temple, Early Dynastic II contexts).

79. For a seal with four rows of remarkably lively turtles in the Iraq Museum, Baghdad, see Amiet 1961, no. 303. Apparently stylized, and later(?), versions occur on a seal from the Warka area (ibid., no. 355).

80. Amiet 1961, no. 365 (with two rows, not staggered; Brussels, Musées Royaux du Cinquantenaire).

81. Ovals, however, appear only on the extant seals, which are indistinguishable from the normal reduced Jemdet Nasr type.

their execution is by no means reduced to the unretouched drill holes and gouges that prevail later. Fish (pl. 138:C) and an analogous impression from Susa[82] and quadrupeds (pl. 138:E) are rendered with a greater elegance of detail than in the standard Jemdet Nasr rows.[83] It might, in fact, be a misplaced emphasis to speak of the staggered rows and the other designs in question as Jemdet Nasr themes; rather the later occurrences of them should probably be considered as simplified versions of designs that had flourished earlier.

The appearance in the same contexts at Chogha Mish of standard early Protoliterate impressions and those that anticipate the Jemdet Nasr style of glyptic indicates both the contemporaneity of the two categories and the considerable range of variations in the glyptic. Moreover, the presence already in the early period of what can be called Jemdet Nasr type seals is an indicator of the unity of the artistic tradition of the Protoliterate period. Within it there was at no point a sharp break or shift in character cutting simultaneously across the different categories of material culture. Although the changes in specific cultural manifestations are sufficient for the characterization of, for example, markedly different styles of early and late Protoliterate art, these are only outstanding poles linked, both synchronously and consecutively, by intermediate versions. It is thus understandable that difficulties sometimes arise in attributing works undated by their contexts to a particular phase of the Protoliterate period. The Chogha Mish seal impressions anticipating features of the Jemdet Nasr glyptic style provide a good example of the underlying consistency of Protoliterate civilization. There is, however, a very significant complication which must be at least briefly discussed.

The glyptic falls into place alongside the other major categories of evidence discussed above, such as the pottery and the economic records with numerical notations, to show that the inhabitants of Chogha Mish shared in the mainstream of Protoliterate civilization. In general, during the early Protoliterate period the entire Susiana plain formed part of the central area of Protoliterate civilization, providing finds so homogeneous with those from southern Mesopotamia that one chronological and cultural term applies to both areas. This is not, however, the case in the later part of the Protoliterate period (phases c–d). Then, despite the tremendous number of earlier elements continuing in changing forms, significant indications of marked regional individuality emerge, above all in the appearance of the Proto-Elamite script reflecting a language altogether distinct from Sumerian. It is a striking circumstance that in the phases following the cultural koiné of the early Protoliterate period the Susiana area displays

so much individuality in script and in glyptic art that the term Protoliterate would be a misnomer. Although the Jemdet Nasr types of seals do appear commonly at Susa, they represent the simplification of antecedents (types) that are typical for the preceding period at Chogha Mish and fade into insignificance alongside the striking developments of the Proto-Elamite style. Major historical events must lie behind the emergence of Proto-Elamite writing and glyptic. Such specialized and elaborate cultural manifestations might well mirror political and dynastic struggles that brought to power groups of people who, while sharing a common heritage with the peoples of southern Mesopotamia, were now able to express their own individuality and to lay the foundations of their own characteristic political institutions. The extent, if any, to which the translocation of populations was involved can hardly be specified, but it seems justifiable to speculate that Chogha Mish was deserted during a time of turmoil at the end of the early Protoliterate period.

In the great phase of Protoliterate expansion during the early part of the period, colonies in the west along the Euphrates (Strommenger 1980a) and enclaves such as that at Godin on the Iranian plateau (Young 1974:80–90; Weiss and Young 1975) were probably the vehicle of influence on regions far from Susiana and southern Mesopotamia.[84] The seals, as easily portable and also highly attractive objects, and sealings were certainly important carriers of elements of Protoliterate iconography. Some of the best evidence for Protoliterate influence is provided by seals or sealings, often representing local versions of Protoliterate originals, from the Iranian plateau and Syria.[85] Glyptic, perhaps borne directly by boats from the Persian Gulf, was undoubtedly the medium through which some knowledge of Protoliterate art reached as far afield as Egypt.[86] The adoption of a number of characteristic early Protoliterate motifs by Predynastic Egyptian craftsmen testifies to the impact of Protoliterate art in a country that had already been developing its native traditions for many centuries. Moreover, the example of Protoliterate art seems to have exerted a profound catalytic influence that resulted in the appearance in the Gerzean period of new themes of a historical character (Kantor 1974:227–56).

84. For southern Anatolia, see Burney 1980. For the Iranian plateau, see Majidzadeh 1976.

85. In addition to Godin, Sialk IV, see Ghirshman 1938, pl. 31:5. For western Syria, see Amiet 1963b:57–83; Buchanan 1966, nos. 703–16.

86. Graves at Naga ed-Der, an Upper Egyptian site located close to the Wadi Hammamat, which connects the Red Sea and the Nile Valley, contained a Protoliterate stamp and cylinder seal (Lythgoe and Dunham 1965:75, fig. 31; p. 318 f., fig. 142:e; Kantor 1952, pl. 25:B). Several other seals of Jemdet Nasr style, either imports or close imitations, are known from Egypt (Kantor 1952:243, fig. 1:A–F; Boehmer 1974:495–514).

82. Amiet 1972, no. 769 (Susa, old excavations).

83. For fish, see Mackay 1931, pl. 73:6, 20, 23 (Jemdet Nasr).

Table 16. Conspectus of the Iconography of the Protoliterate Glyptic at Chogha Mish
(* = designs with two registers of equal importance)

MOTIF	Stamp Seal	Row or File Uniform	Mixed	Single-Register Cylinder Seal Groups Normal	Heraldic	Subsidiary Element	Design Incomplete	Multiple-Register Cylinder Seal Standard Type Main Register	Subsidiary Register	Jemdet Nasr Type	Free-Field Cylinder Seal
GEOMETRIC											
Triangles (heaps of grain?)	—	—	—	—	—	—	—	—	—	Pls. 35:B; 133:A	—
Checkerboard	—	—	—	—	—	—	III-936 (H14:304)	—	—	—	—
Squares + bag-like filling motif	—	—	—	—	—	—	III-811 (R18:305)	—	—	—	—
Cross with coils; in panel	—	—	—	—	Pl. 43:E	—	—	—	—	—	—
Crescents	—	—	—	—	—	—	—	—	—	III-733 (N9:302)	—
Kidneys	—	—	—	—	—	—	—	—	—	III-842–43 (Q18:312)	—
Interlace	—	—	—	—	—	—	Pl. 43 F; III-844 (Q18:312)	—	—	—	—
Cable (headless snakes?)	—	Pls. 142: A–B; 36:E, G, I	—	—	—	—	—	—	—	III-923 (R18:309)	—
Ovals	—	—	—	—	—	—	—	—	—	Pl. 41:D	—
PLANT											
Plant-like scrolls	—	—	—	—	—	—	Pl. 42:B	—	—	—	—
Vertical stalk	—	—	—	—	Pl. 42:O	Pls. 135:L; 143:A	—	—	—	—	—
Branch	—	—	—	—	—	Pls. 136:F; 42:C; 43:G	—	—	—	—	—
Rosette	—	—	—	—	—	Pls. 36:G, I; 142:A	—	—	—	—	—
ANIMAL											
Scorpion	Pl. 135:K	—	—	—	—	—	—	—	—	IV-280 (H15:405)	—
Spider	Pl. 135:H	—	—	—	—	—	—	—	—	—	—
Ant	Pl. 42:A	—	—	—	—	—	—	—	—	—	—
Fish	—	—	—	—	—	Pl. 138:C	—	—	—	Pls. 41:C; 42 L; 138:A; III-829 (Q18:315)	—
Turtle	Pl. 34:G; 135:J	III-746 (H14:305); III-757 (R18:312)	—	—	—	Pl. 135:J; III-744a (H14:310)	—	—	—	—	—
Snake (cf. Cable)		—	—	—	III-924 (R18:309)	Pls. 36:F; 156:C	—	—	—	Pl. 42:S	—
Bird		—	—	—	—	III-837 (Q18:318)	—	—	—	—	—
Quadruped(s)		III-839 (Q18:307)	—	—	Pl. 34:D	—	III-871 (P18:301)	—	—	Pl. 42:M	—
Ruminant(s)	—	III-812 (Q18:314); Pl. 145:B; III-851 (R17:308)	—	III-800 (R18:305)	III-764 (R18:312); Pl. 43:G, L-O	—	Pls. 42:C; 145:A	—	IV-2* (H15:401 South)	IV-9 (J15:402)	—
Horned with nets	—	Pls. 42:D; 143:B, E		—	—	—	III-920 (R18:305)	—	—	—	—

Table 16. Conspectus of the Iconography of the Protoliterate Glyptic at Chogha Mish (*cont.*)
(* = designs with two registers of equal importance)

MOTIF	Stamp Seal	Row or File Uniform	Mixed	Single-Register Cylinder Seal Groups Normal	Heraldic	Subsidiary Element	Design Incomplete	Multiple-Register Cylinder Seal Standard Type Main Register	Subsidiary Register	Jemdet Nasr Type	Free-Field Cylinder Seal
ANIMAL (*cont.*)											
Bull	—	—	Pl. 34:J	—	—	—	III-918 (P18:301); III-932 (N9:302)	—	—	—	—
Boar	—	Pl. 36:A	Pl. 35:J	—	—	—	—	IV-9 (J15:402)	—	—	—
Carnivore	—	—	—	—	—	—	—	—	Pl. 42:I*	IV-5 (H15:401)	—
Carnivore(s) and ruminant(s)	—	—	Pl. 139:A, C–E	—	Pl. 141:A	III-810 (R18:305)	—	III-743* (H14:310)	—	—	—
Dog	—	—	Pl. 35:J	—	—	—	—	—	—	—	—
Lion(s)	—	Pls. 35:A; 38:C–D; 136:B	—	—	Pls. 36:E, H; 37:A–B; 43 :D–E, H; III-847 (R17:303)	Pl. 38:B	Pls. 38:C, D; 42:G; 43:A; III-770 (R18:312); III-848 (R17:303)	—	—	—	—
Lion(s) and bull(s)	—	—	Pl. 43:C	II-837 (Q18:318); III-917 (P18:301)	—	—	Pls. 37:E; 43:A	—	—	—	—
Lions and jars	—	—	—	—	Pl. 43:J–K; III-809 (R18:305)	—	—	—	—	—	—
Lions with wings	—	—	—	—	—	—	Pl. 42:K	—	—	—	—
Griffin(s)	—	Pls. 32:A; 136:C; IV-394 (R21:407)	—	—	—	—	Pl. 42:H, N; III-931 (N9:302)	—	—	—	—
HUMAN											
Human beings squatting with animals	—	—	—	—	—	—	—	Pl. 138:H; IV-5 (H15:401)	Pl. 37:B, D; 148:F	—	—
Women's activities	—	—	—	Pls. 146:E; 152:G; 153:C							
Men's activities	—	—	—	Pl. 38:A, B	—	—	Pls. 33:G; 44:C; III-828 (P18:301); III-860 (East Area)	—	—	—	Pls. 35:I, J; 45:O
Man standing with animals	—	—	Pls. 34:I–J; 35:H, J; 36:D	—	—	—	—	—	—	—	—
Man guiding animals	—	—	Pl. 145	—	—	—	—	—	—	—	—
Master of animals	—	—	—	—	III-746 (H14:305); cf. pl. 36:F	—	Pl. 34:H	—	—	—	—
Plain	—	III-746 (H14:305)	—	—	—	—	IV-279 (H15:405)	—	—	—	—
Master of animals	—	Pl. 36:F	—	—	—	—	—	—	—	—	—
Activities with granaries	—	—	—	Pl. 44:E–F; III-850 (East of R17:303)	—	—	II-361 (R17:208)	—	—	—	—
Squatting with jars	—	—	—	Pls. 33:E; 147:E–H	—	—	Pl. 33:J; II-351 (R17:212)	—	—	—	—

Table 16. Conspectus of the Iconography of the Protoliterate Glyptic at Chogha Mish (*cont.*)
(* = designs with two registers of equal importance)

MOTIF	Stamp Seal	Row or File Uniform	Mixed	Single-Register Cylinder Seal Groups Normal	Heraldic	Subsidiary Element	Design Incomplete	Multiple-Register Cylinder Seal Standard Type Main Register	Subsidiary Register	Jemdet Nasr Type	Free-Field Cylinder Seal
Squatting	—	—	—	—	—	—	IV-390 (J15:403)	—	—	IV-291 (R18:413)	—
Standing rustic-style figures	—	Pl. 34:F	—	Pls. 35:F; 144:D, F	—	—	—	—	—	—	—
Porters	—	Pls. 33:D; 35:G; 152:D, F	—	—	—	—	—	—	—	—	—
PORTERS OF CLOTH:											
Standard figures	—	Pls. 34:K; 35:C; 45:P; III-761, 764, 770, 778 (all R18:312); IV-293 (R18:413); IV-388 (J15:403 Southeast)	—	Pl. 153:D	—	—	—	—	—	—	—
Rustic-style figures	—	—	Pls. 34:G; 38:B	—	—	—	Pl. 45:M; III-868a (P18:301)	—	—	—	—
PROCESSIONS:											
Standard figures	—	Pls. 35:D–E; 152:B	—	—	—	—	IV-393 (R21:407)	—	—	—	—
Pig-tailed figures	—	Pl. 152:C, E, G; III-919 (R18:Trench XX); III-921(North of Q18:308)	—	—	—	—	—	—	—	—	—
With niched-brick building	—	—	—	Pls. 34:A–B; 154:A	—	—	—	—	—	—	Pl. 155:C
Banquet with music	—	—	—	—	—	—	—	—	—	—	Pl. 155:A
WAR											
Archers	—	Pls. 33:H; 37:F–G; 150:D; III-772 (R18:312); III-842 (Q18:312)	—	Pl. 45:D; 151:A	—	—	—	—	—	—	—
Bows and arrows	—	Pl. 45:C	—	—	—	—	—	—	—	—	—
Battlefield scenes	—	—	—	Pl. 151:A	—	—	—	—	—	—	Pl. 45:D
Siege of city	—	—	—	Pl. 151:C	—	—	—	—	—	—	—
Ruler in boat	—	—	—	—	—	—	—	—	—	—	Pl. 151:B
ISOLATED STRUCTURES OR HEAPS											
Granaries	—	III-767 (R18:312)	—	—	—	—	—	—	—	Pl. 35:K	—
Grain Heaps	—	—	—	—	—	—	—	—	—	Pls. 149; 35:B	—
Niched-brick building	—	Pls. 38:F; 45:R–S; 149:F	—	—	—	—	Pl. 33:B–C; III-857a (R19:302); III-866a–c (P18:301); III-867 (Q17:304); III-922 (R18:309)	—	—	—	—

Table 16. Conspectus of the Iconography of the Protoliterate Glyptic at Chogha Mish (*cont.*)
(* = designs with two registers of equal importance)

MOTIF	Stamp Seal	Row or File Uniform	Mixed	Single-Register Cylinder Seal Groups Normal	Heraldic	Subsidiary Element	Design Incomplete	Multiple-Register Cylinder Seal Standard Type Main Register	Subsidiary Register	Jemdet Nasr Type	Free-Field Cylinder Seal
EMBLEMS											
Standard	—	—	Pl. 154: A–B	—	—	—	—	—	—	—	—
Gate post	—	—	Pls. 34:A; 154:A	—	—	—	III-774 (R18:312)	—	—	—	—
Hut symbol	—	—	—	—	—	—	Pl. 45:Q	—	—	—	—

CHAPTER 8

THE PREHISTORIC AREAS

THE SUSIANA SEQUENCE

Problems concerning the sequence of prehistoric cultures in the Susiana plain have been the concern of archaeologists since the 1890s when the *Délégation Française en Perse* directed by Jacques de Morgan discovered graves with magnificent painted pottery at Susa (de Morgan 1900:183–88, figs. 17–19). For many years this pottery was considered to be the earliest in the entire region and even beyond. Gradually the work of the *Délégation Française en Perse* at small sites near Susa and at Tappeh Musyan in the Deh Luran area to the northwest proved that the discoveries at Susa represented only the latest of several stages in a long prehistoric development. Since the different stages were not found stratified at any single site, it taxed the ingenuity of a number of scholars to arrange them into a valid chronological sequence; comparisons with distantly related pottery from stratified sites outside Khuzestan were sometimes relied on for guidance.[1] In 1957 Le Breton, with the aid of additional soundings, presented a very important and influential synthesis covering both the prehistoric and later periods, and in 1969 Dollfus began large-scale excavations at Jafarabad, Jowi, and Bandebal, which are providing a wealth of documentation (Le Breton 1957; Dollfus 1971; idem 1975).

While the Oriental Institute's main concern in Khuzestan at the beginning of the 1960s was the Protoliterate period, it became apparent that Chogha Mish had been occupied during all the cultural phases discovered in the sites near Susa and that, in addition, it also possessed new types of pottery which were earlier than anything then known in central Khuzestan. Accordingly, the investigation of the stages of development preceding the Protoliterate period, and in particular of the new period which was termed Archaic, became one of the major aims of the expedition. The work has not been limited to problems of stratification and the sequence of cultural phases or of continuity and discontinuity in development. The site has been tested in a

fairly large number of strategically-located areas with the goal of establishing patterns of settlement that might provide clues to the density of the population and the character of the community, thus obtaining some general historical insight into the region as a whole. For this purpose information from other sites, provided not only by surface surveys but also by actual excavation, is important. For instance, the discovery of an Archaic occupation at Boneh Fazili, about 3 km to the northwest of Chogha Mish, suggests a density of settlement at that period which has not been indicated by surface surveys. A general discussion of the prehistoric periods, a brief indication of the chronological sequence obtained, and the terminology adopted facilitate the review of the individual areas that follow.

The Susiana sequence as proposed by Le Breton is, in general, confirmed by the large quantities of stratified material from Chogha Mish. It is both practical and fair, therefore, to retain his term "Susiana" as the general name for all the prehistoric periods. In order to avoid any terminological confusion between the regional Susiana sequence and the phases at Susa itself (e.g., Susiana *e* = Susa A = Susa 1) and also to indicate which of Le Breton's divisions are considered to be subphases within a larger cultural period, his lowercase letter designations were abandoned in favor of "Early," "Middle," and "Late," to which is added Archaic.[2] The main deviation from Le Breton's classification is to consider his three middle phases, namely Susiana *b*, *c*, and *d*, as subdivisions of the Middle Susiana period. The Chogha Mish Early Susiana and Late Susiana correspond to his Susiana *a* and *e* respectively.

In the following review of the prehistoric levels and their features, first the trenches and smaller cuts in the High Mound or in immediately adjacent parts of the terrace are dealt with, next those exposures of Susiana materials on the terrace which are either relatively small or without traces of structures, and then those terrace trenches important for their architectural remains. The discussion concludes with the areas pertinent primarily to the earliest range of the Susiana sequence. There is a certain logic, both spatial and chronological, to this arrangement in that when progressing with considerable

---

1. McCown 1942, table II; Vanden Berghe 1966, table 3; Dyson 1965, fig. 1; idem 1968:310; Dyson's chronology was proposed in conjunction with an important stratigraphic sounding that he made at Susa at the invitation of Ghirshman.

2. See *Editor's Preface* by Alizadeh.

consistency from the north to the south the areas representing the final period of the Susiana sequence are discussed first and those in which the bulk of the material belongs to very early stages are discussed last.

THE HIGH MOUND AND ADJACENT AREAS OF THE TERRACE

Trench II: Trench II was begun in the first season and work on it continued through the second season. It is located in Squares Q10 and R11 on the slope of the southeastern lobe of the High Mound (pl. 11:B, right background). It is divided into six plots, each 4 m long, numbered 1 to 6 from the east to the west. Its upper end, Plot 6, starts slightly to the east of some Old Elamite brickwork with a fragment of a Protoliterate wall; the wall's base was at el. 88.50 and its upper part at the modern surface, el. 89.00 (pl. 46:A). There were two floors with ashes, debris, and beveled-rim bowls against and beneath this wall at el. 88.40 and 88.30 respectively. Where these floors were cut by the slope of the mound the trench proper was begun with a nearly vertical cut that reached a depth of 6.00 m at this point (pls. 46:B; 260; 266). This is the first step in the three-stepped trench.

Many layers of ash and debris succeeded each other at close intervals, but without distinguishable features until the appearance of a hard surface about 2.80 m B.S. (ca. el. 85.50 m), which seems to have been a trodden floor. It is of interest to note that this floor as well as the debris above and below it slant toward the inside of the mound in the opposite direction to the present slope. There seems to have been a second floor about 20 cm below the first one, but it could be traced for only about 2.00 m. At a depth of just over 4.00 m from the surface, a ca. 80 cm thick layer of sandy clay mixed with ashes extended for almost 8.00 m through Plots 4–5. They, too, slanted slightly down toward the northwest, that is toward the inside of the mound. In Plot 4, at el. 83.50 m, this layer covered a pile of clay lumps, perhaps used in a pisé wall, and abutted against a pile of broken mudbricks. Both seemed to rest on a floor at an approximate elevation of 82.30 m. Above the pile of bricks and close to the surface in Plots 3 and 4 there was a debris layer reaching a depth of more than 1.30 m B.S. in Plot 3 and even deeper in Plot 2. Apparently at one time this debris constituted the surface of the mound since above it a very distinctive deposit of wash material, consisting of a mixture of pottery and clay from various levels higher up in the mound, is clearly recognizable.

About 1.30 m below the floor of the pisé lumps in Plot 4 there is another distinct floor at el. 80.80, and on this was found an oven about 1.10 m in diameter and preserved to a height of about 0.90 m. The plaster of a second floor could be recognized 10 cm over this original floor. About 3.50 m below the surface of Plot 2, at el. 89.60, there was a fairly regular rectangle measuring 0.40 m in height and 1.20 m in width. No individual bricks could be distinguished in this patch but presumably it indicated the presence of a wall at this point. No floor could be associated with it. At ca. el. 77.00, traces of a fireplace full of ashes were traced in Plot 2. It was only in this plot that virgin soil was reached, at el. 71.60. The dry riverbed of the Gelal-e Kohnak floodplain, 928.00 m to the east, is about 1.30 m lower at el. 70.30 (pl. 282). In the northeastern part of Plot 2, the discovery at ca. el. 79.10–78.90 of a complete jar, a fragmentary sauceboat, and some sherds suggested the existence of a Late Middle Susiana burial, but no clear traces of bones could be seen (pls. 165:A; 183:L; 184:A; 189:I).

Trench III: Another trial trench was located on the lobe of the High Mound to the north of Trench II and the gully of Trench IV, in Squares R–S8 (pl. 260). Just below the surface at the upper end, regular brickwork of the Old Elamite period was found. In cleaning the slope eastward, prehistoric levels were penetrated and are represented by sherds of the Late Susiana 2 phase.[3] There were no architectural features and the trench was discontinued while it was still relatively shallow.

Trench IV: Immediately to the northwest of Trench II, in Squares Q9–10, is a gully where the modern surface is 10 m lower than the top of Trench II (Plot 6), which suggested the possibility of reaching early phases quickly. Accordingly, a small U-shaped trench was begun in Q9 in the first season (pls. 260–61). However, the upper part of it proved to be full of washed-down debris containing Protoliterate and Late Susiana 2 sherds. The accumulation of rainwater bringing in new fill stopped excavation in Trench IV before virgin soil was reached.

Trial Areas in the Northeastern Promontory: To the northwest of Trench III, across still another gully, lies Trench XXVIII, also known as Q6:301 (pls. 260–61). This locus was primarily a surface clearance except for a small pit at its northeastern end, which was dug to about 3.00 m B.S.; in it Late Susiana 2 sherds already occurred a little below the surface and continued in the lowest level reached (pl. 161:C). The northernmost of the trial cuts on the eastern slopes of the High Mound is P6:301 (pl. 261). Work in that area began as surface clearance in the search for brickwork (P6:302 and 303), but to the east where the slope of the mound became steeper a small trench was cut, as in Q6:301. Locus P6:301 reached a depth of 5.50 m B.S. (el. 86.50); from el. 90.20 down Late Susiana 2 sherds were in the majority.

The Central Area of the High Mound: In the systematic exploration of the High Mound during the third sea-

---

3. See *Chapter 12* for the discussion on the subdivision of the Late Susiana period into the Late Susiana 1 and Late Susiana 2 phases. AA

son, three parts of the eroded central depression in Square O7 were tested. Locus O7:303 was discontinued while relatively shallow, but 301 and 302 were continued far above virgin soil since they were too small to provide adequate and safe working conditions as they became deeper. The pottery samples recovered from these two small loci were naturally rather modest but did provide a general sequence of considerable interest. Below over 2.00 m of debris dominated by Parthian and Old Elamite sherds and 2.00 to 3.50 m of earth with Protoliterate sherds, the tops of coherent Late Susiana 2 deposits were reached at el. 87.70 in O7:301 and at el. 88.30 in O7:302

The Southwestern Slope of the High Mound: Slightly to the southwest of the Protoliterate brickwork and room of N9:301 and 302 respectively, the lowest slopes of the High Mound level off toward the surrounding fields. There, in a narrow and fairly shallow excavation, M10:301, ranging between the modern surface at el. 84.00 and a greatest depth of ca. 1.30 m, portions of a brick wall or walls with a well-defined eastern face and several right-angle turns were traced in the final days of the third season (pl. 261). The wall is well dated by excellent samples of Late Susiana 2 sherds found alongside it, from the modern surface down (pls. 56:B–C, AA; 159:R–S; 162:A).

Trench XXIII: After Trench II, Trench XXIII is the most substantial cut into the High Mound. Located in N10, it is about 11.00 m long and 2.50 m wide and is situated northeast-southwest in the southwestern flank of the High Mound where the slope is still considerable. Thus Trench XXIII's northeastern corner is at el. 86.37 while its southeastern corner is more than 2.00 m lower at el. 84.28. The highest floor at the northern end of the trench was about 0.50 m below the surface (el. ca. 85.87) and extended for about 1.50–1.75 m to the south before petering out at the modern surface. It is the only floor in the trench associated with Protoliterate remains. When this area was slightly enlarged and deepened, a decayed burial without objects was found immediately below the level of the Protoliterate floor and must have been dug in from a higher level at some unknown later date. Aside from this grave, all the remains below the Protoliterate floor belong to the prehistoric period.

A second floor appeared about 0.90 m below the Protoliterate one, at el. 85.00. A third floor only 0.28 m below this one, at el. 84.72, had a pile of stones and some fragments of baked bricks in it. At the depth of 2.00 m B.S. (el. 84.37), a floor was associated with some brickwork that disappeared under the eastern side of the trench and was not traced further. About 2.00 m below this (el. 82.40) was another floor with fragmentary brickwork on it. Finally, a corner of a wall and two superimposed floors appeared some 8.00 m below the surface (el. 78.37). Although Trench XXIII reached a depth of ca. 12.50 m B.S. (el. 73.87) at its northern end, virgin soil did not appear.

Since the strata observed in the narrow trench did not have sufficient architectural associations to provide clear divisions into chronological phases, the pottery must be relied on for this propose. The sherds indicate that the accumulation of Late Susiana debris was at least 6.00 m deep, with the transition to Middle Susiana occurring between el. 80.00–79.00. By the close of the third season it seemed likely that the excavations had reached the beginning of the Middle Susiana period. An additional 4 m of deposit might exist, to judge by the occurrence of virgin soil at el. 70.40 in Trench II. The possibility that Late Susiana, Middle Susiana, and Early Susiana deposits lie stratified in a single trench has not, however, been checked. During the interval between the third and fourth seasons, rain washed debris into the bottom of the trench and greatly weakened its sides. The considerable preliminary cleaning and widening of the trench needed to make further deep excavation in it safe, although begun in the fourth season, had to be discontinued because of the pressure of work in other areas.

Trench XXII: The area of Trench XXII is not on the High Mound but somewhat to the south of Trench XXIII on the higher slopes of the terrace in Square N11. Trench XXII is oriented from northwest to southeast and is about 12.00 m long and 4.00 m wide (pl. 261). The terrace surface slopes slightly here, from el. 82.13 at the northwestern point of the trench to el. 82.59 at the southeast.

Trench XXII contained a fair amount of building remains at different levels (pl. 270:B). On the eastern end, about 2.00 m B.S. (el. ca. 80.54), traces of bitumen plaster on mud some 1.20×1.50 m in extent adjoined a wall constructed of unusually large mudbricks, ca. 0.50 m wide and more than 0.70 m long. In an extension of the trench to the west, this wall was followed for another 4.00 m to the end of the trench and was bordered there by a floor covered with scattered pebbles that might have been associated with it. A small pit ca. 0.60 m in diameter had pierced the floor from above. Below and at right angles to the large east-west wall was an earlier one of much smaller bricks, some of which appeared to be roughly plano-convex in shape. The lower wall is preserved to nearly 1.00 m in height and was apparently associated with a patch of floor visible at its base. A small segment of a wall encountered at the foot of the main steps leading out from the trench was at the same level and presumably belonged to the same structure.

In the northern part of the trench the remnants of a badly decayed skeleton, pelvis, long bones, and a completely disarticulated skull were found at 5.90 m B.S. (el. 76.44), a Middle Susiana level. The skull had a marked artificial deformation.[4] The deepest point reached in Trench XXII was in the northern part, ca. 7.35 m B.S. (el. 75.01), still well above virgin soil.

Trench XVIII: Although similar to Trench XXII in the central section of the terrace, Trench XVIII is located some distance farther from the High Mound at the intersection of Squares M–N13–14 (pl. 6:A, dark square in middle background). It was dug in the third season and had a ca. 0.40 m deep ashy deposit full of Protoliterate pottery just below the modern surface (pl. 16:A). Below this was brownish earth without any marked ashy layers or traces of construction, although a possible door socket and several large boulders occurred. Sherds were rare, even by prehistoric standards, and all belonged to the Middle Susiana period. Only a limited area in the eastern part of the trench was dug as deep as 4.80 m B.S. (el. 76.41), where the earth was as sterile as virgin soil. Not far to the west, in J14:301, virgin soil occurred over 1.00 m lower, at el. 75.20, but it is quite possible that the Trench XVIII area was originally a hillock slightly higher than other parts of the site and was never densely occupied.

Terrace Areas of Relatively Small Size or Without Architecture: On the surface of the terrace with its various promontories and gullies, Protoliterate and prehistoric sherds lie side-by-side together with a scatter of later sherds. The majority of the prehistoric sherds from the surface represent the Middle Susiana period with one variation, namely, that along the slanting slopes of the southeastern flank of the terrace Early Susiana sherds are particularly prominent. However, only by penetrating well below the surface and by observing the stratigraphy down to the earliest occupational debris in a number of areas could it be established whether such surface indications are of any significance or could detailed information be obtained. The present picture is built on the basis of information from many different areas, with the more modest of the cuttings also making significant contributions.

The East and West House Areas: The two terrace areas of greatest extent, in the east in Squares Q–S17–19 and in the west in Squares H–K14–15, have Protoliterate house remains of such depth and complexity as to require much time and effort; they are not yet completely dealt with (pls. 264–65). However, in vari-

ous spots in both the east and west, the bottom of the Protoliterate levels was reached. In most cases excavations were not continued in order to complete work on the Protoliterate remains. Clearly, though, Middle Susiana levels underlie the Protoliterate city. This is shown by the scattered prehistoric sherds that quite normally appear in the lowest Protoliterate levels on both sides of the terrace, by four stratigraphic pits, two on each side, and by an extensive deposit of Middle Susiana sherds in Q18:313.

Locus R17:209, a small sounding sunk below the large Protoliterate pit R17:208, in the northeastern corner of the East Area revealed Middle Susiana debris beginning at about el. 81.90 and continuing down several meters. The second pit, P18:204, was sunk just to the west of the Circular Structure from ca. el. 80.40–77.70 and also contained Middle Susiana sherds. In neither pit was virgin soil reached.

The promontory of the West Area slopes downward on the west and north so that the Protoliterate structures are there even more eroded than to the east. Accordingly, in Trench XVII and the adjacent North Slope in J13–14, the change from Protoliterate to prehistoric already comes about 0.70 m below the modern surface. Also in the western edge of Trench IX Middle Susiana sherds were plentiful and relatively close to the surface. As in the East Area, the primary concern here was the Protoliterate remains, but the underlying levels were tested in two narrow pits. The smaller one, J14:301 East, ca. 1.00 × 3.00 m, was driven down through the packing of the platform in Trench XVII. Here from the bottom of the packing at el. 80.47 there were over 5.00 m of debris before compact yellow soil without any trace of artifacts was reached at el. 75.20. There were no traces of structures, but a clear sequence of Middle Susiana sherds overlying Early Susiana structures.

The second stratigraphic pit of the West Area, H14:306, was somewhat larger, ca. 2.50 × 4.00 m at the top. It was laid out in the southwestern end of Trench IX where the surface sloped from el. 81.60 at the northeastern corner of the locus down to el. 80.50 at the access steps to the south, H14:310. There were neither architectural remains in the uppermost debris nor any surface separating Protoliterate and prehistoric levels. Some Middle Susiana sherds occurred just below the surface (pls. 179:I; 192:E). A clear floor with a stump of wall on it and traces of a kiln or fireplace came to light some 4.70 m below the surface (el. 76.90). Nearly 1.00 m below this there seemed to be traces of brickwork, which disappeared into the southern edge of the pit. The maximum depth of this pit was some 6.00 m below the surface near the southern edge and about 6.30 m in the center (el. 74.85 measured from 81.15). By then the steep sides were becoming unsafe and before the locus could be enlarged, rain washed so much debris into it that further work became impractical. Even though virgin soil

---

4. Similarly deformed skulls have been found in the Deh Luran plain in earlier phases; see Hole, Flannery, and Neely 1969:248–53, pl. 12:b (Ali Kosh, Ali Kosh phase); Hole 1977:91–93, pls. 30:a–b, 31:a–b (Chogha Sefid, Sefid phase). Early Susiana figurines with flattened, elongated heads perhaps portray similar cranial deformations (pl. 66:B; Kantor 1976:192, fig. 24). In Mesopotamia figurines of the Samarra (Oates 1969, pls. 25:A–F; 26:A–F; 27:A–C) and Ubaid (Woolley 1955, pl. 24:Ur 15399) periods have elongated heads.

was not reached, the more than 6.00 m deep deposits in H14:306 provided a good sequence with an Early Susiana level underlying the Middle Susiana ones.

Trenches VIII, X, and XV: Three small trial digs strung along the western slope of the terrace from the north to the south in the second season did not provide architectural features of the prehistoric period and were not developed to any considerable degree.

Trench VIII in Squares H–J21 had remnants of some disintegrated late burials of uncertain date sheltered under an irregular gable of small stones and re-used baked-brick fragments. There was very little intact Protoliterate deposit here. The upper 0.60 m of debris contained a mixture of Protoliterate and Middle Susiana sherds. Below, the pottery was consistently of the Middle Susiana period for ca. 2.50 m down to el. 81.00, where the excavation ended, presumably still high above virgin soil.

Trench X in Squares G26–27 revealed primarily Protoliterate material. In the western half of the trench, where most of the digging was done, there was a concentration of sherds and complete beveled-rim bowls at el. 79.60, and in the access steps to the west a pile of twenty-five beveled-rim bowls and four conical bowls between el. 80.40 and 79.60. The transition between Protoliterate and Middle Susiana debris was at about el. 79.50. Digging in Trench X stopped at that level, except in a small Protoliterate pit, the bottom of which was at el. 77.60, and in the southwestern corner of the trench, which was carried down to el. 78.35 and yielded Middle Susiana sherds (pls. 163:AA; 188:G).

Trench XV in Square F27 at the southwestern corner of the terrace, at a very low point where the slope has almost leveled off into the fields, was begun in the second season because Middle Susiana sherds were particularly noticeable on the surface. A small area of ca. 2.00 × 4.00 m was carried down to a sloping from 2.65 B.S. (el. 76.35) in the western end to 3.20 B.S. (el. 75.80) in the east. The sherds corroborated the surface finds, showing that if any Protoliterate or other later deposits that were once present, they had been totally eroded, leaving Middle Susiana debris at the modern surface.

Trenches XVI and XXXI (pls. 260, 277): Two trenches were located at the southeastern corner of the terrace, the first in Square O27 where there is a rather sharp slope and the second slightly to the northeast in Square P27 on a lower and more gentle slope (pl. 260). Trench XVI is T-shaped and its northern stalk provided the majority of the finds, with good Middle Susiana material appearing underneath the below-surface mixture of Protoliterate and Susiana sherds.[5] The middle of the northern part of the trench had traces of considerable

masses of brickwork, but they were so poor as to defy articulation. They resembled an irregular packing rather than a real structure. In the eastern end of the southern part of the trench a small test pit was dug to about 5 m B.S. (ca. el. 75.00), where the soil was sterile. It is likely that virgin soil was reached here, but the results should be checked in a larger exposure.

Trench XXXI, begun several years later than Trench XVI, provided not only stratified pottery of the Protoliterate, Middle Susiana, and Early Susiana periods but also contained segments of well-built walls. In the western part of the trench, P27:501, 502 and 507 had ashy deposits with large amounts of Protoliterate sherds and some complete beveled-rim bowls immediately below the surface (pl. 277). To the east in P27:504 was a pit of the Protoliterate period 1.00 m in diameter and about 2.00 m deep, as well as some scattered vessels, but most of the Protoliterate material had been eroded away. Prehistoric remains, such as the well-constructed Middle Susiana wall with post holes in P27:503 appear about 0.70 m below the surface. The roughly east-west walls and the hard surface at 78.29–78.27 in P22:501 North and 503–505, similar to the post-hole wall, represent the Early Middle Susiana phase. In P27:505 very substantial walls appeared about 0.30 m below the Middle Susiana floor and continued into the unexcavated northeastern side of the trench. Lack of time prevented the clearance of these walls to their base. They can be assigned to Early Susiana by the pottery. The less well-defined wall of P27:506 was probably part of the same structure as the walls of P27:505.[6] The segments of walls already found suggest that Trench XXXI, if enlarged, would provide architecture comparable to that in the trenches now to be considered.

TRENCH XIII

The Digging of the Trench (pls. 47–50; 267–69): In the second season (1963), a small trench was started at a nearly flat part of the terrace in Square K22 (pl. 260). At the surface, ca. 83.60 m above datum, it measured ca. 17.00 sq. m. It reached a maximum depth of 6.60 m (el. 77.00 m) in a much reduced area of only ca. 4.00 sq. m (pl. 269, K22:201). Its purpose was to test the character and dates of the deposits in the central part of the terrace and in that season it yielded primarily informa-

---

5. It is difficult to determine which prehistoric period was intended here; however, judging by the wide distribution of

Late Middle Susiana pottery on the mound, it is assumed that "Susiana sherds" belonged to this phase. AA

6. The roughly rectangular feature that appeared in the eastern extension of locus P27:504 at el. 77.63 seems to represent a pebble-paved hearth of a type that a later season proved to be typical for the Early Susiana period. This feature is, therefore, probably associated with the fragmentary Early Susiana structure recovered in loci P27:505 and 506. For examples of hearths from Early Susiana levels at Jafarabad, see Dollfus and Hesse 1977, pl. 2:b–c, figs. 3–4.

tion concerning the Susiana phases. The only building remains encountered were fragments of a mudbrick wall between ca. 1.50 m and 2.00 m below the surface. Directly under the present surface of the terrace was a rather thin accumulation of mixed debris containing Late period and Protoliterate sherds. No traces of Late Susiana 2 pottery were present. Middle Susiana pottery appeared immediately below the mixed debris and continued for a considerable depth. About 3.60 m below the surface (ca. el. 80.00) mixed Middle Susiana and Early Susiana sherds were recorded. Consistent Early Susiana deposits extended from about 5.00 to 6.50 m B.S. (el. 78.60–77.10).

During the fourth and fifth campaigns Trench XIII was enlarged first to ca. 200.00 sq. m and then to 265.00 sq. m, so that it covered parts of four squares, L22–23 and K22–23. The northeastern edge of the enlarged trench is nearly level at el. 83.59–83.56, while the lowest of the four corners, the southwestern one, is only 50 cm lower than the northwestern corner.

The results of the excavations in Trench XIII insofar as they concern later remains, those of the Late Cemetery and the Achaemenid and Protoliterate periods, are summarized in *Chapters 1* and *2*. The prehistoric remains provide, however, the great bulk of the material from this area, the stratification of which are described next and then the architectural structures are considered in more detail (pls. 268–69).

The Prehistoric Stratification: The upper Susiana levels in Trench XIII had been greatly disturbed throughout the trench by the graves of the Late Cemetery and by some deep Protoliterate deposits (K23:502) and a pit (K23:503 South). Accordingly, it is not surprising that mixtures of Late, Protoliterate, and Middle Susiana sherds occurred as low as 0.85–1.35 B.S. in K23:400 (el. 82.35–82.05 and 81.95–81.75), while an extensive group of Middle Susiana sherds was found as high as 0.40–0.50 B.S. in L22:400 (el. 83.24–83.14), although the highest structural remains with which they could originally have been associated were the wall stumps of L22:402 (el. 82.59–82.20).

The much disturbed upper levels in Trench XIII have preserved in the west, K22.400, some scattered and disjointed stumps of walls sufficient only to indicate the orientation and level of the constructions, but the only integrated plan is provided by the fairly substantial walls of the rectangular room L22:402 in the eastern part of the trench. The bases of its walls at el. 82.20–82.30 correspond well with the bases of the brickwork in K22:400, Wall 1 at el. 82.32 and Wall 2 at el. 82.20. Accordingly, the walls in the northern part of the trench provide the first definite level, I, at 82.20 (pl. 269).

The walls of L22:402 were built directly over Kiln 1 and 2 of L22:403 (pl. 269). The burnt floors of this cluster of kilns varied somewhat in depth from el. 82.30 to

el. 81.90. The base of the kiln layer corresponds to a floor and the tops of some wall stumps in the southern part of L22:404 and at the northwestern corner of L22:405 are preserved to a height of ca. 0.45–0.50 (el. 81.65–82.10). These stumps had belonged to fairly substantial structures with walls nearly 75 cm wide and were themselves sufficiently distinct to indicate the presence of floors at their bases and also that they had been leveled off for later constructions, in the case of L22:404 and the kilns of L22:403. These kilns constitute Level II, and its beginning at ca. el. 82.00 is indicated by the floor at the top of the leveled walls. Level III consists of these wall stumps; their bottoms and the floors that correspond to them indicate that it began at about el. 81.60.

The Level III remains had covered earlier walls with tops at ca. el. 81.60 (L22:502; K22:406; K23:403). These walls had either a footing or floors ranging from approximately el. 81.00 to 80.70, which determine the beginning of Level IV (marked as el. 81.00 in plate 268). In the southwestern end of the trench, badly disturbed by Protoliterate remains, the low-lying walls of K23:509–511 might have originally continued up to heights corresponding to the Level IV occupation in rooms K22:403, 406 and L22:405.

Still lower floors, apparently connected with the same building complex, were reached in K23:403 = K23:507 at el. 80.61 (Level V)[7] and 80.27 (Level VI).[8] A series of closely spaced thin transverse walls with "slots" between them appeared late in the fifth season in Room K23:507 (pl. 50:B–C) and just at the close of the season similar transverse walls began to appear in the next room to the west, K23:402 (K23:506). They are only 30–40 cm wide, much narrower than the normal walls of the rooms. Color differences in the surface of the still unexcavated ground indicated that such walls are present in a larger area than dug so far. Their relation to the walls above them is still not clear, but in any case, they are distinguished as Level VII. The lowest point in a slot between two dwarf walls, apparently a floor, was at el. 80.00, a little over 3.50 m B.S. To the west, rooms K23:509, 511, and probably 510 represent Level VII.[9]

At ca. el. 80.00, Level VII, the lowest point reached in the southwestern rooms, is still about 3.00 m above the deepest point reached in the original small trench

---

7. Indicated by the floor covering the narrow north-south wall at el. 80.61. The uppermost of the three hearths belongs to this stage.

8. A rounded-off elevation corresponding to the floor of the middle hearth of K23:507.

9. Such grill-like structures appear to be widespread both chronologically and geographically and have been interpreted as platforms for drying grain. For stone-built examples in southeastern Turkey, see Braidwood, Çambel, Schirmer, et

dug during the second season, el. 77.10 (pl. 268, K22:201). As yet little is known concerning the earliest phases of occupation in the area of Trench XIII. A hint of how much remains to be discovered is provided by a few intrusive Archaic Susiana sherds in the upper levels (pl. 208:G and 4.572 [K22:409]).

The Architecture of Levels IV–VII: The best-preserved building remains of Trench XIII, which began to appear beneath the scattered stumps of the Level III walls, were not all excavated to the same level. Rooms K22:403 and 406 were dug down only to an average depth of ca. 60 cm, where there were some associated floors at ca. el. 81.00. However, this is only an approximate depth for the base of Layer IV. In K22:406 a lower floor was noticed at ca. el. 80.70, but the corresponding walls remain unexcavated; Rooms K22:406 and 403 were both refilled at the end of the fourth season (pl. 47). All through the area somewhat higher and lower occupation floors could be observed, as well as partial rebuildings, alterations, and additions within what might be considered as one major phase of occupation in which Level IV represents a rebuilding of the earlier Levels V and VI traced in K23:403 (= K23:507). Further excavation beneath still standing walls of Level I (K22:402) and Level IV (K22:403 and 406) is needed to clarify the exact relationships of successive walls and various details of the plan. At present there is only a composite plan of the architectural remains in Trench XIII below Level III and above Level VII (pl. 269).

The central features of the structures of Levels IV–VI are the two large oblong rooms, K23:403 and L22:405, each ca. 3 m wide and over 5 m long. The long walls are oriented southeast-northwest at about 15° declension from magnetic north.[10] These large rooms share a continuous northwestern cross wall which is not at right angles to the long walls but deviates from the right angle by about 10°. This irregularity is not carried over into the smaller rooms on either side of the large central rooms but does reappear in the northern wall of K22:406. Except for some narrow wedge-like rooms, such as K23:510 to the west and L22:504 to the east, which perhaps indicate the limits of architectural units, all the rooms are rectangular. The walls were on the whole fairly well preserved and at some points even the mud plaster on them could be traced. However, with the exception of an apparently secondarily blocked doorway opening from the southeastern corner of K22:403 into the northwestern corner of K23:403, no doorways

were traceable. Although the architectural units cannot be determined on the basis of circulation, it is likely that Rooms K22:403 and K23:402 belong to the same unit as the two large rooms. The presence of an extraordinarily well-preserved kiln, K22:405, to the west of Room K22:403 (pl. 48) and a partitioned bin in the southwestern corner of that room (pl. 47) would indicate that the western end of the unit was given up to domestic purposes.

The large Room K23:403 (the lower phase of which was marked K23:507) contained a hearth that in its first version was round and approximately in the center of the room (pls. 47; 50:B). At a somewhat higher level of occupation (VI) this hearth was a truncated ovoid structure attached to a partition wall on the east. Finally when the partition wall was covered by the floor of Level V at ca. el. 80.60, the hearth became a roughly rectangular structure forming a kind of bench against the eastern wall (pl. 50:B). In the southern part of the room the tops of the dwarf walls, at el. 80.27, can be taken as underlying the Level VI floor of the middle hearth. Though both the lowest hearth and the dwarf walls apparently rest on the floor of Level VII at el. 80.00, their relationship and the character of the room at that time are still unclear.

To the northeast of the wedge-like space, L22:504, which might mark the limit of the architectural unit, were some very small and very regular chambers, L22:506, with an oven against its northern wall, and L22:508, the northern wall of which was not traced. On the east and west they were flanked by compartments only 40–50 cm wide. In their narrowness the walls of this group of chambers resembled the dwarf walls of Level VII rather than the wider walls of the Levels IV–VI rooms. However, L22:506 and 508 might have been merely spaces partitioned off within a larger unit. They were found beneath kilns of Level II in the northeastern part of the trench (L22:403, nos. 3, 6); their continuation to the south is still concealed by the as yet unremoved later walls of L22:402.

The main building, represented by the composite plan of Levels IV–VI in Trench XIII, is an important enlargement of present knowledge about the Middle Susiana period. It proves the existence of well-conceived buildings planned as units, as indicated by the regular alignment of the rooms and the party walls. Moreover, some of the rooms are of impressive sizes and their distribution and the variety of features in them suggest that they were planned to perform predetermined functions. It is difficult at the moment to reconstruct these in detail or even to ascertain with certainty the character of the main building, whether it was a standard house or one belonging to an important or wealthy member of the community. To answer such questions additional structures are needed for comparison; in the meantime, the main building of Trench XIII

al. 1981, figs. 3–4 (Çayönü, aceramic). For examples with mud walls in northern Iraq, see Munchaev and Merpert 1981:38, fig. 12:1. Square 37, Complex 37 (Yarim Tepe I, Level 10, Hassuna period) and ibid., p. 32, fig. 7:I (Square 37, Complex 26 = p. 39, fig. 13:2; Square 57, Buildings 296–97 = p. 53, fig. 16:3; Level 9, Hassuna period).

10. Magnetic north as given by the Heidemy survey of 1963.

stands as an exemplar of substantial architecture at a fairly early period of the Susiana sequence. In a more general context, the association of pottery and other objects with the successive architectural phases provides good evidence for the Susiana cultural sequence, despite the considerable disturbance of the area by its Protoliterate inhabitants and, much later, by burial activities. As is shown in the following chapters, Level VII represents a transitional Early Susiana-Middle Susiana phase, Levels VI–IV the Early Middle Susiana and Levels II–I the Late Middle Susiana.

TRENCH XXI

In the slope of the terrace, Trench XXI, to the east of Trench XIII, an area of approximately 400.00 sq. m was dug (pls. 51; 274–75). It developed from an initial trench ca. 2.00 m wide and ca. 9.50 m long cut during the third season into the eastern side of the terrace at a point where the modern surface slopes from ca. el. 82.50 down to ca. el. 80.00. The purpose was to test the character and to establish the relative dating of the occupational remains of the site at this point, especially to elucidate the stratigraphic and archaeological associations of the newly discovered Archaic pottery found slightly to the north in Trench XII in 1963 during the second season (pl. 51:A). In the third season the original Trench XXI reached what appears to be the earliest occupation at ca. el. 76.50 (ca. 5.50 B.S. in P23:301), where a series of irregularly and closely spaced depressions were cleared. They were far too random in shape and arrangement to be anything except animal burrows and holes. No similar concentration of depressions was encountered elsewhere on the site.

At the northeastern end of the trench very hard soil consisting of closely laminated layers of clay was first taken to be a water-laid deposit. However, though the layers were thin and seemed horizontal there was apparently only a pocket of this material. At the edges of this hard clay distinct outlines of fairly large mudbricks could be recognized. Only in the fourth season was it possible to articulate such bricks into fragments of walls. By this time the examination of the sherds from Trench XXI indicated clearly that the latest material *in situ* was Middle Susiana preceded by Early Susiana, which in turn occurred above the new Archaic Susiana culture at the bottom. Reconstructible vessels of the Early Susiana and Middle Susiana periods were washed out from the edges of the trench by heavy rains in the third and fourth (P23:401, Q23:401) seasons.

During the fifth season the area of Trench XXI was extended in order to recover architectural remains contemporary with the stratified pottery found previously. The enlarged area had the original trench as its southern limit in Square P23 and was expanded to the east and north at somewhat different levels corresponding to the

modern slope of the mound. Two distinct architectural complexes came to light. The lower (eastern) one had floors varying between el. 79.60 and 79.55 and the second one on the west had floors nearly 2.00 m higher, varying between el. 81.25 and 81.45 in room P23:505 and at el. 81.04 in room P23:504 (pl. 275). In addition to the main structure, a burnt apsidal hearth(?) enclosed by brickwork, P23:502, provided traces of occupation at the modern surface, el. 81.75. The analysis of the pottery from the two architectural complexes clearly dates the western rooms to the Early Middle Susiana phase and the lower, eastern complex to the Early Susiana period.

The Middle Susiana Remains: Of the architectural remains at the higher level, an apsidal structure at the modern surface, el. 81.75, P23:502 (1.70 × 1.60 m), had miraculously survived rain and modern plowing. A narrow, shallow channel separated the burnt platform and the well-built thin wall around it. These elements presumably formed the base of a carefully constructed kiln/hearth. In P23:507 to the east were remnants of a fragmentary wall that had been mostly destroyed by the downward slope of the mound. To the south of P23:502 and at a little lower level a substantial east-west wall, between 50 and 70 cm thick, was situated along the northern edge of P23:503; its eastern end was lost in the slope and its western end was not excavated. Two oblong narrow spaces delimited on the north by thin walls separate the substantial wall from the two rooms to the north, P23:504 and 505 (both 2.50 m long and 2.30 m wide); a bin filled the southwestern corner of the latter.

About 2.50 m to the south of the thick east-west wall in P23:503 was an opening into a hollow in the ground that was not completely excavated. Its character remains uncertain and it might not have been manmade. To the west a child's skeleton lay only a few centimeters below the modern surface. Even without the evidence of some late sherds among the Middle Susiana pieces found here, its character as a late burial unrelated to any of the prehistoric finds would have been clear.

The Early Susiana Building: The lower group of rooms apparently belonged to one architectural unit (pls. 51:B; 52:A; 275). It consisted of a long, wide room or court on the eastern side (Q22:504; 4.0 × 7.5 m) with rooms to the north and west. Originally there had been two oblong rooms to the west, each about 2.00 m wide and about 4.50 m long, with walls varying in thickness between 50 and 60 cm. At some later time these two rooms were divided into four by a thin partition wall made of lumps of clay and broken bricks (Q23:501, 503, 505, 506). One of these small rooms was almost filled by a large fireplace (pl. 275). At the southwestern side of this unit was a narrow, oblong corridor or lane (Q23:502) and at the northwestern side the beginning of a similar narrow space (Q23:507 Northeast). Just to the south of this lane there was found *in situ*, dug in from a somewhat higher level, the first large deposit of complete and semi-complete Early Susiana pots (pl. 52:C). Large quantities of carbon samples were found in and between these vessels.

Two larger rooms (Q23:508, 511) were excavated in the northeastern end of the trench. The corners of all these rooms deviated to some degree from the rectangular, and their walls were not precisely aligned or parallel. The thickness of the walls also varied considerably from the 20–30 cm of the thin partition wall to over 60 cm. The quality of the brickwork was also uneven; some of it was excellent and afforded the possibility of articulating and measuring single bricks and studying the bricklaying methods (pl. 52:A–B). In some cases it was miserable, as in the partition wall where no regular brickwork could be distinguished. The lack of doorways leaves the circulation in doubt; nonetheless, it seems apparent that the rooms just described belonged to a single architectural unit, with the exception, perhaps, of Q23:502. This might have been a lane or blind alley outside of the houses.

The majority of the rooms of the eastern complex had more than one floor and, in addition, indications of earlier walls, which appeared as benches alongside the walls of the main level. In many cases these earlier remains were parallel to those above them, indicating that they represent only an earlier phase of the same architectural complex, but occasionally, as in Room Q23:506, they were oriented at an angle to the main walls (pl. 275). On the eastern end of the complex in Q23:504 below the main floor at el. 79.10, earlier occupation was represented by about 50 cm of deposit, some of it consisting of ash layers.

The finds in Trench XXI, in addition to establishing a stratified sequence of Middle Susiana, Early Susiana, and Archaic Susiana sherds in one area, are now also providing well-dated evidence for the Early Middle Susiana and Early Susiana architecture. The upper, Early Middle Susiana structures, in so far as can be judged on the basis of their partially excavated states seem to have been composed of rooms smaller than those of the Early Susiana house in its unpartitioned phase. Moreover, the Middle Susiana rooms were bordered on the south by a thick wall, apparently the division between a dwelling complex and an adjacent open area (P23:501, 503). The Early Susiana unit seems to have had narrow dead-end lanes on two sides. The one on the south, Q23:502, separated the house from an area of brickwork of uncertain character, Q23:512. The original top of the brick mass has been lost in the eroded modern slope of the terrace.

The Early Susiana architecture and the frequency of semi-complete or complete vessels of the period in Trench XXI show that erosion of the eastern slope of the terrace has cut into the remains of a substantial settle- ment that is closer here to the modern surface than apparently anywhere else on the site. This circumstance explains why Early Susiana sherds are particularly prominent along the eastern sides of the terrace. However, the exposures of low levels on the western terrace were not large enough to indicate the true extent of the Early Susiana settlement in that direction or to support the claim that it was located for the most part in the east. Both of the two deepest loci in the West Area provided Early Susiana material (H14:306, J14:301 East).

TRENCH XXV (pls. 53–54; 55:A; 260; 271–73)

In the third season a trench was established in Squares R20–21 with the same purpose as Trench XXI, namely, to obtain better evidence for the earliest occupation of Chogha Mish than that yielded by Trench XII (pl. 260). By the end of the fifth season Trench XXV had been enlarged to an area of 275.00 sq. m and its stratification was very disturbed and complex. The uppermost levels had segments of parallel walls probably marking the sides of a Protoliterate lane (R21:300; bases at el. 78.20; cf. pl. 272). A relatively well-preserved Protoliterate kiln and its ash heap were found in the southwestern corner of the trench (R21:404; pls. 272–73). However, the most ubiquitous remains of the Protoliterate occupation were the pits sunk deep into the earlier levels, whose stratification and walls they had either destroyed or greatly disturbed. In R21:509 complete Protoliterate vessels occurred 1.00 m deeper (el. 74.50–74.40) than the bottom of the lower of the adjacent Archaic Susiana walls of R21:409 (el. 75.46) or of the sterile sandy clay underlying the thin black layer with Archaic Susiana sherds that was particularly evident in the southeastern corner of the trench (el. 75.50; cf. test pit in R21.300 Southeast, [pl. 272], enlarged as R21:410 [pl. 271]). The plan of Trench XXV shows the shape of the more regular of the Protoliterate pits by broken outlines, but only the positions of large, sprawling pit areas such as R20:402, 509, and 510 are indicated (pls. 271–72). For the sake of clarity some pits sunk into Archaic Susiana rooms are not indicated on the plan (R20:505 South; R21:414, 510 area).

Trench XXV, with the possible exception of the kiln of R20:516, provided no structures of the Middle Susiana and Early Susiana periods, but a considerable amount of Archaic Susiana brickwork did escape the ravages of the Protoliterate inhabitants. The structures now extend more than 21.00 m in length and over 5.00 m in width. They apparently represent three architectural units and several building phases, which are combined in the plan (pls. 271–72). One unit extending from R20:502 in the north to R21:502 in the south contains a series of fairly large rooms; the three in the north are limited by a perfectly straight wall on the east over 9.00 m long and apparently 0.80 m wide (pls. 53:A–B; 271–72). South of these three rooms a projection to the east, R21:414, formed a tower-like structure (pl. 54:B). Its western side is the double wall of R21:409, which appears on two levels, the western one of which might belong to an earlier phase (pl. 54:C). This double wall runs to the south until cut by the Protoliterate pits R21:503 and 505. Just at this point, on the eastern side, were three large stones embedded between long bricks, perhaps the remnants of steps to an entrance (R21:502; pl. 54:D).

The second Archaic unit began with R20:507. It projected farther to the west than the room to the south (pl. 55:A) and had no walls in common with it. Instead there were double walls with a narrow, wedge-like space between them. The first room of this unit was about 2.40 m wide on the inside and 3.40 m long; it was of fairly regular rectangular shape. The eastern wall was about 0.80 m wide. To the north was part of another room, R20:505 South, separated from the first by a narrow wall.

A third architectural unit is apparently represented by massive brickwork to the east of the second unit. The direction of this wall differs from that of the second unit and the space between them is a long triangle (pl. 53:C). Presumably, this unit once extended to the eastern and to the north. All the architectural remains of the Archaic Susiana period were constructed of exceptionally shaped bricks usually between 0.80 and 0.95 m long, ca. 12 cm wide, and 9–10 cm thick (pl. 54:A). These bricks were most often laid in stretchers with mortar containing ashes between them, but headers were also freely used (pls. 53:A–B; 54:B). On the assumption that the headers were of the same length as the stretchers and were not shortened in construction, the walls must originally have been at least 0.80 m thick. The preponderance of stretchers resulted in at least the upper parts of the walls when first discovered, appearing to be much narrower than they had originally been as the shape and the great weight of the long bricks caused the stretchers to roll off the tops of crumbling walls at a fast rate, still leaving a "wall face" behind them. For instance, when the "outer face" of the straight wall separating Room R20:501 from the area of R20:514 on the east was first discovered, the thickness on top was only that of two bricks. Later, traces of the lower part of the wall were found farther to the east so that it can be restored as shown on plate 272. When a row of headers was found exposed, as at the northern edge of pit R21:503, the true thickness of a wall was apparent.

When the surfaces of these extraordinary bricks were first cleaned for measurement, parallel longitudinal grooves that were originally thought to be reed impressions were found on their surface. The cleaning of additional examples soon proved that these were instead rather complicated series of finger marks forming a number of patterns (pl. 54:A, C). Some were within a

"frame" drawn around the edges of the bricks. Usually these patterns occurred only on the upper side of the bricks. Their practical function, if there was such, would have been to hold the mortar. However, the consistency of the mortar, as observed so far, was on the whole so crumbly and friable that these finger patterns might have had very little practical effect. In one stretch of wall where the bricks had been placed with the finger-marked side down, a workman was able to clear the imprint of the brick patterns remaining in the mortar after the majority of the bricks that had made them had been weathered away anciently (pl. 54:C).[11]

Despite the disturbed stratification of Trench XXV, the Archaic Susiana structures can be assigned with considerable confidence to the third, final, phase of the period. Sherds of that phase scattered at various elevations prove that the area was occupied at that time.[12] In addition, a fragment of a close-line bowl found just outside the southeastern corner of Room R20:507 among pebbles and ashes can be taken as *in situ* evidence for the dating of the walls of long bricks (pl. 208:C). Confirmation of the Archaic Susiana 3 date is provided by the relative scarcity of Archaic Susiana 1 material *in situ* well below the level of the walls (pl. 272).

AREAS PRIMARILY IMPORTANT FOR THE EARLIEST RANGES OF THE SUSIANA SEQUENCE

Four areas in the low, gradual slopes of the terrace to the east of Trenches XXX, XII, and XXV were dug as complements to them, to increase knowledge of the Archaic Susiana period and its relationship to the following periods.

Soundings G and H (pls. 260, 278): Two stratigraphic soundings located in Squares S–T21 and T22 respectively were too small to provide any coherent plans of structures. However, traces of floors and walls occurred in the ca. 3.00 × 4.50 m Sounding G, as indicated on the plan (pl. 278). About 15 cm below the surface was a patch of mud-plastered pebble floor at el. 77.35.

---

11. Bricks of comparable long shape laid with the finger-impressed side at the top were found at Chogha Sefid in a phase that can be dated to the Archaic Susiana 3 phase (Hole 1977:75); unimpressed long bricks were found there in earlier and later phases (ibid.). In general, bricks of long dimensions seem to have been typical in various areas at early periods, but they are not all of identical type nor as similar to Chogha Mish bricks as those found in Deh Luran; see Smith 1976:14–15 (Ganj Dareh, Level D, Early Neolithic); Masuda 1974:25 (Sang-e Chakhmaq East, Archaic); Malek-Shahmirzadi 1979:184, fig. 3 (Zagheh, Zagheh period); Mellink and Filip 1974, fig. 78a (Chogha Mami); el-Wailly and Abu es-Soof 1965:21, fig. 56 (Tell es-Sawwan, Samarra period); Lloyd and Safar 1948:121 (Eridu XV, Ubaid 1).

12. Cf. *Index of Loci and Finds,* R20:404 East, 502, 510, 512; R21:402 + 411, 410, 509.

Two somewhat lower patches, a white-plastered mud floor with a raised edge at el. 76.75 in the northwestern corner and a trodden earth surface at el. 76.60 at the eastern edge, might mark an occupation level just subsequent to that of the mud walls which are the main elements in the upper part of Sounding G. The corner walls on the north had a preserved top at el. 76.70 and an associated pebble floor at el. 76.44. A stub projecting to the south does not appear to have been bonded into the corner walls. In the southeastern corner of the sounding a much thicker wall had its preserved top at el. 76.55, the earth floor at el. 76.23 associated with it covered the southern part of the sounding and presumably underlay the irregularly curving patch of earth with pebbles and traces of fire lying at el. 76.43. Middle Susiana pottery is associated with these fragmentary installations.

The transition from the Early to Late Middle Susiana phase came at about el. 76.00. The only feature of the Early Middle Susiana phase was a small patch of pebble and sherd pavement at el. 75.84 at the eastern edge of the sounding. Some 30 cm lower was the bottom course of a wall over 80 cm wide, with an orientation completely different from that of the upper wall, resting on a trodden floor at el. 75.40. This wall marked the upper part of the Early Susiana occupation, which went down for over 1.00 m, to a pebble floor at el. 74.45 that extended over most of the southern half of Sounding G. This floor, which had a thickness of ca. 15 cm, represented the beginning of the Early Susiana occupation and was the lowest feature traced. Below it the area of excavation was reduced to only the central part of the sounding that was carried down through 3.00 m of Archaic Susiana debris until virgin soil was reached at el. 71.25.

There was no sharp delimitation of one phase from another in the lower part of Sounding G. At el. 74.30–74.20 the pottery was predominantly Archaic Susiana straw-tempered smoothed ware with two close-line sherds and a few Early Susiana sherds, the latter presumably intrusive from above. The shift from Archaic Susiana 2 to Archaic Susiana 3 occurred around el. 72.50, below which point dense-sandy red-line and red-washed sherds of the Archaic Susiana 2 phase occurred. From el. 71.70 down to virgin soil at 71.25 sherds were very sparse. Sounding G contained no *in situ* remains of Archaic Susiana 1, although a single, and intrusive, painted-burnished sherd occurred in Archaic Susiana 3 debris.

Sounding H, some 13.00 m to the east of Sounding G and ca. 1.00 m lower at the surfaces had as its only structural elements small portions of two mudbrick platforms, each some 50 cm high, their tops at el. 75.75 and 75.35 respectively. The general stratigraphic sequence is almost the same as that of Sounding G except that in Sounding H the sherd groups tended to be more mixed. For example, the debris of el. 74.40–74.20 was transi-tional between Early Middle Susiana and Early Susiana, but it also contained a few Archaic Susiana straw-tempered sherds and one close-line sherd. Unlike Sounding G, in Sounding H the Early Susiana remains were shallow. In the small group of sherds recovered from el. 73.90–73.30, Archaic Susiana straw-tempered smoothed ware was dominant, but a few Early Susiana sherds appeared, presumably intrusions. Although el. 72.80–72.20 marked the transition between Archaic Susiana 3 and 2, a few close-line sherds occurred even lower. Pottery stopped occurring around el. 71.95 and virgin soil was reached at el. 71.35–71.25.

Soundings G and H provided evidence for the location of the eastern edge of the settlements in various periods. In the Late Middle Susiana phase and Early Susiana period the built up area of the town clearly extended as far as Sounding G while Sounding H appears to have been at the edge of the settlement. Likewise in the Archaic Susiana 2 and 3 phases, while both soundings were considerably to the east of the Archaic structures in Trench XXV, the difference in the thickness of the deposits suggests that Sounding G was part of a much used open-air working and dumping area while Sounding H was at the periphery.

Trench XXXII (pls. 55:B; 260; 276)

A small trench of ca. 70.00 sq. m was opened in Square R23 in the fifth season. It is located to the east of Trench XXI where the steep slope of the terrace levels off toward the plain. Throughout the trench Protoliterate sherds predominated in the top 75 cm of debris, mixed, however, even just below the surface, with some Middle Susiana, Early Susiana, and Archaic Susiana sherds. In the northeastern part of the trench two floors appeared, an upper floor of hard earth and pebbles at el. 77.64 and a lower floor of hard earth at el. 76.57. The latter marked the bottom of the Protoliterate remains that here went down deeper than in the other parts of the trench, where already at 77.55 the sherds were consistently of the Archaic Susiana 3 phase. Two extended skeletons at el. 77.08 (Grave 5.16) and el. 76.31 (Grave 5.17) had no grave goods to date them. In the absence of any better evidence, Grave 5.16 can be considered as contemporary with the Archaic Susiana 3 sherds near it. Grave 5.17 lay 77 cm deeper. The only two diagnostic sherds nearby, at el. 76.20, were red-line and dense-sandy gray fragments; they suggest that Grave 5.17 lay in Archaic Susiana 2 debris; this was also the date of the comparable levels in R23:503 and 504. On the other hand Grave 5.17 might have been an Archaic Susiana 3 interment dug into a deeper level.

The tops of the walls at el. 77.28 and 77.18 delimited two loci, R23:503 and 504, in the southern part of the trench (pl. 55:B). No bricks were distinguishable in the hard upper part of these walls, which seem to have consisted of pisé resting upon long Archaic bricks similar to those in Trench XXV. The continuation of the east-west walls of R23:503 and 504 to the east was traced for about 1.00 m in R23:402, at which point part of a north-south wall appeared (pl. 276), presumably the eastern wall of room R23:504. Its southeastern corner was missing, but might well have been destroyed by a Middle Susiana pit that straddled the border of R23:503 and 502 from el. 77.11 down to ca. 76.00. If the reconstruction proposed for R23:504 is correct, it was a room of rather imposing dimensions. Sherds were sparse between the tops of the east-west walls at el. 77.28 and 77.18 and their bases at 76.05; the only representative of the painted wares specific to Archaic Susiana 3 was at el. 77.25, a close-line fragment which joined another from R23:501 (pl. 212:D). Otherwise, aside from a few intrusive fragments, the sherds were straw-tempered smoothed accompanied by a few dense-sandy examples. An earlier building level was represented by irregular remnants of north-south walls with their tops at ca. el. 76.20 and their bases on a floor at 75.49. Again sherds were rare but between el. 76.05 and 75.49 dense-sandy, red-washed, and red-line fragments occurred. Thus the ceramic evidence, though scanty, points to an Archaic Susiana 2 date for the fragmentary structures of Trench XXXII. Six isolated painted-burnished sherds, mostly small and abraded, found in R23:503 at el. 76.83 and in R23:504 at el. 76.85, 78.15 (pl. 223:M), and 75.90 suggest that Archaic Susiana 1 remains exist at a lower level in Trench XXXII.

The Gully Cut (pls. 55:C–D; 279–81): In the fourth season a narrow trench was begun in Square S22 to check the cultural sequence of the low eastern slope of the mound along a gully eroded by rainwater from the terrace, hence the name Gully Cut. It proved to have substantial early deposits that made it a particularly promising area for establishing the successive phases of the Archaic Susiana period. In the fifth season the trench was enlarged to the east and attained a size of ca. 140.00 sq. m. The parts of the Gully Cut dug in the fourth and fifth seasons had few features and consisted primarily of layers of soil, ashy earth, and variously colored patches of clay (pl. 280). In the absence of architectural elements, locus numbers were assigned according to the exigencies of excavation (pl. 280).

Protoliterate debris occupied the uppermost levels of the Gully Cut. On the western side, near the modern gully, in loci S22:401–04, such debris lay under some 50 cm, and at some spots more, of pebbles and worn sherds washed down from the terrace during the millennia of desertion between the Protoliterate and the Achaemenid periods. On the eastern side of the trench there was no gravel and Protoliterate sherds began directly under the surface. Three Protoliterate features were found. In S22:402 a pit ca. 3.00 m in diameter lay below the

gravel, which at this point had an exceptional thickness of 1.20 m. The southern side of this pit was cut by a second much narrower and deeper one, with its top under a cluster of disjointed baked bricks (pl. 280). The southern edges of both pits overlapped into S22:403. The soft greenish soil of the second pit indicated that it had been a cess pit. It had cut through the Archaic Susiana layers down to a point only some 60 cm above compact sterile sand. The third Protoliterate feature consisted of reused baked brick fragments in the northeastern corner of the trench, S22:501, at el. 76.77–ca. 76.50; they had presumably once been part of a drain.

S22:501 was the most disturbed locus in the eastern half of the Gully Cut. Below the homogeneous Protoliterate debris was a ca. 40 cm thick layer in which the Archaic Susiana deposits had been disturbed during the Protoliterate period (el. 75.81–75.41). Both Protoliterate and prehistoric sherds appeared, the latter mostly Archaic Susiana in date. Still deeper, below el. 75.13 in the middle and western parts of the locus, there were traces of a pit filled with dense, water-laid layers of clay and a jumble of mudbricks at el. 74.48–74.43 (pl. 55:C). The individual bricks were ca. 40 × 12 × 10 cm; many had a central groove and six or eight finger imprints on a slightly convex upper surface (pl. 55:D). Unfortunately, there is no direct evidence to date the jumbled bricks. The clay above and around them was almost sterile and provided no diagnostic sherds. The ashy debris with Archaic Susiana 2–3 sherds immediately adjacent in the eastern part of the locus cannot be used to date them, nor are they similar to the long Archaic bricks from Trench XXV. Accordingly, it is likely that they belong to a considerably later period, presumably Middle Susiana, and had been tumbled down into a depression at the edge of the settlement.[13]

The higher Archaic Susiana levels, in S22:504, 507 + 508, and 512, consisted of soft black ashy earth mixed with many pebbles and contained a wealth of close-line and matt-painted sherds. A small patch of burnt, ashy material at el. 75.78 in the southeastern corner of the much-disturbed locus S22:501 marked the top of the Archaic Susiana layer, which was better preserved immediately to the east where the top was ca. 75.85. In S22:508 the bottom of the latest phase of Archaic Susiana was marked in the northwestern corner by a pebbly surface at el. 74.65–74.63 and at the eastern edge by a shallow pit full of large pebbles and sherds with a surface sloping north-south from el. 74.92 to

13. For a possible parallel to these bricks (pl. 55:D), see Ghirshman 1938, pl. XI:4 (Sialk, Period II). Another possible parallel consists of perhaps similar bricks from Eridu, Level 15, which are described as "square in section and extremely long, having a conspicuous row of double thumb impressions on the upper side" (Lloyd and Safar 1948:121).

74.69. It was probably an open-air cooking pit filled with stones to retain heat. An analogous conglomeration of ashes, pebbles, and sherds lay in S22:502 at a lower level, 74.26, and represents the middle phase of the Archaic Susiana period. The lowest floor in the Gully Cut was an irregularly round, hard surface, S22:510 in the area of S22:405, with some traces of burning; it was about 4.00 m in diameter. No sherds were associated with it, but it can be assigned to the Archaic Susiana 1 phase on the basis of its depth and the stratified sherds of the S22:405 area in which it lies.

Four poorly preserved skeletons were found in the Gully Cut. They had no grave goods and their dates remain problematic. In S22:507 some long bones of a child, Grave 5.10, and the skeleton of an adult, Grave 5.11, were found in Archaic Susiana 3 debris at el. 75.43 and 75.23 respectively (pls. 279–80). Over 1.50 m lower in mixed debris of Archaic Susiana 1–2 in S22:502 the bones of two adults, Graves 5.13 and 5.14, appeared at el. 73.60 and 73.50. The bones lay in levels that can be dated, but they could have been dug down from above; it is uncertain whether the close-line sherds lying close to the bones in S22:507 (pl. 210:B) were actually in association with them. Both sets of bones were covered by masses of hard packed clay. The clay in S22:507 rested on a floor just over the top of Grave 7.10 at el. 75.43 and was preserved as high as el. 76.24 in the western half of the locus, but only up to el. 75.43 in the east; presumably on that side it had been cut into during the Protoliterate occupation. In S22:502 the skeletons were immediately below a layer of hard clay present between el. 73.83 and 73.60 in most of the locus but apparently rising as high as el. 74.40 in the east directly above the bones. Each of the two clay layers was limited to its own small area, appearing respectively over and near the two sets of skeletons. This circumstance suggests that the skeletons might have been, despite the absence of gifts, real burials intentionally sealed with clay. Their date remains uncertain, though in the absence of any contrary evidence, they can with due reservation, be taken as belonging to the Archaic Susiana period.

The stratified layers of Archaic Susiana debris constitute the most important evidence obtained from the Gully Cut (pl. 279). As the profile of the northwestern edge of the trench illustrates (pl. 281) the top of the Archaic Susiana 2 layer, consisting of reddish-brown plaster, was at ca. el. 75.33, directly below the Protoliterate accumulation. In S22:402 the Archaic Susiana 2 layer had been destroyed by the two Protoliterate pits. The Archaic Susiana 2 layer ended at ca. el. 74.93. The highest part of the Archaic Susiana 1 material consisted of a layer of black ashy earth. Below was an extensive mass of dark brown earth, sinking into a pit in S22:404. Archaic Susiana 1 sherds were fewer and more sporadically distributed than those in higher and later levels; they were present only in the dark-colored earth and not

in the outcrops of clay or of compact sand. The top of virgin soil varied somewhat. In S22:402–04 it was at ca. el. 72.33 with some thin layers of hard red or sandy clay above the virgin sand. In the small test pit S23:509 sterile red or brown clay appeared from el. 73.74 to 72.35, corresponding to the outcrops of analogous material in S22:403 and 404, and the top of the sand was at 71.19.

There is an outstanding stratigraphic difference between the western and eastern parts of the Gully Cut. Protoliterate debris lies directly above the Archaic Susiana 2 level in the west; in the east it sits on a soft black ashy earth containing a wealth of pottery dated by the painted wares characteristic of Archaic Susiana 3. Only below the ca. 1.00 m thick layer of Archaic Susiana 3 did the Archaic Susiana 1–2 layers appear. Furthermore, the absolute heights at which contemporary Archaic Susiana strata appear in the western and eastern sides of the Gully Cut differ considerably. In the west Protoliterate deposits occur at the same depths as the Archaic Susiana 3 deposits in the east. The top of Archaic Susiana 2 came at ca. el. 75.33 in the west (S22:404), at ca. el. 74.63/60 in the middle (S22:401, 405 Middle), and at ca. el. 74.60 and 74.26/22 in the east (S22:405 East, 502, 508). There was likewise a slant in the top of the Archaic Susiana 1 debris from ca. el. 74.93 in the west (S22:403, 404, 405 West), and ca. el. 73.83 and 73.45 in the middle (S22:401, 405 Middle), to ca. el. 73.70, 73.44, and 73.30 in the east (S22:405 East, 508, 502). Clearly, the Archaic Susiana strata sloped from the west downward toward the east. This slope makes the absence of an Archaic Susiana 3 level in the western Gully Cut understandable. Any such remains that might have once existed there must have been eroded by the ancient predecessor of the modern gully before the Protoliterate occupation. The same was presumably true for any Middle Susiana or Early Susiana remains once present, which explains why there were no layers of that date between the Protoliterate and Archaic Susiana levels but only occasional stray sherds in the lower part of the Protoliterate debris. Comparisons with Trench XXXII and Sounding G, respectively to the west and east of the Gully Cut show that the slope of the Archaic Susiana layers was general for the early settlement on the lower flanks of the northeastern terrace.

In Trench XXXII Archaic Susiana 3 materials are found *in situ* as high as el. 77.55, while in Sounding G they occur only from ca. el. 74.30 down. There is thus a difference of 3.25 m in height in a distance of 45.00 m. Nowhere in the Archaic Susiana strata of the Gully Cut was there a layer indicating any destruction or abandonment of the area. It seems, rather, to have served continuously as an open space where ordinary activities were carried on and debris was dumped. The characteristic straw-tempered smoothed ware was in use in all levels. On the other hand, the consistent stratification of the sharply divergent classes of painted pottery establishes firmly both the existence and the sequence of the three phases of the Archaic Susiana period.

The survey of the soundings and trenches in which Susiana materials were exposed during the first five seasons of excavation at Chogha Mish has shown that the earliest and latest major prehistoric periods, Archaic Susiana and Late Susiana 2, are well documented by stratified debris. The Early Susiana period and the Early Middle Susiana phase are represented both by stratified debris and by excellent architecture. For the definition of the Late Middle Susiana phase the excavators had to rely during the first five seasons on the ceramic evidence from occupational debris without architecture.[14] A detailed consideration of the sequence of Susiana pottery, beginning with that of the Late Susiana 2 phase, is given in the next chapter.

14. During the ninth season at Chogha Mish an important structure of the Late Middle Susiana phase was excavated on the eastern side of the East Area. AA

CHAPTER 9

THE PREHISTORIC POTTERY

The pottery of the prehistoric Susiana sequence is represented by many more sherds than whole forms and is often characterized by elaborate painted decoration. Nonetheless, insofar as possible, the Susiana ceramics are dealt with in the same fashion as the Protoliterate pottery, that is, by basing the classification on an analysis of the shapes according to Delougaz' system (Delougaz 1952). In the absence of large numbers of complete shapes, such as are available from the Protoliterate period, complete classification numbers indicating body shape, proportions, and accessory elements cannot always be determined. On the other hand, it is evident from the finds that the tremendous variety of body and rim forms so characteristic of the Protoliterate pottery did not exist in the Susiana periods. This makes it easier to use the relatively small number of complete or semi-complete forms to define families of shapes within which the sherd material can be placed. Throughout this chapter almost every individual sherd is associated with a family of shapes. The inevitable risk of some mistaken attributions, especially when dealing with small fragments, seems preferable to a presentation of many discrete items.

Design or design elements have not been used as the basis for primary classification since the vessel shape, as the field or context in which the designs exist, must take primacy (Delougaz 1952:3–4). This is particularly true for styles such as those of prehistoric Susiana, which are markedly tectonic. The close correlations between pattern and shape often make it possible, once specific families have been defined, to attribute relatively shapeless body sherds to certain vessel forms with considerable likelihood. Accordingly, such sherds are shown in the plates together with those semi-complete or complete forms, to which they are considered comparable.

In analyzing the decoration, the individuality of the total composition—consisting of specific combinations of elements on specific shapes—is retained wherever possible. Individual motifs are classified according to their role in the total composition (e.g., tectonic framing elements; major motifs establishing symmetry or asymmetry, and the axes or "faces" of a composition; simple or complex bands or friezes; directional elements in which individual motifs through their asymmetry pro-duce the effect of movement; subsidiary or filling motifs).

As in the description of the prehistoric trenches and architecture, the latest material is described first and the earliest is described last. Thus, this discussion begins with that stage of the Susiana sequence which has been longest known, the pottery which has been variously termed Susa 1, Susa A, or Susiana *e*, and which has been famous since its discovery on the surface of Susa in 1891 and in the graves at the "Nécropole" there in 1906/07 (de Morgan et al. 1900:183; de Mecquenem 1912).

LATE SUSIANA POTTERY

THE WARES

Late Susiana pottery can be divided into two major categories, the standard buff wares and the orange and red wares. Despite the prominence and frequency of the latter, they are clearly specialized wares appearing in a limited number of forms. In contrast, the buff wares are the standard constituents of the ceramics, appearing in a wide range of shapes. In addition, two rare wares are attested, a gray-burnished ware and an apparently imported red ware with simple designs in black paint, the latter represented by only one example.

The Standard Buff Wares: The greater part of the Late Susiana pottery was made of what is basically a single ware, even though it ranges through innumerable gradations from relatively coarse to extremely fine. It is dense and tempered with mineral inclusions normally so small and evenly diffused through the paste as to be hardly noticeable. Thicker, coarser variations of the ware have visible grits and sometimes traces of vegetal tempering. The color varies considerably, ranging from brown to apricot or pink tones, but buff shades are the commonest. Greenish buff examples are relatively rare. There are no gray cores.

The manufacture of the vessels is good, even in the cases of the large and thick vessels. Very regular horizontal striations sometimes occurring on necks suggest that such specimens were turned rather rapidly on some kind of a wheel; but on the whole the pottery is still handmade. The paint varies in color from purplish brown to almost black. It tends to be glossy, though matt versions appear. In places where the paint has flaked away, its traces clearly can be seen on the surface.

The Red Wares: There is considerable diversity among the Late Susiana wares although all varieties resemble each other in having a dense paste and in being highly fired, with often a metallic ring. Sometimes a few scattered small grits and air pockets occur but often there is no visible tempering. The interior and exterior colors of the paste vary through many shades of buff, brown, brownish red, orange, or brick red. Despite their basic identity, the red ware sherds can be divided into two main categories by the absence or presence of a gray or black core. The sherds of the latter group have a thick dark core with only a thin layer of red on each side, except for some examples where the red layers are thicker. The dark core does not seem to be indicative of low firing; such sherds have a high ringing clink. Both the plain red and the dark-core categories can be subdivided according to variations in the treatment of the surface.

The plain red ware occurs either with or without a red wash, which varies from dense to unevenly smeared. In some cases the wash is plum or brownish, a color variation that might be a result of firing. The red-washed surface might be either matt or stroke-burnished, sometimes to a considerable sheen. The third subdivision of the plain red ware is characterized by a whitish surface film, sometimes fairly dense and sometimes so slight that the red color of the paste remains visible. The white surface does not appear to be a slip but rather the result of chemical interaction during firing. A variation of the white-film ware has either a dense or a smeared red wash added on top of the white surface.

Dark-core ware occurs also either with or without a red wash. The surfaces of the uncoated group can be either matt or stroke-burnished. The stroke-burnishing usually leaves a typically rippled surface and sometimes has produced a very high sheen. Such sherds occur in red or in a light tan or cream variant. In the coated group of the dark-core ware, the red wash is usually fairly dense, but frequently uneven. Sometimes the wash is only thinly smeared. Dark-core, red-washed sherds were sometimes burnished, either so slightly as to hardly be apparent or enough to produce a considerable sheen.

Gray Ware. In Late Susiana contexts gray ware is very rare. It is uniformly dense and usually without visible tempering. Both the interior and exterior surfaces of bowls are burnished with irregular horizontal strokes (pl. 162:K). The short neck of a jar, unburnished, proves that closed forms were also made in gray ware (pl. 162:U).

Black-on-red Ware. A distinctive ware is represented at Chogha Mish by only one example (fig. 21). The red brick fabric is granular, dense, and without vis-

ible tempering. The matt surface bears simple geometric decoration in a dull, grayish black paint. In all respects this vessel is alien at Chogha Mish. It has parallels at Jafarabad and Susa in Late Susiana and perhaps later contexts.[1] The ware has been found in various parts of Luristan, which might have been the eventual source for the stray example from Chogha Mish.[2]

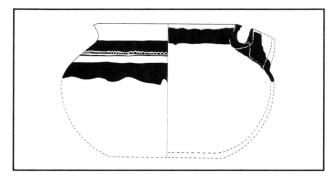

Figure 21. Fragment of an Imported Spouted Vessel, 2.567, from R8–S8:Trench III, Late Susiana

THE FAMILIES OF LATE SUSIANA POTTERY
(Fig. 23)

Though the Late Susiana period is well represented on the High Mound of Chogha Mish, only a relatively limited amount of material was excavated during the first five seasons. It comes primarily from two narrow but deep trenches (Trenches II and XXIII), supplemented by other small areas (Trenches IV and XXVIII). In order to make the typology more complete, pottery from Susa has also been used in defining the Late Susiana families. Only four of these are still unrepresented at Chogha Mish, but in some other cases complete forms from Susa are illustrated to represent the families instead of relatively small sherds from Chogha Mish.

Late Susiana Family I

A.01, .03, .04; standard buff ware, painted exterior

Figure 23; plates 56:A; 159:A–D

Miniature bowls are rather rare. They occur in either shallow or deep versions. One example has a square base (pl. 159:C). Another is unusual for its

---

1. For parallels, see Dollfus 1971:47, fig. 12:16–24 (this ware forms 1% of the Levels 1–3 ceramics; Jafarabad, Levels 1–3, Late Susiana); de Mecquenem 1912, pl. 19:10 (Susa A, Nécropole); Le Breton 1947:212, fig. 52:7–10, particularly 8 (Susa, "Intermediate Susa 1–2"); de Mecquenem 1912, pl. 25:2 (Susa, "Susa 2").

2. See Vanden Berghe 1973:51–52, 58 (Pusht-e Kuh, Late Chalcolithic); Mortensen 1976:56, fig. 5:b–c (Hulailan Valley, Late Chalcolithic); Goff 1971:141, fig. 5:3–5, 8–11, 51 (Pish-e Kuh, "Uruk").

everted ledge rim (pl. 159:D) The painted decoration is always simple.[3]

Late Susiana Family II

B.03, .04; standard buff ware, painted exterior

Figure 23; plate 159:G

Small convex bowls with simple geometric decoration such as horizontal bands occasionally occur. Complete examples show that such bowls could have ring bases.[4]

Late Susiana Family III

B.03, .04, .07; standard buff ware, painted exterior

Figure 23; plate 159:E–F

Small undecorated bowls or cups with convex walls are accommodated in Family III. Only two restorable profiles were recovered.

Late Susiana Family IV

B.03, .04, .07; standard buff ware, painted exterior

Figure 23; plates 56:B–C; 159:H–I

Family IV, containing small beakers, is the first of five Late Susiana families made up of examples of the same basic shape. Such vessels form a major component of Late Susiana pottery. They can be subdivided according to size and, secondarily, the shapes of their profiles. All five families can be considered as descendants of Middle Susiana categories: the small Family IV beakers are descendants of the tall examples of Middle Susiana Family I-3 (pl. 163:F–L) and the larger Families XII, XVIII–XX beakers are descendants of Middle Susiana Subfamily XVd vessels (pl. 175:F–G).[5] Like their Late Middle Susiana prototypes, the Late Susiana beakers are characterized by flat bases and by certain recurring decorative motifs. Another similarity is the appearance

of slightly flaring lips on both the Middle Susiana and Late Susiana beakers.[6]

Late Susiana Family V

B.20; standard buff ware, painted exterior

Figure 23

Cylindrical vessels with slightly flaring bases and rims appear to be fairly common at Susa but so far are not attested at Chogha Mish.[7]

Late Susiana Family VI

B.54, .55; standard ware, flaring neck, painted exterior

Figure 23; plate 159:J–M

Three groups of small jars can be distinguished by the position of their greatest diameter: in the upper part of the body in Family VI, in the middle in Family VII, and in the lower body in Family VIII. Each of these three families is subdivided on the basis of the (a) presence or (b) absence of a carination, but Subfamilies VIa and VIIIa are not represented at Chogha Mish.[8] Antecedents for these Late Susiana families of small jars can be found in the small vessels of Middle Susiana Families XXVIII and XXIX. Flaring necks seem to be standard for the small jars of Subfamily VIb. Tubular spouts were added to some examples (pl. 159:L–M). The upper part of the bodies and sometimes the necks bear painted decoration, usually horizontal bands.[9]

Late Susiana Family VII

B–C.60, B.64, .65; standard or fine buff ware, rims or short necks, painted exterior

Figure 23; plate 159:N–Q

Chogha Mish provided an intact example of a carinated Subfamily VIIa jar; it has geometric decoration on the upper body (pl. 159:N).[10] One Subfamily VIIb fragment has a vertical neck (pl. 159:O). Two other fragments have very slight everted necks (pl. 159:P–Q). Other accessories were sometimes added, such as the four pierced lugs (pl. 159:Q) or the straight tubular

---

3. For Late Susiana Family I in general, see Le Breton 1947:200, fig. 46:17 (Susa, old excavations); de Mecquenem 1912, pl. 19:6 (Susa, Nécropole). For parallels to plate 159:C, see Le Breton 1947, fig. 46:21 (squatter, painted triangles; Susa, old excavations); Weiss 1976, fig. 25:6–7 (Qabr-e Sheykheyn).

4. For parallels to plate 159:G, see de Mecquenem 1912, pl. 10:6 (Susa, Nécropole); Steve and Gasche 1971, pl. 39:12–13 (Susa, Acropole, 1965 Sounding, Phase A 2); Dollfus 1971, fig. 13:5 (Jafarabad, Level 2); Le Breton 1947:144, fig. 14:5 (Jafarabad, surface, -2.00); Dollfus 1983, fig. 74:2 (Bandebal, Level 16).

5. Middle Susiana Family XIV vessels, despite their rather similar body shape, cannot be taken as antecedents for Late Susiana beaker families. As a class, they seem to have been consistently squatter than the Late Susiana beakers. Moreover, they have ring bases and a simple, vertically aligned painted decoration quite different from that of the later beakers.

6. For parallels to plate 56:B, see de Mecquenem 1912, pls. 7:3; 8:1 (Susa, Nécropole).

7. See ibid., pls. 3:1–2; 9:1, 5 (Susa, Nécropole).

8. For Late Susiana Subfamily VIa, see figure 23. AA

9. For parallels to plate 159:J–K, see Le Breton 1947, fig. 46:3 (Susa, "Couche intermédiare"); Dollfus 1971, fig. 16:17–18 (Jafarabad, Level 2). For a parallel to plate 159:L, see de Mecquenem 1912, pl. 20:5 (Susa, Nécropole); cf. also Le Breton 1947, fig. 46:1 (no spout; Susa, "Couche intermédiare").

10. For motif similar to plate 159:N, see de Mecquenem 1912, pl. 16:4 (on interior of Late Susiana X bowl; Susa).

spouts on complete vessels from Susa (de Mecquenem 1912, pls. 20:9; 22:b). The amount of painted decoration varies. On one example (pl. 159:O) painted decoration occurs only on the neck; on another (pl. 159:Q) solid wash covers the neck and frames a vertical panel of ornament that must have covered at least half of the body.[11] The same tectonic scheme of panels framed by four pierced lugs appears on larger jars (pl. 161:C).

Late Susiana Family VIII

> B.70, .75; standard buff ware, very low flaring neck or rim, painted or unpainted

> Figure 23

Small vessels with their greatest diameter in the lower body have not been traced at Chogha Mish. At Susa carinated examples of Subfamily VIIIa were very common,[12] but rounded specimens of Subfamily VIIIb were rare.[13]

Late Susiana Family IX

> C.03; proportion "0," standard buff ware, painted interior

> Figure 23; plate 159:V–X

Large shallow bowls with rounded bases and interior decoration constitute a specific class of Late Susiana pottery. An occasional example might have a diameter of more than 30 cm. These shallow bowls do not seem to be nearly as common as the bowls of higher proportions.[14]

Late Susiana Family X

> B–C.00, .01, .04, .05; proportions "1–2," standard buff ware, painted interior

> Figure 23; plates 56:SS–TT; 160:A–F

Convex bowls with disc or ring bases, a painted lip band on the exterior, and the main decoration on the interior form one of the larger and one of the more elabo-rately painted series of Late Susiana pottery. Some intact examples from Susa indicate that occasionally such bowls were supported by high cylindrical pedestal bases; the high pedestals found at Chogha Mish (pl. 159:R, T) and Jafarabad are conical so that it is not altogether certain that they once supported Family X bowls. The bases are decorated with horizontal bands (pl. 159:R–U) and in one case also zigzags (pl. 159:R).[15] The incomplete Family X bowls from Chogha Mish document various motifs, such as the "comb" (pl. 160:A, E–F), meander (pl. 160:C), and center patterns (pl. 159:A, D), well known on complete bowls from the Late Susiana cemetery at Susa.[16]

The bowls of Family X appear to be the descendants of Middle Susiana Subfamily IXb bowls that always have ring bases and their main decoration on the interior. The Family X repertory of designs, however, seems to have been derived from the general Middle Susiana tradition rather than from specific patterns that occur on Middle Susiana Subfamily IXb bowls from Chogha Mish.

Late Susiana Family XI

> B–C.00, .01, .03, .04, .05; proportions "1–2"; fine buff ware, painted exterior, designs include hatched friezes

> Figure 23; plates 56:F–M, P–V; 160:G–Q

In sharp contrast to the preceding group, the bowls of Family XI are painted only on the exterior. Another distinction is the ware, which in this family is usually fine. However, as in Family X, both disc and ring bases occur. Bowls with their upper walls approaching the vertical (.04) appear to be dominant. The ware and shapes of the Family XI bowls mark them as descendants of thin-walled bowls of Middle Susiana Families III and XI.

The predominant decorative scheme of Family XI is a narrow frieze of Xs above wider, vertically or diagonally hatched friezes that frame the central field of the bowl. Hourglasses frequently divide the field into segments occupied by birds with outstretched wings (pl. 160:H–J; 2.189) or, less commonly, dogs (pl. 160:Q).

11. For an example related to plate 159:O, see Dollfus 1971, fig. 16:19 (Jafarabad, Level 2). For an example with the same shape but different decoration as plate 122:Q, see ibid., fig. 16:16, 9, 10 respectively (Jafarabad, Levels 2, 3).

12. For the Late Susiana Family VIIIa in general, see de Mecquenem 1912, pls. 19:1–5, 8–9; 20:1–3 (Susa, Nécropole).

13. Subfamily VIIIb (fig. 23) must be dated to the Late Middle Susiana phase; see Le Breton 1947, fig. 25:17; Dollfus 1983, fig. 32:10–11.

14. For a small version of the shape of plate 159:V–X, see Dollfus 1971, fig. 9:2 (diameter only 11.4 cm; Jafarabad, Level 2). For a probable Late Middle Susiana antecedent to plate 159:X, see Gautier and Lampre,1905:105, fig. 166 right (Musyan). For birds similar to those shown on plate 159:X, see Canal 1978:174, fig. 25:1 (beaker; Susa, Acropole 2).

15. For Family X bowls on high cylindrical pedestals, see de Mecquenem 1912, pls. 11:4, 12:1 (Susa, Nécropole). For unpainted bowls on high pedestals, see Steve and Gasche 1971, pl. 39:18–19 (Susa, Acropole, 1965 Sounding, Phase A 2). For parallels to plate 159:R–U, see Dollfus 1971, fig. 9:9, 12 respectively (Jafarabad, Level 1 and no level).

16. For a parallel to plates 56:TT and 160:A, see de Mecquenem 1912, pl. 2:4 (Susa, Nécropole). For motif similar to plates 15:4 (center motif) and 17:3 (crude "comb"), see de Mecquenem 1912, pls. 2:3, 9:8, 17:4, 41:2, 42:1 (motif of a standard). For a parallel to plate 160:D, see Le Breton 1947, fig. 46:8 (Susa, old excavations); for motif, see de Mecquenem 1912, pl. 15:7 (Susa, Nécropole). For motif similar to plate 160:F, see ibid., pl. 14:2.

The Maltese crosses preserved on small sherds might have either filled panels demarcated by hourglasses or formed a continuous frieze (pl. 56:P–R). Occasionally a motif consisting of four lines pendant from an oval splotch was set at intervals in the central field (pl. 56:J–L) or used to form a basal frieze replacing the usual hatched frieze (pl. 56:M). Usually a solid wash covers the lowermost part of the body and the base.[17]

An alternative and rarer scheme of decoration has no hatched friezes but only narrow geometric bands delimiting the field in which the main motifs appear. These can be augmented circles alternating with pairs of subsidiary splotches plus pendant lines (pl. 160:M) or spread-winged birds placed on their sides to form continuous horizontal friezes (pl. 160:P). The simpler of the Family XI designs from Chogha Mish are horizontal zigzags reserved in broad wash (pl. 160:L).[18]

A sherd with bands of Xs and hatching has a slightly everted lip and a relatively straight profile (pl. 160:K). Although it appears to be a beaker fragment it is decorated atypically with motifs characteristic for Family XI bowls.

Late Susiana Family XII

C.0; standard or fine buff ware, unpainted

Figure 23

Sherds of thin buff ware bowls and beakers, often of eggshell thinness, found in Late Susiana debris were usually too small to indicate shapes with certainty. The one complete example comes from a transitive Late Middle Susiana–Late Susiana level and could as well belong to the Late Middle Susiana phase. It is probable that such vessels continue in the Late Susiana period.

Late Susiana Family XIII

.54, .56; standard buff ware, painted exterior

Figure 23; plate 161:A–B

Ovoid jars without any marked change of angle are only rarely exemplified at Chogha Mish (pl. 161:B). On the basis of examples from Susa, the necks of the Fam-

ily XIII jars should be short; nonetheless the sherd of a high and elaborately painted neck is tentatively placed here (pl. 161:A).[19]

Late Susiana Family XIV

B–C.64; standard buff ware, painted exterior

Figure 23; plates 56:N–O, Y, PP, WW; 161:C–D, F

Among the more typical vessels of the Late Susiana period are fairly squat jars with wide or fairly wide flaring necks, four pierced lugs, and a dense net of painted decoration on the upper body (pl. 161:C–D, F). The four lugs, each set in a vertical black band, divide the main register of the composition into panels. The vessels of Family XIV can be considered as descendants of the jars of Middle Susiana Family XXXII.[20]

Late Susiana Family XV

C.7; standard ware, painted

Figure 23; plate 161:E

Medium-sized jars with their greatest diameter in the lower body seem to have been very rare. There is, however, one sherd that can be considered as a representative of Family XV and restored by analogy with smaller, Subfamily VIIIa, specimens from Susa with the same motif.[21]

Late Susiana Family XVI

D.00; standard buff ware, unpainted

Figure 23; plate 161:G–H

Sherds of relatively thick or coarse buff ware prove the existence of straight sided, unpainted bowls of fairly large size. Family XVI might also be used to accommodate any unpainted convex bowl sherd that might eventually appear.[22]

17. For parallels to plate 56:P–R, see de Mecquenem 1912, pl. 7:1, and Le Breton 1947, fig. 47:22 (concentric circles instead of Maltese crosses), 24 (isolated crosses; all from Susa, Nécropole); Le Brun 1971, fig. 36:7 (spectacle spirals; Susa, Acropole I, Level 27); Dollfus 1971, fig. 11:4 (Jafarabad, Level 2); Gautier and Lampre 1905, fig. 136 (disc; Musyan). For parallels to plate 160:G, see Steve and Gasche 1971, pl. 39:21 (Susa, Acropole 1965, Phase A 2); Dollfus 1971, fig. 11:5 (Jafarabad, Level 2). For parallels to plate 160:H–J, see Le Breton 1947, fig. 51:17 (for bird only; Susa, old excavations); Dollfus 1971, fig. 13:6 (Jafarabad, Level 1). For continuous friezes of dogs similar to plate 160:N and Q, see de Mecquenem 1912, pls. 3:7; 9:1 (Susa, Nécropole).

18. For the same design as that in plate 160:P on a beaker, see de Mecquenem 1912, pl. 41:5 (Susa, Nécropole).

19. For a parallel to plate 161:A, see Dollfus 1971, fig. 17:15 (Jafarabad, Level 2). For a parallel to plate 161:B, see ibid., fig. 16:12.

20. For a parallel to plate 56:PP, see Steve and Gasche 1971, pl. 39:14 (Susa, Acropole 1965, Phase A 2). For a parallel to plate 161:C, see Dollfus 1971, fig. 17:6 (Jafarabad, Level 3). For a design comparable to plate 161:F, see de Mecquenem 1912, pl. 21:4 (on a four-lugged jar; Susa, Nécropole).

21. For a parallel to plate 161:E, see de Mecquenem 1912, pl. 21:3, 6 (Susa).

22. For parallels to plate 161:G–H, see Le Brun 1971, fig. 38:8 (Susa, Acropole I, Level 25); Dollfus 1971, fig. 10:9 (Jafarabad, Level 1); idem 1983, fig. 88:1 (Bandebal, Level 10).

Table 17. Pottery, Similar to Chogha Mish Late Susiana Families I–XXX, Present at Other Sites

OTHER SITES	I	II	IV	V	VIb	VIIa	VIIb	VIIIa	VIIIb	IX	Pedestal	X	XI	XIII
SUSA														
Old Excavations	X	—	—	—	X	M	—	—	—	—	X	X	X	—
Nécropole	X	—	X	—	X	—	X	X	X	—	—	X	X	—
Acropole I:25, 27	—	—	—	—	—	—	—	—	—	—	—	—	X	—
Acropole II:11–10	—	—	—	—	—	—	—	—	—	M	—	—	—	—
Acropole 1965 A 1–2	—	X	—	—	—	—	—	—	—	—	X	—	—	—
JAFARABAD														
Level 1	—	—	—	—	—	—	—	—	X	—	M	—	—	—
Level 2	—	X	—	—	X	—	S	—	—	S	—	—	X	X
Level 3	—	—	—	—	—	—	S	—	—	—	—	—	—	—
Old Excavations	—	X	—	—	—	—	—	—	—	—	—	—	—	—
BANDEBAL														
Level 10	—	—	—	—	—	—	—	—	—	—	—	—	—	—
Levels 16–11	—	X	—	—	—	—	—	—	—	—	—	—	—	—
QABR-E SHEYKHEYN	X	—	—	—	—	—	—	—	—	—	—	—	—	—
MUSYAN	—	—	—	—	—	—	—	—	—	—	—	—	M	—
NOKHODI III-b	—	—	—	—	—	—	—	—	—	—	—	—	—	—
BAKUN A	—	—	—	—	—	—	—	—	—	—	—	—	—	—

Late Susiana Family XVII

> C–D.04, .07; standard buff ware, painted exterior
>
> Figure 23

Susa provides examples of a deep bowl with the upper part of the exterior decorated by a major register of design set off by narrow and wide horizontal bands, but the type seems to be rare.[23] It is not represented at Chogha Mish. It is both in shape and in the general scheme of the decoration a Late Susiana successor to the craters of Middle Susiana Family XXIV.

Late Susiana Family XVIII

> C–D.02, .03c, .04; fine to standard buff ware, painted exterior
>
> Figure 23; plate 161:I

Late Susiana Family XIX

> C–D.07; fine to standard buff ware, painted exterior
>
> Figure 23; plate 161:J–N

Late Susiana Family XX

> C–D.20, .22, .24; fine to standard buff ware, painted exterior
>
> Figure 23; plate 56:Z–AA, CC, EE–LL, NN–OO

Tall beakers, normally of proportions "6"–"7," are among the better known of the Late Susiana vessels. They are divided into three families distinguished according to their profiles: concave or convex in Family

XVIII, convex below and concave above in Family XIX, and cylindrical in Family XX. The sophisticated designs of bold zigzags, ibexes with huge sweeping horns, friezes of long-necked birds, and other motifs have long been famous.[24] At Chogha Mish no restorable examples were found, but there were many sherds, particularly lips with a row of wading birds depicted (pls. 56:EE–GG, II–LL; 161:K, N). Much more unusual is a frieze of flying birds (pl. 161:M). A small fragment has what are probably the tips of ibex horns that originally encircled a patterned circle (pl. 56:Z). Several sherds had a common composition, hourglasses dividing the frames of rectangular panels that are either sparsely (pl. 56:QQ–RR) or densely (pl. 56:NN–OO) filled with geometric motifs. Several designs, although stylistically typical for Late Susiana, have no specific parallels: a composition of equilateral and concave-sided triangles (pl. 56:AA), the head and forearm of a human figure (pl. 161:L), and, particularly striking, two birds with spiky plumage (pl. 56:HH).[25]

23. See de Mecquenem 1912, pl. 6:2 (Susa, Nécropole); Le Brun 1971, fig. 36:4 (Susa, Acropole I, Level 25).

24. See Groenewegen-Frankfort 1951:6, 146–47; pls. 1, 50.

25. For a parallel to plate 56:Z, see de Mecquenem 1912, pl. 4:1–2 (Susa, Nécropole). For a parallel to plate 56:GG, see Le Breton 1947, fig. 48:5 (Susa, old excavations). For spiky plumage similar to that in plate 56:HH, see Weiss 1976, fig. 22:139 (Qabr-e Sheykheyn). For a parallel to plate 56:KK, see Goff 1963, fig. 11:13 (heads facing opposite direction; Tall-e Nokhodi, Level IIIb). For diagonally slashed vertical divider similar to plate 56:MM, see de Mecquenem 1912, pls. 5:1–2; 8:5; Pottier 1923, pl. 2:31 (Susa, Nécropole); Dollfus 1971, fig. 14:7 (Jafarabad, Level 3). For a parallel to plate 56:QQ, see de Mecquenem 1912, pl. 8:1 (Susa, Nécropole). For a parallel to plate 56:RR, see de Mecquenem 1912, pl. 6:5; Pottier 1923, pl. 2:32 (Susa, Nécropole). For a parallel to plate 161:I, see de Mecquenem 1912, pl. 5:1, 6 (Susa, Nécropole). For a parallel to plate 161:K and N, see Steve and Gasche 1971, pls. 36:5, 40:10

Table 17. Pottery, Similar to Chogha Mish Late Susiana Families I–XXX, Present at Other Sites (*cont.*)

OTHER SITES	XIV	XV	XVI	XIX–XX	XXI	XXII	XXIIIb	XXIV	XXV	XXVI	XXVII	XXVIII	XXIX	XXX
SUSA														
Old Excavations	—	—	—	X	—	—	M	—	S	—	—	—	—	—
Nécropole	—	M	—	X	—	—	—	—	—	—	—	—	—	—
Acropole I:25, 27	—	—	X	—	—	X	X	—	—	—	—	X	—	X
Acropole II:11–10	—	—	—	—	—	—	—	—	—	—	—	—	—	—
Acropole 1965 A 1–2	X	—	—	X	—	—	X	X	—	—	—	—	—	—
JAFARABAD														
Level 1	—	—	X	—	—	—	—	—	—	—	—	—	X	X
Level 2	—	—	—	X	X	X	M	—	X	X	—	—	—	X
Level 3	X	—	—	—	—	—	X	—	X	X	—	X	—	X
Old Excavations	—	—	—	—	—	—	X	—	—	—	X	X	—	—
BANDEBAL														
Level 10	—	—	X	—	—	—	—	—	—	—	—	—	—	—
Levels 16–11	—	—	—	—	—	—	—	—	—	—	—	—	—	—
QABR-E SHEYKHEYN	—	—	—	M	—	—	—	X	—	—	—	—	—	—
MUSYAN	—	—	—	—	—	—	—	—	—	—	—	—	—	—
NOKHODI III-b	—	—	—	M	—	—	—	—	—	—	—	—	—	—
BAKUN A	—	—	—	—	—	—	—	—	—	—	X	—	—	—

X = Both shape and design (when applicable) present; M = Motif is attested, shape not necessarily related; S = Shape is present but, if painted, motif might differ

Antecedents for the Late Susiana beakers are to be found in Middle Susiana Family XV. For example, a beaker decorated by a snake anticipates vessels found at Susa in both shape and decoration size (pl. 175:F, H) and a squat beaker provides a prototype for the great extended zigzags so typical of the Late Susiana period (pl. 174:A).

Late Susiana Families XXI–XXII

C.5, .6; standard buff ware, unpainted

Figure 23; plate 162:B–C

Unpainted jars represented at Chogha Mish by small sherds that could belong to either .5 or .6 shapes. Those with plain hole mouths are assigned to Family XXI and those with unobtrusive low necks to Family XXII. The latter are comparable to some examples of the red ware Family XXVIII (pl. 162:P–Q). In general, the sherds of Families XXI and XXII exemplify types more commonly found in red ware and are ultimately derived from the red ware hole-mouthed cooking pots of Middle Susiana Family XXXIX.[26]

Late Susiana Family XXIII

C–D.5, .6; standard buff ware, painted exterior

Figure 23; plates 56:UU–VV; 162:D, F–H

Ovoid or globular storage jars make up Family XXIII. Examples with relatively wide and short necks can be distinguished as Subfamily XXIIIa (pl. 162:D) and those with narrower and higher necks as Subfamily XXIIIb (pl. 162:F, H), but the division is blurred by necks of intermediate proportions.

The decoration is usually limited to the upper part of the body and often consists only of simple geometric elements, such as clusters of squiggles (pl. 162:H) or of two or three vertical lines bordered by scallops, spaced in a band below the neck. Friezes of vertical wavy lines of crosshatched lozenges and of stepped triangles separated by a recessed zigzag band also occur (pls. 56:UU–VV; 162:D).[27] Occasionally a representational element appears in the register at the root of the neck, as on a sherd with a dog similar to those of the fine ware bowls except that it is stouter.[28]

(Susa, Acropole 1965, Phases A 1 and A 2). For human figures similar to plate 161:L, see Pottier 1923, pl. 8:15, 18 (Susa, Nécropole); de Mecquenem 1934, figs. 11:1; 12 (old excavations). For parallels to plate 161:N, see de Mecquenem 1912, pl. 9:2, 7–9 (Susa, Nécropole); Dollfus 1971, fig. 14:4 (Jafarabad, Level 2). For a parallel to plate 162:A, see Weiss 1976, fig. 12:4 (Qabr-e Sheykheyn).

26. For forms related to plate 162:B, see Dollfus 1971, fig. 15:1–2 (Jafarabad, Level 2). For parallels to plate 162:C, see Le Brun 1971, fig. 39:5 (Susa, Acropole, Level 27); Dollfus 1971, fig. 15:8 (Jafarabad, Level 2).

27. For a parallel to plate 56:UU, see Steve and Gasche 1971, pl. 40:9 (Susa, Acropole 1965, Phase A 2). For parallels to plate 162:F–G, see Le Brun 1971, fig. 37:9 (Susa, Acropole I Sounding, Level 25); Le Breton 1947, fig. 15:9–10 (Jafarabad, surface to 2.0 m); Dollfus 1971, fig. 18:4, 7 (Jafarabad, Level 2). For forms similar to plate 162:H, see Le Brun 1971, fig. 37:3 (neck only; Susa, Acropole I Sounding, Level 27); Dollfus 1971, fig. 17:4 (Jafarabad, Level 3).

28. For example, see Dollfus 1971, fig. 17:5, 7 (Jafarabad, Levels 2–3). For dog motif, see Le Breton 1947, fig. 49 (Susa, old excavations).

Figure 22. Fragment of a Late Susiana Family XXV Jar, 1.236,
from Trench IV:Q9 South, el. 82.80–81.95

Late Susiana Family XXIV

C–D.5, .6; standard buff ware, low neck with interior ledge, painted exterior

Figure 23; plate 162:E

The feature distinguishing the Family XXIV jars from those of the preceding family is the inward-projecting ledge of the neck. The neck on one example (pl. 162:E) is vertical and the ledge slightly concave. It had vertical perforations spaced at wide intervals. The ledge must have served a specific function; it would have been well suited for supporting a lid. The purpose of the perforations is not certain.[29]

Late Susiana Family XXV

D.5; standard buff ware; four lugs, painted exterior

Figure 22; plate 56:PP

Large-sized versions of the Family XIV jars with four lugs and dense decoration are designated as Family XXV. The vessels of this family differ from those of Family XIV in sometimes having the four lugs placed above the main register of decoration. There is also a tendency to increase the importance or the number of the subsidiary registers. The few surviving sherds of a very sloppily painted example from Chogha Mish indicate that groups of horizontal wavy lines were placed at intervals close to the neck, while the main register was occupied by multiple zigzags on a reserved field, a well-known Late Susiana motif (fig. 22).[30] The fabric of this

vessel is unusual in being intermediate between the buff and red wares. The dense paste has some small to medium grits and air pockets. Although the basic color of the paste is light orange, on both the exterior and interior it grades to yellowish buff edges, which are sometimes about 1 mm thick, but sometimes so thin as to resemble a slip.

Late Susiana Family XXVI

C.01, .03, .04; red and gray wares, unpainted

Figure 23; plate 162:I–L

The first family of the red wares contains medium-sized bowls of simple shapes. One of the two convex-sided examples is of burnished dark-core ware (pl. 162:I). The other has an orange-colored paste with a cream slip on both sides, on top of which a filmy red wash has been applied in streaks (pl. 162:J). A third sherd (pl. 162:K), of gray ware, appears to have a markedly vertical stance and might have had a wide flat base similar to those of red-washed bowls from Jafarabad.[31]

Late Susiana Family XXVII

D.00, .03, .05; red wares, unpainted

Figure 23; plate 162:M–N

Large bowls with straight or convex sides are some of the more frequent and characteristic vessels of the red wares. They occur in plain red ware and its tan variant, in red-washed ware, and in dark-core ware. The surfaces are frequently burnished to a high gloss, with the irregularities left by individual burnish strokes producing a rippled effect. Despite the frequency of lip and body sherds, relatively few restorable forms were recovered. At present it appears that the thicker-walled bowls (e.g., pl. 162:N–O) were commoner than thinner-walled bowls (e.g., pl. 162:M). The latter's incurving lip also seems to have been more rare than the flaring lips.[32]

Late Susiana Family XXVIII

C–D.5, .6; red wares, unpainted

Figure 23; plate 162:O–T

At Chogha Mish this family is known only from mouth and upper body sherds; they suggest that the vessels were globular in shape. The mouths were not left

29. For examples similar to those in plate 162:E, see Steve and Gasche 1971, pl. 41:27 (Susa, Acropole 1965 Sounding, Phase A 2); Weiss 1976, figs. 27:237; 30:5 (Qabr-e Sheykheyn).

30. For parallels to figure 22 and plate 56:PP, see Dollfus 1971, fig. 18:8 (Jafarabad, Level 3; ibid., fig. 17:6 is a Late Susiana Family XXV jar with almost exactly the same decoration as on pl. 161:C); for multiple zigzags on smaller jars, see Dollfus 1971, fig. 16:5, 22 (Jafarabad); de Mecquenem 1943, pl. 7:1–2 (with different motifs; Susa, old excavations).

31. For shapes possibly analogies to plate 162:L, see Dollfus 1971, fig. 19:9–10 (Jafarabad, Levels 2–3).

32. For parallels to plate 162:N, see Le Breton 1947, fig. 45:1 (Jafarabad, surface to 2.0 m); Dollfus 1971, fig. 19:7 (Jafarabad, Level 2).

LATE SUSIANA

Scale 1:5

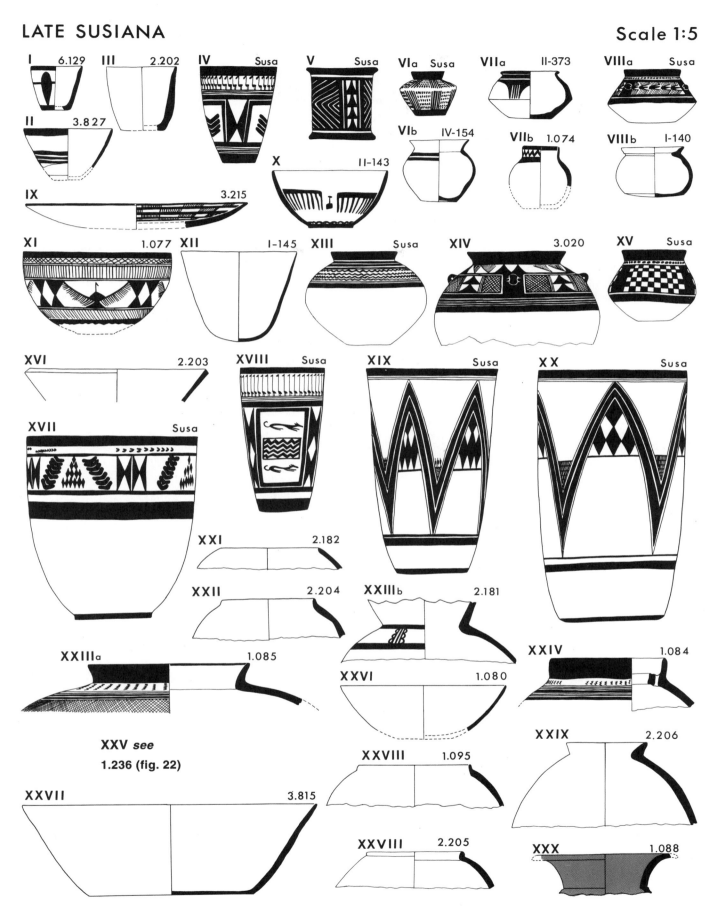

Figure 23. Late Susiana Families I–XXX

plain but have either a slight blunt rim (pl. 162:O–Q) or a separately-made globular or triangular rim. In the latter, the join of the rim and the body shows clearly on the interior (pl. 162:R–T). Both types of rims are so low and the mouth opening so wide that the vessels can still be considered as essentially hole-mouthed and comparable in both shape and function to the hole-mouthed round-bottomed cooking pots of the Middle Susiana period (pl. 193:H–I, U–V, X). Corroboration that the Late Susiana bases were round is provided by complete and semi-complete examples from Jafarabad.[33] The vessels of Family XXVIII were the direct descendants of the Middle Susiana cooking pots. In view of their function it is understandable that, unlike many of the bowls of Families XXVI and XXVII, the surfaces of Family III were not burnished. In addition, the Family XXVIII sherds are frequently smudged or stained.[34]

Late Susiana Family XXIX

C–D.5, .6; red wares, unpainted

Figure 23; plate 162:U–Y

In contrast to the sherds of the preceding family, the Family XXIX vessels have a well-differentiated neck. They usually flare quite sharply and might have perforations at the base analogous to those of Family XXIV. No restorable examples have been found, but it is likely that in shape the Family XXIX jars resembled the almost certainly flat-based buff ware jars of Family XXV.[35]

Late Susiana Family XXX

C–D.5, .6; red wares, unpainted

Plate 162:Z–AA

A relatively narrow and tall neck with a rim is the diagnostic feature of the last Late Susiana family. Such necks occur in both plain and dark-core red-washed wares and belonged to rather large jars that were probably similar in shape to those of the buff ware Family XXIII. Jafarabad provides parallels for both the splayed

and vertical necks; one example combines a vertical neck with four lugs on the uppermost part of the body.[36]

MIDDLE SUSIANA POTTERY

As in the Late Susiana period, the two main categories of pottery are the buff wares and, appearing for the first time in the Middle Susiana period, the red-brown wares. The former constitute the greater bulk of the material. Each of the two major categories can be subdivided into several subgroups that blend into one another.

THE WARES

Standard Buff Ware: The paste varies in color from varieties of brownish yellow, through cream, to greenish buff. The tempering is mineral with variations in both the amount of grit and the size of the individual grains. Sometimes larger grits, though scattered rather sparsely in the paste itself, were worked up to the surface in clusters during the shaping and smoothing of the vessels. The texture of the paste varies from granular to dense.

The vessels are handmade and frequently show marks of shaping and scraping, as well as somewhat uneven surfaces. In some cases surfaces remain relatively rough; in others there has been smoothing, though usually not enough to obliterate all the scrape marks or to produce a polish. Often smoothing of still moist vessels produced a "slip" that was difficult to distinguish from actual slips added separately unless the latter were of a different shade than the body paste.

The paint grades from brown to black and not infrequently has a definite greenish tinge. The thickness of the paint deposited in the course of a single brush stroke can vary considerably. Often crossing or impinging brush strokes can be distinguished; they are indicated in the drawing by a convention of white reserve borders (e.g., pls. 165:A; 167:F; 169:L; 171:L; 177:G; in contrast to the artificial white lines that indicate varying shades, compare the actual white reserved areas in many designs, e.g., pl. 183:Y–BB). The thicker paint is darker in color, often granular, and tends to flake. The disappearance of the paint reveals that it had often eaten into the paste of the vessels forming slightly sunken beds. In cases where the paint is entirely gone, the decoration can still be drawn by careful observation of the sunken areas. In other cases the areas once covered and protected by paint are lighter in color than the adjacent, always exposed surfaces, which have weathered to darker tones.

Fine Buff Ware: The finer range of the buff ware is distinguishable by a dense paste, the absence of any visible grit tempering, and thin body walls, about 6 mm or

---

33. For example, see Dollfus 1971, fig. 15:12, 14 (Jafarabad, Levels 1 and 3).

34. For a parallel to plate 162:P–Q, see Le Brun 1971, fig. 39:4 (Susa, Acropole I Sounding, Level 27). For parallels to plate 162:R–U, see Le Breton 1947, fig. 8:8 (Jafarabad, surface to 2.0 m); Dollfus 1971, fig. 19:4 (Jafarabad, Level 3); for the same shape in buff, see Le Brun 1971, fig. 39:5 (Susa, Acropole I Sounding, Level 27).

35. For a parallel to plate 162:U, see Le Brun 1971, fig. 39:9–10 (Susa, Acropole I Sounding, Level 25). For parallels to plate 162:W, see Le Brun 1971, fig. 39:11 (Susa, Acropole I Sounding, Level 25); Dollfus 1971, fig. 17:12 (buff ware; Jafarabad, Level 1); Langsdorff and McCown 1942, pl. 20:13 (Bakun A).

36. For a parallel to plate 162:Z, see Dollfus 1971, fig. 19:1, 2 (Jafarabad, Levels 3 and 2 respectively). For a parallel to plate 162:AA, see ibid., fig. 19:3 (Jafarabad, Level 1).

less. The fine buff ware tends to be more highly fired than the standard varieties. Although the fine ware was used for smaller vessels, in one of the commoner groups of unpainted vessels, Middle Susiana Family XX, the walls are sometimes notably thin for the large size of the bodies and often of a very dense paste; the ware is either fine or intermediate between the fine and standard buff wares.

Gritty Buff Ware: A variety of buff ware distinguished by the considerable amount of grit in the paste and by the relative thickness of the vessel walls is particularly characteristic for the first phase of the Middle Susiana period and, in fact, represents the survival of the very gritty buff ware of the Early Susiana period. The best examples of the gritty variant of the buff ware are some of the deep vessels of Middle Susiana Family XXI. However, paste with more grit than in the standard Middle Susiana buff ware also occurs in other shapes, even in painted vessels.

Straw-tempered Buff Ware: A buff ware variant is defined by its vegetal tempering and also by the relative thickness of the walls of the vessels made of it. The ware was used for some of the coarser domestic vessels, which were usually unpainted. They form a relatively small proportion of the total ceramics of the Middle Susiana period.

Plain Red Ware: In all the Middle Susiana varieties of red ware the paste is essentially the same: dense, granular in the breaks, with the mineral tempering for the most part too small to be easily visible, and high fired with a clinky ring. Sometimes there were mica or white inclusions and sometimes small or occasionally larger grits. The basic color is a brick red, but light orange-red and brown shades occur. Sometimes a sherd grades from red on one side to light-orange buff or brown on the other. There are a few examples of a gray core (pl. 193:L, T), but hardly enough to form a group comparable to the dark-core class of the Late Susiana period. Variations in the treatment of the surface provide the criteria for subdividing the Middle Susiana red wares. It is notable that, in contrast to the prominence of burnishing on the Late Susiana red wares, this treatment does not occur on their Middle Susiana antecedents.

The plain red ware vessels are those that, aside from the scraping and paring incidental to their shaping, had no special surface treatment such as a coating. The exteriors were, however, sometimes smoothed. The surface color of some examples, for the most part the smoothed sherds of hole-mouthed cooking pots, ranges from red through brown to black shades (pl. 193:K–M). The different colors can appear on the same vessel and are presumably due to the circumstances of firing.

Red-washed Red Ware: Red or orange-red washes frequently appear on both exterior and interior surfaces, often as a uniform and quite thick coating distinct in color from the paste.

White-film Ware: A tenuous white film sometimes covers either the exterior or both surfaces of vessels that are otherwise of plain red or, rarely, of red-washed ware. The sherds are lighter or darker according to whether the primary surface color is red, brown, or mottled. When the sherds are moistened the light film becomes unnoticeable, but it reappears as they dry, making them look as if they had been carelessly washed. The white film is probably a result of chemical action during firing, as was noted above in the description of Late Susiana continuation of this ware.

Buff-slipped Red Ware: Sometimes a buff slip was added so uniformly that the unbroken vessels would have appeared to be of buff ware (pl. 193:P–Q, T, X). Rare and atypical is a thick, coarse variant with vegetal tempering, but nonetheless still quite dense and high-fired (2.704, R10–11:Trench II, Plot 2, el. 79.70).

Gray Ware: A few sherds are characterized by their dense, uniformly gray paste, with only occasional scattered grits visible. Their burnished surfaces underline their identity as representatives of a specific ware distinct from the red wares that are never burnished in the Middle Susiana period. At Chogha Mish, the shapes appear to be limited to simple convex bowls (cf. pl. 193:A; 4.482). The gray ware seems to be typical for the Late Middle Susiana phase but is extremely rare at Chogha Mish. It is known from several sites in central Khuzestan.[37]

THE FAMILIES OF MIDDLE SUSIANA OPEN FORMS
(FIGS. 26, 30–31)

An attempt has been made to divide the ceramics of the Middle Susiana period into groups, each of which is defined by a cluster of specific characteristics. Some families, however, include a variety of individual types. This is particularly the case among families devoted to open forms, which constitute the majority of the ceramic assemblage and are often simple, undifferentiated shapes (e.g., Families X–XI). Other families are limited to one distinctive type of vessel (e.g., Families XII-1, XIII-2, XVII, XXV, XXVI) or to only a few very similar types (e.g., Families XVIIIc–f, XIX).

Occasionally, a family contains specimens of generally similar shape grouped together provisionally until

---

37. Examples include Dollfus 1975, fig. 53:11–13 (Jafarabad, Levels 3m–n); Dollfus 1983, figs. 68:3–4, 8; 79:8; 83:3, 5 (Bandebal, Levels 16, 14–13); Le Breton 1947, fig. 33:7 (Susa); Weiss 1976, fig. 11 (Qabr-e Sheykheyn). For presumably analogous burnished black ware, see Hole, Flannery, and Neely 1969:168–69 (Deh Luran, Tappeh Sabz, Bayat phase).

such time as further or more complete examples enable more exact attributions to be made (e.g., Middle Susiana Family XV). The initial subdivision of the Middle Susiana pottery has already been amplified,[38] and what is now to be presented is a working classification to be refined and supplemented as additional material accumulates.

Some families are exemplified throughout the Middle Susiana period. Certain types might represent a middle phase [between Early Middle Susiana and Late Middle Susiana phases] that should remain tentative since they do not possess a stratified niche at the site (see *Introduction* by Alizadeh).

Middle Susiana Family I-1

A.04, .13, .20 .79; standard buff ware, unpainted

Figure 26; plate 163:A–D

Miniature vessels so roughly made that there is no regularity of form among them were, when first found, considered simply as accidentally misshapen. Now enough examples have been recovered to indicate that they represent a definite class, albeit widely different in shape and of questionable function. Frequently the walls of such vessels are very thick in proportion to their size. The ware might be straw-tempered (pl. 163:B), gritty with a few accidental pieces of straw (pl. 163:A) with fine grits (pl. 163:C), or without visible tempering (pl. 163:D).

Middle Susiana Family I-2

B.03, .04; standard buff ware, unpainted

Figure 26; plate 163:E

A small, rather crude shallow bowl of fairly coarse standard ware so far remains an isolated specimen rather than the representative of a frequent type. However, such an undifferentiated shape would be difficult to recognize from small fragments.

Middle Susiana Family I-3

B.03, .04, .07; standard to fine buff ware, painted

Figure 26; plates 57:B; 163:F–L

Small saucers and bowls occur with varying profiles. They are painted with geometric designs on either the interior or exterior. Such small vessels do not seem to have been nearly as common as larger bowls.[39] The reconstruction of one vessel (pl. 163:J) with tall proportions is hypothetical. The part preserved resembles another (pl. 163:K) in the width of its base and relatively vertical wall; it could have been a similarly shallow bowl.

Middle Susiana Family II

B.03, 04; fine to eggshell buff ware, unpainted

Figure 26; plate 163:M–N

Few restorable examples of the small thin-walled cups have been recovered, but many of the fine ware sherds in Middle Susiana sherd groups might have belonged to such vessels.

Middle Susiana Family III

B or small C.03, .04; fine buff ware, painted exterior

Figure 26; plates 58:C, T–U; 163:O–BB

Elegant small cups or bowls with painted decoration are represented only by lip and body fragments, except for one (pl. 163:P). The bases were probably slightly convex, similar to an unpainted example (pl. 163:M), or flattened. The painted motifs are often drawn with a delicacy in consonance with the eggshell thinness of many of the sherds. Both geometric and representational motifs were used, with the latter being particularly prominent. The commoner motifs are goats and bucrania; birds and linked human beings also occur. The motifs appear most frequently in friezes, sometimes without accessories (pl. 163:O, T, and probably BB), once as alternating pairs (pl. 163:U) and sometimes supported by horizontal geometric bands (pl. 163:R, V–W). It is possible that the friezes of small motifs were placed near the lip and near the base of the bowls (pl. 163:AA). The bucrania are always placed upside down and might be combined into two or three tiers; they were probably used as isolated elements spaced at intervals (pl. 163:X–Z). Only one example of all-over patterning was found, diagonal rows of crosses below an inconspicuous lip frieze of squiggles (pl. 163:P).[40]

Middle Susiana Family IV

B–C.03, .04; standard and gritty buff ware, painted or unpainted, tab handle

Figure 23; plates 59:A–B; 163:CC–DD; 164:A–D

Tab-handled ladles appear in painted and, very rarely, unpainted versions. The smaller ladles tend to

---

38. Families not yet recognized at the time of the original classification are inserted in their proper corpus order, that is, according to their forms in Delougaz' system of classification by combining roman and arabic numbers. For example, Middle Susiana Families XII-1 and XII-2 designate independent families. Subdivisions within a family are indicated, as usual, by lowercase letters.

39. For parallels to plate 163:G, see Dollfus 1983, fig. 35:2 (Jowi, Level 9); Weiss 1976, fig. 22:140 (Qabr-e Sheykheyn).

40. For a parallel to plate 163:Q, see Dollfus 1983, fig. 31:14 (Jowi, Level 11).

have longer, tapered handles and the larger ladles shorter, broader handles. The edges of the handles are outlined with paint and both sides are usually completely covered with simple arrangements of straight or wavy bands. The blank side of one ladle (pl. 164:C) is an exception. The body of the only complete example was painted all over (pl. 163:CC).[41]

The tab-handled ladles occur only in the Early Middle Susiana phase and represent the final phase of a type of utensil typical for the Early Susiana period (pl. 194:L–N). In the case of the larger, unpainted examples the continuity is evident not only in the shape but also in the grittiness of the ware (pl. 164:C).

Middle Susiana Family V

B.20, .31; standard buff ware, painted exterior

Figure 26; plate 164:E–F

Two examples were found of objects with a central perforation and decoration only on the exterior. These characteristics indicate that they are lids. Unfortunately, neither example is dated by context, and there are no means of determining whether the differences in shape and decoration preclude their contemporaneity. The closest parallels at Chogha Mish for the decoration of the cylindrical lids (pl. 164:F) are provided by Late Susiana spindle whorls (pls. 65:Y; 232:D), but the design is too simple and long-lived to be a conclusive chronological indicator.[42]

The best parallel for the shape of the convex lid (pl. 164:F) is a somewhat squatter example, from Bandebal, also perforated in the center. The decoration on another (pl. 164:E) is paralleled on lids from Ras al-ʿAmiya and Haji Muhammad, which have a very different, squat, flat-topped cylindrical shape. One of the Ras al-ʿAmiya lids also has a perforation, although not in the middle. Tell Halaf, in addition to the more frequent squat flat-topped lids, also has some examples somewhat closer in shape to the Chogha Mish lids.[43]

Middle Susiana Family VI

B.05; standard or fine buff ware, buff-slipped, red ware

Figure 26; plate 164:G–K

The small bowls with incurving lips can be subdivided according to the absence (Subfamily VIa) or presence (Subfamily VIb) of painted decoration. Few restorable profiles of the unpainted bowls were recovered; it is likely, however, that many small, unclassifiable lip and body sherds belonged to such shapes. Only one of the examples (pl. 127:G) is made of standard ware. The other (pl. 164:H) is of buff-slipped red ware; if it should eventually prove to be the representative of a definite class, not merely an aberrant example, a family of B-sized red ware vessels would have to be added to the Middle Susiana corpus.

The painted subclass of Family VI includes a standard type characterized by a specific decoration near the lip: pendant scallops with bulbous tips (pl. 164:K). Trough spouts are also typical for these bowls. They are small-scale versions of larger vessels of Subfamily XVIb with the same decoration (pl. 176:C–E, L). Two individual specimens also assigned to Subfamily VIb are a small bowl with an almost imperceptibly incurved lip and another on a low foot (pl. 164:I–J). Both the scallops at the lip, a pattern well known from the large bowls of Family XXII and the jars of Family XXXII, and the debased center pattern (pl. 164:I) place it in the Late Middle Susiana phase. On the other hand, the contexts of two examples (pl. 164:J–K) of this pottery family place them in the Early Middle Susiana phase; they both have a fugitive red wash, apparently a secondary coating applied after firing.

Middle Susiana Family VII-1

B.11; standard or fine ware, painted exterior
Figure 26

Small carinated bowls seem to exist only as individual, and unusual, specimens and do not at present represent a standard family of forms. Larger-sized examples are not quite as uncommon.

Middle Susiana Family VII-2

B–C.80; standard or fine ware, painted or unpainted
Figure 26; plates 164:L–M; 165:A

Vessels with oval horizontal sections are so rare that the B and C sizes are included in one family in which each example is a type unto itself. A small only slightly oval bowl is decorated on the exterior with a zigzag band (pl. 164:L). Two examples of more elongated ovoid forms were recovered, but one is a very coarsely made unpainted fragment and the other is well shaped and painted on the exterior (pls. 164:M; 165:A). Both have a broken projection at the preserved end. It is possible that they are both boat models, in general com-

41. For parallels to plate 163:CC–DD, see Le Breton 1947, fig. 22:2 (Jowi, old excavations); Hole, Flannery, and Neely 1969:143, fig. 53:e–f (Tappeh Sabz, Mehmeh phase). For parallels to plate 164:A–B and D, see Hall and Woolley 1927, pl. 17:1588, 1593, 1765 (Ubaid); D. Stronach 1961, pl. 57:3–4 and concave-sided variants 2, 5 (Ras al-ʿAmiya).

42. For an Early Middle Susiana occurrence, see Dollfus 1983, fig. 16:6 (Jowi, Level 4).

43. For parallels to plate 164:E, see Dollfus 1978, fig. 17:7 (Bandebal, Levels 16–11); D. Stronach 1961, pl. 57:7–9 (Ras al-ʿAmiya); Ziegler 1953, pl. 25:c (Haji Muhammad); Von Oppenheim 1943, pls. 23:1–8; 24:1–7 (Tell Halaf). For general approximation to the form in plate 164:F, see Von Oppenheim 1943, pl. 24:9, 11 (Tell Halaf).

parable to an explicit model from Eridu and a fragment from Buhallan.[44] All three fragments of Family VII-2 can be dated to the Late Middle Susiana phase.

Middle Susiana Family VIII-1

C.00; fine ware; proportion "2" or less unpainted

Figure 26; plate 165:B–C

The first group of medium-sized Middle Susiana vessels consists of shallow unpainted bowls with substantially straight walls. The few examples whose shapes can be reconstructed are of thin ware and in general character resemble the thin-walled bowls of Subfamily XVIIIa. The rarity of Family VIII-1 bowls might be, at least in part, due to accidents of preservation and the difficulty of reconstructing the forms of small sherds of unpainted fine ware vessels.

Middle Susiana Family VIII-2

C.00, .03; proportion transitional "1" to "2," standard ware, painted both sides

Figure 26; plate 165:D

Family VIII-2 was originally defined by both shape, namely relatively straight sides and a wide, slightly convex base, and interior decoration, namely a main register divided into panels by clusters of vertical lines. Evidence is accumulating, however, that the clusters of vertical lines diagnostic for Family VIII-2 can also appear on fragments of large bowls with somewhat convex walls, which are thus comparable in shape to the medium- and large-sized convex-sided bowls of Family XIX. As an additional complication, some of the Family XIX bowls have almost straight sides (pl. 181:K, P). On the other hand, the arc friezes and broad wash standard for Family XIX contrast with the clusters of vertical lines of Family VIII-2. Thus design becomes the criterion for assigning to their respective families bowls that overlap in sizes and shapes. Examples of Family VIII-2 are by far rarer than those of Family XIX. Both families are characteristic for the Late Middle Susiana phase.

Middle Susiana Family VIII-3

C.02,.07 [atypical]; fine ware, painted exterior

Figure 26; plate 165:E–H

A rare but distinctive type of bowl is characterized by its fine ware, concave walls, and specific decoration in which wide horizontal bands divide the entire exterior surface into registers filled with large solid circles. Only small sherds were found during the first seasons, so an almost complete specimen (VII-15) excavated during the seventh season at Chogha Mish is included in order to represent the family adequately. A fragment found in the eighth season is assigned to Family VIII-3 because of its decoration, even though it has a .07 shape diagnostic for Family XV (8.181). The bowls of Family VIII-3 are characteristic for the Early Middle Susiana phase.[45]

Middle Susiana Family IX

C.00, .03; standard buff ware, painted, low or high ring base

Figure 26; plates 57:G; 58:W; 59:L, R–S; 165:I–K; 166:A–D

The defining characteristic of Family IX is the combination of a ring or pedestal base with a medium-sized straight or convex-sided bowl. Two subfamilies of such bowls can be distinguished. The first, Subfamily IXa, includes bowls with both ring and pedestal bases and with considerable variation in their painted decoration. Two examples represented by fragments of their bases are painted on the flattened interiors with a row of goats (pl. 58:W) or a single animal (pl. 165:I); in each case the central pattern appears to have been enclosed by a cusped border. Both sherds belong to the Late Middle Susiana phase, but ring-based bowls occurred already in the Early Middle Susiana phase. Two sherds (pl. 59:F) can be identified as parts of convex-sided bowls with a ring base by comparison with a semi-complete example found in the seventh season. All three share a specific scheme of decoration: on the exterior a zigzag frieze of vertical and diagonal bands and on the interior a broad wash into which wavy bands are scratched. The technique is diagnostic for the Early Middle Susiana phase.[46]

The bowls of Subfamily IXb appear to form a consistent group characterized by standardized size, shape, and decorative syntax, as is well exemplified by a semi-complete example (pls. 57:G; 165:J). Mouth diameters range from ca. 22.50 to 24 25 cm and height from ca. 8.00 to 9.00 cm. Walls are usually convex, but on one example (pl. 165:K) the walls are unusually straight. The presumption is that the ring base was always low. The exterior is undecorated except for a lip band. The main decoration appears on the interior and consists of large scale motifs organized with reference to the lip of the bowl. This is a procedure that contrasts strongly with the standard Susiana scheme in which the interior decoration is focused on a main pattern in the center of the bowl and ripples out from there. In contrast, the center

---

44. For parallels to plate 164:M, see de Mecquenem 1943, fig. 112:9 (unpainted, flat base; Buhallan, 10.50–7.00 m); Safar, Mustafa, and Lloyd 1981, fig. 111 (Eridu, Ubaid Cemetery, near surface).

45. For parallels to plate 165:E–H, see Le Breton 1947, fig. 28:1–2 (Jowi, old excavations); D. Stronach 1961, pl. 46:4 (circles surrounded by dots; Ras al-ʿAmiya, but see also ibid., pl. 47:8 for a C.14 bowl with row of large, plain circles).

46. Some examples of this family have also a lip frieze of reserved crescents, another characteristic Early Middle Susiana design. AA

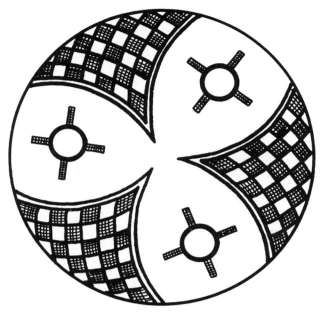

Figure 24. Restored Decoration of Middle Susiana IXb Bowl, 2.067, Trench XVI:Q27, el. 80.70

Figure 25. Diagram Showing the Construction of the Pattern on Middle Susiana X-1, 5.239, P27:501 Southeast, el. 78.34

of one example (pl. 165:J) remains unpainted; three large triangles, subdivided in typical Late Middle Susiana manner, hang from the lip. One sherd (pl. 166:A) represents a similar composition in which three concave-sided triangles were pendant from the lip and the space between them was filled by rayed circles (fig. 24). On other fragments the motifs, alternating with small pendant triangles (pl. 165:K) and bucrania (pl. 166:C–D), are placed adjacent to the lip in paratactic and hypotactic rows respectively. The example with goat decoration (pl. 166:B) might have been similarly arranged. In all these cases it is likely that the center of the bowls remained unpainted. Bowls of Subfamily IXb, although not extremely common, are among the more outstanding types of the Late Middle Susiana phase.[47]

Middle Susiana Family X-1

.03, .04; standard and fine ware, main decoration on exterior

Figure 26; plates 59:K; 166:E

Rare, but characteristic, are forms distinguished from ordinary shallow bowls by the appearance of the main decoration on the exterior and only simple crossing lines on the interior. Sherds representing about half of such a lid testify to another important characteristic, the

presence of a pair of perforations at the lip (pl. 166:E). Although only one of the holes is preserved, the second can be restored without hesitation by analogy with lids of the Early Susiana period (pl. 195:C).[48] They are characterized by a pair of holes and the same decorative scheme: crossing lines on the interior and the main decoration on the exterior. The very rare examples of Family X-1 are the continuations of the Early Susiana lids, some of which provide prototypes for the convex shape of one of the examples representing this pottery family (pl. 166:E; cf. pl. 194:R).

The crosshatched squares that often decorate the flattened tops of the Early Susiana lids provide prototypes for the design on a small Family X-1 fragment (pl. 59:K). The painting on another (pl. 166:E) is more elaborate. The cross of the interior is formed by triple lines and a seemingly organic branching pattern covers the exterior. The pattern is actually strictly geometric, consisting of a rosette of eight narrow triangular rays; to the apex of each is attached the apex of a squatter triangle extending to the border (fig. 25). At Chogha Mish such branched rosette patterns are typical for the Early Middle Susiana phase. Examples are also to be found in southern Mesopotamia.[49]

---

47. For the bowls of the same family as those in plates 165:J–K and 166:A, mostly with related designs, see Le Breton 1947, fig. 23:11 (rayed circles, goat horn, and pendant triangles; Jowi, old excavations); Le Breton 1947, fig. 35:14 (three pendant and torsional bands of designs; Bandebal); Weiss 1976, fig. 29 (small pendant triangles and torsional clusters of lines; Qabr-e Sheykheyn); Egami and Masuda 1962, figs. 17:1 (floating lozenges) and 3 (pendant checkered triangle; Bakun B).

48. Additional examples, each with a completely preserved pair of holes, were found after the fifth season. AA

49. For example, see Ziegler 1953, pls. 4:b = 17:b (base plate probably of Middle Susiana Family XVIII; Haji Muhammad). For another base plate with the same basic pattern but the attached triangle elaborated, see ibid., pls. 4:g = 17:a. For further examples, see D. Stronach 1961, pl. 49:3, 6 (base plates of Middle Susiana Family XVIII; Ras al-ʿAmiya); Safar, Mustafa, and Lloyd 1981, fig. 91:8 (fragment of straight-sided lid with rather flattened top; Eridu XIV).

Middle Susiana Family X-2

> C.03, .04, .05; proportions "0–1," normally fine buff ware, painted both sides

> Figure 26; plates 59:F; 166:F; 167:A–F; 168:A–D, F–I

A closely integrated and common family is made up of shallow bowls with low, relatively vertical walls and wide, rounded bases. Usually a definite angle marks the junction of wall and base, but some uncarinated examples exist (pl. 167:E–F). The Family X-2 bowls share their distinctive scheme of decoration with the larger bowls of Family XVIII. On the exterior the painting is limited to the body proper and frequently consists of a zigzag band so broad as to cover the sides with a solid wash of color except for small triangles of ground pointing alternately up and down (pls. 166:F; 167:B, D–E). Occasionally the wall is solidly covered (pl. 167:C) or the zigzag band is thin (pl. 167:A). One bowl is exceptional in having only the narrowest of lip bands on the exterior (pl. 167:F).

The interiors are densely painted with a tripartite scheme that corresponds to the structure of the vessel. The focal, central field of design on the broad bases is enclosed by two concentric bands, the inner one cusped and the outer one plain. A solid broad wash of paint covers the vertical walls or at least their upper parts. The transition between these two main zones is located at or close to the junction of base and wall; it consists of a reserved band of ground filled by groups of carob-like vertical strokes (pls. 166:F; 167:A, C–D)[50] or, more rarely, continuous wavy bands (pl. 167:B) or a row of Xs (pl. 167:E). On one vessel (pl. 166:F) the filling motif of the reserved band seems to have been painted with exceptional care; it consists of a central circle with five carobs on either side. Another vessel (pl. 167:F) is unusual in that the transitional reserved band is reduced to almost nothing. This bowl is also unusual for the appearance of two cusped bands, very sloppily painted, and for the rather inchoate pattern of the central circle of the base. Normally this area is occupied by one of a considerable variety of patterns, the majority of which are variations on the division of a circle into quadrants. The same patterns were also used on the centers of Family XVIIIa–f (pls. 177–79) bowls and are discussed in more detail below.

Despite the similar patterns, on the whole there is little difficulty in attributing base fragments to Families X-2 or XVIII. The ware of the former is normally quite fine and the thickness of the base plate varies from about 5 to 9 mm whereas the Family XVIII bowls are

usually of standard ware and the base plates vary from about 12 to 16 mm. Occasionally some uncertainty arises if a sherd is about 10 to 11 mm thick and of not as fine a paste as most of the examples of Family X-2. One example (pl. 168:E), though illustrated with the Family X-2 bases, almost certainly belonged to a Family XIX bowl. Family X-2 is diagnostic for the Early Middle Susiana phase. The characteristics of the family are so clear cut that the identity of even quite small fragments is usually evident.[51]

Middle Susiana Family X-3

> C.00, .03, .04, .05, .11; standard to fine buff ware, unpainted

> Figure 26; plate 168:J, L–N

Unpainted low bowls, of proportion 2 or less, occur in varying profile shapes and grades of buff ware. They presumably formed a larger constituent of the pottery assemblage than indicated by the examples of reconstructible form. As more information accumulates, it might become advisable to distinguish two subfamilies, Subfamily X-3a for the thinner-walled vessels and Subfamily X-3b for the thicker-walled vessels.

The two complete forms have concave bases (pl. 168:J, N). They resemble some small examples of Family XX (cf. pl. 182:A, C), except for their squatness. Since Family XX bowls are by definition rather deep, these two complete examples (pls. 168:J, N) are, despite the similarity, better placed in Family X-3 among the relatively shallow bowls of assorted shapes. Although the reconstructions of the incurved-rim bowls (pl. 168:L–M) are tentative, it is unlikely that they could have had deeper proportions than those suggested. A fifth vessel stands out because of its thick, coarse ware, slightly oval shape, and size (pl. 168:K).

Four of the examples of Family X-3 are dated to the Early Middle Susiana phase by their contexts (pl. 168:J–K, M–N). Another (pl. 168:L) was found with only a few other sherds, several of them of rather gritty unpainted buff ware. There is not much doubt that all of them belong to the Early Middle Susiana phase, particu-

---

50. Such clusters of blobs or squiggles can be considered as distantly reminiscent of carob tree pods, distended at intervals by their seeds; for the sake of brevity these motifs are henceforth termed "carobs."

51. For a parallel to plate 167:B, see D. Stronach 1961, pl. 49:7 (upper wall more flaring; Ras al-ʿAmiya). For a parallel to plate 167:C, see Dollfus 1983, fig. 23:6 (Jowi, Level 14). For related vessels to that in plate 167:D, see ibid., fig. 13:3 (Jowi, Levels 15). For certain parallels to plates 60:G and 168:A, see D. Stronach 1961, pl. 49:7 (Ras al-ʿAmiya). For a similar pattern, see also Von Oppenheim 1943, pl. 11:9 (Halaf). For a parallel to plate 168:B, see D. Stronach 1961, pl. 59:35 (in pl. 59 the reserved spaces between the quadrants do not taper toward the periphery, and they remain straight in fig. 53:D–E; Ras al-ʿAmiya); Ziegler 1953, pls. 5:g–h, k; 18:b–c (quadrants separated by reserved star, but judging by 7.0–7.5 mm thickness of sherds, are probably parts of large bowls analogous to the painted Middle Susiana Family XVIII examples; Haji Muhammad).

larly since Early Middle Susiana sherds and even two Early Susiana sherds (cf. pl. 196:D) were already found at higher levels.

Middle Susiana Family X-4

> C.00, .03, .04, .08; standard to fine ware, painted interior
>
> Figure 26; plates 59:Q, U–V; 169:A–G; perhaps 58:E, R

Three families, X-4, X-5, and XI, are closely related in that each includes a variety of bowls of relatively undifferentiated and in some cases common shapes. The characteristic that distinguishes Families X-4 and X-5 from Family XI is the proportion, the first two families having a ratio of 2 or less and the latter a ratio of 3 or more. As is natural, the deeper forms of Family XI are painted only on the exterior, with at most a lip band on the interior, while the shallower forms can be divided into those that are painted on the interior (Family X-4) or on the exterior (Family X-5). Family X-4 can be subdivided into examples with tapered or blunt lips (Subfamily X-4a) or those with flat or channeled lips (Subfamily X-4b). The latter are much rarer as the majority of such lips belong to vessels with a diameter larger than 30 cm (cf. Subfamilies XXIII-1b–d).

Family X-4 shallow bowls of standard ware and sparsely painted with a few plain bands seem to have been ubiquitous in the Late Middle Susiana phase (pl. 169:B–E). One example is particularly important since it still preserves part of its base, which was covered by birds in a free-field arrangement (pl. 169:G). A base-plate chip preserving almost identical birds with spread wings, suggests that this pattern was a standard one (pl. 169:F). Two other chips with simple bird-like motifs might perhaps be Family X-4 bases even though they are of fine ware rather than of the standard buff ware normal for the plain-banded bowls (pl. 58:E, R).[52] Three base plates of standard ware are more likely to have belonged to Family X-4 bowls; two are decorated by a scalloped circle (pl. 59:U–V) and the third by a rosette of pompon-tipped rays (pl. 59:Q).

Quite distinct from the Late Middle Susiana bowls with simple bands are some fragments with more complicated decoration. One has a reserved-crescent frieze, a design diagnostic for the Late Middle Susiana phase, and comes from a good context (pl. 59:J). Another, from a mixed context, can be dated to the Late Middle Susiana phase with certainty in view of the triangles pendant from the lip and the quadrant pattern in the central field (pl. 169:A).

Middle Susiana Family X-5

> C.00, .03, .04; proportion "2" or less, standard to fine ware, painted exterior
>
> Figure 26; plate 169:I–P

Shallow bowls painted on the exterior can also, similar to those decorated on the interior, be subdivided on the basis of lip shape into a group with tapered or blunt lips, Subfamily X-5a (pl. 169:I–O), and rarer groups with flat lips, Subfamily X-5b (pl. 169:P).

The decoration, or at least the more important part of it, is concentrated on the upper walls of the bowls. A simple pattern of horizontal borders enclosing a wavy band appears to be standard. It occurs on vessels of both standard (pl. 169:J–K, N–O) and fine ware (pl. 169:L–M). A debased version of the decoration that also lacks the subsidiary band on the lower body can be recognized on one of the bowls (pl. 169:J). The bowls with the wavy bands are characteristic for the Late Middle Susiana phase.[53]

A variety of other patterns appears on sherds whose stance suggests that they might have belonged to Subfamily X-5a bowls rather than to deeper bowls (pl. 169:Q–W).[54] The stepped designs of crosshatched squares or rectangles are closely related to one of the motifs frequent on Middle Susiana jars (pl. 191:E).[55]

Middle Susiana Family X-6

> C.02, .03, .07, .22; proportion "2" or less, standard to fine ware, painted and unpainted
>
> Plate 170:A–E

A specialized interior ledge rim, presumably always with vertical perforations at intervals, is the defining feature for both Family X-6 bowls and the jars of Subfamily XXXIa (pl. 190:C–H). The inner ledge rim might have served to hold a lid. Bowls so equipped are rare. Although almost all of the examples are represented only by small sherds, it is clear that the inner ledge rims were set on vessels of varying profiles.

Subfamily X-6a consists of a single unpainted example that provides a complete profile. It is conical and

---

52. For an analog to plate 58:R, see Le Breton 1947, fig. 39:2 (Bandebal, old excavations).

53. For vessels related to those in plate 169:K–O, see Dollfus 1983, figs. 30:3, 31:12, 33:2 (Jowi, Levels 11 and 10). For a parallel to plate 169:P, see Safar, Mustafa, and Lloyd 1981, fig. 87:24 (Eridu XI).

54. Object 2.263 (pl. 169:R) is a fragment of a tortoise vessel and is therefore misplaced here. AA

55. For a parallel to plate 169:Q, see Safar, Mustafa, and Lloyd 1981, fig. 88:23 (Eridu XII). For a similar design to plate 169:T–U, see Gautier and Lampre 1905, fig. 168 (Musyan). For a parallel to plate 169:V, see Weiss 1976, fig. 17:80 (Qabr-e Sheykheyn); for related designs, see Le Breton 1947, fig. 27:2 (Jowi, old excavations); Hole, Flannery, and Neely 1969, fig. 62:m (Tappeh Sabz, Mehmeh and Bayat phases).

has a trough-shaped rim with the inner side practically as high as the outer side. In Subfamily X-6b the inner ledge rim is approximately horizontal and the profiles are tentatively reconstructed as .04 (pl. 170:D), a very slight .07 (pl. 170:B–C), and .22 (pl. 170:E), a shape characteristic for Family XVI. On the painted examples the decoration seems to be concentrated on the upper part of the body, but on a Subfamily X-6b example (pl. 170:D) it goes down to the middle of the vessel.

The Subfamily X-6a bowls known so far from Chogha Mish can be assigned to the Late Middle Susiana phase. The general class, however, might have originated earlier, as both conical and barrel-shaped vessels with inner ledge rims are known from Ras al-ʿAmiya.[56]

Middle Susiana Family XI

> C.00, .03; proportion "3" or "4," standard to fine ware, painted exterior
>
> Figure 26; plate 171:A–B, D–T

Medium-sized bowls of deeper proportions than those of Family X-5 are placed in Family XI. When sherds represent only a small portion of the original vessels it is frequently impossible to reconstruct with certainty the ratio of diameter to height. It is thus with considerable reservation that some sherds (pl. 171:E, H–K, M–R) are assigned to Family XI and others (pl. 169:Q–W) to Family X-5. Family XI bowls, apparently, always have blunt or tapered lips. Many Middle Susiana sherds at first glance seem assignable to Family XI because of their flattened lips, relatively thick walls, and fairly vertical stance. This is particularly the case if the sherds are relatively small. However, such flattened lip sherds normally turn out to have diameters of over 30 cm, which indicates that they are fragments of the large-sized crateriform vessels of Family XXIV.

The decoration of the Family XI bowls varies from very simple horizontal bands to more elaborate geometric designs such as hatched zigzags, lozenge bands, and polka dots. Three of the fine ware examples bear representational motifs. The human figure in a panel formed by vertical bands of triangles is tentatively restored (pl. 171:G). Some designs (pl. 171:B, D) are comparable in structure to the tiered bucrania of Family III bowls (cf. pl. 163:Y), but the elements here seem to be superimposed human torsos.[57] Linked human figures with similar triangles are illustrated (pl. 171:C) for comparison

even though they do not occur on a Family XI bowl but on an enigmatic straight-sided chip of pottery with paint on all sides.[58]

Most of the examples of Family XI are dated to the Late Middle Susiana phase by either context or the character of the design. The wavy band (pl. 171:E), the polka dots (pl. 171:I, K, M–N), and the multiple swag (pl. 171:R) are characteristic. The more unusual ridged arcs (pl. 171:E) might be an abstraction from a frieze of goats with ridged horns. Some motifs point forward to the Late Susiana period. The tiered triangles (pl. 171:G) are antecedents for an element widely used in Late Susiana design. A frieze (pl. 171:J) is very close in shape to one on a goblet attributed to the Late Susiana period (pl. 161:M). Very different is a bold pattern of hatched zigzags on a fragment from an Early Middle Susiana context (pl. 171:A).[59]

Middle Susiana Family XII

> C.00, .03, .04; proportions transitional "3–4," buff ware, flat base, unpainted
>
> Figure 26; plate 172:A–C

Unpainted bowls with simple convex profiles and of medium depth make up Family XII. They are subdivided according to their ware, those of standard buff ware with rather thick walls and blunt lips constituting Subfamily XIIa and those of fine or eggshell ware with tapered lips constituting Subfamily XIIb. Though the simple convex profile is probably commoner, bowls with their upper walls approximately vertical also occur. Although restorable forms were very rare, it is assumed that Family XII bowls were originally fairly common. Thicker examples were probably current in the Early Middle Susiana phase and thinner examples later.

---

56. For parallels to plate 170:A, see Dollfus 1975, fig. 48:10 (unpainted light gray fragment; Jafarabad, Levels 3m–n); for a similar shape with painted decoration, see D. Stronach 1961, pl. 53:8 (Ras al-ʿAmiya). For a related(?) barrel-like form to plate 170:E, see ibid., pls. 53:9, 54:6.

57. For design similar to that in plate 171:B, perhaps a little later, see Alizadeh 1988b, fig. 6:I.

58. For triangular torso parallel to plate 171:C, see Le Breton 1947, fig. 30:16 (Jowi, old excavations); ibid., fig. 27:18 (Bandebal). For motifs related to plate 171:D and G, see Gautier and Lampre 1905, figs. 261–64 (Tappeh Khazineh); Hole, Flannery, and Neely 1969, fig. 62:c (Tappeh Sabz, Mehmeh and Bayat phases).

59. For designs similar to plate 171:A, see Le Breton 1947, fig. 27:18 (Jowi, old excavations); Dollfus 1983, fig. 25:6 (Level 12). For possible prototype for the design of plate 171:E, see Gautier and Lampre 1905, fig. 229 (Tappeh Khazineh). For a motif similar to plate 171:I and M, see Le Breton 1947, fig. 28:7 (Jowi, old excavations); Gautier and Lampre 1905, fig. 180 (Musyan). For a variation of the motif on plate 171:J, see Dollfus 1983, figs. 60:12, 64:9, 73:6 (Bandebal, Levels 22, 17–16). For related design consisting of triangles projecting alternately from either side of a horizontal line, see Le Breton 1947, fig. 27:3 (Jowi, old excavations); Weiss 1976, fig. 20:109 (Qabr-e Sheykheyn); Gautier and Lampre 1905, fig. 153 (Musyan). For lozenge frieze similar to plate 171:Q, see Weiss 1976, fig. 18:87 (Qabr-e Sheykheyn). For shape similar to plate 171:T, see Gautier and Lampre 1905, fig. 264 (Tappeh Khazineh); Hole, Flannery, and Neely 1969, fig. 62:a–f (Tappeh Sabz, Mehmeh and Bayat phases).

MIDDLE SUSIANA

Scale 1:5

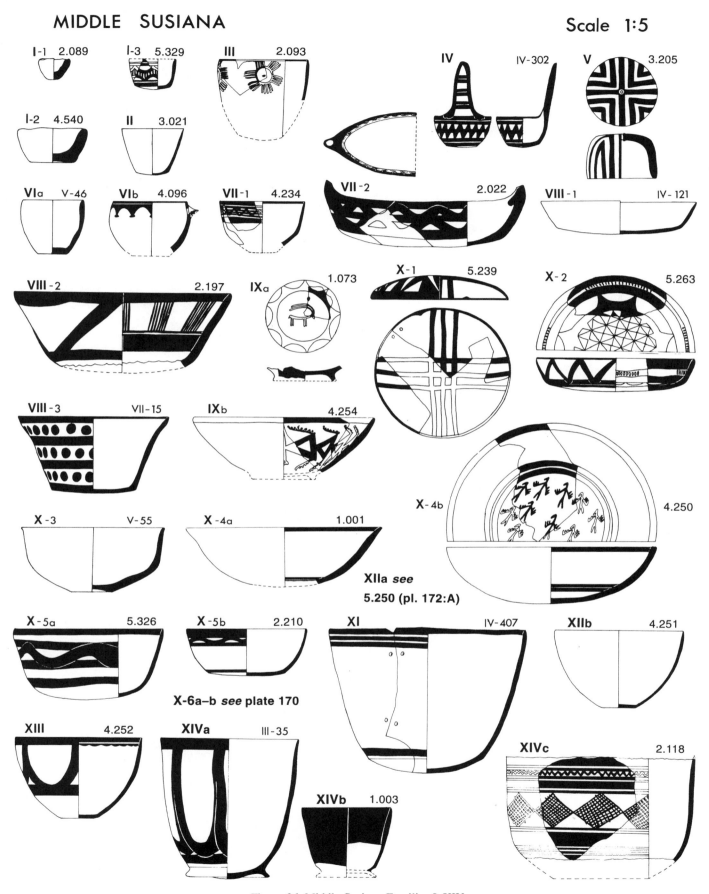

Figure 26. Middle Susiana Families I–XIVc

Middle Susiana Family XIII

C.03; proportions "3," fine to eggshell ware, painted
Figure 26; plate 172:D–G

This family contains the painted versions of the thin-walled bowls of Subfamily XIIb. Not only is the range of ware and shape very slight, but there is also only one scheme of decoration: on the exterior large arcs between horizontal borders and on the interior a lip band separated from a scalloped band by a narrow reserved line. Exactly the same decoration occurs on the one variant example of the family, which is unusually squat and has a ring base instead of a flat base (pl. 172:F). Though its total proportions are normal, the body is squatter than those of the standard bowls of the family.[60]

Middle Susiana Family XIV

C.03, .04, .07, .24; usually proportion "4" or "5,"
standard or fine ware, ring base, painted
Figure 26; plates 172:H–I; 173:A–D, G, L; 174:A–F

Ring-based open vessels of fairly high proportions, usually in the 4–5 range and only rarely as squat as 3, make up Family XIV. Often the curvature of the relatively vertical walls is so slight that the different profile shapes blend into one another. The vessels of this family are distinguished from the other prominent groups of footed vessels, Subfamilies IXa and b, by higher proportions and by the corresponding placement of the main decoration on the exterior, in contrast to the shallower vessels where the primary decoration is on the interior.

For some time only ring-based sherds or semi-complete beakers were assigned to Family XIV, but with the accumulation of evidence from later seasons at Chogha Mish and from other sites it is now possible to recognize designs standard for the family and accordingly to assign to it with confidence various lip sherds. The division of Family XIV into three subgroups is based upon the treatment of the exterior.

Subfamily XIVa beakers are painted on the exterior with bold vertical bands. On one vessel these end in basal arcs comparable to those on Family XIII bowls (pl. 172:H), but on most examples the bands run directly down to a basal border or a painted ring base (pl. 173:A–C).[61] The interiors have either a plain or a scalloped lip band. There seems to be no rule as to the treatment of the bases. They can be either unpainted or painted.

The Subfamily XIVb vessels are those on which the greater part of both the exterior and interior is covered by a broad wash of paint, which leaves only the lower body uncovered.[62] Such beakers are of fine ware and probably normally smaller in size and also rarer than the other beakers of Family IV.

Unlike Subfamilies XIVa–b, each limited to a single decoration, the third subfamily, XIVc, contains beakers with a variety of designs. Although the absence of complete or restorable examples during the first five seasons prevented the identification of many lip and body sherds as the upper parts of ring-based beakers, evidence from later seasons as well as from other sites has now made such attributions possible with a high degree of certitude.[63]

The shapes vary with .03, .04, .07, and .24 profiles occurring. Fairly deep beakers of proportion "4" appear to be more common, but some "3" examples exist. About half or more of the exterior surface is decorated by wide and narrow bands framing other elements. These often consist of narrow friezes of wavy lines, lozenges, or chevrons (pl. 174:C–F).[64] Representational motifs such as a file of birds (pl. 174:B), which preludes the characteristic Late Susiana lip friezes of birds, appear to be extremely rare in beakers.[65] Sometimes the specialized frieze area accommodates enlarged motifs. Simplest is the frieze of crosshatched lozenges (pl. 173:G–I).[66] More complicated is a large and bold zigzag (pl. 174:A), a descendant of those adorning Early

---

60. For a parallel to plate 172:D–G, see Dollfus 1983, fig. 59:5 (Bandebal, Level 20).

61. For parallels to plate 173:A–C, see Dollfus 1975, fig. 51:6, 11–12 (Jafarabad, Levels 3m–n); Le Breton 1947, fig. 13:14 (Jafarabad, old excavations, 2.0–3.5 m); Dollfus 1983, fig. 37:3 (Jowi, Level 7); Le Breton 1947, fig. 21:8 (Jowi, old excavations); Dollfus 1983, figs. 57:4, 75:4 (squat; Bandebal, Levels 23, 16); for same pattern on different shapes, see Dollfus 1975, figs. 51:11 (flat-based beaker), 12 (probably squat form similar to pl. 172:F here); 52:5, 9 (jars; all Jafarabad, Levels 3m–n).

62. For a parallel to plate 173:D, see Dollfus 1983, fig. 37:8 (Jowi, Level 7).

63. Two vessels (pl. 174:E–F) have a less vertical stance than the other Middle Susiana Subfamily XIVc examples and could perhaps be taken as the upper parts of .07 Middle Susiana Subfamily XVe beakers. On the other hand, their decoration is typical for Middle Susiana Subfamily XIVc.

64. For parallels to plate 174:C, see Dollfus 1975, fig. 54:4 (Jafarabad, Level 3m); Le Breton 1947, fig. 13:9 (Jafarabad, old excavations, 2.0–3.5 m); ibid., fig. 27:10 (Jowi, old excavations). For design similar to plate 174:D, see Dollfus 1975, fig. 60:3 (Bandebal, Level 22). For a parallel to plate 174:E–F, see Hole, Flannery, and Neely 1969, fig. 61:1 (Tappeh Sabz, Bayat phase).

65. For birds similar to plate 174:B, see Dollfus 1975, fig. 50:6 (C.03; Jafarabad, Level 3n); see also Egami and Sono 1962, fig. 24:8, 10–11 (Tall-e Gap).

66. For parallels to plate 173:G, see Le Breton 1947, fig. 13:5–6 (Jafarabad, old excavations, 2.0–3.5 m); Dollfus 1983, figs. 56:11, 60:13 (C.05 profile) and 2 (C.07 profile) respectively (Bandebal, Levels 24, 20–19). For pattern of a complete ring-based beaker similar to that on plate 173:H, see Le Breton 1947, fig. 21:9 (Jowi, old excavations). For analogous shape and design to plate 173:I, see Dollfus 1975, fig. 50:8 (Jafarabad, Level 3n).

Table 18. Pottery, Similar to Chogha Mish Middle Susiana Families I-3–XIVc, Present at Other Sites

OTHER SITES	I-3	III	IV	V	VII-2	VIII-3	IXb	X-1	X-2	X-5a	X-6	XI	XIII	XIVa	XIVb	XIVc
JOWI																
5–10	X	—	—	—	—	—	—	—	—	—	X	—	—	X	—	X
11–12	—	X	—	—	—	—	—	—	—	—	X	—	M	—	—	—
13–17	—	—	—	—	—	—	—	—	X	—	—	—	—	—	—	—
Old Excavations	—	—	X	—	—	X	X	—	—	—	—	—	M	—	X	—	X
JAFARABAD																
3M–N	—	—	—	—	—	—	—	—	—	—	X	—	—	X	—	X
Old Excavations	—	—	—	—	—	—	—	—	—	—	—	—	—	X	—	X
BANDEBAL																
13–18	—	—	—	X	—	—	—	—	—	—	—	—	—	X	—	X
19–27	—	—	—	—	—	—	—	—	—	—	—	X	—	X	—	X
Old Excavations	—	—	—	—	—	—	X	—	—	—	—	—	—	—	—	—
BUHALAN	—	—	—	—	X	—	—	—	—	—	—	—	—	—	—	X
QABR-E SHEYKHEYN	X	—	—	—	—	—	X	—	—	—	—	M	—	—	—	X
TAPPEH SABZ																
Khazineh	—	—	—	—	—	—	—	—	—	—	—	—	—	—	—	—
Mehmeh	—	—	X	—	—	—	—	—	—	—	—	S	—	—	—	—
Bayat	—	—	—	—	—	—	—	—	—	—	—	S	—	—	—	X
KHAZINEH	—	—	—	—	—	—	—	—	—	—	—	S	—	—	—	—
MUSYAN	—	—	—	—	—	—	—	—	—	—	—	M	—	—	—	—
BAKUN B	—	—	—	—	—	—	X	—	—	—	—	—	—	—	—	—
GAP	—	—	—	—	—	—	—	—	—	—	—	—	—	—	—	—
IBLIS	—	—	—	—	—	—	—	—	—	—	—	—	—	—	—	M
ERIDU																
Cemetery	—	—	—	—	X	—	—	—	—	—	—	—	—	—	—	—
VIII–IX	—	—	—	—	—	—	—	—	—	—	—	—	—	—	—	—
XI–XIII	—	—	—	—	—	—	—	—	—	—	X	—	—	—	—	—
XIII–XIV	—	—	—	—	—	—	—	—	—	—	—	—	—	—	—	—
XVI	—	—	—	—	—	—	—	X	—	—	—	—	—	—	—	—
UBAID	—	—	X	—	—	—	—	—	—	—	—	—	—	—	—	—
HAJI MUHAMMAD	—	—	—	X	—	—	—	—	—	—	—	—	—	—	—	—
WARKA Survey 042	—	—	—	—	—	—	—	—	—	—	—	—	—	—	—	—
WARKA Survey 267	—	—	—	—	—	—	—	—	—	—	—	—	—	—	—	—
RAS AL-ʿAMIYA	—	—	X	X	—	X	—	—	X	—	X	—	—	—	—	—
GAWRA																
XIX	—	—	—	—	—	—	—	—	—	—	—	—	—	—	—	—
XVII–XVIII	—	—	—	—	—	—	—	—	—	—	—	—	—	—	—	—
HALAF	—	—	—	X	—	—	—	—	—	—	—	—	—	—	—	—

X = Both shape and design (when applicable) occur; M = Motif attested, but shape not necessarily related; S = Shape attested, but if painted, motif may be or is different.

Middle Susiana cups (pl. 175:A–B).[67] Triplets of triangles fill the interstices of the zigzag; those on the upper side are the crosshatched triangles typical for the

G, K). Examples from Archaic Susiana 2 (pl. 218:F–H) seem to be a variation on this design. An example from Archaic Susiana 3 (pl. 213:B) shows great similarity with the later versions. For later versions see de Mecquenem 1943, fig. 112:24–25; Vanden Berghe 1973, p. 56 (lower left fig.); Dollfus 1975, fig. 22:2; ibid., 1978, fig. 14:2; Pottier 1922, no. 15; Alizadeh 1992, fig. 28:D.

In Mesopotamia, the design first appears in Samarra pottery but does not seem to have continued into later periods. See Lloyd and Safar 1945, fig. 16:9–10, 14 (Hassuna, Samarra level); Herzfeld 1930, figs. 85, 158–59, 161, 181, 185, 202; pls. 32:212, 244a; 35:207b, 209, 213 (Samarra). AA

67. The similarity of the zigzags shown on plate 174:A to those shown on pl. 175:A–B notwithstanding, bold zigzags (sometimes in reserve), the interstices of which are filled with triangles that are usually broken up into three smaller triangles, are one of the more persistent, and presumably favorite, designs throughout the prehistoric sequence of Iranian pottery. A rudimentary version of this design appears in the Archaic Susiana 1 phase at Chogha Mish (pl. 229:E,

Late Middle Susiana phase (pls. 165:J; 191:A), but below the pattern is obscured by the small lozenges filling one triangle and the fusion of the other two because the tips of the zigzag do not touch the lower border (pl. 174:A).[68]

In still another type of design the motifs of the specialized register are crosshatched rectangles stretched between the small solid squares at their corners by which they are attached to each other and to framing elements (pl. 173:K–L). A complete vessel from Bandebal provides a prototype for the reconstruction of another (pl. 173:L).[69] Stretched rectangles appear to be particularly characteristic for eastern Iran, as, for example, the Bardsir painted ware of Tall-e Iblis.[70] Certainly the motif does not seem to be at home at Chogha Mish and these (pl. 173:K–L) might well be the remnants of beakers imported from other sites.

Middle Susiana Family XV

> C–D.07, .11, .12, .14; varying proportions, standard to fine buff ware

> Figure 30; plates 174:G–L; 175:A–H

The feature unifying the vessels of Family XV is the double curvature of their walls, concave above and convex below (.07). However, the family is not rigidly limited to .07 shapes, but also includes examples with either borderline or somewhat similar profiles that can be better accommodated in Family XV than elsewhere. Differences in proportions and body treatment divide the Family XV vessels into four subfamilies varying widely in appearance.

The canonical types of Subfamily XVa are fine ware .07 vessels of shallow proportions ("1") painted on the exterior (pl. 174:G–H).[71] A frieze of alternating butterflies and crosshatched rectangles appears to be typical.[72] In addition to the standard .07 vessels, some shallow bowls with various slightly carinated shapes have been assigned to Subfamily XVa (pl. 174:I–K). The butterfly and rectangle frieze on one vessel (pl. 174:I) links it with a sinuous-sided vessel (pl. 174:G). The bowls of Subfamily XVa are typical for the Early Middle Susiana phase, although some of the somewhat coarser examples might be later.

Finally, Subfamily XVb, similar to Subfamily XVa, consists of fine ware bowls but they are distinguished from those of the first group by higher proportions, ranging from "2" to lower "3" ratios (pl. 175:A–B). In addition, the entire outer surface is covered by painting. The standard motif appears to be a boldly outlined, hatched zigzag framed by horizontal bands or groups of carobs and with elongated ovals in the reserved band. Such vessels are typical for the Early Middle Susiana phase.[73]

In the third subfamily, XVc, the vessels are defined by their quite deep proportions, namely ratios of "3" to "5," and the absence of painted decoration. They are made of fine ware or of standard ware verging on fine. The walls of these beakers tend to be fairly straight, but not very sharply defined, hovering on the border lines of .00, .03, or a very slight .07. As the complete example shows, opposite sides of the same beaker can have different profiles, providing a choice of classification numbers (pl. 175:C). The bases are either flattened or rounded. The Subfamily XVc beakers are characteristic for the Late Middle Susiana phase and were probably fairly common, although they cannot be distinguished with certainty when represented only by small lip sherds.[74]

The last subfamily, XVd, is for tall painted beakers. Such vessels seem to have been very rare, but fortunately, sherds from Trench XIII are sufficient for the restoration of both the shape and decoration of a .076 beaker (pl. 175:F). T-shaped elements divide the surface into two panels, each filled by a snake coiling vertically upward and antithetical to each other (pl. 175:H). Although the fragments were found in disturbed debris just below a late grave, there is hardly any doubt that they belong to the Late Middle Susiana phase. They provide a striking and direct antecedent for the Late Susiana snake beakers found at Susa many years ago.[75]

---

68. For parallels to plate 174:A, see de Mecquenem 1943, fig. 108:1 (Buhallan); Dollfus 1983, figs. 73:2 (C.03; Bandebal, Levels 16, 12–11); Weiss 1976, figs. 12:3, 20:107 (with ring base; Qabr-e Sheykheyn).

69. For a parallel to plate 173:L, see Dollfus 1983, fig. 82:1 (Bandebal, Level 14).

70. Caldwell 1967, figs. 5:126, 9; see also Giyan Vc for a stretched rectangle serving as a dividing panel next to a goat (Ghirshman 1935, pl. 51:7).

71. The shape of one vessel (pl. 174:H) is similar to that of an unpainted bowl (pl. 177:C); however, the latter has a definite angle that is taken as the dividing point between a concave wall (.02) and a round base. The more sinuous wall (pl. 174:H) is classified as .07 profile with a flat base.

72. For parallels to plate 174:G, see D. Stronach 1961, pl. 47:9 (Ras al-ʿAmiya); for the design, on different shapes, see Dollfus 1983, fig. 25:1 (Jowi, Level 12); Gautier and Lampre 1905, fig. 155 (Musyan).

73. For parallels to plate 175:A, see D. Stronach 1961, pl. 46:9 (Ras al-ʿAmiya; see ibid., 1–3, for bowls very similar to pl. 175:A–B in shape and proportions, but with different patterns).

74. For parallels to plate 175:C, see Dollfus 1983, fig. 34:2–3 (Jowi, Levels 8, 7); ibid., figs. 55:5, 66:4 (gray ware; Bandebal, Levels 24, 16); Dollfus 1975, fig. 47:6 (gray ware; Jafarabad, Levels 3m–n). For parallels to plate 175:D, see Dollfus 1983, figs. 55:3–4, 58:5 (.00; Bandebal, Levels 24, 21, 16) and 66:1 (gray ware, .00; ibid.); de Mecquenem 1943, fig. 108:3 (Buhallan); Weiss 1976, fig. 29:13 (Qabr-e Sheykheyn).

75. For parallels to plate 175:E, H, see de Mecquenem 1928, pl. 4:1–2 (Susa, Acropole); idem 1934, figs. 9–10; Pottier 1912, fig. 158; Le Breton 1947, fig. 51:19; Steve and Gasche 1971, pl. 40:19 (Susa, Acropole 1965 Sounding, Phase A 2).

A few slightly concave lip sherds are tentatively placed in Subfamily XVd (pl. 175:E, G). So little is preserved of them that insofar as the shape goes, they could also be placed in Subfamily XIVc. On the other hand, their designs are atypical for that group, particularly the isolated branch-like motif (pl. 175:E).[76]

Middle Susiana Family XVI

C–D.22, .24; standard and fine buff ware

Figure 30; plate 176:A–P

In shape the vessels and sherds designated as Family XVI are barrel-like. They fall into two distinct groups distinguished by the presence or absence of painted decoration and also, to a considerable extent, by size. Subfamily XVIa consists of medium-sized vessels (C), for the most part of standard ware, decorated sparsely around the mouth (pl. 176:A–L). There is frequently a simple band on the interior. The repertory of designs on the exterior is very limited consisting mostly of variations on the theme of scallops: linear (pl. 176:A, F),[77] filled in (pl. 176:H–I, K),[78] or elaborate (pl. 176:C, E, J, L).[79] In the last the scallop tips, which are sometimes elongated, end in blobs. This simple but characteristic motif has already been seen on a small, trough spouted bowl, see Family VI-2 from an Early Middle Susiana context (pl. 164:K). Another vessel (pl. 176:C) is also dated to the Early Middle Susiana phase, but the motif was well known in the Late Middle Susiana phase (pl. 176:D, L) and appears in degenerate form on Late Susiana jars.[80] The simple solid scallops (pl. 176:K) separated by a narrow reserved line from the solid lip band is exactly the same combination that occurs on the interior lips of Family XIII bowls (pl. 172:D–G). The wavy band (pl. 176:G) is unusual for Subfamily XVIa[81] and the isolated scalloped circle (pl. 176:B) even more so. It is a motif at home on the upper body of jars (pl. 191:J, L, R, T). The isolated scalloped circle motif and the sherd's fine ware could be used to attribute the fragment (pl. 176:B) to Family XVII if it were not for the out-sized diameter of the mouth.

The lips of Family XVI vessels might be slightly tapered or blunt, but channeled ones, sometimes inbeveled, are particularly characteristic (pl. 176:A, D, G–H, K–L). This feature, in addition to the general shape, links Subfamilies XVIa and b. However, vessels of Subfamily XVIb are with one exception (pl. 176:M) much larger than those of XVIa; they tend to have at least some straw tempering and are without decoration (pl. 176:M–P). A 1 m high vat from Jowi might be taken as a prototype for the reconstruction of one of the vessels (pl. 176:P) representing Subfamily XVIb.[82]

Middle Susiana Family XVII

C.224; fine to eggshell buff ware, painted exterior

Figure 30; plate 176:Q–Z

Very thin walls slanting inward toward the lip and characteristic designs define an outstanding category of Middle Susiana pottery. Small sherds can be unmistakably identified as parts of Family XVII vessels. A complete example (VI-42) found in the sixth season and the fragmentary example (pl. 176:V) show that their lower bodies taper inward to a relatively narrow, approximately flat base.

The surface decoration can be organized in several fashions, but the commonest scheme stresses the horizontal. Two rows of contiguous or almost contiguous circles filled by various simple motifs border the lip and lower part of the body; between is a row of masks (pl. 176:S, U). The latter vary in the stylization of facial features, but the hair always streams toward the left of the viewer. A small fragment shows that birds, instead of masks, can appear between the rows of circles (pl. 176:Z). The vertical compositions consist of columns of alternating motifs, either geometric and representational as in the case of groups of human figures and squiggly lines (pl. 176:T) or all geometric as in crosshatched band and circles (pl. 176:X). A third type of composition is dominated by large representational motifs that divide the vessel surface into fields. In one case the motif is a panther; the fragment does not preserve any framing elements, which could, however, have existed (pl. 176:R). Another example is more elaborate (pl. 58:D). The surface of the vessel is divided into three main fields each filled by twinned birds with outstretched wings. Small segmented circles spaced between the paired bird necks can be taken as fillers hinting at the division of the vessel's surface into fields. A geometric frieze encircles the lip. If it were originally matched by another on the lower part of the vessel, the composition could be claimed as an elaborate version of the horizontal scheme of composition.

To a great extent the motifs on the Family XVII vessels are combined in a fashion specific to that family.

---

76. For a parallel to plate 175:G, see Le Breton 1947, fig. 28:5 (Jowi, old excavations).

77. For a parallel to plate 176:A and F, see Dollfus 1983, fig. 57:5 (inbeveled channeled lip and single scallops; Bandebal, Level 24). For a parallel to plate 176:F, see ibid., fig. 75:6–7 (Bandebal, Level 16).

78. For decoration similar to plate 176:I and K, see D. Stronach 1961, pl. 51:5 (related shape), 14 (Ras al-ʿAmiya).

79. For analogous pattern to plate 176:E, see Le Breton 1947, fig. 24:2 (neck of jar; Jowi, old excavations).

80. See Pottier 1923, pl. 11:21, 23, 26, 30–33, 36, 40.

81. For a parallel to plate 176:G, see Dollfus 1983, fig. 23:6 (Bandebal, Level 23).

82. For a parallel to plate 176:N, see ibid., fig. 24:7 (Jowi, Level 11). For a parallel to plate 138:P, see ibid., fig. 28:4 (Jowi, Level 12).

Moreover, it provides the only habitat for the masks at Chogha Mish, although this was not the case at all other sites.[83] Family XVII is a family of rather rare luxury vessels in use during the Late Middle Susiana phase, as shown by six examples from good contexts (pl. 176:T–Y).

Middle Susiana Family XVIII

C–D.02; standard to fine buff ware, painted except for XVIIIa

Figure 30; plates 60:A–M; 177–79; 180:A–F

Concave walls and wide, gently convex bases are the essential defining features of Family XVIII. This extensive family can be subdivided into a number of groups, the first two of which, Subfamilies XVIIIa–b, stand apart from Subfamilies XVIIIc–f. The latter differ among themselves only in details of the painted decoration on their interiors and are a closely linked cluster forming the bulk of the family.

Subfamily XVIIIa consists of relatively small, unpainted bowls of fine ware (pl. 177:A–D). They form, similar to the fine ware bowls of Families VIII-1 and X-2, one of the categories of small, delicate, open vessels suitable for serving food. Unfortunately, the sherds providing relatively complete profiles came from mixed contexts, but it seems likely that such vessels were in use throughout the Middle Susiana period.[84]

The Subfamily XVIIIb bowls are characterized by their fine ware, shallow proportions, and painting on the exterior (pl. 177:E–F). There is no sharp demarcation between these bowls and examples of Subfamily XVa (pl. 174:H), since shallow .07 forms without a definite basal angle can easily grade into .02 shapes. Both examples of Subfamily XVIIIb are decorated by a single motif, goats and rosettes respectively, executed on a scale that is quite large in proportion to the size of the bowls. They are from Early Middle Susiana contexts.

Bowls of this shape occur at Ras al-ʿAmiya, in one case painted with large discs somewhat analogous to rosettes (pl. 177:F) and in two others with continuous friezes.[85]

The bowls of Subfamilies XVIIIc–f are distinguished from those of the first two subfamilies by their larger size, standard ware, and elaborate painting on the interior. The decoration of both sides represents the same tectonic scheme found on Family X-2 bowls, except that the greater depth of the Subfamilies XVIIIc–f vessels provides larger wall surfaces for painting. As in Family X-2, the standard treatment for the exterior is a zigzag so broad as to produce the effect of a wash with reserved triangles (cf. pl. 177:G). The decoration of the interior is in two parts; the central patterns of the base are enclosed by a cusped band, while registers of various thickness adorn the inner wall. Only occasionally, however, are sherds found that are large enough to provide correlations between wall and base patterns.

An interior lip frieze of reserved crescents, sometimes grading into triangles, defines the bowls of Subfamily XVIIIc (pls. 177:G–I; 178:A, G). Below most of the wall is covered by a broad register of solid paint. Often, as in Family X-2 bowls, the broad wash of the wall is separated from the cusp-encircled pattern of the base by a transitional reserved register with varying filling motifs. As in Family X-2, the commonest of these is the carob (pls. 60:B; 177:I), but dots (pls. 60:A; 177:I) and short wavy lines (pl. 178:A) also appear. These are subsidiary elements usually arranged in clusters. Proof that the center patterns include whirligigs and a composite axial band is provided by a bowl from Jowi and a seventh-season sherd from Chogha Mish (fig. 27:C).[86] It seems likely that the cross and quadrant pattern common on contemporary Family X-2 bowls (pl. 178:G) also occurred. Subfamily XVIIIc bowls are characteristic for the Early Middle Susiana phase. They are particularly useful chronological indicators since they are common and even small fragments of their walls are distinctive. They belong to a class of bowls that was also common in Mesopotamia, but there examples with a reserved crescent border are very rare.[87]

83. For circles with solid center, apparently forming a network on an Middle Susiana Family XVII vessel, similar to plate 176:S and V, see Dollfus 1983, fig. 35:6 (Jowi, Level 8[?]); for a probable Middle Susiana Family XVII design with an analogous network, see Weiss 1976, fig. 27 top right (Qabr-e Sheykheyn). For circles and masks similar to plate 176:S and V, flanked by a human figure, see Le Breton 1947, fig. 30:15 (Jowi, old excavations); Weiss 1976, fig. 27:227 center (Qabr-e Sheykheyn); for masks not on Middle Susiana Family XVII vessels but on the interior of bowls and the exterior of a sherd of unknown profile, see Gautier and Lampre 1905, figs. 172–73 (Tappeh Khazineh). For linked figures similar to plate 176:T, see Dollfus 1983, fig. 31:18 (Jowi, Level 11). For general analogy to circles with quatrefoil center (cf. pl. 176:U, W), see ibid., fig. 31:6 (Jowi, Level 11). For Middle Susiana Family XVII sherds with simplified motifs, see ibid., fig. 30:6, 11 (Jowi, Levels 11–12[?] and 11); see also ibid., fig. 33:12 for sketchy rows of circles on a bowl (Jowi, Level 10).

84. For a parallel to plate 177:A–B, see ibid., fig. 19:1–2 (Jowi, Level 14).

85. For a parallel shape to plate 177:E–F, with different motifs, see D. Stronach 1961, pl. 47:8–10 (Ras al-ʿAmiya).

86. See Le Breton 1947, fig. 23:4 (also Ziegler 1953, fig. 7) from Jowi old excavations, and unpublished Chogha Mish sherd 7.093.

87. For parallels to plate 60:A, see Dollfus 1983, figs. 13:8 (Jowi, Level 15), 21:3 (sherd with dots in the reserved crescents; Jowi, Level 13). For parallels to plates 60:B and 177:I, see Le Breton 1947, fig. 23:4, 7 (Jowi, old excavations); Hole, Flannery, and Neely 1969, figs. 56:a, 57:n–o (Tappeh Sabz, Khazineh phase); Safar, Mustafa, Lloyd 1981, fig. 88:15 (Eridu XII); for reserved crescent borders on bowls of Middle Susiana Family XVIII and other shapes, see Ziegler 1953, pl. 12:i, y (Haji Muhammad); Safar, Mustafa, and Lloyd 1981, figs. 84:13, 86:4 (Eridu IX and X); Hall and Woolley 1927, pl. 18:1810 (al-Ubaid).

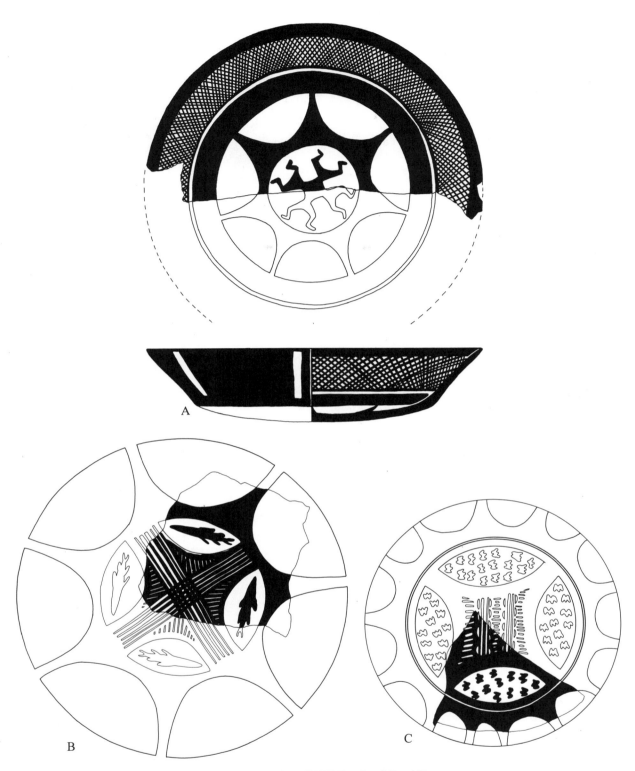

Figure 27. Middle Susiana XVIII Bowl and Bowl Fragments

Subfamily XVIIId bowls are distinguished from those of the preceding subfamily by the appearance of a solid black border and a wide crosshatched register instead of the reserved crescent border and broad wash (pls. 60:G; 178:B–C, H). Often the crosshatched lines were painted so closely together that the pigment has spread, leaving little of the unpainted surface showing through (pl. 178:C). The register reserved between the wall and center patterns, typical for Family X-2 and

Subfamily XVIIIc, is reduced to a narrow reserved line, while the solid band around the cusps of the base is thickened. Three types of center patterns are documented for Subfamily XVIIId bowls. An example from the small mound of Boneh Fazili, about 2 km to the northwest of Chogha Mish, has a central square from which spring quadrants with two appendages (fig. 27:A). Enough remains of one vessel to reconstruct a hollow cross with hatched quadrants (pl. 178:C), while at Haji Muhammad whirligigs are combined with a crosshatched wall (Ziegler 1953, pls. 14:32b). The exterior decoration is similar to that of Subfamily XVIIIc except that sometimes less of the surface is covered by wash, producing the effect of a positive zigzag rather than of reserved triangles. Subfamily XVIIId bowls are common in the Early Middle Susiana phase, but some examples linger on later. In Mesopotamia such vessels seem to have been quite common.[88]

In Subfamily XVIIIe the even lattice grill is replaced by clusters of two to five lines between which considerable background is visible. The exterior can have either the standard broad wash with reserved triangles (pl. 178:D) or large arcs (pl. 178:I). The latter are atypical for Family XVIII but form one of the diagnostic features of the convex-sided Family XIX bowls. It is symptomatic that one example (pl. 178:I) no longer has the concave walls normal for Family XVIII but is practically straight-sided. The decoration of Subfamily XVIIIe bowls is clearly a simplified version of that of the preceding subfamily and it is tempting to interpret the difference in chronological terms. Unfortunately, Subfamily XVIIIe sherds are both rare and from mixed contexts. The question of whether they belong to a transitional phase between the Early Middle Susiana and Late Middle Susiana phases must be left open until there is additional evidence.[89]

The decoration of the final subfamily, XVIIIf, brings a simplification of the lattice even greater than in Subfamily XVIIIe. Now the grill has become still more open and the four- or eight-line clusters cross each other completely only once, in the middle of the register (pls. 60:D–E; 178:E; 179:A). Two fragments from Late Middle Susiana contexts show a complete degeneration of the open lattice, as well as a loss of the concave sides, and end the typological series of Subfamilies XVIIIc–f (pl. 178:F, J).[90]

The sherds of one Subfamily XVIIIf bowl are sufficient to show that in its case the open lattice was accompanied on the base by a variant of the cross and quadrant design (pl. 179:A; for restoration cf. pl. 168:A). However, the four normally empty ovals reserved between the quadrants at the center and the cusped band are now filled with stylized birds. A second innovation is the change in the cusped band; the "bodies" of the cusps are attenuated and their tips enlarged into straight strokes. The origins of the arcs on the exterior of the Subfamily XVIIIf example (pl. 179:A) can be found on Subfamily XVIIIc examples (pl. 177:G), where overlapping brush strokes show that part of the paint was applied in a zigzag.

Most of the examples of Middle Susiana bases with elaborate interior decoration occur as isolated fragments, so that the problem of associating them with the correct type of wall arises. The three main families in question are Families X-2, XVIII, and XIX.[91] The first two, which share the same decorative scheme, can usually be distinguished with a considerable degree of certainty by their ware. Sherds of fine ware or of a thickness less than 10 mm can be assigned to Family X-2. The thick base plates are presumed to have belonged to Subfamilies XVIIIc–f bowls. The general scheme for the decoration of Family X-2 and Subfamilies XVIIIc–f bases was a center pattern bordered by a cusped band, itself often encircled by a solid border. Only in the Late Middle Susiana phase, by which time Family XVIII bowls had been for the most part replaced by those of Family XIX, was this scheme largely abandoned in favor of a single free-field motif in the center of the base. The individual motifs on the centers of the bases, as well as their familial context, are indicated in table 19.

The base patterns of the wide bowls come in many variations, but three schemes of composition can be differentiated: squared (fig. 28:A–N), diaper (fig. 28:O–Q), and radial (fig. 28:R). The first, the designs which square the circle, are by far the most common. They develop directly out of the standard Early Susiana scheme for decorating circular fields, namely, a central square with its corners tipped by triangles whose broad sides are attached to the circular border (pls. 194:C; 195:B; 199:B). This type of composition developed in several ways. In one group the triangles are emphasized; they are painted solid and the central square is usually smaller in proportion to them than in the Early Susiana period. The broad sides of the triangles no longer abut the circular frame as in Early Susiana patterns but have become the usually concave sides of quadrants. The tips of the quadrants can either touch the cusp border, thus creating four reserved ovals (fig. 28:E), or be detached, in which case their outer tips might have either one or two appendages, producing respectively torsional (fig.

88. For parallels to plates 60:C and 178:C, see Dollfus 1983, fig. 14:5 (Jowi, Level 15); Ziegler 1953, pls. 3:d; 4:a; 6:e; 11:h–i, s; 14; 32:a (Haji Muhammad); D. Stronach 1961, pl. 49:2 (Ras al-ʿAmiya); Safar, Mustafa, and Lloyd 1981, figs. 83:9, 86:30, 88:22, 90:3–4 (Eridu VIII, X, XII, XIV); for a related type, see Hole, Flannery, and Neely 1969, fig. 57:p (Tappeh Sabz, Khazineh phase). For parallels to plate 178:H, see Ziegler 1953, pl. 11:a (Haji Muhammad); Safar, Mustafa, and Lloyd 1981, fig. 90:5 (Eridu XIV).

89. For parallels to plate 178:D and I, see Dollfus 1983, fig. 54:11 (Bandebal, 9.40–9.00 = Period I); perhaps Gautier and Lampre 1905, fig. 165 middle (no indication of shape; Musyan).

90. For a parallel to plate 60:D–E, see Ziegler 1953, pl. 32:b (Haji Muhammad). For a degenerated lattice on the interior, similar to that in plate 178:J, see Hole, Flannery, and Neely 1969, figs. 56:f; 57:q (Tappeh Sabz, Khazineh and Early Mehmeh phases).

91. That such elaborate decoration was also used in the bases of Middle Susiana Family VIII-2 bowls is shown by sherds found during the seventh season at Chogha Mish (7.165).

Table 19. Base Patterns on Middle Susiana Bowls of Families X-2, XVIIIc–d, f, unassigned, and XIX

MOTIFS	Hypotactic X-2	XVIII c	d	f	Unassigned	Free-field XIX
TRIANGLES: ANTITHETICAL						
Within cusped bands	Pl. 167:F	—	—	—	—	—
With patterned cross	—	—	—	—	Pl. 180:A	—
With quadrants at corners	—	—	—	—	—	Pl. 180:G
DIAPERS						
Whirligigs	Pls. 166:F; 126:A	Pl. 60:J–L	Pl. 60:J–L	—	—	—
Triangles	—	—	—	—	Pl. 180:E	—
Checkerboard	—	—	—	—	Pl. 180:C	—
QUADRANTS						
Attached	Pl. 168:B	—	—	—	—	—
With one appendage	Pl. 168:G	—	—	—	—	—
With two appendages	Pl. 168:C, I	—	Fig. 27	—	—	Pl. 180:H
Hatched + filled ovals	—	—	—	Pl. 179:B, H	—	—
With cross	Pls. 60:G; 168:A, F, H	—	Pl. 178:C	—	—	—
CROSSES						
Patterned	—	—	—	—	Pl. 180:B	—
Vestigial	—	—	—	—	—	Pl. 181:C
RADIAL						
Rosette: rounded petals	—	—	—	—	Pl. 180:D	—
Rosette: straight edged (blunt) petals = tails	Pl. 168:D	—	—	—	—	—
Pine cones	Pl. 168:E*	—	—	—	—	—
BANDS						
Axial swags	—	—	—	—	Pl. 180:F	—
Zizags or swags in concave-sided rectangle	—	—	—	—	Pl. 179:G, J	—
Composite axial band	—	Fig. 27	—	—	Fig. 27	—
REPRESENTATIONAL						
Fish in ovals	—	—	—	Pls. 58:X; 179:C–I	—	—
Birds in ovals	—	—	—	Pls. 58:Q, S; 179:A	—	—
Fish + birds in ovals	—	—	—	Fig. 27	—	—
Quadrupeds in ovals	—	—	—	Pl. 179:J	—	—
Fish in groups	—	—	—	—	—	Pl. 181:D, E
Turtle	—	—	—	—	—	Pl. 179:K
Birds = geometricized line	—	—	—	—	—	Pl.181: A
Bucranium	—	—	—	—	—	Pl. 181:O
Leopard head	—	—	—	—	—	Pl. 181:F, P
Human head	—	—	—	—	—	Pl. 181:B

*Family attribution tentative

28:D) or relatively static effects (fig. 28:C). However, when quadrants with two appendages spring asymmetrically from a small central square, as was probably the rule in Family X-2 bowls (pl. 168:C), even they give some impression of circular movement. In the torsional designs the center rectangle tends to be reduced to practically nothing and the broad side of the quadrants might be straight. A radial torsional design results from the splitting of each quadrant into two (fig. 28:B). The designs that stress solidly painted quadrants at the expense

of other elements of the basic pattern are found at Chogha Mish on Family X-2 bowls. However, a large fragment from Boneh Fazili proves that quadrant motifs were also used on Subfamily XVIIId bowls (fig. 28:C).

Although solid quadrant designs are particularly characteristic for the Early Middle Susiana phase, they remained in use later. A free-field design of simple quadrants centered in a pair of antithetical triangles was almost certainly part of a Family XIX vessel of the Late Middle Susiana phase (fig. 28:A). By that time quadrant

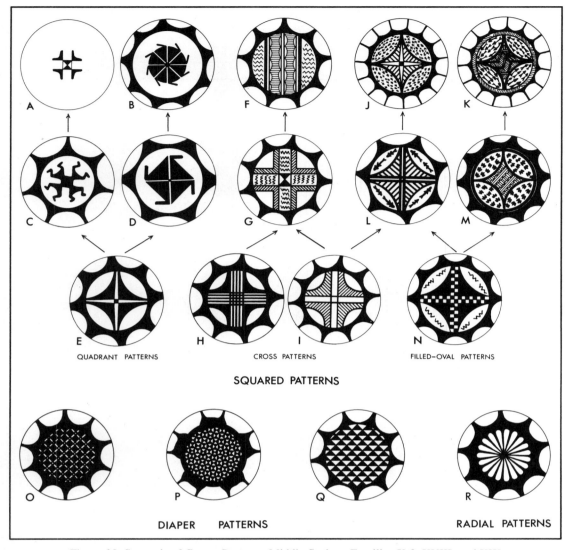

QUADRANT PATTERNS   CROSS PATTERNS   FILLED–OVAL PATTERNS

SQUARED PATTERNS

DIAPER   PATTERNS   RADIAL PATTERNS

Figure 28. Synopsis of Center Patterns: Middle Susiana Families X-2, XVIII, and XIX

cross, but in addition two fish appear in the ovals. The next typological stage reduces the reserved cross to a negative star with pointed rays and fills the ovals with many small fish, birds or, in one case, quadrupeds. Usually all the ovals of one bowl were filled by the same kind of animal (pl. 179:A–C). The only example (fig. 28:I) whose setting is known was framed by attenuated cusps and belonged to a Subfamily XVIIIf bowl (pl. 179:A). In an alternative pattern occurring not only at Chogha Mish but also at KS 112 (in central Khuzestan) to the southeast (fig. 27:C),[92] the inner division delimiting the quadrants were omitted, leaving a quadrangular area in which bands of zigzags or hatched swags substitute for the simple hatching of the quadrants (fig. 28:K, M). In both cases an extra element appears between the ovals and the cusped frame, in the first a solid border separated from the cusps by a thin reserved line and in the second a band with opposed clusters of lines.

The third manner in which the squared patterns developed was by stressing the cross elements at the expense of the quadrants (fig. 28:F–I). Precedents for segmenting of a circular field by a cross formed of multiple lines (fig. 28:H) can be found on Early Susiana Family XV bowls (pls. 62:K–O, Q–R; 199:E–F). On a Family X-2 bowl the cross is not implicit or reserved as shown in figure 28:C, L, N, but is given equal weight with the solid quadrants by a checkerboard filling (fig. 28:N). This example also has the simplest-known version of filled ovals, which makes it pertinent to the patterns illustrated in figure 28:J–M. In the next typological stage, illustrated in figure 28:G, a wide-armed cross filled with

designs had migrated from the interior of bowls to other habitats where they appear as subsidiary elements. On the exteriors of Families XVII and XXXIII vessels quadrants fill simple (pl. 176:Q) or scalloped (pl. 191:S) circles; the rosette on one fragment (pl. 191:T) is a doubled version of another (pl. 168:C), comparable in general to the torsion of a circular field (pl. 191:N).

The first group of squared designs is characterized by the contrast between solidly-painted positive motifs and unpainted background (fig. 28:A–E). In the second group the circular field, always segmented into outer ovals and inner quadrangular area, is covered by a more even web of pattern, without markedly contrasting dark and light sections (fig. 28:J–N). This effect was achieved by filling the reserved ovals with representational motifs, thus changing them into positive elements of the design. The hatching of the quadrants, which seems to have been fairly standard, also contributed to the even effect. The design of hatched quadrants (fig. 28:I), which can be taken as a starting point for the series, is elsewhere (fig. 28:L) separated by a reserved

92. This sherd was found on the surface of KS 112 during an informal survey by Daniel Shimabuku and Shan Winn at the beginning of the eleventh season at Chogha Mish.

wavy lines is the dominant motif; the quadrants have disappeared as recognizable elements although the hatched borders of the cross can be interpreted as vestiges of hatched quadrants similar to those shown in figure 28:I. The cross design gives rise by the atrophy of one pair of arms to a wide composite axial band. One fragment, probably from a Subfamily XVIIIc bowl,[93] can be restored as a design consisting of four reserved ovals and a central swag flanked by bands with pairs of incised wavy lines (fig. 29). Another axial pattern has two hatched swags bordered by thick and thin lines (fig. 28:F). The hemispherical areas reserved on either side were probably filled with short wavy lines; although this cannot be established with certainty because of the sherd's eroded surface, the analogy with filled ovals (fig. 28:J–M) makes it unlikely that such large spaces were left empty.[94]

The other two categories of base patterns, the diaper designs (fig. 28:O–Q) and the radial designs (fig. 28:R), display less variety than do the compositions that square the circle. The basic framework for constructing the overall designs was a square grid or combinations of grids. A simple version (fig. 28:O), a single grid, demarcated by borders in reserve is found on a sherd that is unusual in having a slight indication of a ring base.[95] Whirligigs are the commonest overall pattern; they result from filling in alternate elements in the network of triangles created by two complete grids placed at right angles to each other (fig. 28:P).[96] If, instead of a complete second grid, there is only one line diagonally

Figure 29. Sherd from Base of Bowl, probably Belonging to Middle Susiana Family XVIIIe or f, Found by Daniel Shimabuku on the Surface of KS 112 during the Eleventh Season

bifurcating the squares of the primary grid a series of triangles is produced, each alternate one of which is likewise filled in solidly (fig. 28:Q).[97] Aside from these patterns developed by splitting quadrants (fig. 28:B), radial designs are represented by simple rosettes, presumably with rounded petals by analogy with comparable designs from Haji Muhammad and Ras al-ʿAmiya (fig. 28:R).[98]

The circular patterns just reviewed flourished in the Early Middle Susiana phase on Family X-2 and Subfamilies XVIIIc–d bowls. Solid quadrant designs are particularly prominent on the former according to the

93. This identification can be made on the basis of a fragment (7.093) found during the seventh season at Chogha Mish, with an allied pattern on the base and the lower part of the wall of a Middle Susiana Subfamily XVIIIc vessel.

94. On a Late Ubaid sherd from Eridu IX, with the same general composition, the large hemispheres are filled respectively with small Vs and clusters of short lines (Safar, Mustafa, and Lloyd 1981, fig. 84:3).

95. For a similar pattern to plate 180:C, see Ziegler 1953, pl. 37:25 = Heinrich and Falkenstein 1938, pl. 38:b (Haji Muhammad).

96. For parallels to plate 60:J–L, see Le Breton 1947, fig. 23:4 = Ziegler, 1953, fig. 4 (Jowi); Hole, Flannery, and Neely 1969, fig. 57 (elaborated version with irregular whirligigs separated from two concentric cusp borders, each with a border line in white reserve, by a wavy line in a reserved band; Tappeh Sabz, Khazineh phase); Ziegler 1953, pls. 14, 16:b (Haji Muhammad); Heinrich and Falkenstein 1938, pl. 38:e (Haji Muhammad); Safar, Mustafa, and Lloyd 1981, figs. 82:11; 85:4; 86:22; 90 (actually fig. 91):24; 91 (actually fig. 90):6 (oval; Eridu VIII–X, XIV).

97. For a parallel to plate 180:E, see Ziegler 1953, pl. 4:h (Haji Muhammad); sherds found at Haji Muhammad were also decorated by simple "one and one-half" and double grids (ibid., pls. 9:a, c; 21:a; 37a:20 [exterior of .02 bowl]; 5:m; 37a:22 [base sherd] respectively); for pattern, see also Safar, Mustafa, and Lloyd 1981, fig. 83:26 (Eridu VIII).

98. For rosettes with round-tipped petals similar to those in plate 180:D, see Ziegler 1953, pl. 16:a (Haji Muhammad); D. Stronach 1961, pls. 48:2; 49:1–2, 4 (Ras al-ʿAmiya); Adams and Nissen 1972, figs. 34:7, 60:6 (Warka Survey, Sites 042 and 267); Safar, Mustafa, and Lloyd 1981, figs. 89:20; 91 (actually fig. 90):9, 7 (triangular tips); 96:11 (Eridu XIII–XIV, XVI); Hall and Woolley 1927, pl. 16:2123, 2133, 2146, 2155, 2160 (Ubaid). For rosettes with straight tips, see Hole, Flannery, and Neely 1969, fig. 56b (straight tips; Tappeh Sabz, Khazineh and later[?] phases); Ziegler 1953, pl. 25:e (Haji Muhammad).

Table 20. Pottery, Similar to Chogha Mish Middle Susiana Families XVa–XXIIb, Present at Other Sites

OTHER SITES	XVa	XVb	XVc	XVd	XVIa	XVIb	XVII	XVIIIa	XVIIIb	XVIIIc	XVIIId	XVIIIe	XVIIIf	XVIII bases	XIX	XXI	XXII	XXIIb
SUSA, Old Excavations	—	—	—	X	—	—	—	—	—	—	—	—	—	—	—	—	—	—
JOWI																		
5–10	—	—	X	—	—	—	R	—	—	—	—	—	—	—	—	—	X	—
11–12	M	—	—	—	—	X	R	—	—	—	—	—	—	—	X	—	X	—
13–17	—	—	—	—	—	—	—	X	—	X	X	—	—	—	—	—	X	—
Old Excavations	—	—	—	—	M	—	M	—	—	X	—	—	—	M	X	—	X	—
JAFARABAD																		
3M–N	—	—	X	—	—	—	—	—	—	—	—	—	—	—	—	—	X	—
Old Excavations	—	—	—	X	—	—	—	—	—	—	—	—	—	—	—	—	—	—
BANDEBAL																		
13–18	—	—	X	—	—	—	—	—	—	—	—	—	—	—	—	—	X	X
19–27	—	—	X	—	X	—	—	—	—	—	—	—	—	—	—	—	—	—
Old Excavations	—	—	—	—	—	—	—	—	—	—	—	—	—	—	—	—	—	—
BUHALAN	—	—	—	—	—	—	—	—	—	—	—	—	—	—	—	—	—	—
QABR-E SHEYKHEYN	—	—	X	—	—	—	R	—	—	—	—	—	—	—	—	—	—	—
TAPPEH SABZ																		
Khazineh	—	—	—	—	—	—	—	—	—	X	—	—	M	M	—	—	—	—
Mehmet	—	—	—	—	—	—	—	—	—	—	—	—	M	—	—	—	—	X
Bayat	—	—	—	—	—	—	—	—	—	—	—	—	—	—	—	—	—	X
KHAZINEH	—	—	—	—	—	—	M	—	—	—	X	—	—	—	—	—	—	—
MUSYAN	—	M	—	—	—	—	—	—	—	—	—	—	M	—	—	—	—	—
BAKUN B	—	—	—	—	—	—	—	—	—	—	—	—	—	—	—	—	—	—
GAP	—	—	—	—	—	—	—	—	—	—	—	—	—	—	—	—	—	—
IBLIS	—	—	—	—	—	—	—	—	—	—	—	—	—	—	—	—	—	—
ERIDU																		
Cemetery	—	—	—	—	—	—	—	—	—	—	—	—	—	—	—	—	—	—
VIII–IX	—	—	—	—	—	—	—	—	X	X	—	—	—	M	—	—	—	—
XI–XIII	—	—	—	—	—	—	—	—	X	X	—	—	—	M	—	—	—	—
XVI	—	—	—	—	—	—	—	—	—	—	—	—	—	M	—	—	—	—
UBAID	—	—	—	—	—	—	—	—	—	X	—	—	—	M	—	—	—	—
HAJI MUHAMMAD	—	—	—	—	—	—	—	—	X	X	—	M	M	M	X	—	—	M
WARKA Survey 042	—	—	—	—	—	—	—	—	—	—	—	—	—	M	—	—	—	—
WARKA Survey 267	—	—	—	—	—	—	—	—	—	—	—	—	—	M	—	—	—	—
RAS AL-ʿAMIYA	X	X	—	—	M	—	—	S	X	X	—	—	—	M	—	—	—	—
GAWRA																		
XIX	—	—	—	—	—	—	—	—	—	—	—	—	—	—	—	—	—	—
XVII–XVIII	—	—	—	—	—	—	—	—	—	—	—	—	—	—	—	—	—	—
HALAF	—	—	—	—	—	—	—	—	—	—	—	—	—	—	—	—	—	—

X = Both shape and design (when applicable) occur; M = Motif attested, but shape not necessarily related; S = Shape attested, but if painted, motif can be or is different; R = Same shape, but motif only related.

material available. They also appear on an example of Subfamily XVIIId, but in general the painted Family XVIII bowls seem to favor designs emphasizing cross elements or reserved ovals. In the Early Middle Susiana phase the cusped borders framing the center patterns are substantial. They are elements characteristic of Middle Susiana pottery with only one good example from Mesopotamia despite the occurrence there of quadrant, whirligig, and rosette patterns in the centers of bowls.[99] By the Late Middle Susiana phase the cusps, when they

still appear, have reduced bodies and attenuated tips. Such cusps are known on Families VIII-1 and XIX vessels as well as combined with filled ovals on an example of Subfamily XVIIIf from a mixed context (pl. 179:A). The smaller fragments of ovals filled with many small animals are also, unfortunately, from mixed or surface deposits that do not provide precise dating evidence. It should be noted, however, that the primary Late Middle Susiana contexts excavated after the fifth season yielded no sherds decorated by ovals filled with many small representational motifs. They are also absent from the Middle Susiana levels of Jafarabad and Jowi. Accordingly, it seems possible that this motif, pre-

99. For an example, see D. Stronach 1961, pl. 49:7 (Ras al-ʿAmiya); for a probable second example, see Safar, Mustafa, and Lloyd 1981, fig. 92:15 (Eridu XV).

sumably continued with Subfamilies XVIIIe or f walls, might have belonged to a transitional phase between the Early and Late Middle Susiana phases. In any case, the painted Family XVIII bowls and their allies are clearly important chronological markers, even though additional material is needed to delimit the exact range of some of the types.

Middle Susiana Family XIX

C–D.03.; proportions "1–2," standard buff ware, painted both sides

Figure 30; plates 180:G–H (probably); 181:A–P

The bowls of Subfamilies XVIIIc–f were the direct ancestors of those of Family XIX. The primary distinction between Families XVIII and XIX is the convex form of the latter. Occasionally bowls with rather straight walls, intermediate between the forms canonical for the two families, but with Subfamily XVIIIf interior patterns occur (pls. 178:J; 179:A). The decoration is also diagnostic for Family XIX vessels. Their exterior walls are normally covered by sweeping arcs fully comparable to those on Family XIII bowls, but distinct from the angular zigzags of Subfamilies XVIIIc–f (pls. 177:G; 178:H). On three examples of the intermediate Subfamilies XVIIIe–f which probably overlap chronologically with Family XIX, the arcs are already present (pls. 60:E; 178:I; 179:A).[100] The decoration of the interior also contrasts with that of Subfamilies XVIIIc–f (pl. 181:M). A broad wash might cover almost the entire inner wall above the basal carination (pl. 181:K–L, O). On one of the atypically small examples the broad wash is interrupted by a reserved band containing widely spaced clusters of short wavy lines (pl. 181:H). In other cases the wash is limited to the upper wall (pl. 181:J) or the lower wall with above pendant triangles (pl. 181:N) or an arc frieze (pl. 181:M). Sometimes the arc frieze covers the entire interior wall, repeating there the decoration standard for the exteriors of full-sized Family XIX bowls (pl. 181:I, P). Pendant loops, a subsidiary element typical for the Late Middle Susiana phase, sometimes border the lower edge of the broad wash (pl. 181:H, K, M). The base patterns of Subfamilies XVIIIc–f, when they do persist on Family XIX bowls, are simplified.

The cusp bands common on Families X-2 and XVIII, if they appear at all, are of the developed form, already seen on one example of Subfamily XVIIIf, in which the tips of the cusps are elongated at the expense of their bodies (pls. 59:F; 167:F). An almost unrecognizable example occurs on an atypically small Family XIX

sherd (pl. 59:P). In many cases the cusped border has disappeared altogether. Sometimes the central circular area remained unpainted (pl. 181:I–J), but often it combined detached motifs placed freely in the field, as illustrated by a fragmentary example with a bucranium and traces of an unidentified motif (pl. 181). Base sherds with groups of fish can be safely assigned to Family XIX, and probably also small sherds with a schematic line of birds (pl. 181:A) and a human head (pl. 181:B). The small part of a base (pl. 181:P) has the head of a carnivore, depicted with both profile and full view elements, namely, gaping jaws well supplied with teeth and an extended tongue, but also two eyes. In the detailed drawing of the motif short brush strokes that fused together to provide a solid attachment to what was presumably a concentric band (pl. 181:F). A few sherds with geometric motifs are probably also from the centers of Family XIX bowls (pls. 180:G–H; 181:C).

Middle Susiana Family XX

C–D.03, .04, .07; proportions "2–3," thin standard or fine buff ware, unpainted

Figure 30; plates 60:X, Z–AA; 182:A–J

This family consists of relatively deep, unpainted bowls, sherds of which were common. There was a considerable range in size. The smaller examples would have been useful vessels for table-service while the larger examples were presumably storage jars. The ware is always dense and frequently quite fine. In most cases the walls are notably thin in proportion to the size of the vessels. There was an effort to make them watertight, as indicated by the black, bitumen stain on the interiors of most examples. The profiles vary but double-curved, .07, types are particularly frequent. Asymmetrical, tapered lips predominate, although blunt lips also occur (pl. 182:H). Bases are normally concave, but the lower part of the body is sometimes (pl. 182:I, J) very evenly convex so the bases have been tentatively restored as round; perhaps they were almost imperceptibly concave (cf. pl. 182:A–C).

The vessels of this family developed from the Early Middle Susiana types subsumed under Family XXI and appear alongside of them. Family XX vessels continue to be common in the Late Middle Susiana phase.

Middle Susiana Family XXI

C–D.03, .08; gritty ware predominant, proportion "3"

Figure 30; plates 60:N–W; 182:K–P

The defining feature of Family XXI is the vestigial flange slightly above the concave base. As the name indicates, the vestigial flanges are the final development of those typical for the major group of Early Susiana unpainted vessels (pls. 199–200) and testify to the transi-

---

100. What appear to be local Deh Luran types are intermediate between the painted Middle Susiana Family XVIII subfamilies, and Middle Susiana Family XIX (Hole, Flannery, and Neely 1969, fig. 56:c–e). AA

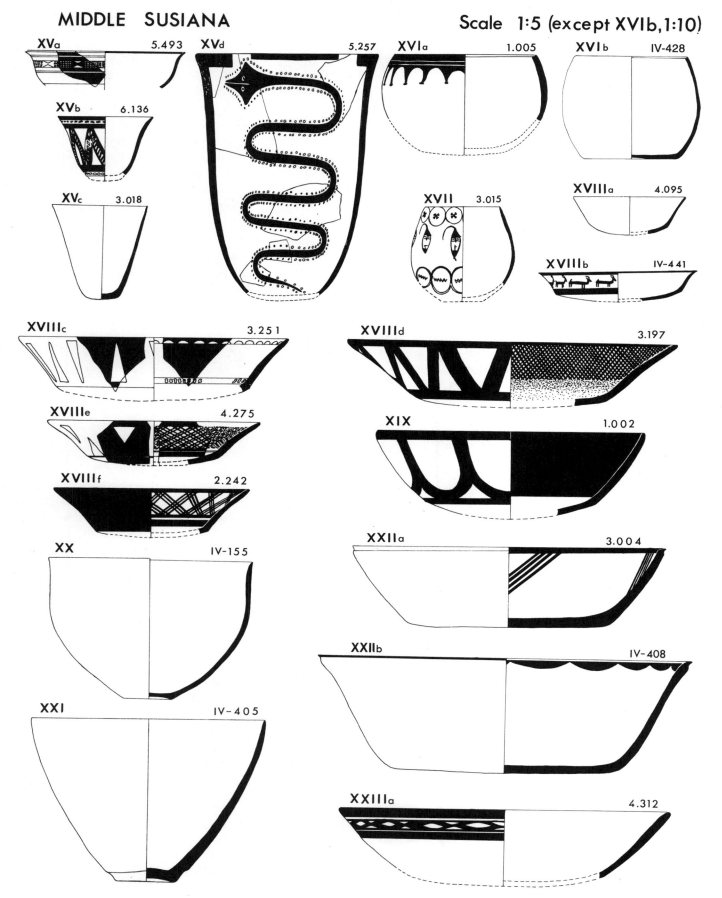

Figure 30. Middle Susiana Families XVa–XXIIIa

tional character of the Early Middle Susiana phase. They differ from their ancestors in their contracted position, being frequently amalgamated with the base into a single thick element (pl. 182:K, M–N) and in their diminished shape, often appearing as only a slight overhang without the swelling convexity of the Early Susiana flanges. Sometimes the vestigial flange is reduced to a slight, rough groove (pl. 182:N) or to a barely perceptible line (pl. 182:P). As in Early Susiana, potters' marks appear fairly often just above the basal angle; they tend to be smaller and more neatly executed than their Early Susiana antecedents (tables 21–23; pls. 60:N–W; 182:K). The ware of the majority of examples of Family XXI is considerably grittier than the standard Middle Susiana buff ware. This is another characteristic linking Family XXI with Early Susiana pottery. Relatively thick blunt lips of gritty ware comparable to the fabric of the bases with vestigial flanges can be taken as belonging to Family XXI vessels. However, atypical examples do occur, for example, in which the ware is standard with only a slight amount of grit (pl. 182:P). The reconstructible examples show that Family XXI vessels were fairly deep (pl. 182:N–P), corresponding in this characteristic to the majority of the ancestral Early Susiana flanged vessels. However, there does not seem to have been variation in profile shape that was found earlier.

Family XXI is one of the distinctive categories of the Early Middle Susiana repertoire. Though complete examples are rare, the vestigially-flanged bases are quite common and constitute an unmistakable diagnostic feature.[101]

Middle Susiana Family XXII

D.00, .01, .03, .07; usually shallow proportion, i.e., lower "1" or "0," lip usually flat or channeled, standard buff ware, painted interior

Figure 30; plate 183:A–F

A very uniform group of vessels is made up of large bowls and basins on which the painted decoration consists primarily of simple motifs suspended from the lip on the interior. The exterior has at most a lip band, the carryover of the paint from the interior and top of the wide lip. Subdivisions can be made on the basis of the simple designs.

Subfamily XXIIa consists of vessels with three sets of curved or triangular festoons[102] and Subfamily XXIIb

of those with a continuous band of scallops.[103] Both subfamilies are typical for the Late Middle Susiana phase, the examples of the former apparently somewhat more frequent than those of latter. Several semi-complete Subfamily XXIIa bowls from the concentration of Late Middle Susiana pottery in Q18:312 and Q18:313 North prove that the curved and triangular festoons were used side-by-side (pl. 183:A–D). However, an indication that the triangular festoon began earlier is provided by an atypical example in a bowl from an Early Middle Susiana context; on it the festoon lines are thin and hang directly from the lip, the thick band normal there being absent.

Middle Susiana Family XXIII

D.03, .04, .05; shallow proportion "1"–"0," standard ware, exterior usually painted

Figures 30–31; plates 59:M–N; 183:G–AA

Fairly shallow large bowls painted on the exterior except for Subfamily XXIIId were common during the Middle Susiana period. They are, however, almost always represented only by sherds, which leave the height and the exact proportions of the vessels uncertain. The group is subdivided by the shapes of the profiles and lips by general proportion, and secondarily by painted motifs. The first two subfamilies belong to the Late Middle Susiana phase and the others to the Early Middle Susiana phase.

Bowls with either fairly straight[104] or convex walls and either tapered or blunt lips are classified as Subfamily XXIIIa (pl. 183:G–L, T) and those with flat or channeled lips as Subfamily XXIIIb (pl. 183:M–R). A second pair of subfamilies, XXIIIc and d(?), also have convex or sometimes convex changing to vertical walls but are distinguished from the first pair by the very shallow proportions ("0"). The lips are flat or channeled. Subfamily XXIIIc bowls are painted (pl. 183:U, X) and Subfamily XXIIId bowls are plain (pl. 183:W). The final major subfamily, XXIIIe, is characterized by an incurved lip, sometimes very slight (pl. 183:Y–AA). The most completely preserved example has a unique feature, a hollow vertical omphalos the use of which is unknown.

A unique sherd belonging to a large open form is illustrated (pl. 183:BB) with the Family XXIII vessels. It

---

101. For a parallel to plate 182:K, see Dollfus 1983, fig. 19:6 (Jowi, Level 14). For a parallel to plate 182:N, see ibid., fig. 19:11 (Jowi, Levels 13–14[?]). For a parallel to plate 182:P, see ibid., fig. 19:3 (Jowi, Level 13).

102. For parallels to plate 183:A–B and D, see Dollfus 1983, figs. 31:7, 36:2 (Jowi, Levels 11, 7); Le Breton 1947, fig. 23:13 (Jowi, old excavations); Dollfus 1975, fig. 49:5, 7 (Jafarabad, Level 3n); Dollfus 1983, figs. 70:3, 81:6 (Bandebal, Levels 16, 14); Weiss 1976, fig. 22:142 (Qabr-e

Sheykheyn); Ziegler 1953, pl. 10:g (Haji Muhammad). For a parallel to plate 183:C, see Dollfus 1975, fig. 49:8 (Jafarabad, Level 3m).

103. For parallels to plate 183:F, see Dollfus 1983, fig. 70:5 (Bandebal, Level 16); Hole, Flannery, and Neely 1969, fig. 60:a–b (Tappeh Sabz, Mehmeh and Bayat phases); Ziegler 1953, pl. 10:e (Haji Muhammad).

104. Small sherds (pl. 183:H–I) might have been the straight upper ends of .03 profiles.

consists of a wide ledge rim presumably set on either a .04 or .22 body. It cannot be satisfactorily classified until further discoveries allow the reconstruction of a complete form. The decoration, a broad wash on the exterior and bold triangles on the ledge rim, is also atypical. The sherd was found in a transitional Middle Susiana to Late Susiana level and presumably belongs to the Late Middle Susiana phase.[105]

The painted decoration of Family XXIII bowls was applied in a zone around the lip and normally consisted of a single geometric frieze in a horizontal frame.[106] The contrast between the motifs and their setting characteristic for Subfamilies XXIIIa–b on the one hand and c and e on the other mirrors the different dates of the two groups. Thick outer and very thin inner bands frame the main motif on Subfamilies XXIIIa–b sherds, except for an example with a rather sloppily drawn wavy line (pl. 183:Q), which is comparable to the decoration of a Family X-5a bowl dating to the Late Middle Susiana phase (pl. 169:K).[107] Single (pl. 183:H, Q) or antithetical (pl. 183:I, M, T–U) wavy bands appear to be common motifs, but neatly hatched zigzags (pl. 183:L), swags (pl. 183:N), lozenges (pl. 183:O), and stepped rectangles (pl. 183:P) also occur. In Subfamilies XXIIIc and e the inner framing bands, if present, are wider than those of the first two subfamilies. In addition, the repertory of main motifs is limited. An early version of the frieze of antithetical wavy bands is characterized by neat brush strokes that are very narrow at the crossing points and thicker where the ovals touch the horizontal borders (pl. 59:M); sometimes the outer edges of the loops are quite straight (pl. 183:U) so that parts of a loop vary in thickness.[108] The contrast between motifs of the Early Middle Susiana phase (pls. 59:M; 183:U) and of the Late Middle Susiana phase (pl. 183:R) is clear. An intermediate version (pl. 183:T) appears to be a Late Middle Susiana sherd out of place in a Protoliterate context. The other main motif found on Subfamilies XXIIIc and e is a frieze of one or more scalloped bands (pl. 183:Y), which appear most frequently on an area reserved in a broad wash of paint (pls. 59:N; 183:Z–AA).

A closely related pattern, a frieze forced by clusters of wavy bands on a reserved ground, is characteristic for the Haji Muhammad period in Mesopotamia.[109] The top of an omphalos (pl. 183:Y) is adorned by a simple version of a cusped diaper pattern in which the center is crosshatched. A sherd attributable by its shape to Subfamily XXIIIc has a frieze of notched triangles, possibly representing birds; it was found on the surface and its date remains uncertain.[110] Unpainted versions of Subfamily XXIIIc bowls seem to have been very rare. They can, however, be attributed to the Early Middle Susiana phase without hesitation.[111]

Middle Susiana Family XXIV

> D.01, .03, .04, .07; proportions "3–4," standard buff ware, painted exterior

> Figure 31; plates 57:H–J; 58:Z–AA, DD–FF; 184:A–T

An important category of large crateriform vessels is defined by deep proportions—far greater than those of Families XXII and XXIII, rather sharp basal angles, and slightly convex or occasionally flat bases. Painted decoration always encircles the lip zone, as on Subfamilies XXIIIa–b bowls but can extend about halfway down the body. Some examples also have a single wide band close to the basal angle (pl. 184:S), which enables otherwise unidentifiable bases to be recognized as parts of Family XXIV vessels. Although the individual character of the crateriform vessels is clear, simple friezes such as zigzags (pls. 183:L; 184:H), swags (pls. 183:N; 184:B), and lozenges (pls. 183:O; 184:D–E) are common to both Families XXIV and XXIII, so that the attribution of some sherds might seem doubtful. Usually, however, even small sherds can be identified by means of their stance and by their relatively thick walls combined with flat or channeled lips.

The simpler decoration of the crateriform vessels corresponds in both the frame of thick and thin bands and the motifs to that of Subfamilies XXIIIa–b bowls and developed boldly on craters (pls. 57:H–I; 184:F–G). One lattice of the type characteristic for Subfamily XVIIIf, but, unknown on Subfamilies XXIIIa–b, occurs

---

105. Similar decoration occurs on a structurally different type of ledge from Jowi (Level 15; Dollfus 1983, fig. 17:8). In view of the different form and early context of the Jowi sherd, the resemblance is presumably accidental.

106. The presence of two friezes, antithetical wavy bands, and a hatched zigzag(?) (pl. 183:J) is atypical and weakens the attribution of the sherd to Middle Susiana Family XXIII.

107. For a parallel to plate 183:Q, see Dollfus 1983, fig. 30:3 (Jowi, Level 11).

108. For parallels to plates 59:M and 183:U, see ibid., fig. 22:9 (Jowi, Level 13). For design, see Le Breton 1947, fig. 26:3 (Jowi, old excavations); Dollfus 1983, fig. 15:9–10 (Jowi, Level 16); D. Stronach 1961, pls. 44:7, 9; 46:7; 54:6 (Ras al-ʿAmiya).

109. For a parallel to plate 183:Y, see Le Breton 1947, fig. 26:7 (Jowi, old excavations); for a similar shape, see Dollfus 1983, figs. 15:9, 22:7 (as well as the rim and related design; Jowi, Levels 16, 13); D. Stronach 1961, pl. 44:5 (related design; Ras al-ʿAmiya); for related design, see Ziegler 1953, pl. 34:k (Haji Muhammad). For design of peaked wavy lines similar to plate 183:Y–AA, see Dollfus 1983, fig. 25:7 (Jowi, Level 11).

110. For triangles similar to plate 183:V, see ibid., fig. 31:15 (Jowi, Level 11).

111. For a parallel to plate 183:W, see ibid., fig. 20:11 (Jowi, Levels 13–14[?]).

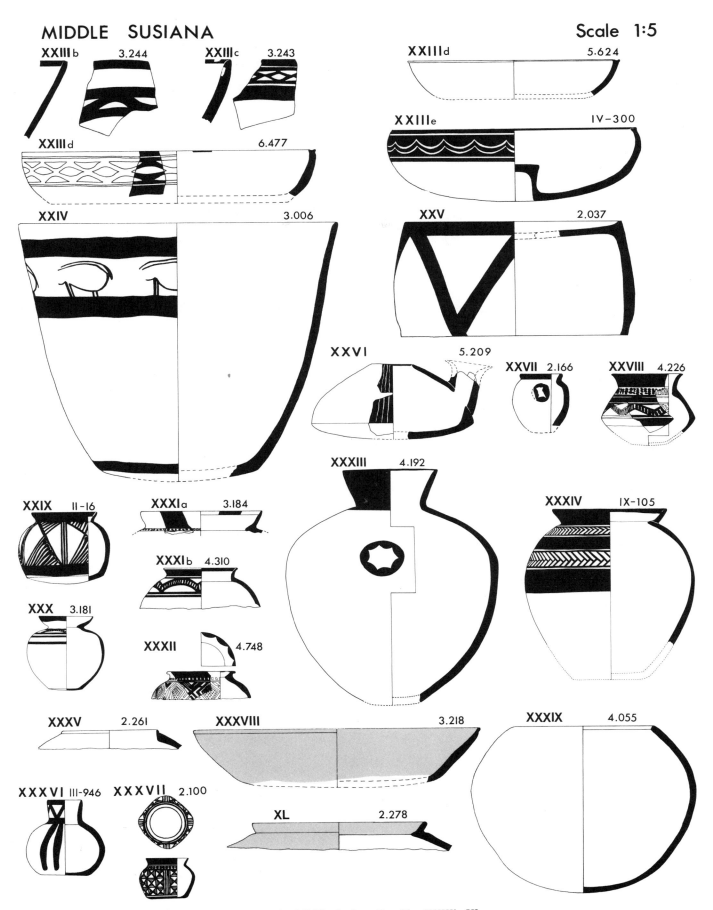

Figure 31. Middle Susiana Families XXIIIb–XL

(pl. 184:N).[112] The use of representational motifs is characteristic for Family XXIV. Bucrania (pl. 184:I) and flying birds (pl. 184:S) were placed sideways to form friezes. The latter occur on a vessel sufficiently complete to show that the frieze was not continuous but broken at one point by a vertical branch. In a more abstract variation of the frieze of flying birds, they appear as wings strung along a median line (pl. 58:O). The more complicated decoration on Family XXIV vessels is formed by multiple friezes. One crater has a greatly enlarged hatched zigzag as the main frieze; the narrower band above is filled by a motif that can be interpreted as a highly geometricized version of bird friezes (pls. 58:N; 184:R; cf. also pl. 171:F). Two body sherds with equal-sized bands of zigzags (pl. 184:O) and swags (pl. 194:P) can be tentatively assigned to Family XXIV.

The most frequent, as well as the largest, representational motif on the craters is the long-horned goat. The animals are all formed by a few lines—three long lines for the body and horns, short lines for the head and tails, and straight lines for the legs. Although the pattern of the brush strokes remains the same, the wide variation in their character suggests the hands of different craftsmen. Some goats are rendered with bold sweeping curves and with less steady lines (cf. 58:AA, EE). Goats of the same structure also occur on small bowls of Family III (pls. 58:U; 163:V–W). The goats sometimes occupy the only frieze on a vessel (pls. 58:Z, DD–FF; 184:T). They are framed by thick borders; in most instances the upper band is set an appreciable distance below the lip, a stylistic detail found also on some Subfamily X-5a bowls (pl. 169:J, L).[113] In multiple frieze compositions geometric motifs appear with the goats. They are framed by two narrow geometric registers in the most complete example (pl. 184:M), as might also have originally been true of two fragments (pls. 58:AA; 184:K–L). A variation in which a wavy band separates two friezes of goats is illustrated by a small sherd (pl. 184:J).[114]

112. For a parallel to plate 184:B, see Le Breton 1947, fig. 27:9 (Jowi, old excavations). For a swollen swag similar to plate 184:F, see Egami and Sono 1962, fig. 22:5 (C.075.200 beaker from Tall-e Gap). For a parallel to plate 184:G, see Dollfus 1983, fig. 56:12 (Bandebal, Level 23). For a parallel to plate 184:H, see ibid., fig. 171:17 (Bandebal, Level 16).

113. For a parallel to plate 58:Z, see Le Breton 1947, fig. 40:3, 8 (Bandebal, old excavations). For a parallel to plate 58:BB, see ibid., fig. 29:5 (Jowi, old excavations). For parallels to plates 58:EE–FF and 184:T, see ibid., fig. 29:1–2, 6 (Jowi, old excavations); ibid., fig. 40:2–3 (Bandebal, old excavations).

114. For a shape similar to plate 184:M, see Weiss 1976, fig. 16:67 (with tailed zigzag; Qabr-e Sheykheyn). For goat and wavy band, see Le Breton 1947, fig. 29:4 (Jowi, old excavations). For a solid zigzag and a goat on a .03 tapered lip bowl, presumably Middle Susiana Family XI, see Dollfus 1983, fig. 60:8 (Bandebal, Level 22).

So far craters with a single frieze of goats have been found in the East Area and those with multiple friezes of goats and geometric motifs farther north in Trenches I and XXII. Whether this distinction is an accident of discovery, a question of the preferences of individual craftsmen or households, or even of some chronological distinction remains an open question. For the present, however, all the craters of Family XXIV stand as representatives of the Late Middle Susiana phase.

THE FAMILIES OF MIDDLE SUSIANA CLOSED FORMS

The closed vessels are less numerous than the open vessels and do not present as large a variety of families. The first two groups contain highly specialized types and are followed by a number of other families, the members of which are ovoid or globular in form. The standard closed vessels are often represented only by fragments of convex body walls or of the shoulder and neck. Thus, although ovoid bodies seem to be more common than globular ones, it is frequently difficult to define families by exact body shape and proportion or to attribute bases to specific types of closed forms. In many cases, other elements such as decoration or accessories have served as defining features. Thus, the classification of eleven families of standard closed vessels, Families XXVII–XXXVII, depends on the type of neck taken in combination with other features. Low necks are distinguished as those whose height is 25% or less of their diameter (that is, ranging from the upper half of ratio "0" through the lower half of ratio "1"). In the majority of cases a solid broad wash of color covers the exteriors of necks, but painted patterns sometimes occur.

Middle Susiana Family XXV

C–D.22, .30, .31; standard buff ware, painted exterior

Figure 31; plates 185:A–D; 186

One of the more highly specialized and unmistakable forms of the Susiana sequence has a concave top with a hole in the center and an open base. Although most examples appear to have been large with a greatest diameter over 30 cm, a few smaller examples occur (pl. 185:A–B). The elaborate overall decoration on the tops indicates that they were the most prominent part of the objects. Presumably they were stands; if porous vessels were placed in them, the holes could have served to drain moisture away, perhaps into a bowl placed underneath. It is less likely that the perforations were simply hand holes.

The decoration of the Family XXV stands is organized in a different manner than that of the Families X-2, Subfamilies XVIIIc–f, and even Family XIX bowls, which is not surprising since the latter develop from the center where the stands have only a hole. Thus it was logical to encircle the hole with concentric registers (pl. 185:B–C) or with one main register and solid borders (pls. 185:A; 186). Familiar geometric motifs of the Late Middle Susiana phase, such as hatched zigzags and swags, occur. In one example (pl. 185:C) the swags alternate with opposed clusters of hatching, the whole bordered with scallops similar to those of Subfamily XXIIb basins. In another example (pl. 185:B) the registers are noteworthy for introducing representative motifs and for the use of both birds and a zigzag in one band, presumably in panels produced by clusters of vertical lines. The most rococo of the platform designs consists of a large hatched zigzag fringed with swags; the larger interstices are filled by rosettes (pl. 186). The sides of the stands have simpler decoration, a zigzag band covering the entire height apparently being standard.[115]

The need met by Family XXV stands must have been fairly widespread as fragments of them are quite common. At Chogha Mish they are typical of the Late Middle Susiana phase but the presence at Jowi in Level 15 of an Early Middle Susiana stand with an .06 profile suggests that the origins of the group go back earlier (Dollfus 1983, fig. 17:8).

Middle Susiana Family XXVI

B–C.31; fine to standard buff ware, painted exterior

Figure 31; plates 58:K; 187:A–I; 188:A–B

Tortoise vessels are so well known in Mesopotamia that their defining features—lentoid body, hole mouth, and large flaring spout—need hardly be mentioned. At Chogha Mish such vessels were common. The bodies vary in their proportions, the higher forms being typical of the Early Middle Susiana (pls. 187:I; 188:A–B) and the squatter forms belonging to the Late Middle Susiana phase (pl. 187:A). The evidence for making such a distinction in Mesopotamia is more equivocal.[116] Many Chogha Mish examples are represented by small fragments from which the proportions cannot be reconstructed with certainty (pl. 187:B–D, F, H).

The decoration of the tortoise vessels varies according to their date. In the Early Middle Susiana phase, a broad wash of paint covers the spout and the entire body above the carination with the exception of narrow vertical bands frequently reserved so as to divide the body into zones. On one vessel the strength of the painter's tectonic feeling is indicated by the reserved line bisecting the front of the spout (pl. 188:A). Sometimes the broad wash runs below the carination. Patterns painted in reserved areas or incised through the wash are always arranged so as to set off a zone centered on the spout. In it a reserved rectangle with carobs appears regularly between the spout and the mouth; it might be the only decoration of a spout zone set off by vertical lines in reserve (pl. 188:B) or flanked by incised vertical elements. In one case these are slightly wavy lines that also fill the zone opposite the spout (pl. 188:A). It appears to have been more common, however, for the decoration of that zone to run horizontally, as shown by the carob-filled borders and incised wavy lines on one example (pl. 187:I). The design of another vessel (pl. 187:E) can be completed by analogy with the larger fragments; a zigzag fills the rectangle of the spout zone, the borders of its horizontal design (cf. pl. 188:B) are filled with carobs (cf. pl. 187:I) instead of concave triangles.[117]

By the Late Middle Susiana phase, the tortoise vessels are not always decorated by designs reserved or scratched in a broad wash covering all the body except the base. Although spouts are normally still covered by a broad wash (pl. 187:C–D, H), sometimes the body remained as an open field for painting. Large solid triangles decorate two fragments (pl. 187:F–G). On another a bucranium, the most elaborate on Chogha Mish pottery, with both ears and the pupils of the eyes shown, was probably one of several scattered freely in the field (pl. 187:B). A relatively complete composition can be reconstructed from sherds on which most of the paint has flaked away, leaving only its bedding (pl. 187:A). The unpainted area above the spout is framed by vertical lines reserved in patches of broad wash contiguous to the spout. Goats of the same type as on the Family XXIV craters adorned the body. Three are preserved; the file might have been two symmetrical files proceeding from the spout zone to a dividing element opposite the spout.[118]

---

115. For a shape similar to plate 185:B, see Le Breton 1947, fig. 23:10 (register with vertical lines and frieze of triangles; Jowi, old excavations).

116. At Eridu some thirty, mostly fragmentary, tortoise vessels occur in Levels XIII and VIII. However, only a few were published, so it is not possible to distinguish between earlier and later examples (Safar, Mustafa, and Lloyd 1981, figs. 72–73). For the taller, earlier variety, see Dollfus 1983, fig. 23:7, 10 (Jowi, Level 13); D. Stronach 1961, pl. 56:3–5 (Ras al-ᶜAmiya).

117. For a parallel to plate 187:E, see Dollfus 1983, fig. 23:7, 9 (Jowi, Level 13). For very slight upturned and tapered rim, see D. Stronach 1961, pl. 56:3 (Ras al-ᶜAmiya). For an shape similar to plate 188:A, see ibid., pl. 56:3 (wider mouth). For a design similar to plate 188:B, see Ziegler 1953, pls. 21:b–c, 27:a, 34:e–i (Haji Muhammad); Safar, Mustafa, and Lloyd 1981, figs. 83:14; 85:2, 8, 18; 86:23; 88:21; 90:6, 8; 98:34 (Eridu VIII–X, XII, XIV–XV, XVII).

118. For vertical dividers similar to plate 187:A, but on tortoise vessels from Mesopotamia, see D. Stronach 1961, pl. 56:3, 5 (Ras al-ᶜAmiya); Safar, Mustafa, and Lloyd, figs. 73, 87:13 (Eridu XIII–VIII); Tobler 1950, pl. 69b:24 (Gawra XIX).

Middle Susiana Family XXVII

A–B.31, .55, .64; standard or fine buff ware, painted

Figure 31; plate 188:C–G

Small vessels with either ovoid or broad-based conical bodies and low flaring necks form a relatively rare but characteristic group ancestral to Late Susiana Subfamily VIb (pl. 159:J–M). Necks vary from thick and blunt (pl. 188:G) to more tapered examples (pl. 188:C, E). The decoration can consist either of elements covering the entire body, such as rows of hatched triangles or cones (pl. 188:C–D), or of a single motif in a panel (1.009a–b), or of an individual scalloped circle in an otherwise empty field (pl. 188:E–G). The latter seem to be particularly typical. The small jars of Family XXVII appear to belong primarily to the Late Middle Susiana phase of which the scalloped circle is a hallmark.[119]

Middle Susiana Family XXVIII

C.50, .60, .74; standard to fine buff ware, painted

Figure 31; plate 189:A–F

The diagnostic feature distinguishing Family XXVIII from the preceding family is the carination that defines a shoulder area. The neck is short and flaring; in one case it ends in a slight rim (pl. 189:C). The paint was applied tectonically with the main elements on the shoulder unless it was particularly high (pl. 189:A, F). Continuous friezes of geometric motifs prevail, but on one example clusters of vertical strokes divide wavy lines into panels (pl. 189:C). The patterns on another example (pl. 189:D) stand out because of their boldness: they include groups of splotches on the interior of the neck, comparable to the clusters of splotches or carobs filling reserved bands on the interiors of the Family X-2 bowls of the Early Middle Susiana phase, and a frieze of carobs, a motif typical for the Early Middle Susiana phase. The vessel differs from the other examples in the lowness of its carination, which bisects the body. Although it is from a mixed context, it can be assigned to the Early Middle Susiana phase, while others (pls. 189:A–C, E, F) can be dated to the Late Middle Susiana phase. Family XXVIII jars were the ancestors of the small medium-sized carinated vessels of the Late Susiana period (Late Susiana Families VIa, VIIa, XV).[120]

Middle Susiana Family XXIX

B–C.54, .64; predominantly fine ware, painted

Figure 31; plate 189:G–O

A characteristic combination of features—squat proportions, a flaring neck, a sharp basal angle, a convex base, and a specific decorative scheme—define the Family XXIX jars. Except for an atypical unpainted example (pl. 189:K), the entire body was covered by a limited repertory of motifs. Even when a motif is shared with other families, it appears in a version characteristic for Family XXIX; the swag, for example, was repeated so as to form a netting with reserved ovals (pl. 189:L–M, O). This all over pattern is extremely rare in other families (pl. 171:R). Hatched triangles are probably the most frequent motif in Family XXIX jars, often in metopes. In the simplest version a large hourglass fills each panel (pl. 189:I). Hourglasses and butterflies alternate in registers (pl. 189:J) or in panels (pl. 189:H, N). Enough is preserved of one vessel (pl. 189:N) to show that the one point common to all four pairs of triangles is precisely in the middle of the panel; if the design is taken as centered on that point it appears as an excerpt from a whirligig diaper. In any case, the relationship between the hatched triangle patterns of the Family XXIX jars and the whirligig diapers of the Early Middle Susiana phase, which can also be looked at as rows of alternating butterflies and hourglasses, is clear. In addition to the hatched triangle motifs, solid butterflies separated by vertical strokes occur (pl. 189:G); the design might be related to that typical for Subfamily XVa bowls of the Early Middle Susiana phase (pl. 174:G, I). The globular jars of Family XXIX are characteristic for the Late Middle Susiana phase.[121]

Middle Susiana Family XXX

B–C.54; fine buff ware, painted

Figure 31; plate 190:A–B

Two small vessels of distinctive character constitute Family XXX. They are both of strikingly thin fine fabric and have the same simple decoration on the upper body, but it is the elegant curvature of their bodies and their markedly flaring bow necks that give them their specific character. They seem to be a very rare type. A bow

---

119. For a shape similar to plate 188:E, see Dollfus 1983, fig. 79:1 (unpainted; Bandebal, Level 14). For a parallel to plate 188:G, see ibid., fig. 61:1 (almost straight neck, hollow star; Bandebal, Level 20).

120. For panel design similar to plate 189:C, see ibid., fig. 60:11 (Bandebal, Level 20). For shape and carob frieze somewhat similar to that in plate 189:D, see ibid., fig. 18:12 (vertical neck with slight rim, high shoulder; Jowi, Level 15).

121. For similarities of design between plate 189:G and those of Qabr-e Sheykheyn, see Weiss 1976, fig. 17:74 (.04). For a parallel to plate 189:H, J, see Le Breton 1947, fig. 25:5 (Jowi, old excavations). For a parallel to plate 189:K, see ibid., fig. 25:17 (all-over wash). For a parallel to plate 189:L, see Dollfus 1983, fig. 75:21 (Bandebal, Level 16). For parallels to plate 189:M, O, see ibid., fig. 57:10–11 (Bandebal, Level 24); Dollfus 1975, fig. 51:9 (Jafarabad, Level 3n). For a parallel to plate 189:N, see Gautier and Lampre 1905, fig. 154 (Tappeh Musyan).

neck of similar shape, although larger and squatter, from Jowi probably had a body similar to the bodies of the two vessels representing this pottery family (pl. 190:A–B), which came from Late Middle Susiana contexts.[122]

Middle Susiana Family XXXI

B–C.5, .6; normally standard buff ware, painted or unpainted

Figure 31; plate 190:C–O

Jars with low necks but without the characteristics diagnostic for the four preceding families are placed in Family XXXI. The group can be subdivided by means of the shape of the neck. Jars whose necks are sufficiently concave on the interior to produce a ledge are assigned to Subfamily XXXIa (pl. 190:C–I) and those with ledgeless, slightly flaring necks to Subfamily XXXIb (pl. 190:J–O). The ledges of the former often have vertical or diagonal perforations, the purpose of which remains uncertain (pl. 190:D–E, H). The inner collar itself might, when it was pronounced, have served to support a lid. The necks without ledges vary in their stance and height, four of which (pl. 190:J–M) can be considered as average examples. The neck of one vessel (pl. 190:N) is rather high approaching the proportions of Family XXXIII necks; the large size and rudimentary neck of another (pl. 190:O) is typical.

Unpainted examples of Subfamily XXXIa occur in standard buff ware (pl. 190:D–E) and also in plain red ware (pl. 193:Z). On Subfamily XXXIb jars the painting ranges from a minimal band at the root of the neck (pl. 190:J) to several registers of geometric designs covering a considerable part of the upper body (fig. 31). Often, however, decoration was limited to the uppermost part of the body (pl. 190:K–O). The swag diaper motif (pl. 190:C) is as atypical for Family XXXI as it is characteristic for Family XXIX; only the rather straight slope of the upper body, as well as a parallel from Jowi, prevents this sherd from being reconstructed as a typical Family XXIX jar. The motifs used are for the most part standard and already known from other families, such as the broken zigzag and wide friezes found on a Family XI bowl (pls. 171:H; 190:I) and the knobbed scallops typical for Family VI-2 and Subfamily XVIa (pls. 164:K; 176:C–E, L; 190:M). More unusual are hatched arches (pl. 190:K) and the tiny lozenge frieze between thick bands (cf. pl. 190:N).[123]

The majority of the examples of Family XXXI are from Late Middle Susiana contexts, but a small fragment of a neck with a typical carob frieze indicates that the antecedents of the family go back to the Early Middle Susiana phase.

Middle Susiana Family XXXII

C.5, .6; standard to fine buff ware, painted

Figure 31; plates 190:P–T; 191:A

Vessels varying in size, to some degree in shape, and in decoration, share a specific type of neck. It is flaring, very short, and often so flattened as to become an overhanging rim (pls. 190:P, S; 191:A). The flat upper surface is painted with a band of scallops. Although many examples are represented only by the mouth and uppermost body, the Family XXXII jars were evidently squat and globular, similar to those of Family XXIX. The greatest diameter was probably in most cases in the middle of the body,[124] but there is at least one example in which it is lower (pl. 191:A).

The decoration ranges from broad washes (pl. 190:P–Q) to geometrical patterns extending over half of the body. Patterns of lozenges bordered by triangles are characteristic; they might have covered the body (pl. 190:R [reconstructed[125]]) or have been limited to a single frieze of large lozenges (pl. 191:A). The lozenges and triangles are variegated, producing an ornate effect. The triangle (pl. 191:A) broken up into three crosshatched triangles has already been seen on Subfamilies IXb and XVc vessels (pl. 57:C, G). The scalloped decoration of the mouth is shared with the basins of Subfamily XXIIb. The jars of Family XXXII are diagnostic for the Late Middle Susiana phase and were quite common.[126]

---

form related to that in plate 190:H, apparently unpainted, see ibid., fig. 58:a, profile on right. For a parallel to plate 190:M, see Le Breton 1947, fig. 24:2 (neck vertical but flaring at lip; Jowi, old excavations).

124. This is indicated by complete examples found after the fifth season at Chogha Mish and also by examples from Jafarabad; see note 126, below.

125. This reconstruction is corroborated by a fragmentary vessel found during the ninth season at Chogha Mish (9.677).

126. For parallels to plate 190:P, Q, see Dollfus 1975, fig. 52:4 (Jafarabad, Level 3n); Dollfus 1983, figs. 57:12, 77:9 (Bandebal, Levels 24, 16); Le Breton 1947, fig. 25:14 (Jowi, old excavations); Hole, Flannery, and Neely 1969, fig. 58:m (Tappeh Sabz, Bayat phase). For a parallel to plate 190:R, see Dollfus 1983, fig. 76:1 (Bandebal, Level 16); for related design on a .03 bowl, see Weiss 1976, fig. 19:102 (Qabr-e Sheykheyn). For a parallel to plate 190:T, see Dollfus 1983, fig. 57:12 (Bandebal, Level 24). For the triangle divided into three crosshatched triangles similar to plate 191:A, see Le Breton 1947, fig. 25:15 (Jowi, old excavations).

---

122. For bow neck similar to that in plate 190:A–B, see Dollfus 1983, fig. 38:1 (Jowi, Level 7).

123. For a parallel to plate 190:C, see ibid., fig. 35:9 (Jowi, Level 8). For a parallel to plate 190:D–E, see Le Breton 1947, fig. 24:13 (Jowi, old excavations). For a decoration similar to that in plate 190:G, see Gautier and Lampre 1905, fig. 144 (shape of neck not given; Tappeh Musyan); for similar shape and decoration, see Hole, Flannery, and Neely 1969, fig. 58:a (Tappeh Sabz, Mehmeh phase). For a

Middle Susiana Family XXXIII

C–D.5; standard to fine buff ware, painted or unpainted

Figure 31; plates 191:B–U, W–X; 192:A–F

The largest of the closed form families comprise those medium- and large-sized ovoid vessels possessing as their defining feature a high-flaring neck. While the low-necked jars of the preceding families are for the most part small or medium in size, Family XXXIII includes many large storage jars (pl. 191:R–U). Completely restorable shapes unfortunately remain rare, but a relatively tall ovoid body with a flat base considerably narrower than the greatest diameter appears to have been standard (pl. 191:J). The majority of Family XXXIII jars are of standard ware with at least some painted decoration. The fine ware jars might be either unpainted (pl. 191:B) or painted (pl. 191:J). Neckless sherds, which in ware, size, and curvature could belong to Family XXXIII jars, are included under that rubric with the realization that some of them might have actually been part of Families XXXI or XXXIV jars.

The painting is limited to a solid wash on the neck and to designs on the upper part of the body. The latter can be arranged either hypotactically or paratactically. The more common representatives of the first type of composition are horizontal bands creating registers, the upper registers left empty and the lower registers filled with stepped clusters of vertical hatching (pl. 191:E) or an unbroken frieze of a single motif (pl. 191:Q). Other varieties of horizontal friezes formed by geometric elements occur (pl. 191:G–H, O). A simple panel arrangement of narrow bands is framed by numerous horizontal ones (pl. 191:F). There is also a quite different kind of panel containing quadrants (pl. 191:N). In the paratactic type of composition, individual motifs are spaced freely around the upper body. The most ubiquitous of these, the scalloped circle, can be derived with considerable confidence from the circular patterns of the Early Middle Susiana phase (fig. 31, Family XXXIII). The motif is nothing but the negative ground of the cusped border now changed into a positive design. The relationship with the older patterns can be seen in an example (pl. 191:S) where four quadrants appear in the middle of the scalloped circle, a good analogy for which is the design on the base of a footed bowl, except that there the scallops are still negative and the cusps positive (pl. 165:I). A small fragment of a large-scale motif can be restored as a doubled quadrant motif (cf. pl. 168:C–D); it was undoubtedly surrounded by a scalloped circle (pl. 191:T). Other elements such as a cross, a star, and a dotted circle are also to be found inside scalloped circles (pl. 191:K–L, P). However, often the motif appears alone without any filling (pl. 191:I–J, R, W). An almost perfectly matched pair of practically complete jars proves that the scalloped circles were spaced around the

body in sets of three, not four (pl. 191:J). This is not an accidental feature, but marks a specific preference of the pottery painters of the Late Middle Susiana phase for spacing three bold motifs in the field to be decorated. Excellent examples are the three pairs of swirling bands on another Family XXXIII jar (pl. 192:A), the straight bands on a Family XXXIV jar (pl. 192:M), and the patterned triangles on Subfamily IXb bowls (fig. 24; pl. 165:J). Scalloped circles were the favorite motif on medium- and large-sized storage jars. Also characteristic for pithoi is the hollow, rayed circle (pl. 191:U). In addition, a solid circle with a reserved cross was probably used in the same way as the scalloped circles and can be taken as an antecedent for the typical Maltese crosses of the Late Susiana period (pl. 191:N).

Several sherds with representations of animals are shown by their profiles to have come from the upper bodies of jars. The bucranium has already been seen on Family III bowls, where it hangs upside down from the lip (pl. 163:S, X–Z) and on a tortoise vase where it is right side up (pl. 187:B; cf. pl. 192:F). Three other animals are a bird, a stag, and an equid-like head (pl. 192:B, D–E). Not enough of these four sherds is preserved to show whether the animals were isolated, similar to the scalloped circles, or in a file, but parts of two animals widely spaced in a frieze are preserved (pl. 192:C) close to the root of the neck. The spots on the curved feline tail and on the neck identify the animals as leopards. The representation is striking for its combination of profile jaws and tongue with "front-view" eyes and ears (pls. 58:H; 192:C). A similar head occurs on the interior of Family XIX bowls (pl. 181:F, P). The missing body can be visualized by comparison with the leopards on sherds of Subfamily X-5a and Family XVII vessels (pl. 50:F–G). A sherd of a large jar preserves two forelegs and presumably testifies to a large-scale and relatively roughly painted version of the leopard motif (pl. 58:J).[127]

Family XXXIII jars were used during the entire Middle Susiana period. The decoration of narrow bands

127. For a parallel to plate 191:E, see Dollfus 1983, fig. 18:9 (Jowi, Level 3). For a motif similar to plate 191:I–J and R, see Le Breton 1947, fig. 24:15 (Jowi, old excavations); Dollfus 1983, fig. 33:17 (Jowi, Level 10); Tobler 1950, pl. 69a:6 (Gawra XIX). For a motif similar to plate 191:L, see Hall and Woolley 1927, pl. 16:1636 (Ubaid). For a motif related to plate 191:M, see ibid., pl. 16:1644, 1646 (Ubaid). For a parallel to plate 191:P, see Dollfus 1983, fig. 76:10 (Bandebal, Level 16). For a parallel to plate 191:Q, see ibid., fig. 23:18 (carobs instead of Ws; Jowi, Level 13). For a motif similar to plate 191:U, but on vessels of other families, see ibid., figs. 30:13, 61:1, 78:4 (Jowi, Level 11 and Bandebal, Levels 20, 16); Weiss 1976, fig. 28:240 (Qabr-e Sheykheyn). For leopards similar to plate 192:C, see Le Breton 1947, figs. 28:14, 41:10–10a; Dollfus 1983, fig. 13 (Jowi and Bandebal, old excavations and Level 16).

delimiting registers left empty, with some exceptions (pl. 191:E, Q), is characteristic for the Middle Susiana period but appears to persist later to a certain extent. The vessels with paratactic decoration can be safely attributed to the Late Middle Susiana phase.

Middle Susiana Family XXXIV

C–D.5, .6; standard buff ware, painted

Figure 31; plates 191:V; 192:G–I

The only distinction between the shapes of Families XXXIII and XXXIV jars is the inward projection at the join of neck and body, which in some cases is large enough to form a ledge. Such collared necks do not seem to have been as common as the plain ones. They can be dated to the Late Middle Susiana phase. The vessels to which they belonged were probably for the most part decorated paratactically with the same motifs as on Family XXXIII jars. A sherd that apparently had a collared neck bears the knobbed triangle frieze already seen in Subfamily XVIa (pl. 192:I; cf. pl. 176:E, L).[128]

Middle Susiana Family XXXV

C.6; coarse ware, painted or unpainted

Figure 31; plate 192:J

This family accommodates a sherd that does not fit into other categories. The body shape was probably globular, similar to that of the red ware hole-mouthed vessels of Family XXXIX (pl. 193:H–X), but is surmounted by a tiny vertical neck. This feature was to recur on some red ware vessels of Late Susiana Family XXVIII (pl. 162:O–P).

Middle Susiana Family XXXVI

B–C.6; standard buff ware, painted

Figure 31; plate 192:K–N

The feature unifying a group of somewhat disparate types is a relatively vertical neck of either medium or high proportions. The complete shapes of the vessels represented by two fragments from Early Middle Susiana contexts are uncertain, particularly in the case of one known only from a small part of the neck juncture (pl. 192:K–L). Both remain as isolated pieces. A neck with a rather vertical exterior profile comes from a Late Middle Susiana context (pl. 192:N). The only complete example of the family is also the only one possessing close parallels elsewhere (pl. 192:M). Its decoration of three pairs of pendant bands on the body (cf. pl. 192:A)

exemplifies the Late Middle Susiana predilection for tripartite decorative schemes.[129]

Middle Susiana Family XXXVII

B .03; standard to fine buff ware, painted

Figure 31; plate 192:O–P

Small vessels of square or rectangular section occur very rarely. One example (pl. 192:P) has both the profile and the butterfly/hourglass decoration frequent on Family XXIX vessels, among which the panels of one example (pl. 189:N) provide the closest parallel. However, on the small square jar the decoration is even more tectonic since the vertical bands defining the panels are placed on the corners. The same motifs ran continuously around a small footed container of which only one corner remains (pl. 192:O). It was probably an open tray rather than a closed form.[130]

THE FAMILIES OF RED WARES

In contrast to the numerous shapes made in buff wares, only a limited number of bowl and hole-mouthed jar forms are provided by the red wares. They are accommodated in three families, Family XXXVIII for the open forms and Families XXXIX and XL for the more closed ones. Normally the walls of red ware vessels are unpainted, but there are instances in which the addition of a slip and paint allows them to masquerade as buff ware specimens. The better examples were found in late seasons.

Middle Susiana Family XXXVIII

C–D.00, .01, .03; usually proportions "0"–"1," plain and red-washed red wares, unpainted

Figure 31; plate 193:A–G

Shallow bowls with profiles varying from rather straight-sided (pl. 193:D) to convex are for the most part represented by lip and body sherds. However, some reconstructible forms indicate that the basal angle could be sharp and that the bases were either slightly convex or fairly flat. The lips are usually blunt. These bowls vary from medium-sized bowls with a diameter of about 19.0 cm to large bowls of some 60.0 cm in diameter and a greatest thickness of about 1.5 cm (pl. 193:G). Both the interior and the exterior are usually well coated with

---

128. For parallels to plates 191:V and 192:G, see ibid., figs. 57:13, 61:13, 78:2–3 (Bandebal, Levels 24, 21, 16); Weiss 1976, fig. 25:210 (Qabr-e Sheykheyn); Dollfus 1975, fig. 52:17 (Jafarabad, Level 3m).

129. For parallels to plate 192:M, see ibid., figs. 61:3–4 (wider necks); 76:4, 8; 77:4 (closest parallel for shape, but about three times larger; clusters of four pendant bands; Bandebal, Levels 21–20, 16); Weiss 1976, fig. 26:221 (zigzag on neck; clusters of three pendant bands; Qabr-e Sheykheyn).

130. For shape similar to plate 192:O, see Le Breton 1947, fig. 22:11 (Jowi, old excavations).

CHOGHA MISH I

Table 21. Loci with Middle Susiana Pottery Marks

Area	Locus	Level	Locus Description	Family	Type	Sherd List	Number
West Area	H15:402	80.16	Protoliterate Debris. Out of context	XX	8	4.1071	1
	J15:403	79.98–79.03	Occupational debris (Protoliterate). Out of context	XVd	13	4.1034	1
	J15:403	80.73–80.38	(No records)	XX	16	4.1032	1
East Area	R18:403	80.40	Occupational debris. Out of context	XX	1	4.1031	2
	R18:403	80.40	Occupational debris. Out of context	XXXVIII	14	4.1033	
	S17:901	80.76	Occupational debris	XX	2	9.781	1
Trench XIII	L22:502	82.00	Occupational debris	XX	5	5.420	1
Trench XXV	R20:515	78.50–77.50	Occupational debris	XXXIX buff ware	16	5.275	1
Gully Cut	S–T21:Sounding G	76.15	Occupational debris (Late Middle Susiana)	XX (?)	6	4.306	1
Trench XIII	K22:403	81.19–80.99	Room (Early Middle Susiana)	XXI	3	4.395	1
	K22:409	81.94–81.64	Occupational debris	XXI	5	4.952	1
	K23:502	82.42–81.72	Disturbed, occupational debris. Middle Susiana-Protoliterate-Late	XXI	1	5.439	3
	K23:502	81.77	Disturbed debris, Middle Susiana-Protoliterate	XXI	16	5.445	
	K23:502	81.05	Disturbed debris, Middle Susiana-Protoliterate	XXI	18	5.441	
	K23:503	80.56	Disturbed occupational debris Protoliterate-Early Middle Susiana-mixed	XXI	9	5.442	1
	K23:507	81.50	Room (Early Middle Susiana)	XXI	4	5.443	1
	K23:509	80.30	Room (Early Middle Susiana)	XXI	15	5.444	1
	L22:501	82.45	Disturbed occupational debris. Middle Susiana-Protoliterate-Late	XXI	12	5.419	1
	L22:504	81.62	Narrow room or corridor (Early Middle Susiana)	XXI	10	5.372	1
Trench XVIII	M–N/13–14:Trench XVIII	77.91	Occupational debris	XVIII	8	3.175	1
Trench XVI	O27:Trench XVI	Surf.	Surface	XXI	17	5.146	1
Trench XXXI	P27:501 Southwest	79.04	Occupational debris	XXI	11	5.821	1
Trench XXXI	Q23.512	81.09	B.S.	XXI	7	5.440	1
Gully Cut	S–T21:Sounding G	74.95	Occupational debris	XXI	6	4.1038	1
TOTAL							24

wash. The Family XXXVIII bowls are the direct ancestors of those of Late Susiana Family XXVII.[131]

Middle Susiana Family XXXIX

C–D .5; plain, red-washed, and buff-slipped red wares, unpainted

Figure 31; plate 193:H–X

Medium- to large-sized hole-mouthed vessels with globular bodies that vary only slightly in shape constitute Family XXXIX. The round bases and characteristic highly-fired paste indicate that these vessels were cooking pots, which would explain their frequent occurrence. However, the body sherds do not show extensive traces of burning. The hole-mouthed vessels occur frequently in buff-slipped ware, but in addition, very rarely in straw-tempered buff ware (pl. 193:K) or in standard buff ware.

The lips of the cooking pots are normally flattened, either diagonally (pl. 193:H, J–K, Q–R, U, W–X) or vertically (pl. 193:I, N–O). Grooving, either slight or pronounced, is also quite standard. Some blunt lips (pl. 193:T, V) are less usual. Some lips are of the same thickness as the upper body wall (pl. 193:O), others are thickened wedges (pl. 193:I, P), and still others swell asymmetrically in the inner side (pl. 193:J, W). Occasionally accessorial elements such as trough spouts (pl. 193:R–S) or small, crude ledge handles (pl. 193:T) were added to the hole-mouthed vessels.[132]

131. For parallels to plate 193:D, see Dollfus 1975, fig. 53:10 (Jafarabad, Level 3n); Le Breton 1947, fig. 20:8 (Jowi, old excavations); Dollfus 1983, fig. 68:5 (Bandebal, Level 16); Hole, Flannery, and Neely 1969, fig. 67:a (Tappeh Sabz, Bayat phase). For a parallel to plate 193:E, see Dollfus 1983, fig. 80:7 (Bandebal, Level 14). For a parallel to plate 193:F, see Weiss 1975, fig. 10:3 (Qabr-e Sheykheyn). For parallels to plate 193:G, see Dollfus 1983, fig. 32:13 (channeled lip; Jowi, Level 10); ibid., fig. 58:16 (Bandebal, Level 20).

132. For parallels to plate 193:H, P, and U, see ibid., figs. 27:4, 32:9 (Jowi, Levels 12, 10); ibid., fig. 68:9 (Bandebal, Level

Table 22. Middle Susiana Pottery Marks: Types and Number of Examples

Type	Middle Susiana Family XXI			Middle Susiana Family XX			Middle Susiana: Other Families				Total
	Number	Locus	Level	Number	Locus	Level	Family	Number	Locus	Level	
1	5.439	K23:502	82.42–81.72	4.1031	R18:403	80.40	—	—	—	—	2
2	—	—	—	9.781	S17:901	80.76	—	—	—	—	1
3	4.395	K22:403	81.19–80.99	—	—	—	—	—	—	—	1
4	5.443	K23:507	81.50	—	—	—	—	—	—	—	1
5	4.952	K22:409	81.94–81.64	5.420	L22:502	82.00	—	—	—	—	2
6	4.1038	S-T21:Sounding G	74.95	4.306	S-T21:Sounding G	76.15	—	—	—	—	2
7	5.440	Q23.512	81.09	—	—	—	—	—	—	—	1
8	—	—	—	4.1071	H15:402	80.16	XVIII	3.175	M–N/13–14	77.91	2
9	5.442	K23:503	80.56	—	—	—	—	—	—	—	1
10	5.372	L22:504	81.62	—	—	—	—	—	—	—	1
11	5.821	P27:501 Southwest	79.04	—	—	—	—	—	—	—	1
12	5.419	L22:501	82.45	—	—	—	—	—	—	—	1
13	—	—	—	—	—	—	XVd	4.1034	J15:403	79.98–79.03	1
14	—	—	—	—	—	—	XXXVIII	4.1033	R18:403	80.40	1
15	5.444	K23:509	80.30	—	—	—	—	—	—	—	1
16	5.445	K23:502	81.77	4.1032	J15:403	80.73–80.38	XXXIX	5.275	R20:515	78.50–77.50	3
17	5.416	O27:Trench XVI	Surface	—	—	—	—	—	—	—	1
18	5.441	K23:502	81.05	—	—	—	—	—	—	—	1
Totals	14			6				4			24

Middle Susiana Family XL

C–D .5; red-washed ware, normally unpainted

Figure 31; plate 193:Y–AA

The defining feature for Family XL is the presence of a low neck with an inner ledge, usually with perforations. The same type of collared neck was seen as one of the defining characteristics of the buff ware Subfamily XXXIa (pl. 190:G–H). A thick red-brown wash on the exterior and on the interior of the neck appears to be typical for Family XL. An example found in the seventh season has in addition a band of black paint on the upper body (7.164). It is fairly complete and indicates that the bodies of the Family XL vessels were similar to those of Family XXXIX. In fact, the vessels of this group are cooking pots with a neck.[133]

---

16); Hole, Flannery, and Neely 1969, fig. 67:c (blunt lip; Tappeh Sabz, Bayat phase). For a parallel to plate 193:I, see Weiss 1975, fig. 10:10 (Qabr-e Sheykheyn). For hole-mouthed vessel in buff ware similar to plate 193:K, see Dollfus 1983, fig. 20:13 (Jowi, Level 13). For a parallel to plate 193:M, see Dollfus 1975, fig. 53:1 (Jafarabad, Level 3n). For parallels to plate 193:Q, see Dollfus 1983, fig. 24:8 (Jowi, Level 11); ibid., fig. 67:3 (gray ware; Bandebal, Level 16). For a parallel to plate 193:R, see ibid., figs. 55:20, 80:4 (Bandebal, Levels 24, 14). For profile similar to plate 155:T, but without handle, see ibid., fig. 20:14 (gray burnished surface; Jowi, Level 14); for later, Late Susiana, handled example, see Dollfus 1971, fig. 20:6–7 (Jafarabad).

133. For parallels to plate 193:Y–AA, see Dollfus 1975, fig. 53:3 (Jafarabad, Level 3n); Dollfus 1983, fig. 32:11 (Jowi, Level 10).

EARLY SUSIANA POTTERY

THE WARES

The bulk of Early Susiana pottery is made of a ware combining great quantities of grit and finely divided vegetal tempering. The individual grits of various colors and sizes are very prominent, appearing in clusters on the surface and bulging out of the broken edges of sherds. Fragments of very soft sandstone made up of such multicolored grits were found in the excavation and might have been brought to the site to be pulverized for tempering. This standard ware was used for unpainted larger vessels (Early Susiana Family XVI) and also for many of the families of painted vessels (Early Susiana Families I–II, V, VIII, X–XI). Some unpainted (Early Susiana Family XVIII) and painted vessels (Early Susiana Families VI, XI, XV) have a denser paste without vegetal tempering and with only sparsely scattered grits of a uniform size. There is no hard and fast line between the standard and dense pastes; examples with varying amounts of grit and vegetal tempering can be arranged in a graduated series between the two extremes.

THE FAMILIES OF EARLY SUSIANA POTTERY

Early Susiana Family I

B .00 or .03; standard ware, painted

Figure 33; plate 194:A–E

Small bowls when shallow were decorated on the interiors and when deeper on the exterior. One example is painted on both sides. On the inside of a shallow sau-

Figure 32. Sherds of Early Susiana Family VI Bowls Found after the Fifth Season

lines on one of the examples (pl. 194:E) were probably part of a compartment pattern of a second register.[134]

Early Susiana Family II

B.05, .22; standard ware, painted or unpainted

Figure 33; plates 61:A; 194:F–K

The defining features of the Family II bowls are their small, B size and incurved lip. The majority of the examples can be considered as conical in shape, but one squat bowl is cylindrical (pl. 194:F). As more examples accumulate it might be useful to subdivide the family into two groups, unpainted and painted. An accessory commonly added to the painted examples is the trough spout (pl. 194:I–K). The individual treatment of the area below the spout of one of the examples (pl. 194:I) illustrates the tectonic feeling of Early Susiana potters; at that point the broad wash on the upper body is interrupted by an x and two small triangles painted on a reserved rectangle.[135]

Early Susiana Family III

B–C.00 and .22; grit tempered ware, tab handle, painted or unpainted

Figure 33; plate 194:L–N

The characteristic feature of Family III is the vertical tab handle. Usually the ladles or scoops are small, with relatively straight sides and a narrow flat base. The handles of the small ladles appear to have been slender; the example preserved is painted on both sides with the same simple pattern of horizontal and vertical lines. A wavy band reserved in a broad wash decorates the exterior of the small ladles. Larger ladles are represented by an unpainted example from the pottery deposit in

cer two pairs of widely-spaced parallel lines crossing at right angles produced segments, some of which were filled with wavy lines (pl. 194:C). The end result, a square in the center and triangles attached to its corners, is a simple version of the "squared circle" pattern characteristic of the Early Susiana period and basic for the development of more complex circular patterns in the Middle Susiana period (fig. 28). Bold contrasts between negative and positive elements are also typical for the Early Susiana period, as is the habit of painting the wavy lines in alternate triangles of the squared-circle pattern at right angles. The decoration on the exterior of the deeper bowls relies for its effect on the contrast between broad washes of color and reserved areas (pl. 194:D–E). The partially preserved groups of vertical

134. For shapes similar to plate 194:C–D, see Dollfus 1975, fig. 16:4, 11 (Jafarabad, Level 5a).

135. For parallels to plate 194 I, see ibid., fig. 24:8 (taller; Jafarabad, Level 5a). For trough spouts on different shapes, see Le Breton 1947, fig. 9:1–3 (Jafarabad, old excavations, 3.5–6.0 m); Dollfus 1975, figs. 23:9–11, 12:14–16, 24:1–7 (Jafarabad, Levels 6–4).

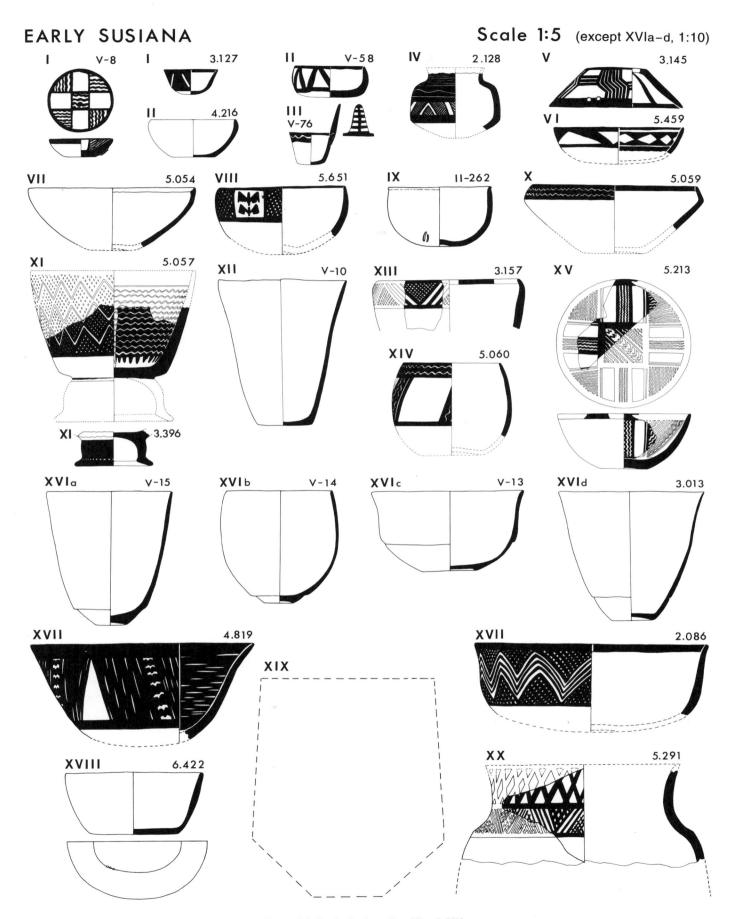

Figure 33. Early Susiana Families I–XX

Q23:502 (pl. 194:N). Evidence from later seasons shows the larger ladles had broader, shorter handles.[136]

Early Susiana Family IV

B–C.5, .63, .7; standard ware, painted exterior

Figure 33; plates 61:B; 194:O–P

Small jars are rarer than open vessels. An almost complete profile, the neck of which can be restored (cf. pl. 194:O), is provided by a sherd painted in the Early Susiana closed style (pl. 194:P). It is densely covered with paint down to the lower carination. Reserved horizontal lines cover the lower neck and shoulder, the upper register of the body has a wavy line in reserve, and the lower, reserved, register has crosshatched triangles and diagonal bands that are set off by reserved bands. A neck sherd (pl. 194:O), despite its smallness, testifies to the importance of reserved elements in Early Susiana painting and the predilection for tectonic arrangement.[137]

Early Susiana Family V

C.30, .31, .32; standard ware, primary painting on exterior

Figure 33; plates 61:C–L; 194:Q–V; 195:A–G

One of the more distinctive and frequent of the Early Susiana families consists of objects that obviously had a specific function. Diagnostic are the flaring and shallow shapes, the presence of a pair of perforations near the lips and the distribution of the decoration. The more elaborate designs are on the exterior while the interior has only a pair of crossed lines (pl. 61:D, H, J). The type is so specialized that even small fragments not preserving all of the features of the family can be attributed to it with confidence. The elaborate decoration of these objects would have been hidden if they had been used as shallow bowls. Accordingly, we are tentatively terming them lids, with the reservation that it is very uncertain as to what they could have covered; most of the pottery vessels of the Early Susiana period have mouths wider in diameter than those of the presumptive lids. Also problematic is the function of the pair of holes; it would be anachronistic to suggest that they might have been used to peg the lids to walls.

The more typical patterns for the tops of the lids are variations of the squared-circle design already seen on an Family I saucer (pls. 61:H–I, L; 194:S–U; 195:B, E). Rows of reserved lozenges with dots (pl. 195:A) are unique. Radial compositions predominate on the outer walls of the lids. Clusters of wavy lines appear (pl. 194:S), but groups of zigzags are more common radial elements (pl. 61:I–K); they often alternate with other motifs such as clusters of small zigzags (pl. 195:A), antithetical zigzags (pl. 194:T), or a cluster of chevron lines (pls. 61:L; 195:F). A design, seen elsewhere (pls. 61:L; 195:F) except that a zigzag panel substitutes for the simple zigzag cluster, fills one zone of an elaborately decorated lid (pl. 195:E) and can be used as a likely model for reconstructing a composition of which only the zigzag panel is preserved (pl. 194:V). Sometimes the radial zigzags are linked by roughly horizontal bands (pl. 194:U; 195:C–D). In addition to geometrical motifs, birds with spread wings served as fillers between radial elements (pl. 61:D). An unusual design of truncated crosshatched rectangles can also be considered radial because of their slant (pl. 195:G). Antithetical triangles (butterflies) fill a radial band (pl. 194:Q) and also appear as free-field motifs made into torsional radii by their diagonal placement (pl. 194:R).

Designs more complicated than the radial compositions are rare. One is a variant of the squared-circle design in which four checkerboard triangles alternating with radial bands of lozenges surround the round top of the lid (pl. 195:B). The crosshatched rectangles on a small sherd might have belonged to a similar composition (pl. 61:E). In the most complicated example of all, the walls of the lid are divided into two zones, the upper zone consisting of two concentric registers of lozenges and the lower zone being the alternating zigzag panel and chevron already mentioned (pl. 195:E). This composition is an outstanding example of the sophisticated use of negative and positive areas by Early Susiana pot painters. In quite a different style are the bold triangles, perhaps part of a concentric register on a small sherd (pl. 61:C).

The lids are so frequent at Chogha Mish that their apparent rarity elsewhere in Khuzestan is surprising. Jowi provides an example in a level transitional between Early Susiana and Middle Susiana periods and Jafarabad provides a rare rectangular variant not found at Chogha Mish until after the fifth season (6.101).[138] In Mesopotamia proper one certain and two possible fragments are known from Eridu.[139] At Chogha Mish, some rare Early Middle Susiana lid fragments, although much

---

136. For narrow handles similar to plate 194:L, see ibid., fig. 30:9 (Jafarabad, Level 5a); Hole, Flannery, and Neely 1969, fig. 53:e–f (Deh Luran sites, Mehmeh phase); D. Stronach 1961, pl. 57:4 (Ras al-ʿAmiya); for similar decoration on broad handle, see Dollfus 1975, fig. 30:8 (Jafarabad, Level 5a); for broad handles, see Hole, Flannery, and Neely 1969, fig. 53:a–d (Deh Luran sites, Sabz and Khazineh phases); D. Stronach 1961, pl. 57:2–3, 56 (Ras al-ʿAmiya).

137. For a parallel to plate 194:O, see Dollfus 1975, fig. 28:12 (Jafarabad, Level 5a).

138. For a parallel to plate 194:U, see Dollfus 1983, fig. 16:5 (Jowi, Level 4); for rectangular lid, see Dollfus 1975, fig. 30:3 (Jafarabad, Level 4).

139. See Safar, Mustafa, and Lloyd 1981, figs. 97:12, 99:6, 94:1 (Eridu XVII and possibly XVIII and XVI).

flatter in shape than those of the Early Susiana period, reveal their ancestry by perforations at the lip and by crossing lines on the interior (pl. 166:E).

Early Susiana Family VI

C.03, .04, .07; dense ware, painted exterior and interior

Figure 32; plates 61:V–BB; 196:A–B

One of the more outstanding Early Susiana families consists of shallow bowls bearing a set of patterns so specific that even small chips are recognizable. Family VI bowls are made of a dense paste in which the grits are of a more uniformly small size than in the standard Early Susiana ware and vegetal inclusions are sometimes completely absent. The exteriors always have a horizontal register, sometimes extending over more than half of the body, containing a zigzag band often wider at the upper border than at the lower one (pls. 61:Y; 196:A). The interiors are completely covered by more elaborate decoration consisting of narrow and wide concentric registers encircling the circular field of the base. Although few of the base designs are preserved, it is certain that squared-circle patterns were typical, as shown by the boldly structured decoration on sherds found after the fifth season (fig. 32:A).

The contrast between painted and reserved areas plays a prominent role in the decoration of the Family VI bowls. Thus, the next painted element outside the central pattern, a narrow concentric band filled by a zigzag is set off on each side by a register in reserve (pl. 196:A–B). The choice of motifs for the wide register above was considerable: approximately vertical hatching presumably filling the entire area (pl. 61:X); diagonal hatching alternating with butterflies (pl. 196:B) or perhaps sometimes with triangles; crosshatching presumably filling the entire area (pls. 61:Y–Z); a wide lattice (pl. 61:U); a negative zigzag (pl. 61:V); an hourglass frieze in which the negative lozenges are as prominent as the positive elements (pl. 196:A); and a band of whirligigs (fig. 32:B).

Family VI bowls are a very important group for establishing the continuity of the Susiana tradition of pottery making. In shape and decoration they are the direct antecedents of the prominent Families I and X-2, and, despite the difference in shape, the decoration of Family XVIII bowls is equally dependent on them. The zigzags on the exterior of Family VI bowls have thickened so much on Families X-2 and XVIII vessels that the negative triangles are often more prominent than the now massive zigzags. The Early Susiana center pattern (fig. 32:A) shows all of the elements that were developed in different directions during the Middle Susiana period.

At Chogha Mish, Family VI bowls are both prominent and standard elements of the ceramic assemblage.

Thus, it is surprising that no examples seem to occur at Jafarabad and only one fragment at Jowi.[140] On the other hand they are particularly significant for the relative chronology of the Chogha Mish sequence and southern Mesopotamia. Important as is this aspect of the Family VI bowls, their significance for chronology and the strength of connections with southern Mesopotamia is even greater. At Eridu bowls of this type form one of the more prominent classes of pottery. They are typical for the Eridu phase (Ubaid 1), although they continue to appear in later levels, whether as survivals or accidental intrusions. Thus, both the synchronism of the Early Susiana period with the Eridu phase of southern Mesopotamia and also the intensity of the contacts between the two areas at that time are established by the Family VI bowls.[141]

Early Susiana Family VII

C.03, .04; standard ware, unpainted

Figure 33; plate 196:C

Fragments of simple conical bowls without decoration or other well-defined features are assigned to Family VII. The lips vary from thick horizontally-flattened lips to those which are inbeveled.

Early Susiana Family VIII

C–D.04; standard ware, painted exterior

Figure 33; plates 61:M–N; 196:D–G

Shape and decoration combine to define a specific type of relatively small bowls. They are globular and have incurving or occasionally vertical lips, being in shape very similar to the unpainted bowls of Family VIII. In this group, however, the upper part of the body is covered by a broad register divided into panels by crosshatching. The reserved metopes are filled by one

---

140. See Dollfus 1983, fig. 15:2 (Jowi, Level 16).

141. For a parallel to figure 32:A, see Safar, Mustafa, and Lloyd 1981, figs. 91:14, 92:28 (base fragment with concentric bands, one in reserve separating solid bands from another with a narrow zigzag; Eridu XV–XIV). For wavy band and exterior pattern similar to figure 32:A–B, see Dollfus 1983, fig. 15:2 (Jowi, Level 16). For a parallel to plate 61:U, see Safar, Mustafa, and Lloyd 1981, fig. 85:10 (Eridu IX). For reserved zigzag similar to plate 61:V, see ibid., figs. 86:35, 92:21 (Eridu XV, X). For a parallel to plate 61:W, see ibid., figs. 94:11, 14; 92:8, 10–11; 89:24; 85:15; 83:13 (Eridu XVI–XV, XIII, IX–VIII). For parallels to plate 61:Y–Z, see ibid., figs. 99:19, 97:16, 96:4, 92:2, 85:14 (Eridu XVIII, XVI–XV, IX); Hall and Woolley 1927, pl. 18:1669, 1675, 1606, 1667, 1600, 1905 (al-Ubaid); Ziegler 1953, pl. 24:b (variant with continuous diagonal hatching on exterior in place of zigzags; Haji Muhammad). For hourglass frieze similar to plate 196:A, see Safar, Mustafa, and Lloyd 1981, figs. 99:3, 92:26, 89:21 (Eridu XVI, XIII). For parallels to plate 196:B, see Woolley 1955, pl. 50 (Ur); see also Shahideh 1979, fig. 19:a (Chogha Pirchestan, Izeh plain).

or two birds with outstretched wings. Despite the specific character of the Family VIII bowls they are not recorded from other sites, although the motif of flying birds, in rather sketchy renderings, does occur.[142]

Early Susiana Family IX

C.05; standard ware, unpainted

Figure 33; plates 62:EE; 196:H–J

Small- or medium-sized bowls are distinguished from the unpainted vessels of Families II and VII by their markedly hemispherical shape and incurving lip and from those of Family VIII by the absence of paint. The lips are usually noticeably incurved (pl. 196:H), although not always (pl. 196:I). Characteristic for the family, even though not present on every example, is a slight rim (pl. 196:H, J). The Family IX bowls appear to have normally a neat, dimple-like concavity in the center. Pottery marks were sometimes incised on the lower body.[143]

Early Susiana Family X

C–D.05; standard ware, painted exterior

Figure 33; plates 61:O–T; 196:K–M; 197:A–C

One of the commoner groups of Early Susiana pottery consists of medium- to large-sized bowls with flaring walls, incurved lips, and a register of simple geometric designs encircling the lip, but normally leaving most of the body plain. When preserved, the base is broad and at least slightly concave. The curvature of the lip varies from gently convex (pls. 196:M; 197:B–C) to sharper (pl. 196:L) and carinated examples (pls. 196:K; 197:A). The repertory of the painted friezes is limited: crosshatched (pls. 61:Q; 196:L; 197:B–C) or solid lozenges (pl. 197:A); a pair of reserved wavy lines (pls. 61:R; 196:K, M); diagonal lines combined with crosshatched triangles or lozenges (pls. 61:P; 196:M); and antithetical clusters of chevrons (pl. 61:T). Registers with lozenges are the most frequent. Double registers occur very rarely; wavy lines are combined with solid lozenges (pl. 61:R) and triangles bordered by diagonal lines with a single wavy line (pl. 196:M). The Family X bowls are well known at the Early Susiana sites in the vicinity of Susa.[144]

Early Susiana Family XI

B–D.36, .37; standard ware, pedestal, painted exterior and interior

Figure 33; plates 61:CC–HH, KK–MM; 197:D–J

The diagnostic feature for Family XI is the presence of a substantial pedestal supporting a rather deep, slightly convex bowl that is almost completely painted on both sides. The majority of the vessels conform to a standard type in both shape and decoration. Their walls are relatively thick, particularly those of the pedestals whose wide upper ends are often irregularly ribbed so as to produce a better weld between the separately made parts (pl. 61:KK). The base plate of a Family XI bowl has a rough ring where the pedestal has broken away (pl. 61:FF). The standard pedestals vary considerably in proportions from quite squat (pl. 197:J) to fairly high (pl. 197:F).

All parts of the Family XI vessels are decorated. The walls provide outstanding examples of the Early Susiana close style (pls. 61:CC–EE; 197:D). On the exterior reserved zigzags demarcate crosshatched lozenges and triangles. The interior, below a solid lip band, is covered by wavy lines in reserve; a fringe hangs from the bottom of the painted area. A lip sherd with the exterior pattern of an Family XI vessel has vertical bands on the interior and hence cannot be assigned with certainty to this family. It was probably normal for the flat floor of the Family XI bowls to have one or more free-field motifs, but few are preserved, a windmill (pl. 197:F) and a quadruped and bird (pl. 61:FF). The pedestals were covered on the exterior with a wash of paint. Sometimes one or two bands of reserved rectangles form the only decoration (pls. 61:GG; 197:G). Excised triangles or lozenges appear often cut either partially into the pedestal walls (pls. 61:LL; 197:F, J) or completely through so as to form windows (pl. 61:HH, MM).[145]

---

142. For parallels to plates 61:M–N and 196:D–E, see Hole, Flannery, and Neely 1969, figs. 50:i, 54:i, 55:d (Tappeh Sabz, Sabz phase).

143. For a parallel to plate 196:H, see Dollfus 1975, fig. 11:3–4 (Jafarabad, Level 5a). For a parallel to plate 196:J, see ibid., fig. 11:2, 5, 15 (Jafarabad, Levels 5, 5a, 6).

144. For a parallel to plates 61:R–S and 196:K, see ibid., figs. 21:9; 23:3 (Jafarabad, Levels 5b, 5); for related bowl with vertical lip, see Dollfus 1983, fig. 15:1 (Jowi, no level). For a parallel to plate 61:O, see Dollfus 1975, fig. 23:8 (Jafarabad, Level 4). For a parallel to plates 61:Q and

158:M, see ibid., fig. 23:7 (Jafarabad, Levels 5 and 4). For a parallel to plate 61:T, see ibid., fig. 22:6 (Jafarabad, Level 4). For shape and design related to plate 197:A, see ibid., fig. 22:8 (Jafarabad, Level 5a). For shape similar to plate 197:B, see ibid., fig. 23:8 (Jafarabad, Level 4). For a parallel to plate 197:C, see ibid., fig. 21:11 (Jafarabad, Level 5). For an analogous combination of a primary register with a reserved wavy line below, similar to plate 196:M, see ibid., fig. 22:7 (Jafarabad, Level 5[?]).

145. For parallels to plates 61:CC–EE and 197:D, see Dollfus 1971, fig. 30:6, and idem 1975, fig. 19:2–3 (Jafarabad, Levels 5, 5a, and no context); Le Breton 1947, fig. 11:4, 7 (Jafarabad, old excavations, 3.5–6.0 m); Dollfus 1983, fig. 21:7 (Jowi, Level 14). For a parallel to plate 61:GG, see Dollfus 1975, figs. 18:7, 19:9 (Jafarabad, Levels 5a, 6). For a parallel to plate 61:HH and MM, see Le Breton 1947, fig. 11:11 (Jafarabad, old excavations, 3.50–6.00 m). For parallels to plates 61:LL and 197:F and J, see Dollfus 1971, fig. 30:11, and idem 1975, figs. 18:67; 19:1, 3–6 (Jafarabad, Levels 5, 5b, 5a); Le Breton 1947, fig. 11:11–12 (Jafarabad, old excavations, 3.50–6.00 m).

Two pedestal bowls diverge widely from the standard Family XI type. One is made of a denser paste than the ordinary Early Susiana fabric and is unusually small (pl. 197:E). The shape and decoration are even more atypical: a high pedestal surmounted by a shallow incurved lip bowl painted with only a meager zigzag. The other example, the painted base of a bowl, rests on two supports that are cylindrical in their horizontal section (pl. 197:H).

Early Susiana Family XII

C.07; standard ware, unpainted

Figure 33; plate 198:A

The vessels of Family XII are defined as being fairly large and deep and, though unpainted, without the flanges diagnostic for most of the unpainted pottery (Family XVI). Since the lip and body sherds are indistinguishable from those of Family XVI, members of this family can be recognized only when the base and enough of the lower body are preserved to prove the absence of a flange. The complete, beaker-like vessel from the pile of vessels in Q23:502 represents the type, which was clearly very rare.[146]

Early Susiana Family XIII

C.00, .03, .05; proportion "3"–"4," painted

Figure 33; plates 61:II, NN; 198:B–C

The existence of deep bowls or beakers with steep sides, varying somewhat in profile, painted on the exterior, is indicated by some lip sherds. It is characteristic for the lips to bend inward. Similar forms in B sizes occur in Family I (pl. 194:E). The decoration, though not covering large areas solidly, provides good examples of the close style. The main register encircling the lip is often supplemented by a reserved wavy line and by vertical elements carrying the decoration lower. A hollow lozenge frieze (pl. 61:II) provides an Early Susiana antecedent for similar friezes used in the Early Middle Susiana phase (pls. 59:M; 183:R, U). Antithetical zigzags filled with dots (pl. 198:C) and crosshatched triangles separated by diagonal bands, one of the most frequent Early Susiana patterns (pl. 198:B), also appear in the lip friezes. Although rare at Chogha Mish, Family XIII vessels are a standard Early Susiana class, as indicated by examples from Jafarabad.[147]

Early Susiana Family XIV

C.22; standard ware, painted exterior

Figure 33; plates 61:JJ, OO–PP; 198:D–F; 202:C

Fairly deep barrel-shaped vessels painted on the exterior in the close style form a distinct group. Normally the designs probably covered somewhat more than half of the body, but not always with a solid net of pattern. Diagonal bands with pairs of reserved wavy lines spaced at intervals below a horizontal band of the same kind delimit large blank trapezoidal panels (pl. 198:D). A much larger version of the barrel-shaped vessel has vertical bands of crosshatched lozenges spaced around the body (pl. 202:C). Rather different is a pattern in which Xs and crosshatched rectangles alternate in the lip register while the incompletely preserved register below is divided by vertical bands into panels (pl. 61:OO). The typical close-line motif of diagonal bands and crosshatched triangles, here arranged antithetically on a mid-rib, probably originally covered the greater part of the vessels with a dense net of pattern (pls. 61:JJ, PP; 198:F).[148]

Early Susiana Family XV

C–D.00, .03; standard ware, painted interior

Figure 33; plates 62:A–U; 198:G–J; 199:A–I

One of the more important and frequent Early Susiana families consists of medium- and large-sized shallow bowls in which all the decoration is concentrated on the interior except for an exterior lip band. The bases are broad and might be either flat or somewhat concave. Occasionally a potter's mark was imprinted at the basal angle (pl. 198:J).

Family XV bowls provide one of the more frequent early habitats for squared-circle designs. Several different methods were used to quadrate their circular interiors. Often the apices of four triangles hanging from the lip are attached to the corners of a square painted in the flat center of a bowl. A completely restorable composition is the same as that on a Family VI bowl (fig. 32:A), differing only in the details of individual elements. The central square is divided diagonally by a band with flying birds and the two triangles remaining, as well as the pendant triangles, are filled with wavy lines (pl. 198:I). In addition, bands with wavy lines are centered in the space between the triangles. The design on a base frag-

148. For pattern related to plates 61:JJ and PP and 198:F, see Dollfus 1975, fig. 28:3 (Jafarabad, Level 5b); Hole, Flannery, and Neely 1969, fig. 52:a (Tappeh Sabz, Sabz phase). For a parallel to plates 61:OO and 198:E, see Dollfus 1975, fig. 28:5 (Jafarabad, Level 5b). For a parallel to plate 198:D, see ibid., fig. 30:12 (Jafarabad, Level 5b). For shape analogous to plate 198:D–F, see ibid., figs. 25:1, 28:1–5 (Jafarabad, Levels 6, 5a, 5b). For shape and vertical band with lozenges similar to plate 202:C, see ibid., fig. 25:1 (Jafarabad, Level 6).

146. For a painted version of apparently the same form as plate 198:A, see Dollfus 1975, fig. 25:10 (lower body only; Jafarabad, Level 5a).

147. For a parallel to plate 198:B, see Dollfus 1975, fig. 25:8 (antithetical triangles and diagonal lines; Jafarabad, Level 5a). For patterns related to plate 198:C, see ibid., fig. 22:4, 7–8 (Jafarabad, Levels 5, 5[?], 5a).

ment with diagonal clusters of wavy lines crossing the space between the pendant triangles (pl. 199:B) has been tentatively restored by analogy with the more complete example. A small fragment probably belonged to a similar composition (pl. 62:T). In addition to the patterns with a strictly rectilinear central square, there are others in which multiple bands, with either a slightly convex or concave curvature form the square. The designs once contained inside are for the most part not preserved. Triangles are attached to the corners of the multiple bordered squares, as in the first group (pls. 62:C, J; 199:G, I).

In the patterns so far described a central square and its four attached triangles dominate the circular field. In another group the cross elements are primary and the triangles only subsidiary filling motifs hanging free (pls. 62:E, P–Q; 199:A). When the circle is a quadrated cluster of lines, its center becomes a square of crosshatch (pls. 62:P–Q; 199:A). In one example (pl. 199:A) two zones—the floor and the wall of the bowl—are created by a pair of concentric bands. Only a trace of the outer zone remains. In other versions, broad bands divided into squares or rectangles cross the entire inner surface of the bowls. Each individual segment has a dense pattern, varying in detail from bowl to bowl, but usually consisting of positive and negative elements combined so as to produce a central lozenge and four triangles (pls. 62:L–O, Q–R; 198:J; 199:E–F). Sometimes bands of crosshatched lozenges (pl. 61:H) or the familiar motif of paired wavy lines (pls. 62:U and probably 198:G) form the cross.

Certain details of the rendering of the triangles on the Family XV bowls are worthy of note. Crosshatching (pls. 62:P–Q; 199:A, F) or wavy lines (pls. 62:H, J; 198:I–J; 199:B–C) appear as filling. The lineage of other triangles with blank strips interrupting the filling, usually of wavy lines (pls. 62:A–F; 199:G) but occasionally of straight lines (pl. 161:I), goes back to the Archaic Susiana period (pl. 207:D, L–M). An unobtrusive feature, a line projecting from the apex of a triangle, is probably not an accidental drip since carefully painted analogies occur on sherds from Eridu.[149]

Early Susiana Family XVI

   C–D.03, .04, .05, .07, .22; usually standard ware,
   unpainted

   Figure 33; plates 62:FF–KK; 199:J–M; 200:A–G;
   201:A–F

The largest category of Early Susiana pottery consists of unpainted vessels with an overhanging carination a short distance above a concave base. These

carinations are a type specific to the Early Susiana period and are termed "flanges." The vessels themselves vary considerably in size and in the details of the body curvature. The majority of examples have high proportions ("4–5").

Although some of the flanged vessels occur in gritty ware, the majority are of the standard paste mixed with large quantities of both grit and chaff. The sherds are extremely crumbly. In some cases a pronounced white slip appears on the exteriors, which is particularly noticeable when the paste is pink or reddish in color. The majority of the flanged vessels probably had a thin slip, but the coating is hard to distinguish when both it and the paste are the same color. The interiors are frequently stained black from bitumen, presumably applied to produce less porous containers. The flanged vessels must have been the basic domestic containers; the smaller, rarer, vessels would have been useful in preparing or serving food and the larger vessels for storage.

The flanged vessels are for the most part represented by sherds that do not provide all the details necessary for exact restoration of the shape. However, the complete or semi-complete examples available allow the definition of four subfamilies: a, vessels with either flaring (.03) or relatively straight upper walls (.04); b, deep vessels with incurving lips (.05 or .22); c, squat vessels of proportion 2 with varying profiles (.03, .07); and d, vessels with recurved walls (.07). Examples of Subfamilies XVIa and d are more frequent than those of the other two groups.[150]

Marks made on vessels before firing are characteristic for only a few families of Early Susiana pottery; most occur on examples of Family XVI, but some Family IX bowls and occasional Families XV, XVII, or XVIII vessels have marks (pl. 203). They are painted on the pedestals of Family XVII[151] but imprinted or incised on the unpainted surfaces of the other families. The marks are normally placed at the lowest part of the vessels, either near (pl. 62:EE, HH) or at (pl. 62:GG, JJ) the basal angle. Occasionally they were incised on the underside of the base at the basal angle (pl. 62:II) or in the middle (pl. 62:KK), and rarely just above the flange.

---

149. For projections pendant from the apices of triangles similar to plate 62:E, see Safar, Mustafa, and Lloyd 1981, figs. 92:16; 97:8, 11, 13; 99:16; 100:11 (Eridu XV, XVII–XIX).

For a parallel to plates 62:U and 160:G, see Dollfus 1975, figs. 16:3; 12 (Jafarabad, Levels 5a, 4). For decorative scheme distantly related to plate 198:J, see Adams and Nissen 1972, fig. 60:9 (sherd from WS 267). For a parallel to plate 199:E–F, see Dollfus 1975, fig. 17:6 (Jafarabad, Level 5a).

150. For a parallel to plate 199:J, see Dollfus 1983, fig. 11:18 (Jowi, Level 3). For a possible parallel to plate 200:A, see Dollfus 1975, fig. 14:3 (Jafarabad, Level 5a). For a parallel to plate 200:B and E, see ibid., fig. 14:1 (Jafarabad, Level 5a). For a parallel to plate 200:F, see ibid., fig. 14:7 (Jafarabad, no level).

151. Painted pottery marks appear to be rarer at Chogha Mish than at Jafarabad (Dollfus and Encreve 1982).

In two instances marks occur on opposite sides of the base, Types 13 and 6 (pl. 199:M) and 13 and 63 (pl. 200:G). Many more examples might originally have had double markings, since their presence can only be established if at least the basal parts of the vessels are completely preserved. Among the base and basal angle sherds only a small proportion bore marks; for example, from S22:808 at el. 75.60, 18.1%; and from S22:823 Middle at el. 75.43, 11%. However, these statistics might well be misleading, since the basal part of each vessel must often have broken into several plain sherds in addition to the one with the mark. Among the small number of complete or semi-complete vessels from the third to sixth seasons, eight are marked and five plain. Out of these thirteen examples six were piled together in Q23:502 and four had marks. Accordingly it is quite possible that at least half of the Family XVI vessels were marked.

The corpus of Early Susiana marks from Chogha Mish, represented by full-sized facsimiles (pl. 203), includes those excavated after the fifth season.[152] The marks are arranged in an order starting with punctations and continuing from simple incised strokes to more elaborate combinations of elements, for example, Ws, lozenges, and tridents. All types, except for the few examples located in the center of bases, are oriented according to the horizontal line of the base, as vertical, diagonal, or horizontal marks. Thus, Vs appear as vertical in Type 63 and horizontal in Type 72. Types 6 and 7, 15 and 17, 23 and 24, and 31 and 32 are vertical-diagonal pairs. Some prints of Types 2 and 7 and the single or multiple strokes of Types 15 and 16, 20 and 21, 25 and 26, 65 and 66, and 85 to 87. Types 41 and 42, although similar in size, are distinguished by the narrow or squat shape of the imprints. Various examples given separate type numbers (pl. 203) were probably considered anciently as one type.

The limited use of pottery marks, for the most part on Family XVI, their form, and the frequency and distribution of individual types must be considered in attempting to determine their function. That they were made before firing is not sufficient to establish them as the hallmarks of individual potter, workshop, or presumptive owner unless supported by some systematic pattern of distribution. However, many of the types (pl.

152. Plate 203:Type 28, reproduced from a sketch in the sherd register, is not to scale. The collection of pottery marks began during the fourth season at Chogha Mish; Charles M. Adelman compiled a corpus of marks that provided the basis for the drawing of the first versions of plates 203–04. During the twelfth season at Chogha Mish Guillermo Algaze extended the corpus and later prepared table 22. Carolyn Livingood prepared table 21, which lists all the Early Susiana pottery marks in order of the types. The field numbers of the examples drawn in plate 203 are marked by an asterisk. AA

203) occur only once and others only up to four times (table 21). The only common types are vertical strokes, a single line (Types 13–14) occurs eleven times, two strokes (Types 15–17) thirty-two times and three strokes (Types 20–22) twelve times. Dollfus and Encreve (1982) have suggested that these and other simple marks occurring in different multiples might have formed a primitive numerical notation. Volume would seem to be a likely feature for such recording but the occurrence of different marks on Family XVI vessels of similar size precludes such an interpretation (e.g., pls. 161:L; 162:G).

In groups of pottery with several marks, each one is usually a different type (table 22). However, some types (pl. 203) might be over-refined. Anciently only the number of punctations or slashes might have been important, without regard to their size or shape. Only the shape of the Vs might have been significant, but not their orientation. When various types (pl. 203) are clustered together to form general types some of these do reoccur several times in a few loci, always with other types (table 23).

The six vessels of the Q22:502 deposit were clearly in use together since they had been stacked while still complete. The four marked examples bear respectively three punctations, three slashes, two slashes opposite a single one, and a V (pls. 199:J, L–M; 200:C). Whether the marks on three of the vessels should be considered as essentially the same, namely "three," remains an open question.

The examples just cited are not sufficient to establish a meaningful pattern of distribution of the marks, leaving their function uncertain. Perhaps varying exigencies of daily life prompted potters to give individuality to some vessels by marking them before firing. At Chogha Mish the unpainted Family XVI vessels and some Family IX bowls carry the majority of the marks, rather than the vessels that derived some individuality from variations in their painted designs. However, the position of the marks would have made them practically invisible when the containers were in use.

Despite our unsatisfactory understanding of the pottery marks, it is evident that they were a characteristic and well-established feature of Early Susiana culture. The same standard repertory of signs occurs at Jafarabad with relatively few individual variations (Dollfus and Encreve 1982).

Pottery marks are another feature carried over from the Early Susiana to Middle Susiana periods; fourteen occur on the descendants of Family XVI, the vestigial flanged vessels of Family XXI (pls. 60:N–W; 182:K). The mark on a Family XVIII vessel also belongs to the Middle Susiana period (pl. 180:E). A sherd from Late Middle Susiana debris (table 24 [4.306, pl. 203:6]) and three others out of context, but of Late Middle Susiana types (table 24 [4.1034, pl. 203:13; 4.1033, pl. 203:14;

Table 23. Early Susiana Pottery Marks in Order of Type Number

Type	Early Susiana XVI			Early Susiana IX			Early Susiana XV			Early Susiana XVIII			Early Susiana: Undetermined			Total
	Number	Locus	Level	Number	Locus	Level	Number	Locus	Level	Number	Locus	Level	Number	Locus	Level	
1	6.798	S20:607	78.94	—	—	—	—	—	—	—	—	—	—	—	—	1
2	6.328	P22:611	80.50	—	—	—	—	—	—	—	—	—	8.1063	—	—	3
	5.106	Q23:504	79.33													
3	9.734	S22:904	77.26	—	—	—	—	—	—	6.422	P22:606	80.86	—	—	—	2
4	6.331	P22:629	80.16	8.962	S22:830	75.69	—	—	—	—	—	—	—	—	—	3
	V-15	Q23:502	79.70–79.56													
5	9.766	S22:921	74.95	—	—	—	—	—	—	—	—	—	—	—	—	1
6	—	S22:902 Northeast	76.82	—	—	—	—	—	—	—	—	—	8.1100	—	—	4
	9.733	S22:921	75.13										8.1101	—	—	
7	8.819	S22:827	74.78	—	—	—	—	—	—	—	—	—	—	—	—	1
8	8.444	S22:828	75.30	—	—	—	—	—	—	—	—	—	—	—	—	1
9	5.427	Q23.504 North	80.20	—	—	—	—	—	—	—	—	—	—	—	—	1
10A	6.749	Q22.608	79.95–79.57	—	—	—	—	—	—	—	—	—	—	—	—	1
10B	—	—	—	—	—	—	3.123	R21:300 Center West	77.35–77.30	—	—	—	—	—	—	1
11	6.249	P22:606 West	81.14	—	—	—	—	—	—	—	—	—	—	—	—	2
	3.166	R20:300 East	78.46													
12	4.905	—	Surface	—	—	—	—	—	—	—	—	—	—	—	—	1
13	6.759	P22:605 South	81.34	—	—	—	—	—	—	—	—	—	8.1062	—	—	10
	6.757	P22:606	80.86										8.1067	—	—	
	6.807	P22:616	81.43										8.1128	—	—	
	5.430	Q23:504	79.92–79.52													
	8.895	S22:825	75.95													
	8.864	S22:826	75.02													
	8.892	S22:827	74.93													
13, 63	4.043	Q23:401	80.45	—	—	—	—	—	—	—	—	—	—	—	—	2
	V-11	Q23:502	79.70–79.56													
14	8.517	S22:823 Middle	75.43	—	—	—	—	—	—	—	—	—	6.171	P22:611	80.50	2
15	4.955	K22:400	82.29–82.09	8.354	S22:823	74.98	—	—	—	—	—	—	8.520	S22:823 Middle	75.43	19
	2.659	P22:202	81.20	8.964	S22:830 South	74.99							8.1048	—	—	
	3.1257	P23:301	80.85										8.1049	—	—	
	5.437	Q23:504	79.92–79.52										8.1054	—	—	
	6.796	S20:607	78.74										8.1099	—	—	
	8.355	S22:823	74.98										11.220	—	—	
	8.449	S22:823 West	75.94													
	8.971	S22:827	75.51													
	8.930	S22:827	74.78													
	8.443	S22:828	75.30													
	9.735	S22:914	75.32													
16	8.828	S22:808 North	75.47	—	—	—	—	—	—	—	—	—	—	—	—	5
	8.518	S22:823	75.65													
	8.607	S22:823 North	75.81													
	8.865	S22:826	75.02													
	8.973	S22:827	75.51													
17	6.172	P22:611	80.50	II-262	Q22:203	78.66	—	—	—	—	—	—	—	—	—	9
	5.424	Q23:504	80.34													
	5.428	Q23:504	79.40													
	8.764	S22:823	75.98													
	8.554	S22:823	75.84													
	8.608	S22:823 North	75.81													
	8.910	S22:826	75.02													
	9.258	S22:914	75.76													
18	8.1068	—	—	—	—	—	—	—	—	—	—	—	—	—	—	1
19	6.321	P22:606	82.18	—	—	—	—	—	—	—	—	—	—	—	—	2
	VI-35	P22:606	80.86													

Table 23. Early Susiana Pottery Marks in Order of Type Number (*cont.*)

Type	Early Susiana XVI			Early Susiana IX			Early Susiana XV			Early Susiana XVIII			Early Susiana: Undetermined			Total
	Number	Locus	Level	Number	Locus	Level	Number	Locus	Level	Number	Locus	Level	Number	Locus	Level	
20	6.758	P22:606	80.42	—	—	—	—	—	—	—	—	—	8.1054	—	—	8
	6.318	P22:620	81.81										B.F. 1.015	Boneh Fazili		
	5.421	P27:503	78.90													
	V-12	Q23:502	79.70–79.56													
	8.519	S22:823 Middle	75.43													
	5.829	—	—													
21	8.867	S22:826	75.02	—	—	—	—	—	—	—	—	—	8.1059	—	—	4
	8.900	S22:827	74.60													
	8.416	S22:830 South	75.23													
22	8.399	Q23:827 East	78.82	—	—	—	—	—	—	—	—	—	8.1092	—	—	3
	8.550	S22:823	74.98													
23	6.326	P22:606	80.42	—	—	—	—	—	—	—	—	—	—	—	—	2
	6.217	Q23:601	80.90													
24	5.423	Q23:508	79.73	—	—	—	—	—	—	—	—	—	—	—	—	1
25	8.814	S22:827	74.76	—	—	—	—	—	—	—	—	—	8.1053	—	—	2
26	8.884	S22:808	75.60	—	—	—	—	—	—	—	—	—	—	—	—	1
27	8.487	S22:823	75.51	—	—	—	—	—	—	—	—	—	—	—	—	1
28	4.1037	S-T21:Sounding G	73.45	—	—	—	—	—	—	—	—	—	—	—	—	1
29	6.755	P22:606 West	81.14	—	—	—	—	—	—	—	—	—	—	—	—	1
30	[lost]	—	—	—	—	—	—	—	—	—	—	—	—	—	—	1
31	4.939	S-T21:Sounding G	75.95	—	—	—	—	—	—	—	—	—	—	—	—	1
32	6.325	P22:606	80.42	—	—	—	—	—	—	—	—	—	—	—	—	1
33	5.418	P23:501	82.49	—	—	—	—	—	—	—	—	—	—	—	—	1
34	3.790	Q23:301 Steps	80.85–78.65	—	—	—	—	—	—	—	—	—	8.1059	—	—	2
35	—	—	—	—	—	—	—	—	—	—	—	—	8.1130	—	—	1
36	—	—	—	—	—	—	—	—	—	—	—	—	8.1069	—	—	1
37	—	—	—	8.183	S22:823	75.84	—	—	—	—	—	—	—	—	—	1
38	—	—	—	—	—	—	—	—	—	—	—	—	9.731	S22:914	75.57	1
39	4.489	Q23:401	79.40	—	—	—	—	—	—	—	—	—	—	—	—	1
40	8.965	—	—	—	—	—	—	—	—	—	—	—	—	—	—	1
41	8.143	Q23:803 Southwest	80.14	—	—	—	—	—	—	—	—	—	—	—	—	2
	8.893	S22:827	74.93													
42	4.954	S17:401	ca. 83.10	8.563	S22:823 N	75.81	—	—	—	—	—	—	—	—	—	2
43	8.612	S22:823 North	75.81	—	—	—	—	—	—	—	—	—	—	—	—	1
44	8.552	S22:823 Middle	75.43	—	—	—	—	—	—	—	—	—	B.F. 1.013	Boneh Fazili	—	2
45	9.887	S22:923	74.85	—	—	—	—	—	—	—	—	—	—	—	—	1
46	8.960	S22:830	75.69	—	—	—	—	—	—	—	—	—	—	—	—	1
47	3.165	Q23:301	80.35–80.05	8.553	S22:823	—	—	—	—	—	—	—	—	—	—	2
48	5.432	Q23:504	80.34	—	—	—	—	—	—	—	—	—	—	—	—	1
49	—	—	—	—	—	—	—	—	—	—	—	—	8.1069	—	—	1
50	8.566	S22:823 West	75.90	—	—	—	—	—	—	—	—	—	8.1126	—	—	2
51	8.886	S22:808	75.67	—	—	—	—	—	—	—	—	—	—	—	—	1
52	—	—	—	5.433	Q23:504	80.34	—	—	—	—	—	—	—	—	—	1
53	6.808	P22:606	81.77	—	—	—	—	—	—	—	—	—	8.1066	—	—	3
	8.410	S22:823 West	76.35													
54	8.866	S22:826	75.02	—	—	—	—	—	—	—	—	—	—	—	—	1
55	—	—	—	—	—	—	—	—	—	—	—	—	8.1055	—	—	1
56	8.516	S22:823 Middle	75.43	—	—	—	—	—	—	—	—	—	—	—	—	1
57	6.319	P22:607	81.91	—	—	—	—	—	—	—	—	—	—	—	—	1
58	8.356	S22:823 North	74.98	—	—	—	—	—	—	—	—	—	6.289	R23:601 South	76.96	3
	8.963	—	—													

Table 23. Early Susiana Pottery Marks in Order of Type Number (*cont.*)

| Type | Early Susiana XVI | | | Early Susiana IX | | | Early Susiana XV | | | Early Susiana XVIII | | | Early Susiana: Undetermined | | | Total |
	Number	Locus	Level	Number	Locus	Level	Number	Locus	Level	Number	Locus	Level	Number	Locus	Level	
59	6.330	P22:606 West	81.14	—	—	—	—	—	—	—	—	—	—	—	—	1
60	9.767	S22:919	75.61	—	—	—	—	—	—	—	—	—	—	—	—	1
61	5.417	—	—	—	—	—	—	—	—	—	—	—	—	—	—	1
62	—	—	—	—	—	—	—	—	—	—	—	—	5.435	Q23:512	81.09	1
63	4.953	Southeast L22:402	82.54–82.14	—	—	—	—	—	—	—	—	—	—	—	—	8
	6.320	P22:606	81.06													
	6.323	P22:606 West	82.18													
	V-16	Q23:502	79.70–79.56													
	8.807	S22:808	75.60													
	8.488	S22:823	75.51													
	8.1500	S22:830 South	75.23													
	8.1056	—	—													
64	8.514	S22:823 Middle	75.43	—	—	—	—	—	—	—	—	—	8.1053	—	—	4
	8.415	S22:830 South	75.23													
	9.303	S22:912	74.73													
65	8.381	S22:830 Middle	75.28	—	—	—	—	—	—	—	—	—	—	—	—	2
	8.959	S22:830 Middle	75.28													
66	4.491	K22:400	78.99–78.49	—	—	—	—	—	—	—	—	—	—	—	—	2
	8.710	S22:823	75.30													
67	—	—	—	—	—	—	—	—	—	—	—	—	8.1051	—	—	1
68	6.317	P22:625	81.88	—	—	—	—	—	—	—	—	—	—	—	—	1
69A	8.931	S22:827	74.78	—	—	—	—	—	—	—	—	—	—	—	—	1
69B	6.324	P22:606 North	81.06	—	—	—	—	—	—	—	—	—	—	—	—	1
70	8.972	S22:827	75.51	—	—	—	—	—	—	—	—	—	—	—	—	1
71	8.510	S22:823	75.08	—	—	—	—	—	—	—	—	—	—	—	—	1
72	6.322	P22:616	81.43	—	—	—	—	—	—	—	—	—	—	—	—	3
	8.564	S22:823 West	75.94													
	8.615	S22:823 North	75.03													
73	6.537	S20:610	77.48	—	—	—	—	—	—	—	—	—	8.1060	—	—	2
74	6.797	S20:607	78.74	7.230	R23:710	77.02	—	—	—	—	—	—	—	—	—	2
75	—	—	—	—	—	—	—	—	—	—	—	—	B.F. 1.011	Boneh Fazili	—	1
76	6.332	P22:611	80.08	—	—	—	—	—	—	—	—	—	—	—	—	1
77	5.426	Q23:503	80.10–79.52	8.512	S22:823	75.43	—	—	—	—	—	—	—	—	—	4
	8.829	S22:808 North	75.47													
	8.521	S22:823 Middle	75.43													
78	5.431	Q23:501	80.27	—	—	—	—	—	—	—	—	—	8.1129	—	—	4
	8.613	S22:823 North	75.47													
	4.547	S–T21:Sounding G	74.70													
79	6.460	P22:606	81.92	—	—	—	—	—	—	—	—	—	—	—	—	2
	8.614	S22:823	75.62													
80	8.616	S22:823 North	75.03	—	—	—	—	—	—	—	—	—	—	—	—	1
81	8.515	S22:823 Middle	75.43	9.725	S22:914	75.57	—	—	—	—	—	—	8.555	S22:823	75.84	3
82	8.511	S22:823	75.08	—	—	—	—	—	—	—	—	—	—	—	—	1
83	9.732	S22:914	75.57	—	—	—	—	—	—	—	—	—	—	—	—	1
84	8.961	S22:830 South	74.99	—	—	—	—	—	—	—	—	—	—	—	—	1
85	6.329	P22:606 West	81.14	—	—	—	—	—	—	—	—	—	—	—	—	3
	8.883	S22:808	75.60													
	8.706	S22:823	75.30													
86	2.413	K22:201	78.60	—	—	—	—	—	—	—	—	—	8.1057	—	—	6
	2.421	P22:202	—										8.1178	—	—	
	VI-34	P22:606 North	81.75													
	6.754	P22:606 West	81.14													
87	3.164	R21:300 Northeast	78.31	—	—	—	—	—	—	—	—	—	8.1052	—	—	3
													8.1135	—	—	
88	5.434	Q23:503	80.10–79.52	—	—	—	—	—	—	—	—	—	—	—	—	1

Table 23. Early Susiana Pottery Marks in Order of Type Number (*cont.*)

| Type | Early Susiana XVI | | | Early Susiana IX | | | Early Susiana XV | | | Early Susiana XVIII | | | Early Susiana: Undetermined | | | Total |
	Number	Locus	Level	Number	Locus	Level	Number	Locus	Level	Number	Locus	Level	Number	Locus	Level	
89	—	—	—	5.425	Q23:504	80.34	—	—	—	—	—	—	—	—	—	1
90	8.417	S22:830 South	75.23	—	—	—	—	—	—	—	—	—	—	—	—	1
91	8.880	S22:827	75.13	—	—	—	—	—	—	—	—	—	—	—	—	1
92	2.414	Q23:203	78.96	—	—	—	—	—	—	—	—	—	—	—	—	1
93	6.327	P22:611	80.50	—	—	—	—	—	—	—	—	—	—	—	—	1
94	—	—	—	6.273	P22:611 South	80.15	—	—	—	—	—	—	—	—	—	1
95	—	—	—	7.152	R23:701	77.59	—	—	—	—	—	—	—	—	—	1
96	—	—	—	—	—	—	—	—	—	—	—	—	8.1050	—	—	1
97	8.513	S22:823	75.43	—	—	—	—	—	—	—	—	—	—	—	—	1
98	6.809	P23:606	80.40	—	—	—	—	—	—	—	—	—	—	—	—	1
99	—	—	—	—	—	—	—	—	—	—	—	—	B.F. 1.012	Boneh Fazili	—	1
100	—	—	—	—	—	—	6.250e	P22:601	81.83	—	—	—	—	—	—	1
101	8.565	S22:823 West	75.90	—	—	—	—	—	—	—	—	—	—	—	—	1
102	—	—	—	—	—	—	—	—	—	—	—	—	8.1093	—	—	1
103	—	—	—	—	—	—	7.103	R23:701	77.53	—	—	—	—	—	—	1
104	N/A	—	—	VI-23	Q22:602	80.47	—	—	—	—	—	—	—	—	—	1
TOTAL																221

5.275, pl. 204:16]) prove that a few vessels were still being marked in the Late Middle Susiana phase. Five marks on Family XX sherds from Protoliterate or mixed contexts might belong to either the Early Middle Susiana or Late Middle Susiana phases (table 24 [4.1031, pl. 203:1; 4.1032, pl. 203:16; 4.1071, pl. 204:8; 5.420, pl. 203:5; 9.781]). In any case, with fifteen out of the twenty-four marks dated to the Early Middle Susiana phase, it is clear that phase the pottery marks were no longer important elements after that. Already in the Early Middle Susiana phase the marks are too rare to constitute any evidence as to function.

Almost all the marks in the limited Middle Susiana repertory repeat those already known in the Early Susiana period, or are closely related variants (cf. pls. 204:7 and 203:60, 79; 204:9 and 203:65; 204:10 and 203:89). Only a disorganized mark (pl. 204:18) is without an earlier parallel.

Early Susiana Family XVII

D.07; gritty ware, painted

Figure 33; 62:V–BB; 201:G–I; 202:A

Large sinuous-sided bowls with close-style decoration form a relatively rare but outstanding group. The profiles are either flaring with walls almost completely covered by designs on both sides (pl. 201:G–H [with slight rim]) or more vertical, sometimes even cylindrical, with painted decoration on the exterior wall and only a lip band on the interior (pls. 201:I; 202:A). The latter, particularly one example (pl. 201:I), are closely related to convex-sided bowls from Jafarabad with the same decoration.

A standard scheme of decoration for the flaring bowls consists of strokes painted so closely together that they form almost a solid mass (pl. 201:G). On the interior, they are horizontal; on the exterior, they appear as pairs of diagonal clusters separated by reserved diagonal bands filled with schematic flying birds. Such bowls, both in shape and decoration, are directly descended from an Archaic Susiana type (pl. 206:M). Sometimes the exterior pattern was executed with solid bands rather than multiple coalescing strokes and was combined with an interior design of chevrons and crosshatched triangles (pl. 201:H). Several small sherds can be attributed with considerable likelihood to Family XVII. On one a reserve panel has wavy lines that might be anorectic versions of birds (cf. pls. 62:AA; 201:G–H). Chevron and crosshatched triangles recur (pl. 62:BB). Reserved wavy lines and a painted pottery mark appear on a base angle sherd (pl. 62:X). Another base sherd is painted on the interior with crossing lines (pl. 62:Z), the same pattern as on some Family XV sherds (pls. 62:P–Q; 199:A). The exterior has the lowest part of a multiple chevron-band and the base is speckled. This sherd indicates that some at least some of the Family XVII bowls had concave bases.[153]

153. For decorations similar to plates 62:V–W, BB, 201:I, and 202:A, see Dollfus 1975, figs. 17:11; 21:14, 17; 22:2 (Jafarabad, Levels 4–5). For a parallel to plate 201:G, see ibid., figs. 17:10, 18:5, 20:2 (Jafarabad, Levels 5b, 5a, 6). For .03 bowls of character similar to plate 201, see ibid., fig. 21:14, 17 (Jafarabad, Level 4).

Table 24. Loci with Early Susiana Pottery Marks

Locus	Level	Locus Description	Family	Type	Reg. No.	Number
K22:201	78.60	Sounding	XVI	86	2.413	1
K22:400	78.99–78.49	—	XVI	66	4.491	2
	82.29–82.09	Occupational debris (Middle Susiana level, out of context)	XVI	15	4.955	
Southeast of L22:402	82.54–82.14	Occupational debris (Middle Susiana level, out of context)	XVI	63	4.953	1
P22:202	—	—	XVI	86	2.421	2
	81.20	Occupational debris	XVI	15	2.659	
P22:601	81.83	Occupational debris	XV	100	6.250e	1
P22:605 South	81.34	Occupational debris	XVI	13	6.759	1
P22:606	82.18	Occupational debris	XVI	19	6.321	9
	81.92	Occupational debris	XVI	79	6.460	
	81.77	Occupational debris	XVI	53	6.808	
	80.86	Pottery deposit	XVI	13	6.757	
	80.86	Pottery deposit	XVI	19	VI-35	
	80.86	Pottery deposit	XVIII	3	6.422	
	80.42	Surface and occupational debris above	XVI	20	6.758	
	80.42	Surface and occupational debris above	XVI	32	6.325	
	80.42	Surface and occupational debris above	XVI	23	6.326	
P22:606 North	81.75	Occupational debris	XVI	86	VI-34	3
	81.06	Pottery deposit	XVI	69B	6.324	
	81.06	Pottery deposit	XVI	63	6.320	
P22:606 West	82.18	Occupational debris	XVI	63	6.323	6
	81.14	Pottery deposit	XVI	11	6.249	
	81.14	Pottery deposit	XVI	85	6.329	
	81.14	Pottery deposit	XVI	59	6.330	
	81.14	Pottery deposit	XVI	86	6.754	
	81.14	Pottery deposit	XVI	29	6.755	
P22:607	81.91	Occupational debris (mixed Middle Susiana-Early Susiana)	XVI	57	6.319	1
P22:611	80.50	Occupational debris	XVI	93	6.327	5
	80.50	Occupational debris	XVI	2	6.328	
	80.50	Occupational debris	XVII(?)	14	6.171	
	80.50	Occupational debris	XVI	17	6.172	
	80.08	Occupational debris	XVI	76	6.332	
P22:611 South	80.15	Occupational debris	IX	94	6.273	1
P22:616	81.43	B.S.	XVI	13	6.807	2
	81.43	B.S.	XVI	72	6.322	
P22:620	81.80	Courtyard area	XVI	20	6.318	1
P22:625	81.88	Occupational debris	XVI	68	6.317	1
P22:629	80.16	Hearth area	XVI	4	6.331	1
P23:301	80.85	Occupational debris	XVI	15	3.1257	1
P23:501	82.49	Occupational debris (Early Middle Susiana level, out of context)	XVI	33	5.418	1
P23:606	80.40	—	XVI	98	6.809	1
P27:503	78.90	Early Middle Susiana room (out of context)	XVI	20	5.421	1
Q22:203	78.96	Occupational debris	XVI	92	2.414	2
	78.66	Occupational debris	XVI	17	II-262	
Q22:602	80.47	Pottery deposit	IX	104	VI-23	1
Q22:608	79.95–79.57	Mixed debris	XVI	10A	6.749	1
Q23:301	80.85–78.65	Occupational debris	XVI	34	3.790	2
	80.35–80.05	Occupational debris	XVI	47	3.165	
Q23:401	80.45	Pottery deposit	XVI	13, 63	4.143	1
Q23:401 Middle	79.40	Occupational debris	XVI	39	4.489	1
Q23:501	80.27	Early Susiana room	XVI	78	5.431	1
Q23:502	79.70–79.56	Pottery deposit	XVI	13, 63	V-11	4
	79.70–79.56	Pottery deposit	XVI	20	V-12	
	79.70–79.56	Pottery deposit	XVI	4	V-15	
	79.70–79.56	Pottery deposit	XVI	63	V-16	
Q23:503	80.10–79.52	Early Susiana room	XVI	88	5.434	2
	80.10–79.52	Early Susiana room	XVI	77	5.426	
Q23.504	80.34	B.S.	XVI	17	5.424	8
	80.34	B.S.	IX	89	5.425	
	80.34	B.S.	XVI	48	5.432	
	80.34	B.S.	IX	52	5.433	
	79.92–79.52	Early Susiana room	XVI	13	5.430	
	79.92–79.52	Early Susiana room	XVI	15	5.437	
	79.40	Early Susiana room	XVI	17	5.428	
	79.33	Early Susiana room	XVI	2	5.106	
Q23:504 North	80.20	B.S.	XVI	9	5.427	1

Table 24. Loci with Early Susiana Pottery Marks (*cont.*)

Locus	Level	Locus Description	Family	Type	Reg. No.	Number
Q23:508	79.73	Early Susiana room	XVI	24	5.423	1
Q23:512	81.09	B.S.	?	62	5.435	1
Q23:601	80.90	Early Susiana room	XVI	23	6.217	1
Q23:803 Southwest	80.14	B.S.	XVI	41	8.143	1
Q23:827 East	78.82	Early Susiana room	XVI	22	8.399	1
R23:601 South	76.42	—	(?)	58	6.289	1
R23:701	77.59	Mixed debris	IX	95	7.152	1
R23:710	77.02	Mixed debris	IX	74	7.230	1
R23:711	77.53	Mixed debris	XV	103	7.103	1
R20:300 East	78.46	Mixed debris	XVI	11	3.166	1
R21:300 Northeast	78.31	Mixed debris	XVI	87	3.164	1
R21:300 Center West	77.35–77.30	Sherd pavement	XV	10B	3.123	1
S17:401	ca. 83.10	Early Susiana room	XVI	42	4.954	1
S20:607	78.74	Sherd pavement	XVI	15	6.796	3
	78.74	Sherd pavement	XVI	74	6.797	
	78.74	Sherd pavement	XVI	1	6.798	
S20:610	77.48	—	XVI	73	6.537	1
S–T21:Sounding G	75.95	Occupational debris (Middle Susiana, out of context)	XVI	31	4.939	3
	74.70	Occupational debris	XVI	78	4.547	
	73.45	—	XVI	28	4.1037	
S22:808	75.67	Early Susiana Circular Structure, Building(?)	XVI	51	8.886	4
	75.60	—	XVI	26	8.884	
	75.60	—	XVI	63	8.807	
	75.60	—	XVI	85	8.883	
S22:808 North	75.47	—	XVI	16	8.828	2
	75.47	—	XVI	77	8.829	
S22:823	75.98	Ashy black layer	XVI	17	8.764	16
	75.84	Ashy black layer	IX	37	8.183	
	75.84	Ashy black layer	IX	47	8.553	
	75.84	Ashy black layer	XVI	17	8.554	
	75.84	Ashy black layer	(?)	81	8.555	
	75.65	Ashy black layer	XVI	16	8.518	
	75.62	Ashy black layer	XVI	79	8.614	
	75.51	Ashy black layer	XVI	63	8.488	
	75.51	Ashy black layer	XVI	27	8.487	
	75.30	Ashy black layer	XVI	66	8.710	
	75.30	Ashy black layer	XVI	85	8.706	
	75.08	Ashy black layer	XVI	71	8.510	
	75.08	Ashy black layer	XVI	82	8.511	
	74.98	Ashy layer (Early Susiana-Archaic Susiana)	IX	15	8.354	
	74.98	Ashy layer (Early Susiana-Archaic Susiana)	XVI	15	8.355	
	74.98	Ashy layer (Early Susiana-Archaic Susiana)	XVI	22	8.550	
S22:823 Middle	75.43	Hearth area and associated plastered surfaces	XVI	77	8.512	10
	75.43	Hearth area and associated plastered surfaces	XVI	97	8.513	
	75.43	Hearth area and associated plastered surfaces	XVI	64	8.514	
	75.43	Hearth area and associated plastered surfaces	XVI	81	8.515	
	75.43	Hearth area and associated plastered surfaces	XVI	56	8.516	
	75.43	Hearth area and associated plastered surfaces	XVI	14	8.517	
	75.43	Hearth area and associated plastered surfaces	XVI	20	8.519	
	75.43	Hearth area and associated plastered surfaces	(?)	15	8.520	
	75.43	Hearth area and associated plastered surfaces	XVI	77	8.521	
	75.43	Hearth area and associated plastered surfaces	XVI	44	8.552	
S22:823 North	75.81	Ashy black layer	IX	42	8.563	8
	75.81	Ashy black layer	XVI	16	8.607	
	75.81	Ashy black layer	XVI	17	8.608	
	75.81	Ashy black layer	XVI	43	8.612	
	75.47	Ashy black layer	XVI	78	8.613	
	75.03	Ashy layer (Early Susiana-Archaic Susiana)	XVI	80	8.616	
	75.03	Ashy layer (Early Susiana-Archaic Susiana)	XVI	72	8.615	
	74.98	Ashy layer (Early Susiana-Archaic Susiana)	XVI	58	8.356	
S22:823 West	76.35	Ashy black layer	XVI	53	8.410	5
	75.94	Ashy black layer	XVI	15	8.449	
	75.94	Ashy black layer	XVI	72	8.564	
	75.90	Ashy black layer	XVI	101	8.565	
	75.90	Ashy black layer	XVI	50	8.566	
S22:825	75.95	Ashy layer (= S22:823)	XVI	13	8.895	1

Table 24. Loci with Early Susiana Pottery Marks (*cont.*)

Locus	Level	Locus Description	Family	Type	Reg. No.	Number
S22:826	75.02	Collapse, mixed debris (Early Susiana)	XVI	13	8.864	5
	75.02	Collapse, mixed debris (Early Susiana)	XVI	16	8.865	
	75.02	Collapse, mixed debris (Early Susiana)	XVI	54	8.866	
	75.02	Collapse, mixed debris (Early Susiana)	XVI	21	8.867	
	75.02	Collapse, mixed debris (Early Susiana)	XVI	17	8.910	
S22:827	75.51	Inside room (Early Susiana)	XVI	15	8.971	11
	75.51	Inside room (Early Susiana)	XVI	70	8.972	
	75.51	Inside room (Early Susiana)	XVI	16	8.973	
	75.13	Inside room(?)	XVI	91	8.880	
	74.93	Inside room(?)	XVI	13	8.892	
	74.93	Inside room(?)	XVI	41	8.893	
	74.78	Occupational debris below room	XVI	7	8.819	
	74.78	Occupational debris below room	XVI	15	8.930	
	74.78	Occupational debris below room	XVI	69A	8.931	
	74.76	Occupational debris below room	XVI	25	8.814	
	74.60	—	XVI	21	8.900	
S22:828	75.30	Inside room (Early Susiana)	XVI	8	8.444	2
	75.30	Inside room (Early Susiana)	XVI	15	8.443	
S22:830	75.69	Outside of Early Susiana room (828)	IX?	4	8.962	2
	75.69	Outside of Early Susiana room (828)	XVI	46	8.960	
S22:830 Middle	75.28	Outside of Early Susiana room (828)	XVI	65	8.381	2
	75.28	Outside of Early Susiana room (828)	XVI	65	8.959	
S22:830 South	75.23	Outside of Early Susiana room (828)	XVI	64	8.415	6
	75.23	Outside of Early Susiana room (828)	XVI	21	8.416	
	75.23	Outside of Early Susiana room (828)	XVI	90	8.417	
	75.23	Outside of Early Susiana room (828)	XVI	63	8.1500	
	74.99	Outside and under(?) Early Susiana room (828)	XVI	84	8.961	
	74.99	Outside and under(?) Early Susiana room (828)	IX	15	8.964	
S22:902 Northeast	76.82	—	XVI	6	—	1
S22:904	77.26	B.S. mixed debris	XVI	3	9.734	1
S22:912	74.73	Ashy layer (= 823?)	XVI	64	9.303	1
S22:914	75.76	Stone paving (street?) (Early Susiana)	XVI	17	9.258	5
	75.57	Stone paving (street?) (Early Susiana)	IX	81	9.725	
	75.57	Stone paving (street?) (Early Susiana)	(?)	38	9.731	
	75.57	Stone paving (street?) (Early Susiana)	XVI	83	9.732	
	75.32	Stone paving (street?) (Early Susiana)	XVI	15	9.735	
S22:919	75.61	Outside of Early Susiana room (= 830) stone and pebble pavement	XVI	60	9.767	1
S22:921	75.13	Ashy layer (= 823)	XVI	6	9.733	2
	74.95	—	XVI	5	9.766	
S22:923	74.85	Inside Early Susiana buttressed building occupational debris(?)	XVI	45	9.887	1
S17:401	83.10	Room (Protoliterate, out of context)	XVI	42	4.954	1
East Area	—	—	—	—	—	46
TOTAL						219

Early Susiana Family XVIII

C–D.20, .23, .80; proportion ca. "2," standard or gritty ware, occasionally painted

Figure 33; plates 62:CC–DD; 202:B

The oval basins are best known from materials excavated after the fifth season. Their ware is usually denser than that of the Family XVI vessels and their walls are fairly vertical and relatively thick. The lips are frequently flattened and some examples have semicircular indentations, two on one side on the most complete specimen, presumably balanced by another pair on the other side (VI-39 and pl. 202:B). Although the oval basins are primarily an undecorated category, occasional examples have a lattice painted on the exterior (pl. 62:CC–DD). The basins, unlike the flanged vessels of Family XVI, are not stained with bitumen on the interior, either because their denser paste made it unnecessary or because they served different functions. The basins could have been used as mixing bowls or feeding troughs or portable charcoal hearths. The semicircular indentations might have held skewers. However, fire smudges have not been found on the basins. The unpainted and painted varieties might have had different functions. Parallels for both types occur at Jafarabad.[154] A bowl from an Early Middle Susiana context in Trench XIII might be a debased descendant of the basins (pl. 168:K).

154. For a parallel to plate 62:CC–DD, see ibid., fig. 27:6 (not oval), 8–9 (not oval, wider lattices; Jafarabad, Levels 5b, 5a, 4). For a parallel to plate 202:B, see Dollfus 1975, fig. 13:8–9 (Jafarabad, Level 5b).

Table 25. Multiple Occurrences of Early Susiana Pottery Marks in Individual Loci

Mark	Type Clusters (cf. pl. 203)	Locus	Number of Examples	Accompanied by Other Types	Number of Examples	Total Number of Types
ᴐᴑ	15, 17	Q23:504	3	2, 13, 48, 52, 89	5	8
	15, 16, 17	S22:823	5	22, 27, 37, 47, 63, 66, 71, 79, 81, 82, 85	11	16
	15, 16	S22:827	3	7, 13, 21, 25, 41, 69A, 70, 91	8	11
⋀⋀	53	P22:606	1	3, 13, 19 (2 exx.), 20, 23, 32, 79	8	9
	63	Q23:502	1	4, 13+63, 20	3	4
Total			13		35	48

Early Susiana Family XIX

D.7; unpainted

Figure 33

This family number has been reserved for large vessels with their greatest diameter in the lower part of the body. However, no unmistakable example occurs at Chogha Mish, although the type is known in Level 5 at Jafarabad (Dollfus 1975, fig. 14:5).

Early Susiana Family XX

D.65; standard ware, painted exterior

Figure 33; plate 202:D–E

Large closed vessels are very rare, and no completely restorable body shapes have yet been found. However, painted neck and shoulder sherds indicate that jars with convex upper bodies and high vertical necks existed (pl. 202:D–E).

A neck sherd painted with typical Early Susiana designs proves that large closed vessels were made (pl. 202:E). However, they are extremely rare. The designs on the second example (pl. 202:D) are not specific for the Early Susiana period, although the wide neck and carination at the juncture of the neck and shoulder suggest a shape analogous to that of the small-closed jars of Family IV.[155]

ARCHAIC SUSIANA POTTERY

THE WARES

In the Archaic period, three basic categories of fabric can be distinguished according to tempering: straw or chaff, sand, or small grits. Naturally there are gradations between the categories; some chaff or straw might appear in the primarily mineral-tempered classes and vice versa. The three categories of fabric can be further subdivided into specific wares according to surface treat-

ment, presence of wash or slip, and type of decoration. The stratigraphic distribution of the more elaborate of these wares, in particular those with painted decoration, defines three distinct stages in the Archaic Susiana period. The most frequent category is the vegetal-tempered one, varieties of which occur as the standard pottery throughout this period.

Accordingly, the straw and chaff-tempered wares (smoothed, the dominant Archaic ware; coarse; red-washed; red-banded; painted-burnished, and matt-painted) are described first. Of these the painted-burnished ware is distinctive for the Archaic Susiana 1 phase, and the matt-painted for the Archaic Susiana 3 phase. The dense-sandy fabric, which occurs as plain red-washed and decorated red-line and dark-painted wares, is limited primarily to the Archaic Susiana 2 phase. The third category, the grit-tempered, consists of a single class of decorated pottery, the close-line ware of the Archaic Susiana 3 phase.

Straw-tempered Smoothed Ware: In this ware the paste was mixed with masses of vegetal tempering, usually rather large and coarse straw, making for a very porous fabric. The black stains on the interiors of many vessels indicate that bitumen was often used to decrease their porosity. In color the paste ranges from buff to a reddish orange and might have a gray or brownish core. Sherds with a uniform color on the exterior are rarer than those with the surface mottled buff through light orange to almost red. In the majority of cases the mottling must have been produced by the firing. Another important characteristic defining this ware is the smoothing of the exterior surface so that it is soft to the touch. This is true even though there might be many small cavities of burnt-out tempering. In some vessels the surface has been polished to a considerable sheen, at least in patches. Sometimes a thick white slip was applied and then smoothed.

An outstanding feature of this class of Archaic Susiana pottery, as well as of the related red-washed ware, is its manufacture in layers. Some vessels have three layers. The middle one was built up by superim-

---

155. Jafarabad, Level 4, provides one example of a large jar, but of a different, narrow-necked type (ibid., fig. 28:14).

posing strips of clay that were carefully dovetailed by fitting the concave lower edges over the rounded upper edges and pressing them together, then outer and inner layers of clay were added, and all three layers so successfully fused that they can only be distinguished in the few sherds broken along planes of cleavage (pls. 65:G; 205:B). Both the outer and inner surfaces were smoothed. Sometimes only two layers can be distinguished, an inner layer of strips and a thick outer layer (pl. 205:A). A wash of red pigment was added on the exterior (cf. pls. 65:G; 205:A).

A massive base of straw-tempered smoothed ware consists of two horizontal layers of clay, to whose rounded ends the thick body wall was attached; thin outer layers of clay massed the inner structure (pl. 205:G). A smaller base was made in two parts: a slab of clay attached to a lower one with a triangular profile, thus producing a concavity in the center (pl. 205:F). On the whole, however, painted vessels and small vessels of plain ware do not show layers and were presumably shaped by paddling and pinching. Occasionally a basket was used as a mold for the inner layer of a vessel; when dry enough, this was lifted out and an outer layer of clay was pressed into the basketry imprints, producing vessels indistinguishable from strip-made examples (pl. 205:C–D). Presumably most of the smoothed and red-washed vessels were built up in parts, which were then so tightly welded together that only a tiny minority of examples show their inner structure.

Straw-tempered smoothed pottery is the standard ware of the Archaic Susiana period. It was in use throughout all three phases of the Archaic Susiana and seems not to have changed appreciably during what might have been a considerable extent of time. This ware is thus of outstanding importance as an indicator of continuity in the Archaic Susiana period.

Straw-tempered Coarse Ware: Fundamentally this ware is the same as the preceding, the difference being the omission of the smoothing so that the surface remains slightly bumpy and rough. There are some cases, however, where there is also an actual difference in fabric: namely, sherds so filled with straw that they are noticeably lighter than smoother sherds of comparable size. The coarse ware sherds are of a relatively drab brownish-buff color and have no mottled surfaces. As a rule, they are somewhat thicker than the smoothed sherds. Presumably they belonged to the rougher domestic utensils, though it is odd that they are considerably rarer than smoothed ware sherds.

Straw-tempered Standard and Fine Red-washed Wares: The standard red-washed ware is essentially the same as the ordinary smoothed ware except for the pigment on the exterior. However, the paste is sometimes more porous and lighter in weight because of a great amount of straw tempering. The color of the paste is fre-

quently brown or grayish buff rather than the reddish orange common in the smoothed ware. The sherds are fairly thick and come from large vessels. The red wash tends to be fugitive and is normally matt without any traces of burnish. Occasionally a standard red-washed vessel is found with all of its color detached and adhering to the soil.

The fine red-washed ware is rarer and more specialized, consisting of vessels somewhat smaller and thinner than those of the standard red-washed ware. The paste is often quite dense, with a limited amount of straw. In color it ranges from light orange to buff, probably a function of firing as both colors can occur on a single sherd. Normally both exterior and interior are thickly covered with the wash, which is deeper in color than that of the standard red-washed ware, sometimes approaching a brown or purple hue and often mottled in the same sherd. Another important characteristic is the frequency of burnishing: the fine red-washed sherds often have a considerable sheen.

The fine red-washed ware is characteristic for the Archaic Susiana 1 phase. The standard red-washed ware was also in use at that time, but is more prominent in the Archaic Susiana 2 phase. A matt red wash still occasionally covers an entire vessel in the Archaic Susiana 3 phase, although by then it was usually used only on the lower parts of some carinated matt-painted vessels.

Straw-tempered Red-banded Ware: This group is distinguished from the smoothed and standard red-washed wares only by its surface treatment, namely, the application of red pigment to part of the surface, usually in bands but occasionally in more complex patterns. Sometimes the paint seems to have been smeared with irregular or hazy edges; in other cases the sharp edges suggest that the patterns were painted with a brush.

The size and thickness of the sherds indicate that the vessels of the red-banded ware were fairly large, but few reconstructible forms have yet been obtained. Fortunately one of the better-preserved fragments proves that a continuous red wash over the upper body could be combined with red bands below (pl. 220:F). It is a reminder that sherds classified respectively as standard red-washed and red-banded ware might in reality have been upper and lower parts of vessels with the same combination of features. The red-banded ware flourished during the middle phase of the Archaic Susiana period, occurring in the same levels as the red-line ware described below.

Straw-tempered Painted-burnished Ware: The fabric of this ware, too, is essentially the same as that of the straw-tempered smoothed ware, supplemented by refinements in the surface treatment. The color of the paste varies from light buff to yellowish tan, brown, or orange. It often has a marked gray or black core. A slip was needed over the straw-filled paste to provide a uniform and smoothed surface for the painted decoration. In the majority of cases the interiors as well as the exteriors were slipped. Normally the slip is a light yellowish buff. The bonding of the slip to the fabric was not always sufficiently firm to survive millennia in the earth; sometimes even restorable forms retain only a few tiny specks of their original slip. In such cases the numerous cavities left by large segments of straw are prominent and make the basic identity of the painted-burnished and the other straw-tempered wares particularly evident. The designs were executed in a dark brown paint; a few examples are black. After painting the entire vessel was burnished on the exterior to a high gloss. The surfaces of the interiors vary from a full burnish to slightly burnished or matt. The gloss, when well preserved, and the creamy slip are so characteristic that sherds can be identified as painted-burnished ware even when they come from the undecorated parts of the vessels.

In addition to the standard painted-burnished sherds, others without the normal creamy slip appear. On these the surfaces were either self-slipped or given a thin coating of the same kind of clay that was mixed with straw to form the paste. Sometimes straw cavities show through on the surface. The color of the surface is either orange or, more often, mottled orange and yellowish-buff. On these sherds the burnished surface is not always as shiny as on the standard painted-burnished fragments. This is particularly noticeable on the paint, which sometimes has relatively little sheen and, when worn, none at all. This variant of the painted-burnished ware is characteristic for Family XLVIII. The painted-burnished ware is found in the lower occupation levels at Chogha Mish and is the most prominent ceramic indicator of the Archaic Susiana 1 phase.

Matt-painted Ware: Unlike the vegetal tempering of the wares so far described, that of the matt-painted ware consists for the most part of finer particles. As a result the fabric is often somewhat denser than that of the regular straw-tempered wares. There is, however, considerable variation in the amount of chaff present, so that some sherds are lighter in weight and more porous than others. The standard color is yellow buff; the paste might be somewhat browner. The surfaces might show a slight pink or light orange suffusion. Gray cores do occur, particularly in the thicker walls (ca. 1.00–1.50 cm); they are not markedly distinct median cores as in the painted-burnished ware but wide areas, sometimes amounting almost to the total sherd. Often it is difficult to determine whether a separate slip was added or whether the surfaces of the vessels were merely well smoothed before painting. The latter is likely in the majority of cases. The ware takes its name from the thin dull gray or black paint used to decorate the upper parts of the vessels. However, occasionally a vessel was smoothed sufficiently after painting to produce at least some patches with sheen (pls. 64:G–H; 215:D–E).

A special variety of the matt-painted ware is represented by sherds or vessels on which the normal painted zone is supplemented by a red wash on the lower part of the body and sometimes on the lip. The red wash is rather fugitive and as preserved is probably of a duller color than originally. Some of the bichrome sherds have a finer, denser fabric than the standard fragments and often a cream slip. The matt-painted ware is one of the distinguishing characteristics of the final phase of the Archaic Susiana period.

The Dense-sandy Wares: Typical of this group is the absence of any tempering visible to the naked eye. The paste is dense, giving the impression of having been made from sandy silt or from well-levigated clay without obvious grains of mineral tempering. Sometimes the imprints of small amounts of chaff remain. The color is a rather pinkish brown or orange, sometimes ranging into gray in the core. The surfaces are rather even although there are no visible signs of wet smoothing or polishing, nor of slips. The dense-sandy ware vessels are usually relatively small and thin-walled.

Four dense-sandy wares can be distinguished on the basis of their surface treatment: (1) plain ware with no wash now visible; (2) red-washed ware covered by a continuous red fugitive coating; (3) red-line ware on which the same fugitive red pigment appears as paint; and (4) dark-painted ware on which the pigment is fast. Among these categories the dark-painted ware is the rarest, represented by only a few sherds distinctive not only for their dark paint but also for their simple decoration, the windowpane motif (pl. 217:E), unrelated to that of the red-line ware (see Families XIV, XVI). The red-line ware is the most frequently found of the dense-sandy group and occurs in a number of shapes with a variety of painted motifs (Families XIII, XVII). Occasionally red-line vessels have a red wash (pl. 218:F, H) or red bands (pl. 219:A, C) below the carination (pl. 218:F–H). The stratigraphic distribution of the dense-sandy wares indicates that they are typical for the middle phase of the Archaic Susiana period.

Close-line Ware: Among the Archaic Susiana wares, one stands out from all the others because of its grit tempering. The grits are clearly visible but small and of uniform size, in great contrast to the irregular sizes of the Early Susiana grits. It is accordingly possible to distinguish the normal Early Susiana wares from the close-line ware by the character of the grits alone. The close-line ware does not have the large admixture of straw tempering found in the Early Susiana standard ware. On the other hand, the close-line ware is similar to the fine gritty ware of the Early Susiana period, in that both are dense and have very fine grits, but those of the close-line ware are more uniform in size and the paste of individual specimens is more uniform in color. The paste of the close-line ware is often a light grayish or greenish buff but might sometimes be rather yellowish or, rarely, light orange buff. In some cases a slip of almost the same color as the paste is visible, but on many sherds the presence of a slip is not certain.

The close-line ware vessels were normally painted with a black or dark brown pigment, apparently applied in dilute form so that it flowed on evenly without forming thick droplets or crackling. It does not have variations in tint comparable to those of Middle Susiana paints. The paint did not sink into the vessel paste similar to a stain. Occasionally part of a vessel was stained with the same fugitive red pigment used on the bichrome variety of the matt-painted ware. Like that ware, the close-line ware is a feature for the Archaic Susiana 3 phase, being a common constituent of the assemblage.

THE FAMILIES OF ARCHAIC SUSIANA POTTERY
(Figs. 34–35, 37)

In analyzing the forms of the Archaic Susiana pottery, there is both a simpler and a more complicated situation than in dealing with those of the later periods. It is simpler since the range of forms is more limited. The majority are open; true closed forms are almost nonexistent. On the other hand, the task is complicated first by the undifferentiated character of some shapes, with attendant difficulties in classifying the forms, and, secondly, by the greater diversity of the wares. For example, the bulk of the pottery of the later Susiana periods, aside from the red ware groups, could be subdivided by shape into single sequences of families without reference to the variations of the buff ware. In contrast, in defining the Archaic Susiana families, the distinctive wares of which the vessels are made necessarily play a major role. Thus, in the case of the close-line, matt-painted, dense-sandy, and painted-burnished wares, the classification of the shapes are applied within the framework of the individual wares rather than across the whole range of the Archaic Susiana pottery. The vessels made of the variants of the standard straw-tempered ware, namely smoothed, coarse, red-washed, and red-banded, are arranged in a single sequence of forms. The families of the Archaic Susiana pottery are presented in the following order: close-line ware (Families I–IV), matt-painted ware (Families VII–XII), dense-sandy plain, red-washed, and dark-painted wares (Families XIII–XVII), dense-sandy red-line ware (Families XVIII–XXIV), straw-tempered wares except the painted-burnished (Families XXV–XLIV), and the painted-burnished ware (Families XLV–LIV).

Archaic Susiana Family I

> B–C.05; close-line ware, proportion "2," painted exterior

> Figure 34; plates 63:A; 206:A–C

The bowls with incurving lips, either blunt or inbeveled, are rare. They bear distinctive decoration, hatched triangles placed symmetrically along a horizontal band so as to form a frieze of lozenges. A bowl with a basket handle provides an elegant example of tectonic design (pl. 206:A). Its handle is decorated with horizontal bands that are carried down to the upper wall as pairs of horizontal lines. The two "root" panels of the handle bisect the band of lozenges so that the painted composition echoes the bilateral shape established by the handle. In the Early Susiana period bowls of Early Susiana Families VIII and IX carry on the shape of this family and occasionally variants of its decorative scheme occur (pl. 61:T).

Archaic Susiana Family II

> C.07, .14; close-line ware, painted exterior and interior

> Figure 34; plates 63:B–D; 206:D–M

Bowls with flaring lips and a sinuous profile, sometimes sharpened to a definite angle, can be established as a specific family by their shape and divided into subfamilies consisting of shallower (proportion 1) and deeper (proportion 2) examples respectively. Specific decorative patterns are associated with each subclass.

The shallower vessels, Subfamily IIa, have on the exterior only a few thick bands, sometimes quite widely spread. On some sherds the interior decoration is limited to horizontal wavy lines clustered near the lip (pls. 63:C; 206:E); there were almost certainly patterns in the center. Sometimes the interiors were covered with a dense network of meander-like bands (pls. 63:B, D; 206:H, J) or registers of hatched triangles producing a negative zigzag (pl. 206:D, F–G). These concentrically arranged motifs originally enclosed a central circular pattern. The small portion of one motif (pl. 206:I) can be restored as crossing lines and crosshatched triangles; it is surrounded by lines and a narrow hatched band. In addition, this small sherd is of particular importance as proof that the Subfamily IIa bowls could have pedestals. The sherd's lower break shows clearly the smoothly finished base of the bowl and some of the clay solder by which the foot had been scoured. Another fragment with the juncture of the pedestal is unpainted on the interior (pl. 206:K). The paint on the bottom of a foot has been destroyed by wear; the absence of interior decoration and the exterior peg design are characteristic (pl. 206:L).

Characteristic for the deeper bowls, Subfamily IIb, is the markedly close spacing of bands that almost coalesce into solid masses of color (pl. 206:M). Most of the

ARCHAIC SUSIANA

Scale 1:5

CLOSE-LINE WARE

MATT−PAINTED WARE

Figure 34. Archaic Susiana Families I–VI (Close-line Ware) and VII–XII (Matt-painted Ware)

exterior is covered by opposed groups of diagonal strokes leaving reserved triangles. On the interior a wavy line separates the wide lip band from the narrower bands that cover most of the surface.

The bowls of Family II are so far represented only by fragments. A few establish that some Subfamily IIa bowls had pedestals. Perhaps the two categories of interior decoration of IIa, the clusters of wavy lines at the lip and the overall painting, were specific respectively for bowls with slightly concave bases and those with pedestals. It is also possible that the Subfamily IIb bowls were mounted on pedestals; an Early Susiana bowl from Jafarabad with a design derived from that of the Subfamily IIb bowls has a pedestal.[156] A comparison shows clearly the lineage of some of the Early Susiana Family XVII bowls (cf. pls. 201:G; 206:M), as well as the debased Early Susiana rendering of the taut strokes of the close-line prototypes.[157] Exact parallels for the Family II bowls occur in the Deh Luran plain. Much farther away, a somewhat similar type was found on the surface of an early mound in the Warka area.[158]

Archaic Susiana Family III

> A–D.11, .12, .14, .39; usually proportion "1," close-line ware
>
> Figure 34; plates 63:E–F, K–L; 207:A–M; 208:A–G; 209:A–E; 210:A

Angled shapes, sometimes sharply carinated, squat proportions, and prominent painted decoration on both exterior and interior characterize the commonest close-line family. Several subfamilies are distinguished by size, shape, or the designs on their exteriors. Subfamily IIIa accommodates some atypical small specimens; the larger carinated bowls, the most frequent representatives of the close-line ware, are divided by their exterior motifs into those with alternating panels of crosshatching and linked vertical lines (Subfamily IIId). Subfamily IIId is also distinguished by its shape; the upper walls slope at least slightly inward.

Subfamily IIIa (B.14; pls. 65:E–F; 207:A–C): The two smaller examples have unpainted interiors, and outside triangles, an atypical motif for the exterior (pls.

63:E; 207:A, C). Although the location of the motifs is conventional, on the larger example the triangle on the interior is unusual for its crosshatching (pls. 63:F; 207:B).

Subfamily IIIb (C.11, .12, .14; exterior with Xs; pls. 63:I, K–L; 207:D–M; 208:A–C): The majority of the numerous Subfamily IIIb bowls are "C" sizes, with only rare larger examples (pls. 63:I; 208:B–C). The dominant shape is convex below the carination and concave above (.14). The bases when preserved are concave: the low proportions provided scope for painted decoration inside and out. On the exterior continuous friezes of simple Xs are the most frequent (pls. 63:G; 207:D–H, K–M; 208:A–B; 5.096) but Xs of double (pls. 63:I–J; 207:I; 208:C) or triple (pl. 207:J) lines also occur. The three-line Xs are used as individual groups rather than a continuous frieze. The same is true of the four-line Xs of a miniature Family III bowl (pls. 63:F; 207:B). Three motifs are standard for the interior walls. By far the commonest are the triangles suspended from the lip, these being normally hatched except for a reserved band with dots (pls. 63:G; 207:D, L–M); the filling of the reserved band by a "butterfly" is unique (pl. 207:F). Occasionally more than one dotted band appears (pls. 63:K; 207:E), or the hatching of the triangles are completely filled by braided hatching (pl. 207:G–H). The hatched triangles on a coarsely painted bowl are typical and probably represent a final stage of the cross-line ware (pl. 208:A). The other standard, but rarer, motifs of the interior are horizontal wavy lines (pl. 208:B) similar to those on some Subfamily IIa bowls (pl. 206:E) and groups of three or four straight vertical lines, usually linked by cross strokes (pls. 63:I, L; 207:J; 208:C; 6.056), but sometimes independent (pl. 207:I). In at least some cases, the center of the bowl was also painted, as on an example with windmill motifs (pl. 207:K).[159]

Subfamily IIIc (C–D.12, .14; exterior with diagonal bands; pls. 208:D, F–G, possibly E; 209:A–B): Cari-

156. See Dollfus 1975, fig. 19:5 (Jafarabad, Level 5b).

157. See ibid., fig. 20:2 (Jafarabad, Level 6) for an Early Susiana Family XVII sherd similar to Archaic Susiana Subfamily IIb prototypes on the interior, but with only solid wash, instead of diagonal strokes, on the exterior.

158. For parallels to plates 63:C and 206:E, see Hole 1977, fig. 50:a, pl. 34:d (Chogha Sefid, Chogha Mami Transitional phase); ibid., pl. 34:a, f (out of context). For a parallel to plates 63:B, D and 206:H, J, see ibid., fig. 51:c, f. For parallels to plate 206:I, see ibid., pls. 36:j, 36:k. For a type possibly related to plate 206:M, see Adams and Nissen 1972, fig. 66:6 (Warka survey, Site 298).

159. For parallels to plates 63:G and 207:D, L–M, see Dollfus 1975, figs. 17:1, 29:3 (Jafarabad, Level 6); Hole 1977, fig. 50:d (Xs more attenuated; Chogha Sefid, Chogha Mami Transitional phase), pl. 35:a (for interior design only), b; for interior interrupted triangles only, see Oates 1969, pl. 32:3–4 (Chogha Mami Transitional phase). For a parallel to plate 207:G–H (interior design only), see Hole 1977, pl. 35:e (Chogha Sefid, out of context). For a parallel to plate 207:I, see ibid., pl. 34:c (exterior single Xs). For parallels to plates 63:I–J, 207:I (double Xs), and 207:J (shape), see ibid., fig. 50:c (hatched triangle on interior); Wright et al., 1981, fig. 11:6 (single X exterior; Farukhabad, out of context). For a parallel to plate 208:A, see Dollfus 1975, fig. 29:3 (Jafarabad, Level 6); for same designs in standard close-line style, see Hole 1977, fig. 50:c (interior design only), pl. 35:f (Chogha Sefid, Chogha Mami Transitional phase). For parallels to plate 208:B, see ibid., fig. 50:b; Wright et al., 1981, fig. 11:a (without dots on exterior; Farukhabad, out of context).

nated bowls decorated on the exterior by groups of diagonal lines are rarer than those with Xs. The alternating slant of blocks of diagonal lines is typical for close-line painting and was also used to form designs on other families (Families V–VI). The treatment of the interior varies according to the stance of the upper walls. The more flaring examples have designs comparable to those of Subfamily IIIb bowls: linked groups of vertical lines (pl. 208:F), horizontal bands clustered below a solid and a wavy lip band (pl. 208:G), and some rare interrupted triangles found after the fifth season. When the upper walls are fairly vertical the interior painting is limited to a solid and a wavy lip band (pls. 208:D; 209:B) and probably to only a solid band on an example where the lip is missing (pl. 209:A).

The thickening still preserved at the lower break of one example (pl. 208:D) shows that it had a pedestal foot that would presumably have resembled another (pl. 208:E) since all the pedestal fragments of close-line ware are bulbous and have identical hatched bands at the base (pl. 206:L).[160]

Subfamily IIId (C–D.39; dominant exterior motif, alternating panels of crosshatching and vertical linked lines; pls. 209:C–E; 210:A): The rarest of all the carinated bowls are those whose upper walls slant inward. One of the examples is much larger than the normal Family III bowls (pl. 209:E). Two exterior designs occur, both unknown on the other subfamilies of Family III. One design consists of closely crosshatched rectangles alternating with linked vertical lines obviously related to one type of interior decoration (pls. 207:I–J; 208:C, F). However, on the Subfamily IIId bowls, each of the vertical groups consists of only two bands, which are broad and almost contiguous. Moreover, the groups are linked by chevrons more elaborate and placed at a higher level than most of the linking strokes of Subfamilies IIIb–c. The resulting frieze of bilateral elements can be, with some imagination, visualized as a row of human figures holding hands in a fashion impossible in the case of the interior linked designs of Subfamilies IIIb–c.[161]

The second exterior design of Subfamily IIId is unique, diagonal bands densely filled with hatching and

hourglasses (pl. 210:A). In its interior design of interrupted triangles, the bowl resembles Subfamily IIIb bowls more than the other Subfamily IIId bowls, which have either simple lip bands or no painting at all.

Archaic Susiana Family IV

C.142; close-line ware, primary painting on exterior

Figure 34; plates 63:M–N; 210:B–E

Bowls allied in shape to Subfamilies IIIc–d vessels with fairly vertical concave upper walls have a distinctive exterior decoration (pls. 63:M–N; 210:B–E; 6.077). Three elements fill the space between lip and carination: a solid band, a double register with alternating groups of paired and multiple lines, and a zone in which a wide reserved zigzag, or in one case wavy (pl. 210:B) zone is filled with from one to three narrow black lines. The interiors have a lip band more often than not banded below by a wavy line. The workmanship ranges from an even profile and taut painting (pl. 210:B–D) to a sloppy lip and brushwork (pl. 210:E).[162]

Archaic Susiana Family V

C.20, .21, .22, .23, .31; close-line ware, painted exterior

Figure 34; plates 63:O–P; 210:F–J; 211:A–F

Cylindrical shapes of definitely higher proportions than the bowls of the preceding close-line families and with characteristic decoration make up Family V. The only interior painting is a lip band. On the exterior the painting, as is normal for the close-line ware, covers the entire surface above either the carination or the basal angle. Normally, a horizontal band bisects the space to be decorated and the designs are placed symmetrically on either side of it. Areas of reserved background function as actively in the designs as the painted elements. Friezes of opposing chevrons, either of single lines or clusters, separated by hourglasses and lozenges, were produced in two ways, by combining symmetrically two registers of either interrupted triangles and single diagonal lines (pls. 210:G–I; 211:A) or of clusters of opposing diagonal lines (pls. 210:F; 211:D–F). The latter are the design of Subfamily IIIc except that there the triangles separating the opposing diagonal lines remain only as negative reserved background, while in the doubled versions of Family IV they have become positive, either completely hatched (pl. 211:D) or equipped with small solid triangles (pl. 211:E–F). In addition to the standard patterns of Family IV, a unique composition of vertical elements occurs (pl. 210:J).

---

160. For parallels to plate 208:E, see Hole 1977, fig. 50:f (Chogha Sefid, Chogha Mami Transitional phase); Oates 1969, pl. 32:6 (with trace of pedestal and vertical-line clusters linked by chevrons; Chogha Mami, Chogha Mami Transitional phase). For a coarser version of the exterior only related to plate 209:A, see ibid., pl. 32:2 (Chogha Mami, Chogha Mami Transitional phase).

161. For parallels to plate 209:D–E, see Hole 1977, pl. 44:a–d (linked elements separated by vertical bands, presumably no interior lip band; Chogha Sefid, out of context); Dollfus 1975, fig. 25:4 (Jafarabad, Level 5a, Early Susiana); Le Breton 1947, fig. 12:809 (Jafarabad, 3.50–6.00 m, Early Susiana).

162. For a parallel to plates 63:M–N and 210:B–E, see Hole 1977, pls. 38:i, s, v–x (out of context); 38:k, n–o, q, u; 39:g–c (Chogha Sefid, Chogha Mami Transitional levels); for related examples, see Ippolitoni 1970/71, fig. 5:5, 7 (Tell es-Sawwan, Levels IIIa, IIIb).

Archaic Susiana Family VI

> C.23, B–C.24, C.74, C.75; close-line ware, main decoration exterior; neck band interior

> Figure 34; plates 63:Q–W; 211:G–S; 212:A–J

Family VI is divided into two subfamilies that differ rather considerably in shape but share certain design elements. Examples of Subfamily VIa are rare, while Subfamily VIb is, after Subfamily IIIb, the more common category of the close-line ware.

Subfamily VIa (C.23:B–C.24; pls. 63:Q; 211:G–K): The shapes vary from fairly squat carinated bowl type (pl. 211:G) to more rounded and apparently deeper forms (pl. 211:H–K). Although one example (pl. 211:G) is similar in shape to an Archaic Susiana bowl (pl. 210:H), it has the distinctive decoration of Subfamily VIa. The wide, everted mouths are surrounded by a peg pattern, a simplified version of the upper decoration of Family IV, which marks this part of the vessels off sharply from the lower part (pl. 211:G–I). Clusters of opposed diagonal lines separated by crosshatched triangles (pl. 211:G) are shared with Subfamily VIb. Solid horizontal bands at intervals with a narrow hatched band, a combination applied to the interior of an Archaic Susiana bowl sherd (pl. 206:I), seem to have been typical for Subfamily VIa. A sherd with a variant of this type of decoration probably belonged to a large Subfamily VIa vessel (pl. 211:K).

Subfamily VIb (C.60, .74, .75; pls. 63:R–W; 211:L–S; 212:A–J): In Subfamily VIb the segmentation of the body adumbrated in the decoration of Subfamily VIa is now marked. This is the only group of closed vessels in the close-line ware. They have fairly wide and usually flaring necks and fairly squat bodies. These are often sharply carinated but sometimes curve more roundly toward the base. The decoration was applied tectonically, with three main registers, on the neck and on the body at or near the root of the neck and near the carination, unified by groups of horizontal bands. The lower body was left unpainted. The normal neck decoration consists of the familiar groups of opposed diagonal lines (pls. 63:S–T; 170:L–N, Q; 212:A–E); vertical bands and Xs (pl. 212:F) are exceptional. Subfamily VIb necks do not carry the peg patterns typical for the lip frieze of Family IV and Subfamily VIa bowls and the basal frieze of the Subfamily IIa pedestals. Thus small sherds can be identified as necks or feet of their respective families. Characteristic for necks, but not for feet, is the interior lip band, sometimes finished at the bottom by scallops or a second, narrower, band (pl. 211:L–N, Q).

The main register of the body is decorated by either a zigzag reserved in a solid or crosshatched field and houses one or more positive zigzags (pl. 212:B–C, G–H) or variations on the theme of opposed clusters of diagonal lines. The simplest is an enlarged version of the

neck pattern (pl. 212:I), in others the triangular spaces between the diagonal spaces are crosshatched (pl. 212:A, D), and in still other variations the diagonal bands are also crosshatched (pl. 212:E, J).

The third register, the white reserved one on the upper body, is the most variable. When narrow it contains simple geometric filling motifs (pls. 211:M, Q–R; 212:A, C–D) and when larger it contains representational motifs. The stylized quadruped and flying bird are easily recognizable (pls. 63:U–V; 211:O–P); a more complicated motif (pl. 211:S) is harder to identify with certainty but is probably a scorpion. It has the same three parts, tail, body, appendages, including large projecting claws, as scorpions represented on the somewhat later Samarra ware but is less realistic. The scorpions from Samarra itself even have the correct number of legs, four pairs, and other naturalistic details. A simpler Samarra version on a sherd from Chogha Mish provides a somewhat closer parallel.[163] A detail on its tail, the oval enclosing two dots, remains enigmatic. On its lowest part there appears to be a second reserved register with a representational motif. The presence of two reserved registers is so far unique.

Despite the prominence of the Subfamily VIb jar sherds at Chogha Mish, there are hardly any contemporary parallels.[164] The group is important in the ceramic sequence at Chogha Mish as ancestors both in shape and decoration of the Early Susiana Family IV vessels and, in a wider context, for connections with the Samarra pottery of northern Mesopotamia.

Archaic Susiana Family VII

> C.04, .05, .11; matt-painted ware

> Figure 34; plate 213:A–D

This family is the least coherent of the matt-painted families since it was set up to accommodate sherds belonging to conical bowls of varying shapes and sizes. The exteriors were painted down to the carination or to somewhat below the greatest diameter. Footed rectangles, a motif specific to the matt-painted wares, decorate a small carinated bowl (pl. 213:B) and a large vessel whose shape can be conjecturally restored (pl. 213:D). The latter represents a standard type since a number of sherds of similar thickness and design have been found. A carinated bowl (pl. 213:C) has polka-dot accents in white paint on the angles of its chevron bands. This is a rare elaboration of the matt-painted

---

163. For examples, see Herzfeld 1930, pls. 1:2, 5; 2:3; 3; 4; 5:4 (Samarra); Oates 1968, pl. 8:15 (Serik); Oates 1969, pl. 31:d (Chogha Mami).

164. For parallels to plates 63:S and 212:C, G–H, see Hole 1977, pl. 41:h–i (Chogha Sefid, out of context). For design and presumably shape analogous to plate 212:D, H, see ibid., pl. 41:j.

technique, which reappears on an Family VIII bowl (pl. 213:F). The interiors are unpainted except for the scallops at the lip of one example (pl. 213:A). Such interior lip bands are standard for the matt-painted ware.[165]

Archaic Susiana Family VIII

B.22, C.20, .22; matt-painted ware

Figure 34; plate 213:E–K

A rather common group of matt-painted vessels is characterized by its relatively shallow cylindrical form and decoration of chevron friezes. These frequently consist of only one wide band, either solid or crosshatched. When there is more than one chevron band, they are narrower (pl. 213:F, K). The reserved triangles delimited by the chevron bands might be left empty or occupied by small filling motifs. On the whole, the decoration on the Family VIII bowls tends to be fairly open, with considerable amount of the background unpainted, but this was not always the case (pl. 213:F).

Some Family VIII bowls are mounted on three blunt-edged legs. The entire shape of an example from Boneh Fazili (pl. 213:H) can be restored and serves to identify sherds from Chogha Mish (6.087). A red wash covers the lower part of the Boneh Fazili bowl and parts of its legs. This is the first example of the bichrome treatment typical for a number of matt-painted vessels.

Archaic Susiana Family IX

C.22, D.22; matt-painted ware

Figure 34; plates 64:A–B, D, H; 214:A–D; 215:B–D

In shape the vessels of this family are essentially the same as those of the preceding group, that is globular bowls with no carinations interrupting the smooth curvature of their walls, but they are frequently larger. A relatively small bowl (pl. 214:A) preserved almost to the base, can be used as a model for reconstructing lip sherds of larger vessels of the family. Usually the lips curve markedly inward. They vary in shape from blunt to flattened inbeveled forms.

The decoration provides the primary distinction between Families VIII and IX vessels. In place of the chevron friezes of Family VIII, the greater part of the body of Family IX bowls is decorated by a bold checkerboard of crosshatched and reserved rectangles. Normally the unpainted rectangles are filled by a geometric motif, the commonest element being the hollow cross. It appears singly (pls. 64:A; 214:B) or in vertical (pls. 64:B; 214:A, C–E) or in diagonal (pl. 214:F) chains of varying length. Other filling motifs are crosshatched lozenges and triangles (pl. 214:G), solid lozenges (pls. 64:F; 214:J; 215:D); pairs of chevrons (pls. 214:H; 215:C) or vertical lines (pl. 215:D), butterflies (pl. 215:A) and a tripartite design (pl. 215:B). A row of scallops or triangles usually decorates the interior of the lip. The Family IX bowls form a major category of the matt-painted ware.

Archaic Susiana Family X

C.24; matt-painted ware

Figure 34

Vessels with somewhat sinuous sides are so far represented only by an example found in the sixth season. The base is rounded and unfinished, which indicates the presence originally of a separately-made foot. The chevron bands, so closely spaced as to blend together into almost completely solid wide ribbons encircling the body, break at one point to admit a single vertical motif, a zigzag. The lower body and the lip of the vessel are covered by red wash.

Archaic Susiana Family XI

C.39; matt-painted ware

Figure 34; plates 64:J; 215:H–J; 216:A–B

Carinated vessels consisting of two conical elements joined at their widest points have relatively straight or somewhat convex lower walls. The center of gravity is either nearer the base than the mouth or about midway between them. The upper body, the more prominent part of the vessels, bears the decoration. The lower body and sometimes the flattened lip were covered by a red wash.

Although Family XI vessels are rare, they can be divided into two groups by variations in their shape. In Subfamily XIa the upper walls are straight or convex (pl. 215:H, J). The vessels of Subfamily XIb have somewhat concave vertical upper walls and are higher in their proportions than those of Subfamily XIa (pl. 216:A–B). Both groups are decorated by chevron friezes bordered by triangles at the lip and carination. This is one of the two dominant patterns of the matt-painted ware; it occurs also on Families VII and X vessels. Apparently, it was standard for the friezes to be interrupted at one point by a vertical element, although only a few examples are preserved; for example, frontal human figures rendered in a simple geometric style (pl. 215:H–I). One is female; the gesturing figure might be male. Similar, but by no means identical, figures occur on a unique sherd found at Chogha Mami in a mixed deposit of transitional and Samarra sherds.[166]

165. For a parallel to plates 213:D and 195:F, see Dollfus 1975, fig. 29:5–6 (Jafarabad, Levels 5b, 6).

166. For a parallel to plate 215:H–I, see Oates 1969, pl. 31:b (Chogha Mami, mixed Chogha Mami Transitional).

Archaic Susiana Family XII

> C–D.44; matt-painted ware

> Figure 34; plate 216:C–G

Sherds of one vessel sufficient to indicate its shape from the mouth to the concave base suggest a definition of Family XII as a family of large vessels, transitional between C and D sizes, with an incurving upper body and a definite, though rounded, carination (pl. 216:G). Family XII shares its decoration of filled checkerboard designs with the vessels of Family IX. The latter are distinguished from Family XII by their barrel-like bodies without carination, which provided no precise lower boundary for the painting. In contrast, in Family XII the carination, even though rounded, gives a definite limit, higher up on the vessel, below which the painting could not be extended without violating the tectonic relationship between it and the form. Unfortunately, most of the Families IX and XII vessels are represented only by sherds small in proportion to the total body area. In the plates an attempt has been made to assign lip sherds to their respective families, but this can sometimes only tentatively be done. Two vessels (pl. 215:E–F) in particular, which by shape could belong to Families IX or XII, do not have the checkerboard pattern standard for these families and remain unattributed; the decoration of one (pl. 215:F) is identical with that of another (pl. 213:D) and the filling motif of the other (pl. 215:E) probably represents a bird.

Archaic Susiana Family XIII

> B.00, C.03, .04; dense wares, sandy or vegetal tempering, unpainted or painted

> Figure 35; plate 217:A–E

The sherds included in this family are examples of simple conical shapes, either straight-sided or somewhat convex. Otherwise they do not form a unified group. When sufficient examples are recovered, it might well be possible to break up the present "family" into more coherent groups, such as small unpainted cups (pl. 217:A) and shallow bowls (pl. 217:B) or larger bowls with simple diagonal line or ladder patterns in red paint (pl. 217:C–E).

Archaic Susiana Family XIV

> B–C.04, .05, .39; dense ware with vegetal tempering, black paint sometimes combined with red wash

> Figure 35; plate 217:F–K

Family XIV accommodates rare sherds that are given a special character by their small size, well smoothed or burnished exteriors, and refined painting. Usually, the greatest diameters are at most only somewhat over 12 cm. Two fragments of small bowls are painted with vertical or diagonal windowpane designs on a mottled surface or over a red wash (pl. 217:G–H). A red-washed, burnished pedestal base supported a bowl (cf. pl. 217:A) with a ladder design on a plain ground (pl. 217:F). A parallel from Chogha Sefid for the two windowpane bowls is classified by Hole as "Sialk Black-on-Red" ware because of its similarity to sherds that he collected from the surface of the North Mound at Sialk.[167] At Chogha Mish the rarity of sherds with windowpane pattern might indicate that they are not indigenous. If they were imports, the contrast must have been of long duration, as they occur in both the Archaic Susiana 2 and 3 phases.

With the typical windowpane examples might be associated, at least provisionally, three fragments, each the only one of its kind. On a bowl sherd (pl. 217:J; cf. pl. 217:F), the painted decoration is placed on the reserved ground of the vessel with the area below red-washed. The upper part of what was probably a cylindrical vessel had two registers of stepped rectangles and on the interior a zone of decoration at the lip (pl. 217:K). The third fragment (pl. 217:I) preserves part of the floor of a bowl and its foot (cf. pl. 217:F). The paint has flaked away, but its matt bed can be clearly seen in the brownish-buff burnished surface of the sherd. The exterior of the foot had simple linear decorations; in contrast, the elaborate pattern in the center of the bowl consists of eight women closely knotted into a group by a single set of shared triangular legs and thighs. In their geometric stylization these figures are related both to those on matt-painted sherds (pl. 215:H–I) and on a sherd from Chogha Mami cited above. The Chogha Mami figures have the same triangular lower extremity as the matt-painted sherds (pl. 215:H–I).

The context of one example (pl. 217:I) does not allow a precise date for it, but suggests that it probably belongs to the Archaic Susiana 3 phase, which would fit well with its similarities to matt-painted designs.[168] The cylindrical fragment (pl. 217:L) comes from an Archaic Susiana 2 context. The position of the final example (pl. 217:K) is more ambiguous; it has a possible range of the Archaic Susiana 1–2 phases and might be earlier than the windowpane fragments. There seems no impelling reason to consider these three sherds as imports.

---

167. For a parallel to plate 217:G–H, see Hole 1977:134f., 141, fig. 53:a (Chogha Sefid, Chogha Mami Transitional).

168. Object 4.1026 (pl. 217:I) was found to the east of Protoliterate kiln R21:404, at an elevation of ca. 76.25. Thus it must have been either in the debris of a Protoliterate pit that was completely excavated the following season, R21:509, or in the mixed debris of R21:409, where Archaic Susiana brickwork appeared at el. 75.81; cf. plate 272. AA

Archaic Susiana Family XV

B–C.1; dense wares

Figure 35

A family number has been reserved for unpainted carinated or cylindrical vessels similar in form to those of the red-line Family XIX. It seems likely that unpainted versions of such shapes existed although they have not yet been found.

Archaic Susiana Family XVI

C.20; dense with straw tempering, painted

Figure 35; plate 217:L

A sherd of a small cylindrical vessel with broad washes of dark brown or grayish paint bordering the lip and base and a faded, undefinable pattern in between is so far unique. Additional evidence is needed to prove whether this sherd is merely an aberrant specimen or represents a rare family. It comes from a context with Archaic Susiana 1–2 and intrusive Protoliterate sherds.

Archaic Susiana Family XVII

C.22, .39, .41; dense wares, sandy or vegetal tempering, painted or unpainted

Figure 35; plate 217:M–P

This family shelters a few sherds varying considerably among themselves. One can be restored as a bulging cylinder (pl. 217:M) and two as bowls with the upper body inclined inward (pl. 217:N–O). The exteriors are variously treated. The painted ladders depicted on one example (pl. 217:O) are reminiscent of that on another (pl. 217:E) but have an extra set of panes. A relatively large vessel represented only by a small sherd was unusual for the presence of a neck covered by a broad wash of black paint; the shoulder below has horizontal bands (pl. 217:P). The combination of elements is similar to that on the upper part of the Family XVI bowl (pl. 217:L).[169]

At present Family XVII is only a pragmatic collection of sherds placed together because of generally comparable paste and somewhat concordant body shapes, but in detail they are quite diverse. If they were representative of groups of vessels, rather than being only individual examples, three of the examples (pl. 217:M, O–P) could be members of three separate families.

---

169. For form similar to plate 217:P, painted with two wide horizontal bands, see Wright et al., 1979, fig. 14:f (Izeh area survey, Archaic period).

Archaic Susiana Family XVIII

C.03; dense-sandy red-line ware

Figure 35; plate 218:A–B

In the prominent category of pottery decorated with fugitive red paint simple bowls are much rarer than other shapes, particularly the angled or carinated bowls. Even in the convex bowls of Family XVIII the walls flare only slightly, so that at the top the stance is almost vertical, approaching the .04 shape. Several different designs appear.

Archaic Susiana Family XIX

C.11; dense-sandy red-line ware, painted

Figure 35; plates 64:M–O; 218:C–E

Sherds assigned to this family have relatively straight or slightly everted walls meeting at a definite angle. However, this juncture is frequently not sharp enough to be counted as a true carination. In size the bowls range up to a diameter of some 16 cm but are not normally larger; they thus fall into the smaller range of the "C" size. In addition to shape, Family XIX is defined by decoration with considerable patches of open background. Chevron friezes are characteristic (pls. 64:M; 218:D–E); diagonal bands with basketry-like hatching and pairs of stepped lines also occur (pls. 64:O; 218:C). The densest Family XIX pattern is the frieze of hourglasses, but even there the lozenge-shaped reserve areas are prominent (pl. 64:N). The lower part of the Family XIX bowls were probably normally covered by a red wash (pls. 64:N–O; 218:D).

Archaic Susiana Family XX

B–C.20, .23; dense-sandy red-line ware, painted

Figure 35; plates 64:R–S; 218:F–H

Vessels similar in shape to those of Family XIX but with their main walls fairly vertical are either definitely carinated or rounded. The lips are flattened. In Family XX the painted decoration covers the space between the lip and the lower angle more evenly and densely than in Family XIX. The design is always the same: chevron friezes framed at the top and bottom by solid triangles continuing as an overall wash below the carination. When the paint is well preserved the patterns are bright and bold. Family XX sherds are the commonest representatives of the red-line ware. Their decoration, including the red wash below the carination, is an antecedent for that on many matt-painted vessels.

Archaic Susiana Family XXI

C.20, .22; dense-sandy red-line ware, painted

Figure 35; plates 64:T; 218:I–L

The basic shape of Families XX and XXI is the same. The distinctions between them, insofar as can be judged from the small sherds at hand, are in proportion, size, and decoration. The bowls of Family XXI tend to be shallower and often larger than those of Family XX. Instead of the neat chevron friezes of Family XX, there are carelessly executed versions (pl. 218:I, L) or other patterns that only sparsely cover the surface: clusters of vertical bands (pl. 218:J) and hollow rectangles alternating with small triangles (pl. 218:K).

Archaic Susiana Family XXII

B.24, .27; dense-sandy red-line ware, painted

Figure 35; plates 64:U; 219:A

A so far unique sherd has a shape that can be considered as an upper cylinder combined with a lower, wider cylinder. It is decorated tectonically with a roughly painted chevron frieze above the carination and wide vertical bands below it. They replace the solid red wash common on the lower bodies of Families XIX and XX bowls.

Another sherd assigned to Family XXII can be reconstructed as a squat vessel with a light neck (fig. 35:6.427). Both it and another example of this pottery family (pl. 219:A) are unique and have been placed together in one family because, despite their variation in shape, they are both relatively cylindrical and do not fit well elsewhere.

Archaic Susiana Family XXIII

C.39; dense-sandy red-line ware, painted

Figure 35; plates 64:V; 219:B

Sherds from rather small vessels, the upper walls of which incline inward to a greater or lesser degree and are either approximately equal to or higher than the lower walls, make up Family XXIII. The overhanging carination of one example (fig. 35:6.140) is unusual. The decoration consists of linear patterns, usually rather neatly painted, arranged horizontally, diagonally, or vertically. They sometimes cover only a small part of the upper surface. A red wash below the carination was apparently quite normal.

Archaic Susiana Family XXIV

C.39; dense-sandy red-line ware, painted

Figure 35; plates 64:W; 219:C–D

The general shape of Family XXIV is the same as that of Family XXIII, namely, two conical parts joined approximately at the middle of the body. However, in Family XXIV the walls tend to be somewhat concave. The main distinction between the two families is one of size, with Family XXIV reserved for the larger vessels. All of the other families contain only small-sized vessels. Among the few examples of Family XXIV recovered is a concave base, which probably illustrates the type of base standard for the red-line ware (pl. 219:C). The decoration above the carination can be restored as a chevron frieze with solid triangles in the interstices. The carination is marked by a broad band from which vertical bands fall to the base. This treatment of the lower body has already been seen in Family XXII (pl. 219:A) and is also to be found on straw-tempered, smoothed vessels. Another example of Family XXIV was apparently decorated by a large scale version of the hourglass frieze known from Family XIX (pls. 64:W–X; 219:D; cf. pl. 64:N).

Archaic Susiana Family XXV

B.02; straw-tempered, red-washed ware, unpainted

Figure 35; plate 219:E

The rarity of restorable forms has led to the definition of a number of families of the straw-tempered wares on the basis of one or two examples (Families XXIV–XXIX, XXXII–XXXVI, XXXVIII). The assumption is that originally more examples existed. Family XXV accommodates small, concave-sided cups. The one example is red-washed.

Archaic Susiana Family XXVI

B 03; straw-tempered red-washed ware, unpainted

Figure 35; plate 219:F

A convex-sided bowl represents a simple shape, more examples of which presumably existed.

Archaic Susiana Family XXVII

B.14; straw-tempered smoothed ware, painted

Figure 35; plate 219:G

A fragment of a carinated vessel decorated with vertical red bands has been assigned its own family number since it is such a well-defined type. It remains however, an isolated example.

Archaic Susiana Family XXVIII

B.39; straw-tempered red-washed ware, unpainted

Figure 35; plate 219:H–I

Small carinated bowls of restorable shape so far remain very rare in the straw-tempered ware. One of the two examples has a slightly outcurving lip.

Archaic Susiana Family XXIX

C.00, .02; straw-tempered, standard red-washed ware, proportion 0–1

Figure 35

Two complete vessels form the basis for distinguishing Family XXIX. Their shallowness and their pronounced flare distinguish them from the majority of the shapes of the straw-tempered ware. It is likely that they belong to a late stage of the Archaic Susiana period.

Archaic Susiana Family XXX

C.03; straw-tempered fine red-washed ware, beaded rim

Figure 35; plate 219:J

Bowls with splaying, convex sides and beaded rims are represented by a complete example with a slightly concave base (pl. 219:J). The vessel's thin walls and dense red wash, burnished on both sides, are also characteristic. Beaded-rim sherds covered by a similarly dense red wash and varying in color from dark- or purple-red to light orange belonged to the same type of bowl. They are unmistakable indicators of an Archaic Susiana 1 date.

Archaic Susiana Family XXXI

C.03, .04; straw-tempered smoothed, red-washed, and red-banded wares, painted or unpainted

Figure 35; plates 219:K, probably L–M; 220:A–D

Thick-walled open vessels of medium or large "C" sizes appear to have been fairly common in the Archaic Susiana period. The restorable forms vary from a relatively shallow bowl (pl. 219:K) to rather deep convex-sided vessels (pl. 220:A–B). The latter were the standard types, judging by similar flat red-washed (pl. 220:C–D) and red-banded (pl. 219:L–M) bases (cf. pl. 220:B). A low footed base (pl. 219:N) probably had a profile similar to a flat red-washed example of this family (pl. 220:C) but cannot be assigned with certainty.

Archaic Susiana Family XXXII

C.05; straw-tempered ware, painted

Figure 35; plate 220:E

Medium-sized bowls with an incurved lip are very rare, although some large deep vessels with incurved lips occur (cf. Family XLII). One example was decorated by vertical bands, probably in clusters. A sherd unusual both for the trace of a trough spout and for its spiral painted decoration can be restored as a bowl with recurved lip (pl. 220:E). Its pattern is so unusual that a concave base with comparable painting can be associated with it (pl. 219:P). The two fragments indicate that there is much to learn concerning the painted repertory of the Archaic Susiana 2 phase.

Archaic Susiana Family XXXIII

C.08; straw-tempered red-banded ware, painted

Figure 35; plate 220:F

A sherd (pl. 220:F) from the upper part of a deep vessel with sinuous sides is so far unique. It remains to be seen whether it represents a specific type or whether, as is probably more likely, it can be associated with the deep vessels of Family XXXI.

Archaic Susiana Family XXXIV

C.11, .12, .14; straw-tempered, red-washed, and coarse wares

Figure 35; plate 220:G–K

Family XXXIV is reserved for angled bowls. The upper wall can vary from less than half of the total height to considerably more than half. Two examples have a red-washed interior and are either definitely or probably earlier than the Archaic Susiana 3 phase (pl. 220:G, I). In shape one of the vessels (pl. 220:I), except for its everted lip, resembles a much larger Family XXXIX vessel dated to the Archaic Susiana 2 phase (pl. 222:I). In contrast, two other vessels (pl. 220:J–K), both of coarse ware despite their sharply profiled forms, are allied in shape to various close-line vessels of the Archaic Susiana 3 phase (for pl. 220:J cf. pl. 207:G; for pl. 220:K cf. pl. 207:L).[170]

Archaic Susiana Family XXXV

C.23, .39; straw-tempered coarse, smoothed, and red-banded wares

Figure 35; plate 221:A–E

Carinated bowls with either fairly vertical or slightly inclined upper walls are assigned to Family XXXV. One example (pl. 221:A) is the coarse ware equivalent of unpainted and painted dense-sandy vessels (pls. 217:M; 218:H–I) and perhaps belongs to the Archaic Susiana 2. The carination of another example (pl. 221:C) though of different proportions, overhangs the lower body as in a red–line ware vessel (fig. 35:6.140). Other carinated fragments with broad strokes in clusters of three are excellent examples of the red-banded decoration (pl. 221:D–E).

Archaic Susiana Family XXXVI

C.5; straw-tempered coarse, smoothed, and red-washed ware, unpainted

Figure 35; plate 221:F

A hole-mouthed lip sherd of straw-tempered coarse ware presumably belonged to a vessel with a globular body. A red-washed lip sherd from a vessel with a mouth about 30 cm in diameter does not have as much of an overhang as this vessel (pl. 221:F). Both sherds are probably aberrant types rather than representatives of well-established types.

---

170. For a form similar to plate 220:H, found in an Early Susiana context, see Dollfus 1975, fig. 10:5 (Jafarabad, Level 4).

Archaic Susiana Family XXXVII

> C.80; straw-tempered coarse, smoothed, and red-washed wares, unpainted

> Figure 35; plate 221:G–J

Rare, but apparently quite typical for the Archaic Susiana period are vessels that are not circular in horizontal section. Oval bowls with a red wash (pl. 221:I) and a matting imprint on the base (pl. 221:J) belong to the end of the Archaic Susiana 1 phase and to the Archaic Susiana 2 phase. In the same periods, squat rectangular bowls occur in red-washed (pl. 221:I) and coarse (pl. 221:G) wares; the latter had low feet at the corner.

Archaic Susiana Family XXXVIII

> C–D.11; proportion "1," straw-tempered smoothed ware, unpainted

> Figure 35; plate 222:E–F

Large, shallow carinated bowls are represented by only a few sherds. One example has a white slip on an orange paste and might have been oval (pl. 222:F).

Archaic Susiana Family XXXIX

> C–D.11, .12; proportion "2–4," straw-tempered smoothed ware, unpainted

> Figure 37; plate 222:G–L

Characteristic for Family XXXIX are the pronounced angles and approximately vertical stance of the upper walls. They constitute at least half, and frequently more, of the total height of the vessels that can be quite deep (pl. 222:K). Sometimes the upper walls might flare slightly (pl. 222:H, J). The lower walls might be straight (pl. 222:G), slightly concave (pl. 222:H–J, L), or somewhat convex (pl. 222:K). Usually the lips are flat either of the same thickness as the body below or slightly thinned. Rather blunt lips also occur (pl. 222:K). In the complete vessels the bases are concave (pl. 222:H, J–K).

In the pottery groups of all three Archaic Susiana phases the bulk of the sherds, namely, the straw-tempered smoothed lips, the body angles, and the concave bases, as well as the corresponding body sherds, can be attributed to Family XXXIX. The majority are mottled and originally even many of the monochrome sherds probably belonged to mottled vessels, although on the whole the mottling seems to be caused by firing, in some cases it might be a stain left by a red wash.

Many of the containers needed for the ordinary purposes of daily life must have been variously sized Family XXXIX vessels. They were also, as is clear from some examples (pl. 222:J–K), the ancestors of the equally ubiquitous Early Susiana Family XVI vessels.[171]

Archaic Susiana Family XL

> C–D.39; proportion [4], straw-tempered coarse, smoothed red-washed, and red-banded wares

> Figure 37; plate 222:M–P

The outstanding diagnostic feature of Family XL is the inclined upper wall. By analogy with Family XXXIX, the bases are presumed to have been concave, although no example is sufficiently preserved to establish this. In two restorable examples the lips are blunt and the bases concave. Two red-washed fragments are tentatively attributed to the family (pl. 222:M–N). One is the carination of a large vessel and the other the highly unusual club rim of a large container presumed to have been similar in shape and size to a Family XXXVIII vessel (pl. 222:E). A red-banded sherd (pl. 222:L) extending from the carination to the base probably belonged to a vessel similar to one of this family (pl. 222:M). Family XL vessels appear to have been rare, although some examples might possibly be hidden among sherds whose stance is uncertain because so little of the lip is preserved.

One representative of Family XL comes from a Protoliterate pit dug into Archaic Susiana debris (pl. 222:M) and two others from transitional Archaic Susiana-Early Susiana levels (pl. 222:P), while the red-washed rim (pl. 222:M) fragment is from Archaic Susiana 2 contexts. Although the range of the family might begin then, assuming that the two pieces are correctly assigned, the unpainted, standard examples constitute a late group that was probably characteristic for the transition between the Archaic Susiana and Early Susiana periods. A closely related form occurs in an Early Susiana level at Jafarabad.[172]

Archaic Susiana Family XLI

> D.03, .04; straw-tempered ware

> Figure 37

No certain examples of large-sized vessels with convex profiles have yet been identified. Since such types are well known in medium sizes (Family XXXI), it seems likely that larger examples will eventually be found and a family number has been reserved for them.

---

171. For shapes similar to plate 222:I–J, from Early Susiana contexts, see Dollfus 1975, figs. 10:11, 14:4 (Jafarabad, Levels 5b, 5a).

172. For shape related to plate 222:O, see Dollfus 1975, fig. 12:2 (Jafarabad, Level 5b). For a taller variant on the example in plate 222:P, from an Early Susiana context, see ibid., fig. 14:5 (Jafarabad, Level 5). For a fragment similar to plate 222:M, see Hole 1977, fig. 44:bb (Chogha Sefid, Surkh phase).

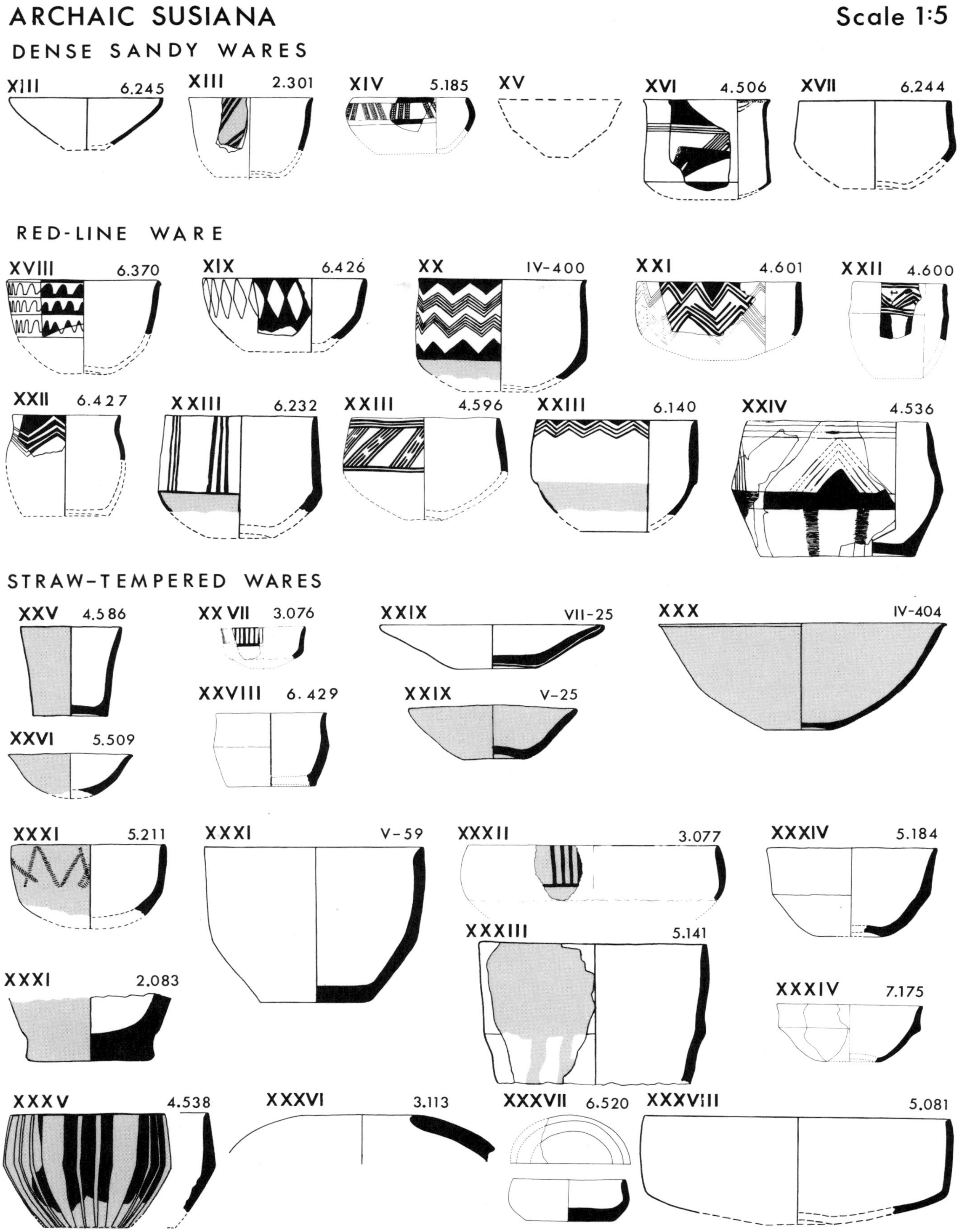

ARCHAIC SUSIANA

Scale 1:5

DENSE SANDY WARES

XIII 6.245	XIII 2.301	XIV 5.185	XV	XVI 4.506	XVII 6.244

RED-LINE WARE

XVIII 6.370 · XIX 6.426 · XX IV-400 · XXI 4.601 · XXII 4.600

XXII 6.427 · XXIII 6.232 · XXIII 4.596 · XXIII 6.140 · XXIV 4.536

STRAW-TEMPERED WARES

XXV 4.586 · XXVII 3.076 · XXIX VII-25 · XXX IV-404

XXVI 5.509 · XXVIII 6.429 · XXIX V-25

XXXI 5.211 · XXXI V-59 · XXXII 3.077 · XXXIV 5.184

XXXI 2.083 · XXXIII 5.141 · XXXIV 7.175

XXXV 4.538 · XXXVI 3.113 · XXXVII 6.520 · XXXVIII 5.081

Figure 35. Archaic Susiana Families XIII–XVII (Dense-sandy Ware), XVIII–XXIV (Red-line Ware), and XXV–XXXVIII (Straw-tempered Ware)

Archaic Susiana Family XLII

> D.05; straw-tempered smoothed and red-banded
> wares, painted and unpainted

> Figure 37; plate 222:A–D

Large vessels with incurving lips appear to have been a standard type. An almost complete deep bowl, perhaps with a flat base, in straw-tempered smoothed ware (pl. 222:D) illustrated the complete forms to which various lip sherds belonged (pl. 222:A–C). A body sherd that appears to be from a vessel of this family is highly unusual in that the three vertical bands preserved differ in color, being brown, red, and black respectively (4.719, R21:401 Middle South).

Archaic Susiana Family XLIII

> D.11; proportion "1" or less, straw-tempered ware

> Figure 37

Family XLIII is defined as the family of large-sized and shallow carinated bowls. The one example recovered is a squat variant of the Family XXXIX vessels and is oval in section. It probably belongs to a late part of the Archaic Susiana 3 phase. In the absence so far of other examples, it is uncertain whether the example (fig. 37:8.155) represents a class of vessels or is merely an aberrant piece.

Archaic Susiana Family XLIV

> D.8; straw-tempered ware

> Figure 37

A family number has been reserved to accommodate special forms that either do not fit into other families or are so incomplete that their shape cannot be even tentatively restored. A fragment (fig. 37:5.944) resembles the neck of a large jar, but since such a form seems to be alien to the Archaic Susiana repertory, it should perhaps be considered as a pedestal foot.

Archaic Susiana Family XLV

> B.04, C.03, .04; painted-burnished ware

> Figure 37; plate 223:A

The first family of the painted-burnished ware consists of conical bowls. An example of flaring shape is unusual for its use of paint on the exterior, only a broad lip band, and inside an overall wash (pl. 223:A). In dealing with small fragments of simple, not sharply profiled forms it is sometimes difficult to distinguish sherds with relatively straight upper walls (.04) from those with an incurved lip (.05). The latter form is one of the main families of the painted-burnished ware, Family XLVI. In contrast, Family XLV has only isolated pieces.

Archaic Susiana Family XLVI

> C.05; painted-burnished ware

> Figure 37; plates 223:B–E, G–H, J–O

A number of small fragments are sufficiently distinctive to be recognized as parts of bowls with incurving lips. Some can be tentatively reconstructed as medium deep, with proportions of "2" or "3" (pl. 223:C, M). Quite large-sized examples existed (pl. 223:J, O). The decoration ranged from discontinuous blocks of ornament such as fringed panels (pl. 223:C–D), vertical zigzags (pl. 223:M), and rickrack zigzags (pl. 223:O) to the apparently more common continuous bands of design. Zigzag registers are combined with a narrower band filled by small elements suggesting florets (pl. 223:H) or horizontally placed birds (pl. 223:E); in both cases the representational interpretation is not certain. A small sherd preserves only two bands of "florets" (pl. 223:G). Pendant semicircles normally appear only on the interiors of lips so that their presence in two exterior registers (pl. 223:J) is atypical. Two body sherds that might have belonged to the Family XLVI bowls have unique patterns, plaiting (pl. 223:I) and a net (pl. 223:F). Also unusual is a stepped design (pl. 223:N). The rickrack so prominent on the largest family of painted-burnished ware (Family XLVII) occurs on two small sherds whose designs cannot be reconstructed with certainty (pl. 223:K–L).

Archaic Susiana Family XLVII

> C–D.41, .44; painted-burnished ware

> Figure 37; plates 64:AA–BB, KK–LL, NN–QQ;
> 65:A–D; 224:A–P; 225:A–J; 226:A–C, E–G

Family XLVII is the dominant group of the painted-burnished ware. In contrast to the unsegmented shapes of the first two painted-burnished families, those of Family XLVII are carinated, often quite sharply. Two subfamilies can be distinguished according to the shape of the upper body, which is frequently either fairly straight or slightly convex (Subfamily XLVIIa) but sometimes concave (Subfamily XLVIIb). The vessels were made in two grades of depth, the standard-sized ones of proportion "2" and the large, D, sizes of proportion "3." In almost all cases the lower part of the body is taller than the upper part. A complete vessel (pl. 224:B) and a semi-complete vessel (pl. 225:B) indicate that the bases were concave. The shapes of the lips vary from blunt (pls. 224:D–E; 225:L), through slightly (pl. 225:C) or markedly (pl. 225:F) inbeveled, to definitely thickened, almost club-like (pl. 224:C).

The decoration is remarkably consistent. The upper body was the primary zone for painting (pls. 224:B–F; 225:C). Sometimes lower borders of triangles with "hooks" (pl. 225:A, G; 226:C) fall below the carination (pl. 226:A; cf. 64:EE for an analogous example on a sherd of uncertain shape). The patterns, with a few exceptions (pl. 224:H–J), are constructed of asymmetrical rickrack bands, that is bands with the upper edge scalloped. These must have been made by two brush strokes, the first a plain one and the second, perhaps painted with a thin brush, to add the scalloping. The rickrack bands were closely spaced so that the structure of the designs depends completely upon the minute reserved areas of light-colored ground. These sophisticated patterns could not have been successful without very specific prior visualization of them by the painters and an equally accurate execution.

The rickrack bands were used to construct the following designs, all of them rectilinear:

1. Overlapping steps in which the individual steps can be either broad solid strokes (fig. 36:C; pl. 226:A) or a cluster of narrow strokes within a large white reserve step (fig. 36:A–B; pl. 226:C, G).

2. Panels of horizontal rickrack linked together on at least one side by a vertical band that might project to the upper or lower border or both (fig. 36:G; pls. 64:JJ, probably LL and QQ; 224:B, F).

3. Continuous meanders with solid (fig. 36:D; pls. 65:C = 226:E; 224:M) or rickrack (fig. 36:H; pl. 224:K–L) filling.

4. Wide blocks of vertical zigzags separated by a relatively narrow zigzag of solid paint (pls. 65:A; 225:A, C; 226:B).

5. Vertical or slightly diagonal lines arranged individually (pl. 64:BB) or in linked groups (pls. 65:D; 224:P).

6. Vertical pinnate sprays (pls. 64:OO; 225:E, H, J).

7. Pairs of horizontal zigzags arranged symmetrically and enriched by subsidiary filling motifs (pls. 65:B = 225:F and presumably 224:N).

8. Fragmentary compositions of triangular groups of rickrack (pl. 225:D, G, I).

The Family XLVII vessels stand out for the variety and sophistication of their rickrack motifs. The very rare rickrack bands on vessels of other painted-burnished families are less elaborate. The standard decoration on the interiors of Family XLVII vessels is a wide lip band with pendant loops. These are more commonly double (pls. 224:B–D, F, M; 225:C, E) but triple (pls. 224:G; 226:E) or quadruple (pls. 225:A; 226:A) examples also appear. Occasionally simple broad lip bands (pl. 224:P; 225:D) or solid scallops (pl. 224:E, N) occur.

Archaic Susiana Family XLVIII

C.80; painted-burnished ware

Figure 37; plate 226:D

Vessels with noncircular sections are not characteristic of the painted-burnished ware. So far only one ex-

ample, a bowl with a squared base, has been found. It is also unusual in that almost the entire body was painted. Though badly abraded, the entire design can be made out (cf. fig. 36:F). Between the broad lip band and the pendant scallops near the base are three registers with continuous meanders, a broad band supporting pendant triangles, and six horizontal rickrack bands respectively. The only other example of the use of this interior lip motif on the exterior is provided by a Family XLVI sherd (pl. 223:J), the family to which this example (pl. 226:D) would be assigned if it did not have a square base.

Archaic Susiana Family XLIX

D.55 or .64; painted-burnished ware

Figure 37; plate 226:H

The last category of the standard painted-burnished ware shapes is represented by a single lip sherd. It curves inward much more markedly than the lips of Families XLVI and XLIX vessels and can be taken as belonging to a hole-mouthed vessel. The body was probably fairly globular, with a concave base. The decoration is exactly comparable to that on a Family XLVI bowl (pl. 223:M), on the interior of the lip are solid scallops of a minimal character consonant with the sherd's inward stance and on the exterior blocks of vertical wavy lines. Additional painted registers might have existed below the broad border.

Archaic Susiana Family L

C–D.03, .04, .05, .07; painted-burnished ware

Figure 37; plate 227:A–O

Although represented only by sherds, the combination of forms and designs distinctive for Family L is clear. The vessels were obviously large, probably for the most part D-sized, bowls without sharp angles in their contours but curving in roundly toward the base (pl. 227:F–G, K, O). The upper walls were relatively vertical (pl. 227:A, C), although the lips might curve out (pl. 227:D) or in (pl. 227:E) somewhat. The light, yellowish-buff slip normal for the painted-burnished ware provides a splendid foil for the decoration executed in dark brown or black paint: wide lip bands and below a web of ornament on the exterior. Horizontal undulating lines are the commonest element, either alone or combined with zigzags (pl. 227:B, G), or Vs, Hs, or meanders (pl. 227:K–M). Patterns in which the wavy lines form concentric rectangles (pl. 227:H) or appear vertically in panels below, probably meanders (pl. 227:O), are less usual. Also unusual is a frond-like motif (pl. 227:I). In their prominence and heaviness, chevron bands (pl. 227:A) contrast with the spidery character of the normal Family L designs. The bottom of the decorated zone, approximately at the point where the body

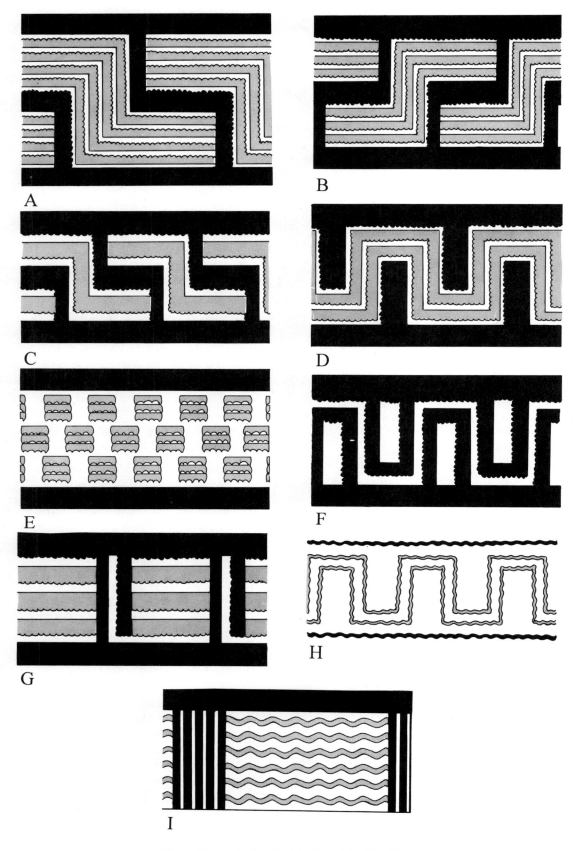

Figure 36. Analysis of Painted-burnished Motifs

begins to curve inward toward the base, small pendant triangles or scalloped bands appear (pl. 227:F–G).

In ware, Family L is similar to the normal painted-burnished families, but not in its decoration. Neither do the Family L sherds occur alongside standard painted-burnished sherds. They are all, except for one found on the surface but probably dropped out of excavated earth on the way to the dump (pl. 227:N), from the lowest level of occupation traced in Trench XXV. They are associated with other sherds (e.g., fig. 36:E) that also do not fit into the standard painted-burnished families. Thus, it appears that the black ashy level at the bottom of Trench XXV antedates the Archaic Susiana 1 phase proper and should be placed, at the latest, at the very beginning of that period. The question of the chronological sequence is returned to later, but in the meantime it is clear that the Family L sherds, not only in their ware but also in such details as the subsidiary pendant elements at the bottom of the field of decoration, are direct antecedents of the standard painted-burnished ware.[173]

Archaic Susiana Family LI

C.03, .04, .05, .20, .22; painted-burnished variant

Figure 37; plate 228:A–E

Sherds of shallow bowls decorated by evenly undulating horizontal lines constitute a second group found only in the lowest level of Trench XXV. The amount of vegetal tempering varies; some examples are porous while others are dense, with either little or no visible traces of straw. A color range from yellowish buff to orange is characteristic; some sherds are mottled. Slips, when discernible, are of the same colors as the bodies and appear to result from the careful smoothing of interior and exterior surfaces; the differently colored buff slip characteristic for the standard painted-burnished ware does not occur. Although always well-smoothed, not all of the surfaces have a high sheen. The paint also varies from a shining black to a faded matt gray. The Family LI bowls have cylindrical and apparently quite shallow shapes. The decoration is limited to horizontal wavy lines, which on the whole undulate more evenly than those on Family L vessels and form either continuous friezes (pl. 228:B) or are divided into metopes by vertical bands (fig. 36:I; pl. 228:E).[174] Exact parallels for

the Family LI vessels occur in Khuzestan itself and similar forms are known from northeastern Iran.[175]

Archaic Susiana Family LII

C.31, .39; painted-burnished variant

Figure 37

A family number has been reserved for vessels of the same ware and with the same decoration as those of Family LI, but with their upper walls turned inward.

Archaic Susiana Family LIII

C.03, .04, .05; painted-burnished variant

Figure 37; plates 228:F–L; 229:A–D, H, J

The ware of Family LIII is essentially the same as that of Family LI with one difference; the surfaces of the vessels were smoothed but often not enough to produce a high sheen. There is considerable variation from vessel to vessel; the ground might be matt and the brown-black paint glossy or vice versa. The shapes, in so far as they can be visualized on the basis of lip sherds, seem to have been simple varieties of conical bowls.

Four subfamilies can be distinguished by the painted decoration. Each of three groups is characterized by only one motif: Subfamily LIIIa with a wide, solid band of paint below the lip (pls. 228:J–L; 229:A, J); Subfamily LIIIb with a negative chevron band reserved in the solid zone of paint (pl. 228:F); and Subfamily LIIIc with most of the body covered by registers of pendant triangles (pl. 228:G–I). The sherds of Subfamily LIIId are not limited to a single motif. Relatively simple are roughly painted horizontal zigzags (pl. 229:D) and a dotted lattice (pl. 229:B, H), the latter a design recurring, though disguised by thick brush strokes, on a standard painted-burnished sherd (pl. 223:F). The most complicated of the Subfamily LIIId designs consists of "four-legged" meanders whose interstices are filled by horizontal bands (pl. 229:C). The upper horizontal edge of each band and some of the vertical edges are scalloped, giving a rickrack effect. In this and in the large scallops on the interior of the lip, this vessel anticipates features of the standard painted-burnished ware (pls. 223:N; 224:E, N).[176]

---

173. For a sherd possibly related to plate 227:C–D, see Wright et al., 1979, fig. 14:e (Izeh area survey, Archaic period).

174. Two examples (pl. 228:A, D) are reconstructed from small sherds that might have originally been part of paneled compositions. The two fragments on which the reconstruction of 3.009a (pl. 228:B) rests are large enough to indicate that the wavy lines were continuous.

175. For parallels to plate 228:A–B and D, see Hole 1975, figs. 5:k–l, n; 8:a (Tappeh Tula'i); Masuda 1972, fig. 7, and idem 1974, fig. 5:5–7 (Sang-e Chakhmaq). For a parallel to plate 228:C, see Hole 1975, figs. 5:m, o, q; 8 b (Tappeh Tula'i); Masuda 1972, fig. 7, and idem 1974, fig. 5:5–7 (Sang-e Chakhmaq).

176. For decoration similar to plate 228:E, see Hole 1974, fig. 6 (Tappeh Tula'i). For a parallel to plate 228:J–L, see Hole 1977, fig. 46:g (Chogha Sefid, Sefid phase); for decoration, see ibid., fig. 7:a–g (Tappeh Tula'i). For a decoration similar to plate 228:I–K, see ibid., fig. 7:l.

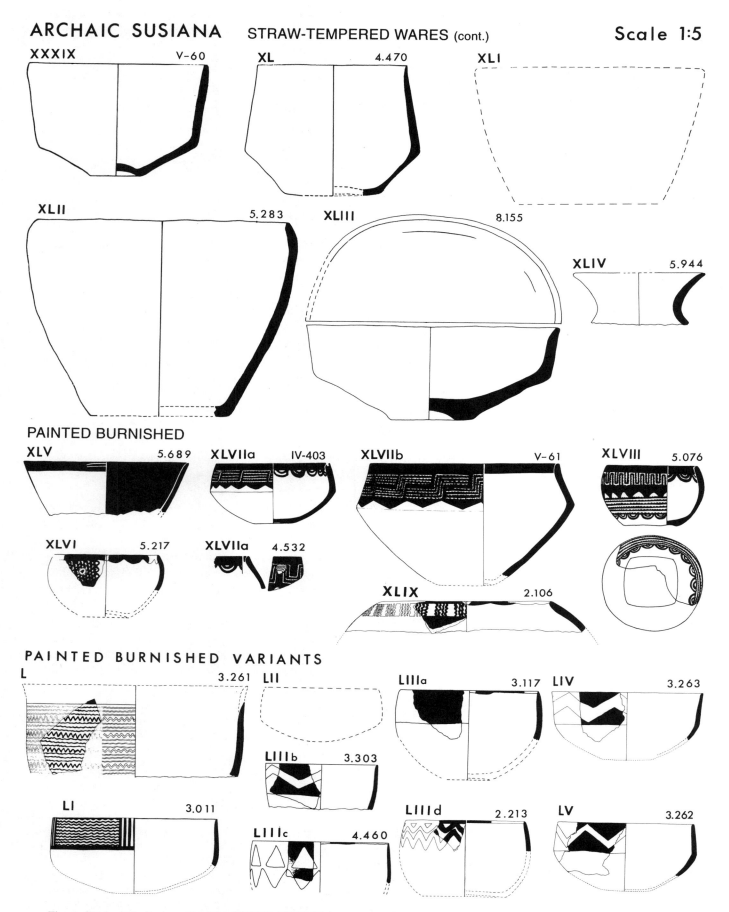

Figure 37. Archaic Susiana Families XXXIX–XLIV (Straw-tempered Ware) and XLV–LV (Painted-burnished Ware)

Archaic Susiana Family LIV

C.13; painted-burnished variant

Figure 37; plate 229:E

A sherd preserving both lip and carination has a distinctive shape but remains so far an isolated specimen so that it is not yet certain whether it is merely an aberrant example or the representative of a family of bowls. Its ware is the same as that of the Family LIII bowls and its decoration is the same as that which defines the Subfamily LIIIb.

Archaic Susiana Family LV

C.39; painted-burnished variant

Plate 229:F–G, K–L

Fragments that appear to have belonged to approximately biconical bowls, with their upper and lower parts roughly equal in height, have been assigned to a family of their own. Their upper walls are relatively straight and they are either carinated or rounded at the equator. The decoration varies from reserved zigzags, either simple as on some Subfamily LIIIb and Family LIV sherds (pls. 228:F; 229:E) or filled by thin positive zigzags (pl. 229:K), to a more complicated pattern in which diagonally-hatched vertical bands divide the field into panels with a diagonal filling of a crosshatched band and triangles (pl. 229:F, L). The narrow hooks suspended from the lower border of the decorated field point forward to one of the typical elements of the standard painted-burnished ware.[177] Family LV is the last of the families of pottery known only from the lowest level of Trench XXV. Families L, LI, and LIII–LV represent the earliest period of occupation known at Chogha Mish.

The pottery of the individual Susiana periods is described above, the Susiana objects are surveyed in the following chapter, and the relationship of the various periods among themselves and with the cultures of other areas is considered in *Chapter 12*.

177. For decoration parallel to plate 229:G, see Hole 1974, fig. 6 (Tappeh Tula'i). For a parallel to plate 229:K, see ibid., fig. 8:c.

CHAPTER 10

OBJECTS OF THE PREHISTORIC PERIODS

In addition to pottery, Chogha Mish has yielded a wide variety of prehistoric objects. Prominent among these are the numerous ground and hammered stone objects (pls. 238–52) that are discussed by Daniel Shimabuku in *Chapter 11*. The other categories of small objects, namely the stone vessels (pl. 230), a copper pin (pl. 65:P), baked and unbaked clay implements (pl. 231), spindle whorls (pl. 232), bone implements (pl. 233), ornaments (pl. 234), glyptic (pls. 67, 234), and figurines (pls. 235–37) are presented in this chapter.[1]

STONE VESSELS

The small number of stone vessel fragments found during the first five seasons of excavations might be an accident of discovery. Part of a large vessel imitating in stone the flanged vessels of Early Susiana Family XVI, found in the third season on the surface at the edge of Trench XXI, proves that already in the Early Susiana period the craft of stone vessel cutting was remarkably well developed (pls. 65:Q; 230:B). The thick flange is well cut and so unmistakable in shape that the entire vessel can be easily visualized by means of the pottery prototypes (pl. 199:J–M). It was a considerable feat to produce such a shape in stone. Three fragments of stone vessels can be dated to the Middle Susiana period. Of the two examples with beaded rims, the one of bituminous stone comes from an Early Middle Susiana context (pl. 230:D); that of gray limestone probably belongs to the same period (pl. 230:C). Finds made in later seasons suggest that both in shape and the use of bituminous stone the two beaded-rim vessels continue an Early Susiana tradition. A fragment of a shallow bowl unfortunately comes from a context of uncertain date, a deep level in Trench XVI with few finds but probably belonging around the transition from the Early Susiana to Middle Susiana periods (pl. 230:A). The shallow concave shape of this vessel is similar to that of one of the pottery families typical for the Early Middle Susiana

phase; the stone fragment might be tentatively attributed to the same period.

STONE IMPLEMENTS

Polished stone celts, made of various stones, are more prominent in the first two phases of the Archaic Susiana period than at any other time. Of the seven Archaic Susiana celts, two are unusual in having retouch, presumably stemming from secondary usage, around the edges (pls. 65:NN–SS; 230:E–H). The shapes vary from rectangular to trapezoidal. Only one piece, presumably the narrower end of a trapezoidal celt, can be attributed to the Middle Susiana period. Although at Chogha Mish celts are hardly to be found between the Archaic Susiana and Protoliterate periods, elsewhere in Khuzestan they appear in the intervening periods.[2]

Mace-heads were extremely rare. A small example of elongated shape came from an Archaic Susiana context in the Gully Cut (pl. 230:K).[3] A similarly elongated but larger example from an Early Susiana level in Trench XXI has two depressions at one end (pl. 230:I). The narrowness of the central perforation makes it unlikely that a stick stout enough for a mace handle could have been inserted. A small globular mace-head was found in the northern corner of a Middle Susiana room in Trench XIII (pl. 230:L).

An Archaic Susiana 1 context provided a rather straight-sided perforated stone, smooth at the ends and in the interior of the perforation (pl. 230:N). Its large size suggests that it was not a mace-head, but rather one of the perforated stones of Type PF 4 (pl. 247:O–P), described below by Shimabuku.

A pounding or rubbing stone of red conglomerate is unusual in having two depressions to serve as finger holes (pl. 230:M). It comes from a context in Trench XIII that probably belongs to the Early Middle Susiana phase. A square block of gray stone from the surface of Trench XVI, possibly dating to the Late Middle Susiana phase, has a concavity on one side; it could have served

---

1. A chapter on the flint industry was to have been written by James S. Phillips, but he has only been able to prepare the illustrations (pls. 253–56), leaving a serious gap in the documentation. It was decided, however, to publish the evidence for reference purposes. The flints and other evidence not analyzed in this volume will be dealt with in the final report of Seasons 6–12. AA

2. For celts ranging from the Sabz through the Bayat phases, ca. Early Susiana-Middle Susiana, see Hole, Flannery, and Neely 1969:189, 192, fig. 82 (Tappeh Sabz); for Middle Susiana celts, see Dollfus 1975, fig. 27:20 (Jafarabad, Level 2).

3. See ibid., fig. 35:2–3 (Jafarabad, Levels 6, 4).

as a small mortar (pl. 230:J). Scratches on a finely polished tan-colored pebble suggest that it might have been used as a "cutting board" (pl. 230:O). It comes from a Late Susiana context in the High Mound.

METAL IMPLEMENTS

The only metal object recovered from the prehistoric levels is a corroded and bent pin from a Late Middle Susiana context (pl. 65:P). The material of the pin has not been analyzed but is almost certainly copper. The object is important as proof that copper was known. It was rare, however, to judge by the sparsity of metal fragments recovered in the excavations.

BAKED AND UNBAKED CLAY IMPLEMENTS

During the Susiana periods sherds were frequently shaped into tools. Simplest are round scrapers, ranging in diameter from ca. 3 to 11 cm, which have at least one edge worn smooth from use and sometimes the entire periphery. Examples in unpainted wares range from the Early Susiana (pl. 231:DD), through Middle Susiana (pl. 231:CC, FF), to Late Susiana periods (pl. 231:EE). The Middle Susiana scrapers were also made from painted sherds (pl. 231:BB, II); on another example the characteristic crosshatching of Middle Susiana bowls can still be recognized (pl. 231:JJ).

Trapezoidal scrapers appear to have been much rarer than round scrapers. Both a red-washed Archaic Susiana 1 scraper (pl. 231:GG) and an Early Middle Susiana example made from the sherd of a Middle Susiana bowl (pl. 65:J) have a perforation at one end. These perforations probably remain from attempts to mend the vessels before they were irretrievably broken. A Late Susiana trapezoidal scraper is without a perforation (pl. 231:HH).

Perforated roundels shaped out of unpainted sherds cover the same chronological range as the scrapers.[4] The roundels tend to be somewhat smaller than the scrapers (pl. 231:X–Z). The largest example does not seem to have been completely trimmed (pl. 231:AA).

Small perforated roundels ranging in diameter from ca. 1 to 2 cm occur in the Middle Susiana (pl. 231:T) and Late Susiana periods, the latter made from fine ware sherds (pl. 231:U–V). The perforated roundels differ among themselves in size and weight. They probably had a variety of functions that remain uncertain. On the whole, they seem to be too light to have served as net sinkers or weights of some sort.

Small roundels with large perforations (e.g., pl. 231:T) are transitional in shape to a recognizable group of pottery "rings" cut from fine ware sherds and found in Middle Susiana and Late Susiana contexts (pl. 231:Q–S). They range in exterior diameter from 1.1 to 2.5 cm and in internal diameter from 0.7 to 1.5 cm. Their use is uncertain although perhaps they might have been personal ornaments.

Considerably rarer and more specialized than the scrapers and roundels are violin-shaped sherd tools ranging in length from 2.0 to 3.5 cm and made of fine or almost fine buff ware. They seem to have been in use during the Late Middle Susiana phase and the Late Susiana period.[5] They vary in shape; some are elongated with one or two of the long sides concave and at least one of the short sides convex. Other sherd tools of the Late Middle Susiana phase are of a more regular and simple ovoid shape (pl. 65:K); all the edges have been worn smooth. These small sherd implements were probably shaping and burnishing tools used by potters.

In addition to the tools made secondarily from sherds, there are also terra-cotta objects of various types. A disc with a small central perforation, almost certainly of the Late Middle Susiana phase, is painted with a rosette of broad-tipped petals (pl. 65:I); perhaps, it was also a lid. Broad petals occur on a small Middle Susiana bowl painted on the convex side and therefore presumably a lid (pl. 164:E). Also from a Late Middle Susiana context is the fragment of a crude, straw-tempered round plaque with a knob that fitted it to be a lid (pl. 231:KK).

Thick roundels, the tops of which are either slightly concave or flat and painted with designs typical for the Late Susiana period (pl. 235:A–B), are paralleled in contemporary contexts at Susa and Jafarabad[6] and, outside Khuzestan, at Tall-i Bakun A in Fars (Langsdorff and McCown 1942. pl. 82:38–39). The Chogha Mish roundels have perforations, suggesting that they might have been strung as ornaments, but not all of the parallels elsewhere are pierced; the solid Tall-i Bakun A discs were termed pawns. The function of these objects remains uncertain.[7] The same is true of a gable-shaped

---

4. Two examples from Early Susiana contexts are made from Archaic Susiana straw-tempered ware (4.1215 [pl. 231:Y], 4.1217). It is unclear whether they represent survivals or, as is more likely, the utilization of older sherds.

5. One example was found in a Protoliterate pit and was probably out of context (pl. 231:N). A second was discovered in a mixed Late Middle Susiana-Late Susiana deposit. Solid evidence for a Middle Susiana date came in the seventh season (VII-14, VII-17, VII-13).

6. For parallels to plate 235:A–B, see de Morgan 1912, fig. 20 (Susa, Nécropole); Dollfus 1971, fig. 21:18 (two slight depressions on upper side, but unperforated; Jafarabad, Level 2). For unpainted examples, see de Mecquenem 1943, fig. 3:19–20 (Susa, old excavations); for a related(?) object, found out of context at Ur, see Woolley 1955, pl. 16:U.17689a.

7. Alizadeh (1988b), however, argues that most of these tokens were associated with administrative practices at Bakun.

object with a central perforation and painted decoration on all four sides (pl. 235:C). It comes from a Protoliterate context in the East Area but must be a intrusion from the underlying Late Middle Susiana level. Its overall painting can be considered as an antecedent for that covering the two Late Susiana roundels.

Two terra-cotta objects dating to the Late Susiana period are a terra-cotta knob unparalleled elsewhere (pl. 235:E) and the fragment of a stalked ring (pl. 235:H). The latter represents a type of object well known at other sites but nonetheless of uncertain function.[8]

SPINDLE WHORLS

The typology of the spindle whorls at Chogha Mish, as finally determined, is given in table 26; for the sake of completeness, the spindle whorls of the historical periods as well as those from mixed and undated contexts are included.[9] Shape is the basic criterion. The following types are distinguished: flat, low- and high-domed, convex-topped, discoidal, biconical, and solid and hollow conical. There are, inevitably, intermediate examples between the various categories. The convex shapes are distinguished from the conical ones by squatness. The conical shapes rise to more pointed tops than the Protoliterate domed shapes and in profile vary from straight to concave or convex but do not have the gently rounded curvature typical of the domed shapes. The discoidal and biconical categories are self-evident. Subdivisions within the major categories are sometimes based on surface treatment, for example, the plain, painted, or impressed conical spindle whorls, and sometimes on a combination of size and surface treatment, for example, the small-, medium-, or large-sized plain biconical whorls. The convex and discoidal categories provide an added complication. The flat edge of the convex spindle whorls and the equator of the discoidal whorls might be decorated by small imprints, but when these notches are deeper they affect the actual shape of the objects, creating either a series of close-set cogs (pl. 232:M–N, FF, HH–II) or wider-spaced teeth (pl. 232:O, EE). The categories of shapes are characteristic for different periods. Thus, the flat and domed whorls, which stand out from the prehistoric whorls, are typical for the Protoliterate period. The discoidal and cogged whorls of the Early Susiana period stand out from the solid and hollow coni-

cal whorls, with their varying types of decoration, predominant in the Middle Susiana period.

In addition to the spindle whorls of normal size, there are objects that look similar to miniature spindle whorls but seem too small to have been functional (pl. 232:A–C, F–L). Their shapes fit in fairly well with the spindle whorl typology, but nonetheless they might perhaps have only been beads.

No spindle whorls datable without question to the Archaic Susiana period have been recovered; although an example was found in an Archaic context, it is a rather nondescript bead-like "spindle whorl" (pl. 232:I) of ordinary Susiana buff ware and must be intrusive. The earliest indubitable spindle whorls belong to the Early Susiana period; their ware is standard for the period, gritty with traces of chaff temper. They are for the most part discoidal, usually with a denticulated edge (pls. 65:FF–GG; 232:FF, HH–II). Often the denticulations are big enough to look similar to cogs. Low-domed examples with denticulated edges also occur (pl. 232:GG). Sometimes the whorls are painted with a cross design. The straw-tempered ware, the cog-shaped edge, and painted cross of a discoidal example points to an Early Susiana date, although it was found in a Protoliterate context (pl. 65:GG). Similar spindle whorls occur in Early Susiana levels elsewhere.[10]

The Early Susiana tradition was continued in the Early Middle Susiana phase by a convex spindle whorl with pinched edges and a roughly painted cross (pls. 65:DD; 232:O) and an unpainted example of the ninth season (9.907). Other examples from disturbed areas probably also belong to the Early Middle Susiana phase (pls. 65:BB–CC; 232:M–N). In addition, the first of the bead-like spindle whorls occurs in the Early Middle Susiana phase (pl. 232:G).

A new range of shapes, the conical spindle whorls, and new decorative techniques, appear in the later part of the Middle Susiana period. The hollow conical spindle whorls are the dominant types in the Late Middle Susiana phase, the solid conical whorls being much rarer. There seems to be a fairly consistent distinction in ware between the painted and unpainted conical spindle whorls. The unpainted examples are usually made in a light to brownish buff ware, commonly rather dense and with few grits. The painted examples are of the standard greenish-buff Middle Susiana ware.

Many of the unpainted spindle whorls are altogether plain; others have some sort of plastic decoration. Very rare are two examples that carry on the old tradition of the Early Susiana notched spindle whorls (pl.

---

8. For parallels to plate 235:H, see Le Breton 1947, fig. 42:3 (Susa, old excavations); de Mecquenem 1943, fig. 111:5 (Buhallan, old excavations); Le Breton 1947, fig. 7:5 (Jafarabad, old excavations); Dollfus 1971, fig. 21:13–14, 21 (Jafarabad, Level 3 and unstratified).

9. A number of individuals have worked on the classification of the Chogha Mish spindle whorls: in the field, Mary Carolyn McCutcheon, Aghil Abedi, and Guillermo Algaze; in Chicago, Guillermo Algaze and Abbas Alizadeh.

10. For a parallel to plates 65:FF and 232:FF, see Dollfus 1975, fig. 31:4 (Jafarabad, Level 5a). For a parallel to plate 232:EE, see Dollfus 1983, fig. 43:4 (Jowi, Level 10). For a parallel to plate 232:FF, see Dollfus 1975, fig. 31:4 (Jafarabad, Level 5a).

Table 26. Typology of the Protoliterate and Susiana Spindle Whorls

CON-TEXT	FLAT	DOMED:LOW Plain	Incised	Punctated	Imprinted	DOMED HIGH	CONVEX-TOPPED Notched	Denticulate	DISCOIDAL Pinched	Denticulate	Notched	BICONICAL Plain sm	Plain md	Plain lg	Punct.
Elamite						1			1			1			
Elam.-PL		1				1							1		
PL	9	117	10	9	1	5	8		1	28		3	35	25	1
PL–MS		6				2	2			8		3	15	4	
LS		1				1	1	1	2	8		5	12	2	
LS–MS															
MS	1					8	15	3	7	30+4*		3	29	23	2
Late MS						2	2		3	9	1	1	8	4	2
Early MS							5	3					3	1	
MS–ES							1								
Early MS–ES						1	1		1	1*			1	2	
ES							4+3*	1+1*	2+2*	1+7*					
ES–AS													1		
AS							1	1	1*				3		
Mixed		3					2						4	2	
Undated	1	5	1			3	5	1	4	12+1*		4	6	10	1
Surface		4				1	5		2	13		2	11	2	
Total by Type	11	137	11	9	1	25	55	11	26	122	1	22	129	75	6
		158					66		149			232 (226)			

* = Painted

232:U, W). New are imprinted circles, which occur either in clustered patterns or all over (pls. 65:V; 232:AA); they are quite rare. Commoner are punctations, also found either in clusters (pls. 65:S; 232:S, V) or all over (pl. 65:V). Another new technique is incision, similar to imprinting used only occasionally. The incisions are either Xs (pl. 65:R), stars (pl. 232:W), or long lines converging on the center (pl. 232:T).

The painted spindle whorls are the most common. Their decoration is usually fairly simple: often crossing lines dividing the surface into quadrants filled with a subsidiary motif (pl. 232:U, Z, BB–DD); more rarely, torsional lines (pl. 232:X), overall dots (pl. 232:P), or free-field quadrants (pl. 232:Q). The majority of the painted spindle whorls are hollow, but a few have slightly concave or solid bases (pl. 65:Z).

Undecorated biconical objects occur in several sizes, the largest are comparable to the conical spindle whorls just discussed, but the medium- and small-sized objects appear to be more similar to beads. The function of these smaller "spindle whorls" remains uncertain. The earliest known example dates to the Early Middle Susiana phase, but they are much more in evidence in the later part of the period and they also occur in the Late Susiana period, a range which corresponds well with the range of these types at other sites.[11] However, even more were recorded from mixed Middle Susiana-Protoliterate contexts and from straight Protoliterate

loci; in addition, Protoliterate loci provided twenty-five of the large biconical spindle whorls and twenty-one plain conical hollow ones. This distribution of Susiana types creates a problem since the low-domed type is well established as the typical Protoliterate spindle whorl. Perhaps the answer is to be found in the establishment of the Protoliterate settlement directly on top of the Middle Susiana layers of the terrace, which would have made it easy for the spindle whorls to have intruded into the later settlement, or even to have been purposely collected and reused.

In the Late Susiana period, some of the typical Late Middle Susiana types continued, such as plain biconical and hollow conical (pls. 65:LL; 232:B; 232:D–E). Notably absent, however, are the unpainted conical spindle whorls, either undecorated or with some sort of plastic decoration. Among the painted examples, quadrants seem common (pls. 65:Y; 232:D). As already mentioned, the bead-like "spindle whorls" are common in Late Susiana. It should be remembered that the exposure of that period at Chogha Mish is much smaller than that of the earlier periods.

The types of spindle whorls characteristic for the individual periods seem to be as follows: in Early Susiana the convex-topped with marked cogs and denticulations; in the Early Middle Susiana phase some convex-topped and a number of discoidal examples, still carrying on the cog or denticulated Early Susiana tradition; in the Late Middle Susiana phase the hollow and solid conical types, either plain or with imprinted or painted decoration, and the bead-like whorls; and in Late Susiana period the bead-like whorls probably dominate, with the various conical Late Middle Susiana types continuing. If the mixed loci or the considerable number of examples dated only to the Middle Susiana period are disregarded, this sequence of types stands out clearly and fits

11. For a parallel to plate 232:A, see Dollfus 1971, fig. 21:2, 6 (Jafarabad, Level 3). For parallels to plate 232:B and F, see Dollfus 1971, fig. 21:12; Dollfus 1975, fig. 54:4 (Jafarabad, Levels 2, 3n). For a parallel to plate 232:C, see Dollfus 1971, fig. 21:4 (Jafarabad, Level 3). For a parallel to plate 232:G, see Dollfus 1971, fig. 21:8 (Jafarabad, Level 3). For a parallel to plate 232:H, see Dollfus 1975, fig. 54:1 (Jafarabad, Level 3m).

Table 26. Typology of the Protoliterate and Susiana Spindle Whorls (*cont.*)

CONICAL: SOLID					CONICAL: HOLLOW							Unas-signed	Total by Context
Plain	Painted	Incised	Impressed	Punctated	Plain	Painted	Painted	Notched	Incised	Impressed	Punctated		
													3
							1						4
3	1			1	21	5	8		1	1	2	3	298
2	1	1	1	1	7	1	10				2	1	67
1					3	1	3					1	42
			1								1		2
8	1	1	1	2	35	3	28	3	2	4	12	6	231
	3	1		1	11	6	13		2		6		75
1					2								15
	2				1	1					1	1	7
1												1	9
					1						1	6	29
							1					1	2
				1			2						9
					1	2	15					1	30
	1		1	1	7	2	7			1	3	3	80
	1	1			2				1		6		51
16	10	3	4	7	91	21	88	3	6	6	34	24	954
40					249								

in well with the dating of comparable types of spindle whorls at other sites.

SLINGSHOTS

No slingshots have been found in Archaic Susiana levels, but they are common at Chogha Mish from the Early Susiana period onward (pls. 65:L; 231:I–M). They range in length from 3.5 to 6.0 cm and vary in shape from rather globular to more elongated. In both shape and size they are indistinguishable from Protoliterate examples. Slingshots are found individually in most loci, but occasionally they occur in clusters, as for example the cache of fifty-three slingshots in the Early Middle Susiana room, K23:506 in Trench XIII.[12]

STRUCTURAL ELEMENTS

Two fragments of perforated terra-cotta plaques, one very uneven (pl. 231:LL) and one regular (pl. 231:MM), come from Middle Susiana contexts. They probably belonged to grillwork separating the fire pits and firing chambers of kilns. It should be noted that one example (pl. 231:LL) came from a locus immediately adjacent to P23:502, an Early Middle Susiana kiln or

hearth. Similar grillwork fragments occurred at Chogha Mish in the Protoliterate period (pl. 127:K–L).

PREHISTORIC TOKENS

Small unbaked clay objects of simple geometric shapes occurred in the Susiana levels (pl. 231:A–G). Their similarity in shape and size to the more numerous and varied tokens of the Protoliterate period suggests that they were antecedents. By far the most common shape is the sphere, occurring in the Archaic Susiana, Early Susiana, and Middle Susiana periods (pl. 231:B–F). Less common are hemispherical tokens (pl. 231:A) and conical tokens with concave or flat bases (pl. 231:G). Table 27 indicates the Susiana tokens found during the fourth season, with a few additions from the third season. Such objects are widely distributed in the prehistoric sites of the ancient Near East (cf. Schmandt-Besserat 1977a:4ff.; 1992).

BONE OBJECTS[13]

Bone tools were not numerous at Chogha Mish, but almost all periods are represented except for Late Susiana, for which the area excavated was small. The bones of gazelles, goats-sheep, and equids were used for making tools.

Archaic Susiana 1 levels provide three bone tools. From the small deep pit in Trench XII comes part of a haft, almost certainly of a sickle; flint blades (pl. 254) would have been set in bitumen into the socket.[14] Two

---

12. For parallels, see Dollfus 1975:34 (Jafarabad, Levels 4–6); ibid., pp. 56–57 (Jafarabad, Levels 3m–n); ibid., p. 51, fig. 27:8 (Jafarabad, Levels 1–3); Le Breton 1947:175 (Bandebal, old excavations); de Mecquenem 1943:148 (Buhallan, old excavations); Hole, Flannery, and Neely 1969:213 (Tappeh Sabz, Khazineh and Bayat phases); Hole 1977:233–34, pl. 51:c–e (Chogha Sefid, Surkh and Sefid phases); Ghirshman 1938:24, 33, pl. 52:35–36 (Sialk I–II); Langsdorff and McCown 1942:75, pl. 85:5–7 (Bakun A, Level 4); Mallowan and Rose 1935:88 (Arpachiyah, Ubaid and Halaf periods); Tobler 1950:173, pls. 86:b; 87 (Gawra XVI and XIII).

13. Some of the examples included were excavated after the fifth season. The bone identifications and some of the descriptions in the plate lists for plates 257–59 were provided by Jane Wheeler.

14. For a parallel to plate 65:N, see Ghirshman 1938, pl. 8:2 (Sialk I).

Table 27. Tokens Recorded from Susiana Levels during the Third and Fourth Seasons

Period	Locus	Elevation	Spherical	Hemispherical Conical
Late Middle Susiana	N11:Trench XXII	81.11–88.88	1-	—
Late Middle Susiana	N11:Trench XXII	N/A	2-	—
Late Middle Susiana	S–T21:Sounding G	77.50	1-	—
Late Middle Susiana	S–T21:Sounding G	77.15	—	1+
Middle Susiana	F27:Trench XV	Dump	1-	—
Middle Susiana	N11:Trench XXII	76.46	—	1-*
Middle Susiana	K22:400	82.74–82.54	2-	—
Middle Susiana	K22:400	82.54–82.44	1-	—
Middle Susiana	K22:400	82.44–82.24	2-	—
Middle Susiana	K22:400	82.39–82.09	1-	2+
Middle Susiana	K22:402	82.74–82.44	9-	—
Middle Susiana	K22:402	82.54–82.44	2-	—
Middle Susiana	K22:402	82.34–81.94	1-	1+
Middle Susiana	K23:400	82.25–82.15	3-	—
Middle Susiana	L22:400	82.99–82.79	3-	—
Middle Susiana	L22:400	82.49–82.39	1-	—
Middle Susiana	South of L22:402	81.89–81.69	1-	—
Middle Susiana	L22:403	82.14–81.94	2-	—
Middle Susiana	S–T21:Sounding G	76.15	—	1
Middle Susiana	S–T21:Sounding G	76.00	—	1-
Early Middle Susiana	K22:400	81.84–81.64	1-	—
Early Middle Susiana	K22:409	82.04–81.74	1-	—
Early Middle Susiana	K22:409	81.84–81.64	3-	—
Early Susiana	P23:301	79.35	1+	—
Early Susiana-Archaic Susiana	P/Q23:301	78.30	—	1
Archaic Susiana	P23:301	76.35	2-	—
Archaic Susiana 1–2	S22:405	74.60	1-	—
Archaic Susiana 1	S22:403	72.88	5-	4+
Archaic Susiana 1	S22:404	72.88	2-	1+

* = stone   - = under 15 mm   + = over 15 mm

other Archaic Susiana 1 tools are broad, rather flat-sided, and polished "reamers" (pl. 233:W–X). Their use is uncertain, but they might have been potters' tools for burnishing the surface of the painted-burnished ware of the Archaic Susiana 1 phase. Awls recognizable by their narrow pointed tips and mostly made from metapodals or tibias with epiphysis are known from Archaic Susiana 2 (pl. 233:I), Archaic Susiana 3 (pl. 233:G–H, V), and Archaic Susiana-Early Susiana transitional (pl. 233:K, U) contexts. A small Archaic Susiana 2 fragment could be either an awl or a pin (pl. 233:D). The three most complete awls come from Early Susiana (pl. 233:P), Early Susiana-Early Middle Susiana (pl. 233:Q), and Early Middle Susiana (pl. 233:O) contexts. Also from the Early Middle Susiana phase is a tool with a pointed end, which if an awl, is atypical (pls. 65:M; 233:F). It is too thin to have withstood much pressure and high polish on one side suggests that it might have been a burnisher.

In addition to awls, several other types of bone tools occurred in the Early Susiana period. One has, instead of the pointed tip of the awls, a broad working edge (pl. 233:R). Another is a pin with a carefully finished head

(pl. 233:E). A needle with a hole has a stubby point and could have been used for only coarse sewing (pl. 233:A). A pointed tip fragment could have belonged to a pin, a needle, or an awl (pl. 233:B).

Several tools can be attributed to the Middle Susiana phase: a pin (pl. 233:C); an ovoid point and fragmentary pointed tip (pl. 233:S–T); and two implements with broad edges polished through use, presumably fleshers (pl. 233:Y–Z).

PERSONAL OBJECTS OR ORNAMENTS

Beads are rare and for the most part of simple shapes. Archaic Susiana contexts provided a small tubular bead of white stone (pl. 234:AA) and a large, crude disc of unbaked clay (pl. 234:CC). A small globular carnelian bead could be either the Early Susiana period or Early Middle Susiana phase (pl. 234:W). Two small disc beads cut from shell and white stone respectively were found in Middle Susiana levels of Trench XIII (pl. 234:X–Y). A single bead is attributable to the Late Susiana period: it is tubular, of a green stone with white veins. Only one bead stands out as more sophisticated, a tiny Middle Susiana example cut in the shape of a quadruped (pl. 67:N). Although the bush tail over the back suggests certain types of dogs, the animal intended cannot be identified.

To the Late Middle Susiana phase can be attributed a relatively large terra-cotta pendant in the shape of a bull's head (pl. 67:M). One remaining stump indicates that originally the horns projected considerably. The mouth and the nostrils were imprinted. The eyes are painted in the same way as on the head of a Late Susiana animal figurine (pl. 66:H). Paint was also used for accents, such as the vertical strokes under the eyes. In its general shape and the rendering of the eyes, the pendant resembles bucranium motifs on pottery, which provides analogies for the shape of the missing horns (pl. 187:B). The appearance of the bucranium as a pendant, together with its prominence among the representational motifs of the painted pottery of the Middle Susiana period (pls. 163:X–Z; 181:O; 187:B), suggests that it might have been an important emblem, perhaps even one with religious connotations.

Three beads distinctive for their lentoid shapes and incised decoration were found in the East Area, one from the interior of a Protoliterate wall (pl. 234:EE) and two fairly deep in the area of R19:302/401, where Protoliterate deposits directly overlay Late Middle Susiana ones (pl. 234:FF–GG). The incised decoration of these beads allies them with Susiana stamp seals (pl. 234:GG–II), but nonetheless their Susiana date cannot be established beyond doubt. Although they could have easily been accidental intrusions or reused objects, they were found in Protoliterate contexts. Although some prehistoric parallels exist, there are also others from Protoliterate contexts in Mesopotamia.[15] The question of their date must remain open.

Small objects made of unbaked or baked clay, stone, and bituminous stone might be considered as studs or labrets (pl. 234:F–V). However, four slightly conical examples from Archaic Susiana levels are of uncertain use (pl. 234:B–E). Much more certainly identifiable as studs or labrets are objects of either pronounced or slight T-shape. They range in date from the Archaic Susiana through the Middle Susiana periods. Their function can be partly established by their shape, the T-shaped base would hold them in place, but better by an

Early Susiana terra-cotta head from Chogha Mish with a representation of a labret (pl. 234:A) and by the discovery at Ali Kosh in the Deh Luran plain of one in place against the mandible of a male skeleton (Hole, Flannery, and Neely 1969:235–36, fig. 109). Two Archaic Susiana examples made of unbaked, polished clay have a characteristic bulbous stem (pl. 234:F–G).[16] No actual Early Susiana labrets were found at Chogha Mish in the first five seasons, but that represented on the terra-cotta head just mentioned proves their existence.[17] Labrets and studs were used throughout the Middle Susiana period. The T-shape started in the Archaic Susiana period, continued in several versions. Stout examples equivalent in size and proportion to their Archaic Susiana antecedents now have cylindrical, flatended stems (pl. 234:H [Early Middle Susiana]; pl. 234:I–J [Late Middle Susiana]).[18] Other Middle Susiana T-shaped labrets are smaller, tend to have larger shafts, and in addition to clay, can be made of fired clay or bituminous stone (pl. 234:O, R). The stem of one has a pointed end (pl. 234:R) and the stems of two others are so long that they probably could not have been used in the same manner as the short-stemmed examples (pl. 234:S–T).[19] The examples of a third group of T-shaped ornaments are cut from white-veined black stone in such a way as to produce a black stalk ending in a white "eye" with a black "iris" (pls. 67:F–I; 234:K–N). This group appears to be characteristic for the Late Middle Susiana phase.[20]

Two small objects of white stone are isolated examples. One is spool-shaped and found on the surface (pl. 234:U).[21] The other has a narrow cylindrical stem with a large and small conical head at each end (pl. 234:V). It is probably Early Middle Susiana in date, and after the fifth season similar examples were found in

15. For a parallel to plate 234:EE, see Woolley 1955, pl. 28:U.15606 (Ur, Pit F, Late Protoliterate). For an example more elongated than plate 234:GG, see Le Breton 1947, fig. 32:17 (Bandebal, old excavations); for related examples, see Woolley 1955, pl. 28:U.17923 (Diqdiqqeh); Tobler 1950, pl. 171:8, 10 respectively (Gawra XV and XII). For a general parallel for plate 234:EE–GG, see Delougaz and Lloyd 1942:267, Ag. 36:354 (cut from limestone as opposed to translucent stone; Tell Aqrab, Shara Temple, Early Dynastic II level).

16. For parallels to plate 234:F–G, see Hole, Flannery, and Neely 1969, fig. 102:e (Ali Kosh, Muhammad Jafar phase); Hole 1977, fig. 92:o, q–t, table 78 (Chogha Sefid; Sefid, Surkh, and Chogha Mami Transitional phases).

17. Terra-cotta figurines of the Samarra period from Chogha Mami also have appliqué decoration suggesting the use of labrets (Oates 1969). In addition, two appliqué pellets on the nose suggest that studs were also in use.

18. For parallels to plate 234:H, see Dollfus 1975, fig. 46:4 (Jafarabad, Level 5a); Le Breton 1947, fig. 32:10 (Bandebal, old excavations); Hole, Flannery, and Neely 1969:236, fig. 102:c (Ali Kosh or Tappeh Sabz, Muhammad Jafar/early Khazineh phases).

19. For parallels to plate 234:T, see Dollfus 1983, fig. 44:4–5 (Jowi, Levels 4 and 12); Hole, Flannery, and Neely 1969:236, fig. 102:g (shorter; Tappeh Sabz, Mehmeh phase).

20. For stone and terra-cotta labrets or studs of similar shape to plate 234:K–N but without the "eye," see Oates 1969, pl. 30:a–b (Chogha Mami, Samarra levels).

21. For parallels to plate 234:U, see Hole 1977, pl. 54:e–f (Chogha Sefid, Surkh phase).

Archaic Susiana 3-Early Susiana transitional levels (VIII-42, Q23:821; VIII-52, S22:827).

The most commonly found ornaments are bracelets made of bituminous stone or baked clay. They are almost always represented only by small segments. Insofar as can be judged by these, the bracelets ranged in diameter from less than 6 cm to about 8 cm.[22] There was considerable variation in the shape of the section and the width of the band. So far no bracelets have been found in good Archaic Susiana contexts. The examples from mixed Archaic Susiana-Early Susiana deposits should almost certainly be assigned to the Early Susiana period, the first major period for bracelets. All of the examples recovered (forty-three) are made of bituminous stone. Most common, altogether ca. 28% of the Early Susiana bracelets, are wide examples divided by shallow incisions into two to four bands or, more rarely, five (5.927). Second in terms of popularity, ca. 21%, were bracelets with square sections. Less popular, but still quite frequent, were bracelets of trapezoidal, ca. 14%, or rectangular, ca. 12%, sections. Also attested are bracelets with barrel, oval, biconvex, or triangular sections.

In the Early Middle Susiana phase all of the twenty-two bracelet fragments recovered are made of bituminous stone except for one gray stone example, biconvex in section and decorated by transfer incisions (4.1196). Among the bituminous examples the range of shapes is smaller than those of the Early Susiana period. Bracelets with rectangular sections constitute about 40%. Those with square, 28%, and trapezoidal, 18%, sections are also common. A single example with a barrel-shaped section occurred.

By the Late Middle Susiana phase an important change has taken place. Bituminous stone bracelets have decreased in popularity, constituting only 36% of the total of twenty-five Late Middle Susiana specimens. Among the bituminous stone bracelets, those of biconvex section are commonest, along with some rectangular and one trapezoidal example; examples with two or three bands still occur. The terra-cotta bracelets have plano-convex, rectangular round sections, the first being more frequent. No bracelets have been recovered from Late Susiana levels, and the eight examples from Protoliterate levels are intrusive.

Table 28 summarizes the shapes and materials of the prehistoric bracelets found at Chogha Mish during the first nine seasons of excavation. For the percentages, only loci securely dated to the Early Susiana period, the Early and Late Middle Susiana phases, have been utilized. A considerable number of the examples included under Middle Susiana comes from loci of later seasons and will eventually be datable with more precision. Bracelets similar to those found at Chogha Mish occur at other sites in Susiana and elsewhere.[23]

GLYPTIC

The earliest evidence from Chogha Mish indicating the existence of stamped seals comes from Middle Susiana contexts. A rectangular stamped seal in light orange stone found on the surface of the terrace has a perforated midrib on the reverse and a geometric design of hatched quadrants on the obverse (pl. 234:GG).[24] Its design is paralleled in general by that on a red stone button seal with a broken loop handle on the reverse; its decoration is closely paralleled elsewhere (pl. 234:II).[25] The latter seal comes from a context in Trench XXV that was severely disturbed by Protoliterate pits. A second button-shaped seal of white stone, also with a broken loop handle, appears to be unfinished (pl. 234:JJ). It was found out of context in Protoliterate debris immediately below the surface in the southwestern corner of Trench XX in the East Area. Although the context for these Chogha Mish stamp seals are not primary, the parallels indicate that they must belong to the later part of the Susiana sequence.

Three impressions on unbaked clay sealings of a rosette design have better contexts (pl. 67:A–B and 4.658, K22:402). One comes from the dump of Trench XVI, a

22. A pair of complete examples (VI-32–33) found during the sixth season have diameters of 6.00 and 6.15 cm. A fragment from the same season might have come from an example with a diameter of 9.50 cm.

23. Jafarabad has produced a total of six bituminous stone bracelets in Levels 5 and 4 dated to the Early Susiana period (Dollfus 1975:44, pl. 46:12–17); these have parallels at Chogha Mish. In the Deh Luran plain, similar bracelets are also reported. Band bracelets identical to those from Chogha Mish but said to be of "polished limestone" were found. At Tappeh Sabz, they are concentrated in the levels of the Sabz phase, but at least one example comes from a Bayat phase context. At Ali Kosh, very early examples also of the same material and with irregular rounded or plano-convex sections, come from Muhammad Jafar phase levels (Hole, Flannery, and Neely 1969:237, 240, fig. 104). Similar examples with rounded or plano-convex sections are reported in "Sefid" and Chogha Mami Transitional period levels at Chogha Sefid (Hole 1977:240, pl. 55:a–b). Outside of Susiana, similar bracelets have been reported from Sialk, Periods I and II, and are reportedly made of "gray stone." Examples with multiple bands, triangular and oval sections, are represented there (Ghirshman 1938:31, pl. 52:2, 5, 10, 15–16, 20–23).

24. For a seal with similar shape and design to plate 234:GG, see Oppenheim 1943, pls. 38:14, 114:17 (Tell Halaf, Halaf period).

25. For parallels to plate 234:II, see de Mecquenem 1934, fig. 17:4, and Amiet 1972, pl. 38:8, 25, 35; pl. 43:98 (Susa, old excavations); Le Breton 1947, fig. 32:21 (Bandebal, old excavations); Ghirshman 1938, pl. 86:S.259, S.117, respectively (Sialk, Levels III-4 and III-5). For a related design but no loop handle, see Dollfus 1971, fig. 23:3 (Jafarabad, Level 2); Tobler 1950, pl. 4:49 (Gawra XII).

Table 28. Typology of the Susiana and Protoliterate Bitumen and Terra-cotta Bracelets

(Material: B = Bitumen, T = Terracotta)

TYPE	Round Reg. B	Round Reg. T	Round Irr. B	Round Irr. T	Oval B	Oval T	Barrel B	Plano-convex B	Plano-convex T	Bi-convex B	Bi-convex T	Triangular Apex out B	Triangular Apex out T	Triangular Apex in B	Square B	Rectangular Horiz. B	Rectangular Vert. B	Rectangular Vert. T	Trape-zoidal B	Grooved 1 Groove B	Grooved 2 Grooves B	Grooved 3 Grooves B	Grooved 4 Grooves B	TOTAL
TOTALS BY PERIOD																								
PL		1		2					1	1						2	1							8
LS																								0
MS-PL		1												2	1	1	3		1	1				10
Late MS		1		2					9	4							2	4	1	1	1			25
Early MS							1								6	5	4		4	2				22
MS	2	4	1	3	4			3	7	16		5			7	19	1	10	9	5	1		2	99
ES-MS					1		1		1	1					4	3	1		3	1				16
ES					2		4			3		2			9	1	4		6	6	1	3	2	43
AS-ES							1								1		4		1					7
TOTAL	2	7	1	7	7		7	3	18	25		7		2	28	31	20	14	25	16	3	3	4	230
TOTALS BY PERCENTAGE																								
Late MS		4		8					36	16							8	16	4	4	4			100%
Early MS							4.5								27.3	22.7	18.2		18.2	9.1				100%
ES					4.7		9.35			7		4.7			20.9	2.35	9.35		14	14	2.35	7	4.7	100%

(Grooved combined percentage for ES: 27.95)

small test area that yielded an abundance of Late Middle Susiana sherds, a second from Trench VI, which produced some Middle Susiana material in addition to the Protoliterate finds, and the third in an ashy pit, cutting into the Early Middle Susiana rooms in Trench XIII. Thus these impressions can be dated to the Late Middle Susiana phase. They prove that the button seals were actually used as seals. Parallels for the rosette design occur in Halaf contexts.[26] In addition, both stamp seals and impressions with similar designs occur at Tall-i Bakun A in Fars at a slightly later period contemporary with the Late Susiana period.[27] In the Susiana area itself, button seals occur in Late Susiana levels at Susa and Jafarabad.[28]

The High Mound yielded one complete and one fragmentary example of a type of stamp seal typical for the Late Susiana period (pl. 67:D–E). They are made of baked clay and rectangular in shape. Both have perforated handles on the back and excised geometric patterns on the base. Susa and Jafarabad provide parallels.[29]

The most elaborate seal that can be attributed to the Late Susiana period is made of stone, hemispherical in shape, and transversely perforated (pl. 67:C). It was found on the surface of the High Mound near the southern edge of Plots 5–6 of Trench II. On the base are carved several animal figures; one with horns seems to be attacked by the animal above it. For the shape of the seal and for its decoration there are good parallels from Susa and from Mesopotamia.[30] Both the terra-cotta seals

26. See Homès-Fredericq 1970:144, fig. 300 = Oppenheim 1943, pls. 38:15, 114:13 (Tell Halaf, Halaf period); Homès-Fredericq 1970:146, fig. 307 = Mallowan 1936:25, fig. 7:6 (Chagar Bazar, Halaf period).

27. See Langsdorff and McCown 1942, pls. 8:1–10, 81:16–33, 82:1–20.

28. For parallels to plate 234:II, see de Mecquenem 1934, fig. 17:1 (Susa, old excavations); Dollfus 1971, fig. 23:3, pl. 9:12 (Jafarabad, Level 2).

29. For parallels to plate 67:E, see Amiet 1972, pl. 52:251 (Susa, old excavations); Dollfus 1971, fig. 23:6 (Jafarabad, Level 3).

30. For seals related to pl. 67:C, see de Mecquenem 1934, fig. 19 = Amiet 1972, pl. 45:143, and Le Breton 1947, fig. 44:4 (Susa, old excavations); Tobler 1950, pl. 164:100 (Gawra XIII, well); Frankfort 1935:29, fig. 31 (somewhat ovoid; Tell Gomel, unstratified).

and the more elaborate one of stone are excellent indications of the complexity of life that had already been attained by the Late Susiana period.

HUMAN AND ANIMAL FIGURINES

Chogha Mish has yielded a considerable number of prehistoric figurines. It is striking that human figurines predominate in the earlier part of the sequence (Archaic Susiana and Early Susiana) and animal ones in the later part (Middle Susiana and Late Susiana). The finds are sufficiently consistent and numerous to indicate that this contrast is not a mere accident of discovery but reflects rather a shift in the preoccupations of the makers of the figurines.

Three categories of human figurines appear in the Archaic Susiana period. The earliest example known, from an Archaic Susiana 1 context, represents the "naturalistic" type (pl. 237:C). The slightly conical lower part the figure can be interpreted as a long skirt with incisions indicating the patterns or fringes at the top and bottom of the textile, and on the front and back, the division of the legs. There is hardly any modeling, except for depressions indicating the navel and the small of the back. Other examples dating to the Archaic Susiana 2 and 3 phases taper at the waist more than the first example described above, but, as on it, vertical incisions at the base suggest a fringe and are standard for this type of figurine (pl. 237:A–B, D–E). The rest of the skirt can be plain or with only a few incisions. The long skirts mark the figures as female.[31] One fragment indicates what the upper part of these figurines was probably like (pl. 237:F). It is narrow at the broken waist and broadens out across the shoulders, which are rounded off without any indication of arms. The "head" consists of a conical stump with a "necklace" of incisions. Vertical incisions presumably mark the backbone of the figure. Another example (pl. 237:G) begins to flare out in the shoulders (cf. pl. 237:F), but unlike the other examples, it lacks the basal incisions. It has a division between the legs and horizontal incisions similar to another example (pl. 237:B).

A second type of figurine has an abstract chessman shape. One of the best preserved examples was found low in the Archaic Susiana 2 levels of the Gully Cut (pls. 66:D; 237:K). It is an irregular, squat cylinder with a slightly concave top and bottom; three punctations represent the eyes and either the nose or mouth. The vertical lines incised at the base can be taken as representing a fringed skirt by analogy with the less abstract conical figurines. The function of the punctation in the top is unknown. Several such figures, often rather irregular in shape or incomplete, have been found in Archaic Susiana 2 or 3 contexts (pl. 237:I–J).

A third distinctive type of figurine attributable to the Archaic Susiana period consists of an elongated ovoid base, essentially flat at the bottom, from the center of which rises a narrow thorn-like projection. Such figures were made of baked clay or, occasionally, stone. The best example, found out of context in the East Area, shows that the "thorn" is an extremely simplified human figure (pl. 236:G). Incisions demarcate the head and suggest its features. A single vertical incision marks the back and two others the front. The latter suggest clothing enveloping the body, but this might be too realistic an interpretation.

In addition to the almost complete examples, several bases of thorn figures were recovered (pl. 236:F). Of these, two were found in Trench XXV, where the Susiana levels were thoroughly disturbed in the Protoliterate period, and one in the Gully Cut in an Archaic Susiana 2 level. There is every likelihood that the thorn figures belong to the earlier part of the Archaic Susiana period.

The thorn figures show some relationships with the larger-sized conical-skirted figures. Thus, the upper part of the almost complete thorn figurine (pl. 236:G) is similar in shape to the shape of the torso presumed to have had a conical skirt (pl. 237:F). The use of incision (pl. 236:G) is reminiscent of that on conical-skirted fragments (pl. 237:B, G). The splayed ovoid base fragment of a conical-skirted figurine (pl. 237:H) might have been influenced by the shape of the bases of the thorn figurines. It seems certain that the thorn and conical-skirted figurines overlap, but also that the former began earlier. In fact, thorn figurines have a wide range from the northwestern Zagros to the northeastern corner of the Iranian plateau.[32]

The figurines of the Early Susiana period appear to have developed from Archaic Susiana figurines without any break. For example, two terra-cotta fragments carry on the tradition of the conical-skirted Archaic figures,

---

31. Finds made after the fifth season corroborate this conclusion. AA

32. In Deh Luran, a large number of these figurines have been found. The majority come from the early phases of Chogha Sefid and Ali Kosh. One example is also reported from Tappeh Sabz. There, these figurines have been called "T-shaped figurines." At Ali Kosh they are reported from both Ali Kosh and Muhammad Jafar phase levels They are by far more common in the latter phase (Hole, Flannery, and Neely 1969:226, tables 47–48, fig. 98). The single example reported from Tappeh Sabz comes from Sabz phase (ibid., tables 47–48). At Chogha Sefid, they were recovered in all phases from the Ali Kosh to the Surkh phase. They are most common in the Sefid and Surkh phases (Hole 1977:229–32, fig. 91:g–n). Examples of thorn figurines have also been found at Sang-e Chakhmaq in the Iranian central plateau (Masuda 1974, fig. 3:10, 12); related, but not identical, examples were found at Jarmo in Iraqi Kurdestan (Braidwood and Howe 1960, pl. 16:14–15).

substituting painted lines instead of incisions to indicate the skirt. One fragment is fairly evenly covered on all sides by vertical bands crossed near the base by an irregular horizontal band (pl. 236:A).[33] Another fragment, found out of place in a Protoliterate context, represents half of the lower part of a figurine (pl. 235:I). The buttock projects markedly and, together with the contours of the figure, shows a shift toward a more naturalistic rendering than that of Archaic Susiana conical-skirted figures (pl. 237:A–E, G). The simple decoration consists of two broad bands on the side and a vertical band, bifurcating at the top, on the front and back.

The smoothness of the inner side of one figurine (pl. 235:I) indicates that it was made in two lateral halves that were then pressed together. Another example made in two parts found in the sixth season shows that this was a quite standard technique. It was one that rose independently in widely separate areas. It appears in Neolithic Greece where Talalay (1987:161–69) has interpreted it on the basis of much later written evidence as a surprisingly sophisticated technique of recording agreements.

The type of head that might have belonged to some of the headless bodies (cf. pl. 235:I; 236:A) is illustrated by an example without provenience (pl. 66:A). The neck apparently projected forward diagonally to support a discoidal head, slightly concave in the back. All of the main facial features are rendered. Although much of the large nose has been broken, the nostrils, indicated by slight indentations and emphasized by neat dabs of brown paint, remain. The mouth is shown in the same way but less neatly. Pairs of flattened pellets represent the ears. Long appliqués form the eyes and eyebrows; one of the latter is missing, but its emplacement is still visible. After the application of the pellets the entire head was covered by a green slip that fastened them down and partly filled the cleft that runs from the top of the nose across the head and down to the nape of the neck. The hair is indicated by paint that carries over to the front to form a continuous border around the face. Paint also outlines the forehead cleft and continues down as two prominent diagonal bands. The remaining eyebrow and the center of the eyes are accentuated by paint. Three diagonal lines on the back of the neck are difficult to interpret in their fragmentary state. On the front of the neck a thick bit of paint looks as if it had accumulated against a now missing pellet, perhaps one of several that once formed a necklace encircling the neck. Comparable heads are typical for the Samarra culture of northern Mesopotamia.[34]

A second, larger, head is executed in a different technique from the first one (pls. 66:B; 234:A). It has fewer facial features and only an overall red wash instead of painted details.[35] On the other hand, it makes considerable use of volume to produce its effect. Though the back of the head is irregularly concave (cf. pl. 66:A), the face in profile forms a swelling hemisphere (2.3 cm thick), the curve of which is repeated by the large projecting nose. The eyes are big oval swellings with deep slits. There is some modeling of the lower part of the cheeks. Incisions mark the nostrils, but there is no indication of the mouth. Instead, a flattened pellet projects from the chin, rendering a labret. The projecting ear lobes have two perforations reminiscent of a pair of pellets forming ears (pl. 66:A). The larger perforations on the forehead might in themselves represent hair or a headdress or have served for the attachment of perishable elements. When the face is vertical the stub of the neck projects back horizontally; it is likely that the neck projected diagonally from the body so as to tilt the head back. The head might render an artificially deformed skull such as the later, Late Middle Susiana, one found in Trench XXII and the earlier skulls from the Deh Luran sites. A body fragment (pl. 235:I) broken at the waist can be used to obtain a very rough estimate of ca. 8.0 cm for the height of the entire figure. It would have been large enough with its huge unseeing eyes to have embodied an important force. Similar to the painted head (pl. 66:A), the red-washed one also has an analogy from the Samarra period.[36]

In addition to the painted or red-washed figurines, several examples of unbaked clay can be assigned to the Early Susiana period even though three come from Trench XXV, where the stratigraphy has been disturbed by Protoliterate pits. Two others were found in the Gully Cut in a mixed Archaic Susiana-Early Susiana context above undisturbed deposits. The clay examples tend to be smaller than the terra-cotta figurines. They have a circular base, cylindrical stem, and markedly projecting buttocks (pls. 235:I; 236:D). Simple incisions substitute for painted decoration of the terra-cotta figurines (cf. pl. 236:B). One fragment with the same general shape, though less pronounced buttocks, has a projection in front that appears to be an exaggerated rendering of the navel (pl. 236:C). Perhaps a link with the notion of fertility or pregnancy gave rise to the unnatural form and emphasis given to a relatively inconspicuous anatomical feature.

The rendering of squatting figures was an innovation of the Early Susiana period. Two small unbaked

---

33. For a parallel to plate 236:A, see Dollfus 1975, fig. 32:1 (Jafarabad, Level 5a).

34. For parallels to plate 66:A, see Oates 1969, pl. 26:A–F, especially A (Chogha Mami).

35. Another Early Susiana figurine head covered with red wash was discovered during the sixth season (see Kantor 1974; 1972:192, fig. 24); it is smaller and of less elaborate shape.

36. For a parallel to plate 66:B, see Oates 1969, pl. 27:a–c (Chogha Mami).

figurines represent squatting females with the lower legs rounded off and swelling buttocks separated by a large cleft (pl. 236:B, E). The better modeled one has large breasts. In addition to the squatting pose, the naturalism with which swelling natural shapes could be rendered was a new characteristic not seen in the Archaic Susiana figurines.

The number of human figurines from the Archaic Susiana and Early Susiana periods contrasts with their almost complete absence in the later Susiana levels at Chogha Mish. There is only one example that appears to be later than Early Susiana, a violin-shaped figurine from a transitional Early Susiana-Middle Susiana context in Trench XXXI (pl. 235:G). Its shape and decoration of dots painted around the periphery and sides are so different from the features normal for Early Susiana figurines that it can be attributed to the succeeding phase, Early Middle Susiana. The figurine was probably rounded off below and could have had a simple conical head similar to that of an Archaic Susiana 2 figurine (pl. 237:F). In general, various types of violin-shaped figurines are widely distributed geographically and chronologically. It is unlikely that they can all be placed in a single series (Korfmann 1972). There seems to be no close relative for the violin-shaped figurine.

The problem remains as to whether the dearth of human figurines in the Middle Susiana period is an accident of discovery or a sign of a cultural change. Although it is possible that human figures were used or kept only in limited areas and thus might be easily missed, the size of the sample provided by the trenches distributed over Chogha Mish makes the second alternative more likely. From now on the animal figurines, which had not been very frequent in the Archaic Susiana and Early Susiana levels, predominate.

Many of the animal figurines are represented by small almost shapeless fragments whose character as quadrupeds is barely recognizable. Both unbaked clay and terra-cotta examples occur, the latter usually with painted decoration. The species is often difficult to determine, particularly since the horns are frequently broken. Presumably both oxen and sheep are represented. A surface find is one of the best examples of the unbaked figurines; its curving muzzle resembles that of a sheep (pl. 66:E). Another example (pl. 66:K) could be either an ox or a sheep. It is boldly painted with a ring around the neck and stripes on the back and legs. It also illustrates the normal shape with hind and forelegs projecting down from the solid body in a single concave curve. There is no division between the individual hind or forelegs. Another example has only a painted neck band (pl. 66:G). Although usually the body was a solid mass, in an atypical example it has been formed from a flattened piece of clay bent so that the whole underpart is concave and each of the legs projects separately (pl.

66:J). The elongated neck, small head, and lattice design are also unusual. Sometimes incisions mark eyes, nostrils, and mouth as on a head found on the surface of the terrace and presumably belonging to the Late Middle Susiana phase (pl. 66:F). A head from a Late Susiana context is painted with three median lines and dotted eyes (pl. 66:H). The eyes of the Late Middle Susiana bull pendant from the West Area (pl. 67:M) are rendered in the same way, this being a feature linking the animal figurines of the Late Middle Susiana phase and Late Susiana period. Bird figures are much rarer than those of quadrupeds. In one case the base of the figure is flat; the body is decorated with splotches of paint (pl. 66:I). It was found on the surface of the terrace and presumably belongs to the Late Middle Susiana phase. Another figure has the stalk typical for Late Susiana birds (pl. 235:D).[37] The traces of paint remaining on the denuded surface indicate that the entire figure was originally covered by splotches (cf. pl. 66:I).

A terra-cotta painted snake head is unique at Chogha Mish (pl. 235:F). It is made of solid buff ware, red-washed, and painted solid black on the neck. Two pellets form the eyes and incisions form the nostrils and mouth. It was located in the sherd yard of the West Area, in a pile of discards from the second season, so unfortunately its exact context is lost. However, it must have been found among the Late Middle Susiana sherds that were prominent in that area. The neck has a rough break, which suggests that originally it was attached to a body. This is supported by the partial analogy provided by the body fragments and head of a snake found in the Late Ubaid Temple VII at Eridu (Safar, Mustafa, and Lloyd 1981, fig. 110). The Eridu head differs in being perforated through the neck and mouth. The body to which it was originally joined is hollow. In view of its findspot, it was certainly a cult object. The Chogha Mish snake head likewise might have been part of a snake figure and it was found in an area that later in the Protoliterate period yielded cult objects, among them, the jar with two spouts and appliqués of snakes biting the neck of goats.

37. See the examples in Dollfus 1971, fig. 22:4, 6–7, 9, 12 (Jafarabad). Another type of terra-cotta object typical for the Late Susiana period, the spike with a ring head, occurs at Chogha Mish (cf. I-18 [pl.235:H]; Dollfus 1971, fig. 21:13–14, 21); see also Woolley 1955, pl. 15:U.18297 (Ur).

CHAPTER 11

THE GROUND STONE TOOLS FROM CHOGHA MISH

Daniel M. Shimabuku

The 1,087 stone objects that make up this study are organized into thirteen categories of stone tools.[1] On the basis of four criteria (1) shape and size, (2) function, (3) mode of utilization, and (4) relative temporal distribution, a total of 101 tool types and subtypes are differentiated. The typology is based principally on features relating to general descriptive characteristics such as shape and size and is secondarily dependent on particular features of the work area of the tool. Considerable energy was spent in attempting to determine from wear/use patterns the function and mode of utilization of each stone artifact. Chronological considerations were generally of minor importance in distinguishing tool types. The classification scheme is given in table 29.

Table 29. Ground Stone Tools: The Categories and Their Types

Category	Type
Grinding Stones	G 1–8
Handgrinders	HG 1–3
Pestles/pounders	P 1–12
Finger Stones	F 1–3
Slicing Slabs	SS 1
Waisted Pebbles	WP 1
Stone Hoes	H 1–9
Perforated Stones	PF 1–6
Stones with Depressions	D 1–7
Pivot Stones	PV 1–3
Stone Discs	DS 1–6
Grooved Stones	GR 1–3
Rubbing/polishing Stones	R 1–4

As suspected, shape and size conditions usually offered logical explanations for differences in function, but the mode of utilization was often less discernible. Detailed analyses of the wear/use patterns showed that the mode of utilization was highly variable, even for tools with basically the same function or purpose. A dis-

cussion of the mode of utilization for each tool-type is included throughout this chapter.

The chronological sequence covered is from the Archaic Susiana through the Protoliterate periods of Chogha Mish. Following a discussion of each category of stone tools, a chart illustrates the relative temporal distribution of each tool type (see table 30). The relationship of tool types to each cultural period is indicated by four bars that refer to ranked degrees of significance: (1) characteristic, (2) relatively well represented, (3) represented (by at least one example), and (4) uncertain whether represented.

Table 30. Key to the Temporal Distribution Charts for Stone Objects

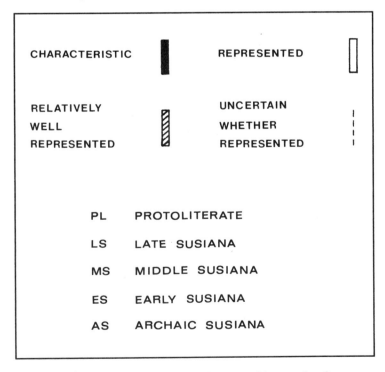

A chart of this nature emphasizes notable trends of continuity or change that might otherwise go unobserved if the tool type counts were presented simply as statistical data arranged in time-correlated numerical listings or graphs.

A variety of stones had been selected for the manufacture of ground stone tools. The range of types are generally classified into hard and soft stones, and fur-

---

1. A report on a category of possible stone weights by Daniel M. Shimabuku, "The Beveled Rim Bowls and Stone Spheroids Found at Chogha Mish: Possible Ancient Systems of Weights and Measures," was to appear in *The Proceedings of the Vth Annual Symposium on Archaeological Research in Iran* (1977), but that volume was never published.

ther distinction is based on the geologic character or natural color of stones. All types of stones, with the exception of chert and granite, can still be found in relative abundance, especially along river channels in the near vicinity of the site of Chogha Mish. Vesicular basalt might, however, have been at times imported from the Zagros Mountains. The main source of chert, granite, and flint for the Susiana region is about 40 km to the northwest of Chogha Mish, in the area of Ivan-e Karkheh. The following is a list of the different types of stones that were represented in the Chogha Mish corpus of ground stone tools.

CONGLOMERATES

Conglomerate	Rock composed of considerable amounts of grits of various sizes and colors in a limestone base
Conglomerate-sandstone	Conglomerate with an abundance of sand-size grits
Sandstone-conglomerate	Basically sandstone with some large grits
Quartzite	Quartzite rock formation; quartz chips/grits densely mixed in a base that is probably of limestone

HARD STONES

Buff stone	Very similar to chert in the manner of flaking, but a bit too grainy; probably a form of limestone; buff in color
Chert	Chert; probably essentially fibrous chalcedony
Granite	Granite; intrusive igneous rock. Along with chert, the hardest type of stone utilized
Gray stone	Hard limestone; perhaps andesite, gray to black colored
Sandstone/greenish	Very compact sandstone; grits visible; usually greenish
Slate	Common fine-grained metamorphic rock; light grayish
Slate/greenish gray	Like slate, but more gritty; greenish gray
Vesicular	Vesicular basalt; black basalt filled with basalt numerous small cavities
White stone	Hard limestone, white to cream colored, sometimes marbled

SOFT STONES

Limestone	Relatively chalky limestone; whitish colored
Sandstone	Sedimentary rock of compressed particles that are similar to those of the conglomer-

	ate stones, but with grits that are sand-size to dust-size; grit is mainly light colored, but sometimes reddish
Dense sandstone	Fine-grained sandstone; very compact; usually grayish

GRINDING STONES

TYPE G 1. OVOID-SHAPED GRINDING SLAB

This classification of grinding stones comprises six variant forms of ovoid-shaped slabs with one relatively flat grinding surface. In one form or another this type of grinding slab has been found throughout the cultural sequence at Chogha Mish.

Unlike other types of grinding stones, G 1-types are never stained from color pigment or from bitumen. It is most probable that this type of grinding slab was for the grinding of foodstuffs. Because of the use of conglomerate type stones, the presence of some grit in the food was unavoidable, but as the grits in the types of conglomerates usually selected for G 1 grinding stones were predominately rather large, they could have been removed from food while eating (much as chips of bone might be removed).

G 1a. Common Ovoid (stone, some form of conglomerates; 98 samples) (pl. 238:A–D). This group represents by far the most common subtype of ovoid grinding slabs. The outlines of the G 1a slabs vary from almost circular to a rather irregular but ovaloid shape. The work surfaces are usually approximately level along both the long and short axes of the oval, but they might also be either slightly concave or slightly convex along either axis (with all combinations possible). The bases or undersides appear to be the natural irregular convex surfaces of the stones. Occasionally the convex sides have been deliberately rounded, but usually the irregular undersides have been only somewhat smoothed by the rocking of the slabs during use. The sides or edges of the grinding slabs have been definitely modeled to form an ovoid outline. A general uniformity in size appears to cut across temporal barriers. The approximate average size is rather small, 20 to 25 cm in length and 15 cm in width.

The amount of concavity or convexity of the grinding surfaces probably indicates variations in the degree of utilization; however, examination of the striations on some of the larger grits seems to suggest that the varying condition of a grinding surface is also a product of varying predominating modes of utilization. Although the most common direction of grinding was parallel to the long axis, resulting in a concave surface after prolonged usage, some of the slabs were clearly ground from side to side, that is, along the short axis. Grinding along the short axis caused the grinding surfaces to be convex along the short axis but level along the long axis. Grinding slabs of the latter type were perhaps used more as top stones, in the manner of handgrinders, rather than as bottom stones.

G 1b. Large Ovoid (stone, conglomerate; 12 samples) (pl. 238:E). G 1b grinding slabs have the same shape as the G 1a types but are considerably larger and have somewhat thicker proportions. Wear marks indicate a grinding movement mainly along the long axis but at a slight angle. The grinding surfaces are very smooth and even rather glossy, suggesting fine grinding.

G 1c. Rectangular (stone, usually some form of conglomerate; 10 samples) (pl. 238:F–H). Aside from the rectangular outline, a flattish cross section distinguishes the stones of G 1c from those of G 1a. Most G 1c type grinding stones are about twice as long as they are wide. The grinding surfaces are markedly concave along the long axis but only slightly convex or level along the short axis. Both the edges and undersides usually appear to have been completely modeled.

Very fine striations reveal grinding mainly in one direction along the long axis, but there are some crisscrossing striation marks as well. The narrow width of the grinding surface suggests utilization in conjunction with a small handgrinder, and the use of only one hand to perform the actual grinding. The other hand would then be free to add and collect the material being ground. The handgrinders were pushed down and along in one direction, resulting in more pronounced wear of the end farthest from the user. The curved shape of the grinding surfaces was desirable, as it facilitated the pattern of grinding. The areas of most intense wear correspond with the areas of thickest dimension, indicating that the manufacturers and/or users anticipated the wear pattern.

G 1d. Ridged (stone, conglomerate; 2 samples) (pl. 239:A–B). The grinding surfaces are unusual. The surfaces that were actually worked are level along both axes, but the narrow ends of the slabs are raised ridges that are probably the result of intentional modeling rather than the result of gradual formation in the course of utilization. The ridged ends, although of stylistic import, seem to be functionally irrelevant.

G 1e. Oblong (stone, conglomerate, most typically greenish; 18 samples) (pl. 239:C). In comparison with G 1a, the widths are much narrower, while the lengths remain about the same. The cross sections are almost triangular. The grinding surfaces are at least slightly convex along the short axis and usually level along the long axis.

Perhaps G 1e types are actually the top stones. Heavily worn areas on some examples hint at a rocking motion on the long axis; the stones would have been laid lengthwise, perhaps on top of grinding stones with flat work surfaces such as G 1a or G 1b, and rocked back and forth.

G 1f. Hemispheroid (stone, conglomerate-sandstone; 5 samples) (pl. 239:D). G 1f types have an ovoid outline, but a hemispherical cross section along both axes. The edges and undersides clearly appear to have been shaped intentionally. Except for being unusually thick, hemispheroids are relatively rather small.

These grinding stones seem much too large (and heavy) and the grinding surfaces too flat to have been used effectively as handgrinders. The domed undersides might have been sunk in earthen floors or pebble layers in order to secure the stone.

TYPE G 2. FLAT GRINDING SLAB

Stone, conglomerate, but more typically conglomerate-sandstone; 15 samples; plate 239:E–F

These are generally ovoid to circular in shape. Both the upper and under sides are flat and relatively smooth. The edges are rounded but form distinct corners. The overall appearance is that of a manufactured tool.

Both sides have been used. One side is usually smoother than the other. The smoother side often has a somewhat glossy central area, suggesting rubbing rather than grinding. The stones are hand-sized, usually light in weight, and thus could have been conveniently held in one hand while being worked with the other. It might well be that G 2 grinding slabs were used for sharpening or shaping (softer stones, wood and/or bone implements) rather than for crushing (foodstuffs or other materials).

TYPE G 3. GRINDING SLAB OF VESICULAR BASALT

The cavities in the stone comprise approximately one third to one half of the work surfaces. Some pocks are as large as 10×10 mm and 7 mm deep; most are smaller holes, 2–4 by 2–4 mm and about 2 mm deep. The type of stone employed probably has some functional significance. As the stone is very hard with a naturally rough, pocked surface, it is ideal for pounding and rubbing tough material such as chaff or leather/skins as well as softer stones or wood. The large deep holes in the surface, however, render the stone unsuitable for work with small particles such as seeds, powdery material such as pigments and chalk, and also moist material such as fresh vegetables and nuts.

G 3a. Flat-topped (4 samples) (pl. 239:G). The shape is usually a roughly modeled circular form, but one example is somewhat egg-shaped with irregular sides. The working surfaces are level and, aside from the deep pocks, very smooth. The cross sections are rather thin. The bases are the original natural surfaces and are coated in places with thick calcium deposits. The average size is 20–30 by 30 cm.

There appears to be no fixed orientation to the striations on the grinding surfaces. There are slight indications that the grinding motion might have been primarily a circular one, but wear marks on vesicular basalt are difficult to see.

G 3b. Shallow-hollow (5 samples) (pl. 239:H). G 3b slabs are similar to G 3a, except that the work surfaces are markedly concave along either one or both axes; in this respect the shallow-hollow grinding slabs of G 3b resemble those of G4. Preserved edges of the slabs are rather thin and sharp, indicating that the slabs were flaked from large boulders.

The concave work surfaces of G 3b do not appear to have been simply the result of the grinding down of the flat surfaces of G 3a. Concave surfaces certainly excluded the use of some types of handgrinders and facilitated the employment of others. That the slabs of G 3a and G 3b had identical functions is indicated by the fact that they were manufactured from the same unique type of stone; however, due to the shape of the work surface, the manner of utilization of the G4 types (rather than G 3a) was probably more suitable for the G 3b grinding stones.

TYPE G 4. SHALLOW-HOLLOW GRINDING SLAB

These are distinguished by their concave grinding surfaces and crescent-shaped cross sections. There are, unfortunately, not many well-preserved examples. As a result, it is difficult to generalize about shape and size and the degree to which the modeling of the periphery was meaningful; however, an attempt was made to separate the G 4 slabs into two subtypes on the basis of the regularity or irregularity of their outline.

G 4a. Regular Outline (stone, typically sandstone-conglomerate or conglomerate-sandstone; some are made of sand; 20 samples) (pl. 240:A). The outline has definitely been modeled into an ovoid or circular shape. The general appearance is that of concave trays or shallow basins. The G 4a slabs are exceptionally thin, about 5 cm thick on the average. The grinding surfaces are very even and smooth. The base surfaces are lumpy and coarse but have been modified, at least partially, to conform to the curvature of the grinding surfaces.

The work surfaces are usually so smooth that it appears certain that hard, rough handgrinders could not have been used with typical G 4a slabs and that hard, coarse materials could not be readily or efficiently ground by this stone. Often preserved on the grinding surfaces are light reddish-colored stains of chalky pigment and some other kind of stain of a much darker color, which might be from vegetable matter such as fruits or tree saps. Striations are primarily in line with the long axis, but they are also along the short axis at an oblique angle, indicating a rather irregular grinding motion, perhaps slightly circular.

G 4b. Irregular Outline (stone, same as G 4a; 12 samples) (pl. 240:B–C). The shape is ovoidal, but the

sides are natural. The concave grinding surfaces are not as centrally placed as those of the G 4a type and the work surfaces of G 4b do not have even-surfaced contours. The cross sections are thicker than those of G 4a, and the undersides more closely resemble G 1a rather than G 4a types.

The differences between G 4a and G 4b seem to be more stylistic than functional. The wear pattern of G 4b appears to be identical with that of G 4a, and red stains are equally prevalent on G 4b grinding surfaces.

TYPE G 5. HOLLOWED SQUARISH SLAB

Stone, dense sandstone; 12 samples; plate 240:D

These are squarish-shaped slabs with deeply hollowed grinding surfaces. As the hollowed areas begin at the edge of the slabs, there are no ridges around the periphery. The sides are vertical, forming sharp corners with the top and bottom surfaces.

The G 5 grinding stones were probably used with spherical handgrinders or small pestles for crushing and mixing relatively soft materials. Hammer marks scattered over the grinding hollows indicate some pounding as well. Hollowed areas are almost entirely stained with red pigment. Perhaps Type G 5 was primarily for mixing rather than for grinding.

TYPE G 6. ROUND MORTAR-LIKE STONE

Stone, typically a variety of conglomerate composed of loosely packed buff-color grits; 10 samples; plate 240:E–F

The sides have clearly been modeled to form round stone slabs with thick cross sections. The work areas are relatively deep circular depressions; the edges of the hollow are characteristically thick, forming a definite ridge around the hollow area. The diameters of the circular work area are approximately 18 cm, while the outer diameters of the stones vary from 25 to 40 cm.

It is evident from the wear patterns that G 6 types were both ground and pounded. Red chalky material is preserved in thick coats and lumps within the deep work surfaces. The grinding surfaces and condition of the stones make this slab particularly suited for the preliminary grinding of soft, chalky material; the type of stone is too friable to permit heavy pressure while grinding or pounding, and the surface of the stone is too coarse and porous to be used for producing a fine powder or for work with moist materials. These grinding slabs were probably used with small handgrinders or pestles.

TYPE G 7. GRINDING BOWL

Stone, dense sandstone; 11 samples; plate 241:A–G

Grinding bowls are very similar to stone vessels but have thick, heavy walls. They vary in size and in the ratio of height to rim diameter, but the proportions are

Table 31. Temporal Distribution of the Grinding Stones

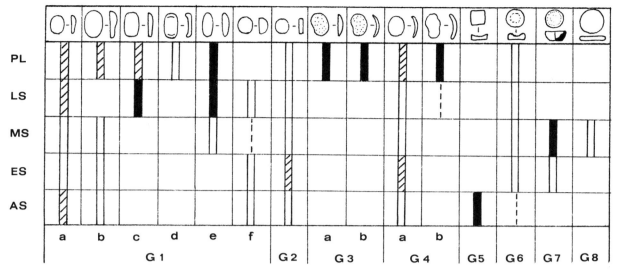

usually rather shallow, and the average rim diameter is about 35 to 40 cm. There is a distinctive rim form, although the rims of some examples seem rudimentary. It might be that the rim was less developed in the Early Susiana period and attained its characteristic appearance sometime during the Middle Susiana period. The bowls are modeled both inside and out. The interior surfaces are smooth and finely ground; the exterior surfaces retain chisel marks. These marks, which average only 1.2 cm in length, were made by narrow points no wider than 2.5 mm. It is evident from the direction and angle of the marks that the bowls were base up at the time of the final modeling of the exterior surfaces, and that the chisels were held in the left hand and struck by the right hand. The bases are flat; there is a single example with a low ring base.

The shape and type of stone make these grinding bowls especially suitable for use with smooth stone balls or wooden pestles with blunt, rounded work ends.

TYPE G 8. LARGE CIRCULAR DISCOID (MILLSTONE)

Stone, dense sandstone; 1 sample; plate 241:H

The entire flat stone slab has been modeled into what appears to be a functional millstone. The grinding surface is particularly smooth and well shaped. This stone perhaps represents the most important piece of indirect evidence for the manufacture of flour during the Middle Susiana period.

HANDGRINDERS

TYPE HG 1. SHAPED HANDGRINDER

There are definite signs that these handgrinders were manufactured into stone implements of specific shape and size. The three subtypes are all very similar in shape and size as well as in the types of stone uti-

lized, but certain features pertaining to the shape of the work surfaces make the subtypes distinctive. These stones can be held conveniently in one hand.

HG 1a. Flattened Spheroids (stone, two main types: gray or white stone and some form of conglomerate; 13 samples) (pl. 242:A–C). Flattish river pebbles have been pecked around the periphery to form symmetrically balanced, squat spheroids. The two opposing wide sides constitute the work surfaces. There is usually a smooth band, ca. 3 to 4 cm wide and 7 to 8 cm long, which extends from one pecked side into a portion of the other side of the stone. The method of utilization thus appears to be a consistent short rocking and sliding motion along a fixed line. HG 1a handgrinders seem especially suited for use with G 3a and G 4 types of grinding stones.

HG 1b. Truncated Spheroid (stone, gray stone, slate, and quartzite; 5 samples) (pl. 242:D–F). All surfaces of the stones have been hammered into shape. A section of the spheroids has been ground to a smooth, flat surface, which was the main work surface. The flat surfaces have been worn by a circular grinding motion. The domed part of the stones was also employed for grinding and pounding, especially near the flat sides. HG 1b handgrinders have been found with G 3a grinding slabs.

HG 1c. Large Balls (stone, typically conglomerate-sandstone; 7 samples) (pl. 242:G–H). The entire surfaces of these almost perfect spheroids are covered with hammer marks. These balls are generally about 8 cm in diameter. These spheroids are best suited for use with softer grinding stones that have hollow grinding surfaces, such as G 4, G 5, and G 7. The stones are uniformly worn over all surfaces, indicating that the balls were primarily rolled rather than pushed or rocked during grinding operations.

Type HG 2. Natural River Pebble (unshaped)

Ordinary river-smoothed pebbles were frequently used for both grinding and pounding. These hand-sized pebbles seem to have been used principally for grinding and were divided into two subtypes.

HG 2a. Roundish River Pebbles (stone, a variety of stones ranging from hard stones, e.g., white stone, to soft stones, e.g., sandstone; 38 samples were studied in detail and identified; many more are unrecorded) (pl. 242:I–L). The surfaces of these naturally shaped ovoid or roundish river pebbles are smooth with even curvatures. The stones are flattish in cross section. HG 2a pebbles were used in a variety of ways for grinding, pounding, and mixing. Only a few examples have pronounced facets. In general, the narrower ends were used for pounding and scraping, while the flatter surfaces were used for rocking and push-grinding. The majority of HG 2a handgrinders have red pigment stains.

HG 2b. Irregular River Pebbles (stone, a variety of river stones; 20 samples were studied; scores more still need to be examined for definite signs of wear) (pl. 242:M–P). This class of handgrinders incorporates a wide variety of different shapes, including squarish, diamond-shaped, and pear-shaped. Usually one area was more intensively utilized. While wear was mainly the result of grinding, at least some indication of pounding has been observed. Many of the recorded HG 2b stones were stained with red pigment.

Type HG 3. Spheroid or Grinding Ball

The shape of these spheroids appears to be the result of the method of utilization. HG 3 spheroids have been divided by size into two subtypes. Grinding was primarily accomplished by rather short rolling or rocking movements with slight twists. These stone balls were rolled roughly 30° to 45° (i.e., 4.0 to 5.5 cm along a total circumference of about 18.0 to 25.0 cm). This manner of utilization required a somewhat roundish stone to begin with, and the method of grinding tended to enhance the spheroid shape. In addition to the rocking motion, pounding and push-grinding are evidenced by battered and faceted surfaces on the stones.

HG 3a. Spheroids, "hand-sized"; ca. 7 to 9 cm in diameter (stone, typically quartzite conglomerate; 18 samples) (pl. 242:Q–S).

HG 3b. Spheroids, small; ca. 5 to 7 cm in diameter (stone, same as HG 3a; 21 samples) (pl. 242:T–V).

PESTLES/POUNDERS

Type P 1. Shaped, Two-handed Pounder

All are relatively large stones that could be utilized only by holding and lifting with both hands. The stones were hammered and pecked into shape. Three subtypes

Table 32. Temporal Distribution of the Handgrinders

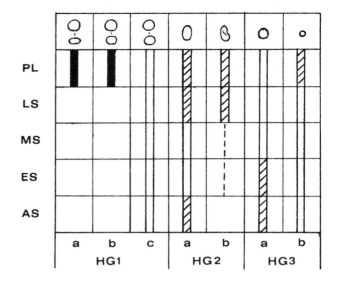

of large pounders have been distinguished on the basis of the shape of the head, that is, the utilized end. The various types of work ends correspond with expected differences in the pattern of utilization.

P 1a. Wedge-headed (stone, slate; 3 samples) (pl. 243:A). The body is a long cylindrical trunk. The head is flattened on two opposing sides, forming a wedge-shaped work end. The wedge shape of the work end is undoubtedly the result of the manner of utilization.

P 1b. Flat-headed (stone, characteristically gray stone; 5 samples) (pl. 243:B–C). The body is slightly conical. The work end is flat, but with smooth, rounded edges. Although these pounders are very large and could best be employed by using both hands, P 1b were manipulated very similar to hand-sized pestles. A twisting and rocking of the stone accompanied pounding and grinding. The wear pattern reveals that the center of the head was used for intensive pounding and the edges of the head for grinding.

P 1c. Round Head (stone, slate/greenish gray; 4 samples) (pl. 243:D–E). These are long, almost cylindrical stones with a domed, sometimes slightly pointed work end. Only the central area of the domed head appears to have been utilized. The wear pattern argues for intensive pounding. The weight and type of stone would have permitted very heavy impacts.

Type P 2. Shaped, Slender Conical Pestle with Rounded Head and Pointed End

Stone, slate and slate/greenish; the latter is more typical; 27 samples; plate 243:F–G

The slender trunks and parts of the edges around the heads are covered by peck marks. The unworked end of the trunk is characteristically rather sharply pointed. P 2 pestles could have been manipulated with the use of one or both hands. Marks on the head end were caused by pounding around the center of the head and rocking or pushing the stone about the perimeter of the head. Twisting motions are not indicated. The head sections of a number of examples are stained with red pigment.

TYPE P 3. SHAPED, SQUAT, CONICAL CRUSHING STONE

Stone, a variety of hard stones; no characteristic type; 7 samples; plate 243:H–I

These are proportionally thick conical stones with domed heads. These tools have the general appearance of stone objects that have been fashioned with special care; the contours are gentle and symmetrical; the surfaces are polished. There is some variation in size, but all can be held and lifted in one hand. P 3 types were used more like handgrinders than pounders or pestles. Striations about the head section reveal a rocking movement. The conical trunks also seem to have been used for grinding; apparently the stones were laid lengthwise and rolled, so that the squat shape had a definite functional purpose. One stone has red pigment preserved about the head. It seems likely that a wide range of materials could have been crushed by the rocking and rolling motion of these heavy stones.

TYPE P 4. SHAPED, SLENDER, CONICAL PESTLE WITH FLAT HEAD

Stone, mainly softish limestone; 8 samples; plate 243:J–K

The flat head sections form rather marked junctures with the long, slender trunks. The wear pattern on the flat heads gives evidence of typical "hit-and-twist" movements. The stone is suitable only for work with soft materials. The opposite end of some of the pestles also bear signs of some light pounding.

TYPE P 5. SHAPED, WIDER HEAD SECTION

These are unusual types of pestles/pounders, characterized by work ends that are wider in diameter than the trunks. This type of pestle is divided into two subtypes.

P 5a. Nail-shaped Head Section (stone, gray stone; 1 sample) (pl. 243:L). The tool is nail-like in appearance, with a conical trunk and a disc-shaped head section. Surfaces are fairly well polished. This stone evidently was used mainly as a pounder. The work surface of the head has been chipped and battered by much pounding on hard surfaces; there is only limited evidence of grinding.

P 5b. Cylindrical Head Section (stone, slate or limestone; 4 samples) (pl. 243:M–O). Both the trunk and the head section of the P 5b types are cylindrical. The head sections vary from approximately the same length of the

trunk to much shorter than the trunk. There is no clear evidence that these hand-sized tools were ever used for pounding. The wear pattern is predominately the result of grinding and rubbing.

TYPE P 6. SHAPED, SMALL CONICAL PESTLE

Stone, typically slate/greenish gray; slate is also represented; 12 samples; plate 243:P–R

These are finely modeled finger-sized pestles of "classical" shape and size. Some examples are highly polished. The manner of utilization was the typical "hit-and-twist" pestling action. The smooth surfaces of the work areas indicate that the materials that were crushed and mixed were rather soft. Residues from red pigments were found on many of the head sections. P 6 pestles are sufficiently small and delicate to have been used in combination with hand-held stone palettes such as the flat rubbing stones of the R 3 type.

TYPE P 7. SHAPED, SMALL CYLINDRICAL PESTLE/ POUNDER

Three subdivisions were made on the basis of functionally dependent variation in shape and size.

P 7a. Hand-sized (stone, slate /greenish gray; 3 samples) (pl. 243:S). All have clearly been shaped into a cylindrical pounding tool by light hammering over the entire surface. P 7a pestle/pounders are similar to P 10 (natural oblong pounding stones) in terms of size and general appearance, except that P 10 have not been trimmed, for reasons that might be aesthetic or functional. Both ends have been used for pestling, but one end is usually more worn than the other. The trunks of these stones might have been used for rolling or rocking (similar to a rolling pin). The markedly different manner of utilization suggests service for different functions, so that these stone cylinders could be considered multipurpose tools.

P 7b. Barrel-shaped (stone, white stone; 3 samples) (pl. 243:T). The opposing ends have been flattened, either by the toolmaker or as a result of the mode of utilization, giving the stone a bitruncated ovoid appearance. The sides of the stones retain their original surfaces. Both ends have been used for pounding and grinding. These stones were never used as rolling handgrinders. They are small implements that would have served more efficiently if held with the ends of the fingers rather than in the palms of the hands.

P 7c. Slender (stone, slate; 2 samples) (pl. 243:U). All surfaces have been pecked into slender cylinders. Both ends are domed. These small stones were best handled by being grasped with the ends of the fingers. They were possibly used in a craft requiring precision in striking the butts of chiseling and piercing tools or in

Table 33. Temporal Distribution of the Pestles/Pounders

	P1 a	P1 b	P1 c	P2	P3	P4	P5 a	P5 b	P6 a	P6 b	P7 a	P7 b	P7 c	P8	P9	P10	P11	P12 a	P12 b	P12 c
PL	▨				■										■	▨	■		▨	▨
LS					■												▨			
MS				■			▨													
ES				■					▨											
AS		▨																	▨	▨

hammering other objects. Both ends have been lightly tapped about the center of the domes.

TYPE P 8. NATURAL, TWO-HANDED POUNDER

Stone, slate or sandstone; 7 samples; plate 244:A

These are natural long stones that were perhaps roughly hewn but not carefully shaped. These large stones are well suited for heavy pounding. Although both ends were used, one end is usually more battered than the other. Two hands are needed to wield these stones.

TYPE P 9. NATURAL, LONG STONE WITH FLAT CROSS SECTION

Stone, slate; 10 samples; plate 244:B

The long trunks have flat, rectangular cross sections. The shapes and sizes are such that the stones could have been conveniently manipulated with one hand.

These are multipurpose tools. The ends were used for pounding, and the wide sides for grinding. The selection of stones with such broad surfaces must have been for some special reason.

TYPE P 10. NATURAL, SMALL, OBLONG RIVER STONE

Stone, a variety of river stones; slate is most common; 12 samples have been recorded, but numerous additional examples are still to be examined for signs of use; plate 244:C–F

Smooth river stones of various shapes have been included in this class of tool-types; some are oblong, others are squat, while some are pear-shaped or sausage-shaped. The sizes vary from hand-sized to fingertip-sized.

These oblong stones represent crude multipurpose pounding and grinding implements. It is evident from the wear pattern that the ends were used for pestling and also rubbing, while the sides were used in various ways for grinding.

TYPE P 11. NATURAL, SMALL, IRREGULAR STONE

Stone, slate is characteristic, but a variety of other stones, ranging from very hard to rather soft also were utilized; 45 samples were recorded from a much larger collection; plate 244:G–J

This type class includes all other longish hand-sized stones with at least a single battered area. Occasionally, broken stones and rough stone splinters have been utilized for pounding and/or pestling.

These crude implements were utilized in a variety of ways, recalling P 10 pestles/pounders. There might be some sociological rather than functional explanation for the use of natural stones, when well-made stone tools were available for apparently the same purposes.

TYPE P 12. NATURAL, SMALL HAMMERSTONE

These river pebbles are usually battered through use in one or two separate areas only. P 12 hammerstones are subdivided into three size groups.

P 12a. Ovoid Pebbles (stone, slate; 4 samples) (pl. 244:K). These are hand-sized pebbles of an egg shape. The wider ends are battered laterally over a relatively large area. There are no indications of other means of utilization.

P 12b. Large Pebbles (ca. 5 to 8 cm) (stone, usually a hard stone [white stone or buff stone]; 24 samples recorded, but many more need to be studied for wear) (pl.

244:L–N). These are hand-sized stones of a general spheroid shape. Hammering in several places about a single limited area of the pebble resulted in a wear pattern that suggests a "one-hold" utilization; the stones were grasped, positioned in the hands, and used without a shift in the grip, and then discarded. Some stones bear a band of wear due to hammering. The band might have been formed while the stone was rotated in the hand during utilization; apparently a fresh surface was desirable for the hammering operation.

P 12c. Small Pebbles (less than 5 cm) (stone, hard stones [white stone or buff stone]; 36 samples recorded; many more await examination) (pl. 244:O–P). The diameters of these round pebbles range from 2.5 cm to 5.0 cm. The wear on these small hammerstones consists of very light peck marks, usually at the more pointed areas of the pebbles. The size of the stones and mode of utilization strongly suggest that many of these pebbles were "precision" hammerstones, perhaps used to strike the butt ends of chisel-like tools. Some pebbles were struck only a few times, suggesting "onetime" utilization, that is, the pebbles were selected, used for one specific hammering purpose, and then discarded.

FINGER STONES

The entire surface of these long, slender, naturally-shaped stones is characteristically very smooth. Therefore, it is not difficult to differentiate finger stones from small natural pounders such as P 1O. Finger stones are divided into a number of types and subtypes, reflecting differences in function and size.

TYPE F 1. BITUMEN POUNDER OR STIRRING ROD

Stone, usually slate or dense sandstone; 27 samples; plate 244:Q–T

These slender stones vary from 10 to 20 cm in length. Bitumen stains usually are concentrated about one end only, but traces extend over more than half of the stone.

There are often some battering marks about the bitumen-stained ends. Other wear marks justify the label "stirring rods." Some examples are also stained with red pigment, indicating a wider utilization of these finger stones.

TYPE F 2. SLENDER RIVER-SMOOTHED STONE

F 2 types are identical with F 1, except for the absence of bitumen stains on F 2 stones. These finger stones are separated into two size groups.

F 2a. Large (11 to 22 cm in length) (stone, usually slate or dense sandstone; 39 samples) (pl. 244:U–W). These finger stones are the most versatile multipurpose tools in the ground stone inventory. The F 2a type bears

evidence of use not only as pestles/pounders, but also as tools for many other purposes: (1) as rolling handgrinders—wear from grinding was commonly seen along the length of the stone; (2) as whetstones—narrow areas along the sides have been rubbed; (3) as club-like hammers—battering appears near one end; (4) as rubbing/polishing tools—polished facets about the ends suggest intensive rubbing; (5) as small slicing stones occasionally—cut marks similar to those found on SS 1 slicing slabs occur near the ends; and (6) as stirring rods—they are slender enough to have been suitable for this purpose.

F 2b. Small (less than 10 cm in length; average is 7 to 8 cm) (stone, hard stones such as buff stone and slate stone; 9 samples) (pl. 244:X). These small finger stones might have been used as small pestles, but no prominent signs of utilization—except for red pigment stains—appear on any example. Perhaps these tiny stones were stirring rods for the mixing of small amounts of pigment with water.

TYPE F 3. RUBBING ROD

These finger stones are characterized by highly polished areas about the ends or over the entire surface. F 3 types are divided into two groups according to size.

F 3a. Large (10 to 15 cm in length) (stone, hard stones such as gray stone, buff stone, or slate; 10 samples) (pl. 244:Y–AA). The direction of very subtle striations at the ends reveals two separate rubbing motions—semi-rotary downward and side to side. Perhaps these hard stones were used in the shaping of other stone objects, such as finer stone vessels, and they also could have served in the dressing of hides.

F 3b. Finger-sized (ca. 8 cm in length) (stone, hard stones; 5 samples) (pl. 244:BB). Several patterns of

Table 34. Temporal Distribution of the Finger Stones

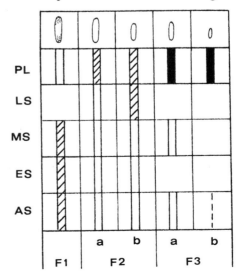

wear have been observed on individual specimens; wear was predominantly from rubbing but was also from pestling and hammering.

SLICING SLABS

TYPE SS 1. LONG, FLATTISH PEBBLE

Stone, very hard stones [gray stone or buff stone]; 7 samples identified; plate 244:CC–DD

There is nothing unusual about the general appearance of these stones. However, careful examination of the surfaces near the ends reveals numerous distinct striae varying in length and crisscrossing in every direction, very similar to slice marks on a cutting board. The slice marks are concentrated near both ends, and perhaps the stones might have been inserted into carcasses to serve as slicing slabs for flint blades in the cutting of meat and sinew. The ends of most slicing slabs have also been used for pounding, conceivably to break up bones as part of the butchering process.

The temporal distribution of SS1 slicing slabs was rather even: three for the Protoliterate, one for the Middle Susiana, one for the Early Susiana, and two for the Archaic Susiana periods.

WAISTED PEBBLES

TYPE WP 1. FLAT WAISTED PEBBLE

Stone, a variety of common river pebbles; 23 samples; plate 245:A–H

Two opposing sides of these oval pebbles are usually flaked fairly symmetrically at the middle. The size of the pebbles averages about 8 to 9 by 6 to 7 cm and 2 cm thick.

Waisted pebbles were probably suspended weights. One example, made of softer stone (sandstone), has a small groove about 4 mm wide at the edges of both waisted areas (pl. 245:D). The groove might have been caused by cord or twine that was wrapped around the middle of the stone. Five waisted pebbles were found together in a single excavation locus (pl. 245:A–E). The occurrence of waisted pebbles in clusters suggests a use as loom weights or as net sinkers.

WP 1 waisted pebbles were found in Protoliterate, Middle Susiana, and Early Susiana levels; they appear to increase in popularity during the Late Middle Susiana phase. A group of five waisted pebbles (see above) was excavated in a good Protoliterate context.

STONE HOES

Nearly all stone hoes were originally flakes removed from large cobbles. The edges were crudely chipped into shape, forming tang and blade sections. Only a few types of stone hoes were further refined by retouch flaking or grinding. The work edge of the blades was shaped by flaking and/or grinding the natural outer surfaces or the broken inner surfaces (sometimes both). The shape of the tang in most cases was conducive to easy hafting; traces of bitumen on the tang section offer concrete evidence for the manner of hafting. It should be emphasized that the term "hoe" refers to the morphological similarities of the stones included in this category of stone tools and not to a specific determination of function.

TYPE H 1. COMMON NORMAL TANG

H 1 stone hoes are the most common type, both in number and in terms of temporal distribution. Normal tang hoes are divided into four subtypes; the divisions are based on such typological features as the size of the blade, the width of the tang, and the overall size of the tool.

H 1a. Splayed Semicircular Blade (stone, sandstone/greenish and slate most common; 30 samples) (pl. 245:I–L). The tang sections are well made sturdy shafts with roughly parallel sides. In general the blade sections are not as carefully formed. It is probable that as long as the tangs provided firmness in mounting, the frequent irregularities of the blade sections had no effect on the functionality of the hoes. The symmetrical appearance of most H 1a hoes was probably due to aesthetic preference rather than practical necessity.

Traces of bitumen are preserved over the entire tang section and reach as far as the splayed end of the blade. The use of bitumen for hafting undoubtedly facilitated the replacement of worn hoes.

Considering the broadness of the blades, the type of stone from which H 1a hoes were manufactured is relatively too soft for chopping or cutting hard material such as wood but is best suited for constructing earthworks and for hoeing operations. The edges of the blades are usually partially chipped and often have dulled, shiny surfaces. Digging earth would not appreciably dull the edge of a stone blade, but hitting stones would eventually wear the edge down, and working against sandy soil and roots of brush and weeds would produce a gloss on the blade.

It might well be that the agricultural fields around Chogha Mish were periodically left fallow for a time, allowing weeds and brush to spread. When planting was resumed, tough, hard stone hoes would have been needed to break up the hardened ground and to dig out the unwanted vegetation. After this initial clearing and turning of the soil, other types of implements could have been used to complete the preparation of the fields.

H 1b. Larger Blade Section (stone, sandstone/greenish; 8 samples) (pl. 245:M). H 1b hoes are similar in shape and size to H 1a types, except for the more spade-like blade section of the H 1b types. H 1b hoes would have made more effective digging and earth-moving implements by virtue of their large blade sections and overall size.

H 1c. Larger Tang Section (stone, sandstone/greenish; 7 samples) (pl. 245:N). The tang sections actually seem too large in proportion to the blades; much effort would be required to secure the stones to handles. No trace of bitumen has been found on any example of this type. Perhaps such hoes could have been used as hand-held implements. Undoubtedly, hoes with tangs that varied markedly in shape and/or size would have dictated different hafting methods and possibly different types of hafting material.

Since their blade sections resemble those of types H 1a and H 1b, it seems probable that the hoes of type H 1c served similar purposes, although the manner of utilization was necessarily different due to the size of the tangs.

H 1d. Smaller-sized Hoes (stone, a wide variety of hard stones; 8 samples) (pl. 245:O–P). H 1d hoes average 12 cm in length, while H 1a types are about 15 cm. Due to the small size of H 1d hoes and the manner of hafting, only the edge of the blade would have lacked a coating of bitumen.

In an experiment conducted with one stone hoe of this type, it was found that wood could be chopped with this tool, but with much difficulty, as the stone tended to mash rather than cut the wood. On the basis of this single trial, it is estimated that 3 to 4 hours of chopping would be required to cut through a branch of poplar wood with a thickness of 10 to 15 cm. The hoe would no longer be serviceable after this one operation.

TYPE H 2. WIDE TANG AND BROAD BLADE

Tangs are wide and short. The shoulders of the blade sections range from stooped to broad, and the blade sections vary in length. The edges of the blades were made by grinding down the inside surfaces. The cross sections of these hoes are relatively flat; they are typically thicker at the tangs and narrower toward the

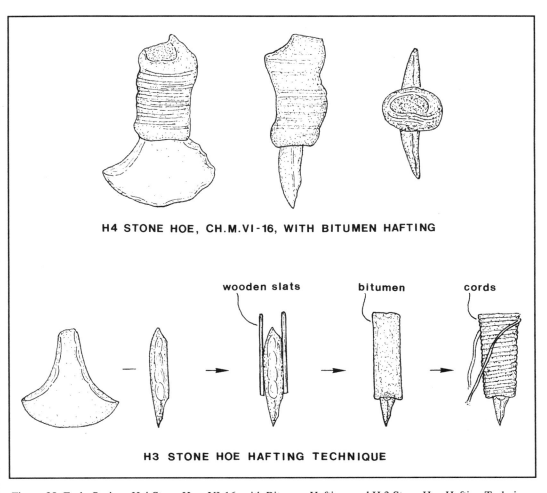

H4 STONE HOE, CH.M.VI-16, WITH BITUMEN HAFTING

H3 STONE HOE HAFTING TECHNIQUE

Figure 38. Early Susiana H 4 Stone Hoe, VI-16, with Bitumen Hafting; and H 3 Stone Hoe Hafting Technique

ends of the blades. These hoes are somewhat larger in size than other types; H 2 range from 13 to 18 cm in length.

H 2a. Standard Wide Tang (stone, typically sandstone/greenish; 20 samples) (pl. 245:Q–S). The entire tang section down to the shoulder of the blade shows evidence of bitumen coating. Because of the size and thinness of the blades these tools are especially suited for digging and hoeing. An experiment using a typical H 2a hoe, held in the hand, was conducted on a 1.00 m square section of a small garden. The plot was cleared of weeds and large pebbles and a narrow channel for water was dug, proving the effectiveness of the hoe as an earth mover.

H 2b. Elongated Blade (stone, sandstone/greenish; 9 samples) (pl. 245:T). The blade sections of H 2b hoes are longer and have slightly broader shoulders than H 2a types. Although the work sections of H 2a and H 2b hoes are morphologically distinctive, the wear patterns for both subtypes indicate that there was probably no difference in function or manner of utilization between H 2a and H 2b. Thus, the elongated blade of H 2b hoes could be viewed as a stylistic variant.

Table 35. Temporal Distribution of the Stone Hoes

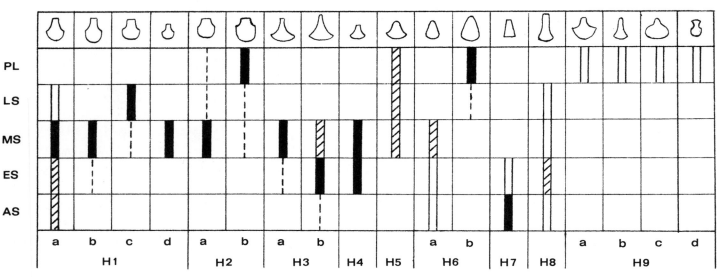

TYPE H 3. NARROW TANG AND SPLAYED BLADE

The distinctive features of these hoes are relatively narrow tangs and markedly splayed blade sections. The edges of the blades are wedge-shaped, as a result of the flaking of both the outer and inner surfaces. There is characteristically no refinement of the crudely flaked surfaces; these hoes have a general appearance of chipped stone tools of rough quality. The two subtypes reflect what seem to be temporally significant variations in the tang.

Originally, bitumen coated all surfaces except for the thin crescent-shaped edge of the blade. In a few cases this hafting material is well enough preserved to reveal details of the method of mounting the blade onto a wooden shaft (fig. 38).[2]

Apparently, two wooden slats, ca. 3.5 cm wide, were placed along both the outer and inner sides of the tang. Bitumen was then used to hold the slats in place, and cords were wrapped around the bitumen to strengthen the arrangement. The stone, thus secured to wooden pieces, could be tied by additional pieces of cord (or the same cord) to a handle. Conceivably, the more complex parts of the hafting along with the stones were removable.

H 3 hoes were probably employed for chopping rather than for hoeing. Because of the shortness of the blade, these worked stones are unsuited for use as heads of digging or earth-moving implements. Instead, they have stout blade sections and long tangs, which enable firm hafting, and are made from hard stones that seem sufficiently flinty to retain a sharp edge through repeated heavy blows against such hard objects as wood or softer stones. In most cases the blade sections of H 3 types were found extensively chipped or fragmented. The use-life of these choppers was probably rather short.

2. For photograph, see Kantor 1976:191, fig. 21 (P22:622, 80.50; Early Susiana).

H 3a. Standard Narrow Tang (stone, granite and chert typical; 16 samples) (pl. 245:U–V).

H 3b. Long Tang (stone, granite and chert typical; 13 samples) (pl. 245:W–X).

TYPE H 4. SHORT TRIANGULAR TANG

Stone, granite (a few buff stones); 29 samples; plate 246:A–D

The tangs of H 4 hoes were basically formed by a single blow on each side with only rather minor retouching. The blade sections are short and stubby, and the blade edges are wedge-shaped. These stones are comparatively small in overall size and have thick cross sections.

Almost the entire hafting of bitumen was preserved in one example. The tang is covered by a cylinder of bitumen, ca. 7.5 cm long and from 4.8 to 6.0 cm in diameter. Between either side of the tang and the layer of bitumen are two earth-filled cavities, presumably left by decayed wooden slats. Impressions of string around the exterior of the bitumen coating indicate at least ten windings.

The hafting technique is similar to that illustrated in figure 38. These stones were probably the heads of chopping rather than tilling implements. Definite sheen is visible on the edges of the blades. Perhaps these stones were parts of implements for cutting and breaking up tough vegetal matter (e.g., brush and straw), possibly to form compounds (e.g., in the manufacture of brick or the preparation of animal feed). These triangular heads, when mounted, could have served as combination chopping and pounding tools. An experiment using H 4 hoes to chop thick beams showed that the blade is shaped in such a way that it mashes the wood instead of cutting cleanly through it. H 4 hoes would not have been efficient choppers for the felling of timber.

TYPE H 5. STUB TANG

Stone, slate and slate/greenish gray typical; 16 samples; plate 246:E–F

The tangs are triangular and widen gradually toward the semicircular blade sections. Bitumen stains are only on the tangs and do not dip down onto the area of the blades. H 5 tools seem suitable for hoeing. The edges of the blades are often glossy.

TYPE H 6. TRIANGULAR WITH CURVED EDGE

H 6 hoes are basically triangular-shaped stones; the wider ends have been modified into curved edges. There is little differentiation between the tang and blade section. Although the size of these hoes varies considerably, two basic size groups can be identified.

H 6a. Small (8 to 12 cm height, 5 cm long) (stone, a variety of hard stones; 7 samples) (pl. 246:G–H). Apparently only a small strip of the work end was not covered with bitumen. Tools of this type are probably chopping or cutting stones.

H 6b. Large (ca. 16 cm long) (stone, slate and slate/greenish gray; 7 samples) (pl. 246:I–J). H 6b hoes are sufficiently larger in size than H 6a types to suggest strongly there must be some functional difference between the two subtypes.

TYPE H 7. AX-LIKE

Stone, slate most common; sandstone/greenish also used; 11 samples; plate 246:K–L

H 7 tools have no distinction between the tang and working edge. These stones are long, triangular, and relatively narrow, with flat cross sections. None have any trace of bitumen.

H 7 types seem of suitable shape and size for woodworking. They are made from stones that are comparatively resistant to fracturing when struck against hard objects. The edges of most blades clearly show use; some work edges are smooth and shiny.

TYPE H 8. POUNDER-LIKE

Stone, slate and sandstone/greenish; 10 samples; plate 246:M–N

These tools resemble large pounders in their long shape and rather thick cross sections, but differ in that their work ends are somewhat splayed and formed into an edge. They vary considerably in size; the smallest example is 12.5 cm in length and the largest is 28.7 cm.

H 8 tool types were probably used as hand-held implements. The tang area seems clearly to have been shaped for clutching in the hands rather than for attachment to a handle. The shape of the stone and the sharp edge of the blade suggest that H 8 hoes were hand tools used for breaking up hard substances. One example has bitumen stains around the blade area.

TYPE H 9. SPECIAL FORMS

These special hoes are individual examples that exhibit some unusual features; perhaps they are unique tools designed for singular purposes. All four examples were found in Protoliterate contexts.

H 9a. Polished Hoe (stone, gray stone; 1 sample) (pl. 246:O). This stone is remarkably well modeled, and the surfaces on both sides have been polished to a shine. The blade section seems exaggeratedly splayed. This example might have represented an ideal form of hoe, functioning as a prestige object or as a model.

H 9b. Hoe with Rod Handle (stone, sandstone/greenish; 1 sample) (pl. 246:P). The tang section is a modeled handle with an oval cross section. This stone might have been a hand-held digging tool.

H 9c. Hoe with Vestigial Tang (stone, buff stone; 1 sample) (pl. 246:Q). The blade is large and splayed and the tang is a mere stump. Because the tang is so small, the stone could not have been hafted in the usual manner. There is no trace of bitumen. Apparent use of this stone is demonstrated by the blade edge, which is worn down and has a distinct sheen.

H 9d. Waisted Pebble Hoe (stone, slate; 1 sample) (pl. 246:R). The tang has been forced by flaking the opposite sides near one end. There are no other signs of shaping. The sharp edge of the blade is a natural feature; the tool was made from a flake struck off a larger stone. The method of utilization is not evident.

PERFORATED STONES

TYPE PF 1. PERFORATED GEODE

Stone, geode stones of a variety of ordinary river pebbles, usually hard stones, such as buff stone or white stone; 16 samples; plate 247:A–D

The soft inner material of these geodes has been removed, and the edges around the openings have been chipped, apparently to widen and/or blunt the edges of the hole. There is but slight variation in size, which ranges from $3.4 \times 5.1 \times 5.5$ to $4.4 \times 5.8 \times 10.0$ cm.

There are no wear marks to suggest whether these perforated stones were used for hammering or rubbing or similar purposes. They were most probably suspended weights (e.g., loom weights, net sinkers, etc.).

TYPE PF 2. DISCOIDAL RING

These flat stones were at least partially hammered about the sides to form a discoidal ring. PF 2 types are divided into two size groups: PF 2a and PF 2b. PF 2c and PF 2d subtypes are individual morphological variants of PF 2a.

Table 36. Temporal Distribution of the Perforated Stones

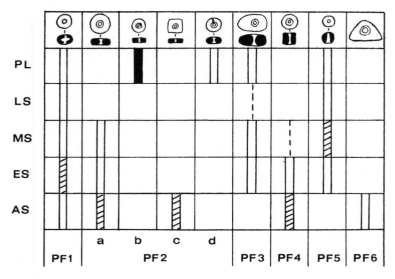

PF 2a. Normal Size (average diameter ca. 1.5 cm) (stone, sandstone; 7 samples) (pl. 247:E–H). In most cases the cross sections of the perforations are spool-shaped. No obvious wear patterns are evident on the outer or inner surfaces of these rings. Although PF 2a perforated stones were carefully shaped, they might have been merely suspended weights of some kind.

PF 2b. Small (average diameter ca. 9 cm) (stone, sandstone; 5 samples) (pl. 247:I). The perforations are hourglass-shaped in cross section. The holes are about 3.5 cm wide at the rims and 1.5 cm at the centers. The manner in which the perforations were made is indicated by the hourglass-shaped section; initially, a rod with a conical bit bored a conically-shaped hole in one side of the stone; after a time, perhaps due to the increasing depth of the hole, the rod apparently spun with less efficiency, for the stone was then inverted and a fresh hole was bored from the other side.

The wear pattern within the perforations of these stones reveals that a rod of some kind was spun at both ends of the holes. The small size of the stones and width of the holes indicate that these perforated discoidals might have been pivot stones for potter's wheel shafts. The holes seem too wide for hand drill rods and too small for doorposts.

PF 2c. Special Form, Perforated Squarish Slab (stone, sandstone; 1 sample) (pl. 247:J). Striation marks from a spinning shaft are especially clear within the perforation.

PF 2d. Special Form, Doughnut-like Ring (stone, sandstone; 1 sample) (pl. 247:K). A single thin groove on the exterior surface runs from one side of the hole to the other side. This groove might have been a notch in which twine or leather strips could be wound in order to suspend the stone.

TYPE PF 3. PERFORATED LARGE COBBLE

Stone, sandstone; 6 samples; plate 247:L–N

PF 3 stones are large cobbles with an hourglass-shaped perforation. Usually one or more places on the natural outer surfaces appear to be battered from use. These large cobbles could certainly have been clubheads. However, the rather friable nature of the stones would have restricted the kinds of objects or materials that could be repeatedly struck without breaking the implement.

TYPE PF 4. CYLINDROID

Stone, very hard stones (white stone or buff stone); 7 samples; plate 247:O–P

These stones are tall cylinders with a proportionally large hole through the center. The outer surfaces were shaped by hammering; the inner surfaces of the holes are finely polished.

Cylindroids were possibly used as rolling grinders or rolling pins. The wide outer surfaces make these stones excellent tools for crushing materials on flat grinding slabs or planks of wood. A short wooden rod could have been inserted through the holes and held with the hands on both ends. The user would push down on the rod and allow the stone to roll back and forth.

TYPE PF 5. MACE-HEAD

Stone, hard stones such as white, buff, and gray stone; 7 samples studied; plate 247:Q–T

The shape of these highly polished stones is definitely the result of some degree of modeling. The holes are typically conical in cross section. The size varies markedly, ranging from 5.6 to 16 cm in diameter.

In the drilling process, the perforation began with the pecking out of a small depression. The bit of the drill was then set into this depression. The direction of the boring was consistently from the wider opening to the smaller opening. The drill shaft usually was spun in a clockwise direction. The sides of the holes are corrugated, probably the result of rather unstable high speed drilling. There are no wear marks on the outer surfaces. PF 5 mace-heads probably served as parts of symbolic or prestige objects.

TYPE PF 6. LARGE STONE WITH LOOP HANDLE

Stone, dense sandstone; 1 sample; plate 247:U

This large stone has a wide perforation forming a semicircular ring or loop. The loop is shaped all around by hammering and grinding. One part of the stone is much wider and seems to be some kind of base.

There are a number of possible uses for this unusual stone. It might have been an anchor stone for the securing of objects or the harnessing of animals. The stone also might have served as a floor compressor. The weight, size, and flatness of the underside, plus the handle-like appearance of the loop enable the stone to function as a large pounder. Earthen or plaster surfaces could have been compacted and leveled by the frequent lifting and dropping of this stone. The stone is about three fourths complete and weighs approximately 1.5 kg.

STONES WITH DEPRESSIONS

TYPE D 1. BOULDER MORTAR

D 1 types are large, roundish cobbles with at least one circular depression made by pounding. Three subtypes, which might reflect differences in function or mode of utilization, were readily identified on the basis of variation of size.

D 1a. Large, more than 1.5 cm long (stone, —; 3 samples) (pl. 248:A–C). The wear pattern within the depression was probably the result of pestling with a hand-sized pestle. There is usually a small, rather shallow depression on both sides of the stone. When the mortar hole reached a certain depth the stone was turned over and the other side used; this might indicate that a deep working surface was undesirable. One could speculate that certain materials such as nuts or large seeds were easily flicked out of the shallow depression and over the sides of the stone and therefore did not become mashed; additional materials could have been continually added with one hand, while the other hand worked with the pestle and mortar to crack the shells and pods.

D 1b. Normal Size, 10–15 cm (stone, white stone; 7 samples) (pl. 248:D–F). Some stones are rather pointed on the bottom side; these must have been set into earth or pebbles for stability. One example appears to have served also as a pounder.

D 1c. Pebble Size, 5–9 cm (stone, white stone; 3 samples) (pl. 248:G–I). These stones were possibly miniature mortars that were used in association with small pestles, such as P 6, or with pebble pounders, P 12.

TYPE D 2. HOLLOWED GEODE

Stone, white stone geodes; 4 samples; plate 248:J–K

These hollowed geodes are similar to shallow oval-shaped vessels. The inside surfaces clearly seem to have been used for pounding and pestling.

TYPE D 3. COMBINATION MORTAR AND GRINDING STONE

Stone, conglomerate and conglomerate-sandstone; 2 samples; plate 248:L

D 3 types resemble G 1 grinding stones but have a small, fairly deep depression in the center of the grinding surface. Examination of the surfaces of the depressions reveals limited evidence of pounding; most of the wear is from grinding and rubbing.

TYPE D 4. SLAB WITH ELLIPTICAL DEPRESSION

Stone, gray stone; 2 samples; plate 248:M–N

D 4 are flat, naturally shaped stones with an elliptical hollow on one side. The depression was made by first hammering and subsequently refined and smoothed by rubbing. Although the stones vary considerably in size, from 16.6 to 34.0 cm in length, the depressions are about the same dimensions.

Striations within the elliptical depressions show a rubbing movement along the long axis. The inner area, ca. 5 cm long and 2 cm wide, is highly polished. The wear pattern certainly suggests the working and sharpening of wood or bone awls and/or spatulas.

TYPE D 5. SQUARISH BLOCK WITH DEPRESSION

Stone, sandstone and dense sandstone; 2 samples; plate 249:A–B

These flat blocks have been shaped by hammering and grinding the entire surface. Two opposing sides have been ground so that they appear smooth and level. In the center of each wide surface is a relatively narrow but deep boring. The stones range in size from 9 to 15 cm square.

The symmetry and depth of the two opposing holes suggest that the stones might have been hafted. The two smooth sides might have been used for grinding and rubbing. Perhaps they were used in various construction operations, for example, packing down or smoothing earthen floors or plaster surfaces.

Table 37. Temporal Distribution of the Stones with Depressions

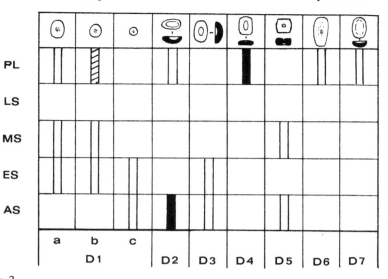

TYPE D 6. LARGE STONE ANVIL

Stone, gray stone; 1 sample; plate 249:C

This very large stone has a shallow, hammered area near the middle of one side. The surfaces of the stone are naturally smooth. The battered area on this stone is the result of heavy pounding. Each hammer mark is relatively large. Numerous stray hammer marks are found about the depression; evidently there was a considerable lack of control over the hammerstone or pounder.

TYPE D 7. LARGE OVAL STONE WITH DEEP HOLLOW

Stone, dense sandstone; 1 sample; plate 249:D

This single specimen is large and roughly shaped, with a deep, ovalish depression. The underside has been flattened by hammering and grinding to prevent the stone from rocking when in use. The deep hollow of this stone was produced by intensive pounding and grinding, implying its use as a large mortar.

PIVOT STONES

TYPE PV 1. COBBLE

Stone, slate and white stone; 6 samples; plate 249:E–H

Each of these river cobbles has a single wide hole. After being hollowed out by hammering, the hole was enlarged by the rotation of a shaft, making a pivot socket. The stones vary in size and their sockets range from approximately 5 to 8 cm. No correspondence between the overall size of the cobble and the width of the socket has been observed.

Striation marks within the hole clearly show the pivoting of a post. The stones are rather irregularly shaped, and one imagines that they must have been set into the ground, with only the socket area exposed.

TYPE PV 2. ROUGH STONE BLOCK

Stone, dense sandstone; 2 samples; plate 250:A–B

These crudely hewn rectangular blocks have a socket on both broad sides. Although these stones differ in size (ca. 20 to 44 cm in length) the sockets have about the same width and depth.

These large stone blocks were undoubtedly door-socket stones. Their overall size and weight, plus the leveled underside, must have made these socket stones very stable and capable of bearing large doorposts and heavy doors. From an examination of the wear pattern a brief history of each stone can be reconstructed (see pl. 250:A). The placement of the socket toward one end provides information concerning the construction of the doorway. If the doorpost were set close to the doorjamb,

Table 38. Temporal Distribution of the Pivot Stones

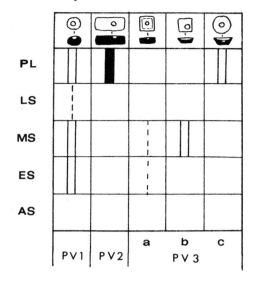

the pivot stone—a long block—would have been part of the threshold (pl. 250:B). The hole on one side is made up of two overlapping pivot sockets. The original socket was centrally located on the stone; apparently the doorpost shifted and a second hole was formed near the right edge of the block. The position of the second hole appears to have caused the stone to break. One can imagine the distress of the house occupants when it was discovered that the door had fallen.

TYPE PV 3. SPECIAL FORMS

PV 3a. Polished Stone Plaque (stone, conglomerate; 1 sample) pl. 250:C. This skillfully made square slab with a ridge around the edges has a socket in the center of the more markedly bordered side. All surfaces are highly polished. Characteristic facets within the socket verify the movement of a doorpost, which was apparently fitted loosely in the socket to prevent the door from sticking when the wooden post expanded on moist days. The fine workmanship of this plaque might indicate that it was but secondarily used as a pivot stone.

PV 3b. Reused Stone Tray (stone, dense sandstone; 1 sample) pl. 250:D. The pivot area is at one corner of this finely made rectangular tray. Traces of red coloring remain within the hollow and about the sides on the exterior surface of the tray, indicating use of this stone for the mixing of pigments. Although the sequence of use cannot be exactly ascertained, it seems likely that this stone was secondarily used as a door socket. A shift in the position of the doorpost resulted in two distinct sockets; because the last socket was near the edge, the corner of the tray broke.

PV 3c. Reused Stone Basin (stone, dense sandstone; 1 sample) pl. 250:E. This shallow stone vessel has a tapering rim and a flat base. The doorpost socket was placed inside the vessel. The wear pattern is clearly due to the pivoting of the rounded end of a post.

STONE DISCS

TYPE DS 1. STONE VESSEL SHERD ROUNDEL

Stone, usually fine white stone; 5 samples; plate 251:A–C

Sherds from different parts of stone vessels were chipped and ground around the periphery to form roundels. Although the overall size of these roundels varies considerably from small to large (3.7 to 8.8 cm in diameter), the thickness of the sherds consistently measure about 1 cm.

There are many contiguous facets around the edges of the sherds. The roundels clearly have been used for scraping and rubbing. In two examples the convex sides also were worn from rubbing. In one case bore marks are found on the concave side; evidently this roundel was used as the pivot stone for a small hand drill (pl. 251:A).

TYPE DS 2. SHAPED FLAT ROUNDEL

Stone, various; 11 samples; plate 251:D–E

The edges and occasionally the flat surfaces of these pebbles have been modified. The size varies from 3.4 to 12.4 cm in diameter. There are usually no pronounced facets. These flat discs were probably used primarily for rubbing rather than scraping. In most cases, both flat surfaces have been rubbed.

TYPE DS 3. PERFORATED STONE ROUNDEL

Stone, gray, buff, or white stone; 16 samples, 4 are blanks; plate 251:F–K

All surfaces have been smoothed and polished. Although their outlines are not always perfect circles, these finely made roundels have the general appearance of stone ornaments. They are of a uniform size, ca. 4–5 cm in diameter. The drilled perforations usually have a cylindrical shape and are about 1 cm in diameter.

Judging by the consistent width of the perforations of DS 3, the borings were probably made by drills of a standard size. A number of examples lack perforations, but since they are otherwise identical to DS 3 discs, they are probably blanks of this type of perforated roundel.

There are a number of possible uses; DS 3 stone discs might have served as: (1) spindle whorls, (2) some form of rubbers, (3) suspended weights, or (4) weight measures. The high polish within the holes requires explanation.

TYPE DS 4. UNSHAPED FLAT PEBBLE

Stone, various; 17 samples were examined for wear; plate 251:L–O

No shaping or modeling of any kind has been observed. Pebbles of this group vary in size from about 4

Table 39. Temporal Distribution of the Stone Discs

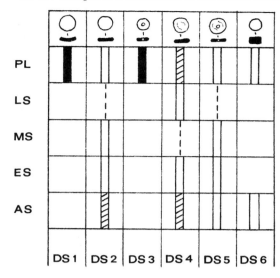

to 10 cm. Many appear to have been used as rubbing stones, others as hand-held mixing palettes.

TYPE DS 5. PERFORATED FLAT PEBBLE

Stone, ordinary river stone pebbles; 5 samples; plate 251:P–Q

This type is similar to DS 4 unshaped pebbles but has a centrally drilled hole. The cross sections are typically rather thin. The size ranges from 5 to 8 cm. The perforations have hourglass-shaped cross sections. The points of the drills used for these borings were most probably conical. These perforated pebbles were possibly spindle whorls or suspended weights.

TYPE DS 6. DISCOID

Stone, conglomerate and quartzite; 2 samples; plate 251:R–S

These discs have been completely shaped. DS 6 were probably used as small handgrinders. The wear pattern over both the flat surfaces and sides indicates light pounding and grinding.

GROOVED STONES

TYPE GR 1. SMALL GROOVED PEBBLES

Stone, typically hard stones such as buff stone or slate/greenish gray; 16 samples; plate 252:A–H

These ovaloid river pebbles range in length from 9 to 12 cm. In each case there is a single straight groove running across one side of the stone. The reverse sides of these stones are often coated or stained with bitumen.

The dimensions of the grooves are remarkably consistent: length, 7.2 to 8.7 cm; width, 1.1 to 1.8 cm; depth, 0.7 to 0.9 cm. There is but one exception; here the groove is 0.5–.06 × 1.5 × 4.5 cm. Grooves are usually U-

Table 40. Temporal Distribution of the Grooved Stones

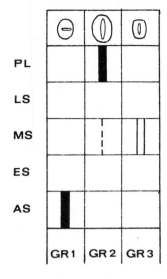

	GR 1	GR 2	GR 3
PL			
LS			
MS			
ES			
AS			

shaped in cross section, but in two examples were V-shaped. In one case (pl. 248:H) the groove has a U-shaped lower section and an upper section with straight sides (sloped at about a 4° or 5° angle).

Striations in the grooves are clearly the result of a rubbing motion along the length of the groove. The inner areas of the grooves are especially shiny and polished. In one case, individual striation lines are distinct; each stroke is about 5 cm long and 0.3 to 0.5 mm wide. The heating of the stone, possibly in conjunction with molten bitumen, would have facilitated the shaping and the sharpening of points. These grooved stones might also have been used for the straightening of thin rods such as arrow shafts.

TYPE GR 2. LARGE GROOVED SANDSTONES

Stone, sandstone; 3 samples; plate 252:I–J

The grooves are considerably larger, but proportionally shallower, than those of GR 1. The GR 2 grooves have been worn by a linear rubbing motion along their lengths. The abrasive quality of the stone would have made GR 2 stones suitable for the initial grinding of the points of awls and spatulae.

TYPE GR 3. SPECIAL FORM

Stone, slate/greenish gray; 1 sample; plate 252:K

This is a well-made, well-proportioned object, shaped by hammering and then improved by grinding. The groove is 8.0 cm long, 1.4 cm wide, and 0.3 cm deep. An area 4.0 cm long and 0.6 cm wide within the groove is especially well polished. The stone fits comfortably in one hand. This special form appears to have been used in the same manner as GR 1 types.

RUBBING/POLISHING STONES

TYPE R 1. LARGE OVAL

Stone, white stone or buff stone; 4 samples; plate 252:L–M

The entire surfaces of these apparently naturally shaped stones are highly polished. The stones vary in size but are all about hand-sized. These stones were certainly polished by human hands. Their actual function as rubbers, however, is rather dubious. They could have served to soften leather. They might have been prestige or symbolic objects.

TYPE R 2. SMALL PEBBLES

Stone, various; 10 samples; plate 252:N–Q

R 2 stones are either roundish or flat disc-shaped. The entire surface is smooth, but there is usually one area that appears more polished. These small pebbles might have been burnishing stones used in the treatment of ceramic surfaces.

TYPE R 3. FLAT STONES

Stone, mainly slate and buff stone; 12 samples; plate 252:R–T

These stone tablets are of various shapes and sizes. At least one of the two flat surfaces shows signs of having been used for rubbing or fine grinding. Some appear to have been used as whetstones or rubbing stones. Others were probably cosmetic palettes; red pigment adheres to the surfaces of a few examples.

TYPE R 4. VARIOUS FACETED STONES

Stone, various hard stones; 20 samples; plate 252:U–Z

Included in this classification are rubbing stones of various shapes and sizes, with at least one faceted area. There is no sign of wear other than the faceted areas. The stone hoe (Subtype H 2a; pl. 252:Z) was secondarily used as a rubbing stone.

Table 41. Temporal Distribution of the Rubbing Stones

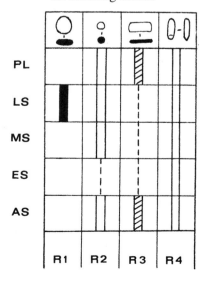

	R1	R2	R3	R4
PL				
LS				
MS				
ES				
AS				

CHAPTER 12

THE GROWTH OF THE SETTLEMENT AT CHOGHA MISH AND SUSIANA FOREIGN RELATIONS

This chapter considers various general aspects of the Susiana period at Chogha Mish; namely, the changing extent of the settlement on the mound, the questions of ceramics continuity and discontinuity, the comparison of the Susiana sequence as known at Chogha Mish with that at other Susiana sites, and the parallels and relationships of the Susiana sequence with cultures in other areas. Moreover, it seems appropriate to report briefly on the earliest cultural sequence in Susiana as known only from Chogha Banut.

THE FORMATIVE SUSIANA PERIOD

The major problems in the Archaic Susiana period deal with origins, continuity, and foreign connections. In the first place, Archaic Susiana 1 pottery is remarkably sophisticated in its painted decoration and also in the variety of surface treatment applied to the one basic straw-tempered ware. Even the painted-burnished variants of Trench XXV (pl. 272) hardly represent the beginnings of pottery in the Susiana area.

During the later seasons when the area of the Gully Cut was considerably enlarged, no examples similar to the pottery found just above virgin soil in Trench XXV occurred. This seemed at first like an anomaly, but it is clear now that an important chronological distinction is involved. In the third season Trench XXV provided a sample of materials that were obtained on a much larger scale in the rescue excavation of the small site of Chogha Banut, 6 km to the west of Chogha Mish. At that site there are stratified sherds of painted-burnished ware variants similar to those found in Trench XXV, both the type with a light cream slip and various wavy line motifs and that with a red background and metopes filled with straight or wavy lines. In addition, Trench XXV yielded some less highly burnished sherds with, near the lip, rows of black triangles or wide solid black bands that are paralleled by a number of complete or semi-complete bowls from Banut. This material represents a phase intermediate between the Archaic Susiana 1 phase as known at Chogha Mish and the earlier Formative Susiana period as known at Chogha Banut.[1]

FORMATIVE SUSIANA FOREIGN RELATIONS

The painted-burnished variants of Chogha Mish and Chogha Banut are also known from the excavations at Tappeh Tula'i conducted by Hole, who considers it to be a camping site since the archaeological materials are widely scattered over a flat surface (Hole 1974, 1975, 1987:39). The pottery of this initial painted-burnished phase is associated with other artifacts, for example, the tiny T-shaped figurines, which occur both at Chogha Mish and at the Deh Luran sites. However, striking parallels can be found in the pottery and figurines from the distant site of Sang-e Chakhmaq, in the northeastern corner of Iran (Masuda 1972, 1974). The T-shaped figurines are frequently interpreted as belonging to a Zagros complex (Braidwood et al. 1983:369–424; Morales 1990), but they have a wider distribution since there is closely similar material far to the northeast of Iran (Masuda 1972, 1974).

These close parallels from widely separated sites in southern Turkmanestan (Jeitun) (Masson and Sarianidi 1972), the Zagros (Jarmo), and Susiana can be interpreted as regional variety of a single incipient cultural horizon that can be taken as common ancestors of many later regional traditions in Iran. It should be noted, however, that the great problem in accepting such a proposal is that there are no known representatives of an analogous cultural phase in any of the sites in between. For example, at Sialk the early straw-tempered pottery of Levels 1 and 2 is quite different. In the northwest, at Tepe Zagheh, nothing has been published antedating the Zagheh phase (Malek-Shahmirzadi 1977, 1980; Negahban 1973, 1977). In the northwest, the Neolithic site of Haji

---

1. Below the Archaic Susiana levels at Chogha Banut was found 1.5 m of darkish earth deposit with sherds unknown

from the lowest levels at Chogha Mish. Some of the sherds were similar to the painted-burnished ware of the Archaic Susiana 1 phase, but their simple designs did not parallel those found at Chogha Mish. These levels at Chogha Banut also contained examples of wares, such as the film-painted, not found at Chogha Mish. The simple painted-burnished sherds became rare in lower levels and the film-painted became prominent. In the basal levels, pottery altogether disappears and the deposit alternates with brown clay surfaces and ashy layers, containing animal bones, fragments of stone vessels, simple clay figurines, and bullet-shaped flint cores and blades. AA

Firuz has nothing similar, although it has produced very primitive pottery (Voigt 1983). Accordingly, the comparisons for the transitional Formative/Archaic Susiana phase implies that it might have been a widely distributed primeval culture. If such was actually the case, then it can be taken as the common ancestor of many of the regional cultures in Iran.

THE ARCHAIC SUSIANA PERIOD

The earliest occupation at Chogha Mish can be identified by the presence of painted-burnished variants (pls. 227–29) and associated pottery found only in Trench XXV, where the sherds occurred in a thin black ashy level lying directly on virgin soil (fig. 39). They indicate the existence of a tiny settlement antedating the floruit of the Archaic Susiana 1 phase, when the settlement had expanded somewhat; a few meters east of Trench XXV, in the Gully Cut, sherds of the standard Archaic Susiana 1 painted-burnished ware (pls. 223–26) appear immediately above virgin soil, as they do in Trench XII and in Trench XXI (P23:301). They are found also in Trench XXV, where the Susiana deposits have been greatly disturbed by Protoliterate pits.[2] The red-line ware and other Archaic Susiana 2 pottery diagnostics have the same distribution as the standard Archaic Susiana 1 wares and, in addition, occur above virgin soil in Soundings G and H. Despite this slight growth in size, the settlement was probably a small hamlet (fig. 39; pl. 260).

By the Archaic Susiana 3 phase the settlement must have, at the least, doubled in size, to a minimum of ca. 1.05 hectares (fig. 40). Characteristic Archaic Susiana 3 pottery occurs in the area occupied in the Archaic Susiana 2 phase and also in the expanded area of Trenches XXI and XXXII. Substantial walls of 0.80 to 1.00 m long bricks occurred in Trench XXV and, more denuded, in the Trench XXI area. Moreover, the existence of the Archaic Susiana 3 phase some 15(?) m to the south of Trench XXI was established after the fifth season (Trench XXXVIII excavated in the eighth season). Thus, a settlement of approximately 90 × 100 m can be established for the Archaic Susiana 3 village, but it might well have been larger. Two close-line ware sherds were found worked up into higher levels in Trench XI (pl. 212:H) and XIII (pl. 208:G), suggesting the existence of a contiguous occupation. Thus, Trench XIII, about 90 m to the west of Trench XXXVIII, might quite possibly have been part of the continuous Archaic Susiana 3 settlement.[3]

THE EARLY SUSIANA PERIOD

The Early Susiana period is more extensively represented on Chogha Mish than the Archaic Susiana 3 phase. Trenches XII, XXI, XXXII, and the Gully Cut yielded good buildings, floors, hearths, and pottery deposits (fig. 41). Early Susiana levels also appeared in Trench XXV and Soundings G and H, and to the south in Trenches XXXI and XXXVII. A continuous settlement on the southeastern slope of the terrace can thus be postulated with some confidence. On the southwestern promontory of the terrace Early Susiana sherds occur in the lowest part of Trench XXXVI. In the middle of the terrace, characteristic Early Susiana pottery occurred in the lowest part of the original Trench XIII (K22:201) and was obviously not far below the Early Middle Susiana structures excavated in the enlarged Trench in seasons IV and V. The whole of the southern part of the terrace might have belonged to one continuous village. In addition, the two small pits sunk in the West Area to test the materials below the Protoliterate occupation ended above virgin soil with good Early Susiana material (H14:306, J14:301). None of the small test areas between the western side and the southern part of the terrace (Soundings B, D–E and Trench VIII) were carried deep enough to reach Early Susiana levels, so it is impossible to know whether there was one continuous occupation or a small cluster of houses separate from the main village in the south. In the latter case, the areas occupied during the Early Susiana period would have amounted to at least ca. 3.6 hectares.

THE MIDDLE SUSIANA PERIOD

THE EARLY MIDDLE SUSIANA

This phase is represented by good architecture in Trenches XIII and XXI. The known settlement is much the same as for the Early Susiana period and the presence of substantial rooms in both Trenches XIII and XXI supports the assumption of a continuous occupation between them. Thus, in the Early Middle Susiana phase the minimum area of occupation might have increased to at least 4.6 hectares. Moreover, it is possible that in the West Area the settled area was larger than shown in figure 42. It is also likely that Early Middle Susiana material exists in deeper elevations of the East Area than have yet been reached.

---

2. In Sounding A, on the western side of the terrace, about 190 m to the northwest of the Gully Cut, one sherd of painted-burnished ware (pl. 226:H) was found in a mixed context, which cannot be indicative of a westward expansion of Archaic Susiana 1 settlement.

3. At Chogha Mish the Archaic Susiana levels are well below the present plain level and are not to be found weathered

out on the surface. Although the Archaic Susiana levels at the small site of Boneh Fazili, some 3 km to the northwest of Chogha Mish, are also below the modern surface, sherds of all three phases of the period were found in the spoil heap of a deeply-dug porcupine burrow (pl. 213:H, matt-painted). This suggests that small Archaic Susiana villages might have been more numerous than can be established on the basis of survey data. AA

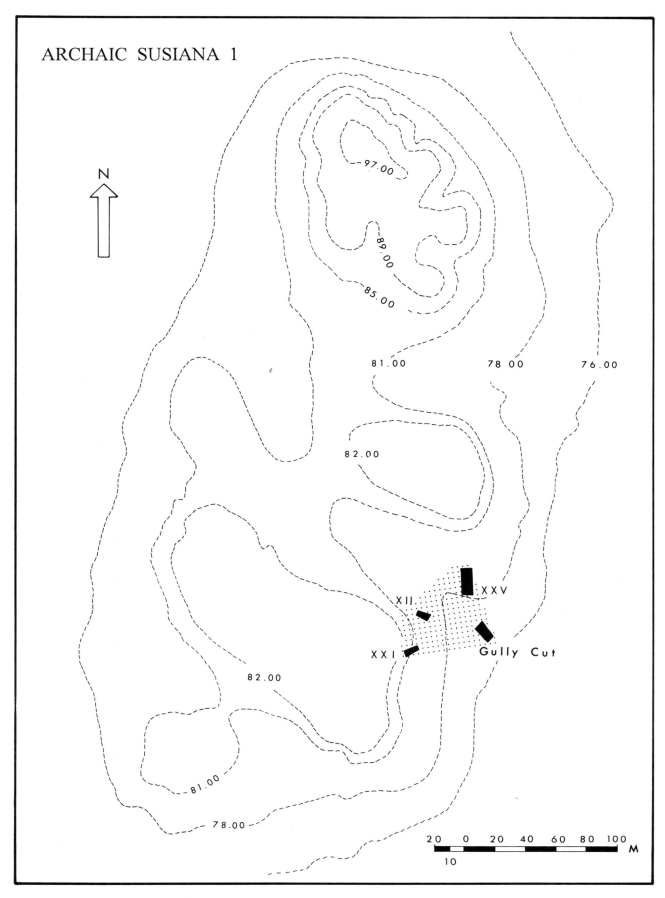

Figure 39. Minimum Extent of Archaic Susiana 1 Settlement at Chogha Mish

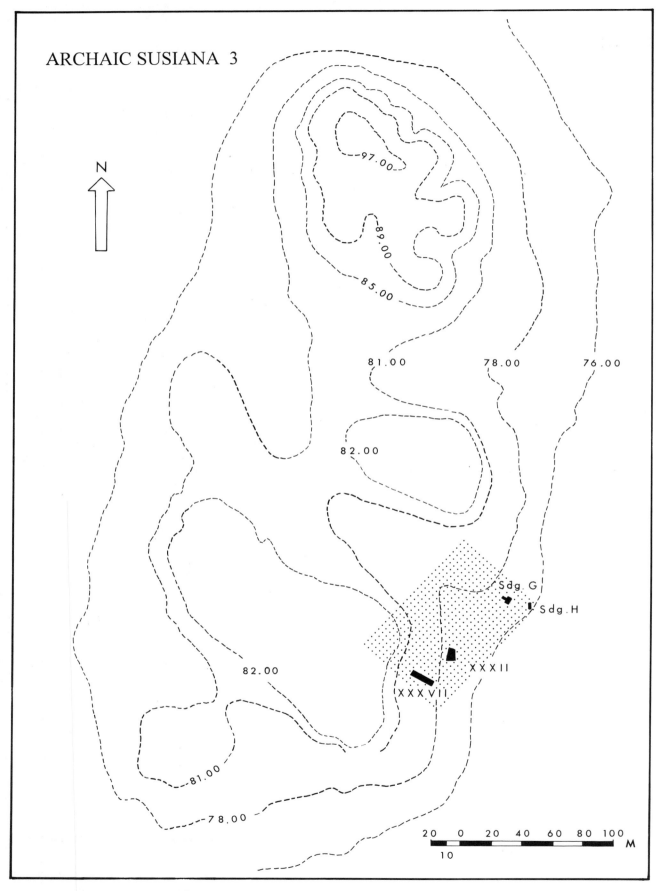

Figure 40. Minimum Extent of Archaic Susiana 3 Settlement at Chogha Mish

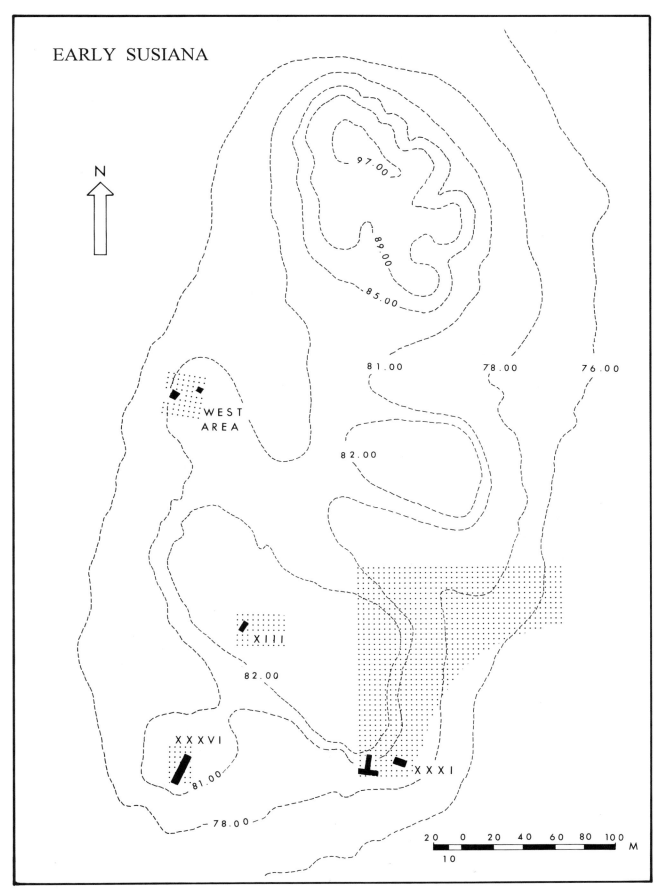

Figure 41. Minimum Extent of Early Susiana Settlement at Chogha Mish

THE LATE MIDDLE SUSIANA

The Late Middle Susiana phase is the most extensive occupation of the prehistoric period (fig. 43). Evidence for this phase occurs in every area that has been carried deep enough, both on the High Mound and the terrace, and on the surface all over the terrace. Late Middle Susiana material exists in abundance in the southern half of the High Mound. It almost certainly occurred in the untested northern part of the High Mound, as there is no reason why it should have suddenly stopped. Late Middle Susiana materials also occurred in Trenches I–II and XXIII. The density of the Late Middle Susiana occupation indicates that the entire mound was a continuous settlement of about 15 hectares. The realization that a center of such size existed in the Late Middle Susiana phase is one of the more important contributions made by Chogha Mish to present knowledge of the prehistoric period in Khuzestan, and parallel development in southern Mesopotamia. Then the discovery of the Burnt Building (see p. 168, fn. 14, above) on the down-sloping northeastern edge of the East Area provided Late Middle Susiana pottery in a splendid architectural context, which confirmed the definition of the ceramic assemblage that been developed in previous seasons (Kantor 1975/76:15).

THE LATE SUSIANA PERIOD

A vastly altered situation is presented by the next stage of settlement. Two thirds of the site was abandoned and the Late Susiana settlement was limited to the northern part of the site (fig. 44). The Late Susiana occupation must have endured for a considerable time since about 6 m of debris were deposited, creating the "High Mound," which thereafter remained such a dominating feature of the site. The reduction in size of the settlement at Chogha Mish is paralleled by the absence of Late Susiana material at the neighboring sites of Boneh Fazili and, possibly, Chogha Banut. This desertion and contraction was part of an overall regional drop in the number of sites that remained occupied in the Susiana plain during the later phase of the Late Susiana period (Hole 1987:42–43; Alizadeh 1992:57) and a general westward movement of settlements (Hole 1987:84).

THE DEVELOPMENT OF THE SUSIANA SEQUENCE AND ITS FOREIGN RELATIONS

THE ARCHAIC SUSIANA PERIOD

In general the earliest period of occupation at Chogha Mish, the Archaic Susiana, with its tradition of vegetal-tempered pottery represents a widespread general stage of development that can be traced not only in other parts of Iran,[4] but also in Mesopotamia to the west

4. Cf. Dyson's "Soft Ware" and "Jarmo-related" horizons discussed in Ehrich 1965:217f.

(cf. Kirkbride 1972:8f.; Braidwood and Howe 1960:43f.; Braidwood et al. 1983), and Turkestan to the east (cf. Masson and Sarianidi 1972:36, 40). Ceramics of the same general character occur in Mesopotamia at Umm Dabaghiyah and Jarmo and in Turkestan at sites of the Early Jeitun periods. At Chogha Mish this period was evidently a long one, with three phases characterized by well-differentiated painted wares. The painted-burnished ware of the Archaic Susiana 1 phase was specific to Khuzestan; however, Chogha Sefid in Deh Luran provides a parallel, dated to the Surkh phase, close enough to suggest that the ware existed there (Hole 1977:116, fig. 44:bb). Elsewhere there are only a few general analogies from early phases, such as the interlocked designs on Kutahi (Sumner 1977, fig. 4) and Mushki (ibid., pl. III) wares in Fars or the rickrack bands on a sherd from Tappeh Guran in Luristan (Meldgaard et al. 1963), which are insufficient to establish any connections.

Another problem is that of the extent to which the three phases of the Archaic Susiana period represent the gradual development of a single cultural tradition. In all phases most of the vessels are of the same basic straw-tempered smoothed ware. The major shapes, in particular the carinated open vessels, remain the same throughout. Another indication of continuity in the pottery is the use of red wash in both the Archaic Susiana 1 and 2 phases, although in different shapes. In the Archaic Susiana 3 phase the red wash below the carination continues on the matt-painted ware, which is itself a variety of the standard straw-tempered ware.

However, in addition to the standard straw- or chaff-tempered categories that continue, the two later phases saw the appearance of wares of substantially different fabric, namely the dense-sandy red-line ware in the Archaic Susiana 2 phase and Archaic Susiana 3 close-line ware. Since the red-line ware is linked by both shape and chevron decoration with the straw-tempered smoothed and painted-burnished wares, it can be considered a later development within the same cultural tradition as the earlier pottery.

Archaic Susiana 1: The earliest cultural phase occurring at Chogha Mish is represented by the sherds just above virgin soil in Trench XXV. The relatively simple variants found there (pls. 227–29) illustrate the beginning of the painted-burnished ware that is one of the main features diagnostic for the Archaic Susiana 1 phase. The other outstanding category produced by the surface treatment of the basic straw-tempered ware is the red-washed and burnished bowls with beaded rims, which likewise is precluded by red-washed sherds from Trench XXV.

In the Archaic Susiana 1 phase the surface treatment of the basic straw-tempered ware produced two categories diagnostic for the phase, one the red-washed and burnished bowls with beaded rims and the other the cream-slipped painted-burnished vessels with their re-

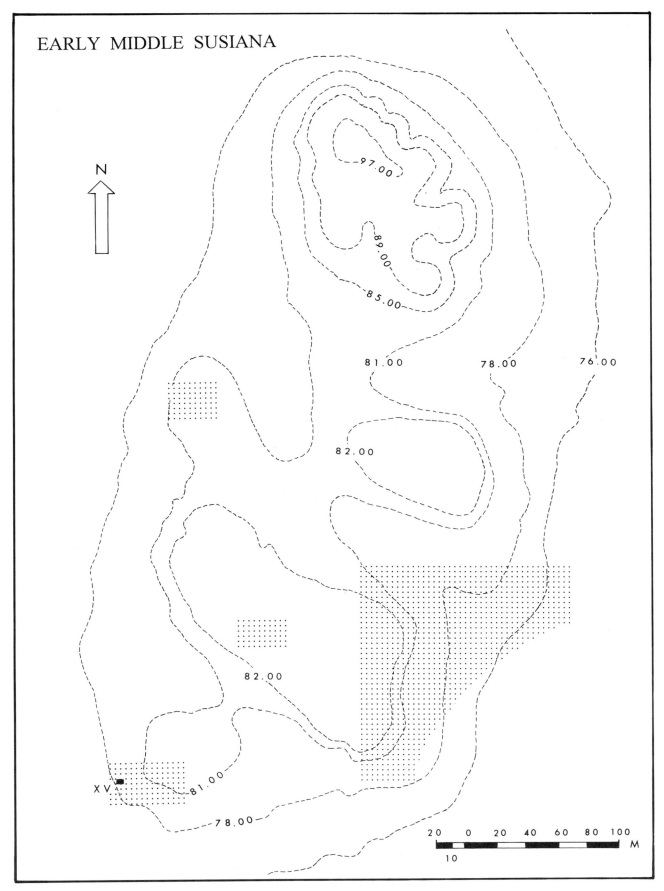

Figure 42. Minimum Extent of Early Middle Susiana Settlement at Chogha Mish

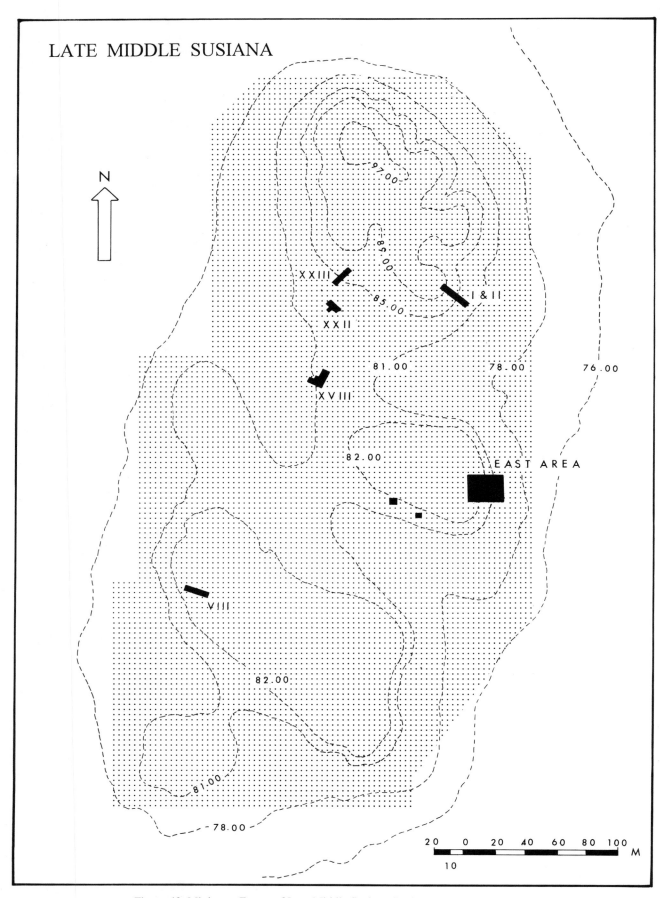

LATE MIDDLE SUSIANA

N

XXIII

I & II

XXII

XVIII

81.00   78.00   76.00

82.00

EAST AREA

VIII

82.00

81.00

78.00

20 0 20 40 60 80 100
                                    M
10

Figure 43. Minimum Extent of Late Middle Susiana Settlement at Chogha Mish

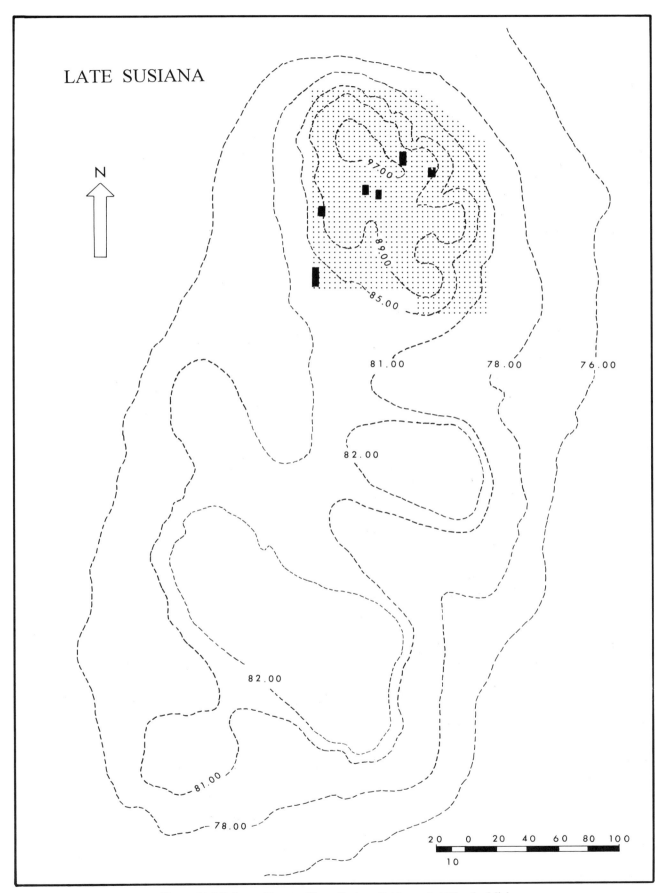

Figure 44. Minimum Extent of Late Susiana Settlement at Chogha Mish

markably sophisticated designs. The sherds just above virgin soil in Trench XXV are antecedents for both categories. However, even the painted-burnished variants of Trench XXV are too developed to represent the beginnings of the ceramic tradition, so antecedents for the earliest cultural phase occurring at Chogha Mish must be sought elsewhere. The bulldozing in 1976 of a site 6 km to the west, Chogha Banut, provided an opportunity to do this in the eleventh and twelfth seasons. There the Formative Susiana wares and the transitional painted-burnished variants provide the ancestors of the standard Archaic Susiana ceramic tradition. Throughout the Archaic Susiana period the picture is one of a homogeneous Susiana culture, with the exception of the close-line ware characteristic for the Archaic Susiana 3 phase, steadily increasing in complexity.

In the Archaic Susiana period the bulk of the pottery hardly changed in either ware or shape. Carinated open vessels made of the straw-tempered smoothed ware dominate the repertory and give an overall unity to the period. It is the more specialized wares (varieties of the basic straw-tempered ware), particularly the painted ones, that are diagnostic for phases within the period and, in one major case, raise problems of cultural continuity and homogeneity probably more pronounced than in any of the later periods.

Archaic Susiana 2: The paint and patterns of the red-line ware diagnostic for this phase (pl. 218) have parallels in the Jafar painted ware from Ali Kosh and Chogha Sefid in the northwestern Deh Luran plain (Hole et al. 1969, fig. 44). Similarly shaped vessels bear the designs, but have some difference in the paste.

The disappearance of the painted-burnished ware in the Archaic Susiana 2 phase is better interpreted as a change in fashion rather than a break in continuity since the bulk of the pottery remains the same. One innovation is the use of red pigment not only for allover washes but also for simple designs (pl. 219:C–D, K–M). Another is the appearance of a different fabric, namely the dense-sandy ware, alongside the standard straw-tempered ware. It is a development within the same ceramic tradition. The ware, though markedly dense, does possess some finely divided, chaff temper. Archaic Susiana 1 pottery provides prototypes for the shapes (pls. 218:C–E; 219:A; 222:E–F) and for the commonest pattern of the dense-sandy red-line vessels (cf. the painted-burnished design of a wide negative zigzag containing thin positive zigzags [pl. 229:K]).

Archaic Susiana 3: In the Archaic Susiana 3 phase the situation is more complex, particularly because of the use at the same time of two well-defined and sharply contrasting painted wares. Continuity can be seen in the unpainted smoothed vessels and in the chaff-tempered matt-painted ware. The chaff temper of the latter represents a version of the straw-tempered standard ware in which the vegetal inclusions have been more minutely pulverized. The matt-painted decoration continues red-line ware features: the chevron friezes, the elongated hourglass (pls. 214:J; 215:F–G), and the fugitive red wash on the lower body. In contrast, the close-line ware differs markedly from the other Archaic Susiana wares in its fabric, shapes, and painted decoration. It is the only grit-tempered Archaic ware (even the dense-sandy has a bit of chaff). The upper bodies of the vessels tend to flare out, and lower bodies to incurve markedly, frequently as a carination, toward the base. Its carinated bowls bring the first Archaic Susiana vessels with important interior decoration (pl. 207); the other painted Archaic Susiana wares have at most a lip band on the interior. The close-line ware brings the first examples of relatively closed vessels with necks clearly differentiated from the body by both shape and tectonic decoration (pl. 211:L–S).

The individual motifs and their syntax are specific to the ware; they are quite unrelated to the decoration of the other Archaic Susiana painted wares, aside from some very rare instances of motifs shared with the contemporary matt-painted ware. Unlike the matt-painted ware, which in its paste, shapes, and decoration appears as a lineal descendant of earlier Archaic Susiana pottery, the close-line ware has no comparable Susiana roots, a circumstance which forces us to look abroad for parallels. Although the close-line ware stands out as a foreign ingredient added to the Susiana repertory, the uninterrupted continuation of the standard straw-tempered wares and the flourishing of the matt-painted ware alongside the close-line ware rule out any population displacement by the end of the Archaic Susiana 2 phase.

The decided sophistication of the earliest painted pottery as well as the variety of painted wares developed during the three Archaic Susiana phases are matched by the variety of figures modeled in clay, which range from the highly stylized thorn figures and simple geometric "chessmen" to the recognizably human figures of Archaic Susiana 3. The ground stone industry was developed to the point where elegant small polished stone celts and various plugs or labrets were made; although the stone hoes do not begin until the Early Susiana period. The presence of querns and grinding stones, the massive admixture of straw, including an occasional imprint of an individual grain, in the pottery, and the bones of domesticated goats indicate the existence of a mixed economy combining agriculture and animal husbandry. A further index of the caliber of the Archaic Susiana period is the architecture with its remarkably long bricks documented at Chogha Mish in Trench XXV for the final phase of the period. This architectural element , however, seems to have developed much earlier in the Archaic Susiana phase.[5]

---

5. At Chogha Banut similar walls of long bricks belonging to the transitional Formative Archaic phase also occur (see Kantor 1976–77:21). AA

ARCHAIC SUSIANA FOREIGN RELATIONS

Archaic Susiana 1 and 2: In general the earliest period of occupation at Chogha Mish, the Archaic Susiana, with its tradition of vegetal-tempered pottery represents a widespread general stage of development that can be traced not only in other parts of Iran,[6] but also in Mesopotamia to the west (cf. Kirkbride 1972; Braidwood and Howe 1960; Braidwood et al. 1983) and Turkestan to the east (cf. Masson and Sarianidi 1972, 36, 40).

For the painted-burnished ware of Archaic Susiana 1 Chogha Sefid in Deh Luran provides a parallel, dated to the Surkh phase (ca. 5700–5400; Hole 1987, table 2), close enough to suggest that the ware existed there (Hole 1977:116, fig. 44:bb). Elsewhere there are only a few general analogies from early phases, such as the interlocked designs on Kutahi (Sumner 1977, pl. 3) and Mushki (Fukaii 1973) wares in Fars or the rickrack bands on a sherd from Guran in Luristan (Thrane et al. 1963:116, fig. 17:g), which are insufficient to establish any connections. Clearly, the painted-burnished ware was specific to Khuzestan, and perhaps was centered chiefly in the Susiana plain.[7]

While at Chogha Mish the red-line ware paste is primarily dense-sandy, with only sometimes a smaller or greater admixture of fine chaff, in Deh Luran the Jafar painted ware is described as mainly chaff-tempered and porous.[8] The difference in ware can presumably be considered a local variation that does not invalidate the correspondence established by the other features just cited. The red-line ware has distant parallels that appear at Guran in Luristan (Thrane 1964; Mortensen 1974:36, figs. 7–8) and at Sarab in Kurdestan (Braidwood 1960:696, fig. 12) in the form of chaff-tempered vessels painted in red, most frequently with variously-shaped drop-like elements "strung" along diagonal lines. The parallels just cited indicate that the Archaic Susiana 2 phase of the Susiana sequence existed also in the Deh Luran plain in a regional variant, to judge by the differing details of the fugitive red chevron patterns frequent

in both areas. Related cultural phases are traceable in the Zagros valleys of Luristan and Kurdestan.

Farther afield in northwestern Mesopotamia, Umm Dabaghiyah provides some good analogies for Archaic Susiana 2 pottery, most likely representing an approximately contemporary occupation. Thus the second phase of the Archaic Susiana period is related, closely or more distantly, to a number of other cultures stretching to the northwest. Diana Kirkbride's description of the extreme fragility of the red paint with which some of the Umm Dabaghiyah straw-tempered pottery is decorated can be applied exactly to the red-line ware. Among the designs are chevrons reminiscent of some of the simpler examples at Chogha Mish. Umm Dabaghiyah also yielded the greater part of a vessel whose shape and red-painted vertical bands parallel features of Archaic Susiana 2 pottery at Chogha Mish (Kirkbride 1972:9–10, pl. 10).

Archaic Susiana 3: The stratification at Chogha Mish is pertinent to some major problems of the comparative chronology in Mesopotamia. With the accumulation of a tremendous amount of new data during the 1970s and 1980s, the complexity of development in Mesopotamia has become more evident. A continuous cultural tradition, whose gradual development can be followed for several millennia, as it can also be followed in the Susiana tradition, is documented only in the south. The great development in the south is the revelation at el-'Oueili of a phase antecedent to Eridu (Ubaid 1). The new phase, Ubaid 0, displays striking similarities to the close-line ware at Chogha Mish (Calvet 1983).

In contrast to the south, the rest of Mesopotamia falls into a number of provinces. In the center of Mesopotamia, two major areas can be distinguished, the area around Samarra and the area slightly to the northeast, the Hamrin. For the latter there is a great deal of evidence provided by an international rescue effort, while in contrast in the Samarra area there are only three sites, making for a great disparity in the evidence. The two central areas cannot simply be combined together since the Hamrin has not only sites with the Samarra sequence but also some other sites that are primarily Halaf in material culture. One of the more discussed questions in recent years has been the character and date of the Chogha Mami Transitional ware that has been dated by Oates to a phase intermediate between the Samarra and Halaf (Oates 1968, 1969, 1986, 1987).

In northern Mesopotamia the sites to the west of the Tigris River such as Yarim Tepe cluster and Umm Dabaghiyah display a sequence beginning with a prepottery Neolithic on to a pottery Neolithic with apparently a gradual transition to the Archaic phase of the Hassuna/Samarra culture that is eventually superseded by the Halaf phase. In contrast, the sites to the east of the Tigris, as known so far, do not have the Hassuna sequence but instead begin with early Halaf comparable to

---

6. Cf. R. H. Dyson's "Soft Ware" and "Jarmo-related" horizons discussed in Ehrich 1965:217f.

7. The geographical distribution of Archaic Susiana 1 pottery of Chogha Mish is much wider than expected. In the summer of 1993, on a visit to the mobile pastoralist tribes of the Bakhtyari mountains, several small mounds were observed near Aligudarz, to the northeast of Esfahan, with pottery very similar to that of Sang-e Chakhmaq and Archaic Susiana 1 painted-burnished variants of Chogha Mish and Chogha Banut; similar pottery was also reported from an extensive survey in eastern Bakhtyari by Mr. Chegini of the Cultural Heritage Organization, Iran (personal communication). AA

8. Hole (1977:31) described the Jafar plain and the Jafar painted wares as porous and pitted.

that known in the Khabur region of northeastern Syria. The situation as known now has an odd geographical division of early Halaf on either side of a Hassuna/ Samarra cultural area, almost as if the Halaf culture were coming southward from a focus somewhat to the north or northwest. The problem of the origin of Halaf is still debated, although a northwestern origin seems likely. Despite all the uncertainties, a provisional relative chronology can be worked out.

These problems have been raised in various publications. The close-line ware of Archaic Susiana 3, whose similarity to the Ubaid 0 pottery is clear, is well stratified below Early Susiana levels. The same is true at the Deh Luran sites. The prominent Early Susiana family of convex-sided bowls (pl. 196:A–B) is identical with typical bowls of the Eridu phase, creating an excellent synchronism. In addition, the figurines at Chogha Mish are closely comparable to Samarra examples from the Mandali area (Oates 1968, pls. 1–3).

Of the two painted wares diagnostic for Archaic Susiana 3, one, the matt-painted ware, remains almost without parallels away from Chogha Mish. Examples of it cannot be expected from Jowi and Jafarabad, which are later, or from Tula'i, which is much earlier. In the Deh Luran plain the contemporary levels at Chogha Sefid do not have any close parallels to the matt-painted ware.

In striking contrast, the other diagnostic painted pottery of Archaic Susiana 3, the close-line ware, stands out from all the other Archaic Susiana wares in its fabric, forms, and decoration. It is the only Archaic Susiana ware with marked grit tempering and without the straw or chaff admixture found in some sherds of the dense-sandy ware of Archaic Susiana 2. The close-line forms show no evident relationship with those of the other Archaic Susiana wares but are consistent among themselves, namely in the tendency for the upper parts of vessels to flare outward and for the lower part to taper markedly, frequently from a definite carination, toward the base. For the first time in the Archaic Susiana period there are families of shallow bowls in which the interior decoration is at least as important as the exterior painting. The other painted Archaic Susiana wares have no interior decoration other than a lip frieze. In addition, the decoration of the close-line ware, both its individual motifs and its syntax, is specific to the style, without any significant relationship to the painted wares of the Archaic Susiana 1 and 2 phases.

As reported above, unlike the matt-painted ware, which appears as a lineal descendant of earlier Archaic Susiana pottery in its paste, shapes, and decoration, the close-line ware has no comparable roots in the Archaic tradition of Chogha Mish. Also in contrast to the matt-painted ware, the close-line ware possesses an array of parallels that reveal a complex nexus of connections. Prominent among these are its relationships with the

Samarra ware of northern Mesopotamia, which is reviewed below along with the evidence from other sites in Khuzestan, from Chogha Mami in the Mesopotamian border province of Mandali, and from southern Mesopotamia.

Samarra Comparisons: Some Samarra vessels are so similar in both shape and decoration to close-line vessels that they can be classified under the same family designations as follows:

—The flaring-lip bowls with multiple wavy lines on the interior (pl. 206:D–H; fig. 45:A–B)

—The pedestal bases (pls. 206:L; 208:D–E; fig. 45:D, I, M)

—Archaic Susiana Subfamily IIa base pattern (fig. 45:G–H)

—The carinated bowls with exterior patterns of Xs (fig. 46:C–F), braided triangles (fig. 46:A–B), or groups of multiple diagonal lines (fig. 46:G–J), and groups of pendant vertical lines, sometimes linked (pls. 207:I–J; 208:C, F; figs. 46:E–H)

—The carinated bowl variant with "pegs" above a register with a reserved zigzag pattern (fig. 46:M, O, Q) combines shape with the decoration (cf. pl. 210:B–E)

—The vessels with various zigzag patterns below "peg" register (fig. 47:C–G)

—The vessels with zigzag or zigzag-derived designs on the exterior (fig. 47:I–L); cornets (fig. 47:Q–S; pl. 212:L);[9] motifs: vertical lines with scallops (fig. 47:A–B), friezes of simplified birds in neck or shoulder zones (fig. 47:O–P), and quadrupeds (fig. 47:M–N)

The close-line ware at Chogha Mish is found in the layers underlying those of the Early Susiana period and must antedate any cultures contemporary with that period. As discussed below, there are excellent parallels that equate the Early Susiana period in Khuzestan with the Eridu (Ubaid 1) period in southern Mesopotamia. This correlation might preclude the contemporaneity of the close-line and Samarra wares but calls for an explanation of the many similarities between them. A review of additional parallels for the close-line ware, some of them only recently excavated, is necessary to provide such an explanation.

Despite the clear relationship between the Samarra and close-line wares, they are by no means the same. The Samarra ware shows development of elaborate representational compositions without the technically-demanding closeness of line of the close-line ware. In addition, the Samarra ware demonstrates a more complex, developed style than does the close-line ware. These characteristics indicate that the standard Samarra ware was not the direct source of the close-line ware despite the number of similarities they share.[10]

9. For Tell es-Sawwan parallels, see Ippolitoni 1970/71, fig. 10:21–22.

10. The comparison of the close-line and Samarra wares shows a good number of similarities. Nonetheless, as a whole, major distinctions between the two wares remain. In the Samarra ware most forms analogous to close-line vessels

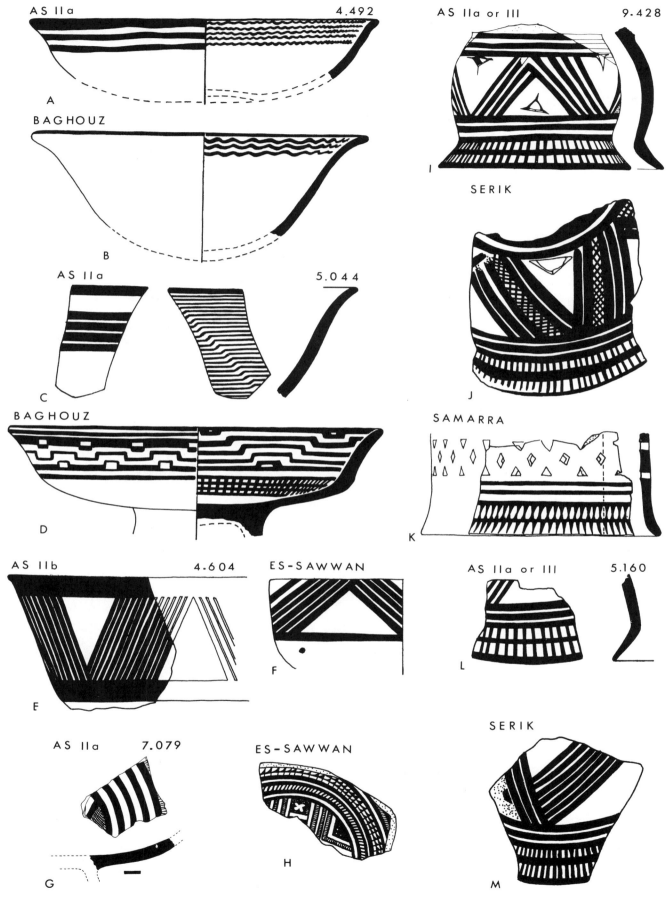

Figure 45. Similarities Between Archaic Susiana 3 and Samarra Pottery

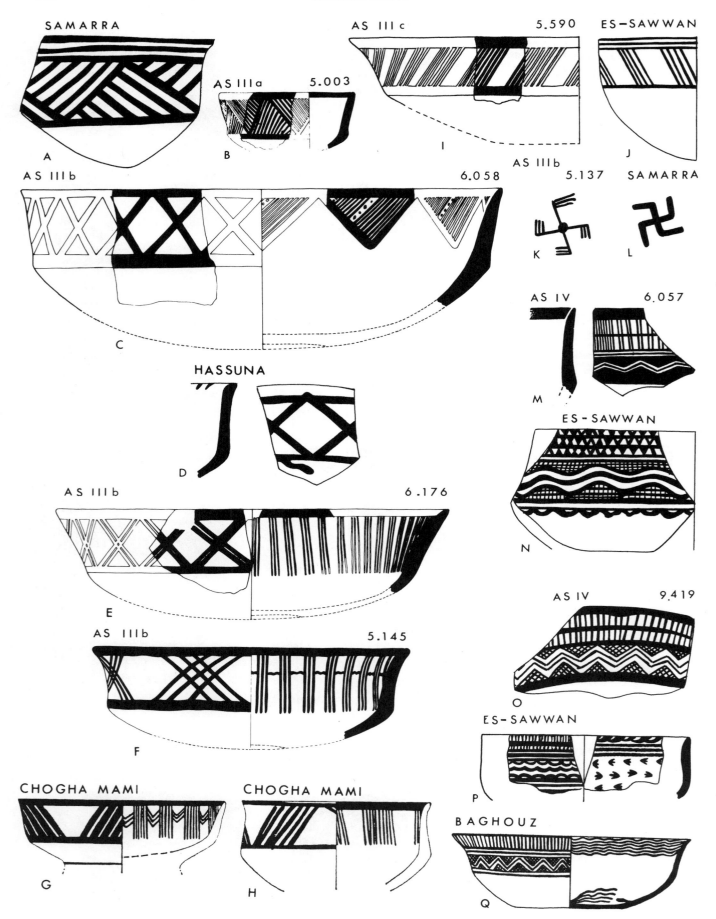

Figure 46. Similarities Between Archaic Susiana 3 and Samarra Pottery

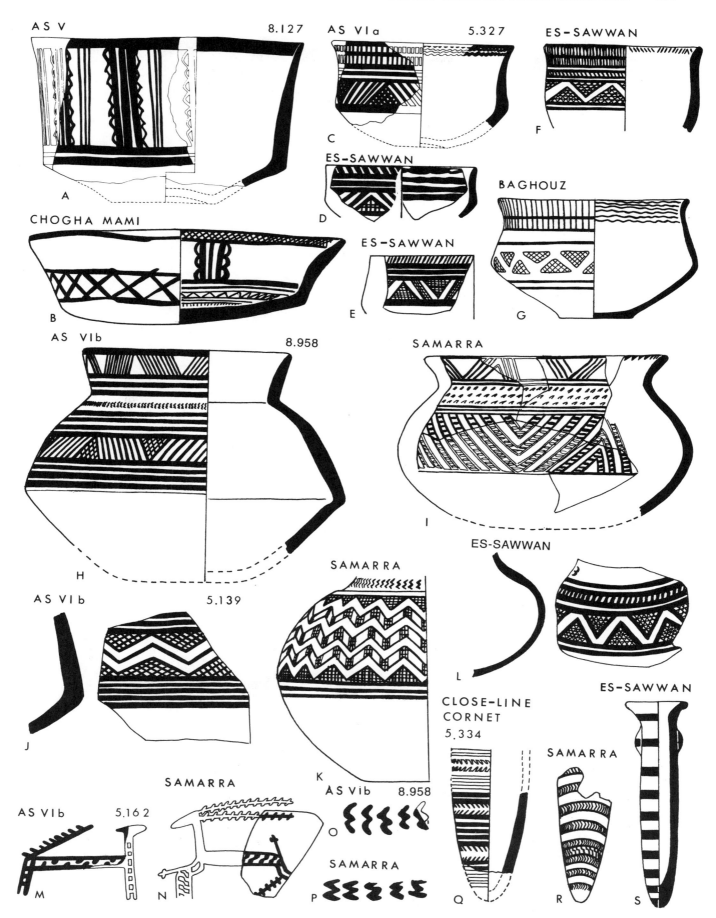

Figure 47. Similarities Between Archaic Susiana 3 and Samarra Pottery

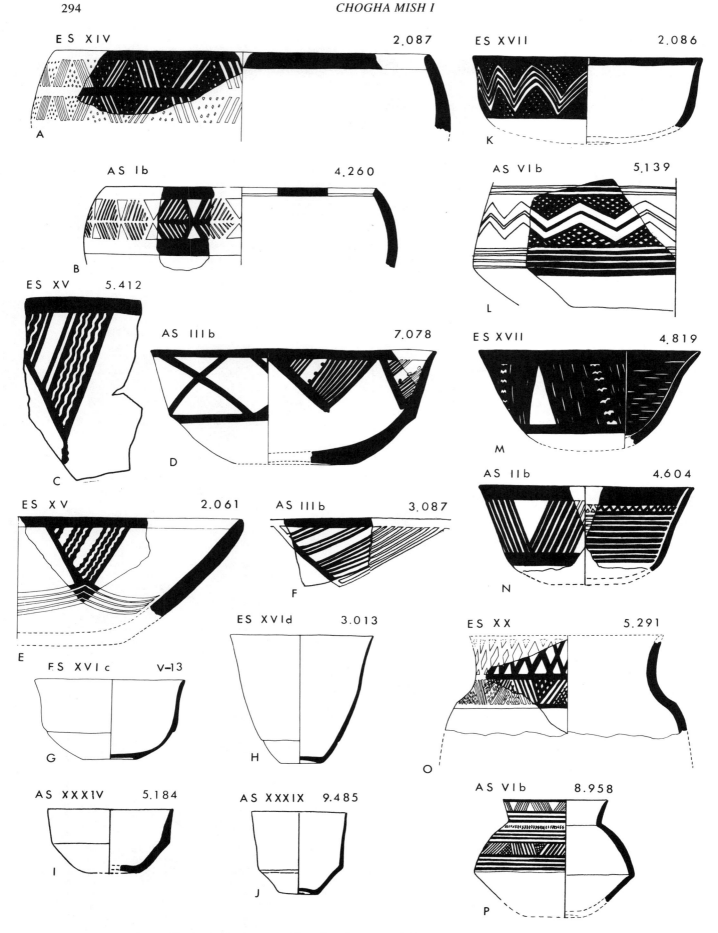

Figure 48. Continuity Between Close-line Ware of Archaic Susiana 3 to Early Susiana Pottery

Susiana Connections: At Jafarabad, Early Susiana levels provide some sherds, apparently of carinated bowls, decorated with Xs (Dollfus 1975, fig. 26). They lack, however, the interior interrupted triangles standard for the close-line ware and resemble late, debased descendants of the close-line Archaic Susiana Family III bowls that occur at Chogha Mish in levels immediately below Early Susiana levels.[11] In the Susiana plain true close-line ware is still known only from Chogha Mish and Boneh Fazili.

Deh Luran and Chogha Mami Transitional Comparisons: In contrast, Chogha Sefid in the Deh Luran plain provides sherds identifiable, with the exception of some too small to be assigned with certainty, as examples of close-line families Archaic Susiana Ia, II, IV, VI. Not far to the northwest of the Deh Luran plain, in the Mesopotamian border province of Mandali, the Chogha Mami Transitional ware provides good parallels for the close-line ware, although not the striking identity evident in Deh Luran. (Local differences in paste and color of the paint are to be expected.)[12] The Chogha Mami Transitional ware is considered by Oates to be both stratigraphically and stylistically intermediate between the Samarra and Halaf periods, placing the ware in a period later than that of the close-line ware at Chogha Mish. At Chogha Sefid in Deh Luran, the pottery in question, equated with the Chogha Mami Transitional ware by Hole but here considered as identical with close-line ware, is also stratified below the Early Susiana/Sabz levels.

A standard type of the close-line ware at Chogha Mish, the carinated bowls with interrupted triangles on the interior and Xs on the exterior (pl. 207:D–E, K–M), has parallels, but not exact parallels at Chogha Mami. There, interrupted triangles on the interior are paired with groups of multiple diagonal lines.[13] A bowl with contiguous Xs on the exterior combines them with clusters of vertical lines on the interior; neither the almost straight-sided shallow basin form (Oates 1987:172, fig. 4:18) nor the simple flaring bowl forms with hatched triangles on the interior and simple or no decoration on the exterior (ibid., fig. 4:17 [triangles crosshatched], 19–21) are represented in close-line ware. However, the hatched triangles on the interior are similar to those on a bowl fragment (pl. 167:A); it varies in its coarsened shape and painting and thick walls from normal close-line ware. It is one of the debased final examples of the close-line ware occasionally found in Early Susiana contexts.

Small sherds of Archaic Susiana Subfamily IIa bowls with a prominent interior register of hatched triangles (pl. 206:D, F–G) are paralleled by a large fragment from Chogha Mami.[14] Archaic Susiana Subfamily IIb (pl. 206:M) does not seem to occur at Chogha Mami, nor do the families with their exterior designs organized around a horizontal median line (pls. 206:A–C; 210:F–I). Chogha Mami has two candidates for Archaic Susiana Family IV (pl. 210:B–E; Oates 1987:173, fig. 5:30–31). Vessels classifiable as Archaic Susiana Subfamilies VIa (pl. 211:G–K)[15] and VIb (pl. 211:L–S); occur at Chogha Mami (Oates 1986:173–74, figs. 5:36, 37, 41; 6:54, 57), along with others that do not fit comfortably into close-line categories.

Southern Mesopotamian Comparisons: At last the gap in knowledge of southern Mesopotamia before the Eridu period is being filled. The existence of a pre-Eridu period in southern Mesopotamia, predicated on the basis of the Warka survey finds,[16] has been documented at el-'Oueili by the discovery of sherds of a pre-Eridu "Ubaid 0" period stratified below the Eridu levels

---

are less sharply defined; the typical close-line carinations are rare so that the rounded, and prevailing, forms cannot be fitted comfortably into the close-line repertoire. On the other hand, various differentiated Samarra shapes, such as the vessels with rather narrow and high necks, do not occur in the close-line ware. The style of the Samarra painted decoration is distinct from that of the close-line ware. In general, lines are less taut and not so tightly spaced. The lively and distinctively Samarra motifs painted on the interior base of plates are entirely missing in the close-line ware. Analogous designs often vary in their details; compare, for example, the treatment of the "pegs," linked pendant lines, or reserved zigzags. Alongside the trend for the simplified rendering of standard geometric designs, is the use of representational motifs to construct the complex circular patterns characteristic for the Samarra style. Excavations at a number of sites, particularly at Tell el-'Oueili, indicate that these differences might be both chronological and spatial. AA

11. Evidence for this intermediate category of the close-line ware will be presented in *Chogha Mish II*. (Such carinated bowls also occur at 'Oueili Layer 12 [Calvet 1985–86, pl. 17:1], a stratigraphic position comparable with the Susiana examples.) AA

12. This is true of the few Chogha Mami sherds that have been examined.

13. This appears only as an isolated case at Chogha Mish (6.070; braided triangles on its interior). It is, of course, a standard design for the exterior of Samarra ware bowls (Oates 1987:172, fig. 4:15–16).

14. Ibid., pp. 169–70, figs. 1–2. Narrow frieze with bird-like squiggles and hatched hourglasses seems rather advanced in type.

15. Oates 1968:1–20; idem 1969:115–52. Archaic Susiana Family IIIb: idem 1968, pls. 4, 12:1–3; idem 1969, pl. 32:2 (hatched triangles on interior), 3–4. Archaic Susiana Family VIa: idem 1969, pl. 32:5, 10; 1986:174, fig. 6:48; p. 175, fig. 7:59.

16. A site near Warka surveyed by Adams and Nissen in 1967, W 298, produced sherds representing a new ware; one had an interrupted triangle similar to those of close-line Archaic Susiana IIIb at Chogha Mish (Adams and Nissen 1972:98, 105, 174–75, fig. 66:1–3, 6, 9; 177, fig. 67:18). Cf. Oates 1986:165, where this ware is considered "a local—and conceivably earlier—variant of Ubaid 1." AA

(Lebeau 1985/86). The pottery decoration displays in general the same taut, closely painted lines that characterize the close-line ware (ibid., pls. 1:1, 8; 2:5–6). Parallels for close-line shapes and decoration occur as follows: Archaic Susiana Subfamily IIa lip sherds (pl. 206:D–L; Calvet 1985/86, pl. 22:1–4; Lebeau 1985/86, pl. 1:1); pedestals (pl. 208:D–E; ibid., pls. 7:2; 18:2–3); carinated bowls (pl. 208:A–C; ibid., pl. 3:4–5); and Archaic Susiana Family VI variants (pl. 211:G–S; ibid., pl. 7:1–6; 8:18; Calvet 1985/86, pl. 25:1–2).

The bowls with Xs are plain on the interior, which is most likely an indication that they are late; one of them is from Layer 12 of the deep Sounding X 36, which is intermediate between Ubaid 1 and 0 (Calvet 1985/86, pl. 17:1). The interrupted triangle motif is found at el-'Oueili on the interior of an Archaic Susiana Subfamily IIa bowl (ibid., pl. 24:3 [Sounding X 36, Layer 18]). In addition, el-'Oueili has sherds that do not parallel Chogha Mish forms. As more material accumulates from there, the roster of similarities will undoubtedly grow. Meanwhile, the Ubaid 0 sherds are, after the close-line ware of Deh Luran, the closest relatives of the close-line ware of Chogha Mish.

The Ubaid 0 of el-'Oueili provides a ceramic tradition firmly stratified between Eridu (Ubaid 1) layers and a basal layer (Sounding X 36, layer 19) containing a few vegetal-tempered and burnished sherds, but only one painted sherd, a bowl lip with roughly-executed Xs (Calvet 1985–86, pl. 25). There, too, the gritty painted ware had earlier, vegetal antecedents.

The similarities between the Ubaid 0 ware of el-'Oueili and the Chogha Mami Transitional and close-line wares indicate clearly the close relationship of the three traditions. Ubaid 0 was probably the central stem of which the contemporary Chogha Mami Transitional ware in the Mandali area and the close-line ware in Khuzestan were variants. The Ubaid 0 ware and the close-line ware can be regarded as the antecedents for the pottery of the immediately succeeding periods in each area: in southern Mesopotamia the Ubaid 0 ware developing into that of Ubaid I and in Susiana the close-line ware into Early Susiana painted pottery.

The affinities of the close-line ware indicate that it was a new cultural ingredient that came into the Susiana area from the west and was absorbed into the Archaic Susiana tradition.[17] There was no major displacement of the population, to judge by the uninterrupted continuation of the standard straw-tempered wares of the Archaic Susiana period and the flourishing of the matt-painted ware alongside the close-line ware. The final phase of the Archaic Susiana 3 was a flourishing period, as indicated by the increased size of the settlement at Chogha Mish and the increasing complexity of the culture.

17. See Hole 1977:12–16 for a discussion of this phase in Deh Luran.

THE EARLY SUSIANA PERIOD

The Early Susiana period, though it brought many changes, does not provide any problems in continuity. There is no stratigraphic hiatus between the latest Archaic Susiana and Early Susiana deposits. This became particularly clear during the sixth and seventh seasons in the eastern part of Trench XXI. The basic straw-tempered ware of the Archaic Susiana period was replaced by the friable grit-and-chaff-filled paste characteristic of Early Susiana, with purely straw-tempered vessels becoming a marked minority. The close-line ware was the antecedent for the fabric, dense and without vegetal tempering, of some of the finer Early Susiana vessels.

Pottery shapes and decoration provide excellent links with the preceding period. In shape, the concave base so typical of Early Susiana ceramics was a carry-over from the Archaic Susiana period, when it was a standard feature (fig. 48:G–J). The ridged or carinated Archaic Susiana forms developed into the outstanding flanged family of Early Susiana vessels (pls. 199:J–M; 200:A–G). Early Susiana pedestal bowls (pl. 197:D–G, J) were the direct descendants of the footed bowls of the Archaic Susiana 3 phase (fig. 45:I; pl. 208:D–E). The squat jars (pl. 194:O–P) continue the Archaic Susiana Subfamily VIb of the close-line ware (fig. 48:P; pl. 211:L–S). Moreover, similarities in vessel shapes are paralleled by continuity in decorative traditions.

The decoration of the close-line ware appears as the ancestor of the Early Susiana "close style." The tightly spaced horizontal lines on various Early Susiana vessels are sometimes practically indistinguishable from those on the Archaic Susiana 3 phase (fig. 48:N; pls. 211–12). The typical Early Susiana reserved zigzag separating crosshatched triangles (fig. 48:K; pl. 201:H–I) is descended from the decoration of close-line ware (cf. fig. 48:L; pl. 212:A–B). The close-line interrupted triangle sometimes appears in Early Susiana versions (fig. 48:E–F; pl. 199:G, I). The vertical zigzag bands to be found on the Archaic Susiana matt-painted ware (cf. pl. 216:C–F) probably inspired those used very commonly in Early Susiana design (pls. 194:T–V; 199:I), while the bird motifs of the close-line ware (pl. 211:O) were the prototypes of similar Early Susiana designs (pls. 196:D–G).

Among the non-ceramic objects dating to the Early Susiana period the products of the ground stone industry were no longer as prominent as in the Archaic Susiana period. It is in this period that the pebble hoe of the type characteristic also for the Hassuna and Samarra levels of Mesopotamia was introduced (Lloyd and Safar 1945, figs. 19–20). Celts went almost completely out of use and in their stead the typical tool was the hoe made from a large pebble, retaining the original cortex on one side and chipped and pounded on the other. This remained the standard agricultural tool through the later

Susiana sequence. Querns, grinding stones, and rounded pounding stones are ubiquitous in the Early Susiana period. Simple stone vessels and bracelets of bituminous stone were in use. Spindle whorls with painted decoration appear. The rarity of Early Susiana figurines in the first five seasons was an accident of discovery. The red-washed head (pl. 234:A) found in the fifth season is well modeled with elaborate features, including what can be interpreted as a stud or labret (pl. 234:B–V).

Early Susiana Foreign Relations: Susiana *a* was the earliest period known to Le Breton; he defined it on the basis of finds from soundings at Jafarabad and elsewhere, which he correlated with materials from the Hassuna and Samarra periods in Mesopotamia (Le Breton 1957:84–87). The finds at Chogha Mish have yielded much new evidence for the complexity of the period and also enable a close relationship between it and the preceding Archaic Susiana 3 phase to be established.

The direct evolution of Early Susiana painted pottery from the close-line ware is discussed above. The geographical range of the ceramics of this period covers both the Susiana and the Deh Luran plains (Sabz phase), with the materials in the latter area corresponding closely to those from the Susiana plain.

The Early Susiana ceramic evidence provides excellent links between Susiana and Mesopotamia. The ceramics of the Eridu period (Ubaid 1) of southern Mesopotamia have vessel shapes, individual decorative motifs, and compositions in common with those of the Early Susiana period in Susiana. Outstanding examples are the bowls of Early Susiana Family VI. They are paralleled exactly in shape and painted decoration by the wide, shallow bowls with broad diagonal bands on the exterior and dense registers completely covering the interior from the earliest levels at Eridu and low levels at el-'Oueili. Note, for example, the use of a broad register of dense crosshatching surrounding narrow registers of wavy lines (Safar et al., 1981, figs. 84:6, 9, 11; 97:16; 99:19; Calvet 1985/86, pl. 8:1) or of reserved lozenges as the main motif of the interior decoration (pl. 196:A; cf. Safar et al. 1981, fig. 94:3). The reserved zigzags at Chogha Mish and the "zigzag" of detached ovals at Eridu resemble each other in general (ibid., fig. 96:1). The importance of reserved areas in the composition of designs is characteristic for the pottery of the Early Susiana, Eridu, and Samarra periods.

A particularly outstanding link between Susiana and southern Mesopotamia is provided by the compositions in which the circular surface on bowl bases are "squared" by placing in the center a rectangle to each corner of which is attached the apex of a triangle. The bases of the four triangles abut on the lip, delimiting the circular field of the bowl's interior. The unpainted, "negative" space between the triangles becomes a pattern in its own right, a kind of reserved cross (pls. 198:H–I; 199:B, I; Safar et al. 1981, fig. 97:6). This squared-circle pattern is basic and frequent in Early Susiana pottery decoration. In addition to the compositional scheme, certain specific details occur in both areas. The triangles are filled with closely-spaced wavy lines always arranged at right angles to each other in adjacent triangles, a ubiquitous feature of Early Susiana painting. Another detail is the slender plant-like spray variegating the "arms" of the reserved cross.

The circular field in the interior of Samarra bowls is often patterned according to the scheme just described. This composition is, in fact, an important feature linking the ceramics of the Early Susiana, Eridu, and Samarra periods. A somewhat more general link between Samarra and Early Susiana is the use of negative zigzags between crosshatched triangles. This is one of the more prominent Early Susiana motifs and occurs frequently, in a somewhat different fashion, on Samarra ware. The negative-zigzag motif, however, could well be a feature each tradition had inherited from an earlier period rather than with a contemporary connection. The same is true of the pedestals, often fenestrated, supporting open bowls (pl. 197:J) prominent in both Early Susiana and Samarra. Le Breton (1957:84–88, figs. 5–6) considered the pedestals as a reliable link between Early Susiana (his Susiana *a*) and Samarra. Another Early Susiana/Samarra connection is the high neck painted with a lattice pattern (pl. 202:E).

A very strong link with the Samarra period is provided by the head of a figurine found in Trench XXI (pl. 234:A). Its effect relies mainly on modeling but is, nevertheless, close in shape to the figurine heads from Chogha Mami, which have more painted detail. It provides excellent corroborative evidence for the contemporaneity of the Early Susiana period with the Samarra period of central and northern Mesopotamia.

In considering the relationships of the Susiana and Mesopotamian cultures at this time, it must be remembered that the ceramic similarities appear primarily in specific decorated forms, while the ordinary domestic vessels, the bulk of the pottery in each area, remain quite distinct.[18] Early Susiana has its great class of flanged vessels (pl. 200), occurring in a wide range of sizes to serve different domestic functions. No parallels for such vessels have been found in Mesopotamia.[19] The situation is one of distinct cultures in which contacts were sufficient to allow the interchange of information about the specialized features, such as painted pottery or figurines, as well as, presumably, raw materials.

18. This situation suggests that perhaps these vessels had symbolic significance shared inter-regionally. AA

19. Unless some of the Hassuna jars of the Archaic Coarse ware (Lloyd and Safar 1945, fig. 6:1–12) are considered distant parallels. AA

The questions of the directions and mechanisms of the connections are more difficult to consider with the present state of knowledge. They are likely to have been complex. At Chogha Mish the Early Susiana Family VI bowls (pl. 196:A–B), the primary links with southern Mesopotamia, are fairly common elements in the pottery. In surprising contrast, they seem to be completely absent in the other Early Susiana sites. This might simply be an accident of discovery or perhaps an indication that Chogha Mish served as a central site in a regional trade network. Chogha Mish sits astride a major route skirting the Zagros foothills where bitumen is easily available. The material was in common use at Chogha Mish in the Early Susiana period and the site could well have controlled trade in bitumen and in that way had access to Mesopotamian objects not available, at least normally, to other Early Susiana sites (Marschner and Wright 1978).

THE MIDDLE SUSIANA PERIOD

Early Middle Susiana: This is an intermediate phase in which the links with the past remain prominent alongside outstanding new ceramic features. The latter demonstrate that there was a greater cultural difference between the Early Susiana period and Early Middle Susiana phase than between that phase and the following phases. To use just one example, but a very important one, the ordinary ware of the period is no longer that typical for Early Susiana, namely bulging with grits and showing the traces of vegetal tempering, but is a considerably denser ware without vegetal tempering.

Ceramic forms and designs are elaborate and various high fired red or reddish wares are prominent. Certain pottery classes of Early Susiana, such as the bowls with incurving lip, the shallow lids, and the ladles, have now disappeared, together with the gritty buff ware. On the other hand, numerous links with typical Early Middle Susiana pottery testify to the continuity and consistency of the Middle Susiana period. Outstanding examples of the continuity of Early Middle Susiana pottery with that of Early Susiana are the deep vessels with vestigial flanges (pl. 182:K–L). They represent the final stage of the flanged vessels characteristic of the Early Susiana period and carry on the use of potters' marks that had been typical of the earlier vessels. Furthermore, the vestigial-flanged vessels frequently have a paste markedly grittier than the standard buff ware of the period, in this case also continuing an Early Susiana tradition.

Rare examples of pottery lids with their elaborate painted decoration on the exterior, sparse crossing lines on the interior, and a pair of holes are the final representatives of one of the more outstanding categories of Early Susiana pottery (pls. 59:K; 166:E). The Early Susiana painted ladles (pl. 194:L–N) continue in much the same shape but with somewhat expanded painted

decoration (pl. 164:C–D). The Early Susiana shallow rounded bowls (pl. 196:A–B) are the direct prototypes in both shape and some of the decoration (e.g., the exterior zigzags) for characteristic Middle Susiana bowls (pl. 174:G–H). The Early Susiana predilection for incurved-lip bowls too continues in the Early Middle Susiana phase.

Normally made of somewhat thinner ware are the equally characteristic Middle Susiana shallow bowls (pl. 167:B–D). Though their painted decoration links them with Early Susiana pottery, they are as shapes a new departure. Also new are the relatively small Middle Susiana Family XV beakers with sinuous profiles. More generalized in shape and hence less marked as innovations are the rather large bowls with fairly vertical sides and frequently a ledge-shaped lip (Middle Susiana Family VI-1).

In addition to various pottery shapes, some of the painted patterns that began in the Early Susiana period became of great importance later. The standard Early Susiana center design, in which a circle was quartered so as to produce a negative cross (pls. 61:L; 194:C, S; 195:B), continues in elaborated forms as one of the primary Early Middle Susiana center motifs (pls. 60:G; 168:A–B, F, H; 180:A–B). The wavy lines so frequently reserved in the Early Susiana close style (pls. 194:L–M, P; 61:R–S, II, NN; 196:K, M; 198:D) are also typical for the Early Middle Susiana phase, though executed in a less demanding technique—not reserved, but incised through a broad wash of paint. They are particularly common on tortoise jars (pls. 59:O) but also occur on a variety of other Early Middle Susiana vessels (pls. 59:L; 60:I). The broad zigzags on the exterior of Early Susiana bowls are the ancestors of those on some Middle Susiana bowls (pls. 166:F; 178:B–C). There is thus a mass of evidence to indicate the continuity between the ceramics of the Early Susiana and the Middle Susiana periods.

Closed forms now become common for the first time. Medium-sized jars with a definite neck and decoration on the upper body must have been of ovoid or spherical shapes, but as yet no completely restorable examples have been found. Far more specialized are the lentoid tortoise vessels with hole mouths and large flaring spouts.

Despite the evidence of continuation just listed, the Early Middle Susiana phase ushers in a characteristic assembly of new plain and painted shapes, made in the standard Middle Susiana buff ware or sometimes in a thinner, fine ware variant. Outstanding are the distinctive Middle Susiana Family XVIII bowls, including the rare examples painted on the exterior—Middle Susiana Subfamily XVIIIa (one showing one of the very few representational motifs attributable to the Early Middle Susiana phase), the common Middle Susiana Subfamily XVIIIc with the interior lip band of reserved crescents distinctive for the Early Middle Susiana, and Middle

Susiana Subfamily XVIIId with the interior crosshatching that in the Early Middle Susiana phase tends to be very close with the paint running over to fill the interstices almost completely (pls. 177–78).

The broad washes of pigment covering large portions of the body surface, which are particularly prominent on the tortoise vessels, though conceivably developed from the Early Susiana close style, are different in appearance. Very characteristic for Early Middle Susiana pottery is the reservation of a group of thin sweeping curves in a broad wash of color (pl. 178:G). Other typical motifs are friezes of hollow lozenges, large and boldly-hatched zigzags, groups of "carobs," and the "railroad" designs of the jars. Representational designs occur only with the greatest rarity.

Late Middle Susiana: The levels of this phase characteristically contain a great bulk of sherds. Ceramic forms and designs are elaborate and various high-fired red or reddish wares are prominent. On the other hand, numerous links with typical Early Middle Susiana pottery testify to the continuity and consistency of the Middle Susiana period. Although the vestigial-flanged vessels are now extinct, they have given rise to a class of deep wide-mouthed vessels represented by many examples (pl. 183:A–F). The late varieties of the large carinated bowls have now lost their carination (pl. 181). The tortoise vessels are now squatter and tend to be larger in diameter than their Early Middle Susiana ancestors. Although large washes of paint were still used, wavy lines scratched through them have disappeared in favor of more widely spaced painted designs.

Amid the open vessels with relatively thick walls, in addition to the shallower (pl. 167) and deeper (pl. 171:A–B, D–T) bowls, a new and outstanding class appears, the deep crateriform bowl (pl. 184). Though these vessels often bear only geometric friezes, they were also the favorite habitat for goats boldly painted with sweeping brush strokes. Such goats are a diagnostic motif for the Late Middle Susiana phase. In general, the use of representational motifs is characteristic for the phase. In addition to the goats, friezes of highly stylized flying-birds occur on the crateriform vessels.

Although large shallow bowls existed in the Early Middle Susiana phase, they do not seem to have been as common as the large painted basins typical for the Late Middle Susiana phase (pl. 183:A–F). Also relatively thick-walled are the vessels of a highly specialized and unknown function, the "stools" (pls. 185–86).

Particularly prominent in the Late Middle Susiana phase are low ring bases. In Middle Susiana Family IX they support wide flaring bowls with fairly elaborate painted decoration on the interior (pls. 165:J–K; 166:D). Middle Susiana Family XIV consists of rather tall beakers on ring bases, which can be subdivided according to their decoration. One group (pl. 172:H) sometimes has

the large arcs characteristic of the fine ware Middle Susiana Family XIII but more frequently reduces them to simple vertical bands (pl. 173:A–C). A solid wash of paint over a greater part of the exterior characterizes Middle Susiana Subfamily XIVb (pl. 173:D), and a number of horizontal registers of simple geometric patterns characterizes Middle Susiana Subfamily XIVc (pl. 173:G–L).

The Early Middle Susiana phase already had the beginning of fine ware, for example, the Middle Susiana Subfamily XIIa bowls and some Middle Susiana Family XV beakers, but one of the more characteristic developments of the Late Middle Susiana phase is the proliferation of fine ware vessels, both unpainted and painted. Smaller unpainted bowls and cups are sometimes very thin. Even the deep bowls of Middle Susiana Family XX, the descendants of the Early Middle Susiana vestigial-flanged vessels (Middle Susiana Family XXI) as the standard open household containers, are often of a dense ware unusually thin for their size (pl. 182). Some shapes, particularly those of the thinner ware, can appear either unpainted or painted. The more prominent of these paired groups are the unpainted Middle Susiana Families II and XII (pl. 172:B–C), the painted Middle Susiana Families III and XIII (pl. 172:D–G), and Subfamily XIVa (pl. 172:H–I). The new high-fired red or reddish wares, though providing a considerable variety in color and surface treatment, were used for only a limited repertory of shapes, fairly shallow open bowls and hole-mouthed pots varying from medium to large sizes. These were undoubtedly the cooking pots of the period.

The Late Middle Susiana repertory of painted decoration is very rich. It includes many elements inherited from the preceding period. Geometric friezes such as the hatched zigzag, swags, lozenges, and wavy bands continue to be common, though sometimes with at least slight changes. The markedly hollow Early Middle Susiana lozenges have gone out of fashion, but Early Middle Susiana geometric patterns, e.g., "railroad," used on the shoulders of jars continue. Another major category of designs derived from Early Middle Susiana repertoire is the circular patterns on the interior of bowls such as Middle Susiana Families IX, X, XVIII, and XIX. The circular area, delimited by a cuspated border, at the bottom of all of these bowls could be treated in a number of ways. It might be bilaterally segmented by axial designs, covered by a diaper pattern, or divided into quadrant patterns, in which negative areas such as large ovals or a central cross might be as significant as the painted elements. Particularly characteristic for the phase is the use of individual motifs "floating" on the ground rather than locked into a tight decorative syntax as in the Early Middle Susiana phase (pl. 165:J).

The painted decoration of Late Middle Susiana pottery seems to vary widely. On the one hand, there is apparently a tendency toward simplified, bolder, or even coarsened designs, as in vertical bands (pl. 173:A–C). On the other hand, in some of the smaller forms such as ledge-rimmed vessels (pl. 191:A), the designs are fairly ornate and meticulously painted. One sinuous-sided beaker (Middle Susiana Family XV) has most of its surface covered by a geometric design, a large zigzag filled by sets of three crosshatched triangles (pl. 174:A). This particular design is very close to one of the standard Late Susiana patterns. In general the use of triangular areas subdivided into three smaller crosshatched triangles appears in the Late Middle Susiana phase and becomes characteristic in the Late Susiana 1 phase.[20]

New motifs and types of compositions give Late Middle Susiana ceramic decoration its distinctive cast. A major new geometric design, the scalloped circle, was probably directly derived from the older circular patterns, translating the small negative arcs of the cusp border into a simple positive pattern used primarily as an isolated motif (pl. 191:I–J). Above all, however, the Late Middle Susiana phase is marked by the proliferation of representational designs that had previously been both rare and markedly geometric in form. Now the repertory of animals includes goats, leopards, bulls or more commonly the heads of bulls with down-curving horns, and birds (pls. 58; 176:R; 181:B, D–E, O; 187:B; 192:B–F). Complete human figures are rare but heads or masks with strands of hair streaming to one side are frequently used on fine ware vessels with somewhat incurving upper walls (pl. 176:S, U).

The representational motifs vary in their degree of abstraction; noteworthy are tiers of triangles to which are added heads and appendages so stylized as to leave unclear whether they represent birds or human beings (pl. 171:D). The painters felt free to use segments of a complete motif in isolation, as in the case of the head of a carnivorous animal appearing as a filling motif on an Middle Susiana bowl (pl. 181:F) and not easily recognizable until it is compared with more complete figures such as those on some jars (pl. 192:B–C). The theme of a bird with outstretched wings, rendered in considerable and to a degree naturalistic detail despite the double necks on a Family XVII vessel (pl. 58:D), could be simplified, turned on its side, and used as an element repeated at very close intervals to form a horizontal frieze (4.224 [pl. 184:S]). The abstraction of the motif is taken a step farther when, instead of individual elements, the frieze consists of a continuous median line to which the "wings" are attached (pl. 58:O).

The variety of compositional schemes is considerable and always tectonically applied. Aside from the circular surfaces of the interiors of bowls, the composi-

tional patterning of which goes back eventually to Early Susiana, the only other round surfaces that Late Middle Susiana potters were called upon to decorate were the tops of the Middle Susiana "stools." Since these had a cutout hole in the center, it was almost inevitable for them to bear concentric registers of geometric motifs (pls. 185–86).

The schemes developed by Late Middle Susiana potters to adorn the cylindrical or conical surfaces provided by outer or inner vessel walls can be summarized as follows:

1. One individual motif freely spaced at wide intervals but at approximately the same horizontal level. Excellent examples are the rayed circles of an Middle Susiana cup (pl. 163:T) or the three scalloped circles common on jars (pl. 191:I–L).

2. Informal friezes or columns of individual motifs set closely together but without any border lines. Such informal lines of motifs are frequent on Middle Susiana Family XVII vessels (pl. 176:Q–Z).

3. Horizontal friezes of motifs enclosed by bordering bands. These are probably the most traditional of the Late Middle Susiana schemes of composition. The filling motifs of the friezes are either geometric or, less commonly, representational, and the decoration usually appears only on the upper part of the vessels. However, registers of geometric and ibex motifs are combined on some crateriform vessels so as to cover a considerable part of the walls.

4. Overall decoration of the body between the neck and the basal carination. Such decoration seems to be limited to small closed jars and consists fittingly of diaper designs such as alternating butterflies and hourglasses (pl. 189:G–N).

5. Division of the area to be decorated (usually consisting of the greater part of the vessel walls) into panels by clusters of vertical lines or other geometric motifs. The metopes so created can be either densely filled by geometric motifs or depend for their effect on the contrast between the free space and a single motif placed in the center.

Although the products of the potter form the largest single category of Late Middle Susiana materials, the phase also provides a variety of other artifacts, such as flints, hoes, some bone tools, a wide range of spindle whorls, and various beads, usually fairly simple. Figurines are represented by a number of types, of which the most common are simply modeled animals, sometimes with painted decoration. More elaborate are terra-cotta bull-head pendants; they parallel in conception and execution (e.g., the reserved triangle on the forehead) some of the painted bucrania on the pottery.

Middle Susiana Foreign Relations: The cultural assemblage of the Middle Susiana period developed directly from that of the preceding period and became a rich and varied manifestation of a flourishing and expanding population. It is clear from the work of the

---

20. For a detailed discussion of pottery forms and painted motifs attributable to the Late Susiana 1 phase, see Alizadeh 1992:21–25; for much earlier examples of positive and negative triangles, see footnote 26, below.

French Mission, from surveys beginning with the pioneering survey of Sir Aurel Stein and from later works of Adams and Wright, that the area of modern Khuzestan shared a common culture. In the west, the Deh Luran plain provides many comparisons for Chogha Mish materials as do sherds collected by Aurel Stein in the eastern part of Khuzestan in the area of Behbahan and Malamir (Stein 1940). A more recent survey and sounding in that area provide some hints that a regional variation of the Susiana culture might have existed there (Dittmann 1984).

The relationship of Middle Susiana culture to other parts of Iran is a large subject that cannot be thoroughly discussed within the scope of this report. It is sufficient to recall that McCown (1942) introduced the comprehensive term "Buff Ware Cultures" for the allied traditions of southwestern Iran. The stages of the development in Fars to the southeast are becoming clearer as evidence accumulates (Goff 1963, 1964; Egami and Sono 1962; Gotch 1968, 1969; Egami 1967; Miroschedji 1972; Sumner 1977; Alizadeh 1988a, 1988b). To the north and northeast in Luristan allied traditions existed (Wright et al. 1979; Dittmann 1984; Zagarell 1975, 1982). Here, however, the significant point to emphasize is that, although Middle Susiana culture belongs to a western Iranian family, its relations with Mesopotamia are more intimate than with those of any of its cousins.

Rooted in the pottery of the Early Susiana period, the ceramics of the Early Middle Susiana phase show a striking degree of similarity with the pottery of the Haji Muhammad (Ubaid 2) period in southern Mesopotamia. This affinity had already been recognized by Le Breton despite the limited material available to him (Le Breton 1957). The close relationship is illustrated by a series of forms and designs from Chogha Mish identical to those discovered at Haji Muhammad (Ziegler 1953), Ras al-ʿAmiya (D. Stronach 1961), and Eridu (Safar et al. 1981). Prominent shapes in common are concave-sided bowls with convex bases (pl. 178:A–C, E–H) and the tortoise vessels (pls. 187:A–I; 188:A–B). Also appearing, but less prominent, are the crateriform vessels (pl. 184:A–T) and the cups or beakers (pl. 175).

The families of pottery forms from Chogha Mish, which are described in previous chapters, have specific designs, and the same coordination between form and pattern is found in the pottery from Mesopotamian sites. One of the outstanding patterns that Chogha Mish had in common with Mesopotamia is that of reserved sinuous lines, which occurred at Haji Muhammad on incurved-lip bowls. The Middle Susiana Family XVIII bowls in Mesopotamia can be divided into two subdivisions: those with a reserved crescent border (Middle Susiana Subfamily XVIIIc) and those with a lattice border (Middle Susiana Subfamily XVIIId; Ziegler 1953, pl. 14; Safar et al. 1981, fig. 88:15–22). Also, the base decorations of these bowls are the same, relying on a

cusp border and on rosette (D. Stronach 1961, pls. 48:2; 49:1–2, 4), whirligig (Ziegler 1953, pls. 14; 16:b; 33:a–f), or "bamboo" (ibid., pls. 4:d, g; 17:a–b; D. Stronach 1961, pl. 49:6) central patterns. The close-style decoration of tortoise vessels at Chogha Mish is typical for this shape in Mesopotamia also (ibid., pl. 56:3–5). In both areas the close-style painting, including narrow zigzag lines scratched through the paint, occurs on other shapes. Various geometric motifs such as hatched zigzags or swags occur on bowls and beakers from Haji Muhammad and Ras al-ʿAmiya. The information concerning the unpainted vessels of the Haji Muhammad period is less extensive. However, the characteristic Early Middle Susiana deep vessels with vestigial flanges (pl. 182:K–P) are absent from Mesopotamia.

Though they are relatively rare, indubitable Early Middle Susiana-Haji Muhammad types exist in the form of very closely crosshatched lip sherds (pl. 178). More common are sherds with simple geometric motives or combinations of types to be found in both the standard Ubaid phase and in the Late Middle Susiana phase.

The relations of Early Middle Susiana with the western-based Halaf culture now appearing in northern Mesopotamia were more distant than those with the south. Nonetheless, there are several parallels in the composition of the interiors of bowls, even though the vessel shapes themselves are not as closely comparable as those of Middle Susiana and southern Mesopotamia. Central rosettes are a hallmark of the developed Halaf style (Mallowan and Rose 1935, frontispiece; pls. 13–16), and, in fact, their appearance on the pottery of the southern culture might have been a northern influence. An altered version of the quartered-circle pattern typical for the south and the Susiana plain appears on one of the famous Halaf polychrome plates (ibid., pl. 18), while the same general composition in reverse, with the "cross" as the positive pattern, also occurs (ibid., p. 120, fig. 58:1). Particularly reminiscent of Early Middle Susiana are bowls with a thin wavy line in a close style surrounding cusp-and-quadrant centers. Halaf also shared with the other two cultures individual motifs such as the swags and "butterfly" separated by multiple vertical bands, the whirligig diaper (ibid., p. 166, fig. 78:8), and the crosshatched lozenge frieze. The latter often occurs on wide-based, concave-sided bowls (pl. 173:G–I), a shape found both at Chogha Mish and at Ras al-ʿAmiya decorated with solid circles (D. Stronach 1961, pl. 46:4).

Southern Mesopotamia has nothing that parallels the widespread use of representational motifs in the Late Middle Susiana phase. For example, a form still common to both areas, the developed type of tortoise vase, can appear at Chogha Mish with bucrania or ibex (pl. 187:A–B); these motifs, although not unknown in Mesopotamia, are rare there. The outstanding Early Middle Susiana families of fine ware (Middle Susiana Families III, XII, XIII, XVII) with their variety of motifs are unparalleled in Mesopotamia. The important Chogha Mish group of crateriform vessels (pl. 184) has only one or two cousins in Mesopotamia. On the other hand, many of the simple geometric motifs and compositions used on late Ubaid pottery were sometimes paralleled in the Late Middle Susiana phase. Examples are the wavy band or zones with horizontal friezes.

The increased importance in the Late Middle Susiana phase of boldly painted and relatively simple elements such as thick vertical bands (pl. 173:A–C) or solid triangles (pl. 183:K) corresponds in a general way with the use by late Ubaid potters of a few large simple elements thrown across a mostly blank surface. The generalized similarity in relatively simple, undifferentiated features and in some stylistic approaches to pottery decoration, which can be suggested for the Late Middle Susiana phase and standard Ubaid, represent a situation removed from what occurred earlier.

New motifs and types of compositions give Late Middle Susiana ceramic decoration its distinctive cast. A major new geometric design, the scalloped circle, was probably directly derived from the older circular patterns, translating the small negative arcs of the cusp border into a simple positive pattern used primarily as an isolated motif.

Unlike the Early Middle Susiana phase, when there was such a striking similarity between much of the pottery of Chogha Mish and that of Mesopotamian sites, by the time of the Late Middle Susiana phase the ceramics of the Susiana area and southern Mesopotamia were following divergent lines of development. In the standard Ubaid culture (Ubaid 3) of Mesopotamia, now acclimatized in the northern part of the country, the pottery decoration was progressing toward a simplification of motif and pattern (that differs strikingly from the elaborate composition and enriched repertoire characteristic of the Late Middle Susiana phase), using one or a few large simple elements decorating a mostly blank surface.

Though Mesopotamia does not provide parallels for the elaborately and sometimes delicately painted vessels of this period, it was not completely out of step. The increased importance in the Late Middle Susiana phase of boldly painted and relatively simple elements, such as thick vertical bands or solid triangles, corresponds in a general way to the usage of Ubaid potters. Haji Muhammad provides examples of simple geometric motifs and compositions that parallel typical Late Middle Susiana pottery: interior base plate with thin-outlined rosette (Ziegler 1953, pl. 10:p), rayed disc (ibid., pl. 6:i.), and bowl sherds with festoons on the interior (pl. 183:A–D; ibid., pls. 10:g; 12:i).

The generalized similarity in relatively simple, undifferentiated features and in some stylistic approaches to pottery decoration that can be suggested for Late Middle Susiana and standard Ubaid represent a situation far removed from what occurred earlier.

Recent research along the coastline of Saudi Arabia has brought to light the existence there of pottery representing the simpler Ubaid types that are common to both the Susiana plain and Mesopotamia. Such sherds have been found on the surface of a number of sites and also in trial excavations (Burkholder 1972; Burkholder and Golding 1971; Oates 1983:255–56). It is already clear that the sherds in question are not scattered examples but representatives of well-established settlements of at least two phases, though at present relatively rare Early Middle Susiana-Haji Muhammad types exist in the form of very closely crosshatched lip sherds (pl. 178:C, H). Much more common are sherds with simple geometric motifs or combinations of types found in both the standard Ubaid phase and in the Late Middle Susiana phase.

The discoveries in Saudi Arabia add an extremely important new dimension, literally, to the Middle Susiana-Ubaid cultural complex. This culture was established, presumably in regional variants, on three sides of the Persian Gulf by the time of the Late Middle Susiana phase and its expansion must have begun in the Early Middle Susiana-Haji Muhammad period. The settlement over this large area of people whose ceramics shared so many common features was certainly of basic importance for later cultural exchanges between the lands at the head of the Persian Gulf as well as those even farther away.

THE LATE SUSIANA PERIOD

Originally it was thought that Chogha Mish provided a complete sequence of the Susiana phases. Recent surveys and excavations in southwestern Iran have indicated that Le Breton's Susiana *d* represents not one phase (Late Middle Susiana) but two succeeding phases represented by two stylistically distinct classes of pottery.[21] Moreover, excavations at Farrukhabad and Qabr-e Sheykheyn have provided a stratigraphic niche for the earlier phase, variably called "Farukh Phase" (Wright 1981), "Bandebal II" (Dollfus 1983), and "Late Susiana 1" (Alizadeh 1992:21–26). Here this earlier phase is referred to as Late Susiana 1 to be consistent with the terminology for the Susiana sequence.

Late Susiana 1: The Late Susiana 1 phase is characterized by highly refined pottery ornamented with many

---

21. In the course of preparing and writing a monograph on the Gremliza survey collection (Alizadeh 1992), Helene Kantor and Abbas Alizadeh extensively discussed the evidence for an intermediate phase between the Late Middle Susiana phase and Susa A. Although she had no problem with the Late Susiana 1 phase and the materials attributed to it, Kantor was reluctant to accept its absence at Chogha Mish. Her reluctance rested on a couple of sherds she found on the site; she was searching to find stronger evidence for the presence of this phase when she died. AA

dotted elements, with concentric circles or concentric rectangles and elegantly stylized animal motifs. Late Susiana 1 pottery is well made and evenly fired with little sand or, in most cases, no visible inclusion. The ware has a typical creamy buff appearance, resembling a slip. The repertoire of the painted motifs is large and varied. Naturalistic, stylized, and geometric motifs occur. Characteristic examples of this class are bowls with a sharp carination near the base and numerous dots as a subsidiary design element. At Farrukhabad and Bandebal, sherds of this ceramic type overlie the levels with characteristic Late Middle Susiana ceramics (Wright 1981:8, 57–60; Dollfus 1983). At Chogha Mish the materials from the first five seasons include only one example of such pottery.[22]

Although a few sherds do appear, there is not enough material from Trenches II and XXIII to establish that Chogha Mish had a real settlement belonging to the Late Susiana 1.[23] The prevalence in this phase of thin fine ware vessels, the general elegance of the painted style, and specific motifs shared with Late Susiana 2 pottery suggest that Late Susiana 1 pottery is an early stage of the standard Susa A material. To be sure, there are important motifs, for example, the chevron/cross-hatched triangle designs that are shared with Late Middle Susiana pottery. However, the difference in the style of rendering, namely the boldness of the Late Middle Susiana contrasted with the elegance of the dotted material, is clear. Furthermore, many of the standard Late Middle Susiana forms and motifs disappeared in the Late Susiana 1 phase.[24]

It makes much better sense if there is a break in the occupation of Chogha Mish between the Middle Susiana and Late Susiana periods. It is clear in any case that drastic changes took place at the end of the Middle Susiana period, since the flourishing and large settlement gave way to the much smaller occupation limited to the northern part of the mound. The re-occupation of Chogha Mish probably took place at the same time, if not somewhat earlier, as the earliest settlement at Susa. The Late Susiana 2 occupation there was large and sophisticated, with the platform and associated structures marking the special importance of the site (Wright 1984). The contrast between the size of the Chogha Mish and Susa settlements cannot be taken, however, as simply the concentration of population at a site achieving political and/or economic hegemony. Evidence for an overall decrease in population, not only in Susiana but also in Luristan, has been yielded from a number of

surveys in the areas in question. The Late Susiana 1 phase, though not extensively represented at these two major sites,[25] was recovered at many sites, as established by the Gremliza Survey (Alizadeh 1992).

Late Susiana 2: The continuity between the Late Middle Susiana phase and the long-known Late Susiana period (Susa 1/Susa A) is marked, even though the latter's corpus of shapes seems rather limited in contrast to that of the earlier assemblage. Certain categories, for example, the convex fine ware bowls painted on the outside (Late Susiana Family X derived from Middle Susiana Family XIIb), the convex bowls with a ring base and their major decoration inside (Late Susiana Family IX continuing Middle Susiana Family X), and the series of tall cups or beakers (Late Susiana Families III, XVIII, XIX, and XX continuing Middle Susiana Family XV) are extremely common, forming a large and obvious proportion of the total ceramic assemblage. Typical are small cups (pl. 159:A–D) that continue an earlier group (pl. 163:M–N). Other earlier Middle Susiana types still prominent are the high-necked jars (pl. 162:F). Among the smaller jars, the carinated examples (pls. 159:N; 161:E) also have Middle Susiana antecedents (pl. 189:A–F). The outstanding Middle Susiana crateriform vessels (pl. 184) seem to have almost disappeared (see Late Susiana Family XVII, fig. 23).

The red and brown wares are now appearing in various shallow bowl shapes (pl. 162:K–N) and the hole-mouthed cooking pots (pl. 162:O–T) continue to be common. In the Late Susiana 2 phase the red-brown globular vessels appear rather frequently with necks (Late Susiana Family XXVIII). The characteristic Middle Susiana large painted bowls (Middle Susiana Families XIX, XXII, XXIII), the stands (Middle Susiana Family XXV), and the large, deep bowls of relatively fine ware (Middle Susiana Family XX) all seem extinct. There appear to be very few really new forms. One, so far not yet known at Chogha Mish, is a small cylindrical vessel (Late Susiana Family IV). Noteworthy also are the jars with four lug handles (Late Susiana Family XIV). The decorative patterns of the Late Susiana 2 pottery have been the subject of interest and debate for practically a century and the detailed analyses that have been made (Groenewegen-Frankfurt 1951:146–47; Frankfort 1954:202–03; Porada 1965:28–30) need not be repeated here.

The materials from Chogha Mish allow both continuity and change in the Late Susiana painted decoration to be traced from the vantage point of a long cultural sequence. Two main points can be made. First, the patterns placed in a circular field, that is those of the Late Susiana Family IX bowls, represent the main innova-

---

22. One small dotted sherd was found in the West Area (pl. 59:AA). AA

23. See Alizadeh 1992:24–25 for the characteristic shapes and motifs of the Late Susiana 1 phase.

24. For examples see Middle Susiana Families IV, VIII, X, XIV-1a, XVIII, XXIV–XXV. AA

25. See Alizadeh 1992:25 for a discussion of the presence of Late Susiana 1 pottery at Susa. AA

tions of the period. Second, the long line of patterns that began in the Early Susiana period and developed extensively during the Middle Susiana period have for the most part ended. It is true that certain links can be seen. For the most part, however, the grammar of the designs has developed a new syntax.

On the whole, the use of new designs is characterized by their simplicity. For example, many of the Late Middle Susiana shoulder designs of jars have disappeared. In their place is a motif consisting of vertical lines flanked by solid area of paint or interspersed with fields of dots. Also new is the reserving of arcs or wavy bands in broad washes of color. Other new geometric designs are, on the fine ware bowls of Late Susiana Family XI, the narrow lip borders filled with Xs and the registers with thin vertical lines (pl. 160:I, K) and, on the four-lugged jars of Late Susiana Family XIV, panel motifs consisting of crosshatched rectangular fields flanking superimposed triangles (pl. 161:C).

Characteristic Middle Susiana geometric motifs—the scalloped circle, the swag, large arc bands, and overall patterns built up of hourglass and butterfly elements—have disappeared from the Late Susiana repertory. However, the encircled Maltese cross of Late Susiana is a descendant of the quartered-circle patterns typical for earlier periods. These motifs, though occasionally appearing on the interior of a bowl, are now most frequently found as individual elements spaced in the middle register of some Late Susiana vessels (pl. 56:B–C, G, P–Z, SS) or as filling elements in ibex patterns. The large continuous zigzag, its corners filled by small solid lozenges that cover many beakers, has one Late Middle Susiana antecedent.[26]

On the whole, representational motifs are fairly limited in number and in position. Birds, frequently with very long necks, normally occur as a frieze at the lips of beakers; there is one Middle Susiana prototype (pl. 174:B).[27] Otherwise, birds appear only as horizontal friezes directly continuing Late Middle Susiana designs or as individual, vertically-placed figures, for which there is a good Late Middle Susiana antecedent (pl. 58:D). The ibex are now very elegantly stylized, their bodies being formed by opposing triangles rather than by the long brush strokes of their Late Middle Susiana ancestors.

Typical of Late Susiana are compositions in which butterfly or hourglass motifs divide the space into pan-

els, wide or narrow depending on the shape of the vessel into which representational or geometric motifs are inserted. Aside from the complexities of the patterns on the interiors of Late Susiana Family IX bowls or on the large beakers, however, the painted decoration of Late Susiana, for all its great refinement and subtlety of composition, seems more limited in scope than that of the Late Middle Susiana phase.

LATE SUSIANA FOREIGN RELATIONS

Late Susiana 1: Starting with the Late Middle Susiana phase, Susiana's interest shifted from Mesopotamia to the highlands. The reorientation of Susiana foreign relations could have been due to a number of interrelated factors, such as population growth, the development and rise of a new elite class, and increasing demand for highland raw material. Although it is not evident at Chogha Mish, the question of Susiana foreign relations is primarily based on comparative analysis of the ceramics of Mesopotamia, Susiana, Deh Luran, and Fars during the Late Susiana 1 phase (see Alizadeh 1992:25, 57, 59–61), and inferences from some other archaeological materials (see Hole 1987:41–43; Wright 1987:141–45; Alizadeh 1992:25–26, 57, 59–61). During the Late Susiana 1 phase, as far as pottery is concerned, Susiana, Bakhtyari Mountains, and Fars exhibit the closest relation in the prehistoric periods.

By the end of the Middle Susiana period, the interregional contact between southwestern Iran and Mesopotamia seems to have diminished. There appears to have been a reorientation in the inter-regional contact. The Late Susiana was a period of increasing contact with the highlands, as suggested by the general similarities among the regional ceramics of southwestern Iran. A general westward shift of the settlements in Susiana also occurred. Large communal burials of Hakalan and Parchineh, and the cemetery and stone foundations of some simple architecture at Kalleh Nesar, all in the Zagros Mountains, appeared during this period or shortly thereafter (Vanden Berghe 1970, 1973, 1975). These cemeteries were not associated with any settlement and are thought to have been built by the mobile pastoralists of the highlands. Similar cemeteries of later historical periods in this region reinforce this attribution. It is, therefore, tempting to link the destruction of the Late Middle Susiana Burnt Building at Chogha Mish, its desertion, the westward movement of the population in the lowland, the similarities among the regional ceramics in southwestern Iran, and the appearance of the highland communal burials. Admittedly, the evidence is not strong and much research is needed to warrant such linkage.

The presumed relation between the increased activities of mobile pastoralists and the westward shift of Susiana settlements becomes more attractive when it is

---

26. The use of large, continuous positive or negative zigzags is a cherished Susiana tradition that dates back to the Archaic Susiana period (pls. 212:B; 218:F–G; 228:F). For examples from the Early Susiana and Middle Susiana periods, see plates 163:J; 174:A; 178:H; 184:R; 201:H–I; 202:A. This design even appears in its archaic form in the Late Susiana 2 phase (pl. 161:A). AA

27. See also Tall-e Gap (Egami and Sono 1962, fig. 24:10–11; pl. 36:4–5, 7–8).

realized that the eastern part of the Susiana plain traditionally has been, and still is, the locus of the winter pasture for the mobile pastoralists of the region. If this environmental niche was also used in antiquity, as one might expect, then the westward shift of the settled community might also indicate an increase in the activities of such transhuman groups in the area.

In the Late Susiana period, Susa replaced Chogha Mish as the largest site on the plain, a status that Susa retained for several millennia. A massive mudbrick platform was constructed probably after a short period of occupation. It was topped by a monumental building of uncertain nature. Whether this project was completed in the course of several generations or in one attempt is not known, but such an undertaking required a tremendous amount of labor and a relevant social organization to mobilize and administer it.

The founding of Susa, according to the analysis presented here, occurred sometime during the latter part of the Late Susiana 1 phase, when contacts between the lowland and the highland increased rapidly. This proposition is based partly on the similarities among regional ceramic traditions. These similarities might have been the result of increased interaction between the lowland and highlands, which probably developed out of increasing demand for various local commodities of both regions. This development might have been the result of the growth of a regional elite in both the lowland and the highlands.

The change in the ceramic tradition seems to coincide with, or was the result of, changes in the settlement pattern and some regional developments. Chogha Mish was abandoned after the conflagration of its "Burnt Building," marking the end of the Middle Susiana period.[28] It was reoccupied sometime during the Late Susiana period, probably when Susa had already been founded as a full-fledged town. Evidence from archaeological surface surveys indicates that during the period between the desertion of Chogha Mish and the founding of Susa, no one site attained, as far as size is concerned, a central position, as did Chogha Mish before and Susa later. Moreover, there was a slight decrease in the size of the regional population and a general tendency for the settlements to move to the west of the plain (Hole 1987:85–86).

Late Susiana 2: The final phase of the Susiana sequence, in terms of ceramics, is characterized by the fa-

mous bowls and beakers in which the decorative traditions so long developing in the area reached the culmination of their elegance and sophistication. Now the points of comparison with the Late Ubaid in Mesopotamia are of minor importance, and it is almost hard to remember that, earlier, the two traditions had so much in common. By now Ubaid had become a culture ranging over a wide geographical area and even reaching communities as far away as the Mediterranean coast of northern Syria, while Late Susiana was a much more regionally limited culture. Underlying these developments was a host of complex socioeconomic interactions that greatly contributed to historical developments of both regions.

CONCLUSION

The Susiana culture, the development of which has been discussed above, constitutes one of the major prehistoric cultural traditions of western Asia. In this brief survey of its immediate relationships, it is distinguished among Iranian cultures by its numerous and at times particularly intimate links with Mesopotamia. Already during the long sequence of prehistoric phases, it played what was to be one of its main historical roles, that of an intermediary between the lowlands of Mesopotamia and the highlands of the Iranian plateau.

At the close of the Susiana period, Chogha Mish was again deserted and was not resettled until the Protoliterate b phase, whereas the Protoliterate a phase is represented at Susa. There has already been much discussion of the momentous developments that ended in the hegemony of a civilization rooted in southern Mesopotamia. One of the major questions has been the retrenchment of settlement in the Late Susiana period, correlated in part at least with the rise of the great settlement at Susa, probably on the basis of elaborate socioeconomic factors. These have been previously discussed in detail.[29] Another major question is the extent to which the Susiana culture was a partner with the Ubaid of Mesopotamia in the developments leading to the Protoliterate period. The complexity already characteristic for the Late Middle Susiana phase at Chogha Mish, which was made particularly clear by finds made after the fifth season, cannot have simply disappeared. The continuity between the Middle Susiana and Late Susiana periods is remarkable and, difficult though it is to trace at this time, experiments with record-keeping and the organization of society in the Susiana area must have gone side-by-side with comparable developments in Mesopotamia.

The discussion of such developments lies beyond the range of this publication. It is sufficient to point out

---

28. There is probably a Late Susiana 1 occupation at Chogha Mish on the High Mound, of which there is relatively little material recovered (Helene Kantor, personal communication, see also plate 59:AA). Although the question of a general conflagration resulting in the total abandonment of the site by the end of the Middle Susiana period should remain open, there is no question that Chogha Mish lost its status as the largest site in the Susiana plain after the Late Middle Susiana phase.

29. Johnson 1973; Wright and Johnson 1975; see also Algaze 1989 for a summary of this development.

that, from the vantage point of the Late Susiana period, the preceding sequence can be seen as a deep rooted Iranian manifestation with parallel developments on the plateau. For example, as a contemporary of the Late Susiana period in Fars, the Bakun culture in its elaborate pottery decoration and in some specific motifs (Alizadeh 1992:25–26) demonstrates a community of basic background and taste that along with the many specific differences sets these cultures apart from that prevailing in Mesopotamia. The Susiana culture, whose development the finds from Chogha Mish now enable us to follow in detail, constitutes one of the major prehistoric cultural traditions of western Asia.

As indicated above in this brief survey of its relationships, the Susiana region is distinguished among the various regions of Iran by its numerous and at times particularly intimate links with Mesopotamia. One of its main historical roles must have been that of an intermediary between the lowlands of Mesopotamia and many parts of the Iranian plateau.

Table 42. Comparative Chronology of the Prehistoric Susiana Periods*

Mesopotamia		Susiana					Deh Luran
Periods		Sites					Sites
		Chogha Mish	Jafarabad	Bandebal	Jowi	Susa Acropole	Farrukhabad
	Late Susiana 2			III		25	
Ubaid 4		Late Susiana	1–3	Level 10		27	Gap
	Late Susiana 1	Gap(?)	Gap	II Levels 11–17	Gap	(?)	
Ubaid 3							A 23–31 B 37–47
		Late Middle Susiana	3m–n		II Levels 4–10		A 33–36
				Levels 18–27			Tappeh Sabz
Ubaid 2	Middle Susiana	Early Middle Susiana	Gap		I Level 11		
				I Level 28	Level 17		
Ubaid 1	Early Susiana	Early Susiana	6–4	(?)			Chogha Sefid
Ubaid 0	Archaic Susiana 3	Archaic Susiana 3					(Chogha Mami Transitional)
Samarra							
Hassuna	Archaic Susiana 2	Archaic Susiana 2					
Jarmo	Archaic Susiana 1	Archaic Susiana 1					

*Table 42 by A. Alizadeh.

CHAPTER 13

EARLY AGRICULTURE AT CHOGHA MISH

Anne I. Woosley

The prehistoric occupation of Chogha Mish from Archaic Susiana through Late Susiana levels spans the crucial period of incipient agriculture in the Near East. Evidence in the form of carbonized macrobotanic remains recovered from the site can contribute substantially to the knowledge of changes in resource exploitation patterns associated with the beginning of farming. The development of a diverse complex of plant domesticates based on irrigated agriculture at Chogha Mish and other contemporary sites became the economic cornerstone that characterized later Mesopotamian societies. An understanding of plant husbandry at Chogha Mish, in addition to other lines of archaeological inquiry, can provide much needed information concerning this era of fundamental cultural change.

THE NATURE AND RECOVERY OF SAMPLES

Carbonized macro-remains of plants, silica skeletons of seeds, grain impressions in clay bricks and pottery sherds, and a limited number of soil samples extracted for their pollen content were examined. Of these botanic samples, the analysis of carbonized seeds, nutlets, and the fragments of cereal spikelets and rachis segments proved to be the most rewarding in terms of furthering present knowledge of prehistoric agricultural practices. In comparison, seeds surviving only as silica skeletons were extremely difficult, indeed, often impossible to identify. The identification of plant impressions from bricks and sherds was also inconclusive. Unfortunately, the morphological characteristics were not precise enough to allow any but a family level identification of such specimens. Preliminary pollen analysis successfully established the presence of pollen grains and indicates that further pollen studies could furnish a more complete picture of plant life and how it was affected and utilized by the inhabitants of Chogha Mish. It would be premature to interpret the limited sample thus far examined.

All carbonized plant material was recovered by the excavators through flotation in the field. The samples were then dried out of direct sunlight and stored in glass vials for subsequent analysis. The flotation technique employed closely follows that developed by Helbaek at the Deh Luran sites of Ali Kosh and Tappeh Sabz (Helbaek 1969). At Chogha Mish samples were taken

from archaeologically significant contexts: from storage pits, charcoal lenses, hearths, from under house walls and floors, and from the interior of bowls. More than 2,700 seeds or identifiable seed fragments were examined from thirty such samples.

PRESERVATION AND EXAMINATION OF SAMPLES

The preservation of the carbonized plant material was satisfactory to adequate in most cases and identification was possible to the generic level. When preservation was good, such macro-botanical material could provide information concerning the general economy of prehistoric farmers, whether they manipulated wild plants or domesticated them, which plants were selected over others also available, and, to some extent, how plants were processed.

In many of the Archaic Susiana samples, however, preservation was of only marginal quality. Seeds from Archaic Susiana contexts often exhibited a fine coating of lime obscuring the morphological characteristics necessary for identification. Salt crystals played havoc with many seeds, particularly the grasses. Deposited in the ventral furrow and under seed coats, crystals expand during the formation of the crystalline structure, ultimately shattering or distorting the delicate seed. The destruction of carbonized seeds by salt crystal formation is noted in the Chogha Mami botanical collection (Helbaek 1972:37). There it was produced artificially during the flotation process. Salt was added to the water to make it buoyant, allowing any carbonized material to float to the surface more easily. Salt crystals were the ruinous result. At Chogha Mish destructive salt crystals occurred naturally, probably due to the high saline content of existing soils and the annual mixing with rainwater over time. Fortunately, this destruction was not characteristic of the entire botanic collection.

Marginal preservation was evident only in Archaic Susiana samples. Identification of remains from later contexts was more successful. Protoliterate samples, unless overly fragmented by mechanical abrasion, displayed a high degree of preservation and produced no problems in identification of individual specimens. The richest group, both in number of seeds and diversity of

Table 43. Percentage of Shrinkage in Fresh and Carbonized Modern Seeds

	Modern Fresh Length in mm	Modern Carbonized Length in mm	Percentage of Shrinkage
Cereals			
Hordeum vulgare	7.81–8.20	6.64–7.22	12–15
Hordeum vulgare var. *nudum*	7.32–7.50	6.21–6.65	12–15
Legumes			
Medicago	2.00–3.00	1.72–2.64	12–16
Prosopis	2.54–7.00	2.13–5.95	11–16
Vicia	1.53–7.00	1.27–5.95	12–15
Flax			
Linum usitatissimum (cultivated)	4.00–5.21	3.42–3.83	12–15

domestic plant species represented, came from Proto-literate samples.

A binocular zoom-lens dissecting microscope (American Optic Corporation) was used to identify all carbonized material. Photographs were made using a 35 mm. Nikon camera mounted on the scope. Magnification from 4× to 20× facilitated examination of all but the smallest specimens.

Because carbonization frequently distorts or alters the size of plant material, all seeds were compared with fresh reference material. To control for size variation, fresh seeds were placed in an oven at 190 C degrees for ten hours and then again compared with fresh counterparts. This artificial carbonization of fresh seeds provided dramatic evidence for the changes in seed size due to partial burning and also furnished a definite index range of size differences between burned and modern reference material of the same species (table 43).

CARBONIZED PLANT MATERIAL

Carbonized plant material was first grouped into major categories: seeds, seed fragments, cereal rachis segments and spikelets, and so forth. All seeds were isolated from other plant material and separated according to plant family. Distinctive seed fragments were also separated in this manner. Once major categories of carbonized seeds, seed fragments, and other plant parts were defined, more detailed determinations with the aid of reference material were made. Badly fragmented remains were left until last and identified when possible. Poorly preserved plant material and that with which the author was unfamiliar were noted. Pieces of charcoal were removed from each sample and weighed. Because of the small size of the individual pieces, none of the charcoal was identifiable. The Chogha Mish carbonized seed collection is summarized in table 44.

THE ARCHAIC SUSIANA PERIOD

The earliest occupation levels from which carbonized plant remains were recovered date to the Archaic Susiana times, ca. 7000 B.C. Carbonized seeds of cereals

and legumes suggest an early agricultural community on the threshold of plant domestication. The archaeological material culture, too, reflects a farming economy. Vessels of simple unpainted ware were used for food storage and probably in food preparation. Ovens could have been employed not only for pottery firing, but for the roasting of cereal grains or the seeds of wild grasses. Artifacts include flint sickle blades so common to other Near Eastern agricultural sites.

CEREALS

When describing early agricultural villages, those plants most often discussed in terms of their economic importance belong to the grass family. Large seeded *Hordeum* (barley), *Triticum* (wheat), and *Avena* (oat) are particularly cited as being favored by the first farmers. The wild grasses *Aegilops* (goat face grass) and *Lolium* (rye grass) are said to grow in association with the domestic cereals. At Chogha Mish these wild grasses as well as *Phalaris* (canary grass) and *Festuca* (fescue) accounted for the majority of grass seeds identified. Domestic varieties including *Hordeum* and *Avena* occurred less frequently in the samples while *Triticum* appeared as a single grain of *Triticum aestivum/durum* (bread wheat) in one sample only. The apparent lack of *Triticum* at this time is puzzling and might in part be a reflection of sampling distribution. More certain, however, is the predominance of the seeds of wild grasses over those of early domestic cereals.

LEGUMES

Seeds belonging to a variety of leguminous species were counted in greater numbers than any other group of seeds in the Chogha Mish Archaic Susiana plant assemblage. Though cereals have been stressed for their economic significance at most other sites, the Chogha Mish farmers apparently cultivated or exploited legumes over other plants. Both wild and domestic types are identifiable. Small seeded legumes attributed to *Alhagi*, *Astragalus* (milk vetch), *Medicago* (medick), *Trifolium* (clover) occur in large amounts. *Prosopis* (screw bean) and *Vicia* (vetch) are frequently counted.

Table 44. Chogha Mish Carbonized Seed Collection

	Archaic	Early Susiana	Middle Susiana	Late Susiana	Protoliterate	Total Seed Counts
TOTAL SAMPLES EXAMINED						
Fabaceae (Leguminosae)						
Alhagi	—	—	—	—	—	—
Astragalus	—	—	—	—	—	—
Medicago	—	—	—	—	—	—
Trifolium	167	160	113	108	21	569
Lens	34	24	31	33	54	176
Pisum	47	38	53	40	70	248
Prosopis	58	54	50	42	34	238
Vicia	69	61	59	60	49	298
Poaceae (Gramineae)						
Aegilops	27	9	14	12	20	82
Festuca	15	—	16	18	3	52
Lolium	45	—	17	17	31	110
Phalaris	19	—	12	—	—	31
Avena	17	10	7	16	53	103
Hordeum	20	13	13	17	285	348
Triticum	1	—	—	—	30	31
Anacardiaceae						
Pistacia	4	—	25	20	35	84
Asteraceae (Compositae)						
Cirsium and others	7	—	—	10	15	32
Boraginaceae						
Echium	7	—	11	9	15	42
Brassicaceae (Cruciferae)						
Capsella and others	4	—	15	7	4	30
Capparidaceae						
Capparis	5	15	15	13	41	89
TOTAL SAMPLES EXAMINED						
Chenopodiaceae						
Atriplex						
Suaeda and others	12	—	11	10	21	54
Cyperaceae						
Scirpus	25	23	20	13	19	100
Fumariaceae						
Fumaria	—	3	9	11	16	39
Lamiaceae (Labiatae)						
Ajuaga						
Marrubium and others	13	—	29	21	31	94
Liliaceae						
Muscari	13	—	—	4	12	29
Linaceae						
Linum	13	7	9	8	80	117
Malvaceae						
Unknown species	8	—	5	8	9	30
Papaveraceae						
Unknown species	2	4	5	7	8	26
Plantaginaceae						
Plantago	9	9	18	11	29	76
Polygonaceae						
Rumex	21	—	8	8	3	40
Rubiaceae						
Galium	29	27	28	22	17	123
Urticaceae						
Urtica	1	—	20	16	22	59
Unknowns	18	25	13	19	23	98
TOTALS	710	482	626	580	1,050	3,448

Pisum (pea) and *Lens* (lentil) seeds are the most interesting members of the seed collection because they exhibit morphological traits implying actual plant domestication during the Archaic Susiana period.

Of the numerous carbonized seeds identified as *Pisum* or *Lens*, some display obvious indentations in the seeds. Such indentations suggest a closely packed pod, the seeds held tightly together producing visibly flattened sides where they have pressed against each other. Seeds are not easily released and generally require forceful mechanical removal, *i.e.*, by hand so that they might propagate. This type of pod indicates domestic varieties, plants which depend on man for their survival. The pods of wild legumes, on the other hand, are not tightly closed. When seeds are ripe they split apart easily in a twisting motion, causing the two halves of the pod to curl under. The seeds do not exhibit the indentations or flattened sides characteristic of domestic varieties because they are loosely housed in the pod and do not press against each other. When the pods are ripe, a gentle breeze or animal brushing against the plant is sufficient to explode the pods and scatter the seeds. Both indented and non-indented seeds, as well as the remains of twisted and straight pods, were recovered from Archaic Susiana deposits at Chogha Mish. Unfortunately, the absence of either seed coat or hilum made a species level identification impossible in most cases.

LINUM

Several seeds belonging to the genus *Linum* were identified. Their large size (4.0–5.2 mm) does not indicate the small seeds of wild species (2.5–3.8 mm approximately), but varieties normally associated with domestication or even irrigation. Helbaek has suggested that irrigation was instrumental in the increase in oil content (also the flax fiber output of plants) of flax seeds, which is reflected in larger seed size, 4.39 mm at Ur and 5.30 mm at Assyrian Nimrud (Helbaek 1960:193). If, in fact, large size seeds are the result of irrigation, their presence in the earliest occupation levels of Chogha Mish would be unlikely. Protoliterate inhabitants did, however, dig storage pits into earlier Archaic Susiana habitation levels. Since *Linum* seeds occur frequently in Protoliterate samples, intrusion of seeds from Protoliterate to Archaic Susiana contexts in a few specific instances is probable. This might also account for the single occurrence of *Triticum aestivum/durum* at this early date.

OTHER CARBONIZED SEED REMAINS

Besides legumes, grasses and flax, a variety of other carbonized seeds were identified from Archaic Susiana deposits. Some of these, though generally considered wild, were counted in such large numbers as to imply economic exploitation. Others probably occurred as a part of the naturally existing vegetation or grew as weeds in association with the domesticates. For example, *Lolium*, *Aegilops*, and *Plantago* (plantain), all three of which were observed in Archaic Susiana samples, grow today as common crop weeds. *Scirpus* (rush), *Galium* (bed-straw), and *Suaeda* (sea blite), other components of the carbonized seed collection, could easily have grown after rains, which often left standing pools of water for lengthy periods after the actual rainfall. Constant flooding appears to have been a frequent occurrence on the Susiana Plain, which was one probable source of water for the crops of the first farmers. The mixing of *Scirpus* and cereal seeds at other Iranian sites has been previously noted (Helbaek 1969).

Seeds which might have had specific uses include *Capparis* (caper), members of the *Lamiaceae* family (mint family) many of which are used as condiments, and *Capsella-bursa-pastoris* (shepherd's purse). Other carbonized seeds identified in varying amounts belong to the *Boraginaceae* (borage family), *Chenopodiaceae* (goosefoot family), *Liliaceae* (lily family), *Malvaceae* (mallow family), *Papaveraceae* (poppy family), and *Urticaceae* (nettle family). Some of these plants undoubtedly were of value (consumable or otherwise) to the prehistoric inhabitants of Chogha Mish, though their exact use might never be established.

CARBONIZED PLANT MATERIAL OTHER THAN SEEDS

The remains of carbonized pods of *Pisum* and *Lens* are discussed above. Small fragments of nutlets, probably *Pistacia* (pistachio), were examined. The glumes (*Hordeum*) and stalks from brick fragments stirred into the original clay as tempering agents cannot be identified in other than general terms. Though surviving as carbonized plant fragments, they do not display necessary morphological characteristics for detailed determination.

EARLY AND MIDDLE SUSIANA PERIODS

All seeds present in Archaic Susiana samples are also identified at this time. There is still a suspicious absence of *Triticum* but *Hordeum*, both 2 and 6 row varieties, are counted. *Compositae* and *Fumaria* (fumitory) are also observed. Legume seeds continue to outnumber grass seeds in total sample seed counts.

PROTOLITERATE PERIOD

CEREALS AND LEGUMES

Carbonized seeds from Protoliterate deposits illustrate a developed farming community dependent upon fully domesticated crops. The most dramatic change associated with the established agricultural economy is a reliance on cereal crops, especially on barley cultivation. Carbonized bread wheat seeds (*Triticum aestivum/durum*) are also found but appear to be of less impor-

Table 45. Spatial and Temporal Distribution of Plant and Seed Remains at Chogha Mish

Locus	Level	Content + Weight	Plant Remains	Date
N9:1003	88.38	Baked Brick. 2 samples, 200 grams and 123 grams	*Aegilops* sp. *Festuca* sp. Unidentifiable grasses	Protoliterate
N9:1004	91.68	Ashy debris around Child burial. 22 grams	Small seeded legumes *Cirsium* sp. *Avena* sp. *Rumex* sp.	Sukkalmaḥ
N9:1004	91.34	Soil sample. 33 grams	Small seeded legumes *Atriplex* sp. *Suaeda* sp. *Cirsium* sp.	Sukkalmaḥ
N9:1004	89.00	Ashy debris around Child burial. 10 grams	Small seeded legumes *Cirsium* sp. *Muscari* sp. *Rumex* sp. *Urtica* sp.	Protoliterate
N9:1005	90.47	Black earth associated with beveled-rim bowls. 70 grams	Small seeded legumes *Pisum* sp. *Hordeum* sp. *Capsella* sp. *Scirpus* sp. *Galium* sp.	Protoliterate
N9:1010	89.90	Kiln below Elamite Levels. 19 grams	*Lolium* sp. *Prosopis* sp. *Plantago* sp.	Protoliterate
P27:501 North	n/a	Soil sample. 30 grams	*Avena* sp. *Hordeum* sp.	Middle Susiana
Q23:502	n/a	Soil recovered by hand, not floated. 42 grams	No seeds. Stalks of unidentifiable grasses	Early Susiana
R17:408	Pit	—	*Ajuga* sp. *Avena* sp. *Hordeum* sp. *Lens* sp. *Pisum* sp. *Rumex* sp. *Urtica* sp. *Linum* sp.	Protoliterate
R18:901	81.10	Burnt Building soil sample. 37 grams	*Alhagi* sp. *Astragalus* sp. *Vicia* sp. *Avena* sp. *Echium* sp.	Late Middle Susiana
R18:905	81.90	Base of walls of Room R18:409, soil sample. 50 grams	*Ajuga* sp. *Papaver* sp.	Protoliterate
R18:915	80.78	Protoliterate pit. 62 grams	Small seeded legumes *Lens* sp. *Pisum* sp. *Hordeum* sp. *Lolium* sp. *Tinticum* sp. *Pistacia* sp. *Echium* sp. *Suaeda* sp. *Linum* sp. *Plantago* sp. *Rumex* sp. *Galium* sp.	Protoliterate

Table 45. Spatial and Temporal Distribution of Plant and Seed Remains at Chogha Mish (*cont.*)

Locus	Level	Content + Weight	Plant Remains	Date
R18:921	81.02	Burnt Building soil sample. 37 grams	Small seeded *Lens* sp. *Pisum* sp. *Hordeum* sp. *Pistacia* sp. *Capparis* sp. *Marnibium* sp. *Galium* sp.	Late Middle Susiana
R18:921	80.38	Burnt Building soil sample. 42 grams	Small seeded legumes *Lens* sp. *Pisum* sp. *Vicia* sp. *Pistacia* sp. *Capparis* sp. *Plantago* sp. *Linum* sp.	Late Middle Susiana
R18:921	80.36	Burnt Building floor. 99 grams	Small seeded legumes *Vicia* sp. *Aegilop* sp. *Linum* sp. *Galium* sp.	Late Middle Susiana
R18:921	80.28	Burnt Building soil sample. 57 grams	Small seeded legumes *Aegilops* sp. *Festuca* sp. *Lolium* sp. *Phalaris* sp. *Echium* sp. *Capsella* sp. *Malva* sp. *Plantago* sp. *Urtica* sp.	Late Middle Susiana
R18:925	80.75	Pit soil sample. 50 grams	Small seeded legumes *Urtica* sp. *Malva* sp. *Atriplex* sp. *Avena* sp. *Aegilops* sp.	Protoliterate
R19:903	79.52	Pit soil sample	Small seeded legumes *Lens* sp. *Pisum* sp. *Triticum* sp. *Hordeum* sp. *Capparis* sp. *Atriplex* sp. *Fumaria* sp. *Marrubium* sp. *Rumex* sp. *Galium* sp.	Protoliterate
R19:903	79.52–78.57	Pit soil sample	Small seeded legumes *Lens* sp. *Pisum* sp. *Lolium* sp. *Avena* sp. *Hordeum* sp. *Capsella* sp. *Marrubium* sp. *Linum* sp. *Papaver* sp.	Protoliterate

Table 45. Spatial and Temporal Distribution of Plant and Seed Remains at Chogha Mish (*cont.*)

Locus	Level	Content + Weight	Plant Remains	Date
S18:902	80.91	Burnt Building soil sample. 81 grams	Small seeded legumes *Pisum* sp. *Avena* sp. *Scirpus* sp. *Atriplex* sp. *Fumaria* sp.	Late Middle Susiana
S18:905 West	81.24	Burnt Building soil sample. 53 grams	Unidentifiable seeds and silica skeletons, highly carbonized	Late Middle Susiana
S22:401	Probably between 75.13 and 73.50	Soil sample. 21 grams	*Cirsium* sp. *Marrubium* sp. *Papaver* sp. *Rumex* sp.	Archaic Susiana 2–3
S22:914	74.72	Small area of settlement debris; Early Susiana dark, stone-filled deposit overlying Archaic Susiana 3 without any break; mixed soil sample. 71 grams	Highly weathered unidentifiable small seeded legumes and grasses	Archaic Susiana 3 (highest Archaic Susiana 3 material with transitional Archaic Susiana– Early Susiana debris immediately above)
S22:914	74.47	Soil sample. 112 grams	Small seeded legumes *Aegilops* sp. *Lolium* sp. *Phalaris* sp. *Cirsium* sp. *Ajuga* sp. *Rumex* sp.	Archaic Susiana 3
S22:914	74.10	Soil sample. 102 grams	Highly weathered Silica skeletons of *Papaver* sp.	Archaic Susiana 3
S22:914	73.90	Soil sample. 52 grams	Small seeded legumes *Lolium* sp. *Phalaris* sp. *Scirpus* sp. *Muscari* sp. *Malva* sp. *Galium* sp.	Archaic Susiana 3
S22:914	73.35	Soil sample. 60 grams	Small seeded legumes *Scirpus* sp. *Galium* sp.	Archaic Susiana 3
S22:923	75.89	Soil sample. 33 grams	Small seeded legumes *Lens* sp. *Pisum* sp. *Avena* sp. *Hordeum* sp. *Scirpus* sp. *Plantago* sp. *Fumaria* sp.	Early Susiana
S22:923	74.82	Soil sample. 48 grams	Small seeded legumes *Scirpus* sp. *Aegilops* sp.	Early Susiana
S22:923	74.53	Under Wall. 50 grams	Small seeded legumes *Pisum* *Vicia* *Avena* sp. *Hordeum* sp. *Capparis* sp. *Scirpus* sp. *Linum* sp. *Galium* sp. *Papaver* sp.	Archaic Susiana 3 and Early Susiana mixed

Table 45. Spatial and Temporal Distribution of Plant and Seed Remains at Chogha Mish (*cont.*)

Locus	Level	Content + Weight	Plant Remains	Date
S22:923	73.97	Occupation debris of Early Susiana below level of Early Susiana wall; soil sample. 82 grams	Small seeded legumes *Pisum* sp. *Vicia* sp. *Festuca* sp. *Capsella* sp. *Echium* sp. *Urtica* sp.	Archaic Susiana 3
S22.929	73.28	Pit in S22:923; filled with stones; soil sample. 61 grams (from bottom of pit)	Small seeded legumes *Lens* sp. *Pisum* sp. *Vicia* sp. *Lolium* sp. *Pistacia* sp. *Plantago* sp.	Initial Early Susiana (Early Susiana and some surviving Archaic Susiana 3 3 types)
S23:505	74.92–74.83	Settlement debris in southern end of Gully Cut; soil sample. 30 grams	*Avena* sp. *Hordeum* sp. *Lolium* sp. *Triticum* sp. *Linum* sp.	Archaic Susiana 2–3

*"Small seeded legumes" includes *Prosopis* sp.

tance than barley, which is clearly the most important domestic crop. Oats, too, are represented as carbonized seeds. They are, however, the small seeded variety and might have been grown primarily as fodder while their larger seeded relatives were consumed by the inhabitants of Chogha Mish.

As several varieties of barley including 2 and 6 row, hulled and naked types became the dominant field crops, other previously important food plants were correspondingly de-emphasized. A conspicuous decrease in the number of carbonized leguminous seeds is evident from all the Protoliterate samples. Field peas, lentils, and vetches, though still a substantial part of the subsistence base, have been superseded by barley. The small seeded legumes including *Alhagi*, *Astragalus*, and *Trifolium* occur incidentally in samples and are of significance, presumably, only as animal fodder.

LINUM

Carbonized flax seeds are counted frequently in Protoliterate samples. Even after allowing for a 10 to 15% shrinkage due to carbonization, the seeds are all of the larger variety. Domesticated flax seeds were probably the major source of oil at this time. The fibers must have been commonly exploited for textiles as well.

OTHER CARBONIZED PLANT SEEDS

During the early stages of the botanic analysis, the carbonized seed assemblage from Protoliterate contexts did not seem as diverse as that recovered from previous levels. This is primarily because of an increase in domesticates at the expense of wild small seeded plants. Small seeded grasses and legumes occur sporadically.

Capsella is infrequently found. The time and energy necessary to gather and process these small seeds was perhaps no longer considered feasible as domestic cereals with their higher economic yields became more and more agriculturally viable. Human effort went into the planting and harvesting of these crops while activities relating to the procurement of small seeded plants were abandoned.

GRAIN IMPRESSIONS

A limited number of ceramic sherds and clay bricks were examined. Many grain impressions (as well as glumes of barley) were observed and all samples displayed the imprints of grass stalks. Certainly, grasses provided a major source of temper for prehistoric potters and masons. In no case was a specific identification possible, however. No distinctive identifying traits were visible.

SILICA SKELETONS

Silica skeletons of ancient plants formed a large component of all samples. Some of these were obviously grasses and legumes, while others closely approximated the size of *Papaver* seeds. These, similar to grain impressions, afforded no opportunity to render genera or species level identifications.

PALYNOLOGY AT CHOGHA MISH

Pollen analysis was conducted on twenty-five samples, primarily to discern the presence or absence of pollen in sediment samples. Pollen did occur in sufficient numbers to warrant further investigation in all but three samples. Preservation is fair in both arboreal and non-arboreal plant species, but great care had to be taken during the laboratory extraction procedure so as not to further distort already delicate pollen grains. Detailed pollen studies of soil samples recovered from all levels of the site is forthcoming.

CARBONIZED PLANT MATERIAL

The carbonized remains of plant material at Chogha Mish came from several deposits dated to the Archaic Susiana levels and from a pit, R17:408, of the Protoliterate period. All samples containing identifiable plant remains were recovered by flotation directly on the site, left to dry, and stored in glass test tubes. A single sample (Q23:502, Archaic), recovered by hand, contained no identifiable ancient plant remains other than charcoal, very small bits of charred bone, and a

few bits of modern twigs. The richest and most diverse material came from the Protoliterate sample. This might in part be due to the size of that particular sample.

First, all seeds, no matter what their condition, were isolated. Those having similar morphological characteristics were then grouped together, and, finally, seeds were further separated by their degree of preservation.

Identification of the plant material can be found in the following tables and photographs (pl. 68). It must be emphasized that this is only a preliminary investigation, and that it would be premature to attempt interpretations or to draw conclusions from the evidence thus far examined. The samples were few and, clearly, not an overall representation of plant material existing at prehistoric Chogha Mish. Other samples already recovered from Chogha Mish await investigation. Many questions have been raised. For example, Why is there an apparent lack of wheat on the site? The single grain that has been identified (*Triticum aestivum*) comes from a very early

Table 46. Plant Material Recovered from Chogha Mish

Locus/Level	Period	Method	Common Name	Scientific Name
S23:401 ca. 4 m	Archaic Susiana 7000 B.C.[+]	Flotation	Creeping thistle	*Cirsium arvense* (L.) Scop.
			Common horehound	*Marrubium vulgare* L.
			Oriental poppy	*Papaver orientale* L.
			Sheep's sorrel	*Rumex acetosella* L.
Q23:502	Archaic Susiana 7000 B.C.[+]	Recovered by hand *in situ*	No recognizable plant material recovered; only charcoal, bits of twigs and bone, tiny grains of sand	—
S23:505	Archaic Susiana 7000 B.C.[+]	Flotation	Short oat	*Avena brevis* Roth.
			Small-seeded naked oat	*Avena nudibrevis* Vav. (possibly)
			2 row wild barley	*Hordeum spontaneum* Koch.
			6 row hulled barley	*Hordeum vulgare* L. emend.
			6 row naked barley	*Hordeum vulgare* var. nudum (= var. *coeleste* L.)
			Flax	*Linum bienne* L.
			Sesame seeds	*Sesamum* sp.
			Bread wheat	*Triticum aestivum*
R17:408 (pit)	Protoliterate	Flotation	Common bugleweed	*Ajuga reptans* L.
			Oat	*Avena* sp.
			Fig	*Ficus carica* L.
			2 row wild barley	*Hordeum spontaneum* Koch.
			2 row naked barley	*Hordeum distichon* L. var. *nudum*
			6 row hulled barley	*Hordeum vulgare* L. emend.
			6 row naked barley	*Hordeum vulgare* var. nudum (= var. *coeleste* L.)
			Lentil	*Lens esculenta* Moench
			Field pea	*Pisum sativa* var. *arvense* L.
			(?)	*Rumex* sp.
			Wheat	*Triticum* sp. (?)
			Burning nettle	*Urtica urens* L.
			Flax	*Linum* sp.
P27:501	Archaic Susiana 7000 B.C.[+]	Flotation	Oat	*Avena* sp.
			Barley	*Hordeum* sp.
			(?)	*Euphorbia* sp.

level indeed. Is there really, then, an absence of wheat and a predominance of barley at the site or were the results a reflection of the sampling techniques?

Further work is now being done, including the examination of pottery for grain impressions. A more complete picture of the plant life and how it was used by the inhabitants of Chogha Mish might yet emerge.

CONCLUSIONS

Preliminary analysis of the botanic material from Chogha Mish suggests two interesting, though tentative, conclusions about the prehistoric agriculture practiced at the site. For years, the importance of cereals, viz., emmer and einkorn wheats and barleys, has been cited as the major indicator of plant domestication and thereby beginning farming communities. The examination of carbonized seeds from Chogha Mish does not support the significance of cereals as early domesticates during the first three prehistoric occupation levels at the site. Though barley was probably cultivated on a small scale, the first several thousand years of agriculture seem to have been characterized by an emphasis on legume crops, including *Pisum*, *Lens*, and *Vicia*, over cereals. Since carbonized cereal seeds are among the most readily surviving carbonized remains, their occurrence in small quantities cannot be easily attributed to poor preservation. Legumes are usually not nearly so well preserved as cereals. Indeed, the legumes recovered from Chogha Mish are often quite battered. However, legumes comprise the largest portion of total seeds counted from Archaic Susiana, Middle Susiana, and Late Susiana samples. Only with the coming of a fully established agricultural economy during Protoliterate times do cereals become a significant component of the subsistence exploitation pattern. This suggests that at Chogha Mish the earliest domestic crops of economic importance were the legumes, not the cereals.

Another anomaly in the Chogha Mish carbonized plant collection is the apparent absence of any varieties of wheat in Archaic Susiana (except for a single grain of bread wheat of questionable provenience), Middle Susiana, and Late Susiana deposits, as well as its extremely limited occurrence during Protoliterate times. *Triticum* is one of the crop plants observed at many early agricultural sites in the Near East. Yet at Chogha Mish, it appears to be of incidental economic importance. Whether there is a marked absence of wheat or whether its later limited occurrence can be associated with sampling distribution has not been established. Since the samples recovered from the site represent a diverse chronological and contextual range, it is difficult to imagine that wheat could have been consistently missed, only to appear suddenly in abundant quantities in samples from other sites.

A few closing remarks concerning future palynological work should be made. Pollen studies in conjunction with macro-botanic analysis can greatly increase the understanding of the early farmers at Chogha Mish, and of early agriculture elsewhere in the Near East. Plants which are visible as carbonized remains are usually those which are processed through partial burning. Roasting of cereals, for example, is often necessary to separate seeds from the glumes. Many other plants exploited by man as consumable resources, for medicinal purposes, for dyes, or as oil plants would only rarely survive as carbonized plant material, perhaps only through the fortuitous (for the archaeologist) burning of a house. Processing of these plants precludes a normal carbonization. The roots, leaves, stems, or flowers could be boiled, dried and powdered, or even eaten fresh, with no portion of the plant remaining for archaeological analysis. Consequently, the evidence for many plants extremely useful to prehistoric peoples would not survive. Even today farmers in southwestern Iran exploit a variety of plants as pot herbs or salad greens, especially during the spring season. Nothing remains of these modern plants after they are processed and their prehistoric counterparts would certainly not be visible in the archaeological record.

Such plants might, however, be observable in pollen diagrams since their pollen could be extracted from the soil. In fact, the only evidence available about a great many plant exploitation activities during prehistoric times might be speculative information resulting from pollen analysis. Additionally, pollen can provide information concerning the human impact, particularly that exercised by agriculturists, on the naturally existing environment.

The analysis of pollen and carbonized macro-botanic material is of major relevance to understanding exploitation patterns at Chogha Mish. A knowledge of the socioeconomic changes occurring at this site during incipient and developed agriculture will also help to explain subsequent processes leading to the emergence of Mesopotamian city states with subsistence systems based on complex agriculture.

****

Acknowledgments

I would like to express my gratitude to the late Professor Pinhas Delougaz for his support and consideration and for giving me the opportunity to work with the Chogha Mish carbonized plant material. Thanks also go to [the late] Professor Helene Kantor and Professor Mildred Mathias for their help and criticism. During the final stages of the analysis, Dr. Marcia Fentress aided in some of the carbonized seed identification and confirmation of doubtful specimens.

Table 47. World-wide Distribution of Plant Remains and Their Use

Scientific Name	Distribution	Use
Ajuga reptans L.	Europe, the Near East: meadows, forests, hedges, universally distributed	Weed
Avena sp.	Temperate regions with abundant water	Food source: gruel, animal fodder
Cirsium avense (L.) Scop.	Europe, Asia, North America: fields, roadways, especially where subsoil is deep	Troublesome weed in fields
Euphorbia sp.	Mainly subtropical and warm temperate (2,000 species)	Unknown (genus of herbs and shrubs
Ficus carica L. (*Ficus persica*)	Eastern Mediterranean, Iran, as far as northwestern India	Food source: source of sugar, animal fodder
Hordeum sp.	Temperate regions, warm areas in the Near East	Food source: gruel, bread, animal fodder
Lens esculenta Moench	Mediterranean, western Asia, warm climates	Specific prehistoric use unknown, probable food source: soup, with high protein content
Linum bienne L. and *L. usitatissisum* L.	Temperate and subtropical regions	Human and animal food source: seeds noted for oil content
Marrunium vulgare L.	Europe, Mediterranean area to central Asia; meadows, pastures, completely entrenched in warmer areas	Specific prehistoric use unknown, formerly cultivated as medicinal plant
Papver orientale L.	Asia Minor, Iran	Specific prehistoric use unknown: today green buds are eaten, ornamental plant, seeds not noted for oil content
Pisum sativa var. arvense L.	Mediterranean, western Asia	Specific prehistoric use unknown, probable food source, plant restores nitrogen to soil
Rumex acetosella L.	Cosmopolitan: fields, meadows, along walls, common to clay soils	Food source: foliage, large quantities of leaves can be toxic
Rumex sp.	see *R. acetosella*	See *R. acetosella*
Sesamum sp.	Asia, tropical southern Africa	Food source
Triticum sp.	Europe, Mediterranean, western Asia	Food source: gruel, bread, animal fodder

ARTIFICIAL CRANIAL DEFORMATION OF A HUMAN SKULL FROM CHOGHA MISH

Donald J. Ortner
Department of Anthropology
Smithsonian Institution

INTRODUCTION

In the Near East the discovery of a skull deformed by an antemortem cultural practice at an archaeological site is sufficiently rare, even in geographical areas where the practice is known, that careful study and descriptive analysis is warranted. The skull that is the subject of this report was sent to me by Dr. Helene J. Kantor of the Oriental Institute, the University of Chicago, with the request that I prepare a report for inclusion in the volume on the first five seasons at Chogha Mish, Khuzestan, Iran.

The skull was found in a Late Middle Susiana context (N11:Trench XXII), and its abnormal shape is readily apparent, even with superficial inspection (pl. 69:A–B). While the deformation in this case is clearly the result of antemortem cultural intervention, it is important to stress that many other conditions can produce abnormal shapes of the skull (Ortner and Putschar 1981:90–92, 352–55). Pathological conditions that affect the shape of the skull include premature fusion of the cranial sutures (*craniostenosis*), trauma, and hydrocephaly. Postmortem deformation also occurs as a result of burial conditions.

Antemortem deformation of the skull through culturally patterned intervention occurs in many areas of the world and has been the subject of several reports in the anthropological and medical literature. Dingwall's monograph (1931) provides a helpful worldwide review of this practice, but relies heavily on artistic representations in modern populations and has minimal evidence from archaeological specimens. In the New World the practice of cranial deformation in archaeological specimens is widespread and well-documented (e.g., Stewart 1941, 1950). The practice was particularly common on the west coast of South America and the Northwest coast of North America (Brothwell 1965:72). In the New World the method of artificial cranial deformation was varied and resulted in different shapes of deformed skulls. Occipital flattening of the skull is found in archaeological specimens from the American Southwest but is an indirect result of using a cradle-board and not the result of intentional deformation.

In the Old World, deformation occurs in several modern societies and is associated with many archaeological sites in widely dispersed geographical areas. However, even if the potential bias inherent in archaeological samples is taken into consideration, the trait still does not appear to be as frequent where practiced in the Old World, as it is in major centers of skull deformation in the New World. In the Near East it is attested at Byblos during the Chalcolithic period (Ozbek 1974; Vallois 1937). Extreme cranial deformation has been found in the skeletons excavated at Chogha Sefid in Iran dating to about 6500 B.C. (Hole 1977). This geographical distribution of deformed skulls indicates that deformation was not an isolated practice in the Near East during the Neolithic and Chalcolithic periods. Risdon reports the presence of cranial deformation in both male and female skulls much later in time (ca. 700 B.C.) at Tell Duweir, ancient Lachish (1939:115–16; pl. 6). Risdon describes the deformation as the fronto-occipital type, indicating that the method is different from the circular method associated with the Byblos and Chogha Sefid specimens.

The association that has been made at Byblos, at least, between cranial deformation and female sex is interesting and needs to be clarified for other sites in the Near East. One should emphasize, however, that the sample size for the Byblos skulls is very small and thus highly vulnerable to the possibility of being unrepresentative of the population living at the site in antiquity. Unfortunately, the preservation of the Chogha Sefid skulls is poor, so that it is not surprising no data is available on the sex of the deformed skull.

At Byblos cranial deformation was produced by two methods. In one method, circular cloth bands were applied from the base of the occipital, across the temporal bones and then around the upper portion of the frontal bone. In the second method, another band was added around the chin and top of the skull. The effect of both methods was to produce the appearance of an elongated skull. While the proportions of the skull are modified slightly, Moss (1958:248) indicates that overall growth was not affected in the cases of deformation that he studied. Blackwood and Danby (1956:175) express the subjective opinion that cranial deformation had no effect on intelligence or other abilities among living groups in New Britain. Although deformation is, in some specimens, quite severe there is no skeletal evidence of dysfunction.

DESCRIPTION OF SPECIMEN

The Chogha Mish skull lacks the mandible but is otherwise complete except for a postmortem defect in the rear portion of the right parietal bone. When the skull arrived in the laboratory, as much of the remaining dirt as possible was removed without causing further damage. The bone was very fragile and was treated with a 10% solution of polyvinyl acetate (PVA) in acetone to insure reasonable stability of the bone tissue. The PVA solution was brushed on the exposed bone surfaces of the specimen. This method of application was used rather than immersion of the specimen in order to minimize post mortem deformation that can occur when the entire skull becomes wet. These conservation procedures revealed more of the tissue surfaces, particularly in the region of the face.

The skull itself is very gracile. Anatomical features such as the browridge and mastoid processes are small, creating a high probability that the skull was that of a female. All the permanent teeth have erupted, indicating an age in excess of 18 years. Tooth wear on the premolars is slight, although wear of the first permanent molar has exposed the dentin over most of the occlusal surface. Brothwell (1965:69) has established the association between the degree of molar tooth wear and age in pre-medieval British skulls. Using his criteria, the Chogha Mish skull would be 35–45 years of age. Tooth wear, of course, is heavily dependent on the amount of grit and coarse fiber in the diet so that aging criteria will vary in different societies.

The pattern of suture closure in the skull suggests a somewhat younger individual (ca. 25–35), which raises the possibility that the diet contained more grit and/or fiber than the British sample. The root remnant of the right second molar provides evidence of dental caries that destroyed the crown of the tooth. Another prominent and somewhat unusual feature of the skull is the presence of a metopic suture. The frequency of this trait during the Neolithic and Chalcolithic periods in the Near East is poorly documented. In a sample of skulls from Kish, dated to between 2700 B.C. and 600 B.C., the frequency of metopism in female skulls is six percent (Rathbun 1975:229). The frequency in Predynastic skulls from Naqada, Egypt, ranges from 3.5% to 9.4% (Berry, Berry, Ucko 1967). In Early Bronze Age I skulls from Bab edh-Dhra, Jordan, the frequency is 11.1% (Frohlich, pers. comm.).

The antemortem cranial deformation seen in the Chogha Mish skull is clearly of the type produced by circular cloth binding around the posterior part of the skull beginning at birth or shortly thereafter. This pattern has

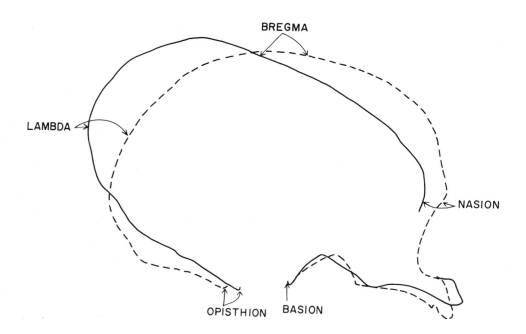

Figure 49. Profile Drawings in the Mid-Sagittal Plane of the Chogha Mish Skull Compared with the Skull from the Early Bronze Age Site of Bab edh-Dhra, Jordan (Tomb Chamber A 102 S, Burial no. 2)

been described for the New World by Stewart (1941) as circular deformation. The appearance of the Chogha Mish skull closely resembles the deformation associated with the Byblos (Vallois 1937; Ozbek 1974) and Chogha Sefid skulls (Hole 1977). The effect of the binding is to produce the appearance of a greatly elongated skull. It is apparent, however, in the measurements given in tables 1 and 2 that this appearance is less the result of the skull being longer-than-normal than of the shape being changed, as seen in the mid-sagittal profile drawing (fig. 49). The normally bulbous frontal region of the skull has been flattened and the occipital region shifted upward and somewhat extruded to create a more bulbous appearance of the superior occipital region.

The deformation in the Chogha Mish skull changed the shape but had less effect on the measurements than one might think. This observation is also supported by Ozbek's data on the unaffected male skulls compared with the deformed female skulls from Byblos (Ozbek 1974). In general, there is slight narrowing of the skull with a resultant decrease in the cranial index. The minimal differences in measurements between male and female skulls at Byblos are at least partly the result of sex-related size variation and support the likelihood that deformation had no affect on the overall growth and development of the skull.

DISCUSSION AND SIGNIFICANCE

The Chogha Mish skull provides additional evidence for the practice of cranial deformation during the Neolithic and Chalcolithic periods in the Near East. The dates of ca. 4500–4000 B.C. for the Chogha Mish skull and ca. 6500 B.C. for the Chogha Sefid ones suggest a considerable time range for the practice in Iran. The Chalcolithic date for deformed skulls from Byblos provides evidence for considerable time depth of the trait in the Near East and also indicates that the trait was probably not restricted to a single geographical area. Clearly, the evidence regarding the frequency as well as the geographical and time distribution of this type of cranial deformation needs to be clarified through the study of burials at other appropriate archaeological sites. It does appear, however, that the circular type of deformation disappears in the Near East by the Early Bronze Age.

Although all adult females at Byblos appear to have deformed skulls (Ozbek 1974), the nature of that sample requires additional data from Byblos as well as other sites before that association can be accepted as typical. The collection of adequate skeletal samples from other related archaeological sites will aid in clarifying both the sex-specific nature and numerical proportions of the population affected by this cultural practice. Good sample sizes would also elucidate a connection between this practice and social status, for example, association with higher ranking, a possibility that might be clarified on the basis of associated grave offerings. Another option to consider, if the proportion varies, is a central geographical focus for the trait and the possibility that females with the trait arrived at the site because of exogamous marriage patterns or perhaps as the result of warfare, whereas local women had undeformed skulls.

****

Acknowledgments

I should like to acknowledge, with deep appreciation, the assistance of Mrs. Janet Beck, who was responsible for the conservation of the Chogha Mish skull. Mrs. Gretchen Theobald and Mrs. Agnes Stix were most helpful with bibliographic searches for relevant reports. Mr. Victor Krantz and Mrs. Marcia Bakry assisted in the preparation of the illustrations. Dr. Bruno Frohlich and Ms. Gillian Bentley read the manuscript and offered helpful suggestions. Research for this report was supported in part by a grant from the National Institutes of Health (Grant No. HHS-IROI AM34250).

Table 48 compares the measurements between anatomical points in the sagittal plane of the Chogha Mish skull with a skull of similar size from the Early Bronze Age site of Bab edh-Dhra, Jordan (Tomb chamber A 102 S, burial no. 2). Despite the deformation in the Chogha Mish skull, the percentage of the arcs between the anatomical points in the two skulls is very similar. The data from a skull from Bab edh-Dhra provide a reference point for understanding the nature of the deformation and is not intended to imply a biological or cultural association with the Chogha Mish skull.

Table 48. Comparative Measurements (in mm) of Anatomical Points in the Sagittal Plane
of the Chogha Mish and Bab edh-Dhra Skulls

	Chogha Mish	Bab edh-Dhra
Nasion-Bregma (Frontal arc)	128 (33%)	130 (35%)
Bregma Lambda (Parietal arc)	130 (34%)	123 (33%)
Lambda-Opisthion (Occipital arc)	125 (33%)	120 (32%)

The cranial measurements of the Chogha Mish skull are compared with a skull of similar size from the Early Bronze Age site of Bab edh-Dhra, Jordan (Tomb A 102 S, burial no. 2) in table 49.

Table 49. Cranial Measurements (in mm) of the Chogha Mish Skull Compared with a Skull of Similar Size from the Early Bronze Age Site of Bab edh-Dhra, Jordan

	Chogha Mish	Bab edh-Dhra
Maximum length	191	186
Maximum breadth	129	133
Biauricular breadth	120	118
Basion-bregma height	132	133
Basion-nasion length	91	98
Basion-prosthion length	99	94
Minimum frontal breadth	89	86
Bizygomatic breadth	N/A	132
Upper facial height	68	67
Nasal height	52	49
Nasal breadth	22	24
Interorbital breadth	N/A	24
Left orbit breadth	39	36
Left orbit height	34	32
Maximum palate length	59	55
Maximum palate breadth	63	61

APPENDIX B

A CARBON 14 DETERMINATION PERTAINING TO SOME PLANT IDENTIFICATIONS FROM CHOGHA MISH

Pinhas Delougaz

A significant supplement to the plant identifications from R17:408, which was dug through and below some private houses of the Protoliterate period, is a ^{14}C determination carried out during the summer of 1972 by the Teledyne Isotopes Laboratories in Westwood, New Jersey. The sample that was submitted to these laboratories was of the same general character as that of the plant specimens obtained by means of flotation. Indeed, it is likely that carbonized grains and other plant remains constituted a large proportion of the carbon used for the age determination.

Since the proportion of carbon in the soil was rather small, a larger sample (by weight) had to be submitted, and a special procedure had to be adopted by the laboratories to obtain the necessary amount of pure carbon by means of combusting the bulk material after HCL decomposition of carbons.

The results as given us by the Isotopes Laboratories are as follows:

When the results were obtained in September 1972, the low date for this material was somewhat surprising. Now, after the work of the scientific team at Applied Science Center for Archaeology at the University of Pennsylvania, with its review of the ^{14}C determination in the light of the dendrochronological cross dating, this date has to be revised. Using the tables that have been published recently (cf. Ralph, Michael, and Han 1973), the date for the specimen would be ca. 3560 B.C., which agrees almost perfectly with the excavator's estimate of the period, based on stratigraphic evidence at sites in the Diyala region of Mesopotamia (see Delougaz and Lloyd 1942:125–35). It should be added that the pit itself, which cuts through the houses, is obviously later than the houses, and presumably the debris that it contains is approximately of the same age as the occupation level from which the pit was dug. Consequently the houses should be dated about a century or so earlier, i.e., ca. 3660 B.C.

Isotope				Age in Years
Sample Number	Sample	^{14}C	B.P.	Date
I-6632	Sample No. 2, from R17:408	455 ± 7	4875 ± 110	2925 B.C.

APPENDIX C

TEST RESULTS OF FIVE BITUMEN SAMPLES FROM CHOGHA MISH

Robert F. Marschner

The following table contains information of five bitumen samples from Chogha Mish that were tested in 1975 by Mr. Robert F. Marschner from Amoco Research Center, Indiana.

Table 50. Description of Bitumen Samples from Chogha Mish

LOCUS	S22:502	S22:502	S23:508	S23:502	R20:513
PERIOD	Archaic Susiana 2	Archaic Susiana 3	Archaic Susiana 3	Protoliterate	Protoliterate
Appearance	Uniform	Fibrous	Striated	Coated	Porous
Color	Steely	Brown	Rusty	Brown	Brown
Heft	Dense	Light	Light	Medium	Light
Class*	Rock asphalt	*	Felt melted	Angular melted	**
Weight, grams	19.9	42.1	13.5	24.9	34.8
Loss of Ignition, %	46.0	32.3	13.5	24.9	34.8
Bitumen, %	0.0	0.1	21.1	26.2	19.5
Ash content, %	—	—	4.8	5.3	2.4
Sulfur content, %	—	—	—	5.35	5.81
Composition:					
Oil %	—	—	—	2.2	—
Resins %	—	—	—	27.7	—
Asphalenes %	—	—	—	49.4	—
Mineral matter %	100.0	99.9	78.9	73.8	80.5
Loss of ignition %	—	—	45.2	43.4	44.7
Size:					
840+ microns	—	—	10.6	3.5	10.4
590–840	—	—	8.5	11.0	10.5
250–590	—	—	13.7	20.4	18.0
149–250	—	—	7.7	9.9	9.1
74–149	—	—	5.8	9.0	7.6
43–74	—	—	14.5	30.7-	36.2-
43 minus	—	—	39.2	15.5+	8.2+
Limestone % (approx.)	105	73	81	73	82

*Sample 2 was lining of a pit or basin.

**Sample 5 was melted material in the bottom of a jar.

INDEX OF LOCI AND FINDS

Abbas Alizadeh

All areas and loci excavated during the first five seasons are recorded here and are presented with full description. In addition, some loci dug in the northeastern corner of the East Area were clarified in the seventh season and their seventh season denominations are included and shown on plate 264.

Locus numbers consist of the square designation followed by three digits, the first of which indicates the season; thus P17:301 is the first locus dug in the third season in Square P17. During the preparation of this volume, it became apparent that some loci should be canceled or their denominations corrected. The loci canceled are so indicated herein.

The long Trench V, dug during the second season before the contour map and grid were available, was divided into plots for which locus numbers have been assigned retroactively. Retroactive locus numbers have also been assigned in various other areas where they were useful. However, some smaller soundings and trenches, for the most part those dug before the grid was established, never received a standard locus number and are denoted by square plus the sounding letter or trench number (e.g., L15:Sounding A or F27:Trench XV). One sounding started as the "Gully Cut" continued to be known only by that name even after the grid was established.

The basic definition of each locus as well as any necessary descriptive details or discussion were provided, mostly, by Helene Kantor. The absolute elevations of the modern surface, and the top and bottom of the locus, are given. In some cases, particularly in the earlier seasons, the lowest point reached in a locus, for a variety of reason, might be uncertain.

The finds of each locus are listed in the *Index* according to their absolute depth, starting from top to bottom. If the object is illustrated, the plate/figure number is given. The date of the objects that are not illustrated are (if known) given.

An alphabetical/sequential list would seem the most serviceable way of organizing and presenting the various loci. This method of organization was not preferred by Kantor. Delougaz' method of excavation can be best described as "organic," therefore, Helene Kantor believed a strictly alphabetical list of loci would break up organic units, for example, interleaving the primarily Protoliterate loci in P17 and R17 in the East Area with the prehistoric loci of P22–23 in the Trench XXI area. Accordingly, various clusters of loci, made up either of those in major areas of excavation or of small test operations in the same general part of the mound, are placed in alphabetical order. For example, Terrace West side part 1 includes Squares E23–J18. Within the general area of the western side, these squares are listed alphabetically regardless of the sequential designated number of the trench in which they are located. The only deviation is a certain amount of backtracking when necessary to avoid breaking up a cluster (e.g., from "K22–L23" back to "L15–O23"). Within a cluster, the loci are in strict alphabetical order. The following key to the order in which the loci are given is provided to guide the reader to locate various loci in the *Index*.

General Area	Description	Loci
Terrace West 1	Various Small Areas	E23–J18 (Trenches VIII, X, XIV, XV; Sounding E)
Terrace West 2	"West Area"	H13–K14 (Trenches VI, IX, XVII, XVIIA)
Terrace Middle 1	"Trench XIII Area"	K22–L23 (Trench XIII Area)
Terrace Middle 2	Various Small Areas	L15–O23 (Trenches VII, XI, XVIII, XXII; Soundings A and F)
High Mound	Various Areas	M8–R11 (Trenches I–IV, XVIIB, XXIII–XXIV. XXVI–XXVIII)
Terrace East 1	"East Area"	P17–R18 (Trenches V A, XIX–XX)
Terrace East 2	Various Small Areas	O27–T22 (Trenches XII, XVI, XXV, XXXI–XXXII; Gully Cut; Soundings G and H)
Terrace East 3	Trench XXI Area	P–Q22–23 (Trench XXI)

TERRACE WEST 1

TRENCH XIV (E23)

This was originally an area of 3.00 × 4.00 m with surface sloping from 79.30 at the southeastern corner to 78.40 at the southwestern corner. At the northern edge of the original trench, eleven beveled-rim bowls and one pouring lip bowl were found in a row at 77.35. The deepest point, ca. 75.80, was reached in a very contracted spot in the original trench. The finds are primarily Protoliterate. Surface elevation: 79.30. Top of locus: 79.30. Bottom of locus: ca. 75.00. See pls. 15:C; 260.

Elevation	Field Number	Description	Plate
—	2.601	Handled jar fragment	cf. 71:B
—	3.352	Painted fragment	58:N
78.20	2.342	Four-lugged fragment	25:C
78.00–77.50	2.193	Ovoid jar fragment; see fig. 9	94:C
ca. 78.00	2.194	Reserved slip jar; see fig. 9	93:D
77.90	2.019	Ladle	82:A
76.80	II-203	Sealing (Protoliterate)	—
79.30	III-656	Spouted jar	102:J
ca. 78.80	III-657	Spouted jar	105:I

NORTHERN EXTENSION OF TRENCH XIV (E23)

This was a 3.00 × 7.00 m area toward the northeast of the second season trench. At the northern end of the extension, rain erosion during the third season revealed that just below the surface was a two-course high wall segment and adjacent to it a cluster of Protoliterate vessels.

Elevation	Field Number	Description	Plate
ca. 78.80	III-658	Swollen spouted jar; like III-247 except slightly wider neck, and no incision	cf. 107:C
ca. 78.80	III-879	Handled jar with notched lip fragment	cf. 98:G
ca. 78.70	III-662	Four-lugged fragment	115:E
ca. 78.70	III-663	Bottle	23:F
ca. 78.60	III-659	Spouted fragment	cf. 107:L
ca. 78.60	III-660	Spouted jar; see fig. 12	106:E
ca. 78.60	III-661	Twisted handle jar, similar to 5.313 except narrower neck with ledge rim and both horizontal and diagonal scoring	cf. 100:E

EAST OF TRENCH XIV (E23)

Elevation	Field Number	Description	Plate
Surface	II-104	Spouted jar; see fig. 12	102:C

TRENCH XV (F27)

An area of 2.00 × 5.00 m, the surface at the northeast was 79.00 and at the northwest ca. 82.20. A depth of 75.80 was reached in a small part of the trench. Surface elevation: 79.00. Top of locus: 79.00. Bottom of locus: 75.80. See pl. 260.

Elevation	Field Number	Description	Plate
79.00	2.326	Painted leopard legs	58:I
76.15	2.150	Bowl fragment	167:A

TRENCH X (G26–27)

This was an area ca. 2.50 × 10.00 m, with the surface sloping from 82.40 at the northeastern corner to 81.60 at the northwest. Excavated in steps: eastern section (2.50 × 3.50 m) dug to only 0.40 B.S.; middle section (1.50 × 2.50 m) dug to 2.00 B.S.; western half (2.50 × 5.25 m) dug to ca. 2.00 B.S. except for a strip along the southern side dug to 2.20 B.S. (79.60); the southwestern corner dug to ca. 3.25 B.S. (78.35), and a small pit, 0.70 m in diameter, dug to 4.00 B.S. Objects in the trench and in the access steps to the west were primarily Protoliterate. In the middle section a pig bone occurred at 80.50 (pl. 257:G). Below the lowest Protoliterate deposits at 2.00–2.20 (79.60–79.40) was the transition to Middle Susiana debris. Surface elevation northeast: 82.40. Top of locus northeast: 82.40. Bottom of locus: 77.60. See pl. 260.

Elevation	Field Number	Description	Plate
Eastern half, surface: 82.40			
82.20	II-42	Bottle stopper	130:X
82.00	II-79	Animal figurine	—
Western half, surface: 81.60			
81.10	2.321	Spouted fragment with appliqué	28:H; 108:K
81.10–80.70	II-160	Bottle stopper (Protoliterate)	—
81.10–80.70	II-161	Conical token (Protoliterate)	—
ca. 81.00	2.769	Fine ware cup fragment	80:J
ca. 81.00	2.770	Fine ware cup fragment	80:K
ca. 80.60	—	4 beveled-rim bowls (Protoliterate)	—
ca. 79.90	II-140	Animal figurine	—
79.80	2.101	Body fragment with painted masks	176:S
ca. 79.60	II-122	Bottle stopper	130:T
79.60	II-247	Domed spindle whorl	—
79.60	II-248	Grinding stone (Protoliterate)	—
79.60	II-249	Stone slab fragment (Protoliterate)	—
79.60	2.314	Stand fragment	86:KK
79.60	2.749	Four-lugged shoulder (Protoliterate)	—
79.60	2.775	Sandstone bowl fragment with chisel marks	125:A
79.60	—	9 beveled-rim bowls (Protoliterate)	—
79.50	2.764	Perforated stone roundel	125:R
79.50	—	Beveled-rim bowl (Protoliterate)	—
79.10	II-280	Stone bowl fragments	124:F
78.35	2.102	Body with painted men	163:AA
78.35	2.166	Miniature jar fragments; see fig. 31	188:G
Access steps, surface: 81.60			
ca. 81.00	II-193	Metal pin fragments (Protoliterate?)	—
ca. 81.00	II-267	Conical token (Protoliterate)	—
81.00	2.797	Terra-cotta grill-work fragment (Protoliterate)	—
80.40–79.60		25 beveled-rim bowls (Protoliterate)	—
ca. 80.35	II-514	Conical bowl (Protoliterate)	—
80.35		3 conical bowls (Protoliterate)	—
79.60	II-496	Beveled-rim bowl (Protoliterate)	—
Position uncertain			
—	II-468	Terra-cotta cone with hollowed end (Protoliterate)	—
—	2.735	Painted spindle whorl fragment	—

TRENCH VIII (H–J21)

This area, ca. 2.50 × 15.00 m, was mostly in J21. The surface slopes from 84.03 at the northeastern corner to ca. 82.80 at the northwestern corner. In the eastern part of the trench, from ca. 83.30 to 82.60, irregular lines of stones and fragmentary baked bricks marked the location of disintegrated burials of late, but uncertain date; the lowest depth in the east was ca. 82.60, while the western end was dug deeper to ca. 80.00. They contained mixed Protoliterate and Middle Susiana sherds until ca. 83.40, below which sherds were consistently Middle Susiana. Surface elevation: 84.03. Top of locus: 84.03. Bottom of locus: ca. 81.00. See pl. 260.

Elevation	Field Number	Description	Plate
84.03	II-123	Perforated stone hemisphere	125:N
84.03	2.238	Sherd scraper	30:Q

Trench VIII (H–J21) (*cont.*)

Elevation	Field Number	Description	Plate
83.93–83.63	2.304	Painted lip fragment	169:M
83.63	II-133	Painted pottery disc fragments	65:I
83.63	2.023	Four-lugged fragment	25:F
83.63	2.060	Eggshell body with painted goats	—
83.33	2.303	Bowl	169:L
82.63	2.278	Red ware jar neck; see fig. 31	193:AA
82.58	2.212	Painted shoulder fragment	191:I
82.20	2.297	Jar fragment	190:D
ca. 82.20	2.273	Jar fragment	193:B
Wash	5.297	Painted bucranium	58:C; 163:S

EAST OF TRENCH VIII (H–J21)

Elevation	Field Number	Description	Plate
83.33	2.041	Tortoise jar fragments	187:A
83.33	2.056	Painted jar fragment	188:F

WEST OF TRENCH VIII (H–J21)

Elevation	Field Number	Description	Plate
—	2.040	Tortoise spout	187:D

SOUNDING E (J18)

Sounding E was ca. 4.00 × 6.00 m, with traces of burnt walls and occupational debris immediately below the surface. The deepest point was the interior of an irregular pit in the middle of the sounding, which contained Parthian with a few Protoliterate sherds. Surface elevation: ca. 81.80. Top of locus: ca. 81.80. Bottom of locus: ca. 80.45. See pl. 260.

Elevation	Field Number	Description	Plate
ca. 81.80	2.215	Jar handle	72:D
ca. 81.80	2.216	Cooking pot fragment	71:B
ca. 81.80	2.219	Jar handle	72:C
ca. 81.80	2.220	Jar handle	72:B
ca. 81.80	2.223	Bowl rim fragment	71:N
ca. 81.80	2.224	Torpedo jar rim	72:K
ca. 81.80	2.225	Jar lip fragment	71:C
81.50	2.164	Painted base fragment	179:B

TERRACE WEST 2
"WEST AREA"

TRENCH XVII A (H13)

This trench, ca. 3.50 × 7.00 m, was dug in northern slope of the West Area to check for the edge of the polygonal platform. It was divided into two loci, H13:301 and J13:301, by a segment of narrow brick wall running parallel to the edge of the platform; top: 81.82; bottom: 81.33. At approximately the base of the wall Middle Susiana debris was found, into which the Protoliterate pit of H13:301 had been dug. The deepest point reached was the bottom of the H13:301 pit. Surface elevation: 82.31. Top of area: 82.31. Bottom of area: ca. 80.00. See pl. 265.

Elevation	Field Number	Description	Plate
Surface	3.1245	Stone celt	125:HH
82.21	—	2 beveled-rim bowls (Protoliterate)	—
81.96	—	5 beveled-rim bowls (Protoliterate)	—

TRENCH XVII A (H13:301)

This portion of Trench XVII A was to the northwest of the brick wall parallel to the polygonal platform. Middle Susiana sherds began ca. 0.70–1.00 B.S.; at 1.25 B.S. two complete Late Middle Susiana vessels were in yellowish earth near the western edge (III-35–36). The ashy debris of a Protoliterate pit extended from the cross wall to ca. 1.50 m to the east of the western edge; the approximate position is indicated on pl. 265. Beveled-rim bowl sherd count in pit: 177 rims + base; 500 rims; 100 bases; 121 bodies. Surface elevation: 82.31. Top of locus: 81.82. Bottom of locus: ca. 80.00. See pl. 265.

Elevation	Field Number	Description	Plate
81.98–81.46	—	Beveled-rim bowls (Protoliterate)	—
81.81–81.76	—	4 beveled-rim bowls (Protoliterate)	—
81.71	3.1201	Hemisphere perforated Stone	125:K
81.41	3.170	Jar base fragment	189:M
81.21	III-749	Impressed ball fragment (Protoliterate)	144:B
81.06	III-35	Footed beaker; see fig. 26	57:E; 172:H
81.06	III-36	Small jar	57:F; 190:B
81.01	3.132	Painted base fragment	58:Y, 181:E
80.61	3.167	Painted fragment	163:G
81.51–81.46	—	4 beveled-rim bowls (Protoliterate)	—
80.21	III-33	Pouring lip bowl	80:Z
Pit	III-597	Miniature beveled-rim bowl	83:J
Pit	III-665	Handled jar; B.635	cf. 100:F
Pit	3.402	Globular jar fragment; see fig. 9	90:B
—	3.1255	Rough-surfaced everted-rim jar fragment	cf. 90:I
80.92	3.571	Cone mosaic	31:V

H14:TRENCH IX

This was the original Trench IX excavated during the second season, an area ca. 4.50 × 13.00 m with surface sloping from ca. 82.20 at northern corner down to ca. 81.00 in northwestern corner. There are three main features: a kiln, H14:201; the remnant of a drain consisting of six vertical and five elapsed baked bricks above the western wall of the kiln; and a floor with a clay ridge, H14:202. There were also two small pits: a round one at the east with the bottom at ca. 80.70 and an irregular one at the west with the bottom at ca. 80.90. Surface elevation: ca. 82.20. Top of locus: ca. 82.20. Bottom of locus: 79.84. See pl. 265.

Elevation	Field Number	Description	Plate
Surface	2.028	Four-lugged jar	122:H
ca. 82.20	II-129	Pyramidal token	134:C 9
ca. 82.20	2.002	Handled bowl fragment; see fig. 8	84:W

H14:Trench IX (*cont.*)

Elevation	Field Number	Description	Plate
82.20–82.00	IV-32	Head of animal figurine (Protoliterate)	—
ca. 82.05	—	1 beveled-rim bowl (Protoliterate)	—
81.90–81.80	—	8 beveled-rim bowls (Protoliterate)	—
ca. 81.85	II-106(?)	Conical bowl and pouring lip fragment; see fig. 8	—
ca. 81.70	—	Metal pin fragment (Protoliterate)	—
81.70–81.55	—	8 beveled-rim bowls (Protoliterate)	—
ca. 81.55	II-147	Clay ball	34:I–K; 146:B; 153:D
ca. 81.25	—	4 beveled-rim bowls (Protoliterate)	—
ca. 80.70	—	1 beveled-rim bowl (Protoliterate)	—
—	II-159	Pill-shaped token	134:D 2
—	IV-267	Terra-cotta figurine	235:F
—	II-200	Perforated biconical clay object	126:S
—	2.416	Perforated stone	247:I
—	2.423	Painted base fragment	60:K

H14:TRENCH IX EAST

Elevation	Field Number	Description	Plate
82.20–81.70	II-434	Four-lugged jar; see fig. 15	114:J
ca. 81.80	II-168	Conical token	134:B 1

H14:TRENCH IX WEST

Elevation	Field Number	Description	Plate
ca. 81.90	II-96	Bale(?) sealing	42:A; 135:G
ca. 81.60	II-406	Stone celt	125:JJ
ca. 81.10	II-435	Spouted jar; see fig. 12	105:C

MIDDLE OF TRENCH IX (H14)

Elevation	Field Number	Description	Plate
ca. 80.90	2.018	Spoon	82:J
80.80–80.70	2.005	Ladle; see fig. 8	17:N; 82:F
Surface	IV-336a	Stone bead	129:X

NORTH OF TRENCH IX (H14)

Elevation	Field Number	Description	Plate
80.83	2.235	Spouted jar fragment	107:H
82.10	3.534	Horizontal twisted handle	21:F

H14–J14

A continuation and extension to the east of Trench IX excavated during the third season, an area of ca. 5.00 × 10.00 m consisting of the eastern end of the original Trench IX, i.e., the area of H14:201 and the space between it and Sounding C, i.e., H14:302, which started from the surface. It sloped from 82.40 at the northwestern corner down to ca. 81.50 at the southern edge. For the northern extension, see H14:303–04. Surface elevation: ca. 82.40. Top of locus: 82.40. Bottom of locus: 79.56. See pl. 265.

Elevation	Field Number	Description	Plate
—	3.555	Terra-cotta cone	31:T

H14:201

A kiln in the eastern section of the original Trench VI, between ca. 81.30 and 81.00, was rectangular, ca. 1.80 × 2.20 m, on a platform with square holes in the southwestern side; top: 81.27, bottom: 80.77. Just to the south of the kiln, there was ashy debris at ca. 81.00. The area was later recleared as H14:307 and 407. Surface elevation: ca. 82.20. Top of locus: 81.27. Bottom of locus: 80.77. See pl. 265.

H14:202

A low ridge of hard clay surrounded a floor at 80.00 and was semicircular in shape as preserved; diameter 2.50 m. A short segment of a baked-brick drain adjoined on the east; probably a Late Middle Susiana feature. Surface elevation: ca. 81.50. Top of locus: ca. 80.30. Bottom of locus: 80.00. See pl. 265.

H14:301

Canceled

H14:302

An ca. 5.00 × 6.00 m extension of the original Trench IX to Sounding C on the east was begun in H14, but the greater part was in J14. The surface at the northwest ca. 82.20, at northeast ca. 82.10. From the surface down the soil was hard with few sherds. A hard fill between 81.61 and 80.77 was underlain by softer ashy debris. A baked-brick drain, covered by slabs, later recleared as J14:401, was found in the east near the western edge of Sounding C. Four vessels (III-37–39; pls. 26, 88:D, 108:F) were found nearby at the border of Sounding C, cf. J15:Sounding C. Surface elevation: ca. 82.10. Top of locus: ca. 82.10. Bottom of locus: 80.20. See pl. 265.

Elevation	Field Number	Description	Plate
ca. 82.10	III-655	Polished pebble (Protoliterate)	—
ca. 81.70	III-18	Clay slingshot	—
ca. 81.10	III-256	Miniature ovoid jar	88:A
ca. 80.90	III-32	Pouring lip bowl (Protoliterate)	—
ca. 80.80	III-49	Conical token (Protoliterate)	—
ca. 80.40	III-29	Strap-handled bowl	95:B

H14:303

This area was an incompletely preserved rectangular Protoliterate room. The eastern wall continued to the south for ca. 1.30 m; top: 81.25. Surface elevation: ca. 82.20. Top of locus: 82.20. Bottom of locus: ca. 80.00. See pl. 265.

Elevation	Field Number	Description	Plate
82.20–80.80	III-9	Trough spout	85:E
80.70	III-12	Perforated stone disc	29:Z
80.70	—	3 beveled-rim bowls (Protoliterate)	—

SOUTH OF H14:303

Elevation	Field Number	Description	Plate
ca. 81.35	III-264	Miniature handled jar	95:D

H14:304

This northern extension, ca. 2.50 × 11.00 m, of the original Trench IX included the access steps excavated during the second season. The northern edge is regular, extending farther in the west than in the east. The surface sloped from ca. 82.20 in the east down to ca. 81.50 in the west. From the surface to a depth of ca. 1.50 B.S., Protoliterate debris with many beveled-rim bowls, perhaps a large pit cutting the northwestern walls of room H14:303 and H14:304 East. In the northwest near pit H14:308 were some traces of wall faces emerging from under the platform. Together with the wall traces in J15:Sounding C and to the south of J15:303, they are the highest Protoliterate walls of the West Area. Below 1.50 B.S. the sherds were primarily Middle Susiana and for the most part were found in the western part of the locus where the Protoliterate debris had been more eroded and where the deepest levels were reached. Surface elevation: ca. 82.20. Top of locus: ca. 82.20. Bottom of locus: ca. 79.70. See pl. 265.

Elevation	Field Number	Description	Plate
82.20–80.20	III-397	Pouring lip bowl	17:C
82.20–81.85	III-398	Clay animal figurine	—
82.05–81.25	—	13 beveled-rim bowls (Protoliterate)	—
ca. 81.90	III-96	Stone bowl fragment	125:C
ca. 81.80	2.767	Perforated stone roundel	125:Q
81.80–81.50	III-26	Clay animal figurine	—
81.75–81.25	—	13 beveled-rim bowls (Protoliterate)	—
81.60–81.25	III-44	Spindle whorl	30:M
81.60–81.25	III-45	Spindle whorl	65:JJ
ca. 81.35	III-747	Clay ball	34:A–B
ca. 81.30	III-30	Copper pin, 17.8 cm long	cf. 29:D
ca. 81.20	III-511	Strap-handled jar scored	cf. 95:B
ca. 81.10	III-138	Conical token (Protoliterate)	—
ca. 81.05	III-936	Clay ball fragment (Protoliterate)	—
ca. 80.90	3.184	Jar neck fragment; see fig. 31	190:F
ca. 80.40	3.169	Painted lip fragment	59:H; 176:B
ca. 80.40	3.185	Jar fragment	189:C
ca. 80.40	3.191	Painted fragment	171:C
ca. 80.40	3.754	Painted lip	178:J
ca. 80.20	III-130	Spindle whorl	65:KK
ca. 80.20	3.553	Clay animal figurine	66:G
ca. 79.70	3.208	Painted lip fragment	173:H
—	III-121	Clay animal figurine (Protoliterate)	—
—	3.183	Jar neck fragment	192:G
—	3.186	Jar rim fragment	190:Q
—	3.182	Beaker lip fragment	175:G
—	3.216	Red ware neck fragment	193:Z
—	3.217	Red ware bowl fragment	193:A
—	3.218	Red ware bowl fragment; see fig. 31	193:E

EAST OF H14:304

Incompletely preserved rectangular room adjacent to room H14:303 on the north. Top of wall: ca. 81.25.

Elevation	Field Number	Description	Plate
—	3.214	Painted lip fragment	174:D

H14:305

An irregularly shaped extension along almost the entire southern side of Trench IX, from H14:306 on the west to the Sounding C steps on the east, was mostly in H14 but extended across the northeastern corner of H15. The lowest depth was in the western part of the locus, ca. 79.80; elsewhere the bottom was 80.70 or less, particularly on the H15 side. A group of six Parthian torpedo jars (see H14:309) found just across the northern edge of H15 must be associated with the Parthian burial pit H15:407. Surface elevation: ca. 81.80. Top of locus: ca. 81.80. Bottom of locus: ca. 79.80. See pl. 265.

Elevation	Field Number	Description	Plate
ca. 81.80	III-46	Spindle whorl	30:L
81.80	III-307	Cylindrical stone bead, crosshatched	cf. 41:K
81.80–81.10	3.177	Painted body fragment (bucranium)	163:X
81.80–81.10	3.204	Miniature jar fragment	188:E
81.80–81.10	3.207	Painted lip fragment	173:J
81.80–81.10	3.212	Painted lip fragment	174:E

Elevation	Field Number	Description	Plate
ca. 81.60	3.422	Trough-spouted fragment	85:G
ca. 81.60	3.478	Stone band rim	124:AA
ca. 81.60	3.875	Hemispherical token	134:E 8
ca. 81.40	III-61	Four-lugged jar	112:F
ca. 81.40	III-91	Spindle whorl	30:J; 126:E
ca. 81.40	3.050	Tortoise jar fragment	58:K; 187:B
81.40–80.80	3.430	Jar fragment	190:P
ca. 81.35	III-188–90	Terra-cotta sickle fragments	cf. 30:T–U, W
ca. 81.35	3.1256	Bowl fragment	178:F
ca. 81.30	III-334	Strap-handled jar; see fig. 9	95:G
ca. 81.30	3.722	Retouched blade	254:E
ca. 81.05	3.725	Truncated blade	255:C
ca. 81.30	III-746	Clay ball	—
ca. 81.00	III-456	Terra-cotta pendant	129:II
ca. 80.80	III-954	Terra-cotta burnisher fragment	—

H14:305 SOUTH

Fragmentary remains of baked-brick and pipe drains at the H14–15 border were followed to the south in a narrow cut until they ended with a few disjointed baked bricks; ca. 80.90–80.40. For the branch of the H14:305 South drain system to the east, see H15:402. The floor at 79.85, dating to Late Middle Susiana, had traces of a wall and a presumed hearth. A lower Early Middle Susiana floor was reached at 80.65. For the access steps, see H14:310. Surface elevation: ca. 81.60. Top of locus: ca. 81.60. Bottom of locus: ca. 74.95. See pl. 265.

Elevation	Field Number	Description	Plate
81.40–81.00	III-107	Stone bead	129:AA
80.69	IV-2	Bale(?) sealing (Protoliterate)	—

H14:306

A stratigraphic sounding from the surface down, its surface slopes from ca. 81.60 at the southeast, with an irregularly-shaped area of ca. 3.50 × 4.00 m, reduced in the lowest 1.50 m to 1.50 × 1.70 m. An upper floor at 79.85, dated to Late Middle Susiana, had traces of a wall and a presumed hearth. A lower Early Middle Susiana floor was reached at 76.45, where mixed Early Middle Susiana-Early Susiana sherds marked the transition between the two periods. For the access steps, see H14:310.

Elevation	Field Number	Description	Plate
81.60	3.382	Jar body fragment	192:E
81.60	3.388	Painted base fragment	179:I
80.90	3.379	Jar body fragment	191:O
ca. 80.40	III-699	Terra-cotta spool	30:B
80.00–79.90	3.393	Painted lip fragment	184:E
80.00–79.90	3.823	Painted lip fragment	183:I
80.70	III-937a–b	Tablet fragments	137:A
80.65	3.194	Beaker lip fragment	174:F
80.65	3.219	Red ware hole-mouthed jar fragment	193:J
80.10	III-393	Spindle whorl	65:R
ca. 80.10	III-394	Bone awl: complete epiphysis; practically with no channel; 11.2 cm long	cf. 233:E
ca. 79.75	III-57	Gritty brown jar; see fig. 9	—
79.75	3.432	Painted body fragment	171:P
ca. 76.90	III-89	Conical notched spindle whorl (Protoliterate)	—
ca. 76.90	III-909	Bitumen bowl fragment	230:C
76.20	3.833	Beaker fragment	174:L
75.60	3.371	Tab handle	164:D
—	3.877	Conical token	134:B 6

SOUTH OF H14:306

Elevation	Field Number	Description	Plate
80.92–80.52	4.304	Bowl fragment	181:N

H14:307

H14:307 was a Protoliterate period kiln and the surrounding area that was cleaned. Surface elevation: ca. 82.20. Top of locus: ca. 81.30. Bottom of locus: ca. 80.50.

H14:308

Protoliterate pit cut into the northwestern edge of the polygonal platform, irregularly round with diameter of 3.00–3.90 m. It was filled with soft earth, ashes, and numerous Protoliterate sherds, the majority beveled-rim bowls. Surface elevation: 81.90. Top of locus: 81.90. Bottom of locus: 80.72. See pl. 265.

Elevation	Field Number	Description	Plate
81.90–80.72	III-687	Convex body sherd into perforated disc	30:X
80.72	III-688	Terra-cotta sickle fragment (Protoliterate)	—
80.72	III-689	Beveled-rim bowl; diameter 21.0 cm; height 9.8 cm (Protoliterate)	—
80.72	III-690	Beveled-rim bowl (Protoliterate)	83:Q
81.00	III-937	Tablet fragment, with numerals (Protoliterate)	—
81.00	III-938	Hut amulet	31:AA

H14:309

A group of six Parthian torpedo jars, ca. 40.0 cm B.S., were found in H14:305, just across the northern edge of H15 and are to be associated with Parthian burial pit H15:407. One jar was almost horizontal, diameter of rim 15.5 cm; height 1.10 m; three vertical with rims up; one vertical with mouth down and another jar inside. Surface elevation: ca. 81.50. Top of locus: ca. 81.10. Bottom of locus: ca. 80.00. See pl. 265.

H14:310

This locus consisted of the north-south extension of the access steps to the stratigraphic sounding H14:306. The uppermost debris contained many fragments of beveled-rim bowls and other vessels. Surface elevation: ca. 80.50. Top of locus: ca. 80.50. Bottom of locus: ca. 76.15. See pl. 265.

Elevation	Field Number	Description	Plate
80.50–79.85	III-795	Door sealing fragment (Protoliterate)	—
80.50–79.85	III-796	Clay ball fragment (Protoliterate)	—
80.50–79.85	III-798a–c	Clay ball fragment (Protoliterate)	—
80.50–79.85	III-799a	Clay ball fragment (Protoliterate)	—
80.50–79.80	III-742	Clay ball (Protoliterate)	154:A
80.50–79.80	III-743	Clay ball (Protoliterate)	—
80.50–79.80	III-744	Clay ball (Protoliterate)	—
80.50–79.75	III-797a–e	Clay ball (Protoliterate)	38:F–G; 137:D; 138:B; 149:F
—	3.368	Tab handle	163:DD
—	3.1080	Metal pin	128:D

H14:401

This area straddled the midpoint of the H14–15 boundary, with portions of a Protoliterate pipe drain. At the northeast one pipe was at 81:08; at the southeast, extending into H15, were three pipes at 81.01. Although the drain sloped down slightly to the southeast, the flow must have been to the northwest because of the way the three pipes were fitted together. The sherds were Protoliterate with some intrusive Middle Susiana. Surface elevation: 81.41. Top of locus: 81.41. Bottom of locus: 80.50. See pl. 265.

Elevation	Field Number	Description	Plate
81.40–81.00	IV-17	Incised bead	234:Q
81.40–81.00	4.041	Footed bowl fragment	183:K

Elevation	Field Number	Description	Plate
81.40–80.66	IV-100	Bone needle	128:V
81.40–80.66	IV-410	Strap-handled bowl	84:U
81.21–80.96	IV-40	Pouring lip bowl	80:BB
80.71–80.51	IV-12	Pyramidal token	134:C 4
80.66	IV-398	Clay ball fragment (Protoliterate)	—
80.66–80.56	4.333	Pouring lip fragment	cf. 80:AA

SOUTHWEST OF H14:401

Elevation	Field Number	Description	Plate
81.40	4.740	Flat base fragment	163:J
81.40	IV-22	Stone pendant	129:HH

H14:402

This area of ca. 2.50 × 3.00 m was in the southwestern corner of H14 just to the northwest of H14:401 and H15:401. At the edge of the locus was a northwest-southeast segment, top at 80.56 and bottom at 80.40, associated with a hard clay surface ca. 30.0 cm thick, in the top of which the outlines of scattered, fallen mudbrick were visible. The upper debris and probably wall stub are Protoliterate, with Middle Susiana sherds from 80.26 down. Surface elevation: 81.41. Top of locus: 81.41. Bottom of locus: 80.03. See pl. 265.

Elevation	Field Number	Description	Plate
81.26–80.03	4.722	Bowl base fragment	180:H
80.26–80.21	IV-155	Deep bowl; see fig. 30	60:AA; 182:E
80.26–80.16	4.912a–b	Jar body fragments	59:HH
81.72	4.861	Bowl fragments	193:C

H14:403

This locus continued Protoliterate pit H14:308 and included the area around the northwestern corner of the polygonal platform. A drain pipe was found below the baked-brick drain excavated during the third season. Top of drain: 81.17; floor under drain: 80.55. The bottom of pit H14:308 was cleared to the floor at 80.61. There were many Middle Susiana sherds from ca. 80.60 down. Surface elevation: 81.72. Top of locus: 81.72. Bottom of locus: ca. 80.05. See pl. 265.

Elevation	Field Number	Description	Plate
80.05	IV-102	Spatula-like bone implement	128:X
—	IV-18	Stone stud	234:R

H14:404

This area consisted of the northwestern section of the long baked-brick drain extending northwest-southeast alongside the polygonal platform. The drain was only fragmentarily preserved. For its southern continuation, see J14:304 and J15:303. Surface elevation: ca. 82.20. Top of locus: 81.37. Bottom of locus: ca. 80.57. See pl. 265.

SOUTH OF H14:404

Elevation	Field Number	Description	Plate
81.37–79.87	4.794	Tray fragment	86:CC
80.85–80.70	IV-109	Spouted fragment	cf. 104:L
—	4.807	Spindle whorl	65:HH

H14:405

This locus was defined by a mass of whole and fragmentary mudbricks irregularly laid to the north of baked-brick drain H14:404 and its continuation in J14. The material represents the eroded southern edge of the polygonal platform, no traces of which occurred to the south of the brick drain. Surface elevation: ca. 82.20. Top of locus: 81.45. Bottom of locus: 80.57. See pl. 265.

H14:406

This was a small area in H14:305 with traces of very poorly built north-south walls founded on rubbish (stairs) that were possibly the western and eastern walls of a small room. Top of eastern wall: 81.38; bricks 6.0 × 11.0 × 25.0 cm. Surface elevation: ca. 82.00. Top of locus: 81.38. Bottom of locus: 79.84. See pl. 265.

Elevation	Field Number	Description	Plate
82.00–81.30	4.756	Painted lip fragment	59:EE; 176:E
—	4.204	Painted lip fragment	171:G

H14:407

This area of kiln H14:201 (Protoliterate), in the eastern end of the original Trench IX (= western part of H14:302) was cleared of the material remaining from excavations during the third season and the area was deepened. At 80.88 an ash layer began. Surface elevation: ca. 82.20. Top of locus: 81.46. Bottom of locus: ca. 80.17. See pl. 265.

H14:408

This was an area in H14:201 and also under its eastern edge. A segment of wall was preserved only by a few courses of brick, 7.0 × 15.0 × 30.0 cm, with one end in J14; top, measured at the southeast: 80.72; bottom, measured at northwest: 80.46. Below was soft, ashy debris ca. 25.0–40.0 cm thick; cf. the ashes nearby in H14:407 at 80.88 and to the south of H14:201 at ca. 81.00. Surface elevation: ca. 82.20. Top of locus: ca. 80.40. Bottom of locus: ca. 79.80. See pl. 265.

H15:401

This roughly rectangular area of ca. 2.5–4.0 cm was adjacent to H14:401 on the south. Beginning at 80.69, ashy debris with many intact beveled-rim bowls and other Protoliterate pottery were found, and just to the west of the ashy debris (at 80.00) was a hard surface with scattered bricks and some Late Middle Susiana sherds. At 79.93 the ashy debris was limited to a regular circular pit, ca. 2.00 m in diameter. Surface elevation: 81.41. Top of locus: 81.41. Bottom of locus: 79.09.

Elevation	Field Number	Description	Plate
80.66–80.51	IV-34	Clay animal figurine	—
80.66–80.46	IV-387	Stone bowl fragment	cf. 124:E
80.66–80.21	IV-6	Door sealing	32:D; 45:M
80.66–80.21	IV-46	Strap-handled jar (Protoliterate)	—
80.60–80.21	IV-60	Strap-handled jar fragment with notched band	cf. 95:H
80.60–80.21	IV-114	Spouted jar	23:B
80.60–80.21	IV-123	Deep bowl	182:C
80.60–80.21	IV-124	Deep bowl	182:G
80.60–80.21	4.068	Globular jar fragment, plain surface	cf. 92:B
80.60–80.21	4.095	Ca. 1/2 of bowl; see fig. 30	177:C
80.60–80.21	4.098	Spouted jar fragment	cf. 105:G
80.60–80.21	4.102	Twisted-handle jar fragment (Protoliterate)	—
80.60–80.21	4.110	Spouted jar fragment	cf. 105:G
80.60–80.21	4.150	Four-lugged fragment (Protoliterate)	—
80.60–80.21	4.167	Spouted jar fragment	cf. 105:A
80.60–80.21	4.195	Spouted jar fragment, plain surface	cf. 107:C
80.60–79.09	4.577	Painted lip fragment	59:AA
80.51	IV-54	Four-lugged vessel; see fig. 15	121:C
80.50–80.40	IV-88	Trough-spouted carinated bowl fragment	85:D

NORTHEAST OF H15:401

This locus was on the western side of the northern end of the drain.

Elevation	Field Number	Description	Plate
80.35	IV-1	Terra-cotta bull's head pendant	67:M

H15:402

This locus is a segment of the Protoliterate baked-brick drain immediately to the east of the southern end of the H14:305 South drain and was probably part of the same system; it was ca. 5.00 m long with the eastern end at H15:403. The western part of the H15:402 drain was disarticulated; the eastern part consisted of a continuous course of baked bricks laid as headers. Top of drain: 80.92. Just to the north of part of the eastern section is a rectangular patch of sherd paving at 80.46, continuing under the drain. The H15:403 diagonal line of vertical baked bricks and the pebble layers of H14:403 South and H15:404 probably belong to the same drainage system. North of H15:402 proper and just to the east of the northern part of H14:305 South are disarticulated baked bricks with tops varying from 81.41 to 81.33. Surface elevation: 81.41. Top of locus: 80.92. Bottom of locus: ca. 80.46. See pl. 265.

Elevation	Field Number	Description	Plate
80.91	IV-439	Terra-cotta sickle fragment	cf. 30:T–U, W
80.56–80.16	IV-61	Ladle	17:M; 82:G
80.41–80.31	IV-204	Metal pin	29:C
80.16	4.1071	Base fragment with potter's mark	204:8
—	IV-58	Strap-handled jar	—

H15:403

This is an irregularly shaped area between H15:402 and J15:402, with layers varying in character in the north and south, but in both spots resting on ashes. The layers in the south can be associated with the drainage system of H15:402 and are somewhat higher than those in the north.

Elevation	Field Number	Description	Plate
—	4.875	Grinding stone	239:B

SOUTH OF H15:403

This locus is immediately adjacent to the eastern end of the H15:402 drain (top, 80.92), with a patch of large pebbles at 81.09. At 80.98 is a lower layer of smaller pebbles ca. 3.0 cm in diameter. Since this layer extended to the southeast of H15:403 proper, where its top was at 81.00, it received its own locus number, H15:404. The small pebble layer was ca. 20.0 cm thick and rested on ashes, with the top at ca. 80.80, surrounding kiln H15:405. Protoliterate and a few Middle Susiana sherds occurred among the pebbles. The pebble layers and the H15:402 drain seem to belong to a later phase of occupation than the industrial layers just to the north.

NORTH OF H15:403

From 80.85 (north) to 80.56 (south) was a sloping red clay floor, 15.0 cm thick at the northern end. At 80.82 a black circular patch was embedded in the red floor, H15:409, the floor of a kiln surrounded by fire-reddened clay and resting on ashes. The highest point of the ashes below the red earth layer (80.70) corresponds well with the top elevations of ashes associated with other kilns in the West Area, ca. 81.00 at the southern side of H14:201; 80.88 in H14:407; 80.46 in H14:408; ca. 80.80 around H15:405. There was apparently a concentration of kilns in the southern part of the West Area. Surface elevation: 81.43. Top of locus: 81.43. Bottom of locus: 80.75. See pl. 265.

H15:404

An irregularly preserved layer, ca. 20.0 cm thick, of small pebbles, ca. 3.0 cm in diameter, was located in H15:403 South, top at 80.98, and immediately to the southeast over kiln of H15:405, top at 81.00. It was presumably a part of the drainage area of H15:402. There were Protoliterate and a few painted Middle Susiana sherds mixed with the pebbles. Below H15:404 was the ashy earth and kiln of H15:405. Surface elevation: 81.43. Top of locus: 81.00. Bottom of locus: ca. 80.75. See pl. 265.

H15:405

This round Protoliterate kiln and associated ashy layer were located at the southern edge of excavation near the H15-J15 border, beneath the H15:404 Protoliterate pebble pavement. It was built of mudbricks 25.0 × 11.0 × 6.0 cm, diameter 1.60 m. The kiln was built upon a plastered floor at 80.29, which extends toward and under the J15:402 bin. Surface elevation: 81.43. Top of locus: ca. 80.75. Bottom of locus: 80.29. See pl. 265.

Elevation	Field Number	Description	Plate
—	IV-280	Flattish sealing (Protoliterate)	—
—	IV-284	Clay ball fragment (Protoliterate)	—

H15:406

A Protoliterate pit, ca. 1.00 m in diameter, located slightly to the west of the southern end of drain H14:305 South. It was filled with an ashy deposit; its greenish-gray tinge and the green stain on some of the sherds indicate the presence of organic wastes. Surface elevation: 81.41. Top of locus: 80.17. Bottom of locus: 79.13. See pl. 265.

H15:407

Parthian burial pit (Grave 4.31) with two partly disarticulated adult skeletons and a child's skull settled into the Protoliterate debris of H15:408. No clear outlines of the pit were detectable, but the positions of Protoliterate vessels established its diameter as ca. 3.00 m. The northwestern skeleton was oriented approximately north-south with legs in a hole and had only one vessel at its head (IV-68). All other vessels were clustered on either side of the head of the second skeleton, oriented approximately southeast-northwest, while its leg bones were gathered on the chest, with the child's skull adjacent. The skeletons and pottery were at 80.19. Surface elevation: 81.62. Top of locus: 81.62. Bottom of locus: 79.77. See pls. 2:C; 265.

Elevation	Field Number	Description	Plate
80.19	IV-68	Glazed handled jar	70:B
80.19	IV-69	Glazed pilgrim flask	70:E
80.19	IV-70	Glazed pitcher	4:B; 70:D
80.19	IV-71	Glazed bowl	4:A; 70:G
80.19	IV-72	Glazed bowl	cf. 70:G
80.19	IV-73	Eggshell bowl	70:F
80.19	IV-74	Eggshell bowl	70:L
80.19	IV-75	Pitcher	71:I
80.19	IV-76	Bronze tool; square sectioned with two sides beveled forming wide cutting edge; length 4.2 cm	—
80.19	IV-77	Bronze pin with pinched and curved top; length 4.2 cm	—
80.19	IV-78	Fragment of tanged iron blade with rivet	—
80.19	IV-79	Fragment of iron blade; bronze rivet at beginning of missing tang; length 10.3 cm	—

H15:408

An irregular area of Protoliterate occupational debris located in the northeastern corner of H15 below H14:305 East and J15:401 West. It contained intrusive Parthian burial pit H15:407 and Protoliterate shallow rectangular pit H15:410 but no structural features and much Protoliterate pottery; see J15:401 West for those examples found at somewhat higher levels. Surface elevation: 81.62. Top of locus: 81.62. Bottom of locus: 79.78. See pl. 265.

Elevation	Field Number	Description	Plate
80.40–80.20	4.989	Gray ware band-rim fragment	—
80.40–80.20	4.126	Jar fragment	cf. 91:K
80.40–80.18	IV-368	Ladle	cf. 82:D
80.40–80.18	IV-414	Spouted jar	cf. 109:H
80.40–80.18	4.067	Jar fragment	cf. 91:K
80 40–79.78	IV-99	Spouted jar (Protoliterate)	—
80.40–79.78	4.048	1/3 vessel	85:HH
80.40–79.78	4.736	Painted base fragment	180:D
80.40–79.78	4.790	Ca. 1/2 bowl; see fig. 8	84:Y
80.40–79.78	—	Beveled-rim bowls (Protoliterate): 7 complete, 34 rims and base, 399 rims, 50 bases, 96 bodies	—
80.28–79.83	IV-225	Jar, spout missing	cf. 105:C

Elevation	Field Number	Description	Plate
80.28–79.83	IV-369	Strap-handled jar	cf. 96:B
80.28–79.83	IV-370	Spouted jar	22:K
80.28–79.83	IV-412	Spouted jar; see fig. 12	cf. 105:C
80.28–79.83	IV-413	Spouted jar (Protoliterate)	—
80.28–79.83	4.109	Spouted jar fragment (Protoliterate)	—
80.28–79.83	4.120	Ca. 1/2 twisted handle jar (Protoliterate)	—
80.28–79.83	4.144	Ca. 1/2 strap-handled jar; see fig. 9	98:D
80.28–79.83	4.166	Upper half spouted jar (Protoliterate)	—
80.20	IV-93	Spouted jar	cf. 103:C
80.18	IV-116	Trough-spouted bowl; see fig. 9	18:E; 85:J
80.18	IV-237	Terra-cotta potter's(?) disc	127:G
80.18	IV-438	Terra-cotta sickle fragment	cf. 30:T–U, W
80.08–79.78	IV-371	Spouted jar; see fig. 12	cf. 105:C
—	IV-285	1/2 clay ball	43:H–I; 140:B

NORTH OF H15:408

Elevation	Field Number	Description	Plate
—	4.023	Funnel	85:GG

H15:409

This circular fire-blackened plastered area ca. 1.35 m in diameter was the floor of a kiln embedded in the red clay pavement of H15:403 North. A rough crucible and slag fragments were found in the area. Surface elevation: 81.62. Top of locus: 80.82. Bottom of locus: 80.82. See pl. 265.

H15:410

A shallow rectangular Protoliterate pit located in the northeastern projection of H15:408 with ashy debris. Surface elevation ca. 81.62. Top of locus: 80.20. Bottom of locus: 79.87. See pl. 265.

Elevation	Field Number	Description	Plate
80.20–80.02	IV-91	Ladle	82:E
80.20	4.762	Cylindrical bowl; see fig. 9	85:U

J13:NORTHERN SLOPE

A narrow, shallow trench dug to trace the outline of the Protoliterate polygonal platform. It began as an extension of the northeastern corner of Trench XVII A and followed the irregular edge of the polygonal platform into J14 and K14, cf. Northern Slope at K14:Trench VI. The surface sloped from 82.13 at the northeastern corner of Trench XVII A, where the top of the platform was at the surface, to 81.20 at the northeastern corner of the platform in J13; see pl. 224 for various elevations. The greatest depth reached was 0.90–1.00; this was the depth of the Protoliterate-prehistoric transition. Stray Susiana sherds occurred at higher levels. The narrow space on the southern side of the eastern extension of the Trench XVII A cross wall had one feature, the curved outline of a kiln or hearth projecting from under the platform at 81.23; at the same level nearby was a cluster of Protoliterate pottery. The lowest depth reached was 0.90–1.00 B.S. Two north-south wall stubs preserved only to a slight height projected to the north from the platform. Top of western stub 81.44. Beveled-rim bowls were scattered between the two stubs. The surface reference point for this part of the Northern Slope is 81.94. The northeastern corner of the platform was found a short distance to the east of the northeastern stub wall and the Northern Slope "trench" continued to the south as a shallow excavation tracing the eastern side of the platform. An eastern stub wall was found in J14. Farther to the south two buttresses projected into K14, cf. K14:Trench VI. The surface reference point for this part of the Northern Slope was 81.20. Surface elevation: 82.13. Top of locus: 82.13. Bottom of locus: ca. 81.00. See pl. 265.

Elevation	Field Number	Description	Plate
—	3.490	Sherd with appliqué bust of woman	5:E
82.13	III-243	Spouted fragment	105:G

J13:Northern Slope (*cont.*)

Elevation	Field Number	Description	Plate
81.53	3.040	Pottery ring	81:W
81.53	3.387	Painted lip fragment	176:K
81.48	3.267	Painted lip fragment	163:U
ca. 81.25	3.021	Ca. 1/3 bowl; see fig. 26	163:M
81.23	3.398	Concave neck fragment	190:E
—	3.209	Painted lip fragment	175:E
81.78	III-65	Spouted jar; see fig. 13	109:F
81.53	—	1 beveled-rim bowl (Protoliterate)	—
81.23	—	4 beveled-rim bowls (Protoliterate)	—
81.23	III-67	Spoon; see fig. 8	17:O; 82:K
81.23	III-282	Spouted jar; see fig. 13	108:G
81.84–81.74	—	4 beveled-rim bowls (Protoliterate)	—
81.54–81.34	—	6 beveled-rim bowls (Protoliterate)	—
80.25	III-97	Clay animal figurine	cf. 31:N
80.25	III-98	Elongated terra-cotta bead	67:J; 234:T
80.25	III-99	Cylindrical terra-cotta bead	129:H
81.20	III-750	Sealing (Protoliterate)	157:F
81.20–81.00	3.290	Beveled-rim bowl (Protoliterate)	83:L
81.20	—	2 beveled-rim bowls (Protoliterate)	—

J13:301

The section of Trench XVII A was located to the southeast of the brick wall parallel to the edge of the polygonal platform and consisted mostly of the hard fill of the platform; along the southern side of the cross wall was Protoliterate and Middle Susiana debris as in H13:301 on the other side of the wall. The deepest point was approximately the same as the base of the wall. Surface elevation: 82.31. Top of locus: 82.31. Bottom of locus: ca. 81.30. See pl. 265.

Elevation	Field Number	Description	Plate
82.31–81.41	3.812	Spike	127:A
82.21	—	Beveled-rim bowl (Protoliterate)	—
81.86	III-748a–b	Sealings (Protoliterate)	—

TRENCH XVII (J14)

A test trench, ca. 4.50 × 6.00 m, in the middle of the polygonal platform. From the surface down, there was only hard soil with few sherds or finds, but on the western side were two Parthian vessels above a rough bowl. The top of the bricky fill of the platform was at 81.63. The excavation was discontinued at ca. 0.80 B.S. except on the eastern side, which became J14:301 North. Surface elevation: 82.13. Top of locus: 82.13. Bottom of locus: ca. 81.35. See pls. 2:D; 265.

Elevation	Field Number	Description	Plate
82.13	III-27	Pitcher	71:F
82.13	III-28	Stone pendant	129:GG
81.83	III-66	Handmade rough pottery bowl	—
81.83	—	Lower body of a torpedo jar (Parthian)	—
—	3.389	Red ware hole-mouthed rim fragment	193:M

J14:301

The eastern side of Trench XVII was excavated in two parts, north and east, the latter outside the limits of the original trench. Surface elevation: 81.85. Top of locus: 81.85. Bottom of locus: 74.65. See pl. 265.

J14:301 NORTH

This locus is the eastern edge of Trench XVII. An intrusive Parthian torpedo jar appeared in the northern edge of excavations at 80.75–80.25 and was deeper below the surface than any other torpedo jar in the West Area. The sherds of eggshell bowl at ca. 80.55 can be associated with it. Excavation discontinued at 78.12.

Elevation	Field Number	Description	Plate
81.85	III-16	Unperforated roundel cut from band-rim stone bowl (Protoliterate)	—
80.75–80.25	—	Torpedo jar (Parthian)	—
80.55	III-58	Eggshell bowl fragment	cf. 70:F
80.55	III-59	Clay slingshot	65:L

J14:301 EAST

This narrow stratigraphic sounding, extending to the east from the southeastern corner of Trench XVII, was excavated from the surface to virgin soil. Top of polygonal platform: 81.63; bottom of bricky packing of platform and top of dark brown earth with Middle Susiana sherds: 80.47; top of Early Middle Susiana debris: 77.10; apparent transition to Early Susiana: 76.15; Early Susiana sherds in light brown earth with sterile soil shortly below: 75.20; bottom of locus: 74.65.

Elevation	Field Number	Description	Plate
79.90	3.385	Painted lip fragment	174:I
78.15	3.375	Ladle handle	164:B
77.55	3.1221	Sherd rubber	231:CC
77.10	III-68	Narrow-tanged hoe	cf. 245:U–X
77.10	3.187	Jar neck fragment	191:D
77.10	3.196	Painted lip fragment	184:N
77.10	3.197	Painted body fragment; see fig. 30	178:H
77.10	3.251	Painted body fragment; see fig. 30	177:I
77.10	3.431	Bowl fragment	168:M

J14:302

A Parthian pit was dug into Protoliterate debris near the southeastern corner of the polygonal platform just to the east of J14:303 and to the north of western end of drain J15:303. It was presumably a burial, but there were no traces of a skeleton. Surface elevation: ca. 81.90. Top of locus: ca. 81.90. Bottom of locus: ca. 80.50. See pls. 2:A; 265.

Elevation	Field Number	Description	Plate
80.07	III-950	Glazed jar	4:C; 71:G

J14:303

Area with two north-south pipe drains at southeastern edge of polygonal platform. The eastern drain consisted of four pipes sloping down to the northwestern end of J15:303, the best preserved fragment of the long northwest-southeast Protoliterate baked-brick drain; top: 81 91, bottom: 80.95. The western drain preserved only two pipes, top: 81.91, bottom: 81.54. Surface elevation: 81.91. Top of locus: 81.91. Bottom of locus: 80.95. See pl. 265.

J14:304

An area along the southwestern side of the polygonal platform located just to the northwest of J14:303 and straddled the H14–J14 boundary with baked bricks laid on edge, the fragmentary northwestern continuation of the drain J15:303. For the equally fragmentary northwestern end of the drain, see H14:404. Bottom of drain in J14:304: 80.79. In the same alignment as the bricks of the drain, but at a higher elevation, were three courses of baked bricks laid flat as stretchers except for some headers forming a corner at the southeastern end. Their sizes varied from 7.0 × 20.0 × 42.0 to 7.0 × 21.0 × 43.5 cm; top 81.46, bottom 81.25. Surface elevation: 82.00. Top of locus: 82.00. Bottom of locus: 80.79. See pl. 265.

J14:305

A narrow trench between Trench VI and Sounding C was continued. The trench was begun during the second season as the southwestern extension to Trench VI but left incomplete (cf. Trench VI Southwestern Extension). The surface varied from 81.64 at the southwestern corner to 81.10 in the northwestern corner. The southeastern end and middle part of the trench were dug from the surface down to ca. 81.30, and elsewhere from the depths reached during the second season. The southeastern end was widened slightly to trace the edge of the polygonal platform; see also J14:403 and J14:404. The drain slopes down to the north toward the long drain, J14:304 + J15:303; at the juncture was a group of rocks. Preserved top of drain at southern end 80.80, at northern end 80.54. Impressed ball fragments III-745a–b were found directly to the east of drain at ca. 80.60. Surface elevation: 81.54. Top of locus: ca. 81.30. Bottom of locus: ca. 80.00. See pl. 265.

Elevation	Field Number	Description	Plate
80.60	III-745a–b	Impressed ball fragment	38:A–B; 40:A; 147:F

J14:401

A Protoliterate baked-brick drain was partially cleaned during the third season as part of the eastern extension of Trench IX, H14:302. J14:401 extends north-south, with its southern end in J15, just to the west of Sounding C. There were bricks standing on edge with others fallen on either side. The top was covered with stone slabs. Surface elevation: ca. 81.80. Top of locus: 80.80. Bottom of locus: ca. 80.60. See pl. 265.

Elevation	Field Number	Description	Plate
81.20–81.05	—	Base sherd with whirligig pattern	—

J14:402

This segment of a Protoliterate drain was oriented northwest-southeast and was completely in J15, consisting of three pipes, 30.0 cm in diameter. The westernmost pipe extends under the southern end of the baked-brick drain, J14:401, to which this pipe drain might have been related. The easternmost pipe was excavated during the third season as part of J15:306, top at 80.70 and bottom at 79.98. Surface elevation: ca. 81.50. Top of locus: 80.70. Bottom of locus: ca. 79.90. See pl. 265.

J14:403

This area, the southwestern end of trench J14:305 plus the small strip between it and drain H14:404, was separated from J14:404 on the northeast by remnants of brickwork (cf. J14:409). The locus seems to consist of the debris of a pit, the upper part of which had been eroded. Three complete vessels were found almost at the surface. Adjacent to the platform beveled-rim bowl sherds, bottle stoppers, and clay ball fragments (IV-399 + two unimpressed fragments) occurred between 0.30–1.00 B.S. (81.24–80.54) in the debris around a cluster of four semi-complete bottles, still fairly vertical as if they had been stacked together. Their bases rested on hard soil at 1.20 B.S. Also part of this group was the body of a bag-shaped jar, 4.429, a form without parallel in the Protoliterate corpus at Chogha Mish and possibly a Parthian intrusion. The hard surface below the pit debris was very uneven, going down to 1.50 B.S. (the deepest point in the locus) on the northeast, and varying from only 1.10–1.20 on the southwest. It remains uncertain whether this stub should be associated with the hard earth at the bottom of the locus and considered as a projecting part of the platform cut away by a pit. Surface elevation: 81.54. Top of locus: 81.54. Bottom of locus: 80.04. See pl. 265.

Elevation	Field Number	Description	Plate
81.54–81.34	—	7 beveled-rim bowls (Protoliterate)	—
81.54	—	Flower pot (Protoliterate)	—
81.34	IV-380	1 mosaic cone, 6.6 cm, red paint	—
81.54–80.74	IV-337b	Polygonal stone bead (Protoliterate)	—
81.54–80.09	IV-337c	Elongated polygonal stone bead	129:N
81.49	IV-81	Flower pot	83:EE
81.49	IV-82	Spouted jar	108:D
81.24–80.74	IV-399	Clay ball fragment	45:R–S; 154:E
80.84–80.34	4.429	Jar fragment	72:G
80.84–80.34	4.431	Bottle body (Protoliterate)	—
80.84	4.432	Bottle body (Protoliterate)	—
80.84–80.34	4.433	Bottle body + rim (Protoliterate)	—

Elevation	Field Number	Description	Plate
80.84–80.34	—	Bottle body (Protoliterate)	—
80.84	—	Beveled-rim bowl fragment (Protoliterate)	—
80.74–80.59	4.159	Ovoid jar fragment	91:H
80.74–80.44	IV-320	Rectangular perforated clay object	126:U
80.74–80.24	4.119	Strap-handled jar fragment	—

J14:403 SOUTHWEST

At the southwestern edge of the locus alongside H14:404, between 0.16 and 0.60 B.S. (81.38–80.94), was a concentration of pottery, including beveled-rim bowls, two flower pots, several bottle fragments, and a spouted vessel fragment. See pl. 265.

Elevation	Field Number	Description	Plate
81.38	IV-214	Flower pot; see fig. 8	83:CC
81.38–80.94	—	11 beveled-rim bowls (Protoliterate)	—

J14:404

This locus originally consisted of the middle part of trench J14:305 and of adjacent areas on the east and on the west, alongside the platform. It was eventually extended to the north next to J14:405 and to the south into the northeastern corner of Square J15. The top of the locus varies from the modern surface in the areas bordering J14:305 to the lowest depths reached in J14:305. The surface sloped down from 81.54 to 81.34 in J14:404 South. The locus proper was a Protoliterate pit cut into brickwork represented by the stubs, surviving as high as 0.40 and 0.70 B.S., at the southwestern edge next to J14:403 and by another stub jutting to the east at an obtuse angle and preserved to 0.30 B.S. This brickwork was traced for at least thirteen courses down to the hard bricky surfaces of the uneven bottom of the pit (1.50 and 1.95 B.S.). Along the pit's eastern edge a ridge of brickwork was preserved to 1.00 B.S. It was not feasible to follow the brickwork to its base, the level of which remains unknown. The pit contained beveled-rim bowls and other pottery normal for Protoliterate debris. Near its eastern edge vessels lay in the ashy earth at ca. 0.40–0.70 B.S. On the southwestern side four beveled-rim bowls rested on the hard bottom, at 1.95 B.S. Surface elevation: ca. 81.54. Top of locus: ca. 81.54. Bottom of locus: ca. 79.45. See pls. 2:F; 265.

Elevation	Field Number	Description	Plate
81.34	IV-223	Spouted jar fragment	—
81.14–80.84	—	4 beveled-rim bowls (Protoliterate)	—
81.04	—	Bottle body fragment	—
81.04–80.84	4.428	Jar fragment (Protoliterate)	94:G
81.04	—	3 beveled-rim bowls (Protoliterate)	—
80.54	—	1 beveled-rim bowl (Protoliterate)	—
80.40–80.05	4.927	Blade core (Protoliterate)	253:D
80.34–80.19	IV-339e	Terra-cotta oval bead	—
80.20–80.05	4.914	Blade core	255:Y
79.59	—	4 beveled-rim bowls (Protoliterate)	—

J14:404 SOUTH

An extension into the northeastern corner of Square J15 revealed that the larger brick stub of J14:404 continued to the south and that the stubs were remnants of a mass of brickwork, probably at least 3.00 m wide, in great part destroyed by two pits in J14:404 South respectively. The eastern part of the second pit remained unexcavated; its curved outline cutting into the brickwork was distinguished on the southeast; on the north it had a relatively straight edge cut into brickwork. At its northwestern corner it seems to have been continuous with the pit of J14:404. The J14:404 South pit extended from the surface, here ca. 81.20, down to a depth of 1.35 m. The lowest 50.0 cm of debris had a great concentration of pottery. The small stub of brickwork abutting the platform at the J14:403–04 line and the brickwork to the south probably formed part of a projection analogous to the buttresses to the north, but wider. The brickwork on the northern side of the J14:404 South pit might have also originally extended to the platform where traces of brick were observed at a point directly opposite it. Here, too, the projection might have been double, as in the north. The brickwork on both the northern and southern sides of J14:404 South was not followed deeper than the bottom of the pit. A Parthian burial, Grave 4.30 at 0.60 B.S., had been dug into the Protoliterate pit. Alongside and slightly below a torpedo jar, the extended (1.75 m long) skeleton of a woman lying on her back was oriented northeast-southwest. A child's skeleton with bent legs lay at the right shoulder of the woman with its skull overlapping hers. Both skeletons were crushed and incomplete. See pl. 2:F.

Elevation	Field Number	Description	Plate
81.54–80.19	4.047	Spouted jar fragment (Protoliterate)	—
81.54–80.14	IV-338d	Cylindrical stone bead (Protoliterate)	—
81.54–79.94	4.191	Strap-handle + pouring lip fragment	21:B
81.04–80.19	IV-340d	Cylindrical unbaked clay bead (Protoliterate)	—
80.54–80.24	4.190	Scrabbled bowl; see fig. 9	86:F
80.44	IV-274	Beveled-rim bowl (Protoliterate)	—
80.19	4.169	Spouted jar fragment (Protoliterate)	—
80.19	IV-335g	Green stone disc (Protoliterate)	—
80.19	IV-207	Bone pin	128:T
80.19	4.915	Flint core	255:Z
80.19	4.062	Handled jar fragment Fine point scoring (Protoliterate)	—
80.19	4.085	Strap + horizontal handled fragment (Protoliterate)	—
80.19	4.141	Strap-handled jar fragment; see fig. 9	98:M
80.19	4.173	Spouted jar fragment (Protoliterate)	—
80.19–80.04	4.292	Bottle fragment	111:I
80.19–80.04	4.293	Spouted jar	103:H
80.14	4.924	Blade core	253:C
80.04	4.032	Strap-handled + pouring lip fragment (Protoliterate)	—
81.24–81.04	—	Torpedo jar	—
80.84	IV-205	Small metal pin	—
80.84	IV-206	Tip of metal pin	—

J14:404 SOUTHWEST

A narrow area was dug to trace the northern face of the J14:404 South projection.

Elevation	Field Number	Description	Plate
81.09	IV-200	Metal adze	29:A
81.04	—	4 beveled-rim bowls (Protoliterate)	—

J14:404 NORTH

Between the northwestern end of J14:404 proper and J14:405 West and East were two ledges where excavation ended during the third season. They were cut down from 0.55–1.95 and 1.40–1.95 B.S. respectively and consisted of bricky material without finds. Surface elevation: ca. 81.60. Top of locus: ca. 81.05. Bottom of locus: ca. 79.65.

J14:405

An area located between the southeastern buttress of the polygonal platform and J14:404 North. Most of the locus is in K14. A mudbrick wall, apparently remaining only about one course high above the floor at ca. 80.54, divided the locus into western and eastern parts, the latter was crossed by the baked-brick drain K14:401. The three courses of mudbricks distinguished on the northern side of the locus and the four courses on the western side, at ca. 80.85–80.55, appear to have been part of the buttress and platform rather than separate walls. The eastern and southern sides of J14:405 East were formed by mudbrick detritus. Four courses of bricks were traced on the southwestern edge of J14:405 West and had once continued to the east, to judge by a small fragment on the southwestern corner of the cross wall. No southern face was articulated and these bricks might not have been part of the hard, bricky material of J14:404 North. Behind the fragmentarily preserved eastern part of this brickwork and in the same orientation was a partly preserved line of baked bricks with top at ca. 81.10. At the best preserved point three bricks, 6.0 × 20.0 × 42.0 cm, were set on edge in three courses. Fragmentary bricks continued the line to the southeast until they reached a 7.0 × 18.0 × 40.0 cm baked brick laid flat on the top of the southern end (K14:401). This line of baked bricks might have been part of the drain installation. The floor of J14:405 West had a beveled-rim bowl in the northwestern corner and a jumble of several vitrified bricks, pottery slag, stones, and hard clay in the middle. Surface elevation: ca. 81.60. Top of locus: ca. 81.10. Bottom of locus: ca. 80.55. See pl. 265.

Elevation	Field Number	Description	Plate
ca. 80.55	—	1 beveled-rim bowl (Protoliterate)	—

SOUNDING C (J14–15)

Area of ca. 4.00 × 6.00 m with northwestern corner in J14. It was excavated during the second season with some additional work done in the third and fourth seasons. The corner walls are badly disintegrated, and only the western and southern faces were articulated, overlying lower corner walls completely different in orientation, with tops at 80.70 and 80.40, and with lane J15:304 on the east. At the southwestern edge are the drain pipes of J14:402. In the northeastern corner are drain pipes belonging to the J14:304 + J15:303 drainage system. Surface elevation: ca. 81.80. Top of locus: ca. 81.80. Bottom of locus: ca. 80.00. See pl. 265.

Elevation	Field Number	Description	Plate
81.80	2.773	Stone bowl fragment	125:B
81.20	2.020	Ovoid jar fragment	92:G
81.20	2.021	Spouted jar fragment	109:E
81.20	2.030	Lid fragment	80:I
ca. 81.00	2.236	Four-lugged jar fragment	112:G
—	III-31	Spouted jar; see fig. 12	105:H
—	3.406	Spouted jar fragment (Protoliterate)	108:L
—	II-379	Clay ball (Protoliterate)	34:F–G; 135:J; 142:B; 144:D; 146:C

SOUNDING C NORTHWESTERN CORNER (J14–15)

Elevation	Field Number	Description	Plate
ca. 81.50	II-295	Spouted jar	22:J; 106:C

SOUNDING C NORTHWESTERN EDGE (J14–15)

Elevation	Field Number	Description	Plate
ca. 81.50	III-37	Strap-handled jar	—
ca. 81.50	III-38	Ovoid jar	88:D
ca. 81.50	III-39	Spouted jar with appliqué	26; 108:F

SOUNDING C NORTHEAST AND EAST (J14–15)

Elevation	Field Number	Description	Plate
ca. 80.90	—	Metal pin fragment (Protoliterate)	—
ca. 80.90	3.1029	Clay jar stopper	130:I
ca. 80.80	3.559	Terra-cotta cone	31:U

SOUNDING C SOUTH (J14–15)

Elevation	Field Number	Description	Plate
ca. 81.50	3.291	Beveled-rim bowl	83:S
ca. 81.00	II-89	Spouted jar	109:C
ca. 81.00	II-90	Spouted jar; see fig. 13	22:I; 109:A
ca. 80.50	II-97	Clay Ball	37:A–D; 135:A–F; 137:C; 141:A
ca. 80.30	3.1028	Jar stopper	130:F
ca. 80.20	III-696	Four-lugged jar	24:D
—	2.766	Perforated stone roundel(?)	125:W
—	3.1086	Metal pin fragment	128:H

SOUNDING C SOUTH CORNER (J14–15)

Elevation	Field Number	Description	Plate
ca. 81.30	3.1012	Spindle whorl	126:F
—	II-384	Lid	80:F

SOUNDING C SOUTH NEAR DRAIN (J14–15)

Elevation	Field Number	Description	Plate
ca. 80.20	II-390	Spherical token	134:A 1
ca. 80.20	II-388	Small bowl; see fig. 8	80:B
ca. 80.00	II-407	Grooved stone mace-head	29:I

SOUNDING C SOUTHWEST (J14–15)

Elevation	Field Number	Description	Plate
—	II-385	Pill-shaped token	134:D 5

SOUNDING C SOUTHWESTERN EDGE (J14–15)

Elevation	Field Number	Description	Plate
ca. 81.10	II-40	Biconical spindle whorl	cf. 232:B
ca. 81.10	II-41	Spindle whorl	cf. 126:C
ca. 80.90	III-42	Terra-cotta sickle	30:U

J15:301

This locus was a Parthian kiln. The diameter of the firing chamber was 1.90 m with plastered walls. There was an intact floor at 80.17 with fourteen semicircular holes spaced around the circumference and five circular holes scattered in the middle; diameter of holes ca. 7.0–10.0 cm. Below the kiln floor a furnace chamber was filled with soft ash, some of which was removed through one of the holes to reach the floor at 79.67. The exterior of the kiln was not excavated. Surface elevation: 81.35. Top of locus: 81.35. Bottom of locus: 79.67. See pl. 265.

Elevation	Field Number	Description	Plate
81.35–80.17	3.305	Jar neck fragment	72:E
81.35	3.306	Bowl rim fragment	71:J
81.35	3.307	Bowl rim fragment	70:J
81.35	3.308	Bowl rim fragment	71:K
81.35	3.309	Bowl rim fragment	71:M
81.35	3.310	Bowl rim fragment	71:L
81.35	3.311	Glazed bowl fragment	70:K
81.35	3.312	Bowl rim fragment	70:H
81.35	3.331	Jar body fragment	72:H
81.35	3.332	Torpedo jar fragment	72:L
81.35	3.333	Torpedo jar fragment	72:I

SOUTHEAST OF J15:301

Small cut with segment of a mudbrick wall; base at 79.67.

J15:302

A shallow circular pit, from the surface down ca. 2.00 m in diameter, located directly to the north of J15:301 kiln (Parthian). Surface elevation: 81.36. Top of locus: 81.36. Bottom of locus: 80.70. See pl. 265.

J15:303

This is the southeastern segment, and best preserved one, of the long baked-brick drain in H14 (H14:404) and J14–15. The sides originally consisted of three courses, the two upper sides much destroyed and mostly made up of broken bricks laid both as headers and stretchers; the lowest course on each side was more regular, consisting of bricks ranging from 7.0 × 20.0 × 42.0 cm to one outsize example of $7.0 \times 21.0 \times 44.0$ cm. The interior measurement was taken at a point where all three courses remained; channel width at base: 28.0 cm; at top: 38.0 cm (top courses set back 5.0 cm); height: 26.0 cm; eastern end, top: 79.87, base: 79.54; western end, top: 80.21, base: 79.81. Surface elevation: ca. 81.60. Top of locus: ca. 81.60. Bottom of locus: ca. 79.50. See pl. 265.

J15:304

This locus was an open area, presumably a street, between two roughly parallel Protoliterate walls. For the most part it was equivalent to the eastern side of Sounding C dug to various depths during the second season. Western wall, top 80.44; eastern wall, base 80.06. Surface elevation: ca. 81.80. Top of locus: ca. 80.50. Bottom of locus: ca. 80.00. See pl. 265.

J15:305

This small area, ca. 0.90×1.40 m, located to the southeast of Sounding C and most of the area between it and the southeastern corner of Sounding G were bordered on the north and south by east-west walls a little below the surface and aligned with and, for the most part, directly above the lower walls of J15:404; the fragmentary remains presumably represent two building phases of one structure. The lower part of J15:305, with its numerous finds, is the eastern end of room J15:404. Surface elevation: 81.36. Top of locus: 81.36. Bottom of locus: ca. 79.40. See pl. 265.

Elevation	Field Number	Description	Plate
80.36	III-84	Pebble hoe	cf. 245:Q–S
80.36	III-127	Pouring lip bowl	80:Y
80.11	III-136	Conical token (Protoliterate)	—
80.11	III-137	Pill-shaped token (Protoliterate)	—
80.11	III-373	Perforated disc	29:S
79.76	3.426	Bowl fragment	85:Q
79.66	III-123	Beveled-rim bowl (Protoliterate)	—
79.66	III-360	Perforated discoidal stone; diameter 7.8–8.0 cm	cf. 247:I
79.66	III-361	Terra-cotta sickle	cf. 30:T–U, W
79.66	3.1045	Disc token; terra-cotta; diameter 3.5 cm	cf. 134:E 3
79.66	3.1237	Pouring lip fragment	cf. 80:Z–EE
79.66	3.1238	Pouring lip fragment (Protoliterate)	—
79.66	3.1239	Pouring lip fragment (Protoliterate)	—
79.36	III-124a–f	Beveled-rim bowls (Protoliterate)	—

WEST OF J15:305

Between the southeastern corner of Sounding C and J15:305.

Elevation	Field Number	Description	Plate
80.96–80.26	3.743	Four-lugged fragments of gray ware (Protoliterate)	—
80.86–80.06	3.039	Four-lugged fragment	122:A
80.76	III-120	Pouring lip bowl (Protoliterate)	—
80.36	III 127	Pouring lip bowl (Protoliterate)	—
80.46	III-147	Carinated bowl + crescent appliqué (Protoliterate)	—
80.46	III-148	Spouted jar	22:G; 109:B
80.46	III-149	Miniature four-lugged vessel	113:B
—	III-374	Stone roundel	—
80.31	III-266	Small four-lugged jar	113:A
—	III-146	Spouted jar	104:E
—	3.720	Dihedral burin	255:W

J15:306

A small area located at the southeastern corner of Trench IX; also the immediately adjacent western edge of Sounding C. Immediately below the surface, disc bases and bodies of three torpedo jars were placed vertically, 81.49–80.81, with a fourth lying diagonally. Just to the northwest of the torpedo jars at a depth of ca. 80.40 were traces of a skull and long bones and several Parthian objects attributable to a burial. Along the southern side of the locus was a brick wall, top at 80.70 and bottom at 79.89, joining the wall on the western side of lane J15:304. Just to the north of the torpedo jars was the easternmost drain pipe of J14:402, top at 80.70

and bottom at 79.98. To the north of this pipe the immediately adjacent space had several baked bricks lying side-by-side with a jumble of objects; several beveled-rim bowls, three grinding stones, and the top of a terra-cotta hut symbol. Surface elevation: ca. 81.50. Top of locus: ca. 81.50. Bottom of locus: 79.89. See pl. 265.

Elevation	Field Number	Description	Plate
80.50	III-884	Glazed jar	70:C
ca. 80.50	III-883	Glazed jar	cf. 70:B
ca. 80.40	III-632	Glazed jar	70:A
ca. 80.40	III-633	Iron lance head	4:D
80.60–80.40	—	3 grinding stones (Protoliterate)	—
ca. 80.00	III-700	Top of terra-cotta hut symbol	31:Q

J15:307

An area located to the east of lane J15:304, to the south of drain J15:303(?), and to the north of kiln J15:301 and Protoliterate room J15.305, surface at 81.36 except somewhat higher to the north. It was excavated only to ca. 0.50 B.S. and contained Parthian pit J15:302, with bottom at 80.70, and another pit cutting the eastern wall of J15:304. It also includes the faces of some fragmentary walls, which together with the wall traces in H14:304 and in J15:Sounding C are the highest Protoliterate walls of the West Area. Surface elevation: 81.36. Top of locus: 81.36. Bottom of locus: ca. 80.90. See pl. 265.

J15:307 EAST

Small, shallow cut without features just to the east of J15:302.

J15:401

A southern extension of the West Area located in the northeast of H15 and to the northwest of J15, from surface down to ca. 1.00 B.S. It was a slightly pelted shaped area of ca. 4.00 × 13.00 m. The western section was above the eastern part of H15:402 and the southeastern part of H15:408; the middle part was above H15:403, H15:405, and J15:402; the eastern part was above the western portion of J15:403. The surface slopes from ca. 81.62 at the southwest to 81.43 at the southeast. There were no significant features and the sherds were primarily Protoliterate with a few Parthian examples. Surface elevation: 81.62. Top of locus: 81.62. Bottom of locus: ca. 80.62. See pl. 265.

Elevation	Field Number	Description	Plate
81.32–81.17	IV-33	Clay animal figurine	cf. 31:M
81.21–81.02	4.800	Spindle whorl	30:K; 126:L
80.87–80.77	4.799	Sherd scraper	30:R
80.87–80.77	4.817a–b	Four-lugged sherds	25:H
81.02–80.87	IV-334d	White stone bead (Protoliterate)	—
81.02	IV-337d	Stone bead	129:I

EAST OF J15:401

Elevation	Field Number	Description	Plate
80.68–80.58	4.818a	Four-lugged body	25:E

J15:401 WEST

Ca. 1.50 m of Protoliterate debris that continued deeper as H15:408.

Elevation	Field Number	Description	Plate
81.37–81.17	IV-50	Stamp seal	41:N
81.17–81.02	IV-98	Small ovoid jar	88:H
81.07	IV-59	Small ovoid jar; see fig. 9	88:R

J15:402

An area below the middle of J15:401 and straddling the H15/J15 border, it extends to H15:403 on the west and north to H15:405 on the south. The central feature is a rectangular bin-like structure outlined by an irregular course of unbaked bricks, 6.0 × 12.0 × 25.0 cm, and containing ashy debris, three beveled-rim bowls, and a clay ball fragment. Top of brick at the northeastern corner: 80.76, base: 80.62; interior dug to depth of 79.83. Projecting from the northwestern corner of the "bin" a short segment of three course high brickwork stepped, perhaps accidentally, toward the northern end of unclear character; preserved top at 81.08. Abutting this brickwork on the south was a small patch of well-constructed floor consisting of a ca. 10.0 cm thick layer of hard clay, top at 80.48, resting on a layer of beveled-rim bowls and ledge-rimmed vat sherds. Abutting the northeastern corner of the "bin" but not bonded to it was a wall, top ca. 81.05 and bottom ca. 79.92, continuing the line of the western wall of J15:304 and bordered on the east by a hard floor surface varying irregularly from 80.30 to 80.24. This is the same floor as that found at 80.29 near the "bin" and H15:405 and which also presumably underlay the clay and sherd floor described above. Surface elevation: 81.43. Top of locus: 80.78. Bottom of locus: 79.83. See pl. 265.

Elevation	Field Number	Description	Plate
80.78	IV-16	Incised stone bead	129:D
80.78	IV-107	Spouted jar	103:E
80.78–80.58	4.1129	Spindle whorl	232:BB
80.70–80.22	4.063	Miniature four-lugged jar	112:D
80.68	IV-9	Clay ball fragment (Protoliterate)	—
80.68	IV-10a–b	Clay ball fragments (Protoliterate)	—
80.68–80.38	4.050	Spouted jar; see fig. 13	108:P
80.53	IV-286	1/2 clay ball (Protoliterate)	—

EAST OF J15:402

Elevation	Field Number	Description	Plate
80.58–80.48	4.093	Jar fragment	75:C
80.53–80.33	4.058	Glazed flask fragment	cf. 70:C

J15:403

This locus was initially a small area of the J15:402 "bin" that appears to be the southern continuation of lane J15:304; scattered fallen bricks began at 80.79 and rested on a hard surface at 80.30, part of the same floor was traced at slightly varying levels in J15:402 and H14:405. Later the locus was expanded to the north to include the entire eastern section of the extension on the southern side of the western area excavated during the fourth season. The locus was bordered on the north by J15:305 and J15:404. The southern part of the lane was delimited by the western face of a wall extending for ca. 10.50 m to the north from the southern edge of the western area near the western access steps; the eastern face of the wall was not preserved; top of wall: 80.55, bottom: 79.55. The orientation of the new wall appeared to be slightly different from that of the eastern wall of J15:304, based at 80.06, and probably represented a late rebuilding of the eastern side of the lane. In the center of the locus was a small test pit starting at 80.08 that had what seemed to be bricks in the top 40.0 cm of its western profile. The test pit was carried to 78.98, the lowest point reached in the locus. Surface elevation: 81.43. Top of locus: 81.08. Bottom of locus: 78.98. See pl. 265.

Elevation	Field Number	Description	Plate
80.73–80.38	4.1032	Base fragment	203:16
80.68–80.58	4.196	Spouted jar fragment	—
80.58–80.18	4.815	Four-lugged incised body fragment	25:O
80.58–80.18	4.057	Handled jar fragment	cf. 72:A
80.58	4.348	Bowl sherd	74:F
80.33–80.18	IV-30	Legs of terra-cotta female figurine	cf. 5:M
80.33–80.03	4.622	Bowl sherds	70:M
80.23	IV-152	Four-lugged jar	cf. 113:C
79.98–79.03	4.748	Jar rim fragment; see fig. 31	190:R
79.98–79.03	4.1034	Base with potter's mark	203:13
79.68	IV-203	Metal pin; rolled head, length 15.4 cm	128:Q

SOUTHEAST OF J15:403

In the eastern part of the locus, in hard earth at 79.98, were several depressions: one large at the southern edge of the excavation and five smaller, ca. 20 cm deep, in an irregular north-south line. Removal of the hard material alongside the small holes revealed underlying ashy earth with, at 79.68, a patch of hard earth forming an irregular and shallow channel with its southeastern end surrounded by a patch of brick-like material. Pin, IV-203 (J15:403), was embedded in the western side of the channel. No slag or other evidence that suggests the function of the channel was recovered.

Elevation	Field Number	Description	Plate
80 43–80.03	IV-94	Spouted jar	cf. 102:J
80.07	IV-390	Small clay ball (Protoliterate)	135:K
79.88	IV-388a–b	Clay ball fragments (Protoliterate)	—

ACCESS STEPS OF J15:403

Elevation	Field Number	Description	Plate
81.23	IV-67	Glazed jar (Parthian?)	—

STAIRS ON EAST OF J15:403

Stairs on the east with complete Parthian vessels.

Elevation	Field Number	Description	Plate
81.03	IV-65	Funnel	70:O
80.90	IV-66	Glazed jar (Parthian?)	—

J15:404

A small rectangular room (Protoliterate) ca. 1.80 × 2.50 m on interior. The eastern end was excavated during the third season (J15:305). The southern wall aligned with and was underneath the higher wall excavated during the third season (West of J15:305). The exterior faces of walls were not articulated. Western wall, top: 80.32; southern wall, top: 80.36; eastern wall, top: 80.21; floor: 79.21. Surface elevation: 81.43. Top of locus: 80.32. Bottom of locus: 79.21. See pl. 265.

Elevation	Field Number	Description	Plate
79.64–79.43	—	13 beveled-rim bowls (Protoliterate)	—

TRENCH VI (K14)

This locus was laid out during the second season as a 3.50 × 10.00 m test trench in the northeastern slope of the West Area, with the surface sloping from 81.10 at the southwestern corner and 81.07 at the southeastern corner to 79.08 at the northeastern corner; it was gradually enlarged in small increments during the second season and later seasons to ca. 6.00 × 13.00 m. Most of the trench proper was excavated during the second season. During the third season only minor irregularities in the trench were dug and most effort was concentrated between its northern edge and the platform buttresses. A narrow extension on the south was begun during the second season and continued briefly in the fourth, being carried down to 1.25 B.S. (79.85) immediately adjacent to the eastern edge of Trench VI and to the steps of 0.40 and 0.15 B.S. beyond. In the northwest was a round bitumen-plastered floor, K14:201, at 79.57. The lowest part of the Protoliterate occupation in the middle and north of Trench VI appears to be a floor at 78.97. During the fourth season the southern end was carried down to 2.25 B.S. (78.85), where there appears to have been a pit. The Trench VI debris was full of Protoliterate sherds, among which flower pots (Protoliterate Family XXIV) were more common than in standard groups. The greatest depth, 2.65 m below the surface point 79.80, was reached in a narrow area at the northern end of Trench VI, where Middle Susiana sherds already appeared ca. 1.00 B.S. Surface elevation: ca. 81.10. Top of locus: ca. 81.10. Bottom of locus: ca. 77.15. See pl. 265.

Elevation	Field Number	Description	Plate
ca. 81.10	2.464	Rim to base bowl fragment	170:A
81.10–78.85	4.100	Vessel fragment	71:D

Elevation	Field Number	Description	Plate
ca. 80.70	II-465	Terra-cotta cone mosaic	31:KK
80.70–80.45	II-154	Gray conglomerate rubbing stone	125:KK
80.70–80.45	2.011	Horizontal-handled jar fragment	101:E
ca. 80.10	2.774	Gray stone tray fragment	125:D
—	II-202	Clay ball	34:C–D; 142:E
—	2.430(?)	Spouted fragment; see fig. 12	—
—	III-48	Spindle whorl	65:MM

TRENCH VI SOUTH (K14)

Elevation	Field Number	Description	Plate
ca. 80.90	II-297	Spouted jar	—
ca. 80.60	3.552	Animal figurine	31:M
ca. 80.20	2.520	Strap-handled fragment	98:A
ca. 80.10	2.504	Four-lugged incised fragment	123:B

TRENCH VI SOUTHEAST (K14)

Elevation	Field Number	Description	Plate
ca. 81.10	II-162	Stone bead	129:J
ca. 80.65	3.338	Jar fragment	71:H

TRENCH VI EAST (K14)

Elevation	Field Number	Description	Plate
ca. 80.70	II-403	Miniature bricks	30:S
ca. 80.70	3.1068	Perforated biconical clay object	126:R

ABOUT TWELVE METERS EAST OF TRENCH VI (K14)

Elevation	Field Number	Description	Plate
—	II-35	Stone bowl fragment	124:DD

TRENCH VI SOUTHWESTERN EXTENSION (K14)

Into J14 alongside polygonal platform.

Elevation	Field Number	Description	Plate
ca. 80.80	II-91	Spouted jar	105:B
ca. 79.65	2.498	Conical cup fragment	81:E

TRENCH VI MIDDLE (K14)

Elevation	Field Number	Description	Plate
ca. 80.80	2.419	Four-lugged fragment	24:B
ca. 79.75	2.032	Bowl fragment; see fig. 9	85:O
ca. 79.10	II-399	Conical token	134:B 7

TRENCH VI NORTHWEST (K14)

Elevation	Field Number	Description	Plate
81.10–80.70	2.025	Four-lugged incised fragment	122:G
ca. 80.70	II-37	Sheep figurine	66:K

TRENCH VI NORTH (K14)

Surface reference point 79.80.

Elevation	Field Number	Description	Plate
ca. 78.90	II-380	Stamp seal impression	67:B
ca. 78.90	II-381	Spindle whorl	65:X
ca. 78.80	II-144	Crude bowl	163:L
—	II-409	Spindle whorl	65:EE

NORTHERN SLOPE AT TRENCH VI (K14)

This locus was an area between the platform buttresses and northern edge of Trench VI. There was a shallow clearance of surface material in order to trace the outline of the polygonal platform. The greatest depth was reached at 0.50 B.S., above J14:404 North. On the western side near the platform buttresses were two parallel segments of brickwork of uncertain character close to the surface. Slightly to the south of the southwestern corner of Trench VI were four drain pipes oriented approximately north-south at a depth of ca. 80.10, about 0.50 m lower than the nearby drain (K14:401).

Elevation	Field Number	Description	Plate
ca. 80.85	3.501	Sherd with appliqué decoration	28:I
ca. 80.85	3.508	Sherd with appliqué decoration (Protoliterate)	28:K
ca. 80.30	3.1018	Bone pin (Protoliterate)	128:U
—	3.410	Fine ware cup (Protoliterate)	80:N

K14:201

A round, bitumen-plastered floor (Protoliterate) at 79.57 in the northwestern part of Trench VI; its diameters ranged from 1.96 to 2.10 m. Surface elevation: ca. 80.20. Top of locus: 79.57. Bottom of locus: ca. 79.57. See pl. 265.

K14:301

This locus (Protoliterate), two parallel pairs of baked bricks with a slot between them, was presumably a toilet and was located immediately at the surface, just above the vertical baked bricks of the northern end of drain K14:401, but with different orientation so that it remained uncertain whether the two belonged to the same installation. Surface elevation: ca. 81.20. Top of locus: ca. 81.20. Bottom of locus: ca. 81.10. See pl. 265.

K14:302

This irregularly rectangular area adjoined the southeastern corner of Trench VI and contained Protoliterate debris in which two Parthian torpedo jars, 0.45 B.S., were found. Slightly below to the east of them a row of three beveled-rim bowls at 0.20 B.S. No traces of burials were found near the torpedo jars. Surface elevation: 81.11. Top of locus: 81.11. Bottom of locus: 80.50. See pls. 2:B; 265.

Elevation	Field Number	Description	Plate
80.91	—	3 beveled-rim bowls (Protoliterate)	—
80.66	—	2 torpedo jars (Parthian)	—

K14:401

This locus, a drain extending to the southeast from a point below the "toilet" (K14:301) across J14:405 East, had a foundation of parallel rows of baked bricks, 7.0 × 18.0 × 40.0 cm, set on edge; above them was a sherd floor bordered by incomplete baked bricks laid horizontally to the line of the drain and flanked on the sides by horizontally laid brick fragments. The entire drain was presumably originally covered by horizontal baked bricks. In line with the horizontal bricks at the southern end of K14:401 and presumably connected with it are the baked bricks laid on edge against the southern side at ca. 81.10; the base of foundation bricks was at ca. 80.65. K14:401 must have belonged to a later phase of the Protoliterate period than J14:405. Surface elevation: ca. 81.30. Top of locus: ca. 81.10. Bottom of locus: ca. 80.65. See pl. 265

K14:402

This was an irregularly rectangular area of ca. 5.00 × 6.00 m just to the south of J14:405 East and K14:401. The surface sloped from ca. 81.30 down to ca. 81.00 near Trench VI. It included the area of K14:302; the eastern part of the locus was dug from the surface down. A corner of rather disintegrated brick walls was at ca. 80.45; northwest-southeast segment had bricks of 9.0 × 13.0 × 20.0 cm. Protoliterate debris was mixed with intrusive late pottery, here consisting apparently of Achaemenid types although in the West Area the late pottery is usually unmistakably Parthian. Surface elevation: ca. 81.30. Top of locus: ca. 81.30. Bottom of locus: ca. 79.80. See pl. 265.

Elevation	Field Number	Description	Plate
81.10–80.90	4.656	Bowl fragment	73:L
81.00–80.00	4.042	Bowl fragments	73:M
80.60–80.00	4.396	Jar fragments	75:A
ca. 80.60	4.655	Bowl fragment	74:H
ca. 80.60	4.632	Trefoil spout (Achaemenid)	—
80.60–80.00	4.694	Handled jar fragment	75:CC
80.50	IV-197	Metal pin	29:F; 128:I

SOUTHWEST OF K14:402

Elevation	Field Number	Description	Plate
ca. 80.70	—	Beveled-rim bowl (Protoliterate)	—

TERRACE MIDDLE 1
"TRENCH XIII AREA"
K–L22–23

Elevation	Field Number	Description	Plate
3.60 B.S.	2.792	Painted body fragment	183:S
—	4.031	Bowl lip and body fragments	182:H
—	5.002	Bowl fragment	74:C

K22:201

This small rectangular terrace, ca. 2.80 × 4.00 m, had access steps on the east and occupational debris with Parthian and Proto-literate sherds near the surface; below were more substantial remains. The western part of the trench was dug to ca. 82.00; the eastern part to ca. 77.00. Surface elevation: 83.60. Top of locus: 83.60. Bottom of locus: ca. 77.40. See pls. 47; 269.

Elevation	Field Number	Description	Plate
83.60–83.10	2.167	Painted base	179:C
83.00	2.315	Jar rim	72:F
82.75	2.710	Trefoil spout	cf. 75:H, K
81.60	2.151	Painted base fragment	168:F
81.10	2.422	Tortoise body	59:II
80.80	II-128	Spindle whorl	65:FF
80.00	2.210	Painted bowl fragment; see fig. 26	169:P
79.60	2.165	Body fragment	58:F; 176:R
78.80	2.139	Painted lip fragment	62:Y; 201:H
78.60	2.242	Painted lip fragment; see fig. 30	178:E
78.60	2.413	Concave base	201:E
78.30	2.411	Concave base	201:C
78.30	2.412	Concave base fragment	201:K
78.00	2.013	Bowl fragment	196:I
Wash	4.822	Painted base fragment	59:V
Wash	4.936	Painted lip fragment	59:M
Wash	4.1222	Sherd rubber	231:II
—	4.372	Painted ring base	180:C
—	4.843	Painted base plate	58:R
—	4.945	Painted body fragment	58:G
—	4.565	Painted lip fragment	175:B

K22:400

This northwestern section of the enlarged Trench XIII was disturbed by a late cemetery: Graves 4.14 (82.84); 4.17 (82.65); 4.21 (northwestern part; 82.74); 4.23 (82.35); 4.29 (82.45). Highest feature, at 82.84, was a kiln floor, ca. 0.75 m in diameter, of mudbrick with two layers of bitumen-like plaster, burnt and partly baked. There were two wall segments of Level I: Wall 1, four courses of bricks, 7.0 × 17.0 × 28.0 cm, top 82.85, bottom 82.20; Wall 2, bricks 7.0 × 17.0 × 28.0 cm, top 82.80, bottom 82.32. In the Wall 1 area, there was ca. 45.0 cm of earth without sherds, 82.20–81.86; below, ashy debris, 81.86–81.64. Slightly to the south of Wall 2 was the burnt clay floor of a hearth or small kiln at 82.15, corresponding to the L22:403 kilns, that is, Level II. Adjacent on the south is the stump of a Level III wall, top 81.96, bottom 81.60. The Protoliterate, Middle Susiana, Late periods were represented. Surface elevation: 83.59. Top of locus: 83.59. Bottom of locus: ca. 81.60. See pl. 269.

Elevation	Field Number	Description	Plate
83.59–82.24	4.312	Painted fragment; see fig. 30	183:G
83.59–82.09	4.038	Unpainted bowl	182:D

Elevation	Field Number	Description	Plate
83.44–83.29	4.296	Bowl fragment	74:E
83.39–83.29	4.276	Crater fragments	184:R
83.14–82.72	4.199	Bowl fragment	169:A
82.84–82.74	4.108	Painted body fragment	62:J
82.74–82.54	4.230	Painted bowl fragments	179:A
82.74	4.235	Painted bowl fragments	174:H
82.54	4.549	Jar body fragment	191:M
82.54	4.1130	Spindle whorl	232:DD
82.64–82.54	4.929	Retouched blade	254:K
82.64–82.54	IV-406	Footed bowl	172:F
82.54	4.202	Jar fragments	189:G
82.54	4.238	Painted goats	58:T; 163:O
82.54–82.44	4.279	Painted bowl fragments	181:O
82.44	4.441	Unpainted jar fragment	191:B
82.45–82.35	4.581	Painted double birds	58:D
82.34	4.865	Stone hoe	245:S
82.29–82.09	IV-334b	Stone bead	234:Y
82.29–82.09	4.250	Bowl fragment; see fig. 26	169:G
82.29–82.09	4.845	Painted base	60:F
82.29–82.09	4.955	Base + angle potter's mark	203:15
82.25–82.05	4.275	Painted fragment; see fig. 30	178:D
81.98	IV-334f	Stone bead	234:Z
81.84	IV-353	Elongated terra-cotta stud	234:S
81.64–81.24	4.1127	Spindle whorl	232:Z
81.34–81.09	4.1217	Perforated terra-cotta roundel	cf. 231:X

K22:401

Large irregular patch of ashy debris on both sides of the K22–L22 boundary and above K22:402 and L22:404. Below the debris was fallen mudbrick material at 82.42. Surface elevation: 83.59. Top of locus: 83.15. Bottom of locus: 82.42.

Elevation	Field Number	Description	Plate
82.74–82.64	4.808	Spindle whorl	65:BB; 232:M
82.54–82.44	4.215	Oval bowl + tray fragment	164:M
82.51	4.868	Stone hoe	246:F

K22:402

This pit (Middle Susiana) had ashy debris below the northern part of K22:401 and was delimited from it by an irregular layer of fallen brick material at 82.42. At the northwestern edge was a corner of brick walls, top at 82.41, that was left in place until the fifth season. Sherds with a range of depth from 82.54 to 82.24, which overlapped K22:401–02, are included under K22:402. The area was continued as K22:501. Surface elevation: 83.59. Top of locus: 82.42. Bottom of locus: 81.08. See pl. 269.

Elevation	Field Number	Description	Plate
82.54–82.24	4.278	Painted lip fragment	57:I
82.54	4.036	Ca. 1/3 unpainted bowl	165:C
82.34–82.14	4.228	Painted body	171:D
82.34–82.14	4.234	Painted bowl fragment; see fig. 26	—
82.34–81.74	4.539	Crude bowl fragment	163:A
82.34–81.74	4.540	Unpainted bowl fragment; see fig. 26	163:E
82.34–81.74	4.541	Unpainted body fragment	163:B
82.34–81.74	IV-334a	Stone bead	234:X
82.34–81.74	IV-407	Painted bowl; see fig. 26	171:T
81.74	IV-408	Painted basin; see fig. 30	183:F
82.34–81.74	4.223	Crater fragments	184:Q

ABOVE K22:402

Elevation	Field Number	Description	Plate
81.98	5.785	Painted body fragment	62:U

WEST OF K22:402

Elevation	Field Number	Description	Plate
82.39–82.09	4.847	Painted bowl base fragment	58:E

K22:403

This room (Early Middle Susiana) had two bins in the southwestern corner; western wall, top: 81.43; southern wall, top: 81.44. Bins, northern wall, top: 81.10; western bin, bottom: 80.94; eastern bin, bottom: 80.83. Floor: 80.72. Surface elevation: 83.59. Top of locus: 81.44. Bottom of locus: 80.70. See pls. 47; 48:A; 269.

Elevation	Field Number	Description	Plate
81.19–80.99	4.358	Painted base fragment	60:I
81.19–80.99	4.395	Vestigial flange with potter's mark	60:T; 182:K; 204:3
81.19–80.99	4.1216	Perforated roundel	231:X

EAST OF K22:403

Elevation	Field Number	Description	Plate
82.06–81.70	4.322	Painted base fragment	168:D

NORTH OF K22:403

Elevation	Field Number	Description	Plate
ca. 80.20	4.381	Painted lip fragment	174:K

K22:404

This small area (Early Middle Susiana) below the northern end of room K22:403 was delimited by a wall of K22:403 and slightly to the south by a lower, differently oriented east-west wall, top 80.72. Surface elevation: 83.59. Top of locus: 80.70. Bottom of locus: ca. 80.20. See pls. 47 (middle foreground); 48:A.

NORTHWEST OF K22:403

Elevation	Field Number	Description	Plate
ca. 80.20	4.281	Jar neck fragment	191:C

WEST OF K22:403

Kiln in K22:407 (Early Middle Susiana) located to the west of K22:403 (under northwestern part of K23:400). Part of flat top and all of arched opening preserved. Exterior diameter 1.06 × 1.10 m. Hard burnt floor slopes slightly downward to the west from the opening. Surface elevation: 83.59. Top of locus: 81.35. Bottom of locus: ca. 80.50. See pls. 48:A–B; 269.

K22:406

Primarily an Early Middle Susiana room to the east of K22:403, but also included a stump of wall, top at 81.96, above northern wall of room. Room walls have tops ca. 81.60; floor 80.67. Surface elevation: 83.59. Top of locus: ca. 82.00. Bottom of locus: N/A. See pls. 47; 49:A; 269.

Elevation	Field Number	Description	Plate
81.73	IV-302	Ladle; see fig. 26	59:A; 163:CC

K22:407

Area surrounding kiln K22:405. Deepest point reached near kiln. Southern part of locus continued as K22:502. Middle Susiana. Surface elevation: 83.59. Top of locus: ca. 81.30. Bottom of locus: ca. 80.20. See pls. 48:B; 269.

Elevation	Field Number	Description	Plate
ca. 80.70	IV-300	Bowl with interior pedestal; see fig. 31	183:Y

WEST OF K22:404 = K22:407

Elevation	Field Number	Description	Plate
ca. 80.70	IV-405	Vestigial flanged base and ca. 1/4 of body; see fig. 30	182:N

K22:408

Hearth in K23:403 at eastern wall; Level V, the uppermost of three hearths; cf. K23:507. Surface elevation: 83.59. Top of locus: 80.88. Bottom of locus: 80.61. See pl. 269.

K22:409

Northwestern corner of Trench XIII: a narrow area between the original trench and western edge. Early Susiana-Middle Susiana transition at ca. 79.50–79.00. Surface elevation: 83.59. Top of locus: 82.04. Bottom of locus: ca. 78.00. See pl. 269.

Elevation	Field Number	Description	Plate
81.94–81.64	4.952	Vestigial flange with potter's mark	204:5
81.84–81.64	4.147	Crude small bowl	163:D
81.34–80.99	4.572	Painted-burnish variant body	cf. 227:B
80.20	4.1227	Bone awl (Early Susiana-Early Middle Susiana)	233:Q
79.59	4.551	Lid fragment	194:T
79.59	4.398	Painted lip fragment	197:B
78.89–78.49	4.721	Bowl fragment	199:C
ca. 78.60	4.319	Bowl fragment	199:F
ca. 78.60	4.356	Bowl fragment	61:V
ca. 78.60	4.854	Pedestal sherd	61:MM
ca. 78.60	4.940	Bowl fragment	61:R
77.15	4.351	Bowl fragment	198:G

K22:501

This locus was a continuation of K22:402; the high corner walls, 82.41–ca. 81.60, of K22:402 were removed. There were no features in the earth below. Surface elevation: 83.59. Top of locus: 81.52. Bottom of locus: ca. 81.00. See pl. 269.

Elevation	Field Number	Description	Plate
ca. 82.00	5.329	Painted bowl fragment; see fig. 26	163:K
ca. 81.40	4.540	Unpainted bowl fragment	163:E

K22:502

Southern part of K22:407 under the access stairs excavated during the fourth season, with continuation to the north of the line of the western wall of K23:509, top: 81.16; cf. northern part of wall traced in K22:407 at 81.26. The K22:407 and K22:502 areas might have been an open court, in which was oven K22:405. A grinding stone and two other stone tools were found on floor at 79.77. Surface elevation: 83.59. Top of locus: 81.52. Bottom of locus: 79.77. See pl. 269.

Elevation	Field Number	Description	Plate
81.07	5.341	Tortoise jar	187:E
81.00	5.250	Bowl fragment	172:A
79.77	5.742	Stone pestle	243:F

K23:400

The southwestern section of the enlarged Trench XIII was extended into the southern part of Square K22. No structural features were found and the Protoliterate deposits were disturbed by a late cemetery, e.g., K23:401. Graves 4.04 (western part; 82.75), 4.05 (82.59), 4.10 (82.74), 4.12 (end; 82.69), 4.19 (82.59), 4.21 (eastern part; 82.74), 4.25 (82.55), 4.26 (82.35), 4.27 (82.40), 4.28 (82.15). The depth of the graves was measured from surface at 83.64. Surface elevation: ca. 83.30. Top of locus: ca. 83.30. Bottom of locus: ca. 81.60. See pls. 3:B–E; 262–63.

Elevation	Field Number	Description	Plate
83.10–82.05	4.846	Lip fragment	59:K
82.80–82.55	4.310a–b	Jar fragment; see fig. 31	190:K
82.80–82.55	4.311	Jar fragment	190:N
82.80–82.55	4.544	Unpainted lip fragment	177:A
82.80–82.55	4.548	Painted base fragment	168:B
82.80–82.55	4.823	Painted lip fragment	183:Z
82.75–82.45	4.1221	Sherd rubber fragment	231:JJ
82.25–82.15	4.550	Sherd scraper	65:J
82.25–82.05	4.029	Bowl lip fragment	74:G
82.25–82.05	4.030	Bowl lip fragment	73:A
82.25–82.05	4.806	Spindle whorl	65:V
82.25–82.05	4.274	Painted lip fragment	174:J
82.25–82.05	4.731	Jug fragment	75:G
82.25–82.05	4.867	Stone hoe	245:V
82.05–81.95	4.543	Unpainted lip fragment	177:B
82.05–81.95	4.803	Perforated stone disc	29:X
82.05–81.95	4.810	Spindle whorl	65:U
82.05–81.95	4.1128	Spindle whorl	232:AA
ca. 81.85	4.210	Footed bowl	164:J
—	4.203	Ca. 1/3 bowl	177:G

GRAVE 4.28 IN K23:400 (ACHAEMENID)

Elevation	Field Number	Description	Plate
82.10	IV-166	Bowl	74:A; 263:1
82.10	IV-167	Bowl	73:I; 263:2
82.10	IV-168	Jar	75:X; 263:3
82.10	IV-169	Jar	263:4
82.10	IV-170	Metal vessel	4:J; 263:5
82.10	IV-171	Metal bowl	3:E; 4:M; 263:6
82.10	IV-172	Spear head	3:E; 4:F; 263:7
82.10	IV-173	Silver band	263:8
82.10	IV-174	Gold strip	4:E; 263:9
82.10	IV-175	Agate bead	263:10
82.10	IV-176	Silver rings	4:K; 263:11
82.10	IV-177	Bronze arrowhead	263:12a
82.10	IV-178	Iron arrowhead	4:L; 263:12b
82.10	IV-179	Iron arrowhead	263:12c

K23:401

Cluster of Protoliterate pottery located between Graves 4.05 and 4.25 to the south, in which four beveled-rim bowls were found right-side up and the sherds of the upper part of an undercut-rim jar. This locus is close to the southern edge of the trench. Surface elevation: ca. 83.30. Top of locus: 83.17. Bottom of locus: 83.17.

K23:402

Northern part of a rectangular room projecting into K22; northern wall, top: 81.44; eastern wall, top: 81.61; floor: 80.46. This locus was continued as K23:508. For southern part of room, see K23:506. Surface elevation: 83.59. Top of locus: 81.61. Bottom of locus: 80.46. See pls. 49:A; 268–69.

K23:403

Early Middle Susiana room almost half in K22; eastern wall, top 81.70; western wall, top 81.61. Hearth K22:408 abuts eastern wall; top: 80.88; uppermost of three hearths, Level V. Locus was excavated to floor at ca. 80.61, where the lip of a middle hearth appeared. It was continued in the fifth season as K23:507. Surface elevation: 83.59. Top of locus: 81.70. Bottom of locus: ca. 80.61. See pls. 47; 48:A; 269.

Elevation	Field Number	Description	Plate
81.61	4.091	Miniature crude bowl fragment	163:C
81.61	4.320	Painted lip fragment	61:II

NORTHEAST OF K23:403

Small patch of earth over the eastern wall segment to the north of the hearth from 82.06 to 81.70; cf. L22:404.

Elevation	Field Number	Description	Plate
82.06	4.866	Stone hoe	245:U
82.06–81.70	IV-441	Painted bowl fragment; see fig. 30	177:E
81.00–80.85	4.096	Trough spouted bowl; see fig. 26	164:K

K23:404

Corner of walls adjoined northeastern corner of K23:510. Top 81.07. Surface elevation: ca. 80.30. Top of locus: 81.07. Bottom of locus: N/A. See pl. 269.

K23:501

This southern extension of the western part of Trench XIII, ca. 3.00 m × 12.70 m at western end, was primarily an area of Protoliterate occupational debris disturbed by late burials: Grave 5.03 (82.79). Close to the surface, at ca. 83.08, was a complete beveled-rim bowl; at 82.98 there were sherds of a large reserve-slip jar and a clay jar stopper; between 82.71 and 82.41 were six complete beveled-rim bowls; eleven clay slingshots; bottle stoppers: one flat, one finger, two grooved; five slingshots; three domed and one flat bottle stoppers; two tokens; one sickle fragment; and one unfired tray rim fragment. Surface elevation: 83.23. Top of locus: 83.23. Bottom of locus: N/A.

Elevation	Field Number	Description	Plate
82.98	V-83	Spouted jar fragment (Protoliterate)	—
82.98	5.911	Ovoid jar	93:B
ca. 82.95	5.723	Wasted pebble	245:A
ca. 82.95	5.724	Wasted pebble	245:B
ca. 82.95	5.725	Wasted pebble	245:C
ca. 82.95	5.726	Wasted pebble	245:D
ca. 82.95	5.727	Wasted pebble	245:E
ca. 82.55	5.257	Painted snake beaker; see fig. 30	175:F, H
82.43	V-109	Metal pin (Protoliterate)	128:G
82.43	5.733	Stone hoe	246:O
82.43	—	1 clay slingshot	—
82.43	—	1 bottle stopper	—

K23:501 (*cont.*)

Elevation	Field Number	Description	Plate
82.37	—	1 slingshot	—
82.23	5.600	Miniature four-lugged jar	112:H
—	5.721	Grinding stone	240:C
—	5.722	Grinding stone	240:E

K23:502

This locus was below the western 4.20 m of K23:501 and above K23:509 and K23:511. The surface at the northwest was at 83.02 and at the southeast 82.96. It contained primarily Protoliterate debris that was mixed with prehistoric sherds in the lower part but was disturbed by late burials: Graves 5.06 (81.56) and 5.09 (81.50). At ca. 82.43 there was an irregular heap of burnt red clay, pebbles, and fragments of baked bricks, undoubtedly debris from the fire pit, ca. 1.10 in diameter with a hardened clay lip at ca. 82.37 and interior at 82.04. At 81.43, between the fire pit and brick wall of Grave 5.06, was a Protoliterate pottery group: two beveled-rim bowls, ovoid jar, base and body sherd of a large vessel, base of a bottle, and a twisted handled jar. Surface elevation: 83.82. Top of locus: ca. 82.40. Bottom of locus: 80.60. See pl. 269.

Elevation	Field Number	Description	Plate
82.63	5.640	Painted base fragment	60:M
82.43	—	7 clay slingshots	—
82.43	—	Bottle stoppers: 3 domed, 1 one-finger	—
82.42	5.338	Painted fragment	166:F
82.42	5.340	Painted fragment	178:C
82.42–81.72	5.439	Vestigial flange with potter's mark	60:S; 204:1
82.38	—	Bottle stoppers: 3 two-finger	—
82.37–81.68	5.208	Stand fragment	186
82.33	5.252	Handled jar	101:A
82.33	5.259	Strap-handled jar	cf. 102:I
82.33	5.363	Painted base fragment	168:C
82.33	—	4 1/2 slingshots	—
82.33	—	Bottle stoppers: 1 five-finger fragment, 1 slotted, 1 two-slotted	—
82.33	5.335	Vestigial flange	182:M
82.33–82.28	—	Bottle stoppers: 4 domed, 1 one-finger, 1 four-finger, 1 five-finger fragment, 1 slotted, 1 two-slotted	—
82.28	—	Bottle stoppers: 1 domed, 1 four-finger	—
82.12–81.48	5.590	Close-line lip fragment; see fig. 46	208:G
81.98	—	3 clay slingshots	—
81.98	—	1 irregular jar stopper	—
81.98–81.43	5.445	Vestigial flange + potter's mark	60:U; 203:13
81.43	5.463	Unpainted ladle fragment	164:C
ca. 81.70	—	4 slingshots	—
ca. 81.70	5.330	Lugged neck jar	194:O
81.43	5.255	Horizontal handled	101:F
81.43	5.313	Twisted handled jar	100:E
ca. 81.32	5.792	Painted lip fragment	61:Z
81.12	—	Slingshot	—
81.12	—	Bottle stoppers: 1 slotted fragment, 1 flat two-fingered	—
81.12	5.717	Stone pestle	244:D
ca. 81.05	5.441	Vestigial flange with potter's mark	60:Q; 204:18
ca. 80.70	5.336	Vestigial flange	182:L
ca. 80.70	5.784	Painted lip fragment	61:P

K23:503

A strip underlying the eastern two-thirds of K23:501 and above K23:506 and K23:507; 8.70 m long; width at the east: 2.50 m, at west: 3.80 m. Surface, at the southeast: 83.23, at the southwest: 82.96. Protoliterate debris was disturbed by late burials and mixed with Susiana sherds in the lower part. Late graves: 5.04 (ca. 82.38); 5.05 (child, no level); 5.07 (81.87). There was a Protoliterate plastered floor, ca. 1.60 m in diameter, with a plastered surface, at 82.12; perhaps it was the base of an oven. A further feature is the very irregularly triangular northern part of a Protoliterate pit, from 82.13 to ca. 80.38, with soft earth and sherds, which cut away part of the southwestern corner of K23:507 (continued from K23:403) and the southernmost part of K23:506 (continued from K23:402). The southern part of the pit was not excavated. Bottom 81.60, except for pit area at ca. 80.38. Surface elevation: 83.23. Top of locus: ca. 82.40. Bottom of locus: 81.60. See pls. 50:C (circular pavement in right background); 269.

Elevation	Field Number	Description	Plate
82.93	5.714	Stone grinder	238:D
82.53	5.307	Lugged-neck fragment (Protoliterate)	—
82.43	5.222	Strap-handled jar; see fig. 9	95:F
82.23	5.680	Vessel fragment	176:P
81.83	—	1 slingshot	—
—	—	2 bottle stoppers	—
80.56	5.442	Vestigial flange + potter's mark	60:R; 204:9

K23:504

This very small area in the northwestern corner of K23:502 was defined by the presence of a wall corner and included the immediately adjacent earth. Surface elevation: 83.02. Top of locus: 81.62. Bottom of locus: 80.82. See pl. 269.

Elevation	Field Number	Description	Plate
81.27	5.209	Tortoise fragment; see fig. 31	188:A
ca. 81.05	5.719	Stone grinder	241:G

K23:505

Access stairs to K23:502 in the southwestern corner of Trench XIII. Surface elevation: 83.02. Top of locus: 83.02. Bottom of locus: 80.82. See pl. 269.

Elevation	Field Number	Description	Plate
81.73	—	Bottle stopper; 1 domed	—

K23:506

The southern part of the room, begun as K23:402, is located under the middle part of K23:503, with the area under the circular floor of K23:503 unexcavated. Most of southern part of the room was occupied by the Protoliterate pit of K23:503, which might have destroyed the southern wall of the room. At the western edge and bottom of this pit were traced a dwarf wall at 80.50 and to the south a bench at 80.38, the bottom of the slot between them being at 80.00. At 80.90, adjacent to the earth supporting the circular floor, was an elongated rectangular cluster of fifty-three slingshots. At 80.59 there was a plastered floor. The narrow space between the southern wall of K23:507 (continued from K23:403) and the edge of the trench, for the most part disturbed by the Protoliterate pit of K23:503, is K23:506 East. Faunal remains included: *Capra-Ovis*: mandible (2); scapula (1); hip fragment (3); humerus (2); radius (2); femur (1); various (1); *Bos*: humerus (2); femur (1); radius (1); vertebrae (1); various (1). *Sus*: skull (1); patella (1); various (1). Unassigned (39). Surface elevation: 82.96. Top of locus: 81.60. Bottom of locus: 80.00. See pl. 269.

Elevation	Field Number	Description	Plate
80.90	—	53 slingshots	—
ca. 80.80	—	1 slingshot	—

K23:507

Deeper part of room K23:403 from ca. 80.61 down. The southern end was under K23:503 East. Eastern wall, southern part, top: 81.58. The exterior of the southwestern corner was damaged by a Protoliterate pit of K23:503 that cut down to 80.38. A narrow wall fragment, top at 81.46, at the southern end, was presumably the remnant of a bin. The hearths indicated three phases. The highest hearth (K22:408; top: 80.88; base: 80.61) rested on a floor covering the middle hearth and the top of a narrow north-south partition on the eastern side of the room; Level V. The middle hearth, top: 80.61; base: 80.27, rested on a floor formed by several layers of strawy mud; Level VI. The lowest hearth, top: 80.27, bottom of interior: 80.11; Level VII. Dwarf walls, tops: 80.27; bases on floor: 80.00; Level VII. Surface elevation: 83.59. Top of locus: ca. 80.61. Bottom of locus: 80.00. See pls. 50:B–C; 269.

Elevation	Field Number	Description	Plate
ca. 81.50	5.443	Vestigial flange with potter's mark	60:O; 204:4
ca. 80.40	—	1 slingshot	—

K23:508

Continuation of K23:402, the northern end of the Early Middle Susiana room, the southern part of which is K23:506. Surface elevation: 83.23. Top of locus: 81.60. Bottom of locus: 80.00. See pl. 269.

Elevation	Field Number	Description	Plate
80.84	—	15 clay slingshots	—
80.66	V-99	Mace-head of grayish black, brown veined stone	230:L
80.47	—	3 clay slingshots	—

K23:509

Room under western part of K23:503. Southern wall top 80.60. Large horns in middle of room at 79.90. Faunal remains: *Capra:* fibula (1); *Capra-Ovis Gazella:* mandible (1); radius (1); various (1); *Capra-ovis:* femur (1); *Bos:* mandible (1); *Sus:* ulna (1); and twenty-nine assorted. Surface elevation: 82.96. Top of locus: 80.60. Bottom of locus: 79.80. See pl. 269.

Elevation	Field Number	Description	Plate
ca. 80.30	5.444	Vestigial flange with potter's mark	60:N; 204:17
ca. 79.90	—	*Capra aegageus:* wild goat skull with two horns	257:A

K23:510

Narrow room under western end of K23:503, northeastern corner. Faunal remains at 80.46. Gazelle horn core. *Capra-Ovis-Gazella:* scapula. Surface elevation: 82.96. Top of locus: 80.60. Bottom of locus: ca. 80.20. See pl. 269.

Elevation	Field Number	Description	Plate
ca. 80.45	—	2 clay slingshots	—
ca. 80.40	5.396	Painted body fragment	62:Z

K23:510

This room, under the western part of K23:502, was incompletely excavated. Walls on the east, north, and south were traced. Surface elevation: 83.02. Top of locus: 80.60. Bottom of locus: ca. 80.00. See pl. 269.

Elevation	Field Number	Description	Plate
ca. 80.60	5.797	Stand fragment	61:EE

L22:400

Northeastern section of the enlarged Trench XIII. There were no structural features except L22:401. The deposits were disturbed by a late cemetery: Graves 4.03 (child; 83.21), 4.06 (82.82), 4.07 (82.64), 4.08 (no level), 4.15 (only head uncovered; Achaemenid; quadratic brick on top; 83.09), 4.16 (82.73), 4.20 (82.59), 4.24 (western part; 82.52). Surface elevation: 83.64. Top of locus: 83.64. Bottom of locus: ca. 82.30. See pls. 262; 269.

Elevation	Field Number	Description	Plate
83.44	4.879	Handgrinder	242:T
83.44–83.24	4.097	Ca. 1/2 glazed bowl (probably Parthian)	73:F
83.24–83.14	4.035	Ca. 1/2 bowl	163:N

Elevation	Field Number	Description	Plate
83.24–83.14	4.037	Ca. 2/3 bowl	172:B
83.24–83.14	4.040	Ca. 1/4 bowl	164:I
83.24–83.14	4.053	Red ware hole-mouthed fragment	193:X
83.24–83.14	4.054	Red ware lip and 1/4 body hole-mouthed fragment	193:U
83.24–83.14	4.055	Red ware hole-mouthed fragments; see fig. 31	193:H
83.24–83.14	4.192	Jar fragment; see fig. 31	191:J
83.24–83.14	4.225	Painted carinated bowl fragment	189:E
83.24–83.14	4.240	Painted fragment	58:U; 163:W
83.24–83.14	4.251	Ca. 2/3 bowl; see fig. 26	172:C
83.24–83.14	4.252	Painted fragments; see fig. 26	172:D
82.99–82.79	4.1115	Spindle whorl	232:J
82.89	4.227	Painted base fragment	180:F
82.79–82.69	4.1131	1 spindle whorl	232:CC
82.79–82.59	4.737	Bowl fragment	169:B
82.70–82.50	4.350	Painted bowl fragment	163:F

L22:401

Small area in the northeastern corner of Trench XIII with patches of two hard floors at 83.27 and 83.16. Achaemenid occupation debris was mixed with Susiana sherds below lower floor. Surface elevation: 83.64. Top of locus: 83.27. Bottom of locus: 82.79. See pl. 269.

Elevation	Field Number	Description	Plate
83.14–82.79	4.027	Loop-handled bowl fragment	75:O
83.14–82.79	4.056	Ring-based plate fragments	75:U
83.14–82.79	4.078	1/3 bowl	73:E
83.14–82.79	4.625	Jar rim fragment	75:Y
83.04–82.89	IV-440	Terra-cotta bull protome	76:A
83.04–82.89	IV-442	Bronze arrowhead	76:E

L22:402

Room with badly preserved, irregular walls. On the north only were some fallen mudbricks; the original northern wall was presumably to the south of the 82.49 high northern edge of kiln L22:403 West. Western wall, top: 82.59; bottom: 82.20. Floor: 82.17–82.14. The northern end of the eastern wall was cut away to reveal L22:402 kiln 2. Surface elevation: 83.64. Top of locus: 82.59. Bottom of locus: 82.14. See pl. 269.

Elevation	Field Number	Description	Plate
82.59	4.874	Perforated stone	247:L
82.59–82.29	4.052	Red ware; ca. 3/4 body hole-mouthed	193:V
82.59–82.29	4.458	Painted lip fragment	172:E
82.59–82.29	4.841	Painted bowl body fragment	59:T
82.59–82.29	4.842	Painted lip fragment	59:BB
82.59–82.29	4.1126	Spindle whorl	232:Y

NORTH OF L22:402

Debris just to the north of room overlying L22:403 kiln 4.

Elevation	Field Number	Description	Plate
82.39–82.29	4.224	Painted crater	184:S
82.54–82.14	4.953	Base with potter's mark	203:63

SOUTHEAST OF L22:402

Debris abutting exterior face of southern wall of L22:402.

Elevation	Field Number	Description	Plate
82.54–82.14	4.545	Lip + convex bowl fragment	177:D
82.39–82.14	4.1116	Spindle whorl	232:K

NORTHWEST OF L22:402

Elevation	Field Number	Description	Plate
81.95	V-141	Conglomerate stone pestle	230:M
81.89–81.69	IV-348	Clay stud	234:H

SOUTHWEST OF L22:402

Elevation	Field Number	Description	Plate
81.89–81.69	4.805	Spindle whorl	65:DD; 232:O

L22:403

This is a group of seven kilns under or near room L22:402 that defines Level II. All but one were roughly circular. Kiln 1 was partly under the western wall of L22:402; rim: 82.49; interior: 82.28. Kiln 2 was partly under the eastern wall of L22:402; 1.0 cm thick white plaster on interior; rim: 82.34; interior: 82.28. The northern part of kiln 3 was under the northern edge of the trench, interior: 82.24. Kiln 4 was irregularly rectangular; interior: 82.14. Kiln 5, interior: 81.94. Kiln 6, interior: 81.90. Kiln 7 was partly under the southeastern corner of L22:402, interior: ca. 81.94. Surface elevation: 83.64. Top of locus: 82.49. Bottom of locus: 81.90. See pls. 49:B; 269.

ABOVE L22:403

Elevation	Field Number	Description	Plate
82.24–81.99	IV-249	Clay stud	—

NORTHEAST OF L22:403

Elevation	Field Number	Description	Plate
82.19–81.99	4.336	Painted jar body fragment	191:P

L22:404

Pit with ashy debris located in the southwestern corner of L22 and extending into K22. It is below Grave 4.06 and the southern part of K22:401 and above L22:405. Bottom of L22:404 at 81.62, slightly deeper than top of western wall of L22:405 at 81.70. At southern edge of locus was a wall stump, top: 82.06, rested on a floor at 81.69 (Level III). Surface elevation: 83.64. Top of locus: 82.68. Bottom of locus: 81.62. See pl. 269.

SOUTHWEST OF L22:403

Elevation	Field Number	Description	Plate
81.84–81.64	IV-339f	Perforated roundel	231:T

L22:405

Room (Early Middle Susiana) under the ashy pit L22:404 and the debris surrounding it (cf. Northeast of K23:403). Western wall (= eastern wall of K23:403) with top at north 81.70, at south 81.58. Eastern wall (= western wall of L22:504) with top at 81.65; narrower than western wall. No southern wall was traced. Locus was continued in L22:507. Surface elevation: 83.56. Top of locus: ca. 81.70. Bottom of locus: ca. 80.90. See pl. 269.

Elevation	Field Number	Description	Plate
ca. 80.90	IV-437	Bone awl	65:M; 233:F

L22:501

This small extension, ca. 2.50 × 6.00 m, of the northeastern corner of Trench XIII was excavated to check for the existence of Achaemenid remains comparable to those of L22:401, which was termed South of L22:501 during the fifth season; it was dug to a depth of ca. 81.60. The features were a wall segment (top 83.00, bottom 82.63 [not indicated on pl. 269]), a baked brick possibly marking an Achaemenid floor at 83.00, and a kiln at the west. From the surface to ca. 1.00 m (83.56–82.56) sherds were predominantly late with some Protoliterate; below the number of Middle Susiana sherds increased. Small fragments of a terrazzo of pebbles in bitumen were found at ca. 83.26. The kiln is slightly conical with an irregular interior in which slight projections ca. 0.80 m below the rim indicate the probable placement of a terra-cotta grill, many small fragments of which were found inside the kiln that was plastered by hand, leaving finger marks, around the mouth; diameter of mouth 0.75–0.90; diameter of base 1.25. Top north, 82.33; top south, 81.13; bottom 81.00. Surface elevation: 83.56. Top of locus: 83.56. Bottom of locus: ca. 82.00. See pls. 3:A (left foreground); 269.

Elevation	Field Number	Description	Plate
83.56	5.001	Bowl fragment	70:N
ca. 82.90	5.715	Finger stone	244:Z
ca. 82.90	5.718	Finger stone	244:S
82.56	5.619	Bowl lip fragment	73:J
82.46	V-3	Bone tool	65:O; 233:Z
ca. 82.45	5.419	Vestigial flange chip with potter's mark	60:P; 204:12
Wash	V-7	Crescentic token	134:F 6

SOUTH OF L22:501

Elevation	Field Number	Description	Plate
Wash	5.617	Jar neck fragment	71:E

L22:502

Below L22:400 on eastern side of L22:402. No structural features were found except for a well-built long wall below the eastern wall of L22:402 but projecting slightly farther to the east: top 81.61. Hard sloping surface (but not a constructed floor) at 81.65. Lowest point reached along western wall ca. 81.30. Surface elevation: 83.56. Top of locus: ca. 82.00. Bottom of locus ca. 81.30. See pl. 269.

Elevation	Field Number	Description	Plate
ca. 82.00	5.420	Concave base with potter's mark	203:5
ca. 80.50	5.471	Painted base fragment	168:G

L22:503

Canceled

L22:504

Narrow wedge-shaped area under eastern part of L22:405. No northern wall was found. The eastern wall extends farther to the south than the western wall, apparently forming the southwestern corner of a mostly unexcavated room extending under L22:402

and termed only "East of L22:504." Western wall, top: 81.65; eastern wall, top of southern corner: 81.61. The eastern wall is bordered on the west by another wall, extending farther to the north; its top is at 81.00–81.15 and it must belong to an earlier phase. The sequence of floors in this locus is not yet fully established, but each of the following elements could be taken as indicating a floor level: bench in southern end at 80.98; an oval basin (5.345) and two bases of pottery vessels, one concave and one very large, were found in the southeastern corner at 80.05. Bottom reached at 79.80. Among the few bones were: *Capra-Ovis*: radis (1), femur (1); *Suidae*: scapula (1). Surface elevation: 83.56. Top of locus: 81.62. Bottom of locus: 79.80. See pl. 269.

Elevation	Field Number	Description	Plate
81.62	5.372	Vestigial flange with potter's mark	204:10
ca. 80.05	5.345	Oval basin fragment	168:K

EAST OF L22:504

Elevation	Field Number	Description	Plate
81.77	5.212	Painted fragment	183:E

L22:505

Continuation of L22:402. Work was limited to cleaning of interior and the demolition of a 1.00 m section of the eastern wall, at a point ca. 1.50 m from the interior southeastern corner, to check stratification. A 25.0 cm thick deposit consisting of three irregular layers of earth mixed with varying amounts of ash separated the hard floor at 82.17 from the top of the wall of L22:502, 81.76 high at this point. Surface elevation: 83.56. Top of locus: 82.17. Bottom of locus: 81.76. See pl. 269.

Elevation	Field Number	Description	Plate
82.17	5.339	Painted base fragment	60:L
82.17	5.492	Painted lip fragment	59:Y
82.17	5.487	Painted body fragment	169:U
82.17	5.697	Body fragment	165:H

L22:506

Small room below kilns 4 and 6 of L22:403. Northern wall, with top at 81.86 continues to the east to a wall parallel with the eastern wall of the room. A narrow wall of stretchers, top at 81.94, abuts the southern face of the southern wall and continues to the east to complete a small compartment. There was an analogous, but longer compartment on the west and an oven against the northern wall with its top at 80.25. Floor 80.00–79.95. Faunal remains: *Capra-Ovis*: mandible (1), ulna (1), various (1); *Bos*: various (3); fifteen miscellaneous bones. Surface elevation: 83.56. Top of locus: 81.94. Bottom of locus: 79.95. See pls. 49:A–D; 269.

Elevation	Field Number	Description	Plate
82.24	4.573	Vestigial flanged vessel fragment	182:O

NORTH OF L22:506

Elevation	Field Number	Description	Plate
ca. 80.00	5.651	Painted lip fragment; see fig. 33	196:E

SOUTH OF L22:506

Elevation	Field Number	Description	Plate
ca. 81.90	5.360	Bowl fragment	176:O

L22:507

Continued from L22:405. In the southern part of the room was a plastered floor at 80.17. Surface elevation: 83.56. Top of locus: 81.60. Bottom of locus: N/A. See pl. 269.

Elevation	Field Number	Description	Plate
80.61	5.732	Rubbing stone	252:P
80.17	5.547	Bone awl	233:J

L22:508

Small room contiguous to L22:506 on the north; top of wall (in common) 81.86. Floor at 79.86. Surface elevation: 83.56. Top of locus: 81.86. Bottom of locus: 79.86. See pls. 49:D (right; not fully excavated); 269.

L23:TRENCH XIII

Elevation	Field Number	Description	Plate
—	5.747	Pestle/pounder	243:D

L22–23:400

Elevation	Field Number	Description	Plate
ca. 83.45	4.077	Pottery vessel	71:A

L23:400

Southeastern section of the enlarged Trench XIII; there were no structural features and the deposits were disturbed by a late cemetery (see L23:402): Graves 4.01 (83.14), 4.02 (Achaemenid quadratic brick used to support exterior of eastern end brick; 83.04), 4.06 (eastern part; 82.82), 4.09 (83.04), 4.11 (83.30), 4.12 (without mudbrick wall; 83.06), 4.13 (consisted only of skull resting vertically, facing to the south; 83.19). Surface elevation: 83.59. Top of locus: 83.59. Bottom of locus: ca. 82.00. See pl. 261.

Elevation	Field Number	Description	Plate
83.59–83.44	4.188	Bowl fragment	73:H
83.26–83.09	4.387	Painted jar body fragment	58:P
83.24	IV-23	Terra-cotta stud or labret	234:P
83.24–83.09	4.613	Bowl fragments	169:D
83.14–83.04	4.061	Jar fragments	75:W
83.14–82.94	4.024	Ca. 1/3 bowl	74:B
82.94	4.226	Jar fragments; see fig. 31	189:D
82.94	4.744	Stand fragment	185:D
82.94–82.74	4.064	Four-lugged incised fragment	122:F
82.86	IV-428	Bowl; see fig. 30	176:N
82.74–82.54	4.1125	Painted spindle whorl	232:X
82.54	4.862	Wasted pebble	245:H
82.54–82.34	4.295	Painted bowl fragment	167:D
82.54–82.34	4.1119	Incised spindle whorl	232:R
82.44–82.24	4.231	Painted lip fragment	60:C; 178:B
82.34–82.14	4.273	Shoulder fragment	191:Q
82.04–81.74	4.814	Spindle whorl	65:CC; 232:N

L23:401

Three groups of stones arranged in a relatively straight east-west line in L23:400. The eastern group contained eight pebbles and two baked-brick fragments; the middle group had two small and two large pebbles, a fragment of a grinding stone, and a rectangular fragment of conglomerate stone; and the western group consisted of one large oblong pebble, one finger stone, and four large pebbles. Surface elevation: 83.59. Top of locus: 83.44. Bottom of locus: 83.44.

L23:402

Protoliterate group of four beveled-rim bowls, two pouring lip bowls, one finger stone, and four handgrinders found just behind the brick wall of Grave 4.09; slightly lower another beveled-rim bowl was found slightly higher than Grave 4.09 at the same spot. Surface elevation: 83.59. Top of locus: 82.89. Bottom of locus: 82.54. See pl. 262 for position of Grave 4.09.

Elevation	Field Number	Description	Plate
82.84	IV-39	Pouring lip	80:CC
82.79	IV-97	Small jar	88:J
82.74	4.877	Handgrinder	242:B
82.74	4.880	Handgrinder	242:A
82.74	4.887	Finger stone	244:CC

L23:501

This southern extension of the eastern part of Trench XIII was an elongated triangle ca. 8.00 m long and ca. 2.00 m wide at the Square K–L border. Surface at west 83.23 (reference point), at east 83.54. Debris had primarily Protoliterate sherds from the surface down. In the southwest was (late) Grave 5.01 at 82.65. The bottom was not marked by a floor, but the locus was closed at ca. 82.50 above debris from an intrusive Achaemenid grave, L23:502, and a Protoliterate deposit, L23:503. Surface elevation: 83.23. Top of locus: 83.23. Bottom of locus: ca. 82.50. See pl. 269.

L23:502

Area of ca. 1.00 × 2.00 m below the southwestern part of L23:501, both beneath and immediately to the northeast of Grave 5.01. Between 82.48 and 82.00 were scattered fragments from an Achaemenid burial, Grave 5.08. A small group of Protoliterate sherds still occurred at 82.38; see the immediately adjacent Protoliterate deposit in L23:503. Middle Susiana debris was found in the lower part of the locus. Surface elevation: 83.23. Top of locus: 82.43. Bottom of locus: ca. 81.00. See pl. 269.

Elevation	Field Number	Description	Plate
82.48	V-130	Shapeless fragment of iron blade	—
82.35–82.23	V-122	Bronze cup	74:P
82.35–82.23	V-123	Corroded phiale	4:N
82.35–82.23	V-124	Bronze bracelet	76:J
82.35–82.23	V-125	Bracelet fragments	cf. 76:I
82.35–82.23	V-126	Cluster of three corroded silver-wire rings	76:I
82.35–82.23	V-127	Silver-wire ring fragment	—
82.35	V-128	Silver foil fragment forming disc 3.3 cm in diameter; two perforations near edge	76:K
82.35	V-129	Silver foil fragment forming a 2.7 × 5.8 cm irregular oval perforated at narrow end	76:L
ca. 82.35	V-131	Beads: 2 silver-wire; carnelian, 13 barrel, 4 biconical, 6 ring; agate, 4 cylindrical	—

POSSIBLY FROM GRAVE 5.08 IN L22:502

Elevation	Field Number	Description	Plate
82.23	5.598	Small jar fragment	73:D
82.13	5.495	Bowl base fragment	168:I

L23:503

Area below L23:501, except for the southeastern corner with remnants of plundered Achaemenid Grave 5.08. Just to the east of L23:502 was a cluster of six Protoliterate vessels and one stone bowl fragment. The western part of L23:400, between L23:503 proper and L22:507, was also included in L23:503. No structure was found, but a hard surface sloped from ca. 81.65 in L23:503 North near L22:507 to 80.90 in L23:502 and apparently represented an ancient surface in an unbuilt area; the same surface occurred in L23:504 and the eastern part of L23:503. Surface elevation: 83.54. Top of locus: ca. 82.50. Bottom of locus: ca. 80.90. See pl. 269.

Elevation	Field Number	Description	Plate
82.37	V-63	Small ovoid jar	88:N
82.37	V-64	Beaker	—

Elevation	Field Number	Description	Plate
82.37	V-65	Jar with two rows of notches on upper body (Protoliterate)	—
82.37	V-66	Bowl	—
82.37	V-67	Four-lugged jar	cf. 113:B
82.37	V-68	Pouring lip bowl	cf. 80:X
82.37	—	Fragmentary gray stone bowl	—

L23:504

Below the eastern part of L23:400. No features were discovered except for a hard surface that sloped down from 81.60 near L22:505 to 81.11 at the southern edge of Trench XIII in L23:503 and represented the same ancient surface found in the western part of L23:503. Surface elevation: 83.54. Top of locus: ca. 82.34. Bottom of locus: N/A. See pl. 269.

Elevation	Field Number	Description	Plate
82.33	V-35	Rough surfaced jar	cf. 90:F
82.33	V-69	Pouring lip bowl	cf. 80:W
82.33	V-70	Pouring lip bowl	cf. 80:W

L23:506

This area of 1.50 × 1.40 m between the eastern side of L23:505 stairs and the southwestern corner of L23:503 was dug to check for additional remains of plundered Grave 5.08, to which a few fragments of apparently human bones at 82.30 can be attributed. Surface elevation: 83.25. Top of locus: 83.25. Bottom of locus: 82.00. See pl. 269

Elevation	Field Number	Description	Plate
ca. 83.25	5.945	Painted body fragment	—
ca. 82.60	5.793	Painted pedestal	61:GG
82.00	5.701	Painted lip fragment	59:X

TERRACE MIDDLE 2

SOUNDING A

L15

This is an area ca. 5.00 × 5.00 m. From the surface to ca. 79.80 only water-laid clay with few sherds was to be found, except in the southwestern corner there was a patch of rough pavement formed by pebbles and sherds of Parthian torpedo jars. Surface slopes from 80.65 down to 80.15 in the north. From ca. 79.80 Protoliterate sherds appear; at ca. 79.65 a complete beveled-rim bowl, a beveled-rim bowl waster, and a complete pseudo-beveled-rim bowl were found, but Parthian and Protoliterate sherds continue to be mixed at the deepest point reached in the enlarged sounding during the fourth season, ca. 79.35. The deepest point of the original, second season, sounding was ca. 78.65, with Middle Susiana sherds occurring. Surface elevation: 80.65. Top of locus: 80.65. Bottom of locus: ca. 78.65. See pl. 260.

Elevation	Field Number	Description	Plate
80.65	2.652	Recurved sided D size bowl (Parthian)	—
78.85	2.106	Painted-burnished lip; see fig. 37	64:CC; 226:H
—	II-62	Stone spacer bead	76:N
—	2.781	Sherd rubber	231:BB

TRENCH XVIII

M–N/13–14

This area, originally 4.00 × 5.50 m with the long axis north-south, contained Protoliterate ashy occupational debris from the surface to ca. 0.40 B.S. (81.21–80.81), but it tapers out in the western end where beveled-rim bowls did not occur. There were thirty-eight complete beveled-rim bowls; one occurred at 0.50 B.S.; below were a sparse number of Middle Susiana sherds. The northern extension, ca. 2.50 × 3.00 m, to the eastern half of the original trench had no ashy deposit and practically no Protoliterate sherds; below 0.55 B.S. were only Middle Susiana sherds, appearing sparsely. Sterile soil perhaps was reached in a limited area in the eastern part of the trench at ca. 4.80 B.S. (76.41). Surface elevation: 81.21. Top of locus: 81.21. Bottom of locus: ca. 76.41. See pls. 16:A; 260.

Elevation	Field Number	Description	Plate
81.21	III-706	Three-spouted fragment	108:H
81.21–80.81	3.425	Trough-spouted bowl	85:L
81.21–80.56	III-79	Spindle whorl	65:S
81.21	3.271	Token (Protoliterate)	—
81.01	III-707	Four-lugged strap-handled jar; see fig. 15	115:B
80.91	III-410	Bottle fragment	111:A
80.91	III-875	Strap-handled cup	95:L
80.86	III-132	Spouted bowl fragment; see fig. 8	85:A
80.81–80.41	3.1095	Metal pin	128:J
80.81	III-421	Tray; see fig. 9	86:P
79.81	3.173	Painted jar body	192:I
79.46	3.372	Tortoise lip	187:F
77.91	3.175	Painted base	180:E
77.61	3.1249	Clay slingshot	231:L
—	3.051	Painted base	180:A

NORTH OF M–N/13–14

Elevation	Field Number	Description	Plate
78.41	3.1250	Clay slingshot	231:K
—	3.176	Bowl fragment	181:M

TRENCH XXII

N11

This locus was originally a rectangle of 2.00 × 4.00 m with the long axis north-south, in the middle of which was an east-west Middle Susiana wall of large mudbricks. To follow this wall, Trench XXII was enlarged to an east-west length of 12.50 m and north-south width varying from 2.00 to 4.00 m. The deepest point was reached only in a restricted area in the northern part of the trench. Surface elevation: 82.36. Top of locus: 82.36. Bottom of locus: ca. 74.86. See pls. 260–61.

Elevation	Field Number	Description	Plate
82.36	3.200	Painted pithos body	191:U
81.86–79.91	3.226	Painted body	171:Q
81.86	3.835	Painted body	189:L
81.11	3.1235	Clay token	231:C
80.46	3.856	Spindle whorl	232:F
80.36–78.86	3.192	Painted body	163:I
80.36–78.86	3.245	Painted jar carination	189:B
80.36–78.86	3.384	Ring base	173:E
79.96	3.737	Flint blade	254:J
79.91	3.202	Red ware hole-mouthed lip	193:W
79.91	3.337	Red ware lip	193:G
78.69	3.256	Painted jar body	191:L
76.46	3.1233	Stone token	231:D
76.46	3.1092	Terra-cotta grill fragments	231:MM
76.16	3.377	Painted shoulder	191:G

WEST OF N11

Elevation	Field Number	Description	Plate
81.23	3.434	Painted body	171:M

MIDDLE OF N11

Elevation	Field Number	Description	Plate
81.01	3.574	Metal pin	65:P

NORTH OF N11

Elevation	Field Number	Description	Plate
79.21	3.433	Painted lip	171:H
78.09	3.370	Crateriform fragments	184:M

NORTHEAST OF N11

Elevation	Field Number	Description	Plate
78.69	3.015	Painted masks; see fig. 30	58:A; 176:U
78.69	3.133	Crateriform lip	58:AA; 184:L
78.69	3.181	Small jar; see fig. 31	190:A
78.69	3.188	Crateriform body	184:J
78.69	3.189	Painted inner concave rim	170:C
78.69	3.198	Crateriform lip	57:H; 184:G
78.69	3.203	Red ware hole-mouthed lip	193:O

SOUNDING F
N22

Approximately 2.00 × 6.00 m area. Sherds were primarily late, apparently mostly Achaemenid. Surface elevation: 82.40. Top of locus: 82.40. Bottom of locus: 78.00. See pl. 260.

Elevation	Field Number	Description	Plate
—	2.594	Jar neck	cf. 75:CC
—	2.577	Horizontal handle	75:M
—	2.608	Jar rim and shoulder	—
—	2.648	Blue glazed handle (Parthian?)	—
—	2.650	Blue-green glazed rim (Parthian?)	—
—	2.490	Bowl fragment	cf. 73:D
—	2.581	Bowl fragment (Achaemenid)	—
—	2.596	Bowl fragment (Achaemenid)	—
—	2.605	Painted jar body (Achaemenid)	—
—	2.611	Bowl fragment (Protoliterate)	—
—	2.641	Bowl fragment (Achaemenid)	—
—	2.655	Handle, cooking pot ware (Achaemenid)	—
—	2.667	Jar neck and rim (Achaemenid)	—
81.00	II-39	Perforated terra-cotta disc. Loom weight	126:EE

TRENCH VII
O20–21

Approximately 2.00 × 7.00 m area. There were no substantial architectural features, only some bricks and possibly traces of a wall. There were late period sherds, including some glazed and presumably Parthian; most were Achaemenid but some might have been Iron III, predating the Achaemenid dynasty (cf. pl. 73:G, H; 2.657). The trench was discontinued at the point where Protoliterate sherds began to appear. Surface elevation: 81.70. Top of locus: 81.70. Bottom of locus: ca. 80.20. See pl. 260.

Elevation	Field Number	Description	Plate
81.70–81.20	2.578	Jar neck	75:BB
81.70–81.20	2.583	Jar rim and shoulder fragment (Achaemenid)	—
81.70–81.20	2.586	Jar rim (Achaemenid)	—
81.70–81.20	2.588	Bowl fragment (Achaemenid)	—
81.70–81.20	2.597	Jar fragment	—
81.70–81.20	2.604	Rim fragment (Achaemenid)	—
81.70–81.20	2.612	Jar rim and handle	cf. 77:D
81.70–81.20	2.613	Jar neck and shoulder (Achaemenid)	—
ca. 80.80	2.614	Ribbed bowl fragment, gray ware	73:G
ca. 80.80	2.657	Ribbed bowl fragment greenish ware	cf. 73:H
—	2.575	Horizontal handle	75:R
—	2.582	Vat rim fragment	—
—	—	Base (Achaemenid)	—

TRENCH XI
O23

This area of 2.00 × 14.00 m at the southwestern end projects into O24. The surface slopes from 84.30 in the southwest to 83.90 in the northeast. There were fragmentary brickwork and pits. The trench was discontinued at a shallow depth, only reaching ca. 1.50 B.S. in a limited area. Primarily Achaemenid. Surface elevation: 84.30. Top of locus: 84.30. Bottom of locus: ca. 82.80. See pl. 260.

Elevation	Field Number	Description	Plate
82.90	II-102	Bowl	74:K
—	2.068	Close-line carinated body	212:H
—	2.482	Bowl fragment	cf. 74:M
—	2.644	Bowl fragment	cf. 74:N
—	2.488	Bowl fragment (Achaemenid)	—

HIGH MOUND

Elevation	Field Number	Description	Plate
Surface	I-18	Terra-cotta object	235:H
Surface	2.779	Pottery roundel	231:V
Surface	IV-162	Stone bead	129:BB
—	1.049	Painted lip fragment	160:E
—	1.050	Painted body	160:H
—	1.100	Painted body	56:O
—	1.129	Blade core	253:J
—	3.1020	Neck + handle	72:A
—	3.1061	Metal arrowhead	76:C
—	5.245	Painted body	191:R

EAST SLOPE

Elevation	Field Number	Description	Plate
Surface	1.085	Jar neck fragment; see fig. 23	162:D

NORTHWEST SLOPE

Elevation	Field Number	Description	Plate
Surface	I-38	Vessel	77:J

WEST SLOPE

Elevation	Field Number	Description	Plate
Surface	1.167	Painted lip	56:RR

SOUTH SLOPE

Elevation	Field Number	Description	Plate
Surface	III-949	Female figurine	5:I

HILL B

Elevation	Field Number	Description	Plate
Level of last brick articulation	1.135	Truncated blade	254:B

HILL B, E

Elevation	Field Number	Description	Plate
Surface	1.138	Retouched blade	254:G

HILL C, E

Elevation	Field Number	Description	Plate
Surface	1.149	Truncated blade	255:B
Surface	1.147	End scraper on blade	255:F
Surface	1.137	Truncated notched blade	254:D
Surface	1.150	Truncated blade	255:H

M8:401

This small, irregular eroded area in the southeastern corner of M8 was tested for the presence of Protoliterate brickwork, which was not established during the two days the locus was dug. There was soft, ashy debris with numerous Protoliterate sherds. Also, in the lower part of the locus were traces of a Late Susiana burial (marked by an oval on pl. 261). Surface elevation: ca. 86.75. Top of locus: ca. 86.75. Bottom of locus: ca. 85.60. See pl. 261.

Elevation	Field Number	Description	Plate
ca. 86.75	IV-154	Jar; see fig. 23	159:J
—	IV-242	Painted animal figurine (Late Susiana)	—

M10:301

Brickwork in the northeastern corner of M10, extending irregularly north-south for ca. 9.00 m, was traced by a narrow and relatively shallow cut along the eastern side. The northern end emerged below the western end of the diagonal line of north-south brickwork of N10:304, at a lower level, and extended 4.60 m to the south, where it turned sharply to the west. At this corner the top of the wall was at 83.35 and its base at 82.61. Another north-south wall, somewhat differently aligned, petered out after ca. 4.20 m. It has an apparent jog on the west, opposite what might be the stump of an east-west wall. No western or northern faces were found for the northern brickwork of the locus. The bricks of heavy gray clay were long and thick, ca. 12.0 × 45.0 cm. Surface elevation: ca. 84.00. Top of locus: ca. 84.00. Bottom of locus: ca. 82.60. See pl. 261.

Elevation	Field Number	Description	Plate
84.00	3.138	Beaker lip	56:AA
84.00	3.143	Beaker lip	162:A
84.00	3.258	Painted lip	56:B
84.00	3.259	Painted body fragment	56:C
84.00–83.00	3.793	Painted conical foot	159:S
84.00–83.00	3.794	Painted conical foot	159:R

N5 SHERD YARD

Elevation	Field Number	Description	Plate
Surface	3.268	Painted pot body	191:W

N5:301

Small area at the southwest of N5 where roughly gabled-shaped alignments of stones and fragmentary baked bricks covered decayed skeletons of uncertain late date. Surface elevation: ca. 93.00. Top of locus: ca. 93.00. Bottom of locus: ca. 92.25. See pl. 261.

N6:301

Northern portion of massive Elamite wall and immediately adjacent western area (= northernmost part of Trench XXIV area). Surface elevation: ca. 95.00. Top of locus: ca. 95.00. Bottom of locus: ca. 93.00. See pl. 261.

N9

Elevation	Field Number	Description	Plate
Dump	3.491	Figurine head (Elamite)	5:D

N9 SOUTH

In the southeastern corner of N9 was a small semicircular test area with traces of brickwork, presumably Protoliterate, at 86.69. This restricted area carried down to ca. 2.60 B.S. The sherds were a mixture of Late Susiana and Protoliterate in the upper part of the sounding; Late Susiana sherds were mixed with Protoliterate as high as 87.00 and were dominant from 86.60 down and included the neck and shoulder of a large Late Susiana jar. Surface elevation: 88.78. Top of locus: 88.78. Bottom of locus: ca. 86.18. See pl. 261.

N9:301

Initial part of Trench XXIV on the western slope of the southwestern spur of the High Mound. Protoliterate brickwork was eroded into "steps" immediately below the N9:301 surface. The surface sloped from 86.57 in northeast to ca. 84.50 in the southwest. In articulating the bricks, only ca. 30.0 cm or less of the debris was removed. Much of locus is in M9. Surface elevation: 86.57. Top of locus: 86.57. Bottom of locus: ca. 86.27. See pls. 10:A; 261.

Elevation	Field Number	Description	Plate
86.57	III-286	Ovoid jar; see fig. 9	89:O
86.57	III-602	Stone hut amulet	31:FF
86.27	III-460	Agate bead	76:P

N9:302

Protoliterate room, 1.80 × 4.50 m, with northern and eastern walls abutting brickwork of N9:301, was eroded between the southern wall and irregular traces of southwest-northeast brickwork of N9:304. Surface sloped from 86.33 at northeastern corner to 84.76 at northwest; from 86.28 at the southeast to 84.82 at southwest. Bottom at northeastern corner 84.77, at northwest 83.53, at the southeast 84.70. Northeastern wall preserved higher and better than elsewhere. Bricks averaged 8.0 × 12.0 × 23.0 cm, mostly laid as stretchers. Under bricks of the northeastern wall yellow soil appeared at 85.29, which might indicate the original floor level. The objects were concentrated between the surface and 0.75 B.S. (86.33–85.58). Surface elevation: 86.33. Top of locus: 86.33. Bottom of locus: 84.7. See pls. 10:A–B; 261.

Elevation	Field Number	Description	Plate
86.33	3.723	Truncated, serrated blade	254:F
86.33–85.58	III-782	Four-lugged fragments	—
86.33–85.58	III-783	Four-lugged, fine ware red-washed, blunt lip	—
86.33–85.58	III-785	Notched lip jar fragments, gray ware	cf. 90:L
86.33	III-786	Fine ware spouted vessel	cf. 105:E
86.33	III-787	Spouted jar	cf. 105:E
86.33	III-788	Spouted jar	cf. 105:F
86.33	III-789	Spouted jar	104:J
86.33	III-790	Spouted jar; see fig. 13	23:D; 110:G
86.33	III-791	Jar, spout missing	109:D
86.33	III-792	Pouring lip bowl	cf. 80:Y
86.33	III-793	Miniature beveled-rim bowl	cf. 83:G
ca. 86.33	III-615	Stone bowl	124:A
86.33	III-616	Fragment stone bowl	124:G
86.33	III-617	Fragments band-rimmed bowl (Protoliterate)	—
86.33	III-618	Fragments band-rimmed (Protoliterate)	—
86.33	III-619	Stone cup fragment (Protoliterate)	—
86.33	III-620	Stamp seal	41:M
86.33	III-621	White stone bead	129:Y
86.33	III-622	Cylindrical frit bead; faded gray; length 1.4 cm; diameter 0.06 cm	129:G
86.33	III-623	Ladle bowl	cf. 82:A
86.33	III-624	Spouted jar body	cf. 102:I
86.33	III-625	Spouted jar body	cf. 103:F
86.33	III-626	Spouted jar; see fig. 12	105:E
86.33	III-627	Narrow-necked flask	cf. 90:C
86.33	III-628	Narrow-necked flask round base	cf. 90:B
86.33	III-629	Inner ledge bowl; see fig. 8	81:Y
86.33	III-630	Small jar with knobs and notches at neck	cf. 88:E
86.33	3.1033	Perforated spherical clay object	126:X
86.33-83.53	III-784	Four-lugged jar with knobs	24:K

N9:302 (*cont.*)

Elevation	Field Number	Description	Plate
86.33–84.77	3.1032	Clay jar stopper	130:C
86.33–84.77	3.1035	Clay jar stopper	130:H
85.63	III-601	Hut amulet	cf. 31:BB
85.63	3.033	"Potter's wheel"	127:J
85.63	3.323	Beveled-rim bowl	83:F
85.63	3.330	Twisted handled jar	100:G
85.63	3.412	Large basin	87:C
85.63	3.512	Notched lip	19:L
85.58	III-931a	Door sealing: lion, griffin + unidentified motifs (Protoliterate)	—
85.58	III-931b–c	Door sealings: same motifs as III-931a (Protoliterate)	—
85.58	III-932	Stopper fragment with imprint (Protoliterate)	—
85.58	III-933	Seal impression (Protoliterate)	—
85.58	III-934	Seal impression (Protoliterate)	—
85.58	III-935	Seal impression (Protoliterate)	—
85.58	3.724	Flint blade	254:I
85.43	III-752	Clay ball	36:A–D; 136:A; 137:B; 158:A–C
—	3.329	Strap-handled jar	96:E
—	3.867	Spherical token (Protoliterate)	—
—	—	25 small beveled-rim bowls; diameters 7.0 cm or less (Protoliterate)	—
—	—	7 medium beveled-rim bowls; diameters 8.0 cm or more (Protoliterate)	—
—	—	3 conical clay stoppers; diameters 9.5–11.0 cm; heights 6.0–10.0 cm (Protoliterate)	—
—	—	6 jar stoppers (Protoliterate): 1 flat, diameter 9.8 cm, height ca. 3.5 cm; 1 flat, diameter 12.0 cm, height ca. 5.0 cm; 1 domed, diameter 9.0 cm, height 5.5 cm; 1 conical truncated, diameter 12.5 cm, height 8.0 cm; 1 conical with 2 finger depressions, diameter 11.0 cm, height 5.0 cm; 1 conical with 2 finger depressions, diameter 6.2 cm, height 5.0 cm	—
—	—	24 rather small slingshots, ca. 3.2–4.0 cm long (Protoliterate)	—
—	—	1 perforated domed clay mace-head(?); diameter 11.0 cm; height 5.5 cm (Protoliterate)	—

N9:303

Western edge of Protoliterate brickwork on the southwestern side of the High Mound actually in the northeastern part of M9 with an indented edge extending into M8. Elevations of corners from those abutting on N9:301: 85.94; 86.10 (northwestern corner of buttress-like projection); 86.06 (southwestern corner of indentation); 86.35 (bricks in indentation); 85.65 (floor of indentation). Surface elevation: ca. 87.00. Top of locus: ca. 87.00. Bottom of locus: 85.65. See pl. 261.

N9:304

Traces of Protoliterate brickwork in the form of several jogged faces traced in the eroded southwestern corner of N9 and the adjacent southeastern corner of M9. Surface sloped from ca. 88.80 in the east to 85.00 in the west. No two-sided walls were recovered; the brickwork might have belonged to a platform with more than one building phase. The tops of the brickwork along the N9–10 boundary varied from 86.70 at the east to 84.77 at the west. The tops of the northeast-southwest segment, which petered out at the M9–10 boundary, varied from 86.77 at the northeast to 84.96 at the southwest, with the base there at 84.19. At this point, at a lower level, an unrelated lower wall extending to the south was found; cf. M10:301. Surface elevation east: 88.80. Surface elevation west: 85.00 (in M9). Top of locus, east: 88.80. Top of locus, west: 85.00. Bottom of locus, east: N/A. Bottom of locus, west: 84.19. See pl. 261.

SOUTH OF N9:304

Elevation	Field Number	Description	Plate
ca. 88.30	3.492	Terra-cotta plaque	5:M

N9:402

Elevation	Field Number	Description	Plate
B.S.	4.1112	Spindle whorl	232:D

TRENCH XXIII
N10

Trench of ca. 2.50 × 11.00 m with surface sloping from 86.37 at the northeast to 84.28 at the southeastern corner. Excavated to a depth of ca. 12.50 m at the northern end, but most of the lower part of the trench was filled by access stairs. Prehistoric debris appeared immediately beneath a Protoliterate surface at 0.50(?) B.S. Late Susiana surfaces or floors occurred at 85.00, 84.72, 84.37, and ca. 82.40. Late Middle Susiana deposits began to appear between 80.00 and 70.00. A corner of a Middle Susiana wall and two superimposed floors were found at ca. 78.40. Surface elevation: 86.37. Top of locus: 86.37. Bottom of locus: 73.47. See pls. 260–61.

Elevation	Field Number	Description	Plate
86.37	III-452	Rectangular bead (probably late)	5:G
86.37	—	1 slingshot	—
86.22–85.22	3.815	Orange ware bowl fragment; see fig. 23	162:M
86.22–84.92	3.830	Orange ware bowl lip	162:J
86.17	3.635	Swollen spout	110:B
86.07–85.67	—	3 slingshots	—
85.92–84.82	3.831	Orange ware bowl fragment	162:L
85.87	—	1 slingshot	—
85.52	III-106	Stone stamp seal	41:L
84.92	3.1251	Clay slingshot	231:M
84.52	III-142	Painted terra-cotta roundel(?)	235:B
84.07	—	14 slingshots	—
83.97	3.1252	Clay slingshot	231:J
83.97	—	8 slingshots	—
83.82	III-126	Spindle whorl	65:LL
83.77	3.163	Jar body	162:H
83.42	3.255	Bowl lip	163:V
83.32	3.829	Gray ware bowl lip	162:K
83.32	—	1 slingshot	—
83.17	3.137	Painted lip(?)	56:MM
83.17	3.668	Painted lip(?)	56:GG
82.62	3.215	Bowl chip; see fig. 23	159:X
82.62	3.394	Bowl body	184:P
82.47	3.853	Spindle whorl	232:A
82.47	3.854	Spindle whorl	232:B
81.92	3.136	Beaker lip	56:OO
81.22	3.827	Bowl; see fig. 23	159:G
80.07	III-943	Pottery tool	65:K; 231:P
80.02	3.195	Rim	183:BB
80.02	3.304	Footed beaker fragment	173:B
80.02	3.828	Red ware jar neck	162:X
79.22	3.301	Small ovoid jar	159:K
78.92	3.190	Beaker body	161:L

N10 NORTHEAST CORNER

Elevation	Field Number	Description	Plate
78.52	3.199	Beaker lip	174:B
78.07	3.210	Bowl fragment	181:H
Wash	3.797	Cup	159:C
Surface	3.168	Jar body	191:S
—	3.532	Horizontal handled jar	21:G
—	3.832	Brown ware jar rim	162:Q

N10 MIDDLE

Elevation	Field Number	Description	Plate
85.77	3.017	Bowl fragment	160:O
85.27	—	21 slingshots	—
84.92	—	4 slingshots	—
84.77	III-90	Spindle whorl	65:Y
84.67	—	4 slingshots	—
82.47	III-717	Animal figurine	66:H
81.42	—	2 slingshots	—
—	—	5 slingshots	—

N10 NORTH

Elevation	Field Number	Description	Plate
82.62–81.92	3.193	Jar fragment	162:H

N10 NORTHWEST

Elevation	Field Number	Description	Plate
81.02	3.572	Beaker fragment	56:D

N10 STEPS

Elevation	Field Number	Description	Plate
85.42	3.855	Spindle whorl	232:C
82.67	—	1 slingshot	—
—	III-887	Painted terra-cotta roundel	235:A

N10 EAST

Elevation	Field Number	Description	Plate
81.22	3.257	Jar body fragment	191:T

O7:301

Ca. 1.00 × 2.00 m test pit with access stairs. Heavily salt-encrusted sherds down to 90.50 and less encrusted sherds down to 94.30 indicate the considerable depth of washed-in debris. At 2.25 B.S. were Parthian and Old Elamite sherds with some Proto-literate; at 2.25–5.00 the majority of sherds were Protoliterate but mixed with Old Elamite and some Late Susiana; at 5.00–5.50 were Protoliterate sherds with some Late Susiana; at 5.50–5.80 were Protoliterate sherds with slightly more Late Susiana; at 5.80–7.00 were Late Susiana sherds. Surface elevation: ca. 93.50. Top of locus: ca. 93.50. Bottom of locus: ca. 86.50. See pl. 261.

NORTH OF O7:301

Slope above O7:301. Surface: ca. 95.00. Probable provenience of III-740.

Elevation	Field Number	Description	Plate
ca. 95.00	III-740	Stone cylinder seal	5:C
ca. 95.00	3.445	Jar fragment	77:L
ca. 95.00	3.450	Vat rim	79:E
ca. 95.00	3.451	Vat rim	79:O
ca. 95.00	3.452	Vat rim	79:T

O7:302

Test pit, ca. 1.60 × 1.60 m. Salt-encrusted sherds still as deep as 4.00 B.S.; at 2.80 were Parthian, Elamite, and some Proto-literate sherds; at 2.40–2.80 were Protoliterate sherds with some Elamite or nondescript late and a few Late Susiana sherds; at 4.00–4.70 were predominantly Protoliterate sherds, with a few late intrusions and some Late Susiana. Surface elevation: ca. 93.00. Top of locus: ca. 93.00. Bottom of locus: ca. 86.50. See pl. 261.

Elevation	Field Number	Description	Plate
ca. 93.00	3.455	Jar neck	78:O
ca. 92.30	3.489	Terra-cotta plaque fragment	5:J
ca. 91.50	3.313	Jar fragment	78:M
ca. 91.50	3.314	Jar neck	79:P
ca. 91.50	3.315	Jar shoulder	78:C
ca. 91.50	3.316	Bowl rim	77:E
ca. 88.40	3.320	Bowl rim	77:F
ca. 88.40	3.443	Bowl fragment	77:C
ca. 88.40	3.444	Bowl rim	77:G

O7:303

This test area, ca. 1.00 × 2.00 m, was discontinued at a depth where the sherds were still predominantly late mixed with some Protoliterate. Surface elevation: ca. 95.00. Top of locus: ca. 95.00. Bottom of locus: ca. 92.50. See pl. 261.

O9:301

Protoliterate cesspit of baked bricks varying slightly in size: 6.0 × 11.0 × 26.0, 7.0 × 12.0 × 26.0, or 6.0 × 12.8 × 26.0 cm. Top course had fifteen or sixteen bricks. Most of the bricks were laid flat, although some in the lower layers were on edge. Beveled-rim bowls: 11 complete; 186 rims-plus-base fragments; 1,650 rims; 128 bases; 650 bodies. Surface elevation: ca. 89.00. Top of locus: 88.38. Bottom of locus: 86.40. See pls. 6:B; 10:C–D; 261.

Elevation	Field Number	Description	Plate
—	III-407	Bowl, pouring lip missing	—
—	3.560	Cone mosaic	31:Y

NORTH OF O9:301

Protoliterate remains occurred on the eastern slope of the southwestern spur of the High Mound at the foot of the disintegrated lowest courses of the Old Elamite brickwork.

O9:302

Cesspit of baked bricks; on brickwork details, see O9:301. Filled with soft greenish earth and green-stained beveled-rim bowls: 8 almost complete; 210 rim-plus-base fragments; 1,896 rims; 612 bases; 3,207 bodies. Surface elevation: ca. 89.00. Top of locus: 88.38. Bottom of locus: 86.58. See pls. 6:B; 10:C; 261.

Elevation	Field Number	Description	Plate
87.88	III-614	Band-rimmed stone bowl	29:AA; 124:U
—	III-751	Sealing (Protoliterate)	—

NORTH OF O9:302

Immediately to the north of O9:302, a spouted jar and a beveled-rim bowl lay at the lower edge of an irregular sloping mass of Protoliterate sherds. See pl. 6:B

Elevation	Field Number	Description	Plate
ca. 80.80	III-206	Spouted jar; see fig. 12	103:A

NORTHWEST OF O9:302

Somewhat farther to the north and west of O9:302. Protoliterate remains occurred close to the surface at the foot of the disintegrated lowest courses of Elamite brickwork. Note in particular a cluster of pottery (III-268, a tray fragment, and four beveled-rim bowls) just downslope from an inverted rim fragment of an Elamite vat, ca. 91.00. See pl. 6:B.

Elevation	Field Number	Description	Plate
ca. 90.60	III-268	Spouted jar	105:A
ca. 90.30	III-210	Pouring líp bowl	cf. 80:Z

P6:301

Small stratigraphic pit slightly down the slope from the pebble pavement of P6:302. The upper part of the pit had mixed nondescript late, Elamite, and Protoliterate sherds, chiefly of beveled-rim bowls. Although some later sherds occurred as low as 88.30, Late Susiana sherds were in the majority at 90.20. Surface elevation: ca. 92.00. Top of locus: 91.70. Bottom of locus: 86.50. See pl. 261.

P6:302

Area between the brickwork of P6:303 and the pit of P6:301. Distinguished by a patch of pebble pavement at 92.45 with a few definite bricks adjacent on the south. Date uncertain. Surface elevation: ca. 93.00. Top of locus: ca. 93.00. Bottom of locus: 92.45. See pl. 261.

P6:303

Exploratory area on the northeastern slope of the High Mound. A patch of brickwork was reached with top at northwestern corner at 95.00 and at the southeastern corner at 93.70; work was then continued down the slope in P6:302 and 301. The date of the brickwork is uncertain, but it is probably of a late period. Surface elevation: ca. 96.50. Top of locus: ca. 96.50. Bottom of locus: 93.70. See pl. 261.

P6:304

This late burial of uncertain date was covered by an irregular "gable" of stones and baked-brick fragments; it was near some very fragmentary bits of brickwork. There was an extended skeleton oriented approximately north-south. Surface elevation: ca. 97.00. Top of locus: ca. 97.00. Bottom of locus: ca. 96.40. See pl. 261.

Elevation	Field Number	Description	Plate
ca. 98.00	III-886	Ornament in shape (near burial) of human head	5:A
ca. 97.40	III-910	Shell bird pendant	5:F

P7:301

Eastern end, ca. 1.00 × 3.00 m, of narrow test trench running from P7 to O7. At 93.66 was a floor with the base of a Parthian vessel still *in situ*. On the floor was a large group of Parthian sherds, including masses of corrugated torpedo jar bodies, some rims and bases, and also glazed sherds, including the neck of a flask. Below the Parthian floor was ca. 1.00 m of relatively sterile soil sealing a particularly numerous and varied group of Protoliterate sherds lying on a floor at 91.74. This same floor, varying between 91.87 and 91.62, but with less profuse sherds, was traced in the rest of the narrow trench. Surface elevation: ca. 95.00. Top of locus: ca. 95.00. Bottom of locus: 91.74. See pl. 261.

Elevation	Field Number	Description	Plate
94.30–93.65	3.1006	"Torpedo jar rim"	72:J

P7:302

Platform or wide wall formed by several courses of large bricks, 11.5 × 12.5 × 48.0–50.0 cm; top at north, 94.40, at south, 94.17; base at 93.89. Presumed to be Parthian. Surface elevation: ca. 95.00. Top of locus: ca. 95.00. Bottom of locus: 93.89. See pl. 261.

P7:303

This locus consists of a fragment of wall traced immediately under the surface and lying between P7:301 and 302. Surface elevation: ca. 95.20. Top of locus: ca. 95.20. Bottom of locus: ca. 95.11. See pl. 261.

P8:301

Elamite wall 4.80 m wide. Surface at east 95.00, at the southwest ca. 90.75. Top of wall at northeast 94.02, at the southeast 93.12, at middle southern edge 91.81, at the southwest ca. 90.70. The wall was followed down for 3.20 m without reaching the bottom. An average brick size of $11.0 \times 34.0 \times 34.0$ cm was distinguishable in the upper seventeen courses. The face was set back 31.0 cm for seventeen courses, i.e., ca. 2.0 cm for each brick course. Twenty-seven courses were clearly distinguished. Cf. P8:303. Surface elevation: 95.00. Top of locus: 95.00. Bottom of locus: 89.92. See pl. 261.

Elevation	Field Number	Description	Plate
ca. 95.00	III-388	Terra-cotta cone	31:S
ca. 94.30	III-653	Stone mace-head	29:M; 125:CC

WEST OF P8:301

Gully below western slope.

Elevation	Field Number	Description	Plate
Surface	III-306	Cylindrical stone bead	41:K

SOUTHEAST OF P8:301

Promontory of survey.

Elevation	Field Number	Description	Plate
Surface	3.804	Vat rim	79:B

P8:302

Trench, ca. 1.00×10.00 m, located to the east of P8:301; the northwestern end extended into P7. Surface at northwest 95.00, at the southeast 82.02. No traces of a continuation of P8:301 occurred. A floor at the western end at 91.98 and brickwork in the middle at 90.55 were both probably Elamite. At 92.50 (2.50 B.S.) the sherds were mixed groups of Parthian and Old Elamite with some Protoliterate and an occasional Late Susiana sherd. Below, Parthian sherds disappeared but as deep as 90.00 a few Elamite and Protoliterate sherds were mixed with Late Susiana sherds. Still lower the few sherds found were Late Susiana. The deepest point reached was 89.65. Surface elevation: 95.00. Top of locus: 95.00. Bottom of locus: 89.65. See pl. 261.

Elevation	Field Number	Description	Plate
Surface	III-741	Cylinder seal	5:B
93.50	3.449	Disc base	77:I
90.85	III-567	Bowl	77:A
90.85	III-568	Bowl	cf. 77:A
90.70	3.795	Painted foot	159:T

P8:303

Segment of wall, destroyed at both ends, at the southwestern corner of P8:301. Although the two walls are not bonded together, they might have originally formed one wide wall. The base of P8:303 was not reached. Surface elevation: ca. 91.00. Top of locus: ca. 91.00. Bottom of locus: ca. 89.00. See pl. 261.

TRENCH XXVII A
P9:301

Face of a Parthian wall with top at 92.76 and base at 92.09. Alongside the wall face were a large number of typical Parthian sherds including torpedo jar rims and corrugated bodies. Surface elevation: ca. 93.00. Top of locus: ca. 93.00. Bottom of locus: 92.09. See pl. 261.

Elevation	Field Number	Description	Plate
Surface	3.493	Terra-cotta plaque fragment	5:L

P9 EAST

Elevation	Field Number	Description	Plate
B.S.	4.689	Jar fragment	4:I

P10

Elevation	Field Number	Description	Plate
B.S.	4.664	Incised body	4:H

P10 SLOPE

Expanse of Elamite brickwork immediately B.S. in a ca. 7.00 m long strip extended to the southwest from P9:401 and between P9:401 and P10:402. The surface sloped down from ca. 89.38 to 89.00 or lower and was dug only sufficiently to articulate the brickwork except at the southwestern end of the 7.00 m strip just beyond the end of the brickwork, where a small area was taken down to 85.44 without reaching the base of the bricks. Surface elevation: 91.38. Top of locus: 91.38. Bottom of locus: 85.44.

Elevation	Field Number	Description	Plate
91.38	4.661	Jar shoulder	78:F
91.38	4.666	Jar neck	78:A
91.38	4.667	Jar neck	78:I
91.38	4.675	Jar neck	79:N
91.38	4.676	Vat ridge	79:L
91.38	4.688	Vat rim	79:D
91.38	4.690	Vat fragment	79:G
88.23	4.685	Jar shoulder	78:L

P10:401

Floor at 88.48–88.39 located at the foot of, and underneath, the westernmost preserved Elamite brickwork of the southeastern spur of the High Mound. A segment of baked-brick and stone drain extended to the northwest and on the east abutted Old Elamite vat sherds (4.659) that paved the floor, which was covered by a 15.0 cm layer of ash and was underneath the lowest courses of the brick mass (seen partly cut away in pl. 7:D). The locus also included the sloping, eroded brickwork with surface at 89.00 immediately alongside or above the floor. Surface elevation: 89.00. Top of locus: 89.00. Bottom of locus: 88.39. See pl. 261.

Elevation	Field Number	Description	Plate
89.00	4.665	Incised body	4:G
89.00	4.693	Vat fragment	79:A
88.56	4.681	Jar base	77:K
88.56–88.39	4.659	2/3 of vat	79:J

P10:402

Area on the southern slope of the High Mound's spur with a decayed mass of bricks (slightly below the surface) only one or two courses high between ca. 88.60 and 88.38. Irregular layers of earth, with varying amounts of ash (ca. 50.0 cm thick at their deepest point), separate the upper mass from irregular masses of bricky material with their tops at ca. 88.00–87.90 (except one spot directly underlying the upper brickwork). The lower bricky mass rested on a ca. 3.0 cm thick irregular floor of hard mud and straw at ca. 87.40. Below was more ashy earth, with the bases of walls at ca. 87.28, not preserved very high, continuing into adjacent squares and demarcating P10:403 from P10:402. In the western part of the locus was an oval pit, beginning at 87.78, with contracted burial Grave 4.32, at 87.23, oriented approximately east-west with head facing to the south; no objects were found, but sherds from the fill of the burial pit were Old Elamite. Of the twenty-six bones from this locus, identified were *Bos*, including scapula (3), rib (1), humerus (1), femur (1), tibia (1), fibula (1), and various (3). Surface elevation: ca. 88.80. Top of locus: ca. 88.80. Bottom of locus: ca. 87.20. See pl. 261.

Elevation	Field Number	Description	Plate
88.03–87.23	4.668	Jar neck	78:H
87.78–87.23	4.670	Jar shoulder	78:B
87.23	4.682	Jar base	77:N
Grave 4.32 pit			
87.64	4.669	Jar neck	78:J
87.64	4.673	Vat ridge	79:K
87.64	4.679	Jar base	77:O
87.61	4.671	Jar shoulder	78:G
87.61	4.672	Vat rim	79:F
87.61	4.674	Vat rim	79:M
87.61	4.680	Jar base	77:P
87.60	4.864	Stone hoe	245:M

NORTH OF P10:402

Small rounded patch of sherd paving lying in ashy soil at 88.33 just to the north of the northeastern part of P10:402 and, as in P10:401, continuing under the adjacent brickwork, top at 83.63.

P10:403

The locus consists of two parts, both outside of Square P10: P10:403 South is in P11 to the south of P10:402 and P10:403 East is in Q11 to the southeast of P10:402. Both share with P10:402 the hard mud and straw floor at ca. 87.38, the ashy earth below, and the wall stumps with bases at ca. 87.28. The latter might demarcate three rooms. In P10:403 South the wall face was fire reddened. Also in P10:403 South at 86.68 was a partly destroyed skeleton, Grave 4.33, extended except for the bent lower legs, oriented slightly southeast-northwest and with the head facing to the south. Surface elevation: ca. 89.00. Top of locus: ca. 89.00. Bottom of locus: ca. 86.68. See pl. 261.

Elevation	Field Number	Description	Plate
89.00	4.691	Vat rim	79:H
87.83	4.662	Jar shoulder	78:D
87.83	4.1080	Vat rim	79:U

TRENCH XXVIII
Q6:301

The surface slopes from ca. 91.00 at the northwestern corner to ca. 89.50 at the northeast. The greater part of the area was cleared only to a short depth B.S., with eleven courses of bricks in the middle, oriented northwest-southeast, sloping down from 90.60 at the southwest to 89.00 at the northeast. A small pit going down to ca. 86.00, and with consistently Late Susiana sherds, was sunk at the edge of the brickwork. The latter's date is uncertain. The B.S. sherds were mixed, consisting of a few late with Proto-literate and Late Susiana sherds; the latter become dominant at 88.70. Surface elevation: ca. 91.00. Top of locus: ca. 91.00. Bottom of locus: ca. 86.00. See pl. 261.

Elevation	Field Number	Description	Plate
89.80–89.10	3.317	Horizontal-handled bowl fragment	75:T
86.10	3.020	Lugged jar fragments; see fig. 23	56:WW; 161:C

TRENCH IV
Q9

U-shaped trench in hollow on the southeastern side of the High Mound. Eastern corners project into R9 and Q10. Surface, at corners at 86.68, except 85.80 at the southeast. Along the northern edge of the trench a number of beveled-rim bowl fragments were just B.S. Within the trench, there was a proper surface wash of mixed late sherds as deep as 2.00 m; below was Late Susiana occupation debris. Surface elevation: 86.60. Top of locus: 86.60. Bottom of locus: 80.60. See pl. 261.

Elevation	Field Number	Description	Plate
Surface	3.260	Orange ware, bowl fragment	162:N
83.40	1.178	Footed bowl base	159:U
83.10	1.093	Lugged jar fragment	161:F
82.30	1.068	Bowl lip	160:L
80.90	1.234	Sherd rubber	231:EE
80.80	1.139	Truncated blade	254:N
—	1.148	Double truncated blade(?)	255:D

Q9 NORTH

Elevation	Field Number	Description	Plate
84.60	I-91	Pebble	230:O
83.70	3.728	Blade	255:R
83.20	1.115	Lugged body fragment	56:PP
81.90	I-83	Terra-cotta object	235:E
81.90	1.055	Bowl fragment	160:G
81.90	1.113	Bowl body fragment	56:L
81.90	1.116	Lugged jar neck	56:N
81.30	I-112	Perforated clay roundel	231:U
81.30	1.114	Bowl fragment	56:M
81.30	1.120	Bowl fragment	56:W
81.30	1.122	Beaker body fragment	56:LL
81.10	1.121	Bowl fragment	56:V

Q9 SOUTH

Elevation	Field Number	Description	Plate
84.30	1.084	Jar neck; see fig. 23	162:E
84.30	1.156	Flint blade	255:L
84.30	1.235	Sherd rubber	231:HH
82.80	1.119	Bowl body fragment	56:R
82.80–81.95	1.236	Jar fragment; see fig. 22	—
81.60	1.074	Jar sherd; see fig. 23	159:O
81.60	1.077	Bowl fragment; see fig. 23	160:I
81.30	1.046	Bowl fragment	56:G; 160:M
81.30	1.112	Bowl fragment	56:J

Q9:301 = TRENCH XXVII B

Continuation of the testing of the slope above Trench IV begun by P9:301 (= Trench XXVII A). Surface sloped from ca. 93.00 to ca. 91.00. It was dug to a depth of ca. 3.70 B.S., ca. 89.30. At that depth there was still a mixture of late sherds; however, Elamite sherds outnumbered Parthian torpedo-jar rims and corrugated bodies. Surface elevation: ca. 93.00. Top of locus: ca. 93.00. Bottom of locus: 89.30. See pl. 261.

Elevation	Field Number	Description	Plate
ca. 89.50	3.319	Bowl lip	77:D
ca. 89.50	3.447	Jar foot	77:H

EAST OF TRENCH XXVII B

Elevation	Field Number	Description	Plate
Surface	IV-354	Terra-cotta stamp seal	234:HH

Q10 SLOPE

Articulation of brickwork from the top of the southeastern spur of the High Mound in Q10 downslope into Q11. Surface sloped from 93.00 to ca. 88.00. It was primarily a B.S. clearance except for a narrow trench through the crest taken down ca. 1.00 m through decayed brick material, and a small cut into the brickwork lower on the slope. A large chunk of wall that fell as a unit was marked on the plan by a darker grid (Q10–Q11). Surface elevation: ca. 93.00. Top of locus: ca. 93.00. Bottom of locus: B.S. See pl. 261.

Elevation	Field Number	Description	Plate
91.79	4.663	Jar shoulder	78:E
91.79	4.677	Vat rim	79:I
91.79	4.678	Jar base	77:M
91.79	4.683	Vat rim	79:C
91.79	4.686	Jar shoulder	78:N

Q10:401

A heavily damaged burial of a child, oriented approximately east-west, extended with head to west; 48.0 cm long (Grave 4.34). Surface elevation: ca. 93.00. Top of locus: ca. 93.00. Bottom of locus: B.S. See pl. 261.

Elevation	Field Number	Description	Plate
Grave 4.34			
—	IV-331a–b	Two green glass bracelets with twisted glass moldings; diameters 4.5 cm	—
—	IV-331c	11 green glass bracelet fragments with red and green glass molding representing at least 2 bracelets. Islamic	—
—	IV-331d	Light blue frit ring bead; diameter 1.7	—
—	IV-331e	52 ring beads of white, black, blue, yellow, and red (only 1) glass and 0.35 cm in diameter;	—
		1 red barrel bead and 1 slightly larger green irregular barrel bead	
—	IV-331f	Bronze globular pendant with loop; diameter 1.4 cm (broken)	—
—	IV-331g	2 pierced and 1 unpierced shells; length 0.9 cm	—
—	IV-332a	Green glass bracelet with wavy molding; diameter 4.8 cm	—
—	IV-332b	Mottled dark green and white glass bracelet with twisted red and green molding; diameter 3.9 cm	—
—	IV-332c	9 fragments of 1 or 2 bracelets	—

Q11:101

Fragments of an Old Elamite vat, with remains of a burial. Surface elevation: ca. 88.00. Top of locus: ca. 88.00. Bottom of locus: B.S.

Q11:102

Eroded remains of a kiln, presumably Old Elamite in date. Surface elevation: ca. 89.00. Top of locus: ca. 89.00. Bottom of locus: B.S.

Q11:103

Segment of brickwork cleared to the northwest of Trench II. Surface elevation: N/A. Top of locus: N/A. Bottom of locus: N/A.

TRENCH III
R8–S8

This trench, ca. 4.00 m wide and 6.00 m long, was cut on the eastern slope of the eastern lobe of the High Mound. On the summit was Old Elamite brickwork over prehistoric deposits. It was not dug deeply. Surface elevation: ca. 89.00. Top of locus: ca. 89.00. Bottom of locus: N/A. See pl. 260.

Elevation	Field Number	Description	Plate
Surface	1.123	Lip fragment	56:BB
ca. 89.00	2.134	Painted sherd	161:B
—	2.567	Imported spouted vessel, black-on-red ware; see fig. 21	—
—	2.570	Recurved sided handled bowl	75:N

MIDDLE OF R8–S8

Elevation	Field Number	Description	Plate
ca. 89.00	II-36	Stamp seal	67:D

TRENCH I
R10–11

Located slightly to the north of and parallel to Trench II, the surface of this area sloped from 89.50 in the west to ca. 81.00 in the east and it was divided into Trench I plots corresponding to those of Trench II; it served as access to the various steps of Trench II, which are not indicated separately on pl. 260.

PLOT 1

Surface elevation: 83.10. Top of locus: 83.10. Bottom of locus: ca. 79.35.

Elevation	Field Number	Description	Plate
82.10	1.054	Straight spout	159:M
82.10	2.159	Bowl base	160:C
82.10	2.174	Beaker lip	161:M
82.10	2.260	Bowl fragment	169:I
82.10	2.332	Painted body	56:Q
ca. 81.60	2.191	Red ware hole-mouthed spout	193:S

PLOTS 2–3

Surface elevation: 83.10. Top of locus: 83.10. Bottom of locus: ca. 80.00.

Elevation	Field Number	Description	Plate
ca. 81.00	2.264	Bowl fragment	172:G

PLOT 3

Surface elevation: 84.40. Top of locus: 84.40. Bottom of locus: ca. 82.00.

Elevation	Field Number	Description	Plate
82.90	2.172	Painted lip	184:K
82.90	2.337	Painted body sherd	56:Z
82.10	2.144	Painted lip	163:Q

PLOT 4

Surface elevation: 86.10. Top of locus: 86.10. Bottom of locus: ca. 82.00.

Elevation	Field Number	Description	Plate
ca. 85.80	II-17	Miniature cup	56:A; 159:D
83.60	2.123	Beaker lip	56:EE
83.60	2.339	Beaker body	56:II
83.60	2.252	Red ware neck	162:V
82.85	2.177	Beaker lip	159:H
82.85	2.178	Jar fragment	159:Q

TRENCH II
R10–11

This step trench was divided into 2.00 × 4.00 m plots; its surface sloped from ca. 90.70 in the west to ca. 81.00 in the east. See pls. 11:B (background right); 260

Elevation	Field Number	Description	Plate
B.S.	1.048	Painted lip fragment	160:F
B.S.	1.130	Blade core	253:L
—	1.133	Flake core(?)	256:L
—	1.136	Retouched blade	254:C
B.S.	1.164	Double snapped blade	254:P
B.S.	1.162	Double snapped blade	254:R
B.S.	1.160	Truncated blade	254:S
B.S.	1.152	Flint bladelet	254:CC
B.S.	1.153	Flint blade	254:DD

SOUTH OF R10–11

Elevation	Field Number	Description	Plate
Surface	II-31	Domed stamp seal	67:C

PLOT 1

Completely occupied by steps. Surface elevation: 82.10. Top of locus: 82.10. Bottom of locus: N/A.

Elevation	Field Number	Description	Plate
81.40	1.146	Flint blade	254:W
80.70	1.165	Flint blade	254:U
80.20	I-72	Slingshot	cf. 65:L
82.10	1.168	Mèche de foret	255:N
79.60	1.016	Painted lip fragment	176:H

PLOTS 1–2

Elevation	Field Number	Description	Plate
78.80	2.293	Painted lip fragment	184:D
79.50	1.014	Painted lip fragment	176:I
79.50	1.062	Painted lip fragment	163:R
79.50	1.069	Painted fragments	163:P
79.00	1.019a	Painted lip fragment	176:L

PLOT 2

Virgin soil was reached in the western third of the plot. Steps filled the eastern two-thirds, the lowest at 72.50. Surface elevation: 83.10. Top of locus: 83.10. Bottom of locus: 70.40.

Elevation	Field Number	Description	Plate
82.10	1.040b	Painted lip fragment	160:P
82.10	1.159	Painted beaker body	56:NN
82.10	1.161	Mèche de foret(?)	255:M
82.00	1.006	Painted lip fragment	171:E
81.90	1.051	Painted lip fragment	56:E
79.70	1.019b	Painted lip fragment	176:L
79.70	1.098	Painted body fragment	176:W
79.10	1.002	Ca. 1/2 painted bowl; see fig. 30	181:L
79.10	1.038b	Painted jar fragments	190:I
79.10	2.282	Painted lip fragment	183:L
79.10	2.290	Painted lip fragment	184:A
79.10–78.60	2.022	Sauceboat fragments; see fig. 26	165:A
78.90	II-16	Sauceboat fragment; see fig. 31	59:G; 189:I
78.85	1.061	Painted bowl fragments	181:F, P
78.60	2.259	Painted bowl fragments	169:J
78.60	2.284	Painted lip fragment	183:N
78.60	2.285	Painted lip fragment	183:O
78.30	1.044	Painted lip fragment	58:BB
77.70	1.001	Painted bowl fragments; see fig. 26	169:C
77.70	1.004	"Box" corner	192:O
77.70	1.011a	Bowl fragments	171:L
77.70	1.073	Ring base; see fig. 26	165:I
75.50	2.196	Painted jar shoulder	191:F
75.50	2.208	Painted jar fragment	189:J

PLOTS 2–3

Mixed Late Middle Susiana-Late Susiana.

Elevation	Field Number	Description	Plate
ca. 83.40	2.780	Perforated roundel	231:Z

PLOT 3

Virgin soil was reached at the eastern edge of the plot; to the west the bottom was at 80.50. Surface elevation: 84.40. Top of locus: 84.40. Bottom of locus: 70.40.

Elevation	Field Number	Description	Plate
82.50	1.040a, c	Painted lip fragment	160:P
82.90	2.204	Unpainted jar fragment; see fig. 23	162:C
82.90	2.205	Red ware jar fragment; see fig. 23	162:R
82.60	1.066	Painted body fragment	163:BB
82.40	1.043	Painted shoulder fragment	58:CC; 192:D
81.90	I-145	Unpainted bowl; see fig. 23	—
80.90	I-140	Unpainted jar; see fig. 23	189:K
80.40–79.20	1.003	Broad wash beaker fragment; see fig. 26	173:D
80.40–79.20	1.038a	Painted jar fragment	190:I
80.30	1.092	Painted body fragment	163:Y
80.30	1.096	Ring base	172:I
80.30	1.097	Ring base	173:F
80.30	1.185	Painted lip fragment	170:B
79.80	1.075	Red ware trough-spouted fragment	193:R
79.80	1.127	Painted base	181:D
79.80	2.022	Sauceboat fragment	165:A

Elevation	Field Number	Description	Plate
79.60	1.009a	Painted jar fragment	—
79.10	1.012	Terra-cotta lid(?)	231:KK
78.80	1.009b	Painted jar fragment	—
79.60–78.70	1.060	Painted lip fragment	176:Y
78.70	1.028	Painted body fragment	163:Z
78.60	1.027	Painted body fragment	59:D
78.60	1.063	Base fragment	168:E
78.40	1.140	Flint blade	254:T
78.20	2.039	Tortoise jar spout	59:KK; 187:C
77.75	1.011b	Painted fragments	171:L
77.75	1.005	Painted lip fragment; see fig. 30	176:D
77.40	1.099	Painted bowl fragment	169:E
77.40	2.271	Unpainted fragment	176:M
77.20	2.037	Stand fragment; see fig. 31	185:C
77.20	2.197	Painted bowl fragments; see fig. 26	165:D
77.20	2.243	Painted lip fragment	178:I
77.20	2.261	Unpainted neck; see fig. 31	192:J
77.20	2.267	Painted lip fragment	169:N
77.20	2.291	Painted lip fragment	184:B
77.20	2.292	Painted lip fragment	184:F
76.60	2.272	Painted lip fragment	176:J
76.60	2.279	Painted lip fragment	183:H
76.00	2.263	Painted lip fragment	169:R
75.40	2.288	Painted lip fragment	183:U
73.65	2.198	Unpainted shoulder fragment	191:X

PLOT 4

Surface elevation: 86.10. Top of locus: 86.10. Bottom of locus: 80.50.

Elevation	Field Number	Description	Plate
86.10–82.60	2.047	Painted bowl base	59:U
84.70	2.188	Painted fragment	160:N
84.70	2.202	Unpainted fragment; see fig. 23	159:F
84.70	2.424	Painted lip fragment	56:QQ
84.10	1.117	Painted lip fragment	56:H
84.10	1.118	Painted lip fragment	56:I
83.32	1.080	Red ware bowl fragment; see fig. 23	162:I
83.30	1.166	Snapped blade	254:O
83.30	1.169	Red ware neck	162:U
83.30	2.256	Ring-base fragment	160:Q
83.30	2.257	Unpainted lip fragment	161:G
83.30	2.294	Painted body fragment	184:O
83.30	2.325	Painted jar body fragment	56:Y
83.30	2.335	Beaker lip fragment	56:CC
83.30–82.70	II-143	Painted base; see fig. 23	56:SS; 160:A
82.90	II-373	Painted jar; see fig. 23	159:N
82.85	2.045	Painted base	160:D
82.70	2.251	Red ware neck fragment	162:AA
82.60	2.171	Painted lip fragment	159:B
82.60	2.203	Unpainted bowl fragment; see fig. 23	161:H
82.60	2.268	Painted lip fragment	174:C
81.36	2.124	Miniature bowl	159:A
81.35	2.131	Beaker lip fragment	56:FF; 161:K
81.35	2.140	Beaker body fragment	56:JJ
81.35	2.149	Lugged jar fragments	161:E
81.35	2.253	Beaker lip fragment	159:I

PLOT 5

Surface elevation: 87.90. Top of locus: 87.90. Bottom of locus: 81.50.

Elevation	Field Number	Description	Plate
87.10	I-54	Stamp seal	67:E
86.90	I-55	Stone bead	234:BB
86.70	1.078	Red ware neck fragment	162:Y
85.40	2.206	Red ware jar fragment; see fig. 23	162:W

PLOTS 5–6

Surface elevation: 80.50. Top of locus: 89.50. Bottom of locus: 81.50.

Elevation	Field Number	Description	Plate
84.34	2.125	Painted body fragment	56:HH
84.34	2.133	Lugged jar fragment	161:D
84.34	2.137	Beaker lip fragment	161:J
84.34	2.182	Buff ware, hole-mouthed; see fig. 23	162:B
84.34	2.328	Painted lip fragment	56:F
84.34	2.329	Painted body fragment	56:K
84.34	2.330	Painted shoulder fragment	56:VV
84.34	2.333	Painted body fragment	56:S
84.34	2.334	Painted body fragment	56:U
84.34	2.425	Painted body fragment	56:P
84.34	2.426	Painted body fragment	56:T
83.90	2.184	Painted lip fragment	160:K
83.90	2.189	Painted body fragment	—
83.90	2.190	Painted body fragment	160:J
83.90	2.331	Painted body fragment	56:X
83.40	2.527	Unpainted fragment	159:E
83.35	2.157	Painted bowl fragment	159:W
83.35	2.179	Beaker lip fragment	161:I
83.35	2.180	Jar fragment	159:P
83.35	2.181	Painted jar fragment; see fig. 23	162:F
82.44	2.175	Beaker lip fragment	161:N
82.44	2.185	Ring base fragment	160:B
82.40	2.322	Painted shoulder fragment	162:G
Steps and balk	2.176	Painted lip fragment	159:V

PLOT 6

Surface elevation: 89.50. Top of locus: 89.50. Bottom of locus: 82.20.

Elevation	Field Number	Description	Plate
88.50	1.007	Painted shoulder fragment	56:UU
88.50	1.163	Flint blade	254:L
87.00	1.088	Red ware neck; see fig. 23	162:Z
87.00	1.094	Red ware lip fragment	162:O
87.00	1.180	Red ware neck	162:S
84.75	1.083	Painted body-bucrania	184:I
84.75	1.095	Red ware lip fragment; see fig. 23	162:P
84.44	2.479	Red ware neck fragment	162:T
Surface	1.124	Painted lip fragment	56:TT
Surface	1.125	Beaker lip fragment	56:KK

TERRACE EAST 1
"EAST AREA"
P17–S18

The East Area and vicinity had scattered finds without specific provenience. See pl. 260.

Elevation	Field Number	Description	Plate
Surface	III-654	Black stone with white veins; mace-head	—
—	3.454	Incised shoulder of jar (Elamite)	78:K
—	III-258	Jar	88:X
ca. 81.00	III-827a–b	Door sealing	43:C; 139:D
—	—	Grinding stone	239:C
—	3.786	Thorn figure	236:G
—	IV-14	Crescent shape token	40:E; 134:F5
—	4.881	Pivot stone	250:A
—	4.882	Pivot stone	250:B
—	II-382	Perforated stone roundel	125:T
—	III-200	Inlay	129:OO
—	III-300	Shell pendant	129:FF
—	III-301	Shell pendant	129:DD
—	III-443a	Stone bead	129:K
—	3.351	Painted body fragment	58:M

P17–S17:TRENCH V

This southwest-northeast test trench, ca. 2.00 × 30.00 m, was divided into 2.00 × 4.00 m plots, A–L and Z, and retroactively given normal locus numbers. See pl. 264.

Elevation	Field Number	Description	Plate
Surface	2.796	Red-washed neck	cf. 75:Y
—	3.549	Animal figurine	31:N
—	2.226	Base fragment	87:L
Surface	2.228	Base fragment; see fig. 9	87:N
Surface	II-98	Flattish sealing	42:H; 136:E
Dump	3.1205	Gray stone disc	125:AA
Dump	II-343	Jar sealing fragment	157:C
Dump	II-372	Jar sealing fragment	143:D
1.00 B.S.	3.353	Incised body	28:G
—	3.709	Pestle pounder	244:C

P17–S17 NORTHEAST EXTENSION:TRENCH V

Elevation	Field Number	Description	Plate
—	2.307	Tray fragment; see fig. 9	86:JJ

P17–S17 EAST END EXTENSION:TRENCH V

Elevation	Field Number	Description	Plate
Cleaning	III-366	"Eye plug"	67:G

P17–S17 NORTHEAST:TRENCH V

Elevation	Field Number	Description	Plate
Cleaning	2.233	Ovoid jar neck	93:C

P17–S17 NORTHEAST END:TRENCH V

Elevation	Field Number	Description	Plate
Surface	III-457	Bead-like stone seal	41:H

NORTH OF P17–S17:TRENCH V

Elevation	Field Number	Description	Plate
Surface	4.385	Painted fragment	59:Z

EAST OF P17–S17:TRENCH V

Elevation	Field Number	Description	Plate
Surface	II-323	Stone bead/seal(?)	129:B

P17:TRENCH V A

The area was begun during the third season as a small sounding, ca. 1.50 × 2.00 m, to the north of the Circular Structure. It was carried down to a depth of 2.20 m and was crossed diagonally by a segment of wall. A short projection to the south branched at the end to the west and to the east into Q17, where there was a pit, ca. 1.50 m in diameter (not indicated on pl. 264) to which can be assigned Achaemenid sherds (e.g., 3.648, 3.866). Otherwise, Achaemenid sherds normally occurred close to the surface. Trench V A was recleared and enlarged during the third season (cf. pl. 264, P17:301–03). Surface elevation: ca. 83.20. Top of locus: ca. 83.20. Bottom of locus: 81.30.

Elevation	Field Number	Description	Plate
ca. 83.20	III-446	Carnelian bead	—
ca. 83.20	3.655	Bowl fragment	—
ca. 83.20	3.889	C.20 jar fragment (Achaemenid)	—
ca. 83.20	3.895	Carinated bowl. Similar fragment (Achaemenid)	—
ca. 83.20	3.897	Jar handle + body (Achaemenid)	—
ca. 83.20	3.902	Jar fragment (Achaemenid)	—
ca. 83.20	3.922	Jar neck fragment (Achaemenid)	—
ca. 83.20	3.923	Carinated bowl. Similar fragment; see fig. 8	—
ca. 83.20	3.995	Flaring jar neck fragment (Achaemenid)	—
83.20–82.30	3.497	Body, incised decoration	28:O
ca. 83.00	—	1 slingshot	—
82.85	—	Beveled-rim bowls: 4 complete	—
ca. 82.70	III-162	Conical bowl	80:S
ca. 82.70	III-174	Four-lugged jar fragment	cf. 122:B
ca. 82.70	III-346	Horizontal-handled fragment; see fig. 9	101:G
ca. 82.70	III-495	Terra-cotta spool	30:E
ca. 82.70	III-496	Terra-cotta spool	cf. 30:G
ca. 82.70	3.811	Terra-cotta spike	127:C
ca. 82.60	3.924	Bowl	73:N
ca. 82.60	3.029	Fine ware cup	80:M
ca. 82.60	3.456	Jar body fragment	88:W
ca. 82.60	3.596–97	Four-lugged jar body sherds (Protoliterate)	—
ca. 82.60	3.973	Jar fragment (Achaemenid)	—
ca. 82.60	—	2 slingshots	—
ca. 82.50	—	Beveled-rim bowls: 11 complete	—
ca. 82.40	—	Spouted jar fragment	—
82.40–82.08	3.1066	Perforated spherical clay object	126:V

Elevation	Field Number	Description	Plate
82.40–82.08	3.729	Four-lugged jar body	25:A
ca. 82.40	—	Beveled-rim bowls: 1 complete	—
ca. 82.25	III-450	Dice-shaped bead (period unassigned)	—
ca. 82.20	—	Beveled-rim bowl: 1 complete	—
ca. 82.00	3.510	Notched lip	19:B
ca. 81.95	—	Beveled-rim bowls (Protoliterate)	—
ca. 81.90	III-364	Spouted jar fragment	107:K
ca. 81.90	III-365	Horizontal handled jar fragment	101:I
ca. 81.90	—	Slingshot	—
ca. 81.80	III-263	Bowl; see fig. 8	84:D
ca. 81.80	3.866	Horizontal handled bowl fragment (Achaemenid)	75:Q
81.78–80.98	3.028	Bowl fragment; see fig. 8	80:L
ca. 81.75	III-265	Four-lugged jar	113:I
ca. 81.75	3.695	Strap-handled jar	cf. 95:J
ca. 81.70	III-134	Ovoid tray with cup; see fig. 9	86:J
ca. 81.70	3.888	Bowl fragment	—
ca. 81.50	3.648	Ledge rim, recurved sided bowl fragment (Achaemenid)	—
—	3.710	Stone hoe	246:I
Sifting	III-869a–b	Sealing fragments	45:P; 153:Fa–b
—	3.336	Jar spout fragment	75:L
—	III-927	Flattish sealing	43:K; 147:A

SOUTH OF P17:TRENCH V A

Elevation	Field Number	Description	Plate
ca. 82.90	III-176	Beveled-rim bowl 1 complete	—
ca. 82.30	III-175	Spouted jar fragment; see fig. 13	108:E
ca. 82.00	3.538	Three-strand twisted handle	20:R
ca. 81.70	3.459	Strap-handled jar	95:N
ca. 82.00–81.75	III-528	Spouted jar fragment	—
ca. 81.75	III-675	Knobbed beveled-rim bowl fragment	—

P17 EAST END EXTENSION:TRENCH V A

Elevation	Field Number	Description	Plate
Cleaning	II-398	"Nose plug"	67:F

P17 NORTHWEST:TRENCH V A

Elevation	Field Number	Description	Plate
ca. 82.70	III-352	Stone celt	125:II

P17:401

This locus, a strip ca. 4.75 m long located slightly to the north of the Circular Structure, Q18:305, adjoined the original Trench V A on the southwest. The surface sloped from 82.62 at the northwestern corner to ca. 83.00 at the northeastern corner. Mixed Achaemenid and Protoliterate. Surface elevation: ca. 83.00. Top of locus: 83.00. Bottom of locus: 81.63. See pl. 264.

Elevation	Field Number	Description	Plate
ca. 83.00	IV-101	Bone tool	128:Y
ca. 83.00	4.025	Carinated bowl fragment	73:O
ca. 82.40	4.028	Bowl with horizontal handle	75:S
ca. 82.40	4.626	Trefoil spout	75:I

P17:401 EAST

Area of ca. 2.50 × 5.00 m. There was debris from B.S. to ca. 82.60 (baked-brick fragments, a few semi-complete beveled-rim bowls, and other sherds). From ca. 82.08 to 81.63 was an irregular and shallow pit of ca. 1.40 × 2.00 m with beveled-rim bowls.

Elevation	Field Number	Description	Plate
ca. 83.00	IV-20	Frit scaraboid (Achaemenid)	76:M
ca. 83.00	—	Beveled-rim bowls: 16 rims + base, 325 rims, 107 bases, 127 bodies	—
ca. 82.60	—	Beveled-rim bowls: 3 almost complete, 150 rims + base, 900 rims, 207 bases, 325 bodies	—
ca. 82.40	IV-426	Bituminous stone bowl fragment	74:Q
ca. 82.40	4.081	Beaker, incomplete	83:E
81.76–81.63 (Pit)	—	Beveled-rim bowls: 1 almost complete, 3 rims + base, 132 rims, 27 bases, 47 bodies	—

P17:401 WEST

Area of ca. 2.25 × 4.00 m. It included both soft debris and a patch of hard surface associated with an irregular line of baked-brick fragments, the westernmost one of which abutted a round baked brick ca. 30.0 cm in diameter and 5.0 cm thick at ca. 81.27 (i.e., ca. 35.0 cm B.S.). Two other round bricks were also found at about the same depth; they and the hard floor were traces of the Achaemenid occupation. A small Protoliterate pit, P17:404, was in the northwestern corner.

Elevation	Field Number	Description	Plate
82.42–82.12	—	Beveled-rim bowls: 3 almost complete, 21 rims + base, 194 rims, 35 bases, 48 bodies	—

P17:402

Continuation of Trench V A, i.e., P17:402 West and Southeast. Surface elevation: 83.16. Top of locus: 83.16. Bottom of locus: ca. 81.00.

Elevation	Field Number	Description	Plate
83.16	4.886	Stone pestle	244:B
82.96	4.075	Jar neck	75:V
82.76	IV-377	Bone awl	128:AA
82.76–82.26	4.059	Jar neck and handle	75:D
82.31	IV-194	Metal arrowhead	76:H
82.01	IV-195	Metal arrowhead	76:F

P17:402 WEST

Rectangular area, ca. 3.75 × 4.50 m, consisted of the ca. 2.00 × 2.00 m Trench V A sounding from the third season and its periphery. When continued, the original sounding was found on the north, between ca. 0.90 and 1.30 B.S. (82.26–81.86), to be bounded by hard packed clay and fallen bricks, and on the other three sides by brickwork.

Elevation	Field Number	Description	Plate
83.16	—	Beveled-rim bowls: 9 rims + base, 574 rims, 127 bases, 186 bodies	—
82.86	IV-157	Pottery top of hut amulet	31:Z
82.56	—	Beveled-rim bowls: 2 rims + base, 78 rims, 22 bases, 36 bodies	—
82.41	IV-8	Sealing fragment with impression traces	144:A
82.41	IV-13	Pyramidal token	134:C 3
82.41	—	Flat-topped clay stopper; top diameter 11.0 cm, bottom diameter (= jar mouth) 8.5 cm	—
82.36–81.96	4.186	Body fragment of strap-handled jar	—
82.31	IV-7	Clay ball fragment	147:D
80.96	—	Beveled-rim bowls: 8 complete, ca. 16 almost complete, 112 rims + base, 464 rims, 179 bases, 202 bodies (Protoliterate)	—

P17:402 NORTHEAST

Area of ca. 3.50 × 4.00 m with hard yellow clay surfaces pitted by, within a ca. 1.00 × 2.00 m space, shallow depressions filled with dark gray-black earth, probably fire holes (Pits 1 and 2: oval, 20.0 × 50.0 cm; Pit 3: circular, diameter 50.0 cm; 82.66–82.36), and a larger hole filled with ashy earth (Pit 4: diameter 1.25 m; 82.66–81.92). Pits 3 and 4 were dug from the hard surface of 82.66–82.61 and Pits 1 and 2 from a slightly higher one; the lowest point reached was a hard surface at 82.34. The rarity of sherds and the arrowheads (see IV-194–95; P17:402, above) from Pit 4 indicate that the pits and associated "floors" belonged to Achaemenid installations dug into Protoliterate deposits.

Elevation	Field Number	Description	Plate
82.76	IV-21	Perforated black stone hemisphere	125:M
82.76–82.36	—	Beveled-rim bowl: 3 rims	—
82.41	—	Beveled-rim bowls: 6 rims, 3 bases, 2 bodies	—

P17:402 SOUTHEAST

Area of ca. 2.50 × 4.00 m with beveled-rim bowl deposit, 82.96–82.76, above an uneven mass of brickwork and a hard surface at 82.15; the lowest point was reached in the southeast.

Elevation	Field Number	Description	Plate
83.16	—	Beveled-rim bowls: 1 complete, 3 almost complete, 98 rims + base, 957 rims, 98(?) bases, 332 bodies	—
82.96–82.76	IV-47	Twisted handled jar; height 12.1 cm; diameter 14.3 cm	—
82.96–82.76	4.089	Rim and horizontal handles	101:D
82.96–82.76	4.294	Convex bowl	84:J
82.96–82.76	4.300	Buttressed jar	92:F
82.96–82.76	4.301	Four-lugged pithos; see fig. 15	123:H
82.96–82.76	—	Beveled-rim bowls: ca. 39 complete, 88 rims, 19 bases, 23 bodies	—
82.66–82.46	—	Beveled-rim bowls: 1 complete, 8 rims + base, 117 rims, 41 bases, 69 bodies	—

P17:403

An irregular area of 2.00 sq. m alongside Pl7:402 Southeast on the west and slightly to the north of the Circular Structure; the only feature was an irregularly rectangular pit of ca. 1.00 × 1.50 m with both ashy and red earth, possibly the remnant of a kiln. Surface elevation: ca. 82.50. Top of locus: ca. 82.50. Bottom of locus: ca. 81.30. See pl. 264.

Elevation	Field Number	Description	Plate
82.10–81.70	—	Beveled-rim bowls: 29 rims, 6 bases, 6 bodies	—
ca. 81.70	—	Beveled-rim bowls: 4 rims + base, 74 rims, 13 bases, 16 bodies	—
ca. 81.40	—	Beveled-rim bowls: 5 rims + base, 45 rims, 6 bases, 19 bodies	—

P17:404

Area of ca. 1.00 × 2.00 m at the northwestern corner of P17:401 with Protoliterate debris. Just below IV-117 and two beveled-rim bowls, was a small shallow pit with many flints. Surface elevation: 82.62. Top of locus: 81.82. Bottom of locus: ca. 81.40. See pl. 264.

Elevation	Field Number	Description	Plate
81.82	IV-117	Large pouring lip bowl	80:FF
81.82	—	2 beveled-rim bowls	—

P18:201

Trench V, Plot Z; 2.00 × 5.00 m long extension of Trench V to the west of Plot A. No structural features. Protoliterate debris. Surface elevation: ca. 81.50. Top of locus: ca. 81.50. Bottom of locus: ca. 79.40. See pl. 264.

Elevation	Field Number	Description	Plate
ca. 81.20	II-83	Jar stopper	—
ca. 79.60	II-335	Stone tool	125:L
ca. 79.40	2.399	Strap-handled jar body fragment	—
—	2.404	Lip of crude handmade bowl	—

P18:202

Trench V, Plot A; 2.00 × 5.00 m. There were no structural features. Near the surface was some Achaemenid occupational debris overlying Protoliterate deposits. It was dug to a maximum depth of ca. 1.50 B.S. at the northeastern corner. Surface elevation: 81.78. Top of locus: 81.78. Bottom of locus: ca. 80.30. See pl. 264.

Elevation	Field Number	Description	Plate
80.58	II-43	Spindle whorl	—

MIDDLE OF P18:202

Elevation	Field Number	Description	Plate
80.78–80.63	—	4 beveled-rim bowls (Protoliterate)	—

NORTH OF P18:202

Elevation	Field Number	Description	Plate
80.58	—	2 beveled-rim bowls (Protoliterate)	—

P18:202 OR 203

Elevation	Field Number	Description	Plate
—	2.016	Stick ladle	81:H

P18:202 + Q18:202

Elevation	Field Number	Description	Plate
—	2.417	Pestle/pounder	243:E

P18:203

At eastern end, part of a circular wall was found. It belonged to the Circular Structure, Q18:305, cleared the following season. In the west was found part of the great deposit of beveled-rim bowls, which was fully cleared the following season. Surface elevation: ca. 82.00. Top of locus: ca. 82.00. Bottom of locus: 80.00. See pl. 264.

Elevation	Field Number	Description	Plate
ca. 82.00	2.007	Strap-handled jar fragment; see fig. 9	95:K
ca. 82.00	2.029	Four-lugged jar body	25:L; 123:A
ca. 82.00	2.506	Tall four-lugged jar	—
81.30–80.90	2.556	Bowl fragment	—
ca. 80.40	—	Beveled-rim bowls: 7 complete (Protoliterate)	—
80.33	—	Beveled-rim bowl: 1 complete (Protoliterate)	—
—	II-476	Clay cone	cf. 31:S–Y
80.30	III-8	Stone stud	234:O
—	2.255	Oval high-walled tray fragment	—
—	2.437	Bowl fragment	—
—	2.447	Jar neck and body fragment	cf. 89:V
—	2.537	Band rim bowl fragment	17:I
—	2.545	Perforated plaque	127:M
—	2.642	Carinated bowl fragment	cf. 73:P
—	2.646	Bowl fragment (Achaemenid)	—
—	2.647	Jar fragment (Achaemenid)	—
—	—	Beveled-rim bowls: 6 complete	—

WEST OF P18:203

Elevation	Field Number	Description	Plate
82.00–81.50	2.640	Jar neck and body (Achaemenid)	—
ca. 81.40	II-18	Beveled-rim bowl (Protoliterate)	—

STEPS OF P18:203

Elevation	Field Number	Description	Plate
ca. 81.60	2.229	Carinated jar fragment	75:B
—	1.402	Strap-handled jar fragment	cf. 95:J
—	2.444	Vat rim fragment	—
—	2.491	Band rim bowl	cf. 84:O
—	2.626	Orange ware bowl fragment	cf. 74:C
—	2.635	Bowl fragment	—
—	2.643	Bowl fragment (Achaemenid)	—
ca. 80.30	III-304	Stone stud	234:N
—	II-429	Sealing (Protoliterate)	—

P18:203–Q18:202

Elevation	Field Number	Description	Plate
—	2.415	Grinding stone	239:A

P18:204

Small test sounding, ca. 2.00 × 2.00 m, into Susiana levels dug in P18:203, to the southwest of the Circular Structure. Surface elevation: ca. 82.10. Top of locus: ca. 80.40. Bottom of locus: 77.70. See pl. 264.

Elevation	Field Number	Description	Plate
79.90	2.103	Painted bowl base	181:B
79.90	2.544	Jar rim fragment	190:T
79.90	2.535	Red ware jar rim (Middle Susiana)	—

P18:301

Area to the southwest of the Circular Structure with huge deposit of Protoliterate pottery, including numerous sealings and jar stoppers, concentrated between 81.33 and 80.48. For the eastern extension of the deposit, see Q18:301. Surface elevation: ca. 82.00. Top of locus: ca. 82.00. Bottom of locus: ca. 80.00. See pl. 264.

Elevation	Field Number	Description	Plate
ca. 82.00	3.441	Tray fragment	86:EE
ca. 82.00	3.464	Tray fragment	86:N
ca. 82.00	3.465	Tray fragment	86:O
ca. 82.00	3.467	Tray fragment	86:R
ca. 82.00	3.468	Tray fragment	86:T
ca. 82.00	3.472	Tray fragment	86:X
ca. 82.00	3.475	Tray fragment	86:AA
ca. 82.00	3.476	Tray fragment	86:BB
ca. 82.00	3.517	Notched lip	19:Q
ca. 82.00	3.535	Horizontal handle	21:H
ca. 82.00	—	Beveled-rim bowls: 95 rims + base; 3,221 rims; 577 bases; 2,003 bodies. Bottle stoppers: 1 small miscellaneous; 1 flat head; 4 domed; 1 grooved; 4 one finger; 5 three finger, 2 four finger	—
82.00–81.65	3.495	Jar body with appliqué pellets	28:M
—	—	Beveled-rim bowls: 1,400 rims; 500 bases; 6,705 bodies	—

P18:301 (*cont.*)

Elevation	Field Number	Description	Plate
82.00–81.20	3.530	Strap handle	20:D
82.00–81.20	—	Beveled-rim bowls: 141 rims + base; 2,665 rims; 651 bases; 696 bodies	—
82.00–81.10	III-823	Conical door sealing (Protoliterate)	—
82.00–80.90	III-69	Metal fibula	76:B
82.00–80.80	—	Beveled-rim bowls: 80 rims + body; 275 rims; 1,479 bodies	—
ca. 81.65	III-613	Stone bowl fragment	—
ca. 81.60	3.1082	Metal pin fragment	128:P
ca. 81.55	III-105	Stamp seal	41:T
ca. 81.50	III-731	Figurine fragment	235:I
ca. 81.50	—	Beveled-rim bowls: 1,371 rims + base; 750 rims; 250 bases; 250 bodies. Bottle stoppers: 5 small miscellaneous; 7 flat head; 10 domed; 5 grooved; 11 one-finger impressed; 5 two-finger impressed; 8 three-finger impressed; 4 four-finger impressed; 9 five-finger impressed	—
ca. 81.40	—	Beveled-rim bowls: 40 rims + base; 286 rims; 57 base; 188 bodies	—
81.33–80.40	3.440	Tray fragment	86:DD
ca. 81.30	3.1014	Spindle whorl	126:H
ca. 81.30	—	Beveled-rim bowls: 14 rims + base; 333 rims; 70 bases; 9 bodies	—
ca. 81.20	3.533	Horizontal handle	21:A
ca. 81.20	III-825e–f	Sealings (Protoliterate)	—
ca. 81.20	III-828b	Door sealing (Protoliterate)	—
ca. 81.20	III-828c	Bale(?) sealing (Protoliterate)	—
ca. 81.20	3.1077	Coiled head metal pin	128:S
ca. 81.20	—	Beveled-rim bowls: 79 rims + base; 1,178 rims; 261 bases; 977 bodies	—
ca. 81.10	III-825c–d	Sealings (Protoliterate)	—
ca. 81.10	—	Metal rod fragment (Protoliterate)	—
ca. 81.00	III-824	Door sealing	43:A; 139:C
ca. 81.00	III-825a–b	Sealings (Protoliterate)	—
ca. 81.00	III-826	Bale(?) sealing (Protoliterate)	—
ca. 81.00	III-828a	Door sealing (Protoliterate)	—
ca. 81.00	III-866b	Door sealing (Protoliterate)	—
ca. 81.00	III-928a	Sealing (Protoliterate)	—
ca. 81.00	—	Beveled-rim bowls: 135 rims + base; 943 rims; 378 bases; 449 bodies. Bottle stoppers: 12 small miscellaneous; 85 all varieties of finger-impressed; undetermined type, 78 complete, 535 fragments	—
ca. 80.90	—	Beveled-rim bowls: 50 rims + base; 190 rims; 302 bodies	—
ca. 80.60	III-736	Animal figurine	66:J
ca. 80.60	3.334	Bridge spouted jar fragment	75:F
ca. 80.50	3.1087	Star shaped metal stud (Achaemenid)	—
ca. 80.50	III-881	Tray	86:GG
ca. 80.50	III-882	Tray incomplete	cf. 86:DD
ca. 80.50	3.536	Horizontal handle	21:E
ca. 80.50	3.938	Carinated bowl fragment (Achaemenid)	—
ca. 80.50	—	Beveled-rim bowls: 452 complete; 2,875 rims + base; 16,464 rims; 3,091 bases; 1,328 bodies	—
ca. 80.40	III-828d	Sealing (Protoliterate)	—
ca. 80.00	III-830a–c	"Orchestra" sealing	155:A

NEAR Q18:315

Elevation	Field Number	Description	Plate
ca. 80.40	III-829	Door sealing	42:M; 138:D
ca. 80.00	III-913a–c	"Orchestra" sealing	45:N; 155:A
ca. 80.00	III-871	Bale(?) sealing (Protoliterate)	—
ca. 80.00	—	Bottle stoppers: 19 flat heads; 21 domed; 2 grooved; 6 one-finger impressed; 10 two-finger impressed; 5 three-finger impressed; 8 four-finger impressed; 5 five-finger impressed; uncertain type, 57 fragments	cf. 130
ca. 80.00	—	Beveled-rim bowls: 452 complete; 2,875 rims + base; 16 rims, 3,091 bases; 1,328 bodies	—

Elevation	Field Number	Description	Plate
ca. 80.00	—	Bottle stoppers: 19 flat heads; 21 domed; 2 grooved; 6 one-finger impressed; 10 two-finger impressed; 5 three-finger impressed; 8 four-finger impressed; 5 five-finger impressed; uncertain type, 57 fragments	cf. 130
ca. 80.00	III-825g–j	Sealings (Protoliterate)	—
ca. 80.00	III-837c	Clay ball fragment (Protoliterate)	—
ca. 80.00	III-870	Sealing fragment	44:E; 149:B
ca. 80.00	III-872	Clay ball fragment (Protoliterate)	—
ca. 80.00	III-873	Bale sealing (Protoliterate)	—
ca. 80.00	III-911a, c	Bulla fragment (Protoliterate)	—
ca. 80.00	III-914	Door sealing (Protoliterate)	—
ca. 80.00	III-916a, d–g	Sealings (Protoliterate)	—
ca. 80.00	3.288	Spherical token	134:A 2
ca. 80.00	3.876	Hemispherical token (Protoliterate)	—
ca. 80.00	—	Bottle stoppers: 5 flat heads; 9 domed; 12 one-finger impressed; 8 two-finger impressed; 1 three-finger impressed; 1 six-finger impressed; undetermined type, 104 fragments	—
Sifting	III-835a–b	Door sealing	43:A; 139:C
Sifting	III-866a	Door sealing (Protoliterate)	149:E
Sifting	III-868a	Sealing (Protoliterate)	—
Sifting	III-916c	Sealing (Protoliterate)	—
Sifting	III-917	Bale sealing (Protoliterate)	—
Sifting	III-918	Bale sealing (Protoliterate)	—
Sifting	III-928b	Sealing (Protoliterate)	—
Sifting	III-929	Sealing	43:J; 147:C

Q17:201

Trench V, Plot E; 2.00 × 5.00 m. This locus contained Protoliterate occupational debris and no architectural features. Surface elevation: ca. 82.90. Top of locus: ca. 82.90. Bottom of locus: ca. 81.70. See pl. 264.

Elevation	Field Number	Description	Plate
ca. 82.40	II-32	Spouted jar; see fig. 12	106:D
ca. 82.40	II-33	Spouted jar	22:F
ca. 82.40	II-34	Slingshot (Protoliterate)	—

MIDDLE OF Q17:201

Elevation	Field Number	Description	Plate
ca. 82.20	2.341	Lug, coarse ware (Protoliterate)	—
ca. 81.70	2.347	Spoon handle	cf. 82:H–L

Q17:202

Trench V, Plot F, with northern wall of Protoliterate room later clarified as Q17:304 and Q17:402. At the eastern end of the locus was a cluster of beveled-rim bowls at 82.30. Near surface were some Achaemenid finds. Surface elevation: ca. 83.10. Top of locus: ca. 83.10. Bottom of locus: 82.00. See pl. 264.

Elevation	Field Number	Description	Plate
ca. 82.85	2.562	Carinated bowl	74:M
ca. 82.85	2.563	Bowl rim (Achaemenid)	—
ca. 82.80	II-305	Metal pin (Protoliterate)	29:G
ca. 82.20	II-421	Door sealing (Protoliterate)	42:B; 135:L
ca. 82.00	II-518	Blade set in bitumen	—
—	2.620	Bowl fragment (Achaemenid)	73:K

Q17:203

Trench V, Plot G; 2.00 × 6.00 m area with the northeastern end extending into R17. The northeastern half of the plot was occupied by the corner walls of a Protoliterate room; it was further excavated during the seventh season as R17:712 and finally cleared during the ninth season as R17:912. Surface elevation: ca. 83.60. Top of locus: ca. 83.60. Bottom of locus: 83.00. See pl. 264.

Elevation	Field Number	Description	Plate
ca. 83.10	II-510	Beveled-rim bowl (Protoliterate)	—
82.60	II-478	Clay cone (Protoliterate)	—
ca. 82.40	2.379a	Tray fragment	cf. 86:W

Q17:301

Canceled

Q17:302

Canceled

Q17:303

Occupational debris was found from the surface down in the southeastern corner of Q17 and also in the northwestern corner of the Protoliterate room straddling squares Q17–18 and R17–18. Together with R17:306, it was recleaned and clarified as R17:406. Top of the southwestern wall: 83.04, floor: 82.53. Above the northern wall of the Protoliterate room, one radial brick of the Achaemenid village was found. Surface elevation: ca. 83.20. Top of locus: ca. 83.20. Bottom of locus: 82.53. See pl. 264.

Elevation	Field Number	Description	Plate
ca. 83.05	3.504	Jar lip with double rope molding	28:U
ca. 82.60	3.1010	Spindle whorl	126:M
ca. 82.60	3.1247a–q	Beveled-rim bowl sherds squared off into miniature model bricks	cf. 30:S

Q17:304

Uppermost debris and a fragmentarily preserved rectangular Protoliterate room straddling Q17–18. Upper floor at 82.18, lower at 81.74. It was later continued as Q17:402. Surface elevation: ca. 82.90. Top of locus: ca. 82.90. Bottom of locus: ca. 81.30. See pl. 264.

Elevation	Field Number	Description	Plate
ca. 82.90	3.416	Bowl	83:Y
ca. 82.80	3.544	Animal figurine	31:I
ca. 82.80	—	Animal figurine	—
82.60	3.730	Four-lugged body with pellets	25:G
ca. 82.50	III-578	Four-lugged jar	24:H
ca. 81.80	III-867	Ball fragment sealing	149:E
81.70	3.731	Four-lugged body	25:B
ca. 81.50	III-649	Tabular rubbing stone	29:L
ca. 81.40	III-668	Spouted jar	105:D
82.35	3.328	Miniature handled vessel	95:C

SOUTH OF Q17:304

Elevation	Field Number	Description	Plate
ca. 82.40	3.505	Jar neck + body with notched molding	28:Q

WEST OF Q17:304

Elevation	Field Number	Description	Plate
ca. 82.90	3.644	Carinated fragment	cf. 74:H
ca. 82.90	III-862	Clay ball fragment (Protoliterate)	—

Q17:305

This locus consisted of B.S. debris and a rectangular Protoliterate room; it was located in Q18 except for the northeastern corner. There was a semicircular hard earth floor in the eastern end at 81.53. In the southwestern corner there were traces of a "closet." A small pit was dug into the southern wall. Surface elevation: ca. 82.70. Top of locus: ca. 82.70. Bottom of locus: 81.54. See pl. 264.

Elevation	Field Number	Description	Plate
ca. 82.00	—	Beveled-rim bowls: 14 complete	—
—	3.507	Jar body, notched molding	28:R

AREA OF Q17:305–Q18:301

Elevation	Field Number	Description	Plate
—	3.287	Spherical token	134:A 3

Q17:306

Canceled

Q17:307

Part of small Protoliterate trapezoidal room, located partly in R17. Surface elevation: ca. 83.40. Top of locus: ca. 83.40. Bottom of locus: N/A. See pl. 264.

Q17:308

An irregularly shaped Protoliterate room; in the northeastern corner was an oval bitumen floor at 82.53; there was a drain in the southwestern corner. Surface elevation: ca. 83.20. Top of locus: ca. 83.20. Bottom of locus: N/A. See pl. 264.

Q17:401

Area to the north of the Circular Structure and to the southeast of P17:402 with inner faces of brickwork. The top of an ashy pit was at ca. 82.20. Surface elevation: ca. 83.30. Top of locus: ca. 83.30. Bottom of locus: N/A. See pl. 264.

Q17:402

Cleaning of Q17:304. Surface elevation: ca. 82.90. Top of locus: ca. 82.90. Bottom of locus: ca. 81.30. See pl. 264.

AREA OF Q18

Elevation	Field Number	Description	Plate
—	IV-307a	Token	134:G 9

R18:TRENCH XIX

Begun as a 3.50 × 3.50 m trench in the southeastern corner of Q18, the area of Q18:307 and Q18:308 continued to the north as a series of adjacent areas not conforming to a regular trench outline. The northern extension included R18:307 and beyond. The surface ranged from ca. 82.80 in the northeast to ca. 80.70 in the southwest. Surface elevation: ca. 82.80. Top of locus: ca. 82.80. Bottom of locus: 81.80. See pl. 264.

Elevation	Field Number	Description	Plate
ca. 82.80	3.718	Blade core	253:B
ca. 82.80	III-433	Stone stamp seal	234:JJ
ca. 82.65	III-169	Perforated disc	29:Y
ca. 82.60	III-154	Strap-handled jar	95:I
ca. 82.05	III-110	Cylinder seal	41:I
ca. 81.80	III-242	Spouted jar	cf. 105:A

R18 EAST:TRENCH XIX

Elevation	Field Number	Description	Plate
ca. 82.10	III-548	Bottle	111:B

R18 NORTH EDGE:TRENCH XIX

Elevation	Field Number	Description	Plate
ca. 82.25	3.236	Painted lip sherd	173:I

R18:PROBABLY TRENCH XIX

Elevation	Field Number	Description	Plate
82.50–82.40	III-448	Square stamp seal	41:P

R18:TRENCHES XIX–XX

Area of Trenches XIX–XX. See pl. 264.

Elevation	Field Number	Description	Plate
—	3.712	Handgrinder	242:P
—	3.708	Pestle/pounder	244:A
—	3.714	Stone with depression	248:F

Q18:201

Trench V, Plot C, consisted for the most part of the southwestern wall of the Circular Structure, Q18:305, and hard debris in the western interior of the building. It was not excavated to any great depth, and there were few finds. Surface elevation: ca. 82.50. Top of locus: ca. 82.50. Bottom of locus: ca. 82.00. See pl. 264.

Elevation	Field Number	Description	Plate
ca. 82.50	II-424	Conical bowl; see fig. 8	80:U
ca. 82.00	III-53	Pottery animal figurine head	—
—	II-13	Round agate bead (probably Achaemenid)	—

TWO METERS TO THE EAST OF Q18:201

Elevation	Field Number	Description	Plate
ca. 82.00	III-417	Handled vessel fragment	96:F

Q18:202

Trench V, Plot D, located on eastern side, contained part of the southeastern wall of the Circular Structure, Q18:305. The western side of plot had fill in the interior of the structure. Surface elevation: ca. 82.50. Top of locus: ca. 82.50. Bottom of locus: ca. 80.50. See pl. 264.

Elevation	Field Number	Description	Plate
81.70–81.45	2.598	Jar fragment (Achaemenid)	—
81.70–81.45	2.599	Jar fragment (Achaemenid)	—
ca. 81.60	2.618	Jar neck (Achaemenid)	—
ca. 81.60	2.623	Barrel-shaped fragment	—
ca. 81.60	2.638	Jar neck (Achaemenid)	—

Elevation	Field Number	Description	Plate
ca. 81.60	3.646	Carinated fragment	cf. 74:E
ca. 81.50	2.584	Bowl	73:C
81.10–80.70	2.483	Carinated fragment	cf. 74:E
81.10–80.70	2.639	Body with handle, cooking pot ware (Achaemenid)	—
ca. 80.65	—	Beveled-rim bowl (Protoliterate)	—
—	2.373	Tray fragment	cf. 86:R
—	2.377	Tray fragment	—
—	2.438	Vat rim (Protoliterate)	—
—	2.547	Body with horizontal handle (Achaemenid)	—
—	2.572	Body with trefoil spout	75:K
—	2.589	Jar rim fragment (Achaemenid)	—
—	2.591	Carinated fragment	cf. 74:K
—	2.595	Jar fragment (Achaemenid)	—
—	2.600	Jar rim	cf. 75:K
—	2.603	Jar fragment, joins repaired in antiquity with bitumen	—
—	2.668	Jar body	cf. 75:B
—	2.669	Jar body (Achaemenid)	—

Q18:301

Continuation of P18:301 pottery deposit into Square Q18 directly to the south of the Circular Structure, Q18:305. Above pavement was Q18:315. There was a stub of a northwest-southeast wall; top at 81.40. Surface elevation: ca. 82.00. Top of locus: ca. 82.00. Bottom of locus: 79.15. See pl. 264.

Elevation	Field Number	Description	Plate
ca. 82.00	III-641	Strap-handled jar fragment; see fig. 9	98:C
ca. 82.00	3.473	Tray rim	86:Y
ca. 82.00	3.474	Tray rim	86:Z
ca. 82.00	3.931	Bowl lip (Achaemenid)	—
ca. 82.00	—	Perforated stone roundel	cf. 29:Q–Z
ca. 82.00	3.466	Tray fragment	86:Q
ca. 82.00	—	Beveled-rim bowls: 50 rims + base; 281 rims; 219 bodies	—
ca. 82.00	—	Beveled-rim bowls: 150 rims + base; 850 rims; 378 bases; 170 bodies	—
82.00–81.35	—	Beveled-rim bowls: 62 rims + base; 503 rims; 1,203 bases; 660 bodies	—
82.00–79.70	—	Beveled-rim bowls: 5 rims + base; 40 rims; 6 bases; 30 bodies	—
ca. 81.75	3.650	Fine ware cup	cf. 80:L
ca. 81.75	—	Beveled-rim bowls: 1 complete; 454 rims + base; 24 rims; 130 bases; 530 bodies	—
ca. 81.70	—	Beveled-rim bowl: 1 complete (Protoliterate)	—
ca. 81.60	3.415	Beveled-rim bowl: 1 complete	83:N
ca. 81.55	—	Beveled-rim bowls: 28 rims + base; 137 rims; 25 bases; 143 bodies	—
ca. 81.55	3.1069	Biconical terra-cotta disc	cf. 30:O
ca. 81.50	III-25	Notched spindle whorl	65:II
ca. 81.50	—	Stoppers: 2 plain flat; 1 domed; 1 miscellaneous	—
ca. 81.40	—	Beveled-rim bowls: 3 complete	—
81.40–81.10	—	Beveled-rim bowls: 20 rims + base; 2,001 rims; 55 bases; 80 bodies	—
ca. 81.30	—	Beveled-rim bowl: 1 complete	—
81.30–79.65	—	Beveled-rim bowls: 62 rims + base; 570 rims; 157 bases; 322 bodies	—
ca. 81.25	—	Beveled-rim bowls: 3 complete	—
ca. 81.20	3.515	Notched lip	19:O
ca. 81.20	3.518	Jar rim (appliqué) body	19:I
ca. 81.20	—	Animal figurine fragment (Protoliterate)	—
ca. 81.15	—	Beveled-rim bowls: 25 rims + base; 150 rims; 72 bases; 200 bodies	—
81.10–79.65	—	Beveled-rim bowls: 40 rims + base; 283 rims; 55 bases; 110 bodies	—
ca. 81.05	III-338	Spouted jar fragment (Protoliterate)	—
ca. 81.05	III-405	Jar	91:J

Q18:301 (cont.)

Elevation	Field Number	Description	Plate
81.00–80.00	3.506	Jar body, notched bands	28:S
81.00–80.00	—	Beveled-rim bowls: 8 rims + base; 102 rims; 26 bases; 35 bodies	—
ca. 81.00	III-652	Gray stone mace-head(?)	125:BB
ca. 80.80	3.405	Spouted jar; see fig. 12	102:I
ca. 80.70	—	Animal figurine fragment (Protoliterate)	—
ca. 80.50	III-64	Spouted jar; see fig. 12	22:C, 106:F
ca. 80.20	—	Beveled-rim bowls: 83 rims + base; 362 rims; 80 bases; 886 bodies	—
ca. 80.20	—	Stone lip (Protoliterate)	—
—	III-833f–g	Sealings (Protoliterate)	148:A
—	—	Animal figurine fragment	—

Q18:301 NORTH

Elevation	Field Number	Description	Plate
ca. 81.75	—	Beveled-rim bowls: 33 rims; 7 bases; 8 bodies	—
ca. 79.70	—	Beveled-rim bowls: 3 rims + base; 17 rims; 9 bases; 176 bodies	—
ca. 79.15	—	Beveled-rim bowls: 52 rims; 9 bases; 53 bodies	—

Q18:301 NORTHEAST

Elevation	Field Number	Description	Plate
ca. 81.55	—	Beveled-rim bowls: 320 rims + base; 30 rims; 70 bases; 430 bodies	—
ca. 81.40	—	Beveled-rim bowls: 37 rims + base; 530 rims; 70 bases; 430 bodies	—

Q18:301 SOUTH

Elevation	Field Number	Description	Plate
81.50–81.10	—	Stoppers: 1 plain flat; 2 domed; 2 one-finger impressed, 2 six-finger impressed	—
ca. 81.10	—	Beveled-rim bowls: 10 rims + base; 76 rims; 26 bases; 60 bodies	—
80.80–79.15	—	Stoppers: 4 plain; 8 finger impressed	—

Q18:301 WEST

Elevation	Field Number	Description	Plate
ca. 82.00	—	Beveled-rim bowls: 34 rims + base; 430 rims; 190 bases; 350 bodies	—

NORTH OF Q18:301

Elevation	Field Number	Description	Plate
80.40–79.65	III-598	Spouted jar fragment	23:A
80.40–79.65	—	Beveled-rim bowls: 15 rims + base; 180 rims; 17 bases; 24 bodies	—

NORTHEAST OF Q18:301

Elevation	Field Number	Description	Plate
—	—	Beveled-rim bowls: 40 rims + base; 170 rims; 50 bases; 80 bodies	—

SOUTHEAST OF Q18:301

Elevation	Field Number	Description	Plate
ca. 81.75	III-642	Jar fragment; see fig. 9	89:K
ca. 81.75	—	Beveled-rim bowls: 600 rims + base; 2,500 rims; 1,035 bases; 850 bodies	—

WEST OF Q18:301

Elevation	Field Number	Description	Plate
ca. 81.40	III-465	Spouted pithos	110:M

Q18:302

Area on the eastern side of square Q18, with Protoliterate debris and a Protoliterate pit, Q18:312. Surface elevation: 82.70. Top of locus: 82.70. Bottom of locus: N/A. See pl. 264.

Elevation	Field Number	Description	Plate
81.30–80.25	3.892	Jar rim fragment	—

Q18:303

Canceled

Q18:304

Area between kiln Q18:316. Surface elevation: ca. 82.00. Top of locus: ca. 82.00. Bottom of locus: ca. 80.70. See pl. 264.

Elevation	Field Number	Description	Plate
ca. 81.50	3.1009	Spindle whorl and pit Q18:312	126:K
Sifting	III-831	Sealing fragment	143:A

Q18:305

Circular Structure straddling P17–18 and Q17. The western wall was traced in Q18:201, and the eastern wall was traced in Q18:202. Top of wall, B.S. Floor and bottom of large deposit of bones at 81.28. Wall of crumbly brickwork containing ashes, pebbles, and small sherds. Surface elevation: 83.29. Top of locus: 83.29. Bottom of locus: 81.28. See pl. 264.

Elevation	Field Number	Description	Plate
ca. 83.30	3.914	Cooking pot ware handle	cf. 71:B
ca. 83.30	3.927	Bowl fragment	cf. 73:I
ca. 83.30	3.911	Body, vertical handle	cf. 75:D
ca. 83.30	—	Beveled-rim bowls: 57 rims; 6 bases; 27 bodies	—
83.30–82.95	III-260	Carinated bowl	73:P
83.30–82.95	3.030	Carinated bowl fragment	74:J
83.30–82.95	3.885	Jar fragment, loop	—
83.30–82.95	3.904	Jar neck	cf. 75:BB
83.30–82.95	3.993	Jar neck fragment (Protoliterate)	—
83.30–82.95	—	Beveled-rim bowls: 57 rims; 6 bases; 27 bodies	—
83.30–82.80	—	5 bottle bodies; 4 bases (Protoliterate)	—
83.30–82.80	—	Spouts: 2 curved; 6 conical; 2 straight; 1 trumpet; 1 swollen	—
83.30–82.80	—	Horizontal handle (Protoliterate)	—
83.30–82.80	—	9 vertical strap handles (Protoliterate)	—
83.30–82.80	—	2 finger-impressed body fragments (Protoliterate)	—
83.30–82.80	—	3 body fragments, diagonally crossed scoring	cf. 97:C
83.30–82.80	—	7 string-cut bases (Protoliterate)	—

Q18:305 (*cont.*)

Elevation	Field Number	Description	Plate
83.30–82.80	—	4 clay cones (Protoliterate)	cf. 31:S–Y
83.30–82.80	—	3 terra-cotta sickles (Protoliterate)	cf. 30:T–U
83.30–82.80	—	Spindle whorls (Protoliterate)	—
83.30–82.80	—	Beveled-rim bowls: 50 rims; 24 bases; 50 bodies	—
ca. 82.20	III-50	Terra-cotta spool	30:A; 126:CC
ca. 82.95	3.930	Jar neck (Achaemenid)	—
82.95	3.990	Bowl fragment (Protoliterate)	—
82.90	III-7	Carinated bowl fragment	74:D
82.90	—	Beveled-rim bowls: 4 rims + base; 119 rims; 29 bases; 250 bodies	—
ca. 82.85	3.986	Jar neck fragment	cf. 90:E–F
ca. 82.85	—	Beveled-rim bowls: 53 rims; 7 bases; 28 bodies	—
ca. 82.80	III-62	Stand(?) fragment	cf. 75:U
ca. 82.80	3.664	Carinated bowl fragment	cf. 74:M
ca. 82.80	3.980	Jar fragment (Protoliterate)	—
ca. 82.80	3.989	Bowl fragment (Protoliterate)	cf. 83:DD
ca. 82.80	—	Terra-cotta sickle	cf. 30:T–V
82.80–82.30	—	Bottles: 6 bodies; 1 base (Protoliterate)	—
82.80–82.30	—	Spouts: 1 curved (Protoliterate)	—
82.80–82.30	—	10 string-cut bases (Protoliterate)	—
82.80–82.30	—	Clay cones (Protoliterate)	—
82.80–82.30	—	Jar neck (Achaemenid)	—
ca. 82.60	—	Beveled-rim bowls: 5 rims + base; 42 rims; 17 bases; 18 bodies	—
82.58	3.335	Trefoil spout	75:H
82.58	3.407	Jar neck + spout; see fig. 13	—
82.58	3.469	Tray fragment	86:U
82.58	3.470	Tray fragment	86:V
82.58	3.471	Tray fragment	86:W
82.58	3.624	Jar neck + spout (Protoliterate)	—
82.58	3.631	Jar neck + spout (Protoliterate)	—
82.58	3.981	Jar neck + body (Protoliterate)	—
82.58	—	Tray fragment	cf. 86:U
82.58–82.48	3.346	Buttressed spout	—
ca. 82.35	3.656	Carinated bowl fragment	cf. 73:P
82.30–82.05	3.653	Carinated bowl fragment	cf. 74:G
82.50–82.30	III-103	Elongated terra-cotta barrel bead	129:M
82.50–82.30	3.926	Red-washed burnished bowl fragment (Achaemenid)	—
82.50–82.30	3.933	Rolled rim fragment (Achaemenid)	—
82.50–82.30	3.934	Jar neck fragment	cf. 75:Y
82.50–82.30	3.935	Red ware bowl fragment (Achaemenid)	—
82.50–82.30	—	Vat fragment (Protoliterate)	—
82.50–82.30	—	Carinated bowl fragment	cf. 74:J
82.50–82.30	—	Carinated bowl fragment	cf. 74:G
82.50–82.30	—	Carinated bowl fragment	cf. 74:F
—	—	5 string-cut cups (Protoliterate)	—
—	—	Spouts: 5 curved; 3 straight; 2 swollen (Protoliterate)	—
82.30–80.80	—	2 water spouts (Protoliterate)	cf. 87:L-N
82.30–80.80	—	6 terra-cotta cones	cf. 31:S–Y
ca. 82.10	III-838	Impressed bottle stopper (Protoliterate)	131:B
ca. 82.05	3.400	Lid fragment; see fig. 8	80:G
ca. 81.50	3.453	Jar fragment (Elamite)	79:Q
ca. 81.50	3.928	Jar fragment (Achaemenid)	—
ca. 81.50	3.937	Ledge-rim bowl fragment (Achaemenid)	—
ca. 81.50	—	Beveled-rim bowls: 5 rims + base; 9 rims; 3 bases; 9 bodies	—
ca. 81.30	—	Beveled-rim bowls: 2 rims + base; 83 rims; 154 bodies	—
ca. 81.30	—	Lip of stone bowl (Protoliterate)	—
ca. 81.30	III-635	Lower part of hut amulet	31:DD

Elevation	Field Number	Description	Plate
—	III-423	Bowl fragment	73:Q
—	3.972	Bowl fragment (Achaemenid)	—
—	—	Beveled-rim bowls: 24 rims + base; 20 bodies	—

Q18:305 WEST

Elevation	Field Number	Description	Plate
ca. 81.30	—	Beveled-rim bowls: 5 rims + base; 72 rims; 17 bases; 55 bodies	—
ca. 82.60	—	Beveled-rim bowls: 36 rims + base; 168 rims; 233 bodies	—

Q18:306

Canceled

Q18:307

Southeastern corner of Q18, together with Q18:308 East, comprise the southern end of Trench XIX. There were traces of brick-work. Surface elevation: ca. 81.80. Top of locus: ca. 81.80. Bottom of locus: ca. 80.10. See pl. 264.

Elevation	Field Number	Description	Plate
ca. 81.80	3.047	Scrabbled lip	86:C
ca. 81.80	3.899	Potter's tool	81:U
ca. 81.80	3.1002	Basket handled fragment	101:M
81.80–81.50	III-556	Cylindrical jar; see fig. 9	94:E
ca. 81.40	3.486	Stone bowl	124:I
ca. 81.40	3.487	Stone bowl	124:J
ca. 81.40	—	Tapered lip stone bowl fragment (Protoliterate)	—
ca. 81.20	3.1015	Spindle whorl	126:A
ca. 81.10	—	Terra-cotta sickle	cf. 30:T
ca. 80.95	III-183	Animal head spout (Protoliterate)	—
ca. 80.95	III-184	Terra-cotta object	235:C
ca. 80.80	III-839	Domed stopper, impressed	—

SOUTH OF Q18:307

Elevation	Field Number	Description	Plate
ca. 81.35	III-575	Small carinated jar; see fig. 9	88:Y
ca. 81.35	III-816	Flattish sealing, stamp sealed (Protoliterate)	—
ca. 81.35	—	Terra-cotta sickle	cf. 30:T

WEST OF Q18:307

Elevation	Field Number	Description	Plate
ca. 81.00	—	Animal figurine fragment (Protoliterate)	—

NORTH OR NORTHWEST OF Q18:307

Elevation	Field Number	Description	Plate
ca. 81.45	III-580	Trough spouted jar	108:I
ca. 81.45	3.521	Twisted handle vessel	20:L
ca. 81.20	III-577	Squat strap-handled bowl; see fig. 9	85:T
ca. 81.20	3.350	Four-lugged incised body fragment	28:F
ca. 81.20	3.814	Spike	127:B

Q18:307 SOUTHWEST

Between Q18:307 and R19:301. See pl. 264.

Elevation	Field Number	Description	Plate
ca. 81.15	3.1204	Gray stone scraper	125:FF

Q18:308

Area in the southeastern part of Q18, consisting of two superimposed walls separated by a 14.0 cm layer of ash and in part by another, lower layer of pebbles, 22.0 cm thick. Upper wall with preserved top at 81.76, base at 80.77; lower southern wall with preserved top at 80.63, base at 80.19. A pottery deposit contained mostly beveled-rim bowls. Surface elevation: ca. 82.10. Top of locus: ca. 82.10. Bottom of locus: 80.77. See pl. 264.

Elevation	Field Number	Description	Plate
ca. 82.10	3.719	Blade core	253:H
ca. 81.90	—	Animal figurine fragment (Protoliterate)	—
ca. 81.80	III-280	Four-lugged vessel	121:F
ca. 81.55	3.520	Twisted handle (Protoliterate)	20:M
ca. 81.30	3.546	Animal figurine	31:O
ca. 81.30	III-209	Spoon fragment	82:I
ca. 81.30	III-292	Ovoid jar	91:I
ca. 81.25	III-275	Spouted jar; see fig. 13	107:J

Q18:308 MIDDLE

Elevation	Field Number	Description	Plate
ca. 81.60	III-671	Ovoid pot	19:F

NORTH OF Q18:308

Elevation	Field Number	Description	Plate
ca. 82.10	III-840	Bottle stopper, impressed	131:A
ca. 81.75	III-239	Strap-handled jar; see fig. 9	96:B
ca. 81.30	III-841a–c	Clay ball	38:C–E; 136:F
ca. 81.15	3.421	Trough spouted bowl fragment	85:F
ca. 81.00	III-869c	Sealing fragment	153:F
ca. 81.00	III-921	Flattish sealing (Protoliterate)	—

SOUTH OF Q18:308

Elevation	Field Number	Description	Plate
ca. 81.65	—	Stone roundel	cf. 29:Q–Z

Q18:308 SOUTH

Elevation	Field Number	Description	Plate
ca. 82.10	3.1016	Terra-cotta biconical disc	126:T

Q18:308 EAST DRAIN

Elevation	Field Number	Description	Plate
—	3.295	Spherical token, two sets of three punctations	cf. 134:A 6

SOUTH OF Q18:313

Elevation	Field Number	Description	Plate
ca. 81.15	3.721	Backed flint blade	254:A

SOUTH OF Q18:309–311

Canceled

Q18:312

Protoliterate pit, 2.50 × ca. 3.50 m. Surface elevation: 82.70. Top of locus: ca. 82.40. Bottom of locus: ca. 80.15. See pl. 264.

Elevation	Field Number	Description	Plate
82.40	—	Slingshot (Protoliterate)	—
82.20	III-817	Flattish sealing (Protoliterate)	—
82.20–81.70	III-845	Sealing (Protoliterate)	—
82.10	III-197	Stand; see fig. 9	86:H
82.05	III-274	Ovoid jar	89:M
81.90	III-310	Cylindrical stone bead	129:S
81.80	III-211	Stone roundel	125:O
81.80	III-335	Small jar	19:H; 88:P
82.41	3.872a	Hemispherical token	134:E 7
81.60	3.878e	Pill-shaped token	134:D 6
81.60	III-202	Conical token (Protoliterate)	—
81.60	III-203	Pyramidal token; height 2.1 cm (Protoliterate)	—
81.60	III-863	Clay ball fragment (Protoliterate)	—
81.50	3.878a	Conical token; height 2.5 cm (Protoliterate)	—
81.40	3.878c	Spherical token (Protoliterate)	—
81.40	3.541	Animal figurine	31:F
81.30	3.392	Bowl fragment	183:A
81.20	III-842	5 clay ball fragments (Protoliterate)	138:I
81.20	III-843a	Sealing, flat base (Protoliterate)	138:I
81.20	III-843b–c, g	Jar neck sealings (Protoliterate)	138:I
81.20	III-843d–f, h–u	Sealings (Protoliterate)	138:I
81.20	III-844	Flattish sealing (Protoliterate)	—
80.95	—	Slingshot (Protoliterate)	—
80.70	—	Slingshot (Protoliterate)	—
—	III-308	Stamp seal	41:J
—	3.878d	Spherical token (Protoliterate)	—
—	3.283	Conical token; height 2.2 cm	134:B 2
—	—	Animal figurine fragments 2 (Protoliterate)	—

BETWEEN Q18:312 AND R19:310

Elevation	Field Number	Description	Plate
ca. 81.40	III-861a	Ball fragment with cloth offering bearer (Protoliterate)	—

Q18:313

Area to the southwest of a Protoliterate wall stub cut by pit Q18:321. At the southwestern side of this wall, and under it, were traces of a Late Middle Susiana pit. Middle Susiana sherds already occurred as high as 81.81. Surface elevation: 82.51. Top of locus: 82.51. Bottom of locus: 80.10. See pl. 264.

Elevation	Field Number	Description	Plate
82.51	3.632	Buttressed spout and body fragment	110:C
82.51	—	Animal figurine fragment (Protoliterate)	—
82.51	—	Stone bowl lip (Protoliterate)	—

Q18:313 (*cont.*)

Elevation	Field Number	Description	Plate
82.51	—	Stone roundel	cf. 30:Q–Z
82.51	—	Slingshot (Protoliterate)	—
82.06	III-276	Conical cup	80:V
82.06	3.872b	Spherical token (Protoliterate)	—
82.06	3.278	Crescentic token	134:F 3
81.81	3.220	Painted jar fragment	190:O
81.51	III-537	Beaker	85:W

Q18:313 NORTH

Elevation	Field Number	Description	Plate
81.31	3.575	Metal pin	29:B; 128:N
81.30–81.00	3.002	Large convex bowl	181:I
81.30–81.00	3.003	Bowl with festoons	183:B
81.30– 81.00	3.004	Bowl with triangular festoons; see fig. 30	183:C
81.30–81.00	3.005	Bowl with festoons	183:D
81.30–81.00	3.006	Crateriform vessel; see fig. 31	57:J; 184:T
81.30–81.00	3.007	Unpainted vat	182:J
81.30–81.00	3.669	Crateriform vessel	58:FF
81.30–81.00	3.670	Crateriform vessel	58:EE
81.30–81.00	3.672	Painted lip fragment	58:Z
81.30–81.00	3.673a	Painted lip fragment	58:DD
80.31	III-235	Strap-handled ladle; see fig. 8	82:C
—	3.872c	Spherical stone token (Protoliterate)	—
—	3.460	Miniature spouted jar	102:B
—	—	Terra-cotta sickles 2 (Protoliterate)	—

SOUTH OF Q18:313

Elevation	Field Number	Description	Plate
82.51	III-400	Four-lugged, strap-handled jar	24:C; 115:A
82.51	III-401	Small four-lugged jar	114:C
82.51	III-565	Beaker; see fig. 9	85:Y
82.51	III-708	Tabular flint scraper fragment	cf. 29:J
81.96	III-237	Spouted jar	108:M
81.51	—	4 slingshots	—

NORTH OF Q18:313

Elevation	Field Number	Description	Plate
81.81	3.269	Token: irregular	134:G 4
81.21	—	1 slingshots (Protoliterate)	—

Q18:314

Large Protoliterate pit, ca. 4.00 m in diameter, immediately to the south of room Q17:305. Surface elevation: 82.32. Top of locus: 82.32. Bottom of locus: 81.28. See pl. 264.

Elevation	Field Number	Description	Plate
82.30	3.548	Animal figurine	31:P
82.07–81.67	3.046	Tray with notched lip	86:K

Elevation	Field Number	Description	Plate
81.97	3.909	Pedestal base common ware fragment (Achaemenid)	—
81.82	—	Stone roundel	cf. 29:Q–Z
81.62	III-534	Spouted jar	110:E
81.62	III-552b	Spouted jar	107:N
81.62	III-553	Spouted jar; see fig. 13	107:M
81.62	III-587	Spouted jar	102:H
81.62	III-836	Door sealing (Protoliterate)	—
81.38	III-818	Tablet	33:D; 152:D
81.12	III-725	Animal-shaped token	134:G 12
81.12	3.280	Spherical token	134:A 7
81.03	III-819	Bulla	33:H; 150:A
—	3.871	Spherical token (Protoliterate)	—
—	III-803b	Sealing	153:A
—	III-832	Door sealing (Protoliterate)	—
—	III-833a–e	Bale(?) sealing	148:A
—	III-834	Bale(?) sealing	143:F
Sifting	III-835a–b	Door sealing	139:C
—	III-866	Door sealing	—
—	3.542	Animal figurine	31:E

Q18:315

Baked-brick paving with lower pebble paving, located at the southeastern edge of the Circular Structure, below Q18:318 and Q18:301 East. The baked-brick strips sloped from 80.99 at the north to 80.50 at the south; likewise, the pebble pavement sloped from 80.89 on the north to 80.39 on the south. Many Protoliterate tokens were on the upper pavement at ca. 80.40. Details of pavements added to plan according to recleaning of the area during the ninth season. Surface elevation: 82.50. Top of locus: 80.99. Bottom of locus: 80.80. See pl. 264.

Elevation	Field Number	Description	Plate
81.15	3.565	Terra-cotta cone	31:II
ca. 80.00	III-724	Animal-shaped token	134:G 11
ca. 80.00	3.025	Handled vessel fragment	97:B
ca. 80.00	3.281	"Pot"-shaped token	134:G 6
ca. 80.00	3.282	Pyramidal-shaped token	134:C 5
ca. 80.00	3.285	Spherical token; punctated	134:A 5
ca. 80.00	3.858a	Spherical token (Protoliterate)	—
ca. 80.00	3.858b	Spherical token (Protoliterate)	—
ca. 80.00	3.859a–d	4 pill-shaped tokens	134:D 1
ca. 80.00	3.860	Pyramidal token; diameter 1.8 cm; punctated	134:C 8
ca. 80.00	3.861a–g, j, l–m	Pyramidal tokens: (a–c) height 0.8–0.9 cm; (d–g) height 1.0–1.2 cm; (j) height 1.5 cm (pl. 134:C 6); (l–m) height 1.5 cm; notched (pl. 134:C 2, 7)	134:C 2, 6–7
ca. 80.00	3.1043	Spherical token; diameter 1.5 cm; punctated	cf. 134:A 8
ca. 80.00	3.1044	Spherical token; diameter 1.8 cm; punctated	cf. 134:A 8

Q18:316

Small oval kiln in middle of Q18; 0.90 × 1.30 m. Floor of kiln: 80.73. Surface elevation: ca. 82.00. Top of kiln wall: 81.76. Bottom of locus: 80.73. See pls. 13:B; 264.

Elevation	Field Number	Description	Plate
—	III-678	Terra-cotta spool	30:G; 126:Y

Q18:317

Small oval kiln immediately to the south of Room Q17:304; ca. 1.20 × 1.70 m. Surface elevation: ca. 83.00. Top of locus: ca. 81.80. Bottom of locus: 81.35. See pls. 13:A; 264.

Elevation	Field Number	Description	Plate
ca. 81.80	III-524	Pithos	94:A

Q18:318

Area of Protoliterate debris just to the south of Q18:301 and contiguous to P18:301, from surface down to about the level of the Q18:315 pebble pavement. Surface elevation: ca. 82.00. Top of locus: ca. 82.00. Bottom of locus: ca. 81.00. See pls. 13:B; 264.

Elevation	Field Number	Description	Plate
81.50	III-912	Seal impression fragment	42:K; 136:D
81.30–80.20	3.026	Bowl fragment	80:O
81.00	—	Spherical token + clay ball fragments	—
—	III-837a–b	2 punctations (Protoliterate)	—
—	III-911b	Bulla fragment (Protoliterate)	—

Q18:401

Below Q18:308, this locus was divided into northern and southern parts by the wall segment with adjacent pottery drain pipe excavated during the third season. In Q18:401 South, an irregular ashy layer with beveled-rim bowl sherds continued at southern edge as a shallow pit ca. 1.00 m in diameter, piercing a hard surface at ca. 80.20. Surface elevation: ca. 81.39. Top of locus: ca. 81.39. Bottom of locus: ca. 80.00. See pl. 264.

Elevation	Field Number	Description	Plate
81.39	4.871	Stone hoe	246:R
80.47–80.37	4.092	Bowl fragment	73:B
80.19	4.290	Spouted pithos; see fig. 13	110:N–O
Wash	4.254	Bowl fragment; see fig. 26	166:D

Q18:402

Originally an area to the west-southwest of the Q18:316 kiln; it was later expanded to include recleaning and further clarification of the kiln itself. The kiln rested on top of a baked-brick platform and plastered floor that extended to the west. At the edge of the platform was a large broken vat at 81.22. To the south of the kiln area was the bed of a curving water channel made of Protoliterate rain spouts with one preserved at the southern end. There was also a series of small mud-plastered water channels, Q18:403, perhaps connected with kiln P18:316. Below them was soft, ashy debris containing numerous beveled-rim bowl sherds and a cluster of complete vessels including IV-139–45 and 148; apparently an irregular pit extended southward into unexcavated ground. This locus was probably a workshop area. Surface elevation: 82.23. Top of locus: 82.23. Bottom of locus: ca. 80.30. See pls. 16:B; 264.

Elevation	Field Number	Description	Plate
82.23	IV-139	Spouted jar (Protoliterate)	—
82.23	IV-140	Stick ladle	cf. 81:G–L
82.23	IV-141	Spouted jar fragments (Protoliterate)	—
82.23	IV-142a	Handled pithos	16:B; 99:C
82.23	IV-142b	Beveled-rim bowl	16:B; 99:A
82.23	IV-143	Beveled-rim bowl (Protoliterate)	—
82.23	IV-144	Beveled-rim bowl (Protoliterate)	—
82.23	IV-145	Beveled-rim bowl	cf. 83:P
82.23	IV-146	Flower pot	cf. 83:CC–DD
82.23	IV-147	Four-lugged jar	cf. 113:E
82.23	IV-148	1/2 spouted jar	107:F
82.23	4.446	Interior painted bowl fragment	199:B
82.23–81.63	IV-118	Strap-handled jar	97:J
81.73	IV-233	Oval jar	19:G; 91:C

Elevation	Field Number	Description	Plate
81.70	4.872	Stone hoe	246:Q
80.83–80.33	IV-288	Sealing	45:Q; 155:C

Q18:403

Mud-plastered water channels in southern part of Q18:402. Top: 81.31. Base of channels: 81.23. Surface elevation: ca. 81.50. Top of locus: 81.31. Bottom of locus: 81.23. See pl. 264.

Q18:404

A Protoliterate pit continued from Q18:314. Surface elevation: 82.23. Top of locus: ca. 81.23. Bottom of locus: 81.23. See pl. 264.

Elevation	Field Number	Description	Plate
81.23	IV-165	Miniature pot	88:Z

Q18:406

Canceled

Q19:301

Area with pipe drain; southern end 81.09; northern end 81.21. Three fragmentary baked bricks flanked the southernmost, partly destroyed pipe. Beginning with the seventh pipe from the south, the drain was overlaid by a segment of collapsed baked-brick drain ca. 2.00 m long; at the top 81.38; at the north 81.41 (cf. pl. 12:C). After a gap in which nothing remained, the line of the Q19:301 pipe drain was continued in the southwestern part of R18 by incompletely preserved segments of a baked-brick drain, the longer one with two layers of baked bricks; top 81.43 and bottom at 81.23. Apparently these R18 bricks were part of the same installation as the baked bricks overlying the northern part of the Q18:301 pipe drain. Although pipes were not discovered with the baked bricks in the southwestern part of R18, it is possible that the various remnants in Q19:301 and R18 Southwest might have belonged to one major drain with baked bricks protecting pipes and an alignment corresponding to that of the houses to the north until it curved to the south at the edge of the East Area. During the fourth season an area of 2.30 × 4.00 m immediately to the south of Q19:301 was tested, Q19:403. Here at 81.15 some scattered baked bricks now only about 0.40 m below the surface suggested that the drain had originally continued for at least 2.00–3.00 m. In addition to the main drain segments in this area, some fragmentary installations at a higher level were also indicated to the southwest of R18:301 on pl. 264, namely a line of four baked bricks, parallel to the lower drain at 81.85, and a differently aligned drain segment with its inside channel at 81.66 at the north and 81.64 at the south. Surface elevation: ca. 81.80. Top of locus: ca. 81.80. Bottom of locus: ca. 80.80. See pls. 12:C; 264.

Elevation	Field Number	Description	Plate
ca. 81.80	3.345	Handled cup; see fig. 9	97:A
ca. 81.55	III-253	Large ovoid jar; see fig. 9	91:A
ca. 81.55	3.868	Spherical token (Protoliterate)	—
ca. 81.55	—	Band rim stone bowl fragment (Protoliterate)	—
ca. 81.40	III-241	Spouted jar	cf. 104:A
80.60	3.380	Jar neck	191:V

BETWEEN Q19:301 AND P19:401

Elevation	Field Number	Description	Plate
ca. 81.25	3.201	Painted lip fragment	166:C

Q19:303

Elevation	Field Number	Description	Plate
0.45 B.S.	III-451	Die; bone	5:H

Q19:401

Area delimited from Q18:401 by a wide wall excavated during the third season and from R19:401 by Q19:301 pipe drain. Surface elevation: 81.39. Top of locus: 81.39. Bottom of locus: ca. 79.90. See pl. 264.

Elevation	Field Number	Description	Plate
79.89	IV-56	Spouted jar; see fig. 12	cf. 104:J
—	IV-51	Cylinder seal	41:F

WALL BETWEEN Q19:401 AND Q18:401 SOUTH

Elevation	Field Number	Description	Plate
—	IV-15	Cylinder seal	41:A

Q19:402

Small area immediately to the west of Q19:401, almost entirely in Q18 and blending into Q18:402. Two pisé installations: one a channel with water spout fragment at the southern end, presumably remaining from original lining (northern end 81.05; southern end 81.03); the second a subdivided depression, top at 81.31, connected with the two runnels of Q18:403 at 81.23. Surface elevation: 81.52. Top of locus: 81.52. Bottom of locus: ca. 80.60. See pl. 264.

Elevation	Field Number	Description	Plate
81.12	IV-149	Ovoid jar; see fig. 9	89:P
81.12	IV-44	Corrugated conical cup	cf. 80:L
81.12	IV-193	Short metal pin	—

Q19:403

Southern extension of Q19:301 dug to trace extent of the Q19:301 drain. Surface elevation: 81.56. Top of locus: 81.56. Bottom of locus: N/A. See pl. 264.

Elevation	Field Number	Description	Plate
—	4.101	Jar lip fragment	75:Z

R17 AREA

Elevation	Field Number	Description	Plate
—	4.101	Jar lip fragment	75:Z

R17:201

Trench V, Plot H, 2.00 × 5.00 m. Its debris was primarily Protoliterate and located above Protoliterate room R17:313, with beveled-rim bowls on "shelf." Surface elevation: ca. 83.80. Top of locus: ca. 83.80. Bottom of locus: ca. 83.00. See pl. 264.

Elevation	Field Number	Description	Plate
83.60–83.40	2.564	Bowl	74:L
ca. 83.55	II-23	Theriomorphic spout (Protoliterate)	—
ca. 83.05	II-274	Spouted vessel fragment	103:B
—	II-313	Conical token (Protoliterate)	—

R17:202

Trench V, Plot I, 2.00 × 5.00 m, northern walls of Protoliterate rooms excavated at a later date. Rooms R17:410 and 413 were traced. Surface elevation: ca. 84.00. Top of locus: ca. 84.00. Bottom of locus: ca. 82.40. See pl. 264.

Elevation	Field Number	Description	Plate
ca. 83.80	—	Spouted jar	cf. 107:N
ca. 83.80	II-462	Strap-handled jar fragment	cf. 95:J
ca. 83.80	2.355	Spouted jar body fragment (Protoliterate)	—
ca. 83.70	II-26	Ring bead (Protoliterate)	—
ca. 83.70	II-479	Clay cone (Protoliterate)	—
ca. 83.70	2.366	Base and lower part of vessel	—
ca. 83.70	2.508	Spouted fragment (Protoliterate)	—
ca. 83.60	II-19	Square stamp seal	41:O
ca. 83.60	2.009	Strap-handled jar	95:M
83.30–83.15	2.027	Vat fragment; see fig. 9	87:I
ca. 82.50	III-317	Jar; see fig. 9	88:L
ca. 82.40	II-477	Clay cone (Protoliterate)	—

R17:203

Trench V, Plot J, 2.00 × 5.00 m, contained Protoliterate debris and in the western part were three walls of room R17:414. At the southern edge was kiln R17:210. The eastern end and most of adjacent Plot K, R17:204, were occupied by the southwestern part of a large pit, R17:208. Surface elevation: ca. 84.00. Top of locus: ca. 84.00. Bottom of locus: N/A. See pl. 264.

Elevation	Field Number	Description	Plate
ca. 84.00	II-22	Stone bowl fragment (Protoliterate)	—
ca. 84.00	II-29	Conical cup	80:T
ca. 84.00	2.033	Bowl fragment	85:N
ca. 84.00	2.012	Spouted jar	cf. 105:C
ca. 84.00	2.396	Strap-handled jar	cf. 95:J
ca. 84.00	2.503	Four-lugged jar (Protoliterate)	cf. 113:C
ca. 84.00	2.532	Rim with socket	85:EE
84.00–83.60	2.035	Bowl fragment	73:R
84.00–83.60	2.561	Carinated bowl fragment	74:N
84.00–83.50	II-93	Door sealing	143:C
ca. 83.75	II-8	Beveled-rim bowl	cf. 83:F–S
ca. 83.70	II-5	Beveled-rim bowl (Protoliterate)	—
83.61	II-484	Beveled-rim bowl (Protoliterate)	—
83.46	—	Beveled-rim bowl (Protoliterate)	—
83.36	—	Beveled-rim bowl (Protoliterate)	—
ca. 81.90	2.391	Strap-handled jar fragment	cf. 95:J
—	II-204b	Sealing reverse flat	45:H; 152:C
—	2.372	Tray fragment	cf. 86:DD
—	2.187	Four-lugged fragment with painted decoration	123:F

R17:203 WEST

Area of fragmentary Protoliterate room, later continued as R17:414. See pl. 264.

Elevation	Field Number	Description	Plate
ca. 82.65	II-437	Pouring lip bowl	cf. 80:Y–FF
ca. 82.65	2.534	Rod handled cup fragment	cf. 82:F
82.11	2.368	Tray fragment	cf. 86:Y

NORTH OF R17:203

Objects listed here could not be assigned specifically to loci R17:206–08 and 213 but were from this general area of Proto-literate pits and deposits. (Since these object were of the Protoliterate period, it seemed warranted to consider all of them as coming from the Protoliterate pits in R17—AA.) Surface elevation: 84.31. Top of locus: 84.31. Bottom of locus: ca. 82.00. See pl. 264.

Elevation	Field Number	Description	Plate
84.31	II-76	Flint blade	—
84.31	II-163	Spindle whorl	65:W
84.31	2.345	Spouted jar fragment	cf. 109:C
84.31	2.362	Strap-handled jar fragment	cf. 95:J
84.31–83.91	II-425	Conical cup (Protoliterate)	cf. 80:J–R
84.31–83.71	II-431	Tubular bead (Protoliterate)	—
84.31–83.61	II-189	Biconvex bead (Protoliterate)	—
84.21	II-444	Flower pot	cf. 83:BB
84.21	II-458	Handled vessel; see fig. 9	100:D
84.06	II-316c	Sealing	—
84.01	II-49	Slingshot (Protoliterate)	—
84.01	II-449	Flower pot	cf. 83:BB
84.01	II-453	Flower pot	cf. 83:BB
84.01–82.81	II-346	Clay fragment with punctations + possible traces of a sealing	—
83.91	2.227	Trough drain; see fig. 9	87:M
83.71	II-315a–c	Assorted beads	129:U–W
83.71	2.351	Bottle fragment	cf. 111:F
83.71–83.61	II-255	Conical token (Protoliterate)	—
83.71–83.61	II-256	Pill-shaped token (Protoliterate)	—
83.71–83.61	II-257	Miniature globular pot (Protoliterate)	—
ca. 83.70	2.311	Beveled-rim bowl waster	83:AA
83.61	II-258	Shell bead (Protoliterate)	—
83.61	II-259	Pill-shaped token (Protoliterate)	—
83.61–82.71	2.308	Globular jar	89:R
83.61–82.21	2.309	Bottle fragment	111:K
83.31	II-194	Metal pin (Protoliterate)	—
83.31	II-216	Oval shaped token; cloth imprint on one side	cf. 134:G 5
83.30–82.50	2.017	Stick ladle	81:K
83.11	II-422	Conical cup; see fig. 8	81:D
83.11	II-271	Animal figurine (Protoliterate)	—
—	II-357	Barrel shaped token	cf. 134:D 8–11
—	II-366	Perforated stone (Protoliterate)	—
—	II-419	Shouldered jar	89:S
—	2.318	Ovoid jar	88:F
—	2.378	Tray fragment (Protoliterate)	—
—	2.441	Vat rim fragment	cf. 18:J
—	2.449	Vat rim fragment	cf. 18:J
—	2.515	Bowl fragment	cf. 84:I
—	2.714	Spindle whorl	126:I
—	2.765	Perforated stone roundel	125:P

R17:203–204

Surface elevation: ca. 84.00. Top of locus: ca. 84.00. Bottom of locus: N/A. See pl. 264.

Elevation	Field Number	Description	Plate
84.00–83.00	2.574	Bowl	75:E
ca. 83.70	III-70	Metal pin fragment; length 16.2 cm	cf. 29:H
Sifting	II-273	Sealing (Protoliterate)	44:A; 145:B
Sifting	II-324	Sealing (Protoliterate)	—
Sifting	II-339	Conical token	134:B 8
Sifting	II-466	Clay cone	31:LL
Sifting	2.743	Crescentic implement	126:HH

NORTH OF R17:203–204

Surface elevation: 84.31. Top of locus: 84.31. Bottom of locus: N/A. See pl. 264.

Elevation	Field Number	Description	Plate
—	II-46	Conical token (Protoliterate)	—
—	II-448	Flower pot	cf. 83:BB
—	II-463	Strap-handled jar; see fig. 9	98:F
—	2.014	Stick ladle	17:H; 81:G
—	2.201	Beveled-rim bowl; see fig. 8	83:O

R17:204

Trench V, Plot K, area of Protoliterate debris mostly occupied by the southeastern part of large pit R17:208. At the southern edge was an upper phase Protoliterate wall with preserved top at ca. 83.90 (= northern wall of small room R17:703). At right angles to it, but at a lower level, was another Protoliterate wall with preserved top at 83.06. To the east of it was pit R17:212. Surface elevation: ca. 84.00. Top of locus: ca. 84.00. Bottom of locus: ca. 82.65. See pl. 264.

Elevation	Field Number	Description	Plate
ca. 84.00	II-12	Cylinder seal	41:D
ca. 84.00	II-21	Stone bowl fragment (Protoliterate)	—
ca. 84.00	II-464	Strap-handled jar	cf. 95:J
ca. 84.00	2.317	Jar shoulder with impressed decoration	28:T; 92:A
ca. 83.70	II-7	Beveled-rim bowl (Protoliterate)	—
ca. 83.60	2.359	Strap-handled jar fragment	cf. 95:J
ca. 83.10	II-205	Stick sealing (Protoliterate)	—
Sifting	II-217	Cylinder seal fragment	129:C
Sifting	II-239	Sealing (Protoliterate)	—
Sifting	II-240	Plano-convex lump of clay with punctations (Protoliterate)	—

NORTH OF R17:204

Surface elevation: 84.31. Top of locus: 84.31. Bottom of locus: N/A. See pl. 264.

Elevation	Field Number	Description	Plate
84.31–83.71	II-243	Miniature goblet; see fig. 8	80:D
ca. 83.60	II-196	Metal pin	128:R
ca. 83.60	II-197	Metal pin	—
83.31–82.71	2.186	Four-lugged fragment with painted decoration	123:F
ca. 83.30	II-245	Spindle whorl (Protoliterate)	—
83.30–82.40	II-314a–b	Pill-shaped tokens (Protoliterate)	—
ca. 82.65	2.382a–d	Tray fragments	cf. 86:DD
—	II-426	Pouring lip bowl	cf. 80:Z–FF
—	2.354	Spouted bottle fragment	cf. 111:F
—	2.505	Four-lugged jar body	cf. 122:B
—	2.521	Beveled-rim bowl (Protoliterate)	—

R17:204–205

Ash layer. See pl. 264.

Elevation	Field Number	Description	Plate
—	2.232	Lip fragment	87:H
—	2.036	Bowl fragment; see fig. 9	85:R

R17:205

Trench V, Plot L, an area with its western end in R17, but lying mostly in S17, contained Protoliterate debris with an isolated segment of a wall. Surface elevation: 83.42. Top of locus: 83.42. Bottom of locus: ca. 82.17. See pl. 264.

Elevation	Field Number	Description	Plate
83.42	2.015	Stick ladle	81:J
82.17	2.410	Spouted jar	cf. 105:F
—	II-215	Cashew-shaped token	134:F 1
—	2.533	Stone bowl	124:S
—	2.494	Conical cup	80:Q

R17:206/714

Protoliterate debris, in the northwestern corner of the northern extension of R17:203 (= Trench V, Plot J). Below was a narrow rectangular room R17:714. Surface elevation: 84.31. Top of locus: 84.31. Bottom of locus: ca. 82.50. See pls. 11:B; 264.

Elevation	Field Number	Description	Plate
83.71–83.61	II-254	Conical token	134:B 10
83.66	II-404	Small four-lugged jar	114:A
83.35	7.289	Finger stone	244:V
82.65	7.279	Grinding stone	239:G
82.65	7.298	Handgrinder	242:F
82.65	7.299	Handgrinder	242:C
82.65	7.386	Clay ball fragment	152:A; 154:B–C
82.64	7.276	Grinding stone	238:A
82.64	7.280	Stone with depressions	248:N
82.64	7.286	Pestle/pounder	244:F
82.64	7.287	Pestle/pounder	244:G
82.64	7.288	Finger stone	244:U
82.64	7.290	Finger stone	244:W
82.64	7.291	Stone disc	251:A
82.64	7.293	Stone disc	251:H
82.64	7.295	Stone disc	251:J
82.64	7.296	Stone disc	251:K

R17:207

Small area immediately to the west of the northern end of pit R17:208 and above R17:714. Just below surface were two courses of a north-south Protoliterate wall (not shown on pl. 264; cf. pl. 11:D) with a pottery deposit lying alongside it on the east above the southern wall of R17:414 (top at 83.47). The lowest elements of the R17:207 deposit were alongside the R17:414 wall. Surface elevation: ca. 84.31. Top of locus: ca. 84 31. Bottom of locus: ca. 83.00. See pls. 11:D; 264.

Elevation	Field Number	Description	Plate
84.31	—	Beveled-rim bowls: 2 complete (Protoliterate)	—
84.01	—	1 beveled-rim bowl (Protoliterate)	—
83.81	—	Beveled-rim bowls: 4 complete (Protoliterate)	—
83.71	II-364	Fish-shaped mother-of-pearl inlay fragment	129:LL
83.61	—	2 beveled-rim bowls (Protoliterate)	—
83.61–83.11	II-412	Bowl; see fig. 8	18:A; 84:Q
83.56	—	Beveled-rim bowls: 9 complete (Protoliterate)	—
83.56	—	Spouted bottle fragment	cf. 111:A
83.41	2.358	Reserve slip jar fragment (Protoliterate)	—
83.41	—	Spouted bottle base (Protoliterate)	—
83.41	—	Beveled-rim bowls: 15 complete (Protoliterate)	—
83.36	II-184	Twisted handled jar	cf. 100:A–E, G
83.36	2.531	Spouted jar fragment	110:K
83.28	II-423	Conical bowl	81:C

Elevation	Field Number	Description	Plate
83.28	—	Beveled-rim bowl: 1 complete (Protoliterate)	—
83.06	II-108a–g	Sealings	44:G; 146:E
83.06	II-461	Coarse ovoid jar	91:B
—	II-109	Door sealing	42:Q; 138:E
—	II-110	Bale(?) sealing	42:O; 144:E
—	II-111	Jar stopper	130:U
—	II-112–119	Jar stoppers (Protoliterate)	—
—	II-120	Kneaded clay for sealing (Protoliterate)	—
—	II-121	Jar stopper (Protoliterate)	—
—	II-204a	Bale(?) sealing (Protoliterate)	45:H; 152:C
—	II-269	Door sealing (Protoliterate)	—
—	II-397	Sealing	42:L; 138:A
—	II-416	Miniature jar	88:M
—	II-459	Twisted handled jar	20:B; 100:A
—	—	Beveled-rim bowls: 20 complete (Protoliterate)	—
—	2.746	Perforated plaque	127:L

R17:208

Large pit in R17:203–04 (Trench V, Plots J and K and their northern extension) with numerous complete or semi-complete vessels and seal impressions. The bottom of the pit was marked by a hard surface at 82.63–82.60. Some sterile layers below were designated as R17:213. On the east a northwest-southeast Protoliterate wall with top at 83.06 separated R17:208 from pit P17:212. In the northern part of R17:208 a small sounding was dug from the bottom of the big pit to test the underlying levels, R17:209. To the north this pit had cut the southern end of a rectangular mass of brickwork, R17:704 East. Below the rectangular brickwork to the southeast were rooms R17:703 and 715. Surface elevation: 84.31. Top of locus: 84.31. Bottom of locus: 82.60. See pl. 264.

Elevation	Field Number	Description	Plate
84.31	II-229	Beveled-rim bowl waster	17:E
84.31	II-391a	Pill-shaped token	134:D 3
84.31	II-391b	Small spherical tokens, 22 (Protoliterate)	—
84.31	2.365	Everted rim jar fragments	cf. 90:E–J
84.31	2.630	Jar neck + body (Achaemenid)	—
84.31	2.651	Band rimmed bowl fragment (Achaemenid)	—
84.31	2.548	Perforated plaque; window(?)	127:K
84.31–83.91	II-95	Bale(?) sealing	42:C
84.31–83.71	II-99	Door sealing (Protoliterate)	—
84.31–83.61	II-206f–h	Sealing (Protoliterate)	—
84.31–83.61	II-206i	Door sealing (Protoliterate)	—
84.31–83.61	II-206j	Door(?) sealing	43:O
84.31–83.61	II-206l	Bale(?) sealing	43:N
84.31–83.61	II-207	Bale(?) sealing (Protoliterate)	157:H–J
84.31–83.61	2.001	Twisted handled jar fragment; see fig. 9	100:F
84.21	II-294	Deep bowl	18:F; 85:AA
84.21	II-457	Strap-handled jar	96:C
84.16	2.406	Strap-handled jar fragment	cf. 95:J
84.06	II-54	Stopper	130:V
84.06	II-56	Pyramidal token	134:C 10
84.06	II-94	Bale(?) sealing	44:D; 146:E
84.06	II-287	Sealing (Protoliterate)	—
—	II-497	Beveled-rim bowl: 1 complete (Protoliterate)	—
84.06–83.41	II-288d	Sealing	153:B
84.06–83.41	II-316b	Door sealing	145:C
84.06–83.41	II-317	Sealing	142:D
83.96	II-277	Strap-handled jar (Protoliterate)	—
83.96	2.350	Bottle fragment	cf. 111:A
83.96	—	Beveled-rim bowls: 9 complete (Protoliterate)	—
83.96	—	Pivot stone (Protoliterate)	—

R17:208 (*cont.*)

Elevation	Field Number	Description	Plate
83.96	—	Grinding stone (Protoliterate)	—
83.91–83.61	2.428	Double-angled jar fragment	88:U
83.81	II-101	Animal figurine	31:C
83.81	II-222	Tallying slab	132:C
83.81	II-223	Crescent-shaped terra-cotta	126:II
83.81	II-233	Double-angled jar	19:E; 89:U
83.81	II-234	Horizontal handled jar	21:I
83.81	—	Flower pots: 4 complete (Protoliterate)	—
83.81	—	Beveled-rim bowls: 5 complete (Protoliterate)	—
83.81–82.61	II-331	Stopper	130:W
83.71–82.81	II-237	Sealing fragment (Protoliterate)	—
83.61	II-174	Conical token	—
83.61	II-209a–b	Sealing fragment	45:F, I; 152:G
83.61	II-210	Stopper	130:R
83.61	II-211	Stopper	130:S
83.61	II-231	Small disc bead (Protoliterate)	—
83.61	II-250	Conical bowl	17:A; 80:P
83.61	II-263	Flat clay lump with punctations (Protoliterate)	—
83.61	II-264	Conical token	134:B 9
83.61	II-265	Pottery bead(?)	—
83.61	II-266	Plano-convex bead	—
83.61	II-278	Strap-handled jar fragment	cf. 95:J
83.61	II-279	Terra-cotta lid	30:V
83.61	II-436	Bowl	84:L
83.61–82.81	II-171	Spindle whorl (Protoliterate)	—
83.61–82.81	II-172	Spindle whorl (Protoliterate)	—
83.61–82.81	II-173	Conical token (Protoliterate)	—
83.61–82.81	II-208	Sealing, reverse flat	42:P; 138:C
83.61–82.81	II-261	Bowl	83:A
83.61–82.81	II-272	Flattish sealing (Protoliterate)	139:B
83.61–82.81	II-276	Conical token (Protoliterate)	—
83.61–82.81	2.340	Four-lugged jar fragment	cf. 122:B
83.61–82.81	—	Beveled-rim bowls: 4 complete, 1 waster (Protoliterate)	—
83.61–82.81	—	Flower pots: 6 complete (Protoliterate)	—
83.56	II-336	Metal pin (Protoliterate)	—
83.54	7.283	Stone hoe (R17:704 West)	246:P
83.51	II-309	Animal figurine	31:J
83.51	II-316a	Sealing fragment	145:C
83.51	II-360a	Door sealing	32:C, F–G; 33:A; 144:C; 145:C
83.51	—	Beveled-rim bowls: 3 complete (Protoliterate)	—
83.51	—	Flower pots: 3 complete; 1 waster (Protoliterate)	—
83.51	—	Conical cups: 1 complete (Protoliterate)	—
83.51–83.11	II-270	Cylindrical bead (Protoliterate)	—
83.51–83.11	II-360k–q	Door sealing	145:C
83.51–83.11	II-392	Sealing fragment (Protoliterate)	146:D
83.51–83.11	II-393a–b	Fragments flattened clay with punctation (Protoliterate)	—
83.51–82.81	II-206r	Door sealing	43:L
83.51–82.81	II-290	Bale(?) sealing	32:E; 42:I; 138:G
83.46	II-360b	Door sealing	32:C, F–G; 33:A; 144:C; 145:C
83.46	II-360e	Door sealing	32:C, F–G; 33:A; 144:C; 145:C
83.46	II-360i	Door sealing	32:C, F–G; 33:A; 144:C; 145:C
83.46	II-360j	Sealing fragment	32:C, F–G; 33:A; 144:C; 145:C
83.46	II-360c–d, f–g	Door sealing fragments	—
83.46	II-361	Sealing fragment (Protoliterate)	147:G
83.46	II-362	Sealing fragment	157:E
83.46	II-363	Sealing fragment	145:D

R17:208 (*cont.*)

Elevation	Field Number	Description	Plate
83.46	—	Beveled-rim bowls: 5 complete (Protoliterate)	—
83.46	—	Flower pots: 3 complete (Protoliterate)	—
83.46	—	Bottle fragments (Protoliterate)	—
83.41	II-415	Strap-handled jar	20:S
83.41	2.783	Gray stone celt	125:EE
83.36	II-338	Violin shaped potter's tool	231:N
83.31	II-206a–b	Door sealing (Protoliterate)	—
83.31	II-206c	Bale(?) sealing (Protoliterate)	—
83.31	II-206d	Bale(?) sealing	43:M
83.31	II-206e	Door sealing (Protoliterate)	—
83.31	II-286	Door sealing (Protoliterate)	157:G
83.31	II-289	Door sealing	157:B
83.31	—	Beveled-rim bowls: 8 complete (Protoliterate)	—
83.31	—	Flower pots: 5 complete (Protoliterate)	—
83.31	—	2 bottle fragments (Protoliterate)	—
83.31	—	1 spouted jar fragment (Protoliterate)	—
83.27	II-206n	Door sealing (Protoliterate)	—
83.27	II-218	Ovoid clay lump with incised lines and punctations (Protoliterate)	—
83.27	—	Beveled-rim bowls: 7 complete (Protoliterate)	—
83.27	—	Flower pots: 4 complete (Protoliterate)	—
83.27	—	1 pouring lip conical bowl fragment (Protoliterate)	—
83.21–83.11	II-321	Terra-cotta sickle (Protoliterate)	—
83.21–83.11	—	Beveled-rim bowls: 4 complete (Protoliterate)	—
83.21–83.11	—	Flower pots: 1 complete (Protoliterate)	—
83.21–83.11	—	1 bottle fragment (Protoliterate)	—
83.16	—	Beveled-rim bowls: 3 complete (Protoliterate)	—
83.11	—	Flower pots: 3 complete (Protoliterate)	—
83.11	II-213	Sealing fragment (Protoliterate)	—
83.11	II-214	Jar neck sealing (Protoliterate)	157:A
83.11	II-219	Clay tallying slab	132:A
83.11	II-220	Clay tallying slab	132:B
83.11	II-221	Clay tallying slab	cf. 132
83.06	—	Beveled-rim bowls: 7 complete (Protoliterate)	—
—	—	Flower pots: 6 complete (Protoliterate)	—
83.01	II-288a	Door sealing	45:K; 153:B
82.96	—	Beveled-rim bowls: 8 complete (Protoliterate)	—
—	—	Flower pots: 1 complete (Protoliterate)	—
—	—	2 bottle fragments (Protoliterate)	—
82.86	II-206t	Jar neck sealing	143:I
82.86	II-318	Jar neck sealing (Protoliterate)	—
82.86	II-394a	Flattish sealing	44:B; 145:B
82.86	—	Beveled-rim bowls: 6 complete (Protoliterate)	—
82.86	—	Flower pots: 2 complete (Protoliterate)	—
82.86	—	Bottle fragment (Protoliterate)	—
82.81	II-206o	Sealing fragment (Protoliterate)	—
82.81	II-212a–b	Door sealing	42:E–F; 143:E
82.81	II-235	Flattish sealing	135:H–I
82.81	II-236	Disc token (Protoliterate)	—
82.81	II-238	Sealing (Protoliterate)	—
82.81	—	Beveled-rim bowls (Protoliterate)	—
82.81	—	Flower pots: 2 complete (Protoliterate)	—
82.81	—	Strap-handled jar fragment (Protoliterate)	—
82.71	—	Beveled-rim bowls: 1 complete (Protoliterate)	—
82.56	II-332	Stone hoe (Protoliterate)	—
82.56	II-333	Terra-cotta slingshot (Protoliterate)	—
82.56	II-358	Sealing fragment (Protoliterate)	—

R17:208 (*cont.*)

Elevation	Field Number	Description	Plate
82.56	II-405	Pouring lip bowl	80:DD
Sifting	II-206s	Door sealing (Protoliterate)	—
Sifting	II-268	Sealing fragment (Protoliterate)	—
Sifting	II-288b–c	Door sealing	45:L; 153:B
Sifting	II-394b	Door sealing (Protoliterate)	—
Sifting	II-396	Door sealing fragment (Protoliterate)	147:B
—	II-326	Biconical perforated clay object; diameter 6.0 cm; height 3.5 cm	126:O
—	II-328	Animal figurine (Protoliterate)	—
—	II-329	Spindle whorl (Protoliterate)	—
—	II-376	Door sealing	42:D; 143:B
—	2.772	Gray stone bowl fragment	125:E
—	II-377	Sealing, reverse flat (Protoliterate)	—
—	II-378	Jar neck sealing	157:D
—	II-283a–b	2 flattened clay lumps with incisions and punctation (Protoliterate)	—
—	II-428a	Clay ball fragment	44:C; 148:C
—	II-430	Miniature handled jar; see fig. 9	95:E
—	2.209	Flaring jar neck (Achaemenid)	—
—	2.385	Strap-handled jar body fragment	cf. 95:J
—	2.400	Handled-jar fragment (Protoliterate)	—
—	2.559	Carinated bowl fragment (Achaemenid)	—
—	2.637	Jar neck + body (Achaemenid)	—
—	2.649	Blue glazed bowl fragment (period unassigned)	—
—	—	Flower pots: 2 complete (Protoliterate)	—
—	—	Beveled-rim bowls: 13 complete (Protoliterate)	—
—	—	Bottle fragments (Protoliterate)	—

WEST OF R17:208

Elevation	Field Number	Description	Plate
83.76	III-514	"Potter's wheel"	127:I

R17:209

Sounding into Late Middle Susiana levels begun at the bottom of the relatively sterile earth (= R17:213) underlying Protoliterate pit R17:208. R17:209 is below the northern part of R17:208. Surface elevation: 84.31. Top of locus: ca. 81.90. Bottom of locus: ca. 80.30. See pl. 264.

Elevation	Field Number	Description	Plate
80.31	2.100	Small squarish jar; see fig. 31	192:P

R17:210

A Protoliterate, small oval kiln, ca. 0.80 × 1.00 m, in R17:203 (Trench V, Plot J). In its interior were many fragments of overfired pottery, including beveled-rim bowls. Surface elevation: ca. 84.00. Top of locus: ca. 84.00. Bottom of locus: 83.67. See pl. 11:C–D.

Elevation	Field Number	Description	Plate
ca. 84.00	II-28	Jar stopper	130:Q
ca. 84.00	II-275	Flower pot, waster	cf. 83:BB
ca. 84.00	2.386	Open vessel (Protoliterate)	—
ca. 84.00	2.492	Flower pot	cf. 83:Z-DD
ca. 84.00	—	Spouted jar fragment (Protoliterate)	—

EAST OF R17:210

Elevation	Field Number	Description	Plate
83.65	—	Flower pot (Protoliterate)	—
83.35	—	Flower pot (Protoliterate)	—
83.35	—	Strap-handled jar fragment	—
83.30	—	Beveled-rim bowl (Protoliterate)	—
83.15	—	Beveled-rim bowl (Protoliterate)	—
83.15	—	2 flower pot wasters (Protoliterate)	—
83.10	—	Beveled-rim bowl waster (Protoliterate)	—
83.05	—	Beveled-rim bowl waster (Protoliterate)	—
83.00	—	1 flower pot, 1 waster (Protoliterate)	—
82.95	—	Flower pot (Protoliterate)	—
82.90	—	Beveled-rim bowl (Protoliterate)	—
81.75	—	2 beveled-rim bowls (Protoliterate)	—

SOUTH OF R17:210

Elevation	Field Number	Description	Plate
—	II-30	Small four-lugged pot (Protoliterate)	—

WEST OF R17:210

Elevation	Field Number	Description	Plate
—	2.633	Bowl fragment	cf. 81:J
84.00–83.67	II-85	Beveled-rim bowl waster	17:L
83.67	II-86	Beveled-rim bowl waster (Protoliterate)	—

R17:211

Deposit of Protoliterate pottery in the northeasternmost part of the Trench V Northern Extension. Surface elevation: ca. 84.00. Top of locus: ca. 84.00. Bottom of locus: N/A. See pl. 264.

Elevation	Field Number	Description	Plate
ca. 83.05	—	Beveled-rim bowl (Protoliterate)	—
ca. 82.95	—	Beveled-rim bowl (Protoliterate)	—
ca. 82.85	—	Beveled-rim bowl (Protoliterate)	—
ca. 82.70	—	Beveled-rim bowl (Protoliterate)	—
—	II-401	Perforated roundel made from stone bowl fragment	125:X

R17:212

Protoliterate pit separated from large pit R17:208 by northwest-southeast wall with preserved top at 83.06. Directly to the east of the wall at 82.68, a patch of floor remained, apparently at the base of the wall, on which a cluster of four complete clay balls was found. For another example of a clay balls cache at the base of a wall, see R18:312. The patch of floor at 82.68 corresponded well with the floor at 82.63, cut by pit R18:208. Surface elevation: 84.31. Top of locus: 84.31. Bottom of locus: ca. 82.60. See pl. 264.

Elevation	Field Number	Description	Plate
84.31	II-225	Conical token (Protoliterate)	—
84.31	II-226	Conical token (Protoliterate)	—
84.31	II-227	Animal figurine (Protoliterate)	—
84.31	II-228	Animal figurine	—
84.31	2.363	Strap-handled jar fragment	cf. 98:B
84.31	2.364	Jar fragment (Protoliterate)	—
84.31	2.370	Tray fragments	cf. 86:Z

R17:212 (cont.)

Elevation	Field Number	Description	Plate
84.31	—	2 strap-handled jar fragments (Protoliterate)	—
84.31	—	Four-lugged jar fragment (Protoliterate)	—
84.31	—	Storage-sized jar fragment with rope molding (Protoliterate)	—
84.31	—	Vat fragment (Protoliterate)	—
84.01–83.71	2.199	Spouted jar	108:A
83.71	—	Jar fragment (Protoliterate)	—
83.91	II-182	Animal figurine (Protoliterate)	—
83.91	2.319	Spouted vessel fragment (Protoliterate)	111:F
83.91	—	Beveled-rim bowl (Protoliterate)	—
83.81	II-183	Animal figurine (Protoliterate)	—
83.61	—	Pseudo beveled-rim bowl	cf. 83:T
83.56	—	Beveled-rim bowl (Protoliterate)	—
83.51	II-198	Miniature four-lugged jar; see fig. 15	24:A; 112:B
83.51	—	2 beveled-rim bowls (Protoliterate)	—
83.51–83.11	II-352	Inlay fragment greenish gray paste (Protoliterate)	—
83.46	—	Beveled-rim bowl (Protoliterate)	—
83.11	2.310	Spouted jar body	108:J
82.96	2.387	Tray fragment	cf. 86:CC
82.68	II-345	Door sealing (Protoliterate)	42:G
82.68	II-347	Clay ball	34:L; 138:H
82.68	II-348	Clay ball	34:E; 39:B; 138:H
82.68	II-349	Clay ball	34:M; 39:A; 138:H
82.68	II-350	Clay ball	34:H
82.68	II-351	Bale(?) sealing (Protoliterate)	—
82.68	II-353	Miniature spouted jar; see fig. 12	22:E; 102:D
82.68	II-354	12 miscellaneous stone beads (Protoliterate)	—
82.56	—	Terra-cotta sickle (Protoliterate)	—
82.41	—	2 spoon fragment	cf. 82:H–L

SOUTHWEST OF R17:212

Elevation	Field Number	Description	Plate
83.71	—	Beveled-rim bowl (Protoliterate)	—

R17:213

Relatively sterile layers of first gray, then yellowish brown earth sandwiched between Protoliterate pit R17:208 and the top of the Late Middle Susiana debris in test pit R17:209. Surface elevation: 84.31. Top of locus: ca. 82.60. Bottom of locus: ca. 81.90. See pl. 264.

R17:214

Round Protoliterate pit, ca. 1.95 m in diameter, cut into the northeast-southwest wall that formed the southern border of loci R17:401–03. Surface elevation: ca. 84.00. Top of locus: ca. 84.00. Bottom of locus: 83.36. See pl. 264.

Elevation	Field Number	Description	Plate
83.36	II-11	Spouted jar; see fig. 12	103:G

R17:215

Extension to the south of R17:207–08 (Trench V, Plots J and K). Rather large area of Protoliterate debris cut into the east by pits S17:202–03 and R17:710 and 715 in the east. Surface elevation: ca. 83.70. Top of elevation: ca. 83.70. Bottom of locus: 82.50. See pl. 264.

Elevation	Field Number	Description	Plate
ca. 83.70	2.538	Fine ware bowl fragment	cf. 80:L
ca. 83.70	2.782	Stone implement	—
83.61	II-209c	Sealing fragment	45:G; 152:G
ca. 83.60	2.495	Conical cup	81:A
ca. 83.25	2.726	Clay jar stopper	130:B
—	II-395	Jar-neck sealing	43:B; 139:E

R17:215 EAST

Elevation	Field Number	Description	Plate
ca. 83.70	II-63	Incised token	40:B
ca. 83.70	2.026	Unique pottery type; see fig. 9	87:J
ca. 83.70	—	Beveled-rim bowl (Protoliterate)	—
83.70–83.50	2.429	Jar neck + shoulder	88:T
83.70–83.20	II-150	Rubbing stone (Protoliterate)	—
83.70–83.20	II-151	Spindle whorl (Protoliterate)	—
83.70–83.20	II-152	Spindle whorl (Protoliterate)	—
83.70–83.20	2.003	Horizontal-handled jar fragment	101:C
83.70–83.20	2.004	Horizontal-handled jar fragment	101:B
ca. 83.60	II-105	Strap-handled jar	20:C
ca. 83.60	—	2 beveled-rim bowls (Protoliterate)	—
ca. 83.60	—	1 bottle fragment (Protoliterate)	—
ca. 83.30	II-84	Beveled-rim bowl (Protoliterate)	—
ca. 83.30	II-483	Beveled-rim bowl (Protoliterate)	—
ca. 83.30	II-498	Beveled-rim bowl (Protoliterate)	—
ca. 83.30	II-499	Beveled-rim bowl (Protoliterate)	—
ca. 83.10	II-100	Jar stopper	130:P
ca. 83.10	2.031	Bowl fragment (Protoliterate)	84:R
ca. 82.50	II-50	Jar stopper (Protoliterate)	—
ca. 82.50	II-414	Large bowl (Protoliterate)	—
ca. 82.50	2.392	Jar fragments	cf. 88:L
—	II-165	Animal figurine (Protoliterate)	—
—	II-486	Pseudo beveled-rim bowl	cf. 83:T
—	2.010	Four-lugged jar	114:F
—	2.389	Tray fragment	cf. 86:CC

R17:215 WEST

Elevation	Field Number	Description	Plate
ca. 83.70	II-68	Spindle whorl (Protoliterate)	—
ca. 83.70	II-473	Clay cone (Protoliterate)	—
ca. 83.70	2.397	Strap-handled jar fragment	cf. 95:J
83.70–83.30	2.230	Trefoil spout (Achaemenid)	75:J
ca. 83.55	II-148	Perforated stone or mace-head fragment (Protoliterate)	—
ca. 83.55	II-149	Rubbing stone (Protoliterate)	—
ca. 83.55	II-418	Horizontal and vertical handled jar; see fig. 9	21:J; 101:J
ca. 83.55	—	Beveled-rim bowl (Protoliterate)	—
ca. 83.45	II-298	Bottle	111:C
ca. 83.45	II-299	Bottle	23:E; 111:D
ca. 83.45	II-300	Bottle; see fig. 13	111:E

R17:215 West (cont.)

Elevation	Field Number	Description	Plate
ca. 83.45	—	Bottle (Protoliterate)	—
ca. 83.45	—	Pithos rim (Protoliterate)	—
ca. 83.35	II-374	Jar neck sealing	45:J; 152:E
ca. 83.35	II-375	Clay ball fragment (Protoliterate)	—
ca. 83.30	II-413	Bowl	84:H
ca. 83.30	2.376	Tray fragment	cf. 86:V
ca. 83.20	2.741	Terra-cotta spool	126:BB
ca. 82.90	II-369a–b	Clay ball fragments	45:A–B; 150:F
ca. 82.90	II-370	Clay ball fragment	45:C; 150:B–C
ca. 82.90	2.381	Tray fragment (Protoliterate)	—
—	2.393	Handled jar fragment	cf. 97:C

R17:301

Fragmentary skeletal remains found at the southern edge of R17:215 East in the area of later R17:709. Surface elevation: ca. 83.70. Top of locus: ca. 83.70. Bottom of locus: ca. 83.50. See pl. 264.

R17:302

Southern part of a large Protoliterate pit straddling Squares R17–18 at the northwestern corner of room R18:411. The northern part of this pit, directly to the south of the long drain R17:310 + 314, was dug as R17:408. Surface elevation: ca. 83.70. Top of locus: ca. 83.70. Bottom of locus: ca. 81.70. See pl. 264.

Elevation	Field Number	Description	Plate
ca. 83.70	III-135	Conical token; height 2.1 cm (Protoliterate)	cf. 134:B 4
ca. 83.70	III-283	Bottle	111:G
ca. 83.70	3.726	Flint tool	255:U

NORTH OF R17:302

Elevation	Field Number	Description	Plate
ca. 83.70	III-820	Impressed stopper	32:A–B; 136:C

WEST OF R17:302

Elevation	Field Number	Description	Plate
ca. 83.00	III-201	Miniature four-lugged jar	113:D

R17:303

Ovoid Protoliterate pit in the southeastern corner of R17 cutting into the walls of rooms R18:411 and S17:404. Surface elevation: ca. 83.30. Top of locus: ca. 83.30 (drain). Bottom of locus: ca. 81.60. See pl. 224.

Elevation	Field Number	Description	Plate
ca. 83.30	III-111	Cylinder seal	41:G
ca. 83.30	3.044	Large four-lugged jar	25:K; 122:J
ca. 82.80	III-312	Terra-cotta bead	129:Q
ca. 82.10	3.032	Small bowl; see fig. 8	81:T
ca. 82.10	III-822	Bale(?) sealing	42:N; 138:F
ca. 81.30	3.880	Conical token; height 2.6 cm	cf. 134:B 5
—	III-442	Stone bead	129:R
—	III-821	2 clay ball fragments (Protoliterate)	—
—	3.485	Stone bowl	124:E

R17:303 EAST

Elevation	Field Number	Description	Plate
ca. 81.80	III-847	Bale(?) sealing (Protoliterate)	—

NORTH OF R17:303

Elevation	Field Number	Description	Plate
ca. 83.30	III-848	Bale(?) sealing (Protoliterate)	—
ca. 83.30	III-849	Bale(?) sealing (Protoliterate)	—
ca. 83.30	III-850	Clay ball fragment (Protoliterate)	—

NORTHEAST OF R17:303

Elevation	Field Number	Description	Plate
ca. 82.80	III-313	Terra-cotta spool	cf. 30:D, F
ca. 82.80	III-314	Terra-cotta spool	30:F; 126:Z
ca. 82.80	3.511	Notched lip	19:A

R17:303 EAST

Elevation	Field Number	Description	Plate
ca. 81.80	III-847	Bale(?) sealing (Protoliterate)	—

EAST OF R17:303

Elevation	Field Number	Description	Plate
ca. 82.90	III-387	Terra-cotta spool	cf. 30:F

R17:304

Area on the eastern side of a northwest-southeast baked-brick drain, roughly at a right angle to the long drain R17:314. Top of drain at the northern end was at 83.42. A sherd pavement near the northern end of drain was at 82.67. There was a pottery deposit from the surface down to ca. 83.00. Surface elevation: ca. 83.50. Top of locus: ca. 83.50. Bottom of locus: ca. 82.00. See pl. 264.

Elevation	Field Number	Description	Plate
ca. 83.50	III-295	Tubular lugged jar; see fig. 12	24:J; 121:I
ca. 83.10	III-296	Four-lugged jar	114:E
ca. 83.10	III-297	Four-lugged jar; see fig. 15	113:G
ca. 83.10	III-298	Four-lugged jar	120:A
ca. 83.05	III-299	Small ovoid jar	88:K

R17:305

Area to the south and southeast of R17:201 (= Trench V, Plot H), located at the northwestern corner of a room with internal buttresses. Against one buttress was a fireplace at 82.62, presumably marking the floor. R17:305 West was above R17:403–04. R17:305 East was equivalent to a lower level. Surface elevation: ca. 83.80. Top of locus: ca. 83.80. Bottom of locus: ca. 81.80. See pl. 264.

Elevation	Field Number	Description	Plate
ca. 83.80	III-186	Conical token; height 2.2 cm (Protoliterate)	—
ca. 83.80	3.339	Goblet	cf. 80:D
ca. 83.80	3.1024	Jar stopper	130:E
ca. 83.80	—	Animal figurine (Protoliterate)	—

R17:305 (*cont.*)

Elevation	Field Number	Description	Plate
ca. 83.25	3.809	Beaker-like vessel	89:F
ca. 83.20	III-180	Large bowl	87:A
ca. 83.10	3.437	Handled fragment	97:E
ca. 83.00	III-179	Spouted jar	cf. 108:O
ca. 82.90	III-178	Spouted jar; see fig. 13	108:N
ca. 82.90	III-234	Ladle	82:D
ca. 82.90	3.045	Tray	86:L
ca. 82.80	3.272	Disc token	134:E 3
ca. 82.60	III-571	Small ovoid jar	88:B
ca. 82.60	III-572	Goblet	83:B
ca. 81.90	—	Terra-cotta sickle	cf. 30:T
ca. 81.80	3.739	Miniature bowl	80:C
Dump	3.1017	Blue paste cylindrical bead	76:O
—	3.869	Spherical token (Protoliterate)	—

R17:305 NORTH

Elevation	Field Number	Description	Plate
—	3.477	Stone bowl	124:X

R17:305 EAST

Elevation	Field Number	Description	Plate
ca. 83.80	3.420	Bowl	84:S

EAST OF R17:305

Elevation	Field Number	Description	Plate
83.00	3.482	Stone bowl	124:R

SOUTH OF R17:305

Elevation	Field Number	Description	Plate
ca. 83.30	III-194	Pyramidal token; height 2.2 cm (Protoliterate)	—
ca. 83.30	III-195	Spoon bowl	82:L

R17:306

Northeastern part of a Protoliterate room extending from the southwestern corner of R17 into Squares Q17–18 and R18. Together with Q18:303, it was designated as R19:406 during the fourth season. Surface elevation: ca. 83.50. Top of locus: ca. 83.50. Bottom of locus: ca. 82.90. See pl. 264.

Elevation	Field Number	Description	Plate
83.50	3.1206	Semi perforated stone disc	125:V
ca. 83.50	—	Stone roundel	cf. 29:Q–Z
ca. 83.05	III-607	Stone bowl	124:Q
ca. 83.00	3.898	Loop handle (Achaemenid)	—

INSIDE WALL BETWEEN R17:306 AND R18:424–425

Elevation	Field Number	Description	Plate
ca. 83.10	IV 159	Stone bead with incised decoration on one side	234:EE

R17:307

Canceled

R17:308

Area to the south of R17:202–03 (Trench V, Plots I and J). To the west, a small room or closet was clarified during the fourth season as R17:401, and the area adjacent to it in the east with pit R17:412. Surface elevation: ca. 84.00. Top of locus: ca. 84.00. Bottom of locus: ca. 83.00. See pl. 264.

Elevation	Field Number	Description	Plate
ca. 84.00	III-851	Bale(?) sealing (Protoliterate)	—
ca. 84.00	III-853	Bale(?) sealing (Protoliterate)	—
ca. 83.00	III-600	Hut amulet	31:GG

R17:309

Continuation of Protoliterate pit R17:214. Surface elevation: ca. 84.00. Top of locus: ca. 84.00. Bottom of locus: 83.36. See pl. 264.

R17:310

Area immediately to the south of R17:215 East along the northern side of the middle part of the long baked-brick drain in R–S17. It was later continued as R17:709. To the north of this locus was area R17:710. Surface elevation: ca. 83.60. Top of locus: ca. 83.60. Bottom of locus: ca. 82.00. See pl. 264.

R17:311

Canceled

R17:312

Canceled

R17:313

Irregularly rectangular room in area of R17:201 (Trench V, Plot H). Its northern wall was probably represented by fragmentary brickwork between R17:701 West and R17:313. The western wall was destroyed. Along the southern wall was a mud "shelf," 83.14 at its eastern end. On it from east to west was a row of eleven upside-down beveled-rim bowls, one grinding stone, and one more beveled-rim bowl. Behind the grinding stone and the adjacent beveled-rim bowls, along the southern wall, was a subsidiary row of one pouring lip bowl and four beveled-rim bowls. In the room at a slightly lower level than the "shelf," were eight more complete beveled-rim bowls upside-down. Upper floor at 82.35; lower floor at 82.11. Surface elevation: ca. 83.90. Top of locus: ca. 83.90. Bottom of locus: 82.11. See pls. 15:A; 264.

Elevation	Field Number	Description	Plate
83.14	—	Pouring-lip bowl	cf. 80:Y–FF
83.14	—	16 beveled-rim bowls	cf. 83:F–V
83.14	—	Grinding stone (Protoliterate)	—
ca. 83:00	—	8 beveled-rim bowls (Protoliterate)	—

R17:314

Southwestern section of long baked-brick drain. See R17:310 for middle portion and S17:407 for the northeastern end. It was later continued as R17:709. Surface elevation: ca. 83.50. Top of locus: 82.38. Bottom of locus: ca. 82.00. See pls. 12:A–B; 264.

R17:401

Continuation of a small room or closet of R17:308. Top of southern wall at 83.62 and a pebble floor at 83.41. Surface elevation: ca. 83.75. Top of locus: ca. 83.75. Bottom of locus: 83.41. See pl. 264.

Elevation	Field Number	Description	Plate
ca. 83.75	4.761	Small bowl (Protoliterate)	—
ca. 83.75	4.071	Jar sherd (Protoliterate)	—

R17:402

Probably a Protoliterate room in area of R17:305 between R17:401 and 403. Floor at 82.71. Surface elevation: ca. 83.90. Top of locus: ca. 83.00. Bottom of locus: 82.71. See pl. 264.

R17:403

Small "closet" below R17:305 West. Floor sloped from 82.62 in the southeast down to 82.40 in the northeast. Surface elevation: ca. 83.70. Top of locus: 83.00. Bottom of locus: 82.40. See pl. 264.

Elevation	Field Number	Description	Plate
—	4.130	Ovoid strap-handled jar	cf. 98:A

R17:404

"Closet" below R17:305 West and adjoining R17:403 on the southwest. Surface elevation: ca. 83.70. Top of locus: 82.43. Bottom of locus: 82.04. See pl. 264.

Elevation	Field Number	Description	Plate
—	4.084	Strap-handled jar (Protoliterate)	cf. 96:G

R17:405

Baked-brick installation; southeastern corner found in R17:304. On the southern edge of a baked-brick wall, nine courses high, stood a one-course pavement of baked brick. The flush surface of the wall on the southern end suggested that this was the original face. On the northern side of the locus one course of bricks stood on the pavement at right angles to the northeast-southwest wall. This course was probably the base of a cross wall forming the southeastern corner of a small cubicle 1.00 × 1.80 m. The slope of the pavement from 82.73 on the north to 82.64 at the south and the baked-brick construction suggested that R17:405 was an ablution area draining to the south. Nearby, just to the south of P17:404, was a pottery pipe draining to the south. Surface elevation: ca. 83.50. Top of locus: 83.36. Bottom of locus: 82.64. See pl. 264.

R17:406

Protoliterate room straddling corners of Squares Q–R17–18 (= R17:306 + Q17:303). The preserved top of the southern wall was 83.06; the preserved top of the western wall was 83.04. The floor was at 82.42 in the northeast and at 82.53 in the southwest. Surface elevation: ca. 83.50. Top of locus: 83.06. Bottom of locus: 82.42. See pl. 264.

Elevation	Field Number	Description	Plate
—	IV-324	Metal pin with swollen head, 8.9 cm long	—
—	4.1180	20+ beveled-rim bowl sherds squared off into model bricks	cf. 30:S

R17:407

Room preserved in fragmentary condition in the southern part of R17. Only the northwestern and northeastern walls were preserved; within the room was a quern. Floor at 82.12. Surface elevation: ca. 83.50. Top of locus: N/A. Bottom of locus: 82.12. See pl. 264.

Elevation	Field Number	Description	Plate
ca. 82.30	VI-89	Perforated discoidal stone; socket(?)	—

R17:408

Northern part (Protoliterate) of the large pit directly to the south of the southwestern part of the long drain R17:314 + 310. For the southern part of the pit, see R17:302. Between 82.10 and 80.90 the following seeds were recovered: *Lens* sp. (pl. 68:G); *Pisum* sp. (pl. 68 H); *Hordeum distichon* (pl. 68:I); *Hordeum vulgare* (pl. 68 J); *Fumaria* sp. (pl. 68:K); *Linum* sp. Surface elevation: ca. 83.40. Top of locus: ca. 83.40. Bottom of locus: 80.90. See pl. 264.

Elevation	Field Number	Description	Plate
83.40	4.298	Spouted pithos fragment; see fig. 13	23:C; 110:I
82.15	IV-391	Clay ball fragment	37:E; 140:A
—	IV-392	Sealing; reverse flat (Protoliterate)	—
—	IV-359	Fragment of clay tablet(?), divided in quadrants and finger nail impressed	—
—	IV-418	Ovoid jar	90:H
—	4.177	Spouted jar	107:E

R17:408 NORTHWEST

Elevation	Field Number	Description	Plate
82.90–80.90	4.1241	2/3 pouring lip bowl	cf. 80:Y–EE
82.10–80.90	IV-417	Strap-handled jar	98:B
82.10–80.90	IV-419	Ovoid jar	cf. 90:H
82.10–80.90	IV-420	Ovoid jar	cf. 90:E–J

R17:408 SOUTHEAST

Elevation	Field Number	Description	Plate
82.10–80.90	4.170	Spouted jar	107:I
82.10–80.90	IV-423	Barbotine notched lip jar	cf. 90:K
82.10–80.90	4.283	Bowl; see fig. 8	84:T

R17:409

Canceled

R17:410

A Protoliterate rectangular room with its floor at 82.84. It was later continued as R17:707. A small Protoliterate pit was located beneath the floor of this room, with its bottom at 82.15. Surface elevation: ca. 84.00. Top of locus: ca. 84.00. Bottom of locus: 82.84. See pl. 264.

R17:411

Continuation of pit R17:214, cut into long southern wall of R17:401–04. Surface elevation: ca. 84.00. Top of locus: ca. 84.00. Bottom of locus: 83.36. See pl. 264.

R17:412

Ovoid Protoliterate pit adjacent to pit R17:214 and also cutting into southern wall of R17:401–04. Length: ca. 2.60 m. Surface elevation: ca. 84.00. Top of locus: ca. 84.00. Bottom of locus: N/A. See pl. 264.

R17:413

Rectangular room belonging to the highest phase of Protoliterate walls in the eastern area. It shared orientation and formed a unit with rooms R17:401 and 402. A pit was cut into the southern and eastern walls. Within R17:413 was an ovoid bin 0.65 × 0.80 m. To the north was R17:702, a fairly circular kiln 1.50 m in diameter. Surface elevation: ca. 84.00. Top of locus: N/A. Bottom of locus: N/A. See pl. 264.

R17:414

Fragmentarily preserved room cut into by a large Protoliterate pit, R17:208. Top of southern wall: 83.50. It was continued as R17:706. Above it was a small area, R17:711, contiguous to the east of R17:701 East. Surface elevation: ca. 84.10. Top of locus: ca. 83.50. Bottom of locus: ca. 82.70. See pl. 264.

R17:415

Small area with segment of wall between northern wall of room S17:404 and long drain R17:310. Surface elevation: ca. 83.30. Top of locus: N/A. Bottom of locus: N/A. See pl. 264.

TRENCH XX
R18:TRENCH XX NORTHEAST

Elevation	Field Number	Description	Plate
B.S.	—	Perforated spherical clay object	—

R18:TRENCH XX SOUTH

Elevation	Field Number	Description	Plate
0.60 B.S.	3.1023	Clay jar stopper	130:M

R18:TRENCH XX EAST EDGE

Elevation	Field Number	Description	Plate
0.35 B.S.	III-463	Bowl	84:I

EAST OF R18:TRENCH XX

Elevation	Field Number	Description	Plate
Surface	III-71	Sealing fragment	41:E

R18:301

Protoliterate pit with burned soil and numerous sherds. Just below the surface at its southwestern edge were traces of a hard floor and undefined brickwork. To the west was an area without features, located to the northwest and southwest of R19:301, but with extensive pottery deposits. Surface elevation: ca. 82.60. Top of locus: ca. 82.60. Bottom of locus: 81.93. See pl. 264.

Elevation	Field Number	Description	Plate
ca. 82.60	**III-221	Bowl	83:R
ca. 82.60	*III-223	Bowl	17:P–Q
ca. 82.60	III-225	Incised four-lugged jar; see fig. 16	27; 115:C; 116–119
ca. 82.60	**III-228	Twisted handle fragment	cf. 100:F
ca. 82.60	**III-248	Strap-handled jar; see fig. 9	97:D
ca. 82.60	**III-329	Spouted jar	cf. 102:I
ca. 82.60	**III-339	Strap-handled jar	98:E
ca. 82.60	**III-341	Vessel fragment	111:J
ca. 82.60	*III-550	Lugged, handled jar; see fig. 14	115:D
ca. 82.60	3.326	Bowl	84:C
ca. 82.60	3.651	Fine ware cup	cf. 80:M
ca. 82.60	3.667	Bowl	17:F
82.60–82.30	**III-133	Oval tray	18:H

* Trench XX; ** R18:301.

SOUTHEAST OF R18:301

Elevation	Field Number	Description	Plate
ca. 82.30	*III-100	Terra-cotta cylindrical bead	129:F
ca. 82.30	**III-226	Four-lugged vessel	120:D
ca. 82.30	*III-340	Strap-handled notched-lip jar	98:G
ca. 82.20	*III-222	Bowl	83:Z
ca. 82.15	III-638	Bowl with pellets on rim	85:DD
ca. 82.10	**III-259	Beaker	85:Z
ca. 82.10	**III-608	Stone bowl	124:Y
ca. 82.10	3.498	Four-lugged jar	25:M
ca. 82.10	3.1078	Metal pin	128:M

* Trench XX; ** R18:301.

PROBABLY R18:301 (OR ADJACENT AREA TO THE SOUTH)

Elevation	Field Number	Description	Plate
ca. 82.60	3.529	Twisted handle	20:K
ca. 82.10	3.1013	Spindle whorl	126:D
ca. 82.00	3.496	Shoulder sherd with appliqué	28:D
ca. 81.95	**III-250	Bottle	111:H
ca. 81.85	*III-227	Spouted jar	104:K
ca. 81.85	3.031	Bowl; see fig. 8	81:M
ca. 81.60	IV-231	Everted rim jar	cf. 90:G–H

* Trench XX; ** R18:301.

SOUTH OF R18:301 "TRENCH XX SOUTH"

Elevation	Field Number	Description	Plate
ca. 82.25	III-152	Spouted jar	cf. 102:I
ca. 82.60	*III-181	Tall ovoid jar	88:I
ca. 82.60	*III-229	Strap-handled jar	97:H
ca. 82.60	*III-549	Spouted jar	107:L

* Trench XX; ** R18:301.

SOUTH OF R18:301, B.S.

Elevation	Field Number	Description	Plate
ca. 82.60	3.567	Rim fragment	19:C
ca. 82.35	*3.528	Three-strand handle	20:Q
82.30	*III-101	Globular bead (Protoliterate)	—

* Trench XX; ** R18:301.

SOUTHEAST OF R18:301

Elevation	Field Number	Description	Plate
ca. 81.40	3.436	Painted-burnished body	227:K

NORTH OF R18:301

Elevation	Field Number	Description	Plate
Wash	4.021	Squat jar	88:AA
—	—	Trilobite bronze arrowhead (Achaemenid)	—

NORTHWEST OF R18:301 (APPROX. R18:301/310)

Elevation	Field Number	Description	Plate
ca. 82.60	*III-230	Strap-handled, notched-lip jar	98:I
82.60–82.30	3.1074	Metal pin	128:E
81.40	3.1096	Metal pin head (Protoliterate)	—

* Trench XX; ** R18:301.

EAST OF R18:301 AND R19:301

Elevation	Field Number	Description	Plate
ca. 82.60	III-382	Perforated stone disc	29:U

BETWEEN EAST OF R18:301 AND NORTH OF R19:303

Elevation	Field Number	Description	Plate
ca. 81.35	III-285	Spouted vessel	109:H

R18:302

Area of a baked-brick drain immediately below the surface. The eastern part of the locus was above R18:312. Top of drain: 83.06. Surface elevation: ca. 83.10. Top of locus: 83.10. Bottom of locus: ca. 82.60. See pl. 264.

Elevation	Field Number	Description	Plate
ca. 83.10	—	Tapered lip stone bowl fragment (Protoliterate)	—
ca. 82.80	—	Tapered lip stone bowl	—
ca. 82.60	III-861	5 clay ball fragments (Protoliterate)	—

EAST OF R18:302

Elevation	Field Number	Description	Plate
ca. 83.10	3.1007	Spindle whorl	126:C
ca. 83.10	3.1008	Spindle whorl	126:B
ca. 82.60	III-261	Small bowl	81:S
ca. 82.50	III-544	Ovoid jar	90:J
ca. 82.50	—	Band rim stone bowl	cf. 29:AA
82.35–81.20	3.205	Lid fragment; see fig. 26	164:F

WEST OF R18:302

Elevation	Field Number	Description	Plate
ca. 82.60	III-356	Clay loom weight	30:H; 126:GG
ca. 82.50	III-357	Clay loom weight	cf. 30:H
ca. 82.50	III-358	Clay loom weight	cf. 30:I
ca. 82.50	III-359	Clay loom weight	30:I
ca. 81.60	III-582	Terra-cotta spike	127:F

NORTHEAST OF R18:302

Elevation	Field Number	Description	Plate
ca. 83.10	III-155	Spouted jar; see fig. 13	110:D
ca. 82.80	III-108	Stamp seal	41:R
ca. 82.75	3.356	Sherd scraper	30:P

R18:303

An approximately round depression above the twinned pair of pits, R18:303 West and R18:303 East. Surface elevation: ca. 82.80. Top of locus: ca. 82.80. Bottom of locus: 82.13. See pl. 264.

Elevation	Field Number	Description	Plate
Cleaning	IV-304	Fragmentary stone hut amulet	cf. 31:BB

EAST OF R18:303

Elevation	Field Number	Description	Plate
ca. 82.80	III-165	Cylinder seal	41:C

R18:303–04

Area of cleaning during the fourth season.

Elevation	Field Number	Description	Plate
ca. 81.90	4.1077	Jar fragment	90:G

R18:304

Area delimited on the west by northwest-southeast wall (preserved top, northwest: 83.26; southeast: 82.81; preserved height: 0.40 m) and on the northeast by corner walls overlying a pit with numerous pottery fragments. There were Protoliterate remains mixed with Achaemenid. Surface elevation: ca. 83.50. Top of locus: ca. 83.50. Bottom of locus: ca. 82.30. See pl. 264.

Elevation	Field Number	Description	Plate
ca. 83.50	III-945	Tablet	5:K
ca. 83.50	3.642	Bowl fragment; diameter 40.0 cm	cf. 74:I
ca. 83.00	III-545	Strap-handled jar	98:L
ca. 83.00	3.913	Handled jar fragment	cf. 75:CC
ca. 82.70	III-161	Pouring-lip bowl	—
ca. 82.45	III-543	Spouted vessel	102:G
—	III-164	Spouted vessel	102:A

R18:304 SOUTH

Elevation	Field Number	Description	Plate
83.50	—	Animal figurine fragment (Protoliterate)	—

NORTH OF R18:304

Elevation	Field Number	Description	Plate
ca. 83.00	—	Flattish sealing (Protoliterate)	—

R18:305

Area on western side of a wall in R18:304 consisting of below surface debris and one feature, a pit, ca. 1.50 m, cutting into a large Protoliterate pit, R18:310. Surface elevation: ca. 83.50. Top of locus: ca. 83.50. Bottom of locus: 80.20. See pl. 264.

Elevation	Field Number	Description	Plate
ca. 83.15	3.558	Clay cone	31:X
ca. 83.00	III-153	Ledge rim bowl	85:B

R18:305 (*cont.*)

Elevation	Field Number	Description	Plate
ca. 83.00	—	Animal figurine (Protoliterate)	—
83.00–82.75	3.041	Four-lugged jar, incised	122:B
83.00–82.30	III-880	Potter's wheel fragment	127:H
83.00–82.00	III-702	Basket handled scoop	101:H
83.00–82.00	III-703	Basket handled scoop; see fig. 9	101:L
ca. 82.85	3.419	Band-rim bowl fragment	84:P
82.82	3.717	Stone with depression	248:D
ca. 82.80	III-404	Four-lugged jar; see fig. 15	122:C
ca. 82.80	3.019	Buttressed jar; see fig. 9	28:V; 92:E
ca. 82.80	3.494	Miniature spouted jar	22:D
ca. 82.75	3.901	Jar fragment (Protoliterate)	—
ca. 82.75	3.1026	Clay jar stopper	130:A
ca. 82.75	3.1081	Metal pin	128:L
82.70–82.30	3.049a	Scrabbled bowl fragment	28:A; 86:E
ca. 82.50	III-807a–c	Sealings (Protoliterate)	—
ca. 82.50	III-807d	Door sealing	42:R
ca. 82.50	III-809	Clay ball fragment	—
ca. 82.50	—	Metal rod fragment (Protoliterate)	—
ca. 82.40	III-800	Door sealing fragments (Protoliterate)	—
ca. 82.40	III-801	Door sealing fragment	153:A
ca. 82.40	III-802	Clay ball fragment	153:A
ca. 82.40	III-803a	Sealing fragment; reverse with basketry imprint	153:A
ca. 82.40	III-804	Sealing fragment	153:A
ca. 82.40	III-808	Door sealing	42:S; 142:C
ca. 82.40	3.545	Animal figurine	31:D
ca. 82.40	3.1022	Clay jar stopper	130:O
ca. 82.30	III-251	Bottle	111:L
ca. 82.30	III-811	Tablet fragment	155:B
ca. 82.30	III-812	Bulla (Protoliterate)	—
ca. 82.30	III-861b	Flattish sealing (Protoliterate)	—
ca. 82.30	3.292	Strainer fragment; see fig. 8	81:N
ca. 82.30	3.348	Scrabbled bowl fragment	86:B
ca. 82.30	3.526	Twisted handle	20:J
ca. 82.30	3.1065	Terra-cotta biconical perforated object	126:Q
ca. 82.25	III-738	Terra-cotta spool	30:C; 126:AA
ca. 82.25	III-806	Tablet fragment	43:D; 141:C
ca. 82.25	3.550	Animal figurine	31:L
ca. 82.25	3.1079	Metal pin	128:B
ca. 82.25	—	Tapered lip stone bowl fragment (Protoliterate)	—
ca. 82.25	—	Animal figurine fragment (Protoliterate)	—
ca. 82.10	3.022	Stick ladle, incised	81:L
ca. 82.10	3.531	Twisted handle (Protoliterate)	20:E
ca. 82.10	3.808	Handled cup fragment	81:P
ca. 82.00	3.293	Scored bowl fragment	81:Q
ca. 82.00	3.1001	Basket handle fragment	101:K
ca. 81.90	3.427	Scrabbled bowl fragment	86:A
ca. 81.90	3.661	Recurved bowl fragment (Achaemenid)	—
ca. 81.90	—	5 terra-cotta sickles	cf. 30:T
ca. 81.85	—	Band-rimmed bowl fragment	cf. 29:AA
ca. 81.80	3.887	Carinated ledge rim bowl fragment (Achaemenid)	—
ca. 81.75	III-814	Tablet	33:G
ca. 81.75	3.1063	Terra-cotta biconical clay object	126:N
ca. 81.75	—	Tapered lip stone bowl fragment (Protoliterate)	—
ca. 81.75	—	Terra-cotta sickle	cf. 30:T
ca. 81.70	3.243	Bowl fragment; see fig. 31	183:T
ca. 81.70	3.509	Notched lip fragment	19:J

R18:305 (*cont.*)

Elevation	Field Number	Description	Plate
ca. 81.70	—	Shallow stone tray	—
ca. 81.70	—	Tapered-lip stone bowl fragment (Protoliterate)	—
ca. 81.35	3.480	Stone bowl fragment	124:T
ca. 81.25	3.537	Horizontal handled jar fragment	21:D
Sifting	III-813	Bulla	33:I–J; 153:C
Sifting	III-815	Tablet fragment	33:F
Sifting	III-854	Tablet fragment	33:B–C
—	III-920	Jar neck(?) sealing (Protoliterate)	—
—	3.540	Animal figurine	31:G
—	3.727	Flint blade	255:S
—	3.1064	Terra-cotta biconical perforated object	126:P
—	—	Animal figurine fragment (Protoliterate)	—
—	III-810	Sealing (Protoliterate)	139:A
—	3.1072	Spherical token	134:A 4

WEST OF R18:305

Probably from upper part of R18:310.

Elevation	Field Number	Description	Plate
ca. 83.50	III-805	Jar neck sealing	44:F; 131:C; 149:A
ca. 83.50	3.824	Lamp (Parthian?)	—
ca. 83.10	3.732	Four-lugged body fragment	25:I
ca. 83.00	III-269	Trough spouted bowl	85:I

BETWEEN R18:305 AND R18:307

Elevation	Field Number	Description	Plate
ca. 82.00	3.349	Vat lip fragment	28:J

R18:306

Small area to the north of fragmentary corner walls of R18:304. Surface elevation: ca. 83.50. Top of locus: ca. 83.50. Bottom of locus: N/A. See pl. 264.

R18:307

At the southern end of a long drain, R18:314 (an incompletely preserved room), southern wall partially destroyed and western wall missing. On floor at 81.99 was a large pithos (III-289) and two large vats (3.1088–89). Surface elevation: ca. 83.34. Top of locus: ca. 83.34. Bottom of locus: ca. 81.85. See pl. 264.

Elevation	Field Number	Description	Plate
83.34–82.99	3.038	Four-lugged jar fragment	123:G
83.34–82.59	3.1011	Spindle whorl	126:J
ca. 82.55	3.524	Twisted-handle fragment	20:O
ca. 82.55	3.413	Bowl, scrabbled, reserve slip	28:C; 86:G
ca. 82.55	3.733	Four-lugged body fragment	25:J
ca. 82.30	III-525	Socketed rim bowl fragment; see fig. 9	85:BB
ca. 82.15	3.286	Cashew-shaped token	134:F 2
ca. 82.15	3.879a	Truncated conical token	134:E 9
ca. 82.15	3.879b	Spherical token	134:A 8
ca. 82.15	—	Stone roundel	cf. 29:Q–Z
81.99	III-289	Pithos	94:B

R18:307 (*cont.*)

Elevation	Field Number	Description	Plate
81.99	III-288c	Spouted jar	cf. 105:H
81.99	3.1088	Vat (Protoliterate)	—
81.99	3.1089	Vat (Protoliterate)	—
—	IV-230	Everted rim jar	cf. 90:G–H
—	IV-232	Everted rim jar	cf. 90:G–H
—	3.408	Miniature bowl fragment	80:A
—	3.417	Bowl fragment	83:BB
—	3.418	Bowl fragment	84:K
—	3.479	Band rim stone bowl	124:V
—	3.1091	Long metal pin	128:C
—	3.1241	Metal arrowhead	76:G
—	—	Trilobite metal arrowhead	cf. 76:E–F

SOUTHWEST OF R18:307

Open area, mostly in Q18, directly to the southwest of R18:307 and to the south of room Q17:304. It was at a higher level than Room R18:307. It was not associated with a concentration of pottery, including several pithoi (III-516, 517, 521), a vat (III-515), and a large four-lugged jar (III-519). It was dug to the depth of 81.90.

Elevation	Field Number	Description	Plate
ca. 83.00	3.369	Bowl base	179:H
ca. 82.60	III-150	Small jar; see fig. 9	88:O
ca. 82.60	III-515	Vat	18:J
ca. 82.60	III-516	Pithos; everted rim	cf. 93:G
ca. 82.60	III-517	Pithos; everted rim; rocker incision	cf. 93:G
ca. 82.60	III-519	Four-lugged jar fragments with two registers of crosshatched triangles	cf. 122:D
ca. 82.60	III-520	Reserve slip jar; see fig. 9	92:D
ca. 82.55	3.404	Ovoid jar fragment; see fig. 9	91:F
ca. 82.50	III-523	Four-lugged jar	122:D
ca. 82.50	III-290	Spouted vessel	107:D
ca. 82.20	III-518	Strap-handled jar; see fig. 9	21:K; 99:B
ca. 82.20	III-521	Pithos	93:H
ca. 81.90	3.813	"Spike"	127:D
ca. 81.90	3.1058	Stone bead	129:T

WEST OF R18:307

Continuation to the west of the open area to the southwest of R18:307. At 0.45 B.S. there was a surface with many small vessels, mostly four-lugged, *in situ*. It was dug to a depth of 81.80.

Elevation	Field Number	Description	Plate
ca. 82.55	III-467	Spouted jar	106:B
ca. 82.55	III-468	Small jar	89:J
ca. 82.55	III-469	Strap-handled jar	cf. 97:H
ca. 82.55	III-470	Four-lugged jar	114:G
ca. 82.55	III-471	Goblet; see fig. 9	89:G
ca. 82.55	III-472	Four-lugged jar; see fig. 15	113:F
ca. 82.55	III-473	Small ovoid jar	cf. 88:B
ca. 82.55	III-474	Miniature four-lugged	cf. 112:C
ca. 82.55	III-475	Strap-handled jar	97:G
ca. 82.55	III-476	Handled cup; see fig. 8	17:D; 81:O
ca. 82.55	III-477	Four-lugged vessel; see fig. 15	120:C
ca. 82.55	III-478	Four-lugged vessel; see fig. 15	121:H
ca. 82.55	III-479	Four-lugged vessel	113:E
ca. 82.55	III-480	Small four-lugged jar	cf. 114:A
ca. 82.55	III-481	Four-lugged vessel	112:E

Elevation	Field Number	Description	Plate
ca. 82.55	III-482	Four-lugged vessel	114:D
ca. 82.55	III-484	Conical cup	80:R
ca. 82.55	III-485	Conical cup	—
ca. 82.55	III-486	Ovoid jar; see fig. 9	90:K
ca. 82.55	III-488	Four-lugged jar	114:B
82.55–82.20	III-487	Four-lugged jar	—
ca. 82.35	III-483	Miniature four-lugged vessel; see fig. 15	112:J
ca. 81.80	III-944	Stone object	29:N

SOUTH OF R18:307

Elevation	Field Number	Description	Plate
ca. 83.00	3.562	Terra-cotta cone	31:JJ
ca. 82.10	III-939	Hut amulet	31:CC
—	III-856	Flattish sealing (Protoliterate)	145:A

EAST OF R18:307

Elevation	Field Number	Description	Plate
82.60–82.25	3.557	Terra-cotta cone	31:W
ca. 82.55	III-489	Small ovoid jar	88:C

NORTH OF R18:307

Elevation	Field Number	Description	Plate
ca. 83.00	III-168	Trough spouted bowl	85:M

NEAR R18:307

Elevation	Field Number	Description	Plate
—	III-720	Animal figurine	31:A

BETWEEN R18:307 AND Q18:308

Elevation	Field Number	Description	Plate
ca. 83.00	3.523	Combination strap and twisted handle	20:P

BETWEEN R18:307 WEST AND Q17:304 EAST

Elevation	Field Number	Description	Plate
ca. 82.00	3.1094	Broken metal chisel	128:A

BETWEEN R18:307 AND Q17:304

Elevation	Field Number	Description	Plate
ca. 83.00	3.996	Vertical handled jar fragment (Achaemenid)	—

BETWEEN R18:307 AND Q18:302

Elevation	Field Number	Description	Plate
ca. 82.05	III-151	Convex bowl; see fig. 8	84:M

BETWEEN R18:307 AND WEST OF Q18:303

Elevation	Field Number	Description	Plate
ca. 82.30	III-670	Spouted pithos (Protoliterate)	—

BETWEEN R18:307 AND Q18:312

Elevation	Field Number	Description	Plate
ca. 82.40	III-493	Strap-handled jar; see fig. 9	20:A; 97:I

BETWEEN R18:307 AND WEST OF Q18:313

Elevation	Field Number	Description	Plate
ca. 82.30	III-694	Spouted vessel fragment	102:F
ca. 82.35	III-491	Small tray	18:C; 86:I

R18:308

Originally an area, ca. 2.00 × 6.00 m, at the eastern edge of a third season excavation; the northern part became R18:313. The main features were two parallel walls; the eastern one cut by a pit, the eastern part of which was dug during the fourth season, R18:405. Top of eastern wall: 82.35. Surface elevation: ca. 82.60. Top of locus: ca. 82.60. Bottom of locus: 81.19. See pls. 16:D–E; 264.

Elevation	Field Number	Description	Plate
ca. 82.60	III-109	Lapis lazuli(?) bead/pendant fragment (Protoliterate)	—
ca. 81.20	III-293	Ovoid jar; see fig. 9	92:H
—	III-187	Irregular conical token; height 1.4 cm (Protoliterate)	—

SOUTH OF R18:308

Located ca. 2.00 m to the south and just B.S. was the northern end of a line, ca. 3.00 m long, of sherds covering drain pipes; cf. pl. 16:D–E. Many of the sherds joined to form III-344 and III-345.

Elevation	Field Number	Description	Plate
ca. 82.60	III-344	Reserve-slip jar	16:D; 91:L
ca. 82.60	III-345	Spouted reserve slip jar fragment	16:E
—	III-302	Stamp seal	41:Q
—	III-303	Cylindrical stone bead	129:E

EAST OF R18:308

Elevation	Field Number	Description	Plate
ca. 82.15	3.154	Beaker fragment	57:C; 174:A
—	—	Animal figurine (Protoliterate)	—

R18:309

Small area immediately to the north of R18:308 and to the east of R18:312; equivalent to the southwestern corner of room R18:410. The only feature was a segment of a pipe drain with the northeastern end at 82.61 and the southwestern end at 82.40. Surface elevation: ca. 83.00. Top of locus: ca. 83.00. Bottom of locus: ca. 82.40. See pl. 264.

Elevation	Field Number	Description	Plate
ca. 83.00	III-922a–b	Bale(?) sealing	154:D
ca. 83.00	III-923	Bale(?) sealing	—
ca. 83.00	III-924	Bale(?) sealing	142:F
ca. 83.00	3.300	Scored lip jar fragment	90:M
ca. 82.80	—	Band rim stone bowl lip	cf. 29:AA
ca. 82.55	III-497	9 conical tokens (Protoliterate)	—
ca. 82.55	III-498g	Conical token	134:B 4
ca. 82.55	III-498	9 conical tokens (Protoliterate)	—
ca. 82.55	III-499	5 pill-shaped tokens	—
ca. 82.55	III-500	6 pill-shaped tokens (Protoliterate)	—
ca. 82.55	III-501	Pyramidal tokens: 11 of 0.9–1.2 cm height; 6 of 1.5–1.9 cm height	134:C 1
ca. 82.55	III-502	18 pyramidal tokens (Protoliterate)	—
ca. 82.55	III-503	12 spherical tokens (Protoliterate)	—
ca. 82.55	III-504	Spherical tokens: 7 of ca. 1.4 cm diameter; 5 of ca. 0.9 cm diameter (Protoliterate)	—
ca. 82.55	III-505	Triangular token	134:F 7
ca. 82.55	III-506	"Petal"-shaped token	134:G 2
ca. 82.55	III-507	"Petal"-shaped token	134:G 1
ca. 82.55	III-508	Irregular disc token (Protoliterate)	—
ca. 82.55	III-509	2 disc-shaped tokens (Protoliterate)	—

R18:309 EAST EDGE

Elevation	Field Number	Description	Plate
ca. 83.00	—	Band rim stone bowl lip	cf. 29:AA

EAST EDGE OF R18:309 AND 308

Elevation	Field Number	Description	Plate
ca. 82.65	3.042	Pseudo beveled-rim bowl; see fig. 8	83:V
ca. 82.65	3.566	Jar fragment	28:P

SOUTH OF R18:309 AND R18:310

Elevation	Field Number	Description	Plate
ca. 81.40	III-554	Pseudo beveled-rim bowl	83:T

R18:310

Large irregular pit, ca. 4.00 × 6.00 m, without clear demarcation on the southwest. Bottom: ca. 2.00 B.S. at deepest. There was a small subsidiary pit, ca. 0.75 in diameter, at bottom in the north. At the top, in the northeast, the edge was cut into by the pit of R18:305. Surface elevation: ca. 83.00. Top of locus: ca. 83.00. Bottom of locus: ca. 81.00. See pl. 264.

Elevation	Field Number	Description	Plate
ca. 82.60	III-294	Small four-lugged jar	112:C
ca. 82.60	III-569	Strap-handled jar	95:J
ca. 82.60	3.340	Small jar fragment; see fig. 9	87:G
ca. 82.60	3.910	Vertical handle (Achaemenid)	—
82.60–81.50	3.551	Animal figurine	31:K

R18:310 (*cont.*)

Elevation	Field Number	Description	Plate
ca. 82.60	—	Animal figurine	—
—	—	Slingshot (Protoliterate)	—
ca. 82.25	III-692	Spouted jar; see fig. 12	—
ca. 82.20	3.279	Conical Token	134:B 3
ca. 82.10	III-278	Conical cup	81:B
ca. 82.10	III-315	Terra-cotta spool, one end narrower	—
ca. 82.10	III-858	Seal impression	143:G
82.10–81.90	III-535	Four-lugged jar	24:I; 114:L
ca. 81.90	3.023	Stick ladle; see fig. 8	81:I
ca. 81.80	III-254	Goblet	89:E
ca. 81.70	III-413	Small four-lugged jar; see fig. 15	113:C
ca. 81.60	—	1 slingshot (Protoliterate)	—
ca. 81.50	III-355	Stone mace-head fragment	125:DD
ca. 81.40	III-316	Terra-cotta spool, one end narrower (Protoliterate)	—
ca. 81.40	—	1 slingshot (Protoliterate)	—
ca. 81.30	III-236	Large bowl	88:Q
ca. 81.30	III-640	Spouted jar; see fig. 12	22:H; 107:G
ca. 81.30	3.342	Rocker-incised jar fragment	91:D
ca. 81.30	—	Animal figurine fragment	—
81.21	3.564	Clay cone	31:HH
ca. 81.05	III-533	Spouted jar; see fig. 12	107:B
ca. 81.00	III-354	Biconical terra-cotta disc	30:O
ca. 81.00	—	2 slingshots (Protoliterate)	—
—	—	Animal figurine	—

R18:310 SOUTH

Elevation	Field Number	Description	Plate
ca. 82.25	3.276	"Pot"-shaped tokens	134:G 10

R18:310 NORTH

Elevation	Field Number	Description	Plate
ca. 81.00	III-381	Spindle whorl	65:Z
ca. 81.00	—	Animal figurine	—

R18:310 NORTHWEST

Elevation	Field Number	Description	Plate
ca. 81.60	3.035	Stone bowl fragment	124:L
ca. 81.60	3.036	Stone bowl fragment	124:C

NORTH OF R18:310

Elevation	Field Number	Description	Plate
ca. 81.60	III-247	Spouted jar	107:C
ca. 81.60	III-566	Four-lugged jar	114:K

NORTHWEST OF R18:310

Elevation	Field Number	Description	Plate
ca. 81.60	III-564	Shallow bowl	84:E
81.60–81.40	III-331	Strap-handled notched lip jar; see fig. 9	21:C; 98:J

SOUTH OF R18:310

Elevation	Field Number	Description	Plate
ca. 81.90	III-281	Spouted jar	104:I

SOUTHEAST EDGE OF R18:310

Elevation	Field Number	Description	Plate
ca. 83.00	III-157	Bowl	80:W

WEST OF R18:310

Elevation	Field Number	Description	Plate
ca. 81.90	3.500	Decorated fragment	28:E

BETWEEN R18:310 AND Q18:312

Elevation	Field Number	Description	Plate
ca. 82.20	3.483	Stone bowl fragment	124:N

R18:311

Canceled

R18:312

Rectangular Protoliterate room immediately to the southwest of R18:412 and to the north of rooms R18:313 and 309. Its north-western wall was destroyed; other walls were preserved only about two courses high. There was a deposit of clay balls in a shallow pit, top at 82.44 and bottom at 81.93, immediately under the southeastern wall. Surface elevation: ca. 83.10. Top of locus: ca. 82.60. Bottom of locus: 81.93. See pl. 264.

Elevation	Field Number	Description	Plate
82.44–81.93	III-753	Clay ball (Protoliterate)	—
82.44–81.93	III-754a–b	Clay ball	35:I, K–L; 133:D–F; 148:D; 149:C–D
82.44–81.93	III-755	Clay ball	35:A–B; 136:B; 149:C
82.44–81.93	III-756	Clay ball (Protoliterate)	—
82.44–81.93	III-757	Clay ball (Protoliterate)	—
82.44–81.93	III-758	Clay ball (Protoliterate)	—
82.44–81.93	III-759	Clay ball (Protoliterate)	—
82.44–81.93	III-760	Clay ball	151:C
82.44–81.93	III-761	Clay ball	151:B
82.44–81.93	III-762	Clay ball	35:G–H, J; 133:A–C; 146:A; 149:C; 152:F
82.44–81.93	III-763	Clay ball	36:E–I; 141:B; 142:A; 156:C
82.44–81.93	III-764	Clay ball (Protoliterate)	—
82.44–81.93	III-765	Clay ball (Protoliterate)	—
82.44–81.93	III-766	Clay ball	35:D–F; 39:D; 152:B; 156:B
82.44–81.93	III-767	Clay ball with medium-sized spherical token (Protoliterate)	—

R18:312 (*cont.*)

Elevation	Field Number	Description	Plate
82.44–81.93	III-768	Crushed clay ball (Protoliterate)	—
82.44–81.93	III-769	Damaged clay ball with small spherical token (Protoliterate)	—
82.44–81.93	III-770	Damaged clay ball with small conical token (Protoliterate)	—
82.44–81.93	III-771	Clay ball	35:C
82.44–81.93	III-772	Clay ball (Protoliterate)	—
82.44–81.93	III-773	Fragments of clay ball (ca. 5/6) (Protoliterate)	—
82.44–81.93	III-774	Clay ball fragments (Protoliterate)	—
82.44–81.93	III-775	Clay ball fragments (Protoliterate)	—
82.44–81.93	III-776	Ca. 1/4 of clay ball with tokens	39:C; 148:D; 149:C–D
82.44–81.93	III-777	Ca. 1/2 of clay ball (Protoliterate)	—
82.44–81.93	III-778a–c	Fragments of clay ball (ca. 3/4) (Protoliterate)	149:G; 153:E
82.44–81.93	III-779	Small fragments of clay balls (Protoliterate)	—
82.44–81.93	III-780	Clay ball fragments without impressed surfaces (Protoliterate)	—
82.44–81.93	III-781	Body of stone hut amulet	31:EE
82.44–81.93	III-925a	Clay ball fragment	40:D
82.44–81.93	3.275	Conical token	134:B 5
82.44–81.93	3.862	3 large spherical tokens; diameters 0.7, 1.5, 1.9 cm (Protoliterate)	—
82.44–81.93	3.863	9 small spherical tokens; diameters 0.7–0.9 cm (Protoliterate)	—
82.44–81.93	3.864	Pyramidal token; height 0.9 cm (Protoliterate)	—
82.44–81.93	3.865	2 conical tokens; 2.4 cm (Protoliterate)	—

R18:313

This locus was continued from R18:419. There was a small room or storage area to the southwest of R18:410 and it was separated from it by a partition wall. Floor: 81.90. Surface elevation: ca. 82.80. Top of locus: ca. 82.80. Bottom of locus: 81.90. See pl. 264.

Elevation	Field Number	Description	Plate
—	III-876	Strap-handled jar unscored; fire-smudged (Protoliterate)	—

R18:401

Northern part of R19:302, which extended into R18. It was located on the southeastern side of southwest-northeast baked-brick drain, R18:426. From ca. 79.80–79.20 there was an ashy deposit with some Middle Susiana sherds in the lower part. Surface elevation: ca. 82.00. Top of locus: ca. 80.10. Bottom of locus: ca. 79.20. See pl. 264.

Elevation	Field Number	Description	Plate
80.25–80.00	4.793	Spouted pithos (Protoliterate)	—
80.20–79.80	IV-212	Beveled-rim bowl	83:H
80.20–79.80	IV-299	Bowl	57:G; 165:J
80.15–79.55	4.288	Jar fragment	189:F
ca. 79.60	4.926	Flint core	253:G
79.45–79.20	IV-89	Small bowl; see fig. 8	80:E
79.45–79.20	IV-113	Spouted jar	104:L
79.45–79.20	IV-119	Thickened rim bowl	84:F
79.45–79.20	4.012	Strap-handled jar	96:D
79.45–79.20	4.076	Thickened rim bowl; see fig. 8	84:G
79.45–79.20	4.284	Jar	191:A
ca. 79.40	IV-64	Spouted jar	104:B
—	IV-115	Jar, spout missing	cf. 105:F

R18:402

Area in the southeastern part of R18 along eastern side of a one-course high northwest-southeast wall. It was equivalent to the northern part of R19:305. Surface elevation: ca. 82.00. Top of locus: ca. 80.80. Bottom of locus: below 80.00. See pl. 264.

Elevation	Field Number	Description	Plate
80.02	4.885	Rubbing stone	252:U

R18:403

Area in the southeastern part of R18 along the western side of one-course northwest-southeast wall. Surface elevation: ca. 82.00. Top of locus: ca. 81.00. Bottom of locus: N/A. See pl. 264.

Elevation	Field Number	Description	Plate
ca. 80.75	IV-138	Strap-handled jar (Protoliterate)	—
80.48	4.1033	Body fragment with potter's mark	203:14
80.48	4.206	Bowl base fragment	180:G
80.48	4.1031	Body fragment with potter's mark	203:1

R18:404

General area of Protoliterate debris to the north of R19:305 wall and to the south of R18:405 pit above Protoliterate pit R18:407. There were traces of a late burial with a bronze arrowhead. Surface elevation: ca. 82.50. Top of locus: ca. 82.50. Bottom of locus: ca. 81.70. See pl. 264.

R18:405

The eastern part of a large Protoliterate pit to the north of R18:407–08. The western part was dug in the third season as R18:308. The bottom of the pit sloped from 81.50 in the east to 81.19 in the west. It was cut into the eastern wall of R18:308. Surface elevation: ca. 82.50. Top of locus: ca. 82.50. Bottom locus: 81.50. See pl. 264.

Elevation	Field Number	Description	Plate
ca. 82.50	4.079	Bowl fragment	85:P
ca. 82.50	IV-131	Spindle whorl	126:G
82.25–82.05	IV-185	Four-lugged jar; see fig. 15	24:F; 121:A
82.20–82.00	IV-132	Sherd roundel	cf. 30:X
82.20–82.00	4.612	Stone trough	124:EE
82.20–82.00	4.789	Beveled-rim bowl	83:P
82.20–82.00	4.796	Stone bowl	124:B

NORTH OF R18:405

Elevation	Field Number	Description	Plate
ca. 82.50	IV-220	Four-lugged jar	112:A

R18:406

Small area of Protoliterate debris to the east of pit R18:405. At 81.64 was a deposit of pottery, including beveled-rim bowls, spouted jars, and bowls with pouring lips. Surface elevation: 82.32. Top of locus: 82.32. Bottom of locus: ca. 81.40. See pl. 264.

Elevation	Field Number	Description	Plate
82.07–81.72	4.113	Miniature spouted vessel	22:B
81.82–81.62	4.409	Carinated vessel	89:A
81.46	IV-191	Stone bowl	124:BB
ca. 81.25	4.798	Stone bowl fragment	124:CC

R18:407

Protoliterate pit in the southwestern corner of R18 below R18:404 and cutting into southern end of eastern wall of R18:308. It had an ashy fill with sherds. Surface elevation: 82.32. Top of locus: 82.32. Bottom of locus: ca. 81.50. See pl. 264.

R18:408

Surface debris over shallow Protoliterate pit beginning at 81.70 and containing bones, ashes, and sherds. Near the top of the pit was a concentration of animal bones with the possible fragments of four human skulls. Directly below was a concentration of jar stoppers on top of a layer of broken pottery, including beveled-rim bowls. Surface elevation: 82.32. Top of locus: 81.70. Bottom of locus: 81.50. See pl. 264.

Elevation	Field Number	Description	Plate
82.05–81.80	IV-226	Four-lugged jar	121:D
82.05–81.80	IV-229	Twisted handled jar	cf. 100:C
82.05–81.80	4.255	Jar, spout broken	104:G
82.05–81.80	4.291	Ovoid jar	93:A
81.80	IV-188	Small globular jar	90:A
ca. 82.00	IV-252	Animal figurine (Protoliterate)	—

R18:411

Large rectangular Protoliterate room, 2.30 × 5.00 m, at the intersection of Squares R17–18 and S18. The northeastern corner was destroyed by pit R17:303. Top of northern wall: 82.60. The floor sloped from 82.34 at the northeast to 82.12 at the south. A rectangular well, S18:404, near the northwestern wall, was dug from the floor down. Surface elevation: ca. 83.20. Top of locus: ca. 82.60. Bottom of locus: 82.12. See pls. 14:B; 264.

R18:412

Rectangular Protoliterate room in new strip opened along eastern edge of area; directly to the north of R18:410 and to the southeast of R18:302 (top of the northern end of the northern part of the R18:302 drain pipes: 82.63; bottom: 82.44; southern end, bottom: 82.37). The drain belonged to a higher level than the room. Its walls stood only few courses high, with a floor at 82.30. Surface elevation: ca. 83.00. Top of locus: ca. 83.00. Bottom of locus: ca. 82.30. See pl. 264.

Elevation	Field Number	Description	Plate
ca. 82.50	IV-189	Ovoid jar	cf. 88:L

R18:413

Area to the north of R18:312 and West of R18:411. It was possibly originally a room. Surface elevation: ca. 83.10. Top of locus: ca. 83.10. Bottom of locus: ca. 81.90. See pl. 264.

Elevation	Field Number	Description	Plate
82.85–82.75	IV-291	Clay ball (Protoliterate)	138:J
82.85–82.75	IV-292a, c–e	Clay ball fragments (Protoliterate)	148:B
82.85–82.75	IV-292b	Clay ball fragment	45:O
82.85–82.75	IV-293	Clay ball fragments (Protoliterate)	138:J
ca. 82.35	4.183	Miniature spouted jar	22:A
ca. 81.90	IV-224	Spouted jar	106:A

R18:414

Shallow Protoliterate pit underneath the northeast-southwest wall separating R18:308 from pits R18:405 and 407. Surface elevation: ca. 82.60. Top of locus: 82.35. Bottom of locus: 81.54. See pl. 264.

Elevation	Field Number	Description	Plate
—	4.792	Ovoid jar fragment	91:G

R18:415

Protoliterate pit slightly to the northeast of pit R18:301 and immediately to the west of fragmentary western walls of R18:308. Surface elevation: ca. 82.60. Top of locus: 82.23. Bottom of locus: 80.20. See pl. 264.

Elevation	Field Number	Description	Plate
82.35–81.90	4.286	Small jar fragment	89:C

R18:416

Ovoid Protoliterate pit tangent to the northern edge of pit R18:415 and below corner walls on western side of R18:308. Surface elevation: ca. 82.90. Top of locus: ca. 82.23. Bottom of locus: 81.15. See pl. 264.

R18:417

Kiln with incompletely preserved lip, top at 82.08, surrounding a circular plastered floor at 81.98. Surface elevation: ca. 82.50. Top of locus: 82.08. Bottom of locus: 81.98. See pl. 264.

NORTHEAST OF R18:417

The immediately adjacent debris was dug to a depth of ca. 0.50 m (81.58) below the kiln rim.

Elevation	Field Number	Description	Plate
81.90	IV-383	One half of band rim stone bowl	cf. 29:AA

R18:418

Ashy deposit, probably in a pit and containing many sherds, under pit R18:301, to the southeast of kiln R18:417. Surface elevation: ca. 82.50. Top of locus: 82.08. Bottom of locus: 81.51. See pl. 264.

Elevation	Field Number	Description	Plate
82.00	4.888	Pestle	244:L
81.80–81.51	IV-227	Four-lugged jar; see fig. 15	114:M

R18:419

Continuation of small room R18:313, to the southwest of larger room R18:410 and separated from it by a partition wall. Floor: 81.90. Surface elevation: ca. 82.80. Top of locus: ca. 82.80. Bottom of locus: 81.90. See pl. 264.

Elevation	Field Number	Description	Plate
—	IV-201	Straight metal pin shaft	—
—	IV-253	Terra-cotta animal figurine	—

R18:420

Area between pits R18:303 and 301 on the west and pits R18:416 and 415 on the east. R18:420 contained a short segment of a drain of baked bricks laid flat; one side with about eight broken bricks, the other with a mixture of fragments and at least one complete brick. Top of western end: 81.86. Top of eastern end: 81.84. Surface elevation: ca. 82.90. Top of locus: ca. 82.00. Bottom of locus: ca. 81.70. See pl. 264.

Elevation	Field Number	Description	Plate
81.86	—	3 beveled-rim bowls (Protoliterate)	—

R18:421

A small Protoliterate area between two wall segments, presumably part of a room, directly to the south of the western end of the long drain R17:314/S17:407. Surface elevation: ca. 83.30. Top of locus: ca. 82.90. Bottom of locus: 82.13. See pl. 264.

Elevation	Field Number	Description	Plate
ca. 82.30	—	Clay stopper fragment with traces of impression (Protoliterate)	—
—	4.870	Handgrinder	246:J

R18:422

Canceled.

R18:423

Small area separated from R18:421 by a segment of wall with preserved top at 82.92. Continuation of part of R18:304. Surface elevation: ca. 83.30. Top of locus: ca. 82.90. Bottom of locus: ca. 81.90. See pl. 264.

Elevation	Field Number	Description	Plate
ca. 81.90	4.170	Spouted jar	107:I

R18:424

Rectangular room at the southern side of room Q17:303/R17:306. Northern wall, top: 83.06; western wall, top: 82.88; floor: 82.41. Southern end of room was left unexcavated. Surface elevation: ca. 83.30. Top of locus: ca. 82.90. Bottom of locus: 82.40. See pl. 264.

Elevation	Field Number	Description	Plate
82.52	IV-425	Stone bowl, much of rim missing	124:O

R18:425

Incompletely excavated small room adjoining R18:424 on the northeast. Surface elevation ca. 83.30. Top of locus: 82.90. Bottom of locus: 82.40. See pl. 264.

Elevation	Field Number	Description	Plate
ca. 82.80	4.907	Stone perforated disc	29:V
ca. 82.50	IV-303	Hut amulet fragment (Protoliterate)	—
ca. 82.50	IV-381	Shallow stone bowl	—
ca. 82.50	4.139	Miniature strap-handled jar	cf. 95:J
ca. 82.50	4.883	Stone disc	251:C

R18:426

Protoliterate baked-brick drain in the southwestern corner of Square R18. Surface elevation: ca. 82.00. Top of locus: ca. 80.75. Bottom of locus: ca. 80.75. See pl. 264.

Elevation	Field Number	Description	Plate
ca. 80.75	IV-325	Metal pin fragments bent head, 12.1 cm long	—
ca. 80.75	IV-326	Metal pin fragment	29:D; 128:F
ca. 80.75	IV-327	Metal pin fragment	cf. 29:D
ca. 80.75	IV-328	Metal adze: 10.4 cm long; 4.0 cm wide	cf. 29:A

R19:301

Debris scattered in the northwestern corner of R19. The area to the south of drain R18:426 in the southeastern corner of R18 was also included in the locus. Surface elevation: ca. 82.00. Top of locus: ca. 82.00. Bottom of locus: ca. 80.90. See pl. 224.

Elevation	Field Number	Description	Plate
ca. 82.00	3.519	Notched lip fragment	19:K
82.00–81.60	III-232	Blunt-lipped bowl; see fig. 8	83:W
82.00–81.60	III-233	Pseudo-beveled-rim bowl	83:U
82.00–81.60	3.997	Stand fragment	86:II
ca. 82.00	3.354	Sherd with knobs	28:N
82.00–81.40	III-737	Beveled-rim bowl	17:J; 83:I
ca. 81.60	III-422	Carinated bowl	85:S
ca. 81.60	3.516	Notched lip fragment	19:P
ca. 81.60	3.522	Twisted handle	20:N
—	3.882	Conical token; height 2.2 cm (Protoliterate)	—
—	—	Animal figurine (Protoliterate)	—
ca. 81.40	3.1027	Clay jar stopper	130:G
ca. 81.10	3.539	Animal figurine	31:B

R19:301 NORTH

Elevation	Field Number	Description	Plate
ca. 82.00	3.525	Twisted handle fragment	20:I
ca. 82.00	3.634	Spouted jar fragment	—

NORTH OF R19:301

Elevation	Field Number	Description	Plate
—	III-859	Jar stopper with seal impression	45:D; 151:A

R19:301 SOUTH

Elevation	Field Number	Description	Plate
ca. 81.45	3.439	Strap-handled jar, handle missing	96:A

R19:301 SOUTHWEST

Elevation	Field Number	Description	Plate
ca. 81.50	3.424	Trough spouted bowl fragment	85:K

SOUTH OF R19:301

Elevation	Field Number	Description	Plate
ca. 82.00	III-395	Tanged bone arrowhead	128:Z
ca. 82.00	III-666	Four-lugged flask (Protoliterate)	—

EAST OF R19:301

Elevation	Field Number	Description	Plate
ca. 82.00	III-432	Cylindrical terra-cotta bead	129:O

BETWEEN R19:301 AND Q18:307

Elevation	Field Number	Description	Plate
ca. 81.50	3.1034	Jar stopper	130:K
ca. 81.40	III-192	Tabular flint scraper	29:J
ca. 81.10	III-196	Piriform jar; see fig. 9	88:E
ca. 81.10	3.484	Stone bowl fragment	124:H
ca. 80.75	III-216	Buttress-spouted fragment	106:H
ca. 80.75	3.374	Bowl lip fragment	85:CC

BETWEEN R19:301 SOUTH AND R19:303

Elevation	Field Number	Description	Plate
82.00–81.55	III-704	Spoon fragments	82:H

R19:302

Continuation of R19:301, from 1.10 B.S. down. Surface elevation: ca. 82.00. Top of locus: ca. 80.90. Bottom of locus: ca. 79.70. See pl. 264.

Elevation	Field Number	Description	Plate
ca. 80.60	III-240	Spouted jar	cf. 105:A
ca. 80.60	III-272	Spouted jar	cf. 105:A
ca. 80.60	III-940	Stone bead with incised decorations on one side	234:FF
ca. 80.40	III-650	Stone trough	29:BB; 124:FF
ca. 80.30	III-857a	Sealing	149:E; 154:F

WEST OF R19:302

Elevation	Field Number	Description	Plate
ca. 81.60	3.636	Buttressed spout	110:H

WEST OF R19:302 AND NORTH OF R19:303

Elevation	Field Number	Description	Plate
80.70	3.016	Jar body and neck	192:A

R19:303

Area of debris to the east of R19:301–02. There was a large jar base at 81.41 and clusters of beveled-rim bowls. Small segment of a wall built of large bricks ("patzen"); top: 81.19; trodden surface on the north: 80.50. In the southeastern corner was a sounding carried down in Protoliterate debris to ca. 79.30. Surface elevation: ca. 82.00. Top of locus: ca. 82.00. Bottom of locus: ca. 79.70. See pl. 264.

Elevation	Field Number	Description	Plate
ca. 82.00	III-159	Pouring lip bowl fragments	80:EE
ca. 82.00	III-160	Pouring lip bowl stacked upside-down below III-159	—
ca. 82.00	III-182	Pipe; see fig. 9	87:K
ca. 82.00	III-244	Spouted jar	104:F
82.00–81.70	III-372	Pod-shaped token	134:G 8
82.00–81.50	III-112	Terra-cotta barrel-shaped bead	129:P
ca. 81.80	III-330	Trough spouted bowl	18:D
ca. 81.80	III-386	Stone spindle whorl	30:N
ca. 81.80	3.438	Strap-handled jar	97:F
81.80	3.1075	Metal pin	128:O

Elevation	Field Number	Description	Plate
ca. 81.70	III-363	Sickle	30:T
ca. 81.70	3.409	Lid fragment	80:H
81.70–81.50	3.423	Trough spout fragment	85:H
ca. 81.60	3.401	Jar fragment; see fig. 9	89:Q
ca. 81.50	III-198	Small ovoid jar	19:D; 88:G
ca. 81.50	3.302	Ladle handle fragment	164:A
ca. 81.30	III-371	Stone perforated disc	29:Q
ca. 81.30	—	Animal figurine (Protoliterate)	—
ca. 81.15	3.048	Bowl fragment with scrabbled decoration	28:B; 86:D
ca. 81.10	III-685	Spouted jar, spout missing	105:F
ca. 80.95	III-541	Basin	87:B
ca. 80.85	—	Stone perforated disc	cf. 29:Q–Z
ca. 80.70	III-409	Basin	87:D
80.50–80.10	III-673	Beveled-rim bowl; see fig. 8	17:K; 83:G

R19:303 SOUNDING

Elevation	Field Number	Description	Plate
79.95–79.55	3.513	Notched lip fragment	19:M
ca. 79.70	III-636	Terra-cotta sickle	30:W
ca. 79.70	III-637	Terra-cotta sickle fragment	cf. 30:T–W
Sifting	—	Stone band rim bowl lip fragment	cf. 29:AA
—	3.395	Painted lip fragment	184:H

R19:303 WEST

Elevation	Field Number	Description	Plate
ca. 80.80	3.381	Jar body fragment	192:B

R19:303 SOUTHEAST

Elevation	Field Number	Description	Plate
80.50–80.10	III-682	Jar; see fig. 9	94:D

EAST OF R19:303

Elevation	Field Number	Description	Plate
ca. 81.55	3.206	Beaker body; small and large zigzag friezes bordered by narrow and broad bands (Middle Susiana)	—
ca. 81.55	3.386	Bowl lip fragment	176:F
ca. 81.50	III-424a	Mother-of-pearl inlay	129:MM
ca. 81.50	III-424b	Mother-of-pearl inlay	129:NN

NORTH OF R19:303

Elevation	Field Number	Description	Plate
ca. 81.75	3.043	Incised four-lugged body fragment	25:N; 123:C
ca. 81.35	III-593	Strap-handled jar	95:H
ca. 80.70	III-574	Spouted jar; see fig. 12	104:D

R19:304

Extension of R19:301–02 area to the south. There was a deposit of pottery at 81.10–80.80, a low trough-like mud structure with interior at 80.43, and fallen bricks on the southeastern corner of the "trough." Surface elevation: ca. 82.00. Top of locus: ca. 82.00. Bottom of locus: ca. 80.80. See pl. 264.

Elevation	Field Number	Description	Plate
ca. 81.80	III-215	Miniature handled ladle	17:G
ca. 81.60	III-399	Bowl	84:N
ca. 81.20	III-546	Spouted jar, spout missing	cf. 105:A
81.10–80.80	III-318	Spouted jar	104:A
81.10–80.80	III-320	Strap-handled jar	96:G
81.10–80.80	III-321	Beaker; see fig. 8	83:D
81.80–80.80	III-322	Spouted jar, spout missing	104:H
ca. 81.00	3.034	Tray fragment; see fig. 9	86:M
ca. 81.00	III-323	Spouted jar, spout missing	—
80.90–80.60	III-319	Pouring lip bowl	80:AA

R19:305

Area at eastern edge of R19 and R18 alongside the only preserved course of a thick mudbrick wall; top: 82.58. Surface elevation: ca. 82.00. Top of locus: ca. 82.00. Bottom of locus: ca. 80.80. See pl. 264.

Elevation	Field Number	Description	Plate
ca. 81.20	—	Band rim stone bowl fragment	cf. 29:AA
ca. 81.00	3.018	Unpainted beaker fragment; see fig. 30	175:C
ca. 81.00	—	Stone hoe	—
ca. 80.80	III-946	Jar; see fig. 31	192:M

NORTH OF R19:305

Elevation	Field Number	Description	Plate
ca. 81.40	III-955	Body with bird appliqué (Protoliterate)	—

EAST OF R19:305

Elevation	Field Number	Description	Plate
ca. 81.50	III-384	Perforated stone disc	29:T

R19:401

The locus consisted of two parts: R18:401 West, the cleaning of debris washed into R19:304 and the adjoining area to the west (Q19:301) dug during the third season, and R19:304 East, a new strip opened up just to the east of the R19:303 sounding. Immediately to the east of the sounding, at 81.22, R19:401 East had fourteen beveled-rim bowls in a north-south alignment. The surface elevation of R19:401 West at the southern edge was 81.56. For other R19:401 elevations, see R19:304. For R19:401 East elevations, see the following. Surface elevation: 82.00. Top of locus: 82.00. Bottom of locus: ca. 80.45. See pls. 15:B; 264.

Elevation	Field Number	Description	Plate
81.56–81.31	4.259	Coarse bowl fragment	84:B
81.16–80.96	4.051	Red ware bowl fragment	193:F
ca. 80.86	IV-314	Stone bead with incised decoration on one side	234:DD

SOUTH OF S17

Elevation	Field Number	Description	Plate
Surface	III-311	Stone bead	129:CC

S17:201

Irregularly circular shallow Protoliterate pit above room R17:701. Between 10.0 and 40.0 cm B.S were twenty-six beveled-rim bowls and a few other types of vessels. Surface elevation: ca. 84.00. Top of locus: ca. 84.00. Bottom of locus: ca. 83.00. See pl. 264.

Elevation	Field Number	Description	Plate
84.00–83.00	2.768	Stone spindle whorl	125:U
ca. 83.40	II-420	Ovoid jar; see fig. 9	89:N
ca. 83.40	2.722	Clay jar stopper	130:N
ca. 83.40	2.723	Clay jar stopper	130:D
ca. 83.40	2.725	Clay jar stopper	130:J

S17:201 NORTH PERIPHERY

Elevation	Field Number	Description	Plate
—	II-344	Tablet fragment	45:E; 144:F
—	II-400	Stamp seal	41:S

EAST OF S17:201

Elevation	Field Number	Description	Plate
—	III-305	Hut amulet	31:BB

S17:202

Irregularly circular pit, ca. 2.00 m in diameter, dug through long drain R17:310. Surface elevation: ca. 84.00. Top of locus: ca. 84.00. Bottom of locus: 81.56. See pl. 264.

Elevation	Field Number	Description	Plate
ca. 83.35	—	Bottle base (Protoliterate)	—
82.34	II-491	Beveled-rim bowl (Protoliterate)	—
ca. 82.00	II-432a–b	Tablet	33:E; 147:H
ca. 82.00	II-433	Sealing fragment	43:G; 143:H
ca. 82.00	2.323	Tray fragment	18:B
ca. 82.00	2.324	Tray fragment	18:G
ca. 82.00	2.551	"Spike"	127:E
Sifting	II-512	Sealing with flat reverse	147:E
—	II-330	Spindle whorl	cf. 30:K
—	II-513a–b	Cylindrical beads	—
—	II-513c	Clay pendant	—

S17:203

Protoliterate pit adjacent to S17:201 on the northeast. To the south was S17:702, a Protoliterate, fragmentarily preserved, room with eastern and western walls missing. Surface elevation: ca. 83.20. Top of locus: ca. 83.20. Bottom of locus: 81.58. See pl. 264.

Elevation	Field Number	Description	Plate
ca. 82.15	—	Beveled-rim bowl (Protoliterate)	—
ca. 82.15	—	Spouted jar fragment	—
ca. 82.15	—	2 beveled-rim bowls (Protoliterate)	—

NORTH OF S17:203

Elevation	Field Number	Description	Plate
ca. 82.35	—	Beveled-rim bowl (Protoliterate)	—
ca. 82.25	—	2 beveled-rim bowls (Protoliterate)	—

S17:301

Extension of the southern area to the south of S17:201 (Trench V, Plot L) and to the east of S17:203. There were no features. Surface elevation: ca. 83.00. Top of locus: ca. 83.00. Bottom of locus: ca. 82.50. See pl. 264.

Elevation	Field Number	Description	Plate
ca. 83.00	III-396	Corrugated bowl	80:X
ca. 83.00	III-428	Spherical token	cf. 134:A 6
ca. 83.00	III-864	Stick sealing (Protoliterate)	—
ca. 83.00	III-679	Terra-cotta spool	30:D
83.00–82.60	III-680	Terra-cotta spool	cf. 30:D
ca. 82.60	3.874b	Spherical token (Protoliterate)	—
ca. 82.60	3.874c	Spherical token (Protoliterate)	—
ca. 82.50	III-214	Barrel-shaped token	134:D 8
ca. 82.50	3.874a	Spherical token (Protoliterate)	—
ca. 82.50	3.874d	Spherical token (Protoliterate)	—
ca. 82.50	—	Quadruped figure fragment (Protoliterate)	—
ca. 82.35	III-674	Knobbed beveled-rim bowl fragment	cf. 83:I
—	III-369	Whetstone	125:Y
—	III-865	Bale(?) sealing (Protoliterate)	—
—	3.274	Disc shape token	134:E 2

S17:401

Presumed room to the northeast of S17:404 but with no trace of the northeastern wall. In the center of the area, 0.25–0.40 B.S., was an ashy deposit with intact beveled-rim bowls, many beveled-rim bowl sherds, and other vessels. Top of southwestern wall: 82.63; for base of wall, see floor level of S17:404 (82.23). Surface elevation: ca. 83.10. Top of locus: ca. 83.10. Bottom of locus: 81.58. See pl. 264.

Elevation	Field Number	Description	Plate
ca. 83.10	IV-296	Flower pot	83:DD
83.10–82.90	IV-273	Four-lugged jar incised	121:G
83.10–82.90	4.019	Ovoid jar; see fig. 9	89:T
ca. 83.10	4.954	Base fragment with potter's mark	203:42
83.00–82.80	4.340a	Spouted jar fragment	110:J
ca. 82.90	4.121	Twisted handle notched lip jar fragment	98:K
ca. 82.65	IV-236	Vat; see fig. 9	18:I; 87:E
ca. 82.60	—	Spouted bottle	cf. 111
82.60–82.40	IV-298	Footed beaker	57:D; 173:C
82.45–81.85	4.299	Painted four-lugged jar body fragment	24:E
—	4.437	Divided tray fragment	cf. 86:HH

S17:402

Scattered deposit of Protoliterate debris north-northeast of S17:401 room and of S17:407, the preserved end of baked-brick drain, as well as pit S17:403. Surface elevation: ca. 83.20. Top of locus: ca. 83.20. Bottom of locus: N/A. See pl. 264.

S17:403

Large, shallow Protoliterate pit cut into S17:402 just to the northeast of S17:407, the eastern end of the long baked-brick drain. Surface elevation: ca. 83.20. Top of locus: ca. 83.20. Bottom of locus: N/A. See pl. 264.

S17:404

Rectangular room between R18:411 and S17:401. Top of thick northeastern wall: 82.63. Floor: 82.23. There was a doorway in the northwestern wall. Surface elevation: ca. 83.20. Top of locus: ca. 83.20. Bottom of locus: 82.23. See pl. 14:B.

S17:405

Small area in northwestern corner of S17. It was located to the north of S17:201 (Trench V, Plot L) and the material immediately adjacent on the north. There was a large group of Protoliterate sherds. Surface elevation: ca. 83.00. Top of locus: ca. 83.00. Bottom of locus: ca. 81.40.

Elevation	Field Number	Description	Plate
ca. 81.80	IV-202	Metal pin	—
81.80–81.40	IV-389	Flattish sealing (Protoliterate)	—
—	4.127	Ovoid jar fragment	91:K

S17:406

Area of Protoliterate deposits adjacent to the northwest of S17:405, that is to the north of Trench V, Plot L, including the western edge of S17, but mostly in R17. Surface elevation: ca. 83.20. Top of locus: ca. 83.20. Bottom of locus: ca. 82.60. See pl. 264.

Elevation	Field Number	Description	Plate
83.20–82.60	IV-275	Complete bowl	cf. 87:E

S17:407

Easternmost preserved section of a long Protoliterate baked-brick drain extending from R17 (R17:310 and 314) into S17, where it might have ended in a sump. Surface elevation: ca. 82.50. Top of locus: ca. 82.50. Bottom of locus: 81.84. See pl. 264.

S18:401

An incompletely preserved rectangular Protoliterate room. Top of southwestern wall: 82.39; top of northwest: 82.35; floor: 81.80. Small, shallow pit dug from the floor down in the northeastern corner of room. Bottom of pit: 81.60. Surface elevation: ca. 82.50. Top of locus: ca. 82.50. Bottom of locus: 81.60. See pl. 264.

Elevation	Field Number	Description	Plate
82.50–82.30	4.811	Biconical disc	65:AA
82.27–82.10	IV-199	Metal pin	29:E

S18:402

Area to the north of R18:410 and S18:401. It is possible that it was originally a room or courtyard. Against the northern wall was pit S18:403. Top of northern wall: 82.34. Surface elevation: ca. 82.80. Top of locus: ca. 82.80. Bottom of locus: ca. 82.00. See pl. 264.

Elevation	Field Number	Description	Plate
82.80–82.60	IV-134	Miniature jar, handle missing	95:A
82.80–82.60	IV-385	Stone bowl fragment	—
82.80–82.55	IV-125	Miniature handled jar	—
82.80–82.55	IV-126–28	Clay spools	cf. 30:D, F
ca. 82.80	IV-135	Stone bead	129:Z

S18:403

A Protoliterate small pit (perhaps a hearth) at northern wall of S18:402, ca. 0.35 m deep. There was red, burnt clay at the western end. It contained ashes, sherds, and ca. thirty flint blades. Identifiable bones included—*Bos*: tooth (1), tibia (1). Surface elevation: ca. 82.80. Top of locus: ca. 82.00. Bottom of locus: ca. 81.65. See pl. 264.

Elevation	Field Number	Description	Plate
81.80–81.60	IV-323	Flint blade set in bitumen	—

S18:404

A Protoliterate rectangular well dug from the floor of R18:411 along the northern wall. Excavation stopped ca. 4.00 m below the R18:411 floor; its original depth was unknown. Identifiable bones included—*Bos*: tooth (1), tibia (1), and eleven unassigned. Surface elevation: ca. 83.20. Top of locus: 82.12. Bottom of locus: ca. 78.12. See pls. 14:B; 264.

Elevation	Field Number	Description	Plate
81.72–80.92	IV-235	Everted jar rim	93:G
80.47	IV-424	Pouring lip goblet; see fig. 8	81:R
78.12	4.233	Body fragment with leopard	58:H; 192:C

TERRACE EAST 2

TRENCH XVI

O27:201

Northern stalk of the T-shaped Trench XVI on the southeastern corner of the terrace; a cut of ca. 2.50 × 11.00 m sloped down from ca. 81.60 at the north to 80.00 at the south. It was dug to varying levels. The middle elements of decayed brickwork or hard packing were left in place. One with top at 2.60 B.S. (ca. 79.00) was 0.50–1.00 m wide; the other with top at 3.00 B.S. (78.60) was 1.00–2.50 wide. Between them an irregular patch of soft debris was dug to 4.50 B.S. (77.10), the deepest point reached in this locus. Protoliterate and Middle Susiana sherds were mixed from the surface down with Late Middle Susiana types dominant from ca. 0.50 m (ca. 81.10). An Early Susiana sherd, pl. 202:A, at ca. 81.60, was out of context, but another, pl. 194:P, at ca. 77.75, suggested a Middle Susiana/Early Susiana transition depth that corresponded well to the situation in P27:505 in the nearby Trench XXXI. Surface elevation: ca. 81.60. Top of locus: ca. 81.60. Bottom of locus: ca. 75.00. See pl. 260.

Elevation	Field Number	Description	Plate
Sherd yard	5.416	Vestigial flange + potter's mark	60:V; 204:16
Surface	2.163	Painted body fragment	179:D
Surface	2.289	Painted lip	183:V
Surface	2.771	Gray stone	230:J
ca. 81.60	2.088	Jar fragment	189:O
ca. 81.60	2.090	Painted body fragment	163:H
ca. 81.60	2.091	Painted body fragment	176:Z
ca. 81.60	2.092	Painted body fragment	171:N
ca. 81.60	2.095	Sauceboat fragment	164:L
ca. 81.60	2.098	Painted body fragment	60:E
ca. 81.60	2.099	Painted body fragment	60:D
ca. 81.60	2.116	Painted lip fragment	62:V; 202:A
ca. 81.60	2.246	Painted body fragment	169:W
ca. 81.60	2.249	Painted lip fragment	169:Q
ca. 81.60	2.250	Painted rim fragment	170:D
ca. 81.60	2.258	Jar body fragment	191:H
ca. 81.60	2.262	Jar body fragment	192:N
ca. 81.60	2.283	Painted lip fragment	183:M
ca. 81.60	2.287	Painted lip fragment	183:R
ca. 81.10	II-185	Animal-shaped bead	67:N
ca. 81.10	II-190	Eye plug	cf. 67:H
ca. 81.10	2.093	Painted lip fragment; see fig. 26	163:T
ca. 81.10	2.270	Painted lip fragment	176:G
ca. 81.10	2.281	Painted lip fragment	183:J
ca. 81.10	2.286	Painted lip fragment	183:P
ca. 81.10	2.313	Jar neck fragment	192:H
ca. 81.00	2.118	Painted body fragment; see fig. 26	57:A; 173:G
ca. 81.00	2.541	Painted bowl fragment	—
81.00–80.90	2.130	Painted base	179:G
81.00–80.90	2.211	Tortoise jar fragment	187:G
81.00–80.90	2.274	Red ware lip	193:L
80.90–80.40	2.275	Red ware lip	193:N
80.80–80.70	II-282	Spindle whorl, notched disc	—
ca. 80.70	2.067	Painted lip fragment; see fig. 24	166:A
ca. 80.70	II-365	Clay stud	234:I
ca. 80.60	2.162	Painted base	179:F
ca. 79.80	2.038	Tortoise jar fragment	187:H
ca. 79.45	II-303	Stone plug	67:I
ca. 79.20	II-337	Perforated sherd	—
ca. 79.20	2.170	Painted base	169:F
ca. 78.00	II-304	Elongated stone stud	234:V

O27:201 (*cont.*)

Elevation	Field Number	Description	Plate
ca. 77.75	2.128	Jar sherd; see fig. 33	194:P
ca. 77.35	II-359	Stone bowl fragment	230:A
—	II-191	Stone stud	234:M
Dump	II-192	Stone plug	—
Dump	II-334	Stone eye plug	67:H
Dump	2.565	Clay sealing	67:A

O27:201 SOUTH

Surface ca. 80.50.

Elevation	Field Number	Description	Plate
ca. 80.50	II-195	Bone awl fragment	cf. 65:M
ca. 79.75	II-251	Stone hoe	—
ca. 79.75	II-252	Perforated sherd	231:Q

O27:202

The southern crossbar of Trench XVI was an east-west cut of ca. 2.0 × 14.5 m with a surface of ca. 80.50 at its northwestern corner, and ca. 79.40 at its northeastern corner. Most of the locus was dug only a few centimeters except for a small test pit in the east that was dug 5.00 m down to ca. 75.00, presumably virgin soil. It had practically no sherds and this point was clearly at the edge of the settlement. The few objects found in the locus were on the western side. Surface elevation: ca. 80.50. Top of locus: ca. 80.50. Bottom of locus: N/A. Bottom of test pit: ca. 75.00. See pl. 260.

Elevation	Field Number	Description	Plate
ca. 80.50	II-355	Bitumen ball; diameter ca. 5.0 cm (Middle Susiana)	—
ca. 80.10	II-356	Bitumen ball; diameter ca. 5.0 cm (Middle Susiana)	—
ca. 79.90	II-455	Stone peg	—
ca. 79.75	2.777	Pottery roundel	231:W

TRENCH XII
P–Q22:NEAR TRENCH XII

See pls. 260; 267.

Elevation	Field Number	Description	Plate
—	2.344	Painted-burnished fragment	223:L
—	3.139	Painted-burnished various body fragments	227:O

P22:201

Narrow extension (ca. 1.40 m wide) of Trench XII turning to the southwest from Q22:203. Surface elevation: ca. 80.00. Top of locus: ca. 80.00. Bottom of locus: ca. 70.50. See pls. 260; 267.

Elevation	Field Number	Description	Plate
79.30	2.087a	Lip fragment; see fig. 48	61:JJ; 198:F
ca. 77.50	2.384	Painted-burnished body fragment	225:I
ca. 77.25	2.107	Painted-burnished fragment	64:KK; 226:A
77.05	II-307	Clay stud	234:B
75.30	II-342	Bone sickle fragment	65:N

P22:202

Narrow southwestern end of Trench XII; over half filled by access stairs. Early Susiana-Archaic Susiana. Surface elevation: ca. 81.20. Top of locus: ca. 81.20. Bottom of locus: ca. 78.40.

Elevation	Field Number	Description	Plate
81.20	2.659	Base fragment with potter's mark	—
ca. 80.20	2.074	Straw-tempered smoothed fragment	222:G
ca. 80.20	2.084	Straw-tempered carinated body fragment	222:N
ca. 77.25	2.343	Painted-burnished body fragment	223:K
—	2.421	Concave base fragment + potter's mark	203:86

Q22:201

Original Trench XII, ca. 3.00 × 6.00 m. Surface, northwestern corner: 79.21; northeastern corner: 78.78. Archaic Susiana. Surface elevation: 79.21. Top of locus: 79.21. Bottom of locus: 74.89.

Elevation	Field Number	Description	Plate
78.81	2.240	Red-banded lip fragment	222:C
78.81–78.31	2.302	Dense-sandy lip fragment	217:J
78.31	2.383	Painted-burnished lip fragment	225:D
78.31	2.306a–c	Painted-burnished body fragment	226:F
78.21	2.213	Painted-burnished various lip fragment; see fig. 37	229:D
77.76–77.61	2.109	Matt-painted lip fragment	213:G
77.61	2.138	Close-line fragment; see fig. 34	206:B

Q22:201 WEST

Elevation	Field Number	Description	Plate
77.99	2.108	Painted-burnished various body fragment	229:I
74.21	2.305	Painted-burnished various body fragment	229:H

Q22:202

Small (ca. 2.00 × 2.00 m) extension of Q22:201 to the southeast with access steps. The earth was without sherds. At the southern end were traces of hard surfaces at ca. 77.30 and ca. 76.90. Floor: ca. 76.70. Surface (southeastern corner): 79.32. Top of locus: 79.32. Bottom of locus: ca. 76.60.

Q22:203

Narrow (width 1.20–1.50 m) extension of southwestern corner of Q22:201. Surface elevation: 79.86. Top of locus: 79.86. Bottom of locus: ca. 75.21. See pl. 267.

Elevation	Field Number	Description	Plate
79.86	2.058	Trough spout	194:K
79.86	2.433	Lip fragment	62:AA
79.56	2.087b	Lip fragment; see fig. 48	61:JJ; 198:F
79.16	2.432	Lip fragment	61:Q
79.36	2.083	Red-washed base fragment; see fig. 35	220:C
78.96	2.086	Lip fragment; see figs. 33, 48	62:W; 201:I

Q22:203 (*cont.*)

Elevation	Field Number	Description	Plate
78.96	2.414	Chaff-tempered concave base fragment with potter's mark	201:F; 203:92
78.96	2.427	Lip fragment	61:U
78.66	II-262	Bowl with potter's mark; see fig. 33	62:EE; 196:H; 203:17
78.21	2.241	Dense-sandy lip fragment	217:C
77.71	2.301	Dense-sandy lip fragment; see fig. 35	217:D

TRENCH XXXI

P27:TRENCH XXXI

General area. See pls. 260; 277.

Elevation	Field Number	Description	Plate
B.S.	5.744	Stone with depression	248:B

P27:501

Rectangular trench, ca. 4.00 × 8.00 m. Surface, at northwest: 80.14, at southwest: 80.09, at the southeast: ca. 79.60. At the surface of the western side was ashy Protoliterate debris with a well-defined bottom sloping from ca. 80.00 at the northwest to ca. 79.70 at the southwest. In the northeast similar ashy debris was B.S. Below the ashy debris were twelve complete beveled-rim bowls scattered over the locus in hard reddish earth between 79.64 and 79.24. Surface elevation: 80.14. Top of locus: 80.14. Bottom of locus: 77.39. See pls. 260; 277.

P27:501 NORTHWEST

Excavation stopped at the bottom of the Protoliterate level, except for small area along the northern edge dug somewhat lower.

Elevation	Field Number	Description	Plate
79.04	5.741	Stone pestle/pounder	243:R

P27:501 SOUTHWEST

Dug below the bottom of the Protoliterate level at ca. 79.20 to a hard Early Middle Susiana floor at 78.17.

Elevation	Field Number	Description	Plate
80.09	V-116a	Token	—
80.09	V-116b	Spherical token	—
80.09	V-116c	Token: irregular	134:G 3
79.04	5.821	Concave base fragment	—
78.87–78.17	5.525	Beaker fragment	—

P27:501 SOUTHEAST

Below the Protoliterate level was a dense accumulation of large and small pebbles with the top at 78.65; it extended down unevenly to a greatest thickness of ca. 50.0 cm and must have been purposely deposited, perhaps for a pathway. Below was sterile earth, dug down to 77.39. In the north, a small extension was separated from the original locus by a segment of an east-west wall; top at 78.82. Early Middle Susiana. Floor: 78.27. Slightly lower, at 78.10, was the top of a small shallow pit with black ashy fill.

Elevation	Field Number	Description	Plate
79.35–78.70	5.626	Painted lip fragment	169:V
78.70	5.627	Painted lip fragment	169:S
78.34	5.239	Painted lid fragments; see figs. 25–26	166:E
78.34	5.563	Painted bowl fragment	169:T

Elevation	Field Number	Description	Plate
78.34	5.567	Painted lip fragment	176:A
78.34	5.568	Painted lip fragment	181:G
79.14	5.365	Broad-wash lip fragment	181:K
78.57–78.27	5.214	Tortoise jar fragment	188:B
78.10	5.926	Stone bowl fragment	230:D

P27:502

A small extension to the south of southwestern part of P27:501 revealed an ashy Protoliterate deposit with numerous bones, concentrated between 79.14 and 78.65, and included the following: *Ovis*: horn cores (3), various (1); *Capra*: various (1); *Capra-Ovis*: horn core (3), mandible (5), scapula (1), femur (1), fibula (1), tibia (6), radius (2), various (2); *Bos*: mandible (3), scapula (1), femur (4), humerus (2), various (11); *Sus*: radius (1), various (2); *Gazella*: fibula (1); and 197 unassigned bones. Surface elevation: ca. 79.70. Top of locus: ca. 79.70. Bottom of locus: ca. 78.45. See pl. 277.

Elevation	Field Number	Description	Plate
79.29	—	Beveled-rim bowl (Protoliterate)	—
79.14	—	Beveled-rim bowl (Protoliterate)	—
79.14	5.748	Painted lip fragment	60:A
ca. 79.05	5.561	Painted lip fragment	165:K

P27:503

Original eastern end of P27:501, distinguished as a small area to the east of what might be a very decayed north-south pisé wall immediately B.S., top at 79.49, and presumably Protoliterate. To the east was a lower north-south wall, top ca. 78.64–78.99, with three postholes ca. 30.0 cm wide. An upper entry-associated floor or hard surface at 78.29 on the west of the lower wall continued on the other side at 78.27 to the eastern edge of P27:505; this floor also continued to the west in P27:501 North. Lower wall and floor were dated to Early Middle Susiana. Surface elevation: 79.45. Top of locus: 79.45. Bottom of locus: 78.29. See pl. 277.

Elevation	Field Number	Description	Plate
ca. 78.90	5.494	Painted bowl fragments	178:G
ca. 78.90	5.681	Painted lip fragment	177:H
ca. 78.90	5.690	Painted lip fragment	171:A
78.90–78.34	5.421	Concave base + potter's mark	203:20
78.64–78.34	5.469	Painted lip fragment	167:B
78.64–78.34	V-101	Violin-shaped figurine	235:G
78.41	5.735	Perforated stone	247:N

P27:504

Extension, ca. 2.00 × 4.00 m, to the east from P27:503. A hard, irregular surface at 78.76 was cut by a Protoliterate pit, 1.00 m in diameter, with soft ashy fill; bottom at 76.81 with pebbles and bones, including the following: Capra-Ovis-Gazella: vertebrae (16); *Capra-Ovis*: mandible (1), femur (1), radius (1), humerus (1), tibia (1), various (2); *Bos*: mandible (1), various (2); *Sus*: vertebrae (1); *Gazella*: skull fragment (parietal) (1), scapula (3) and humerus (1). Surface elevation: 79.14. Top of locus: 79.14. Bottom of locus: 76.81. See pl. 277.

Elevation	Field Number	Description	Plate
79.11	—	Strap-handled fragment (Protoliterate)	—
79.11	—	4 beveled-rim bowls (Protoliterate)	—
79.14–78.10	V-39	Basin, atypically small; diameter 14.0 cm	cf. 87:C
78.10	5.265	Ca. 1/2 everted-rim jar; see fig. 9	90:I
ca. 77.30	V-121	Bone needle fragment	128:W

P27:504 EAST

Easternmost part of the locus with two beveled-rim bowls ca. 20.0–60.0 cm B.S. at the eastern edge of the trench. It also included the eastern entry of the trench, with a rectangular structure paved with pebbles at 77.63; the "bin" was presumably related to Early Susiana walls in P27:505 and 506. This locus also contained Grave 5.15; a skull appeared in the eastern edge of the trench at 78.56, leading to an extended, partly destroyed skeleton, 1.74 m long; its feet were to the northeast and its head was to the southwest and faced to the northwest; there was a Late Middle Susiana bowl at its head.

Elevation	Field Number	Description	Plate
ca. 78.60	V-46	Unpainted bowl; see fig. 26	164:H

P27:505

A strip, ca. 2.00 × 6.50 m, to the north of P27:503 and 504. Surface at west: 79.68, at east: 78.84. It included the northern part of the post-hole wall of P27:503; at 78.27 the northeastern continuation of the Early Middle Susiana floor of P27:501 North; and, below the floor, thick walls, apparently of Early Susiana rooms; top: 77.80; it was possibly related to the east-west wall at 77.69 in P27:506. There were incompletely excavated stubs, perhaps of a bin. Lowest level: 77.50. The northwestern corner of the locus was dug only to ca. 79.13. See P27:507. Surface elevation: 79.68. Top of locus: 79.68. Bottom of locus: 77.50. See pl. 277.

Elevation	Field Number	Description	Plate
ca. 79.10	5.624	Unpainted lip fragment; see fig. 31	183:W
ca. 79.10	5.679	Painted lip fragment	178:A
ca. 79.10	5.702	Bowl base fragment	58:S
ca. 79.10	5.704	Bowl base fragment	60:G
ca. 78.35	5.356	Painted bowl fragment	199:I
ca. 78.35	5.364	Painted bowl fragment	—

P27:506

Southeastern corner of Trench XXXI, ca. 1.30 × 2.50 m. Surface at east: 78.72. There was an east-west wall segment with its top at 77.69; it was presumably Early Susiana and related to walls in P27:505 to the north. The lowest level reached was 77.24. Surface elevation: 78.72. Top of locus: 78.72. Bottom of locus: 77.24. See pl. 277.

Elevation	Field Number	Description	Plate
ca. 79.00	5.574	Painted lip fragment	183:X
ca. 78.35	5.745	Pivot stone	249:F
ca. 78.20	5.290	Painted lip fragment	58:V; 171:S

P27:507

Northwestern corner of Trench XXXI, ca. 2.0 × 4.5 m. Protoliterate ashy debris began near the surface and continued down to 79.96 on the west and 79.47 on the east. Below it was hard earth with scattered Middle Susiana sherds. Excavation stopped in this layer at 79.13. Surface elevation: 80.27. Top of locus: 80.27. Bottom of locus: 79.13. See pl. 277.

Elevation	Field Number	Description	Plate
ca. 79.60	5.520	Painted lip fragment	196:D
79.34	5.367	Unpainted fragmentary bowl	168:L

TRENCH XXV
R20–21 AREA

For the original Trench XXV, see R21:300 South and North. A few objects from the Trench XXV area, without specific provenience, are listed under this general area. See pl. 260.

Elevation	Field Number	Description	Plate
2.10 B.S.	3.127	Small bowl fragment; see fig. 33	194:D
ca. 1.00 B.S.	III-191	Jar; see fig. 9	88:S

Elevation	Field Number	Description	Plate
Surface	III-449	Stone stud	234:U
—	3.367	Segmented tray fragment	86:HH
—	3.364	Painted-burnished body fragment	224:N
—	3.365	Painted-burnished body fragment	225:G
—	3.716	Grooved stone	252:J
—	3.713	Pestle pounder	243:A

R20–21 SOUTH

Elevation	Field Number	Description	Plate
77.82	—	Four-lugged vessel	122:I

R20:300

This northern extension of Trench XXV was located above the southern part of R20:503 and was part of R20:507. Finds from R20:300 East and R20:300 West were collected separately, but since no structural features separated them, they were listed together. Surface elevation: 79.71. Top of locus: 79.71. Bottom of locus: 77.50. See pls. 271–72.

Elevation	Field Number	Description	Plate
—	3.074	Painted-burnished fragment	227:G

R20:300 EAST AND WEST

East: A strip, ca. 2.00 × 6.50 m, in the middle of the eastern edge, ca. 79.60–79.00, contained a ca. 1.30 × 2.00 m shapeless mass of compacted clay, presumably fallen brick. There was mixed debris throughout, with Middle Susiana, some Early Susiana, and isolated Archaic Susiana sherds. From the surface to 79.20 were some Protoliterate sherds mixed with the dominant Middle Susiana sherds. Below 78.50, sherds were rarer, but still a mixture of Middle Susiana and Archaic Susiana. West: An area ca. 1.50–2.50 m × 4.00 m. In the southern part was a long segment of an east-west wall with the top at 78.29 and the bottom on a floor at 76.68. From the surface down to ca. 78.00 were Protoliterate sherds, particularly numerous at ca. 79.00–78.60, mixed with Susiana sherds. Early Susiana sherds occurred as high as 79.20; individual straw-tempered Archaic Susiana sherds as high as 78.65.

Elevation	Field Number	Description	Plate
79.71	3.244	Painted lip fragment; see fig. 31	183:Q
79.71–79.21	3.383	Bowl fragment	59:R; 166:B
79.01	3.110	Painted lip fragment	59:DD
79.01	3.112	Stand fragment	185:A
79.01	3.113	Straw-tempered fragment; see fig. 35	—
79.01	3.131	Painted lip fragment	184:C
79.01	3.428	Jar neck fragment	190:J
78.46	3.166	Concave base, with potter's mark	201:D
78.35	3.122	Bowl fragment	199:H
78.81	3.024	Ovoid jar fragment	90:F
78.56	3.101	Vertical lug	201:J
77.10	3.071	Painted-burnished various lip fragment	227:D
76.70	3.073	Painted-burnished lip fragment	224:E
76.70	3.180	Painted-burnished lip fragment	229:A

R20:301

Area below R21:300 Northwest with parts of the east and southern walls of an Archaic Susiana room completely defined in later seasons (see R20:405 and 501). Wall elevations, as recorded during the third season: eastern wall (i.e., the northern part of the long diagonal Archaic Susiana wall): top 77.94; bottom 77.20; base and floor: 77.01; southern wall, top: 77.20 at the east and 77.58 at the west. Part of the area was dug deeper than the Archaic Susiana walls. The upper elevations had Protoliterate sherds mixed with Susiana sherds. The group from 77.10 consisted mostly of Protoliterate sherds with about fifty beveled-rim bowls, but it included a few Middle Susiana, ten Early Susiana, and nineteen straw-tempered Archaic Susiana fragments. Below this depth pottery became rarer; the proportion of Protoliterate sherds decreased markedly and straw-tempered Archaic Susiana sherds dominated the small groups, in some cases with no appreciable contamination. Surface, southwestern corner: 79.30. Surface elevation: 78.80(?). Bottom of locus: N/A.

R20:401

Remnant of baked-brick drain consisting of fourteen headers bordered on the south by seven stretchers. At eastern end an additional stretcher on the south and two stretchers on the north projected to the east of the preserved headers. Top of first header on the west: 78.94. Top of eighth header from the west: 78.98. Bricks measured 8.0 × 18.0 × 37.0 cm. Below the easternmost stretchers of the drain and projecting ca. 23.0 cm to the east was an irregular mass of hard earth with top varying from 78.53 to 78.24 and an irregular shallow depression with bottom at ca. 78.00. Surface elevation: 79.23. Top of locus: 79.23. Bottom of locus: ca. 78.86. See pls. 271–72.

R20:402

Protoliterate pit dug down into Archaic Susiana levels. It was located below the area "East of R20:401," but it was not sharply separated from it. A small patch of plastered floor at 78.03 might be an indication of the surface from which the pit was dug. R20:402 extended to ca. 2.00 m. The western continuation of the stub wall was destroyed by the pit; top of stub was at 77.64, with two beveled-rim bowls at 77.76 close to its western end; bottom of stub was at 77.41. In a cutting into the southern side of the stub were a pin and terra-cotta cone. Surface elevation: 79.23. Top of locus: 78.03. Bottom of locus: 75.69. See pls. 271–72.

Elevation	Field Number	Description	Plate
78.23	4.118	Strap-handled but not sharply separated from fragment with four lines of fine scoring (Protoliterate)	—
78.07	IV-86	Jar with notched strap handle	97:C
77.73	4.516	Painted-burnished various lip fragment	227:L
77.63	IV-158	Incised base	cf. 236:G
77.53	4.470	Straw-tempered coarse fragment; see fig. 37	222:O
77.38	IV-85	Conical cup	17:B
77.23	IV-198	Metal pin	29:H; 128:K
76.88	IV-83	Conical cup	—
76.88	IV-84	Conical cup	—

R20:403

Narrow strip, oriented approximately north-south, ca. 0.70–1.00 m wide and 9.00 m long. At the southern end were some bricks, averaging 13.0 × 23.0 × 30.0 cm, but no faces to substantiate the existence of a wall. Surface elevation: 79.23. Top of locus: 79.23. Bottom of locus: 77.58. See pls. 271–72.

Elevation	Field Number	Description	Plate
78.70–77.60	—	Beveled-rim bowl sherds: 835 rims; 555 bodies; 172 bases (Protoliterate)	—
ca. 77.80	—	1 beveled-rim bowl (Protoliterate)	—

R20:404

Continuation of R20:300 (R20:404 East = R20:300 East and R20:404 West = R20:300 West) to remove material still standing higher than the deepest point reached during the third season at the southern end of the R20:300 East and West juncture. The eastern part of the locus was dug deeper than the west. The sherds were primarily Protoliterate, but in the north from ca. 78.00 down they were mixed with Susiana sherds, including Archaic Susiana. Surface elevation: 79.71. Top of locus: West ca. 78.70. Top of locus: East ca. 78.00. Bottom of locus: west ca. 78.00. Bottom of locus: east ca. 77.00. See pls. 271–72.

Elevation	Field Number	Description	Plate
Wash	4.795	Painted base fragment	179:J

R20:404 EAST

Elevation	Field Number	Description	Plate
78.71	4.208	Lid fragment	61:H; 194:S
77.76	4.146	Partitioned bowl fragment	83:X
77.46	4.695	Close-line fragment	63:I; 208:C

R20:404 WEST

Elevation	Field Number	Description	Plate
77.64	IV-306	Terra-cotta figurine base	237:H

SOUTH OF R20:404

Elevation	Field Number	Description	Plate
79.91	4.711	Rim and shoulder, no reserve slip	cf. 89:V
77.63	4.1064	Painted-burnished various body fragment	227:M

R20:405

Small, roughly L-shaped area consisting of the unexcavated strip between R21:300 Northwest, R20:300 West, and a north-south strip along the western side of R20:300 West. Above it was the southern part of Archaic Susiana room R20:507. Surface elevation: 79.71. Top of locus: 79.71. Bottom of locus: ca. 77.00. See pls. 271–72.

WEST OF R20:405

Elevation	Field Number	Description	Plate
79.06	4.198	Strap-handled jar fragment (Protoliterate)	—

R20:406

Archaic Susiana walls in R20:404 East appearing at 2.35 B.S. and 2.40 B.S. It was clarified during the fifth season as R20:503. Surface elevation: 79.71. Top of locus: 77.36. Bottom of locus: ca. 77.00. See pls. 271–72.

Elevation	Field Number	Description	Plate
77.36	4.503	Painted-burnished various body fragment	227:N
77.11	IV-402c	Painted-burnished various fragment	229:L
77.01	4.498	Painted-burnished various lip fragment	229:F

R20:501

Archaic Susiana room partially excavated as R20:301 and R20:405 South. The northern wall at the northeastern corner had eight courses, 85.0 cm high; the eastern wall had six courses, top 77.32, bottom 76.72; the southern wall had four and one-half courses, top 77.16, bottom 76.71; the western wall had six courses, five of them headers, top 77.65, bottom 76.90. A two-course high stub of brick projected from the lower part of the surviving eastern edge of the eastern wall. Surface elevation: 79.32. Top of locus: 77.65. Bottom of locus: 76.72. See pls. 271–72.

R20:502

Small remnant of unexcavated material over the northern wall of R20:501 (i.e., the southern part of R20:405). This locus also included some material lying slightly below the top of the western wall of R20:501. The main feature was a triangular floor fragment, formed by several layers of bitumen, lying over the northeastern corner of R20:501 at 77.99–77.82. Below the bitumen floor, at 77.73, was a shapeless cluster of bricks, possibly Protoliterate, and still lower, at 77.25, the trace of a floor, possibly Middle Susiana. Surface elevation: 79.32. Top of locus: ca. 79.32. Bottom of locus: 77.25. See pls. 271–72.

Elevation	Field Number	Description	Plate
78.17	5.738	Handgrinder	242:I
78.00	5.168	Close-line fragment; see fig. 34	209:C
78.00	5.285	Deep bowl fragment	169:O
—	5.291	Jar neck(?) fragment; see figs. 33, 48	202:E

R20:503

Continued from R20:406. The Archaic Susiana walls enclosing a triangular area were clarified. On the east, the western face of an Archaic Susiana wall consisted of six, and at one point seven, courses of stretchers; the eastern face was obscured by unexcavated debris; top of wall ca. 77.70, bottom ca. 77.00. Projecting to the west from under the eastern wall was one course of headers originally covered by thick plaster; top ca. 77.00. A ledge between the eastern wall of R20:503 and the eastern wall of R20:507 was two courses high and three-bricks wide; its lower course was at about the same level as the one-course headers. At the southeastern corner of R20:507 was a similar ledge, two, or perhaps three, courses high and four bricks wide. The soil in the narrow triangle between R20:503 and R20:507 consisted mostly of sterile sand. Surface elevation north: 79.71. Surface elevation south: 79.32. Top of locus: ca. 77.70. Bottom of locus: ca. 76.50. See pls. 53:C; 272.

Elevation	Field Number	Description	Plate
76.97	5.691	Painted-burnished lip fragment	223:G

R20:504

Eastern part of Archaic Susiana room, R20:507 (below eastern parts of R20:404 West and R20:405 North) from about 77.80 to 77.40. Locus designation used briefly until superseded by R20:507, when the circuit of the walls became clear. Surface elevation: ca. 79.70. Top of locus: ca. 77.80. Bottom of locus: ca. 77.40. See pls. 271–72.

R20:505

A strip, ca. 0.60 × 4.15 m, begun at the surface. This locus was dug to even out the northern edge of Trench XXV on the west. There was Protoliterate debris with some Susiana sherds. In addition, contiguous material below R20:404 West and to the north of R20:507 was dug as R20:505 South from ca. 78.00 down. Surface elevation: 79.60. Top of locus: 79.60. Bottom of locus: ca. 76.90. See pls. 271–72.

Elevation	Field Number	Description	Plate
79.28	5.920	Spindle whorl	232:II
78.48	5.326	Ca. 1/2 of painted bowl; see fig. 26	169:K
78.48–77.88	5.370	Red ware hole-mouthed jar	193:I
78.24	V-117	53 pyramidal tokens	cf. 134
78.24	V-118	52 pyramidal tokens and 1 cashew-shaped token	cf. 134
78.24	—	7 animal figurines	—
78.10	5.284	Incised rim fragment	85:C
—	5.351a–d	Spouted fragment	110:F

R20:505 SOUTH

Small area below R20:404 West and between R20:505 and R20:507, beginning ca. 78.00. It contained part of a mostly destroyed Archaic Susiana room.

R20:506

Protoliterate debris mixed with a few Susiana sherds above the western part of Archaic Susiana room R20:507. Surface elevation: ca. 79.70. Top of locus: 79.21. Bottom of locus: 77.87. See pls. 271–72.

Elevation	Field Number	Description	Plate
79.21	5.279	Potter's tool	81:V
78.46	5.295	Painted pedestal fragment	197:H
78.46	5.731	Rubbing stone	252:N

R20:507

Archaic Susiana room corresponding to R20:504 and R20:506 and to the north of R20:501. The northern wall had seven courses, top 77.50, bottom 76.80; the eastern wall had seven courses, top 77.85, bottom 77.15; the southern wall had eight courses, top 77.93, bottom 77.13; the western wall had seven courses, top 77.75, bottom 77.05. A close-line sherd found outside the southern end of the eastern wall of R20:507 at 77.46, among large pebbles and black ashes, could be taken as evidence for the wall's date. No hard floor was encountered and digging continued lower than the bases of the walls. Surface elevation: ca. 79.70. Top of locus: 77.87. Bottom of locus: 76.80. See pls. 271–72.

SOUTH OF R20:507

Elevation	Field Number	Description	Plate
78.70	V-120	Token	40:I

R20:508

Narrow strip, 4.80 m long, on the eastern edge of Trench XXV and parallel to the southern half of R20:503 and the northeastern corner of R20:501. At 78.48 was a floor with burnt pebbles and sherds, lying at angles. Below, a wall was so badly destroyed that only its western face with about seven courses could be traced; top ca. 78.00, bottom ca. 77.48. Surface elevation: 79.32. Top of locus: 79.32. Bottom of locus: ca. 77.48. See pls. 271–72.

R20:509

Narrow strip, 0.84 × 5.30 m at the top. It was located at the western edge of Trench XXV, alongside R20:505 South and R20:507. The southern part of the locus became R20:511; beginning at 77.96 there was ashy Protoliterate debris belonging to the extensive Protoliterate pit already partly excavated in the south as R20:402 and continued to the west as R20:510. A fragment of bone was found: *Bos taurus*, metapodial, 76.03–74.74, Protoliterate (see pl. 258:BB). Surface elevation: 79.28. Top of locus: 79.28. Bottom of locus: ca. 77.96. See pls. 271–72.

Elevation	Field Number	Description	Plate
79.28	V-33	Rough-surfaced, horizontal-handled, fire smudged jar + round base	cf. 101:G
78.59	5.079	Carinated bowl fragment	220:I
78.59	5.795	Carinated jar fragment	88:V

R20:510

Strip, 2.00 × 6.50 m, to the west of R20:509. With R20:509 it constituted the northern part of the extensive and deep Protoliterate pit, the southern section of which was dug as R20:402. The surface sloped from 79.70 in the north to 79.37 in the south. In the northern end of R20:510, Protoliterate sherds became rarer at 78.41 and the locus number there was changed to R20:512. Surface elevation: 79.70. Top of locus: 79.37. Bottom of locus: ca. 76.00. See pl. 271.

Elevation	Field Number	Description	Plate
79.32	5.555	Carinated bowl fragment	85:X
79.23	V-26	Spouted jar fragment	103:D
79.23	5.167	Close-line ware lip fragment	208:B
78.71	—	3 beveled-rim bowls (Protoliterate)	—
78.68	5.694	Four-lugged jar fragment with painted decoration; see fig. 15	123:D

R20:510 (*cont.*)

Elevation	Field Number	Description	Plate
78.31	V-60	Straw-tempered smoothed carinated bowl; see fig. 37	222:H
78.17	—	7 beveled-rim bowls (Protoliterate)	—
78.11	5.292	Painted-burnished various body fragment	227:J
78.00	V-107	Rubbing/polishing stone; two highly smoothed sides with their long axes at right angel to each other	cf. 252:L
77.64	V-25	Straw-tempered bowl; see fig. 35	—
77.64	5.178	Red-line ware body fragment	—
77.64	5.224	Twisted handle jar	100:C
77.64	5.253	Ovoid jar fragment	92:B
77.64	5.256	Spouted pithos fragment	110:L
77.64	5.716	Finger stone	244:Y

WEST OF R20:510

Strip, ca. 1.30 × 7.80 m, extended to the west from the middle part of R20:510 and contained the continuation of the Proto-literate debris of R20:509 and R20:510. It was originally cut to provide steps, but after the discovery of pit R20:513, the steps were cut in a ca. 0.90 × 1.70 m northern extension. A fragment of bone was found: *Bos taurus*, mandible, 79.48, Protoliterate (see pl. 258:F).

Elevation	Field Number	Description	Plate
79.70	5.213	Painted bowl fragment; see fig. 33	198:I
79.04	V-71	Spouted jar fragment; see fig. 12	103:F

R20:511

Strip, ca. 1.10 × 2.80 m, at the southern end of R20:509. It consisted of Protoliterate debris above the southwestern corner of room R20:507 and immediately adjacent to the northeastern part of R20:402. The exterior of the western end of the southern wall of R20:507 showed six courses of stretchers lying on a course of headers, resting in turn on a bottom course of stretchers (pl. 55:A). This arrangement was a means of bonding the southern and western walls of the room. Surface elevation: 79.37. Top of locus: 77.96. Bottom of locus: ca. 76.00. See pls. 55:A; 271–72.

R20:512

Northern end of R20:510. This new locus number was assigned when Protoliterate sherds became rarer. The debris was mixed with Early Susiana and some Archaic Susiana sherds. Surface elevation: 79.70. Top of locus: 78.41. Bottom of locus: 75.48. See pls. 271–72.

Elevation	Field Number	Description	Plate
78.41	5.153	Matt-painted ware lip fragment	216:D

R20:513

Irregularly oval Protoliterate pit, ca. 1.25 × 1.30 m and beginning at 78.68, and the ca. 1.00 m of debris overlying it. A fragment of bone was found: *Bos taurus*, metatarsal, 79.04 (see pl. 258:AA). Surface elevation: 79.70. Top of locus: 79.70. Bottom of locus: ca. 77.80. See pls. 271–72.

Elevation	Field Number	Description	Plate
79.40	V-43	Ca. 2/3 of fine ware jar	cf. 90:B
79.40	5.229	Ladle fragment	82:B
79.36	—	Obsidian blade	—
79.04	—	Beveled-rim bowl sherds: 33 rims + base; 146 bodies; 115 bases	—
78.89	5.225	Spouted jar fragments	109:G
78.86	V-51	Beveled-rim bowl	83:M
78.84	—	Beveled-rim bowl sherds: 27 rims + base; 144 rim; 75 base (Protoliterate)	—
77.86	—	Large beveled-rim bowl; diameter 26.0 cm (Protoliterate)	—

SOUTH OF R20:513

A long narrow strip with Protoliterate debris along the southern edge of West of R20:510.

Elevation	Field Number	Description	Plate
79.36	5.369	Ca. 1/2 of spouted jar	107:A
78.94	V-44	Fine ware jar	cf. 88:L

SOUTHWEST OF R20:513

The area immediately to the southwest of pit R20:513, namely the western ends of West of R20:510 and South of R2O:513. It contained a chunk of brick debris, 70.0 × 90.0 cm, 50.0 cm thick, with top at 59.57, which partly overlaid a cluster of pottery vessels.

Elevation	Field Number	Description	Plate
ca. 79.00	V-36	Rough-surfaced, everted rim jar	cf. 90:H
78.81	V-96	Mottled buff-orange stone celt; triangular; length 7.5 cm	—
78.81	—	Beveled-rim bowl sherds: 13 rims + base; 202 rims; 20 bases	—
78.66	V-42	Fine ware spouted jar	cf. 105:B
78.66	V-53	Coarse ware bowl	cf. 84:A
—	—	Beveled-rim bowl sherds: 24 rims + body; 306 rims; 120 bodies; 215 bases (Protoliterate)	—
78.60	5.249	Globular jar painted neck	90:D
78.60	—	Beveled-rim bowl sherds: 24 rims + body; 228 rims; 120 bodies; 215 bases (Protoliterate)	—
78.40	V-75	Strap-handled jar	cf. 96:D

R20:514

Area just to the east of rooms R20:501 and R21:501, and merging into R21:508 at the south. At the north, below the southern end of R20:508, the continuation of the wall of R20:503 was traced. Surface elevation: 79.32. Top of locus: 76.27. Bottom of locus: ca. 75.10. See pls. 271–72.

R20:515

Northern extension of Trench XXV. The surface sloped from 80.04 at the northwest to 79.73 at the southwest and from 79.84 at the northeast to 79.64 at the southeast. This was primarily an area of Susiana debris, with very little Protoliterate material, in contrast to the Protoliterate pits and deep trenching just to the south. Oven R20:516 was in the northeastern corner. A fragment of bone was found: *Bos taurus*, metapodial, 79.15, Middle Susiana (see pl. 258:Z). Surface elevation: 80.04. Top of locus: 80.04. Bottom of locus: ca. 76.50. See pls. 271–72.

Elevation	Field Number	Description	Plate
79.69	5.512	Jar fragment	189:A
79.60–79.15	5.370	Red ware hole-mouthed fragments	193:I
79.40	5.513	Jar body fragment	188:D
79.15	5.317	Painted body fragment	58:B; 176:T
78.97	5.278	Trough spout	194:J
78.97	5.728	Stone hoe	245:K
78.77	5.276	Buff ware hole-mouthed lip fragment	193:K
78.50–77.50	5.275	Buff ware hole-mouthed lip with potter's mark	204:16

R20:516

A round floor, perhaps of an oven, 71.0 cm in diameter in the northeastern corner of R20:515. Just to the south was a 10.0 cm wide mud ridge and on the east were traces of brickwork. The oven is probably Late Middle Susiana. Surface elevation: 79.84. Top of locus: 78.19(?) Bottom of locus: 78.19(?). See pls. 271–72.

R21:TRENCH XXV

Elevation	Field Number	Description	Plate
77.75	4.013	Jar fragment	19:R; 90:L

R21:300

Trench XXV began as a 2.50 × 14.00 m strip divided into two parts, north and south, and was gradually enlarged to the west and north. The northern end was extended 3.00 m into Square R20. The denominations used for the different parts of the trench during the third season, "Trench XXV North, Northwest," etc., have been replaced by "R21:300 North, Northwest," etc. In the western extensions architectural units were reached in lower levels but were not completely defined until later seasons (R20:301 was continued as R21:501; R21:301 and R21:302 were continued as R21:501 and R21:510; northern part of R21:300 Southwest was continued as R21:511). Discrepancies between elevations recorded in the third season (pl. 271) and later (pl. 272) were due to some attrition of wall tops and to the complete definition of loci in later seasons. Surfaces at the corners: northwestern 79.30; northeast 79.26; southwest 78.29; southeast 78.36. See the subdivisions of R21:300 for the individual elevations.

R21:300 SOUTHEAST

Area ca. 2.50 × 7.00 m. There were no structures except for the southern end of a Protoliterate wall on the western side of Trench XXV. A few sherds were accompanied by Susiana sherds; the outline of a Protoliterate pit with gray ash and vessels was between 76.72 and 75.82; it was not dug until the fourth season (see R21:407). Its presence explains the mixed character of the sherds. The elevation level at ca. 76.12–75.82 was marked by an undisturbed deposit of dark black ashy earth, sometimes extremely thin, thickening into little pockets of debris in which sherds were rare. They represent the initial phase of Archaic Susiana 1. A small pit, 2.35 m deep, was dug down from the level of the black ash layer but yielded only virgin soil. Surface elevation: 78.72. Top of locus: 78.72. Bottom of locus: 73.07.

Elevation	Field Number	Description	Plate
78.72	3.120	Lid fragment	61:I
78.62	III-362	Inner ledge rim bowl fragment	81:X
78.22	III-212	Barrel-shaped token	134:D10
78.22	III-612	Bitumen bowl fragment	124:K
77.82	III-349	Four-lugged vessel	123:E
77.72	III-348	Vat (Protoliterate)	—
77.72	III-350	Four-lugged jar	25:P
77.57	3.411	Goblet fragment	89:D
77.52	III-213	Conical token; height 2.8 cm	—
77.22	III-376	Stone spindle whorl	29:W
76.52	3.1203	Stone disc	125:S
76.07	3.224	Painted-burnished various lip fragment	228:L
76.07	3.262	Painted-burnished various bowl fragment; see fig. 37	229:G
76.07	3.263	Painted-burnished various bowl fragment; see fig. 37	229:E
76.07	3.264	Painted-burnished various bowl fragment	229:K
76.07	3.303	Painted-burnished various lip fragment; see fig. 37	228:F
75.82	3.116	Painted-burnished various lip fragment	229:J
75.82	3.118	Painted-burnished various lip fragment	227:A
75.82	3.792	Dense ware body fragment	228:H
75.82–75.72	3.011a	Painted-burnished various bowl; see fig. 37	64:Y; 228:E
75.82–75.72	3.261	Painted-burnished various lip fragment; see fig. 37	227:B

R21:300 SOUTHWEST

Area ca. 2.50 × 7.00 m. Protoliterate remains were prominent: the southern parts of the diagonal walls had bases at 78.20 (northern parts in R21:300 Center West) and pottery deposits. In the steps at the southern end, the Protoliterate pit traced in R21:300 South was continued (see R21:407). Only a small area approximately in the middle of the locus was dug as deep as 5.82 m. At the northern end walls of an Archaic Susiana room were not given a separate locus number during the third season (see R21:413). Surface elevation: 78.72. Top of locus: 78.72. Bottom of locus: 75.82. See pl. 271.

Elevation	Field Number	Description	Plate
78.80	3.736	Flint blade	254:H
78.72	III-890	Stone vessel	125:G
78.00	—	4 beveled-rim bowls (Protoliterate)	—
78.00	—	Strap-handled jar (Protoliterate)	—
78.00	—	Four-lugged jar (Protoliterate)	—
77.99	3.527	Twisted handle	20:H

Elevation	Field Number	Description	Plate
77.94	3.514	Notched lip sherd	19:N
77.90	—	Four-lugged jar (Protoliterate)	—
77.82	3.1222	Pottery roundel	231:R
77.79	3.488	Rubbing stone	29:K
77.47	—	Four-lugged jar containing III-891–97	—
77.47	III-891	Miniature stone jar	125:J
77.47	III-892	Miniature stone jar	125:I
77.47	III-893	Miniature stone jar	125:F
77.47	III-894	Miniature stone jar	125:H
77.47	III-895a	Squat stone bead or cylinder seal	129:A
77.47	III-896a	Stone fish pendant	129:EE
77.47	III-896b	75 squat cylindrical white frit and black stone beads	31:R
77.47	III-896c	Black stone disc bead	31:R
77.47	III-896d	Black stone tubular bead	31:R
77.47	III-896e	10 small shells	31:R
77.47	III-896f	6 large shells	31:R
77.47	III-896g	Chunk of friable ocher	31:R
77.47	III-897	Stone inlay	129:KK
77.30	—	2 pottery sickles	—
76.92	3.1244	Miniature celt	125:GG
76.90	3.070	Painted-burnished sherd	223:I
76.15	3.076	Bowl fragment; see fig. 35	219:G
76.00	3.078	Straw-tempered lip fragment	228:I
76.00	3.009a	Painted-burnished various lip fragment	228:B

R21:300 NORTH

Area ca. 2.50 × 7.00 m. Surface measuring points: 79.26 and 78.80. There were no structural features and much less Protoliterate disturbance than in R21:300 South and Southwest. At ca. 77.00 the lowest Protoliterate sherds were found, but Archaic Susiana sherds were already prominent. A few close-line and one matt-painted sherd might denote an Archaic Susiana 3 occupation level at 77.50–77.30. The black earth layer with sherds of the initial phase of Archaic Susiana 1, continuous with that in R21:300 South, was at 76.30–75.90; a floor at 75.70. Surface elevation: 79.26. Top of locus: 79.26. Bottom of locus: 75.50.

Elevation	Field Number	Description	Plate
79.26	3.130	Bowl fragment	168:H
78.96	3.104	Concave base chip	62:T
78.81	III-634	Cylinder seal	41:B
78.81	III-735	Figurine	236:D
78.76	3.126	Stand fragment	61:HH
78.41	3.738	Stand fragment	61:DD
78.36	3.172	Lip and body fragment	202:C
78.36	3.106	Jar body fragment	61:B
78.36	3.121	Lid fragment	61:L
78.31	3.164	Concave base fragment	62:KK
77.96	3.157	Painted lip fragment; see fig. 33	198:B
77.96	3.358	Lip fragment	29:P
77.76	3.057	Smoothed ridged fragment	222:L
77.70–77.65	3.396	Stand fragment; see fig. 33	197:G
77.30	3.397	Bowl fragments	196:J
76.30	3.055	Smoothed lip fragment	222:A
76.30	3.140	Painted-burnished various lip fragment	64:Z; 229:B
76.30–76.15	3.008	Painted-burnished bowl fragment	229:C
75.90	3.009b	Painted-burnished various lip fragment	228:C
75.90	3.010	Painted-burnished various lip fragment	228:D
75.90	3.011b	Painted-burnished various body fragment; see fig. 37	64:Y; 228:E

R21:300 CENTER WEST

A strip, ca. 2.50 × 4.80 m, to the west of the southeast two-thirds of R21:300

Elevation	Field Number	Description	Plate
78.00	3.284	Disc token	134:E1
77.90	3.359	Stone vessel fragment	29:O; 124:M
77.35–77.30	3.123	Bowl fragment	198:J; 203:10b

R21:300 EAST

The surface level at the north was approximately the same as that of the trench on the east, i.e., 78.80. The only features were the northern ends of the Protoliterate walls of R21:300 Southwest with bases at 78.20. From the surface down to 77.30 the pottery was almost exclusively Protoliterate; at 77.35 four intact beveled-rim bowls were found in the southwestern corner and must have formed a group with the two sickles found in the immediately adjacent northwestern corner of R21:300 Southwest at the same depth. Underlying R21:300 Center West were two Archaic Susiana rooms, R21:301 and R21:302. The elevation 77.30 could be taken as the division between these loci even though the walls of R21:301 and R21:302 project higher. Surface elevation: 78.80. Top of locus: 78.80. Bottom of locus: 77.30.

Elevation	Field Number	Description	Plate
77.30	3.128	Stand fragment	61:FF

R21:300 NORTHWEST

Northwestern corner of the original Trench XXV. This strip, ca. 2.20 × 2.50 m, was located entirely in square R20 and above R20:301. There were no features except for the upper part of an Archaic Susiana wall at 77.94 on the eastern side (cf. R20:301). Surface elevation: 79.30. Top of locus: 79.30. Bottom of locus: ca. 77.50. See pls. 271–72.

Elevation	Field Number	Description	Plate
79.00	3.1120	Sherd rubber	231:AA
78.80	3.102	Straw-tempered layered body	65:E; 205:B
78.70	III-610	Stone bowl fragment	124:P
78.70	3.111	Painted rim fragment	190:S
77.80	3.053	Ladle handle fragment	59:B
Surface	3.270	Pill-shaped token	134:D 4

R21:301

Archaic Susiana room (later R21:501) below northern part of R21:300 Center West, but overlapping slightly into R20. It was crossed on the east by a long north-south Archaic Susiana wall. The north narrow R21:301/R20:301 party wall had a preserved top at 77.58; base and floor at 77.01. In the southwestern corner was a bin-like feature: base of northern wall 76.90; of southern wall at east 77.50, at the west 76.90. The deepest point reached in the locus was in a small area just to the south of the room's southern wall. Surface elevation: 78.80. Top of locus: 77.30. Bottom of locus: 75.30. See pls. 271–72.

R21:302

An Archaic Susiana room, recleared during the fifth season (R21:510), under the southern two-thirds of R22:300 Center West, except for its southern wall below the northern end of R21:300 Southwest. A segment of the long north-south Archaic Susiana wall (top at southern end: 77.74; base: 77.50) crossed the room walls (tops: ca. 77.20; bases: ca. 76.50). Between the long north-south wall and the eastern wall of the room, excavation ended at ca. 77.47–77.37 but was carried down elsewhere to the ash layer. Surface elevation: 78.80. Top of locus: 77.30. Bottom of locus: 75.35. See pls. 271–72.

Elevation	Field Number	Description	Plate
76.20	3.077	Straw-tempered smoothed lip fragment; see fig. 35	220:E
75.80	III-898	Clay figurine	236:B
75.80	3.012	Painted-burnished various lip fragment	228:A
75.80	3.072	Painted-burnished various lip fragment	227:C
75.80	3.117	Painted-burnished various lip fragment; see fig. 37	228:K

Elevation	Field Number	Description	Plate
75.80	3.119	Painted-burnished various body fragment	227:P
75.80	3.178 + 3.179	Painted-burnished lip	228:J

R21:401

Strip, ca. 2.00 × 9.00 m, between eastern edge of the original Trench XXV and the north-south wall (R21:403). The northern part of the locus was in R20. The surface sloped from ca. 79.23 in the north to ca. 78.60 in the south. Protoliterate ashy debris was intermixed with layers of harder earth.

Elevation	Field Number	Description	Plate
78.87–78.47	IV-36	Terra-cotta disc, perforated	126:FF
78.63	4.104	Upper half of strap-handled jar	—

R21:401 NORTH

Hard mud surface (or floor) with pottery deposit, 78.29–78.08. An irregularly shaped kiln, 4.75 × 1.50 m, was traced, mostly under the northern end of the long north-south wall ("East of R20:401"); lip: 77.23; bottom: 76.95 (not shown on plan).

Elevation	Field Number	Description	Plate
78.95	IV-53	Ca. 3/4 of a four-lugged jar	113:H
78.58	IV-245	Clay animal figurine	—
78.58	IV-345	Pot-shaped token	134:G 7
78.23	4.151	Rim and shoulder fragment	122:E
77.63–77.44	IV-318–19	Bitumen cone fragments (Protoliterate)	—

R21:401 MIDDLE SOUTH

From 78.08 to 77.95 at the south there was an irregular patch of mudbrick, presumably fallen. Surface elevation: 79.23. Top of locus: 79.23. Bottom of locus: ca. 77.43.

Elevation	Field Number	Description	Plate
78.03	4.175	1/2 of spouted jar (Protoliterate)	—
78.03	4.719	Straw-tempered red-banded body fragment (Protoliterate)	—
77.93	4.009	Fragment; see fig. 9	87:F
ca. 77.70	—	16 slingshots	—

R21:402

Along the western side of Trench XXV, between drain R20:401 and kiln R21:404, an area of Protoliterate debris, ca. 3.50 × 7.50 m, was dug down to Archaic Susiana levels. As in R20:402, contiguous on the northeast, no regular pit outlines were traced, but irregular cuttings, Pits A–D, in the uneven compact earth, ca. 76.90–76.78, that forms the general bottom of the locus, were probably the bottoms of individual refuse holes blended together. Joining fragments of an Archaic Susiana bowl, IV-402, scattered in the locus (in Pits A, C–D; between Pits C and D; and also in R20:406, some distance away), showed the thoroughness of the disturbance in the Protoliterate period. Surface elevation north: 79.23. Surface elevation south: 78.60. Top of locus: 79.23. Bottom of locus: 76.35.

Elevation	Field Number	Description	Plate
79.08–78.78	IV-180a	Bowl fragments	84:Z
79.03	4.069	Red-slip jar	89:V
78.51	IV-19	Black and white stone stud	234:L
78.23	IV-161	Clay animal figurine	—
78.13	IV-246	Clay animal figurine	—
77.93	IV-343	Stone pendant	129:JJ
77.63	IV-401a	Matt-painted ware bowl fragment; see fig. 34	215:J
76.78	IV-313	Stone stamp seal	234:II

R21:402 NORTH

That portion of the locus in Square R20. In the northeast was Pit A (bottom: 76.51). At the southern edge of Pit A, at 77.43–77.23, pebbles, fire-reddened brick fragments, and mud reed impressions, probably from a roof, lay over Protoliterate sherds. In the northwest, ashes and a group of large tokens at ca. 77.43, probably part of Pit D, bottom at 76.35, the lowest point in the locus.

Elevation	Field Number	Description	Plate
78.27	IV-37	Spindle whorl fragment	65:GG
77.78	IV-49	1/3 of jar with three-strand twisted handle	101:N
77.53	4.1084	Painted-burnished various	227:H
77.43	IV-443	Half of a group of large tokens	40:G
77.43	IV-443t	Miniature ovoid token	134:G 5
77.43	IV-443d	Disc ovoid token	134:E 4
77.43	IV-443a	Disc ovoid token	134:E 5
77.43	IV-443q	Barrel ovoid token	134:D 9
77.43	IV-443j	Triangular token	134:F 8
77.43	IV-444a–v	Half of a group of large tokens	cf. 134
76.73	IV-402a	Painted-burnished various fragment	229:L
76.50	4.512	Painted-burnished lip fragment	64:HH; 227:E

R21:402 SOUTH

Small Pits B and C (not shown on plan): bottoms at ca. 76.63.

Elevation	Field Number	Description	Plate
77.43	IV-105	Disc token	40:C; 134:E 6
76.63	IV-402b	Painted-burnished various lip fragment	229:L
76.63	—	Beveled-rim bowl (Protoliterate)	—

R21:403

General area of the southern end of Trench XXV, including the removal of the steps in R21:300 Southwest and the excavation from the surface down of the new southwestern extension (R21:405 South). As soon as specific elements were found, new locus numbers were assigned (R21:405–08). Surface elevation north: ca. 78.35. Surface elevation south: 78.19. Top of locus: 78.35. Bottom of locus: 77.84. See pls. 271–72.

Elevation	Field Number	Description	Plate
78.35	IV-35	Bitumen animal figurine	—
78.25	IV-333a	Stone bead	—
78.25	IV-335a	Whitish stone bead	129:L
78.15	4.207	Neck fragment + pierced lug	—

R21:404

Protoliterate kiln and the area immediately surrounding it just to the south of R21:402. Exterior measurements of the kiln were 1.31 × 1.96 m; reserved top: 77.93; base of interior: 77.04. Part of its upper wall was destroyed a considerable time ago. The arched opening low on the southeast was smoothed on the inside and fire-hardened. The hole opened into the floor of the kiln. The lower part of the kiln was possibly originally separated off as a fire chamber. As found, it was filled with hardened ash, reddened earth, and brick fragments in the lower one-third, which blocked the stoke hole. On the west an irregular layer of mudbrick (top: 77.48, bottom: 77.33) lay on reddish brown earth. On the east at about the same depth was an irregular line of brick and an uneven hard surface, which had been removed, revealing another hard surface at 76.88, before the cross section of the kiln was drawn (pl. 273). Surface elevation: 78.25. Top of locus: 78.25. Bottom of locus: 76.88.

Elevation	Field Number	Description	Plate
77.38	IV-48	Twisted handle	20:G
77.38	4.128	Strap-handled jar fragment	—
77.38	—	2 beveled-rim bowls (Protoliterate)	—

EAST OF R21:404

Elevation	Field Number	Description	Plate
76.25	4.1026	Base fragment	217:I

SOUTH OF R21:404

An area, ca. 3.25 × 3.50 m, in the southwestern corner of the enlarged trench. There was an irregular line of hard earth or pisé at 77.11; an irregular patch of hard earth, perhaps with some pisé chunks, at 77.64; and a heap of ash and debris 50.0 cm to the south of the kiln with the top at 77.20. Lumps of purified clay, five fragments of unbaked pottery, and just to the south of bricks on west of kiln, three beveled-rim bowls and one globular jar, all at 76.66, were found. Bottom of area: ca. 76.40. See pls. 271–72.

Elevation	Field Number	Description	Plate
77.16	IV-156	Handled bowl fragment	84:V

R21:405

Protoliterate pit below the southern part of R21:403, which contained part of the Protoliterate debris that filled the southern end of the trench. Its outline was clarified and the lowest part was dug during the fifth season (R21:503) on the east. Surface elevation: 78.19. Top of locus: 77.84. Bottom of locus: ca. 75.70.

Elevation	Field Number	Description	Plate
77.84	IV-150	Four-lugged jar; see fig. 15	120:G
77.74	4.816	Four-lugged sherd	25:D
77.59	IV-63	1/2 of four-lugged jar	120:B
77.19	IV-180b	Bowl fragments	84:Z
76.19	IV-104	Terra-cotta disc	126:DD
76.19	IV-92	Jar	—

WEST OF R21:405

The debris continued in the southwestern corner of the trench to the west of R21:405 proper and to the south of the ash heap of kiln R21:404. See pls. 272–73.

Elevation	Field Number	Description	Plate
77.84	IV-52	Ca. 2/3 of strap-handled jar (Protoliterate)	—
77.54	4.791	Cylindrical bowl fragment	85:V
77.52	IV-287	Jar sealing	42:J; 148:F
77.52	4.287	Reserve-slip jar	89:B
77.38	IV-382	1/2 gray stone bowl	124:D
77.38	4.760	Band-rim bowl fragment; see fig. 8	84:O
76.89	IV-112	Spouted jar	cf. 104:J

R21:406

Area of steps at the southern end of R21:300 South. Protoliterate debris was found down to a hard surface at 77.41, at which point the locus number was changed to R21:407. Surface elevation: 78.36. Top of locus: 78.36. Bottom of locus: 77.41. See pls. 271–72.

Elevation	Field Number	Description	Plate
77.61	4.906	Stone perforated disc	29:R
77.59	4.088	Strap-handled jar fragment	cf. 95:L

R21:407

Protoliterate debris below R21:406, the transition being marked by a hard surface at 77.41 with vessel fragments. The locus also had a similar curved line, ca. 2.50 m long, of Archaic Susiana brick fragments at 77.09 at the southern edge of a Protoliterate pit traced in the fifth season, R21:505. Surface elevation: 78.36. Top of locus: 77.41. Bottom of locus: ca. 77.00. See pls. 271–72.

Elevation	Field Number	Description	Plate
77.41	IV-151	Four-lugged jar	24:G; 120:E
77.41	IV-181	Four-lugged jar; see fig. 15	121:E
77.41	IV-182	Spouted fragment; see fig. 12	—
77.41	IV-183	Oval tray (Protoliterate)	—
77.41	IV-184	Spouted fragment	106:G
77.03	IV-395a–b	Clay ball fragments	43:E–F; 141:D–E
77.03	IV-396	Small clay ball fragment (Protoliterate)	—
77.03	IV-393a–c	Clay ball fragments (Protoliterate)	—
77.03	IV-394	Clay ball fragment (Protoliterate)	—

R21:408

A 2.50 m square area, consisting primarily of a Protoliterate pit, in the corner between the southern wall of R21:414 and the north-south wall of R21:409. It destroyed the Archaic Susiana remains except at the periphery of the locus. Most of the area had already been excavated to 75.82 as the northern half of R21:300 Southwest. The top of the R21:409 wall at 76.90 marked the top of the locus. In the northwest some irregular fallen brickwork obscured part of the eastern face of the R21:409 wall. In the southwest the brickwork of R21:502 was traced. The pit area of R21:408 was dug to a depth of 73.98, but from ca. 75.40 down, the material was hard yellow sand without sherds. Surface elevation: 78.35. Top of locus: 76.90. Bottom of locus: 73.98. See pls. 271–72.

R21:409

The area between kiln R21:404 and the western edge of the original Trench XXV, beginning ca. 1.00 m below the modern surface. This locus consisted of three elements: (1) The double Archaic Susiana wall forming the western side of room R21:414 that extended to the south until destroyed by Protoliterate pits R21:403 and R21:505; top measured as 76.90 during the fourth season and 76.67 during the fifth season; bottom: 75.81. The top of the north-south wall, 76.90, was taken as the top of the locus; (2) near the southern end of the north-south Archaic Susiana wall, there was lower brickwork with well-preserved finger impressions; top 75.81; bottom 75.46; and (3) the space between kiln R21:404 and the north-south Archaic Susiana wall contained mixed debris excavated to ca. 75.90 and overlay the Protoliterate pit, R21:509, defined during the fifth season. Surface elevation: 78.35. Top of locus: 76.90. Bottom of locus: 75.46. See pls. 54:C; 271–72.

Elevation	Field Number	Description	Plate
76.49	IV-219	Miniature four-lugged jar (Protoliterate)	—
75.93	IV-217	Beaker	83:C

R21:410

Enlargement of the R21:300 South test pit by a ca. 1.00 m square to the north and a ca. 1.00 × 2.00 m strip to the south. It was carried down to 73.85 without yielding any Archaic Susiana 1 sherds. An access ledge was preserved at the southern end at 76.25 under R21:407. Surface elevation: ca. 78.62. Top of locus south: ca. 77.00. Top of locus north: ca. 75.42. Bottom of locus: 73.85. See pls. 271–72.

Elevation	Field Number	Description	Plate
75.63	4.604	Close-line fragment; see figs. 45, 48	206:M
73.92	4.460	Tapered dense ware; see fig. 37	228:G

R21:411

The area below R21:401 North plus the bottom of R21:402 North. The western part of the locus was dug to ca. 76.90 as R21:402 North, and the only new features were the two cesspits, R21:413. In the eastern side patches of brick debris still remained as high as

77.70. During its removal part of the western face of the Archaic Susiana wall at the southwestern corner of R21:501 was traced. Surface elevation: 79.23. Top of locus: ca. 77.70. Bottom of locus: 76.34. See pls. 271–72.

Elevation	Field Number	Description	Plate
77.43	IV-401b	Matt-painted jar; see fig. 34	215:J
77.23	4.876	Stone grinder	240:B
76.73	IV-309	Thorn figurine	236:F
76.63	4.515	Painted-burnished various fragment	227:I

R21:412

Area adjacent to R21:404 on the north and below R21:402 South. A corner wall fragment with top at 76.64 stood on a floor at 75.85 with beveled-rim bowls and other pottery. Below ashy soil in the northern end of the wall corner was an irregular pit with pottery going down to another floor at 75.04. Surface elevation: ca. 78.50. Top of locus: ca. 77.00. Bottom of locus: ca. 75.00. See pls. 272–73.

Elevation	Field Number	Description	Plate
75.56	4.326	Ovoid jar	93:F
75.56	4.1132	Pouring lip bowl fragment	—
75.56	—	String-cut bowl base fragment (Protoliterate)	—
75.56	—	Ca. 18 beveled-rim bowls (Protoliterate)	—
75.85–75.04	4.014	Strap-handled jar fine scoring (Protoliterate)	—
75.04	4.132	Strap-handled jar fine scoring (Protoliterate)	—
75.04	4.163	Small strap-handled jar fragment (Protoliterate)	—
75.04	4.111	Spouted jar; see fig. 12	103:I
75.04	—	Unrecorded number beveled-rim bowls (Protoliterate)	—

R21:413

Two small cesspits in the bottom of R21:411 West. Bottom of R21:413: 75.94; bottom of R21:413 North: 75.71. The southern pit had a white lime lining and contained some green stained sherds and brick fragments. The pits were probably only the lower parts of a cess area, the presence of which higher up in R21:402 North had been betrayed by green stained sherds and earth. Surface elevation: 79.23. Top of locus: 76.34. Bottom of locus: 75.71. See pl. 272.

R21:414

The Archaic Susiana room in R21:300 Southwest (continued as R21:511). The fill from the third season was removed and the inner face of the western wall (R21:409) was traced. Northern wall, top: 77.20; bottom: 76.60. The room's interior was occupied by a later pit, with bottom at 74.10. Surface elevation: ca. 78.55. Top of locus: 76.97. Bottom of locus: 74.10. See pls. 271–72.

R21:501

Continued from R21:301 (Archaic Susiana room). The fill from the third season was removed and the clearance of the western end, begun in the previous season (cf. R21:411 East), was completed under the denomination R21:507. No western side for the bin had survived. Four and one half courses of the northern wall were preserved with probably some headers in the second from the top; top: 77.16, bottom: 76.71; the eastern wall had five courses of stretchers; top 77.38, bottom 76.70; the southern wall had five courses of stretchers; top: 77.29. Floor: 76.56. Surface elevation: 78.80. Top of locus: 77.50. Bottom of locus: 76.56. See pls. 271–72.

Elevation	Field Number	Description	Plate
77.50	5.185	Dense-sandy ware lip fragment; see fig. 35	217:G

R21:502

Ca. 1.00 m square construction of Archaic Susiana bricks and three stones just to the south of the pit of R21:408 at the southeastern edge of the R21:409 wall. Surface elevation: 78.35. Top of locus: 76.13. Bottom of locus: ca. 75.90. See pls. 54:D; 272.

R21:503

Protoliterate pit that cut the southern end of the R21:409 brickwork on the west and fused with pit R21:505 on the east. A small part of the pit in the southeast, between 76.15 and 76.01, was briefly termed R21:504. Surface elevation: 78.21. Top of locus: 77.81. Bottom of locus: 75.25. See pls. 271–72.

Elevation	Field Number	Description	Plate
76.95	5.737	Handgrinder	242:O
76.21	5.223	Spouted jar fragment	—
75.93	5.314	Four-lugged flask fragment (Protoliterate)	—
75.65	—	10 beveled-rim bowls (Protoliterate)	—
75.46	V-41	Four-lugged flask	120:F

EAST OF R21:503

Elevation	Field Number	Description	Plate
76.50	V-1	Ball fragment	150:E

R21:504

Canceled; see R21:503.

R21:505

Protoliterate pit to the east and south of R21:502. Its southeastern edge was defined by the fragmentary curved line of Archaic Susiana bricks cut into by this pit, R21:407; the western side blended into R21:503. Both pits were part of the disturbance that filled the southern part of Trench XXV with Protoliterate debris, as first noticed in the southern steps during the third season. Aside from some scattered brick fragments, the only feature of the area was a brick basin, 55.0 cm square on the exterior and 30.0 cm on the interior; top: ca. 76.25, bottom: 76.07. Its character and date were unclear—whether a feature built in the bottom of the pit or left undisturbed by it. The former seemed more likely since the pottery group from 76.28 is Protoliterate. Surface elevation: 78.36. Top of locus: ca. 76.00. Bottom of locus: 76.07. See pls. 271–72.

R21:506

Area between R21:408 and R21:410 in R21:300 Southeast. There were no features. Surface elevation: ca. 78.62. Top of locus: 76.66. Bottom of locus: ca. 75.50. See pls. 271–72.

R21:507

Western end of R21:301 (continued as R21:501), just beyond the western edge of the third season trench, located under R21:401 and R21:411 East. Surface elevation: 78.80. Top of locus: 76.86. Bottom of locus: 76.59. See pls. 271–72.

R21:508

Below the southern two-thirds of R21:300 Southeast, to the east of the Archaic Susiana rooms R21:501 and R21:510. This area of debris was contiguous with R20:514 and below the northern one-third of R21:300 Southeast. Surface elevation: 78.74. Top of locus: 76.70. Bottom of locus: ca. 75.00. See pls. 271–72.

Elevation	Field Number	Description	Plate
76.12	5.273	Four-lugged fragment	114:I
75.75	V-74	Spouted fragment (Protoliterate)	—

R21:509

Well-defined circular Protoliterate pit below R21:409 West, slightly to the south of the corner wall of R21:412 and immediately to the east of kiln R21:404. The western edge of R21:409 was extended a short distance under the kiln. The top of the pit was ca. 1.00 m lower than the interior of kiln R21:404 and 78.0 cm lower than the top of the higher wall of R21:409. The beaker (IV-217; pl.

83:C) found in R21:409 at the eastern edge of the kiln at 75.93 was almost certainly in the upper part of pit R21:509. Surface elevation: 78.35(?). Top of locus: ca. 76 00. Bottom of locus: 74.40. See pls. 271–72.

Elevation	Field Number	Description	Plate
ca. 76.00	V-40	Ca. 1/2 buttress spouted reserve slip jar; see fig. 13	—
ca. 76.00	5.349	Inner ledge rim bowl fragment	81:Z
76.86	5.351	Spouted jar fragment	110:F
75.75	V-20	Spouted jar fragment (Protoliterate)	—
75.75	V-22	Spouted jar fragment	cf. 102:A
75.67	V-87	Spouted jar fragment (Protoliterate)	—
75.67	5.700	Four-lugged jar fragment	114:H
ca. 75.40	V-19	Spouted jar fragment	cf. 104:C
ca. 75.40	V-24	Twisted-handle cup	20:F; 100:B
ca. 75.40	V-78	Ovoid jar fragment	90:E
ca. 75.40	V-84	Beaker	89:H
ca. 75.40	V-94	Bituminous stone beaker fragment	—
ca. 75.40	5.215	Beveled-rim bowl (Protoliterate)	83:K
ca. 75.40	5.266	Beaker-like vessel fragment; see fig. 9	89:I
ca. 75.40	5.271	Spouted jar fragment	103:C
ca. 75.40	5.921	Pouring lip bowl (Protoliterate)	—
75.17	V-23	Spouted jar	104:C
75.17	V-140	1/2 clay ball	37:F–G; 150:D
75.17	V-143	Spouted jar	cf. 106
75.17	5.166	Matt-painted ware bowl fragment	215:I
75.17	5.248	Deep bowl	85:FF
75.17	5.270	Strap-handled notched lip fragment	98:H
75.17	5.693	Spouted bowl; see fig. 8	84:X
75.10	V-45	Jar with Protoliterate bitumen plug for missing spout	—
74.74	V-93	Stone bowl	29:CC; 124:W
74.74	5.254	Spouted jar fragment	108:O
74.74	5.282	Four-lugged jar fragment (Protoliterate)	121:B
ca. 74.50	V-18	Ovoid jar	19:S
ca. 74.50	V-32	Ovoid jar	cf. 88:B
74.40	5.321	Small strap-handled jar fragment (Protoliterate)	—

R21:510

Archaic Susiana room; most of it was dug during the third season (R21:302) and then refilled. During the fifth season the fill was removed and the small amount of remaining earth was dug, but there were no new finds. Northern wall (= southern wall of R21:501), top: 77.29, bottom: 76.59; eastern wall, top: 77.19, bottom: 76.49; southern wall (= northern wall of R21:511) had six courses: 72.0 cm high, top: ca. 77.20, bottom: ca. 76.58; western wall, had seven courses, the two upper courses had headers, 80.0 cm high, top: ca. 77.38, bottom: ca. 76.58; floor: 76.68. Surface elevation: 78.80. Top of locus: ca. 76.86. Bottom of locus: 76.49. See pls. 271–72.

R21:511

Continued from R21:414 (Archaic Susiana room). The northern wall (= southern wall of R21:510) had six courses, 72 cm high, top: ca. 77.20, bottom: ca. 76.58; eastern wall had five courses, 85 cm high, top: ca. 77.00, bottom: ca. 76.15; southern wall had eight courses; the top two headers, top: 77.00, bottom: 76.10; western wall had six courses, top: 76.67, bottom: 75.97. Surface elevation: ca. 78.55. Top of locus: ca. 77.20. Bottom of locus: 75.97. See pls. 271–72.

TRENCH XXXII
R23:501

Irregular rectangle, 3.50 × ca. 10.30 m. Surface at southwest: 78.30; at the southeast: 77.86; at northwest: 78.00. The locus was covered by surface wash debris with salt-encrusted sherds, mostly Protoliterate, to a depth of ca. 0.75 B.S. In the northeastern corner there was a patch of hard earth with pebbles at 77.64. Also traced in the northern part of the locus was a hard surface at 76.57 marking the bottom of the Protoliterate occupation there. Elsewhere Archaic Susiana 3 sherds appeared at ca. 75.0 cm B.S. and lower. In middle of locus were two extended skeletons, lying on their backs with heads to the south; Grave 5.16 was oriented north-south, 1.73 m long, probably male with well-worn teeth, at 77.08; Grave 5.17 was oriented slightly southwest-northeast, 1.62 m long, probably young adult female by broad pelvis and unworn teeth, at 76.31. No gifts were found with either skeleton, but sherds near Grave 5.16 suggested an Archaic Susiana 3 date, and it seemed likely that Grave 5.17 might also have belonged to that period, but had been dug down into earlier debris. The northern part of the locus was dug to a depth of ca. 76.20. R23:503 and R23:504 lay below the southern part of this locus, from 77.28 down. Surface elevation: 78.30. Top of locus: 78.30. Bottom of locus: ca. 76.20. See pl. 276.

Elevation	Field Number	Description	Plate
78.30	5.159	Close-line fragment	209:A
77.70	5.944	Straw-tempered neck fragment; see fig. 37	—
77.55	5.156	Close-line bowl fragment; see fig. 34	207:D
77.08	5.327	Close-line fragment; see figs. 34, 47	63:Q; 211:G
77.08	5.328a	Close-line fragments	212:D
77.08	5.334	Close-line fragment (cornet)	212:L
76.95	5.736	Perforated stone	247:O

R23:502

An extension, ca. 2.50 m wide, to the east of the southern part of R23:501 made after the appearance of Middle Susiana sherds at an unexpectedly low level in the southeastern corner of Protoliterate debris in the locus. From 75.11 to 76.31 the predominance of Middle Susiana sherds, though mixed with some Early Susiana and Archaic Susiana sherds, indicated the existence of a Middle Susiana pit. It presumably tapered out between 76.31 and ca. 76.00, where Middle Susiana sherds still occurred but with a larger admixture of earlier sherds. The southern face of the northern wall of R23:504 appeared in the northwestern edge of R23:502. Projecting to the south from it was the stub of a north-south wall. Although the latter's preserved top was some distance below the top of the R23:504 wall, the walls might have originally been part of the eastern end of a room. Surface elevation: 77.86. Top of locus: 77.86. Bottom of locus: ca. 75.90. See pl. 276.

Elevation	Field Number	Description	Plate
77.11	5.713	Close-line neck fragment	211:N
76.91	5.642	Terra-cotta figurine	236:C
76.91–76.31	5.739	Pestle	243:B
76.31	5.743	Pestle	243:L
76.31	5.244	Close-line carinated bowl fragment; see fig. 34	210:F

R23:503

A small area below the southernmost part of R23:501. It was divided from R23:504 by an east-west wall with top at 77.18 and bottom at 76.05. Floor: 75.72. Bones: *Capra Ovis*, mandible (1), tibia (1); *Capra Ovis Gazella*, humerus (1), various (1); unidentified (12). Surface elevation: 78.30. Top of locus: 77.18. Bottom of locus: 75.72. See pl. 276.

R23:504

Below the southern part of R23:501. An area, originally ca. 2.50 × 3.50 m, was delimited from R23:501 North and R23:503 by east-west walls. The top of the northern wall at 77.28 was the real top of the locus, but materials from access steps exterior to the northeastern corner of the locus and beginning at 78.15 were included under R23:504. The walls consisted of hard material, presumably pisé, in which no bricks could be articulated, rested on three courses of long bricks laid as stretchers (for southern wall between R23:505 and R23:503, see pl. 55:B). The continuation of the northern wall to the east was visible at the northern edge of R23:502 for at least 1.00 m, at which point its lower part was abutted by a north-south wall. There were also traces of the continuation of the southern wall to the east. It is possible that R23:504 was a room, the southeastern corner of which was destroyed by the Middle Susiana pit of R23:502. Northern wall, top: 77.28; top of bricks: 76.75; bottom of bricks: 76.46. Southern wall, top: 77.18; bottom: 76.05. Below the northern and southern walls were irregular remnants of north-south brickwork, from ca. 76.20 to 75.49, presumably representing an earlier building phase. A rectangular stone with a circular depression found at 75.96 below the eastern part of the northern wall might have been a door socket but was apparently not *in situ*. The diagnostic sherds among the few found at the levels of the walls suggested that they were Archaic Susiana 2 in date. Bones: *Capra Ovis*, mandible (3), scapula (1), hip fragments (ilium and ishium) (2), tibia (1), and various (4); *Capra Ovis Gazella*, skull fragment (frontal) (1), mandible (1), humerus (1); *Bos*, various (2); *Sus*, mandible (1), various (1). Surface elevation: 78.30. Top of locus: 77.28. Bottom of locus: 75.49. See pls. 55:B; 276.

Elevation	Field Number	Description	Plate
78.15	5.344	Painted-burnished fragment	223:M
75.90	5.230	Straw-tempered red-burnished base fragment	219:L

Elevation	Field Number	Description	Plate
75.90	5.283	Straw-tempered smoothed fragment; see fig. 37	222:D
75.90	5.362	Dense-sandy lip fragment	217:K

R23:504 NORTH

Elevation	Field Number	Description	Plate
77.25	5.328b	Close-line fragments	212:D

GULLY CUT

Elevation	Field Number	Description	Plate
—	5.449	Painted-burnished lip fragment (Archaic Susiana)	225:H

S22:401

Rather irregular strip at the bottom of the eastern terrace alongside gully between Trenches XII and XXV; ca. 7.00 m long; width varying from 1.25 m at the north to 1.46 m at the south. The upper 2.00 m of debris contained Protoliterate sherds. At 55.0 cm B.S. in the northern part of the locus were three baked bricks, all in the same alignment but not touching, with one inverted beveled-rim bowl nearby. From 2.00 m down Archaic Susiana sherds were predominant although some Protoliterate sherds still occurred between 2.00 and 2.50 B.S. (75.13–74.23) Irregular layers of brownish earth underlaid by a layer of black ashy earth had predominantly Archaic Susiana 2 sherds with a few intrusive Archaic Susiana 3 and one painted sherd. In the mottled brown and black earth below 73.83, painted-burnished sherds diagnostic for Archaic Susiana 1 occurred until ca. 72.33, below which was sand without sherds. Excavation continued as deep as 71.33 in the locus; most of the southern part was filled by access steps. Surface elevation: 77.13. Top of locus: 77.13. Bottom of locus: 71.23. See pls. 260; 279–80.

Elevation	Field Number	Description	Plate
77.13	4.099	Spouted jar fragment (Protoliterate)	—
76.58	—	1 beveled-rim bowl (Protoliterate)	—
75.13	4.910a	Red-line lip fragment	64:X
75.13–74.63	—	13 beveled-rim bowls (Protoliterate)	—
74.88	IV-238	Animal figurine	—
74.88	IV-360	1/2 perforated stone (probably Archaic Susiana 2)	cf. 247:L
74.88	4.1230	Sandstone pestle; length 13.5 cm	cf. 243:P
ca. 74.85	4.750	Close-line jar body	211:K
74.63–74.55	IV-329	Clay stud (Archaic Susiana)	67:L; 234:F
74.23	IV-239	Animal figurine	—
74.23	IV-240	Animal figurine	—
73.93	4.1242	Painted-burnished fragments	cf. 225:B
73.83	4.526	Painted-burnished lip fragment	65:B; 225:F
73.63	IV-316	Ring bead	—
73.63	IV-363	Ca. 1/8 perforated stone	cf. 247:O
73.63	4.501a–b	Painted-burnished lip fragment	224:J
73.63	4.571e	Painted-burnished fragments	225:A
73.63	4.933	Flint blade	255:P
73.13	4.535a–b	Painted-burnished fragments	224:C
72.88	4.535d	Painted-burnished fragment	224:C
72.88	4.499	Painted-burnished lip	64:AA; 224:G
73.13	4.884	Stone disc	251:S
ca. 72.70	IV-403	Painted-burnished fragment; see fig. 37	224:B
72.53	4.528a	Painted-burnished lip	65:A; 225:C
—	4.504	Painted-burnished fragment	223:E
—	4.1229	Painted-burnished fragment	224:D

WEST OF AREA OF S22:401

Elevation	Field Number	Description	Plate
76.13	4.1231	Sandstone pestle	cf. 243:F–G

S22:402

An extension, 2.00 × 2.00 m, to the west of the northern section of S22:401. The gravel screen of the gully occupied about 40.0 cm at the top with loose wash below based on pebbles at ca. 75.80. An apparently roughly circular pit, 1, with an estimated diameter of 3.00 m began at ca. 75.50. Presumably about three-quarters of it remained unexcavated. It was a source of Protoliterate contamination in later seasons, when rain eroded the northwestern steps corner of the Gully Cut. Its bottom was at ca. 74.60 and had been cut into the top of the Archaic Susiana 1 levels, as was clear from the sherds found and by comparison with less disturbed adjacent layers in S22:403 and S22:404. The southern edge of pit 1 was cut by another Protoliterate pit, 2, dug from a higher level, just below a jumble of baked bricks, 76.41–75.65. Pit 2 had a soft greenish fill, suggesting that it was a cesspit. It continued down to ca. 73.85, that is well down into the Archaic Susiana 1 layers. Below, sherds were relatively sparse and did not occur lower than 72.33, where sterile sand began. However, the deepest point reached, 71.33, revealed dark brown earth with many dark brown clay patches, burned red clay, charcoal and gray clay lumps, and pebbles. Surface elevation: 77.00. Top of locus: 77 00. Bottom of locus: 71.33. See pl. 260.

Elevation	Field Number	Description	Plate
76.48	IV-427	Terra-cotta spool (Protoliterate)	—
76.03	4.922	Flint core	253:E
76.03	4.925	Flint core	253:F
75.33	4.921	Flint core	255:V
74.93	4.507	Painted-burnished fragment	—
74.93	4.919	Flint core	255:X
74.93	4.920	Flint core	256:O
74.88	4.1214	Straw-tempered red-washed perforated burnisher(?)	231:GG
74.80	4.1083	Straw-tempered lip fragment	221:F
74.13	4.587	Dense-sandy lip	217:P
74.13	4.523	Painted-burnished fragment	64:NN; 224:F
73.58	4.532	Painted-burnished fragment; see fig. 37	224:M
73.58	IV-436	Bone awl fragment	—
73.56	IV-404	Beaded rim bowl; see fig. 35	219:J
72.88	IV-315	Clay bead (Archaic Susiana 1)	234:CC
72.88	4.873	Perforated stone	247:J

S22:403

An extension, ca. 2.00 × 2.00–2.40 m, to the west of the middle portion of S22:401. Pit 2 of S22:402 overlapped into the western part of the locus, but to the east the layers were relatively undisturbed. Below the gravel wash were layers of brown and yellowish earth with Protoliterate sherds, 76.50–75.33. A relatively thin layer of reddish-brown earth between 75.33 and 74.93 had straw-tempered red-washed and dense-sandy red-washed and red-line sherds typical for Archaic Susiana 2, as well as four intrusive sherds of the painted-burnished ware of Archaic Susiana 1. From 74.93 down the dominant decorated ware was painted-burnished with sherds becoming increasingly rarer at the lower depths, until they disappeared completely when compact sand was reached at ca. 72.33. Surface elevation: 77.13. Top of locus: ca. 77.00. Bottom of locus: ca. 72.53. See pls. 260–61.

Elevation	Field Number	Description	Plate
75.33	IV-431	Celt fragment	65:SS
75.33	4.592	Red-line fragment	218:D
75.33	4.596	Red-line lip; see fig. 35	64:V; 219:B
75.33	4.602	Dense-sandy fragment	218:C
75.33	4.910b	Red-line lip	64:X
75.33	4.918	Black flint core	253:K
75.33	4.1236	Red-line body, layered	205:E
75.13	IV-312	Stone stud	234:E
74.93	IV-429	Celt fragment	65:OO
74.88	4.566	Straw-tempered oval tray	221:G

Elevation	Field Number	Description	Plate
74.23	—	1 beveled-rim bowl, Pit 2 (Protoliterate)	—
74.13	4.506	Pottery fragment; see fig. 35	217:L
74.13	4.517	Painted-burnished body	64:MM; 224:L
74.13	4.531	Painted-burnished lip and body fragments	224:O
74.13	4.571a, c–d, f	Painted-burnished fragment	225:A
74.13	4.931	Flint blade	254:BB
74.13	4.1050	Painted-burnished lip	cf. 227:A
74.13	4.1232	Painted-burnished lip	223:B
73.53	IV-307b	Figurine	237:F
73.13	IV-374	Terra-cotta animal figurine	—
73.13	4.932	Flint blade	255:E

S22:404

An extension, ca. 2.5 × 3.0 m, to the west of the southeastern section of S22:401. The stratification showed the sequence already traceable in S22:402 and S22:403. The gravel and wash from the surface to ca. 76.40 was underlaid by brownish and yellowish earthen layers with Protoliterate painted sherds, mixed with a few Middle Susiana buff and red ware fragments, between 76.03 and 75.33. The reddish brown Archaic Susiana 2 layer, 75.33 to ca. 74.93, is relatively level on top, but irregular at the bottom. The Archaic Susiana 1 layers, dated by painted-burnished sherds beginning at 74.93, were more irregular and diverse. Black ashy debris lay above dark earth, with patches of yellow clay, and filled an irregular pit sunk into the clay and compact sand. Sherds occurred only in the darker debris and became very sparse in the lower levels. Below this thin red and hard sandy clay levels sterile sand began at ca. 72.33. Only part of the locus was cut as low as 71.43; much of the southern end being occupied by steps. The eastern and southern portions overlay S22:506 and S23:505, S23:507, and S23:509. Surface elevation: 77.13. Top of locus: ca. 77.00. Bottom of locus: ca. 72.83. See pls. 260; 279–80.

Elevation	Field Number	Description	Plate
75.33	IV-308	Figurine	236:E
75.33	4.910c	Red-line fragment	64:X
75.13	IV-400	Red-line fragment; see fig. 35	218:G
75.13	4.1228	Stone-hoe(?)	230:H
75.13	4.505	Painted-burnished lip	64:DD; 223:H
75.13	4.588	Red-line lip	64:W; 219:D
75.13	4.597	Red-line lip	218:E
75.13	4.600	Red-line fragments; see fig. 35	64:U; 219:A
74.93	IV-433	Figurine fragment	237:I
74.93	4.513	Painted-burnished body	227:F
74.93	4.518	Painted-burnished fragments	225:J
74.93	4.521a	Painted-burnished lip	224:P
73.00	4.913	Straw-tempered coil-made lip	65:F
72.83	4.528b	Painted-burnished lip	225:C

S22:405

Area, ca. 7.00 × 7.00 m, to the south of S22:401 and S22:404 and extending farther to the east than S22:401. The southern part of the locus lay in S23. Dug in western, middle, and eastern strips, the middle strip being about twice as wide as the others, which were not all carried down to the same elevation. Much of the eastern strip was occupied by right-angled access steps flanking the southeastern corner of the trench. Surface elevation: 76.70. Top of locus: 76.70. Bottom of locus: ca. 73.30. See pls. 260; 279–80.

Elevation	Field Number	Description	Plate
75.33	4.916	Flint blade	255:J
75.00	IV-310	Stone stud	234:D
74.60	IV-311	Stone stud	234:C
74.60	4.917	Flint core	255:I
73.70	IV-334c	Stone bead	234:AA
ca. 73.40	4.519	Painted-burnished body	223:F
72.88	4.934	Flint blade	254:Q

S22:405 WEST

Gravel and sparse Protoliterate sherds from the surface to 74.90. Between 74.90 and 74.60, some sherds of mixed dates—Protoliterate, Middle Susiana buff chips, painted and unpainted—were found; one close-line lip; three red-line bodies; straw-tempered smoothed; red-banded; and red-washed. Below 74.60 was Archaic Susiana 1 debris. In the southern end a pit, S23:509, was dug during the fifth season to test for virgin soil. The elevation of the figurine IV-435 was misrecorded as 77.80; the actual elevation might have been 73.80. Bottom: ca. 73.30.

Elevation	Field Number	Description	Plate
ca. 74.20	4.529	Painted-burnished lip	64:JJ
73.70	4.522	Painted-burnished lip	64:LL
74.20–73.70	4.535c	Painted-burnished lip	224:C
ca. 73.50	4.567	Painted-burnished lip	223:D
ca. 73.50	4.571b	Painted-burnished lip	225:A
ca. 73.50	4.586	Red-washed bowl fragment; see fig. 35	219:E
—	IV-435	Figurine	66:C; 237:A

S22:405 MIDDLE

Below the top Protoliterate debris were 10.0 cm, 75.05–74.95, with primarily forty-five sherds, including a matt-painted Archaic Susiana IX or XII lip, and several red-line fragments, along with about fifteen beveled-rim bowl sherds. Debris from 74.95 to 74.60 was mixed; with both Archaic Susiana 3 and 2 painted wares and one intrusive and very worn Archaic Susiana 1 painted-burnished sherd. The debris of 74.60–73.35 had a large proportion of straw-tempered red-washed and red-banded sherds as well as dense-sandy red-washed and one red-line sherd; four painted-burnished fragments could be regarded as intrusive. From 73.45 to 72.60 painted-burnished fragments were prominent among the sparse sherds found. The northern half above a round earthen floor at 73.38 became S22:510. The southern end was occupied by part of the access steps, removed during the fifth season as S23:505. East material dated by sparse Protoliterate sherds, consisting of brown earth from the surface (76.70–75.45) and hard clay (from 75.45–75.15), lay directly on a black ashy deposit with Archaic Susiana sherds. It was in turn underlaid by Archaic Susiana 2 debris between 74.60 and 73.70, below which sherds became rare, but included Archaic Susiana 1 painted-burnished examples. In the northern end (above S22:505) at ca. 74.80 were traces of a skeleton (cf. two skeletons nearby in S22:507); two close-line sherds were in the vicinity. Much of the locus was occupied by access steps, which remained at considerably higher elevations than the lowest point reached in this strip, and was dug later as S22:505–07. Bottom: ca. 72.80.

Elevation	Field Number	Description	Plate
ca. 76.05	—	Matt-painted body	—
ca. 74.95	4.757	Painted-burnished lip	223:O
74.90	4.594	Red-line lip	64:K; 218:A
ca. 74.90	4.935	Red-line body	64:S
74.85	4.492	Close-line fragment; see figs. 34, 45	63:C; 206:E
—	4.493	Close-line lip	cf. 207:J
—	4.494	Close-line body (Archaic Susiana)	—
74.85	4.495	Matt-painted body	215:C
74.85	4.536	Red-line fragment; see fig. 35	219:C
74.85	4.538a	Red-banded fragment; see fig. 35	221:D
74.85	4.928	Flint blade	255:A
74.80–74.50	4.930	Flint blade	254:M
73.70	IV-330	Clay stud	67:K; 234:G
73.70	IV-373	Figurine	237:D
73.57	4.1225	Beaded rim (Archaic Susiana)	—
73.57	4.1226	Perforated roundel; dense-sandy + chaff red-wash, burnished(?)	—
73.45	4.520	Painted-burnished fragment	65:D
73.30	IV-445	Celt	65:NN
—	IV-430	Celt	65:RR
ca. 75.40	4.241	Close-line body	211:S
ca. 75.40	4.755	Matt-painted lip	214:J
ca. 74.85	4.751	Close-line body	212:J
ca. 74.85	4.752	Matt-painted fragment	213:I
ca. 74.85	4.753	Matt-painted fragment	213:K
ca. 74.70	4.496	Matt-painted lip	64:D; 215:B

Elevation	Field Number	Description	Plate
ca. 74.60	4.589	Red-line fragment	64:R; 218:F
ca. 74.60	4.595	Red-line lip	218:K
ca. 74.60	4.601	Red-line lip fragment; see fig. 35	64:T; 218:I
ca. 74.60	4.746	Straw-tempered red-washed	222:B
74.60	4.1167	Straw-tempered red-burnished	221:E
74.50–73.80	4.538b	Red-banded fragments; see fig. 35	221:D
74.20	IV-361	Buff stone	230:N
ca. 73.80	4.747	Red-washed; thickened rim	222:M
73.45	IV-432	Celt	65:PP
—	4.591	Red-line lip	64:L; 218:B

S22:501

An extension of approximately 2.5 × 4.0 m to the east of S22:401. From the surface to ca. 75.80 there was Protoliterate debris. From 76.77 to ca. 76.50 reused baked bricks in three layers and still partly aligned were found, and probably marked the position of a drain. In the profile of the trench at the southeastern corner of the locus, a layer of black ashy earth with pebbles was visible and extended into the trench as a very small patch at 75.78; it was part of the Archaic Susiana debris so prominent in the adjacent area of S22:504 and S22:512. At 75.58, the southern half of the locus, except at the eastern edge, was covered by a surface with embedded pebbles and burnt spots; although this appeared to be an occupation surface, its period remained uncertain. The eastern side of the locus had debris without sherds between 75.13 and 74.78 and with a mixture of Archaic Susiana 3 and 2 fragments between 74.78 and 74.43. In the western part of the locus from 75.13 down were traces of a pit with scattered mudbrick fragments in alternating bands of dense reddish or greenish clay and at the bottom, 74.78–74.43, a jumble of mudbricks (these probably extended somewhat farther west into S22:401, but, if so, they were not distinguished in the fourth season). Intact examples were ca. 25.0 × 12.0 × 8.0 cm; several had a central groove and six, seven, or eight finger imprints on a slightly convex surface. No sherds occurred in the clay of the irregular pit and the Archaic Susiana 3 and 2 sherds in the ashy earth just to the east could not be used to date the bricks. They were distinct from the standard Archaic Susiana bricks of Trenches XXV and XXXII and must have fallen or been dumped, presumably in the Middle Susiana period, into a depression intrusive into Archaic Susiana 3 debris. The locus ended at the bottom of the bricks. Surface elevation: 77.11. Top of locus: 77.11. Bottom of locus: ca. 74.43. See pls. 279–80.

Elevation	Field Number	Description	Plate
77.11–75.80	—	Beveled-rim bowls: 78 rims + base; 1,923 rims; 1,294 bodies; 600 bases	—
76.71	5.269	Tray, ca. 1/2	86:S
76.71	—	5 beveled-rim bowls (Protoliterate)	—
76.51	—	1 beveled-rim bowl (Protoliterate)	—
76.11	—	3 beveled-rim bowls (Protoliterate)	—
76.11	—	1 slingshot (Protoliterate)	—
76.11	—	Grinding stone	—
75.96	5.937	Ladle handle fragment	cf. 163:CC
75.81	5.913	Clay figurine	—
74.78	V-111	Clay figurine	231:H

S22:502

The area below S22:501 from the bottom of the jumbled bricks, 74.73, down. On the northeastern side of the locus at 74.35 was a mass of hard clay, perhaps also fallen brick material, although no individual bricks were articulated and the relationship, if any, to the S22:501 brick mass was uncertain. Between 74.43 and 73.83 the prevailing specialized wares were the dense-sandy red-washed and red-line wares of Archaic Susiana 2. The presence of a few painted-burnished sherds of Archaic Susiana 1 did not invalidate the dating; an illustration of how sherds could stray from their proper levels was provided by three painted-burnished fragments which joined, although each was from a different locus and level: S22:502 at 73.96; S22:507 at 74.96; and S22:508 at 73.29. At 74.26 the entire locus, except for the clay strip along the eastern side, was covered by an earthen surface with an irregularly oval area ca. 2.00 m long located approximately in the center of the locus having a concentration of ash, pebbles, sherds, and bones. The identifiable animals among the forty-eight bones cataloged between 74.26 and 74.01 were: *Capra-Ovis, Ovis, Gazella, Bos,* and *Equus.* Between ca. 73.83 and 73.60 and the oval working area at 74.26 was an underlayer of hard bricky clay. Soft blackish earth, between 73.60 and 73.30, contained a considerable number of sherds, of both Archaic Susiana 2 and 1 types, and many flint chips (73.50). At 73.60 in the northeastern corner was Grave 5.13, the extended skeleton of an adult on its back, oriented southeast-northwest with the head at the southeast; at 73.50 in the northern part of the locus was another skeleton of an adult, Grave 5.14, in the same orientation, extended into the balk (unexcavated area). Neither had grave goods; they seemed to be sealed by the clay mass underlying the Middle Susiana surface at 74.26. From 73.30 to 72.47, below which the sherds petered out, the diagnostic pottery was consistently Archaic Susiana 1. In the northeastern corner of the locus the soft fill gave way to clay below 72.89. Surface elevation: 77.11. Top of locus: 74.43. Bottom of locus ca. 72.18. See pls. 55:C–D; 279–80.

Elevation	Field Number	Description	Plate
74.43	5.179	Red-line lip (Archaic Susiana)	—
74.43	5.181	Red-line lip carination (Archaic Susiana)	—
74.43	5.182	Dense-sandy red-washed or red-line fragment (Archaic Susiana) abraded	—
74.43	5.730	Grooved stone	252:A
74.43	5.754	Figurine (Archaic Susiana)	237:E
74.43	—	Red-line carination	—
ca. 74.40	—	Painted-burnished lip	cf. 224:G
74.29	5.686	Dense-sandy bowl	217:A
74.26	5.084	Bowl lip	217:E
74.26	5.104	Straw-tempered bowl carination red-washed (Archaic Susiana)	—
74.26	5.144	Dense-sandy foot	217:F
ca. 74.20	5.083	Red-line carination	—
74.20	5.087	Red-line base (Archaic Susiana)	—
ca. 74.20	5.088	Dense-sandy carinated bowl fragment	—
74.11	V-104	White rubbing stone, 2.5 × 3.5 cm, thickness 1.1 cm (Archaic Susiana)	—
74.11	5.029	Dense-sandy lip; cream slip with red splotches (Archaic Susiana)	—
74.11	5.077	Red-banded fragment	221:C
74.11	5.081	Straw-tempered smoothed fragment; see fig. 35	222:E
74.11	5.477	Red-line lip	64:Q
74.11	5.740	Pestle	243:C
74.11	—	Three figurines	cf. 237:J
74.06	5.078	Straw-tempered smoothed fragment	220:A
73.96	5.065	Red-line flat base	—
73.96	5.066	Red-banded concave base	—
73.96	5.069	Red-washed burnished beaded rim fragment	cf. 219:J
73.96	5.073	Red-line body (Archaic Susiana)	—
73.80	5.220	Straw-tempered red-burnished base	219:P
73.60	V-95	Stone celt	230:E
73.50	V-139	Figurine	66:D; 237:K
73.50	5.192	Dense-sandy red-washed	217:M
73.50	5.200	Painted-burnished lip	223:J
73.50	5.361	Oval tray	221:H
73.50	5.478	Red-line fragment	64:P
73.50	5.509	Straw-tempered red-washed fragment; see fig. 35	219:F
73.50	5.943	Straw-tempered smoothed body, layered	205:C
ca. 73.50	5.447	Painted-burnished body	224:H
ca. 73.30	5.171	Red-washed beaded rim	—
ca. 73.30	5.198a	Painted-burnished fragment	64:PP; 226:G
ca. 73.30	5.205	Painted-burnished fragments	64:II
ca. 73.30	5.759	Straw-tempered fragment coiled	65:G
ca. 73.30	5.941	Straw-tempered smoothed ring base layered	205:F
ca. 73.20	5.204	Painted-burnished lip	64:GG
ca. 73.20	5.454	Painted-burnished body	224:K
ca. 73.20	5.689a	Painted-burnished lip; see fig. 37	223:B
ca. 73.00	5.211	Straw-tempered smoothed fragment; see fig. 35	219:K
ca. 73.00	5.450	Painted-burnished lip	64:FF
ca. 73.00	5.752	Figurine	237:C
72.89	V-61	Painted-burnished fragment; see fig. 37	226:C
72.89	5.075	Painted-burnished fragment	224:A
72.89	5.076	Painted-burnished fragment; see fig. 37	226:D
72.89	5.199	Painted-burnished fragment	65:C; 226:E
72.89	5.202–5.203	Painted-burnished carination (Archaic Susiana)	—

Elevation	Field Number	Description	Plate
72.89	5.206	Painted-burnished body (Archaic Susiana)	—
72.89	5.207	Painted-burnished body	64:EE
—	5.760	Flint core	256:N
—	5.761	Flint core	256:J
—	5.762	Flint core	256:C
—	5.763	Flint core	256:B
—	5.764	Flint core	256:F
—	5.765	Flint core	256:I
—	5.766	Flint core	256:D
—	5.767	Flint core	256:G
—	5.768	Flint core	256:H
—	5.769	Flint core	256:K
—	5.770	Flint core	256:M

S22:503

Irregular area, ca. 1.60 × 3.30 m, of an Archaic Susiana 1 deposit remaining at the northern ends of S22:401 and S22:402 and in the eroded northwestern corner of the Gully Cut. At 72.69 in the northwestern corner was a small burned area with red clay, ashes, and a number of bones: *Capra-Ovis, Equus, Sus*, and a medium-sized carnivore are represented. Surface elevation: 77.19. Top of locus: 72.99. Bottom of locus: ca. 71.70. See pls. 279–80.

Elevation	Field Number	Description	Plate
72.69	V-62a–b	Painted-burnished fragments	cf. 226:C
72.49	5.446	Painted-burnished fragment ca. 1/3 of lip and body	224:D

S22:504

Trapezoidal area, ca. 1.50 × 4.00 m, between S22:501 and S22:512. The surface sloped up from 77.11 at northwestern corner to 77.25 at the northeast. At 76.82 were four baked bricks, a cluster of seven beveled-rim bowls, and others found singly. Between 76.00 and 75.85 the reddish earth with Protoliterate sherds changed to the black ashy deposit of Archaic Susiana 3. Excavation stopped shortly after the undisturbed Archaic Susiana 3 level was reached at 75.85. Surface elevation: 77.25. Top of locus: 77.25. Bottom of locus: ca. 75.70. See pls. 279–80.

Elevation	Field Number	Description	Plate
76.82	—	11 beveled-rim bowls (Protoliterate)	—
76.82	V-112	Clay token	231:G
74.76	5.753	Clay figurine	237:B
75.84	5.183	Close-line lip	—
75.84	5.184	Straw-tempered coarse fragment; see figs. 35, 48	220:H
75.84	5.195	Close-line body	212:G
75.84	5.751	Matt-painted body	64:F
75.84	5.935	Bone borer	233:V

S22:505

Small area below the northeastern corner of S22:405 East. At 74.60 a compacted mud layer was found. It was perhaps a floor, with pebbles and imbedded gazelle horn fragments Other bones included: *Capra-Ovis, Gazella*, mandible (1), vertebra (1), various (1); *Bos*, various (1); *Hystrix indica*, various (1); unassigned (11). This period of this locus was presumably Archaic Susiana 2 by level, but there was no sherd evidence. Surface elevation: 76.92. Top of locus: 74.92. Bottom of locus: 74.06. See pls. 279–80.

S22:506

A strip, ca. 2.00 × 4.00 m, at the eastern edge of the trench in the area of S22:405 East, particularly the remaining high material of the fifth season access steps. The northern end was under S22:505. The uppermost part of the locus had ashy debris with two *Capra-Ovis* mandibles, several other *Capra-Ovis* bones and teeth, and a *Gazella* first phalanx. Red-line sherds date the debris between 74.12 and 74.30 to Archaic Susiana 2, although a few stray Archaic Susiana 1 sherds also appeared. From 73.30 down the pottery was consistently Archaic Susiana 1. Surface elevation: 76.79. Top of locus: 74.12. Bottom of locus: ca. 72.80. See pls. 279–80.

Elevation	Field Number	Description	Plate
74.12	5.080	Straw-tempered smoothed fragment	221:J
ca. 73.30	5.103	Straw-tempered red-washed bowl	220:G
ca. 73.30	5.187	Straw-tempered red-burnished base	219:M
ca. 73.30	5.197	Painted-burnished lip	64:OO; 225:E
ca. 73.30	5.451	Painted-burnished lip	cf. 64:FF
ca. 73.30	5.939	Straw-tempered smoothed base, layered	205:G
ca. 73.30	5.993	Painted-burnished lip	cf. 227:A
73.24	5.217	Painted-burnished fragment; see fig. 37	223:C
73.24	5.582	Straw-tempered + grit tripod foot (Archaic Susiana)	—

WEST OF S22:506

Immediately adjacent to the southern end of S22:506 in the area of S22:405 East steps. An inverted vessel, an Archaic Susiana sherd (both untraced in records), and a spindle whorl (5.919) were at 3.23 B.S. The latter provided a problem; although it appeared to be an Early Susiana type, it occurred at an Archaic Susiana 1 depth in an area that even higher had no Early Susiana deposits.

Elevation	Field Number	Description	Plate
72.59	5.919	Painted spindle whorl	232:HH

S22:507

A strip, ca. 2.5 × 4.0 m, contiguous with the southern end of S22:501 and to the east of the southern half of S22:401. Proto-literate debris occurred until the appearance of Middle Susiana and Archaic Susiana sherds at 75.85; from 75.64 down Archaic Susiana 3 sherds predominated. Hard clay masses from 76.24 down in the west and 75.76 down in the east seemed made up (at least in part) of pisé. At this material's base, rested on a mud-plaster surface, were two fragmentary skeletons: Grave 5.10: 75.43, only some long bones, oriented northwest-southeast; and Grave 5.11: 75.23, oriented east-west, extended on its back; 1.80 m long. In the absence of grave goods, the only datable objects adjacent to the bones were some close-line sherds, but it was impossible to prove with certainty that they were actually associated with the burials rather than merely present in the debris into which the bodies might have been dug. By 75.23 the northern end of the locus, below the hard clay mass, had soft ashy earth with many pebbles comparable to the Archaic Susiana 3 debris in S22:504 and S22:512. Elsewhere in the locus, the debris was alternately harder and softer. Surface elevation: 76.79. Top of locus: 76.79. Bottom of locus: 75.14. See pls. 279–80.

Elevation	Field Number	Description	Plate
76.79	—	1 beveled-rim bowl (Protoliterate)	—
76.24–75.79	—	11 mosaic cones (Protoliterate)	—
75.79	—	Terra-cotta sickle fragment (Protoliterate)	—
76.19	V-2	Bale(?) sealing (Protoliterate)	148:E, G
76.19	—	1 beveled-rim bowl (Protoliterate)	—
75.43	5.005	Close-line carinated fragment (Archaic Susiana)	—
75.43	5.196	Close-line fragment	210:B
—	5.145	Close-line fragment; see figs. 34, 46	63:L; 207:J

S22:508

Below S22:507. At the top the ashy debris with many pebbles, some burnt, was a continuation of the Archaic Susiana 3 material reached in S22:507. Ashes were particularly prominent along the western edge of the locus. At the southeastern edge was a shallow oval pit, about half of it was outside the trench and it was filled with large pebbles and sherds; length: 1.90 m; greatest excavated width: 0.56 m; top sloped from 74.92 at northern edge to 74.69 at the south; bottom 74.72–74.49. In the northwestern corner of the locus was a patch of pebble pavement with slight north-south slant at 74.65–74.63. These two features marked the bottom of the Archaic Susiana 3 level. Below 74.61, although the diagnostic sherds were Archaic Susiana 2, there was no change in the character of the debris; ashy patches continued to occur for some 80.0 cm. The material from 73.44 down was Archaic Susiana 1, with very little pottery below 72.59. Surface elevation: 76.79. Top of locus: 75.14. Bottom of locus: ca. 72.59. See pls. 279–80.

Elevation	Field Number	Description	Plate
75.01	5.544	Bone awl	233:H
ca. 75.00	5.006	Close-line body	211:R
ca. 75.00	5.009	Close-line body	211:I
ca. 75.00	5.011	Matt-painted body fragment	—
ca. 75.00	5.013	Matt-painted lip fragment	—
ca. 75.00	5.015	Matt-painted fragment	64:A; 214:B
ca. 75.00	5.016	Matt-painted lip	64:C; 215:A
ca. 75.00	5.020	Matt-painted body	—
ca. 75.00	5.027	Close-line fragment	207:H
ca. 75.00	5.031	Matt-painted body	—
74.89	V-113	Figurine	237:G
74.89	5.003	Close-line fragment; see figs. 34, 46	63:E; 207:C
74.89	5.004	Close-line neck	63:T; 211:L
74.89	5.024	Dense-sandy matt-painted (Archaic Susiana)	—
74.84	5.545	Bone awl or pin	233:G
74.61	V-114	Figurine	237:J
74.61	5.448	Painted-burnished fragment	224:I
74.61	5.687	Close-line jar body	211:J
74.42	5.546	Bone awl	233:I
74.42	5.474	Red-line carination	—
74.42	5.586	Red-line fragment (Archaic Susiana)	218:H
73.96	V-59	Straw-tempered smoothed bowl; see fig. 35	220:B
73.96	5.070	Red-line flat lip (Archaic Susiana)	—
73.96	5.071	Red-line flat lip (Archaic Susiana)	—
73.96	5.086	Red-washed beaded rim	cf. 219:J
73.96	5.110	Straw-tempered smoothed fragment	222:I
73.96	5.115	Straw-tempered smoothed body	219:O
73.96	5.117	Red-burnished fragment	221:D
73.96	5.201	Painted-burnished fragment	223:N
73.83	5.141	Straw-tempered smoothed red-washed fragment; see fig. 35	220:F
73.83	5.452	Painted-burnished lip	cf. 64:FF
73.83	5.549	Bone pin	233:D
ca. 73.44	—	2 bitumen balls	—
73.29	5.085	Red-washed beaded rim	cf. 219:J
73.29	5.476	Red-line lip	cf. 218:E
73.24	5.485	Painted-burnished fragment (Archaic Susiana)	225:A
73.24	5.490	Sherd (Archaic Susiana)	205:A
ca. 73.20	5.186	Straw-tempered red-burnished flat base	cf. 219:L–M
72.84	5.455a	Painted-burnished body	64:QQ

WEST OF S22:508

Elevation	Field Number	Description	Plate
ca. 72.40	5.692	Painted-burnished body	226:B

NORTH OF S22:508

Elevation	Field Number	Description	Plate
74.22	V-110	Thorn figurine (Archaic Susiana)	—

S22:509

A small area on the western edge of the Gully Cut, beginning at the surface above the baked bricks of Pit 2 and straddling the S22:403–04 line, but also incorporating two shallow cuttings from the fourth season. Additional baked bricks occurred in a jumble ca. 1.00 B.S. The locus also included many Protoliterate sherds from the pit. The locus was closed at 1.40 B.S. See pls. 279–80.

WEST OF S22:509

Surface elevation: 77.11. Top of locus: 77.11. Bottom of locus: 73.30. See pl. 280.

Elevation	Field Number	Description	Plate
Surface	V-103	Haft-end fragment of stone celt (Archaic Susiana?)	—

S22:510

An irregularly round, hard earthen floor, with traces of burning; almost completely in the area of S22:405. No associated sherds were found, but it was datable to Archaic Susiana 1 by comparison with S22:405 levels. Diameter: ca. 4.00 m. Surface elevation: 76.70. Top of locus: 73.38. Bottom of locus: 73.30. See pl. 280.

S22:511

Begun as the area to the west of S22:508, equivalent to the southern part of S22:401, but extended to the west into S22:404 and somewhat to the north alongside S22:502. Occupational debris, still remaining in spots at the bottom of fourth season loci, was removed. Between 72.79 and 72.23 brown clay occurred with the sherds. The soil below was almost completely sterile. Surface elevation: 76.79. Top of locus: 72.79. Bottom of locus: ca. 71.50. See pls. 279–80.

Elevation	Field Number	Description	Plate
72.79	5.551	Bone reamer	233:W
72.79	5.936	Bone reamer	233:X
72.76	5.455b–c	Painted-burnished carination	64:QQ
72.76	5.676	Red-washed; burnished flat lip fragment (Archaic Susiana)	—
ca. 72.40	5.453	Painted-burnished lip	cf. 65:D
ca. 72.40	5.869a	Painted-burnished lip (Archaic Susiana)	—
72.39	5.734	Perforated stone	247:U
72.23	V-97	Stone celt	65:QQ; 230:F

S22:512

Right-angled access steps at the northeastern corner of the Gully Cut. The top 1.00 m of deposits, 77.11–76.10, had reddish earth with Protoliterate sherds and was markedly distinct from the underlying dark ashy debris with numerous Archaic Susiana 3 sherds. Although the top of the ashy debris at 75.88 was clear, mixed Protoliterate and Archaic Susiana 3 sherds between 76.10 and 75.70 indicated some Protoliterate disturbance of the top of the Archaic Susiana 3 debris, which was characterized by large numbers of close-line and matt-painted sherds. It was full of stones, many marked by fire, which were particularly dense at 75.46 and 75.06. It also had many bones; the majority of the 175 cataloged fragments were *Capra-Ovis*, but *Bos*, *Equus*, and *Sus* also occurred. Surface elevation: 77.11. Top of locus: 77.11. Bottom of locus: 74.50. See pls. 279–80.

Elevation	Field Number	Description	Plate
76.51	5.147	Close-line body	212:I
75.96	5.942	Dense-sandy body; layered	205:D
75.96	5.592	Red-line lip	cf. 218:F
75.70–75.30	5.148	Close-line fragments	63:F; 207:B
75.36–74.91	5.137	Close-line fragments; see fig. 46	207:K
74.91	5.151	Matt-painted fragment	64:H; 215:D
74.91	5.161	Close-line neck	63:W; 212:F
75.41	5.483	Close-line neck	211:M
75.16	5.157	Close-line body	63:J
75.16	5.158	Close-line neck + body	63:R; 211:Q
75.16	5.162	Close-line neck + body; see fig. 47	63:U; 211:P
74.91	5.129	Painted-burnished lip (Archaic Susiana)	—

Elevation	Field Number	Description	Plate
74.91	5.462	Straw-tempered smoothed ring base	219:N
74.91–74.71	5.033	Close-line fragment	207:M
74.91–74.71	5.037	Matt-painted body	64:I; 214:H
74.71	5.034	Matt-painted fragment	214:I
74.71	5.040	Matt-painted fragment; see fig. 34	214:C
74.71	5.042	Close-line fragment	63:K; 207:E
74.71	5.043	Matt-painted fragment	64:B; 214:D
74.71	5.044	Close-line body-foot juncture; see fig. 45	63:B; 206:H
74.71	5.045	Matt-painted fragments	64:J
74.71	5.049	Close-line fragment; see fig. 34	207:G
74.71	5.105	Straw-tempered coarse fragment	220:J
74.71	5.688	Matt-painted lip	216:E
74.59	5.142	Straw-tempered smoothed fragment	222:F

S22:512 SOUTH

Slight enlargement to the south of the right-angled turn of the steps with the continuation of the Archaic Susiana ashy debris.

Elevation	Field Number	Description	Plate
77.11	5.048	Close-line fragment	63:H; 210:A
77.11	5.046b	Close-line fragment	63:N; 210:C
75.80	5.154	Matt-painted lip	213:E
75.68	5.046a	Close-line fragment	63:N; 210:C
75.68	5.050	Close-line body; see fig. 34	63:P; 210:H
75.68	5.116	Close-line body-foot juncture	206:K
75.06–74.46	5.131	Close-line basal angle	206:G
75.06–74.46	5.138	Close-line jar neck	63:V; 211:O
75.46	5.124	Matt-painted fragment	216:C
75.46	5.128	Matt-painted lip	64:G; 215:E
75.46	5.135	Close-line bowl	63:G
75.46	5.136	Close-line fragment; see fig. 34	207:A
75.46	5.139	Close-line body; see figs. 47–48	212:B

S23:502

Canceled

S23:503

Southern access steps. The locus also included the southern end of S22:405 lying at the foot of the steps dug from the surface. Down to 75.25 the pottery was Protoliterate, but rather sparse in this outlying part of the mound. Most of the sherds were beveled-rim bowls: 3 rims + base; 151 rims; 178 bodies; and 40 bases. Very few Susiana sherds were found with the Protoliterate sherds. Surface elevation: 76.70. Top of locus: 76.70. Bottom of locus: 74.92. See pls. 279–80.

S23:504

Canceled

S23:505

A strip, ca. 1.35 × 3.90 m, across the southern end of S22:405 and partly below S23:503. It contained hard sand and clay without ashes, and practically no artifacts or bones. Excavation in the eastern and western corners was continued as S23:507 and S23:509. Surface elevation: 76.70. Top of locus: 74.92. Bottom of locus east: 73.86. Bottom of locus west: 73.74. See pls. 279–80.

Elevation	Field Number	Description	Plate
74.92	V-102	Stone mace-head	230:K

S23:506

Canceled

S23:507

Below the eastern half of S23:505 and projecting below the southeastern corner of S22:405. It contained sandy soil with rodent tunnels distinguishable by their reddish fill. There was no ash and practically no sherds, flints, or other traces of human occupation. Surface elevation: 76.70. Top of locus: 73.86. Bottom of locus: ca. 73.50. See pls. 279–80.

S23:508

Canceled

S23:509

A pit, ca. 1.00 × 1.50 m, cut below the western end of S23:505 to test for virgin soil, going through more than 4.00 m of sterile material: At 73.74 was hard reddish clay with some traces of straw and black flecks; at 73.59 was hard brownish clay with some straw; and between 73.38 and 72.35 there were three large mammal vertebrae and one medium mammal vertebra; at 72.35 was hard mottled clay with occasional flecks of charcoal; at 71.20–69.34 was clean sand and clay except, at 70.40, there was one nondescript sherd and a clay lump. Surface elevation: 76.40. Top of locus: 73.74. Bottom of locus: 69.34. See pls. 279–80.

SOUNDING G
S–T21:SOUNDING G

Stratigraphic test pit, 2.00 × 4.00 m. There access stairs and western part were in S21; the eastern part was in T21. Middle Susiana-Archaic Susiana. Surface elevation: 77.50. Top of locus: 77.50. Bottom of locus: ca. 71.50. See pls. 260; 267; 278.

Elevation	Field Number	Description	Plate
ca. 77.50 (steps)	4.261	Jar body fragment	192:F
77.50	4.262	Painted body fragment	58:L
77.50	4.461	Painted lip fragment	59:I
77.50	4.456	Jar body fragment	189:H
77.50	4.480	Painted body fragment	171:I
77.50	4.557	Red ware lip fragment	193:P
77.50	4.558	Red ware lip	193:Q
77.50	4.560	Red ware neck	193:Y
77.50	4.738	Foot beaker	173:A
77.50	4.856	Jar neck	190:H
77.50	4.860	Red ware lip	193:T
77.50	4.863	Stone hoe	245:I
77.50–77.20 (steps)	4.903	Painted lip	59:FF
77.50–76.70 (steps)	4.901	Tortoise body fragment	59:JJ
77.50–76.70 (steps)	—	Pink stone	230:G
77.50	4.1234	Bowl body fragment	173:L
77.15–	4.306	Basal angle potter's mark	203:6
77.15	4.463	Painted body fragment	59:E; 176:X
77.15	4.467	Painted ring base	58:W
77.15	4.475	Painted lip	171:R
77.15	4.857	Jar neck	190:M
77.15	4.859	Bowl fragment	193:D
77.15	4.944	Painted lip	59:S
76.95	4.1122	Spindle whorl	232:U
76.95	4.552	Painted base	176:V
76.95	4.1117	Spindle whorl	232:P
76.95	4.1121	Spindle whorl	232:T
76.70	4.1124	Spindle whorl	232:W
76.50	4.1118	Spindle whorl	232:Q
76.50	4.1120	Spindle whorl	232:S
76.25	4.1123	Spindle whorl	232:V
76.10	4.268	Jar neck	190:G

Elevation	Field Number	Description	Plate
76.10	4.820	Painted body fragment	58:Q
76.10	4.902	Bowl base	59:Q
76.00	4.1220	Sherd rubber	231:FF
75.95	4.804	Painted lip	61:T
75.95	4.939	Concave base + potter's mark	62:JJ; 203:31
75.60	4.938	Basin lip	62:CC
75.00	4.1082	Painted body fragment	62:O
75.00	4.1219	Sherd rubber	231:DD
74.95	4.1038	Concave base + potter's mark	203:6
74.90	4.272	Painted fragment	61:N; 196:F
74.70	4.547	Concave base with potter's mark	203:7
74.50	4.447	Stand foot	61:KK–LL; 197:J
74.50	4.448	Stand base	197:F
74.45	4.937	Painted body	62:BB
74.45	4.941	Painted lip	61:S
74.30	4.450	Trough spout	194:I
74.30	4.451	Trough spout	61:A
74.30	4.819	Bowl fragment; see figs. 33, 48	201:G
74.20	4.533	Painted-burnished lip	64:BB
74.20	4.749	Close-line lip	211:C
73.70	4.260	Close-line lip; see fig. 48	63:A; 206:C
73.45	4.1037	Basal carination + potter's mark	203:28
73.30	4.582	Matt-painted body	215:G
72.90	4.500	Dense-sandy painted lip	217:H
72.50	4.696	Close-line body	63:D; 206:J
72.10	4.590	Red-line lip	218:L

SOUNDING H
T21–22:SOUNDING H

See pls. 260; 267.

Elevation	Field Number	Description	Plate
75.39	4.478	Painted body fragment	171:O
75.39	4.758	Painted body fragment	171:J

T22:SOUNDING H

Stratigraphic test pit, 2.00 × 4.00 m, at northern end in T21. Surface elevation: 76.39. Top of locus: 76.39. Bottom of locus: 71.25. See pl. 267.

Elevation	Field Number	Description	Plate
76.39	4.1114	Spindle whorl	232:I
76.39	4.1233	Bowl, body fragment	173:K
75.85	IV-208	Painted bowl	57:B
75.40	4.236	Jar, body fragment	58:J
75.40	4.900	Painted lip fragment	59:W
75.40	4.911	Painted body fragment	59:C; 176:Q
75.39	4.125	Base plate fragment	—
75.09	4.904	Painted lip fragment	59:CC
74.54	4.472	Jar neck fragment	192:K
74.49	4.1177	Jar fragment	175:D
74.39	4.1237	Pedestal base fragment	206:I
72.20	4.563	Pedestal base fragment	206:L
72.10	4.598	Red-line lip fragment	218:J

TERRACE EAST 3
TRENCH XXI
P–Q23:TRENCH XXI

See pls. 260; 274–75.

Elevation	Field Number	Description	Plate
—	4.878	Handgrinder	242:G
—	5.746	Pivot stone	250:D
82.15	3.857	Spindle whorl	232:EE

NEAR TRENCH XXI

Elevation	Field Number	Description	Plate
—	4.218	Painted base fragment	179:E

NORTHWEST OF TRENCH XXI

Elevation	Field Number	Description	Plate
—	4.216	Bowl fragment; see fig. 33	194:H

P23:301

Western part of original Trench XXI (ca. 2.50 × 15.00 m). The surface sloped from 82.15 at the west to 81.55 at the east. Virgin soil was irregularly pitted with animal holes at ca. 76.50. Surface elevation: 82.15. Top of locus: 82.15. Bottom of locus: ca. 76.58. See pl. 275.

Elevation	Field Number	Description	Plate
ca. 82.15	3.240	Lip fragment	165:F
82.15–81.70	3.376	Bowl fragment	164:G
ca. 80.85	3.1257	Concave basal angle potter's mark	203:15
ca. 79.35	III-141	Stone mace-head	230:I
ca. 79.35	3.250	Close-line body fragment	212:K
78.85	3.153	Painted vessel fragment	196:G
ca. 78.85	3.013	Flanged vessel; see figs. 33, 48	200:E
77.35	3.1236	Clay token	231:B
77.35	3.870a	Clay token	231:F
77.35	3.870b	Clay token	231:E
ca. 77.15	3.054	Red-washed base	220:D

P23:401

Small area immediately to the west of the western end of P23:301. A deposit of an Early Middle Susiana vessel was revealed by rain, just B.S. See P23:506 for vessels, probably belonging to same deposit. Surface elevation: 82.49. Top of locus: 82.49. Bottom of locus: ca. 81.20. See pl. 275.

Elevation	Field Number	Description	Plate
82.49	IV-120	Deep bowl	60:Z; 182:F
82.49	IV-121	Bowl; see fig. 26	60:Y; 165:B
82.49	IV-122	Bowl	60:X; 182:A
82.49–82.00	IV-301	Painted bowl	59:F; 167:F

Elevation	Field Number	Description	Plate
82.49–82.00	4.001	Vestigial flanged vessel	182:P
82.49–82.00	4.297	Deep bowl fragment	182:I
ca. 82.00	4.033	Bowl fragment	168:J

P23:501 EAST

Extension of Q23:401 to the west. It was an open area without any features and contained not only Early Middle Susiana but also some Protoliterate and Early Susiana intrusions. Surface elevation: 82.89. Top of locus: 82.89. Bottom of locus: ca. 81.20. See pl. 275.

Elevation	Field Number	Description	Plate
82.49	5.408	Lid body fragment	61:D
82.49	5.418	Concave base + potter's mark	203:33
82.49	5.493	Lip fragment; see fig. 30	174:G
82.49	5.749	Tortoise lip fragment	59:O
82.39	5.458	Lip fragment	—
82.39	5.486	Lip fragment	59:J
82.04	5.263	Bowl fragment; see fig. 26	167:C
ca. 81.40	5.720	Grinding stone	239:E
81.39	5.918	Spindle whorl	232:G
80.27	5.431	Concave base + potter's mark	203:78
Surface	5.928	Metal arrowhead	76:D

P23:502

Apsidal kiln to the north of P23:501. It had a burnt floor slightly B.S. at ca. 81.70. The thin kiln walls were enclosed by square walls of brick; the western wall merged with the eastern wall of room P23:504; the northern wall was articulated during the eighth season (P23:804) with its base at 81.74; the eastern wall reached down to 81.40 where the excavation stopped. See pls. 274–75.

Elevation	Field Number	Description	Plate
ca. 81.75	5.934	Bone awl	233:O

P23:503

Irregularly shaped area to the north of P23:401 and the western end of P23:301. The surface sloped from 82.78 at the northwestern corner to 82.48 at the northeastern corner. It was a featureless open area. At 81.99, was Grave 5:12, with an incomplete child's skeleton, 58.0 cm long; head to the northeast, facing to the south-southeast; the body on its back; leg bent. At 81.38 was the hard earthen lip of a hollow (ca. 50.0–60.0 cm deep). The context was Middle Susiana (primarily), with a few Early Susiana and late intrusions. Surface elevation: 82.78. Top of locus: 82.78. Bottom of locus, west: ca. 82.00. Bottom of locus: 81.38. See pl. 275.

Elevation	Field Number	Description	Plate
82.78	5.678	Neck fragment	191:N
ca. 82.85	5.457	Lip fragment	59:N; 183:AA
ca. 82.85	5.696	Lip fragment	165:G
ca. 82.85	5.914	Neck fragment	190:L
ca. 82.85	5.932	Terra-cotta grill fragment	231:LL

P23:504

Room to the west of P23:502 and to the north of P23:503 and P23:501. The surface sloped from 82.64 at the southwest to 82.00 at the east. Northern wall, top: 81.96, base: 81.04; eastern wall, top: 81.47, base: 81.01; southern wall, top: 81.77, base: 81.03; western wall, top: 82.00. Faunal remains: *Capra-Ovis*, tibia (1); *Ovis*, fibula (1); *Bos*, ulna (1), tooth (4); *Sus*, scapula (3); *Gazella*, metapodial (1); *Equus*, tooth (1); mammal, indeterminate (2). Surface elevation: 82.64. Top of locus: 82.64. Bottom of locus: 80.95. See pls. 274–75.

Elevation	Field Number	Description	Plate
ca. 82.20	5.472	Bowl fragments	167:E

P23:505

Room with bin in the southwestern corner. The surface sloped from 82.78 (southwest) to 82.64 (southeast). Northern wall, top: 81.88, bottom: 81.45; eastern wall, top: 82.00, bottom: 81.25; southern wall, top: 82.01, bottom: 81.27. Floor: 81.25. Surface elevation: 82.78. Top of locus: 82.78. Bottom of locus: ca. 81.25. See pls. 274–75.

Elevation	Field Number	Description	Plate
82.78	5.703	Painted base fragment	60:J
82.78	5.709	Neck fragment	192:L

P23:506

Access step on southern side. Vessels were found immediately B.S., possibly part of P23:401 deposit. Early Middle Susiana. Surface elevation: 82.49. Top of locus: 82.49. Bottom of locus: ca. 82.20. See pl. 275.

Elevation	Field Number	Description	Plate
82.49	V-55	Bowl; see fig. 26	168:N
82.49	—	Deep open vessel	cf. 182:F

P23:507

Irregularly shaped area immediately to the north and east of kiln P23:502. The surface sloped from 81.75 at the west to 81.39 at the east. It was dug briefly to different depths. The step to the north of P23:502 was dug to 81.11. Directly to the east of P23:502 was a badly preserved segment of a north-south wall with the top at 81.41 and the bottom at 80.98. To the east of the north-south wall segment was a rectangular fragment of a bricky mass, apparently part of a thick wall; top at 81.44 and base at 80.98. To the north, a hard surface or floor was also found at 80.98. Surface elevation: 81.75. Top of locus: 81.75. Bottom of locus: 80.98. See pl. 275.

P–Q23

Original Trench XXI dug during the third season. For details, see P23:301 and Q23:301. Only objects not assigned to one of those loci are listed here.

Elevation	Field Number	Description	Plate
B.S.	3.357	Stone vessel fragment	65:Q; 230:B
81.75	3.1243	Carnelian bead	234:W
78.95–77.15	3.1234	Brown clay token	231:A

Q23:301

Eastern end of original Trench XXI. The surface sloped from 81.55 (southwest) to 80.83 (southeast). The northern half was occupied by steps. Surface elevation: 81.55. Top of locus: 81.55. Bottom of locus: ca. 77.55. See pl. 275.

Elevation	Field Number	Description	Plate
ca. 80.85	3.1223	Pottery roundel	231:S
ca. 80.85	3.790	Base with potter's mark	203:34
80.85–80.65	3.238	1/2 flanged vessel with potter's mark	200:B; cf. 203:39
80.65	3.810	Conical cup fragment	cf. 80:U
ca. 80.35	3.1254	Slingshot	231:I
80.35–80.05	3.706	Concave base and flange	201:A

Elevation	Field Number	Description	Plate
80.35–80.05	3.165	Concave base, with potter's mark	201:B; 203:47
81.55	—	Stone hoe	—
81.55	3.001	Pedestal stand	197:E
80.85–78.65	3.155	Close-line body	210:G
79.65	3.144	Lid fragment	194:U
79.65	3.145	Lid fragment, 2 holes; see fig. 33	61:G; 195:C
79.65	3.146	Lid fragment	195:D
ca. 79.10	3.158	Close-line lip fragment	61:M
79.05	—	Stone hoe	—

Q23:401

Irregularly shaped area just to the north of Q23:301. This locus began in the access steps and the northern edge of Q23:301 when rain washed out a deposit of Early Susiana flanged vessel sherds between ca. 80.45 and 79.75. The area was extended ca. 2.00 m to the west into P23. In the northeastern part of the locus, an irregular mass of bricky material was between 80.55 and 79.35. Brickwork at the southeastern end of the bricky mass was shown during the fifth season to be the southwestern corner of room Q23:501. The small segment of a thick southwest-northeast wall adjacent to a bricky mass was found between ca. 79.54 and 79.35; south of it was the northern part of the flanged vessel deposit. Early Susiana. Surface elevation: 81.75. Top of locus: ca. 81.75. Bottom of locus: ca. 79.35. See pls. 274–75.

Elevation	Field Number	Description	Plate
ca. 81.75	4.486	Lid fragment	194:Q
ca. 81.75	4.1215	Perforated pottery roundel	231:Y
81.75–81.15	4.1076	Body fragment	62:Q
ca. 80.45	4.002	Flanged vessel	200:F
ca. 80.45	4.043	Flanged vessel with potter's marks	200:G; 203:13, 63
ca. 80.15	4.003	Flanged vessel	199:K

Q23:401 EAST

Elevation	Field Number	Description	Plate
ca. 81.75	4.1113	Spindle whorl	232:H
ca. 80.15	4.269	Lip fragment	62:F

Q23:401 MIDDLE

Elevation	Field Number	Description	Plate
ca. 79.50	4.743	Painted lid fragment	195:F
ca. 79.40	4.489	Concave base, with potter's mark	203:39

Q23:501

Western portion of a large room subdivided by a partition; for the eastern portion, see Q23:503. Parts of the western and southern walls lying in Q23:401 were inadvertently cut during the fourth season before the room was distinguished (not indicated in plan, pl. 275, but visible on pl. 52:A; note also the formless pisé-like material abutting the southwestern corner of Q23:501). The northern wall of Q23:501 and Q23:503 was apparently built in two segments; in Q23:501 the thinner segment was preserved to 80.12; the thicker segment to 79.85. The tops of the eastern partition and southern wall were at 80.34. The bottom of the southern wall was at 79.35, on ashy earth. There was an ashy floor at 79.24. Early Susiana. Surface elevation: 80.87. Top of locus: 80.87. Bottom of locus: 79.24. See pls. 51:B; 52:A; 274–75.

Elevation	Field Number	Description	Plate
80.87	5.099	Painted lip fragment	61:PP
—	5.912	Lid fragment	61:K

Q23:502

The lane between rooms Q23:501 and Q23:503 in the north and brick platform Q23:512 on the south. This locus included a stack of eight vessels (V-10–17) dug through the edge of the platform, found complete or semi-complete between 80.43 and 79.56. An isolated segment of brickwork was located slightly to the east of the deposit, with its top at 80.30, and rested on the floor at 79.99 (cf. pls. 51:B, middle foreground; 52:A, left edge). The surface sloped from 81.09 (west) to 80.84 (south). V-8, V-9, and V-76 were found in the lane area. Lane floor, outside Q23:501: 79.36; outside Q23:503: 79.46. Early Susiana. Surface elevation: 81.09. Top of locus: 81.09. Bottom of locus: 79.36. See pls. 51:B; 52:A–B; 275.

Elevation	Field Number	Description	Plate
81.09–79.99	5.095	Lid fragment	194:R
81.09–79.89	5.060	Painted pot fragment; see fig. 33	198:D
81.09–79.89	5.082	Lid fragment	195:B
81.09–79.89	5.755	Body fragment	59:L
80.89	V-8	Small bowl; see fig. 33	194:C
80.89	V-9	Ladle	194:M
80.59	V-76	Ladle; see fig. 33	194:L
80.43–80.23	V-10	Beaker; see fig. 33	198:A
80.10–79.58	5.916	Spindle whorl	232:GG
79.99	5.395	Lid fragment	195:B
79.89	5.056	Lip fragment	197:C
79.73	5.057	Footed bowl fragment; see fig. 33	197:D
ca. 79.70	V-11	Flanged vessel, with potter's marks	199:M; 203:13, 63
79.70–79.56	V-12	Flanged vessel, with potter's mark	199:L; 203:20
79.70–79.56	V-13	Flanged vessel; see figs. 33, 48	200:D
79.70–79.56	V-14	Flanged vessel; see fig. 33	200:A
79.70–79.56	V-15	Flanged vessel, with potter's mark; see fig. 33	199:J; cf. 203:4, 8
79.70–79.56	V-16	Flanged vessel, with potter's mark	200:C; cf. 203:25, 41, 56
79.70–79.56	V-17	Ladle	194:N

Q23:503

Eastern portion of a large room subdivided by a partition; for the western portion, see Q23:501. The diagonal alignment of some brickwork abutting the eastern wall was continued by a thicker mass in Q23:506, but the nature of this presumably secondary material remained unclear. Northern wall, top: 80.04; eastern wall, top: 79.81; southern wall, top: 80.26. Floor: 79.32. Early Susiana. Surface elevation: 80.53. Top of locus: 80.53. Bottom of locus: 79.32. See pls. 51:B; 52:A–B; 274–75.

Elevation	Field Number	Description	Plate
80.10–79.52	5.434	Concave base, with potter's mark	203:88
80.10–79.52	5.782	Bowl body fragment	62:R
80.10–79.52	5.426	Convex base, with potter's mark	203:77

Q23:504

Room to the east of Q23:502–03 and 506. Surface: north: 80.40–80.20; southwest: 80.34; southeast: ca. 79.84. Walls badly preserved, especially in eastern half of locus. Wall elevations: north, top: 79.66, bottom: 79.04; east, top: 79.42, bottom: 79.08; south, top: 79.58, bottom: 79.03; west, top: 79.81, bottom: 79.03. A hardened surface, sloping from 79.92 in the south to 79.86 in the north, blended into the modern surface in the eastern part of the locus. A hard floor at 79.57 (south) and 79.55 (north) was traced in both the eastern and western parts of the locus and in the south it sealed uneven deposits of black ashy earth, which began at 79.52, except at the southern wall, where the top was 79.15–79.10. Figurines V-100 and 5.705 were found in this debris. Their depth was not uniform. In the southeastern part of the locus they continued without a break down to 78.92 below the bases of the walls. Close to the eastern wall in the middle of the locus a patch of hard surface with embedded sherds of a flanged vessel suggested the existence of a floor at 79.33. In the southwest the ashy debris ended at 79.18 on a floor with embedded stones. Surface elevation: 80.40. Top of locus: 80.40. Bottom of locus: 78.92. See pls. 274–75.

Elevation	Field Number	Description	Plate
80.34	5.218	Lip fragment	198:H
80.34	5.397	Body fragment	61:AA
80.34	5.411	Base fragment	62:P; 199:A
80.34	5.412	Lip fragment; see fig. 48	62:E

Elevation	Field Number	Description	Plate
80.34	5.414	Painted body fragment	62:X; 201:L
80.34	5.425	Dimple base, with potter's mark 89	203:89
80.34	5.432	Concave base, with potter's mark	62:GG; 203:48
80.34	5.433	Concave base, with potter's mark	203:52
80.34	5.459	Lip fragment; see fig. 33	196:A
80.34	5.460	Lip fragment	196:B
80.34	5.473	Lip fragment	61:OO; 198:E
80.34	5.779	Lip fragment	62:G
80.34	5.790	Lip fragment	61:X
79.92–79.92	5.430	Concave base, with potter's mark	203:13
79.92–79.52	5.437	Concave base, with potter's mark	203:15
79.86–79.52	5.706	Half of spindle whorl	cf. 65:GG
79.52–78.92	V-58	Small bowl; see fig. 33	194:F
79.52–78.52	5.304	Lip fragment	197:I
79.52–78.92	5.406	Lip fragment	194:E
ca. 79.40	5.058b	Bowl fragment	194:G
ca. 79.40	5.428	Concave base, with potter's mark	203:17
ca. 79.40	5.729	Stone hoe	245:X
ca. 79.40	5.917	Spindle whorl	232:FF
79.33	—	Flanged sherds (Early Susiana)	—
79.33–78.92	5.059	Lip fragments; see fig. 33	196:K
79.33–78.92	5.062	Lid fragment	195:E
79.33–78.92	5.409	Lid fragment	61:J
79.33–78.92	5.413	Bowl fragment	62:K; 199:D
79.33–78.92	5.550	Bone pin	233:E
79.33–78.92	5.712	Bowl fragment	62:L; 199:E
79.33–78.92	5.772	Body fragment	62:B
79.27	V-100	Figurine head	66:B; 234:A
79.23–78.92	5.058a	Bowl fragment	194:G
79.23–78.92	5.705	Figurine	236:A
79.23–78.92	5.794	Lip fragment	61:Y
—	5.777	Body fragment	62:M
—	5.778	Body fragment	62:N

Q23:504 NORTH

Small area consisting of the northern part of Q18:504 and the southern part of Q18:511 at B.S. elevation before the east-west wall delimiting the two loci had been distinguished.

Elevation	Field Number	Description	Plate
ca. 80.20	5.061	Lid fragment	195:A
ca. 80.20	5.298	Lid fragment	194:A
ca. 80.20	5.427	Concave base, with potter's mark	203:23
ca. 80.20	5.707	Lip fragment	61:O

Q23:505

Room to the north of Q23:501. Northwestern corner, top: 80.43; southeastern corner, top: 80.50. Most of the room was filled by an oval area of hard earth, presumably a hearth, top: 80.05. There was somewhat ashy earth with pebbles at 79.95. The base of the walls reached 79.54 during the seventh season. Early Susiana. Surface elevation: 81.05. Top of locus: 81.05. Bottom of locus: 79.62. See pls. 52:B; 275.

Q23:506

Room to the east of Q23:505, and divided from it by a narrow wall. Northern wall, top 79.91; base 79.47. Southern wall, top 80.04; base 79.32. Eastern wall, base 79.41. Floor 79.39. At the eastern end was a bench-like lower brickwork with diagonal orientation; one ledge continued to the south in Q23:503. Early Susiana. Surface elevation: 80.53. Top of locus: 80.53. Bottom of locus: 79.39. See pl. 275.

Q23:507

Area immediately to the west of room Q23:505. The southern end was delimited by an east-west wall stub that continued at a slight angle to the line of the wall between Q23:501/503 and Q23:505/506, with its top at almost exactly the same height, 79.89 (vs. 79.85). The wall stub and the floor at 79.55 represented a continuation of the Early Susiana building. Unrelated was one course of brickwork remaining from a higher southwest-northeast wall, at 80.63, which delimited the western edge of Q23:507. Surface elevation: ca. 81.20. Top of locus: ca. 81.20. Bottom of locus: 79.55. See pl. 275.

Q23:508

Room to the north of rooms Q23:505 and Q23:506. Surface, at the west: 80.53, at east: 80.24. Southern wall, top: 79.91. Eastern wall, top: 79.61. The floor sloped from the northwest to the southeast, 79.13–78.94. Surface elevation: 80.53. Top of locus: 80.53. Bottom of locus: ca. 79.60. See pl. 275.

Elevation	Field Number	Description	Plate
79.73	5.054	Bowl fragment; see fig. 33	196:C
79.73	5.055	Bowl	197:A
79.73	5.404	Lid fragment	61:F; 194:V
79.73	5.407	Lid fragment	61:E
79.73	5.415	Lid fragment	61:C
79.73	5.423	Concave base, with potter's mark	203:24

Q23:509

Area to the south of room Q23:504. This locus began as a small clearance to check the southern face of the southern wall of Q23:504. An enlargement of the area during the seventh season as Q23:702 revealed the western and eastern walls and defined it as a room. Surface, at west: 80.34, at east: 79.70. Party wall with Q23:504, top: 79.58. Western wall, top: 80.14. Lowest level during the fifth season: 79.66. Floor reached during the seventh season: 79.08. Early Susiana. Surface elevation: 80.34. Top of locus: 80.34. Bottom of locus: 79.66. See pl. 275.

Elevation	Field Number	Description	Plate
ca. 79.70	5.402	Body fragment	61:BB
ca. 79.70	5.775	Lip fragment	62:I

Q23:510

Narrow cutting to clear eastern face of the eastern wall of Q23:504. Early Susiana. Surface elevation: 79.84. Top of locus: 79.84. Bottom of locus: 79.00. See pls. 274–75.

Elevation	Field Number	Description	Plate
79.84	5.315	Jar neck fragment	202:D
79.84	5.436	Concave base, with potter's mark	62:II; 203:20
79.84	5.481	Close-line lip fragment	209:D
79.84	5.711	Basin lip fragment	202:B
79.84	5.791	Lip fragment	61:W

Q23:511

Room to the north of Q23:504. Surface, at northwest: 80.10, at southwest: 79.77. Northern wall, top: 79.51; southern wall, top: 79.66, bottom: 79.11. Western wall, top: 79.61. Upper floor: 79.24; lower floor: 79.04. Early Susiana. Surface elevation: 80.10. Top of locus: 80.10. Bottom of locus: 79.04. See pl. 275.

Elevation	Field Number	Description	Plate
ca. 80.10	5.405	Lid fragment	195:G
ca. 80.10	5.771	Lip fragment	62:A

Q23:511 NORTH

Elevation	Field Number	Description	Plate
ca. 80.10	5.305	Lid fragment	195:A
ca. 80.10	5.710	Lip fragment	61:NN; 198:C
ca. 80.10	5.773	Lip fragment	62:D
ca. 80.10	5.774	Lip fragment	62:H
ca. 80.10	5.783	Painted fragment	62:S

Q23:511 WEST

Elevation	Field Number	Description	Plate
ca. 80.10	5.301	Small bowl fragment	194:B

Q23:512

Abraded brick platform immediately at the surface, to the south of lane Q23:502 and to the west of room Q23:509. It contained two courses of bricks, the top course was aligned north-south, and the lower course east-west. Surface, at northwest: 81.09, at southeast: 80.34. The bottom was ca. 10.0–20.0 cm below the top. Surface elevation: 81.09–80.34. Top of locus: 81.09–80.34. Bottom of locus: ca. 81.00–80.14. See pl. 275.

Elevation	Field Number	Description	Plate
81.09	5.435	Body with potter's mark	62:FF; 203:62
81.09	5.440	Vestigial flanged base with potter's mark	60:W; 204:7

Q23:513

Small area between the eastern end of the Q23:512 brickwork and the western wall of Q23:509. Surface, at the southwestern corner: 80.61. From 80.49 down was soft earth, with many Early Susiana sherds. At 79.64 was a floor with Early Susiana XVI fragments *in situ*. Surface elevation: 80.61. Top of locus: 80.61. Bottom of locus: 79.64. See pl. 275.

Elevation	Field Number	Description	Plate
80.49	5.927	Bituminous stone bracelet, five bands	—

Q23:514

Irregularly triangular area between P23:507 and Q23:507. There were no features. Surface elevation: ca. 81.20. Top of locus: ca. 81.20. Bottom of locus: ca. 80.40. See pl. 275.

Q23:515

Narrow area of the northern side of Q23:508 and Q23:511 northern wall. The western part was in Q22. Surface, at west: 80.53, at east: ca. 80.00. It contained Early Susiana sherds in patches of blackish soil. Bottom, at west: ca. 79.70, at east: ca. 79.30. Surface elevation: 80.53. Top of locus: 80.53. Bottom of locus: 79.30. See pl. 275.

Elevation	Field Number	Description	Plate
80.53	5.306	Lip fragment	197:C

Q23:516

Small area to the west of room Q23:501. It was dug to clarify the southwestern corner of the Early Susiana building; it contained no features. Surface elevation: ca. 81.20. Top of locus: ca. 81.20. Bottom of locus: ca. 79.30. See pls. 274–75.

Q23:517

Irregularly-shaped bricky mass in the northeastern part of Q23:401. Further cleaning during the fifth season showed traces of diagonally slanted bricks suggesting that the mass might be part of a collapsed wall. Surface elevation: ca. 81.20. Top of locus: ca. 81.20. Bottom of locus: 80.55. See pls. 274–75.

GENERAL INDEX